STAR WARS VOLUME 1
SUPER COLLECTOR'S WISH BOOK
MERCHANDISE | COLLECTIBLES 1977–2012 2ND EDITION

GEOFFREY T. CARLTON

SCHIFFER PUBLISHING

4880 Lower Valley Road • Atglen, PA 19310

Other Schiffer Books by the Author:
Star Wars Super Collector's Wish Book, Vol. 2: Toys, 1977–2022, 2nd Edition, 978-0-7643-6588-1
Star Wars Super Collector's Wish Book, Vol. 3: Merchandise, Collectibles, Toys, 2011–2022, 978-0-7643-6589-8

Copyright © 2025 by Geoffrey T. Carlton

Library of Congress Control Number: 2025930158

All rights reserved. No part of this work may be reproduced or used in any form or by any means—graphic, electronic, or mechanical, including photocopying or information storage and retrieval systems—without written permission from the publisher.

The scanning, uploading, and distribution of this book or any part thereof via the Internet or any other means without the permission of the publisher is illegal and punishable by law. Please purchase only authorized editions and do not participate in or encourage the electronic piracy of copyrighted materials.

"Schiffer," "Schiffer Publishing, Ltd.," and the pen and inkwell logo are registered trademarks of Schiffer Publishing, Ltd.

Type set in ITC Avant Garde Gothic Std

ISBN: 978-0-7643-6969-8
ePub: 978-1-5073-0597-3

Printed in China

10 9 8 7 6 5 4 3 2 1

Published by Schiffer Publishing, Ltd.
4880 Lower Valley Road
Atglen, PA 19310
Phone: (610) 593-1777; Fax: (610) 593-2002
Email: info@schifferbooks.com
Web: www.schifferbooks.com

For our complete selection of fine books on this and related subjects, please visit our website at www.schifferbooks.com. You may also write for a free catalog.

Schiffer Publishing's titles are available at special discounts for bulk purchases for sales promotions or premiums. Special editions, including personalized covers, corporate imprints, and excerpts, can be created in large quantities for special needs. For more information, contact the publisher.

The Chronology of the Star Wars Super Collector's Wish Book

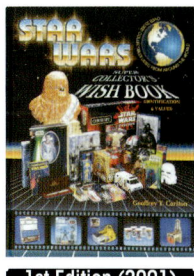    

1st Edition (2001) | 2nd Edition (2003) | 3rd Edition (2005) | 4th Edition (2007) | 5th Edition (2009)

The original series of books was published by Collector Books in Paducah, Kentucky. The title had a run of five editions, each encompassing the collectibles from the previous edition and building upon the content with new merchandise releases. Every book included all categories of toys, collectibles, and merchandise. The first edition in 2001 listed 23,000 items in 384 pages. The fifth edition in 2009 had 50,000 items in 464 pages.

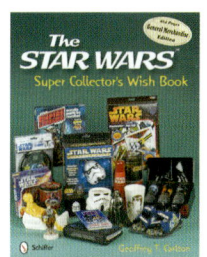 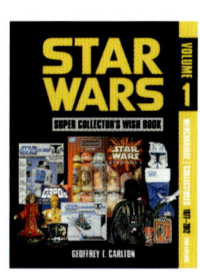 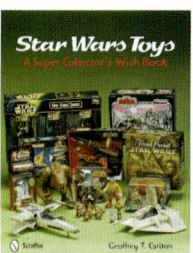 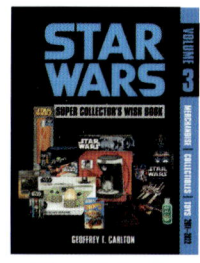

Volume 1: 1st (2012) and 2nd (2025) Editions | Volume 2: 1st (2013) and 2nd (2023) Editions | Volume 3 (2023)

The series changed production to Schiffer Publishing in 2010 and was expanded into two separate volumes to provide space to accommodate the ever-growing selection of merchandise. While values are still included in the content, the primary purpose of the books has evolved to focus on the visual identification of Star Wars merchandise, making each volume timeless.

Volume 1 focuses on non-toy merchandise (1977–2012) and volume 2 is made up of the toy categories exclusively. The first edition of the first two volumes was reprinted through 2021. In 2023, volume 3 was published, resuming where the others had paused and catching up on the identification of 70,000 items manufactured in the 10 years from 2012–2022. Volume 3 also combined the toys and merchandise back under a single cover for the first time since 2009. The collection of the first three volumes, which cover just over 140,000 Star Wars collectibles, provides fans and collectors with the incredible listing of 45 years of Star Wars treasures.

This book is the second edition of volume 1, entirely redeveloped cover to cover. The first edition of volume 1 contained almost 12,000 items from 1977 through 2011. This edition, still focused exclusively on the merchandise, has over 8,000 additional items represented from that time and is the successor to the first edition of volume 1. You can retire your first edition of volume 1, but do not recycle it. This edition offers new selections of photography and refers back to the previous edition for any photography that was not selected for inclusion in this edition. **An informed collector will have every book on their shelf for a complete reference to identifying Star Wars collectibles.**

THIS BOOK: CATEGORY INDEX: VOLUME 1, Second Edition

Non-Toy Merchandise
1977–2012

Address Books	12
Advertising	12
Advertising Displays	15
Air Fresheners	19
Albums, Collecting	19
Answering Machines	20
Arcade: Pinball Machines	20
Arcade: Slot Machines	20
Arcade: Video Games	21
Armor	21
Art	21
Art: Animation Cels	21
Art: Cardbacks	22
Art: Crystal and Glass	22
Art: Lithography	23
Art: Metal	23
Art: Portfolios	23
Art: Prints	24
Art: Prints, ChromeArt	27
Autographs	27
Backpack Tags and Mascots	38
Backpacks and Carry Bags	38
Badges	44
Bags	47
Bags, Drawstring	47
Bags, Shopping Totes	47
Balloons	48
Bandages	48
Bank Books	49
Banks	49
Barware	52
Bath Mats	52
Bathroom Sets	52
Beachpads	52
Bedding: Bed Covers	52
Bedding: Blankets	52
Bedding: Comforters	53
Bedding: Pillowcases	53
Bedding: Pillows	53
Bedding: Sheets	54
Bedskirts	55
Belt Buckles	55
Belt Packs	56
Belts	56
Bicycle Accessories	58
Bicycles	58
Binders	59
Binoculars and Telescopes	59
Blueprints	59
Book Covers	59
Book Ends	59
Book Lists	59
Bookmarks	60
Bookplates	61

BOOKS

• Activity	61
• Art	63
• Audio, Cassette	64
• Audio, CD	65
• Coloring	65
• Cooking	67
• Educational	67
• Galaxy of Fear	68
• Game Guides	68
• Guides	69
• Jedi Apprentice	71
• Jedi Quest	71
• Junior Jedi Knights	71
• Make Your Own Adventure	71
• Music	71
• Non-Fiction	72
• Novels	73
• Pop-Up / Action / Flap	78
• Poster	79
• Science Adventures	79
• Scripts	80
• Star Wars Adventures	80
• Story	80
• Technical	84
• Trivia	84
• Young Jedi Knights	85
• Young Reader	85

Bottle Cap Accessories	87
Bottle Caps	87
Bottle Openers	94
Bowling Ball Bags	94
Bowling Balls	94
Boxes: Ceramic	94
Boxes: Plastic / Resin	94
Boxes: Tin	94
Buckets, Canvas	96
Buckets, Food	97
Bumper Stickers	97
Business Card Holders	97
Business Cards	97
Buttons	97
Buttons, Sewing	103
Cake Decorating Supplies	104
Cake Pans	105
Cakes	105
Calculators	105
Calendar Datebooks	105
Calendar Planners	105
Calendars	105
Calendars, Perpetual	110
Calling Cards, Telephone	110
Cameras	112
Can Holders and Cozys	112
Candles	112
Candlestick Holders	113
Candy Covers	113
Candy Jars	113
Canteens	113

CARDS

• Precious Metals	113
• Trading	113
• 30th Anniversary	114
• 3D, A New Hope	114
• 3D, Empire Strikes Back	114
• 3D, The Phantom Menace	115
• 501st	115
• A New Hope	115
• Attack of the Clones	115
• Bend-Ems	116
• Card Game	116
• Ceramic	116
• Chrome Archives	116
• Clone Wars	116
• DinaMics	116
• Discs	117
• Empire Strikes Back	117
• Empire Strikes Back Giant Photo	117
• Evolution	117
• Evolution Update	118
• Fanclub	118
• Force Attax	119
• Heritage	119
• Mastervision	119
• Mini-Movies	119
• Miscellaneous	119
• Movie Shots	119
• Pack-Ins	119
• Parody	120
• Pilot Licenses	120
• Premiums	120
• Rebel Legion	122
• Return of the Jedi	122
• Revenge of the Sith	123
• Role Playing	123

• Saga	123
• Shadows of the Empire	124
• Signing	124
• Star Wars Finest	124
• Star Wars Galaxy I	124
• Star Wars Galaxy II	124
• Star Wars Galaxy III	124
• Star Wars Galaxy IV	124
• Star Wars Galaxy V	124
• Star Wars Galaxy VI	124
• Star Wars Galaxy VII	124
• Star Wars Galaxy Magazine	124
• Tarot	124
• The Phantom Menace	124
• Tin	126
• Trading Card Game	126
• Trading Card Game, Pocketmodels	127
• TV Week	127
• Vehicle	127
• Wallet	127
• Widevision	127
CCG (Customizable Card Game)	128
CD Wallets	130
Cellular Phone Accessories	130
Cellular Phone Cases and Faceplates	131
Cellular Phone Straps	131
Cellular Phones	133
Certificates	133
Chalkboards	133
Champagne and Wine	134
Checkbook Covers	134
Checks	134
Cigar Bands	134
Clipboards	136
Clippos	136
Clocks	136

Clothing

• Aprons	138
• Baby	138
• Bibs, Baby	139
• Boots	139
• Caps	139
• Earmuffs	142
• Gloves and Mittens	143
• Hats	143
• Hoodies	144
• Jackets	144
• Leg Warmers	145
• Neckties	146
• Outfits, 2-Piece	146
• Overalls	147
• Pants and Shorts	147
• Ponchos	148
• Robes	148
• Scarves	148
• Shirts	148
• Shoes, Sandals, and Slippers	159
• Sleepwear	161
• Socks and Tights	163
• Suspenders	166
• Sweaters and Vests	166
• Swimming Attire	166
• Undergarments	166
• Visors	169
• Warm-Up Suits	169
• Wristbands, Headbands, Sweatbands	169

Coasters	169
Coins	170
Coins: Action Figure	174
Coins: Elongated	177
Coins: Premiums	178
Cologne and Perfume	178
Combs	178

Comic Books	179
Computers	183
Computers: Dust Covers	183
Computers: Keyboards	183
Computers: Mice	183
Computers: Mouse Pads	184
Computers: Software	185
Computers: USB Drives	185
Computers: Wrist Rest	186
Condoms	186
Confetti	186
Construction Paper	186
Containers, Figural	186
Cookie Jars	186
Cooking Cutters	187
Coolers	188
Cork Boards	188
Cosmetics	188
Costume Accessories	188
Costumes	189
Costumes: Makeup Kits	191
Costumes: Masks	191
Coupons	193
Crackers	193
Credit and ATM Cards	194
Crowns, Paper	194
Cup Toppers	194
Cups: Disposable	194
Curtains	197
Danglers	197
Decals	198
Deodorant	198
Desktop Organizers	198
Diaries	199

DISHES

• Bowls	199
• Cups	199
• Dish Sets	205
• Egg Cups	205
• Food Storage	206
• Glasses	206
• Glasses, Shot	208
• Mugs	209
• Pitchers	215
• Plates and Platters	215
• Salt Shakers	215
• Steins	215
• Teapots	216
• Trays	216
• Utensils	216

Dispensers: Candy	217
Dispensers: Food	220
Dispensers: Gum	220
Dispensers: Soap / Lotion	220
Dog Tags	220
Doorknob Hangers	221
Dry Erase Memo Boards	221
Earphones and Headphones	221
Erasers	222
Eyewear: Glasses	225
Fabrics	225
Fans	225
Fans, Hand	225
Figures: Ceramic	226
Figurines: Galactic Village Collection	226
Figurines: Porcelain	226
Film	227
Film Frames	227
Fish Tanks	227
Fishing Accessories	227
Flags	227
Flashlights and Lanterns	227
Folders	228

FURNITURE
- Inflatable 229
- Beds 229
- Bookcases 229
- Chairs and Sofas 229
- Clothes Racks 230
- Desks 230
- Nightstands 230
- Tables 231
- Toy Chests and Storage 231

Game Pieces, Promotional 231
Geocaching Coins and Path Tags 234
Gift Bags 235
Gift Boxes 235
Gift Cards 235
Gift Certificates 237
Gift Tags 237
Gift Wrap 237
Glow In The Dark Decorations 238
Glowsticks 239
Glue 239
Gocarts 239
Golf Bags 239
Golf Ball Markers 239
Golf Club Covers 239
Goodie Bags 239
Greeting Cards 239
Greeting Cards: Valentines, Boxed 246
Growth and Height Charts 247
Guidemaps 247
Guitar Cases 247
Guitar Picks 247
Guitar Straps 248
Guitars 248
Gumball Machines 249
Gym Sets 248
Hair Gel 248
Handbills 248
Handkerchiefs 248
Helmets, Miniature 248
Helmets, Sports 249

HOLIDAY
- Containers 249
- Decoration Crafts 250
- Easter Egg Coloring Kits 250
- Easter Eggs 250
- Easter Grass 251
- Lighting 251
- Ornaments 251
- Stockings 258

Holograms 258
Inflatables 258
Instrument Knobs 258
Iron-On Transfers 259

JEWELRY
- Bracelets 259
- Bracelets, Charm 259
- Charms 259
- Cufflinks 259
- Earrings 259
- Hair Barrettes, Bows, Scrunchies 260
- Necklaces 260
- Rings 261

Journals, Blank 262
Key Covers 263
Keychains 263
Keys, Hotel 274
Lampshades 274
Lamps and Lights 274
Lamps and Lights, Night and Reading 274
Lanyards 275
Laser Light Spinners 275
Laser Pointers 275
Laundry Bags and Hampers 275
License Plates 276
Lip Balm 276
Lotion 277
Lottery Scratch-Off Tickets 277
Luggage 280
Luggage Tags 280
Lunch Boxes 280
Magnets 284
Matchboxes 291
Mats 291
Medallions 291
Medals 291
Media Player Accessories 291
Media Players: CD 291
Media Players: Digital 291
Media Players: Radio, Cassette 292

MEDIA
Audio: Cassettes 292
Audio: CDs 293
Audio: Records 294
Audio: Tapes: 8-Track 296
Audio: Tapes: Reel-to-Reel 297
Movies: Discs: DVDs, Blu-ray 297
Movies: Film 298
Movies: Laser Discs and CEDs 298
Movies: Video Cassette Storage 299
Movies: Video Cassettes 299

Milk Caps 301
Mirrors 301
Mobiles 302
Molds, Candy and Food 302
Movie Cash Certificates 302
Music Boxes 302
Name Badges 303
Newspaper Strips 303
Note Cubes 303
Notebooks, Tablets, and Memo Pads 303
Note Cards 309
Nut Crackers 309
Oil Lamps 309
Oven Mitts 309

PACKAGING
- Bags and Boxes 310
- Beverage 310
- Candy 317
- Cards 325
- Cereal 327
- Cleaners 331
- Cookies 331
- Facial Tissue 334
- Food Trays 334
- Food Wrappers 334
- Fruit Snacks 340
- Gum 342
- Ice Cream 343
- Kids Meals 343
- Margarine 345
- Nuts 345
- Paper Cups 345
- Shoes 346
- Snack Chips 346
- TCG 351
- Yogurt 351

Pads,Sports 352
Pails: Tin 352
Paint 352
Paper Clips and Note Tabs 352
Paper Reinforcements 352
Paper Toweling 353
Paper Weights 353

PARTY
- Bags and Treat Boxes 353
- Banners 354
- Blowouts 354
- Centerpieces 354
- Decorations 355
- Games 356
- Hats 356
- Invitations 356
- Mazes 357
- Napkins 357
- Place Cards 358
- Plates 358
- Ribbons 359
- Supplies 359
- Table Covers 359
- Thank You Cards 360

Passports 360
Patches 360
Patterns 365
Pencil and Pen Toppers 365
Pencil Cases and Boxes 366
Pencil Cups 368
Pencil Sharpeners 368
Pencil Trays 369
Pencils 369
Pennants 371
Pens and Markers 372
Pet Accessories 376
Pewter 376
Photo Albums 378
Photo Frames 378
Piano Rolls, Player 378
Piñatas 378
Pins 379
Pins, Stick and Lapel 390
Placemats 391
Plate Racks 392
Plates: Collector 392
Play Houses 393
Playing Cards 394
Pog Slammers 395
Pogs 395
Poker Chips 396
Popcorn Poppers 396
Postcards 396
Posters 400
Posters: Mini 408
Press Kits 409
Pucks 409
Punch-Out Activities 409
Purses / Carry Bags 409
Purses, Coin 409
Push Pins 410
Refrigerators 410
Remote Controls 410
Replicas 410
Role-Playing Game 413
Role-Playing Miniatures 415
Role-Playing Miniatures: Starship Battles 420
Rubber Bands 420
Rubber Stamps 420
Rugs 421
Rulers 421
School Boxes 422
School Kits 423
Scientific Learning 424
Scissors 424
Scooters 424
Scrapbooking Supplies 425
Scrapbooks 425
Sheet Music 425
Shoe Charms 425
Shoelaces 425
Shower Curtains 426
Signs 426
Skateboards 426
Skates: Ice, Roller, and Inline 426
Slap Bands 427
Sleeping Bags 427
Snow Tubes and Sleds 427
Snow globes and Water Globes 427
Soap Dishes 428
Soap, Sanitizer, and Body Wash 428
Soap: Bubble Bath 429
Soap: Shampoo 430
Speakers 431
Spinners and Fidget Toys 431
Sponges 431
Sprinklers 431
Stamp Collecting Kits 431
Stamps 431
Standees 432
Stationary 433
Statues and Busts 434
Stencils 443

STICKERS 443
- A New Hope 450
- Attack of the Clones 450
- Clone Wars 451
- Empire Strikes Back 451
- Heritage 451
- Parody 451
- Premiums 451
- Return of the Jedi 457
- Revenge of the Sith 459
- Saga 460
- The Phantom Menace 460

Straws 461
String Dispensers 461
Subway Tickets 462
Super Packs 462
Switch Plates and Covers 462
Tape and Dispensers 462
Tattoos, Temporary 463
Tazo 465
Telephones 466
Tents 466
Thermos 466
Thimbles 466
Timers, Kitchen 467
Tissue Covers 467
Toasters 467
Tooth Care 467
Toothbrush Holders 467
Toothbrushes 467
Toothpaste 469
Totes, Record and Tape 469

TOWELS
- Bath 469
- Beach 469
- Hand 471
- Hooded 471
- Washcloth 471

Toy Storage 472
Transfers 472
Travel Kits 473
Umbrellas 474
USB Devices 474
Vases 475
Vehicles, Display 475
Vehicles, Propeller Driven 475
Vending Machine Translites 475
Vitamins 476
Walkie Talkies and Text Messengers 476
Wall Decorations 476
Wallet Chains 476
Wallets 477
Wallpaper 477
Waste Baskets 477
Watches 478
Watches, Digital 481
Watches, Pocket 481
Water Bottles 487
Window Clings 487

OTHER BOOKS IN THIS SERIES

INDEXES OF CATEGORIES FOR VOLUME 2 AND VOLUME 3

Toys 1977–2022 *Merchandise and Toys 2012–2022*

VOLUME 2: Second Edition
Toys 1977–2022

ACTION FIGURES by Scale
- 2″ Scale 10
- 2.5″ Scale 10
- 3.75″ Scale 1977-1986 10
- 3.75″ Scale 1995-1999 26
- 3.75″ Scale 1999-2006 45
- 3.75″ Scale 2006-2015 71
- 3.75″ Scale 2015-2022 110
- 3.75″ Scale Accessories 129
- 3.75″ Scale Creatures 131
- 3.75″ Scale Display Stands 133
- 3.75″ Scale Modern Vintage 119
- 3.75″ Scale Playsets 129
- 3.75″ Scale Storage Cases 136
- 3.75″ Scale Vehicles 136
- 5″ Scale 151
- 5″ Scale Vehicles 153
- 6″ (1:12) Scale 153
- 6″ (1:12) Scale Creatures 163
- 6″ (1:12) Scale Display Stands 164
- 6″ (1:12) Scale Vehicles 164
- 8″ Scale 164
- 10″ Scale 165
- 12″ (1:6) Scale 165
- 12″ (1:6) Scale Creatures 177
- 12″ (1:6) Scale Playsets 177
- 12″ (1:6) Scale Vehicles 177
- 14″ Scale 178
- 18″ (1:4) Scale 178
- 31″ Scale 179
- 42″ Scale 179

Action Fleet Battle Pack 179
Action Fleet Classic Duels 181
Action Fleet Mini Scenes 181
Action Fleet Playsets 181
Action Fleet Series Alpha 182
Action Fleet Vehicles 182
Backpack Tags and Mascots 186
Balls 190
Balls, Beach 192
Balls, Hopper 192
Balls, Punching 193
Baseball Equipment 193
Block Toys 194
Bobble Heads 194
Boomerangs 215
Bop Bags 215
Bubble Toys 215
Building Brick Toys and Figures 216
Coins: Action Figure 232
Collector Fleet Toys 235

CRAFTS
- Art Kits 235
- Beads 237
- Clay 237
- Clip-Alongs 237
- Coloring Sets 238
- Cricut Materials 239
- Doodle Kits 239
- Figure Makers 239
- Latchhook Kits 240
- Meon Light Kits 240
- Paint-By-Number 240
- Paintable Figures 240
- Paper 241
- Poster Art Kits 241
- Sewing Kits 242
- Sun Catcher Kits 243
- Watercolor Paint Sets 243

Crayons and Chalk 243
Dagedar Racers 243
Dagedar Racers Tracks and Accessories 244
Dartboards 244
Darts Accessories 244
Decision Making Toys 245
Dice 245
Dolls: Collector 245
Dolls: Nesting 245

FIGURES
- Action Masters 246
- Angry Birds 246
- Attacktix 247
- Bearbrick 249
- Bend-Ems 250
- Epic Battles 252
- Epic Force 253
- Fighter Pods (Micro Force) 253
- Force Battlers 255
- Galactic Heroes 255
- Hero Mashers 261
- Infinity 3.0 262
- Jedi Force 262
- Kubrick 264
- Metal 266
- Micro Force (Fighter Pods) 267
- Mighty Beanz 268
- Mighty Beanz Accessories 269
- Mighty Muggs 270
- Mini 271
- Mini: Building Brick 277
- Mpire 283
- Plastic / Resin / Vinyl 283
- Rollinz 293
- Totems 293
- Unleashed 295
- Unleashed Battle Packs 296

Fingerboards 298
Flight Controllers 298
Flying Discs 299

GAMES
- Angry Birds 301
- Board 301
- Box Busters 306
- Card 307
- Chess 310
- Consoles, Controllers, Accessories 313
- Dice 314
- Domino 314
- Electronic 315
- Foosball 317
- Midway 317
- Outdoor 317
- Pachinko 317
- Pinball 317
- Star Wars Command 318
- Target 320
- Video 320

Gliders 324
Inflatable Toys 324
Kaleidoscopes 324
Kites 324
Koosh Balls 326
Marbles 326
Micro Collection 327
Micro Collection Figures 328

MICRO MACHINES 329
- Boxed Sets 331
- Epic Collections 332
- Figures 332
- Mega-Deluxe Playsets 334
- Micro Vehicles 334
- Mini-Action Sets 334
- Platform Action Sets 336
- Podracers 337
- Transforming Action Sets 337
- Vehicle / Figure Collections 340
- Vehicle Collections 341
- Vehicles 345
- X-Ray Fleet 361

Models: Metal 361
Models: Paper 353
Models: Plastic 354
Models: Resin 364
Models: Wood / Balsa 364
Paddle Balls 365
Party Toys 365
Play-Doh and Soft Clay Sets 366
Pool Toys 367
Potato Head Character Toys 369
Premium Toys 370
Preschool Ewok Toys 379
Projectors / Viewers 380
Puppets 381
Racing and Diecast Toy Play Sets 382
Racing and Diecast Toys 382
Racing Sets 397
Radio, Remote, App Controlled Toys 397
Rockets, Air 399
Rockets, Model 399
Role Playing Toys 400
Room Alerts 400
Rubber Ducks 401
Sit-and-Spins 401
Slime, Goo, and Putty 401
Slingers 401
Snow Tubes and Sleds 403
Spyware 403
Squeaky Toys 403
Suction Cup Toys 403
Toys and Dolls, Plush 404
Toys, Electronic 420
Toys, Miscellaneous 422
Toys, Miscellaneous Droid 425
Train Cars 425
Transformers 425
Vehicles, Battle Rollers 427
Vehicles, Diecast and Plastic 428
Vehicles, Diecast and Plastic Play Sets 436
Vehicles, Motorized 437
Vehicles, Propeller Driven 437
Voice Changers 437
Walkie-Talkies and Text Messengers 438
Water Guns 439
Weapon Toys 440
Wind-Up Toys 449
Wonder World 451
Yo-Yos 451

VOLUME 3
Merchandise and Toys 2012-2022

SECTION 1: MERCHANDISE

3D Printing Schematic Files 10
Advertising 10
Advertising Displays 13
Air Fresheners 15
Albums, Collecting 15
Arcade: Pinball Machines 16
Arcade: Video Games 16

ART 16
- Animation Cels 16
- Cardbacks 17
- Crystal and Glass 17
- Lithography 17
- Metal 19
- Portfolios 19
- Prints 19

Autographs 34
Automobile Accessories 34
Automobile Mats 35
Automobile Mirror Accessories 35
Automobile Seat Covers 35
Automobile Shades 35
Automobile Steering Wheel Covers 36
Awards 36
Backpack Tags and Mascots 36
Backpacks and Carry Bags 40
Badges 46
Bags 47
Bags, Drawstring 47
Bags, Shopping Totes 48
Balloons 48
Bandages 51
Bandanas 51
Banks 51
Banners: Advertising 53
Barware 53
Bathmats 53
Bathroom Sets 53
Beach Pads 54

BEDDING
- Bedcovers 54
- Blankets 55
- Pillows 57
- Sheets 59

Belt Buckles 59
Belt Packs 59
Belts 59
Bicycle Accessories 61
Bicycles 61
Binders 61
Binoculars and Telescopes 61
Birdhouses 61
Bobble Heads 62
Book Covers 79
Bookends 79
Booklights 80
Bookmarks 80

BOOKS
- Activity 81
- Art 82
- Audio, CD 82
- Coloring 82
- Cooking 83
- E-Book 84
- Educational 84
- Game Guides 85
- Graphic Novels 85
- Guides 85
- Make Your Own Adventure 87
- Music 87
- Non-Fiction 87
- Novels 88

Indexes of Other Books in This Series

• Pop-Up / Action / Flap 91
• Poster 91
• Read-Along 91
• Story 91
• Young Reader 93

Bottle Cap Accessories 95
Bottle Caps 96
Bottle Openers 96

BOXES
• Ceramic 97
• Decorative 97
• Plastic / Resin 97
• Tin 97

Buckets, Canvas 98
Buckets, Food 98
Bulletin Board Supplies 99
Bumper Stickers 99
Business Card Holders 99
Business Cards 99
Buttons 99
Buttons, Sewing 102
Cake Decorating Supplies 102
Cake Pans 102
Calendar Datebooks 102
Calendar Planners 102
Calendars 103
Calendars, Perpetual 106
Calling Cards, Telephone 106
Camera Accessories 108
Cameras 108
Can and Bottle Holders 109
Candles 110
Candlestick Holders 110
Candy Jars 110
Card Sleeves and Holders 110
Cards, Precious Metals 111
Cards, Trading 111

CARDS
• 3D, Revenge of the Sith 111
• 40th Anniversary 111
• 501st 111
• A New Hope 111
• Chrome Perspectives 112
• Chrome Perspectives: Jedi vs Sith 112
• Cosmic Shells 112
• Discs 112
• Discs, Galactic Connexions 113
• Empire Strikes Back 113
• Evolution 2016 113
• Fathead Tradeable 113
• Force Attax 113
• Galactic Files 114
• Galactic Files 2 114
• Galactic Files Reborn 114
• High Tek 114
• Illustrated, A New Hope 116
• Illustrated, Empire Strikes Back 116
• Jedi Legacy 116
• Journey of the Child 116
• Journey to The Force Awakens 116
• Journey To The Last Jedi 117
• Masterwork 117
• Miscellaneous 117
• Pack-Ins 118
• Parody 118
• Perspectives 118
• Premiums 118
• Rebels 119
• Return of the Jedi 119
• Rogue One 119
• Saga 120
• Saga Giant Photo 120
• Solo 120
• Star Wars Galaxy VI 121
• Star Wars Galaxy VII 121
• Star Wars Galaxy VIII 122
• The Force Awakens 122
• The Force Awakens, Chrome 123
• The Last Jedi 123
• The Mandalorian, Season 1 124
• Trading Card Game 125
• Trading Card Game, Pocketmodels 125

Cases, Transit Pass 125
CD Wallets 125
Cellphone Accessories 125
Cellphone Cases and Faceplates 126
Cellphone Straps 127
Cellphones 127
Ceramic and Chalkware, Hobby 127
Chalkboards 127
Chargers: USB 127
Clips, Snack Chip 128
Clocks 129
Clothing Hooks 129

CLOTHING
• Aprons 129
• Baby 130
• Bibs, Baby 130
• Blindfolds 130
• Boots 130
• Caps 131
• Dresses and Skirts 134
• Gloves and Mittens 135
• Hats 136
• Hoodies 140
• Jackets 142
• Leg Warmers 143
• Masks 143
• Neck Gaiters 143
• Neckties 143
• Outfits, 2-Piece 144
• Pajamas 144
• Pants and Shorts 147
• Ponchos 148
• Robes 148
• Scarves 148
• Shirts and Sweatshirts 149
• Shoes, Sandals, and Slippers 156
• Socks and Tights 159
• Sweaters and Vests 164
• Swimming Attire 166
• Undergarments 167
• Wrist Bands and Sweatbands 171

Coasters 172
Coffee Makers 173

COINS 173
• Challenge / Personal 177
• Elongated 177
• Premiums 178

Cologne and Perfume 179
Comic Books 180

COMPUTERS
• Tablets, and Smart Devices 187
• Dust Covers 187
• Mice 187
• Software 187
• USB Drives 187

Confetti 189
Containers, Figural 189
Cookie Jars 189
Cooking Cutters 190
Coolers 191
Cork Boards 191
Cosmetics 191
Costumes 192
Costumes: Masks 193
Coupons 193

CRAFTS
• Art Kits 194
• Beads 196
• Clay 196
• Coloring Sets 196
• Cricut Materials 196
• Doodle Kits 197
• Figure Makers 197
• Meon Light Kits 197
• Paintable Figures 197
• Paint-By-Number 197
• Paper 197
• Poster Art Kits 197
• Sewing Kits 197
• Sun Catcher Kits 198

Crayons and Chalk 198
Credit and ATM Cards 198
Cup Toppers 198
Cups: Disposable 198
Cutting boards 199
Decals 199
Disco Balls 201

DISHES
• Bowls 201
• Cups 202
• Dish Sets 207
• Egg Cups 208
• Food Storage 208
• Glasses 208
• Glasses, Shot 210
• Measuring Cups 210
• Mugs 210
• Pans and Baking 213
• Pitchers and Jugs 214
• Pizza Cutters 214
• Plates and Platters 214
• Salt Shakers 215
• Spatulas 216
• Steins 217
• Teapots 217
• Trays 217
• Utensils 217

Dispensers: Candy 218
Dispensers: Food 220
Dispensers: Soap / Lotion 220
Dog Tags 220
Doorknob Hangers 217
Doormats 217
Dry Erase Memo Boards 222
Earphones and Headphones 222
Easter Egg Coloring Kits 223
Easter Eggs 223
Envelopes 224
Erasers 224
Exercise and Activity Monitors 225
Eyewear: Glasses 225
Eyewear: Glasses, Accessories 227
Fabrics 227
Fans 230
Fans, Hand 230
Fasteners 230
Film Frames 231
Fishing Accessories 231
Flags 231
Flashlights and Lanterns 231
Foam Heads and Stress Dolls 233
Folders 233

FURNITURE
• Beds 234
• Bookcases 234
• Chairs and Sofas 234
• Desks 235
• Inflatable 234
• Pillows and Pads 235
• Stools 235
• Tables 236
• Toy Chests and Storage 236

Game Pieces, Promotional 236
Geocaching Coins and Path Tags 236
Gift Bags 236
Gift Boxes 237
Gift Cards 237
Gift Tags 238
Gift Wrap 238
Glowsticks 238
Goggles 3D 239
Greeting Cards 238
Greeting Cards: Valentines, Boxed 242
Growth and Height Charts 243
Guide Maps 243
Guitar Picks 243
Guitar Straps 244
Guitars 244
Hair Gel 244
Hairbrushes 244
Hand Warmers 244
Handkerchiefs 244

Headbands and Ears 244
Helmets, Sports 245
Hitch Covers 245

HOLIDAY
• Containers 245
• Decor 245
• Decoration Crafts 245
• Lighting 245
• Ornaments 245
• Stocking Hangers 251
• Stockings 251

Humidifiers 253
Ice Scrapers 253
Ice Trays and Blocks 253
Iron-On Transfers 253

JEWELRY
• Boxes 254
• Bracelets 254
• Bracelets, Charm 255
• Charms 255
• Cufflinks 256
• Earrings 257
• Hair Barrettes and Bows 259
• MagicBands 259
• Necklaces 259
• Pendants 261
• Rings 261
• Shirt Studs 262
• Tie Bars 262

Journals, Blank 262
Kaleidoscopes 263
Key Blanks 263
Key Chains 263
Key Covers 266
Keys, Collectible 266
Keys, Hotel 267
Kitchen Appliances 267
Kites 267
Knife Blocks 267
Lamps and Lights 267
Lamps and Lights: Night and Reading Lights 268
Lanyards 269
Laser Pointers 270
Laundry Bags and Hampers 270
License Plate Frames 270
License Plates 270
Lighters 270
Lip Balm 271
Lotion 271
Luggage 271
Luggage Tags 272
Lunch Boxes 273
Magnetic Playsets 274
Magnets 274
Masks 275
Medals 276

MEDIA PLAYERS
• Accessories 276
• CD 277
• Digital 277

MEDIA, AUDIO
Cassettes 277
CDs 277
Records 277

MEDIA, MOVIES
• Discs: DVDs, Blu-Ray, 3D, 4K 278

Menus 279
Metal Detectors 279
Mirrors 279

MODELS
• Metal 280
• Paper 281
• Plastic 282
• Vinyl 284
• Wood / Balsa 285

Indexes of Other Books in This Series

Molds, Candy and Food 285
Money Clips 285
Mouth Wash 285
Mouthwash 285
Name Badges 285
Notebooks, Tablets, Memo Pads 286
Note Cards 288
Novelties, Adult 288
Nut Crackers 288
Oven Mitts 289

PACKAGING
• Beverage 289
• Candy 291
• Cereal 296
• Cookies 299
• Facial Tissue 300
• Food Storage Bags 301
• Food Trays 301
• Food Wrappers 301
• Fruit Snacks 304
• Gum 306
• Ice Cream 306
• Kids Meals 306
• Paper Cups 306
• Shoes 307
• Snack Chips 307
• Yogurt 308

Pads: Sports 309
Pails: Tin 309
Paint 309
Paper 310
Paper Clips and Note Tabs 310

PARTY
• Banners 311
• Blowouts 311
• Centerpieces 311
• Decorations 311
• Games 311
• Hats 311
• Invitations 311
• Masks 311
• Mazes 311
• Napkins 313
• Place Cards 313
• Plates 313
• Ribbons 313
• Supplies 313
• Table Covers 313
• Thank You Cards 315
• Toys 313

Passport Covers 315
Passports 315
Pencil and Pen Toppers 315
Pencil Boards 316
Pencil Cases / Boxes 316
Pencil Sharpeners 318
Pencils 318
Pens and Markers 319
Pet Accessories 321
Pet Toys 322
Pewter 324
Photo Boxes 325
Photo Frames and Desktop Holders 325
Picnic Totes 325
Pillows, Travel 325
Piñatas 325
Pins 325
Pins, Lapel 329
Placemats 329
Planters 329
Playhouses 329
Playing Cards 330
Pocket Knives 330
Poker Chips 330
Pool Toys 330
Pools 331
Popcorn Poppers 331
Postcards 331
Poster Tubes 332
Posters 332

Posters: Mini 333
Power Outlet Controllers 333
Press Kits 333
Pucks 333
Punch-Out Activities 333
Purses / Carry Bags 333
Purses, Coin 335
Push Pins 335
Razors 335
Razors: Disposable 336
Refrigerators 336
Remote Controls 336
Replicas 336
Ribbon 336
Rubber Bands 336
Rubber Stamps 336
Rugs 337
Rulers and Tape Measures 337
School Kits 337
Scientific Learning 338
Scooters 338
Scrapbooking Supplies 338
Scrapbooks 339
Sewing baskets 339
Shoe Charms 339
Shower Curtain Hooks 340
Shower Curtains 340
Signs 340
Skateboards 340
Skates, Roller and In-line 340
Slap Bands 340
Sleeping Bags 341
Snow Globes and Water Globes 341
Soap Dishes 341
Soap, Sanitizer, and Body Wash 341
Soap: Bubble Bath 342
Soap: Shampoo 343
Speakers 343
Spinners 343
Sprinklers 343
Stamps, Postage 343
Stationary 344
Statues and Busts 345
Stencils 345

STICKERS 347
• Angry Birds 349
• Clone Wars 350
• Premiums 350
• The Force Awakens 351
Straws 352
Stylus' 352
Sunscreen 352
Swabs 352
Tape and Dispensers 352
Tattoos 352
Tazo 354
Teacher Supplies 354
Tents 354
Thermoses 354
Tickets 354
Timers, Kitchen 355
Toasters, Pancake, Waffle Makers 355
Tools 356
Tooth Care 356
Toothbrush Holders 356
Toothbrushes 356
Toothpaste 356
Toothpick Holders 356

TOWELS
• Bath 357
• Beach 357
• Hand 358
• Hooded 358
• Wash Cloths 358

Tracking Tags 358
Travel Kits 358
Umbrellas 359
USB Devices 359
Utility Bins 359
Vacuum Cleaners 360
Vitamins 360

Wall Decorations 360
Wallet Chains 361
Wallets 361
Waste Baskets 363
Watches 363
Watches, Digital 365
Watches, Pocket 366
Water Bottles 366
Window Clings 367

VOLUME 3

Merchandise and Toys 2012-2022

SECTION 2: TOYS

ACTION FIGURES by Scale
• 2.5″ Figures 367
• 3.75″ 2011-2015 Figures 368
• 3.75″ 2015-2021 Figures 372
• 3.75″ Accessories 376
• 3.75″ Creatures 376
• 3.75″ Modern Vintage Collection 376
• 3.75″ Modern Vintage Collection Multi-packs 376
• 3.75″ Display Stands 377
• 3.75″ Scale Playsets 377
• 3.75″ Scale Vehicles 377
• 5″ Figures 379
• 5″ Vehicles 379
• 6″ (1:12 Scale) Figures 379
• 6″ (1:12 Scale) Creatures 384
• 6″ (1:12 Scale) Display Stands 384
• 6″ Modern Vintage Collection 384
• 6″ (1:12 Scale) Vehicles 384
• 8″ Figures 385
• 10″ Figures 385
• 12″ (1:6 Scale) Figures 385
• 12″ (1:6 Scale) Creatures 388
• 12″ (1:6 Scale) Playsets 388
• 12″ (1:6 Scale) Vehicles 388
• 14″ Figures 388
• 18″ (1:4 Scale) Figures 389
• 31″ Figures 389
• 42″ Figures 389

Balls 389
Balls, Beach 390
Balls, Punching 390
Baseball Equipment 390
Block Toys 391
Boomerangs 391
Bop Bags 391
Bubble Toys 391
Building Brick Toys and Figures 391
Dagedar Racers 395
Dagedar Tracks and Accessories 396
Dart Boards 396
Decision Making Toys 396
Dice 396
Dolls: Collector 396
Dolls: Nesting 396

FIGURES
• Action Masters 396
• Angry Birds 396
• Bearbrick 397
• Epic Battles 398
• Fighter Pods (Micro Force) 398
• Galactic Heroes 401
• Hero Mashers 401
• Infinity 3.0 401
• Jedi Force 402
• Metal 402
• Micro Force (Fighter Pods) 403
• Mighty Muggs 404
• Mini 404
• Mini: Building Brick 406
• Plastic / Resin / Vinyl 407
• Rollinz 413
• Totems 415

Figurines: Galactic Village 415
Figurines: Wood 415
Fingerboards 415

GAMES
• Angry Birds 415
• Board 416
• Box Busters 417
• Card 417
• Card, Star Wars The Card Game 418
• Chess 418
• Consoles, Controllers, Accessories 419
• Dice 420
• Domino 420
• Electronic 420
• Midway 420
• Outdoor 421
• Pinball 421
• Star Wars Command 421
• Target 423
• Video 423

Gliders 424
Helmets, Miniature 424
Inflatable Toys 425
Light-Up Toys 425

MICRO MACHINES 425
• Transforming Action Sets 425
• Vehicle / Figure Collections 425
• Vehicle Collections 425
• Vehicles 426

Miscellaneous Toys 426
Paddle Balls 427
Play-Doh and Soft Clay Sets 427
Plush Dolls and Toys 428
Potato Head Character Toys 433
Premium Toys 434
Projectors / Viewers 437
Puppets 437
Puzzles 437
Puzzles: Twisting 440
Racing and Diecast Toy Play Sets 441
Racing and Diecast Toys 441
Racing Sets 445
Radio, Remote, App Controlled Toys 446
Rockets, Air 446

ROLE PLAYING MINIATURES 447
• Armada 447
• Imperial Assault 447
• Legion 448
• Starship Battles 448
• X-Wing 448

Role Playing Toys 448
Room Alerts 448
Rubber Ducks 449
Slime, Goo, and Putty 449
Slingers 449
Spy Gear 450
Squeaky Toys 450
Train Cars 450
Vehicles, Battle Rollers 455
Vehicles, Diecast and Plastic 450
Vehicles, Motorized 455
Vehicles, Propeller Driven 455
Voice Changers 455
Walkie Talkies and Messengers 456
Water Guns 456
Weapon Toys 456
Wind-Up Toys 458
Yo-Yos 458
m

Abbreviations and Terms to Know

This book covers the first 35 years of Star Wars non-toy collectibles and merchandise from 1977–2012. Understanding the fan environment an item was produced for or around can be as important as knowing what an item is and its value.

It is not uncommon for more advanced fans or collectors to speak in specific terms or casually resort to abbreviations. Many years have gone by with the hobby undergoing linguistic and appraisal evolutions. Some terms have fallen out of favor, while others have become more standard with newer generations. An easy example of this change was the migration of describing an item on an arbitrary scale of C1 through C10 to now describing items using a 100-point, fully defined grading scale adopted from card, comic, and figure grading organizations.

The information that follows will assist with the decoding of some listings in this guide while also providing a general background around the type of promotions, characters, or series a collectible was produced to support.

IMAGE REFERENCES

Even within the same volume of this title, photo selections and set listings will vary in selection and in size from edition to edition.

When an item is pictured in a previous book and not the current one, a blue photo reference with book number and page number is present.

The book number is either an "edition" of the book from the original Collector Book series, or else a "Volume and edition" number from the current Schiffer series.

Example 1: [5:116]
The photo is in the Collector Books series, 5th edition, page 116.

Example 2: [V1e1:240]
The photo is in the Schiffer Publishing series, Volume 1, 1st edition, page 240.

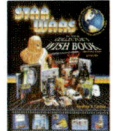

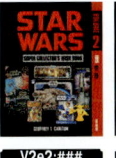

This table shows the cover of the current books in both series and their photo identification prefixes. Larger images of the covers are available on page 3.

GRADING TERMS (Informal)

Loose
An item is loose if no original packaging, instructions, inserts, or documents are included.

Loose / Mint / Complete (LMC)
An item is loose in like-new condition and all original accessories are included.

Open

Loose with Package (LWP)
The item is *loose* and the outer packaging is present. Inserts, applications, or documentation may or may not be included.

Stickers Applied
Stickers Applied is an enhancement description for Loose or LMC or LWP. For any item that includes stickers or decals, they may or not have the stickers applied.

Mint in Box (MIB)
Mint in Package (MIP)
The item may have been removed from the box but has been returned in original condition. Inserts, applications, accessories, and documentation are included. If the seal on a package has been broken, this description applies, even if the item has not ever been removed as it has the potential and ability to be removed and returned.

Mint in Sealed Package (MISP)
Never Removed From Box (NRFB)
Never Removed From Packaging (NRFP)
The seal on the original package is intact.

New with Tag (NWT)
Applies to items sold without exterior packaging, such as clothing, where the product information is supplied on a sticker or tag applied by the manufacturer directly to the item.

Condition 1–Condition 10 (C1–C10)
For the item's current state, a numeric rating from 1 to 10 with C10 being gem mint and C1 being severely broken. A loose action figure can be C1–C10. If the action figure is a C10 but is sealed in a C3 package, it is considered C3. The C-scale is descriptive of condition, not of value.

CONDITION DESCRIPTIONS

Shelf Wear
Corner dings, edge scuffs, and minor surface scratches or surface marring are examples of shelf wear.

Spider / Surface Veins
Thin surface cracks that do not penetrate every layer of the exterior packaging. Usually applies to carded items where stress points on one side do not impact the other side's appearance.

PRODUCTION / SOURCE

Production Error (single instance)
An obvious flaw from the manufacturer. Examples include incorrect aberrant paint application, insert or bubble inserted upside down, or incorrect product in package.

Variation
A change in the production of the actual item, the insert, or the packaging within a single run of the product. The reconfiguration of an action figure within the bubble insert or the changing of numbering, wording, graphics, or UPC on the packaging are examples.

Production Error (variation)
An incorrect detail, misspelled words, incorrect product code, or UPC later corrected in the single run are production error variations.

Bootleg
An item produced by an unlicensed individual, organization, or company specifically designed to appear to be a licensed product, especially an established licensed one. Parody products are excluded from the category label as they are not designed to be sold as actual licensed products, but as art.

Unlicensed
An item produced by an unlicensed individual, organization, or company intended to be sold as a unique product not bearing resemblance to other licensed products.

OOAK: One of a Kind
Any single item bearing a unique trait, not exclusive of other categories. A product with an abhorrent trait (paint application, packaging position, deformity in production, etc.) would be OOAK. The term is also used on occasion to represent unique artistic works not reproduced.

DESCRIPTIVE TERMS

COA: Certificate of Authenticity
A COA is a document that verifies the authenticity and provides important information about the item, such as the date or quantity which were produced.

AP: Artist Proof
An Artist Proof is a test production piece to quality check the process. If it is for a fixed number run, it is not counted in the total.

GRADING

Investment / Certified Grading
When an item has been submitted to an authoritative entity for authentication and documented to be in a certified condition as described and determined by that entity. Usually the item is then sealed within a protective case to deter that certified condition from changing over time.

EPISODIC FILMS

Prequel Trilogy (PT)
EPI:TPM or EPI or TPM or TPM3D
Episode I: The Phantom Menace
EPII:AOTC or EPII or AOTC
Episode II: Attack of the Clones
EPIII:ROTS or EPIII or ROTS
Episode III: Revenge of the Sith

Original Trilogy (OT)
EPIV:ANH or EPIV or ANH
Episode IV: A New Hope
EPV:ESB or EPV or ESB
Episode V: The Empire Strikes Back
EPVI:ROTJ or EPVI or ROTJ
Episode VI: Return of the Jedi

SW:SE or SE or Special Edition
1997 Special Edition theatrical releases of Star Wars, The Empire Strikes Back, and Return of the Jedi

Sequel Trilogy (ST)
EPVII:TFA or EPVII or TFA
Episode VII: The Force Awakens
EPVIII:TLJ or EPVIII or TLJ
Episode VIII: The Last Jedi
EPIX:ROS or EPIX or ROS
Episode IX: The Rise of Skywalker

ADDITIONAL FILMS

Ewoks: The Ewok Adventure
Ewoks: The Battle for Endor
Rogue One: A Star Wars Story
Solo: A Star Wars Story

MEDIA ERAS

Shadows of the Empire (SOTE)
Legends Universe. The time line story that takes place in between The Empire Strikes Back and Return of the Jedi.

The Force Unleashed (TFU)
A media tie-in in the Legends Universe that takes place during the Jedi purge, following Darth Vader and Vader's secret apprentice.

Acknowledgments with Gratitude

Data and Photography Contributors

Patrick Ahern: Collector
Chris Albright: Collector, Costumer
Jeff Allen: Costumer
Jose Arosa: Collector (Spain)
Victor Arriaga: Collector (Mexico)
Ryan Arsenaux: Collector
Dave Arvay: Collector
Gail Ashburn: Friend of the Book
Brittany Auth: Friend of the Book
Edgar Ayala: Son
Brit Barclay: Collector
Pedro Barrios: Collector (Mexico)
Virgil Bauer: Collector
Jad Bean: Collector
Jonathon Bearrie: Collector: Vintage Action Figures
Daniel Berghelli: Collector (Argentina)
Andrew Blazejowski: Collector
Aaron Bock: Collector
James Boryla: Collector / SWSeller.com
Ray Bossert: Collector
Chris Brennan: Collector (Australia)
Lawrence Broden: Collector
Sharon Bronson: Collector
Neil Brown: Collector: Autographs
Buzz Bumble: Collector (New Zealand)
Nathan P. Butler: Timeline Archive
Bill Cable: Collector, Artist
Jose Antonio Macias Ceron: Collector (Mexico)
John Caboco: Collector
Brian Callahan: Collector: Vintage and Glass
Ardith Carlton: Sister
Casey Carlton: Mother
Jose A. Carrera: Collector
Brian Carroll: Collector
Gordon Chan: Collector
Ann Charles: Friend of the Book
Mike Chockley: Collector
MJ Chung: Collector
Robert Clark: Friend of the Book
Cayleigh Coon: Niece
Hunter Coon: Nephew
Jennifer Coon: Sister
Shawn Coon: Brother

Steve Corder: attacktix.wikia.com
Andrew Cox: Collector (New Zealand)
Mike Cramutolo: Friend of the Book
Mark Cravens: Collector
Jeff Craycraft: Disney Collector
Wayne Crews: Collector: LEGOs
Chris Da Costa: Collector (Canada)
Justin Dalby: Collector, Costumer
Wayne Dale: Collector
Anthony Damata: Collector: Vintage
Earl Davis: Super Collector
Steven Davis: Collector, Costumer
Andrew Davison: Collector (United Kingdom)
Chris Dent: Collector
Thomas Derby IV: Collector: Vintage
Sophie Dessiméon: Collector (Belgium)
Ila Edger Dezarn: Collector
Shana Douglas: Sister
Nancy Dickson: Collector (Australia)
Andy Dukes: Collector (United Kingdom)
Darren Dyer: Collector
Brian Earles: Collector, Costumer
Kameron Earles: Collector, Costumer
John Eck: Collector
Sean Eckstadt: Collector
David Elliott: Collector: Cards (Australia)
Monty Elliott: Collector
Dan Emmons: Collector
Jeff Ensor: Collector
David Essex: Friend of the Book
Erica Facer: Collector, Costumer
Gillian Farschman: Friend of the Book
Gina Farschman: Friend of the Book
Chris Fawcett: Collector: Vintage and Pre-Production
Lawrence Fenton III: Son
Guy Fernous: Collector
Robert Fischer: Collector
Jack Flukinger: Collector, Costumer - *In Memoriam*
Riley Flukinger: Friend of the Book
Dave Fox: Collector: Patches
Edgard Villasenor Franco: Collector (Mexico)
Matthew Frey: Collector: Visual Media
David Frost: Collector

Norio Fujimoto: Collector
David Fuller: Owner: Official Star Wars Hummer
Tomás García: Collector
David Gee: Collector
Lori Gifford: Fan
Mike Glover: Costumer
Brian Graham: Collector
Evan Grant: Collector (Australia)
Bill Gray: Collector
Shawneequa Griffin: Friend of the Book
Mariyln Guyote: Collector - *In Memoriam*
Jon Harper: Collector
Jay Harris: Collector
Peter Hauerstein: Collector
Kevin Heffner: Collector (Canada)
Brian Heiar: Collector, Costumer
Jeff Hendrickson: Collector, Costumer
Mike Hessness: Collector
Paul Holstein: Collector: Trading Cards
Gerald Home: Actor, Friend of the Book - *In Memoriam*
Trevor Hopper: Friend of the Book
Scott Horne: Collector
Cole and Catherine Houston: Collectors
Shawn Houze: Collector: Beverage Bottles and Cans
Steve Hovis: Collector
Mark Huff: Gamer
Laura Hughes: Friend of the Book
David Humphries: Collector: Bootleg Action Figures
Mark Ivy: Collector
Warren Jacobsen: Super Collector, Costumer
Keith Jakubowski: Collector
Joel R. Jamison: Collector
Erik Janniche: Collector
Bryan Janorske: Collector
Stephen Jones: Collector (United Kingdom)
Dan Joplin: Collector: Replicas, Costumer
Samantha Juve: Sister
Cathy Kendrick: Collector: Cards / Stickers
Sara Kelley: Friend of the Book
Tim Kennedy: Collector
Alistair Kirkland: Collector
Deborah Kittle: Super Collector
Ryan Koller: Collector

If you read Star Wars books and magazines or follow the collectibles news sites, several names will stand out as people who have established themselves as trusted experts in the community. Also contributing are a combination of experts who walk quietly among us and collectors who took an interest in being a part of the collectibles documentation project.

Some sent in photography. Some researched and reported current values from auctions and sales sources. A couple of them filled in checklists. Several reported items exclusive to their country. It is amazing to learn how every one of them found a unique way to share their time and knowledge. What they have in common is that they all cared enough to do something to improve the awareness and accuracy of Star Wars collectibles for me and for you. Please join me in thanking them for the unique facets and perspective they have each provided.

Acknowledgment for some of these individuals originates as far back as the original database project from 1998. Every contribution to the understanding and completeness of information is treasured and valuable. At the time of this writing, the earliest of the Star Wars collectibles are 45 years old, meaning that what was once a selfless and voluntary contribution of information may have now informed multiple generations.

For those who are no longer with us, this book is a memoriam to honor them.

Acknowledgments with Gratitude

Data and Photography Contributors

"Brother Dave" Krempasky: Collector
Jason Krueger: Collector
Laura Kyro: Collector
Martin Lacy: Collector (United Kingdom)
Stacy Lehn: Friend of the Book
Richard Leigh: Collector
Tait Lifto: Collector
Ian Lindsay: Collector
Becky Lockerby: Collector
Brian Long: Collector
Steve Loos: Fan
Justin Lovelady: Collector
Joe Lynch: Collector: Micro Machines
Geoff Manfre: Collector
Marc Manzo: Collector
Charles Marcus: Collector
Dean Martel: Super Collector
Jim McCallum: Collector (Canada), Author
Marcella McCuiston: Collector
Karen McGoldrick: Collector (Australia)
Michael McGoldrick: Collector (Australia)
Andrew McLennan: Dealer (New Zealand)
Dennis McLeod: Collector
Marc Miller: Collector, Costumer
Tyler Milliman: Collector
Peter Mittag: Collector (Germany)
Phil Mizzi: Collector (Australia)
Sara Ann Mohsin: Friend of the Book
Lance Moran: Collector, Costumer
Brett Morrison: Collector, Friend of the Book
Scot Alan Morrison: Collector
Glen Mullaly: Collector (Canada)
Michael Munn: Son
Patricia Munn: Daughter
Philip Murphy: Collector (United Kingdom)
Peter Myhalenko: Collector
Deb Nelson: Collector
Mark Newbold: Collector
Douglas Neman: Collector
Anne Neumann: Collector, Historical Archives
Moira O'Reilly: Collector (Australia)
Chris Oatman: Super Collector
Barbara Ownbey: Friend of the Book - In Memoriam

Mark Palmer: Collector (United Kingdom)
Charles Parker: Collector
Chuck Paskovics: Collector
Steven Peacock: Collector
Ryan Peterman: Collector
Kristi Pointer: Collector, Costumer
Gary Price: Celebrity Promotions
Maria Pulsonetti: Collector
Eloy Fernandez Quiros: Collector
Charles Radcliff: Collector
Alejandro Radeff: Collector
Brant Raven: Collector
Henry Rembish: Collector
Shanon Reynolds: Collector - *In Memoriam*
Mark Richert: Collector
Sandy Rivers: Collector: Martigras Coins
Mark Roach: Collector
Dave Roberts: Collector, Dealer
Chris and Rachel Robinson: Friends of the Book
Steve Robinson: Collector
David Rockwall: Collector
Rock Rockwell: Collector
Bill Rodgers: Collector (United Kingdom)
Mark Rodnitzky: eBay ID: Playeramusement
Ross Rosemurgy: Collector
Paul Roth: Collector
Robert Russell: Collector
Oscar Saenz: Collector
Dan Salazar: Collector
Gary Saunders: Collector (United Kingdom)
Tom Schaefer: Collector
Sterling Schlangenstein: Collector
Greg Schwalje: Collector
Chris Seabolt: Collector, Costumer
George Seeds IV: Collector
Joseph Setele: Collector
Helen Silver: Collector
Laura Simoneaux: Friend of the Book
Mark Simonetti: Collector
Duane Smith: Collector
Jeff Stagner: Collector
Schon StClair: Collector
Ben Stevens: Collector, Celebrity Promotions

Tré Stratton: Collector
Randy L. Suhre: Collector
Amy Sullivan: Friend of the Book
Brian Switaj: Collector
Adam Sylvester: Collector
Matthew Tave: Collector
Thomas Tave: Fan, Friend of the Book
Jason Thompson: Collector (United Kingdom)
Wayne Thompson: Collector
Martin Thurn: Collector and Historical Archives
Chris Toki: Collector (New Zealand)
Juan Trujillo: Collector
Vectis Auctions, Ltd.: www.Vectis.co.uk
Alonso Vilches: Collector
Corky Visminas: Sister
Curt Vigneri: Collector: Store Displays
Eric Waldmer: Collector
Charles Walker: Collector: Replicas, Costumer
Michael Walters: Friend of the Book
Pearce Weidmer: Fan, Friend of the Book
Cole Weidmer: Fan, Friend of the Book
Samantha West: Friend of the Book
Trent White: Collector: Replicas, Costumer
Scott Will: Costumer
Stuart Wilkshire: Collector (Japan)
Brandon Williams: Son
Kay Williams: Daughter
David and Allen Williams: Grandsons
Brandon Witt: Collector
Philip Wise: Collector, Celebrity Promoter
Bailey Wood: Niece
Logan Wood: Nephew
Matthew Wright: Collector: Media

Lifelong thanks to Sue Cornwell and Mike Kott, who are not contributors to the book but whose work inspired my original collecting journey, over 30 years ago. Thanks also to Anne Neumann, who, from the very beginning, demonstrated to me that collaborative data sharing could be just as bonding as trading bubble gum cards.

Contributing Content / Contacting the Author

Geoffrey Carlton invites you to join in the collecting conversation. Encompassing the global Star Wars merchandise and collectibles market there are thousands of new items produced every year. UPC and packaging updates along with exclusive release items can make locating and documenting every piece of interest a daunting task for individuals who try to go it alone in this hobby.

The Facebook group "Star Wars Collectors - Global" is a social gathering place to discuss new and surprise finds online and in stores. The group is open to the public. www.Facebook.com/Star-Wars-Collectors-Global-105232336239620

Mr. Carlton also maintains the Star Wars collecting database website at www.StarWarsDatabase.com.

For direct contact and image contributions for identification archives, his public email address is info@StarWarsGuide.net.

3D Printing Schematic Files

01-01 | 01-02 | 01-03 | 01-04 | 01-05 | 01-06 | 01-07 | 01-08 | 01-09

01-10 | 01-11 | 01-12 | 01-13 | 01-14 | 01-15 | 01-16 | 01-17

3D Printing Schematic Files
Covered in Volume 3, Page 10

Address Books

The Phantom Menace 3D magnetic phone books.
- ❏ Jar Jar Binks [01-01] 5.00
- ❏ Queen Amidala [01-02] 5.00
- ❏ Yoda [01-03] 5.00

The Phantom Menace tabbed address books.
- ❏ Adventures [01-04] 8.00
- ❏ Heroes [01-05] 8.00
- ❏ Jedi Battles [01-06] 8.00

Antioch
- ❏ Cover art from "The Glove of Darth Vader" [01-07] 5.00

Day Runner
Telephone books, 6-ring binder.
- ❏ Jar Jar Binks 10.00
- ❏ Queen Amidala 10.00
- ❏ Qui-Gon Jinn 10.00

Telephone books, bound spine.
- ❏ Jar Jar Binks [01-08] 5.00
- ❏ Queen Amidala [01-09] 5.00
- ❏ Qui-Gon Jinn [01-10] 5.00

Letts
- ❏ Princess Leia [01-11] 10.00
- ❏ Queen Amidala [01-12] 10.00
- ❏ Stormtrooper [01-13] 10.00

Marks and Spencer (UK)
- ❏ The Phantom Menace with note pad [01-14] 20.00

Yukari (Japan)
Droids / space battle address book with scheduler and 1978/79 pocket calendar.
- ❏ Black [01-15] 50.00
- ❏ White [01-16] 50.00

Hildebrandt art / Tatooine address book with scheduler and 1978/79 pocket calendar.
- ❏ Blue [v1e1-8] 50.00
- ❏ Green [01-17] 50.00

Advertising
Continued in Volume 3, Page 10

- ❏ Return of the Jedi painting competition flyer [v1e1-8] ... 20.00

Where Science Meets Imagination.
- ❏ Exhibit brochure [02-01] 5.00
- ❏ Exhibit map [v1e1-8] 5.00

- ❏ Clone Wars Japan 8.23 flyer [02-02] 5.00

20th Century Fox
- ❏ Empire Strikes Back Christmas re-release "A Better Film Than 'Star Wars'" flyer [02-03] 15.00
- ❏ Imperial Invasion video re-launch flyer [02-04] 10.00

Newspaper advertisements.
- ❏ Star Wars Holiday Special, trimmer 10.00

20th Century Fox (Mexico)
Attack of the Clones invitations.
- ❏ Anakin and Padmé [02-05] 10.00
- ❏ Jango Fett [02-06] 10.00

Abrams
- ❏ 1,000 Collectibles from a Galaxy Far, Far Away, promotion postcard 5.00

Advanced Graphics
- ❏ Holocron Cubi-card, 8.5"x11" flyer 5.00

Star Wars Celebration II. Holocron Cubi-Card.
- ❏ Bounty Hunters [02-07] 8.00
- ❏ Skywalker Family 8.00
- ❏ Villains 8.00

Agfa
- ❏ Free flying disc or yo-yo with film purchase poster [02-08] 25.00

Australia Post (Australia)
- ❏ SWCII 25th Anniversary souvenir stamp sheet ad 8.00

    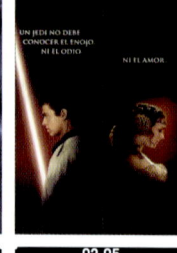 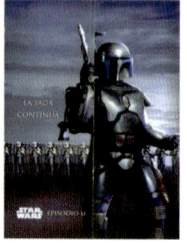  

02-01 | 02-02 | 02-03 | 02-04 | 02-05 | 02-06 | 02-07 | 02-08

02-09 | 02-10 | 02-11 | 02-12 | 02-13 | 02-14 front and back

Advertising

02-15 | 02-16 | 02-17 | 02-18 | 02-19 | 02-20 | 02-21 | 02-22 | 02-23 | 02-24

  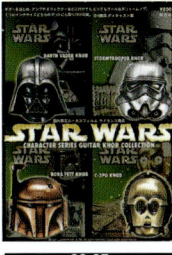    

02-25 | 02-26 | 02-27 | 02-28 | 02-29 | 02-30 | 02-31

Avon
- Relive the magic, Jedi Knights tin card set [2:71] 5.00

Avon (Mexico)
- Attack of the Clones products, 1-sheet flyer [02-09] 12.00

Bakery Crafts
- Star Wars CK-418C 3.00

Bimbo (Mexico)
- Star Cards window poster [v1e1:8] 30.00

Brooklyn Museum of Art
- Magic of Myth, April 5–July 7, 2002 .... 5.00

Burger King
- Glasses Coming Soon C-3PO and R2-D2, Empire Strikes Back [3:100] 350.00
- Play the Star Wars Team Game! flyer [02-10] 15.00

Cartoon Network (Argentina)
- Clone Wars, "Nuevo Show," folded sheet 10.00

Cedco Publishing
Flyer advertisements.
- 2002–2003 17 month locker calendar 5.00
- 2003 Attack of the Clones calendars 5.00
- 2003 Attack of the Clones daily calendar 5.00
- 2003 Classic poster art datebook 5.00

Celebration Japan
- 2008 Flyer [02-11] 5.00

Children's Museum of Indianapolis
- Art of the Starfighter 10.00

Clarks of England (UK)
- Clarks shoe order form [02-12] 65.00

Handbill flyers.
- Clarks shoe line [02-13] 45.00
- Clarks shoe line prices [2:72] 35.00

CMI Toys
Star Wars Celebration VI exclusives.
- Choose Your Side 5.00
- Hello From... .... 5.00

Coca-Cola
- "Ask About Our Keep the Star Wars Plastic Cup Promotion" hanging pyramid 325.00
- Bottle hanger for Star Wars cap game [02-14] 75.00
- Co-bot color and mail card 50.00
- "Match Star Wars Pairs And You Could Win A Cash Prize" bottle cap game promotion [3:101] 145.00

Coca-Cola (Japan)
- Drink Coca-Cola poster, 20"x28.5" [02-15] 850.00
- Fanta flyer 175.00

Code 3 Collectibles
- Millennium Falcon / X-Wing Fighter, free poster inside [02-16] 15.00

Collector Books
- Editions 1-5 ordering sheets, each 5.00

Completest Publications
- Gus and Duncan's Complete Guide to Star Wars Collectibles, promotion postcard 5.00

Dark Horse Comics
- X-Wing Rogue Squadron trade paperbacks 3"x5" card [02-17] 5.00

Deka
- Plastic merchandise flyer [02-18] 145.00

Del Rey
- Cloak of Deception, 11"x11" 8.00
- Vector Prime "You Know Where the Star Wars Saga has been..." 15.00

Disney / MGM
Star Wars Weekends. "Complete your Jedi Training" / "Construct Your Own Lightsaber" flyer. 2004.
- Blue [02-19] 15.00
- Green [02-20] 15.00
- Purple [02-21] 15.00
- Red [02-22] 15.00

   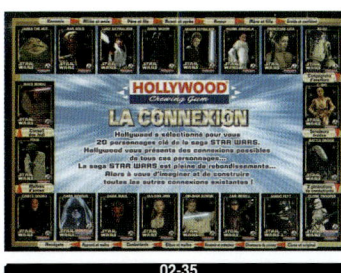 

02-32 | 02-33 | 02-34 | 02-35 | 02-36

  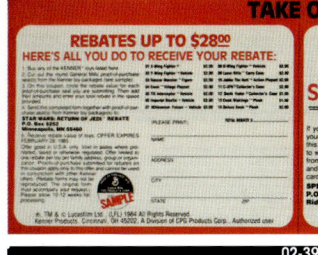    

02-37 | 02-38 | 02-39 | 02-40 | 02-41 | 02-42

Advertising

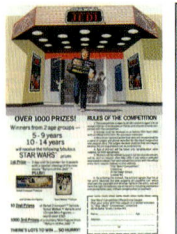     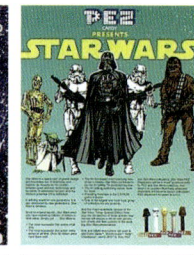  

02-42 | 02-43 | 02-44 | 02-45 | 02-46 | 02-47 | 02-48 | 02-49

     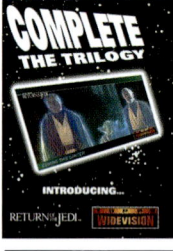 

02-50 | 02-51 | 02-52 | 02-53 | 02-54 | 02-55 | 02-56 Side 1

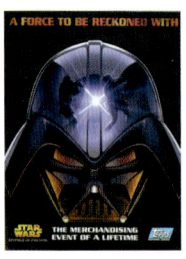  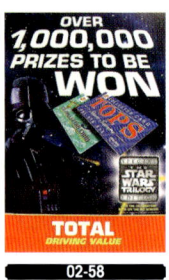    

02-56 Side 2 | 02-57 | 02-58 | 02-59 Front and Back | 02-60 | 02-61

Disney Theme Park Merchandise
- Last Tour to Endor brochure [02-23] 20.00

DK Publishing
- Visual Dictionary 2 page brochure 5.00
- You Can Draw Star Wars 5.00

Electronic Boutique
- Offer guide, free keychain and poster offer 5.00

Encuentros
2004 flyers, Revenge of the Sith.
- Anakin 15.00
- Obi-Wan Kenobi 15.00
- Obi-Wan vs. Vader [4:7] 15.00

Factors, Etc.
- Mail order form 50.00
- Star Wars Fan Club brochure [02-24] 20.00

Fan Club
- Bantha Tracks renewal letter 25.00
- Contest letter 45.00
- Member questionnaire 40.00
- Order form for ink revealing pens and keychain [02-25] 70.00
- Single-page advertisement, clipped from magazine [02-26] 20.00

Fernandes
Character series flyers.
- Guitar Collection: Vader and Stormtrooper [v1e1:10]....5.00
- Guitar Collection: Vader, Stormtrooper, and Boba Fett [v1e1:10] 5.00
- Guitar Knob Collection [02-27] 5.00
- Guitar Pick Collection [02-28] 5.00
- Guitar Strap Collection [v1e1:10] 5.00

Ferrero (Germany)
Star Wars Kinder Hipperium chocolate eggs.
- Dark Laser flyer [02-29] 15.00

Forbidden Zone (Belgium)
- Star Wars exhibition poster 9/10–9/30/98 [2:72] 15.00

Frigo
- La Guerra de las Galaxias [2:72] 95.00

Frito Lay
- A Taste of the Trilogy poster with manufacturer coupon [02-30] 10.00
- The Phantom Menace floor sticker, 18"x24" [4:7] ..85.00

Funko (Japan)
- Wacky Wobbler flyer [02-31] 10.00

GE Consumer Finance
- Star Wars VISA application brochure [02-32] 15.00

Golden Village (Singapore)
- Attack of the Clones charity screening advertisement ...10.00

Gym Dandy
- Scout Walker Command Tower flyer [02-33] 100.00

Hallmark
- Ornament Wish List, 11"x17" black-and-white 12.00
- Use the Force / Keepsake ornaments 10.00

Hamilton Collection
- Wall-mount plate holder brochure [2:73] 10.00

Hasbro
- Fan Choice figure #4 paper ballot 5.00

Heart Art Collection, Ltd. (Japan)
- 30th anniversary collectibles flyer [02-34] 10.00

Hobby Japan (Japan)
- Action Figure Database (book) flyer [v1e1:11] 8.00

Hollywood Chewing Gum (France)
- Attack of the Clones 8.5"x11" folded brochure [02-35]..30.00

Jamie Snell
- Holiday Special Boba Fett, San Diego Comic-Con 10 lobby card / flyer, exclusive to San Diego Comic-Con 75.00

K-Mart
- Exciting Scenes from Star Wars, postcard [02-36] ..15.00

Kenner
- Advertisement, full page glossy [2:73] 5.00
- Nine original POTF2 orange carded figures, tri-logo flyer, fold-out [02-37] 10.00

Speeder bike sweepstakes. Kmart exclusives.
- Entry form for in-store drawing [02-38] 10.00
- Second chance drawing form, with toy rebates [02-39] 40.00

KFC
- Marketing plan media pack, TPM pre-release [2:74]....300.00

Kotobukiya (Japan)
Art FX models.
- Bounty Hunters: Collect All Six postcard 8.00
- Darth Vader, Clone trooper, Anakin flyer 5.00

LucasArts
- Force Unleashed concept art, 12.5"x7" 15.00
- Galaxies 60-day pre-paid cards, flyer 5.00

Lucasfilm
Episode II promotion flyers. 4.25"x5.5".
- www.AcklayComeHome.com [4:8] 5.00
- www.DroidTutor.com [4:8] 5.00
- www.KaminoRentals.com [4:8] 5.00
- www.OutlanderClub.com [4:8] 5.00
- www.PurpleLightsaber.com [4:8] 5.00
- www.uSeekYoda.com [4:8] 5.00

Episode II promotion flyers. 8.5"x11".
- www.AcklayComeHome.com [v1e1:11] 5.00
- www.DroidTutor.com [4:8] 5.00
- www.KaminoRentals.com [4:8] 5.00
- www.OutlanderClub.com [4:8] 5.00
- www.PurpleLightsaber.com [4:8] 5.00
- www.uSeekYoda.com [4:8] 5.00

Marvel Comics
- "The Force That Has Taken America By Storm...", flyer [2:74] 15.00

Advertising Displays

Masterfoods USA
- ❏ Mpire code redemption instructions, flyer 5.00

MBNA
- ❏ Jango Fett chrome premium, flyer 15.00
- ❏ WorldPoints Rewards mailer pack 8.00

Mello Smello
- ❏ Stormtrooper, promotes Vivid Vision, lenticular, exclusive to Star Wars Celebration Europe 12.00

Metallic Images
- ❏ A New Hope metal collector cards, flyer 5.00

Mimoco (Japan)
- ❏ Mimobot series 2 postcard 5.00

Morinaga (Japan)
- ❏ Candy flyer [02-40] 200.00

MPC
- ❏ Plastic model squadron promotes Return of the Jedi model ships, newsprint advertisement from comic book [2:74] .. 5.00

Nikko America
- ❏ R2-D2 webcam / projector advertising sheet 8.00

Nokia
- ❏ Master the True Power of the Force, The Force Unleashed mobile, flyer 5.00

Orquesta Pops De Mexico
- ❏ 2004 Julio flyer [02-41] 5.00

Palitoy (UK)
- ❏ Enter the Return of the Jedi Competition entry brochure [02-42] 65.00

Parker Bros.
- ❏ Return of the Jedi game cartridge magazine advertisement, glossy [02-43] 5.00

Pepsi Cola (Japan)
- ❏ Revenge of the Sith bottle cap stage postcard [02-44] 15.00

Pepsi Cola (UK)
- ❏ Win a Star Wars Family Holiday to the USA flyer [02-45] 10.00

Pepsico, Inc.
- ❏ Star Wars Special Edition invitation [02-46] 20.00

PEZ Candy, Inc.
- ❏ Advertising sheet [02-47] 15.00

Pizza Hut
- ❏ Micromachine heads, flyer [3:103] 15.00

Pizza Hut (UK)
- ❏ Exclusive Star Wars Meal Deal offers menu brochure [02-48] 15.00
- ❏ Star Wars: Special Edition menu, flyer [02-49] 15.00

Rarities Mint
- ❏ Silver and gold coins brochure [2:75] 15.00

Rawcliffe
- ❏ Attack of the Clones keychain flyer 10.00

Runa International Co., Ltd. (China)
- ❏ Mascot strap accessory flyer [02-50] 8.00

Safeway
- ❏ Win a Star Wars family holiday to the USA entry form .. 15.00

Scholastic
- ❏ Jedi Quest / Born to Be A Bounty Hunter flyer 8.00

Sony Classical
- ❏ Revenge of the Sith sound track preview flyer, exclusive to Fan Club 5.00

Sony Ericsson
- ❏ Be the Envy of the Empire, flyer 10.00

Star Jars
- ❏ Cookie jar flyer, 8.5"x11" [02-51] 4.00

Star Wars Celebration III
- ❏ Exhibitor packet [v1e1:9] 25.00

Star Wars Celebration IV
- ❏ Exhibitor folder [v1e1:9] 25.00

Star Wars Celebration Japan (Japan)
- ❏ Photos with the Stars flyer [02-52] 14.00

Star Wars Shop
- ❏ Empire Muggs Back, charity auction promotion postcard 20.00

The Jedi Assembly
- ❏ How To Be A Jedi... [02-53] 5.00

The LEGO Group
- ❏ Star Wars Galactic Challenge building contest entry form 10.00

Tokyo Disneyland (Japan)
- ❏ Star Tours flyer, exclusive to Star Wars Celebration Japan [02-54] 10.00

Topps
- ❏ Return of the Jedi Widevision cards flyer [02-55] 15.00
- ❏ Revenge of the Sith cards advertising sheet [02-56] 15.00
- ❏ "Topps Introduces 15 cent Star Wars Movie Photo Cards!", advertising sheet, 1977 [02-57] 80.00

Total
- ❏ Topps Store Saver Star Wars point promotion brochure [02-58] 15.00

Toys R Us (Japan)
- ❏ Celebration Japan flyer, exclusive to Star Wars Celebration Japan [v1e1:12] 15.00

Tricon Global Restaurants, Inc.
- ❏ Collection page for medallions and official game rules, 8.5"x11" 8.00

Triumvir
- ❏ Stormtrooper mask booth advertisement [02-59] 25.00

United States Postal Service
- ❏ Yoda, "Win a trip", for prepaid Express Mail packs, 1/2 page flyer 20.00

Walkers (UK)
- ❏ Win a Chance to See Star Wars Episode I, leaflet 15.00

Walmart
- ❏ Attack of the Clones Jedi Challenge with participant logos flyer 10.00

Williams
- ❏ The Phantom Menace pinball tips and tricks brochure [4:9] 20.00

Wizards of the Coast
- ❏ Trading Card Game events flyer, exclusive to Star Wars Celebration II 5.00

Yoshitoku Co., Ltd. (Japan)
Star Wars armor flyers.
- ❏ Darth Vader [02-60] 20.00
- ❏ Stormtrooper [02-61] 20.00

Yves Saint Laurent
- ❏ One Love, Queen Amidala cover, brochure 30.00

Advertising Displays
Continued in Volume 3, Page 13

12"x12" cardboard hanging displays.
- ❏ Anakin Skywalker 15.00
- ❏ Darth Maul 15.00
- ❏ Jar Jar Binks 15.00
- ❏ Queen Amidala 15.00

03-01 | 03-02 Front and Back | 03-03 | 03-04 | 03-05 | 03-06 | 03-07 | 03-08

03-09 | 03-10 | 03-11 | 03-12 | 03-13 | 03-14

Advertising Displays

Shelf displays.
- Revenge of the Sith water bottle display box, holds 16 ....10.00

(Japan)
- Star Wars phone card counter display [03-01] 25.00

20th Century Fox
- C-3PO / R2-D2 ceiling dangler [03-02] 270.00
- Darth Maul DVD standee [03-03] 45.00
- Episode I VHS standee [03-04] 35.00
- Shuttle Tydirium hanging display with character danglers [03-05] 325.00
- Yoda standee, "Unlock the Saga" [v1e1:8] 55.00

20th Century Fox (Mexico)
- Star Wars: Special Edition video standee [2:7] 45.00

Applause
- The Phantom Menace 3D shelf display [03-06] 35.00

At-A-Glance
- Hexagonal dump with double-corrugated die-cut header for posters 20.00

Bantam Books
Book dumps with headers.
- R2-D2 Heir to the Empire [03-07] 50.00
- The Courtship of Princess Leia 35.00

Bantam / Spectra
- "Star Wars Where the Adventure Continues," R2-D2 shaped 5.00

Bing Harris Sargood (New Zealand)
- Return of the Jedi: Posters, Badges, Erasers Available Here, set of 2—Return of the Jedi Logo and Characters (Vader, Scout, C-3PO, Solo, Fett, Kenobi) 145.00

Blockbuster Video
Shelf tags.
- Family Guy: It's A Trap! [03-08] 15.00
- Family Guy: Something, Something, Something, Darkside [03-09] 15.00
- LEGO Star Wars III, for Xbox 360 [03-10] 15.00
- LEGO Star Wars III for Nintendo DS [03-11] 15.00
- The Force Unleashed II, for PlayStation 2 ....15.00
- The Force Unleashed II, for Xbox 360 ....15.00

Bulls i Toy
- Power plates gravity feed display 8.00

Burger Chef
- Burger Chef Funmeal tray, table tent 125.00

Burger King
Empire Strikes Back.
- Glasses counter display [03-12] 300.00
- Glasses standee C-3PO and R2-D2 [v1e1:9] 350.00
- Glasses translite display [03-13] 300.00
- Super Scene premium display [3:100] 250.00

Return of the Jedi.
- Glasses counter display [03-14] 250.00
- Glasses counter display, Vader-shaped [03-15] 225.00
- Glasses standee Darth Vader [03-16] 425.00

Star Wars.
- Glasses counter display [v1e1:9] 350.00
- Glasses, hanging [03-17] 200.00
- Collect All Fours, 2-piece hanging [03-18] 650.00

Butterfly Originals
Return of the Jedi.
- Pen display, cardboard box with die-cut header, 36-count pens [3:101] 15.00
- Pencil top eraser counter display [5:7] 30.00
- Royal Guard standee [2:72] 50.00

Vending machine 25 cent headers.
- Erasers, glow-in-the-dark [03-19] 45.00
- Pencil toppers and paper protectors [03-20] 50.00

Candy Rific
- M&Ms light-up lightsaber candy dispenser display 10.00
- M&M's candy bank counter display, holds 15 ....5.00

Chupa Chups
Classic trilogy counter top displays to hold product.
- Fantasy Balls [03-21] 20.00
- Pen Pops [03-22] 20.00
- Port-a-Chups [03-23] 20.00
- Port-a-Chups island [03-24] 25.00

Colgate
- The Phantom Menace toothbrushes floor display [4:7] ...50.00

Deka
- ROTJ "For kids of all ages" display header [03-25] 45.00

Del Rey
- "Reserve Your Copy Now" Attack of the Clones counter sign 10.00

Book dumps with headers.
- Attack of the Clones, Obi-Wan and Jango Fett on blue background 35.00
- Attack of the Clones, Yoda, Jango Fett, Clones, "Collector's Edition" 35.00
- Attack of the Clones, Yoda, Jango Fett, Clones, "Special 12 Page Bonus" 30.00
- Dark Journey 25.00
- Dark Lord, The Rise of Darth Vader 45.00
- Force Heretic 25.00
- Inferno 25.00
- Outbound Flight and Allegiance 25.00
- Revenge of the Sith, Darth Vader, art 30.00
- Revenge of the Sith, advance, Darth Vader 35.00
- Sacrifice 25.00
- Shatterpoint 25.00
- Tatooine Ghost 25.00
- The Cestus Deception 25.00
- The Clone Wars, "In theaters August 15th" 35.00
- The Force Unleashed 25.00
- The Unifying Force 25.00

Dixie / Northern Inc.
- Dixie Cups, Darth Vader header [2:72] 75.00

DK Publishing
- Jango Fett POP 125.00

03-15

03-16

03-17

03-18

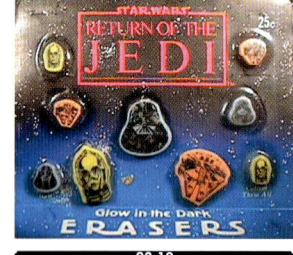
03-19

03-20

03-21

03-22

03-23

03-24

03-25

03-26

03-27

03-28

03-29

03-30

03-31

Advertising Displays

Duncan Heinz
- Empire Strikes Back free poster with purchase display [03-26] 140.00

Factors, Etc.
- Earrings, upright [4:7] 75.00
- Pendant and necklace counter top display rack, rotating [03-27] 80.00

Ferrero (Germany)
Star Wars Kinder Hipperium chocolate eggs.
- Counter display, Luke Eiwalker, Hippoda, Erzwo Hippo [03-28] 25.00
- Floor display, Luke Eiwalker 40.00

Frito Lay
- Clone trooper game piece 25.00
- Experience the Adventure [03-29] 65.00
- Yoda, "May the Fun be with you" 25.00

Fundimensions
- Duel at Death Star shelf talker tag [03-30] 85.00

Fundy Star (Hungary)
- Episode I counter top candy display 125.00

Galerie Chocolates
- M&M collector tins shelf display 10.00

Golden Books
- 20th anniversary book dump with header [03-31] 200.00

H.E. Harris and Company
- Stamp collecting set display bin and 2-piece header 70.00

Harrod's
Sculpted face in 26"x27"x13" black plastic.
- Darth Vader [03-32] 300.00
- Stormtrooper 300.00

Hasbro
- Attack of the Clones lightsabers counter display [v1e1:10] 30.00
- Attack of the Clones action figures floor display 45.00
- Revenge of the Sith action figures floor display [4:7] 35.00
- OTC action figures shelf talker [v1e1:10] 15.00

CommTech counter displays with amplified speaker.
- 1st release—red [03-33] 150.00

Counter displays.
- Fighter Pods, holds 20 .... 15.00

Display cards, 12.5"x48". ROTS action figures.
- Darth Vader / Epic duel art 15.00
- Epic duel art 15.00

Original Trilogy Collection.
- Millennium Falcon with six bonus figures, store display, exclusive to Sam's Club 350.00

Shelf display boxes. Revenge of the Sith.
- Action figures 25.00
- Action figures, stand up 50.00
- Battle Buddies 15.00
- Mini-puzzles, holds 50 .... 15.00

Wall mounted displays. Above AOTC action figures.
- Anakin / Amidala / R2-D2 and C-3PO [2:73] 35.00
- Clone trooper / Mace Windu [2:73] 35.00
- Obi-Wan / Jango [2:73] 35.00
- Padmé Amidala hanging banner [2:73] 30.00

Hasbro (Mexico)
- Ed Poder De Los Jedi [2:73] 30.00

Hanging pegboard banners.
- Power Of The Jedi, Obi-Wan [2:73] 35.00
- Saga, Obi-Wan [2:73] 35.00

HC Ford (UK)
- "Introducing Wicket The Ewok" pencil topper display [03-34] 165.00

Kenner
- Star Wars Lightsaber 35" Inflated [03-35] 650.00
- The Force Lightsaber floor display [v1e1:11] 250.00

Counter displays.
- Collect all 21 [3:101] 1,250.00
- Die-cast space ships [3:102] 1,700.00
- Ewoks plush, holds 2 .... 275.00
- Ewoks Woklings, holds 8 .... 275.00
- Twelve Exciting Figures [3:102] 850.00

Display box headers.
- Collect all 21 [3:101] 1,500.00
- Get a Free Boba Fett Action Figure [3:102] 1,000.00
- Get a Free Boba Fett Action Figure, shows rocket-firing Fett [3:102] 1,600.00
- Toy Center [2:74] 2,500.00

Hanging bell displays.
- Collect all 21 [2:73] 750.00
- Micro Collection, 3 sided [03-36] 600.00
- Toy Galaxy [2:74] 700.00

Standees
- Laser Rifle and Laser Pistol [v1e1:11] 3,000.00

KFC
Outdoor advertising, made of corrugated plasticized cardboard.
- 8-piece meal / flying topper menu topper (straight bottom, shaped top) 100.00
- Cup toppers vertical sign 85.00
- Jar Jar / kid's meal toys vertical sign 100.00

Kotobukiya (Japan)
- Art FX models checklist poster 10.00

La Serenisima (Argentina)
- Clone Wars Yogurisimo, 190g bottles [03-37] 35.00

LucasArts
- Shadows of the Empire Nintendo oversized display box [4:8] 15.00
- Standee, Jedi Power Battles [2:74] 35.00

M1
- Cell phone M1 Top-Up cards counter display [03-38] 35.00

Advertising Displays

03-51 | 03-52 | 03-53 | 03-54 Front and Back | 03-55 | 03-56

 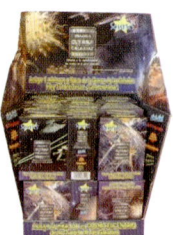   

03-57 | 03-58 | 03-59 | 03-60 | 03-61 | 03-62

03-63 | 03-64 | 03-65 | 03-66 | 03-67 | 03-68

Masterfoods USA
- ❏ M&M Choose Dark Chocolate [03-39] 10.00
- ❏ Shipping carton [03-40] 15.00

McDonald's
- ❏ Clone Wars toy display [v1e1:11] 75.00

McDonald's (UK)
- ❏ R2-D2, Explore the Galaxy standee [03-41] 50.00

Meiji (Japan)
- ❏ Xylish gum dispensers counter display box [03-42] 10.00

Natural Balance
- ❏ Floor display [03-43] 200.00

Omni Cosmetics
- ❏ Bath Collection counter display [3:102] 175.00
- ❏ Darth Vader / Royal Guards bath products display rack [03-44] 550.00
- ❏ R2-D2 bath soap display rack [03-45] 400.00

Oral-B
- ❏ R2-D2 and C-3PO toothbrush display box header [03-46] 150.00

Orchard Books
- ❏ A Pop-Up Guide to the Galaxy book display 20.00

Palitoy (UK)
- ❏ Enter the Return of the Jedi Competition promotion, AT-AT counter display [4:8] 700.00

Panini (UK)
- ❏ Staks counter box [03-47] 10.00

Pepperidge Farms
- ❏ Free Tumbler counter display [2:74] 150.00

Pepsi (UK)
Feel The Force promotion.
- ❏ Defeat the Empire and Win 25,000 .... 35.00
- ❏ Defeat the Empire v2 .... 35.00
- ❏ Win A Family Holiday to Futuroscope [03-48] 35.00

Pepsi Cola
- ❏ Death Star rotating display [03-49] 300.00
- ❏ Display, Walker display [v1e1:12] 150.00
- ❏ "Join the Celebration," Boba Fett shelf talker [3:103] 35.00
- ❏ "Join The Celebration," Vader / Death Star 3D standee [03-50] 90.00

Episode I: The Phantom Menace.
- ❏ "Collect all 24 Star Wars cans," Jar Jar shelf talker [2:74] 25.00
- ❏ Darth Maul 3D wall display [03-51] 35.00
- ❏ "Find Yoda, Win Cash" pole sign [2:74] 25.00
- ❏ "Find Yoda, Win Cash" shelf talker [2:74] 25.00
- ❏ "Find Yoda, Win Cash" window sign [2:74] 35.00
- ❏ "Look for a Limited Edition can" pole sign [2:74] 35.00

Pepsi Cola (Japan)
- ❏ The Phantom Menace special bottle caps counter mat [03-52] 65.00

Pepsi Cola (Mexico)
- ❏ The Phantom Menace Jar Jar Binks, Pepsi / Mountain Dew window sign [2:74] 75.00

Pepsi Cola (UK)
- ❏ "Feel the Force," R2-D2 shelf talker 35.00

PEZ Candy, Inc.
- ❏ Floor display [03-53] 35.00
- ❏ Floor display, header card only 20.00

PEZ Candy, Inc. (UK)
- ❏ Floor sticker [5:9] 100.00

Pizza Hut
- ❏ Kids Pack with mini-transforming play sets counter display 25.00
- ❏ "Welcome to Coruscant, Your senate box is being prepared," building shaped counter display 35.00
- ❏ "Welcome to Coruscant, Your senate box is being prepared," building shaped floor display 95.00

Table-top display cards. 4"x6" 2 sided, plasticized.
- ❏ "Collect Them All!" (toys) [1:49] 35.00
- ❏ "Don't Leave Coruscant Without Them." (6 toys / cup toppers) 35.00
- ❏ "Take A Piece Of Coruscant Home." (cup toppers) [3:103] 35.00

Pizza Hut (Australia)
- ❏ Star Wars: Special Edition premium toys and menu flyer [03-54] 35.00
- ❏ Star Wars Works free with Kids Works hanging sign [03-55] 45.00

Presto Magix / American Publishing
- ❏ Empire Strikes Back rub down transfers counter display [03-56] 25.00

Random House
Book dumps with headers.
- ❏ Jedi Trial, Anakin and Darth Vader 35.00
- ❏ Labyrinth of Evil 35.00

Rawcliffe
- ❏ "Coming to this store May 3, 1999" counter sign [03-57] 15.00

Sigma
- ❏ Empire Strikes Back ceramic figures counter sign [03-58] 250.00

Sonrics (Mexico)
- ❏ 18-package counter display [03-59] 24.00

Sony Classical
- ❏ Attack of the Clones sound track floor display 35.00

Super Live Adventure (Japan)
- ❏ Super Live Adventure standee [03-60] 350.00

Taco Bell
Feel the Force game.
- ❏ Darth Vader THX hanging bell display [03-63] 60.00
- ❏ Drive-thru menu topper display, corrugated plastic, measures approximately 2'x5'. 40.00
- ❏ "Millions of Instant-Win Prizes", floor display vehicle 52"x71" [03-62] 250.00
- ❏ R2-D2 premiums floor display [03-61] 250.00

Albums, Collecting

Takara (Japan)
- ❏ ZETCA display box, empty 85.00

The LEGO Group
- ❏ Enter The LEGO Galactic Challenge Building Contest padded wall display poster [2:74] 40.00
- ❏ Episode I and classic trilogy mural 35.00
- ❏ Naboo Fighter wall display [2:74] 65.00
- ❏ Star Wars / LEGO logos window sticker 35.00
- ❏ Toy Fair promotion: 4"x5"x2" box with Luke and Vader figures and sound chip, labeled "Building a New Galaxy in 1999" 175.00

Theatrical
- ❏ Empire Strikes Back, printed materials at refreshment stand, 22"x28" poster 600.00

Thomas Salter
- ❏ Action rub down transfers, counter display 55.00

Tombola
- ❏ Chocolate eggs counter display [03-64] 15.00

Topps
- ❏ The Topps Vault poster 20.00
- ❏ Return of the Sith cards tin shelf display box, holds 16 tins 15.00

Toys R Us
- ❏ Naboo Sweepstakes, hanging poster [2:75] 30.00

Toys R Us (UK)
- ❏ X-Wing Fighter Tour poster [03-65] 150.00

Tricon Global Restaurants, Inc.
- ❏ The Phantom Menace 2.99 cup toppers menu translite [03-66] 300.00

Wallace Berrie and Co.
- ❏ Pendants and necklaces, Darth Vader counter top display rack [v1e1:13] 350.00

Wells (UK)
- ❏ Battle droid ice pops counter display [v1e1:13] 140.00

WizKids
Pocketmodels.
- ❏ Jumbo X-Wing 3D display 20.00
- ❏ Expansion packs, "Only $4.99!" wall display 25.00

Wonder Bread
- ❏ 16 Free trading cards shelf talker [03-67] 145.00

Yamakatsu Corporation (Japan)
- ❏ Hanging card display, shown with cards, valued as without cards [03-68] 300.00

Air Fresheners
Continued in Volume 3, Page 15

C and D Visionaries, Inc.
- ❏ A New Hope poster [04-01] 8.00
- ❏ Clone trooper collage [04-02] 8.00
- ❏ Darth Vader fighting [04-03] 8.00
- ❏ Darth Vader vs. Luke [04-04] 8.00
- ❏ Darth Vader with lightsaber [04-05] 8.00
- ❏ Jabba and Leia [04-06] 8.00
- ❏ Lightsaber fight [04-07] 8.00
- ❏ R2-D2 and C-3PO [04-08] 8.00
- ❏ Sith Lord [04-09] 8.00
- ❏ Star Wars logo [04-10] 8.00
- ❏ Yoda [04-11] 8.00
- ❏ Yoda collage [04-12] 8.00

Albums, Collecting
Continued in Volume 3, Page 15

- ❏ Movie Shots binder [4:10] 45.00

(Argentina)
- ❏ 1977 Card Collector [05-01] 175.00
- ❏ O Retorno de Jedi card album [05-02] 100.00

(Brazil)
- ❏ El Regreso I Jedi sticker album [05-03] 95.00

(Mexico)
- ❏ 2005 Lottery ticket collecting album 20.00

Activa Consumer Promotions Corp. (Canada)
- ❏ Winnipeg Free Press, holds 20 pin set 15.00

Agence Generale d'Edition (France)
- ❏ L'Empire Contre-Attaque [05-04] 95.00

Burger King
- ❏ Super Scene sticker album, 4 pages [05-05] 45.00

Burger King (Mexico)
- ❏ Episode III: Revenge of the Sith sticker album [05-06] 20.00

Cedibra (Brazil)
- ❏ Star Wars [5:10] 95.00

Costa (Argentina)
- ❏ Holds 40 square stickers [05-07] 75.00

Dark Horse Comics
- ❏ Special collectors album [05-08] 20.00

DinaMics
- ❏ DinaMics sticker album [5:10] 65.00

Eskimo (Japan)
- ❏ Attack of the Clones mail-in premium for Lucky Card 150.00

Fher (Spain)
- ❏ El Imperio Contraataca [05-09] 95.00

FKS (UK)
- ❏ Empire Strikes Back, C-3PO [05-10] 95.00

Frito Lay (Australia)
- ❏ TAZO official collectors album [05-11] 40.00

Frito Lay (Poland)
- ❏ TAZO Album Mocy dla Kolekcjonerow (TAZO collector album) [05-12] 60.00

Albums, Collecting

 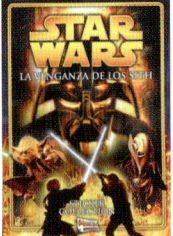 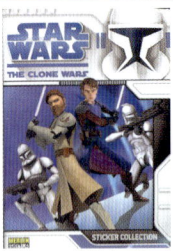 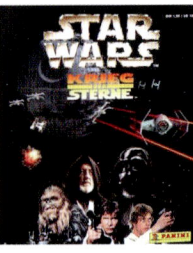   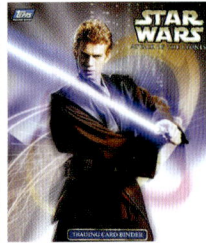

05-14   05-15   05-16   05-17   05-18   05-19   05-20

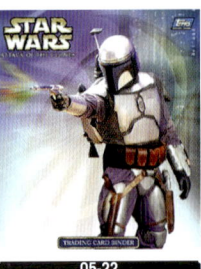 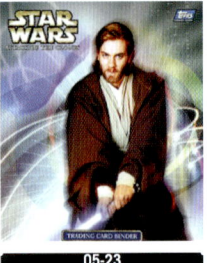   

05-21   05-22   05-23   05-24   05-25   06-01

General Mills
- Wallet, brown with gold border and Star Wars logo; holds 18 cereal premium cards [05-13] 35.00

KFC (Mexico)
- The Phantom Menace sticker collection sheet [05-14] 8.00

Merlin (Germany)
- Clone Wars [5:10] 25.00

Merlin (Spain)
- Revenge of the Sith sticker album [05-15] 25.00

Merlin (UK)
- Clone Wars [05-16] 25.00
- Revenge of the Sith sticker album 25.00

Merlin Publishing International Ltd.
- Episode I sticker collection album 20.00
- Sticker collection plus free saga wall chart 45.00

Panini (Germany)
- Star Wars [05-17] 45.00

Panini (Italy)
- Star Wars [4:10] 45.00

Panini (UK)
- Clone Wars 25.00
- Return of the Jedi, sticker album [05-18] 30.00

Topps
- Episode I Widevision cards 30.00
- Return of the Jedi sticker album, 25 cents [05-19] 35.00

Topps (UK)
Episode II: Attack of the Clones card binders with exclusive trading card.
- Anakin Skywalker [05-20] 35.00
- Count Dooku [05-21] 35.00
- Jango Fett [05-22] 35.00
- Obi-Wan Kenobi [05-23] 35.00

Walkers (UK)
- Episode I: The Phantom Menace sticker collection sheet [05-24] 15.00
- TAZO collector's Force Pack [05-25] 25.00

Answering Machines

Tiger Electronics
- Royal Naboo starship [06-01] 50.00

Arcade: Pinball Machines
Continued in Volume 3, Page 16

A. Hankin and Co.
- Empire Strikes Back [07-01] .... *OSPV*

Data East
- Star Wars [07-02] .... *OSPV*

Sega
- Star Wars special edition trilogy [07-03] .... *OSPV*

Williams
- Episode I [07-04] .... *OSPV*
- Episode I, collector, 100 produced .... *OSPV*
- Star Wars special edition .... *OSPV*

Arcade: Slot Machines

International Gaming Technology
- Star Wars [08-01] 9,500.00

Promatic (Germany)
- Star Wars, plays in Euros [08-02] 8,500.00

07-01   07-02   07-03   07-04   08-01   08-02   08-03

09-01   09-02   09-03   09-04   09-05   09-06

20

Art: Animation Cels

Sankyo Co., Ltd. (Japan)
- ❏ Star Wars video slots [08-03] 6,500.00

Arcade: Video Games
Continued in Volume 3, Page 16

Atari
Coin operated. Value includes coin cabinet intact.
- ❏ Empire Strikes Back [09-01] 3,700.00
- ❏ Return of the Jedi [09-02] 2,500.00
- ❏ Star Wars [09-03] 3,000.00
- ❏ Star Wars, cockpit case [09-04] 3,250.00

Sega
Coin operated. Value includes coin cabinet intact.
- ❏ Star Wars 2 seats, pilot and gunner 9,500.00
- ❏ Star Wars Racer, cockpit case [09-05] 3,250.00
- ❏ Star Wars Trilogy [09-06] 3,600.00
- ❏ Star Wars Trilogy, cockpit case 4,500.00

Armor

Yoshitoku (Japan)
1:4 scale Samurai armor.
- ❏ Darth Vader inspired yoroi (armor), kabuto (helmet), bow, and sword, Tango no Sekku celebration on May 5th.... 4,100.00

Art
Continued in Volume 3, Page 16

- ❏ At Last We Will Have Revenge, neon poster 315.00

2N Enterprise
- ❏ Lacquer L.E.D. (Lite Edition Decor) Series: X-Wing computer game artwork 47.00

ACME Archives
Clone Wars original production drawings.
- ❏ Anakin and Obi-Wan from episode 2 .... 400.00
- ❏ Anakin and Palpatine from episode 1 .... 160.00
- ❏ ARC trooper with chain gun, episode 4 .... 250.00
- ❏ ARC trooper with quad cannon, episode 1.... 250.00
- ❏ Asajj Ventress close-up from episode 19 ..... 200.00
- ❏ Asajj Ventress from episode 17 .... 250.00
- ❏ C-3PO from episode 16 .... 200.00
- ❏ Captain Typho from episode 15 .... 160.00
- ❏ Captain Typho, R2 and C-3PO, episode 15... 250.00
- ❏ Clone trooper close-up from episode 9 .... 200.00
- ❏ Count Dooku from episode 7 .... 250.00
- ❏ Durge from episode 4 .... 200.00
- ❏ Foul Moudama and Palpatine, episode 4 ..... 300.00
- ❏ General Grievous from episode 4 .... 300.00
- ❏ General Grievous, Foul Moudama, and Shaak Ti from episode 4 .... 350.00
- ❏ Ki-Adi Mundi and K'Kruhk from episode 20 ..... 200.00
- ❏ Ki-Adi Mundi close-up from episode 20 .... 160.00
- ❏ Ki-Adi Mundi from episode 20 .... 160.00
- ❏ Kit Fisto using the Force from episode 5 ...... 250.00
- ❏ Kit Fisto, close-up from episode 5 .... 200.00
- ❏ Kit Fisto, lightsaber on left from episode 5 ... 200.00
- ❏ Kit Fisto, lightsaber on right, tendrils down from episode 5 .... 200.00
- ❏ Kit Fisto, lightsaber on right tendrils up, from episode 5 .... 200.00
- ❏ Kit Fisto, lightsaber slashing, from episode 5 ..... 200.00
- ❏ Mace Windu sitting from episode 1 .... 250.00
- ❏ Mace Windu, flowing cape from episode 5 .. 250.00
- ❏ Mace Windu, lightsaber down, episode 12 .. 250.00
- ❏ Mace Windu, lightsaber raised, episode 1 ... 250.00
- ❏ Mace Windu, lightsaber raised, episode 12 .. 300.00
- ❏ Mace Windu, punching from episode 12 ..... 250.00
- ❏ Obi-Wan cuts Durge from episode 8 .... 250.00
- ❏ Obi-Wan Kenobi and Destroyer Droid from episode 9 .... 250.00
- ❏ Roron Corobb and Grievous's Bodyguard from episode 4 .... 250.00
- ❏ Roron Corobb from episode 4 .... 300.00
- ❏ Shaak Ti from episode 4 .... 250.00
- ❏ Shaak Ti behind Grievous's Bodyguard from episode 4 .... 300.00
- ❏ Super Battle Droid from episode 12 .... 200.00
- ❏ Tikkes from episode 5 .... 160.00

Clone Wars. Hand-painted one-of-one created from original production drawings. Laser color reproduced background.
- ❏ Anakin Skywalker vs. Asajj Ventress 520.00
- ❏ Anakin Skywalker, lightsaber down 520.00
- ❏ Anakin Skywalker, lightsaber up 520.00
- ❏ General Grievous attacks Clone trooper 700.00
- ❏ General Grievous, Foul Moudama and Palpatine 700.00
- ❏ General Obi-Wan Kenobi and ARC trooper 520.00
- ❏ Mace Windu 520.00
- ❏ Mace Windu leading Clone troopers with original drawing 820.00
- ❏ Shaak Ti vs. Grievous's Bodyguard 520.00
- ❏ Yoda beside Kybuck 700.00
- ❏ Yoda talking to Kybuck 700.00

Clone Wars. Hand-painted one-of-one created from original production drawings. Original production background.
- ❏ Anakin Skywalker, lightsaber down, approximately 11"x17" matted 800.00

Authentic Images
Matted and framed, 5,000 produced.
- ❏ Darth Vader and Luke in shaft 95.00
- ❏ Luke and Yoda 95.00

Pottery Barn
LED art. 45" wide x 36" high. Digitally printed on canvas.
- ❏ Death Star 300.00
- ❏ Star Wars 300.00

Murals. 4' wide x 6' high, printed on a non-adhesive fabric panel.
- ❏ Millennium Falcon 100.00
- ❏ TIE Fighters 100.00
- ❏ X-Wing Fighters 100.00

Art: Animation Cels
Continued in Volume 3, Page 16

- ❏ Droids series, any with background 225.00
- ❏ Droids series, any without background 175.00
- ❏ Ewoks series, any with background 225.00
- ❏ Ewoks series, any without background 175.00
- ❏ "The Great Heap" feature, any with background 225.00
- ❏ "The Great Heap" feature, any without background... 175.00

ACME Archives
Character keys. 4"x6" (6"x8" matted).
- ❏ Anakin Skywalker, individually numbered, exclusive to Comic-Con [v1e1:15] 75.00
- ❏ ARC Captain, 750 produced, individually numbered, exclusive to Razor's Edge Collectibles [10-01] 95.00
- ❏ Asajj Ventress, individually numbered, exclusive to Razor's Edge Collectibles [10-02] 85.00
- ❏ Boba Fett, individually numbered, exclusive to StarWarsShop.com [v1e1:15] 75.00
- ❏ Boba Fett Holiday Special, individually numbered, exclusive to Hyperspace Members [10-03] 95.00

21

Art: Amimation Cels

 10-16
 10-17
 10-18
 10-19
 10-20

 10-21
 10-22
 10-23
 10-24
 10-25

 10-26
 10-27
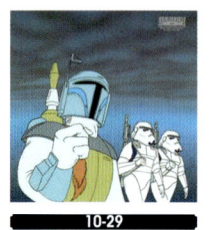 10-28
 10-29
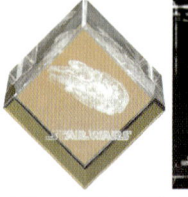 10-30

- ❏ C-3PO, individually numbered, exclusive to StarWarsShop.com [v1e1:15] 95.00
- ❏ Chewbacca, 750 produced, individually numbered, exclusive to Comic-Con [10-04] 85.00
- ❏ Count Dooku, individually numbered, exclusive to Sideshow Collectibles [10-05] 85.00
- ❏ Darth Sidious, individually numbered, exclusive to Comic-Con [v1e1:15] 85.00
- ❏ Darth Stewie (Family Guy), individually numbered, exclusive to Entertainment Earth [10-06] 50.00
- ❏ Darth Vader, individually numbered [10-07] 90.00
- ❏ Durge, individually numbered, exclusive to StarWarsShop.com [10-08] 50.00
- ❏ General Grievous, individually numbered, exclusive to San Diego Comic-Con [10-09] 85.00
- ❏ Grand Moff Tarkin, individually numbered, exclusive to Star Wars Celebration IV [v1e1:15] 75.00
- ❏ Han Solo, individually numbered, exclusive to Hyperspace Members [10-10] 95.00
- ❏ Kit Fisto, individually numbered [10-11] 65.00
- ❏ Luke Skywalker Bespin, 750 produced, individually numbered [v1e1:15] 75.00
- ❏ Mace Windu, individually numbered [10-12] 85.00
- ❏ Maris Brood, signed by Lucasfilm concept artist Amy Beth Christenson and voice actress Adrienne Wilkinson, exclusive to StarWarsShop.com 95.00
- ❏ Mickey Mouse, Jedi, numbered [10-13] 125.00
- ❏ Obi-Wan, Clone Wars, 750 produced, exclusive to StarWarsShop.com [10-14] 95.00
- ❏ Padmé Amidala [10-15] 75.00
- ❏ Princess Leia, 750 produced, individually numbered, exclusive to Comic-Con [10-16] 250.00
- ❏ Princess Leia, prisoner, individually numbered, exclusive to New York Comic-Con [10-17] 90.00
- ❏ R2-D2, individually numbered, exclusive to StarWarsShop.com [10-18] 95.00
- ❏ Roron Corobb, 750 produced, individually numbered, exclusive to Andrews Toys [v1e1:16] 50.00
- ❏ Sandtrooper, individually numbered, exclusive to San Diego Comic-Con [10-19] 75.00
- ❏ Shaak Ti, individually numbered [10-20] 55.00
- ❏ TIE Fighter Pilot, individually numbered, exclusive to Star Wars Celebration Europe [v1e1:16] 80.00
- ❏ Yoda, individually numbered, exclusive to Star Wars Celebration III [10-21] 135.00

Clone Wars 3D.
- ❏ Clone troopers, 8"x10", exclusive to Toy Fair [v1e1:16] 135.00

Clone Wars by Genndy Tartakovsky.
- ❏ Anakin vs. Asajj, 20"x27", 350 produced, individually numbered 300.00
- ❏ General Kenobi, 10.5"x12.5", individually numbered [10-22] 195.00

Clone Wars by Genndy Tartakovsky. Character keys, framed sets.
- ❏ Padmé Amidala, Arc Captain, Darth Sidious, Anakin Skywalker, 32"x9.5" 480.00

Clone Wars by Genndy Tartakovsky. Model sheets. 20"x24", 300 produced each, individually numbered.
- ❏ Anakin 320.00
- ❏ General Grievous 300.00
- ❏ Yoda [4-11] 295.00

Family Guy Pix-cels. 8.5"x11" (13"x16" matted).
- ❏ Here They Come [10-23] 250.00
- ❏ Not So Great Escape [10-24] 250.00
- ❏ Stolen Plans [10-25] 250.00
- ❏ Trash Compactor 250.00
- ❏ Victory 190.00
- ❏ We Meet Again 250.00

Disney / MGM
- ❏ Defend-ears of the Kingdom [10-26] 350.00

Nelvana
- ❏ Ewoks series, hand painted partial, included with 2004 Fan club packet 50.00

Holiday Special.
- ❏ Boba Fett, animated line master 235.00
- ❏ General Ristt, Star Wars Holiday Special 125.00

Royal Animation Art
Limited edition cel series.
- ❏ Droids: Battle Cruiser [v1e1:16] 85.00
- ❏ Droids: Best Friends [v1e1:16] 85.00
- ❏ Droids: Stranded [10-27] 85.00
- ❏ Ewoks: Celebration [10-28] 85.00
- ❏ Ewoks: The Big Hug [v1e1:16] 85.00
- ❏ Holiday Special: Boba Fett: Bounty Hunter, 5,000 produced [10-29] 85.00

Warner Bros.
- ❏ Star Warners [10-30] 275.00

Art: Cardbacks
Continued in Volume 3, Page 17

Hasbro
30th anniversary. Exclusive to Star Wars Celebration IV.
- ❏ Darth Vader 25.00
- ❏ Luke Skywalker 25.00
- ❏ Stormtrooper 25.00

Unleashed.
- ❏ Aayla Secura 25.00
- ❏ Bossk 25.00
- ❏ Tusken Raider 25.00

Art: Crystal and Glass
Continued in Volume 3, Page 17

Bradford Exchange
- ❏ Star Wars stained glass panorama wall decor art, approximately 28"x24" 170.00

Cards, Inc. (UK)
Crystal Cuts.
- ❏ Darth Vader 65.00
- ❏ Jedi Starfighter 65.00
- ❏ Yoda 65.00

Code 3 Collectibles
- ❏ Millennium Falcon, satin lined case, ordering gift at San Diego Comic-Con 2003 [11-01] 135.00

 11-01
 11-02
 11-03
 11-04
 11-05
 11-06
 11-07

Art: Portfolios

Disney / MGM
Star Wars Weekends logo, crystal.
- 2004 .... 250.00
- 2005 .... 250.00
- 2006 [3:326] 250.00

Stiefelmayer-Contento
Laser engraved 3D glass cubes. 3 inches.
- AT-RT with AT-RT driver [v1e1:16] 75.00
- Darth Vader [v1e1:16] 75.00
- Yoda [v1e1:16] 75.00

Laser engraved 3D glass cubes. 5 inches.
- ARC-170 [11-02] 200.00
- AT-RT Driver [11-03] 200.00
- Darth Vader [11-04] 200.00
- R2-D2 [11-05] 200.00
- The Emperor [11-06] 200.00
- Yoda [11-07] 200.00

Art: Lithography
Continued in Volume 3, Page 17

- Empire Strikes Back by Billy Dee Williams, 30"x30", individually numbered [12-01] 125.00
- Episode III: Revenge of the Sith portfolio of 10 prints [4:11] 80.00
- Episode III: Revenge of the Sith premium for EPIII DVD pre-order, exclusive to Best Buy [12-02] 50.00

20th Century Fox
- Episode I premium for pre-ordering The Phantom Menace video [v1e1:17] 25.00
- Jedi Duel, premium for ordering The Phantom Menace video 25.00
- Special Edition Video Covers, free with purchase of Star Wars: Special Edition [12-03] 30.00
- THX Video Covers, free with purchase of THX Star Wars classic trilogy [12-04] 35.00

ACME Archives
- Starfighter Pursuit, 24"x10.75", curved frame 600.00

Animated Animations
Coruscant Skyline framed giclee. 34 1/4"x13". Limited to 1,000 pieces.
- Night in the Galactic Capital 365.00
- Sunset on the Republic 365.00

Cards, Inc. (UK)
- Star Wars movie poster lithograph collection, A3 sized, 6,000 produced 60.00

Disney / MGM
Star Wars Weekends.
- 2000 [12-05] 49.00
- 2001 [12-06] 49.00
- 2003 [12-07] 49.00
- 2005 [12-08] 49.00
- 2006 [12-09] 49.00

Gifted Images Publishing
- Darth Vader from box artwork of Topps Star Wars Galaxy cards, 23.5"x30" signed by the artist, 500 produced, individually numbered 560.00
- Luke and Yoda signed by the artist, 500 produced, individually numbered 410.00

Lucasfilm
- Darth Vader concept, McQuarrie art, 100 lb. linen, 18"x24", 100 produced [4:11] 300.00
- Fett "Like Father, Like Son," 17"x25", 350 produced [4:11] 250.00

Manga
ANH, ESB, ROTJ comic cover trio, 18"x24"
- Framed, unlimited 100.00
- Signed and framed, 500 produced 170.00
- Unlimited [v1e1:18] 50.00

Russell Walks
- Boba Fett, hand-numbered and signed, 100 produced, individually numbered, exclusive to Star Wars Celebration V 80.00

Score Board
- Yoda sitting at his desk by Michael Whelan, 18"x17" signed, 850 produced 170.00

Star Struck
- Return of the Jedi lithograph, 3 X-Wings flying toward Death Star II with planets all around, signed, 3,000 produced, individually numbered 350.00

Art: Metal
Continued in Volume 3, Page 19

- Battle Droid [v1e1:17] 40.00
- Captain Tarpals [v1e1:17] 40.00
- Jango Fett [v1e1:17] 40.00

Bolt Gallery
- Battle Droid, 20", 9 lbs. [v1e1:17] 100.00
- Battle Droid, 9", 4 lbs. [3:104] 80.00
- Boba Fett, 24", 20 lbs. [v1e1:17] 275.00
- C-3PO, 18", 13 lbs. [v1e1:17] 140.00
- Darth Vader, 24", 25 lbs. [v1e1:17] 275.00
- R2-D2, 10", 15 lbs. [3:104] 100.00
- R2-D2, 8", 3 lbs. [v1e1:17] 65.00

Disney / MGM
- Boba Fett, laser cut [13-01] 85.00

Art: Portfolios
Continued in Volume 3, Page 19

Star Wars Episode I: The Phantom Menace.
- Deluxe [v1e1:17] 135.00
- Standard edition [14-01] 60.00

Aardvark-Vanaheim Press
- A collection of 10 prints, 250 produced 165.00

Ballantine
Art portfolios featuring the work of Ralph McQuarrie.
- Empire Strikes Back [14-02] 125.00
- Return of the Jedi [14-03] 125.00
- Star Wars [v1e1:18] 145.00

Bandai (Japan)
- Paintings by Ralph McQuarrie [14-04] 250.00

Art: Portfolios

Black Falcon
- ☐ 2 McQuarrie concept prints in Darth Vader folder, sealed with pewter medallion [4:12] 375.00

Cards, Inc. (UK)
- ☐ Collector's edition, patches and artwork, individually numbered 160.00

Chronicle Books
- ☐ The Art of Ralph McQuarrie (art box) [14-05] 30.00

Classico
- ☐ Star Wars [v1e1:18] 18.00

Zanart Publishing Inc.
Set of eight 11"x14".
- ☐ Trilogy movie cards [v1e1:18] 35.00
- ☐ Vehicle blueprints [14-06] 55.00

Art: Prints
Continued in Volume 3, Page 19

Empire 30th Anniversary Artwork Collection. 100 produced, each, individually numbered. Exclusive to StarWarsShop.com
- ☐ Found Someone You Have, by Nathan Hamill 200.00
- ☐ I Know, by Amy Beth Christenson 200.00
- ☐ Oh My. I Am Terribly Sorry..., by Jamie Snell 200.00
- ☐ Only What You Take With You, by Russell Walks 200.00
- ☐ Never Tell Me The Odds, by Chris Trevas 200.00
- ☐ The Emperor, by Cat Staggs 200.00
- ☐ The Taking of Echo Base by the Sith Lord Darth Vader, by Tom Hodges 200.00
- ☐ This Is No Cave, by JAKe 200.00
- ☐ Ugnaught Retreat, by Michael Flemming 200.00

20th Century Fox
- ☐ "The Force on Blu-Ray" Vader / Yoda, collectible lithographs 35.00

ACME Archives
- ☐ ILM Halloween party: vampire Leia, 300 produced, individually numbered 60.00

Family Guy. 395 produced, individually numbered.
- ☐ Not So Great Escape 75.00
- ☐ Trash Compactor 75.00

Family Guy. Gold matte. Hand numbered in gold. 77 produced, individually numbered. Exclusive to StarWarsShop.com
- ☐ Not So Great Escape 89.00
- ☐ Trash Compactor 89.00

Giclee.
- ☐ A Destiny Unfolds, hand signed, 20.5"x13.5", 200 produced 850.00
- ☐ A Destiny Unfolds, hand signed, 41"x27", 200 produced 1,250.00
- ☐ Anakin vs. Asajj, 20"x27", framed, paper, 350 produced 300.00
- ☐ Anakin vs. Asajj, 20"x27", matted and framed, canvas, 350 produced [15-01] 560.00
- ☐ Boba Fett: Bounty Hunter, 26"x17", framed, canvas, 100 produced 800.00
- ☐ Boba Fett: Bounty Hunter, 26"x17", framed, paper, 350 produced 500.00
- ☐ Darth Vader, 26"x17", framed, canvas, 100 produced 800.00
- ☐ Darth Vader, 26"x17", framed, paper, 350 produced 500.00
- ☐ Jedi and Villains 16"x20", matted, hand numbered, 500 produced [15-02] 125.00
- ☐ Yoda, 26"x17", framed, canvas, 100 produced 800.00
- ☐ Yoda, 26"x17", framed, paper, 350 produced 500.00

Giclees, matted with metal engraved title tag.
- ☐ Arc troopers on Muunilinst, 16"x20", 500 produced, individually numbered [15-03] 95.00
- ☐ Light of the Jedi, Anakin Skywalker, Obi-Wan Kenobi, Ki-Adi-Mundi, Shaak-Ti, Kit Fisto, Mace Windu, and Ronet Corobb with Yoda background, 500 produced, individually numbered [15-04] 95.00
- ☐ Shadow of the Sith, Count Dooku, General Grievous, Asajj Ventress, Durge with Palpatine background, 500 produced, individually numbered 95.00
- ☐ Women of Clone Wars, Padmé Amidala, Aayla Secura, Shaak Ti, Barriss Offee, and Luminara Unduli with Asajj Ventress background, 500 produced, individually numbered [15-05] 95.00

Legends of the Force giclees, 7"x17".
- ☐ Anakin and Obi-Wan, red 50.00
- ☐ Anakin and Obi-Wan, yellow 50.00
- ☐ Dooku and Yoda, blue 50.00
- ☐ Dooku and Yoda, green 50.00

Sketch plates. Individually numbered.
- ☐ AT-AT, exclusive to Star Wars Celebration V [15-06] 50.00
- ☐ C-3PO, 750 produced [15-07] 50.00
- ☐ R2-D2, exclusive to Star Wars Celebration IV [15-08] 50.00
- ☐ X-Wing Fighter [15-09] 50.00

Adam Hughes
- ☐ Last Daughter of Alderaan, 18"x39", 250 produced, individually numbered, exclusive to Star Wars Celebration IV [5:13] 75.00

Allison Sohn
- ☐ The Princess, 250 produced, individually numbered, exclusive to Star Wars Celebration IV [5:13] 35.00

Amy Pronovost
- ☐ Utinni! 30!, 250 produced, individually numbered, exclusive to Star Wars Celebration IV [5:13] 25.00

Brent Woodside
250 produced, each, individually numbered. Exclusive to Star Wars Celebration IV.
- ☐ Clones 25.00
- ☐ Clones, remarqued [5:13] 30.00

Brian Denham
- ☐ Light and Magic, 18"x24", 250 produced, individually numbered, exclusive to Star Wars Celebration IV [5:13] 35.00

Brian Rood
- ☐ A New Hope, 250 produced, individually numbered, exclusive to Star Wars Celebration IV [5:13] 50.00
- ☐ Darkness Falls, exclusive to Celebration III 35.00
- ☐ Where Science Meets Imagination 35.00

Cards, Inc. (UK)
A3 size, lenticular with certificate of authenticity.
- ☐ Jedi Rescue 3D, 2,000 produced 40.00
- ☐ Turn to the Dark Side, 6,000 produced, exclusive to QVC 25.00

Art prints with certificate of authenticity in storage tin.
- ☐ Revenge of the Sith, art 65.00
- ☐ Star Wars Saga, art 65.00

Cat Staggs
- ☐ No Shields, All Guts, 250 produced, individually numbered, exclusive to Star Wars Celebration Europe 150.00
- ☐ Spirit of '77, 250 produced, individually numbered, exclusive to Star Wars Celebration IV [5:13] 50.00

Chris Trevas
- ☐ Thirty Years of the Force, 250 produced, individually numbered, exclusive to Star Wars Celebration IV [5:13] 50.00

Clark Mitchell
- ☐ Darth Vader / Imperial emblem, 24"x18", 250 produced, individually numbered, exclusive to Star Wars Celebration III 45.00
- ☐ Vader, 250 produced, individually numbered, exclusive to Star Wars Celebration IV [5:13] 75.00

Craig Howell
- ☐ 30th Anniversary, 250 produced, numbered, exclusive to Star Wars Celebration IV [5:13] 50.00

Crystal Art Gallery International
16"x20" posters by Trends International, framed.
- ☐ Anakin Skywalker [15-10] 12.00
- ☐ Battle of Geonosis [15-11] 12.00

Cynthia Cummens
- ☐ Celebration print, 250 produced, individually numbered, exclusive to Star Wars Celebration IV [5:13] 25.00

D and L Screen Printing
24"x36", screen printed.
- ☐ Raider, by Dave Kinsey, 350 produced, individually numbered 50.00
- ☐ Scrap Yard Power Droid, by Dave Kinsey, 350 produced, individually numbered 50.00

Dave Dorman
- ☐ Imperial Persuasion, 20"x36", 250 produced, individually numbered, exclusive to Star Wars Celebration IV [5:14] 100.00
- ☐ Revenge of the Sith, 18"x24", 250 produced, individually numbered, exclusive to Star Wars Celebration III 100.00

Star Wars Special Edition. 20"x36"
- ☐ A New Hope 75.00
- ☐ Empire Strikes Back 75.00
- ☐ Return of the Jedi 75.00

David Rabbitte
- ☐ Star Wars, 250 produced, individually numbered, exclusive to Star Wars Celebration IV [5:14] 25.00

David Seeley
- ☐ Rogue Leader, archival print on satin finish, 250 produced, individually numbered, exclusive to Star Wars Celebration IV [5:14] 60.00
- ☐ Rogue Leader, archival print on matte finish, 250 produced, individually numbered, exclusive to Star Wars Celebration IV 150.00

Disney / MGM
- ☐ Donald Duck as Boba Fett, 30 produced, individually numbered [15-12] 150.00
- ☐ Empire Strikes Back poster art 50.00
- ☐ Jedi Mickey 75.00
- ☐ Princess Minnie Leia 75.00
- ☐ Princess Minnie Leia II 75.00
- ☐ Return of the Jedi poster art 50.00
- ☐ Return of the Mouse 75.00
- ☐ Star Wars poster art 50.00

Galoob
Artwork by Ralph McQuarrie, signed, limited to 1,500 and numbered. Toy Fair exclusive.
- ☐ Death Star 45.00
- ☐ Hoth 45.00
- ☐ Star Wars [15-13] 45.00
- ☐ Yavin 45.00

Gifted Images Publishing
- ☐ Darth Vader by Ken Steacy, 500 produced, individually numbered 475.00

Grant Gould
- ☐ A New Hope, heavy gloss stock with full black-border bleed, 250 produced, individually numbered, exclusive to Star Wars Celebration IV [5:14] 35.00

Hans Jensen
- ☐ B-Wing Starfighter, 250 produced, individually numbered, exclusive to Star Wars Celebration IV [5:14] 30.00

Cutaway prints. 500 produced, each, numbered.
- ☐ AT-AT 35.00
- ☐ Millennium Falcon 35.00

Howard M. Shum
- ☐ Animation, 13"x9", 250 produced, numbered, exclusive to Star Wars Celebration IV [5:14] 25.00

Art: Prints

15-01

15-02

15-03

15-04

15-05

15-06

15-07

15-08

15-09

15-10

15-11

15-12

15-13

15-14

Icarus (UK)
Textured 5.5"x7.5" prints mounted in silver wood frames.
- ❏ Boba Fett 28.00
- ❏ C-3PO and R2-D2 [15-14] 28.00
- ❏ Chewbacca [5:14] 28.00
- ❏ Darth Vader [5:14] 28.00
- ❏ Luke Skywalker [5:14] 28.00
- ❏ Yoda [5:14] 28.00

JAKe
- ❏ Star Wars, 16.5"x23", 250 produced, numbered, exclusive to Star Wars Celebration IV [5:14] 50.00

Jan Duursema
- ❏ Legacy, 250 produced, individually numbered, exclusive to Star Wars Celebration IV [5:14] 50.00

Jason Palmer
- ❏ ESB 25th Anniversary, Celebration III exclusive 35.00
- ❏ Padmé, Star Wars Celebration IV exclusive 75.00

Jeff Carlisle
- ❏ 30 years ago, in a galaxy far, far away, 250 produced, individually numbered, exclusive to Star Wars Celebration IV [5:14] 45.00

Jerry Vanderstelt
- ❏ A New Hope, 250 produced, individually numbered exclusive to Celebration III 50.00
- ❏ Forces, 250 produced, individually numbered, exclusive to Star Wars Celebration IV [5:14] 150.00

Joe Corroney
- ❏ Revenge of the Sith, 250 produced, individually numbered, exclusive to Celebration III 45.00
- ❏ The First Thirty Years, 19"x24", 250 produced, individually numbered, exclusive to Star Wars Celebration IV [5:14] 50.00

John Alvin
250 produced of each, individually numbered. Exclusive to Star Wars Celebration IV.
- ❏ Episode IV Decade III [5:14] 250.00
- ❏ If There's a Bright Center [5:14] 300.00

Justin Chung
- ❏ Star Wars 30th Anniversary, 250 produced, indiv. numbered, exclusive to Star Wars Celebration IV [5:15] 45.00

Ken Phipps
- ❏ The First 30 Years, 250 produced, individually numbered, exclusive to Star Wars Celebration IV [5:15] 35.00

Ken Steacy
- ❏ Progression, 250 produced, individually numbered, exclusive to Star Wars Celebration IV [5:15] 100.00

12"x18". 250 produced, each. Individually numbered. Celebration III exclusive.
- ❏ Anakin Skywalker, 1st in sequence 60.00
- ❏ Anakin / Darth Vader, 2nd in sequence 65.00
- ❏ Darth Vader galaxy art, 3rd in sequence 60.00

Kilian Plunkett
- ❏ The First 30 Years, 250 produced, numbered, exclusive to Star Wars Celebration IV [5:15] 50.00

LucasArts
- ❏ The Force Unleashed, preorder premium [5:15] 15.00

Lucasfilm
Lobby cards. Empire Strikes Back 16"x20".
- ❏ Bespin Freezing Chamber 95.00
- ❏ Hoth Rebel trenches 95.00
- ❏ Luke riding Tauntaun 95.00
- ❏ Vader on Hoth 95.00

Lobby cards. Empire Strikes Back 20"x30".
- ❏ Darth Vader / starfield 125.00
- ❏ Falcon fleeing Star Destroyer 125.00
- ❏ Luke and Darth Vader duel 125.00

Lobby cards. Return of the Jedi 16"x20".
- ❏ Droids on Endor 75.00
- ❏ Leia quiets C-3PO 75.00
- ❏ Luke on Sail Barge 75.00

Lobby cards. Return of the Jedi 20"x30".
- ❏ AT-ST attacks 85.00
- ❏ Death Star II 85.00

Malcolm Tween
- ❏ Star Wars Celebration, 250 produced, numbered, exclusive to Star Wars Celebration IV [5:15] 50.00

Marc Wolfe
- ❏ Join the Fight, 250 produced, individually numbered, exclusive to Star Wars Celebration IV [5:15] 60.00

Mark Brooks
20"x30". 250 produced, each. Individually numbered. Celebration IV exclusives.
- ❏ A Long Time Ago, Far Far Away [5:15] 50.00
- ❏ A Long Time Ago, Far Far Away, remarqued 75.00

Mark Chiarello
- ❏ Enlist Now, 250 produced, individually numbered, exclusive to Star Wars Celebration IV [5:15] 50.00

Mark Raats
- ❏ Luke Skywalker, 100 pound paper stock with aqueous coating, 250 produced, individually numbered, exclusive to Star Wars Celebration IV [5:15] 50.00

Matt Busch
Movie anniversary posters, "Villains Style". 24"x36"
- ❏ Empire Strikes Back: 27th 50.00
- ❏ Return of the Jedi: 25th, 500 produced, numbered, exclusive to Motor City Comic-Con 50.00
- ❏ Star Wars: 30th, 250 produced, numbered, exclusive to Star Wars Celebration IV [5:15] 50.00

Matthew Fletcher and Christopher Uminga
- ❏ The Bounty Hunters from The Empire Strikes Back, 200 produced, individually numbered, exclusive to Comic-Con 40.00

Monte Michael Moore
- ❏ Empires of Destiny, 24"x37" 45.00

A Balance of Force series. Individually numbered. Exclusive to Celebration IV.
- ❏ Emperor's edition, 24"x36", archival photo luster paper, 25 produced 225.00
- ❏ Emperor's edition, 24"x36", giclee prints on archival artists canvas, 25 produced 275.00

Art: Prints

15-15

15-16

15-17

15-18

15-19

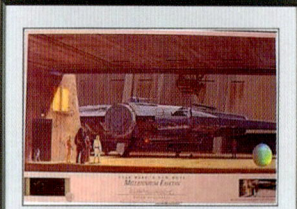
15-20

15-21

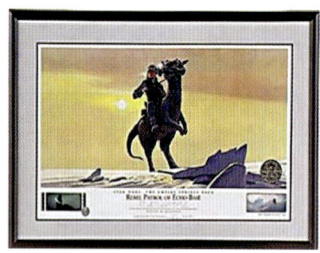
15-22

15-23

15-24

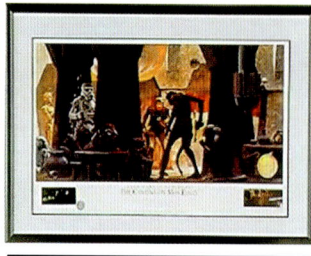
15-25

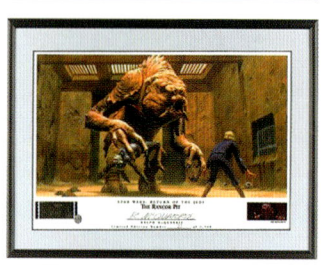
15-26

❏ Jedi edition, 18"x27", archival photo luster paper, 75 produced 90.00
❏ Rebel edition, 13"x19", archival watercolor paper, 125 produced [5:15] 65.00

Paizo Publishing / Fan Club
❏ Episode II, Attack of the Clones, hand signed and numbered, 500 produced, numbered [5:15] 50.00

Phil Noto
❏ Scoundrel, 250 produced, individually numbered, exclusive to Star Wars Celebration IV [5:15] 50.00

Ralph McQuarrie
250 produced of each, individually numbered. Exclusive to Celebration IV.
❏ Droids in the Desert [5:15] 30.00
❏ Laser Duel [5:16] 30.00

Randy Martinez
250 produced of each, individually numbered.
❏ Celebration III, exclusive to Star Wars Celebration III ...35.00
❏ Sith—Live at the Hollywood Bowl, exclusive to Star Wars Celebration IV [5:16] 40.00
❏ Star Wars Celebration, exclusive to Star Wars Celebration IV [5:16] 50.00

Richard Chasemore
❏ TIE Bomber, 250 produced, individually numbered, exclusive to Star Wars Celebration IV [5:16] 30.00

Cutaway prints. 500 produced, each. Numbered.
❏ Sandcrawler 35.00
❏ Slave I 35.00

Robert Hendrickson
❏ In a Galaxy Far, Far Away, 250 produced, individually numbered, exclusive to Star Wars Celebration IV [5:16] 50.00

Russell Walks
❏ Generations diptych, 250 produced, numbered, exclusive to Star Wars Celebration IV [5:16] 50.00

Scott Erwert
❏ Luke and Leia, Death Star chasm, 250 produced, individually numbered, exclusive to Star Wars Celebration IV [5:16] 50.00

Sorah Suhng
❏ Aurra Sing from Star Wars The Clone Wars, signed, 125 produced, individually numbered, exclusive to San Diego Comic-Con 40.00

Star Struck
❏ X-Wing Fighters and Death Star II by Michael David Ward, 3,000 produced 225.00

starwars.com
In 2003 the official Star Wars website offered 13 themed galleries of approximately 12 images in each gallery. Fans could order images through an online merchant in a variety of formats. Considering the number of galleries, images available, and formats to choose from, there are thousands of combinations that were made.

The themed galleries were composed of images from: Bounty Hunters, Clone Wars, Creatures, Droids, Holiday Art, Jedi Logos and Emblems, Padmé, Poster Art, Princess Leia, Rebel, Sith, and Vehicles.

❏ 8"x10" high quality glossy prints 10.00
❏ 8"x10" high quality matte prints 10.00
❏ 16"x20" high quality glossy prints 20.00
❏ 16"x20" high quality matte prints 20.00
❏ 20"x24" high quality glossy prints 25.00
❏ 20"x24" high quality matte prints 25.00
❏ 20"x30" high quality glossy prints 30.00
❏ 20"x30" high quality matte prints 30.00

Steve Anderson
❏ The Dark Avenger, 250 produced, individually numbered, exclusive to Star Wars Celebration IV [5:16] 50.00

Terese Nielsen
❏ Padmé, 250 produced, individually numbered, exclusive to Star Wars Celebration IV [5:16] 50.00

Tom Hodges
❏ One more season, 250 produced, numbered, exclusive to Star Wars Celebration IV [5:16] 50.00

Star Wars Universe Dream Park series. Exclusive to Star Wars Celebration V.
❏ Coruscant 75.00
❏ Death Star Trench Run 75.00
❏ Gungan Bongo Adventure 75.00
❏ Hoth Escape From Echo Base Coaster 75.00
❏ Jabba's Palace Grill 75.00
❏ Star Wars Dream Park Map, 250 produced ...160.00

Tommy Lee Edwards
250 produced of each. Individually numbered.
❏ Darth Vader 40.00
❏ Skywalker 30 Years, exclusive to Star Wars Celebration IV [5:16] 80.00

Topps
10"x14". 99 produced of each, individually numbered. Exclusive to Topps.com
❏ Companions, each 24.00
❏ Companions platinum, each 100.00
❏ Defining Moments, each 30.00
❏ Defining Moments platinum, each 100.00
❏ Masterwork, each 30.00
❏ Scum and Villainy, each 30.00
❏ Scum and Villainy platinum, each 100.00

Tsuneo Sanda
250 produced of each, individually numbered.
❏ Congratulations! 300.00
❏ Star Wars Saga, lithograph and silk, exclusive to Star Wars Celebration IV [5:16] 130.00

William O'Neill
❏ Kill Sith!, 250 produced, individually numbered, exclusive to Star Wars Celebration IV [5:16] 50.00

Willitts Designs
Art work by Ralph McQuarrie, 18"x12", signed, limited to 2,500 and numbered.
❏ Cloud City of Bespin [15-15] 180.00
❏ Darth Vader's Arrival [15-16] 180.00
❏ Death Star Main Reactor [15-17] 180.00

Autographs

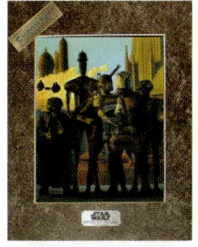
16-01

16-02

16-03

16-04

16-05

16-06

16-07

16-08

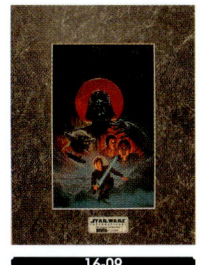
16-09

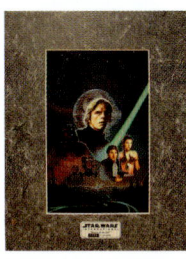
16-10

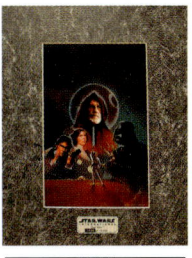
16-11

16-12

16-13

16-14

- ❏ Jabba the Hutt [15-18] 180.00
- ❏ Luke and Darth Vader Duel [15-19] 180.00
- ❏ Millennium Falcon [15-20] 180.00
- ❏ Rebel Attack on Death Star [15-21] 180.00
- ❏ Rebel Ceremony 180.00
- ❏ Rebel Patrol of Echo Base [15-22] 180.00
- ❏ Speeder Bike Chase [15-23] 180.00
- ❏ The Battle of Hoth [15-24] 180.00
- ❏ The Cantina on Mos Eisley [15-25] 180.00
- ❏ The Rancor Pit [15-26] 180.00

Zanart Publishing Inc.
500 produced. Individually numbered.
- ❏ Darth Vader by Williamson, signed 250.00
- ❏ Luke Skywalker, X-Wing Pilot by Williamson, signed 250.00
- ❏ Millennium Falcon with Han and Chewie. Darth Vader with TIE Fighter, Luke with X-Wing. Blueprints used as background. Framed and signed 300.00
- ❏ Stormtroopers by Williamson, signed 250.00

Art: Prints, Chrome Art

O.S.P. Publishing Inc.
- ❏ Star Wars Special Edition Trilogy, exclusive to QVC 45.00

Zanart Publishing Inc.
11"x14" matted.
- ❏ Bounty Hunters [16-01] 50.00
- ❏ C-3PO and R2-D2 [16-02] 50.00
- ❏ Dark Forces cover art 50.00
- ❏ Darth Vader, art [16-03] 50.00
- ❏ Darth Vader, photo [16-04] 50.00
- ❏ Escape from Hoth 50.00
- ❏ Space Battle [16-05] 50.00
- ❏ Stormtrooper, trilogy art 50.00

11"x14" matted. 1995 video cover art.
- ❏ Empire Strikes Back / Stormtrooper [16-06] 40.00
- ❏ Return of the Jedi / Yoda [16-07] 40.00
- ❏ Star Wars / Darth Vader [16-08] 40.00

11"x14" matted. International video cover art.
- ❏ Empire Strikes Back [16-09] 45.00
- ❏ Return of the Jedi [16-10] 45.00
- ❏ Star Wars [16-11] 45.00

11"x14" matted. Movie poster art.
- ❏ Empire Strikes Back [16-12] 50.00
- ❏ Return of the Jedi [16-13] 50.00
- ❏ Star Wars 50.00
- ❏ Star Wars Special Edition [16-14] 50.00

11"x14" matted. Shadows of the Empire.
- ❏ Prince Xizor, 4,500 produced 35.00
- ❏ Shadows of the Empire 55.00

11"x14" matted. Technical drawings.
- ❏ A-Wing 65.00
- ❏ AT-AT 65.00
- ❏ AT-ST 65.00
- ❏ B-Wing 65.00
- ❏ Star Destroyer 65.00
- ❏ TIE Fighter 65.00
- ❏ X-Wing 65.00
- ❏ Y-Wing 65.00

Autographs

Values listed are what the actual signature is worth on common items such as 8"x10" photographs or action figures. Up to $10 more should be added if the photograph is oversized (11"x14" or 16"x20").

Officially licensed photographs are preferred to non-licensed items. Significant deductions in value come into play if photos are grainy, out of focus, or obviously amateur, such as a print from a screen capture. The licensed photos from Official Pix (www.OfficialPix.com) are regarded as the best quality and the more preferred for collectible value.

"Premium" signed items such as official one-sheet posters should be considered more valuable if signed on more recent items, after 1995. Autographs on vintage posters may reduce value of the poster itself to non-autograph collectors.

The addition of a character name is preferable and may assist with resale, but it does not affect value. Quotes or other messages do not affect value and should only be requested if the line was actually uttered by the character. Personalization of the autograph will usually deduct from the value of the signature, unless the actor is deceased.

- ❏ Abbey, Dawn 35.00
- ❏ Ackroyd, David 15.00
- ❏ Acomba, David 25.00
- ❏ Acord, David 25.00
- ❏ Adel, Daniel 85.00
- ❏ Affonso, Barbara 15.00
- ❏ Akindoyeni, Tux 30.00
- ❏ Alaskey, Joe 45.00
- ❏ Alcroft, Jamie 25.00
- ❏ Alessio, Josephine 50.00
- ❏ Alexander, Coinneach 25.00
- ❏ Allen, Amy [17-01] 30.00
- ❏ Allen, Hazel 25.00
- ❏ Allen, Peter 30.00
- ❏ Allen, Roger MacBride 25.00
- ❏ Allen, Tony 25.00
- ❏ Alleneck, Charles 25.00
- ❏ Allie, Scott 25.00
- ❏ Allnutt, Frank 35.00
- ❏ Allred, Michael 25.00
- ❏ Allsopp, Christine 25.00
- ❏ Allston, Aaron 10.00
- ❏ Alsup, Bunny 25.00
- ❏ Altman, John 30.00
- ❏ Alzmann, Christian 30.00
- ❏ Amendt, Paul 45.00
- ❏ Anastassiou, Nicholas 30.00
- ❏ Andersen, Gunnar 60.00
- ❏ Anderson, Bob 30.00
- ❏ Anderson, Franki 30.00

17-01

17-02

17-03

17-04

17-05

17-06

Autographs

❑ Anderson, Kevin J. [17-02] 25.00	❑ Baker, Glyn 25.00	❑ Bell, Patty 30.00
❑ Anderson, Malumba 35.00	❑ Baker, Jerry 150.00	❑ Belleci, Salvatore 'Tory' 25.00
❑ Anderson, Sam 25.00	❑ Baker, Kenny [17-04] 150.00	❑ Bellew, Bernard 25.00
❑ Anderson, Steven D. 25.00	❑ Baker, Rick 40.00	❑ Bellotte, Brigitte 75.00
❑ Anderson, Vass 25.00	❑ Baldry, John 'Long John' 30.00	❑ Benedict, Jay 25.00
❑ Andrews, Todd 30.00	❑ Balin, Marty 25.00	❑ Benjamin, Fenella 25.00
❑ Angel, Jack 25.00	❑ Ballan, Michael Henbury 30.00	❑ Bennett, Alan 30.00
❑ Ankrum, David 30.00	❑ Bambridge, Jolyon 25.00	❑ Bennett, Sarah 30.00
❑ Ansel, Karen 25.00	❑ Bannon, Paul 25.00	❑ Benson, Mike 25.00
❑ Apostalos, Margo [17-03] 30.00	❑ Barbieri, Chantelle 25.00	❑ Berg, Jon 25.00
❑ Appleton, Phil 25.00	❑ Barbour, Peter 25.00	❑ Berg, Ted 20.00
❑ Arbogast, Annie 55.00	❑ Barclay, David Alan [17-05] 30.00	❑ Berk, Ailsa 30.00
❑ Arbogast, Roy 30.00	❑ Bareham, Adam 35.00	❑ Berkey, John C. 30.00
❑ Arkin, Adam 20.00	❑ Barlettani, Brian 25.00	❑ Bernet, Chopper 25.00
❑ Armato, Dominic 25.00	❑ Barnes, Steven 25.00	❑ Best, Ahmed [17-08] 55.00
❑ Armellino, Amanda 45.00	❑ Barnett, Douglas 25.00	❑ Beswick, Doug 30.00
❑ Armitage, Richard 30.00	❑ Baron, Mike 25.00	❑ Betancourt, John Gregory 25.00
❑ Armstrong, Ray 30.00	❑ Barry, John 30.00	❑ Betts, Pamela 30.00
❑ Armstrong, Vic 15.00	❑ Barth, Peter 25.00	❑ Bewley, Tom 25.00
❑ Arnold, Lori 30.00	❑ Bartholomew, Brian 25.00	❑ Bies, Anna 25.00
❑ Aron, Michael 25.00	❑ Barton, Aidan 25.00	❑ Bies, Don [17-09] 35.00
❑ Arthur, Beatrice 300.00	❑ Barton, Chris 40.00	❑ Biggar, Trisha 25.00
❑ Ashley, Graham 80.00	❑ Barton, Roger 25.00	❑ Billington-Marks, Frank 75.00
❑ Ashmore, Brian 100.00	❑ Barton, Sean 30.00	❑ Binder, Steve 20.00
❑ Asner, Ed 40.00	❑ Bateman, Paul 25.00	❑ Bisson, Terry 50.00
❑ Atherton, Jane 25.00	❑ Batsoni, Francis 30.00	❑ Bixman, Jerry 50.00
❑ Atkinson, Lisa 30.00	❑ Bauersfeld, Erik [17-06] 75.00	❑ Blackman, Duncan 30.00
❑ Atwal, Bilu 20.00	❑ Bauman, Marc 50.00	❑ Blackner, Danny 30.00
❑ August, Pernilla 50.00	❑ Bay, Jane 25.00	❑ Blais, Peter 30.00
❑ Ault, John William 30.00	❑ Bayliss, Tace 50.00	❑ Blake, Jerome [17-10] 30.00
❑ Austen, Donald 30.00	❑ Beach, Scott 25.00	❑ Blake, Paul [17-11] 30.00
❑ Austin, Mark 30.00	❑ Bear, Greg 25.00	❑ Blakiston, Caroline [17-12] 30.00
❑ Baena, Carlos 25.00	❑ Bear, Lightning 25.00	❑ Blalack, Robert 25.00
❑ Bagnarol, Anthony 25.00	❑ Beckett, Adam 25.00	❑ Blessed, Brian 35.00
❑ Bailey, Charles 40.00	❑ Beer, Dickey [17-07] 25.00	❑ Bloom, Daniel 25.00
❑ Baillie, Kevin 100.00	❑ Beidler, Jerome 25.00	❑ Bloom, Jim 25.00
❑ Baird, Jason 250.00	❑ Bell, Bobby 30.00	❑ Blundell, Graeme 25.00
❑ Baker, Eileen 30.00	❑ Bell, Michael 25.00	❑ Boa, Bruce [17-13] 55.00

17-07 17-08 17-09 17-10 17-10

17-10 17-10 17-10 17-11 17-12 17-13

17-13 17-14 17-15 17-16 17-17

Autographs

Name	Price
Bocquet, Gavin	25.00
Boekelheide, Todd	25.00
Bonasewicz, Susanna	25.00
Bonehill, Richard	25.00
Bonfils, Khan	30.00
Bonstin, Rob	25.00
Boomansall, Michael	25.00
Botelho, Niki	25.00
Bou-Mansour, Martin	25.00
Bouchard, Matt	25.00
Boukabou, Jamel	30.00
Bourriague, Michonne [17-14]	30.00
Bovill, Robert	25.00
Bowers, David	30.00
Bowles, Bob	30.00
Bowley, Linda	30.00
Boyd, Guy	30.00
Boyle, Steven	30.00
Brace, Peter	25.00
Brannigan, Ray	25.00
Brenneis, Marty	25.00
Brewer, Jeff	25.00
Brill, Maria	75.00
Brimley, Wilford	25.00
Brincat, Paul	25.00
Brissette, Tiffany	35.00
Bronagh, Gallagher	30.00
Brooke, Paul	30.00
Brookman, Anthony	25.00
Brooks, Jill	25.00
Brooks, Terry	25.00
Brooks, William J.	35.00
Brown, Katherine	20.00
Brown, Melleny	25.00
Brown, Phil [17-15]	40.00
Brown, Ralph	30.00
Brown, Ronn	20.00
Bubb, David	45.00
Buchanan, Stephen	25.00
Budz, Mark	50.00
Buff, Conrad	65.00
Bulloch, Jeremy [17-16]	35.00
Burchette, Janice	45.00
Burman Jr., Ellis	30.00
Burman, Thomas R.	75.00
Burnett, Ted	300.00
Burns, Toby	20.00
Burroughs, Jackie	50.00
Burroughs, Peter	30.00
Burton, Corey	25.00
Burtt, Ben	40.00
Busby, Jane	70.00
Busch, Matt	30.00
Bush, Morris	200.00
Butler, Nathan P.	25.00
Butterfield, Trevor	25.00
Button, Roy	75.00
Buza, George	30.00
Byrne, Eddie	30.00
Byrne, Rose	30.00
Calabrese, Thomas	60.00
Calcutt, Stephen	50.00
Calvin Borgo, Deborah	30.00
Campbell, Graeme	50.00
Candice, Orwell	30.00
Canning, Josh	25.00
Cannon, John	75.00
Cantwell, Brian	30.00
Capri, Mark	30.00
Capurro, Scott	30.00
Carano, Gina	125.00
Cardiff, Rodney	25.00
Carlin, Nancy	25.00
Carlton, Geoffrey	10.00
Carney, Art	300.00
Carol, Monroe E.	25.00
Carr, Patricia	25.00
Carrington, Debbie Lee [17-17]	30.00
Carroll, Diahann	25.00
Carson, Dave	25.00
Carson, Silas [17-18]	30.00
Carson, Terrence 'T.C.'	25.00
Carter, Michael [17-19]	30.00
Casady, Chris	25.00
Cass, Mark	25.00
Cassidy, Michael	25.00
Castle-Hughes, Keisha	25.00
Cavelos, Jeanne	30.00
Cebulski, C. B.	75.00
Celia, Imrie	35.00
Chafer, Derek	30.00
Chamberlain, Douglas	25.00
Chan, Kee	25.00
Chancer, Norman	25.00
Chanchani, Dhruv	50.00
Chapman, John	25.00
Chaquico, Craig	25.00
Charlton, Maureen	30.00
Chasemore, Richard	30.00
Chato, Paul	30.00
Chaykin, Mauy	35.00
Chew, Dalyn	30.00
Chew, Richard	30.00
Chiang, Doug	35.00
Chionchio, Dominique	25.00
Chisam, C.B.	50.00
Choles, Nick	30.00
Christensen, Eric D.	200.00
Christensen, Hayden [17-20]	80.00
Christian, Roger	25.00
Chu, Kevin	25.00
Chudasama, Dee	25.00
Church, David	30.00
Church, Ryan	25.00

Autographs

17-30

17-30

17-31

17-32

17-32

17-33

17-34

17-35

- ❏ Ciccarelli, Gary 25.00
- ❏ Cimino, Rick 25.00
- ❏ Clark, Micky 25.00
- ❏ Clarke, Gin 65.00
- ❏ Clay, William 30.00
- ❏ Clayton, Eileen 25.00
- ❏ Clerk, Norton 25.00
- ❏ Cobb, Ron 25.00
- ❏ Cofer, Grady 50.00
- ❏ Coffey, Ian 30.00
- ❏ Cohen, Gilda 25.00
- ❏ Coleman, Rob 35.00
- ❏ Colley, Ken [17-21] 30.00
- ❏ Conboy, Elizabeth 25.00
- ❏ Condren, Tim 25.00
- ❏ Conrad, Rod 25.00
- ❏ Conrad, Roy 15.00
- ❏ Cook, Jeremy 30.00
- ❏ Cooke, Ben 25.00
- ❏ Coombs, Kenneth 25.00
- ❏ Cooper, Emma J. 30.00
- ❏ Cooper, Shirley 25.00
- ❏ Coopwood, Jeff 30.00
- ❏ Cope, Robert 25.00
- ❏ Coppen, Willie 30.00
- ❏ Copping, Barry 75.00
- ❏ Coppinger, John [17-22] 35.00
- ❏ Coppola, Roman 30.00
- ❏ Coppola, Sofia 40.00
- ❏ Corlis, James 25.00
- ❏ Corre, Sadie (as Sadie Corrie) 50.00
- ❏ Corrie, Sadie 30.00
- ❏ Corroney, Joe 25.00
- ❏ Costantino, Stephen [17-23] 40.00
- ❏ Cottrell, Michaela 30.00
- ❏ Cottrell, Mike 40.00
- ❏ Coulier, Mark 30.00
- ❏ Couper, Scott 25.00
- ❏ Court, Alyson 35.00
- ❏ Coveney, Ivo 40.00
- ❏ Cowan, Rob 30.00
- ❏ Cowan, Tom 50.00
- ❏ Cox, H. Ed 30.00
- ❏ Cox, Nathalie 45.00
- ❏ Cox, Tony 30.00
- ❏ Cragg, Dan 25.00
- ❏ Cranna, James 25.00
- ❏ Crary, Keith 25.00
- ❏ Crawford, Sean 45.00
- ❏ Cresswell, Jenny 50.00
- ❏ Crispin, Ann C. 25.00
- ❏ Cristina da Silva, Karol 30.00
- ❏ Croft, Pat 25.00
- ❏ Crooms, Adeal 25.00
- ❏ Crowley, Dermot 40.00
- ❏ Csokas, Marton 30.00
- ❏ Cukr, James 25.00
- ❏ Culver, Michael 35.00
- ❏ Cummens, Cynthia 30.00
- ❏ Cumming, John 30.00
- ❏ Cummings, Jim, voice actor for Weequay pirate chief Hondo Ohnaka in StarWars: The Clone Wars [17-24] 30.00
- ❏ Cunningham, Andy 105.00
- ❏ Cunningham, Dan 25.00
- ❏ Cunningham, Elaine 25.00
- ❏ Currey, Gail 25.00
- ❏ Curtis, Alfie 25.00
- ❏ Cushing, Peter 255.00
- ❏ D'Agostino, Jean 25.00
- ❏ da Silva, Christina 30.00
- ❏ Daisy Ridley [17-25] 165.00
- ❏ Daniels, Anthony [17-26] 50.00
- ❏ Daraphet, Mimi 25.00
- ❏ Darling, Russell 25.00
- ❏ Davenport, Claire 65.00
- ❏ David, Fay 25.00
- ❏ David, Lorelai 25.00
- ❏ Davies, (Billy?) 25.00
- ❏ Davies, Oliver Ford 35.00
- ❏ Davies, Paul 25.00
- ❏ Davis, Charles 25.00
- ❏ Davis, Kim 65.00
- ❏ Davis, Warwick [17-27] 30.00
- ❏ Day, Philippa 25.00
- ❏ Daza, Sagrario 25.00
- ❏ de Aragon, Maria [17-28] 30.00
- ❏ de Haahn, Ray 25.00
- ❏ de Jesus, Luis 30.00
- ❏ de Joux, Jenn 25.00
- ❏ de Souza Correa, Caroline 25.00
- ❏ Dearlove, Jack 25.00
- ❏ DeLisle, Grey [17-29] 35.00
- ❏ Delk, Denny 25.00
- ❏ Dell, Gabriel 40.00
- ❏ Dench, Axel 25.00
- ❏ Denham, Robert A. 35.00
- ❏ Denker, Oliver 25.00
- ❏ Denning, Troy 15.00
- ❏ Dewing, Sebastian 100.00
- ❏ Dharkur, Ayesha 20.00
- ❏ Di Maggio, John 60.00
- ❏ Diamond, Fraser 55.00
- ❏ Diamond, Peter [17-30] 70.00
- ❏ Diamond, Warwick 50.00
- ❏ Dickins, Sebastian 25.00
- ❏ Dicks, John 30.00
- ❏ Dietz, William C. 25.00
- ❏ Dilley, Leslie 30.00
- ❏ Dini, Paul 25.00
- ❏ Dito, Mike 25.00
- ❏ Dix, Justin 25.00
- ❏ Dixon, Debbie Lee 25.00
- ❏ Dixon, Malcolm 35.00
- ❏ Dodson, Mark 25.00
- ❏ Dodwall, Jim 25.00
- ❏ Dona, Eliana Isis 25.00
- ❏ Dondero, Michael 25.00
- ❏ Doran, Matt 30.00
- ❏ Dorman, Dave 25.00
- ❏ Doucette, Andrew 45.00
- ❏ Drees, Zeb 25.00
- ❏ Drisco, Bobby 25.00
- ❏ Driscoll, Richard 25.00
- ❏ Drostova, Lisa 25.00
- ❏ Dry, Tim 30.00
- ❏ Dudman, Nick 25.00
- ❏ Duff, Norwich 30.00
- ❏ Duffy, Mark 30.00
- ❏ Duigan, Patricia Rose 25.00
- ❏ Dukes, Peter 25.00
- ❏ Dunbar, Adrian 25.00
- ❏ Duncan, Lindsay 30.00
- ❏ Durock, Dick 25.00
- ❏ Durrant, Ian 25.00
- ❏ Duursema, Jan 25.00
- ❏ Duxbury, Warren 30.00
- ❏ Dykstra, John 25.00
- ❏ Dyson, Tony 40.00
- ❏ Eager, Malcolm 25.00
- ❏ Earl, Russell 25.00
- ❏ Eason, Phil 35.00
- ❏ Easton, C. Michael 30.00
- ❏ Eccles, Julie 25.00
- ❏ Eckstein, Ashley, voice actress for Ahsoka Tano in Star Wars: The Clone Wars [17-31] 45.00
- ❏ Eddon, Sadie 35.00
- ❏ Eddon, Tracey 25.00
- ❏ Edgerton, Joel 35.00
- ❏ Edgerton, Nash 35.00
- ❏ Edlund, Richard 20.00
- ❏ Edmonds, Mike [17-32] 30.00
- ❏ Edwards, Charles 30.00
- ❏ Egeland, Tom 25.00
- ❏ Eggleton, Bob 30.00
- ❏ Eibra, Robri 25.00
- ❏ Ellenshaw, Harrison 20.00
- ❏ Ellingson, TyRuben 25.00
- ❏ Elliott, Lindsay 25.00
- ❏ Elliott, Stephen 25.00
- ❏ Ellis, Desmond 30.00
- ❏ Ellis, John 30.00

Autographs

Name	Price
Elphick, Michael	25.00
Elross, Robert	25.00
Elsey, Dave	25.00
Emberlin, Randy	30.00
Engelen, Paul	25.00
England, Chrissie	25.00
English, Stephanie	25.00
Ernster, Catherine	25.00
Erwin, Mike	25.00
Evans, Malcolm	25.00
Everson, Roy	25.00
Falk, Ronald	25.00
Falkenburg, Kim	25.00
Fallon, Nina [17-33]	25.00
Fann, Leigh Ann	25.00
Fantini, Michael	25.00
Fantl, Nicole	30.00
Farrar, Katherine	25.00
Felicity Jones [17-34]	135.00
Felix, Jason	25.00
Fell, Stuart	20.00
Fensom, John	35.00
Ferguson, Nicholas	25.00
Fernandez, Margarita	30.00
Ferry, Scott	25.00
Field, David	25.00
Field, John B.	25.00
Field, Nick	30.00
Fielder, Harry	25.00
Finlay, Sandi	25.00
Fisher, Carrie [17-35]	450.00
Fitch, Marina	25.00
Fitzalan, Stephen	25.00
Flanagan, Fionnula	30.00
Fletcher, Colin	25.00
Fondacaro, Phil	30.00
Fondacaro, Sal	30.00
Ford, Harrison	350.00
Forgeham, John	25.00
Forrest, Anthony [17-36]	25.00
Fosselius, Ernie	20.00
Foster, Alan Dean	20.00
Foster, Lawrence	25.00
Fox, Stuart	20.00
Foy, Steven	25.00
Francks, Don	20.00
Frandy, Michael A.	30.00
Franklin, Pat	20.00
Franti, Michael	20.00
Fraser, Ian	20.00
Fraser, Shelagh	55.00
Freddie Prinze Jr [17-37]	40.00
Fredrickson, Cully	20.00
Freeborn, Graham	20.00
Freeborn, Kay	20.00
Freeborn, Stuart	150.00
Freeling, Cynthia [17-38]	15.00
Freer, Chantal	25.00
Friedman, Ira	25.00
Friel, Tony	30.00
Frishman, Daniel	30.00
Fu, Warren	20.00
Fuller, Tex	20.00
Fushille-Burke, Celia	30.00
Gagliano, Ted	20.00
Gale, Paul	20.00
Gallagher, Bronagh	20.00
Galland, Nicole	20.00
Gammill, Kerry	20.00
Gant, Martin	20.00
Gardner, Salo	20.00
Gavigan, Gerry	20.00
Gawley, Steve	20.00
Geddis, Peter	20.00
Gernand, Brian	20.00
Gersh, Howard	20.00
Gescher, Norbert	20.00
Ghavan, John (as John Gayam)	20.00
Gilden, Michael	30.00
Gilding, Tony	20.00
Gillard, Nick	30.00
Gillis, Paulina	20.00
Gilroy, Bennet	20.00
Gleason, Paul	50.00
Glover, Geoff	20.00
Glover, Julian [17-39]	30.00
Glut, Donald F.	20.00
Gnome, Barry	20.00
Goffe, Rusty [17-40]	30.00
Gogos, Basil	20.00
Golden, Christopher	20.00
Goldhar, Marvin	20.00
Gonzales, David	20.00
Goode, Laurie	20.00
Goodman, Ron	20.00
Gould, Grant	20.00
Gower, Joss	20.00
Grand, Isaac	50.00
Grant, Paul	30.00
Grantham, Ken	20.00
Gray, Charles	20.00
Gray, David	20.00
Green, Jenna	50.00
Green, Kes	20.00
Green, Lars	30.00
Green, Lydia	30.00
Greenaway, David	35.00
Greene, Ed	20.00
Grey, Charlie	20.00
Griffin, Nonnie	20.00
Griffiths, Ray	20.00
Grizz, Pamela	30.00
Gross, Sandi	20.00
Grossman, Ted	20.00

17-35

17-36

17-37

Cinthia Freeling as Princess Anne Droid
17-38

Julian Glover as General Veers
17-39

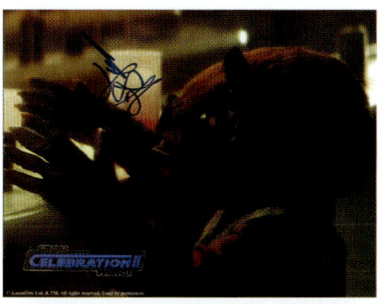
17-40

17-40

17-41

17-42

17-43

17-44

17-45

Autographs

Name	Price
Gruska, Michele	20.00
Guinness, Alec	750.00
Gurland, Robin	20.00
Guyett, Roger	25.00
Haas, Jean-Denis	20.00
Hadley, Kay	20.00
Hagon, Garrick [17-41]	30.00
Haines, Luriene	20.00
Hale, Gavin	20.00
Hales, Jonathan	20.00
Hall, Nelson	30.00
Hambly, Barbara	20.00
Hamill, Mark	80.00
Hamill, Nathan	35.00
Hamilton, Zuraya	20.00
Hammack, Craig	20.00
Hammerman, Howie	20.00
Hand, Elizabeth	20.00
Hanks, Tamzine	20.00
Hann, Gordon	20.00
Harding, Reg	20.00
Harrington, Tim	20.00
Harris, Alan	35.00
Harris, Jez	20.00
Harris, Tom	20.00
Harry, Angela	20.00
Harte, Jerry	30.00
Harvey, Phil	20.00
Harwood, Tim	20.00
Hassett, Ray	30.00
Hattrick, Graeme	35.00
Havord, Mike	20.00
Hawkins, Noel	20.00
Haye, Jack	20.00
Hazelden, Lynne	20.00
Healey, David	20.00
Heckstall-Smith, Nick	20.00
Helman, Pablo	20.00
Helms, John	20.00
Hemion, Dwight	20.00
Henanger, Sigbjørn	20.00
Henbury Ballan, Michael	20.00
Henderson, Don	65.00
Henley, Drewe	55.00
Hennessey, Dan	20.00
Henning, Mary	20.00
Henriques, Darryl	20.00
Henshaw, Jim	20.00
Henson, Frank	20.00
Herbert, Philip	30.00
Herd, Andrew	30.00
Herman, Miki	20.00
Hewitt, Christine [17-42]	55.00
Hey, Jerry	20.00
Hickel, Hal T.	20.00
Hidalgo, Pablo	15.00
Higgins, Colin	20.00
Higgins, Gail	20.00
Hildebrandt, Greg	20.00
Hildebrandt, Tim	20.00
Hill, Thomas	20.00
Hillier, Kit	20.00
Hillios, Sonia	20.00
Hindes, Nifa	30.00
Hindes, Nishan	30.00
Hinds, Scott	20.00
Hinksman, Luke	25.00
Hirsch, Paul	20.00
Hirsh, Michael	20.00
Hoffmann, Daniela	20.00
Hole, Fred	20.00
Holland, Barrie	25.00
Holland, Dave	20.00
Hollis, John [17-43]	55.00
Holman, Tomlinson	20.00
Holt, Larry	20.00
Home, Gerald [17-44]	50.00
Hootkins, William [17-45]	55.00
Horine, Marianne	20.00
Horrigan, Bill	20.00
Hostetter, John	20.00
House, Peter	20.00
Howard, Emma	20.00
Howell, Arthur	20.00
Howson, Hilton	20.00
Hoyland, William	20.00
Hudson, Susie	35.00
Huebler, Dorne	20.00
Hume, Alan	20.00
Humphrey, Vince	20.00
Hunt, Colin	20.00
Hunter, Morgan	20.00
Huston, Paul	20.00
Hutsko, Joe	20.00
Hyatt, Pam	20.00
Hyneman, Jamie	20.00
Ilsley, Tommy	20.00
Imahara, Grant	20.00
Imrie, Celia	20.00
Inch, Rob	20.00
Isaie, Danielle	20.00
Ismay, Steve	20.00
Ives, Burl	200.00
Jackson Mendoza, Rebecca	25.00
Jackson, J.J.	30.00
Jackson, Kerrin	20.00
Jackson, Peter	25.00
Jackson, Samuel L. [17-46]	150.00
Jacob, Jasper	20.00
Jaeger, Alex	20.00
Jafelice, Raymond	20.00
Jaffe, Jennifer	20.00
James, Art	20.00
James, Leroy	20.00
James, Ron	20.00
Jameson, Nick	20.00
Jarvis, Jeremy	20.00
Jensen, Jesse	20.00
Jensen, Zachariah [17-47]	30.00
Jensvold, Lars	20.00
Jerricho, Paul	20.00
Jeter, K.W.	20.00
Jew, Benton	20.00
Jewett, Bethany	20.00
Johns, Milton	30.00
Johnson, Bjorn	20.00
Johnson, Brian	20.00
Johnson, Roger	20.00
Johnson, Taborah	20.00
Johnson, Terrence	20.00
Johnston, Joe	20.00
Joint, Alf	20.00
Jones, Annette	20.00
Jones, Ed	20.00
Jones, Glynn	30.00
Jones, James Earl	600.00
Jones, Jamison	20.00
Jones, Linda	20.00
Jones, Mark	30.00
Jones, Richard	30.00
Jones, Trevor	30.00
Joti, Dipika O'Neill	45.00
Jundis, Ardees Rabang	20.00
Jundis, Elrik	20.00
Juritzen, Arve	20.00
Kahn, Brigitte	30.00
Kamoun, Moez	20.00
Kane, Tom [17-48]	30.00
Kantner, Paul	20.00
Karpyshyn, Drew	20.00
Karvan, Claudia	25.00
Kasdan, Lawrence	20.00
Kastel, Roger	20.00
Katz, Louis	20.00
Katz, Stephen	20.00
Kaye Campbell, Alexi	20.00
Kaye, Joe	20.00
Kazanjian, Howard G.	20.00
Keen, Bob	20.00
Kelly, Andrew	20.00
Kelly, Ken	20.00
Kennedy, Cam	20.00

17-46 · 17-47 · 17-48 · 17-49 · 17-50

17-51 · 17-52 · 17-53 · 17-54

Autographs

☐ Kenny, Shannon	20.00	
☐ Kershner, Irvin	20.00	
☐ Keshavji, Ali	20.00	
☐ Keys, Andre	20.00	
☐ Keys, Jerry	20.00	
☐ Khazzouh, Julian	25.00	
☐ Khendup	20.00	
☐ Khoury, Frank	20.00	
☐ Kingma, Michael [17-49]	25.00	
☐ Kirby, Christopher	25.00	
☐ Kitchens, Colin Michael	20.00	
☐ Kite, Paul	20.00	
☐ Klaff, Jack	35.00	
☐ Klein, Paul	20.00	
☐ Kleut, Goran [17-50]	20.00	
☐ Knightley, Keira	30.00	
☐ Knoll, Alex	30.00	
☐ Knoll, John	35.00	
☐ Knowland, Nicholas	20.00	
☐ Koch, Hilmar	20.00	
☐ Koffi, Gervais	25.00	
☐ Kohen, Zac	20.00	
☐ Korman, Harvey	400.00	
☐ Kramer, Ed	20.00	
☐ Krishan, Nalini [17-51]	30.00	
☐ Kube-McDowell, Michael P.	20.00	
☐ Kuran, Peter	20.00	
☐ Kurtz, Gary [17-52]	50.00	
☐ Kurtz, Melissa [17-53]	30.00	
☐ Kurtz, Tiffany [17-53]	30.00	
☐ Lackersteen, Melissa	20.00	
☐ Ladd Jr., Alan	20.00	
☐ Laga'aia, Jay	30.00	
☐ Lahr, Larin	35.00	
☐ Lampert, Al	20.00	
☐ Lang, Anthony	20.00	
☐ Langdon, Verne	20.00	
☐ Lanning, Steve	20.00	
☐ Larsen, Simon	20.00	
☐ Lau, Kamay	20.00	
☐ Lauren, Jeanne	20.00	
☐ Lawden, Andrew	20.00	
☐ Lawler, Andy	20.00	
☐ Lawson, Denis	70.00	
☐ Lay, Karen	30.00	
☐ Layton, Bob	20.00	
☐ Layton, Joe	20.00	
☐ Le Parmentier, Richard [17-54]	20.00	
☐ Leader, Michael	20.00	
☐ Lean, Aiden	20.00	
☐ Lee, Christopher	400.00	
☐ Leech, George	20.00	
☐ Leech, Wendy	20.00	
☐ Leflore, Julius	20.00	
☐ Lemay, Brian	20.00	
☐ LeParmentier, Richard	30.00	
☐ Letteri, Joe	20.00	
☐ Levi, Olive	25.00	
☐ Levy, Elizabeth	20.00	
☐ Lewin, Janet	25.00	
☐ Lewis, Craig C.	20.00	
☐ Lewis, Dylan	20.00	
☐ Lewis, Garrett	20.00	
☐ Lim, Swee (as Lee, Swim)	45.00	
☐ Lindsay, Alex	20.00	
☐ Ling, Bai	20.00	
☐ Ling, Van	20.00	
☐ Lion, Tim	20.00	
☐ Lippincott, Charles	20.00	
☐ Lipsky, Michael	20.00	
☐ Liska, Laine	20.00	
☐ Liston, Ian [17-55]	30.00	
☐ Lithgow, John	20.00	
☐ Lloyd, Jake [17-56]	250.00	
☐ Lloyd, Madison	35.00	
☐ Logan, Bruce	20.00	
☐ Logan, Daniel [17-57]	25.00	
☐ Lomprakis, Peter	20.00	
☐ Longworth, Toby	30.00	
☐ Loomis, Bernard	20.00	
☐ Lorenz, Michael	20.00	
☐ Loubert, Patrick	20.00	
☐ Louca, Loucas	20.00	
☐ Louez, Jacqui	25.00	
☐ Love, Sue	20.00	
☐ Lucas, Amanda	50.00	
☐ Lucas, George	2,300.00	
☐ Lucas, Jett	50.00	
☐ Lucas, Katie	50.00	
☐ Lucas, Mat	20.00	
☐ Luceno, James	20.00	
☐ Luker, Malcolm	20.00	
☐ Lummiss, John	30.00	
☐ Lynch, Katie	20.00	
☐ Lynch, Michael	20.00	
☐ Lyons, Derek	20.00	
☐ MacDonald, Peter	20.00	
☐ MacInnis, Angus [17-58]	30.00	
☐ Mackie, Bob	20.00	
☐ MacLean, Nancy	30.00	
☐ Macleod, Lewis	30.00	
☐ MacNeill, Peter	20.00	
☐ MacPhee, Jason	25.00	
☐ Madden, Terry	20.00	
☐ Madsen, Daniel	30.00	
☐ Magerkurth, Brian	20.00	
☐ Magruder, Carl	20.00	
☐ Maguire, Oliver	30.00	
☐ Mahjoub	20.00	
☐ Mailer, Lev	20.00	
☐ Maitz, Don	20.00	
☐ Malcolm, Christopher	35.00	
☐ Maley, Nick	20.00	
☐ Maloney, John	20.00	
☐ Maloney, Patty	20.00	
☐ Mancusi, Tim	20.00	
☐ Mandell, Peter	30.00	
☐ Mangan, Alf	20.00	
☐ Mangels, Andy	20.00	
☐ Mann, Sureena	20.00	
☐ Mannion, Tom	40.00	
☐ Mansworth, Ben	20.00	
☐ Mariano, Lee	20.00	
☐ Marini, Sergio	20.00	
☐ Markel, Nicholas	20.00	
☐ Markle, Steven	20.00	
☐ Marquand, Richard	100.00	
☐ Marr, Joseph	20.00	
☐ Marsden, Jason	20.00	
☐ Martin, Fred	20.00	
☐ Martinek, Tom	20.00	
☐ Martinez, Gary	20.00	
☐ Martinez, Randy	20.00	
☐ Masoch, Manuela	20.00	
☐ Masson, Terrence	20.00	
☐ Maurici, Tony	20.00	
☐ Mayhew, Peter [17-59]	150.00	
☐ McAskill, Trish	20.00	
☐ McBryde, James	20.00	
☐ McCaig, Iain	20.00	
☐ McCallum, Mousy	25.00	
☐ McCallum, Rick	45.00	
☐ McCarthy, Kevin	20.00	
☐ McCrindle, Alex	200.00	
☐ McCune, Grant	20.00	
☐ McDiarmid, Ian	100.00	
☐ McEvoy, John	20.00	
☐ McFarlane, Calum	20.00	
☐ McFayden, Iain	20.00	
☐ McGonagle, Richard	20.00	
☐ McGovern, Terry	20.00	
☐ McGowan, Louisa	20.00	
☐ McGrath, Alethea	35.00	
☐ McGregor, Ewan	105.00	
☐ McIntyre, Vonda N.	20.00	
☐ McKenzie, Jack	30.00	
☐ McLaughlin, John	20.00	
☐ McLean, Scott	20.00	
☐ McLeod, Bob	20.00	
☐ McManus, Don	20.00	
☐ McQuarrie, Ralph	950.00	
☐ McRae, Hilton	35.00	

17-55 IAN LISTON as WES JANSON in STAR WARS: THE EMPIRE STRIKES BACK

17-56

17-57

17-58

17-59

17-60

17-60

17-61

17-62

17-63

17-64

Autographs

Name	Price
McRandle, Shannon (Baksa) [17-60]	40.00
McTeigue, James	20.00
McVey, Tony	20.00
Melville, Giles	20.00
Meny, David	20.00
Merry, David	20.00
Metschan, Philip	20.00
Midener, Wendy (aka Wendy Froud)	20.00
Miller, Alvah J.	20.00
Miller, Aubree	20.00
Miller, Carl	20.00
Miller, George	30.00
Miller, Jenny	20.00
Miller, Kerry	20.00
Miller, Pip	35.00
Mills, Mykel	20.00
Mimura, Raven	20.00
Minshull, Keren	20.00
Mitchell, Dean	20.00
Moeller, Christopher	20.00
Moesta-Anderson, Rebecca	20.00
Mollo, John	20.00
Monardo, Domenico 'Meco'	20.00
Moon, Jeff	20.00
Moore, T.V.	25.00
Mooy, Hayley	25.00
Moran, Daniel Keys	20.00
Morgan, Steve	20.00
Morris, Carole	30.00
Morrison, Temuera [17-61]	35.00
Morton, John [17-62]	30.00
Morton, Mandy	20.00
Morton, Mickey	20.00
Mulholland, Declan	20.00
Mullen, Kathryn	35.00
Muncke, Christopher	20.00
Mungarvan, Mike	20.00
Munro, Cathy	80.00
Muren, Dennis	20.00
Murleen, Ru	20.00
Murphy, Sue	20.00
Mustoo, Terence 'Terry'	20.00
Myers, Stuart	20.00
Najem, Sayed	20.00
Natividad, Ed	20.00
Neame, Christopher	20.00
Neeson, Liam	255.00
Nelson, C. Andrew	30.00
Nelvik, Odd Johan	20.00
Newman, Christopher	20.00
Ngoh, Mercedes [17-63]	25.00
Nichol, Rohan	25.00
Nicholls, Stacey	20.00
Nicholls, Stacy	30.00
Nichols, David	20.00
Nichols, Fiona	20.00
Nicholson, Bruce	20.00
Nicholson, Paul	25.00
Nielsen, Jim	20.00
Niles, Steve	20.00
Noble, Trisha	25.00
Noble, Larry	20.00
Norris, Daran	20.00
Northcutt, Brett	20.00
Nunn, Chris	30.00
Nuttgens, Niles	20.00
Nyamwasa, Lily	25.00
O'Laughlin, Barbara	30.00
O'Neill Joti, Dipika	20.00
O'Reilly, Genevieve	20.00
Oates, Kenji	25.00
Oldfield, Richard	30.00
Oliver, Jonathan	35.00
Oltion, Jerry	20.00
Orbik, Glen	20.00
Ordaz, Frank	20.00
Orenstein, Brian	30.00
Orwell, Candice	20.00
Owen, Rena [17-64]	30.00
Owens, Warren	25.00
Oyaya, Mary [17-65]	30.00
Oz, Frank	55.00
Pagan, John	20.00
Pahl, Tish Eggleston	20.00
Paine, David	20.00
Palmer, Jason	20.00
Pampel, Wolfgang	20.00
Panczak, Hans Georg	20.00
Pangrazio, Michael	20.00
Park, Ray [17-66]	30.00
Parker Jr., Harrell	30.00
Parker, Charles E.	20.00
Parker, Jr., Harrell	20.00
Parkinson, Michael	20.00
Parsons, Chris [17-67]	30.00
Parsons, Dan	20.00
Parsons, Leslie	20.00
Pasquarello, Eddie	20.00
Paul, Russell	20.00
Pedrick, John	30.00
Peel, Edward	20.00
Pennington, Michael	35.00
Perez, Omaha	20.00
Perkins, April	30.00
Perry, Steve	20.00
Peterson, Eric	20.00
Peterson, Lorne	30.00
Petrarca, Steven	20.00
Petrides, Andreas	20.00
Phelan, Anthony	30.00
Phillips, Charlie	20.00
Phillips, Ronnie	30.00
Phillips, Siân	20.00
Philpott, Toby	30.00
Pierre, Quentin	20.00
Piesse, Bonnie [17-68]	30.00
Pike, Kelvin	20.00
Pike, Kevin	20.00
Pollak, Kevin	20.00
Polley, Diane	20.00
Pomeroy, Geoff	20.00
Poon, Ellen	20.00
Porter, Susie	30.00
Portman, Natalie	155.00
Post, RK	20.00
Potter, Michael	20.00
Powell, Marcus	20.00
Powell, Nosher	20.00
Power, Dermot	20.00
Preciado, Regina Lynn	20.00
Prestoe, Jeremy	25.00
Pritchard, Michael	20.00
Proops, Greg	35.00
Prowse, David [17-69]	150.00
Purvis, Jack	200.00
Purvis, Katie [17-70]	40.00
Pygram, Wayne [17-71]	25.00
Quarshie, Hugh	30.00
Quinn, Michael [17-72]	30.00
Rabbitte, David	20.00
Rabe, Jean	20.00
Rader, Jack	20.00
Ralston, Ken	20.00
Randall, Michael	20.00
Ratzenberger, John [17-73]	40.00
Raylee, Hal	20.00
Read, Carol	30.00
Read, Nicholas	30.00
Ream, Denise	25.00
Reamer, Tim	20.00
Reaves, Michael	20.00
Reece, Rebecca	20.00
Reitz, Brendan	20.00
Reitz, Peter	20.00
Rekert, Winston	20.00
Rennie, Pauline	20.00
Reubens, Paul	20.00
Revill, Clive [17-74]	60.00
Reyna, Anthony	20.00
Reynolds, Diana	30.00
Reynolds, Jeanne	20.00
Reynolds, Norman	20.00

17-65

17-66

17-67

17-68

17-69

17-70

17-71

17-72

17-73

Autographs

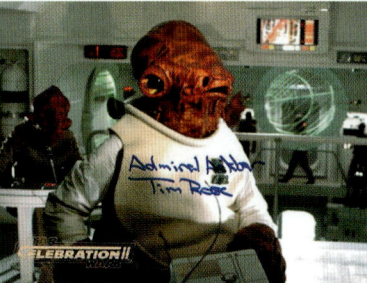
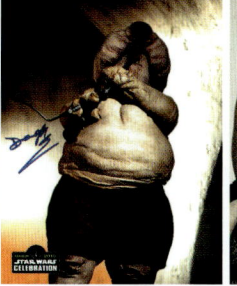

17-74   17-75   17-76   17-77   17-77

17-77   17-78   17-79   17-80   17-81

Name	Price
❑ Rezard, Martin	20.00
❑ Richardson, Kevin Michael	20.00
❑ Riddell, Graham	20.00
❑ Rimmer, Shane	30.00
❑ Rinzler, Jonathan	20.00
❑ Ripps, Leonard	20.00
❑ Risley, Bill	20.00
❑ Rizzi, Gregory	20.00
❑ Roberson, Jennifer	20.00
❑ Roberts, Ian	20.00
❑ Robertson, Barry	30.00
❑ Robinson, Doug	20.00
❑ Robinson, Richard	20.00
❑ Roderick-Jones, Alan	20.00
❑ Rodgers, Daniel	30.00
❑ Rodis-Jamero, Nilo	20.00
❑ Roffman, Howard	20.00
❑ Roloff, Matt	20.00
❑ Romano, Chris	30.00
❑ Romano, Pete	20.00
❑ Roper, Mark	20.00
❑ Rose, Kalki	20.00
❑ Rose, Pam	20.00
❑ Rose, Timothy [17-75]	30.00
❑ Ross, Peter	20.00
❑ Rotich, Kipsang	20.00
❑ Roubicek, George C.	20.00
❑ Rowan, Matthew	20.00
❑ Rowland, James	20.00
❑ Rowling, Kyle	30.00
❑ Rowsell, Stuart	20.00
❑ Rowton, Arthur	20.00
❑ Roxburgh, Hamish	25.00
❑ Roy, Deep [17-76]	35.00
❑ Roy, Peter	20.00
❑ Rusch, Kristine Kathryn	20.00
❑ Ruscoe, Alan [17-77]	30.00
❑ Russell, David	20.00
❑ Russell, P. Craig	20.00
❑ Russell, Peter	20.00
❑ Sach, Terry	20.00
❑ Sackhoff, Katee	40.00
❑ Sally, Joseph Jett	20.00
❑ Salvatore, R. A.	20.00
❑ Sanchez, Juan	30.00
❑ Sanders, Chris	30.00
❑ Sanderson, Tom	20.00
❑ Sanswweet, Steve [17-78]	30.00
❑ Sasso, Marc	20.00
❑ Sauder, Peter	20.00
❑ Sauers, Steve	30.00
❑ Savage, Adam	20.00
❑ Savel, Elizabeth	20.00
❑ Savva, Michael	20.00
❑ Saxon, Nina	20.00
❑ Sayer, Stanley W.	20.00
❑ Scalice, Ray	20.00
❑ Schenk, Udo	20.00
❑ Schofield, Leslie	35.00
❑ Schweighofer, Peter	20.00
❑ Scible Jr., Irving	20.00
❑ Scobey, Robin	40.00
❑ Scott, Esther	20.00
❑ Scott, P. Kevin	30.00
❑ Scott, Rita	20.00
❑ Secombe, Andrew	30.00
❑ Secombe, Andy	20.00
❑ Segura, Veronica	30.00
❑ Selcuk, Zeynup	20.00
❑ Serafinowicz, Peter	35.00
❑ Sexton, David	20.00
❑ Sgorbati, Marco	20.00
❑ Shackelford, Dean	30.00
❑ Shah, Kiran	30.00
❑ Shane, Laurie	20.00
❑ Shank, Jeff	20.00
❑ Shanower, Eric	20.00
❑ Shapi, Hasani	20.00
❑ Shaunessy, Lisa	25.00
❑ Shaw, Sebastian	500.00
❑ Shay, Jeff	30.00
❑ Sheard, Michael [17-79]	45.00
❑ Shenk, Jon	20.00
❑ Sheperd, Steve John	20.00
❑ Sheppard, Larry	20.00
❑ Sherman, Dave	20.00
❑ Shield, Brad	20.00
❑ Shin, Nelson	20.00
❑ Shoshan, Orli [17-80]	25.00
❑ Shuster, Jay	20.00
❑ Silk, Mark	20.00
❑ Silla, Felix [17-81]	30.00
❑ Simmons, Erica	20.00
❑ Simpson, Christian [17-82]	30.00
❑ Sinclair, Sally	20.00
❑ Sinden, Jeremy	80.00
❑ Siner, Guy	20.00
❑ Sitts, William	20.00
❑ Skeaping, Colin [17-83]	30.00
❑ Sleight, Geoffrey	20.00
❑ Sloan, Matt	30.00
❑ Smart, Tony	20.00
❑ Smee, Anthony	20.00
❑ Smee, Katherine	35.00
❑ Smentowski, Jim	20.00
❑ Smith, Adam J.	20.00
❑ Smith, Beau	20.00
❑ Smith, Clarence	30.00
❑ Smith, Clive A.	20.00
❑ Smith, Douglas	20.00
❑ Smith, Gary	20.00
❑ Smith, Howard	20.00
❑ Smith, Matthew	20.00
❑ Smith, Paul Martin	30.00
❑ Smith, Yeardley	20.00
❑ Smits, Jimmy	35.00
❑ Snell, Jason	20.00
❑ Sogliuzzo, Andre	20.00
❑ Solum, Ola	20.00
❑ Sosalla, David	20.00
❑ Sowd, Aaron	20.00
❑ Speirs, Steve	20.00
❑ Spence, Bruce	30.00
❑ Spence, Paul	25.00
❑ Spriggs, Linda	30.00
❑ Springer, Paul	20.00
❑ Squires, Scott	20.00
❑ St. Amand, Tom	20.00
❑ Stackpole, Michael A.	20.00
❑ Staddon, Gerald	30.00
❑ Staddon, Josephine	30.00
❑ Staff, Chris	20.00
❑ Staines, Angela	20.00
❑ Stamp, Terence	45.00
❑ Star, Tony	35.00
❑ Stark, Koo	20.00
❑ Starkey, Steve	20.00
❑ Starr, Gideon	20.00
❑ Starsh, Jeff	20.00
❑ Steacy, Ken	20.00
❑ Stephenson, Ken	20.00
❑ Stevens, Mike	20.00
❑ Stewart, Sean	20.00
❑ Stiff, David	25.00
❑ Stilman, Philip	20.00
❑ Stock, George	20.00
❑ Stocker, John	20.00
❑ Stover, Matthew	20.00
❑ Straite, Roy	20.00
❑ Strane, Marques	20.00
❑ Strasser, Todd	20.00
❑ Stratton, Craig	20.00
❑ Stringer, Holly	25.00
❑ Stromer, Stephanie	20.00
❑ Struyken, Carel	20.00
❑ Struzan, Drew	20.00
❑ Sturgeon, Peter	20.00
❑ Sugiyama, Yuichi	20.00
❑ Sullivan, Mark	20.00
❑ Sullivan, Paul	20.00
❑ Summer, Cree	20.00
❑ Summerford, Barry	20.00

Autographs

❑ Sumner, Peter 35.00	❑ Tighe, Trevor 20.00	❑ Varney, Kelly 20.00
❑ Suotamo, Joonas [17-84] 45.00	❑ Tilman, Bill 20.00	❑ Venerin, Pouchon 20.00
❑ Suschitzky, Peter 20.00	❑ Tim Curry [17-89] 90.00	❑ Victor, Rick 20.00
❑ Sutherland, Gibb 20.00	❑ Tippett, Phil 35.00	❑ Victoria, Carol 20.00
❑ Sutton, Peter 20.00	❑ Tlusty, Bill 20.00	❑ Vilanch, Bruce 20.00
❑ Swaden, Alan 20.00	❑ Toll, Matt 20.00	❑ Vilmur, Peter 20.00
❑ Swaden, Keith 20.00	❑ Tomasetti, Lisa 20.00	❑ Vindenes, Rune 20.00
❑ Swain, Howard 20.00	❑ Tomkins, Alan 20.00	❑ Virgo, Martin 20.00
❑ Swallow, Emily, The Armorer [17-85] .. 50.00	❑ Tong, Derek 20.00	❑ Virtue, Tom 20.00
❑ Swanson, Greg 20.00	❑ Town, Cy 20.00	❑ Viskocil, Joe 20.00
❑ Swindell, Howard 20.00	❑ Towner, Margaret 35.00	❑ Vorsay, Avril 20.00
❑ Sylla, John 30.00	❑ Traviss, Karen 20.00	❑ Waddington, Steve 20.00
❑ Sylla, Tom 30.00	❑ Trevas, Chris 20.00	❑ Wade, Philip 20.00
❑ Tarter, Sacha 20.00	❑ Tricker, Raymond 20.00	❑ Wagner, Danny 30.00
❑ Tatasciore, Fred 20.00	❑ Trimmer, Evelyn 20.00	❑ Wahlgren, Kari 20.00
❑ Tattersall, David 20.00	❑ Trimpe, Herb 20.00	❑ Wakefield, Karina 20.00
❑ Tavoularis, Alex 20.00	❑ Triplett, John 20.00	❑ Wald, Christina 20.00
❑ Taylor, Benedict [17-86] 30.00	❑ Troy, Alan 20.00	❑ Walker, Eric [17-90] 20.00
❑ Taylor, Bodie 'Tindi' 20.00	❑ Truman, Timothy 20.00	❑ Walker, Sydney 20.00
❑ Taylor, Femi [17-87] 30.00	❑ Truswell, Chris 35.00	❑ Wall, Kendra 30.00
❑ Taylor, James 35.00	❑ Tubach, Pat 20.00	❑ Wallace, Daniel 20.00
❑ Taylor, James Arnold 20.00	❑ Tucker, Burnell 40.00	❑ Walpole, Oliver 55.00
❑ Taylor, Michelle 30.00	❑ Tucker, Christopher 20.00	❑ Walpole, Peter 20.00
❑ Taylor, Ronnie 20.00	❑ Tucker, Ezra 20.00	❑ Walsman, Leanna 30.00
❑ Tcimpidis, Tom 20.00	❑ Turk, Marolyn 20.00	❑ Walter, Jerry 20.00
❑ Teach, Jessica 20.00	❑ Turner, Brian 20.00	❑ Wamsley, Hal 20.00
❑ Teiger, Ty 20.00	❑ Turturice, Robert 20.00	❑ Ward, Larry 20.00
❑ Tenggren, Jayne-Ann 20.00	❑ Tyers, Kathy 20.00	❑ Ware, Colin 25.00
❑ Thatcher, Kirk [17-88] 30.00	❑ Tyger, Lucas 80.00	❑ Warren, Rod 20.00
❑ Thiebeaux, Peter 20.00	❑ Udall, Megan 55.00	❑ Wassung, Joshua 20.00
❑ Thomas, Leonard 20.00	❑ Umbarger, Lisa 20.00	❑ Watkin, Ian 30.00
❑ Thompson, Derek 20.00	❑ Unkov, Kosi 20.00	❑ Watts, Robert 35.00
❑ Thompson, Jack 35.00	❑ Upton, Morgan 20.00	❑ Way, Diana Sadley 20.00
❑ Thompson, Kevin 30.00	❑ Valentin, David 20.00	❑ Waye, Anthony 20.00
❑ Thompson, Sandy 25.00	❑ Vallejo, Boris 20.00	❑ Weaver, Judy 20.00
❑ Thorpe, Marc 20.00	❑ Van Fleet, John 20.00	❑ Weaver, Malcolm 20.00
❑ Tiemens, Erik 20.00	❑ Vanderwalt, Lesley 20.00	❑ Webb, Des 20.00
❑ Tierney, Malcolm 35.00	❑ Vargo, Mark 20.00	❑ Weed, Howie [17-91] 20.00

17-82 17-83 17-84 17-85

17-86 17-87 17-88 17-89

17-90 17-91 17-92 17-93 17-94

Autographs

17-95 | 17-96 | 17-97 | 17-98 | 17-99 | 17-100 | 17-101

17-102 | 17-103 | 17-104 | 17-105 | 17-106 | 17-107 | 17-108

17-109 | 17-110 | 17-111 | 17-112 | 17-113 | 17-114 | 17-115

- Weigel, Rafer...20.00
- Weissmuller Jr., Johnny 20.00
- Welch, Ken..20.00
- Welch, Mitzie..20.00
- Weldin, Tommy 20.00
- Welsh, Pat...20.00
- West, Dominic...30.00
- Western, Ted...20.00
- Westman, Gordon 20.00
- Weston, Bill...20.00
- Weston, Paul [17-92].....................................25.00
- Wetherill, Marty 25.00
- Wheeler, Brian...30.00
- Whelan, Paul...20.00
- White, R. Christopher 20.00
- Whitlach, Terryl...20.00
- Whyman, Simon...20.00
- Wildman, Valerie 20.00
- Wilhelm, Butch..30.00
- Wilkinson, Adrienne 20.00
- Williams, Aliyah...25.00
- Williams, Billy Dee [17-93].............................55.00
- Williams, Corey Dee [17-94]..........................30.00
- Williams, Dwayne..30.00
- Williams, John...20.00
- Williams, Roger...20.00
- Williams, Sean...20.00
- Williams, Steve 'Spaz' 20.00
- Williams, Treat..35.00
- Williams, Walter Jon 20.00
- Williamson, Simon 30.00
- Willis, David..20.00
- Wilson, Friday 'Liz' [17-95]............................20.00
- Wilson, Karen..20.00
- Wilson, Lucy Autrey.......................................20.00
- Wingate, Keira 25.00
- Wingert, Wally 20.00

17-116

- Wingreen, Jason 50.00
- Winston, Stan..20.00
- Winters, David..20.00
- Winters, Time..20.00
- Witkin, Jacob...20.00
- Witwer, Sam..20.00
- Wolverton, Dave..20.00
- Wong, Eric...30.00
- Wong, Walden...20.00
- Wood, Fred..20.00
- Wood, Matthew..30.00
- Woods, Bob...30.00
- Woolman, Claude...20.00
- Wragg, Syd..20.00
- Wright, Kristy..25.00
- Wyborn, Peter..20.00
- Yamaguchi, Masa 25.00
- Yankovic, 'Weird' Al.......................................20.00
- Yassukovich, Tatyana 20.00
- Yerkes, Bob...20.00
- Yiamkati, Phoebe...20.00
- Zahn, Timothy [17-96]....................................25.00

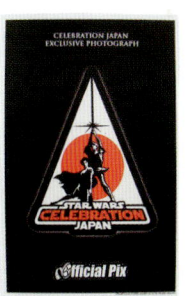 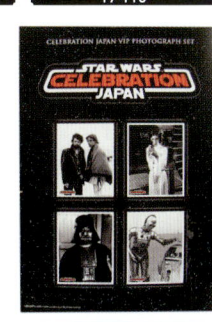

17-117 Front and Back Covers

Crowd Pleasers

- Darth Vader 8"x10", unlicensed appearances in late '70s and early '80s [17-97]..............................25.00

Disney / MGM

Autograph cards, Star Wars Weekends, May 2000.

- Baker, Kenny, hand signed..........................100.00
- Baker, Kenny, preprinted [17-98]...................50.00
- Bulloch, Jeremy, hand signed........................45.00
- Bulloch, Jeremy, preprinted [17-99]..............20.00
- Fisher, Carrie, hand signed.........................350.00
- Fisher, Carrie, preprinted [17-100]................50.00
- Lloyd, Jake, hand signed...............................60.00
- Lloyd, Jake, preprinted [17-101]....................15.00
- Mayhew, Peter, hand signed........................100.00
- Mayhew, Peter, preprinted [17-102]..............50.00
- McCaig, Ian, hand signed..............................25.00
- McCaig, Ian, preprinted [17-103]...................10.00
- Prowse, David, hand signed........................100.00
- Prowse, David, preprinted [17-104]...............35.00
- Quarshie, Hugh, hand signed.........................25.00
- Quarshie, Hugh, preprinted [17-105].............20.00

Autographs

Autograph cards, Star Wars Weekends, May 2001.
- ☐ Baker, Kenny, hand signed 100.00
- ☐ Baker, Kenny, preprinted [17-106] 50.00
- ☐ Brown, Phil, hand signed 30.00
- ☐ Brown, Phil, preprinted [17-107] 15.00
- ☐ Bulloch, Jeremy, hand signed 40.00
- ☐ Bulloch, Jeremy, preprinted [17-108] 20.00
- ☐ Chiang, Doug, hand signed 25.00
- ☐ Chiang, Doug, preprinted [17-109] 10.00
- ☐ Davis, Warwick, hand signed 30.00
- ☐ Davis, Warwick, preprinted [17-110] 15.00
- ☐ Fisher, Carrie, hand signed 350.00
- ☐ Fisher, Carrie, preprinted [17-111] 50.00
- ☐ Mayhew, Peter, hand signed 100.00
- ☐ Mayhew, Peter, preprinted [17-112] 50.00
- ☐ Quinn, Mike, hand signed 30.00
- ☐ Quinn, Mike, preprinted [17-113] 10.00

Autograph cards, Star Wars Weekends, May 2003.
- ☐ Bourriague, Michonne, hand signed 20.00
- ☐ Bourriague, Michonne, preprinted 20.00
- ☐ Bulloch, Jeremy, hand signed [17-114] 45.00
- ☐ Bulloch, Jeremy, pre-signed 20.00
- ☐ Morrison, Temuera, hand signed 55.00
- ☐ Morrison, Temuera, unsigned [17-115] 10.00

Official Pix
- ☐ Darth Vader: David Prowse / James Earl Jones, 11"x14", 100 produced [17-116] 500.00
- ☐ Hayden Christensen as Darth Vader, 200 produced 300.00

Star Wars Celebration Japan.
- ☐ VIP Photograph Set, folder, card, and four photographs [17-117] 20.00

Automobile Accessories
Covered in Volume 3, Page 34

Automobile Shades
Continued in Volume 3, Page 35

Mpire.
- ☐ Boba Fett [18-01] 15.00
- ☐ Count Dooku [18-02] 15.00
- ☐ Darth Vader [18-03] 15.00
- ☐ General Grievous [18-04] 15.00

Backpack Tags and Mascots
Continued in Volume 3, Page 36

Betty Crocker
Episode II: Attack of the Clones fruit snack premiums.
- ☐ Anakin Skywalker [19-01] 8.00
- ☐ Mace Windu [19-02] 8.00
- ☐ Obi-Wan Kenobi [19-03] 8.00
- ☐ Yoda [19-04] 8.00

Hasbro
- ☐ Darth Tater backpack hero [19-05] 10.00

Backpack Heroes. Classic trilogy.
- ☐ Boba Fett [19-06] 10.00
- ☐ Darth Vader [19-07] 10.00
- ☐ Han Solo [19-08] 10.00
- ☐ Luke Skywalker [19-09] 10.00
- ☐ Yoda [19-10] 10.00

The LEGO Group
Exclusive bag charms.
- ☐ Jedi Starfighter [19-11] 35.00
- ☐ Landspeeder [19-12] 20.00
- ☐ Millennium Falcon [v1e1:29] 25.00
- ☐ Slave I [19-13] 35.00
- ☐ Vader's TIE Fighter [v1e1:29] 25.00
- ☐ Y-Wing Fighter [19-14] 30.00

Underground Toys
4" talking plush with clip.
- ☐ Captain Rex 10.00
- ☐ Clone trooper [19-15] 10.00
- ☐ R2-D2 [19-16] 10.00
- ☐ Yoda 10.00

Backpacks and Carry Bags
Continued in Volume 3, Page 40

- ☐ Anakin Skywalker, podracing [20-01] 15.00
- ☐ Anakin Skywalker, podracing [20-02] 15.00
- ☐ Anakin, Obi-Wan, Captain Rex [20-03] 20.00
- ☐ C-3PO and R2-D2, artwork [20-04] 25.00
- ☐ Captain Rex and Clone Commanders [20-05] ...20.00
- ☐ Captain Rex helmet [20-06] 25.00
- ☐ Darth Maul [20-07] 30.00
- ☐ Darth Maul, flap with pouch [20-08] 20.00
- ☐ Darth Maul patch on black and red [20-09] 15.00
- ☐ Darth Vader and Star Destroyer [20-10] 35.00
- ☐ Darth Vader art, with Velcro strapping [20-11] ...20.00
- ☐ Darth Vader with lightsaber [20-12] 25.00
- ☐ Episode I: The Phantom Menace canvas 15.00
- ☐ Epic duel in front of Vader, red and yellow [20-13] 25.00
- ☐ Empire Strikes Back, Millennium Falcon flees Imperial Star Destroyer [20-14] 40.00
- ☐ Imperial black, Darth Vader embossed rubber flap [20-15] 35.00
- ☐ Jedi vs. Sith, Obi-Wan and Darth Maul [20-16] ...15.00
- ☐ Millennium Falcon over Death Star II [20-18] ...30.00
- ☐ Obi-Wan and Anakin, Clone Wars [20-17] 20.00
- ☐ Star Wars / Vader [20-19] 20.00
- ☐ Star Wars / Sith [20-20] 20.00
- ☐ Star Wars Celebration IV tote bag, exclusive to Star Wars Celebration IV 50.00
- ☐ Star Wars logo on black rip proof nylon 20.00
- ☐ Villains, Episode II: Attack of the Clones [20-21] ...20.00
- ☐ X-Wings over Yavin [20-22] 35.00
- ☐ Yoda face on black pack [20-23] 20.00
- ☐ Yoda, Ahsoka, Obi-Wan, Anakin in front of Republic emblem [20-24] 20.00

(Germany)
- ☐ Clone Wars, Commander Fox, Captain Rex, Anakin, Yoda, Obi-Wan [20-25] 40.00

(Japan)
- ☐ Darth Vader canvas 55.00

18-01

18-02

18-03

18-04

19-01

19-02

19-03

19-04

19-05

19-06

19-07

19-08

19-09

19-10

19-11

19-12

19-13

19-14

19-15

19-16

Backpacks and Carry Bags

 20-01
 20-02
 20-03
 20-04
 20-05
 20-06
 20-07

 20-08
 20-09
 20-10
 20-11
 20-12
 20-13
 20-14

(UK)
Clone Wars.
- Captain Rex, Obi-Wan, Anakin, Ahsoka, blue 14" [20-26] 25.00
- Captain Rex, Obi-Wan, Anakin, Ahsoka, blue 16" 25.00
- Captain Rex, Obi-Wan, Anakin, Ahsoka, red [20-27] 25.00

Adam Joseph Industries
Backpacks.
- AT-AT and Speeder bikes 85.00
- Darth Vader and Emperor's Royal Guards [20-28] 75.00
- Return of the Jedi heroes 85.00
- Yoda [20-29] 75.00

Bags.
- Wicket the Ewok [20-30] 235.00

Barrel bags.
- C-3PO and R2-D2 [20-31] 125.00
- Wicket the Ewok [20-32] 125.00
- Yoda [20-33] 125.00

Book bags, carry case.
- Darth Vader and Emperor's Royal Guards [20-34] 130.00

Book bags, strap close.
- Darth Vader and Emperor's Royal Guards [20-35] 90.00
- R2-D2 and C-3PO [20-36] 90.00
- Wicket the Ewok [20-37] 120.00

Book bags.
- C-3PO and R2-D2, blue [20-38] 50.00
- C-3PO and R2-D2, red 50.00
- Darth Vader and Emperor's Royal Guards 50.00
- Wicket the Ewok, blue [20-39] 75.00
- Wicket the Ewok, red [20-40] 75.00
- Yoda [20-41] 50.00

Ditty bags.
- Biker Scout [20-42] 150.00
- C-3PO and R2-D2, Jabba's sail barge [20-43] 150.00

Duffel bags.
- C-3PO and R2-D2 ....120.00
- Darth Vader 120.00
- Empire Strikes Back, silver with logo [20-44] 200.00
- Millennium Falcon 175.00
- Wicket the Ewok 145.00
- Yoda 120.00

Adidas
- "The Force is Strong with This One" carry-on bag [20-45] 70.00

Animations
- Darth Vader "Revenge" with bonus wallet [20-46] 25.00
- Darth Vader with handheld game case [20-47] 30.00
- Darth Vader with bonus pencil case and pencils [20-48] 30.00
- Darth Vader with CD carrier [20-49] 35.00
- Darth Vader with lightsaber [v1e1:31] 20.00
- Darth Vader with lightsaber down [20-50] 25.00
- Darth Vader, lightsaber on front pocket lights up [20-51] 25.00
- Darth Vader, silver and black [20-52] 30.00
- Epic duel [20-53] 20.00
- Epic duel, rolling [20-54] 35.00
- Star Wars / Darth Vader [20-55] 20.00
- Star Wars / Jedi carry bag [20-56] 30.00

Clone Wars. Exclusive to Target.
- Anakin Skywalker and Clone troopers [20-57] 20.00
- Anakin Skywalker, Clone Wars [20-58] 20.00
- Captain Rex [20-59] 20.00
- Captain Rex, lenticular [20-60] 20.00
- Jedi Heroes, lenticular [20-61] 20.00
- Obi-Wan and Anakin, raised art [20-62] 20.00

Pajama pals.
- Darth Vader [20-63] 25.00
- Yoda [20-64] 25.00

Calego International
Episode I: The Phantom Menace.
- Hard-sided with CD wallet [20-65] 40.00
- Queen Amidala, Celebration / Naboo battle, flip action, vinyl [20-66] 60.00
- Queen Amidala, mini backpack [20-67] 25.00

 20-15
 20-16
 20-17
 20-18
 20-19
 20-20
 20-21

 20-22
 20-23
 20-24
 20-25
 20-26
 20-27
 20-28

Backpacks and Carry Bags

20-29 | 20-30 | 20-31 | 20-32 | 20-33 | 20-34

  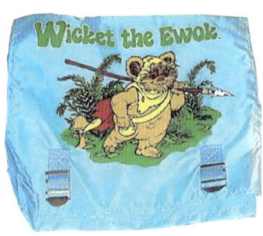    

20-35 | 20-36 | 20-37 | 20-38 | 20-39 | 20-40 | 20-41

Cedco Publishing
- ☐ Star Wars canvas book bag, promotional [20-68] 15.00

Comic Images
Sculpted character backpacks.
- ☐ Chewbacca [20-69] 65.00
- ☐ Darth Vader [20-70] 65.00
- ☐ Darth Vader helmet [20-71] 80.00
- ☐ R2-D2 [20-72] 50.00
- ☐ Rotta [20-73] 60.00
- ☐ Yoda 50.00

Disney / MGM
- ☐ Jedi Mickey 40.00
- ☐ Star Tours [20-74] 17.00
- ☐ Star Wars Weekends 40.00

Walt Disney Weekends. Messenger bags.
- ☐ 2005 logo (Vader Mickey) [20-75] 135.00
- ☐ 2006 logo 125.00

Disney Theme Park Merchandise
- ☐ Jedi Mickey plush, Jedi Training Academy [20-76] 60.00

Editions Atlas
- ☐ Star Wars [20-77] 12.00

Factors, Etc.
- ☐ C-3PO and Luke Skywalker [20-78] 45.00
- ☐ Chewbacca 45.00
- ☐ Chewbacca and Han Solo 45.00
- ☐ "Darth Vadar Lives" *[sic]* 45.00
- ☐ Darth Vader / Stormtroopers 45.00
- ☐ Hildebrandt art [20-79] 45.00

- ☐ "May the Force be with you" 45.00
- ☐ Star Wars logo 45.00

Fan Club
- ☐ Episode I canvas carry bag 35.00

Frankel N Roth (UK)
Empire Strikes Back.
- ☐ Darth Vader [20-80] 165.00

Return of the Jedi.
- ☐ "May the Force be with you", blue [20-81] 135.00
- ☐ "May the Force be with you", red [20-82] 135.00
- ☐ Jabba the Hutt [20-83] 150.00
- ☐ Jabba's palace [20-84] 150.00
- ☐ Rebel hangar [20-85] 150.00
- ☐ Scenes [20-86] 150.00

 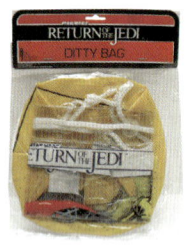   

20-42 | 20-43 | 20-44 Side 1 and Side 2 | | 20-45

20-46 | 20-47 | 20-48 | 20-49 | 20-50 | 20-51 | 20-52

20-53 | 20-54 | 20-55 | 20-56 | 20-57 | 20-58 | 20-59

Backpacks and Carry Bags

20-60 20-61 20-62 20-63 20-64 20-65

20-66 Image 1 and Image 2   20-67   20-68   20-69   20-70   20-71   20-72

Giftware International
Character shaped backpacks.
- C-3PO [20-87] 30.00
- Chewbacca [20-88] 45.00
- Darth Maul [20-89] 30.00
- Darth Vader [20-90] 45.00
- Ewok [20-91] 25.00
- Jar Jar Binks [20-92] 35.00
- R2-D2 [20-93] 40.00
- Yoda [20-94] 40.00

Grosvenor
Episode I: The Phantom Menace mini backpacks.
- Queen Amidala [20-95] 20.00

Episode II: Attack of the Clones mini backpacks.
- Anakin Skywalker [20-96] 8.00
- Jango Fett [20-97] 8.00

Leeds
- Gray and Black, Star Wars Celebration III exclusive [20-98] 40.00

LucasArts
- Star Wars Galaxies, messenger bag 50.00

Pottery Barn
- X-Wing Fighters [20-99] 35.00

Pyramid
Classic trilogy. Dark Side collection. Nylon. Embossed rubber artwork.
- Boba Fett 25.00
- Darth Vader 25.00
- Luke Skywalker 25.00
- Stormtrooper 25.00

Classic trilogy. Destroyer collection. Vinyl. Metallic trim and inset artwork.
- Boba Fett 30.00
- Darth Vader [20-100] 30.00
- Luke Skywalker 30.00
- Stormtrooper [20-101] 30.00

Classic trilogy. Hi-Tech collection. Nylon. All-over artwork.
- Boba Fett 25.00
- Darth Vader [20-102] 25.00
- Stormtrooper 25.00
- Yoda 25.00

Classic trilogy. Imperial collection. Nylon. Rubber patch.
- Boba Fett 30.00
- Darth Vader [20-103] 30.00
- Stormtrooper 30.00

  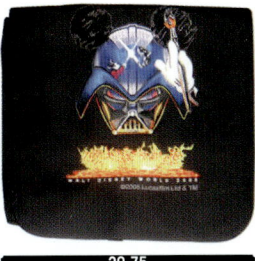    

20-73 20-74 20-75 20-76 20-77 20-78 20-79

20-80 20-81 20-82 20-83 20-84 20-85

20-86 20-87 20-88 20-89 20-90 20-91

Backpacks and Carry Bags

20-92 | 20-93 | 20-94 | 20-95 | 20-96 | 20-97

20-98 | 20-99 | 20-100 | 20-101 | 20-102 | 20-103 | 20-104

Classic trilogy. Interactive collection. Lights and battle sounds.
- ❏ Darth Vader / TIE Fighter [20-104] 35.00
- ❏ Darth Vader, breathes [20-105] 35.00
- ❏ Luke Skywalker / X-Wing Fighter [20-106] 35.00

Classic trilogy. Pilot collection. Vinyl. Schematic artwork.
- ❏ Boba Fett / Slave I [20-107] 30.00
- ❏ Darth Vader / TIE Fighter [20-108] 30.00
- ❏ Luke Skywalker / X-Wing Fighter [20-109] 30.00

Classic trilogy. Star Class collection. Vinyl. Inset artwork.
- ❏ Boba Fett 20.00
- ❏ C-3PO 20.00
- ❏ Darth Vader [20-110] 20.00
- ❏ Stormtrooper [20-111] 20.00

Classic trilogy. Zoom collection. Vinyl. All-over artwork.
- ❏ Boba Fett 25.00
- ❏ Darth Vader [20-112] 25.00
- ❏ Luke Skywalker 25.00

Episode I: The Phantom Menace.
- ❏ Anakin Skywalker and Sebulba [20-113] 15.00
- ❏ Anakin Skywalker in podracer gear with checkerboard, vinyl [20-114] 15.00
- ❏ Anakin Skywalker in podracer gear, canvas 15.00
- ❏ Anakin Skywalker in podracer gear, vinyl [20-115] 15.00
- ❏ Canvas carry bag with handles and over-shoulder strap, black or blue [20-116] 20.00
- ❏ Darth Maul 15.00
- ❏ Darth Maul, character art, quilted [20-117] 15.00
- ❏ Darth Maul art [20-118] 20.00
- ❏ Darth Maul bust, canvas 15.00
- ❏ Darth Maul full-body, canvas 15.00
- ❏ Darth Maul shoulder bag [20-119] 25.00
- ❏ Jar Jar Binks, vinyl [20-120] 20.00
- ❏ Jedi vs. Sith art [20-121] 15.00
- ❏ Jedi, vinyl [20-122] 15.00
- ❏ Obi-Wan lenticular 15.00
- ❏ Podracing art shoulder bag [20-123] 25.00
- ❏ Queen Amidala [20-124] 20.00
- ❏ Queen Amidala, mini [20-125] 25.00
- ❏ Starfighters, vinyl [20-126] 20.00

Episode I: The Phantom Menace. Flip action, vinyl.
- ❏ Darth Maul / Qui-Gon Jinn [20-127] 25.00
- ❏ Starfighters [20-128] 25.00

Episode II: Attack of the Clones.
- ❏ Anakin Skywalker 20.00

20-105 | 20-106 | 20-107 | 20-108 | 20-109 | 20-110 | 20-111

20-112 | 20-113 | 20-114 | 20-115 | 20-116 | 20-117 | 20-118

20-119 | 20-120 | 20-121 | 20-122 | 20-123 | 20-124 | 20-125

Backpacks and Carry Bags

    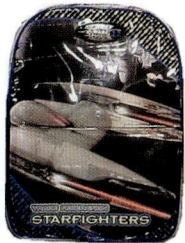  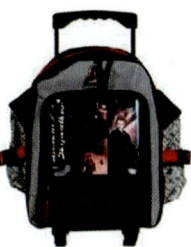

20-126 | 20-127 Image 1 and Image 2 | 20-128 Image 1 and Image 2 | 20-129 | 20-130

20-131 | 20-132 | 20-133 | 20-134 | 20-135

- ❏ Anakin Skywalker blue and orange, side pockets 20.00
- ❏ Anakin Skywalker's destiny, red, gray, and black [20-129] 25.00
- ❏ Anakin Skywalker's destiny, side pockets [20-130] 20.00
- ❏ Heroes 20.00
- ❏ Jango Fett 20.00
- ❏ Jango Fett, blue and gray 20.00
- ❏ Villains 20.00
- ❏ Yoda [20-131] 20.00

Episode II: Attack of the Clones. Plastic with stationary supplies in outer pouch.
- ❏ Anakin Skywalker Jedi, side pockets 20.00
- ❏ Heroes, side pockets 20.00
- ❏ Jango Fett [20-132] 20.00
- ❏ R2-D2 and C-3PO [20-133] 20.00

Duffel bags. Classic trilogy. Dark Side collection. Nylon. Embossed rubber artwork.
- ❏ Boba Fett [20-134] 35.00
- ❏ Darth Vader 35.00
- ❏ Luke Skywalker [20-135] 35.00
- ❏ Stormtrooper 35.00

Duffel bags. Classic trilogy. Destroyer collection. Vinyl. Metallic trim and inset artwork.
- ❏ Boba Fett 40.00
- ❏ Darth Vader 40.00
- ❏ Luke Skywalker 40.00
- ❏ Stormtrooper [20-136] 40.00

Duffel bags. Classic trilogy. Hi-Tech collection. Nylon.
- ❏ Boba Fett 35.00
- ❏ Darth Vader 35.00
- ❏ Stormtrooper [20-137] 35.00
- ❏ Yoda 35.00

Duffel bags. Classic trilogy. Imperial collection. Nylon. Rubber patch.
- ❏ Boba Fett 30.00
- ❏ Darth Vader 30.00
- ❏ Stormtrooper 30.00

Duffel bags. Classic trilogy. Star Class collection. Vinyl. Inset artwork.
- ❏ Boba Fett 30.00
- ❏ C-3PO 30.00
- ❏ Darth Vader 30.00
- ❏ Stormtrooper [20-138] 30.00

Duffel bags. Classic trilogy. Zoom collection. Vinyl. All-over artwork.
- ❏ Boba Fett 35.00
- ❏ Darth Vader 35.00
- ❏ Luke Skywalker [20-139] 35.00

 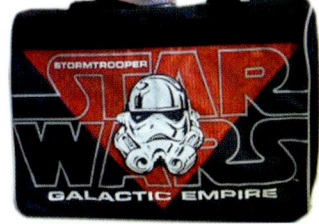  

20-136 | 20-137 | 20-138 | 20-139

20-140 | 20-141 | 20-142 | 20-143

20-144 | 20-145 | 20-146 | 20-147 | 20-148 | 20-149

Backpacks and Carry Bags

Duffel bags. Episode I: The Phantom Menace.
- ❏ Anakin Skywalker [20-140] 30.00
- ❏ Darth Maul [20-141] 30.00
- ❏ Jedi vs. Sith, graphic [20-142] 30.00
- ❏ Jedi vs. Sith, photo [20-143] 30.00
- ❏ Pod Racing [20-144] 30.00

Scholastic
- ❏ Star Wars Junior sign-up bonus [20-145] 50.00

Star Wars Celebration V
- ❏ Boba Fett logo messenger bag 75.00
- ❏ Boba Fett reusable shopping bag [20-146] 35.00
- ❏ I *(heart)* Scoundrels 30.00

The Promotions Factory
Canvas shopping bags.
- ❏ A New Hope / "The Force Is Strong With This One" [20-147] 8.00
- ❏ Empire Strikes Back / "I Am Your Father" [20-148] ... 8.00
- ❏ Return of the Jedi / "I Am A Jedi, Like My Father Before Me" [20-149] 8.00

Zoom Gear
Exclusive to Star Wars Celebration III.
- ❏ Backpack 75.00
- ❏ Messenger bag, gray and black 60.00

Badges
Continued in Volume 3, Page 46

501st Legion
Droid Hunt convention badge game pieces.
- ❏ Celebration III, Indianapolis, IN 10.00
- ❏ Celebration IV, Los Angeles, CA 15.00
- ❏ Comic-Con, San Diego, CA 10.00

Fan Club
Collectible badges are similar size, shape, design as Star Wars Celebration passes. Fan Club exclusives.
- ❏ #1 Imperial / Mara Jade [21-01] 8.00
- ❏ #2 Rebel / Jek Porkins [21-02] 8.00
- ❏ #3 Bounty Hunter / Aurra Sing [21-03] 8.00
- ❏ #4 Tatooine / Wuher the bartender [21-04] 8.00
- ❏ #5 Imperial / Darth Vader [21-05] 8.00
- ❏ #6 Jedi Council / Mace Windu [21-06] 8.00

Star Wars Celebration pass replicas. "Star Wars Insider—Limited Edition" printed on back.
- ❏ All access Sebulba 10.00
- ❏ Backstage Pit Droid 10.00
- ❏ Exhibitors Jar Jar 10.00
- ❏ Exhibitors Jar Jar, autographed by Ahmed Best 75.00
- ❏ Friday Obi-Wan Kenobi 10.00
- ❏ Saturday Qui-Gon Jinn 10.00
- ❏ Staff C-3PO 10.00
- ❏ Staff C-3PO, autographed by Anthony Daniels 150.00
- ❏ Sunday Anakin Skywalker 10.00
- ❏ Three Day Darth Maul 10.00
- ❏ VIP guest Queen Amidala 10.00
- ❏ Volunteer Battle Droid 10.00

Force-Cast
- ❏ Star Wars Celebration, Japan [21-07] 5.00

K B Toys
- ❏ Episode I premiere weekend commemorative badge, May 19–23, 1999 [21-08] 25.00

Marin County
- ❏ Star Wars summit 1996 .... 35.00

Mexico Collector Convention (Mexico)
2001.
- ❏ Comite Organizator, Darth Vader art [21-09] 20.00
- ❏ Domingo, red R2 art [21-10] 20.00
- ❏ Expositor, Watto art [21-11] 20.00
- ❏ Sabado, R2-D2 art [21-12] 20.00
- ❏ Staff, stormtrooper art [21-13] 20.00
- ❏ Tres Dias, Boba Fett art [21-14] 20.00
- ❏ Viernes, blue R2 art [21-15] 20.00
- ❏ VIP, Yoda image [21-16] 20.00

44

Badges

2002.
- ❏ Domingo / Mace Windu [21-17] 15.00
- ❏ Expositor / Watto [21-18] 15.00
- ❏ Invitado VIP / Yoda [21-19] 15.00
- ❏ Organizador / Lightsaber [21-20] 15.00
- ❏ Sabado / Obi-Wan [21-21] 15.00
- ❏ Seguridad / Super Battle Droid [21-22] 15.00
- ❏ Staff / Clone trooper [21-23] 15.00
- ❏ Tres Dias / Jango Fett [21-24] 15.00

2003.
- ❏ Boba Fett / Dos Dias [21-125] 10.00
- ❏ Chewbacca / Domingo [21-26] 10.00
- ❏ Darth Vader / Organizador [21-27] 10.00
- ❏ Gamorrean Guard / Seguridad [21-28] 10.00
- ❏ Han Solo / Sabado [21-29] 10.00
- ❏ Jawa / Expositor [21-30] 10.00
- ❏ Lobot / Prensa [21-31] 10.00
- ❏ Stormtrooper / Staff [21-32] 10.00
- ❏ Yak Face / Fan Club [21-33] 10.00
- ❏ Yoda / Invitado VIP [21-34] 10.00

2004.
- ❏ Fan club [21-35] 10.00
- ❏ Pase Jedi [21-36] 10.00
- ❏ Prensa 10.00
- ❏ Prensa, variation [21-37] 10.00

Star Wars Celebration

1999 Denver.
- ❏ All access Sebulba [21-38] 135.00
- ❏ Backstage Pit Droid [21-39] 50.00
- ❏ Exhibitors Jar Jar [21-40] 25.00
- ❏ Friday Obi-Wan Kenobi [21-41] 25.00
- ❏ Saturday Qui-Gon Jinn [21-42] 25.00
- ❏ Staff C-3PO [21-43] 25.00
- ❏ Sunday Anakin Skywalker [21-44] 25.00
- ❏ Three Day Darth Maul [21-45] 25.00
- ❏ VIP Guest Queen Amidala [21-46] 100.00
- ❏ Volunteer Battle Droid [21-47] 35.00

2002 Indianapolis.
- ❏ Associate [21-48] 25.00
- ❏ Exhibitor [21-49] 25.00
- ❏ Friday Adult [21-50] 25.00
- ❏ Friday Child 25.00
- ❏ Licensee [21-51] 100.00
- ❏ Press [21-52] 25.00
- ❏ Saturday Adult [21-53] 25.00
- ❏ Saturday Child 25.00
- ❏ Staff [21-54] 25.00
- ❏ Sunday Adult 25.00
- ❏ Sunday Child [21-55] 25.00
- ❏ Three Day Adult [21-56] 25.00
- ❏ Three Day Child 25.00
- ❏ VIP Guest [21-57] 175.00
- ❏ Wooden-boxed set 150.00

2005 Indianapolis.
- ❏ 4 day Adult Darth Vader [21-58] 15.00
- ❏ 4 day Child, Anakin Skywalker, animated [21-59] 15.00
- ❏ Associate [21-60] 15.00
- ❏ Exhibitor [21-61] 15.00
- ❏ Friday Adult, Padmé [21-62] 15.00
- ❏ Friday Child, Padmé animated [21-63] 15.00
- ❏ Press [21-64] 15.00
- ❏ Saturday Adult, Yoda [21-65] 15.00
- ❏ Saturday Child, Yoda animated [21-66] 15.00
- ❏ Staff [21-67] 15.00
- ❏ Sunday Adult, Obi-Wan [21-68] 15.00
- ❏ Sunday Child, Obi-Wan animated [21-69] 15.00
- ❏ Thursday Adult, Mace Windu [21-70] 15.00
- ❏ Thursday Child, Mace Windu animated [21-71] 15.00
- ❏ VIP [21-72] 15.00
- ❏ Volunteer [21-73] 15.00
- ❏ Wooden-boxed set 90.00

2007 Los Angeles.
- ❏ 4 Day Adult, Darth Vader [21-74] 15.00
- ❏ 4 Day Child, Wicket [21-75] 15.00
- ❏ All Access, Obi-Wan [21-76] 15.00
- ❏ Associate, Admiral Ackbar [21-77] 15.00
- ❏ Crew, Stormtrooper [21-78] 15.00
- ❏ Exhibitor, Chewbacca [21-79] 15.00
- ❏ Friday Adult, Princess Leia, A New Hope [21-80] 15.00

Badges

- ❏ Friday Child, Princess Leia, captive [21-81] 15.00
- ❏ Media, Emperor [21-82] 15.00
- ❏ Monday Adult, Luke Skywalker [21-83] 15.00
- ❏ Monday Child, Biker Scout [21-84] 15.00
- ❏ Saturday Adult, C-3PO [21-85] 15.00
- ❏ Saturday Child, R2-D2 [21-86] 15.00
- ❏ Staff, Han Solo [21-87] 15.00
- ❏ Sunday Adult, Lando Calrissian [21-88] 15.00
- ❏ Sunday Child, Boba Fett [21-89] 15.00
- ❏ Vendor, Dewback [21-90] 25.00
- ❏ VIP, Yoda [21-91] 40.00

2010 Orlando.
- ❏ 4 Day Adult, Boba Fett [21-92] 10.00
- ❏ 4 Day Child, R2-D2 [21-93] 10.00
- ❏ All Access, Luke Skywalker [21-94] 10.00
- ❏ Collector set, exclusive to Star Wars Celebration V 80.00
- ❏ Crew, Obi-Wan Kenobi [21-95] 10.00
- ❏ Exhibitor, Wampa [21-96] 10.00
- ❏ Friday Adult, Princess Leia [21-97] 10.00
- ❏ Friday Child, Ahsoka Tano [21-98] 10.00
- ❏ Jedi Knight, Aayla Secura [21-99] 10.00
- ❏ Jedi Master, Mace Windu [21-100] 10.00
- ❏ Kids, complimentary, C-3PO [21-101] 10.00
- ❏ Media, General Grievous [21-102] 10.00
- ❏ Saturday Adult, Lobot [21-103] 10.00
- ❏ Saturday Child, Yoda [21-104] 10.00
- ❏ Staff, Han Solo [21-105] 10.00
- ❏ Sunday Adult, Darth Vader [21-106] 10.00
- ❏ Sunday Child, Anakin Skywalker [21-107] 10.00
- ❏ Thursday Adult, Snowtrooper [21-108] 10.00
- ❏ Thursday Child, Captain Rex [21-109] 10.00
- ❏ VIP [21-110] 25.00

Star Wars Celebration (Japan)
2008 Japan.
- ❏ 3-Day [21-111] 10.00
- ❏ 3-Day Child [21-112] 10.00
- ❏ 3-Day Premium [21-113] 10.00
- ❏ Access All Areas 20.00
- ❏ Exhibitor [21-114] 10.00
- ❏ Media [21-115] 10.00
- ❏ Monday [21-116] 10.00
- ❏ Monday Child 10.00
- ❏ Monday Premium [21-117] 10.00
- ❏ Saturday [21-118] 10.00
- ❏ Saturday Child 10.00
- ❏ Saturday Premium [21-119] 10.00
- ❏ Staff [21-120] 10.00
- ❏ Sunday [21-121] 10.00
- ❏ Sunday Child 10.00
- ❏ Sunday Premium [21-122] 10.00

Star Wars Celebration (UK)
2007 London.
- ❏ 3 Day Adult [21-123] 15.00
- ❏ 3 Day Child [21-124] 15.00
- ❏ Adult Friday [21-125] 15.00
- ❏ Adult Saturday [21-126] 15.00
- ❏ Adult Sunday [21-127] 15.00
- ❏ All Access [21-128] 45.00
- ❏ Child Friday [21-129] 15.00
- ❏ Child Saturday [21-130] 15.00
- ❏ Child Sunday [21-131] 15.00
- ❏ Contractor [21-132] 50.00
- ❏ Exhibitor [21-133] 45.00
- ❏ Junior Pass [21-134] 15.00
- ❏ Media [21-135] 20.00
- ❏ Staff [21-136] 30.00
- ❏ VIP [21-137] 45.00
- ❏ Volunteer [21-138] 20.00

Star Wars Conference (Spain)
Sitges Spain 2004. Animated Clone Wars characters on badges.
- ❏ Accesso Total, Yoda [21-139] 15.00
- ❏ Expositor, Count Dooku [21-140] 15.00
- ❏ Invitado, R2-D2 [21-141] 15.00
- ❏ Organizacion, Obi-Wan Kenobi [21-142] 15.00
- ❏ Prensa, C-3PO [21-143] 15.00
- ❏ Socia, Padmé [21-144] 15.00
- ❏ Socio, Anakin Skywalker [21-145] 15.00
- ❏ Visitante, Clone trooper [21-146] 15.00
- ❏ Voluntario, Mace Windu [21-147] 15.00

Star Wars Weekends
- ❏ Staff badge 45.00

Bags, Shopping Totes

 22-01
 22-02
 22-03
 22-04
 22-05
 22-06

 22-07
 22-08
 22-09
 22-10
 22-11
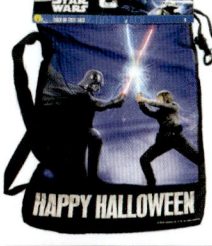 22-12
 22-13 Front and Back

 22-14
 22-15
 22-16
 23-01
 23-02
 23-03
 23-04

 23-05
 23-06
 24-01
 24-02
 24-03 24-04

Bags
Continued in Volume 3, Page 47

- ❑ Celebration II convention fan bag 10.00
- ❑ Celebration III convention fan bag 10.00
- ❑ Celebration IV convention fan bag [22-01] 10.00
- ❑ Space battle, flat paper [22-02] 12.00

Episode III: Revenge of the Sith.
- ❑ Clone trooper [22-03] 15.00
- ❑ Darth Vader 15.00
- ❑ Yoda [22-04] 15.00

Accessory Innovations
Recyclable totes.
- ❑ Clone Wars 12.00
- ❑ LEGO Darth Vader, "I Want You—Io Build the Imperial Army" [22-05] 12.00
- ❑ LEGO Star Wars [22-06] 12.00

Baleno (China)
- ❑ Episode III: Revenge of the Sith plastic carry bag [22-07] 15.00

Cingular
- ❑ Episode III: Revenge of the Sith plastic carry bag 8.00

Disney / MGM
- ❑ Use In Case of Space Sickness [22-08] 35.00

Forbidden Planet
- ❑ Micro Machines promotion printed on plastic bag [22-09] 10.00

Kellogg's (Germany)
- ❑ The Power of Myth 25.00

Penguin Young Readers Group
- ❑ Clone Wars, exclusive to San Diego Comic-Con [22-10] 15.00

Rubies
- ❑ Celebration V convention fan bag 8.00

Reusable trick or treat totes.
- ❑ Darth Vader [22-11] 12.00
- ❑ Luke vs. Darth Vader [22-12] 12.00

Star Wars Celebration V
- ❑ Celebration V logo 35.00

Target
- ❑ Episode III: Revenge of the Sith plastic carry bag ... 10.00

Virgin Atlantic
Air sickness bags. 24 in set. Only 4 are Star Wars theme.
- ❑ Know Your Lightsaber [22-13] 25.00
- ❑ Lightsaber Etiquette [22-14] 25.00
- ❑ Seating Jedi and Sith [22-15] 25.00
- ❑ The Art of Jedi Combat [22-16] 25.00

Bags, Drawstring
Continued in Volume 3, Page 47

- ❑ Anakin Skywalker [23-01] 12.00
- ❑ Jar Jar Binks [23-02] 12.00
- ❑ Queen Amidala [23-03] 12.00

Animations
- ❑ Boba Fett, exclusive to Target [23-04] 10.00
- ❑ Chewbacca, exclusive to Target [23-05] 10.00

Dorling Kindersley (UK)
- ❑ LEGO Figures 15.00

Grosvenor
- ❑ C-3PO and R2-D2, exclusive to Target [23-06] 15.00

Bags, Shopping Totes
Continued in Volume 3, Page 47

Accessory Network
- ❑ Darth Vader [24-01] 30.00

Psycho Bunny
Canvas carry bags.
- ❑ C-3PO [24-02] 25.00
- ❑ Darth Vader 25.00
- ❑ Luke Skywalker [24-03] 25.00
- ❑ Stormtrooper [24-04] 25.00

Balloons

    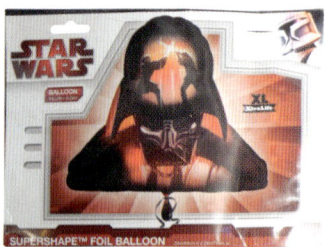 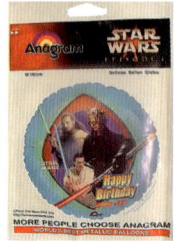 

25-01　　25-02　　25-03　　25-04　　25-05　　25-06　　25-07

25-08　　25-09　　25-10　　25-11　　25-12　　25-13　　25-14　　25-15

   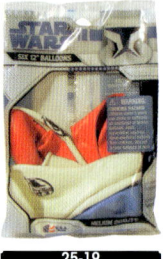  

25-16　　25-17　　25-18　　25-19　　25-19 Inflated　　25-19 Inflated

     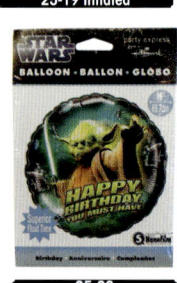 

25-20　　25-20 Inflated　　25-20 Inflated　　25-21　　25-22　　25-23　　25-24

Balloons
Continued in Volume 3, Page 48

Anagram International
Mini Mylar balloons on sticks.
- ❏ Darth Maul 7.00
- ❏ Darth Vader 7.00
- ❏ Jar Jar Binks 7.00
- ❏ Naboo Fighter 7.00
- ❏ R2-D2 .... 7.00

Mylar helium balloons.
- ❏ Anakin Skywalker in podracer [25-01] 8.00
- ❏ C-3PO jumbo shaped 27"x21" 20.00
- ❏ C-3PO mini shaped 10"x12" [4-21] 5.00
- ❏ Classic trilogy characters [25-02] 8.00
- ❏ Darth Maul [25-03] 8.00
- ❏ Darth Maul jumbo shaped 30" 20.00
- ❏ Darth Vader / Millennium Falcon [25-04] 8.00
- ❏ Darth Vader / Millennium Falcon, "Happy Birthday" [3:114] 8.00
- ❏ Darth Vader, super shape [25-05] 25.00
- ❏ Droids, May the Force be with you [v1e1-37] ... 8.00
- ❏ "Happy Birthday Young Jedi" [25-06] 8.00
- ❏ "Happy Birthday" R2-D2 and C-3PO [25-07] ... 8.00
- ❏ Jar Jar Binks [v1e1-37] 8.00
- ❏ Naboo Space Battle [25-07] 8.00
- ❏ Queen Amidala, super shape [25-08] 18.00
- ❏ R2-D2, air walker [25-09] 20.00
- ❏ Yoda, round with ears [4-21] 12.00

Mylar helium balloons. 12" mini shaped.
- ❏ Darth Maul [4-21] 8.00
- ❏ Darth Vader [4-21] 8.00
- ❏ R2-D2 [v1e1-37] 8.00

Ariel
- ❏ Characters or vehicles in assorted colors, 8-pack [25-10] 25.00

Drawing Board Greeting Cards, Inc.
Balloon multi-packs, assorted colors.
- ❏ Empire Strikes Back 10-pack [25-11] 25.00
- ❏ Return of the Jedi 5-pack 20.00
- ❏ Return of the Jedi 6-pack, Ewoks, exclusive to K-Mart [25-12] 30.00
- ❏ Return of the Jedi 10-pack [25-13] 20.00

Overbreak LLC
Hover Discs 2 feet wide, Episode III: Revenge of the Sith.
- ❏ Darth Vader [25-14] 10.00
- ❏ General Grievous [25-15] 10.00
- ❏ Yoda 10.00

Hover Discs 3 feet wide, Episode III: Revenge of the Sith.
- ❏ Darth Vader [25-16] 10.00
- ❏ Yoda [25-17] 10.00

Hover Blimps.
- ❏ Saga [4-21] 12.00

Party Express
- ❏ Darth Vader 42" jumbo [25-18] 25.00

Latex rubber. 12" balloons. 6-packs.
- ❏ Clone Wars [25-19] 8.00
- ❏ Star Wars [25-20] 8.00

Mylar helium balloons, 18" round.
- ❏ Clone Wars [v1e1-37] 10.00
- ❏ Episode II [25-21] 10.00
- ❏ Episode III [25-22] 10.00
- ❏ "Happy Birthday You Must Have" [25-23] 10.00
- ❏ Saga [25-24] 10.00

Bandages
Continued in Volume 3, Page 51

Curad
30 sterile bandages in character box.
- ❏ C-3PO [26-01] 8.00
- ❏ Jar Jar Binks [26-02] 10.00

Episode I: The Phantom Menace. 30 sterile bandages in character box. Collector's edition.
- ❏ Anakin Skywalker [26-03] 10.00
- ❏ Darth Maul [26-04] 10.00
- ❏ Jar Jar Binks [26-05] 10.00
- ❏ Queen Amidala [26-06] 10.00

Episode II: Attack of the Clones. 30 sterile bandages. Lenticular card on front.
- ❏ Heroes [26-07] 10.00
- ❏ Jango Fett [26-08] 10.00

Banks

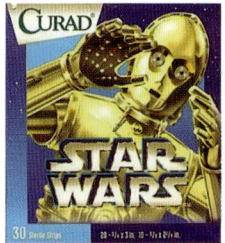      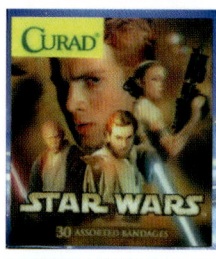

26-01 | 26-02 | 26-03 | 26-04 | 26-05 | 26-06 | 26-07

 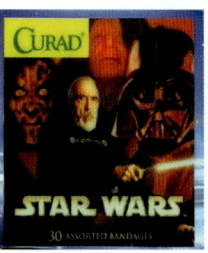 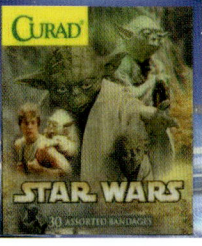    

26-08 | 26-09 | 26-10 | 26-11 | 26-12 | 26-13 | 26-14

❑ Saga villains [26-09] 10.00
❑ Yoda [26-10] 10.00

Nexcare
20 assorted bandages.
❑ Captain Rex [26-11] 8.00
❑ Heroes 8.00
❑ Yoda [26-12] 8.00

Salvemed (Netherlands)
❑ Clone Wars, 16-pack [26-13] 35.00

Salvequick (UK)
❑ Clone Wars, 14-pack [26-14] 25.00

Bank Books

N.S.W. Building Society Ltd.
"Passbook Savings Account"
❑ C-3PO and R2-D2 ....650.00
❑ Wicket 500.00

Banks
Continued in Volume 3, Page 51

Episode I. PVC, approximately 5 1/2".
❑ Battle Droid [27-01] 15.00
❑ Darth Maul [27-02] 15.00
❑ Darth Sidious [27-03] 15.00

❑ Darth Vader [27-04] 15.00
❑ Jar Jar Binks [27-05] 20.00

(China)
PVC, approximately 10" tall.
❑ Darth Vader [27-06] 20.00
❑ Yoda [27-07] 15.00

PVC, approx. 10" tall. Clones with articulated arms.
❑ Blue [27-08] 25.00
❑ Orange [27-09] 25.00
❑ Red [27-10] 25.00
❑ White [27-11] 25.00
❑ Yellow [27-12] 25.00

(Spain)
❑ Droids, cylinder 350.00

(UK)
❑ Chewbacca [27-13] 250.00
❑ Darth Vader [27-14] 250.00

Action
❑ 1999 Jeff Gordon pedal car with trailer 2,508 produced [v1e1:38] 65.00
❑ 2005 #5 Kyle Busch 1:24 clear window 60.00

Adam Joseph Industries
Ewoks. Plastic.
❑ Princess Kneesa [27-15] 35.00
❑ Wicket [27-16] 35.00

Return of the Jedi.
❑ Darth Vader [27-17] 45.00
❑ Emperor's Royal Guard [27-18] 45.00
❑ Gamorrean Guard [27-19] 250.00
❑ R2-D2 [27-20] 45.00

Adam Joseph Industries (Canada)
Return of the Jedi. Bilingual packaging.
❑ Darth Vader [27-21] 50.00
❑ Emperor's Royal Guard [27-22] 50.00

Applause
❑ Darth Maul on Sith Speeder [v1e1:39] 20.00
❑ Jar Jar Binks [27-23] 20.00

Applause (UK)
Boxed banks.
❑ Darth Maul on Sith Speeder [27-24] 20.00
❑ Jar Jar Binks 20.00

Candy Rific
Packaging updated annually with same UPC and new year.
❑ Boba Fett [27-25] 6.00
❑ Darth Vader [27-26] 5.00
❑ Obi-Wan Kenobi [27-27] 5.00

Comic Images
Ceramic.
❑ Darth Vader helmet [27-28] 25.00
❑ Yoda [27-29] 25.00

27-01 | 27-02 | 27-03 | 27-04 | 27-05 | 27-06 Front and Back | 27-07 Front and Back

27-08 | 27-09 | 27-10 | 27-11 | 27-12 | 27-13 Front and Back

Banks

27-14 Front and Back   27-15   27-16   27-17   27-18   27-19   27-20

27-21   27-22   27-23   27-24   27-25   27-26   27-27

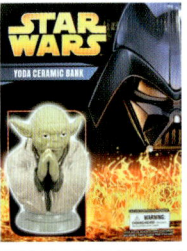     

27-28   27-29   27-30   27-31   27-32   27-33   27-34

Commonwealth Savings (Australia)
- Darth Vader [v1e1:39] 50.00
- R2-D2, dark blue [27-30] 40.00
- R2-D2, light blue 40.00
- R2-D2, white [27-31] 40.00

Diamond Select Toys
- Boba Fett [27-32] 25.00
- Clone trooper [27-33] 25.00
- Commander Cody [27-34] 25.00
- Darth Maul with hologram 45.00
- Darth Maul with lightsaber [27-35] 35.00
- Darth Vader [27-36] 25.00
- Darth Vader unmasked 25.00
- Han Solo [27-37] 25.00
- Jango Fett, exclusive to Toys R Us [27-38] 50.00
- R2-D2 .... 25.00
- Slave I [27-39] 40.00

Disney Theme Park Merchandise
- Mickey and Minnie as Luke and Leia [27-40] 60.00
- Stormtrooper Helmet [27-41] 45.00

Fuji (Japan)
- R2-D2 [27-42] 300.00

Funko
12" Bobble banks.
- Boba Fett [27-43] 50.00
- Darth Vader [27-44] 50.00
- Yoda 50.00

Kinnerton Confectionery (UK)
- Darth Maul, ceramic [27-45] 25.00
- Darth Vader, ceramic [27-46] 25.00
- Darth Vader with chocolate egg [27-47] 25.00
- R2-D2, tin [27-48] 15.00

Merit (UK)
- Return of the Jedi coin sorter [27-49] 400.00

Metal Box Ltd.
- Darth Vader with combination dials [27-50] 45.00
- Empire Strikes Back, octagonal [27-51] 30.00
- Yoda with combination dials [27-52] 45.00

NECA
- Heroes, tin [27-53] 15.00
- Villains, tin [27-54] 15.00
- R2-D2, 5,000 produced [27-55] 35.00

NTD Apparel Inc. (UK)
Plastic bust bank with t-shirt inside.
- Anakin Skywalker [27-56] 20.00
- Darth Maul [27-57] 20.00
- Jar Jar Binks [27-58] 20.00

27-35   27-36   27-37   27-38   27-39   27-40   27-41

27-42 Front and Back   27-43   27-44   27-45   27-46   27-47

Banks

      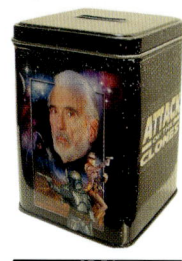

27-48   27-49   27-50   27-51   27-52   27-53   27-54

27-55   27-56   27-57   27-58   27-59 Side 1 and Side 2   27-60   27-61

27-62   27-63   27-64   27-65   27-66   27-67   27-68

  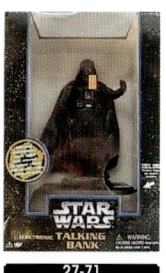    

27-69   27-70   27-71   27-72   27-73   27-74   27-75

 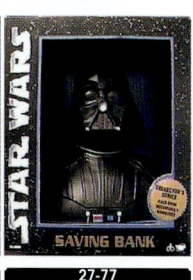   

27-76   27-77   27-78   27-79   27-80   27-81

Pepsi Cola
Episode I: The Phantom Menace soda can body with slit tops. Pepsi Cola premiums.
❏ R2-D2 [27-59] 20.00
❏ Set of 24 with Pepsi wall display stand 175.00

Pepsi Cola (Mexico)
Star Wars: Special Edition soda can with slit top. Pepsi Cola premiums.
❏ Darth Vader [27-60] 100.00
❏ Stormtrooper [v1e1:40] 100.00

Reliable (Canada)
❏ R2-D2 [27-61] 145.00

Roman Ceramics
Ceramic coin banks.
❏ C-3PO [27-62] 150.00
❏ Darth Vader helmet [27-63] 90.00
❏ R2-D2 [27-64] 100.00

Roy Lee Chin
❏ Darth Vader ceramic [v1e1:40] 35.00

Sigma
Ceramic banks.
❏ Chewbacca [27-65] 50.00
❏ Darth Vader [27-66] 190.00
❏ Jabba the Hutt [27-67] 150.00
❏ Yoda [27-68] 65.00

Takara (Japan)
❏ R2-D2 pocket coin (yen) dispenser [27-69] 65.00

Thinkway
Electronic, talking with music.
❏ C-3PO and R2-D2 [27-70] 25.00
❏ Darth Vader [27-71] 25.00
❏ Darth Vader [27-72] 25.00

Electronic. Interact when combined.
❏ Darth Maul [27-73] 30.00
❏ Obi-Wan Kenobi [27-74] 30.00
❏ Qui-Gon Jinn [27-75] 30.00

Plastic bust coin banks.
❏ C-3PO [27-76] 25.00
❏ Darth Vader [27-77] 25.00

Thinkway (Canada)
Electronic, talking with music, bilingual package.
❏ C-3PO and R2-D2 [4:24] 25.00
❏ Darth Vader 25.00

Plastic bust coin banks, bilingual package.
❏ C-3PO [4:24] 30.00
❏ Darth Vader [3:116] 30.00

Vinolos Romay (Mexico)
❏ Darth Vader [27-78] 250.00
❏ R2-D2 [27-79] 250.00
❏ Yoda [27-80] 250.00

Wei Kee Plastic Industrial Ltd. (China)
❏ R2-D2 Mailbox [27-81] 135.00

Banners: Advertising

28-01 Package, Closed and Open 28-02 Closed and Open 28-03 Closed and Open 28-04 Front and Bottom

Banners: Advertising

20th Century Fox
- Episode I: The Phantom Menace [5:28] 200.00
- Episode II: Attack of the Clones [v1e1:40] 200.00
- Episode III: Revenge of the Sith 200.00

20th Century Fox (Mexico)
- Jango Fett, no text [3:116] 200.00
- Jango Fett, Preventa De Boletos 23 De Junio [v1e1:40] 200.00
- Padmé, Estreno Lunes 10 De Julio [v1e1:40] 200.00
- Prerelease theater banner 250.00

Fan Club
- Star Wars original trilogy DVD art, 39" x 27", 2,500 produced 45.00

Grosset and Dunlap
- "Feel the Force" Anakin and Yoda Clone Wars Banner 60.00
- "Feel the Force" Yoda Clone Wars Banner, 54" x 30" ... 50.00

LucasArts
- Knights of the Old Republic, approximately 5'x10' 50.00

Movie City
- Episode I: The Phantom Menace [3:16] 150.00
- Episode IV: A New Hope [3:16] 150.00
- Episode V: The Empire Strikes Back [3:16] 150.00
- Episode VI: Return of the Jedi [3:16] 150.00

Nestlé (Mexico)
- Episode II: Attack of the Clones cereal advertisement banner [v1e1:40] 120.00

Barware
Continued in Volume 3, Page 53

Unique Concepts (UK)
Sculpted barware exclusive pewter collectibles.
- C-3PO foil knife [28-01] 120.00
- Darth Vader corkscrew [28-02] 225.00
- R2-D2 bottle opener [28-03] 200.00
- Yoda wine cork [28-04] 180.00

Bath Mats
Continued in Volume 3, Page 53

- The Clone Wars [29-01] 30.00

Jay Franco and Sons
20" x 30".
- Anakin Skywalker [29-02] 20.00
- Naboo Space Battle [29-03] 35.00

Bathroom Sets
Continued in Volume 3, Page 53

Added Extras, LLC
- Bath and Body Set [30-01] 20.00
- Bath and Body Set with bonus squirting dispenser [30-02] 25.00

Avon (Mexico)
Episode II: Attack of the Clones toothbrush and cup with holder.
- Movie scenes [30-03] 30.00
- Padmé Amidala [30-04] 30.00

Makeup bags.
- Padmé Amidala [30-05] 25.00

Cosrich Group, Inc.
- Bubbling Bath set: bubble bath, Yoda pouf, pouf hanger, lip balm with zipper pull, 3 giant bath fizzies [30-06] 15.00
- Groom n' Go Bath set [30-07] 15.00
- Play shave kit, exclusive to Walmart [30-08] 20.00

Jay Franco and Sons
- Toothbrush holder, soap dish, tumbler all featuring space battle scenes [v1e1:41] 25.00

Beach Pads

Bibb Co.
- Star Wars: Galaxy design [31-10] 135.00
- Star Wars: Space Fantasy design 135.00

Bedding: Bed Covers
Continued in Volume 3, Page 54

Bibb Co.
Empire Strikes Back.
- Boba Fett 95.00
- Boba Fett, exclusive to JCPenney 95.00
- Darth Vader and Yoda 95.00
- Darth's Den 95.00
- Ice Planet 95.00
- Lord Vader 95.00
- Lord Vader's Chamber 95.00
- Yoda 95.00

Return of the Jedi.
- Jabba the Hutt, Ewoks, etc. 80.00
- Logos from all 3 films 80.00
- Luke and Darth Vader Duel, AT-ST, etc. 80.00
- Star Wars Saga 80.00

Star Wars.
- Aztec Gold 150.00
- Galaxy [2:89] 150.00
- Jedi Knights 150.00
- Lord Vader 150.00
- Space Fantasy 150.00

Bedding: Blankets
Continued in Volume 3, Page 55

Stadium blankets.
- Vader in flames, exclusive to Star Wars Celebration III 75.00

29-01

29-02

29-03

30-01

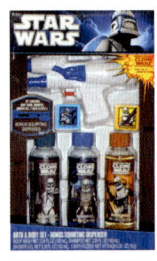

30-02

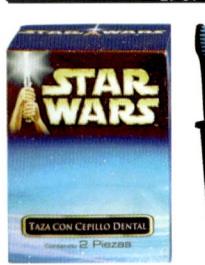

30-03 Package and Open

30-04

30-05

30-06

30-07

30-08

Bedding: Pillows

31-01   31-02   31-03   31-04   31-05   31-06 Side 1 and Side 2

31-07 Side 1 and Side 2   31-08   31-09 Side 1 and Side 2   31-10

Bibb Co.
Empire Strikes Back.
- Boba Fett 100.00
- Boba Fett, exclusive to JCPenney 135.00
- Darth's Den 100.00
- Ice Planet 100.00
- Lord Vader 100.00
- Lord Vader's Chamber 100.00
- Spectre 100.00
- Yoda 120.00

Return of the Jedi.
- Jabba the Hutt, Ewoks 60.00
- Logos from all 3 films 70.00
- Luke and Darth Vader duel, AT-ST 60.00
- Star Wars saga 60.00

Star Wars.
- Aztec Gold 130.00
- Galaxy 130.00
- Jedi Knights 130.00
- Lord Vader 130.00
- Space Fantasy [v1e1:41] 130.00

Franco Manufacturing Company
Clone Wars throws.
- Micro raschel, 50" x 60" [v1e1:41] 30.00
- Throw wrap, 43" x 51" [v1e1:41] 30.00

Idea Nuova
Episode III: Revenge of the Sith camping mat / blanket.
- Clone, white [4:24] 35.00
- Darth Vader, black [v1e1:41] 35.00

Episode III: Revenge of the Sith fleece blanket sack 50" x 60".
- Anakin / Jedi [v1e1:41] 30.00

Jay Franco and Sons
- Darth Vader 20.00

Springs Industries, Inc.
Fleece throw kit, no-sew, 43" x 55".
- A New Hope [v1o1:41] 25.00
- Darth Vader [v1e1:41] 25.00

St. Marys Inc.
- Return of the Jedi 300.00

The Northwest
Multilayered woven jacquard blankets and throws.
- Anakin Skywalker and pod race [2:89] 30.00
- Darth Maul [2:89] 30.00
- Darth Maul and Star Wars logo [2:89] 40.00
- Episode I logo [2:89] 25.00
- Jar Jar [2:89] 30.00

- Jar Jar Binks [2:89] 30.00
- Jedi [2:89] 25.00
- Jedi vs. Sith [2:89] 25.00
- Naboo fighters [2:89] 30.00
- Naboo space battle and Star Wars logo [v1e1:41] 30.00
- R2-D2 [2:89] 35.00
- Star Wars fighters [2:89] 30.00
- The Dark Side [2:89] 25.00

Bedding: Comforters

- Clone Wars 40.00
- Galactic Heroes [4:25] 45.00
- Star Wars Saga 35.00

Caprice
Quilt cover sets.
- Episode I Space Battle 65.00
- Episode II Speeder Chase 65.00
- Episode III Darth Vader 65.00
- Episode III Epic Battle 65.00

Character World Ltd. (UK)
- Episode II Heroes and Villains [2:89] 75.00

Dan River, Inc.
Episode II: Attack of the Clones designs, reversible, twin or full size only.
- Lightsabers 40.00

Jay Franco and Sons
Microfiber comforter, blue with Darth Vader and Stormtroopers.
- Full size 35.00
- Twin size 35.00

Westpoint Stevens
- Classic trilogy characters 25.00

Episode I: The Phantom Menace designs, available in twin or full size only.
- Pod Racing [2:89] 35.00
- Space Battle [2:89] 35.00

Bedding: Pillowcases

- Character Study, 2-sided 15.00
- Empire Strikes Back, 2-sided, heroes and villains 25.00
- Star Wars Saga 15.00

2-pack of characters. Gold, black, and red overlaid on Rebel Alliance emblem.
- Han and Chewbacca [5:30] 20.00

- Luke and Leia [2:89] 20.00
- Yoda and Obi-Wan Kenobi [2:89] 20.00

Return of the Jedi.
- Ewok village 35.00
- Pillow sham [2:89] 30.00
- Tatooine Skiff / Chewbacca with Droids 35.00

Star Wars.
- Poly cotton 35.00

Bibb Co.
Empire Strikes Back.
- Boba Fett / Darth Vader [5:30] 35.00
- C-3PO / R2-D2 [5:30] 35.00
- Chewbacca / Yoda [5:30] 35.00
- The Empire Strikes Back [4:25] 35.00

Star Wars.
- Logo and designs 45.00
- Luke / Leia movie pose 60.00

Dan River, Inc.
- Episode II: Attack of the Clones lightsabers pillow sham 15.00

Pottery Barn
- Star Wars 20.00
- The Empire Strikes Back 20.00

16" square.
- A long time ago in a galaxy far, far away... 25.00
- May the Force be with you 25.00

Pillow shams.
- Star Wars Euro quilted 40.00
- Star Wars quilted 35.00
- The Empire Strikes Back 25.00

Westpoint Stevens
- Space Battle pillow sham [5:30] 25.00
- Space Battle pillowcase [5:30] 20.00

Bedding: Pillows
Continued in Volume 3, Page 57

- Darth Vader, shaped [31-01] 20.00

Episode II: Attack of the Clones. Bed pillows.
- Anakin and Obi-Wan in Speeder / Obi-Wan and Jedi Starfighter 15.00

Square.
- Chewbacca 25.00
- Han Solo 25.00

Bedding: Pillows

 31-10
 31-11
 31-12
 31-13
 31-14

 31-15
 31-16
 31-17
 31-18
 31-19

(UK)
- ❏ Anakin Skywalker / Clone Wars, 16" square 15.00

Adam Joseph Industries
Die-cut.
- ❏ Darth Vader [31-02] 60.00
- ❏ Jabba the Hutt [31-03] 60.00
- ❏ R2-D2 [31-04] 60.00

Comic Images
Convertible, zip and flip.
- ❏ Darth Vader 30.00
- ❏ Yoda 30.00

Dan River, Inc.
- ❏ Darth Vader [31-05] 15.00
- ❏ Darth Vader / Yoda [31-06] 15.00

Episode II: Attack of the Clones.
- ❏ Anakin wielding lightsaber / Star Wars logo, 16" x 16" [31-07] 15.00
- ❏ R2-D2 [31-08] 20.00
- ❏ Republic Gunship / Slave I [31-09] 20.00

Liebhardt, Inc.
16" square.
- ❏ Anakin [31-10] 10.00
- ❏ Darth Maul [31-11] 10.00
- ❏ Jar Jar [31-12] 10.00
- ❏ Queen Amidala [31-13] 10.00
- ❏ Qui-Gon [31-14] 10.00
- ❏ Space Battle [31-15] 15.00

Springs Industries, Inc.
Fleece pillow kit, no-sew, 18" x 18".
- ❏ Battle over Yavin [v1e1:42] 20.00
- ❏ Darth Vader 20.00
- ❏ Star Wars logo [v1e1:42] 20.00

Taito (Japan)
- ❏ Yoda, game prize [31-16] 35.00

Shaped characters. Approximately 12.5" x 10.5"
- ❏ C-3PO [31-17] 40.00
- ❏ Darth Vader [31-18] 40.00
- ❏ Stormtrooper [31-19] 40.00

Bedding: Sheets
Continued in Volume 3, Page 59

- ❏ Classic trilogy bed linen 20.00
- ❏ Clone Wars 25.00
- ❏ Jedi 25.00
- ❏ Saga 25.00
- ❏ Trilogy Home Collection [v1e1:43] 20.00

Revenge of the Sith.
- ❏ Galactic Heroes [v1e1:43] 45.00

Bibb Co.
Empire Strikes Back packaging.
- ❏ Boba Fett 70.00
- ❏ Boba Fett, exclusive to JCPenney 90.00
- ❏ Darth's Den 70.00
- ❏ Ice Planet 70.00
- ❏ Lord Vader 70.00
- ❏ Lord Vader's Chamber 70.00
- ❏ Spectre [v1e1:43] 70.00
- ❏ Yoda 70.00

 32-01
 32-02
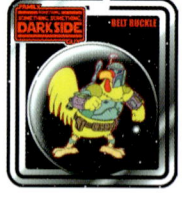 32-03
 32-04
 32-05

 32-06
 32-07
 32-08
 32-09
 32-10

 32-11
 32-12
 32-13
 32-14

Belt Buckles

 32-15
 32-16
 32-17
 32-18
 32-19

 32-20
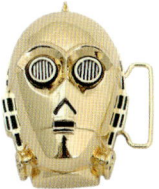 32-21
 32-22
 32-23
 32-24
 32-25
 32-26
 32-27

Return of the Jedi packaging.
- Jabba the Hutt, Ewoks, etc....................60.00
- Logos from all 3 films [v1e1:43]..............60.00
- Luke and Darth Vader Duel, AT-ST, etc........60.00
- Star Wars Saga...............................60.00

Star Wars packaging.
- Aztec Gold...................................85.00
- Galaxy fitted................................85.00
- Jedi Knights.................................85.00
- Lord Vader...................................85.00
- Space Fantasy................................85.00

Black Falcon
- Empire Strikes Back.........................125.00

Dan River, Inc.
- Episode II, Lightsabers twin size............35.00

Hay Jax Manufacturing
- Ewoks twin sheet set.........................80.00

Jay Franco and Sons
Blue vehicles/characters.
- Full Sheet Set, Millennium Falcon, TIE Fighters, X-Wings....................30.00
- Twin sheet set, Millennium Falcon, TIE Fighters, X-Wings....................25.00

Pottery Barn
- Star Wars..................................100.00
- Star Wars, full............................100.00
- Star Wars, queen...........................120.00
- Star Wars, twin.............................70.00
- The Empire Strikes Back, full..............100.00
- The Empire Strikes Back, queen.............120.00
- The Empire Strikes Back, twin...............70.00

Westpoint Stevens
- Episode I twin sheet set [v1e1:43]..........25.00
- Star Wars twin sheet set [2:9]..............25.00

Bedskirts
- Space Battle, Episode I [2:90]..............30.00
- Starships, classic trilogy..................30.00

Belt Buckles
Continued in Volume 3, Page 59

- C-3PO and R2-D2 [32-01].....................35.00

Brass lettering.
- C-3PO [v1e1:43].............................25.00

- R2-D2 [4:26]................................25.00
- Star Wars [32-02]...........................30.00

Family Guy. Something Something Something Dark Side.
- Boba Chicken [32-03]........................30.00
- Darth Stewie [32-04]........................30.00

Basic Tool and Supply
- C-3PO R2-D2 [32-05].........................35.00
- Darth Vader, Oval [4:26]....................35.00
- Star Wars logo [4:26].......................35.00
- X-Wing Fighter with Star Wars logo [32-06]..35.00

Boy Scouts of America
- 1978 Scout-O-Rama Mid-America Council [32-07]........75.00

Leather Shop
- C-3PO and R2-D2 [32-08]....................40.00
- Darth Vader [32-09].........................40.00
- Darth Vader, oval with name on either side of helmet [v1e1:44]...........................30.00
- Darth Vader, oval with name under helmet [32-10]........30.00
- May the Force be with you [32-11]...........35.00
- R2-D2 [32-12]...............................30.00
- Star Wars logo [32-13]......................35.00
- X-Wing Fighter with Star Wars logo [v1e1:44]........30.00

 32-28
 32-29
 32-30
 32-31
 32-32

 32-33
 32-34
 32-35
 32-36

 32-37
 32-38
 32-39
 32-40
32-41

Belt Buckles

 33-01
 33-02
 33-03
 33-04
 33-05
 33-06
 33-07
 33-08
 33-09

Lee Co.
- Darth Vader [v1e1:44] 35.00
- Droids pewter [32-14] 30.00
- Jabba the Hutt [32-15] 35.00
- Yoda [32-16] 40.00

Enameled.
- C-3PO and R2-D2 [32-17] 35.00
- Darth Vader [v1e1:44] 35.00
- Empire Strikes Back logo [32-18] 35.00
- Jabba the Hutt 35.00
- Return of the Jedi logo [32-19] 30.00
- Star Wars logo [v1e1:44] 35.00
- Yoda 40.00

Rock Rebel
- Boba Fett helmet, sculpted [32-20] 25.00
- C-3PO [32-21] 25.00
- Darth Maul [32-22] 25.00
- Darth Maul, painted [32-23] 25.00
- Darth Vader helmet, sculpted [32-24] 25.00
- Imperial emblem [32-25] 25.00
- R2-D2 [32-26] 25.00
- R2-D2, painted [32-27] 25.00
- Rebel emblem [32-28] 25.00
- Star Wars logo [32-29] 25.00
- Star Wars logo, cut out 25.00
- Stormtrooper helmet, sculpted [32-30] 25.00
- Yoda 25.00
- Yoda, painted [32-31] 25.00

Unlicensed
- Star Wars logo on black background, gold trim [32-32] ... 25.00
- Star Wars logo, enamel filled [32-33] 25.00

Prismatic logo, black background, red and black detail.
- Sawtooth [32-34] 20.00
- Stars [v1e1:44] 20.00

Star Wars characters on black prism sticker.
- C-3PO and R2-D2 [v1e1:44] 25.00
- Darth Vader [v1e1:45] 25.00
- Darth Vader, 2-line name [32-35] 25.00
- Luke and Leia [32-36] 25.00

Star Wars characters on blue prism sticker.
- C-3PO [32-37] 30.00

- Chewbacca [32-38] 30.00
- Darth Vader [32-39] 30.00
- R2-D2 [32-40] 30.00

Swirled sun background.
- C-3PO [v1e1:45] 20.00
- Star Wars logo [32-41] 20.00

Belt Packs
Continued in Volume 3, Page 59

The Phantom Menace.
- Anakin Skywalker [33-01] 15.00
- Darth Maul [33-02] 15.00
- Jedi [33-03] 15.00

Disney / MGM
- Star Tours with logo [33-04] 80.00

Pyramid
Dark Side collection, nylon with embossed rubber art.
- Boba Fett 25.00
- Darth Vader [33-05] 25.00
- Luke Skywalker 25.00
- Stormtrooper 25.00

Destroyer collection, vinyl with metallic trim and inset artwork.
- Boba Fett 25.00
- Darth Vader 25.00
- Luke Skywalker 25.00
- Stormtrooper 25.00

Hi-Tech collection, nylon with all-over artwork.
- Boba Fett 25.00
- Darth Vader 25.00
- Stormtrooper 25.00
- Yoda 25.00

Imperial collection, nylon with rubber patch.
- Boba Fett [33-06] 25.00
- Darth Vader 25.00
- Stormtrooper 25.00

Pilot collection, vinyl with schematic artwork.
- Darth Vader / TIE Fighter [33-07] 25.00
- Luke Skywalker / X-Wing Fighter 25.00

Star Class collection, vinyl with inset artwork.
- Boba Fett 25.00
- C-3PO 25.00
- Darth Vader 25.00
- Stormtrooper 25.00

Zoom collection, vinyl with all-over artwork.
- Boba Fett 25.00
- Darth Vader 25.00
- Luke Skywalker 25.00

Q-Stat (UK)
- Podracing 25.00
- Queen Amidala [33-08] 30.00
- Sith Lord [33-09] 25.00

Belts
Continued in Volume 3, Page 59

- Darth Maul 15.00

(Japan)
- Star Wars with characters [34-01] 125.00

(UK)
- Darth Vader, with brushed steel buckle 35.00

American Supply
- Star Wars designs 40.00

El Buen Equipaje
- Dark vinyl silk screened with Empire Strikes Back logo, TIE Fighter, Luke, Leia, R2-D2, TIE Fighter art 70.00

Dark vinyl with enameled character buckle.
- AT-ST 50.00
- Baby Ewoks 50.00
- C-3PO 50.00
- Chewie 50.00
- Darth Vader 50.00
- Jabba 50.00
- Speeder bike 50.00
- Wicket 50.00
- Yoda 50.00

Hot Topic
Art, black-and-white vinyl, adult sizes.
- Dark Side [34-02] 30.00

34-01

 34-02
 34-03
34-04
 34-05

Belts

- ❏ Darth Vader [34-03] 30.00
- ❏ Light Side [34-04] 30.00
- ❏ Rebels and Imperials [34-05] 30.00
- ❏ Star Wars [34-06] 30.00

Lee Co.
Fabric, Droids, pewter buckle with R2-D2, C-3PO, and landspeeder.
- ❏ Blue [34-07] 55.00
- ❏ Spaceships, robots, planets [34-08] 55.00

Fabric, Ewoks.
- ❏ Ewoks with Wicket buckle [34-09] 55.00

Fabric, Return of the Jedi, character buckle with 2 lines of text.
- ❏ Darth Vader, brown / white, red / yellow [34-10] 35.00
- ❏ Darth Vader, red and white [34-11] 35.00
- ❏ Jabba the Hutt, blue belt with brown lettering [34-12] 35.00
- ❏ Wicket the Ewok, tan belt with blue lettering [34-13] 35.00
- ❏ Wicket the Ewok, yellow and brown belt with yellow lettering [34-14] 35.00

Fabric, Return of the Jedi, rectangular buckle with 2 lines of text.
- ❏ Blue and white belt, white and red lettering [34-15] 30.00
- ❏ Red and blue belt, blue and red lettering [34-16] 30.00
- ❏ White and brown belt, red and yellow lettering [34-17] 30.00
- ❏ White belt with blue lettering [34-18] 30.00
- ❏ Yellow and brown belt with brown and yellow lettering [34-19] 30.00

Fabric, Star Wars, magnetic clasp buckle.
- ❏ Blue with white logo [34-20] 40.00
- ❏ White with blue logo [34-21] 40.00

Vinyl, Return of the Jedi, Skiff, Ewoks, Star Wars logo, Jabba, and Return of the Jedi logo art.
- ❏ Brown [34-22] 45.00

Vinyl, Star Wars, Darth Vader, Luke, Leia, Droids, and Star Wars logo art.
- ❏ Blue [34-23] 45.00
- ❏ Brown [34-24] 45.00

Nishimura Seni Kogyo (Japan)
Star Wars designs.
- ❏ Leather 80.00
- ❏ Vinyl with brass buckle 70.00
- ❏ Vinyl with movie photos 70.00

Belts

35-01

35-02

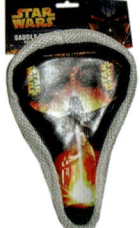
35-03

35-04

36-01

36-02

36-03

36-04

36-05

36-06

36-07

Textile Artesa
- Star Wars designs...30.00

The Leather Shop
- C-3PO and R2-D2, enameled buckle, boxed.................90.00
- C-3PO and R2-D2, enameled buckle, hang tag............75.00
- Darth Vader, enameled brass buckle, boxed.................90.00
- Darth Vader, enameled buckle, hang tag.....................75.00
- Han and Chewbacca, Droids and Luke, Leia and Darth Vader [34-25]..80.00
- Obi-Wan and Darth Vader pattern...............................80.00
- Oval Darth Vader buckle [34-26]......................................95.00

Droids.
- Screened logo and droids in landspeeder....................70.00
- Space emblems, 3D droid busts, brass buckle.............65.00
- Space emblems, 3D droid busts on pewter buckle......65.00

Empire Strikes Back.
- Darth Vader on enameled brass buckle.......................75.00
- Logo on enameled brass buckle..................................75.00
- Yoda 3D on round brass buckle [34-27].........................75.00

Return of the Jedi.
- Circular portraits and logo screened on belt 60.00
- Embossed with logo on rectangular enameled brass buckle..60.00
- Jabba the Hutt on rectangular buckle.........................60.00

Star Wars.
- Logo on enameled brass buckle, boxed [34-28]..............90.00
- Logo on enameled brass buckle, hanging tag 90.00

Bicycle Accessories
Continued in Volume 3, Page 61

(UK)
- Clone Wars handlebar bell [35-01]..................................25.00

Adie
- Bell and Bottle set [35-02]..20.00
- Horn, Darth Vader sculpted...25.00
- Seat (saddle) cover, Episode III art [35-03]....................20.00

Handlebar bells.
- Darth Vader helmet art 25.00
- Darth Vader with lightsaber [35-04]...............................25.00
- Yoda..25.00

Bicycles
Continued in Volume 3, Page 61

- Clone [36-01]..150.00

(Australia)
- Imperial Street Monster..150.00

Episode III: Revenge of the Sith.
- Darth Vader...145.00

(UK)
- Clone Wars, 14"..125.00
- Clone Wars, 16" Rex [36-02]...150.00
- Clone Wars, 16" Star Wars [36-03]................................150.00

Dynacraft
- Darth Maul, boys 16" [v1e1:47].......................................95.00
- Jar Jar, boys 12" [v1e1:47]..95.00
- Queen Amidala, girls' 12"...120.00

Huffy
- Baba Ewok, Baga, Princess Kneesaa first bike, girls'...335.00
- C-3PO and R2-D2 first bike, boys'..............................325.00
- Princess Kneesaa high rise, girls'................................375.00
- X-Wing first bike, boys'/ girls' [v1e1:47]......................385.00

Episode III: Revenge of the Sith.
- Darth Vader, boys' 16" [36-04]......................................95.00

Kenner
- Speeder Bike pedal vehicle, Kmart promotion [36-05]..2,400.00

Lord and Taylor
- Rebel Assault, chrome [36-06]......................................350.00

UrbanX (Australia)
- Lean Machine, Clone Wars [36-07]...............................235.00

37-01

37-02

37-03

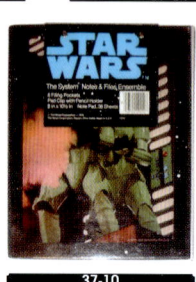
37-04

37-05

37-06

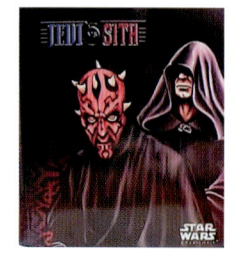
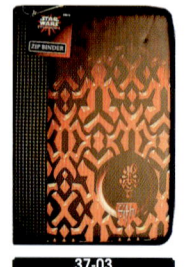
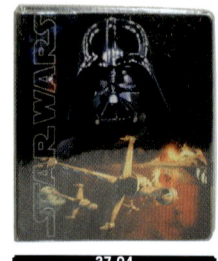

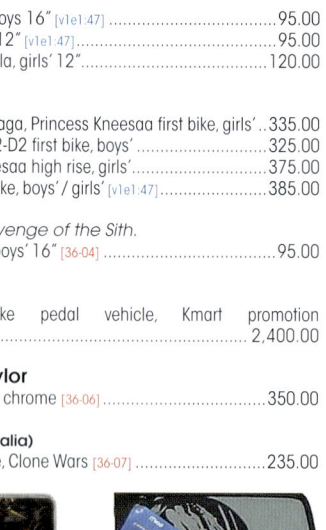

37-07 · 37-08 · 37-09 · 37-10 · 37-11 · 37-12 · 37-13

Book Lists

38-01

39-01 39-02 Detail

40-01

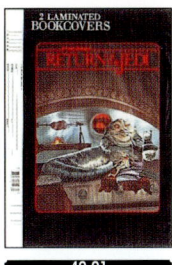
40-02

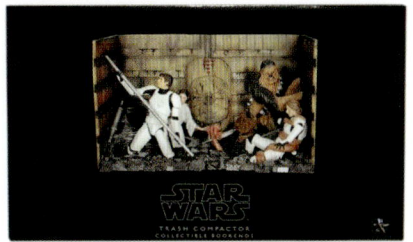
41-01

41-02

41-03

41-04

Binders
Continued in Volume 3, Page 61

Accessory Zone
- Clone Wars [37-01] 10.00

Animations
- Darth Vader 10.00
- Darth Vader lightsaber up 10.00

C2 Ventures
- Autograph / photo binder, exclusive to Star Wars Celebration II 20.00

Cards, Inc. (UK)
- Medalionz storage binder (folder) 15.00

DeAgostini
- Official Figurine Collection [v1e1:48] 30.00

Impact, Inc.
- Anakin Skywalker 8.00
- Anakin, Jar Jar / Tatooine [v1e1:48] 8.00
- Darth Maul, Darth Sidious / Jedi vs. Sith [37-02] 8.00
- Jar Jar 8.00
- Queen Amidala 8.00
- Qui-Gon Jinn 8.00
- R2-D2 / C-3PO 8.00
- Sith [37-03] 8.00

Innovative Designs
1" binders.
- Darth Vader and B-Wings [37-04] 8.00
- Obi-Wan Kenobi and Clones [37-05] 8.00

Letraset
- X-Wing pursues TIE Fighter over Death Star [v1e1:48] 40.00

Mead
- Darth Vader, blue zippered [v1e1:48] 15.00
- Darth Vader, gray zippered [37-06] 15.00

Vintage.
- Ben Kenobi, Han Solo, Luke Skywalker, Princess Leia [37-07] 30.00
- C-3PO and R2-D2 [37-08] 30.00
- Darth Vader / Ben Kenobi [37-09] 30.00
- Han and Chewbacca / Stormtroopers [37-10] 30.00

Merlin Publishing International Ltd.
2 ring binders.
- Empire Strikes Back [37-11] 12.00
- Star Wars [37-12] 12.00

Official Pix
Autograph / photo binders.
- Star Wars Celebration III, exclusive to Star Wars Celebration III 25.00
- Star Wars Celebration IV, exclusive to Star Wars Celebration IV 25.00

Q-Stat (UK)
- Anakin's Podracer / Sebulba's Podracer [37-13] 15.00
- Obi-Wan Kenobi [v1e1:48] 15.00
- Queen Amidala [v1e1:48] 15.00

Stuart Hall
- 2-1B, Bounty Hunters, Probot, Ugnaught 35.00
- C-3PO and R2-D2 .... 35.00
- Darth Vader and Stormtroopers 35.00
- Luke on Dagobah 35.00
- Yoda 35.00

Topps
- Star Wars Finest [v1e1:48] 20.00
- Star Wars Galaxy [v1e1:48] 25.00
- Star Wars Widevision, includes Widevision promo card [v1e1:48] 25.00

Binoculars and Telescopes

Tiger Electronics
- Darth Maul binoculars [38-01] 45.00

Birdhouses
Covered in Volume 3, Page 61

Blueprints

Unlicensed. 4 folded sheets in printed envelope.
- Millennium Falcon 25.00
- Star Destroyer 25.00

Ballantine
- Blueprints, 15 in plastic pouch [39-01] 40.00
- Blueprints, 15 in plastic pouch with Return of the Jedi sticker [39-02] 40.00

DK Publishing
Five double-sided poster-sized plans.
- Blueprints, the ultimate collection [v1e1:48] 20.00

Master Replicas
Artist proofs, limited to 1,000.
- Count Dooku lightsaber [v1e1:48] 175.00
- Darth Maul lightsaber [v1e1:48] 175.00
- Darth Vader lightsaber [v1e1:48] 175.00
- Han Solo blaster [v1e1:48] 175.00
- Luke Skywalker lightsaber [v1e1:48] 175.00
- Obi-Wan Kenobi lightsaber [v1e1:48] 175.00

Matted, framed, limited to 5,000.
- Count Dooku lightsaber 75.00
- Darth Maul lightsaber 75.00
- Darth Vader lightsaber 75.00
- Han Solo blaster 85.00
- Luke Skywalker lightsaber 85.00
- Obi-Wan Kenobi lightsaber 85.00

Bobble Heads
Covered in Volume 2, Page 194

Book Covers

Butterfly Originals
- Jabba the Hutt and Speeder Bikes [40-01] 15.00

Factors, Etc.
- Original Fan Club logo [3:123] 25.00

Impact, Inc.
- Episode I 4-pack of book covers [40-02] 10.00

Bookends
Covered in Volume 3, Page 79

Gentle Giant Studios
- Death Star Trash Compactor [41-01] 600.00
- Jabba's Palace [41-02] 1,250.00
- Jabba's Palace, with unmasked Leia and full-figure jawa, exclusive to Premiere Guild 2,300.00
- Mos Eisley Cantina, Han Solo and Greedo, 3,500 produced, individually numbered [41-03] 475.00
- Star Wars logo, gold colored 150.00

Sigma
- Chewbacca and Darth Vader [41-04] 300.00

Book Lists

Bantam Books
- 1996 Darth Vader / Shadows of the Empire [v1e1:48] 5.00
- 1996, ...await you in the exciting and ever-expanding universe of Star Wars [v1e1:48] 5.00
- 1997 The Adventure Continues / Lightsaber [v1e1:48] ... 5.00

Del Rey
- The Time Line [v1e1:48] 5.00

Bookmarks

Bookmarks
Continued in Volume 3, Page 80

(Thailand)
- ☐ 3 break-apart bookmarks [v1e1:51] 5.00

20th Century Fox
Episode III: Revenge of the Sith.
- ☐ Darth Vader, "Rise Lord Vader" 5.00
- ☐ Epic duel 5.00
- ☐ Yoda 5.00

20th Century Fox (Thailand)
Episode III: Revenge of the Sith.
- ☐ Anakin / Epic duel 5.00
- ☐ Anakin holding Padmé 5.00
- ☐ Anakin and Padmé / Padmé 5.00
- ☐ Bail Organa, Obi-Wan, Anakin, Yoda 5.00
- ☐ C-3PO 5.00
- ☐ Darth Vader 5.00
- ☐ Droids / Anakin (dark side) 5.00
- ☐ General Grievous 5.00
- ☐ Grievous's bodyguard 5.00
- ☐ Jedi ... captured 5.00
- ☐ Mace Windu 5.00
- ☐ Obi-Wan / Epic duel 5.00
- ☐ Obi-Wan Kenobi 5.00
- ☐ Obi-Wan, Anakin, Padmé 5.00
- ☐ Wookiee rage 5.00
- ☐ Yoda 5.00

A.H. Prismatic
Each bookmark shows 3 hologram images.
- ☐ B-Wing Fighter, Millennium Falcon, TIE Fighter [v1e1:51] 10.00
- ☐ Millennium Falcon, Darth Vader, Star Destroyer 10.00
- ☐ X-Wing Fighter, TIE Interceptor, AT-AT [42-01] 10.00

American Library Association
- ☐ Darth Vader, Conquer the Information Universe [42-02] 5.00
- ☐ "Read, You Will!" Yoda, Episode I [42-03] 5.00

Antioch
Book cover art with tassel.
- ☐ The Courtship of Princess Leia [42-04] 5.00
- ☐ The Crystal Star [42-05] 5.00
- ☐ The Glove of Darth Vader [42-06] 5.00
- ☐ The Lost City of the Jedi [42-07] 5.00
- ☐ Truce at Bakura [42-08] 5.00
- ☐ Zorba the Hutt's Revenge [42-09] 5.00

Classic trilogy character with bead on tassel.
- ☐ Luke and Leia [42-10] 10.00
- ☐ R2-D2 and C-3PO [42-11] 10.00

Classic trilogy character with tassel.
- ☐ Ben Kenobi [42-12] 8.00
- ☐ Chewbacca 8.00
- ☐ Darth Vader [42-13] 8.00
- ☐ Han Solo [42-14] 8.00
- ☐ Lando Calrissian [42-15] 8.00
- ☐ Luke Skywalker [42-16] 8.00
- ☐ Mos Eisley Cantina [42-17] 8.00
- ☐ Princess Leia Organa [42-18] 8.00
- ☐ Star Wars special edition [42-19] 8.00
- ☐ Yoda [42-20] 8.00

Classic trilogy die-cut character.
- ☐ Boba Fett [42-21] 8.00
- ☐ C-3PO [42-22] 8.00
- ☐ Chewbacca [4:31] 3.00
- ☐ Darth Vader [42-23] 8.00
- ☐ Han Solo [4:31] 8.00
- ☐ Jawa [42-24] 8.00
- ☐ R2-D2 [42-25] 8.00
- ☐ Stormtrooper [4:31] 8.00
- ☐ Tusken Raider [v1e1:51] 8.00
- ☐ Yoda [42-26] 8.00

Prequel trilogy character with bead on tassel.
- ☐ Anakin Skywalker [v1e1:51] 6.00
- ☐ Clone trooper [42-27] 6.00
- ☐ Destroyer Droid [v1e1:51] 6.00
- ☐ Jango Fett [42-28] 6.00
- ☐ Jar Jar Binks [42-29] 6.00
- ☐ Queen Amidala, Coruscant [42-30] 6.00
- ☐ Queen Amidala, travel gown [v1e1:51] 6.00
- ☐ R2-D2 [42-31] 6.00
- ☐ Sith Villains [42-32] 6.00

Prequel trilogy character with tassel.
- ☐ Anakin Skywalker [42-33] 6.00
- ☐ Anakin Skywalker's destiny [42-34] 6.00
- ☐ C-3PO [42-35] 6.00
- ☐ Count Dooku [42-36] 6.00
- ☐ Darth Maul [42-37] 6.00
- ☐ Obi-Wan Kenobi, Episode I [42-38] 6.00
- ☐ Obi-Wan Kenobi, Episode II [42-39] 6.00
- ☐ Padmé Amidala [42-40] 6.00
- ☐ Qui-Gon Jinn [42-41] 6.00
- ☐ Sith Lords [42-42] 6.00
- ☐ Zam Wesell [42-43] 6.00

Prequel trilogy die-cut character.
- ☐ Darth Maul [42-44] 8.00
- ☐ Jar Jar Binks [42-45] 8.00
- ☐ Queen Amidala [42-46] 8.00
- ☐ Rune Haako [42-47] 8.00
- ☐ Sebulba [42-48] 8.00

Prequel trilogy Gallery Edition.
- ☐ Battle Droids [42-49] 6.00
- ☐ Pod Race [42-50] 6.00
- ☐ Starfighters [42-51] 6.00

Prequel trilogy with punch out page clip.
- ☐ Anakin Skywalker [42-52] 6.00
- ☐ Darth Vader [42-53] 6.00
- ☐ Jar Jar Binks [42-54] 6.00
- ☐ Queen Amidala [42-55] 6.00
- ☐ Trade Federation Droids [v1e1:51] 6.00

Cards, Inc. (UK)
- ☐ Anakin Skywalker [42-56] 5.00
- ☐ Clone trooper [42-57] 5.00
- ☐ Darth Vader [42-58] 5.00
- ☐ General Grievous [42-59] 5.00
- ☐ Obi-Wan Kenobi [42-60] 5.00
- ☐ Yoda [42-61] 5.00

Books: Activity

Dark Horse Comics
- Darth Vader 5.00
- "May The Horse Be With You" [42-62] 5.00
- "Submit to the Dark Side of the Horse!" [42-63] 5.00
- The Saga Continues / graphic novels 5.00

Del Rey
- Sacrifice, advertisement, exclusive to Star Wars Celebration IV..5.00
- Star Wars, Episode I characters [42-64] 5.00

Dreams and Visions Press
The Art of Ralph McQuarrie. Exclusive to Star Wars Celebration, Japan.
- Death Star [42-65] 15.00
- Mos Eisley [42-66] 15.00

The Art of Ralph McQuarrie. Set of 9. Exclusive to Star Wars Celebration IV.
- Arms Extended 10.00
- Asleep 10.00
- Bounty Hunters 10.00
- Catch a Star 10.00
- Darth Vader 10.00
- General McQuarrie 10.00
- Sand People 10.00
- Sitting 10.00
- Stormtrooper 10.00

Fantasma
3D bookmarks, 2" x 6".
- Darth Vader [42-67] 10.00
- Darth Vader and Luke Skywalker [42-68] 10.00

Random House
- #1 Luke Skywalker [42-69] 8.00
- #2 Darth Vader [42-70] 8.00
- #3 Princess Leia (Boushh) [42-71] 8.00
- #4 R2-D2 [42-72] 8.00
- #5 C-3PO [42-73] 8.00
- #6 Lando Calrissian [42-74] 8.00
- #7 Chewbacca [42-75] 8.00
- #8 Yoda [42-76] 8.00
- #9 Ben Kenobi [42-77] 8.00
- #10 Han Solo [42-78] 8.00
- #11 Boba Fett [42-79] 8.00
- #12 Wicket the Ewok [42-80] 8.00
- #13 Emperor's Royal Guard [42-81] 8.00
- #14 Stormtrooper [42-82] 8.00
- #15 Jabba the Hutt [42-83] 8.00
- #16 Admiral Ackbar [42-84] 8.00

Rye by Post
Film cell bookmark.
- A New Hope 10.00
- Attack of the Clones [42-85] 10.00
- Return of the Jedi 10.00
- The Empire Strikes Back 10.00
- The Phantom Menace [42-86] 10.00

Smithsonian Institute
- "The Magic of Myth" display with plastic case [v1e1:52] ..10.00

Trends International Corp.
- Empire Strikes Back 6.00
- Empire Strikes Back, Darth Vader 6.00
- Empire Strikes Back, Luke Skywalker 6.00

Bookplates

Antioch
- C-3PO and R2-D2 [43-01] 10.00
- Dark Empire, 10-pack on hanger card [v1e1:52] 10.00
- Dark Empire, 30-pack boxed [v1e1:52] 10.00
- Hildebrandt Art [43-02] 10.00

3 of each.
- Darth Vader, Boba Fett, Luke in X-Wing gear [43-03] 8.00
- Jedi vs. Sith, Pod Race, Naboo Space Battle 8.00
- Obi-Wan, Darth Maul, Qui-Gon 8.00

Hunter Leisure, Ltd. (Australia)
- School Book Labels, Revenge of the Sith characters [v1e1:52] 8.00

Introduct Holland
- Return of the Jedi scenes 12.00

MAUCCI S.A. (Argentina)
Packets of 6 different designs.
- Characters, art [v1e1:52] 10.00
- Darth Vader [v1e1:52] 10.00
- McQuarrie concept art [v1e1:52] 10.00
- Starships [v1e1:52] 10.00

Random House
- C-3PO and R2-D2 [43-04] 20.00
- Darth Vader [43-05] 20.00
- Wicket the Ewok [43-06] 20.00
- Yoda [43-07] 20.00

Books: Activity
Continued in Volume 3, Page 81

- Activity pad, Boba Fett cover [44-01] 5.00
- Activity pad, Jedi cover [44-02] 5.00

(Argentina)
- Para Pegar, con stickers de regalo [44-03] 8.00

(Japan)
- Return of the Jedi activity book 35.00
- The Star Wars Book of Masks 35.00
- The Star Wars Iron-On Transfer book [44-04] 50.00

Abrams
- Star Wars: Punch Out and Play 15.00

Ballantine
- The Star Wars Iron-On Transfer book [44-05] 50.00

Collins
- Punch-Out and Make It book, Star Wars 25.00

Dalmatian Press
- Clone Wars : Book to Color [44-06] 4.00
- Clone Wars Activity Book to Color 6.00
- Clone Wars sticker, coloring, and activity book, exclusive to Target [44-07] 4.00
- Clone Wars: Paint With Water [v1e1:53] 4.00

Books: Activity

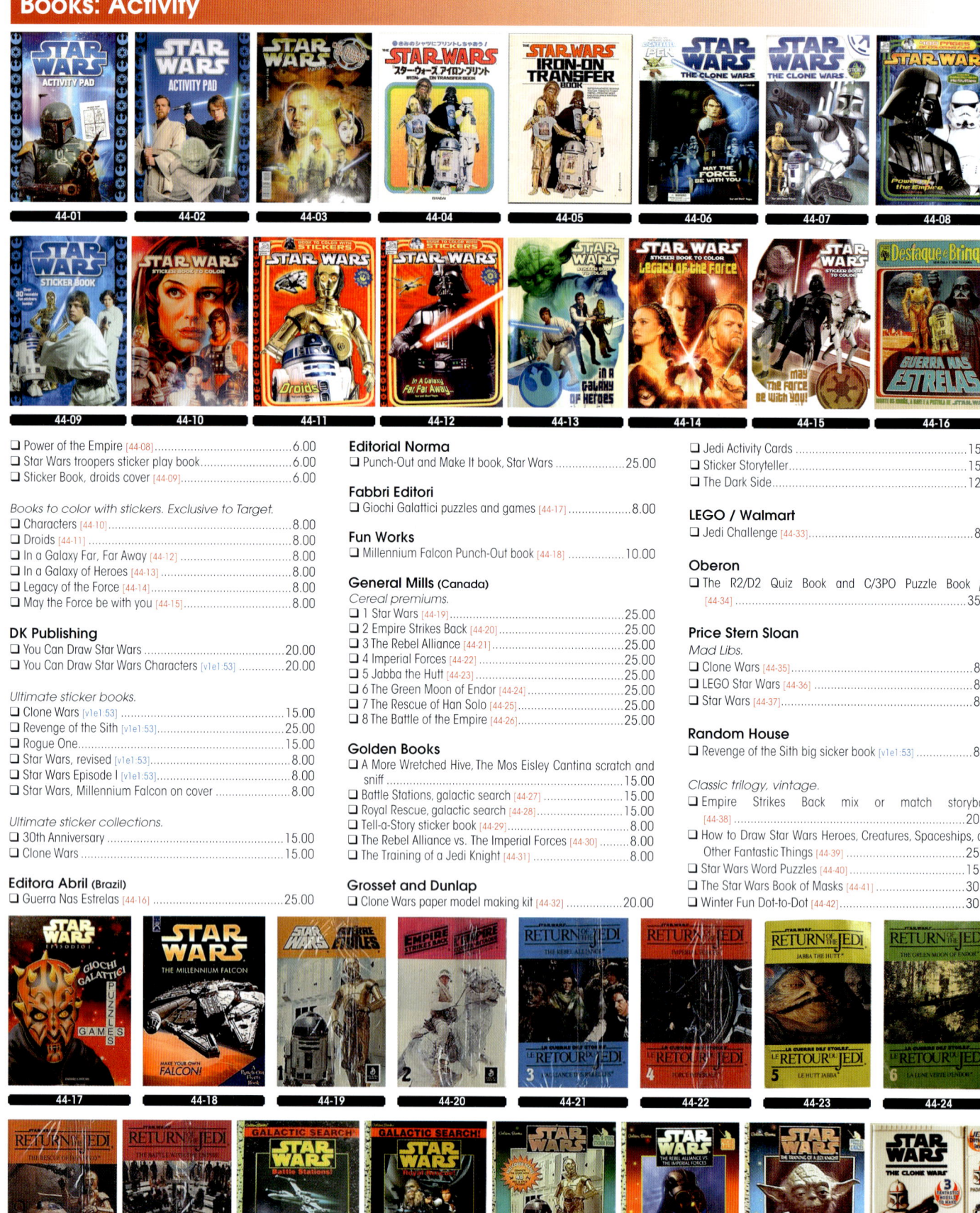

- ❏ Power of the Empire [44-08] 6.00
- ❏ Star Wars troopers sticker play book 6.00
- ❏ Sticker Book, droids cover [44-09] 6.00

Books to color with stickers. Exclusive to Target.
- ❏ Characters [44-10] 8.00
- ❏ Droids [44-11] 8.00
- ❏ In a Galaxy, Far Away [44-12] 8.00
- ❏ In a Galaxy of Heroes [44-13] 8.00
- ❏ Legacy of the Force [44-14] 8.00
- ❏ May the Force be with you [44-15] 8.00

DK Publishing
- ❏ You Can Draw Star Wars 20.00
- ❏ You Can Draw Star Wars Characters [v1e1:53] 20.00

Ultimate sticker books.
- ❏ Clone Wars [v1e1:53] 15.00
- ❏ Revenge of the Sith [v1e1:53] 25.00
- ❏ Rogue One 15.00
- ❏ Star Wars, revised [v1e1:53] 8.00
- ❏ Star Wars Episode I [v1e1:53] 8.00
- ❏ Star Wars, Millennium Falcon on cover 8.00

Ultimate sticker collections.
- ❏ 30th Anniversary 15.00
- ❏ Clone Wars 15.00

Editora Abril (Brazil)
- ❏ Guerra Nas Estrelas [44-16] 25.00

Editorial Norma
- ❏ Punch-Out and Make It book, Star Wars 25.00

Fabbri Editori
- ❏ Giochi Galattici puzzles and games [44-17] 8.00

Fun Works
- ❏ Millennium Falcon Punch-Out book [44-18] 10.00

General Mills (Canada)
Cereal premiums.
- ❏ 1 Star Wars [44-19] 25.00
- ❏ 2 Empire Strikes Back [44-20] 25.00
- ❏ 3 The Rebel Alliance [44-21] 25.00
- ❏ 4 Imperial Forces [44-22] 25.00
- ❏ 5 Jabba the Hutt [44-23] 25.00
- ❏ 6 The Green Moon of Endor [44-24] 25.00
- ❏ 7 The Rescue of Han Solo [44-25] 25.00
- ❏ 8 The Battle of the Empire [44-26] 25.00

Golden Books
- ❏ A More Wretched Hive, The Mos Eisley Cantina scratch and sniff 15.00
- ❏ Battle Stations, galactic search [44-27] 15.00
- ❏ Royal Rescue, galactic search [44-28] 15.00
- ❏ Tell-a-Story sticker book [44-29] 8.00
- ❏ The Rebel Alliance vs. The Imperial Forces [44-30] 8.00
- ❏ The Training of a Jedi Knight [44-31] 8.00

Grosset and Dunlap
- ❏ Clone Wars paper model making kit [44-32] 20.00

- ❏ Jedi Activity Cards 15.00
- ❏ Sticker Storyteller 15.00
- ❏ The Dark Side 12.00

LEGO / Walmart
- ❏ Jedi Challenge [44-33] 8.00

Oberon
- ❏ The R2/D2 Quiz Book and C/3PO Puzzle Book [sic] [44-34] 35.00

Price Stern Sloan
Mad Libs.
- ❏ Clone Wars [44-35] 8.00
- ❏ LEGO Star Wars [44-36] 8.00
- ❏ Star Wars [44-37] 8.00

Random House
- ❏ Revenge of the Sith big sicker book [v1e1:53] 8.00

Classic trilogy, vintage.
- ❏ Empire Strikes Back mix or match storybook [44-38] 20.00
- ❏ How to Draw Star Wars Heroes, Creatures, Spaceships, and Other Fantastic Things [44-39] 25.00
- ❏ Star Wars Word Puzzles [44-40] 15.00
- ❏ The Star Wars Book of Masks [44-41] 30.00
- ❏ Winter Fun Dot-to-Dot [44-42] 30.00

Books: Art

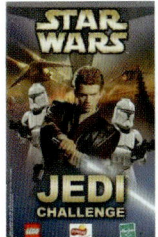 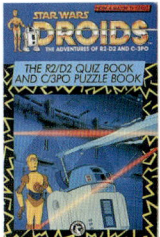  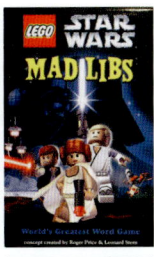 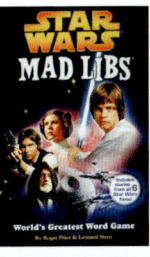  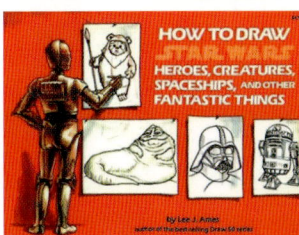 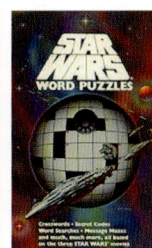

44-33   44-34   44-35   44-36   44-37   44-38   44-39   44-40

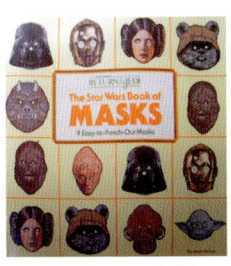 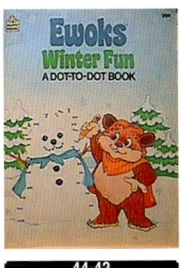 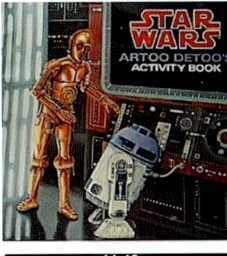 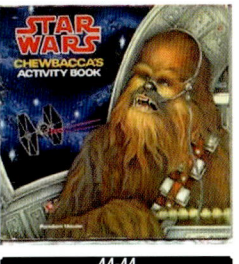  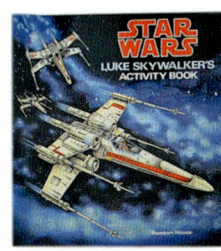

44-41   44-42   44-43   44-44   44-45   44-46

Classic trilogy, vintage. Activity books.
- Artoo Detoo's [44-43] 18.00
- Chewbacca's [44-44] 18.00
- Darth Vader's [44-45] 18.00
- Luke Skywalker [44-46] 18.00

Classic trilogy, vintage. Punch-out and make it books.
- Empire Strikes Back [44-47] 15.00
- Return of the Jedi [44-48] 15.00
- Star Wars [44-49] 15.00

Classic trilogy, vintage. Return of the Jedi activities.
- Dot-to-Dot Fun [44-50] 15.00
- Mazes [44-51] 15.00
- Monster activity book [44-52] 15.00
- Picture puzzle book [44-53] 15.00
- Things to Do and Make [44-54] 15.00
- Word puzzle book [44-55] 15.00
- Yoda's activity book [44-56] 15.00

Episode I: The Phantom Menace.
- Galactic puzzles and games [44-57] 4.00
- Jedi Punch-Outs, full-color backdrop included [44-58] 8.00
- Lightsaber marker activity book, blue [44-59] 6.00
- Lightsaber marker activity book, green 6.00
- Lightsaber marker activity book, red 6.00
- Mask punch-out book 10.00
- Micro Vehicle Punch-Outs [44-60] 10.00
- Podracer Punch-Outs [44-61] 8.00
- Posters to Color, mail-in premium [44-62] 15.00
- Queen Amidala paper doll book [44-63] 15.00

Episode II: Attack of the Clones.
- Big Sticker book [44-64] 8.00
- Jedi Activity book, fabric patch cover [44-65] 8.00
- Padmé Amidala paper doll book [44-66] 15.00
- Ship Schematics punch-out book [44-67] 10.00

Jedi Training and Trials Quiz Book.
- Blue lightsaber pen 6.00
- Green lightsaber pen [44-68] 6.00
- Purple lightsaber pen [v1e1-54] 6.00
- Red lightsaber pen 6.00

Scholastic
Activity magazines.
- Anakin's activity magazine 5.00
- Obi-Wan's activity magazine 5.00

Books: Art
Continued in Volume 3, Page 82

(Japan)
- N. Olai Original Sketch Collection [45-01] 45.00
- The Return of the Jedi Sketchbook 25.00

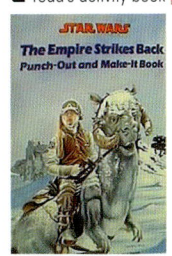 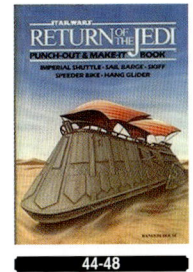     

44-47   44-48   44-49   44-50   44-51   44-52   44-53

 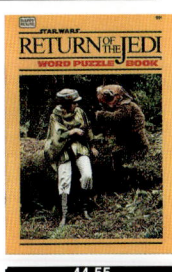   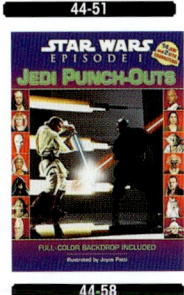 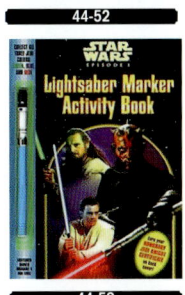 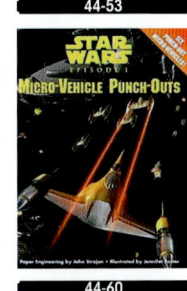

44-54   44-55   44-56   44-57   44-58   44-59   44-60

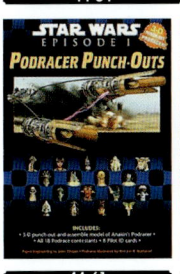 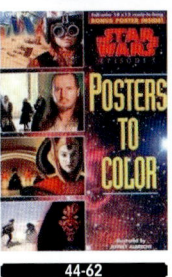 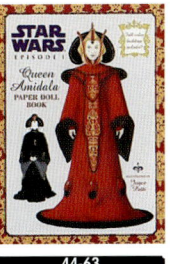  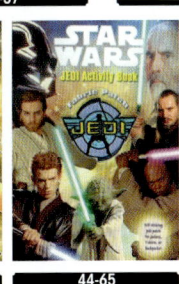  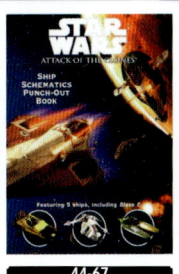 

44-61   44-62   44-63   44-64   44-65   44-66   44-67   44-68

Books: Activity

 45-01
 45-02
 45-03
 45-04
 45-05
 45-06
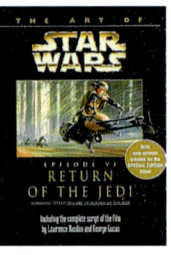 45-07
 45-08
 45-09
 45-10
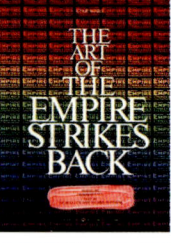 45-11
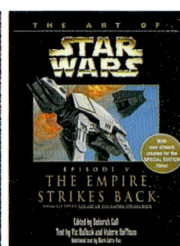 45-12
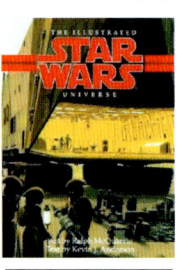 45-13
 45-13
 45-14
 45-15
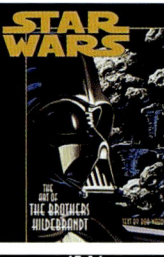 45-16
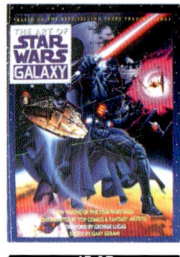 45-17
 45-18

(Spain)
- ❏ Star Wars Fotograms 1977-2005 [45-02] 45.00

Abrams
- ❏ Visions [45-03] 40.00

Amber
- ❏ Gwiezdne Wojny (Art of Star Wars), trade paperback [3:126] 30.00

Ballantine
- ❏ The Art of Revenge of the Sith, hardcover 35.00

Sketchbooks.
- ❏ Empire Strikes Back [45-04] 50.00
- ❏ Return of the Jedi [45-05] 25.00
- ❏ Star Wars [45-06] 70.00

The Art of Return of The Jedi.
- ❏ 1994 cover, trade paperback 30.00
- ❏ 1997 Special Edition section, trade paperback [45-07] 20.00
- ❏ Hardcover 30.00
- ❏ Trade paperback [45-08] 10.00

The Art of Star Wars.
- ❏ 1994 cover, trade paperback 20.00
- ❏ 1997 Special Edition section, trade paperback [45-09] 20.00
- ❏ Hardcover [45-10] 50.00
- ❏ Trade paperback 25.00

The Art of The Empire Strikes Back.
- ❏ 1994 cover, trade paperback [45-11] 10.00
- ❏ 1997 Special Edition section, trade paperback [45-12] 20.00
- ❏ Hardcover 25.00
- ❏ Trade paperback 25.00

Bandai (Japan)
- ❏ Star Wars Book of Blueprints 50.00

Bantam Books
- ❏ The Illustrated Star Wars Universe [45-13] 60.00

Benford Books
The Art of Dave Dorman.
- ❏ Hardcover, numbered and signed 80.00
- ❏ Trade paperback [45-14] 30.00

Cartoon Network
- ❏ Clone Wars, A Collection of Sketches from Cartoon Network [v1e1:55] 15.00

Chronicle Books
- ❏ Episode I: 20 Lithographic Reproductions by Doug Chiang [v1e1:55] 60.00

Dark Horse Comics
- ❏ Panel to Panel [45-15] 20.00
- ❏ Panel to Panel Volume 2: Expanding the Universe 20.00

Del Rey
- ❏ The Art of Star Wars : Attack of the Clones [v1e1:55] 35.00
- ❏ The Art of the Brothers Hildebrandt [45-16] 25.00
- ❏ The Art of The Phantom Menace [v1e1:55] 25.00
- ❏ The Art of The Phantom Menace, trade paperback [v1e1:55] 30.00

Dreams and Visions Press
- ❏ The Art of Ralph McQuarrie, oversized paperback, exclusive to Star Wars Celebration Japan 200.00
- ❏ The Art of Ralph McQuarrie, oversized paperback, exclusive to Star Wars Celebration V 200.00
- ❏ The Art of Ralph McQuarrie, signed, 302 produced, individually numbered 300.00
- ❏ The Art of Ralph McQuarrie, signed leather bound 750.00
- ❏ The Art of Ralph McQuarrie, unsigned 155.00

Hermes Press
- ❏ The Worlds of Matt Busch 20.00

Insight Editions
- ❏ The Art and Making of Star Wars: The Force Unleashed 35.00

Jason Palmer
- ❏ Padmé, a collection of drawings 20.00

SFT Productions
- ❏ The Force in the Flesh Star Wars Inspired Body Art 125.00

Topps
- ❏ The Art of Star Wars Galaxy [45-17] 25.00
- ❏ The Art of Star Wars Galaxy II, foil cover, trade paperback 25.00
- ❏ The Art of Star Wars Galaxy II, trade paperback [45-18] 20.00
- ❏ The Art of Star Wars Galaxy with card sheet, exclusive to QVC 30.00

Underwood-Miller Inc.
- ❏ The Art of Star Wars Galaxy, limited edition (bound and boxed) [v1e1:55] 175.00

Books: Audio, Cassette

Bantam Books
- ❏ Before the Storm 15.00
- ❏ Children of the Jedi 15.00
- ❏ Courtship of Princess Leia 15.00
- ❏ Crystal Star 15.00
- ❏ Dark Apprentice 15.00
- ❏ Dark Empire [2:98] 15.00
- ❏ Dark Empire II [2:98] 15.00
- ❏ Dark Empire trilogy in Millennium Falcon collector's box [2:98] 40.00
- ❏ Dark Force Rising 15.00
- ❏ Dark Saber 15.00
- ❏ Han Solo Omnibus: The Paradise Snare, the Hutt Gambit, Rebel Dawn [2:98] 20.00
- ❏ Heir to the Empire [2:98] 15.00
- ❏ Hutt Gambit [2:98] 15.00
- ❏ Jedi Academy Omnibus [2:98] 20.00
- ❏ Jedi Search [2:98] 15.00
- ❏ Last Command [2:98] 15.00
- ❏ Mandalorian Armor [2:98] 15.00
- ❏ Night Lily, the Lovers Tale 10.00

- ❏ Paradise Snare [2:98] 15.00
- ❏ Planet of Twilight [2:98] 15.00
- ❏ Rogue Planet [2:98] 15.00
- ❏ Shadows of the Empire [2:98] 15.00
- ❏ Shield of Lies 15.00
- ❏ Showdown at Centerpoint 15.00
- ❏ Slave Ship [2:98] 15.00
- ❏ Specter of the Past 15.00
- ❏ Star Wars sampler, 6 stories [2:98] 10.00
- ❏ Star Wars: Episode I 15.00
- ❏ The New Rebellion [2:98] 15.00
- ❏ The Phantom Menace, unabridged [2:98] 15.00
- ❏ Thrawn Omnibus [2:98] 30.00
- ❏ Truce at Bakura 15.00
- ❏ Tyrant's Test 15.00
- ❏ X-Wing 5: Wraith Squadron [2:98] 10.00
- ❏ X-Wing 6: Iron Fist [2:98] 10.00
- ❏ X-Wing 7: Solo Command [2:98] 10.00
- ❏ X-Wing 8: Isard's Revenge [2:98] 10.00
- ❏ X-Wing 9: Starfighters of Adumar [2:98] 10.00

Griffin
- ❏ The Science of Star Wars, unabridged 25.00

Highbridge Company
- ❏ Soldier for the Empire [2:98] 15.00

Random House
- ❏ Ambush at Corellia / Assault at Selonia / Showdown at Centerpoint 20.00
- ❏ Cloak of Deception [2:98] 15.00
- ❏ Dark Journey 15.00
- ❏ Darth Maul Shadow Hunter 15.00
- ❏ Star Wars Episode 2 ....15.00
- ❏ Star Wars Episode 2, unabridged 20.00
- ❏ Survivor's Quest 15.00
- ❏ The Approaching Storm 15.00
- ❏ Yoda, Dark Rendezvous: A Clone Wars Novel 15.00

New Jedi Order.
- ❏ 1 Vector Prime [2:98] 15.00
- ❏ 2 Dark Tide I: Onslaught [2:98] 15.00
- ❏ 3 Dark Tide II: Ruin [2:98] 15.00
- ❏ 4 Agents of Chaos 1: Hero's Trial [2:98] 15.00
- ❏ 5 Agents of Chaos 2: Jedi Eclipse [2:98] 15.00
- ❏ 6 Balance Point [2:98] 15.00
- ❏ 7 Edge of Victory I: Conquest [2:98] 15.00
- ❏ 8 Edge of Victory II: Rebirth [2:98] 15.00
- ❏ 9 Star by Star 15.00
- ❏ 10 Dark Journey 15.00
- ❏ 11 Enemy Lines I: Rebel Dream 15.00
- ❏ 12 Enemy Lines II: Rebel Stand 15.00
- ❏ 13 Traitor 15.00

WB Audio Video
- ❏ Star Wars a New Hope, 2 cassettes 20.00

Books: Audio, CD

Bantam Books
- ❏ Night Lily, the Lovers Tale 15.00
- ❏ Rogue Planet [2:99] 15.00
- ❏ Shadows of the Empire [2:99] 15.00
- ❏ Star Wars, We Don't Do Weddings, The Band's Tale 15.00
- ❏ Star Wars: Episode I [2:99] 15.00

Fantom Films
David Prowse autobiography.
- ❏ Straight from the Force's Mouth, unabridged 35.00
- ❏ The Star Wars Diaries 35.00

Highbridge Company
- ❏ Star Wars Dark Empire 15.00
- ❏ Star Wars Dark Empire II 15.00

Penguin Audiobooks
- ❏ Crimson Empire [2:99] 15.00
- ❏ Dark Forces: The Collector's Trilogy [2:99] 20.00

Random House
- ❏ Clone Wars: Wild Space, unabridged 15.00
- ❏ Dark Nest I, The Joiner King 15.00
- ❏ Dark Nest II, The Unseen Queen 15.00
- ❏ Dark Nest III, The Swarm War 15.00
- ❏ No Prisoners 15.00
- ❏ Outbound Flight 15.00
- ❏ Shatterpoint 15.00
- ❏ Star Wars Cloak of Deception 15.00
- ❏ Star Wars Dark Lords of the Sith 15.00
- ❏ Star Wars Episode 2 ....15.00
- ❏ Star Wars Episode 2, unabridged 15.00
- ❏ Star Wars Labyrinth of Evil 15.00
- ❏ Star Wars Tales of the Jedi 15.00
- ❏ Star Wars, Revenge of the Sith 15.00
- ❏ Star Wars, Revenge of the Sith, unabridged 15.00
- ❏ Star Wars: Episode I, unabridged 15.00
- ❏ Star Wars: Episode I, unabridged limited edition boxed set 20.00
- ❏ Survivor's Quest 15.00
- ❏ Tatooine Ghost 15.00
- ❏ The Approaching Storm [2:99] 15.00
- ❏ The Complete Star Wars Trilogy, the original radio dramas 60.00
- ❏ Yoda, Dark Rendezvous: A Clone Wars Novel 15.00

Clone Wars Novels.
- ❏ Jedi Trial 15.00
- ❏ Medstar I, Battle Surgeons 15.00
- ❏ Medstar II, Jedi Healer 15.00
- ❏ The Cestus Deception 15.00

Fate of the Jedi.
- ❏ Abyss, by Troy Denning 15.00
- ❏ Allies, by Christie Golden 15.00
- ❏ Backlash, by Aaron Allston 15.00

Legacy of the Force.
- ❏ 1 Betrayal 15.00
- ❏ 2 Bloodlines, unabridged 15.00
- ❏ 3 Tempest 15.00
- ❏ 4 Exile 15.00

New Jedi Order.
- ❏ 12 Enemy Lines II, Rebel Stand 15.00
- ❏ 14 Destiny's Way 15.00
- ❏ 15 Force Heretic I: Remnant 15.00
- ❏ 16 Force Heretic II: Refugee 15.00
- ❏ 17 Force Heretic III: Reunion 15.00
- ❏ 18 The Final Prophecy 15.00
- ❏ 19 The Unifying Force 15.00

WB Audio Video
- ❏ Dark Empire The Collectors Edition: Dark Empire I and II; Empires End 35.00

Books: Coloring
Continued in Volume 3, Page 82

Episode II flip books.
- ❏ Anakin and Amidala 10.00
- ❏ Heroes and Villains 10.00

(Argentina)
- ❏ Para Pintar 15.00

(UK)
- ❏ Star Wars A5 Gel journal [v1e1:56] 15.00

Collins
- ❏ The Droid Colouring Book [46-01] 50.00
- ❏ The Ewok Fun Colouring Book [46-02] 50.00

Creative Edge
Giant books to color.
- ❏ Star Wars—Jedi Masters [46-03] 3.00
- ❏ Star Wars—The Empire Begins [46-04] 3.00

Sticker books to color. Exclusive to Target.
- ❏ Darth Vader 10.00

Super books to color. Exclusive to Target.
- ❏ Battle Ready [46-05] 5.00
- ❏ First In Last Standing [46-06] 5.00
- ❏ Follow Me! [46-07] 5.00

| 46-01 | 46-02 | 46-03 | 46-04 | 46-05 | 46-06 | 46-07 | 46-08 |
| 46-09 | 46-10 | 46-11 | 46-12 | 46-13 | 46-14 | 46-15 Front and Back |

Books: Coloring

❏ Know the Power [46-08] 5.00
❏ The Force [46-09] 5.00

Dalmatian Press
❏ Balance of the Force [46-10] 5.00
❏ Beware the Dark Side [46-11] 12.00
❏ Colouring Book [46-12] 5.00
❏ Friends of the Force [46-13] 5.00
❏ Jedi Forces 5.00
❏ Jumbo Colouring Book [46-14] 5.00

Big fun books to color.
❏ Duty and Honor [46-15] 10.00
❏ Hold Your Ground [46-16] 5.00
❏ Master and Apprentice [46-17] 5.00

Clone Wars. Sticker play books to color.
❏ Jedi Forces [46-18] 10.00
❏ Troopers 10.00

Sticker books to color.
❏ Darth Vader [46-19] 7.00
❏ Yoda [46-20] 7.00

Gaviota (Spain)
❏ Heroes Y Villanos Libro de Colorear [46-21] 15.00

Golden Books
❏ A Galaxy of Creatures, Characters, and Droids [46-22] 10.00
❏ An Ewok Adventure [46-23] 10.00
❏ Galactic Adventures [46-24] 10.00
❏ Heroes and Villains [46-25] 10.00
❏ Invisible Forces [46-26] 15.00
❏ Join the Jedi [46-27] 10.00
❏ Mark and See Magic [46-28] 15.00
❏ Posters to Color 15.00

Kenner
Return of the Jedi.
❏ Lando [46-29] 20.00
❏ Lando as skiff guard 20.00
❏ Luke with lightsaber [46-30] 20.00
❏ Max Rebo band [46-31] 20.00
❏ Wicket and Kneesaa 20.00
❏ Wicket the Ewok [46-32] 25.00
❏ Wicket, Kneesaa, and Logray 50.00
❏ Wicket's World [46-33] 35.00

Kenner (Canada)
❏ Wicket the Ewok [v1e1:57] 25.00
❏ Wicket's World [v1e1:57] 35.00

Empire Strikes Back.
❏ C-3PO and Chewbacca 25.00
❏ Chewbacca and Princess Leia [46-34] 25.00
❏ Chewbacca, Han, Lando, and Princess Leia [46-35] ... 25.00
❏ Darth Vader and Stormtroopers [46-36] 25.00
❏ Luke [46-37] 25.00
❏ R2-D2 [46-38] 25.00
❏ Yoda [46-39] 25.00

Star Wars.
❏ C-3PO and Luke 75.00
❏ Chewbacca [46-40] 75.00
❏ Chewbacca and Luke 75.00
❏ R2-D2 .... 75.00

LucasBooks
❏ Episode II 8.00

Oral-B
❏ Dental Health Adventure Book, 4/83 [46-41] 20.00
❏ Dental Health Adventure Book, 8/83 [46-42] 20.00

Random House
❏ Attack of the Clones, Movie Scenes to Color [46-43] 10.00
❏ Attack of the Clones, Movie Scenes to Color, Anakin / Amidala [46-44] 10.00
❏ Attack of the Clones, Movie Scenes to Color, villains / heroes [46-45] 10.00
❏ Battles To Color, The Phantom Menace [46-46] 12.00
❏ Droids, Creatures, and Vehicles [46-47] 12.00
❏ Episode I Anakin's Adventures To Color [46-48] ... 12.00
❏ Episode I Heroes and Villains [46-49] 12.00
❏ Episode I Jedi Missions [46-50] 12.00
❏ Giant Coloring Fun [46-51] 15.00
❏ Jar Jar's Coloring Fun [46-52] 12.00
❏ Jedi Knights and Heroes [46-53] 10.00
❏ Podracer! [46-54] 10.00
❏ Queen Amidala [46-55] 10.00
❏ The Phantom Menace [46-56] 12.00

      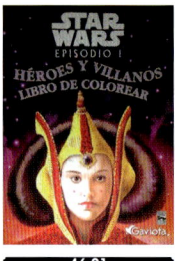 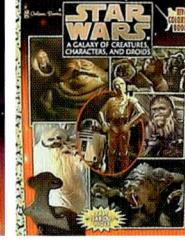

46-16 Front and Back | 46-17 | 46-18 | 46-19 | 46-20 | 46-21 | 46-22

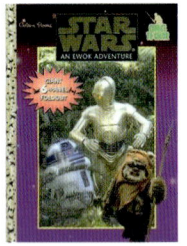 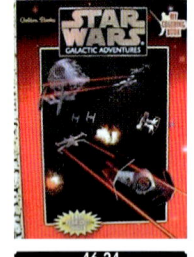 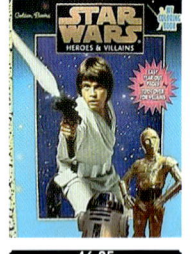 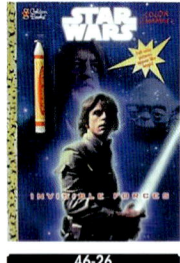 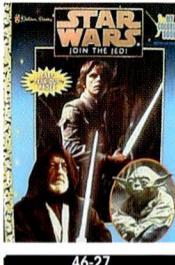  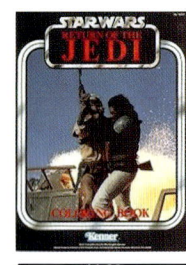

46-23 | 46-24 | 46-25 | 46-26 | 46-27 | 46-28 | 46-29

  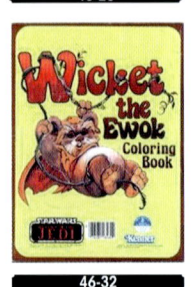 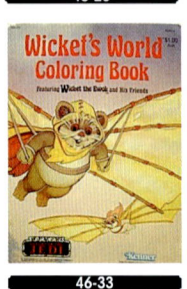 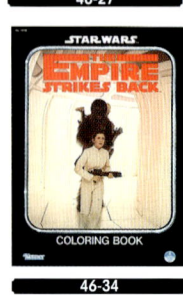 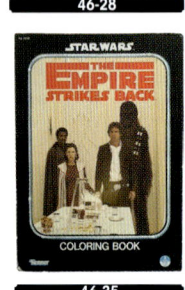 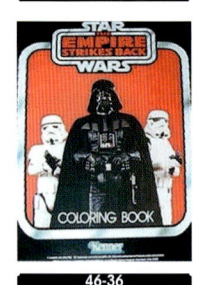

46-30 | 46-31 | 46-32 | 46-33 | 46-34 | 46-35 | 46-36

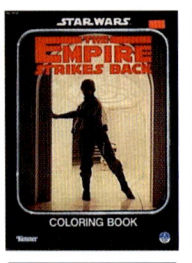 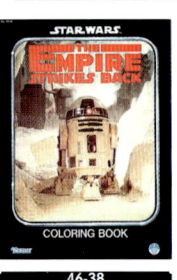   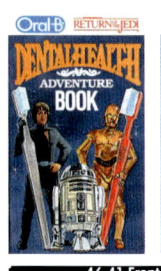 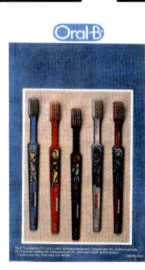  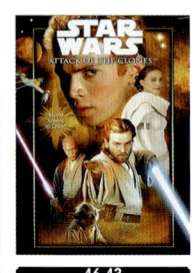

46-37 | 46-38 | 46-39 | 46-40 | 46-41 Front and Back | 46-42 Back | 46-43

Books: Educational

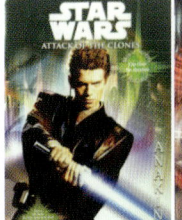   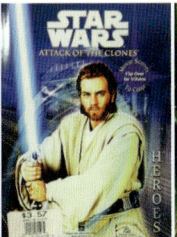    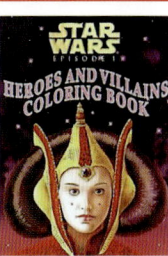

| 46-44 Front and Back | 46-45 Front and Back | 46-46 | 46-47 | 46-48 | 46-49 |

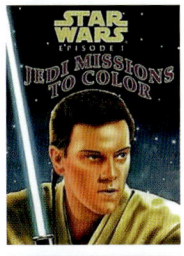   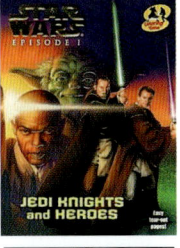   

| 46-50 | 46-51 | 46-52 | 46-53 | 46-54 | 46-55 | 46-56 |

Books: Cooking
Continued in Volume 3, Page 83

Chronicle Books
- Darth Malt and More Galactic Recipes [47-01] 20.00
- Star Wars Party Book—Recipes and Ideas [47-02] 15.00
- Wookiee Cookies and other Galactic Recipes [47-03] 10.00
- Wookiee Pies, Clone Scones, and other Galactic Goodies 20.00

Enterprise Incidents
- The Alien Cook 15.00

Books: Educational
Continued in Volume 3, Page 84

Cortexia Publishing
- Teaching, Learning, and Star Wars 24.00

Golden Books
- Han Solo's Rescue from Jabba the Hutt, math grades 2-3 [48-01] 12.00
- Luke Skywalker's Battle with Darth Vader, reading grades 2-3 [48-02] 12.00
- Princess Leia's Escape from the Death Star, spelling grades 2-3 [48-03] 12.00

Super shape books.
- Chewbacca the Wookiee [48-04] 8.00
- Han Solo, Rebel Hero [48-05] 8.00
- Luke Skywalker, Jedi Knight [48-06] 8.00
- Princess Leia, Rebel Leader [48-07] 8.00
- R2-D2 and C-3PO, Droid Duo [48-08] 10.00

Longman Publishers
- Star Wars, easy reading edition [48-09] 20.00

Random House
- C-3PO's Book About Robots [48-10] 12.00
- Ewok: ABC Fun 15.00
- Ewok: Learn-to-Read 15.00
- Spelling Workbook 20.00
- The Star Wars Book About Flight [48-11] 10.00
- The Star Wars Question and Answer Book About Computers, soft cover [48-12] 10.00
- The Star Wars Question and Answer Book About Space, hardcover 15.00

    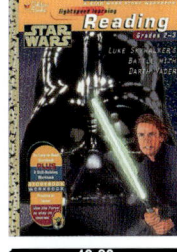  

| 47-01 | 47-02 | 47-03 | 48-01 | 48-02 | 48-03 | 48-04 |

 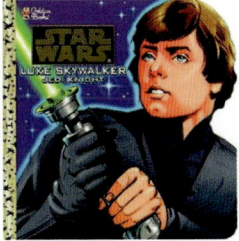   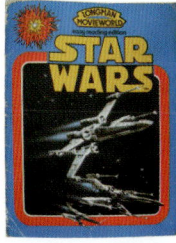 

| 48-05 | 48-06 | 48-07 | 48-08 | 48-09 | 48-10 |

  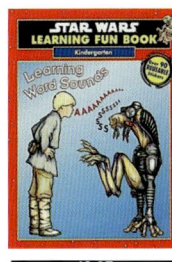    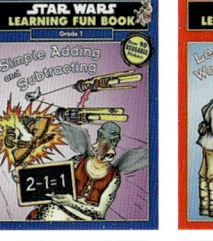

| 48-11 | 48-12 | 48-13 | 48-14 | 48-15 | 48-16 | 48-17 |

Books: Educational

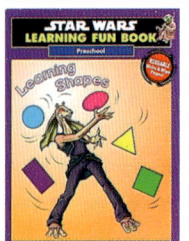 48-18
 48-19
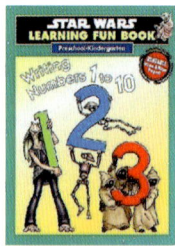 48-20
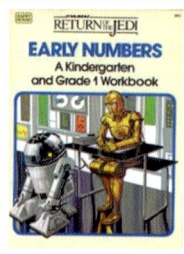 48-21
 48-22
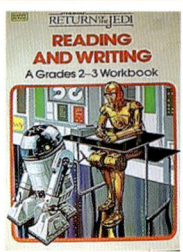 48-23
 48-24

Attack on Reading series.
- ❑ Comprehension 1 [48-13] 40.00
- ❑ Comprehension 2 [v1e1:58] 40.00
- ❑ Study Skills [48-14] 40.00
- ❑ Teacher's Guide 50.00
- ❑ Word Study [48-15] 40.00

Star Wars Learning Fun Books.
- ❑ Grade 1: Simple Adding and Subtracting [48-16] 15.00
- ❑ Kindergarten: Learning Word Sounds [48-17] 15.00
- ❑ Preschool: Kindergarten Counting Numbers 1–20 .... 15.00
- ❑ Preschool: Kindergarten Learning Shapes [48-18] 15.00
- ❑ Preschool: Kindergarten Writing Letters A to Z [48-19] 15.00
- ❑ Preschool: Kindergarten Writing Numbers 1 to 10 [48-20] 15.00

Workbooks.
- ❑ ABC Readiness [v1e1:58] 35.00
- ❑ Addition and Subtraction 35.00
- ❑ Early Numbers [48-21] 35.00
- ❑ Multiplication [48-22] 35.00
- ❑ Reading and Writing [48-23] 35.00

Scholastic
- ❑ The Star Wars Question and Answer Book About Space, soft cover [48-24] 15.00

Sphere
- ❑ Star Wars, easy reading edition 20.00

Books: Galaxy of Fear

Galaxie de la Peur
- ❑ Armee de Terreur 8.00
- ❑ La Cite des Morts [v1e1:58] 8.00
- ❑ La Monstre Cache 8.00

Bantam Books
- ❑ 1 Eaten Alive [v1e1:58] 8.00
- ❑ 2 City of the Dead [5:41] 8.00
- ❑ 3 Planet Plague [v1e1:58] 8.00
- ❑ 4 The Nightmare Machine [v1e1:58] 8.00
- ❑ 5 The Ghost of the Jedi [5:41] 8.00
- ❑ 6 Army of Terror [5:41] 8.00
- ❑ 7 The Brain Spiders [v1e1:58] 8.00
- ❑ 8 The Swarm [v1e1:58] 8.00
- ❑ 9 Spore [5:41] 8.00
- ❑ 10 The Doomsday Ship [5:41] 8.00
- ❑ 11 Clones [5:41] 8.00
- ❑ 12 Hunger [5:41] 8.00

Sperling and Kupfer (Italy)
La Galassia del Terrore.
- ❑ La Citta Dei Morti [5:41] 10.00
- ❑ Mangiati VIVI [v1e1:58] 10.00

VGS
- ❑ Lebendig begraben / Stadt det Toten [5:41] 15.00

Books: Game Guides
Continued in Volume 3, Page 85

- ❑ Battle Masters Guide 8.00
- ❑ Defender of the Empire: Official Secrets and Solutions 10.00
- ❑ Jedi Knight Strategy Guide [4:37] 10.00
- ❑ Secrets of Shadows of the Empire [4:37] 10.00
- ❑ Shadows of the Empire: Official Strategy Guide [4:37] 10.00
- ❑ Star Wars Nintendo Hint Book (Special Offer) 10.00
- ❑ Super Empire Strikes Back Official Game Secrets [2:102] 10.00
- ❑ Super Return of the Jedi Official Game Secrets 10.00
- ❑ Super Star Wars Official Game Secrets 10.00
- ❑ TIE Fighter Collector's CD-ROM: The Official Strategy Guide [2:102] 10.00
- ❑ TIE Fighter: The Official Strategy Guide [4:37] 10.00
- ❑ X-Wing Collector's CD-ROM: The Official Strategy Guide 10.00
- ❑ X-Wing vs. TIE Fighter Strategy Guide 10.00
- ❑ X-Wing: The Official Strategy Guide 10.00

BradyGames Strategy Guides
- ❑ TIE Fighter: Authorized Strategy Guide [4:37] 10.00

Future Publications
- ❑ Episode I: The Phantom Menace, The Unofficial Game Players Guide 12.00

 49-01
 49-02
 49-03
 49-04
 49-05
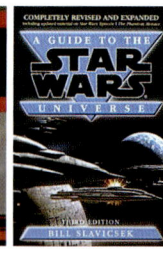 49-06

 49-07
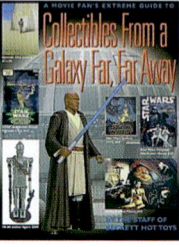 49-08
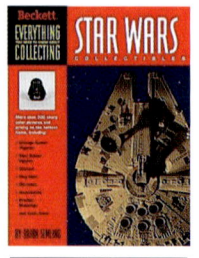 49-09
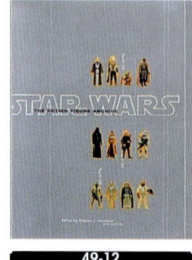 49-10
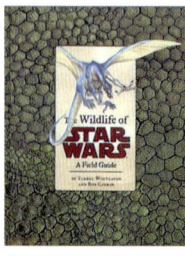 49-11
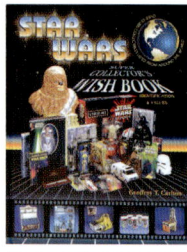 49-12
 49-13

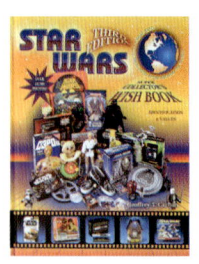 49-14
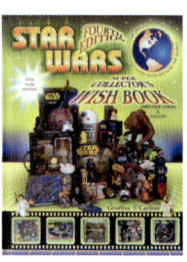 49-15
 49-16
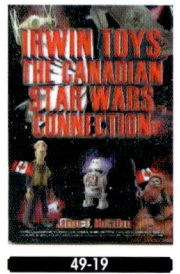 49-17
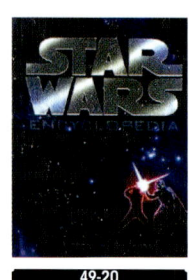 49-18
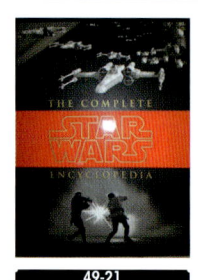 49-19
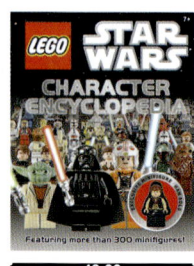 49-20

Books: Guides

Infotainment World Books
- Rebel Assault II: Official Player's Guide 12.00

LucasArts
- Dark Forces: Official Players Guide [4:37] 12.00

Markt Technik (Germany)
- Die X-Wing Piloten - Power 15.00

Nintendo
- Episode I: Racer, Official Nintendo Player's Guide [2:102] 12.00

Prima Publishing
- An Empire Divided, with giant poster [4:37] 15.00
- Battlefront [4:37] 10.00
- Battlefront II 10.00
- Bounty Hunter [4:37] 10.00
- Collector's Guide 20.00
- Demolition [4:37] 10.00
- Empire at War [4:37] 12.00
- Episode I: Racer [4:37] 10.00
- Episode I: The Phantom Menace [4:37] 10.00
- Episode III: Revenge of the Sith 10.00
- Force Commander [4:37] 12.00
- Galactic Battlegrounds 12.00
- Galaxies Map Atlas (Expanded) 5.00
- Galaxies: An Empire Divided (console) 5.00
- Gungan Frontier [4:37] 10.00
- Jedi Power Battles [4:37] 10.00
- Knights of the Old Republic [4:37] 10.00
- LEGO Star Wars 2: The Original Trilogy 15.00
- Lightsaber Duels and Jedi Alliance 10.00
- Map Atlas 10.00
- Masters of Teras Kasi [4:37] 10.00
- Quick Reference Guide 10.00
- Rebel Assault: The Official Insider's Guide 10.00
- Space Expansion 10.00
- Star Wars Galaxies: The Total Experience 5.00
- Star Wars Galaxies: The Complete Guide 5.00
- Starfighter [4:37] 10.00
- X-Wing 10.00
- X-Wing Alliance [4:37] 10.00

Books: Guides
Continued in Volume 3, Page 85

- Force of Star Wars [49-01] 35.00
- Kiddie Meal Collectibles [49-02] 20.00
- The World of Star Wars 15.00
- Vader the Ultimate Guide 15.00

(Japan)
- 2006 Official Star Wars Horoscopes [49-03] 25.00
- Episode II [v1e1:59] 20.00

Abrams
- 1,000 Collectibles: Memorabilia and Stories from a Galaxy Far, Far Away [49-04] 40.00

Antique Trader Books
- Galaxy's Greatest Star Wars Collectibles [49-05] 20.00

Back Bay Books
- Unauthorized Star Wars Companion: The Complete Guide to the Star Wars Galaxy 15.00

Ballantine
A Guide to the Star Wars Universe.
- 1st edition [49-06] 25.00
- 2nd edition [49-07] 20.00
- 3rd edition [49-08] 20.00

- Galactic Phrase Book and Travel Guide: Beeps, Bleats, Boskas, and Other Common Intergalactic Verbiage [49-09] 15.00

Beckett
- Collectibles from a galaxy far, far away [49-10] 15.00
- Everything you need to know about Collecting Star Wars [49-11] 15.00

Boxtree
Essential Guides To...
- Alien Species [v1e1:60] 15.00
- Characters [v1e1:60] 15.00
- Characters, condensed 10.00
- Droids [v1e1:60] 15.00
- Planets and Moons [v1e1:60] 15.00
- Vehicles and Vessels [v1e1:60] 15.00
- Vehicles and Vessels, condensed 10.00

Chronicle Books
- Star Wars Poster Book, The 150.00
- The Action Figure Archive [49-12] 30.00
- The Jedi Path: A Manual for Students of the Force 14.00
- The Wildlife of Star Wars: A Field Guide [49-13] 40.00

Collector Books
Star Wars Super Collector's Wish Book.
- 1st edition [49-14] 35.00
- 2nd edition [49-15] 35.00
- 3rd edition [49-16] 35.00
- 4th edition [49-17] 35.00
- 5th edition [49-18] 40.00

Collector's Guide
- Irwin Toys the Canadian Star Wars Connection [49-19] 325.00

Completest Publications
- Gus and Duncan's Comprehensive Guide to Star Wars Collectibles 100.00

Del Rey
- Jedi vs. Sith, The Essential Guide to the Force, by Ryder Windham 20.00
- Star Wars Encyclopedia [49-20] 35.00
- Star Wars: The Essential Atlas, paperback, by Daniel Wallace and Jason Fry 20.00
- The Complete Star Wars Encyclopedia [49-21] 75.00

Essential Guides To...
- Planets and Moons 20.00
- The Essential Chronology 20.00
- Weapons and Technology 20.00

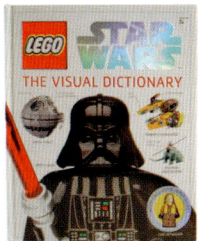 49-23
 49-24
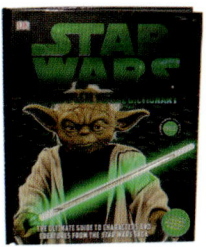 49-25
 49-26
 49-27
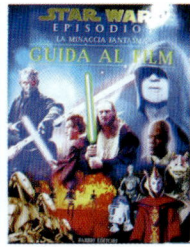 49-28
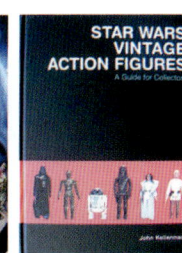 49-29
 49-30
 49-31
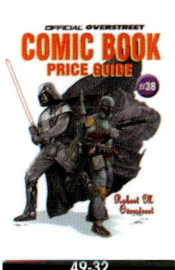 49-32
 49-33
 49-34
 49-35
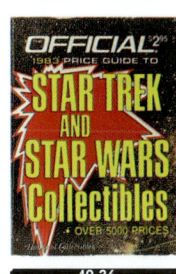 49-36
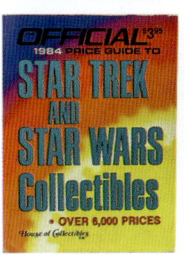 49-37
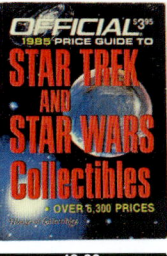 49-38
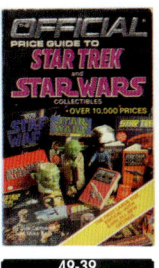 49-39
 49-40
 49-41
 49-42
 49-43
 49-44

Books: Guides

New Essential Guides To...
- Alien Species [v1e1:60] 20.00
- Characters [v1e1:60] 20.00
- Chronology [v1e1:60] 20.00
- Chronology, Droids, and Aliens [v1e1:60] 20.00
- Droids [v1e1:60] 20.00
- Vehicles and Vessels [v1e1:60] 20.00

DK Publishing
- Complete Cross-Sections 35.00
- Complete Locations of Star Wars 20.00
- Complete Locations, Inside the Worlds of the Entire Saga 35.00
- Complete Visual Dictionary 35.00
- Episode II Incredible Cross-Sections 15.00
- Episode II Visual Dictionary 15.00
- Episode III Incredible Cross-Sections [v1e1:60] 15.00
- Episode III Visual Dictionary [v1e1:60] 15.00
- Inside the Worlds of Star Wars Episode I [v1e1:60] 20.00
- Inside the Worlds of Star Wars Episode II 20.00
- Inside the Worlds of Star Wars Trilogy [v1e1:60] 25.00
- LEGO Star Wars: Character Encyclopedia, with exclusive Han Yavin Ceremony mini-figure [49-22] 35.00
- LEGO Star Wars: The Visual Dictionary, with exclusive Luke Yavin Ceremony mini-figure [49-23] 35.00
- Star Wars Clone Wars Character Encyclopedia, hardcover [49-24] 20.00
- Star Wars: The Complete Visual Dictionary [49-25] 25.00
- Star Wars Character Encyclopedia [49-26] 15.00
- Star Wars Incredible Cross-Sections [v1e1:60] 35.00
- Star Wars The Visual Dictionary [v1e1:60] 35.00
- The Phantom Menace Cross Sections [v1e1:61] 20.00
- The Phantom Menace: Cross Sections, inside metal box with combination lock, promotional, 500 produced [3:131] .. 250.00
- The Phantom Menace: The Visual Dictionary [v1e1:61] ..15.00
- Ultimate Visual Guide 25.00
- Ultimate Visual Guide, Special Edition [49-27] 30.00

Edbury Press (UK)
- Attack of the Clones Illustrated Companion 25.00

Fabbri Editori
- Episodio I Guida Al Film [49-28] 20.00

Fantasia Verlag
- Star Heroes #1 .... 20.00
- Star Heroes #2 .... 20.00
- Star Heroes #3 .... 20.00
- Star Heroes #4 .... 25.00

Front Back Books
- Star Wars Vintage Action Figures [49-29] 750.00

FunFax (UK)
Data files.
- Episode I [49-30] 8.00
- Revenge of the Sith 8.00
- Star Wars [49-31] 8.00

Gemstone Publishing
- 2008 Overstreet Price Guide, Darth Vader and Boba Fett Cover [49-32] 25.00

Grosset and Dunlap
- Clone Wars Official Episode Guide - Season 1 [49-33] 10.00

Henderson Publishing
- Star Wars Data File [49-34] 20.00

Funfax Missions.
- 1: Star Wars 5.00
- 2: Empire Strikes Back 5.00
- 3: Return of the Jedi 5.00

Microfax series.
- #1: Darth Vader 5.00
- #2: C-3PO and R2-D2 .... 5.00
- #3: Galactic Empire 5.00
- #4: Jabba the Hutt and Bounty Hunters 5.00
- #5: Princess Leia 5.00
- #6: Luke Skywalker 5.00
- #7: Millennium Falcon 5.00
- #8: Obi-Wan Kenobi 5.00
- #9: Han Solo and Chewbacca 5.00
- #10: Imperial Fleet 5.00
- #11: Rebel Fleet 5.00
- #12: Rebel Alliance 5.00
- Mini-Binder [49-35] 15.00

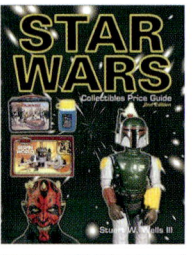
49-45

49-46

49-47

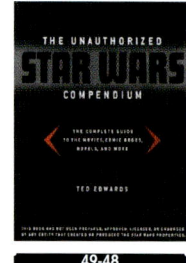
49-48

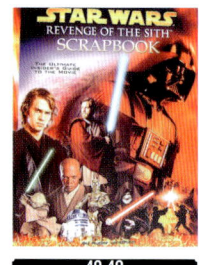
49-49

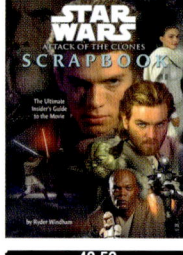
49-50

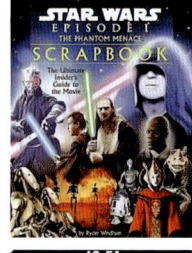
49-51

49-52

49-53

49-54

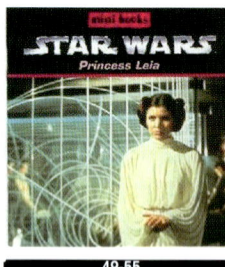
49-55

49-56

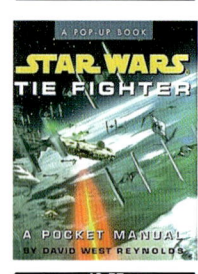
49-57

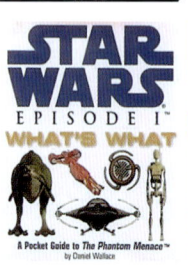
49-58

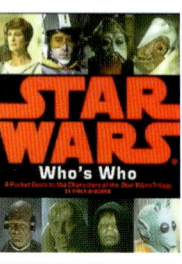
49-59

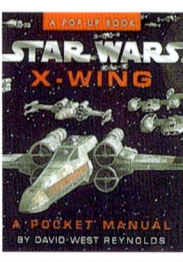
49-60

49-61

49-62

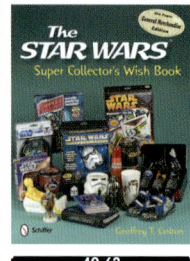
49-63

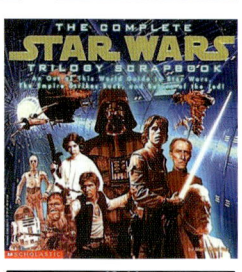
49-64

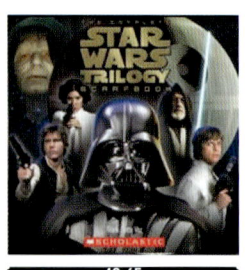
49-65

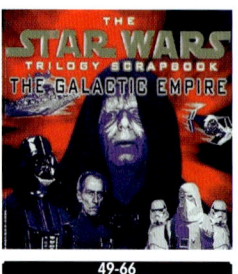
49-66

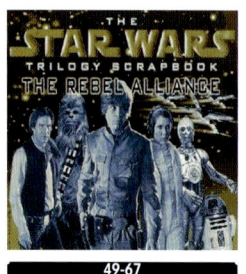
49-67

49-68

49-69

49-70

Books: Music

 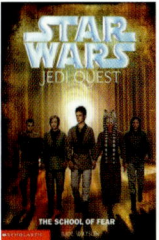  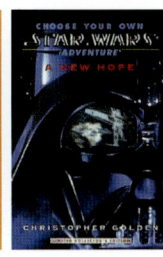 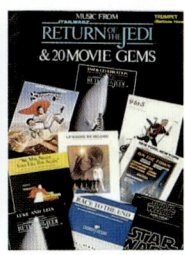 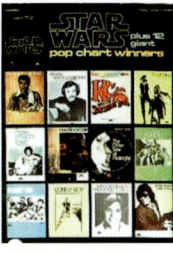 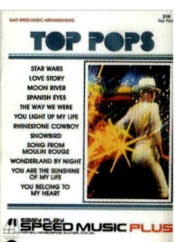 

50-01 51-01 52-01 53-01 54-01 54-02 54-03 54-04

House of Collectibles
Official Price Guide Star Trek and Star Wars Collectibles.
- ❑ 1983 [49-36] 20.00
- ❑ 1984 [49-37] 15.00
- ❑ 1985 [49-38] 15.00
- ❑ 1986 first edition [49-39] 15.00
- ❑ 1987 second edition [49-40] 15.00
- ❑ 1987 third edition [49-41] 15.00

Official Price Guide to Star Wars Memorabilia.
- ❑ 1997 fourth edition [49-42] 15.00
- ❑ 2005 [49-43] 15.00

IDG Entertainment
- ❑ Revenge of the Sith Official Souvenir Guide [49-44] 10.00

Kindai Eigasha (Japan)
- ❑ Star Wars: Return of the Jedi 25.00

Krause Publications
- ❑ Science Fiction Collectibles, star wars listings inside .. 10.00
- ❑ Star Wars Collectibles Price Guide [49-45] 30.00
- ❑ Star Wars Collector's Pocket Companion [49-46] 15.00
- ❑ Warman's Star Wars Field Guide [49-47] 15.00

Little, Brown
- ❑ Unauthorized Star Wars Compendium [49-48] 25.00

LucasBooks
- ❑ Revenge of the Sith scrapbook [49-49] 5.00

Planeta
- ❑ Episode I Incredible Cross-Sections [v1e1:61] 25.00
- ❑ Episode I Visual Dictionary [v1e1:61] 25.00

Random House
- ❑ Attack of the Clones Scrapbook [49-50] 10.00
- ❑ Episode I: The Phantom Menace Scrapbook [49-51] .. 15.00
- ❑ Secrets of the Sith Movie Scrapbook [49-52] 10.00

Reeds
- ❑ Darth Vader mini-book [49-53] 8.00
- ❑ Han Solo mini-book [49-54] 8.00
- ❑ Princess Leia mini-book [49-55] 8.00

Running Press
Pocket guides.
- ❑ Star Wars Collectibles [49-56] 10.00
- ❑ TIE Fighter [49-57] 10.00
- ❑ What's What : The Phantom Menace [49-58] 10.00
- ❑ Who's Who: Characters of Phantom Menace [3:131] .. 10.00
- ❑ Who's Who: Characters of Star Wars Trilogy [49-59] .. 10.00
- ❑ X-Wing [49-60] 10.00

Sankyo Co., Ltd. (Japan)
- ❑ Star Wars Fever, Official Guide Book [49-61] 30.00

Schiffer Publishing
- ❑ Collecting Star Wars Toys 1977-1997: An Unauthorized Practical Guide [49-62] 30.00

Star Wars Super Collector's Wish Book.
- ❑ Volume 1, 1st edition: Collectibles and Merchandise (1977–2011) [49-63] 75.00
- ❑ Volume 1, 2nd edition: Collectibles and Merchandise (1977–2011) 40.00
- ❑ Volume 2, 1st edition: Toys (1977–2012) 60.00
- ❑ Volume 2, 2nd edition: Toys (1977–2022) 45.00
- ❑ Volume 3, 1st edition: Collectibles, Merchandise, and Toys (2012–2022) 45.00
- ❑ Volume 4, 1st edition: Collectibles, Merchandise, and Toys (2022–2025) 40.00

Scholastic
- ❑ The Complete Star Wars Trilogy Scrapbook [49-64] .. 10.00
- ❑ The Complete Star Wars Trilogy Scrapbook [49-65] .. 10.00
- ❑ The Star Wars Trilogy Scrapbook: The Galactic Empire [49-66] 10.00
- ❑ The Star Wars Trilogy Scrapbook: The Rebel Alliance [49-67] 10.00

Shueisha (Japan)
- ❑ All About the Star Wars, Young Jump special edition 30.00
- ❑ Return of the Jedi, Road Show special collection 35.00

Tokuma Shoten (Japan)
- ❑ Star Wars: Empire Strikes Back, TV Land deluxe color graph 25.00

Tomart
Tomart's Price Guide to Worldwide Star Wars Collectibles.
- ❑ 1st edition [49-68] 40.00
- ❑ 2nd edition [49-69] 30.00
- ❑ 2nd edition hardcover [49-70] 75.00

VGS
- ❑ Episode I Die Risszeichnungen [v1e1:62] 35.00

WSOY
- ❑ Episodi I Kuvitettu Opas [v1e1:62] 35.00

Books: Jedi Apprentice

Bonnict
- ❑ Den morka rivalen [5:43] 10.00

Fabbri Editori
- ❑ Il rivale oscuro [5:43] 10.00

Scholastic
- ❑ 1 The Rising Force [v1e1:63] 8.00
- ❑ 2 The Dark Rival [5:43] 8.00
- ❑ 3 The Hidden Past [2:104] 8.00
- ❑ 4 The Mark of the Crown [2:104] 8.00
- ❑ 5 The Defenders of the Dead [2:104] 8.00
- ❑ 6 The Uncertain Path [2:104] 8.00
- ❑ 7 The Captive Temple [2:104] 8.00
- ❑ 8 The Day of Reckoning [2:104] 8.00
- ❑ 9 The Fight for Truth [2:104] 8.00
- ❑ 10 The Shattered Peace [2:104] 8.00
- ❑ 11 The Deadly Hunter [2:104] 8.00
- ❑ 12 The Evil Experiment [2:104] 8.00
- ❑ 13 The Dangerous Rescue [50-01] 8.00
- ❑ 14 The Ties That Bind [2:104] 8.00
- ❑ 15 The Death of Hope [2:104] 8.00
- ❑ 16 The Call to Vengeance [2:104] 8.00
- ❑ 17 The Only Witness [2:104] 8.00
- ❑ 18 The Threat Within [2:104] 8.00
- ❑ Special Edition 1: Deceptions [v1e1:63] 10.00
- ❑ Special Edition 2: The Followers [5:43] 10.00

Books: Jedi Quest

Scholastic
- ❑ 1 The Way of the Apprentice [v1e1:62] 8.00
- ❑ 2 The Trail of the Jedi [v1e1:62] 8.00
- ❑ 3 The Dangerous Games [v1e1:62] 8.00
- ❑ 4 The Master of Disguise [3:132] 8.00
- ❑ 5 The School of Fear [51-01] 8.00
- ❑ 6 The Shadow Trap [3:132] 8.00
- ❑ 7 The Moment of Truth [3:132] 8.00
- ❑ 8 The Changing of the Guard 8.00
- ❑ 9 The False Peace 8.00
- ❑ 10 The Final Showdown 8.00

Books: Junior Jedi Knights

Boulevard
- ❑ 1 The Golden Globe [v1e1:63] 8.00
- ❑ 2 Lyric's World [2:105] 8.00
- ❑ 3 Promises [2:104] 8.00
- ❑ 4 Anakin's Quest [52-01] 8.00
- ❑ 5 Vader's Fortress [v1e1:63] 8.00
- ❑ 6 Kenobi's Blade [2:105] 8.00

Books: Make Your Own Adventure
Continued in Volume 3, Page 87

Bantam Books
- ❑ Empire Strikes Back [4:40] 8.00
- ❑ Return of the Jedi [4:40] 8.00
- ❑ Star Wars [53-01] 8.00

Grosset and Dunlap
- ❑ The Way of the Jedi [v1e1:63] 10.00

West End Games
- ❑ Jedi's Honor [3:132] 15.00
- ❑ Scoundrel's Luck [3:132] 15.00

Books: Music
Continued in Volume 3, Page 87

- ❑ Music from Return of the Jedi and 20 movie gems [54-01] 20.00
- ❑ Star Wars plus 12 giant pop chart winners [54-02] .. 20.00
- ❑ Top Pops, easy play piano [54-03] 20.00

Alfred Publishing
- ❑ Clone Wars: Piano Solos 20.00
- ❑ Episodes I, II & III Instrumental Solos Book and CD (Alto Sax Edition) [54-04] 30.00

Star Wars Instrumental Solos (Movies I-VI). Includes book and CD.
- ❑ Alto Sax 15.00
- ❑ Cello 15.00
- ❑ Clarinet 15.00
- ❑ Flute 15.00
- ❑ Horn in F 15.00
- ❑ Piano 15.00
- ❑ Tenor Sax 15.00
- ❑ Trombone 15.00
- ❑ Trumpet 15.00
- ❑ Viola 15.00
- ❑ Violin 15.00

Fox Fanfare Music
- ❑ Star Wars 15.00
- ❑ Star Wars Picture Book 15.00
- ❑ Star Wars Saga Book 25.00
- ❑ The Empire Strikes Back 15.00

Warner Bros Publications
- ❑ Music from Star Wars Episode I 15.00

Books: Music

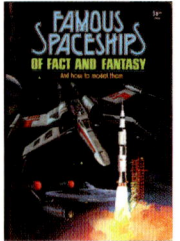   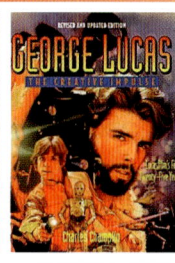 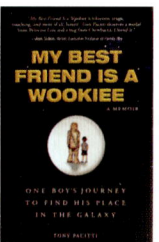  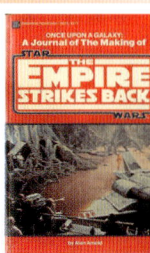 

55-01 | 55-02 | 55-03 | 55-04 | 55-05 | 55-06 | 55-07 | 55-08

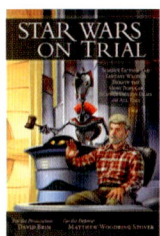     

55-09 | 55-10 | 55-11 | 55-12 | 55-13 | 55-14

    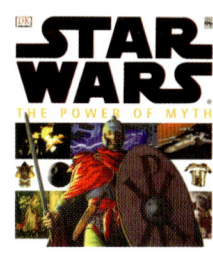  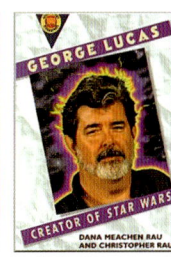

55-15 | 55-16 | 55-17 | 55-18 | 55-19 | 55-20 | 55-21

- ❏ Music from the Star Wars Trilogy for flute 20.00
- ❏ Phantom Menace Clarinet Song book 20.00
- ❏ Phantom Menace Tenor Sax Song book 20.00
- ❏ Phantom Menace Trumpet Song book 20.00
- ❏ Selections from Star Wars for Guitar [4:40] 25.00

Books: Non-Fiction
Continued in Volume 3, Page 87

- ❏ Famous Spaceships and How to Model Them [55-01] 40.00
- ❏ Flying Solo, hardcover with slipcase, signed by Jeremy Bulloch, 2,000 produced [4:41] 55.00
- ❏ Return of the Jedi Official Collector's Album 15.00
- ❏ The Making of The Phantom Menace, Limited First Edition 25.00
- ❏ The Making of The Phantom Menace, Special Collector's limited edition [55-02] 30.00

(Germany)
- ❏ The Making of Return of the Jedi 35.00
- ❏ The Star Wars Album 35.00

(Japan)
- ❏ George Lucas Museum 45.00
- ❏ Industrial Light and Magic 25.00
- ❏ Star Wars Chronicles [55-03] 200.00
- ❏ Star Wars: From Concept to Collectible 35.00
- ❏ The George Lucas Exhibition 45.00
- ❏ The Making of Return of the Jedi 25.00
- ❏ The Star Wars Album 24.00

(Netherlands)
- ❏ The Star Wars Album 30.00

Abrams
- ❏ Creating the Worlds of Star Wars 365 Days, with bonus CD-ROM 30.00
- ❏ Dressing a Galaxy : The Costumes of Star Wars 65.00
- ❏ Dressing a Galaxy: The Costume of Star Wars, limited edition with DVD 355.00

- ❏ George Lucas The Creative Impulse: Lucasfilm's First Twenty Years [55-04] 40.00
- ❏ George Lucas: The Creative Impulse 1st print 35.00
- ❏ George Lucas: The Creative Impulse 2nd print 40.00
- ❏ George Lucas: The Creative Impulse, 2nd edition 35.00
- ❏ Monsters and Aliens from George Lucas [v1e1:63] 25.00
- ❏ The Cinema of George Lucas 50.00

Adams Media
- ❏ My Best Friend is a Wookiee: One Boy's Journey to Find His Place in the Galaxy [55-05] 15.00

Back Stage Books
- ❏ What Were They Thinking—The 100 Dumbest Events in Television History *(Spoiler: Star Wars Holiday Special is listed as the number one event.)* 30.00

Ballantine
- ❏ Making of Return of the Jedi [55-06] 30.00
- ❏ Once Upon A Galaxy, The Making of Empire Strikes Back [55-07] 25.00
- ❏ Star Wars, Star Trek and 21st Century Christians 15.00

Bantam Books
- ❏ The Magic of Myth, hardcover [55-08] 45.00
- ❏ The Magic of Myth, trade paperback 35.00

Benbella Books
- ❏ Star Wars on Trial [55-09] 15.00

British Film Institute
- ❏ Big Picture: Hollywood Cinema from "Star Wars" to "Titanic" (Paperback) 20.00

Chronicle Books
- ❏ From Star Wars to Indiana Jones: The Best of Lucasfilm Archives, hardcover [v1e1:63] 45.00
- ❏ From Star Wars to Indiana Jones: The Best of Lucasfilm Archives, trade paperback 30.00
- ❏ Rogue Leaders: The Story of LucasArts 60.00
- ❏ Star Wars Chronicles [55-10] 175.00
- ❏ Star Wars Chronicles II 175.00

- ❏ Star Wars Scrapbook: The Essential Collection [55-11] 35.00
- ❏ Star Wars: From Concept to Screen to Collectible, hardcover 35.00
- ❏ Star Wars: From Concept to Screen to Collectible, paperback [55-12] 25.00
- ❏ The Sounds of Star Wars, by J.W. Rinzler with forward by Ben Burtt 85.00
- ❏ Yoda, "Bring You Wisdom I Will," book in a box with figure [55-13] 17.00

Postcard books.
- ❏ Aliens and Creatures [v1e1:63] 18.00
- ❏ Behind the Scenes [v1e1:63] 18.00
- ❏ Star Wars Comics: 100 Collectible Postcards 25.00
- ❏ The Toys [55-14] 20.00

Citadel
- ❏ Empire Building: The Remarkable Real Life Story of Star Wars [v1e1:64] 15.00
- ❏ Empire Building: The Remarkable Real Life Story of SW, includes new section on EPI: The Phantom Menace [55-15] 20.00

Continuum Publishing Group
- ❏ Using the Force: Creativity, Community and Star Wars Fans [v1e1:64] 30.00

Del Rey
- ❏ Industrial Light and Magic: Into the Digital Realm [55-16] 65.00
- ❏ Industrial Light and Magic: The Art of Special Effects 75.00
- ❏ Star Wars: The Making of Episode III 35.00
- ❏ The Art of Star Wars: Episode III 35.00
- ❏ The Making of Star Wars Revenge of the Sith [55-17] 15.00
- ❏ The Making of Star Wars: The Definitive Story Behind the Original Film, hardcover [55-18] 75.00
- ❏ The Making of Star Wars: The Definitive Story Behind the Original Film, paperback 35.00

DK Publishing
- ❏ Classic Gift Pack (Visual Dictionary, Cross-Sections, Ultimate Sticker book, Power of Myth book, calendar) [5:44] 85.00

Books: Novels

55-22
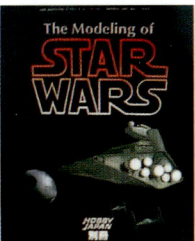
55-23 Front and Back

55-24

55-25

55-26
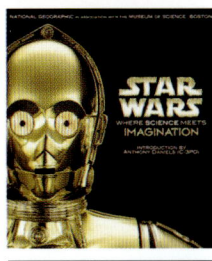
55-27

55-28

55-29

55-30
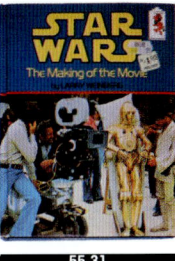
55-31
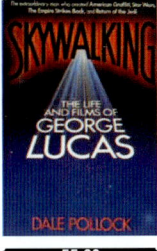
55-32
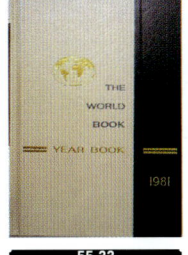
55-33
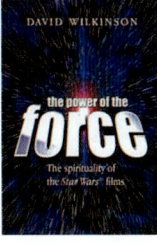
55-34

55-35

- ❏ Episode I gift pack (Visual Dictionary, Cross-Sections, Ultimate Sticker book, Power of Myth book, Calendar) [5:44] 80.00
- ❏ The Power of Myth [55-19] 20.00

Facts on Demand
- ❏ The Incredible Internet Guide to Star Wars [55-20] 10.00

Fictioneer Books, Ltd.
- ❏ David Anthony Kraft's Comics Interview Super Special: Star Wars 15.00

Franklin Watts
- ❏ George Lucas : Creator of Star Wars [55-21] 10.00
- ❏ George Lucas : Creator of Star Wars, hardcover 20.00

Griffin
- ❏ The Science of Star Wars [55-22] 35.00
- ❏ The Science of Star Wars, hardcover 40.00

Hachette
- ❏ The Star Wars Album 20.00

HarperEntertainment
- ❏ The Star Wars Vault: Thirty Years of Treasures from the Lucasfilm Archives 85.00

Harry N. Abrams, Inc.
- ❏ Dressing a Galaxy: The Costumes of Star Wars 65.00
- ❏ Dressing a Galaxy: The Costumes of Star Wars, limited edition with DVD 295.00

Henry Holt and Company
- ❏ A Galaxy Not So Far Away [v1e1:64] 15.00

Hobby Japan
- ❏ The Modeling of Star Wars [55-23] 35.00

Humanics Trade Group
- ❏ Tao of Star Wars [55-24] 15.00

Insight Editions
- ❏ Sculpting a Galaxy, The Models of Star Wars 75.00
- ❏ Sculpting a Galaxy, The Models of Star Wars, limited edition [55-25] 350.00

Jeremy Backett
- ❏ Tatooine Tours: On Location, ebook 5.00

Krause Publications
- ❏ Sci-Fi Movie Freak 10.00

Legacy Books
- ❏ The Secret History of Star Wars 40.00

LucasBooks
- ❏ Generation Star Wars: A Celebration of Fandom 15.00
- ❏ Making of Episode I: The Phantom Menace [4:42] 25.00
- ❏ Making of Episode I: The Phantom Menace, limited 1st edition 40.00
- ❏ The Making of Star Wars: The Empire Strikes Back: The Definitive Story Behind the Film, hardcover 55.00

Mark Dermul
- ❏ Tatooine Reunion 45.00
- ❏ The Force in Finse 30.00
- ❏ Trip to Tatooine 30.00

Marvel Comics
- ❏ The Star Wars Album 20.00

National Geographic
- ❏ Star Wars Where Science Meets Imagination, hardcover 45.00
- ❏ Star Wars: Where Science Meets Imagination [55-26] 20.00

Octopus Books
- ❏ Sci-Fi Now [55-27] 15.00

Open Court Publishing
- ❏ Star Wars And Philosophy, paperback [55-28] 15.00
- ❏ The Journey of Luke Skywalker: An Analysis of Modern Myth and Symbol [55-29] 20.00

Orbit
- ❏ The Making of Return of the Jedi 30.00

Peter Lang Pub Inc
- ❏ Finding the Force of the Star Wars Franchise: Fans, Merchandise, and Critics, hardcover 15.00
- ❏ Finding the Force of the Star Wars Franchise: Fans, Merchandise, and Critics, paperback [55-30] 10.00

Random House
- ❏ Attack of the Clones Postcard Book 25.00
- ❏ Star Wars, The Making of the Movie, step-up [55-31] .. 20.00
- ❏ Stars of Star Wars 10.00

Samuel French Trade
- ❏ Skywalking: The Life and Films of George Lucas [55-32] 15.00
- ❏ Skywalking: The Life and Films of George Lucas; updated edition 1997 .... 15.00

Sphere
- ❏ Once Upon A Galaxy, The Making of Star Wars: The Empire Strikes Back 35.00

Starlog
- ❏ Starlog Salutes Star Wars, 10th Anniversary 15.00

The World Book
Yearbooks.
- ❏ 1978 Motion Pictures [v1e1:64] 25.00
- ❏ 1980 Special report and games 20.00
- ❏ 1981 Motion Pictures [55-33] 20.00
- ❏ 1984 Motion Pictures 20.00

Trafalgar Square
- ❏ The spirituality of the Star Wars films [55-34] 15.00

Virgin Books
- ❏ The Star Wars Archives: Props, Costumes, Models and Artworks from Star Wars 85.00

Wisdom Publications
- ❏ The Dharma of Star Wars, paperback 15.00

Xlibris Corporation
- ❏ Star Wars: The New Myth 20.00
- ❏ Star Wars: The New Myth, hardcover [55-35] 25.00

Books: Novels
Continued in Volume 3, Page 88

- ❏ Star Wars Chronology, hardcover 30.00
- ❏ Star Wars Chronology, trade paperback 15.00
- ❏ Star Wars Trilogy Omnibus Edition [v1e1:65] 10.00
- ❏ Star Wars Trilogy Omnibus Edition, 10th anniversary ... 15.00

(Belgium)
- ❏ Episode III: De wraak van de Sith 15.00

(Finland)
- ❏ Imperiumin Vastaisku (Empire Strikes Back) 15.00
- ❏ Jedin Paluu (Return of the Jedi) 15.00
- ❏ Mustan Lordin Paluu (Splinter of the Mind's Eye) 15.00
- ❏ Tahtien Sota (Star Wars) 15.00

(France)
- ❏ L'Empire Contre-Attaque, hardcover (Empire Strikes Back) 25.00
- ❏ L'Empire Contre-Attaque, paperback (Empire Strikes Back) 15.00
- ❏ L'Heritier de l'Empire (Heir to the Empire) 20.00
- ❏ La Bataille des Jedi (Dark Force Rising) 20.00
- ❏ La Guerre des Etoiles (Star Wars) [v1e1:65] 15.00
- ❏ Le Retour du Jedi (Return of the Jedi) 15.00
- ❏ Les Derniers Ommand (The Last Command) 20.00

(Japan)
- ❏ Return of the Jedi, Darth Vader on cover 25.00
- ❏ Return of the Jedi, droids on cover 25.00
- ❏ Return of the Jedi, hardcover 30.00

Books: Novels

- ❏ Splinter of the Mind's Eye [v1e1:65] 20.00
- ❏ Star Wars, hardcover [3:133] 20.00
- ❏ Star Wars, Hildebrandt cover 25.00
- ❏ Star Wars, space battle cover 20.00
- ❏ The Empire Strikes Back, hardcover [3:133] 20.00

(Korea)
- ❏ Heir to the Empire 25.00

(Netherlands)
- ❏ De terugkeer von de Jedi, illustrated (Return of the Jedi) 25.00
- ❏ De terugkeer von de Jedi, Jabba cover (Return of the Jedi) [v1e1:65] 20.00
- ❏ De terugkeer von de Jedi (Return of the Jedi) 20.00
- ❏ De Wraak van Han Solo (Han Solo's Revenge) 20.00
- ❏ Gevangenen van de Oerwoudplaneet (Splinter of the Mind's Eye) [v1e1:65] 20.00
- ❏ Han Solo in Stars' End [56-01] 20.00
- ❏ Strijd tussen de sterren, Falcon cockpit cover (Star Wars) [56-02] 25.00
- ❏ Strijd tussen de sterren (Star Wars) [v1e1:65] 20.00
- ❏ Wraak uit het heelal, Dagobah cover (Empire Strikes Back) [v1e1:65] 20.00
- ❏ Wraak uit het heelal (Empire Strikes Back) 20.00

(Poland)
- ❏ Atak Klonow 15.00
- ❏ Krysztalowa Gwiazda 15.00
- ❏ Przed Burza 15.00
- ❏ Stadkobiercy Mocy [56-03] 15.00
- ❏ Utracona Fortuna [56-04] 15.00
- ❏ Zagubieki 15.00

(Russia)
- ❏ Empire Strikes Back, hardcover 15.00
- ❏ Return of the Jedi, hardcover 15.00
- ❏ The Courtship of Princess Leia, paperback 20.00

(Singapore)
- ❏ Return of the Jedi, McQuarrie cover 30.00

(Spain)
- ❏ El Imperio Contra ataca, soft cover (Empire Strikes Back) 15.00
- ❏ El Ojo de la Mente 15.00
- ❏ El Retorno del Jedi (Return of the Jedi) 15.00
- ❏ La Guerra de las Galaxis, paperback (Star Wars) 15.00
- ❏ La Guerra de las Galaxis, soft cover (Star Wars) 15.00

(Asia)
- ❏ Heir to the Empire 20.00
- ❏ The Last Command 20.00

Arnoldo Mondadori (Italy)
- ❏ Guerre Stellari, hardcover (Star Wars) 20.00
- ❏ Guerre Stellari, soft cover with slipcase (Star Wars) 45.00
- ❏ Han Solo Guerriero Stellare 25.00
- ❏ L'imperio Colpisce Ancora, hardcover (Empire Strikes Back) 20.00

Ballantine
- ❏ Dark Lord: The Rise of Darth Vader 25.00
- ❏ Dark Nest I: The Joiner King [56-05] 10.00
- ❏ Dark Nest II: The Unseen Queen 10.00
- ❏ Dark Nest III: The Swarm War 10.00
- ❏ Empire Strikes Back, hardcover 16.00
- ❏ Empire Strikes Back, hardcover THX art [3:134] 12.00
- ❏ Empire Strikes Back, illustrated edition [56-06] 10.00
- ❏ Empire Strikes Back [v1e1:65] 10.00
- ❏ Empire Strikes Back, classic edition [v1e1:65] 10.00
- ❏ Empire Strikes Back, medallion art [v1e1:65] 10.00
- ❏ Empire Strikes Back, special edition art [v1e1:65] 10.00
- ❏ Han Solo Adventures, classic edition [3:134] 15.00
- ❏ Han Solo Adventures, compilation [56-07] 15.00
- ❏ Han Solo and the Lost Legacy, hardcover 15.00
- ❏ Han Solo and the Lost Legacy [4:43] 10.00
- ❏ Han Solo and the Lost Legacy, classic edition [56-08] 10.00
- ❏ Han Solo and the Lost Legacy, classic edition 10.00
- ❏ Han Solo at Stars' End [4:43] 15.00
- ❏ Han Solo at Stars' End, classic edition [56-09] 10.00
- ❏ Han Solo at Stars' End, hardcover [56-10] 15.00
- ❏ Han Solo's Revenge [4:32] 15.00
- ❏ Han Solo's Revenge, classic edition [56-11] 10.00
- ❏ Han Solo's Revenge, hardcover [56-12] 15.00
- ❏ Lando Calrissian Adventures, classic edition [3:134] 10.00
- ❏ Lando Calrissian Adventures compilation 15.00
- ❏ Lando Calrissian and the Flamewind of Oseon [56-13] 18.00
- ❏ Lando Calrissian and the Flamewind of Oseon, hardcover 35.00
- ❏ Lando Calrissian and the Mindharp of Sharu [56-14] 18.00
- ❏ Lando Calrissian and the Mindharp of Sharu, hardcover 35.00
- ❏ Lando Calrissian and the Starcave of Thonboka [v1e1:65] 18.00
- ❏ Lando Calrissian and the Starcave of Thonboka, hardcover 35.00
- ❏ Outbound Flight, hardcover 25.00
- ❏ Red Harvest [56-15] 10.00
- ❏ Return of the Jedi 10.00
- ❏ Return of the Jedi, classic edition [56-16] 10.00
- ❏ Return of the Jedi, hardcover, book club with dust jacket [v1e1:66] 20.00
- ❏ Return of the Jedi, hardcover, THX art [3:134] 12.00
- ❏ Return of the Jedi, illustrated edition [3:134] 10.00
- ❏ Return of the Jedi, medallion art [v1e1:66] 10.00
- ❏ Return of the Jedi, special edition art [56-17] 10.00
- ❏ Rogue Planet, paperback [56-18] 10.00
- ❏ Splinter of the Mind's Eye [4:43] 20.00
- ❏ Splinter of the Mind's Eye, classic edition [5:46] 10.00
- ❏ Splinter of the Mind's Eye, hardcover [56-19] 20.00
- ❏ Star Wars Trilogy with introduction by George Lucas, paperback 20.00
- ❏ Star Wars Trilogy, 25th Anniversary Collectors Edition, hardcover 35.00
- ❏ Star Wars Trilogy, hardcover special edition art, library with dust jacket [4:43] 10.00
- ❏ Star Wars Trilogy [v1e1:66] 15.00
- ❏ Star Wars Trilogy, boxed set [3:134] 30.00
- ❏ Star Wars Trilogy, classic edition [v1e1:66] 10.00
- ❏ Star Wars, 1st edition: 1976 (concept cover) [56-20] 100.00
- ❏ Star Wars, "Now a Spectacular Science-Fantasy Adventure From Twentieth Century Fox!" [56-21] 20.00
- ❏ Star Wars, "Over 5 Million in Print" red [v1e1:66] 15.00
- ❏ Star Wars, "Over 5 Million in Print" yellow [v1e1:66] 15.00
- ❏ Star Wars, "The Year's Best Movie" [v1e1:66] 18.00

Books: Novels

- ☐ Star Wars, classic edition [56-22] 10.00
- ☐ Star Wars, medallion art 10.00
- ☐ Star Wars, special edition art cover 10.00
- ☐ Star Wars, hardcover [3:134] 15.00
- ☐ Star Wars, hardcover 1976 [56-23] 95.00
- ☐ Star Wars, hardcover, gold dust jacket 80.00
- ☐ Star Wars, hardcover, THX art [3:134] 10.00
- ☐ The Exploits of Han Solo, boxed set [3:135] ... 25.00

Bantam Books

- ☐ Ambush at Corellia [3:135] 10.00
- ☐ Ambush at Corellia, signed [v1e1:66] 35.00
- ☐ Assault on Selonia [3:135] 10.00
- ☐ Before the Storm [v1e1:66] 10.00
- ☐ Black Fleet Crisis Trilogy, hardcover 25.00
- ☐ Bounty Hunter Wars: 1 Mandalorian Armor [v1e1:66] ... 15.00
- ☐ Bounty Hunter Wars: 2 Slave Ship [4:44] 15.00
- ☐ Bounty Hunter Wars: 3 Hard Merchandise [56-24] ... 15.00
- ☐ Champions of the Force [v1e1:66] 10.00
- ☐ Children of the Jedi, hardcover [v1e1:66] 25.00
- ☐ Children of the Jedi, hardcover, book club edition ... 12.00
- ☐ Children of the Jedi 10.00
- ☐ Corellian Trilogy, hardcover compilation [3:135] ... 15.00
- ☐ Corellian Trilogy, boxed set 25.00
- ☐ Courtship of Princess Leia, hardcover [56-25] ... 25.00
- ☐ Courtship of Princess Leia, hardcover, book club edition ... 20.00
- ☐ Courtship of Princess Leia [v1e1:66] 15.00
- ☐ Crystal Star, hardcover 25.00
- ☐ Crystal Star, hardcover, book club edition 10.00
- ☐ Crystal Star [v1e1:66] 10.00
- ☐ Dark Apprentice [3:135] 10.00
- ☐ Dark Force Rising, hardcover 25.00
- ☐ Dark Force Rising [3:135] 10.00
- ☐ Dark Force Rising, signed and numbered, hardcover with slipcover ... 175.00
- ☐ Darksaber, hardcover [56-26] 20.00
- ☐ Darksaber, hardcover, book club edition 15.00
- ☐ Darksaber [v1e1:66] 10.00
- ☐ Heir to the Empire [v1e1:66] 15.00
- ☐ Heir to the Empire, hardcover [56-27] 25.00
- ☐ Heir to the Empire, hardcover signed and numbered with slipcover ... 175.00
- ☐ Hutt Gambit 10.00
- ☐ I, Jedi [4:44] 10.00
- ☐ I, Jedi, hardcover [v1e1:66] 25.00
- ☐ Jedi Academy Trilogy, boxed set 20.00
- ☐ Jedi Academy Trilogy, hardcover compilation ... 30.00
- ☐ Jedi Search [3:135] 10.00
- ☐ Last Command [4:44] 15.00
- ☐ Last Command, hardcover 25.00
- ☐ Last Command, hardcover, signed and numbered with slipcover ... 175.00
- ☐ New Rebellion [4:44] 10.00
- ☐ New Rebellion, hardcover 25.00
- ☐ New Rebellion, hardcover, book club edition ... 20.00
- ☐ Paradise Snare [3:135] 10.00
- ☐ Planet of Twilight 10.00
- ☐ Planet of Twilight, hardcover [56-28] 25.00
- ☐ Planet of Twilight, hardcover book club edition [v1e1:66] ... 15.00
- ☐ Rebel Dawn [3:135] 10.00
- ☐ Shadows of the Empire [v1e1:66] 20.00
- ☐ Shadows of the Empire, hardcover [56-29] 25.00
- ☐ Shadows of the Empire, hardcover, book club edition ... 20.00
- ☐ Shield of Lies [3:135] 10.00
- ☐ Showdown at Centerpoint [3:136] 10.00
- ☐ Specter of the Past [56-30] 10.00
- ☐ Specter of the Past, hardcover 25.00
- ☐ Star Wars: Episode I The Phantom Menace, hardcover, Anakin Skywalker cover [v1e1:66] ... 25.00
- ☐ Star Wars: Episode I The Phantom Menace, hardcover, Darth Maul cover [v1e1:66] ... 25.00
- ☐ Star Wars: Episode I The Phantom Menace, hardcover, Obi-Wan Kenobi cover [56-31] ... 25.00
- ☐ Star Wars: Episode I The Phantom Menace, hardcover, Queen Amidala cover [56-32] ... 25.00
- ☐ Star Wars: Episode I The Phantom Menace, paperback, Darth Maul cover ... 10.00
- ☐ Tales from Jabba's Palace [v1e1:67] 10.00
- ☐ Tales from Mos Eisley Cantina [v1e1:67] 10.00
- ☐ Tales from the Empire [56-33] 10.00
- ☐ Tales from the New Republic [v1e1:67] 10.00
- ☐ Tales of the Bounty Hunters [56-34] 10.00
- ☐ Thrawn Trilogy, boxed set 40.00
- ☐ Truce at Bakura [v1e1:67] 10.00
- ☐ Truce at Bakura, hardcover 25.00
- ☐ Truce at Bakura, hardcover, book club edition ... 10.00
- ☐ Tyrant's Test 10.00
- ☐ Vision of the Future [3:136] 10.00
- ☐ Vision of the Future, hardcover [56-35] 25.00

X-Wing: Rogue Squadron.
- ☐ 1 Rogue Squadron [v1e1:67] 10.00
- ☐ 2 Wedge's Gamble [3:135] 10.00
- ☐ 3 The Krytos Trap [3:135] 10.00
- ☐ 4 The Bacta War [3:135] 10.00
- ☐ 5 Wraith Squadron [3:135] 10.00
- ☐ 6 Iron Fist [3:135] 10.00
- ☐ 7 Solo Command [3:135] 10.00
- ☐ 8 Isard's Revenge [3:135] 10.00
- ☐ 9 Starfighters of Adumar [3:135] 10.00

Bantam Books (Brazil)

- ☐ Ala-X [56-36] 10.00
- ☐ Amanecer Rebelde 10.00
- ☐ La Maniobra Hutt [56-37] 10.00

Blanvalet

- ☐ Episode I [3:136] 10.00
- ☐ Episode I, hardcover [56-38] 25.00

Cimino

- ☐ The Star Wars Diaries, 84 page with CD-ROM ... 30.00

Del Rey

- ☐ Allegiance 10.00
- ☐ Allegiance, hardcover [56-39] 25.00
- ☐ Cestus Deception 10.00
- ☐ Choices of One [56-40] 55.00
- ☐ Cloak of Deception 10.00
- ☐ Cloak of Deception, hardcover [v1e1:67] 26.00
- ☐ Clone Wars Gambit: Siege [v1e1:67] 12.00
- ☐ Coruscant Nights I: Jedi Twilight 10.00
- ☐ Coruscant Nights II: Street of Shadows 10.00
- ☐ Coruscant Nights III: Patterns of Force 10.00

Books: Novels

- ❏ Coruscant Nights: Jedi Twilight 10.00
- ❏ Crosscurrent 10.00
- ❏ Dark Lord: The Rise of Darth Vader [v1e1:67] 10.00
- ❏ Dark Lord: The Rise of Darth Vader, hardcover [56-41] 25.00
- ❏ Darth Bane: Path of Destruction [56-42] 25.00
- ❏ Darth Bane: Rule of Two 10.00
- ❏ Darth Bane: Rule of Two, hardcover [56-43] 20.00
- ❏ Darth Maul : Shadow Hunter [56-44] 10.00
- ❏ Darth Maul: Shadow Hunter, hardcover 25.00
- ❏ Death Star 10.00
- ❏ Death Star, hardcover 20.00
- ❏ Death troopers 15.00
- ❏ Death troopers, hardcover [56-45] 35.00
- ❏ Deceived [56-46] 25.00
- ❏ Dynasty of Evil [56-47] 15.00
- ❏ Episode I: The Phantom Menace autographed, slipcase, 5,000 produced 65.00
- ❏ Episode II autographed, exclusive to Suncoast [3:136] .. 75.00
- ❏ Episode II: Attack of the Clones [v1e1:67] 10.00
- ❏ Episode II: Attack of the Clones, hardcover [56-48] ...25.00
- ❏ Episode II: Attack of the Clones, hardcover [56-49] ...20.00
- ❏ Episode III autographed, silver foil Vader slipcase 140.00
- ❏ Episode III: Revenge of the Sith............................. 10.00
- ❏ Episode III: Revenge of the Sith, hardcover 25.00
- ❏ Heir To The Empire (20th Anniversary Ed.) [56-50] ... 25.00
- ❏ Imperial Commando 501st 10.00
- ❏ Jedi Trail 10.00
- ❏ Knight Errant 10.00
- ❏ Labyrinth of Evil 10.00
- ❏ Labyrinth of Evil, hardcover [56-51] 25.00
- ❏ Luke Skywalker: Shadows of Mindor [v1e1:67] 15.00
- ❏ Luke Skywalker: Shadows of Mindor, hardcover [56-52] ...35.00
- ❏ Mad About Star Wars 10.00
- ❏ Medstar I: Battle Surgeons [56-53] 10.00
- ❏ Medstar II: Jedi Healer 10.00
- ❏ Millennium Falcon, hardcover [56-54] 25.00
- ❏ No Prisoners 10.00
- ❏ Order 66 .... 10.00
- ❏ Order 66, hardcover [56-55] 25.00
- ❏ Outbound Flight [56-56] 10.00
- ❏ Path of Destruction, Darth Bane [56-57] 25.00
- ❏ Republic Commando: Hard Contact 15.00
- ❏ Republic Commando: Triple Zero [56-58] 15.00
- ❏ Republic Commando: True Colors [56-59] 16.00
- ❏ Revan, hardcover [56-60] 50.00
- ❏ Shatterpoint, hardcover [v1e1:67] 25.00
- ❏ Star Wars Trilogy, The First Ten Years [4:44] 20.00
- ❏ Star Wars: Episode I The Phantom Menace 10.00
- ❏ Survivor's Quest [56-61] 10.00
- ❏ Survivor's Quest, hardcover [v1e1:67] 25.00
- ❏ Tatooine Ghost [56-62] 10.00
- ❏ Tatooine Ghost, hardcover 25.00
- ❏ The Approaching Storm 10.00
- ❏ The Approaching Storm, hardcover [v1e1:67] 20.00
- ❏ The Clone Wars [56-63] 15.00
- ❏ The Complete Vader 60.00
- ❏ The Force Unleashed 10.00
- ❏ The Force Unleashed, hardcover [56-64] 25.00
- ❏ The Force Unleashed 2, hardcover 25.00
- ❏ The Old Republic: Fatal Alliance [56-65] 25.00
- ❏ The Prequel Trilogy 25.00
- ❏ Wild Space 15.00

Clone Wars novels.
- ❏ Jedi Trial [56-66] 15.00
- ❏ Yoda: Dark Rendezvous [56-67] 15.00
- ❏ Yoda: Dark Rendezvous, hardcover 25.00

Fate of the Jedi.
- ❏ 1 Outcast 10.00
- ❏ 1 Outcast, hardcover [v1e1:67] 25.00
- ❏ 2 Omen 10.00
- ❏ 2 Omen, hardcover [56-68] 25.00
- ❏ 3 Abyss [v1e1:68] 10.00
- ❏ 3 Abyss, hardcover [v1e1:67] 20.00
- ❏ 4 Backlash, hardcover [56-69] 20.00
- ❏ 5 Allies, hardcover [v1e1:68] 20.00
- ❏ 6 Vortex, hardcover 20.00
- ❏ 7 Conviction, hardcover [56-70] 25.00

Legacy of the Force.
- ❏ 1 Betrayal 10.00
- ❏ 1 Betrayal, hardcover [56-71] 25.00
- ❏ 2 Bloodlines 10.00
- ❏ 3 Tempest [56-72] 10.00
- ❏ 4 Exile [56-73] 10.00
- ❏ 5 Sacrifice, hardcover 25.00
- ❏ 6 Inferno 10.00
- ❏ 7 Fury 10.00
- ❏ 8 Revelation [v1e1:68] 10.00
- ❏ 9 Invincible 10.00
- ❏ 9 Invincible, hardcover [56-74] 25.00

New Jedi Order.
- ❏ 1 Vector Prime [4:44] 10.00
- ❏ 1 Vector Prime, hardcover [56-75] 25.00
- ❏ 2 Dark Tide I: Onslaught [56-76] 10.00
- ❏ 3 Dark Tide II: Ruin [v1e1:68] 10.00
- ❏ 4 Agents of Chaos 1 : Hero's Trial [56-77] 10.00
- ❏ 5 Agents of Chaos 2 : Jedi Eclipse [56-78] 10.00
- ❏ 6 Balance Point [56-79] 10.00
- ❏ 6 Balance Point, hardcover 25.00
- ❏ 7 Edge of Victory I: Conquest [v1e1:68] 10.00
- ❏ 8 Edge of Victory II: Rebirth [v1e1:68] 10.00
- ❏ 9 Star by Star 10.00
- ❏ 9 Star by Star, hardcover [56-80] 25.00
- ❏ 9 Star by Star, hardcover (misprinted timeline) 28.00
- ❏ 9 Star by Star, hardcover, book club edition 10.00
- ❏ 10 Dark Journey, paperback [v1e1:68] 10.00
- ❏ 11 Enemy Lines I: Rebel Dream [56-81] 10.00
- ❏ 12 Enemy Lines II: Rebel Stand [v1e1:68] 10.00
- ❏ 13 Traitor [v1e1:68] 10.00
- ❏ 14 Destiny's Way 10.00
- ❏ 14 Destiny's Way, hardcover [v1e1:68] 25.00
- ❏ 15 Force Heretic I: Remnant [v1e1:68] 10.00
- ❏ 16 Force Heretic II: Refugee [56-82] 10.00
- ❏ 17 Force Heretic III: Reunion 10.00
- ❏ 18 The Final Prophecy [56-83] 10.00
- ❏ 19 The Unifying Force 10.00
- ❏ 19 The Unifying Force, hardcover [56-84] 25.00
- ❏ Box Set: Vector Prime, Dark Tide I: Onslaught, Dark Tide II: Ruin 35.00

Editora Bruguera (Spain)
- ❏ Genes de Muerte 25.00
- ❏ Guerra Entre los Dioses 25.00
- ❏ Investigador Privado Siglo XXII [56-85] 25.00
- ❏ La Trampa de los Androides [56-86] 25.00
- ❏ Planeta Rebelde 25.00

Books: Novels

Editora Record (Brazil)
- ❏ Guerra nas Estrelas (Star Wars) 15.00
- ❏ O Imperio Contra-Ataca (Empire Strikes Back)............15.00
- ❏ O Returno de Jedi (Return of the Jedi) 15.00

Europa-America (Portugal)
- ❏ A Guerra das Estrelas, paperback (Star Wars) 15.00
- ❏ A Ressurreicao Da Force Negra [56-87] 15.00
- ❏ O Imperio Contra-Ataca, paperback (ESB) 15.00
- ❏ O Imperio Contra-Ataca, soft cover (ESB) 18.00
- ❏ O Regresso de Jedi, paperback (Return of the Jedi) 15.00
- ❏ O Regresso de Jedi, soft cover (Return of the Jedi) 18.00
- ❏ Treguas Em Bakura [v1e1:69] 15.00

FF
- ❏ Star Wars: A New Hope [3:137] 20.00
- ❏ Star Wars: Empire Strikes Back [v1e1:69] 20.00
- ❏ Star Wars: Return of the Jedi 20.00

Fleu Ve Noir
- ❏ Le defi du tyran [56-88] 10.00
- ❏ Un piege nomme Krytos..............10.00

Fredholis Forlag (Norway)
- ❏ Evighetens oye (Splinter of the Mind's Eye) 20.00
- ❏ Imperiet slar tilbake, paperback (ESB) 20.00
- ❏ Jedi Ridderen Vender Tilbake (Return of the Jedi) 20.00
- ❏ Stjerne Krigen, paperback (Star Wars) 20.00

Futura
- ❏ Return of the Jedi [56-89] 15.00
- ❏ Return of the Jedi, junior edition, paperback 10.00

G.K. Hall and Co.
- ❏ Specter of the Past, large print [3:137] 15.00

Granada Publishing, Ltd. (UK)
- ❏ THX 1138, paperback, from the creator of Star Wars [56-90] 12.00

Guild America Books
Hardcover story re-release.
- ❏ Enemy Lines [3:137] 25.00
- ❏ Star Wars Tales 25.00
- ❏ The Corellian Trilogy [3:137] 20.00

Heyne (Germany)
- ❏ Der Hinterhalt [56-91] 15.00
- ❏ Der Kristallstern 15.00
- ❏ Der Pakt von Bakura [56-92] 15.00
- ❏ Entfuhrung nach Dathomir [v1e1:69] 15.00
- ❏ Palpatines Auge [3:137] 10.00
- ❏ Schatten Der Vergangenheit [3:137] 15.00
- ❏ Schatten Des Imperiums (Shadows of the Empire) 15.00
- ❏ Showdown auf Centerpoint [56-93] 15.00

Kozmosz Konyvek (Hungary)
- ❏ A Birodalom visszavag (Empire Strikes Back) 15.00
- ❏ A Jedi visszater (Return of the Jedi) 15.00
- ❏ Csillagok haboruja (Star Wars) 15.00

LucasBooks (Japan)
- ❏ Cloak of Deception 10.00
- ❏ Shadow Hunter [56-94] 10.00
- ❏ The Approaching Storm [56-95] 10.00
- ❏ Truce at Bakura [56-96] 10.00

MacDonald Film Tie-In
- ❏ Return of the Jedi, hardcover 15.00

Martinez Roca
- ❏ El Courtejo de la Princesa Leia [3:137] 10.00
- ❏ Estrella de Cristal [56-97] 10.00
- ❏ La Nueva Rebelion [v1e1:69] 10.00
- ❏ La Tregua de Bakura [3:137] 10.00
- ❏ Los Hijos de los Jedi [3:137] 10.00
- ❏ Sombras del Imperio [3:137] 10.00

Triloga de Academia Jedi.
- ❏ Campeones de la Fuerza [56-98] 10.00
- ❏ El Dicipulo de la Fuerza Oscura [3:137] 10.00

Triloga de Corellia.
- ❏ Ajuste de Cuentas en Centralia [3:137] 10.00

Trilogia de la Flota Negra.
- ❏ Escudo de Mentiras [3:137] 10.00
- ❏ La Prueba del Tirano [3:137] 10.00

Minotaur (Yugoslavia)
- ❏ Zvezdani Ratovi (Star Wars) 15.00

MsfX
- ❏ Aanval op Selonia [3:137] 15.00
- ❏ De droom van de Jedi [56-99] 15.00
- ❏ De Jedi Academe 10.00
- ❏ De Macht van de Duistere Kant [v1e1:69] 15.00
- ❏ De woeste planeet (Rogue Planet) 15.00
- ❏ Erfgenaam van het Rijk (Hier to the Empire) 15.00
- ❏ Het Laatste Bevel [56-100] 15.00
- ❏ Hinderlaag op Corellia [3:138] 15.00
- ❏ Le spectre Du Passe' (Specter of the Past) 10.00
- ❏ Wapenstilstand bij Bakura 10.00

Orion Books (UK)
- ❏ Star Warped (parody) [56-101] 15.00

Pocket
- ❏ Assaut sur Solonia [v1e1:69] 15.00
- ❏ Bras de fer sur Cernterpoint [3:138] 15.00
- ❏ L'etoile de cristal [56-102] 15.00
- ❏ La bataille des Jedi 15.00
- ❏ Traquenard sur Corellia [3:138] 15.00

Random House
- ❏ Jedi Trial [56-103] 10.00
- ❏ Labyrinth of Evil [v1e1:69] 15.00
- ❏ Rogue Planet [3:138] 15.00
- ❏ Shatterpoint [56-104] 10.00
- ❏ Star Wars Trilogy, compilation [3:138] 15.00
- ❏ The Cetus Deception [56-105] 15.00
- ❏ The Ruins of Dantooine [56-106] 10.00

Roman Presses de la Citie
- ❏ L'Etoile De Cristal [3:138] 15.00
- ❏ La Nouvelle Rebellion [3:138] 15.00
- ❏ Le Sabre Noir [56-107] 15.00

Scholastic
- ❏ Jedi Quest—Path to Truth [v1e1:69] 10.00
- ❏ Legacy of the Jedi [56-108] 10.00

Books: Novels

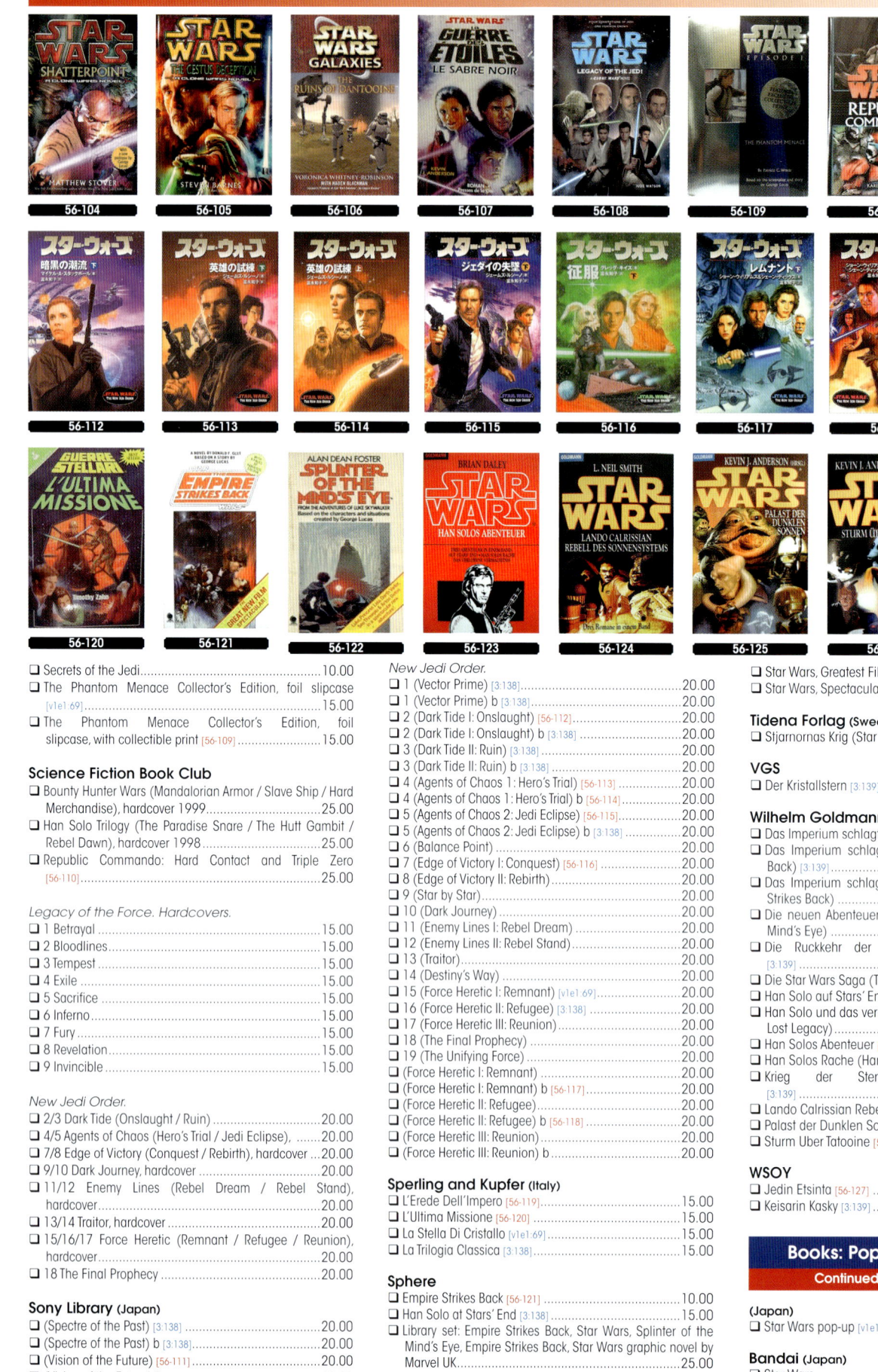

- ❑ Secrets of the Jedi..................................10.00
- ❑ The Phantom Menace Collector's Edition, foil slipcase [v1e1:69] 15.00
- ❑ The Phantom Menace Collector's Edition, foil slipcase, with collectible print [56-109] 15.00

Science Fiction Book Club
- ❑ Bounty Hunter Wars (Mandalorian Armor / Slave Ship / Hard Merchandise), hardcover 1999................25.00
- ❑ Han Solo Trilogy (The Paradise Snare / The Hutt Gambit / Rebel Dawn), hardcover 1998 ....25.00
- ❑ Republic Commando: Hard Contact and Triple Zero [56-110]..25.00

Legacy of the Force. Hardcovers.
- ❑ 1 Betrayal 15.00
- ❑ 2 Bloodlines 15.00
- ❑ 3 Tempest 15.00
- ❑ 4 Exile 15.00
- ❑ 5 Sacrifice 15.00
- ❑ 6 Inferno 15.00
- ❑ 7 Fury 15.00
- ❑ 8 Revelation 15.00
- ❑ 9 Invincible 15.00

New Jedi Order.
- ❑ 2/3 Dark Tide (Onslaught / Ruin) 20.00
- ❑ 4/5 Agents of Chaos (Hero's Trial / Jedi Eclipse), ...20.00
- ❑ 7/8 Edge of Victory (Conquest / Rebirth), hardcover 20.00
- ❑ 9/10 Dark Journey, hardcover 20.00
- ❑ 11/12 Enemy Lines (Rebel Dream / Rebel Stand), hardcover 20.00
- ❑ 13/14 Traitor, hardcover 20.00
- ❑ 15/16/17 Force Heretic (Remnant / Refugee / Reunion), hardcover 20.00
- ❑ 18 The Final Prophecy 20.00

Sony Library (Japan)
- ❑ (Spectre of the Past) [3:138] 20.00
- ❑ (Spectre of the Past) b [3:138] 20.00
- ❑ (Vision of the Future) [56-111] 20.00
- ❑ (Vision of the Future) b [3:138] 20.00

New Jedi Order.
- ❑ 1 (Vector Prime) [3:138] 20.00
- ❑ 1 (Vector Prime) b [3:138] 20.00
- ❑ 2 (Dark Tide I: Onslaught) [56-112]..........20.00
- ❑ 2 (Dark Tide I: Onslaught) b [3:138] 20.00
- ❑ 3 (Dark Tide II: Ruin) [3:138] 20.00
- ❑ 3 (Dark Tide II: Ruin) b [3:138] 20.00
- ❑ 4 (Agents of Chaos 1: Hero's Trial) [56-113] ...20.00
- ❑ 4 (Agents of Chaos 1: Hero's Trial) b [56-114] ..20.00
- ❑ 5 (Agents of Chaos 2: Jedi Eclipse) [56-115] 20.00
- ❑ 5 (Agents of Chaos 2: Jedi Eclipse) b [3:138] ...20.00
- ❑ 6 (Balance Point) 20.00
- ❑ 7 (Edge of Victory I: Conquest) [56-116] ..20.00
- ❑ 8 (Edge of Victory II: Rebirth) 20.00
- ❑ 9 (Star by Star) 20.00
- ❑ 10 (Dark Journey) 20.00
- ❑ 11 (Enemy Lines I: Rebel Dream) 20.00
- ❑ 12 (Enemy Lines II: Rebel Stand) 20.00
- ❑ 13 (Traitor)...20.00
- ❑ 14 (Destiny's Way) 20.00
- ❑ 15 (Force Heretic I: Remnant) [v1e1:69] ..20.00
- ❑ 16 (Force Heretic II: Refugee) [3:138] 20.00
- ❑ 17 (Force Heretic III: Reunion) 20.00
- ❑ 18 (The Final Prophecy) 20.00
- ❑ 19 (The Unifying Force) 20.00
- ❑ (Force Heretic I: Remnant) 20.00
- ❑ (Force Heretic I: Remnant) b [56-117] 20.00
- ❑ (Force Heretic II: Refugee) 20.00
- ❑ (Force Heretic II: Refugee) b [56-118] 20.00
- ❑ (Force Heretic III: Reunion) 20.00
- ❑ (Force Heretic III: Reunion) b 20.00

Sperling and Kupfer (Italy)
- ❑ L'Erede dell'Impero [56-119].....................15.00
- ❑ L'Ultima Missione [56-120] 15.00
- ❑ La Stella Di Cristallo [v1e1:69] 15.00
- ❑ La Trilogia Classica [3:138] 15.00

Sphere
- ❑ Empire Strikes Back [56-121] 10.00
- ❑ Han Solo at Stars' End [3:138] 15.00
- ❑ Library set: Empire Strikes Back, Splinter of the Mind's Eye, Empire Strikes Back, Star Wars graphic novel by Marvel UK...............................25.00
- ❑ Splinter of the Mind's Eye [56-122] 15.00

- ❑ Star Wars, Greatest Film of the Century......15.00
- ❑ Star Wars, Spectacular Motion Picture [3:139] ...15.00

Tidena Forlag (Sweden)
- ❑ Stjarnornas Krig (Star Wars) 20.00

VGS
- ❑ Der Kristallstern [3:139]............................15.00

Wilhelm Goldmann (Germany)
- ❑ Das Imperium schlagt zuruck (Empire Strikes Back) ...10.00
- ❑ Das Imperium schlagt zuruck, 2nd cover (Empire Strikes Back) [3:139] 15.00
- ❑ Das Imperium schlagt zuruck, 2nd cover revised (Empire Strikes Back) 15.00
- ❑ Die neuen Abenteuer des Luke Skywalker, (Splinter of the Mind's Eye) 20.00
- ❑ Die Ruckkehr der Jedi-Ritter (Return of the Jedi) [3:139] 10.00
- ❑ Die Star Wars Saga (Trilogy) [3:139] 20.00
- ❑ Han Solo auf Stars' End 15.00
- ❑ Han Solo und das verlorene Vermachtnis (Han Solo and the Lost Legacy) 15.00
- ❑ Han Solos Abenteuer [56-123] 15.00
- ❑ Han Solos Rache (Han Solo's Revenge)....15.00
- ❑ Krieg der Sterne, paperback (Star Wars) [3:139] 10.00
- ❑ Lando Calrissian Rebell Des Sonnensystems [56-124] ..20.00
- ❑ Palast der Dunklen Sonnen [56-125] 15.00
- ❑ Sturm Uber Tatooine [56-126]..................15.00

WSOY
- ❑ Jedin Etsinta [56-127] 20.00
- ❑ Keisarin Kasky [3:139] 20.00

Books: Pop-Up / Action / Flap
Continued in Volume 3, Page 91

(Japan)
- ❑ Star Wars pop-up [v1e1:70]......................45.00

Bandai (Japan)
- ❑ Star Wars 30.00

Books: Science Adventures

 57-01
 57-02
 57-03
 57-04
 57-05
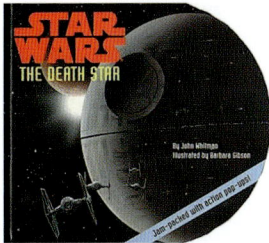 57-06
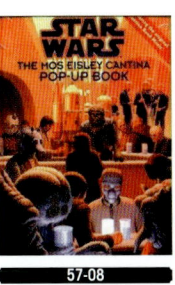 57-07
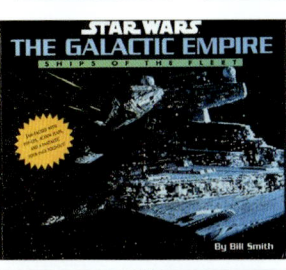 57-08
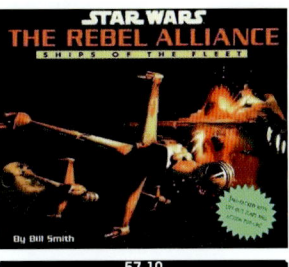 57-09
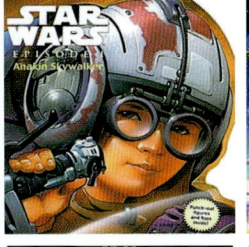 57-10
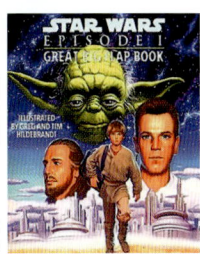 57-11
 57-12
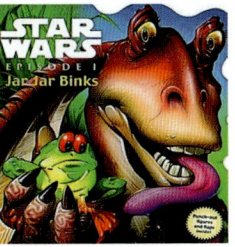 57-13
 57-14
 57-15
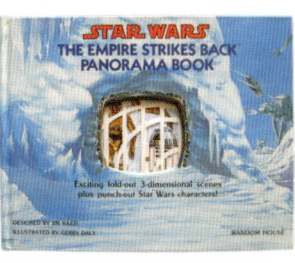 57-16
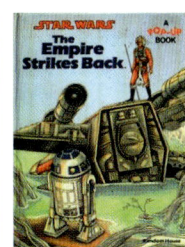 57-17
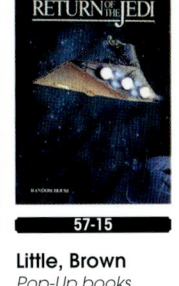 57-18

Collins
- Star Wars Pop-Up 25.00

Dark Horse Comics
- Battle of the Bounty Hunters Pop-Up [v1e1:70] 35.00

Editorial Roma (Spain)
- Droids, Capturados 45.00
- Droids, La Desaparacion de C-3PO [57-01] 45.00
- Droids, Las Adventuras de Mungo Babab [57-02] 45.00
- Droids, Trigon [57-03] 45.00
- Ewoks, Amenaza sobre la Aldea 45.00
- Ewoks, Asha 45.00
- Ewoks, Fuego en el Bosque 45.00
- Ewoks, Latara 45.00

Flammarion (France)
- La Guerre des Etoiles (Star Wars) 25.00

Fun Works
- Heroes in Hiding [57-04] 10.00
- Star Wars, shimmer [57-05] 10.00

Flip books. Classic trilogy mini-series.
- Empire Strikes Back [2:111] 10.00
- Return of the Jedi [2:111] 10.00
- Star Wars [v1e1:70] 10.00

Grosset and Dunlap
- Heroes 25.00

Little, Brown
Pop-Up books.
- Death Star [57-06] 20.00
- Jabba's Palace [57-07] 20.00
- Millennium Falcon [4:46] 25.00
- Mos Eisley Cantina [57-08] 20.00

Ships of the Fleet series.
- Galactic Empire [57-09] 20.00
- Rebel Alliance [57-10] 20.00

Orchard Books
- Star Wars: A Pop-Up Guide to the Galaxy 35.00
- Star Wars: A Pop-Up Guide to the Galaxy, signed, 500 produced, individually numbered 150.00

Random House
- Anakin Skywalker [57-11] 10.00
- Episode I great big flap book [57-12] 15.00
- Han Solo's Rescue [57-13] 20.00
- Han Solo's Rescue, hardcover 15.00
- Jar Jar Binks [57-14] 10.00
- Return of the Jedi pop-up, shuttle Tydirium cover [3:139] 20.00
- Return of the Jedi pop-up, star destroyer cover [57-15] 20.00
- Star Wars Lift the Flap [57-16] 20.00
- Star Wars Pop-Up [v1e1:70] 18.00
- The Empire Strikes Back Panorama [57-17] 25.00
- The Empire Strikes Back Pop-Up [57-18] 20.00
- The Ewoks Save The Day [4:40] 30.00

Sperling and Kupfer (Italy)
- Guerre Stellari (Star Wars) 15.00

Books: Poster
Continued in Volume 3, Page 91

DK Publishing
- Star Wars Blueprints: Rebel Edition 15.00

Kellogg's
- Revenge of the Sith, pull-out poster books, 4 posters [58-01] 10.00

Scholastic
Pull-out poster books.
- Empire Strikes Back [58-02] 16.00
- Return of the Jedi [58-03] 16.00
- Star Wars [58-04] 16.00

Trends International Corp.
- Clone Wars, 4 posters [58-05] 15.00

Books: Science Adventures

Scholastic
- Emergency in Escape Pod Four [59-01] 10.00
- Emergency in Escape Pod Four (pages 45-46 missing, pages 55-56 appear twice) 10.00
- Journey Across Planet-X [59-02] 10.00

 58-01
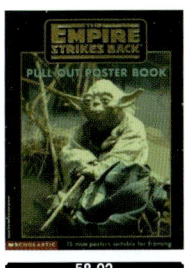 58-02
 58-03
 58-04
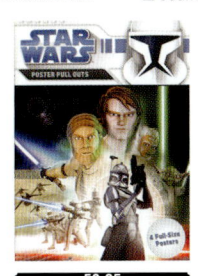 58-05
 59-01
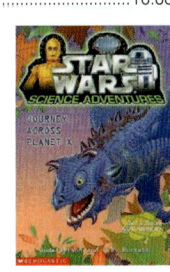 59-02

Books: Scripts

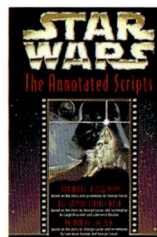 60-01
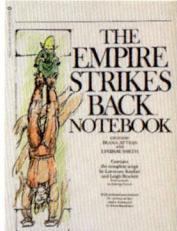 60-02
 60-03
 60-04
 60-05
 60-06
 60-07
 60-08

Books: Scripts

(Japan)
Screenplays.
- Empire Strikes Back 25.00
- Return of the Jedi 25.00
- Star Wars 25.00

Ballantine
- The Annotated Scripts [60-01] 25.00
- The Empire Strikes Back Notebook [60-02] 25.00

National Public Radio Dramatizations.
- Empire Strikes Back [60-03] 25.00
- Return of the Jedi 25.00
- Star Wars 25.00

D.S.P. Publishing, Inc.
- Star Wars Trilogy Original Movie Scripts Collector's Edition [60-04] 40.00

Del Rey
Complete Script with Special Edition Scenes.
- Empire Strikes Back [v1e1:71] 25.00
- Return of the Jedi [v1e1:71] 25.00
- Star Wars [v1e1:71] 25.00

Illustrated Screenplays.
- Empire Strikes Back [v1e1:71] 25.00
- Episode I: The Phantom Menace [60-05] 25.00
- Return of the Jedi [60-06] 25.00
- Star Wars [v1e1:71] 25.00

Ebury Press
- Episode I: The Phantom Menace, the Illustrated Screenplay [v1e1:71] 25.00

LucasBooks
- Episode I: The Phantom Menace [v1e1:71] 20.00

LucasBooks (Japan)
- Episode I: The Phantom Menace, the Illustrated Screenplay [60-07] 20.00

Premiere
- Return of the Jedi 25.00
- Return of the Jedi, recalled for typographical errors 40.00
- Star Wars [60-08] 25.00
- Star Wars Trilogy, boxed set 50.00
- The Empire Strikes Back 25.00
- The Empire Strikes Back, recalled for typographical errors 40.00

Virgin Books (UK)
Complete illustrated scripts.
- A New Hope 25.00
- Empire Strikes Back 25.00
- Return of the Jedi 25.00

Books: Star Wars Adventures

Scholastic
Episode I: The Phantom Menace.
- #1 Search for the Lost Jedi [61-01] 10.00
- #1 Game book 10.00
- #2 The Bartokk Assassins [v1e1:71] 10.00
- #2 Game book 10.00
- #3 The Fury of Darth Maul [61-02] 10.00
- #3 Game book 10.00
- #4 Jedi Emergency [61-03] 10.00
- #4 Game book 10.00
- #5 The Ghostling Children [v1e1:71] 10.00
- #5 Game book 10.00
- #6 The Hunt for Anakin Skywalker [v1e1:71] 10.00
- #6 Game book 10.00
- #7 Capture Arawynne [61-04] 10.00
- #7 Game book 10.00
- #8 Trouble on Tatooine [v1e1:71] 10.00
- #8 Game book 10.00
- #9 Rescue in the Core [61-05] 10.00
- #9 Game book 10.00
- #10 The Festival of Warriors [61-06] 10.00
- #10 Game book 10.00
- #11 Pirates From Beyond the Sea 10.00
- #11 Game book 10.00
- #12 The Bongo Rally [v1e1:71] 10.00
- #12 Game book 10.00
- #13 Danger on Naboo [61-07] 10.00
- #13 Game book 10.00
- #14 Pod Race to Freedom [61-08] 10.00
- #14 Game book 10.00
- #15 The Final Battle 10.00
- #15 Game book 10.00

Episode II: Attack of the Clones.
- #1 Hunt the Sunrunner [v1e1:72] 10.00
- #1 Game book 12.00
- #2 The Cavern of Screaming Skulls [61-09] 10.00
- #2 Game book 12.00
- #3 The Hostage Princess [61-10] 10.00
- #3 Game book 12.00
- #4 Jango Fett vs. The Razor Eaters [61-11] 10.00
- #4 Game book 12.00
- #5 The Shape-Shifter Strikes [61-12] 10.00
- #5 Game book 12.00
- #6 The Warlords of Balmorra [61-13] ...10.00
- #6 Game book 12.00
- #7 The Ghostling Children [61-14] 10.00
- #7 Game book 12.00
- #8 The Hunt for Anakin Skywalker [61-15] 10.00
- #8 Game book 12.00
- #9 Capture Arawynne [v1e1:72] 10.00
- #9 Game book 12.00
- #10 Trouble on Tatooine [61-16] 10.00
- #10 Game book 12.00
- #11 Danger on Naboo [v1e1:72] 8.00
- #11 Game book 8.00
- #12 Pod Race to Freedom [v1e1:72] 8.00
- #12 Game book 8.00
- #13 The Final Battle [v1e1:72] 8.00
- #13 Game book 8.00

Books: Story
Continued in Volume 3, Page 91

- Beyond the Stars, Tales of Adventure in Time and Space 8.00
- Crossfire [62-01] 8.00
- Ewoks Annual [62-02] 20.00
- The Maverick Moon, UK cover [62-03] 20.00

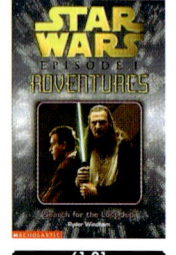 61-01
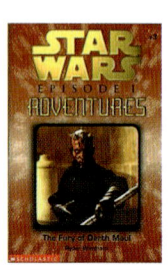 61-02
 61-03
 61-04
 61-05
 61-06
 61-07
 61-08

 61-09
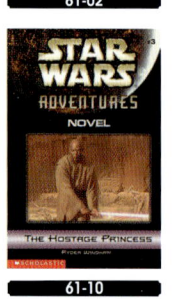 61-10
 61-11
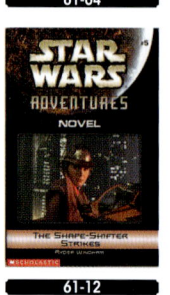 61-12
 61-13
 61-14
 61-15
 61-16

Books: Story

 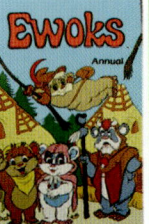 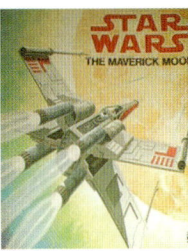     

62-01 | 62-02 | 62-03 | 62-04 | 62-05 | 62-06 | 62-07 | 62-08

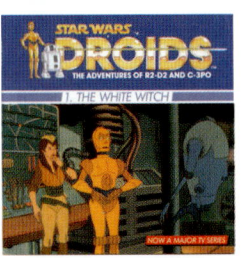 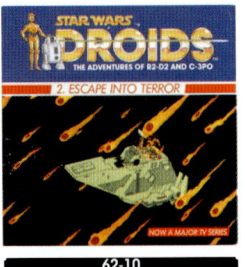 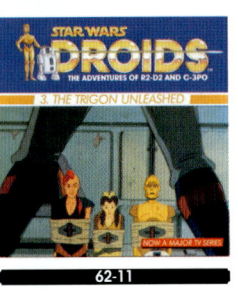 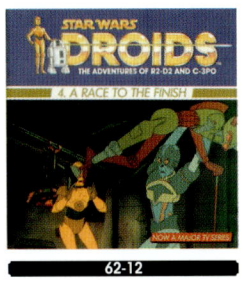 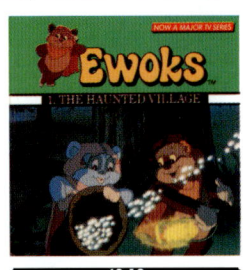

62-09 | 62-10 | 62-11 | 62-12 | 62-13

20th Century Fox
- ❏ Caravan of Courage [62-04] 35.00

Armada (UK)
- ❏ The Star Wars Storybook 25.00

Ballantine
- ❏ Star Wars Album 20.00
- ❏ The Star Wars Storybook, hardcover 20.00

Bandai (Japan)
- ❏ The Star Wars storybook [62-05] 25.00

Brown Watson
- ❏ Annual number 1, hardcover [62-06] 35.00

Cartwheel Books
- ❏ Spaceships 20.00

Chronicle Books
- ❏ The Queen's Amulet [62-07] 15.00

Mini hardcover books.
- ❏ Attack of the Clones 10.00
- ❏ Empire Strikes Back [1:78] 10.00
- ❏ Return of the Jedi [1:78] 10.00
- ❏ Revenge of the Sith 10.00
- ❏ Star Wars [v1e1:72] 10.00
- ❏ The Phantom Menace [62-08] 10.00

Collins
- ❏ Star Wars Storybook with dust jacket 25.00

DK Publishing
- ❏ Inside the Death Star 15.00
- ❏ Join the Rebels, hardcover 15.00

Dragon Picture Books (UK)
Droids series.
- ❏ #1 The White Witch [62-09] 35.00
- ❏ #2 Escape into Terror [62-10] 35.00
- ❏ #3 The Trigon Unleashed [62-11] 35.00
- ❏ #4 A Race To The Finish [62-12] 35.00

Ewoks series.
- ❏ #1 The Haunted Village [62-13] 35.00
- ❏ #2 To Save Deej [62-14] 35.00
- ❏ #3 Sun Star Against Shadow Stone [62-15] 35.00
- ❏ #4 Wicket's Wagon [62-16] 35.00

Fernandez Editores
- ❏ El Imperio Contraataca [62-17] 15.00
- ❏ El Regreso Del Jedi [62-18] 15.00
- ❏ Una Nueva Esperanza [62-19] 15.00

 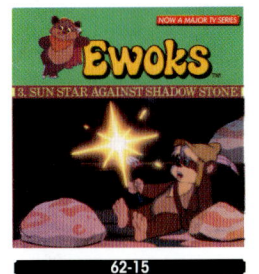 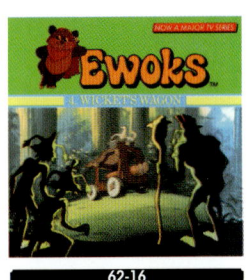 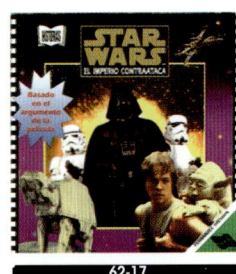 

62-14 | 62-15 | 62-16 | 62-17 | 62-18

62-19 | 62-20 | 62-21 | 62-22 | 62-23

    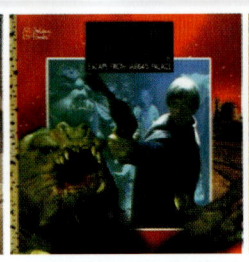  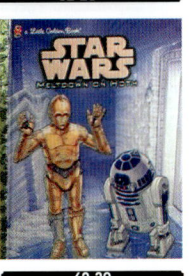

62-24 | 62-25 | 62-26 | 62-27 | 62-28 | 62-29 | 62-30

Books: Story

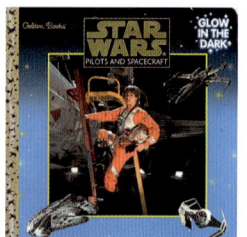 62-31
 62-32
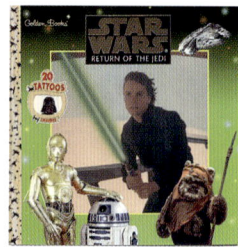 62-33
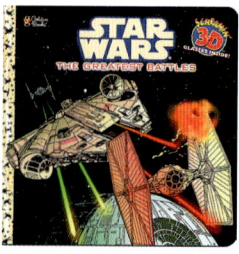 62-34
 62-35
 62-36

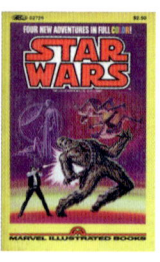 62-37
 62-38
 62-39
 62-40
 62-41
 62-42

Fun Works
Toy bound into spine.
- Darth Vader's Mission: The Search for the Secret Plans [62-20] 20.00
- Han Solo's Rescue Mission [62-21] 20.00
- Luke Skywalker's Race Against Time [62-22] 20.00
- R2-D2's Mission: A Little Heroes Journey [62-23] 20.00

Futura
- Return of the Jedi, "Special Junior Edition" [62-24] 15.00

Golden Books
- A Droid's Tale sound story [62-25] 25.00
- A New Hope [v1e1:73] 10.00
- A New Hope with tattoos [62-26] 15.00
- Adventure in Beggar's Canyon [62-27] 15.00
- Empire Strikes Back [v1e1:73] 10.00
- Empire Strikes Back with tattoos [3:141] 15.00
- Escape from Jabba's Palace [62-28] 20.00
- Journey to Mos Eisley [62-29] 20.00
- Meltdown on Hoth [62-30] 15.00
- Pilots and Spacecraft with glow-in-the-dark pages [62-31] 15.00
- Rebel Heroes and Galactic Villains [62-32] 15.00
- Return of the Jedi 10.00
- Return of the Jedi (with tattoos) [62-33] 15.00
- Star Wars: The Greatest Battles, includes 3D glasses [62-34] 20.00
- The Hoth Adventure [62-35] 20.00

Grosset and Dunlap
- Jar Jar's Big Day 10.00
- Meet Ahsoka Tano 20.00
- R2-D2's Adventure 10.00
- The Clone Wars 10.00

Keibunsha
- Return of the Jedi picture book 25.00

Landoll
- Star Bores, Looney Toons 10.00

Leadsha (Japan)
- Star Wars: Empire Strikes Back, Perfect Memory Deluxe 2 [62-36] 35.00

Marvel Books
- Return of the Jedi Storybook [62-37] 15.00
- Star Wars, Four New Adventures [62-38] 15.00
- World of Fire, Star Wars 2 [1:78] 25.00

Phidal
- Anakin a la conquete de la liberte [62-39] 15.00
- Attention, Jar Jar [62-40] 15.00
- Je suis un droide [62-41] 15.00
- Je suis un Jedi [62-42] 15.00

Plaza Joven Ediciones (Spain)
Children's books on oversized character backer cards.
- Droids: La Bruja Blanca [62-43] 65.00
- Droids: Mission Especial [62-44] 65.00
- Droids: Vacaciones en Tammuz-All [62-45] 65.00
- Ewoks: Kinesa y los korrinas [62-46] 65.00
- Ewoks: La desparicion de Latara [62-47] 65.00
- Ewoks: La fiesta de las maravilas [62-48] 65.00
- Ewoks: Wicket va de pesca 65.00

Publications International
Play-a-sound books.
- Episode I [62-49] 15.00
- Episode I, R2-D2 ....15.00
- Revenge of the Sith [62-50] 15.00
- Star Wars [62-51] 15.00

Random House
- Anakin: Apprentice [62-52] 8.00
- Attack of the Clones Movie Storybook [v1e1:73] 15.00
- Battle in the Arena [62-53] 15.00
- Droid Dilemma 20.00
- Droids 20.00
- Empire Strikes Back Storybook, hardcover [v1e1:73] 15.00
- Empire Strikes Back, classic [62-54] 10.00
- EPI: The Phantom Menace Movie Storybook [62-55] 10.00
- Escape from the Monster Ship [62-56] 20.00
- Fuzzy as an Ewok [62-57] 25.00
- How the Ewoks Saved the Trees 15.00
- How the Ewoks Saved the Trees, hardcover [62-58] 25.00
- I am a Bounty Hunter [62-59] 10.00
- I am a Jedi Apprentice [62-60] 10.00
- I am a Pilot [62-61] 10.00

 62-43
 62-44
 62-45
 62-46
 62-47
 62-48

 62-49
 62-50
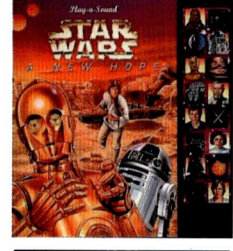 62-51
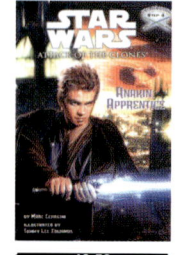 62-52
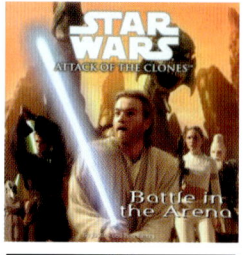 62-53
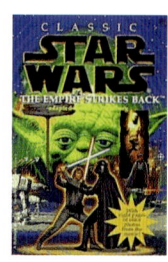 62-54

Books: Story

  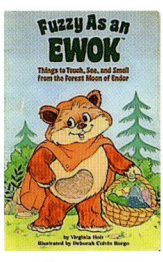 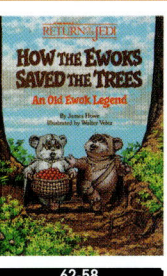 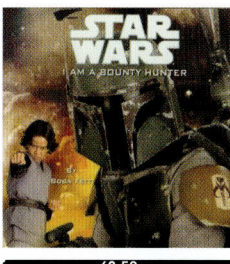 

62-55   62-56   62-57   62-58   62-59   62-60

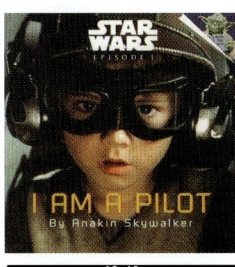    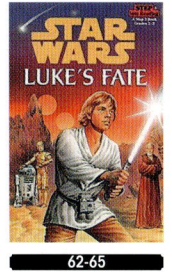 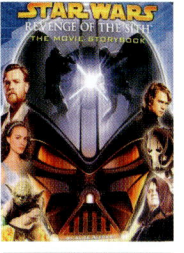 

62-61   62-62   62-63   62-64   62-65   62-66   62-67

- ❏ I am a Queen [62-62] 10.00
- ❏ Jango Fett: Bounty Hunter [62-63] 10.00
- ❏ Luke's Fate [5:50] 10.00
- ❏ Luke's Fate, "Brand New" on cover [62-64] 10.00
- ❏ Luke's Fate, brown cover [62-65] 10.00
- ❏ Return of the Jedi Storybook, hardcover 15.00
- ❏ Revenge of the Sith movie storybook [62-66] 10.00
- ❏ School Days, Ewoks 20.00
- ❏ Shiny as a Droid [62-67] 20.00
- ❏ Skywalker Family Album [v1e1:74] 15.00
- ❏ Star Wars Storybook Trilogy 10 year anniversary [62-68] ... 20.00
- ❏ Star Wars Storybook, hardcover 15.00
- ❏ The Adventures of R2-D2 and C-3PO 25.00
- ❏ The Adventures of Teebo [62-69] 25.00
- ❏ The Baby Ewoks' Picnic Surprise [62-70] 25.00
- ❏ The Ewok Who Was Afraid [62-71] 30.00

- ❏ The Ewoks and the Lost Children [62-72] 20.00
- ❏ The Ewoks Join the Fight [62-73] 20.00
- ❏ The Ewoks' Hang-Gliding Adventure [62-74] 20.00
- ❏ The Lost Prince 20.00
- ❏ The Lost Prince, hardcover [62-75] 25.00
- ❏ The Maverick Moon [62-76] 20.00
- ❏ The Mystery of the Rebellious Robot [62-77] 20.00
- ❏ The Pirates of Tarnoonga [62-78] 25.00
- ❏ The Red Ghost [62-79] 25.00
- ❏ The Ring, The Witch, and the Crystal [62-80] ... 25.00
- ❏ The Shadow Stone [62-81] 25.00
- ❏ The White Witch - A Droid Adventure [62-82] .. 25.00
- ❏ The Wookiee Storybook [62-83] 15.00
- ❏ Three Cheers for Kneesaa [62-84] 20.00
- ❏ Wicket and the Dandelion Warriors [62-85] 25.00
- ❏ Wicket Finds a Way [62-86] 20.00
- ❏ Wicket Goes Fishing [62-87] 20.00

Star Wars storybook with foil stickers.
- ❏ Anakin's Race for Freedom [v1e1:75] 15.00
- ❏ I am a Droid [v1e1:75] 15.00
- ❏ I am a Jedi [v1e1:75] 15.00
- ❏ Watch Out Jar Jar! [v1e1:75] 15.00

Step-Up Movie Adventures.
- ❏ Return of the Jedi [62-88] 15.00
- ❏ Star Wars [v1e1:75] 15.00
- ❏ The Empire Strikes Back [v1e1:75] 15.00

Step-Up Movie Adventures 1995.
- ❏ Return of the Jedi [5:51] 10.00
- ❏ Star Wars [5:51] 10.00
- ❏ The Empire Strikes Back [5:51] 10.00

Scholastic
- ❏ Episode I: The Phantom Menace [62-89] 10.00

 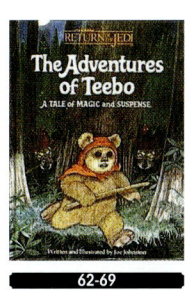    

62-68   62-69   62-70   62-71   62-72   62-73

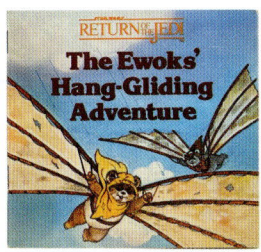 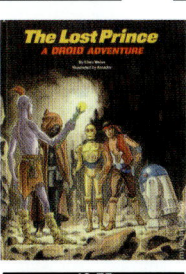   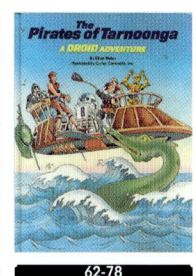 

62-74   62-75   62-76   62-77   62-78   62-79

  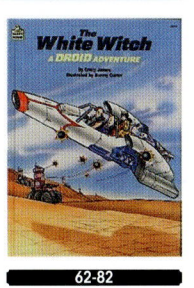   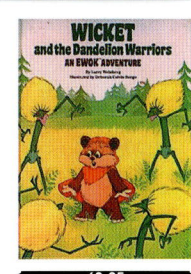

62-80   62-81   62-82   62-83   62-84   62-85

Books: Story

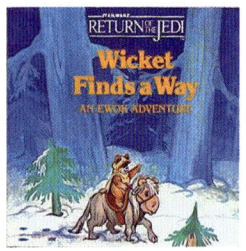  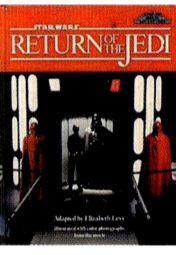 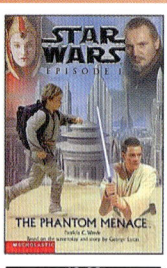   

62-86   62-87   62-88   62-89   62-90   62-91   62-92

  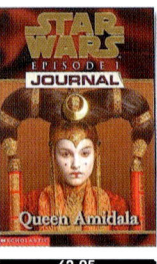 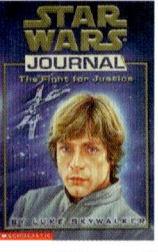 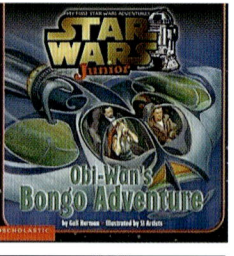  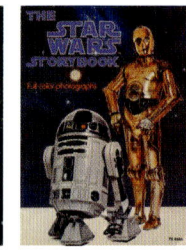

62-93   62-94   62-95   62-96   62-97   62-98   62-99

62-100   62-101   62-102   62-103   62-104   62-105   62-106

- ❏ Episode II: Attack of the Clones..................10.00
- ❏ Save the Galaxy, LEGO [62-90]........................15.00

Journals.
- ❏ Anakin Skywalker [62-91] 8.00
- ❏ Captive to Evil by Princess Leia [62-92] 8.00
- ❏ Darth Maul [62-93] 8.00
- ❏ Hero for Hire by Han Solo [62-94] 8.00
- ❏ Queen Amidala [62-95]..................................8.00
- ❏ The Fight for Justice by Luke Skywalker [62-96] 8.00

Star Wars Junior.
- ❏ Obi-Wan's Bongo Adventure [62-97]............10.00
- ❏ Podrace! [62-98]...10.00

Storybooks, hardcover, trilogy covers.
- ❏ A New Hope 10.00
- ❏ Return of the Jedi.......................................10.00
- ❏ The Empire Strikes Back 10.00

Storybooks, hardcover.
- ❏ Empire Strikes Back [v1e1:75] 15.00
- ❏ Return of the Jedi [3:142] 15.00
- ❏ Star Wars [62-99].......................................15.00

Storybooks, soft cover.
- ❏ Empire Strikes Back [62-100] 10.00
- ❏ Empire Strikes Back [62-101] 10.00
- ❏ Return of the Jedi Storybook [62-102] 10.00
- ❏ Return of the Jedi Storybook [62-103] 10.00
- ❏ Star Wars Storybook 10.00
- ❏ Star Wars Storybook [62-104].....................10.00
- ❏ Star Wars Treasury, all 3 soft cover in a slipcase 30.00

Sperling and Kupfer (Italy)
- ❏ L'Impero Colpisce Ancora [62-105] 15.00

St. Michaels Press
- ❏ Return of the Jedi [62-106] 25.00

Workman Publishing
- ❏ Star Wars: A Scanimation Book, by Rufus Butler Seder 25.00

Books: Technical

Boxtree
- ❏ Star Wars Technical Journal, soft cover 30.00

Del Rey
- ❏ Star Wars Technical Journal, hardcover......35.00

Starlog
Starlog Technical Journals.
- ❏ Volume 1: Tatooine 10.00
- ❏ Volume 1: Tatooine, foil cover 15.00
- ❏ Volume 1: Tatooine, special edition insert..12.00
- ❏ Volume 2: Imperial Forces [v1e1:75] 10.00
- ❏ Volume 2: Imperial Forces, special edition insert 12.00
- ❏ Volume 3: Rebel Forces [v1e1:75]..............10.00
- ❏ Volume 3: Rebel Forces, special edition insert............12.00

Books: Trivia

- ❏ From The Blob to Star Wars - The Science Fiction Movie Quiz Book [v1e1:76]................8.00

Revenge of the Sith trivia quest.
- ❏ Darth Vader cover.......................................10.00
- ❏ Epic duel cover [63-01] 10.00
- ❏ General Grievous cover [v1e1:76] 10.00
- ❏ Yoda Cover...10.00

Ballantine
- ❏ 425 Questions and Answers about Star Wars and Empire Strikes Back....................15.00
- ❏ Diplomatic Corps Entrance Exam [v1e1:76]...................15.00
- ❏ I'd Just as Soon Kiss a Wookiee: The Quotable Star Wars [63-02]....................................15.00
- ❏ I'd Just as Soon Kiss a Wookiee: The Quotable Star Wars, condensed.............................10.00
- ❏ The Jedi Master's Quiz Book, black cover [63-03]..........20.00
- ❏ The Jedi Master's Quiz Book, blue cover [v1e1:76]..........20.00

Carol Publishing
- ❏ The Jedi Academy Entrance Exam: Tantalizing Trivia from the Star Wars Trilogy [v1e1:76].....................15.00

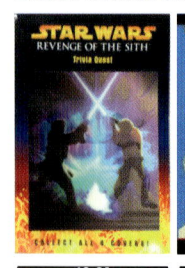 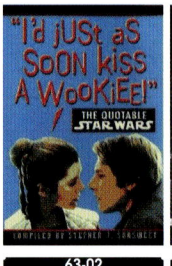     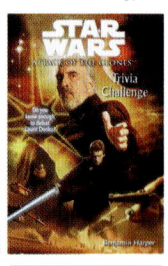 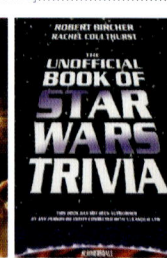 

63-01   63-02   63-03   63-04   63-05   63-06   63-07   63-08   63-09   63-10

Books: Young Reader

Chronicle Books
- ❏ Obsessed with Star Wars [63-04].................................25.00

FunFax (UK)
Quiz Quest.
- ❏ Empire Strikes Back [63-05]......................................10.00
- ❏ Return of the Jedi [63-06]..10.00
- ❏ Star Wars [63-07]..10.00

Kensington
- ❏ Ultimate Unauthorized Star Wars Trilogy Challenge [v1e1:76]...12.00

LucasBooks
- ❏ Attack of the Clones Trivia Challenge [63-08]............10.00

Scholastic
- ❏ Star Wars: Head to Head 15.00

Summersdale Publishing
- ❏ The Unofficial Book of Star Wars Trivia [63-09]..........15.00

Workman Publishing
- ❏ Star Wars Fandex Deluxe [63-10]...............................20.00

Books: Young Jedi Knights

Berkley
- ❏ 1 Heirs to the Force [v1e1:76]...................................10.00
- ❏ 2 Shadow Academy [v1e1:76]...................................10.00
- ❏ 3 The Lost Ones [v1e1:76].......................................10.00
- ❏ 4 Lightsabers [v1e1:76]..10.00
- ❏ 5 Darkest Knight [v1e1:76].......................................10.00
- ❏ 6 Jedi Under Siege [v1e1:76]...................................10.00
- ❏ 7 Shards of Alderaan [v1e1:76]................................10.00
- ❏ 8 Diversity Alliance [v1e1:76]...................................10.00
- ❏ 9 Delusions of Grandeur [v1e1:76]...........................10.00
- ❏ 10 Jedi Bounty [v1e1:76]...10.00
- ❏ 11 The Emperor's Plague [v1e1:76].........................10.00
- ❏ 12 Return to Ord Mantell [v1e1:76].........................10.00
- ❏ 13 Trouble on Cloud City [v1e1:76].........................10.00
- ❏ 14 Crisis at Crystal Reef [v1e1:76]..........................10.00
- ❏ Set of books 1-3, boxed 18.00

Books recompiled under combined names.
- ❏ Books 1-3, "Jedi Shadow" [v1e1:76]........................15.00
- ❏ Books 4-6, "Jedi Sunrise" [v1e1:76]........................15.00

Hardcover compilations.
- ❏ 1–6, Rise of the Shadow Academy [v1e1:76]..........15.00
- ❏ 7–11, The Fall of the Diversity Alliance 15.00
- ❏ 12–14, Under Black Sun 15.00

Omnibus Editions.
- ❏ Books 1–6 ....20.00
- ❏ Books 7–11 ....20.00
- ❏ Books 12–14 ....20.00

VGS
- ❏ Akademie der Verdammten [v1e1:76]......................10.00
- ❏ Allianz der Vergessenen [v1e1:76]..........................10.00
- ❏ Angriff auf Yavin [v1e1:76]......................................10.00
- ❏ Die Huter Der Macht [v1e1:76]................................10.00
- ❏ Die Ruckkehr des Dunklen Ritters [v1e1:76]...........10.00
- ❏ Die Trummer von Alderaan [v1e1:76]......................10.00
- ❏ Die Verlorenen [v1e1:76]...10.00
- ❏ Gefangen auf Ryloth [v1e1:76]................................10.00
- ❏ Lichtschwerter [v1e1:76]...10.00
- ❏ Stimmen des Zorns [v1e1:76].................................10.00

Books: Young Reader

Bantam Books
- ❏ 1 The Glove of Darth Vader [v1e1:77].......................5.00
- ❏ 2 The Lost City of the Jedi [v1e1:77]........................5.00
- ❏ 2 The Lost City of the Jedi, blue logo [64-01]...........8.00
- ❏ 3 Zorba the Hutt's Revenge [v1e1:77]......................5.00
- ❏ 4 Mission from Mount Yoda [v1e1:77].......................5.00
- ❏ 5 Queen of the Empire [64-02]..................................5.00
- ❏ 6 Prophets of the Dark Side [v1e1:77].....................5.00

Gold foil logo.
- ❏ 1 The Glove of Darth Vader [3:143]..........................8.00
- ❏ 2 The Lost City of the Jedi [v1e1:77]........................8.00
- ❏ 3 Zorba the Hutt's Revenge [v1e1:77]......................8.00
- ❏ 4 Mission from Mount Yoda [3:143]..........................8.00
- ❏ 5 Queen of the Empire [64-03]..................................8.00
- ❏ 6 Prophets of the Dark Side 8.00

Hardcover with library binding.
- ❏ 1 The Glove of Darth Vader 15.00
- ❏ 2 The Lost City of the Jedi 15.00
- ❏ 3 Zorba the Hutt's Revenge 15.00
- ❏ 4 Mission from Mount Yoda 15.00
- ❏ 5 Queen of the Empire 15.00
- ❏ 6 Prophets of the Dark Side 15.00

- ❏ Books 1–3, boxed set..25.00
- ❏ Shadows of the Empire [64-04]..............................10.00

Barnes and Noble
- ❏ Books 1–3, hardcover compilation [v1e1:77]..........20.00
- ❏ Books 4–6, hardcover compilation [v1e1:77]..........20.00

Bullseye Books
- ❏ Star Wars: A New Hope [64-05]..............................10.00
- ❏ Star Wars: Empire Strikes Back [64-06].................10.00
- ❏ Star Wars: Return of the Jedi [64-07].....................10.00

Cartwell Books
- ❏ Boba Fett: The Fight to Survive, hardcover............15.00

Cartwheel Books
- ❏ Star Wars ABC 15.00

Del Rey
- ❏ Marvel Comics Illustrated Star Wars [64-08]...........20.00

DK Publishing
- ❏ Beware the Dark Side [64-09]...................................8.00
- ❏ Epic Battles..8.00
- ❏ Feel The Force [64-10]...8.00
- ❏ Galactic Crisis! [64-11]...8.00
- ❏ Journey Through Space [64-12]...............................8.00
- ❏ Obi-Wan's Foe [64-13]...8.00
- ❏ R2-D2 and Friends [64-14].......................................8.00
- ❏ Star Pilot [64-15]..8.00
- ❏ Star Pilot [64-16]..8.00
- ❏ What is a Wookiee? [64-17].....................................8.00
- ❏ What is a Wookiee? [64-18].....................................8.00
- ❏ Yoda In Action!..8.00

Books: Young Reader

Clone Wars.
- Anakin in Action [64-19] ... 10.00

Grosset and Dunlap
- Ambush ... 8.00
- Battle at Teth ... 8.00
- Bombad Jedi ... 8.00
- Bounty Hunter ... 8.00
- Captured ... 8.00
- Children of the Force ... 8.00
- Grievous Attacks! ... 8.00
- Operation: Huttlet ... 8.00
- The Battle for Ryloth ... 8.00
- The Galactic Photobook ... 8.00
- The Holocron Heist [64-20] ... 8.00
- The Hunt for Grievous [v1e1:77] ... 8.00
- The Lost Legion ... 8.00
- The New Padawan ... 8.00

Clone Wars: Secret Missions.
- Breakout Squad ... 10.00
- The Curse of the Black Hole Pirates [64-21] ... 10.00

Personally Yours Books
Episode I story books, personalized.
- Queen Amidala and Me [64-22] ... 25.00
- The Phantom Menace [64-23] ... 25.00

Pocket Junior
- La reine de l'Empire [64-24] ... 20.00
- La vengeance de Zorba le Hutt [64-25] ... 20.00
- Le destin du Prince Jedi [64-26] ... 20.00
- Le Prophete Supreme du Cote Obscur [64-27] ... 20.00

La Saga du Prince Ken.
- Le Gant de Dark Vador [v1e1:77] ... 10.00
- La Cite Perdue les Jedi [64-28] ... 10.00
- Le Prophete Supreme du Cote Obscur [64-29] ... 10.00

Random House
- Anakin to the Rescue [64-30] ... 8.00
- Anakin's Fate [64-31] ... 8.00
- Anakin's Pit Droid [64-32] ... 8.00
- Dangers of the Core [64-33] ... 8.00
- Darth Maul's Revenge [64-34] ... 8.00
- Jar Jar's Mistake [64-35] ... 8.00
- Obi-Wan's Foe ... 8.00
- Queen in Disguise [64-36] ... 8.00

Classic Star Wars.
- A New Hope [v1e1:78] ... 10.00
- Empire Strikes Back [v1e1:78] ... 10.00
- Return of the Jedi [64-37] ... 10.00

Scholastic
- Anakin: Space Pilot with 3D glasses ... 20.00
- Boba Fett: Crossfire [v1e1:78] ... 15.00
- Heroes, board book [64-38] ... 10.00
- Legacy of the Jedi / Secrets of the Jedi [64-39] ... 10.00
- Life and Legend of Obi-Wan Kenobi ... 15.00
- Luke Skywalker Biography ... 15.00
- Return of the Jedi, junior novelization ... 10.00
- Revenge of the Sith junior novelization [64-40] ... 10.00
- Star Wars, young reader edition [64-41] ... 12.00
- The Rise and Fall of Darth Vader ... 15.00

A Clone Wars Novel.
- 1 The Fight to Survive [64-42] ... 8.00
- 2 Crossfire [v1e1:78] ... 8.00
- 3 Maze of Deception [v1e1:78] ... 8.00
- 4 Hunted [v1e1:78] ... 8.00
- 5 A New Threat [v1e1:78] ... 8.00
- 6 Pursuit [v1e1:78] ... 8.00

Adventures in Hyperspace.
- 1 Fire Ring Race [64-43] ... 15.00
- 2 Shinbone Showdown ... 15.00

Rebel Force.
- 1 Target ... 10.00
- 1 Target, hardcover ... 15.00
- 2 Hostage ... 10.00
- 3 Renegade ... 10.00
- 4 Firefight ... 10.00
- 4 Firefight, hardcover ... 15.00
- 5 Trapped ... 10.00
- 6 Uprising ... 10.00

Star Wars Missions.
- 1: Assault on Yavin Four [v1e1:78] ... 10.00
- 2: Escape from Thyferra [v1e1:78] ... 10.00
- 3: Attack on Delrakkin [v1e1:78] ... 10.00
- 4: Destroy the Liquidator [64-44] ... 10.00
- 5: The Hunt for Han Solo [v1e1:78] ... 10.00
- 6: The Search for Grubba the Hutt [v1e1:78] ... 10.00
- 7: Ithorian Invasion [v1e1:78] ... 10.00
- 8: Togorian Trap [v1e1:78] ... 10.00
- 9: Revolt of the Battle Droids [v1e1:78] ... 10.00
- 10: Showdown in Mos Eisley [v1e1:78] ... 10.00
- 11: Bounty Hunters vs. Battle Droids [v1e1:78] ... 10.00
- 12: The Vactooine Disaster [v1e1:78] ... 10.00
- 13: Prisoner of the Nikto Pirates [64-45] ... 10.00
- 14: The Monsters of Dweem [v1e1:78] ... 10.00
- 15: Voyage to the Underworld [v1e1:78] ... 10.00
- 16: Imperial Jailbreak [v1e1:78] ... 10.00
- 17: Darth Vader's Return ... 10.00
- 18: Rogue Squadron to the Rescue [v1e1:78] ... 10.00
- 19: Bounty on Bonadan [v1e1:78] ... 10.00
- 20: Total Destruction [v1e1:78] ... 10.00

Star Wars Trilogy.
- A New Hope ... 8.00
- Empire Strikes Back [64-46] ... 8.00
- Return of the Jedi ... 8.00

The Last of the Jedi.
- 1 The Desperate Mission [v1e1:78] ... 10.00
- 2 Dark Warning [v1e1:78] ... 10.00
- 3 Underworld [v1e1:78] ... 10.00
- 4 Death on Naboo [v1e1:78] ... 10.00
- 5 A Tangled Web ... 10.00
- 6 Return of the Dark Side ... 10.00
- 6 Return of the Dark Side, hardcover ... 15.00
- 7 Secret Weapon ... 10.00
- 8 Against the Empire ... 10.00
- 9 Master of Deception [64-47] ... 10.00
- 10 Reckoning ... 10.00

Sphere
Young reader editions.
- Empire Strikes Back [64-48] ... 15.00
- Star Wars [64-49] ... 15.00

Bottle Caps

65-01 | 65-02 | 65-03 | 65-04 | 65-05 | 65-06

Bottle Cap Accessories
Continued in Volume 3, Page 95

Pepsi Cola (Japan)
- ❏ A New Hope cap stage, holds 5 .... 35.00
- ❏ Empire Strikes Back cap stage, holds 5 .... 35.00
- ❏ Return of the Jedi cap stage, holds 5 .... 35.00
- ❏ The Phantom Menace cap stage, holds 5 .... 35.00
- ❏ Vehicles and Starships cap stage, holds 5 .... 35.00

Cap stages.
- ❏ Episode I: Tatooine [3:145] 350.00
- ❏ Episode II: Arena [65-01] 170.00
- ❏ Episode III: Death Star [65-02] 250.00

Episode I concealment bags.
- ❏ 3D hologram magnet [65-03] 10.00
- ❏ Anakin Skywalker 8.00
- ❏ Artoo-Detoo [v1e1:79] 8.00
- ❏ Darth Maul 8.00
- ❏ Jar Jar Binks 8.00
- ❏ Obi-Wan Kenobi [65-04] 8.00
- ❏ Queen Amidala 8.00
- ❏ Yoda 8.00

Episode II concealment bags.
- ❏ Anakin Skywalker 8.00
- ❏ Barris Offee 8.00
- ❏ Boba Fett 8.00
- ❏ C-3PO 8.00
- ❏ Chancellor Palpatine 8.00
- ❏ Clone trooper 8.00
- ❏ Count Dooku 8.00
- ❏ Kitt Fisto [2:118] 8.00
- ❏ Mace Windu 8.00
- ❏ Obi-Wan Kenobi 8.00
- ❏ Padmé Amidala [2:118] 8.00
- ❏ R2-D2 .... 8.00
- ❏ Shaak Ti [2:118] 8.00
- ❏ Super Battle Droid [2:118] 8.00
- ❏ Yoda [65-05] 8.00
- ❏ Zam Wesell 8.00

Episode III concealment bags.
- ❏ Anakin Skywalker (Jedi) 8.00
- ❏ Anakin Skywalker (Pod Racer) 8.00
- ❏ Battle Droid 8.00
- ❏ C-3PO 8.00
- ❏ Chewbacca 8.00
- ❏ Darth Vader 8.00
- ❏ Emperor Palpatine 8.00
- ❏ General Grievous [v1e1:79] 8.00
- ❏ Han Solo 8.00
- ❏ Luke Skywalker 8.00
- ❏ Padmé Amidala [65-06] 8.00
- ❏ Princess Leia 8.00
- ❏ R2-D2 .... 8.00
- ❏ Stormtrooper 8.00
- ❏ Yoda 8.00

Bottle Caps
Continued in Volume 3, Page 96

(China)
Iced Tea pets. 6-packs in window boxes.
- ❏ C-3PO, R2-D2, Padmé Amidala, Chewbacca, Princess Leia, Luke Skywalker [66-01] 45.00
- ❏ Yoda, Han Solo, Darth Vader, Darth Maul, The Emperor, Anakin Skywalker [66-02] 45.00

Coca-Cola (Canada)
Bottle caps featuring Star Wars characters, peel-off game pieces underneath.
- ❏ C-3PO, Coca-Cola [66-03] 15.00
- ❏ C-3PO, Coke [66-04] 15.00
- ❏ Star Cruiser [66-05] 25.00

66-01 | 66-02 | 66-03 | 66-04

66-05 | 66-06 | 66-07 | 66-08 | 66-09 | 66-10 | 66-11 | 66-12

66-13 | 66-14 | 66-15 | 66-16 | 66-17 | 66-18 | 66-19 | 66-20

66-21 | 66-22 | 66-23 | 66-24 | 66-25 | 66-26 | 66-27 | 66-28

Bottle Caps

Coca-Cola (Japan)
Random scenes under Coca-Cola, Fanta (orange and grape), and Sprite caps.
- Bantha and Tusken Raider [66-06] 20.00
- C-3PO and Luke Skywalker [66-07] 20.00
- C-3PO and Obi-Wan Kenobi [66-08] 20.00
- C-3PO and R2-D2, Death Star control room [66-09] 20.00
- C-3PO and R2-D2, Death Star control room, pink stripe [66-10] 100.00
- C-3PO and R2-D2, Tatooine [66-11] 20.00
- C-3PO, oil bath [66-12] 20.00
- C-3PO, Tatooine standing [66-13] 20.00
- C-3PO, Tatooine walking [66-14] 20.00
- Chewbacca [v1e1:78] 20.00
- Darth Vader (head shot) [66-15] 20.00
- Darth Vader, blockade runner 20.00
- Detention block [66-16] 20.00
- Escape Pod [66-17] 20.00
- Escape Pod, pink stripe [66-18] 100.00
- Grand Moff Tarkin (head shot) [66-19] 20.00
- Grand Moff Tarkin and Darth Vader [66-20] 20.00
- Han and Chewbacca fighting [66-21] 20.00
- Han and Chewbacca standing [66-22] 20.00
- Han Solo (head shot) [66-23] 20.00
- Han Solo, Death Star [66-24] 20.00
- Han Solo, posed [3:145] 20.00
- Han, Chewbacca, Luke at Yavin ceremony 20.00
- Imperial Star Destroyers [66-25] 20.00
- Jawa [66-26] 20.00
- Luke Skywalker [66-27] 20.00
- Luke Skywalker, X-Wing Pilot 20.00
- Luke, landspeeder [66-28] 20.00
- Millennium Falcon [66-29] 20.00
- Millennium Falcon Escapes Tatooine 20.00
- Obi-Wan Kenobi (head shot) [66-30] 20.00
- Obi-Wan Kenobi (head shot), pink stripe [66-31] ... 100.00
- Obi-Wan Kenobi, duel [66-32] 20.00

Bottle Caps

- ☐ Obi-Wan Kenobi, tractor beam [v1e1:78]......................20.00
- ☐ Princess Leia and C-3PO, Yavin [66-33]....................20.00
- ☐ Princess Leia and Luke, Death Star bridge [66-34].........20.00
- ☐ Princess Leia, regal [66-35]...............................20.00
- ☐ Princess Leia, Yavin [66-36]...............................20.00
- ☐ PRIZE [66-37]..200.00
- ☐ Quad turrets, destroying TIE Fighter [66-38].............20.00
- ☐ R2-D2 and C-3PO [66-39]..................................20.00
- ☐ R2-D2, canyon [66-40]....................................20.00
- ☐ R2-D2, canyon, pink stripe [66-41].....................100.00
- ☐ R2-D2, R5-D4, and Luke [66-42]..........................20.00
- ☐ Stormtrooper, mounted [66-43]............................20.00
- ☐ TIE Fighter blasts X-Wing [66-44]........................20.00
- ☐ TIE Fighter, firing [66-45]...............................20.00
- ☐ TIE Fighter, shot at [66-46].............................20.00
- ☐ TIE Fighter, shot at, pink stripe [66-47]..............100.00
- ☐ Tusken Raider, attacking [66-48].........................20.00
- ☐ X-Wing and Vader's TIE Fighter [66-49]...................20.00
- ☐ X-Wing, firing under Death Star [66-50].................20.00
- ☐ Yavin ceremony [66-51]...................................20.00
- ☐ Yavin rebel hangar [66-52]...............................20.00

Random scenes under Coca-Cola, Fanta (orange and grape), and Sprite caps. Collected set.
- ☐ Collected set in display tray..........................750.00

Coca-Cola (Mexico)
Random scenes under Coca-Cola, Boing, and Fanta caps.
- ☐ Artoo-Deetoo [66-53].....................................15.00
- ☐ Artoo-Deetoo escapa [66-54].............................15.00
- ☐ Artoo-Detoo Y See-Threepio [66-55].....................15.00
- ☐ Busqueda de Artoo-Deetoo [66-56].......................15.00
- ☐ Chewbacca [66-57].......................................15.00
- ☐ Combate Galactico [66-58]...............................15.00
- ☐ Darth Vader [66-59].....................................15.00
- ☐ Darth Vader escapa [66-60].............................15.00
- ☐ Grand Moff Tarkin [66-61]..............................15.00
- ☐ Han Solo [66-62].......................................15.00
- ☐ Han Solo y Chewbacca [66-63]..........................15.00
- ☐ Jawas [66-64]..15.00

- ☐ Jawas y Artoo-Deetoo [66-65]...........................15.00
- ☐ Kenobi y Threepio [66-66].............................15.00
- ☐ La Guerra De Las Galaxias [66-67]....................20.00
- ☐ Luke en su nave [66-68]..............................15.00
- ☐ Luke Skywalker [66-69]...............................15.00
- ☐ Luke y Threepio [v1e1:80]............................15.00
- ☐ Nave Imperial [66-70]................................15.00
- ☐ Obi-Wan Kenobi [66-71]...............................15.00
- ☐ Princess Leia [66-72]................................15.00
- ☐ Princess Leia y Luke [66-73].........................15.00
- ☐ Princess Leia y Vader [66-74]........................15.00
- ☐ See-Threepio [66-75].................................15.00
- ☐ Stormtroopers [66-76]................................15.00
- ☐ Stormtroopers atacan [66-77].........................15.00
- ☐ Stormtroopers en el desierto [66-78].................15.00
- ☐ Tarkin y Vader [66-79]...............................15.00
- ☐ Triunfo de la Alianza [66-80]........................15.00
- ☐ Tusken Raider [66-81]................................15.00
- ☐ Tusken Raider y la Bestia [66-82]....................15.00
- ☐ Tusken Raider y Luke [66-83].........................15.00
- ☐ Vader y Stormtroopers [66-84]........................15.00

Pepsi Cola
- ☐ EPI:The Phantom Menace promotion, twist-on [66-85]...10.00
- ☐ EPI:TPM promotion, twist-on Yoda $20 winner [66-86]...40.00

Pepsi Cola (Japan)
Episode I: The Phantom Menace.
- ☐ Anakin Skywalker [66-87]..............................15.00
- ☐ Anakin Skywalker podracer gear [66-88]................15.00
- ☐ Anakin Skywalker podracer gear, head [66-89]..........15.00
- ☐ Battle Droid [66-90]..................................15.00
- ☐ Boss Nass [66-91].....................................15.00
- ☐ Boss Nass, head [66-92]...............................15.00
- ☐ C-3PO [66-93]...15.00
- ☐ Captain Tarpals, head [66-94].........................15.00
- ☐ Chancellor Velorum [66-95]............................15.00
- ☐ Darth Maul, head [66-96]..............................15.00
- ☐ Darth Maul, Jedi duel [66-97].........................15.00
- ☐ Darth Maul, Tatooine [66-98]..........................15.00
- ☐ Darth Sidious [66-99].................................15.00

- ☐ Darth Vader [66-100]..................................15.00
- ☐ Darth Vader, head [66-101]............................15.00
- ☐ Jar Jar Binks [66-102]................................15.00
- ☐ Jar Jar Binks, head [66-103]..........................15.00
- ☐ Ki-Adi-Mundy [66-104].................................15.00
- ☐ Mace Windu [66-105]...................................15.00
- ☐ Mace Windu, head [66-106].............................15.00
- ☐ Nute Gunray [66-107]..................................15.00
- ☐ Nute Gunray, head [66-108]............................15.00
- ☐ Obi-Wan Kenobi Jedi duel [66-109].....................15.00
- ☐ Obi-Wan Kenobi Tatooine [66-110]......................15.00
- ☐ Padmé [66-111]..15.00
- ☐ Princess Leia as Jabba's Prisoner [66-112]............15.00
- ☐ Queen Amidala battle dress [66-113]...................15.00
- ☐ Queen Amidala Coruscant [66-114]......................15.00
- ☐ Queen Amidala Naboo [66-115]..........................15.00
- ☐ Queen Amidala, head [66-116]..........................15.00
- ☐ Qui-Gon Jinn [66-117].................................15.00
- ☐ R2-D2 [66-118]..15.00
- ☐ Sebulba [66-119]......................................15.00
- ☐ Sebulba, head [66-120]................................15.00
- ☐ Senator Palpatine [66-121]............................15.00
- ☐ Tusken Raider [66-122]................................15.00
- ☐ Watto [66-123]..15.00
- ☐ Watto, head [66-124]..................................15.00
- ☐ Yoda [66-125]...15.00
- ☐ Yoda, head [66-126]...................................15.00

Episode I: The Phantom Menace. Special caps with moveable arms.
- ☐ Anakin Skywalker podracer gear........................20.00
- ☐ Boss Nass [66-127]....................................20.00
- ☐ Captain Tarpals.......................................20.00
- ☐ Darth Maul [66-128]...................................20.00
- ☐ Jar Jar Binks [66-129]................................20.00
- ☐ Mace Windu [66-130]...................................20.00
- ☐ Nute Gunray [66-131]..................................20.00
- ☐ Queen Amidala [v1e1:81]...............................20.00
- ☐ R2-D2 [v1e1:81].......................................20.00
- ☐ Sebulba [66-132]......................................20.00
- ☐ Watto [66-133]..20.00
- ☐ Yoda [66-134]...20.00

Bottle Caps

Episode II: Attack of the Clones.
- ❏ Anakin Skywalker [66-135] 10.00
- ❏ Anakin Skywalker / Darth Vader [66-136] 10.00
- ❏ Anakin Skywalker bust [66-137] 10.00
- ❏ Battle Droid [66-138] 10.00
- ❏ Boba Fett [66-139] 10.00
- ❏ C-3PO [66-140] 10.00
- ❏ C-3PO bust [66-141] 10.00
- ❏ Captain Typho [66-142] 10.00
- ❏ Chancellor Palpatine [66-143] 10.00
- ❏ Clone trooper [v1e1:82] 10.00
- ❏ Clone trooper bust [66-144] 10.00
- ❏ Count Dooku [66-145] 10.00
- ❏ Count Dooku bust [66-146] 10.00
- ❏ Darth Sidious [v1e1:82] 10.00
- ❏ Dexter Jettster [66-147] 10.00
- ❏ Dexter Jettster bust [66-148] 10.00
- ❏ Geonosian warrior [66-149] 10.00
- ❏ Geonosian warrior bust [66-150] 10.00
- ❏ Jango Fett [66-151] 10.00
- ❏ Jango Fett / Clone trooper [66-152] 10.00
- ❏ Jango Fett bust [66-153] 10.00
- ❏ Jar Jar Binks senator [66-154] 10.00
- ❏ Kitt Fisto [66-155] 10.00
- ❏ Kitt Fisto bust [66-156] 10.00
- ❏ Lama Su [66-157] 10.00
- ❏ Luminara Unduli [66-158] 10.00
- ❏ Luminara Unduli bust [66-159] 10.00
- ❏ Mace Windu [66-160] 10.00
- ❏ Mas Amedda [66-161] 10.00
- ❏ Mas Amedda bust [66-162] 10.00
- ❏ Obi-Wan Kenobi [66-163] 10.00
- ❏ Obi-Wan Kenobi bust [66-164] 10.00
- ❏ Orn Free Ta [66-165] 10.00
- ❏ Padmé Amidala arena escape [66-166] 10.00
- ❏ Padmé Amidala senator [v1e1:82] 10.00
- ❏ Plo Koon [66-167] 10.00
- ❏ Plo Koon bust [66-168] 10.00
- ❏ Poggle the Lesser [66-169] 10.00
- ❏ R2-D2 [66-170] 10.00
- ❏ RIC-920 [66-171] 10.00
- ❏ Royal Imperial guard [66-172] 10.00
- ❏ Royal Imperial guard bust [66-173] 10.00
- ❏ Saesee Tiin [66-174] 10.00
- ❏ Saesee Tiin bust [66-175] 10.00
- ❏ Shaak Ti [66-176] 10.00
- ❏ Shaak Ti bust [66-177] 10.00
- ❏ Super Battle Droid [66-178] 10.00
- ❏ Taun We [66-179] 10.00
- ❏ Taun We bust [66-180] 10.00
- ❏ Tusken female [66-181] 10.00
- ❏ Wat Tambor [66-182] 10.00
- ❏ Yoda [66-183] 10.00
- ❏ Zam Wesell [66-184] 10.00
- ❏ Zam Wesell bust [66-185] 10.00

Episode II: Attack of the Clones. Set 1 Star Wars.
- ❏ 5-pack, sealed [66-186] 35.00
- ❏ C-3PO and R2-D2 .... 10.00
- ❏ Han Solo 10.00

Bottle Caps

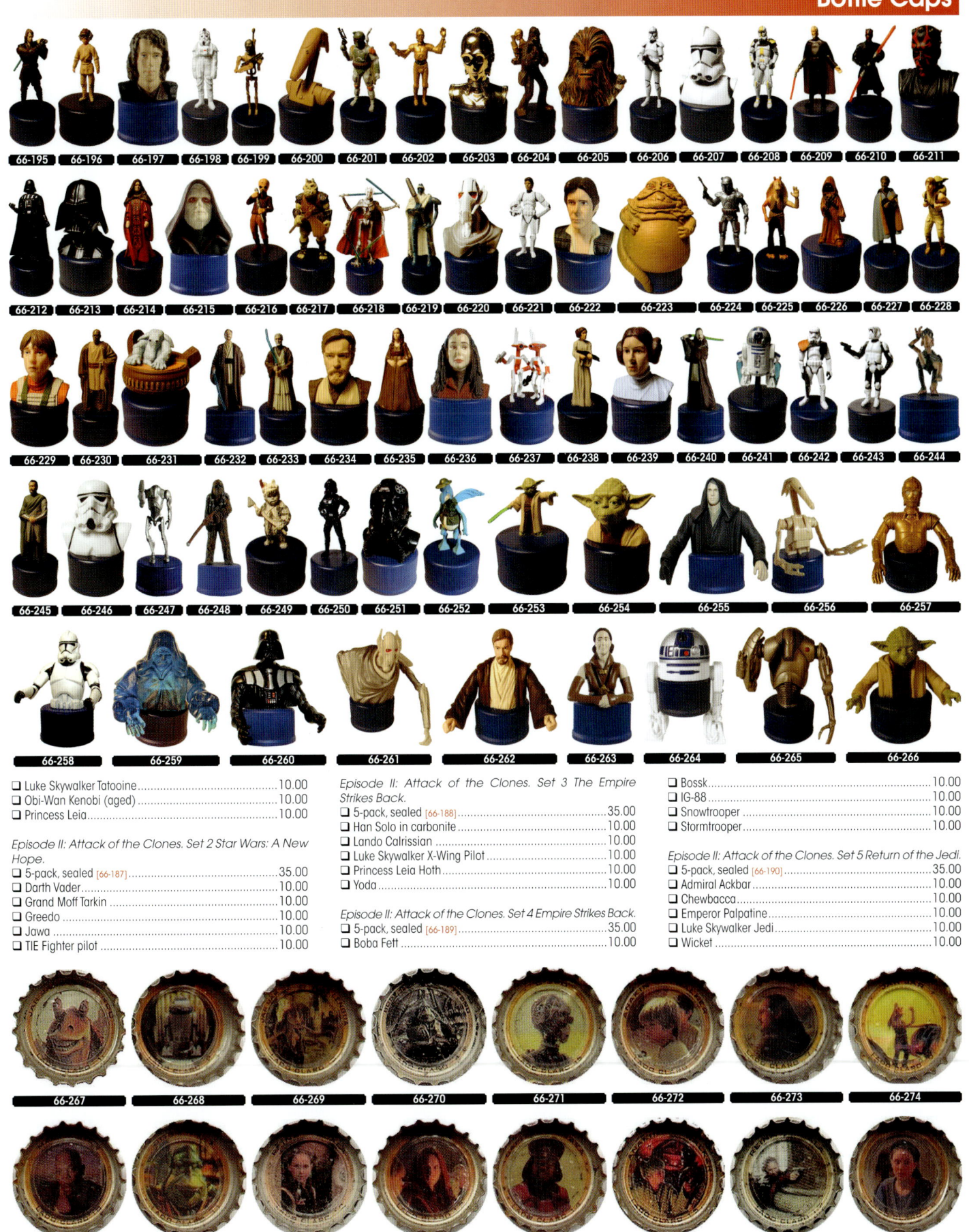

- ❏ Luke Skywalker Tatooine 10.00
- ❏ Obi-Wan Kenobi (aged) 10.00
- ❏ Princess Leia 10.00

Episode II: Attack of the Clones. Set 2 Star Wars: A New Hope.
- ❏ 5-pack, sealed [66-187] 35.00
- ❏ Darth Vader 10.00
- ❏ Grand Moff Tarkin 10.00
- ❏ Greedo 10.00
- ❏ Jawa 10.00
- ❏ TIE Fighter pilot 10.00

Episode II: Attack of the Clones. Set 3 The Empire Strikes Back.
- ❏ 5-pack, sealed [66-188] 35.00
- ❏ Han Solo in carbonite 10.00
- ❏ Lando Calrissian 10.00
- ❏ Luke Skywalker X-Wing Pilot 10.00
- ❏ Princess Leia Hoth 10.00
- ❏ Yoda 10.00

Episode II: Attack of the Clones. Set 4 Empire Strikes Back.
- ❏ 5-pack, sealed [66-189] 35.00
- ❏ Boba Fett 10.00
- ❏ Bossk 10.00
- ❏ IG-88 .... 10.00
- ❏ Snowtrooper 10.00
- ❏ Stormtrooper 10.00

Episode II: Attack of the Clones. Set 5 Return of the Jedi.
- ❏ 5-pack, sealed [66-190] 35.00
- ❏ Admiral Ackbar 10.00
- ❏ Chewbacca 10.00
- ❏ Emperor Palpatine 10.00
- ❏ Luke Skywalker Jedi 10.00
- ❏ Wicket 10.00

Bottle Caps

Episode II: Attack of the Clones. Set 6 Return of the Jedi.
- 5-pack, sealed [66-191] 35.00
- Bib Fortuna 10.00
- Gamorrean Guard 10.00
- Jabba the Hutt 10.00
- Oola 10.00
- Speeder Bike trooper 10.00

Episode II: Attack of the Clones. Set 7 The Phantom Menace.
- 5-pack, sealed 35.00
- Anakin Skywalker padawan 10.00
- C-3PO unfinished 10.00
- Obi-Wan Kenobi 10.00
- Queen Amidala travel gown 10.00
- Qui-Gon Jinn 10.00

Episode II: Attack of the Clones. Set 8 The Phantom Menace.
- 5-pack, sealed [66-192] 35.00
- Battle Droid 10.00
- Darth Maul 10.00
- Destroyer Droid 10.00
- Jar Jar Binks 10.00
- Pit Droid 10.00

Episode II: Attack of the Clones. Set 9 Vehicles.
- 5-pack, sealed [66-193] 35.00
- Darth Vader's TIE Fighter 10.00
- Death Star II 10.00
- Millennium Falcon 10.00
- TIE Fighter 10.00
- X-Wing 10.00

Episode II: Attack of the Clones. Set 10 Vehicles.
- 5-pack, sealed [66-194] 35.00
- Landspeeder 10.00
- Naboo fighter 10.00
- Royal Starship 10.00
- Slave I 10.00
- Star Destroyer 10.00

Episode III: Revenge of the Sith.
- Anakin Skywalker (Jedi) [66-195] 15.00
- Anakin Skywalker (podracer) [66-196] 15.00
- Anakin Skywalker, head only [66-197] 15.00
- AT-AT Driver [66-198] 15.00
- Battle Droid [66-199] 15.00
- Battle Droid, head only [66-200] 15.00
- Boba Fett [66-201] 15.00
- C-3PO [66-202] 15.00
- C-3PO, head only [66-203] 15.00
- Chewbacca with C-3PO [66-204] 15.00
- Chewbacca, head only [66-205] 15.00
- Clone trooper [66-206] 15.00
- Clone trooper, head only [66-207] 15.00
- Commander Bly [66-208] 15.00
- Count Dooku [66-209] 15.00
- Darth Maul [66-210] 15.00
- Darth Maul, head only [66-211] 15.00
- Darth Vader [66-212] 15.00
- Darth Vader, head only [66-213] 15.00
- Emperor Palpatine [66-214] 15.00
- Emperor Palpatine, head only [66-215] 15.00
- Figrin Dan [66-216] 15.00
- Gamorrean Guard [66-217] 15.00
- General Grievous [66-218] 15.00
- General Grievous guard [66-219] 15.00

Bottle Caps

- ❏ General Grievous, head only [66-220] 15.00
- ❏ Han Solo [66-221] 15.00
- ❏ Han Solo, head only [66-222] 15.00
- ❏ Jabba the Hutt [66-223] 15.00
- ❏ Jango Fett [66-224] 15.00
- ❏ Jar Jar Binks [66-225] 15.00
- ❏ Jawa [66-226] 15.00
- ❏ Lando Calrissian [66-227] 15.00
- ❏ Luke Skywalker with Yoda [66-228] 15.00
- ❏ Luke Skywalker, head only [66-229] 15.00
- ❏ Mace Windu [66-230] 15.00
- ❏ Max Rebo [66-231] 15.00
- ❏ Obi-Wan Kenobi (Jedi) [66-232] 15.00
- ❏ Obi-Wan Kenobi (old) [66-233] 15.00
- ❏ Obi-Wan Kenobi, head only [66-234] 15.00
- ❏ Padmé Amidala [66-235] 15.00
- ❏ Padmé Amidala, head only [66-236] 15.00
- ❏ Pit Droid [66-237] 15.00
- ❏ Princess Leia [66-238] 15.00
- ❏ Princess Leia, head only [66-239] 15.00
- ❏ Qui-Gon Jinn [66-240] 15.00
- ❏ R2-D2 [66-241] 15.00
- ❏ Sandtrooper [66-242] 15.00
- ❏ Scout trooper [66-243] 15.00
- ❏ Sebulba [66-244] 15.00
- ❏ Senator Bail Organa [66-245] 15.00
- ❏ Stormtrooper, head only [66-246] 15.00
- ❏ Super Battle Droid [66-247] 15.00
- ❏ Tarfful [66-248] 15.00
- ❏ Teebo [66-249] 15.00
- ❏ TIE Fighter Pilot [66-250] 15.00
- ❏ TIE Fighter Pilot, head only [66-251] 15.00
- ❏ Watto [66-252] 15.00
- ❏ Yoda [66-253] 15.00
- ❏ Yoda, head only [66-254] 15.00

Episode III: Revenge of the Sith. Special caps with moveable arms.
- ❏ Anakin Skywalker [66-255] 20.00
- ❏ Battle Droid [66-256] 20.00
- ❏ C-3PO [66-257] 20.00
- ❏ Clone trooper [66-258] 20.00
- ❏ Darth Sidious [66-259] 20.00
- ❏ Darth Vader [66-260] 20.00
- ❏ General Grievous [66-261] 20.00
- ❏ Obi-Wan Kenobi [66-262] 20.00
- ❏ Padmé Amidala [66-263] 20.00
- ❏ R2-D2 [66-264] 20.00
- ❏ Super Battle Droid [66-265] 20.00
- ❏ Yoda [66-266] 20.00

Pepsi Cola (Mexico)
Episode I: The Phantom Menace. Clario.
- ❏ 1 Jar Jar Sonriendo [66-267] 15.00
- ❏ 2 R2-D2 [66-268] 15.00
- ❏ 3 Jar Jar Sacando La Lengua [66-269] 15.00
- ❏ 4 Boss Nass En Su Trono [66-270] 15.00
- ❏ 5 C-3PO [66-271] 15.00
- ❏ 6 Anakin Skywalker [66-272] 15.00
- ❏ 7 Qui-Gon [66-273] 15.00
- ❏ 8 R2-D2 [v1e1:84] 15.00
- ❏ 9 Jar Jar [66-274] 15.00
- ❏ 10 Mace Windu [66-275] 15.00
- ❏ 11 Boss Nass [66-276] 15.00
- ❏ 12 Reina Amidala [66-277] 15.00
- ❏ 13 Obi-Wan [66-278] 15.00
- ❏ 14 Captain Panaka [66-279] 15.00
- ❏ 15 Anakin Skywalker [66-280] 15.00
- ❏ 16 Padmé (handmaiden) 15.00
- ❏ 17 Reina Amidala [66-281] 15.00
- ❏ 18 Padmé (Tatooine) [66-282] 15.00
- ❏ 19 Qui-Gon En Batalla [66-283] 15.00
- ❏ 20 Shmi y Qui-Gon [66-284] 15.00
- ❏ 21 C-3PO y R2-D2 [v1e1:84] 15.00
- ❏ 22 Qui-Gon y Jar Jar [66-285] 15.00
- ❏ Yoda 1 (facing right) [66-286] 15.00
- ❏ Yoda 2 (facing left) [66-287] 15.00

Episode I: The Phantom Menace. Ladio.
- ❏ 1 Androide De Batalla [66-288] 15.00
- ❏ 2 Watto [66-289] 15.00
- ❏ 3 Darth Sidious y Darth Maul [v1e1:84] 15.00
- ❏ 4 Watto [66-290] 15.00
- ❏ 5 Darth Sidious [66-291] 15.00
- ❏ 6 Sebulba [66-292] 15.00
- ❏ 7 Nute Gunray y Rune Haako [66-293] 15.00
- ❏ 8 Qui-Gon Y Darth Maul [66-294] 15.00
- ❏ 9 Senador Palpatine [66-295] 15.00
- ❏ 10 Darth Maul y Obi-Wan [66-296] 15.00
- ❏ Darth Maul 1 (face only, Tatooine) [66-297] 15.00
- ❏ Darth Maul 3 (face only, Jedi duel) [v1e1:84] 15.00
- ❏ Darth Maul 3 (lightsaber drawn) [66-298] 15.00

Episode I: The Phantom Menace. Lenticular motion caps.
- ❏ 1 Jar Jar Sonriendo [66-299] 10.00
- ❏ 2 R2-D2 [66-300] 10.00
- ❏ 3 Jar Jar Sacando La Lengua [66-301] 10.00
- ❏ 4 Boss Nass En Su Trono [66-302] 10.00
- ❏ 5 C-3PO [66-303] 10.00
- ❏ 6 Anakin Skywalker [66-304] 10.00
- ❏ 7 Qui-Gon [66-305] 10.00
- ❏ 8 R2-D2 [66-306] 10.00
- ❏ 9 Jar Jar [66-307] 10.00
- ❏ 10 Mace Windu [66-308] 10.00
- ❏ 11 Boss Nass [66-309] 10.00
- ❏ 12 Reina Amidala [v1e1:85] 10.00
- ❏ 13 Obi-Wan [66-310] 10.00
- ❏ 14 Captain Panaka [66-311] 10.00
- ❏ 15 Anakin Skywalker [66-312] 10.00
- ❏ 16 Padmé (handmaiden) [66-313] 10.00
- ❏ 17 Reina Amidala [66-314] 10.00
- ❏ 18 Padmé (Tatooine) [66-315] 10.00
- ❏ 19 Qui-Gon En Batalla [v1e1:85] 10.00
- ❏ 20 Shmi y Qui-Gon [66-316] 10.00
- ❏ 21 C-3PO y R2-D2 [66-317] 10.00
- ❏ 22 Qui-Gon y Jar Jar [66-318] 10.00
- ❏ 23 Yoda 1 (facing right) [66-319] 10.00
- ❏ 24 Yoda 2 (facing left) [66-320] 10.00
- ❏ 25 Androide De Batalla [66-321] 10.00
- ❏ 26 Watto [v1e1:85] 10.00
- ❏ 27 Darth Sidious y Darth Maul [66-322] 10.00
- ❏ 28 Watto [66-323] 10.00
- ❏ 29 Darth Sidious [66-324] 10.00
- ❏ 30 Sebulba [66-325] 10.00
- ❏ 31 Nute Gunray y Rune Haako [66-326] 10.00
- ❏ 32 Qui-Gon y Darth Maul [v1e1:85] 10.00
- ❏ 33 Senador Palpatine [66-327] 10.00
- ❏ 34 Darth Maul y Obi-Wan [66-328] 10.00
- ❏ 35 Darth Maul 1 (face only, Tatooine) [66-329] 10.00
- ❏ 36 Darth Maul 3 (face only, Jedi duel) 10.00
- ❏ 37 Darth Maul 3 (lightsaber drawn) [66-330] 10.00

66-331 | 66-332 | 66-333 | 66-334 | 66-335 | 66-336 | 66-337 | 66-338

66-339 | 66-340 | 66-341 | 66-342 | 66-343 | 66-344 | 66-345 | 66-346

66-347 | 66-348 | 66-349 | 66-350 | 66-351 | 66-352 | 66-353 | 66-354

66-355 | 66-356 | 66-357 | 66-358 | 66-359 | 66-360 | 66-361

Bottle Caps

67-01 | 67-02 | 67-03 | 67-04 | 67-05 | 67-06 | 68-01 | 68-02 | 69-01 | 69-02

Star Wars Celebration Japan (Japan)
Metal caps with optional pinback attachment. 30 different plus one "secret" design. Unnumbered. Sold blind-packed, 2 per capsule with checklist sheet.
- ☐ 2 caps in unopened capsule [66-331]..................50.00
- ☐ Aayla Secura [66-332]..................20.00
- ☐ Admiral Ackbar..................20.00
- ☐ Anakin Skywalker [66-333]..................20.00
- ☐ Boba Fett [66-334]..................20.00
- ☐ C-3PO [66-335]..................20.00
- ☐ Chewbacca [66-336]..................20.00
- ☐ Clone trooper [66-337]..................20.00
- ☐ Count Dooku [66-338]..................20.00
- ☐ Darth Maul [66-339]..................20.00
- ☐ Darth Sidious [66-340]..................20.00
- ☐ Darth Vader [66-341]..................20.00
- ☐ General Grievous [66-342]..................20.00
- ☐ Grand Moff Tarkin [66-343]..................20.00
- ☐ Han Solo [66-344]..................20.00
- ☐ Jabba the Hutt [66-345]..................20.00
- ☐ Jango Fett [66-346]..................20.00
- ☐ Jawa [66-347]..................20.00
- ☐ Lando Calrissian [66-348]..................20.00
- ☐ Leia Organa [66-349]..................20.00
- ☐ Luke Skywalker [66-350]..................20.00
- ☐ Mace Windu [66-351]..................20.00
- ☐ Obi-Wan Kenobi [66-352]..................20.00
- ☐ Queen Amidala [66-353]..................20.00
- ☐ Qui-Gon Jinn [66-354]..................20.00
- ☐ R2-D2 [66-355]..................20.00
- ☐ "Secret" [66-356]..................20.00
- ☐ Shaak Ti [66-357]..................20.00
- ☐ Stormtrooper [66-358]..................20.00
- ☐ Tusken Raider [66-359]..................20.00
- ☐ Wicket [66-360]..................20.00
- ☐ Yoda [66-361]..................20.00

Bottle Openers
Continued in Volume 3, Page 96
- ☐ Celebration III logo, magnetic back [67-01]..................20.00
- ☐ Celebration IV logo, magnetic back [67-02]..................15.00
- ☐ Celebration V logo, magnetic back [67-03]..................15.00

Hallmark
- ☐ The Force is Strong with this One [67-04]..................15.00

Rancho Obi-Wan
- ☐ Rancho Obi-Wan World Record Night [67-05]..................35.00

Symbiote Studios
- ☐ Luke Skywalker's lightsaber [67-06]..................20.00

Bowling Ball Bags
Strike Ten
- ☐ Darth Vader [68-01]..................50.00
- ☐ Darth Vader [68-02]..................50.00

Bowling Balls
Strike Ten
- ☐ Boba Fett [v1e1:86]..................125.00
- ☐ C-3PO [v1e1:86]..................125.00
- ☐ Darth Maul [v1e1:86]..................125.00
- ☐ Darth Vader [v1e1:86]..................125.00
- ☐ Padmé / Leia [v1e1:86]..................125.00
- ☐ Stormtrooper [v1e1:86]..................125.00
- ☐ Yoda [v1e1:86]..................125.00

Boxes: Ceramic
Continued in Volume 3, Page 97
Limoges
7 cm tall porcelain boxes, FAO Schwarz exclusives.
- ☐ Queen Amidala [69-01]..................450.00
- ☐ Yoda [69-02]..................500.00

Sigma
- ☐ Yoda in backpack [69-03]..................100.00

Taito (Japan)
Mosquito repellent incense coil holders.
- ☐ Darth Vader [69-04]..................50.00
- ☐ Stormtrooper..................50.00

Boxes: Plastic / Resin
Continued in Volume 3, Page 97

3D Arts
Hologram foil on lid, 2" square.
- ☐ C-3PO and R2-D2..................20.00
- ☐ Darth Vader..................20.00
- ☐ Millennium Falcon..................20.00
- ☐ X-Wing Fighter..................20.00

A.H. Prismatic
Hologram foil on lid, 2" square.
- ☐ AT-AT [70-01]..................20.00
- ☐ B-Wing..................20.00
- ☐ C-3PO and R2-D2..................20.00
- ☐ Darth Vader [70-02]..................20.00
- ☐ Darth Vader with lightsaber [70-03]..................20.00
- ☐ Darth Vader's TIE Fighter..................20.00
- ☐ Dogfight in Space..................20.00
- ☐ Imperial Cruiser [70-04]..................20.00
- ☐ Millennium Falcon..................20.00
- ☐ Millennium Falcon over Death Star [70-05]..................20.00
- ☐ TIE Interceptor [70-06]..................20.00
- ☐ X-Wing Fighter [70-07]..................20.00
- ☐ X-Wing Fighter in combat..................20.00

Olszewski Studios
Disney Pokitpals.
- ☐ Darth Vader / Stormtrooper [70-08]..................75.00
- ☐ Donald Han Solo in Carbonite [70-09]..................75.00

Paper clip boxes.
- ☐ Darth Vader [70-10]..................65.00
- ☐ R2-D2 [70-11]..................65.00

Boxes: Tin
Continued in Volume 3, Page 97

Butterscotch candy tins from the U.K.
- ☐ Anakin Skywalker [71-01]..................8.00
- ☐ Darth Maul [71-02]..................8.00
- ☐ Obi-Wan Kenobi [71-03]..................8.00
- ☐ Qui-Gon Jinn [71-04]..................8.00

69-03 | 69-04 | 70-01 | 70-02 | 70-03 | 70-04 | 70-05 | 70-06 | 70-07

70-08 Side 1 and Side 2 | 70-09 Front and back | 70-10 | 70-11

Boxes: Tin

 71-01
 71-02
 71-03
 71-04
 71-05
 71-06

 71-07
 71-08
 71-09
 71-10
 71-11

 71-12
 71-13
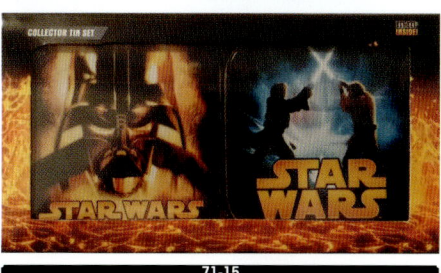 71-14 / 71-15
 71-16

 71-17
 71-18
 71-19
 71-20 Image 1 and Image 2

(UK)
- ❏ Trunk, locking [71-05] 18.00

Chein Industries
- ❏ Return of the Jedi Round Cookie Tin with lid [71-06] 30.00

Carry-all rectangular tins with handles and lid.
- ❏ Ewoks [4:54] 45.00
- ❏ Return of the Jedi [71-07] 40.00

Mini-tins, 3.5" high.
- ❏ C-3PO and R2-D2 [71-08] 15.00
- ❏ Darth Vader 15.00
- ❏ Ewoks 15.00
- ❏ Han Solo, Luke Skywalker, and Princess Leia [71-09] 15.00
- ❏ Jabba the Hutt [71-10] 15.00
- ❏ Max Rebo Band 15.00

Trinket tins, 1" high.
- ❏ C-3PO and R2-D2 .... 10.00
- ❏ Darth Vader 10.00
- ❏ Ewoks 10.00
- ❏ Han Solo, Luke Skywalker, and Princess Leia 10.00
- ❏ Jabba the Hutt 10.00
- ❏ Max Rebo Band [71-11] 10.00

Frito Lay
Episode II promotion. Four Big Grab bags of snack chips inside.
- ❏ 1 of 3, The Life of Anakin [71-12] 10.00
- ❏ 2 of 3, Jedi Heroes [71-13] 10.00
- ❏ 3 of 3, Droids and Clones [71-14] 10.00

Galerie
- ❏ Sith and Jedi collector tin set [71-15] 10.00

Houston Harvest
2 lb. popcorn tin.
- ❏ Revenge of the Sith [71-16] 8.00

Masterfoods USA
- ❏ MPire chocolate [71-17] 15.00

Heart shaped tins filled with M&M minis.
- ❏ Chewbacca, "I'd Just As Soon Kiss A Wookiee" [71-18] 10.00
- ❏ Yoda, "A Happy Valentines Day You Will Have" [71-19] 10.00

Round tins with lenticular characters, filled with M&M minis.
- ❏ Anakin / Darth Vader [71-20] 8.00
- ❏ Yoda / General Grievous [71-21] 8.00

Metal Box Ltd.
Medium sized tins.
- ❏ Chewbacca [71-22] 15.00
- ❏ Darth Vader [71-23] 15.00
- ❏ Han Solo 15.00
- ❏ Luke Skywalker 15.00
- ❏ Princess Leia 15.00
- ❏ Probot [71-24] 15.00
- ❏ Star Destroyer [71-25] 15.00
- ❏ Yoda [71-26] 15.00

Oval tins.
- ❏ Cloud City [71-27] 30.00

Small sized tins.
- ❏ AT-AT [71-28] 10.00
- ❏ Boba Fett [71-29] 10.00
- ❏ Darth Vader and Luke Skywalker duel [71-30] 10.00
- ❏ Lando Calrissian [71-31] 10.00
- ❏ Luke on Tauntaun [71-32] 10.00
- ❏ Yoda tin [71-33] 10.00

Space trunks.
- ❏ Droids / Probot [71-34] 40.00
- ❏ Luke Skywalker 40.00

Movistar (Argentina)
Tin canisters for Nokia 1100 series phones.
- ❏ Darth Vader [71-35] 10.00
- ❏ Yoda [71-36] 10.00

Popcorn Express
18.5 oz. popcorn tins.
- ❏ Blu-Ray 12.00
- ❏ Classics [71-37] 12.00
- ❏ Prequels 12.00
- ❏ Saga 12.00

Boxes: Tin

71-21 Image 1 and Image 2 — 71-22 — 71-23 — 71-24

71-25 — 71-26 — 71-27 — 71-28 — 71-29

71-30 — 71-31 — 71-32 — 71-33 — 71-34

Rand International
Super Power Mints mini tins.
- ❏ Chewbacca [71-38] 8.00
- ❏ Darth Vader [71-39] 8.00
- ❏ Epic duel [71-40] 8.00
- ❏ Yoda [71-41] 8.00

Tin Box Company
- ❏ Locker, 10" with lock [71-42] 20.00

Dome shaped with top latch.
- ❏ Boba Fett [71-43] 20.00
- ❏ C-3PO 20.00
- ❏ Darth Vader [71-44] 20.00
- ❏ R2-D2 [71-45] 20.00

Mini lunch boxes.
- ❏ Darth Vader 15.00

- ❏ Epic Battle 15.00
- ❏ Yoda 15.00

Topps
- ❏ Darth Vader 8.00
- ❏ Darth Vader, flowing cape 8.00

Tin contains 7 packages of Attack of the Clones cards and mega sized foil card.
- ❏ Anakin Skywalker 40.00
- ❏ Count Dooku 40.00
- ❏ Jango Fett 40.00
- ❏ Mace Windu 40.00
- ❏ Obi-Wan Kenobi 40.00

Tin contains 8 packages of Episode I Widevision cards.
- ❏ Anakin Skywalker 40.00

- ❏ Darth Maul 40.00
- ❏ Obi-Wan Kenobi [71-46] 40.00
- ❏ Queen Amidala 40.00
- ❏ Qui-Gon Jinn 40.00

Toumart (Japan)
Mint tin covers. Caricature style.
- ❏ Boba Fett 20.00
- ❏ R2-D2 .... 20.00
- ❏ Yoda 20.00

Buckets, Canvas
Continued in Volume 3, Page 98

Pottery Barn
- ❏ Darth Vader 10" [72-01] 35.00

71-35 — 71-36 — 71-37 — 71-38 — 71-39

71-40 — 71-41 — 71-42 — 71-43 — 71-44 — 71-45 — 71-46

Buttons

72-01

73-01

73-02

73-03

73-04

73-05

73-06

73-07

73-08

73-09

73-10

Buckets, Food
Continued in Volume 3, Page 98

Plastic popcorn pails. Theater promotions.
- ❏ Star Wars special edition [73-01] 25.00
- ❏ Star Wars special edition trilogy scenes [73-02] 25.00

Frito Lay
EPII. Four Big Grab bags of snack chips inside.
- ❏ 1 of 3, The Life of Anakin [73-03] 10.00
- ❏ 2 of 3, Jedi Heroes [73-04] 10.00
- ❏ 3 of 3, Droids and Clones [73-05] 10.00

KFC (Australia)
- ❏ Paper bucket, classic trilogy, Star Wars special edition [73-06] 25.00

Popcorn buckets. Episode I: The Phantom Menace.
- ❏ Anakin Skywalker, large [73-07] 15.00
- ❏ Anakin Skywalker, medium 15.00
- ❏ Battle Droid, large [73-08] 15.00
- ❏ Battle Droid, medium 15.00
- ❏ Jar Jar Binks, large [73-09] 15.00
- ❏ Jar Jar Binks, medium 15.00
- ❏ Queen Amidala, large 15.00
- ❏ Queen Amidala, medium [73-10] 15.00

Bumper Stickers

- ❏ Darth Vader Lives [74-01] 10.00
- ❏ I saw Star Wars at Mann's Chinese Theater 10.00
- ❏ I'm a Star Wars fan, honk if you R2 [74-02] 10.00
- ❏ Star Wars exhibition in Space World [74-03] 30.00
- ❏ Star Wars Lives, R2-D2 [74-04] 10.00
- ❏ Star Wars logo outline [74-05] 10.00

C and D Visionaries, Inc.
- ❏ My other transport is the Millennium Falcon [74-06] 10.00

Creation Entertainment
- ❏ 10th Anniversary bumper sticker [74-07] 35.00

Dark Horse Comics
- ❏ Starfighter crossbones 8.00

Disney / MGM
- ❏ Star Tours, My Other Vehicle is an X-Wing [74-08] 25.00

Fantasma
- ❏ Star Wars logo on holographic foil [74-09] 25.00

Hot Topic
- ❏ May the Force be with you [74-10] 8.00
- ❏ Use the Force [74-11] 8.00

Star Wars Celebration V
- ❏ I Found The Droids I Was Looking For... ....15.00
- ❏ I'd Just As Soon Kiss a Wookiee! 15.00
- ❏ Original Princess Magnet 15.00

Business Card Holders
Continued in Volume 3, Page 99

(Japan)
- ❏ Jedi Training Academy / Episode II: Attack of the Clones [75-01] 15.00

Kotobukiya (Japan)
- ❏ Han Solo in Carbonite [75-02] 40.00
- ❏ R2-D2 [75-03] 40.00

Business Cards
Continued in Volume 3, Page 99

Oral-B
- ❏ Membership / dental appointment [76-01] 10.00

Buttons
Continued in Volume 3, Page 99

- ❏ 20-pack, Die Ruckkehr der Jedi-Ritter 75.00
- ❏ 5/25/1977, exclusive to Star Wars Celebration IV 10.00
- ❏ Badge pack, Four 1.5" classic trilogy characters with phrases [77-01] 15.00
- ❏ Darth Vader's TIE Fighter attacking [77-02] 10.00
- ❏ Droids: On Video Now [77-03] 15.00
- ❏ First 10 Years, pewter 25.00
- ❏ Happy EMPIRE Day [77-04] 12.00
- ❏ I Saw It, 6 movie marathon, exclusive to Star Wars Celebration IV [77-05] 25.00
- ❏ Ice Capades and Ewoks with light-up eyes, 2.25" [77-06] 25.00
- ❏ Ice Capades and Ewoks, 3.5" [77-07] 25.00
- ❏ Join the Force Star Wars Strike Force [77-08] 15.00
- ❏ Luke Skywalker, Dagobah crash 8.00
- ❏ May the Force be with you, Saturday, March 1 [77-09] 15.00
- ❏ Something, Something Something Dark Side pin set [77-10] 15.00
- ❏ Star Wars books on sale now [77-11] 8.00
- ❏ Star Wars Sandpeople [77-12] 8.00
- ❏ starwarscards.net [77-13] 10.00
- ❏ Super Collector's Wish Book [77-14] 10.00
- ❏ The Clone Wars, rectangular [77-15] 8.00
- ❏ Yoda for President [77-16] 15.00

Episode II: Attack of the Clones.
- ❏ Star Wars [77-17] 15.00
- ❏ Star Wars Coming April 23 [77-18] 15.00
- ❏ Train to be a Jedi May 18th 10:00am to Noon [77-19] 15.00

75-01

75-02

75-03

76-01

74-01

74-02

74-03

74-04

74-05

74-06

74-07

74-08

74-09

74-10

74-11

Buttons

 77-01
 77-02
 77-03
 77-04
 77-05
 77-06
 77-07

 77-08
 77-09
 77-10
 77-11
 77-12
 77-13
 77-14

 77-15
 77-16
 77-17
 77-18
 77-19
 77-20

10th anniversary.
- C-3PO and R2-D2 [77-20] 20.00
- Darth Vader [77-21] 20.00
- Leia and Luke [77-22] 20.00
- The First Ten Years, black round [77-23] 20.00
- The First Ten Years, silver rectangle [77-24] 25.00

U.K.
- Darth Vadar Lives [sic] [77-25] 15.00

(France)
Badges Officiels, 4-packs.
- Characters: Anakin, Obi-Wan, Yoda, Clone Wars logo [77-26] 15.00
- Empire Symbols: Darth Vader, Galactic Empire, Stormtrooper. Star Wars [77-27] 15.00
- Rebel Symbols [77-28] 15.00

20th Century Fox
- Space Balls, May The Schwartz Be With You [77-29] 25.00
- The Star Wars trilogy, March 28, 1985 [77-30] 25.00

Classic trilogy video prerelease employee buttons.
- Continue the Adventure on Video [77-31] 15.00
- Han Shoots First—Sept 12, 2006 .... 15.00
- Special Edition Trilogy [77-32] 15.00
- Special Edition Trilogy, August 26 [77-33] 15.00
- Trilogy Video Re-Release August 29 [77-34] 15.00

Episode I DVD prerelease employee buttons. "The Saga Begins on DVD October 16!"
- Darth Maul [77-35] 15.00
- Maul and Kenobi duel [77-36] 15.00
- Queen Amidala [77-37] 15.00

Episode I video prerelease employee buttons.
- Darth Maul, "Ask me how to reserve..." [77-38] 15.00
- Episode I: "The One To Own On Video" [77-39] 15.00

Episode II DVD prerelease employee buttons.
- Yoda, "Unlock the Saga..." [77-40] 10.00

Episode III DVD employee button.
- The saga is complete. Own it on DVD. [77-41] 10.00

A.H. Prismatic
Holograms, series 1.
- AT-AT 20.00
- B-Wing Fighter 20.00
- Darth Vader 20.00
- Darth Vader's TIE Fighter 20.00
- Imperial Cruiser [77-42] 20.00

 77-21
 77-22
 77-23
 77-24
 77-25
 77-26
 77-27

 77-28
 77-29
 77-30
 77-31
 77-32
 77-33
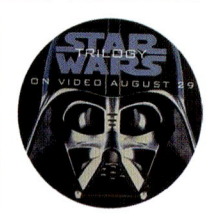 77-34

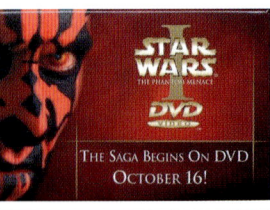 77-35
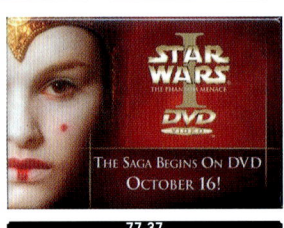 77-37
 77-38
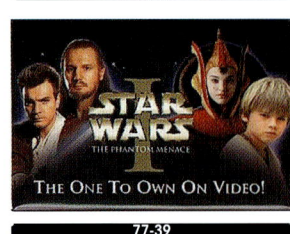 77-39
 77-40

Buttons

   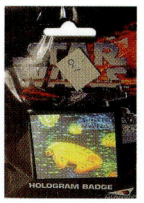     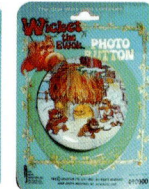

77-41   77-42   77-43   77-44   77-45   77-46   77-47   77-48   77-49

 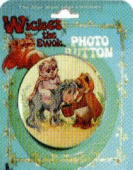 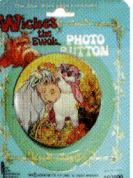   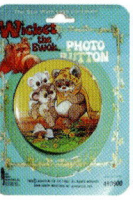    

77-50   77-51   77-52   77-53   77-54   77-55   77-56   77-57   77-58   77-59

    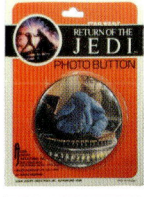    

77-60   77-61   77-62   77-63   77-64   77-65   77-66   77-67   77-68

- ❑ Millennium Falcon......................................20.00
- ❑ Millennium Falcon with Star Wars logo.....................20.00
- ❑ Tie Interceptor..20.00
- ❑ X-Wing Fighter..20.00

Holograms, series 2.
- ❑ C-3PO and R2-D2 [77-43]...............................20.00
- ❑ Darth Vader...20.00
- ❑ Millennium Falcon [77-44]................................20.00

Adam Joseph Industries
Ewoks.
- ❑ Baby Ewoks [77-45]....................................15.00
- ❑ Ewok Daydreaming [77-46]..............................15.00
- ❑ Ewok Flying Glider [77-47].............................15.00
- ❑ Ewok Lessons [77-48].................................15.00
- ❑ Ewok Village in Snow [77-49]...........................15.00
- ❑ Ewok with Basket on Head [77-50].......................15.00

- ❑ Kneesaa and Wicket Feed Baga [77-51]..................15.00
- ❑ Princess Kneesaa [77-52].............................15.00
- ❑ Wicket and R2-D2 [77-53].............................15.00
- ❑ Wicket on a Vine [77-54].............................15.00
- ❑ Wicket Tells a Story [77-55]..........................15.00
- ❑ Wicket the Ewok [77-56].............................15.00

Return of the Jedi.
- ❑ Baby Ewok [77-57]...................................10.00
- ❑ Chewbacca [77-58]..................................10.00
- ❑ Darth Vader [77-59].................................10.00
- ❑ Emperor's Royal Guard [77-60]........................10.00
- ❑ Gamorrean Guard [77-61].............................10.00
- ❑ Heroes on Endor [77-62].............................10.00
- ❑ Jabba the Hutt [77-63]..............................10.00
- ❑ Max Rebo [77-64]...................................10.00
- ❑ R2-D2 and C-3PO [77-65]............................10.00

- ❑ Revenge art [77-66]................................10.00
- ❑ Return of the Jedi Logo [77-67].....................10.00
- ❑ Yoda [77-68].......................................10.00

Burger King
- ❑ "Ask Me For Your Return of the Jedi Glasses" [77-69]....25.00

Burger King (UK)
Episode III: Revenge of the Sith. "Play the Choose Your Destiny Game"
- ❑ Blue [77-70].......................................10.00
- ❑ Red [77-71].......................................10.00

C and D Visionaries, Inc.
- ❑ Adventure... Excitement... A Jedi craves not these things [77-72]..5.00
- ❑ Boba Fett [77-73]..................................5.00
- ❑ Chewbacca [77-74]................................5.00

  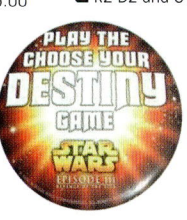    

77-69   77-70   77-71   77-72   77-73   77-74   77-75

77-76   77-77   77-78   77-79   77-80   77-81   77-82

77-83   77-84   77-85   77-86   77-87   77-88   77-89

Buttons

77-90 77-91 77-92 77-93 77-94 77-95 77-96 77-97

77-98 77-99 77-100 77-101 77-102 77-103 77-104

77-105 77-106 77-107 77-108 77-109 77-110 77-111

77-112 77-113 77-114 77-115 77-116 77-117 77-118

- ❏ Clone Helmet [77-75]..........5.00
- ❏ Clone trooper [77-76]..........5.00
- ❏ Darth Vader Sith Lord [77-77]..........5.00
- ❏ "Do… or do not. There is no try," art [77-78]..........5.00
- ❏ "Do… or do not. There is no try," photo [77-79]..........5.00
- ❏ Jedi [77-80]..........5.00
- ❏ Look at me… Judge me by my size do you? [77-81]..........5.00
- ❏ Luke Skywalker..........5.00
- ❏ May the Force be with you [77-82]..........5.00
- ❏ My ally is The Force… and a powerful ally it is [77-83]..........5.00
- ❏ R2-D2 and C-3PO..........5.00
- ❏ Size Matters Not –Yoda [77-84]..........5.00
- ❏ Use the Force [77-85]..........5.00
- ❏ Who's Your Daddy? [77-86]..........8.00
- ❏ Yoda [77-87]..........5.00
- ❏ You have failed me for the last time [77-88]..........5.00

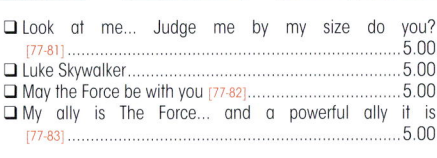   

77-119 77-120 77-121 77-122 Black 77-122 Blue 77-123

  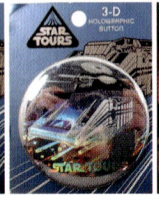   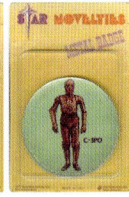

77-124 77-125 77-126 77-127 77-128 77-129 77-130

77-131 77-132 77-133 77-134 77-135 77-136 77-137 77-138 77-139 77-140

Buttons

 77-141
 77-142
 77-143
 77-144
 77-145
 77-146
 77-147
 77-148
 77-149
 77-150
 77-151
 77-152
 77-153
 77-154
 77-155
 77-156
 77-157
 77-158
 77-159
 77-160
 77-161

Large.
❏ Boba Fett [77-89] 8.00
❏ I'd just as soon kiss a wookiee [77-90] 8.00
❏ Princess Leia captive [77-91] 8.00

Small 4-pack button sets.
❏ Classic trilogy [77-92] 12.00
❏ Clone Wars [77-93] 12.00
❏ Join the Dark Side, Who's Your Daddy?, Clone trooper, Star Wars [77-94] 20.00

Small.
❏ Yoda backer card, 5-pack button set [77-95] 12.00

CHOZ F.M.
❏ Star Wars NPR promotional [77-96] 30.00

Coca-Cola
❏ Things Go Better... [77-97] 35.00
❏ Y A Rien Comme Un Coke [77-98] 30.00

Danilo Promotions Ltd. (UK)
Originally packaged with greeting cards.
❏ 6 Today [77-99] 5.00
❏ 7 Today [77-100] 5.00
❏ 8 Today [77-101] 5.00
❏ Jedi [77-102] 5.00
❏ Jedi Starfighter [77-103] 5.00
❏ Jedi Starfighter with Jedi code [77-104] 5.00
❏ May the Force be with you [77-105] 5.00
❏ May the Force be with you (Anakin) [77-106] ... 5.00
❏ Obey Your Master [77-107] 5.00
❏ Use the Force [77-108] 5.00
❏ Use The Force (Darth Vader) [77-109] 5.00
❏ Vader [77-110] 5.00
❏ Who's The Daddy? [77-111] 5.00
❏ Yoda Jedi Master [77-112] 5.00

Dark Horse Comics
❏ Ask Me About Star Wars Comics! [77-113] 15.00

DC Metro Area Star Wars Collecting Club
❏ 30 Years of the Force, exclusive to Star Wars Celebration IV 10.00

Decipher
❏ Imperial cog [77-114] 10.00
❏ Rebel Alliance [77-115] 10.00

Del Rey
❏ "Read, You Will." Yoda 8.00

 77-162
 77-163
 77-164
 77-165
 77-166
 77-167
 77-168
 77-169
 77-170
 77-171
 77-172
 77-173
 77-174
 77-175
 77-176
 77-177
 77-178
 77-179
 77-180
 77-181

Buttons

- ❏ Surrender to the Future of the Force [77-116] 12.00
- ❏ Vader "Join Me ... and Read" [77-117] 10.00
- ❏ Yoda, "Read You Will" [77-118] 10.00

Disney / MGM
- ❏ A short time ahead... Star Tours [77-119] 35.00
- ❏ Star Tours and Disney-MGM logos 35.00
- ❏ Star Tours and Disney-MGM logos with C-3PO and R2-D2 [77-120] 35.00
- ❏ Star Tours Flight Test Team [77-121] 50.00
- ❏ Star Tours logo [77-122] 30.00
- ❏ Star Tours logo with C-3PO and R2-D2 [77-123] 35.00
- ❏ Star Wars Weekends—May 2000 [77-124] 15.00
- ❏ Star Wars Weekends—May 2001 [77-125] 15.00

3D Holographic buttons.
- ❏ R2-D2 and C-3PO [77-126] 50.00
- ❏ Star Tours shuttle [77-127] 50.00

DK Publishing
- ❏ Ask me about the Star Wars Episode I books... [77-128] 10.00

Factors, Etc.
- ❏ Ben (Obi-Wan) Kenobi [77-129] 10.00
- ❏ Boba Fett 10.00
- ❏ C-3PO [77-130] 10.00
- ❏ C-3PO and R2-D2 .... 10.00
- ❏ Chewbacca [77-131] 10.00
- ❏ Darth Vader (photo) [77-132] 10.00
- ❏ Darth Vadar Lives [sic] [77-133] 10.00
- ❏ Darth Vader mirrored keychain 15.00
- ❏ Darth Vader mirrored necklace 15.00
- ❏ Han Solo and Chewbacca [77-134] 10.00
- ❏ Luke Skywalker [77-135] 10.00
- ❏ "May the Force be with you" [77-136] 10.00
- ❏ "May the Force be with you" with Kenner logo 20.00
- ❏ Princess Leia [77-137] 10.00
- ❏ R2-D2 [77-138] 10.00
- ❏ R2-D2 and C-3PO with logo [77-139] 10.00

Punched plastic disc with safety pin on back.
- ❏ Star Wars [77-140] 25.00

Fan Club
- ❏ Artoo [77-141] 15.00
- ❏ Ben Kenobi [77-142] 15.00
- ❏ Chewbacca [77-143] 15.00
- ❏ Darth Vader [77-144] 15.00
- ❏ George Lucas [77-145] 15.00
- ❏ Han Solo [77-146] 15.00
- ❏ Jawa [77-147] 15.00
- ❏ Luke [77-148] 15.00

 77-183
 77-184
 77-185
 77-186
 77-187
 77-188
 77-189
 77-190

 77-191
 77-192
 77-193
 77-194
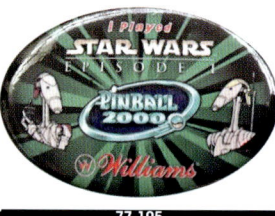 77-195
 77-196
 77-197

 77-198
 77-199
 77-200
 77-201
 77-202
 77-203
 77-204

 77-205
 77-206
 77-207
 77-208
 77-209
 77-210
 77-211

 77-212
 77-213
 77-214
 77-215
 77-216
 77-217
 77-218
 77-219

 77-220
 77-221
 77-222
 77-223
 77-224
 77-225
 77-226

- ❏ Moff Tarkin [77-149] 15.00
- ❏ Official Member [77-150] 20.00
- ❏ Princess Leia [77-151] 15.00
- ❏ Stormtrooper [77-152] 15.00
- ❏ Threepio [77-153] 15.00
- ❏ Tusken Raider [77-154] 15.00

Fox Video
Star Wars Trilogy for the first time on DVD 9.21
- ❏ Darth Vader [77-155] 15.00
- ❏ Heroes [77-156] 15.00

Hallmark
- ❏ Do, or do not. [77-157] 8.00
- ❏ I am your father. [77-158] 8.00
- ❏ I've got a bad feeling about this. [77-159] 8.00
- ❏ Size matters not. [77-160] 8.00

Hallmark Keepsake.
- ❏ Anakin and Ahsoka [77-161] 10.00
- ❏ Boba Fett [77-162] 10.00
- ❏ Captain Rex [77-163] 10.00
- ❏ Han Solo in Carbonite [77-164] 10.00
- ❏ Han Solo, stormtrooper disguise [77-165] 10.00
- ❏ Jedi Master Yoda (Empire Strikes Back) 10.00
- ❏ Landspeeder [77-166] 10.00
- ❏ LEGO Darth Vader 10.00
- ❏ Showdown at the Cantina (Han and Greedo) 10.00
- ❏ Yoda [77-167] 10.00

Hasbro
- ❏ Princess Leia Mighty Mugg [77-168] ...8.00

Hungry Jacks
- ❏ Episode III Revenge of the Sith [77-169] 15.00

K B Toys
- ❏ Destination Episode I, employee button [77-170] 25.00

Kenner
- ❏ Power of the Force, Biker Scout 15.00
- ❏ The Kenner Star Wars Convention, 2" round [77-171] 35.00

KFC (Malaysia)
- ❏ Join the Celebration [77-172] 25.00

Kinnerton Confectionery (UK)
Starfield background.
- ❏ C-3PO and R2-D2 [77-173] 15.00
- ❏ Darth Vader [77-174] 15.00
- ❏ The Force Will Be With You Always [77-175] 15.00

LucasArts
- ❏ BattleFront 2, Coming 11.01.05 [77-176] 10.00
- ❏ BattleFront 2, on 11.01.05 [77-177] 10.00
- ❏ BattleFront 2, on 11.01.05 ....10.00

Mister Badges
- ❏ 2-pack of random buttons 50.00
- ❏ C-3PO 10.00
- ❏ C-3PO and white protocol droid 10.00
- ❏ Chewbacca 10.00
- ❏ Darth Vader 10.00
- ❏ Darth Vader and Stormtrooper 10.00
- ❏ Han Solo 10.00
- ❏ Luke as pilot 10.00
- ❏ Luke as pilot, close-up 10.00
- ❏ Luke in Millennium Falcon gun well 10.00
- ❏ Luke with gun drawn 10.00
- ❏ Millennium Falcon 10.00
- ❏ Princess Leia 10.00
- ❏ R2-D2 ....10.00
- ❏ Star Destroyer 10.00
- ❏ X-Wing 10.00
- ❏ Yoda 10.00
- ❏ Yoda and Luke 10.00

Return of the Jedi photo buttons.
- ❏ AT-ST 10.00

- ❏ Darth Vader 10.00
- ❏ Emperor's Royal Guard 10.00
- ❏ Gamorrean Guard 10.00
- ❏ Jabba the Hutt 10.00
- ❏ Jabba the Hutt, close-up 10.00
- ❏ Luke and Leia 10.00
- ❏ Millennium Falcon 10.00
- ❏ Stormtrooper 10.00
- ❏ Wicket the Ewok 10.00

National Public Radio
- ❏ Darth Vader / Star Wars, any station [77-178] 50.00

Penguin Young Readers Group
Clone Wars. "Read"
- ❏ Asajj Ventress: "Defeat the Dark Side" [77-179] 8.00
- ❏ Captain Rex: "Be First In Command" [77-180] 8.00
- ❏ Grievous: "Plan Your Attack" [77-181] 8.00
- ❏ Obi-Wan Kenobi: "Experience the Force" [77-182] 8.00

Present Needs Ltd.
- ❏ Baby Ewoks 10.00
- ❏ Darth Vader and Royal Guard 10.00
- ❏ May the Force be with you 10.00

Scholastic
- ❏ Darth Maul, lenticular [77-183] 12.00

Skywalkers
- ❏ Don't Give In To The Dark Side [77-184] 15.00

Spirit
- ❏ Celebration V promotion [77-185] 25.00

Star Badges
- ❏ Admiral Ackbar 25.00
- ❏ Bib Fortuna 25.00
- ❏ C-3PO [77-186] 25.00
- ❏ Chewbacca 25.00
- ❏ Darth Vader 25.00
- ❏ Gamorrean Guard 25.00
- ❏ Jabba the Hutt 25.00
- ❏ R2-D2 [77-187] 25.00
- ❏ Shuttle Tydirium 25.00
- ❏ Yoda 25.00

Super Live Adventure (Japan)
- ❏ Event souvenir, giant [77-188] 50.00

Takara (Japan)
- ❏ C-3PO and R2-D2 [77-189] 100.00
- ❏ Star Wars logo, black on silver [77-190] 100.00
- ❏ Star Wars logo, silver on black [77-191] 100.00
- ❏ Stormtroopers stop landspeeder, art [77-192] 100.00

Touchline
- ❏ Admiral Ackbar 8.00
- ❏ C-3PO 8.00
- ❏ Chewbacca 8.00
- ❏ Darth Vader 8.00
- ❏ Ewok 8.00
- ❏ Jabba the Hutt 8.00
- ❏ R2-D2 ....8.00
- ❏ Stormtrooper 8.00

Volkswagon
- ❏ Imperial Emblem 15.00
- ❏ Passat 15.00
- ❏ Star Wars The Complete Saga 15.00
- ❏ Volkswagon Logo 15.00

Walmart
- ❏ 48 Hours of the Force, April 2nd and 3rd [77-193] 20.00
- ❏ Star Wars logo on Episode I background [77-194] 20.00

Williams
- ❏ I Played Star Wars Episode I Pinball 2000 [77-195] 15.00

Yujin
1" buttons dispensed in capsules with insert.
- ❏ 1. Luke Skywalker 10.00
- ❏ 2. Chewbacca [77-196] 10.00
- ❏ 3. Jawa 10.00
- ❏ 4. Qui-Gon Jinn 10.00
- ❏ 5. Boba Fett 10.00
- ❏ 6. Mace Windu 10.00
- ❏ 7. Stormtrooper 10.00
- ❏ 8. Han Solo in Carbonite 10.00
- ❏ 9. Princess Leia 10.00
- ❏ 10. X-Wing Fighter 10.00
- ❏ 11. Try not. Do or do not. There is no Try. 10.00
- ❏ 12. Training to be a Jedi will not be easy. 10.00
- ❏ 13. Mandalorian emblem 10.00
- ❏ 14. Bantha skull 10.00
- ❏ 15. (Mystery button) 10.00
- ❏ 16. Han Solo [77-197] 10.00
- ❏ 17. Obi-Wan Kenobi 10.00
- ❏ 18. Anakin Skywalker podracer 10.00
- ❏ 19. Lando Calrissian [77-198] 10.00
- ❏ 20. Jar Jar [77-199] 10.00
- ❏ 21. Yoda 10.00
- ❏ 22. AT-AT Driver 10.00
- ❏ 23. The Kiss (Empire Strikes Back) 10.00
- ❏ 24. Death Star 10.00
- ❏ 25. Darth Vader on Bespin 10.00
- ❏ 26. May the Force be with you 10.00
- ❏ 27. The Force is Strong with This One 10.00
- ❏ 28. Rebel emblem 10.00
- ❏ 29. Imperial emblem 10.00
- ❏ 30. Empire Strikes Back poster art 10.00
- ❏ 31. Darth Vader 10.00
- ❏ 32. Princess Leia on Hoth [77-200] ...10.00
- ❏ 33. C-3PO, Episode I [77-201] 10.00
- ❏ 34. Salacious Crumb 10.00
- ❏ 35. Battle Droid [77-202] 10.00
- ❏ 36. Tusken Raider [77-203] 10.00
- ❏ 37. Queen Amidala [77-204] 10.00
- ❏ 38. C-3PO and R2-D2 ....10.00
- ❏ 39. Millennium Falcon cockpit 10.00
- ❏ 40. Biker Scout 10.00
- ❏ 41. It's a wonder you're still alive 10.00
- ❏ 42. I have a very bad feeling about this 10.00
- ❏ 43. Rebel emblem [77-205] 10.00
- ❏ 44. Anakin's pod racer emblem 10.00
- ❏ 45. (Mystery button) 10.00
- ❏ 46. C-3PO [77-206] 10.00
- ❏ 47. R2-D2 [77-207] 10.00
- ❏ 48. Darth Maul [77-208] 10.00
- ❏ 49. Jabba the Hutt [77-209] 10.00
- ❏ 50. Obi-Wan Kenobi [77-210] 10.00
- ❏ 51. TIE Fighter Pilot [77-211] 10.00
- ❏ 52. IG-88 [77-212] 10.00
- ❏ 53. Stormtrooper [77-213] 10.00
- ❏ 54. TIE Fighter [77-214] 10.00
- ❏ 55. Boba Fett [77-215] 10.00
- ❏ 56. "Wars not make one great" 10.00
- ❏ 57. "Concentrate on the moment..." 10.00
- ❏ 58. Rebel Alliance Emblem [77-216] ...10.00
- ❏ 59. Republic Emblem [77-217] 10.00
- ❏ 60. (Mystery button) 10.00
- ❏ 61. Jango Fett [77-218] 10.00
- ❏ 62. Anakin Skywalker [77-219] 10.00
- ❏ 63. Obi-Wan Kenobi [77-220] 10.00
- ❏ 64. Padmé Amidala [77-221] 10.00
- ❏ 65. Boba Fett [77-222] 10.00
- ❏ 66. Zam Wesell [77-223] 10.00
- ❏ 67. Count Dooku [77-224] 10.00
- ❏ 68. Clone trooper 10.00
- ❏ 69. Yoda 10.00
- ❏ 70. Super battle droid [77-225] 10.00
- ❏ 71. Begun this Clone War has 10.00
- ❏ 72. The dark side clouds everything. 10.00
- ❏ 73. Republic emblem [77-226] 10.00
- ❏ 74. Lightsaber 10.00
- ❏ 75. (Mystery button) 10.00

Buttons, Sewing

Birchcroft
Porcelain, hand painted. Set 1.
- ❏ Darth Maul [78-01] 10.00
- ❏ Freedon Nadd [78-02] 10.00
- ❏ Naga Sadow [78-03] 10.00
- ❏ Palpatine [78-04] 10.00
- ❏ Too-Onebee [78-05] 10.00
- ❏ Wicket [78-06] 10.00

Buttons, Sewing

 78-01
 78-02
 78-03
 78-04
 78-05
 78-06
 78-07
 78-08
 78-09
 78-10
 78-11
 78-12

Porcelain, hand painted. Set 2.
- C-3PO [78-07] 10.00
- Darth Vader [78-08] 10.00
- Han Solo [78-09] 10.00
- Leia Organa [78-10] 10.00
- R2-D2 [78-11] 10.00
- Yoda [78-12] 10.00

Cake Decorating Supplies
Continued in Volume 3, Page 102

Cupcake toppers, look-alike.
- C-3PO [4:60] 8.00
- R2-D2 [4:60] 8.00

Decopac
- Chewbacca / Han Solo 12.00
- Darth Vader figurine / Vader backpack tag 12.00

- Luke and R2-D2 with candy stars and moons 10.00
- Obi-Wan and Jango Fett figures / Kamino backdrop ...15.00

Episode I: The Phantom Menace edible images.
- Darth Maul figure / Jedi vs. Sith image 12.00
- Jedi vs. Sith 8.00

Episode II: Attack of the Clones edible images.
- Classic 8.00
- Collage 8.00
- Heroes 8.00
- R2-D2 and C-3PO 8.00

Episode II: Attack of the Clones.
- Bakery promo kit. Black box with Saga logo containing: order brochure, lenticular book tag, and figures of Obi-Wan, Vader, and Jango 50.00

Episode III: Revenge of the Sith.
- Cake skirts 10.00

Rings made as cupcake toppers.
- C-3PO [79-01] 3.00
- Darth Vader [79-02] 3.00
- R2-D2 [79-03] 3.00

Meri Meri
Cupcake decorating kits. Exclusive to Williams-Sonoma.
- Galactic Empire 25.00
- Rebel Alliance [79-04] 25.00

MT Creations (France)
- Cake mat / centerpiece 12" x 16" 15.00

Pop Tops
- Darth Vader mask [79-05] 5.00

Williams-Sonoma
- Cupcake stencils [79-06] 25.00

 79-01
 79-02
 79-03
 79-04
 79-05
 79-06
 79-07
 79-08
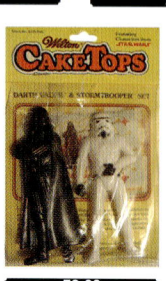 79-09
 80-01
 80-02
 80-03
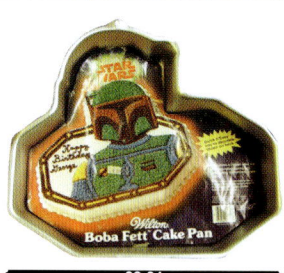 80-04
 80-05
 80-06
 80-07
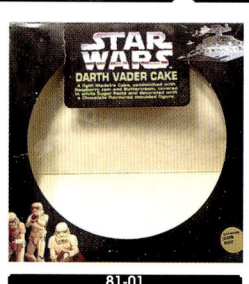 81-01
 82-01
 82-02

Calendars

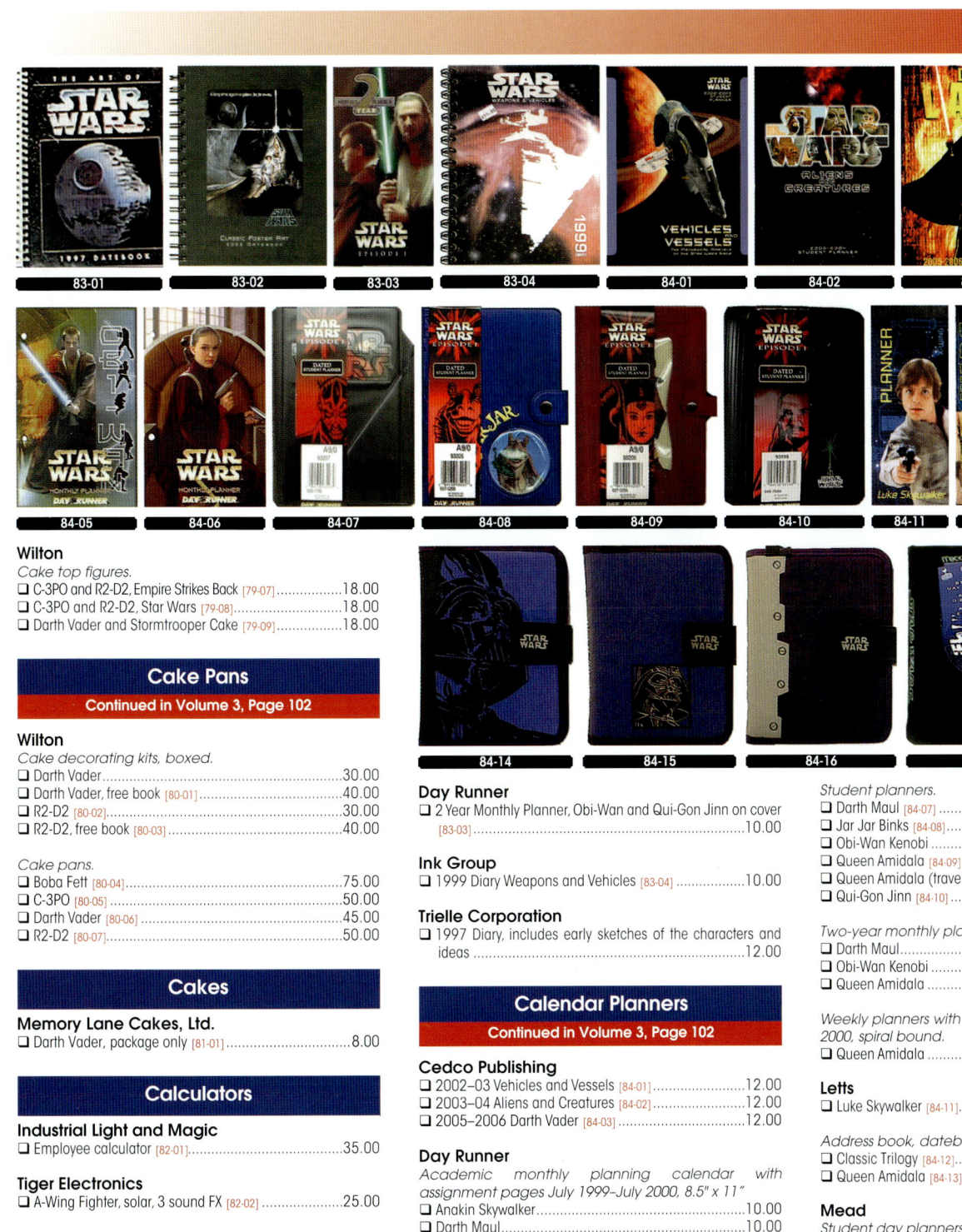

Wilton
Cake top figures.
- ☐ C-3PO and R2-D2, Empire Strikes Back [79-07]..................18.00
- ☐ C-3PO and R2-D2, Star Wars [79-08]..............................18.00
- ☐ Darth Vader and Stormtrooper Cake [79-09]..................18.00

Cake Pans
Continued in Volume 3, Page 102

Wilton
Cake decorating kits, boxed.
- ☐ Darth Vader 30.00
- ☐ Darth Vader, free book [80-01] 40.00
- ☐ R2-D2 [80-02] 30.00
- ☐ R2-D2, free book [80-03] 40.00

Cake pans.
- ☐ Boba Fett [80-04] 75.00
- ☐ C-3PO [80-05] 50.00
- ☐ Darth Vader [80-06] 45.00
- ☐ R2-D2 [80-07] 50.00

Cakes

Memory Lane Cakes, Ltd.
- ☐ Darth Vader, package only [81-01] 8.00

Calculators

Industrial Light and Magic
- ☐ Employee calculator [82-01] 35.00

Tiger Electronics
- ☐ A-Wing Fighter, solar, 3 sound FX [82-02] 25.00

Calendar Datebooks
Continued in Volume 3, Page 102

Antioch
- ☐ 1996 Star Wars "Book of Days" 15.00

Cedco Publishing
- ☐ 1996 Wide Image 12.00
- ☐ 1997 Art of Star Wars [83-01] 10.00
- ☐ 1998 Trilogy Special Edition 10.00
- ☐ 1999 May the Force be with you datebook 14.00
- ☐ 2000 Star Wars Episode I 10.00
- ☐ 2002 Star Wars Style 10.00
- ☐ 2003 Classic Poster Art 16.00
- ☐ 2003 Classic Poster Art, spiral bound [83-02] 10.00
- ☐ 2003 Imperial Forces 10.00
- ☐ 2003 Rebel Alliance 10.00
- ☐ 2004 Star Wars 16.00

Day Runner
- ☐ 2 Year Monthly Planner, Obi-Wan and Qui-Gon Jinn on cover [83-03] 10.00

Ink Group
- ☐ 1999 Diary Weapons and Vehicles [83-04] 10.00

Trielle Corporation
- ☐ 1997 Diary, includes early sketches of the characters and ideas 12.00

Calendar Planners
Continued in Volume 3, Page 102

Cedco Publishing
- ☐ 2002–03 Vehicles and Vessels [84-01] 12.00
- ☐ 2003–04 Aliens and Creatures [84-02] 12.00
- ☐ 2005–2006 Darth Vader [84-03] 12.00

Day Runner
Academic monthly planning calendar with assignment pages July 1999–July 2000, 8.5" x 11"
- ☐ Anakin Skywalker 10.00
- ☐ Darth Maul 10.00
- ☐ Obi-Wan Kenobi 10.00
- ☐ Queen Amidala 10.00

Academic monthly planning calendars with assignment pages July 1999–July 2000, 5.5" x 8.5"
- ☐ Anakin Skywalker 10.00
- ☐ Darth Maul 10.00
- ☐ Queen Amidala 10.00

Dated assignment books.
- ☐ Anakin Skywalker 10.00
- ☐ Darth Maul 10.00
- ☐ Jedi 10.00

Monthly planners, 5.5" x 8.5"
- ☐ Anakin Skywalker 10.00
- ☐ Darth Maul [84-04] 10.00
- ☐ Obi-Wan Kenobi [84-05] 10.00
- ☐ Queen Amidala [84-06] 10.00

Student planners.
- ☐ Darth Maul [84-07] 15.00
- ☐ Jar Jar Binks [84-08] 15.00
- ☐ Obi-Wan Kenobi 15.00
- ☐ Queen Amidala [84-09] 15.00
- ☐ Queen Amidala (travel gown) 15.00
- ☐ Qui-Gon Jinn [84-10] 15.00

Two-year monthly planner Jan 2000–Dec 2001.
- ☐ Darth Maul 10.00
- ☐ Obi-Wan Kenobi 10.00
- ☐ Queen Amidala 10.00

Weekly planners with assignments August 1999 to July 2000, spiral bound.
- ☐ Queen Amidala 10.00

Letts
- ☐ Luke Skywalker [84-11] 12.00

Address book, datebook, and note pad.
- ☐ Classic Trilogy [84-12] 6.00
- ☐ Queen Amidala [84-13] 6.00

Mead
Student day planners.
- ☐ Darth Vader [84-14] 8.00
- ☐ Darth Vader inset art [84-15] 8.00
- ☐ Technology design with Star Wars logo 8.00
- ☐ Technology design with Star Wars logo on Velcro latch [84-16] 8.00
- ☐ Yoda inset art [84-17] 8.00

Q-Stat (UK)
Episode I: The Phantom Menace address book, datebook, and note pad.
- ☐ Jar Jar Binks [84-18] 15.00

Calendars
Continued in Volume 3, Page 103

- ☐ 1998 Classic trilogy [85-01] 12.00
- ☐ 1998 Computer Games Calendar (Star Wars Rebellion on Cover & July) 12.00

Calendars

2006 Episode III: Revenge of the Sith pocket calendar cards.
- Anakin Skywalker..5.00
- Anakin Skywalker against flames........................5.00
- Anakin, Padmé, Dooku, Obi-Wan........................5.00
- Anakin, Padmé, Obi-Wan, Darth Tyranus 5.00
- Darth Vader 5.00
- Darth Vader bust 5.00
- Darth Vader reaching upwards.............................5.00
- Darth Vader, Obi-Wan, Anakin, and Grievous......5.00
- Epic duel 5.00
- Epic duel in front of Vader image 5.00
- Episode III / Darth Vader 5.00
- General Grievous (long) 5.00
- General Grievous (tall) 5.00
- Grievous, Padmé, Anakin, Obi-Wan.....................5.00
- Obi-Wan and Mace Windu....................................5.00
- Obi-Wan, Anakin, Count Dooku, Mace Windu, Padmé, droids 5.00
- Padmé...5.00
- Palpatine, Obi-Wan, Anakin, Padmé....................5.00
- Sith Lords look over epic duel 5.00
- Wookiees..5.00
- Yoda..5.00
- Yoda with lightsaber...5.00
- Yoda with lightsaber in front of flames................5.00

Poster wall calendars, 19" x 35".
- 2002 Darth Vader: Reflections of Darkness [85-02].......24.00
- 2002 The Art of Star Wars Episode I [85-03]...............24.00

(Hungary)
1985 Return of the Jedi pocket calendar cards.
- Luke and Artoo [85-04]..10.00
- Nien Nunb [v1e1:97] 10.00
- Scout Walker [v1e1:97] 10.00
- Skiff prisoners [v1e1:97] 10.00
- The Emperor [v1e1:97] 10.00

(Thailand)
Classic Trilogy poster pocket calendar cards.
- Empire Strikes Back 10th anniversary [v1e1:97] 8.00
- Empire Strikes Back 1982 rerelease [v1e1:97] 8.00
- Empire Strikes Back public radio broadcast [v1e1:97] 8.00
- Empire Strikes Back style A [v1e1:97]..................8.00
- Empire Strikes Back style A advance [v1e1:97] ...8.00
- Empire Strikes Back style B [v1e1:97]..................8.00
- Empire Strikes Back style C art [v1e1:97] 8.00
- Le Retour Du Jedi [v1e1:97]..................................8.00
- Return of the Jedi 10th anniversary advance [v1e1:97] ...8.00
- Return of the Jedi 10th anniversary [v1e1:97] 8.00
- Return of the Jedi 1985 rerelease [v1e1:97] 8.00
- Return of the Jedi horizontal [v1e1:97] 8.00
- Return of the Jedi style A in red [v1e1:97] 8.00
- Return of the Jedi style B [v1e1:97] 8.00
- Star Wars 10th anniversary [v1e1:97] 8.00
- Star Wars concert [v1e1:97] 8.00
- Star Wars lobby poster art [85-05].........................8.00
- Star Wars program art [v1e1:97] 8.00
- Star Wars public radio broadcast [v1e1:97] 8.00
- Star Wars style D [v1e1:97] 8.00

Classic Trilogy Special Edition pocket calendar cards.
- A New Hope [85-06]...8.00
- Empire Strikes Back [v1e1:97] 8.00
- Return of the Jedi [v1e1:97] 8.00

Episode I: The Phantom Menace pocket calendar cards. Characters / Pepsi logo.
- Anakin Skywalker [v1e1:98] 8.00
- C-3PO [85-07]...8.00
- Darth Maul [v1e1:98] 8.00
- Jar Jar Binks [v1e1:98] 8.00
- Queen Amidala [v1e1:98] 8.00
- Qui-Gon Jinn [v1e1:98] 8.00
- Sebulba [v1e1:98] 8.00
- Watto [v1e1:98] 8.00
- Yoda [v1e1:98] 8.00

Episode I: The Phantom Menace pocket calendar cards. Characters.
- Anakin Skywalker [v1e1:98] 8.00
- Darth Maul [v1e1:98] 8.00
- Movie poster [v1e1:98] 8.00
- Obi-Wan Kenobi [v1e1:98] 8.00
- Queen Amidala [v1e1:98] 8.00
- Qui-Gon and Obi-Wan [v1e1:98] 8.00
- Qui-Gon Jinn [v1e1:98] 8.00
- Yoda, Qui-Gon, and Obi-Wan [v1e1:98] 8.00

Episode I: The Phantom Menace pocket calendar cards. Colleges.
- Confrontations [v1e1:98] 8.00
- Entire cast [v1e1:98] 8.00
- Heroes on Tatooine [85-08].....................................8.00
- Heroes over Naboo [v1e1:98] 8.00
- Jedi vs. Sith on Tatooine [v1e1:98] 8.00
- Quartet of destiny [v1e1:98] 8.00
- Tatooine duel / Podracing [v1e1:98] 8.00

Episode III: Revenge of the Sith pocket calendar cards. Characters.
- Anakin Skywalker...5.00
- Clone trooper 5.00
- Epic duel / Jedi 5.00
- General Grievous 5.00
- Mace Windu 5.00
- Yoda...5.00

Episode III: Revenge of the Sith pocket calendar cards. Colleges.
- Anakin 5.00
- Darth Vader 5.00
- Darth Vader lightsaber down................................5.00
- Epic duel / Darth Vader 5.00
- Episode III conflict [85-09].......................................5.00
- Jedi 5.00
- Obi-Wan 5.00
- Sith...5.00

20th Century Fox
- 1999 Fox Movie Release desktop calendar [85-10]........20.00

Abrams
- 1991 Lucasfilm [85-11]..15.00

Andrews and McNeel
- 1995 trilogy 3D [85-12]...20.00

Antioch
- 1995 trilogy [5:61] 15.00

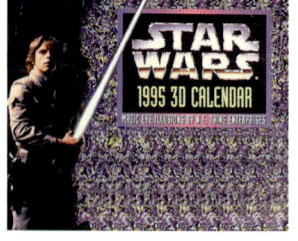
85-12

85-13 Box and Calendar

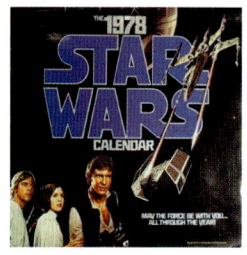

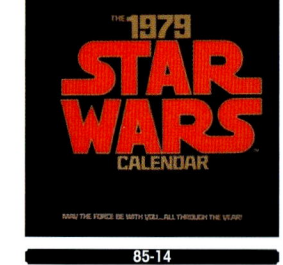
85-14

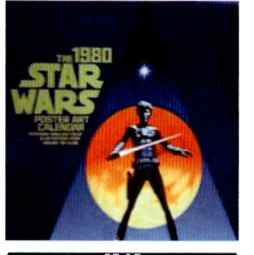
85-15

Calendars

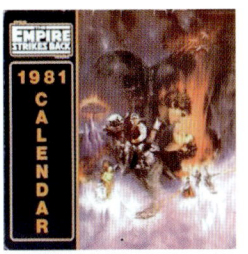 85-16
 85-17
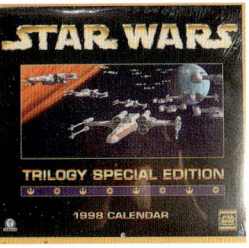 85-18
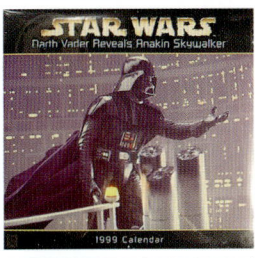 85-19
 85-20

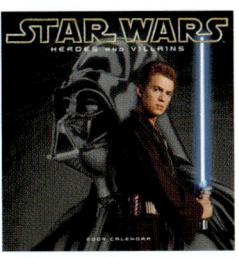 85-21
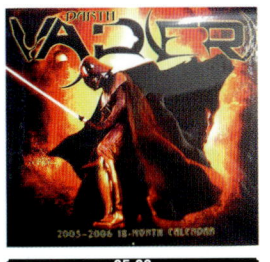 85-22
 85-23
 85-24
 85-25
 85-26

Ballantine
- 1978 Star Wars [85-13] 35.00
- 1979 Star Wars [85-14] 35.00
- 1980 Star Wars Poster Art [85-15] 30.00
- 1981 Empire Strikes Back [85-16] 30.00
- 1984 Return of the Jedi [85-17] 30.00

Bay Street Publishing
- 1998 Trilogy Special Edition [85-18] 20.00
- 1999 Darth Vader Reveals Anakin Skywalker [85-19] 20.00
- 2003 Attack of the Clones, 18 month [85-20] 15.00
- 2003 Star Wars Heroes and Villains [v1e1:99] ... 15.00
- 2004 Star Wars Heroes and Villains [85-21] 15.00
- 2005–2006 Darth Vader 18 month [85-22] 15.00
- 2005–2006 Revenge of the Sith 18 month [85-23] 15.00
- 2006 Poster calendar [85-24] 15.00

Bonbon Buddies (UK)
Advent calendar, milk chocolate.
- Clone Wars [85-25] 18.00
- Episode III: Revenge of the Sith 15.00

Cadbury (UK)
- Jedi-Sith duel, Episode I advent 3D, chocolate [85-26] .. 15.00

Capital
- 1995 distributing titles, June shows Dark Empire II scene [v1e1:99] 20.00

Cedco Publishing
- 1990 Trilogy [85-27] 20.00
- 1991 Trilogy [85-28] 20.00
- 1996 Wide Image 20.00
- 1997 Art of Star Wars [85-29] 20.00
- 1997 Star Wars 20th Anniversary [85-30] 20.00
- 1998 Art of Star Wars: Classic Characters [85-31] 20.00
- 1998 Trilogy Special Edition, Han and Jabba on cover [85-32] 20.00
- 1999 Daily Wisdom of Star Wars [85-33] 20.00
- 1999 Darth Vader Reveals Anakin Skywalker [v1e1:99] .. 20.00
- 1999 Empire Strikes Back [85-34] 20.00
- 1999 May the Force be with you [85-35] 20.00
- 1999 Star Wars [v1e1:99] 20.00
- 1999 Weapons and Technology [85-36] 20.00
- 2003 Daily box calendar [85-37] 15.00
- 2003 Daily Character A-Z 15.00
- 2003 Daily Episode II: Attack of the Clones ... 15.00
- 2003 Droids locker calendar [85-38] 15.00
- 2003 Episode II, 18 month [85-39] 15.00
- 2003 Heroes and Rebels [85-40] 15.00
- 2003 Scum and Villainy [85-41] 15.00

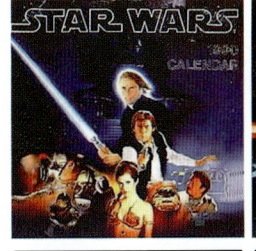 85-27
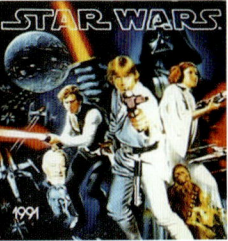 85-28
 85-29
 85-30
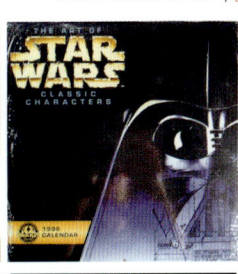 85-31
 85-32

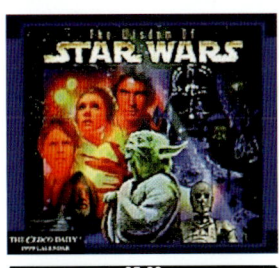 85-33
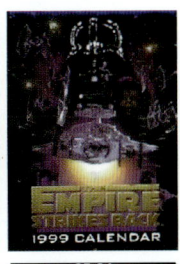 85-34
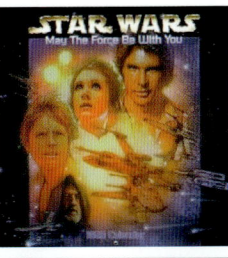 85-35
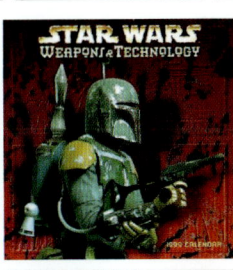 85-36
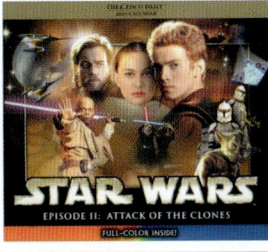 85-37
 85-38

 85-39
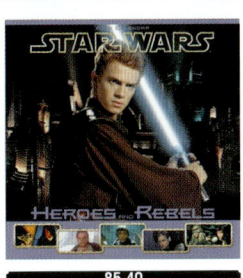 85-40
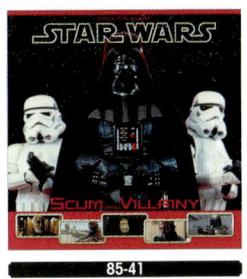 85-41
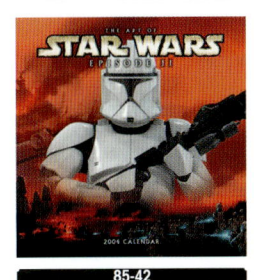 85-42
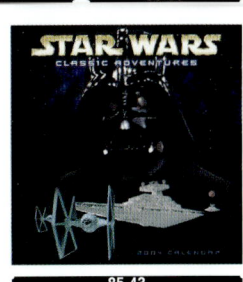 85-43

Calendars

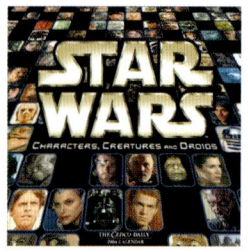 85-44
 85-45
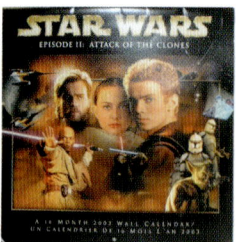 85-46
 85-47
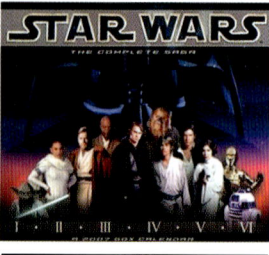 85-48

 85-49
 85-50
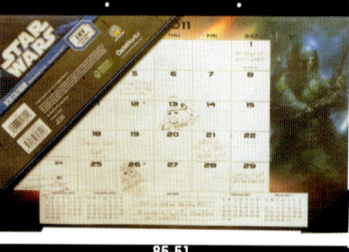 85-51
 85-52
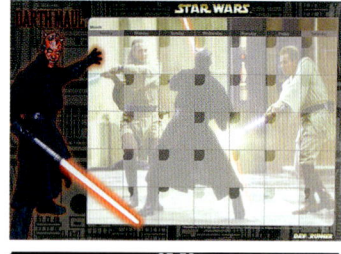 85-53

- ❑ 2003 Daily Characters, Creatures, Droids 15.00
- ❑ 2004 Art of Episode II [85-42] 15.00
- ❑ 2004 Classic Adventures [85-43] 15.00
- ❑ 2004 Daily Characters, Creatures, Droids [85-44] 15.00
- ❑ 2005 Star Wars Evolutions: Characters 15.00
- ❑ 2005 Star Wars Evolutions: Vehicles 15.00
- ❑ 2006 Revenge of the Sith 15.00
- ❑ 2006 The Complete Saga 15.00

Chronicle Books
- ❑ 1997 Vehicles with blueprints 20.00

Code 3 Collectibles
- ❑ 2004 1-sheet with lift-up panels [v1e1:99] 15.00

Cosmic Cat Creations
- ❑ 2005 The Year of the Crumb [85-45] 10.00

DateMaker
- ❑ 2003 Wall calendar [85-46] 15.00
- ❑ 2007 Celebrating 30 Years [85-47] 15.00
- ❑ 2007 The Complete Saga box [85-48] 15.00
- ❑ 2008 The Art of Star Wars [85-49] 15.00
- ❑ 2009 The Clone Wars 15.00
- ❑ 2012 Wall calendar [85-50] 15.00

DateWorks
2011.
- ❑ Clone Wars wall valendar 15.00
- ❑ Clone Wars wall calendar with DVD 16.00
- ❑ Saga box calendar 15.00
- ❑ Saga desk calendar [85-51] 10.00
- ❑ Saga lenticular wall calendar, spiral-bound 16.00
- ❑ Saga oversized wall calendar, spiral-bound 16.00
- ❑ Saga wall calendar 15.00

2012.
- ❑ Saga oversized wall calendar [85-52] 16.00

Day Runner
14" x 16" laminated wipe-off 1-month blank wall calendar.
- ❑ Darth Maul [85-53] 25.00
- ❑ Jar Jar Binks [85-54] 25.00
- ❑ Naboo Fighters [85-55] 25.00
- ❑ Queen Amidala [85-56] 25.00
- ❑ Watto [85-57] 25.00

24" x 35" laminated, 2-sided sheet.
- ❑ Jar Jar Binks 30.00
- ❑ Naboo Fighter 30.00
- ❑ Obi-Wan Kenobi 30.00
- ❑ Podrace 30.00
- ❑ Queen Amidala 30.00

 85-54
 85-55
 85-56
 85-57

 85-58
 85-59
 85-60
 85-61
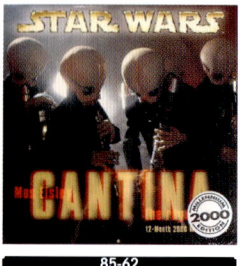 85-62
 85-63

 85-64
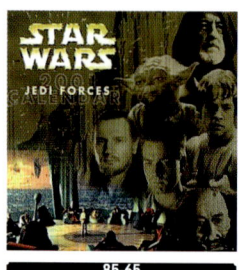 85-65
 85-66
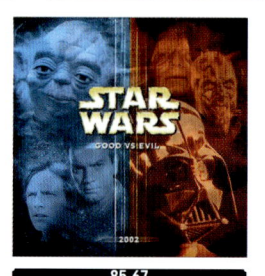 85-67
 85-68

Calendars

85-69

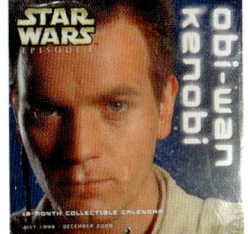
85-70

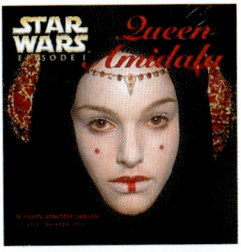
85-71

85-72

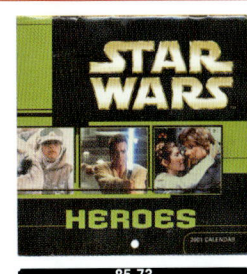
85-73

85-74

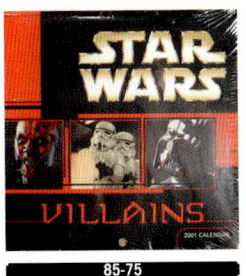
85-75

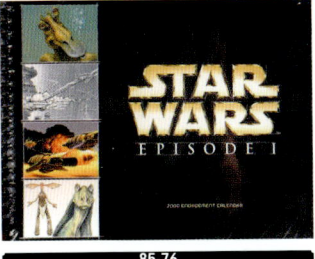
85-76

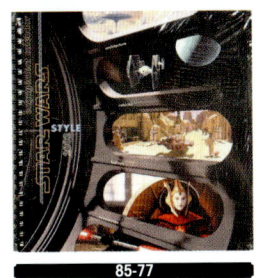
85-77

85-78

Golden Turtle Press
- ☐ 1997 Collector's Edition [85-58] 20.00
- ☐ 1999 Episode I 20 month wall calendar [85-59] 20.00
- ☐ 2000 Characters of Episode I [85-60] 15.00
- ☐ 2000 Han Solo cover [85-61] 15.00
- ☐ 2000 Mos Eisley Cantina Regulars [85-62] 15.00
- ☐ 2000 Yoda cover [85-63] 15.00
- ☐ 2001 Bounty Hunters [85-64] 15.00
- ☐ 2001 Jedi Forces [85-65] 15.00
- ☐ 2001 Podrace [85-66] 15.00
- ☐ 2002 Good vs. Evil wall calendar [85-67] 15.00

1999 18-month mini wall calendars.
- ☐ Darth Maul [85-68] 10.00
- ☐ Jar Jar Binks [85-69] 10.00
- ☐ Obi-Wan Kenobi [85-70] 10.00
- ☐ Queen Amidala [85-71] 10.00

2001 12-month mini wall calendars.
- ☐ Bounty Hunters [85-72] 10.00
- ☐ Heroes [85-73] 10.00
- ☐ Vehicles [85-74] 10.00
- ☐ Villains [85-75] 10.00

52-week engagement calendars.
- ☐ 2000 Episode I [85-76] 20.00
- ☐ 2002 Star Wars Style [85-77] 18.00

Flip animation, trivia calendars, boxed.
- ☐ 2000 podracer cover [85-78] 12.00
- ☐ 2001 TIE Fighters cover [85-79] 12.00
- ☐ 2001 X-Wing Figters cover [85-80] 12.00
- ☐ 2002 saga scenes cover [85-81] 12.00

Hallmark
- ☐ 1996 Star Wars 25.00
- ☐ 1997 The Empire Strikes Back 20.00
- ☐ 1998 Return of the Jedi [85-82] 20.00

Hallmark (Australia)
- ☐ 2000 Episode I, millennium collection [85-83] 15.00
- ☐ 2003 Episode II [85-84] 15.00

Ink Group
- ☐ 1998 The Battles [85-85] 20.00
- ☐ 1998–2000 Star Wars Episode I [85-86] 20.00
- ☐ 1999 Classic Commemorative [85-87] 20.00
- ☐ 1999 Heroes and Villains [85-88] 20.00
- ☐ 2000 Aliens and Creatures [85-89] 15.00
- ☐ 2000 Episode I collector's edition [85-90] 15.00
- ☐ 2000 Episode I: The Adventures [85-91] 15.00
- ☐ 2002 Darth Vader: Reflections in Darkness [85-92] 15.00

85-79

85-80

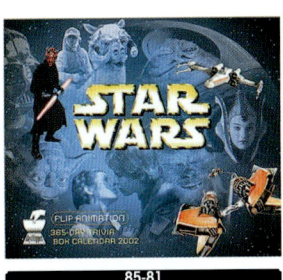
85-81

85-82

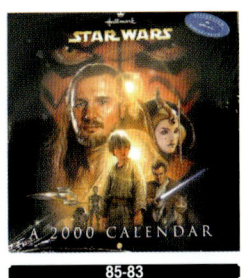
85-83

85-84

85-85

85-86

85-87

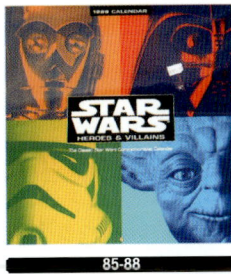
85-88

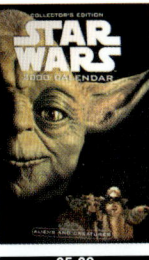
85-89

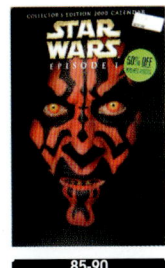
85-90

85-91

85-92

85-93

85-94

85-95

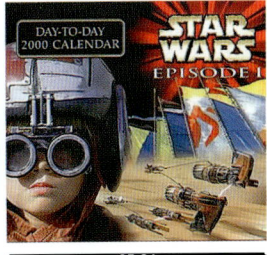
85-96

Calendars

   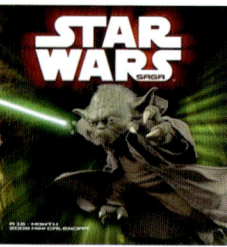  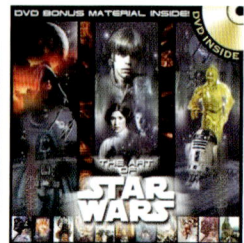

85-97 | 85-98 | 85-99 Front and Back | 85-100 | 85-101 | 85-102

 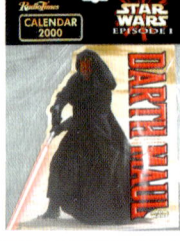    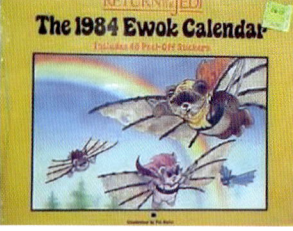 

85-103 | 85-104 | 85-105 | 85-106 | 85-107 | 85-108 | 85-109

   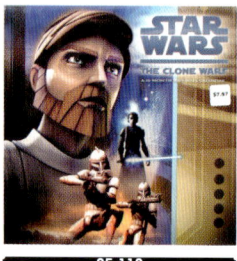 

85-110 | 85-111 | 85-112 | 85-113 | 86-01

- ❏ 2002 The Art of Star Wars Episode I 15.00
- ❏ 2003 Attack of the Clones [85-93] 15.00

Day-to-day calendars, boxed.
- ❏ 1998 [85-94] 15.00
- ❏ 1999 C-3PO and X-Wings cover [85-95] 15.00
- ❏ 2000 Anakin / Podracing cover [85-96] 15.00

Kinnerton Confectionery (UK)
Advent Calendar, 26 chocolates with Star Wars punch-out on back.
- ❏ Mask [85-97] 20.00
- ❏ Mobile [85-98] 20.00

Landmark
- ❏ 1995 trilogy 15.00

Major Cineplex
Episode II: Attack of the Clones pocket calendar cards.
- ❏ 2003 Anakin Skywalker [v1e1:101] 10.00
- ❏ 2003 Jango Fett [85-99] 10.00
- ❏ 2003 Obi-Wan Kenobi [v1e1:101] 10.00
- ❏ 2003 Padmé Amidala [v1e1:101] 10.00

Mega Calendars
- ❏ 2008 Art of Star Wars page-per-day 15.00
- ❏ 2008 mini-calendar [85-100] 10.00
- ❏ 2008 Saga—TV series / movies [85-101] 15.00
- ❏ 2008 The Art of Star Wars with bonus DVD [85-102] 20.00

Radio Times
2000, free-standing.
- ❏ Battle Droid [85-103] 15.00
- ❏ Darth Maul [85-104] 15.00
- ❏ Darth Maul with Sith probe droids [85-105] 15.00
- ❏ Jar Jar [85-106] 15.00
- ❏ Obi-Wan Kenobi [85-107] 15.00

Random House
- ❏ 1984 Return of the Jedi with Ewok stickers [85-108] 35.00

Revell (UK)
Advent calendars. Models, Top Trumps, paint, candy.
- ❏ 2008 [85-109] 45.00
- ❏ 2011 [85-110] 45.00

Shooting Star Press
- ❏ 1997 20th Anniversary 20.00

Slow Dazzle Worldwide
- ❏ 1999 A New Hope / Star Wars 10.00
- ❏ 1999 Empire Strikes Back 10.00
- ❏ 1999 Return of the Jedi 10.00

Starwars.com
In 2003 the official Star Wars website offered 13 theme galleries with approximately 12 images in each gallery. Fans could order calendars from an online merchandiser in a variety of formats. Considering the number if galleries, images available, and formats to choose from, there are thousands of combinations that could have been individually produced.

Galleries were categorized as "Bounty Hunters," "Clone Wars," "Creatures," "Droids," "Holiday Art," "Jedi," "Logo and Emblems," "Padmé," "Poster Art," "Princess Leia," "Rebels," "Sith," and "Vehicles."

- ❏ 10" x 15" glossy, any 15.00
- ❏ 10" x 15" matte, any 15.00
- ❏ 20" x 30" glossy, any 18.00
- ❏ 20" x 30" matte, any 18.00

Thomas Foreman and Sons
- ❏ 1982 Star Wars / Empire Strikes Back 30.00

TPF (Germany)
- ❏ 24 Mal Adventskalender [85-111] 35.00

Trends International Corp.
- ❏ 2008 16-month wall calendar [85-112] 15.00
- ❏ 2009 Clone Wars, 16-month [85-113] 15.00
- ❏ 2009 Clone Wars, mini 15.00
- ❏ 2009 Star Wars Saga, Boba Fett cover 15.00
- ❏ 2009 Star Wars Saga, mini, Darth Vader cover 15.00
- ❏ 2010 Clone Wars 15.00
- ❏ 2010 Clone Wars, mini 15.00
- ❏ 2010 Clone Wars with DVD 15.00
- ❏ 2010 Star Wars—The Saga 15.00
- ❏ 2010 Star Wars—The Saga, boxed 15.00
- ❏ 2010 Star Wars, oversized 15.00
- ❏ 2010 Star Wars, spiral bound 15.00

Calendars, Perpetual
Continued in Volume 3, Page 106

(Japan)
- ❏ R2-D2, theater promotion, Revenge of the Sith [86-01] .. 90.00

Calling Cards, Telephone
Continued in Volume 3, Page 106

- ❏ Anakin Skywalker [3:161] 10.00
- ❏ C-3PO and R2-D2 [4:64] 10.00
- ❏ Darth Maul [v1e1:102] 10.00
- ❏ Jar Jar Binks [v1e1:102] 10.00
- ❏ Lucas Legacy [v1e1:102] 15.00
- ❏ Queen Amidala [v1e1:102] 10.00
- ❏ Qui-Gon Jinn [v1e1:102] 10.00
- ❏ Return of the Jedi, Chewbacca [v1e1:102] 10.00
- ❏ Star Wars special edition, video preorder [v1e1:102] . 10.00
- ❏ Yoda [v1e1:102] 10.00

$10.00, 250 fixed minutes, THX video cover art.
- ❏ A New Hope / Vader [5:64] 15.00
- ❏ Empire Strikes Back / Stormtrooper [3:160] 15.00
- ❏ Return of the Jedi / Yoda [3:160] 15.00

Episode II: Attack of the Clones.
- ❏ Heroes top-up [v1e1:103] 10.00

Asia. Comic book and novel art.
- ❏ Dark Empire 1 [v1e1:103] 10.00
- ❏ Dark Empire 2 [v1e1:103] 10.00
- ❏ Empire's End [v1e1:103] 10.00
- ❏ Empire's End 2 [v1e1:103] 10.00
- ❏ Heirs to the Force [v1e1:103] 10.00
- ❏ Luke Skywalker [v1e1:103] 10.00

Calling Cards, Telephone

Asia. Movie collage art.
- Episode I: characters [v1e1:103] 10.00
- Episode I: heroes [v1e1:103] 10.00
- Episode I: Phantom Menace [v1e1:103] 10.00
- Episode II: Geonosis Jedi [v1e1:103] 10.00
- Episode III: Epic duel / Obi-Wan [v1e1:103] 10.00
- Episode III: Epic duel / Yoda [v1e1:103] 10.00

Japan.
- Super Live Adventure [v1e1:103] 45.00

1-2-Call
- Anakin vs. Obi-Wan [v1e1:103] 10.00
- Darth Vader [v1e1:103] 10.00
- Epic duel [v1e1:103] 10.00
- Yoda [v1e1:103] 10.00

Episode III: Revenge of the Sith Call Time Refill Card. 300 Baht.
- Anakin (dark side) [v1e1:103] 10.00
- Anakin (Jedi) [v1e1:103] 10.00
- Anakin vs. Obi-Wan [v1e1:103] 10.00
- Clone Commander [v1e1:103] 10.00
- Clone trooper (Order 66) [v1e1:103] 10.00
- Clone trooper (standing) [v1e1:103] 10.00
- Darth Vader [v1e1:103] 10.00
- Darth Vader (reaching) [v1e1:103] 10.00
- General Grievous [v1e1:103] 10.00
- Grievous's bodyguard [v1e1:103] 10.00
- Obi-Wan Kenobi [v1e1:103] 10.00
- Yoda [v1e1:103] 10.00

Episode III: Revenge of the Sith Call Time Refill Card. 300 Baht. Series 2.
- Anakin Skywalker / Darth Vader [v1e1:104] 10.00
- Clone Commander [v1e1:104] 10.00
- Clone trooper [v1e1:104] 10.00
- Darth Vader [v1e1:104] 10.00
- General Grievous [v1e1:104] 10.00
- Grievous's bodyguard [v1e1:104] 10.00
- Jedi Starfighters [v1e1:104] 10.00
- R2-D2 and C-3PO [v1e1:104] 10.00

Episode III: Revenge of the Sith. Thailand.
- 40 different images, each 10.00

7-Eleven Inc. (Japan)
- 1000 Minutes, contest premium [v1e1:104] 35.00

BT
Return of the Jedi calling cards with collectible folders.
- #3 Star Destroyer / Death Star II [v1e1:104] 20.00
- #4 Inside Death Star II [v1e1:104] 20.00
- #5 B-Wing Attack [v1e1:104] 20.00
- #6 Boba Fett [v1e1:104] 20.00

Celcom (Malaysia)
Revenge of the Sith.
- Anakin as Darth Vader *RM50* [v1e1:104] 15.00
- Darth Vader *RM30* [v1e1:104] 15.00
- Epic duel *RM10* [v1e1:104] 15.00
- Obi-Wan Kenobi *RM30* [v1e1:104] 15.00
- Yoda *RM30* [v1e1:104] 15.00

Set of four EPII lenticular cards with folder for Malaysia.
- Gold: heroes, villains, droids, Anakin, and Padmé [v1e1:104] 30.00
- Silver: Anakin, Jango, bounty hunters, Boba Fett [4:65] 25.00

Disney / MGM
- C-3PO / Starspeeder 3000, mirrored [v1e1:104] 50.00

Entel (Bolivia)
Episode III: Revenge of the Sith. BS-30 prepaid.
- Anakin Skywalker [4:65] 10.00
- Clone trooper [4:65] 10.00
- Epic duel / Darth Vader [4:65] 10.00
- Epic duel / Emperor [4:65] 10.00
- General Grievous [4:65] 10.00
- Jedi Starfighter [4:65] 10.00
- Obi-Wan Kenobi [4:65] 10.00
- R2-D2 and C-3PO [4:65] 10.00
- Wookies [5:64] 10.00
- Yoda [4:65] 10.00

Globalcall
- $10 Star Wars: Episode I collage [v1e1:104] 10.00

GTI
$10 cards.
- A-Wing 15.00
- A New Hope ceremony 15.00
- AT-AT 15.00
- B-Wings 15.00
- Darth Vader [v1e1:104] 15.00
- Han and Chewbacca [v1e1:104] 15.00
- Jabba and Bib Fortuna [v1e1:104] 15.00
- Luke and Yoda 15.00
- Millennium Falcon 15.00
- Obi-Wan vs. Darth Vader [v1e1:104] 15.00
- TIEs and X-Wing 15.00

$20 cards.
- Ceremonial droids 18.00
- Ceremonial Leia 18.00
- Rebels on Hoth 18.00
- Return of the Jedi ceremony 18.00
- Return of the Jedi duel 18.00
- TIE Bomber 18.00

$5 cards.
- B-Wing Fighter 15.00
- Gamorrean Guard [v1e1:104] 15.00
- Imperial Star Destroyer [v1e1:104] 15.00
- Luke Skywalker in Landspeeder [v1e1:104] 15.00
- Speeder Bike trooper [v1e1:104] 15.00
- Yoda [4:65] 15.00

Intelcom
100 unit cards, lenticular 3D.
- ANH Han promo shot [v1e1:105] 15.00
- ANH R2-D2 [v1e1:105] 15.00
- ANH Stormtrooper promo shot [v1e1:105] 15.00
- ESB Fett [v1e1:105] 15.00
- ESB Yoda [v1e1:105] 15.00
- TPM Anakin [v1e1:105] 15.00
- TPM Battle Droids and tanks [v1e1:105] 15.00
- TPM Darth Maul / Lightsaber battle [v1e1:105] 15.00
- TPM Jar Jar [v1e1:105] 15.00
- TPM Obi-Wan Kenobi [v1e1:105] 15.00
- TPM Queen Amidala [v1e1:105] 15.00
- TPM Qui-Gon Jinn [v1e1:105] 15.00
- TPM Watto [v1e1:105] 15.00

200 unit cards, lenticular 3D.
- ESB international video artwork [v1e1:105] 15.00
- TPM characters [v1e1:105] 15.00

50 unit cards, lenticular 3D.
- ANH desert C-3PO and Luke [v1e1:105] 15.00
- ANH Jawas [v1e1:105] 15.00
- ANH Leia and Luke [v1e1:105] 15.00
- ANH Lightsaber duel [v1e1:105] 15.00
- ANH Vader choking rebel [v1e1:105] 15.00
- ANH X-Wing Fighters [v1e1:105] 15.00
- ESB AT-AT [v1e1:105] 15.00
- ESB Chewie and Leia [v1e1:105] 15.00
- ESB finale scene [v1e1:105] 15.00
- ROTJ AT-AT [v1e1:105] 15.00
- ROTJ B-Wings [v1e1:105] 15.00
- ROTJ Boushh and frozen Han [v1e1:105] 15.00
- ROTJ Death Star II [v1e1:105] 15.00
- TPM Naboo Fighter [v1e1:105] 15.00
- TPM Royal Starship [v1e1:105] 15.00

Kertel
- Anakin Skywalker [v1e1:105] 10.00
- Darth Maul [v1e1:105] 10.00
- Jedi vs. Sith [v1e1:105] 10.00

M1
Revenge of the Sith. Top Up cards, special edition.
- General Grievous [v1e1:105] 10.00
- Obi-Wan Kenobi [v1e1:105] 10.00
- Padmé [v1e1:105] 10.00
- Yoda [v1e1:105] 10.00

Matav
- Anakin Skywalker [v1e1:105] 15.00

- Obi-Wan Kenobi [v1e1:105] 15.00
- Queen Amidala [v1e1:105] 15.00
- Qui-Gon Jinn [v1e1:105] 15.00

Mitsubushi
- C-3PO and R2-D2 [v1e1:105] 50.00

Movistar (Argentina)
Episode III: Revenge of the Sith.
- Anakin Skywalker / Darth Vader [v1e1:106] 10.00
- Anakin Skywalker / Darth Vader [v1e1:106] 10.00
- Chewbacca [v1e1:106] 10.00
- Clone trooper [v1e1:106] 10.00
- Darth Sidious [v1e1:106] 10.00
- Darth Vader helmet [v1e1:106] 10.00
- Darth Vader reaching [v1e1:106] 10.00
- Darth Vader standing [v1e1:106] 10.00
- Epic duel, blue [v1e1:106] 10.00
- Epic duel, red [v1e1:106] 10.00
- General Grievous [v1e1:106] 10.00
- General Grievous with lightsabers [v1e1:106] 10.00
- Obi-Wan Kenobi [v1e1:106] 10.00
- Yoda jumping [v1e1:106] 10.00
- Yoda reaching [v1e1:106] 10.00
- Yoda standing [v1e1:106] 10.00

Movistar (Guatemala)
Episode III: Revenge of the Sith.
- Anakin and Obi-Wan [v1e1:106] 10.00
- Chewbacca [v1e1:106] 10.00
- Clone trooper [v1e1:106] 10.00
- Darth Vader [v1e1:106] 10.00
- Darth Vader and Anakin [v1e1:106] 10.00
- R2-D2 and C-3PO [v1e1:106] 10.00
- Yoda [v1e1:106] 10.00

Movistar (Venezuela)
Episode III: Revenge of the Sith.
- Clone trooper [v1e1:106] 10.00
- Epic duel [v1e1:106] 10.00
- Mace Windu [v1e1:106] 10.00
- Yoda [v1e1:106] 10.00

Orange (Dominican Republic)
- Darth Vader 300 units [v1e1:106] 20.00
- Droids 100 units [v1e1:106] 20.00
- Yoda 60 units [v1e1:106] 15.00

PPS Ltd.
- Anakin and Obi-Wan [v1e1:106] 10.00
- Battle Droid Army [v1e1:106] 10.00
- Obi-Wan and Qui-Gon [v1e1:106] 10.00
- Obi-Wan Kenobi [v1e1:106] 10.00
- Queen Amidala [v1e1:106] 10.00
- Qui-Gon, Jar Jar, and Anakin [v1e1:106] 10.00
- R2 unit, blue [v1e1:106] 10.00
- R2 unit, red [v1e1:106] 10.00

Singapore Telecom (Singapore)
- Jar Jar Binks [v1e1:106] 10.00
- Obi-Wan Kenobi [v1e1:106] 10.00
- Watto [v1e1:106] 10.00

Swift Communications International
- 1 Millennium Falcon over Mos Eisley [v1e1:107] 15.00
- 2 Millennium Falcon over Bespin [v1e1:107] 15.00
- 3 Millennium Falcon over Death Star II [v1e1:107] 15.00
- 4 X-Wings in formation [v1e1:107] 15.00
- 5 Heroes on Hoth [v1e1:107] 15.00
- 6 Yoda in hut [v1e1:107] 15.00
- 7 Princess Leia, Yavin celebration [v1e1:107] 15.00
- 8 Cloud City welcome [v1e1:107] 15.00
- 9 Emperor's throne room [v1e1:107] 15.00
- 10 Heroes in 3263827 [v1e1:107] 15.00
- 11 Chewbacca saves R2 from power outlet [v1e1:107] 15.00
- 12 Logray [v1e1:107] 15.00
- 13 Obi-Wan and Vader duel [v1e1:107] 15.00
- 14 X-Wing and medical frigate [v1e1:107] 15.00
- 15 Millennium Falcon docked next to shuttle Tydirium [v1e1:107] 15.00
- 16 "Help me Obi-Wan Kenobi…" [v1e1:107] 15.00
- 17 Preparing Han for carbon freeze [v1e1:107] 15.00
- 18 Battle above Death Star II [v1e1:107] 15.00

Calling Cards, Telephone

87-01   87-02   87-03   87-04   87-05   87-06

87-07   87-08 Package and Detail   87-09 Detail   88-01 Front and Back   88-02   88-03

- ❑ 19 Ronto in Mos Eisley [v1e1:107] 15.00
- ❑ 20 Cloud City residents [v1e1:107] 15.00
- ❑ 21 Shuttle landing on Death Star II [v1e1:107] 15.00
- ❑ 22 Luke, Han, and Chewbacca entering Yavin ceremony [v1e1:107] 15.00
- ❑ 23 Cloud Cars [v1e1:107] 15.00
- ❑ 24 Bib Fortuna and Boushh [v1e1:107] 15.00
- ❑ 25 Cantina patron reports disturbance [v1e1:107] 15.00
- ❑ 26 Millennium Falcon lands on Cloud City [v1e1:107] 15.00
- ❑ 27 Emperor in his throne room [v1e1:107] 15.00
- ❑ 28 Jabba and Han in Mos Eisley [v1e1:107] 15.00
- ❑ 29 Wampa's meal disturbed [v1e1:107] 15.00
- ❑ 30 Imperial welcome [v1e1:107] 15.00

Teleca (Japan)
Star Wars anniversary set.
- ❑ A New Hope movie poster art [v1e1:107] 10.00
- ❑ C-3PO and R2-D2 [v1e1:107] 10.00
- ❑ Darth Vader [v1e1:107] 10.00
- ❑ Falcon above Death Star II [v1e1:107] 10.00
- ❑ Han and Chewbacca [v1e1:107] 10.00
- ❑ Yoda [v1e1:107] 10.00

Telefonica
- ❑ Anakin Skywalker [v1e1:107] 5.00
- ❑ Battle Droid [v1e1:107] 5.00
- ❑ C-3PO [v1e1:107] 5.00
- ❑ Jedi knights [v1e1:107] 5.00
- ❑ Naboo Fighter [v1e1:107] 5.00

Cameras
Continued in Volume 3, Page 108

Celebration III.
- ❑ Caricature art [87-01] 40.00

(UK)
- ❑ Darth Vader, digital 60.00

JazWares, Inc
- ❑ Clone shaped [87-02] 55.00
- ❑ Clone Wars [87-03] 60.00
- ❑ Darth Vader [87-04] 60.00

Kellogg's
- ❑ Revenge of the Sith, 12 exposure, disposable [4:67] 25.00

Sakar International
- ❑ Clone Wars digital kit [87-05] 50.00

Clone Wars digital kits. Camera has preview screen.
- ❑ Republic forces / clone [87-06] 50.00
- ❑ The Force / Clone Wars [87-07] 50.00

Tiger Electronics
Picture Plus Image camera.
- ❑ Darth Maul with background, "droid" misspelled [87-08] 45.00
- ❑ Darth Maul without background [87-09] 40.00

Can Holders and Cozys
Continued in Volume 3, Page 109

- ❑ Episode III inflatable bottle cozy [88-01] 15.00

Disney / MGM
- ❑ Jedi Training Academy cozy [88-02] 15.00

Pepsi Cola (Japan)
Redemption premiums.
- ❑ Battle Droid [88-03] 75.00
- ❑ C-3PO [88-04] 95.00
- ❑ R2-D2 [88-05] 95.00

Candles
Continued in Volume 3, Page 110

(UK)
- ❑ Clone Wars [89-01] 10.00

Bakery Crafts
- ❑ Darth Vader holder with lightsaber candle [89-02] 10.00

Party Express
- ❑ Darth Vader cake candle [89-03] 10.00

Unique (Canada)
- ❑ Episode I with classic logo [89-04] 10.00

     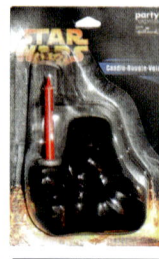    

88-04   88-05   89-01   89-02   89-03   89-04   89-05   89-06   89-07

90-01   90-02   91-01   91-02   91-03   91-04   91-05   91-06   91-07   92-01

Cards, Trading

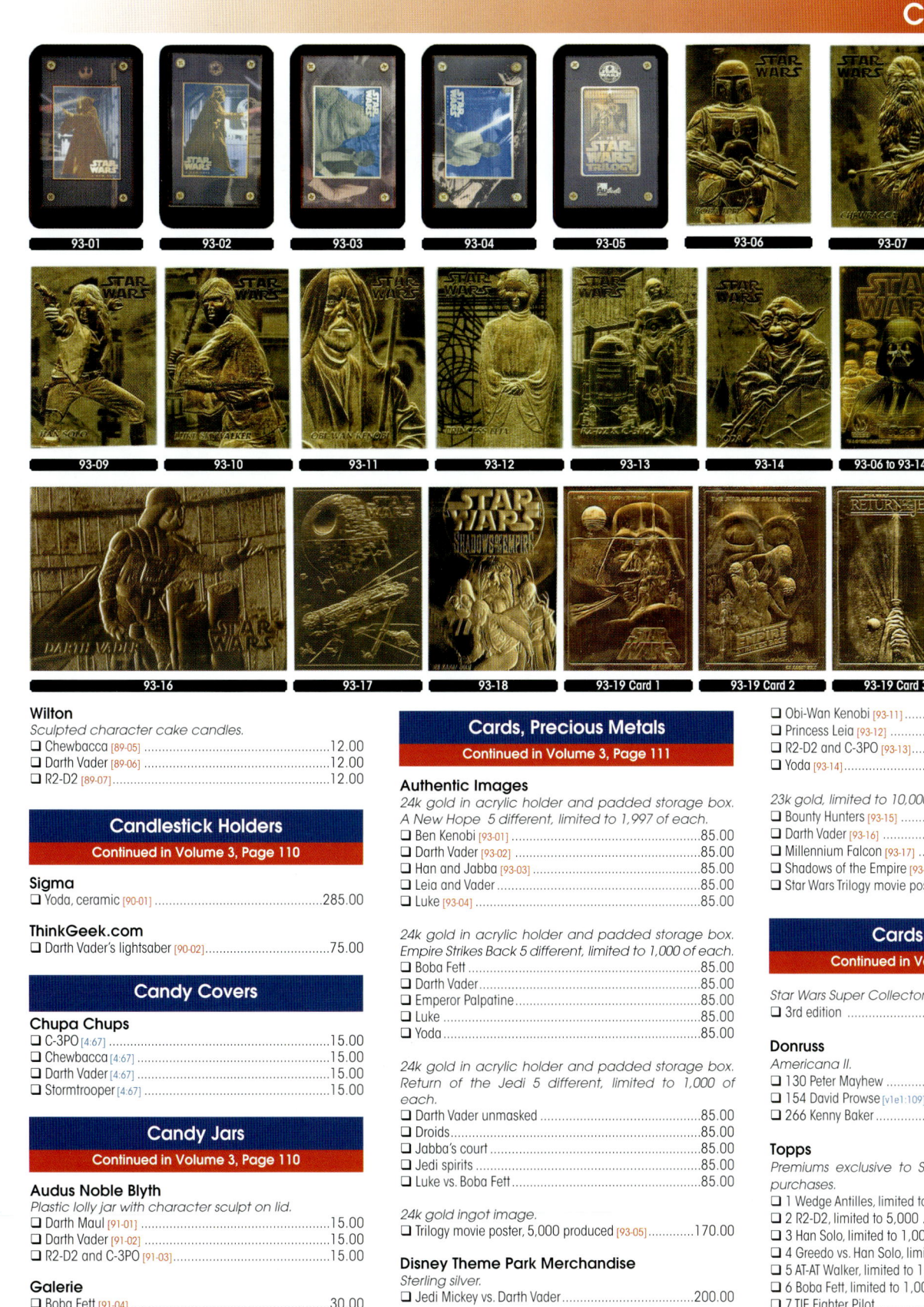

Wilton
Sculpted character cake candles.
- ❏ Chewbacca [89-05] 12.00
- ❏ Darth Vader [89-06] 12.00
- ❏ R2-D2 [89-07] 12.00

Candlestick Holders
Continued in Volume 3, Page 110

Sigma
- ❏ Yoda, ceramic [90-01] 285.00

ThinkGeek.com
- ❏ Darth Vader's lightsaber [90-02] 75.00

Candy Covers

Chupa Chups
- ❏ C-3PO [4:67] 15.00
- ❏ Chewbacca [4:67] 15.00
- ❏ Darth Vader [4:67] 15.00
- ❏ Stormtrooper [4:67] 15.00

Candy Jars
Continued in Volume 3, Page 110

Audus Noble Blyth
Plastic lolly jar with character sculpt on lid.
- ❏ Darth Maul [91-01] 15.00
- ❏ Darth Vader [91-02] 15.00
- ❏ R2-D2 and C-3PO [91-03] 15.00

Galerie
- ❏ Boba Fett [91-04] 30.00
- ❏ C-3PO [91-05] 30.00
- ❏ Darth Vader [91-06] 30.00
- ❏ Stormtrooper [91-07] 30.00

Canteens
- ❏ Darth Vader [92-01] 35.00

Cards, Precious Metals
Continued in Volume 3, Page 111

Authentic Images
24k gold in acrylic holder and padded storage box. A New Hope 5 different, limited to 1,997 of each.
- ❏ Ben Kenobi [93-01] 85.00
- ❏ Darth Vader [93-02] 85.00
- ❏ Han and Jabba [93-03] 85.00
- ❏ Leia and Vader [93-04] 85.00
- ❏ Luke [93-04] 85.00

24k gold in acrylic holder and padded storage box. Empire Strikes Back 5 different, limited to 1,000 of each.
- ❏ Boba Fett 85.00
- ❏ Darth Vader 85.00
- ❏ Emperor Palpatine 85.00
- ❏ Luke 85.00
- ❏ Yoda 85.00

24k gold in acrylic holder and padded storage box. Return of the Jedi 5 different, limited to 1,000 of each.
- ❏ Darth Vader unmasked 85.00
- ❏ Droids 85.00
- ❏ Jabba's court 85.00
- ❏ Jedi spirits 85.00
- ❏ Luke vs. Boba Fett 85.00

24k gold ingot image.
- ❏ Trilogy movie poster, 5,000 produced [93-05] 170.00

Disney Theme Park Merchandise
Sterling silver.
- ❏ Jedi Mickey vs. Darth Vader 200.00

Score Board
10,000 produced of each. Individually numbered.
- ❏ Boba Fett [93-06] 20.00
- ❏ Chewbacca [93-07] 20.00
- ❏ Darth Vader [93-08] 20.00
- ❏ Han Solo [93-09] 20.00
- ❏ Luke Skywalker [93-10] 20.00
- ❏ Obi-Wan Kenobi [93-11] 20.00
- ❏ Princess Leia [93-12] 20.00
- ❏ R2-D2 and C-3PO [93-13] 20.00
- ❏ Yoda [93-14] 20.00

23k gold, limited to 10,000.
- ❏ Bounty Hunters [93-15] 40.00
- ❏ Darth Vader [93-16] 40.00
- ❏ Millennium Falcon [93-17] 40.00
- ❏ Shadows of the Empire [93-18] 40.00
- ❏ Star Wars Trilogy movie poster, set of 3 [93-19] 90.00

Cards, Trading
Continued in Volume 3, Page 111

Star Wars Super Collector's Wish Book.
- ❏ 3rd edition 2.00

Donruss
Americana II.
- ❏ 130 Peter Mayhew 50.00
- ❏ 154 David Prowse [v1e1:109] 50.00
- ❏ 266 Kenny Baker 50.00

Topps
Premiums exclusive to StarWarsShop.com for select purchases.
- ❏ 1 Wedge Antilles, limited to 5,000 ....10.00
- ❏ 2 R2-D2, limited to 5,000 ....10.00
- ❏ 3 Han Solo, limited to 1,000 [v1e1:109] 15.00
- ❏ 4 Greedo vs. Han Solo, limited to 3,000 [v1e1:109] ...10.00
- ❏ 5 AT-AT Walker, limited to 1,000 [v1e1:109] ...15.00
- ❏ 6 Boba Fett, limited to 1,000 [v1e1:109] 15.00
- ❏ 7 TIE Fighter Pilot 10.00
- ❏ 8 Kit Fisto 10.00
- ❏ 9 Boba Fett 10.00
- ❏ 10 Shadow Stormtrooper, limited to 1,000 [v1e1:109] ...15.00

Holiday Special
- ❏ R2-D2 ....15.00
- ❏ Stormtrooper [v1e1:109] 15.00

Cards: 30th Anniversary

94-01

94-02 Sample

94-03 Sample

94-04 Sample

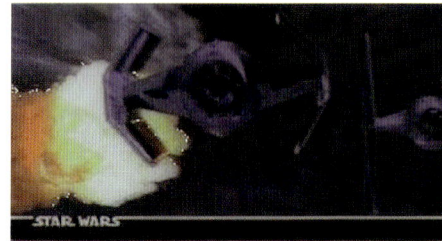
95-01 Sample

96-01 Sample

97-01 Sample

Cards: 30th Anniversary

Official Pix.
Autograph cards, unsigned. Set of 15 plus 2 promos. Star Wars Fan Days. Plano Texas, October 2007.
- Cards unnumbered, unsigned, each [94-01] 10.00
- Cards P1-P2 unsigned, each 15.00

Topps
Base set. 120 cards, foil stamped.
- Cards 1–2, each 1.00
- Cards 3–9 characters, each [94-02] 1.00
- Cards 10–18 A New Hope, each [5:67] 1.00
- Cards 19–27 The Empire Strikes Back, each................1.00
- Cards 28–36 Return of the Jedi, each.....................1.00
- Cards 37–45 special editions, each.......................1.00
- Cards 46–54 The Phantom Menace, each.....................1.00
- Cards 55–63 Attack of the Clones, each...................1.00
- Cards 64–72 Revenge of the Sith, each....................1.00
- Cards 73–81 behind the scenes, each......................1.00
- Cards 82–90 special FX, each.............................1.00
- Cards 91–99 TV live action, each.........................1.00
- Cards 100–108 TV animation, each.........................1.00
- Cards 109–117 deleted scenes, each.......................1.00
- Cards 118–119 sneak preview, each........................1.00
- Card 120 checklist..1.00
- Complete base set of 120 ....45.00
- Unopened card packets, each 15.00

Special insert cards.
- Animation cel clear cards 1–9, each.....................10.00
- Magnet cards, any of 9, each [5:67] 10.00
- Promo cards P1–P3, each 5.00
- Triptych puzzle cards 1–27, die-cut, each 5.00

Foil card sets, parallel to 120 card base set.
- Blue foil cards inserted 1:12 packs, each................15.00
- Red foil cards inserted 1:24 packs, each [5:67] 10.00
- Gold foil cards inserted 1:287 packs, each* (card values are all at-demand by owner).............................N / A

Box toppers. Vintage cards redistributed with 30th anniversary foil logo stamped on them. All 330 cards in circulation; not all reported as found.
- Cards 1–66 Series 1 blue, each [94-03] 45.00
- Cards 67–132 Series 2 red, each [94-04]..................45.00
- Cards 133–198 Series 3 yellow, each......................45.00
- Cards 199–264 Series 4 green, each.......................75.00
- Card 207 C-3PO (Anthony Daniels) rated-R image...500.00
- Cards 265–330 series 5 orange, each......................75.00

Cards: 3D, A New Hope

Topps
63 cards plus promotional, bonus, and multi-motion chase cards. Bonus card.
- Bonus card with envelope.................................60.00
- Cards 1-63, each [95-01] 3.00
- Multi-motion cards, each 10.00
- Promotional cards, each...................................5.00
- Wrappers, each..5.00

Cards: 3D, Empire Strikes Back

Topps
48 cards plus promotional, sketch, and autograph cards.
- Cards 1–48, each [96-01] 3.00

98-01 Sample

98-02 Sample

98-03 Sample

98-04 Sample

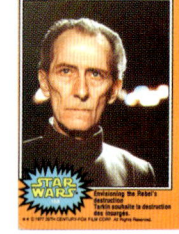
98-05 Sample

98-06 Sample

98-07 Sample

98-08 Sample

98-09 Sample

98-10 Sample

98-11 Sample

98-12 Sample

98-13 Sample

98-14 Sample

98-15 Sample

98-16 Sample

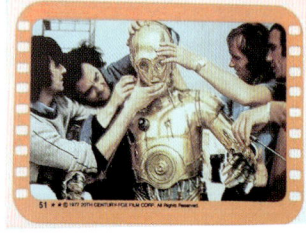
98-17 Sample

98-18 Sample

Cards: Attack of the Clones

   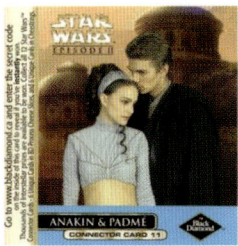 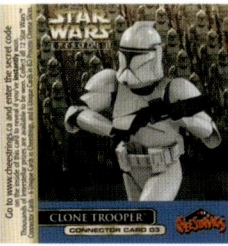  

99-01 Sample 99-02 Sample 99-03 Sample 99-04 Sample 99-05 Sample 99-06 Sample 99-07

99-08 Sample 99-09 Sample 99-10 Sample 99-11 Sample 99-12 Sample 99-13 Sample 99-14 Sample

Cards: 3D, The Phantom Menace

Topps
46 cards plus promotional and multi-motion chase cards. Cards 1–46.
- Cards 1–46, each [97-01] 5.00
- Multi-Motion cards, each 10.00
- Promotional cards, each 10.00

Cards: 501st

501st Legion
Promotional cards distributed exclusively by costuming club members. (Checklist and images are at: www.501st.com/cards.php.)
- Series 1 (2005) cards 1–100, each [4:68] 3.00
- Series 2 (2006) cards 101–150, each 1.00
- Series 3 (2006) cards 151–200, each 1.00
- Series 4 (2006) cards 201–250, each 1.00
- Series 5 (2007) cards 251–300, each 1.00
- Series 6 (2007) cards 301–350, each 1.00
- Series 7 (2007) cards 351–400, each 1.00
- Series 8 (2009) cards 401–550, each 1.00
- Series 9 (2010) cards 451–500, each 1.00
- Special: 10th Anniversary, Celebration Europe exclusive [v1e1:110] 5.00
- Special: Series 9 (2010) card 501 [v1e1:110] 25.00

Cards: A New Hope

(Argentina)
Guerra de las Galaxias. 66 blue border cards, no stickers. Similar to Topps series 1 cards.
- Cards 1–66, each [98-01] 15.00
- Complete set of 66 cards 250.00
- Unopened card packets, each 45.00

Laboratorios y Agencias Unidas (Mexico)
Spanish text. Series 1. 66 blue border cards, no stickers. Similar to Topps series 1.
- Cards 1–66, each [98-02] 15.00
- Complete set of 66 cards 250.00

O-Pee-Chee (Canada)
Series 1. English and French text. 66 numbered blue border cards, 11 numbered stickers.
- Cards 1–66, each [98-03] 10.00
- Complete set of 66 cards 175.00
- Stickers 1–11, each 15.00

Series 2. English and French text. 66 numbered red border cards, 11 numbered stickers.
- Cards 67–132, each [98-04] 10.00
- Complete set of 66 cards 175.00
- Stickers 12–22, each 15.00

Series 3. English and French text. 132 numbered orange border cards, 22 numbered stickers.
- Cards 133–265, each [98-05] 10.00
- Complete set of 132 cards 225.00
- Stickers 13–33, each 15.00
- Unopened card packets, each 80.00

Pacosa Dos / Internacional
187 numbered cards. White borders, no text. (Images in 3rd edition, page 168. Checklist in 3rd edition, page 167.)
- Cards 1–187, each [98-06] 10.00
- Complete set of 187 cards 345.00

Scanlens
72 numbered cards. (Checklist in 3rd edition, page 170.)
- Cards 1–72, each [98-07] 10.00

Topps
Series 1. 66 numbered blue border cards, 11 numbered stickers. (Images in 2nd edition, page 166. Checklist in 3rd edition, page 170.)
- Cards 1–66, each [98-08] 15.00
- Complete set of 66 cards 230.00
- Stickers 1–11, each 18.00
- Unopened card packets, each 100.00

Series 2. 66 numbered red border cards, 11 numbered stickers. (Images in 2nd edition, page 167. Checklist in 3rd edition, page 170.)
- Cards 67–132, each [98-10] 12.00
- Complete set of 66 cards 180.00
- Stickers 12–22, each [98-11] 15.00
- Unopened card packets, each 100.00

Series 3. 66 numbered yellow border cards, 11 numbered stickers. (Images in 2nd edition, page 167. Checklist in 3rd edition, page 170.)
- Cards 133–198, each [98-12] 10.00
- Complete set of 66 cards 135.00
- Stickers 23–33, each [98-13] 15.00
- Unopened card packets, each 100.00

Series 4. 66 numbered green border cards, 11 numbered stickers. Card 207 updated mid-production of series. (Images in 2nd edition, page 169. Checklist in 3rd edition, page 171.)
- Cards 199–264, each [98-14] 10.00
- Card 207 "X-rated" version of C-3PO [5:68] 45.00
- Complete set of 66 cards 150.00
- Stickers 34–44, each [98-15] 15.00
- Unopened card packets, each 100.00

Series 5. 66 numbered orange border cards, 11 numbered stickers. (Images in 2nd edition, page 170. Checklist in 3rd edition, page 172.)
- Cards 265–330, each [98-16] 12.00
- Complete set of 66 cards 225.00
- Stickers 45–55, each [98-17] 15.00
- Unopened card packets, each 100.00

Topps (UK)
Series 1. 66 numbered blue border cards. (Checklist in 3rd edition, page 172.)
- Cards 1–66, each 20.00
- Complete set of 66 cards 400.00
- Unopened card packets, each 125.00

Series 2. 66 numbered red border cards. Numbered 1a–66a.
- Cards 1a–66a, each 25.00
- Complete set of 66 cards 450.00
- Unopened card packets, each 135.00

Yamakatsu Corporation (Japan)
Set of 36 unnumbered cards, text on back. (Images in 3rd ed., page 172. Checklist in 3rd edition, page 173.)
- Cards, each [98-08] 16.00
- Complete set of cards 350.00
- Unopened card packets, each 100.00

Cards: Attack of the Clones

20th Century Fox (Germany)
Episode 2 opening-day cinema foil cards. 4 numbered cards. (Images in 3rd edition, page 172. Checklist in 3rd edition, page 173.)
- Cards, each [99-01] 20.00

7-Eleven Inc. (Japan)
16 unnumbered cards plus 3 winner cards. (Images in 3rd ed., page 173. Checklist in 3rd edition, page 173.)
- Cards, each [99-02] 20.00
- Winner cards, each [99-03] 150.00

Black Diamond (Canada)
Set of 12 numbered Connector Cards. First six by Cheesestrings, last six by Black Diamond. (Images in 3rd ed., page 174. Checklist in 3rd edition, page 174.)
- Cards 7–12, each [99-04] 35.00

Cheesestrings (Canada)
Set of 12 numbered Connector Cards. First six by Cheesestrings, last six by Black Diamond. (Images in 3rd ed., page 174. Checklist in 3rd edition, page 174.)
- Cards 1–6, each [99-05] 35.00

Eskimo (Japan)
30 numbered cards plus 1 lucky winner card. Ice cream premiums. (Images in 3rd edition, page 174. Checklist in 3rd edition, page 174.)
- Cards 1–30, each [99-06] 25.00
- Complete set of 30 cards 300.00
- Lucky Winner card [99-07] 150.00

Cards: Attack of the Clones

100-01 Sample   101-01 Sample   102-01 Sample   102-02 Sample   103-01 Sample   103-02 Sample   103-03 Sample

Habib's Restaurant (Brazil)
8 unnumbered cards. (Images in 3rd edition, page 174. Checklist in 3rd edition, page 174.)
- Cards, each [99-08] 25.00

Mainland Food (New Zealand)
18 numbered cards. (Images in 2nd edition, page 172. Checklist in 3rd edition, page 174.)
- Cards 1–18, each [99-09] 20.00

Topps
100 numbered cards plus 6 promotional, 5 mega-sized foil, 5 panoramic fold out, 8 prismatic foil, and 10 silver foil cards. Silver foil cards. (Images in 2nd edition, page 172. Checklist in 3rd edition, page 174.)
- Cards 1–21 characters, each 1.00
- Cards 22–90 movie scenes, each 1.00
- Cards 91–100 behind scenes, each 1.00
- Complete set of 100 base cards 40.00
- Mega-sized foil cards, each 15.00
- Panoramic fold-out cards, each [99-10] 8.00
- Prismatic foil cards, each [99-11] 5.00
- Promo cards P1–P5, each [99-12] 5.00
- Promo card P6 .... 15.00
- Silver foil cards, each [99-13] 3.00

Collector tins. Contains 7 packs of random movie cards and 1 mega-sized foil card. (Checklist in 3rd edition, page 175.)
- Unopened tin with card intact, each 35.00

Topps (UK)
10 foil cards, 1 card in collector binder. (Checklist in 3rd edition, page 175.)
- Binder card [v1e1:111] 20.00
- Foil cards, each [99-14] 8.00

Cards: Bend-Ems

Just Toys
28 cards numbered alphabetically. A–BB. Images taken from Star Wars Galaxy series of cards. (Images in 2nd ed., page 175. Checklist in 3rd ed., page 175.)
- Cards A–Z and AA–BB, each [100-01] 10.00

Cards: Card Game
(Hungary)
Return of the Jedi matching game. Unnumbered pairs.
- Cards, each [101-01] 10.00

Cards: Ceramic

Hamilton Collection
12 unnumbered cards. (Images in 3rd edition, page 176. Checklist in 3rd edition, page 176.)
- Cards, each [102-01] 30.00

Score Board
3 unnumbered cards, limited to 5,000 each. (Images in 3rd ed., page 176. Checklist in 3rd ed., page 176.)
- Cards, each [102-02] 75.00

Cards: Chrome Archives

Topps
90 numbered chrome foils cards, plus 4 clear chrome, 9 double-sided, and 2 promotional cards. (Images in 2nd ed., page 176. Checklist in 3rd ed., page 176.)
- Cards 1–90, each [103-01] 3.00
- Complete set of 90 cards 65.00
- Clear chrome cards, each 20.00
- Double-sided cards, each [103-02] 25.00
- Promotional cards, each [103-03] 8.00

Cards: Clone Wars

Boston Globe
- Page of 12 cut-apart [104-01] 20.00

Topps
2004. 90 cards, 2 autograph cards, 10 battle motion cards, 3 promo cards, and 10 stickers.
- Cards 1–90, each [104-02] 2.00
- Complete set of 90 base cards 35.00
- Autograph card: Anthony Phelan 35.00
- Autograph card: Jack Thompson 35.00
- Battle Motion cards B1–B10, each [104-03] 8.00
- Promo cards P1–P3, each [104-04] 5.00
- Stickers 1–10, each [104-05] 5.00

2008. 90 numbered cards, 90 parallel foil cards, 10 animation cel cards, 2 promo cards, 10 foil cards (retail), 5 motion cards (retail), 5 Target exclusive animation cel cards.
- Cards 1–90, each [104-06] 1.00
- Complete set of 90 base cards 25.00
- Cards 1–90 parallel foil, each 25.00
- Animation cel cards 1–10, each 5.00
- Animation cel cards, red, Target exclusive, each ... 15.00
- Foil cards 1–10, each 2.00
- Motion cards 1–5, each 5.00

2009. 80 numbered Widevision trading cards, 10 clear cel cards, 10 flix-pix motion cards, 10 foil cards, 10 plastic cards.
- Cards 1–80, each 0.50
- Complete set of 80 base cards 25.00
- Clear cel 1–10, each 10.00
- Flix-pix motion 1–10, each 8.00
- Foil cards 1–10, each 8.00
- Plastic cards 1–10, each 10.00

2010. Season 2. Rise of the Bounty Hunters. 90 base cards, 20 numbered foil cards, 5 motion cards.
- Cards 1–20, each [104-07] 2.00
- Foil cards 1–90, each [104-08] 5.00

Clone Wars. Season 1. Set of 24, numbered. Distributed with matching dog tag. Value is for card alone.
- Cards, each [104-09] 5.00

Cards: DinaMics

DinaMics
168 numbered cards. (Images and checklist in 3rd edition, page 178.)
- Cards 1–168, each [105-01] 1.00
- Complete set of 168 base cards 125.00

104-01   104-02 Sample   104-03 Sample   104-04 Sample   104-05 Sample

 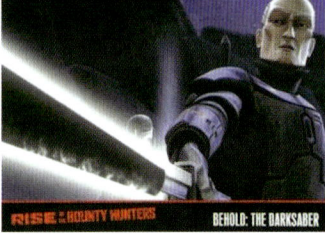   

104-06 Sample   104-07 Sample   104-08 Sample   104-09 Sample   105-01 Sample

Cards: Evolution

   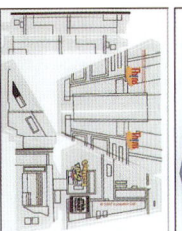 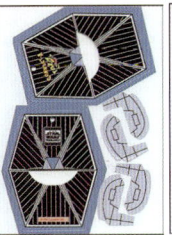 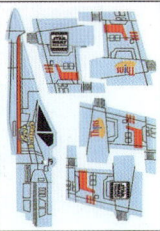 

106-01 Sample | 106-02 Sample | 106-03 Sample | 106-04 | 106-05 | 106-06 | 106-07 Sample

107-01 Sample | 107-02 Sample | 107-03 | 107-04 Sample | 107-05 Sample | 107-06 Sample

107-07 Sample | 107-08 Sample | 107-09 Sample | 107-10 Sample | 107-11 Sample | 107-12 Sample | 108-01 Sample

Cards: Discs
Continued in Volume 3, Page 112

Blix (Spain)
43 numbered plastic chip discs from the Clone Wars.
- Discs 1–43, each [106-01] 4.00
- Complete set of 43 discs 80.00

Tazo (Australia)
80 Tazos numbered 81–160, plus 3 special "Connect-a-Tazo" starship cards. (Images in 2nd edition, page 404. Checklist in 3rd edition, page 405.)
- Tazos 81–100 (3D Motion), each 1.00
- Tazos 101–130 (octagonal), each [106-02] 1.00
- Tazos 131–140 (3D), each [106-03] 1.00
- Tazos 141–160 (hologram), each 1.00
- Shuttle (connect card) [106-04] 8.00
- TIE Fighter (connect card) [106-05] 8.00
- X-Wing (connect card) [106-06] 8.00

Tazo (China)
40 numbered Tazos. 15 holographic foil Tazos numbered variously though out the set. (Checklist in 3rd edition, page 406.)
- Holofoil Tazos, any number, each 10.00
- Regular Tazos, any number, each 3.00

Tazo (Mexico)
50 numbered Tazo, plus one bonus Tazo. (Images in 2nd edition, page 405. Checklist in 3rd edition, page 406.)
- Tazos 1–50, each [106-07] 2.00
- Bonus Darth Vader Tazo 8.00

Tazo (Poland)
50 numbered Tazos. (Checklist in 3rd ed., page 406.)
- Tazos 1–50, each 2.00

Tazo (UK)
50 numbered Tazos. (Checklist in 3rd edition, page 406.)
- Tazos 1–50, each 2.00

Cards: Empire Strikes Back
Continued in Volume 3, Page 113

Greece. 200 white bordered Empire Strikes Back cards with several Star Trek cards printed into the set. Produced with two different logos; 1 large text and the other small text. Text is in the Greek alphabet. (Images and checklist are in 3rd edition, page 188.)
- Cards 1–200 large text, each [107-01] 15.00
- Cards 1–200 small text, each [107-02] 15.00
- Unopened card packets, each [107-03] 45.00

Agence Generale d'Edition
225 numbered L'Empire Contre-Attaque cards. (Checklist in 3rd edition, page 179.)
- Cards 1–225, each 3.00
- Complete set of 225 cards 275.00

Coca-Cola (China)
6 unnumbered Sprite cards. (Images and checklist in 3rd edition, page 180.)
- Cards, each [107-04] 35.00

Editorial Fher
225 numbered El Imperio Contrataca cards. (Images and checklist in 3rd edition, page 180.)
- Cards 1–225, each [107-05] 5.00

FKS (UK)
225 numbered cards. (Checklist in 3rd edition, page 180.)
- Cards 1–225, each [107-06] 3.00

O-Pee-Chee (Canada)
Series 1. 132 numbered red-bordered cards, 33 stickers. English / French text.
- Cards 1–132, each [107-07] 5.00
- Stickers 1–33, each 20.00

Series 2. 132 numbered blue-bordered cards, 33 stickers. English / French text.
- Cards 133–264, each [107-08] 5.00
- Stickers 34–66, each 20.00

Series 3. 88 numbered blue-bordered cards, 22 stickers. English / French text.
- Cards 265–352, each [107-09] 5.00
- Stickers 67–88, each 20.00

Scanlens
132 numbered cards. (Checklist in 3rd ed., pg. 182.)
- Cards 1–132, each 3.00

Topps
- Rack pack, 3 wax packs [v1e1:112] 125.00
- Rack pack, 51 random cards [v1e1:112] 65.00

Series 1.
- Cards 1–132, each [107-10] 2.00
- Stickers 1–33, each [v1e1:112] 10.00

Series 2.
- Cards 133–264, each [107-01] 2.00
- Stickers 34–66, each [v1e1:112] 10.00

Series 3.
- Cards 265–353, each [107-12] 2.00
- Stickers 67–88, each [v1e1:112] 10.00

Cards: Empire Strikes Back Giant Photo

Topps
30 numbered oversized cards. (Images and checklist in 3rd edition, page 178.)
- Cards 1–30, each [108-01] 8.00
- Complete set of 30 cards 90.00

Cards: Evolution

Topps
90 numbered cards, 3 checklist cards, 12 "set A" insert cards, 8 "set B" insert cards, 4 promotional cards, and 25 hand-signed autograph cards.
- Cards 1–90, each [109-01] 2.00
- Checklist cards C1–C3, each [109-02] 2.00
- Insert set A cards A1–A12, each [109-03] 3.00

Cards: Evolution

109-01 Sample

109-02 Sample

109-03 Sample

109-04 Sample

- ☐ Insert set B cards B1–B8, each [v1e1:113] 5.00
- ☐ Promotion cards P1–P2, each [v1e1:113] 5.00
- ☐ Promotion card P3, AlphaCon exclusive, limited to 5,000, each 35.00
- ☐ Promotion card P3, AlphaCon exclusive, limited to 250, autographed, each 90.00
- ☐ Promotion card P4, each [109-04] 5.00
- ☐ Unopened card packets, each 14.00

Autographed cards.
- ☐ C-3PO / Anthony Daniels..1,200.00
- ☐ Princess Leia Organa / Carrie Fisher 1,000.00

Autographed cards, limited to 300 each.
- ☐ Lando Calrissian / Billy Dee Williams 425.00
- ☐ Chewbacca / Peter Mayhew 350.00

Autographed cards, limited to 1,000 each.
- ☐ Andrew Secombe / Watto, voice 45.00
- ☐ Caroline Blakiston / Mon Mothma 30.00
- ☐ Dalyn Chew / Lyn Me 30.00
- ☐ Dermot Crowley / General Crix Madine 35.00
- ☐ Femi Taylor / Oola 40.00
- ☐ Ian McDiarmid / Senator Palpatine 350.00
- ☐ James Earl Jones / Darth Vader, voice 75.00
- ☐ Jeremy Bulloch / Boba Fett 75.00
- ☐ Kenneth Colley / Admiral Piett 35.00
- ☐ Kenny Baker / R2-D2 ....60.00
- ☐ Lewis MacLeod / Sebulba, voice 45.00
- ☐ Mercedes Ngoh / Rystall 45.00
- ☐ Michael Culver / Captain Needa 35.00
- ☐ Michael Pennington / Moff Jerjerrod 35.00
- ☐ Michael Sheard / Admiral Ozzel 35.00
- ☐ Michonne Bourriague / Aurra Sing 45.00
- ☐ Mike Quinn / Nien Nunb 30.00
- ☐ Paul Blake / Greedo 35.00
- ☐ Phil Brown / Owen Lars [v1e1:113] 45.00
- ☐ Tim Rose / Admiral Ackbar 35.00
- ☐ Warwick Davis / Wicket W. Warrick 40.00

Cards: Evolution Update

Topps
90 numbered cards, 2 checklist cards, George Lucas chase autograph, autograph cards at five levels of scarcity, 20 level-A chase cards, 15 level-B chase cards, 2 chase cards level-C (hobby), 9 Crystal Galaxy cards (retail), 6 etched foil cards (hobby), 2 promotional cards, 1 redemption card.
- ☐ Cards 1–90, each [110-01] 1.00
- ☐ Checklist cards, each 1.00
- ☐ Chase cards A1–A20, each 3.00
- ☐ Chase cards B1–B15, each 4.00
- ☐ Chase cards C1–C2, each 12.00
- ☐ Crystal Galaxy cards G1–G10, each 8.00
- ☐ Etched Foil cards 1–6, each 8.00
- ☐ Promotion cards P1–P2, each 10.00
- ☐ Redemption card D1, each 350.00

Autograph cards.
- ☐ Hayden Christensen / Anakin Skywalker 500.00
- ☐ James Earl Jones / Darth Vader 670.00
- ☐ Bob Keen / Jabba the Hutt 25.00
- ☐ David Barclay / Jabba the Hutt 25.00
- ☐ John Coppinger / Jabba the Hutt 25.00
- ☐ Mike Edmonds / Jabba the Hutt 25.00
- ☐ Mike Quinn / Jabba the Hutt 25.00
- ☐ Toby Philpott / Jabba the Hutt 25.00
- ☐ Wayne Pygram / Governor Tarkin 35.00
- ☐ Nalini Krishan / Barriss Offee 25.00
- ☐ Garrick Hagon / Biggs Darklighter 20.00
- ☐ Jesse Jensen / Saesee Tiin 20.00
- ☐ Matt Sloan / Plo Koon 20.00
- ☐ Zach Jensen / Kit Fisto 20.00
- ☐ Maria de Aragon / Greedo 20.00
- ☐ Michael Kingma / Tarfful 20.00
- ☐ Michonne Bourriague / Aurra Sing 20.00
- ☐ Richard LeParmentier / Admiral Motti 20.00

Cards: Fanclub

Norwich and District Star Wars Club (UK)
Norwich Star Wars Costume Gang. Heroes and Villains. Series 1. 24 members, numbered. 600 produced of each.
- ☐ Members 1–24, each 3.00

Skywalkers
- ☐ Chewbacca 8.00
- ☐ Darth Vader 8.00
- ☐ Han Solo 8.00
- ☐ Luke Skywalker 8.00
- ☐ Membership 15.00
- ☐ Princess Leia Organa 8.00
- ☐ Yoda [111-01] 8.00

Cards: Force Attax
Continued in Volume 3, Page 113

Topps (UK)
Series 1.
- ☐ 1–12 Republic Jedi Knight, each [112-01] 1.00
- ☐ 13–16 Republic Droid, each [112-02] 1.00
- ☐ 17–40 Republic Clone trooper, each [112-03] 1.00
- ☐ 41–42 Republic Navy, each 1.00
- ☐ 43–46 Republic Senate, each 1.00
- ☐ 47–57 Republic Vehicle, each 1.00
- ☐ 58–67 Separatist Droid, each 1.00
- ☐ 68–69 Separatist Mandalorian, each 1.00
- ☐ 70–73 Separatist Sith, each 1.00
- ☐ 74–79 Separatist Vehicle, each 1.00
- ☐ 80 Separatist Viceroy 1.00
- ☐ 81–90 Mercenary Bounty Hunter, each 1.00
- ☐ 91 Mercenary Crime Lord 1.00
- ☐ 92–95 Mercenary Droid, each 1.00
- ☐ 96–99 Mercenary Pirate, each 1.00
- ☐ 100 Mercenary Vehicle 1.00
- ☐ 101–110 Republic Jedi Knight Power Up 1.00
- ☐ 111 Republic Senate Power Up 1.00
- ☐ 112–113 Republic Clone trooper Power Up 1.00
- ☐ 114–116 Separatist Sith Power Up 1.00
- ☐ 117 Separatist Mandalorian Power Up 1.00
- ☐ 118–120 Mercenary Bounty Hunter Power Up 1.00
- ☐ 121 Mercenary Droid Power Up 1.00
- ☐ 122–124 Republic Clone trooper Strike Force 1.00
- ☐ 125–133 Republic Jedi Strike Force 1.00
- ☐ 134–140 Separatist Sith Strike Force 1.00
- ☐ 141–145 Mercenary Bounty Hunter Strike Force ...1.00
- ☐ 146–150 Separatist Mandalorian Strike Force 1.00
- ☐ 151–158 Republic Jedi Night Star, foil 2.00
- ☐ 159–161 Republic Clone trooper Star Clone, foil ...2.00
- ☐ 162 Republic Senate Star Senator, foil 2.00
- ☐ 163–165 Separatist Sith Star Sith, foil 2.00
- ☐ 166 Separatist Mandalorian Star Mandalorian, foil 2.00

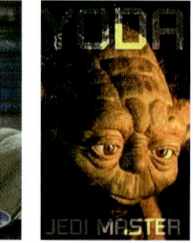
110-01 Sample

111-01 Sample

112-01 Sample

112-02 Sample

112-03 Sample

112-04 Sample

112-05 Sample

112-06 Sample

112-07 Sample

112-08 Sample

112-09 Sample

112-10 Sample

112-11 Sample

112-12 Sample

112-13 Sample

- ❏ 167–169 Mercenary Bounty Hunter Star Bounty Hunter, foil 2.00
- ❏ 170 Mercenary Crime Lord Star Crime Lord, foil 2.00
- ❏ 171–181 Repunlic Jedi Knight Force Master, foil 3.00
- ❏ 182–183 Republic Senate Force Master, foil 3.00
- ❏ 184–187 Separatist Sith Force Master, foil 3.00
- ❏ 188 Separatist Mandalorian Force Master, foil 3.00
- ❏ 189–190 Mercenary Bounty Hunter Force Master, foil 3.00
- ❏ LE1–LE4 Limited Edition, foil 10.00
- ❏ L73 LEGO Limited Edition 25.00

Series 2.
- ❏ 1–89 The Republic, each [112-04] 1.00
- ❏ 90–123 The Separatists, each [112-05] 1.00
- ❏ 124–154 The Mercenaries [112-06] 1.00
- ❏ 155–170 Creatures [112-07] 1.00
- ❏ 171–177 Force Duels [112-08] 1.00
- ❏ 178–192 Strike Forces [112-09] 1.00
- ❏ 193–212 Star Cards [112-10] 2.00
- ❏ 213–224 Power Ups [112-11] 2.00
- ❏ 225–240 Force Masters [112-12] 3.00
- ❏ LE1–LE2 Limited Editions [112-13] 8.00

Cards: Heritage

Topps
120 numbered cards, 6 etched foil cards, 6 promotional cards, 30 stickers. (Images in 4th edition, page 72.)
- ❏ Cards 1–120, each [113-01] 1.00
- ❏ Complete set of 120 cards 30.00
- ❏ Etched foil cards 1–6, each 5.00
- ❏ Promotional cards 1–6, each [v1e1:113] 10.00
- ❏ Stickers 1–30, each 8.00

Cards: Mastervision

Topps
36 numbered cards plus 4 promotional cards. (Images in 2nd edition, page 191. Checklist in 3rd edition, page 191.)
- ❏ Cards 1–36, each [114-01] 5.00
- ❏ Complete set of 36 cards 40.00
- ❏ Promotion cards, each [114-02] 10.00

Cards: Mini-Movies

Interlace 4d
8 unnumbered cards sold individually. 24 frame lenticular animations on each card. (Images in 4th edition, page 184. Checklist in 4th edition, page 183.)
- ❏ Cards, each [115-1] 15.00

Cards: Miscellaneous

- ❏ Married with Children, parody [116-01] 6.00

Blockbuster Video video game promotional card series.
- ❏ #35 Super Star Wars [v1e1:114] 8.00

Comic Images
- ❏ Card #29 of the "Lost Worlds by William Stout" set features Luke, his tauntaun, and a fleet of Twin Pod Cloud Cars on Hoth; artwork for a Varese Sarabande record album from 1980 ....10.00

Gentle Giant Studios
- ❏ 2005 Fan Club promo for Bust-Ups [116-02] 5.00

History Channel
- ❏ Lightsaber 5.00
- ❏ Stormtrooper 5.00
- ❏ X-Wing Fighter 5.00
- ❏ Yoda [116-03] 5.00

Master Replicas
Included with Collector's Society membership kit.
- ❏ 2006 Mace Windu's lightsaber .45 scale 6.00
- ❏ 2007 Qui-Gon Jinn's lightsaber .45 scale 6.00

Packaging Parodies
- ❏ Bar Wars parody [116-04] 4.00

Runnin Bare QSL Cards
Story of Star Wars. 13 numbered story cards, 3" x 5". (Images in 2nd edition, page 192. Checklist in 3rd edition, page 192.)
- ❏ Cards 1–13, each [116-05] 20.00

Sci-Fi Expo and Toy Show
Styled after Topps Star Wars vintage series 4 to commemorate attending actors.
- ❏ P1 Garrick Hagon (Biggs) [2:192] 15.00
- ❏ P2 Peter Mayhew (Chewbacca) [v1e1:114] 25.00

The LEGO Group
Background / character card included with mini-figures. (Images in 3rd edition, page 191.)
- ❏ Cards, each [116-06] 5.00

Topps
- ❏ Gummy Award card [3:191] 25.00
- ❏ Truce at Bakura cover art, Waldenbooks with novel purchase [v1e1:114] 15.00

Convention cards.
- ❏ Millennium Falcon, b/w art 10.00
- ❏ SD1 Darth Vader, 5" x 6" 20.00
- ❏ SD2 Millennium Falcon, 5" x 6" 20.00
- ❏ Star Wars Galaxy Magazine, large 10.00

Dark Horse Comic cards.
- ❏ DH1 War Droids 10.00
- ❏ DH2 Boba Fett 10.00
- ❏ DH3 Millennium Falcon 10.00

Cards: Movie Shots

Movie Shots (Belgium)
50 numbered miniature frame film scenes from all 3 classic trilogy movies. (Checklist in 3rd ed., page 192.)
- ❏ Cards 1–50, each 3.00
- ❏ Complete set of 50 cards 90.00

Movie Shots (Indonesia)
100 numbered miniature frame film scenes from all 3 classic trilogy movies. (Checklist in 3rd edition, page 192.)
- ❏ Cards 1–100, each [117-01] 3.00
- ❏ Complete set of 100 cards 95.00

Movie Shots (Mexico)
40 numbered miniature frame film scenes from all 3 classic trilogy movies. (Images in 2nd edition, page 193. Checklist in 3rd edition, page 193.)
- ❏ Cards 1–40, each [117-02] 3.00
- ❏ Complete set of 40 cards 85.00

Movie Shots (Netherlands)
50 numbered miniature frame film scenes from all 3 classic trilogy movies. (Checklist in 3rd edition, page 192.)
- ❏ Cards 1–50, each 3.00
- ❏ Complete set of 50 cards 90.00

Movie Shots (Spain)
50 numbered miniature frame film scenes from all 3 classic trilogy movies. (Images in 2nd edition, page 194. Checklist in 3rd edition, page 193.)
- ❏ Cards 1–50, each [117-03] 3.00
- ❏ Complete set of 50 cards 90.00

Pelis
40 numbered miniature film scenes from Episode I. (Images in 2nd edition, page 195. Checklist in 3rd edition, page 193.)
- ❏ Cards 1–40, each [v1e1:115] 5.00
- ❏ Complete set of 40 cards 75.00

Cards: Pack-Ins

Kenner
Action Masters from 4-packs.
- ❏ 523296.00 Princess Leia Organa (Star Wars scene) 5.00
- ❏ 523297.00 Obi-Wan Kenobi (Star Wars) 5.00
- ❏ 523298.00 R2-D2 (Dagobah) 5.00
- ❏ 523299.00 C-3PO (oil bath) 5.00

113-01 Sample

114-01 Sample

114-02 Sample

115-01 Sample

116-01 Sample

116-02 Sample

116-03

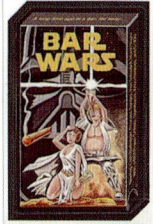
116-04 Sample

116-05 Sample

116-06 Sample

117-01 Sample

117-02 Sample

117-03 Sample

Cards: Pack-Ins

Action Masters from 6-packs.
- 509996-00 Darth Vader (from carbon chamber) 5.00
- 509997-00 Stormtrooper..5.00
- 509998-00 Boba Fett (Empire Strikes Back scene) 5.00
- 511821-00 Han Solo (Star Wars scene) 5.00
- 515859-00 Chewbacca (close-up) 5.00
- 515860-00 Luke Skywalker (Empire Strikes Back scene) 5.00

Action Masters from POTF2 4-packs.
- 511819-00 Princess Leia Organa (Star Wars scene)....5.00
- 511820-00 Obi-Wan Kenobi (publicity shot) 5.00
- 515861-00 C-3PO (close-up) 5.00
- 515862-00 R2-D2 (Cloud City) 5.00

Action Masters from POTF2 6-packs.
- 523290.00 Han Solo...5.00
- 523291.00 Chewbacca (close-up) [118-01]..................5.00
- 523292.00 Stormtrooper (3 troopers) 5.00
- 523293.00 Boba Fett (Empire Strikes Back scene) 5.00
- 523294.00 Darth Vader (in carbon chamber) 5.00
- 523295.00 Luke Skywalker (Empire Strikes Back).......5.00

Action Masters from single packs.
- 509218-01 Darth Vader (reaching out to Luke) 5.00
- 509221-01 Luke Skywalker (duel with Vader) 5.00
- 509223-01 C-3PO (in control room) 5.00
- 509225-01 R2-D2 (in Cloud City) 5.00
- 509227-01 Stormtrooper..5.00

Topps (Ireland)
Set of 10, numbered. Packed in with sculpted candy dispensers.
- Cards 1–10, each [118-02]...10.00

Cards: Parody
Continued in Volume 3, Page 118

Inkworks
Family Guy. 50 numbered cards, 1 case loader card, 3 Droid Chat holographic foil cards, 9 foil puzzle cards, 12 Fox Video bonus cards, 2 promotions cards, 6 scenes from space cards, 9 spaceship cards, 6 What Happens Next cards.
- Cards 1–50, each 0.50
- Complete set of 40 cards...25.00
- Case loader 35.00
- Droid Chat holo foil cards DC1–DC3, each 2.00
- Foil puzzle cards NH1–NH9, each 2.00
- Fox Video bonus cards 1–12, each 2.50
- Promotion cards, each 5.00
- Scenes from Space cards S1–S6, each 3.00
- Spaceships / Transports cards ST1–ST9, each 3.00
- What Happens Next cards WN1–WN6, each 3.00

Pixar
- Cars, 6 numbered, each [119-01] 5.00

Cards: Pilot Licenses

5 unnumbered character cards. (Images and checklist in 3rd edition, page 193.)
- Cards, each [120-01] 10.00

Cards: Premiums
Continued in Volume 3, Page 118

American Premium Corp.
18 numbered cards distributed in General Mills cereal. (Images and checklist in 3rd edition, page 198.)
- Cards 1–6 (yellow), each [121-01] 10.00
- Cards 7–12 (blue), each [121-02] 10.00
- Cards 13–18 (red), each [121-03] 10.00
- Complete set of 18 cards..120.00

Bimbo (Mexico)
19 unnumbered punch-out bread cards. Episode II: Attack of the Clones. (Images and checklist in 3rd edition, page 193.)
- Cards, each [121-04] 10.00

12 unnumbered punch-out bread cards. Episode III.
- Cards, each [121-05] 10.00

Biscuiterie Nantaise
40 unnumbered cards. 36 character and 4 planet cards. (Images in 3rd edition, page 187. Checklist in 3rd edition, page 186.)
- Character cards, each [121-06].................................2.00
- Planet cards, each [121-07] 2.00
- Complete set of 40 cards..65.00

Bluebird (New Zealand)
18 numbered medium cards. (Checklist in 3rd edition, page 212.)
- Cards 1–18, each 1.00
- Complete set of 18 cards..30.00

Set of 18 mini cards with numbering continued from medium-sized set. (Checklist in 3rd edition, page 213.)
- Cards 19–36, each 1.00
- Complete set of 18 mini cards 20.00

Set of 30 large cards. (Images in 2nd edition, page 216. Checklist in 3rd edition, page 213.)
- Cards 1–30, each [121-08] 1.50
- Complete set of 30 cards..15.00

Bondy Fiesta (Mexico)
From Surprise Eggs. Each egg contained 1 lollipop, 10 random memory cards, a charm, and a sticker.
- Memory cards, any 10 [121-09] 3.00

Burger Chef
12 unnumbered character cards; cut out from Funmeal box. (Images in 4th edition, page 74.)
- Cards, each [121-10]..2.00

Burger King
36 cut-apart cards distributed in sheets of 6. Six sheets cut apart at stores to make sheets of 3. Value of cards should take into account precision and quality cuts since all were made by hand. (Images in 3rd edition, page 196. Checklist in 3rd edition, page 194.)
- Individual cards cut apart..1.00
- 3 card cut-apart sheets, each [121-11].......................5.00
- 6 card cut-apart sheets, each 8.00

 118-01 Sample
 118-02 Sample
 119-01 Sample
 120-01 Sample
 121-01 Sample

 121-02 Sample
 121-03 Sample
 121-04 Sample
 121-05 Sample
 121-06 Sample
 121-07 Sample
 121-08 Sample
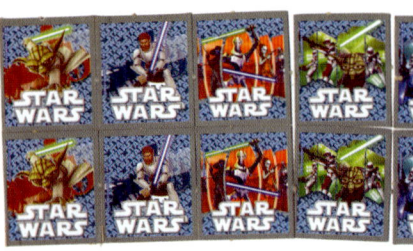 121-09 Sample

 121-10 Sample

 121-11 Sample
 121-12 Sample

Cards: Premiums

Chio (Hungary)
40 unnumbered chip / crisp cards from Episode II. (Images in 2nd edition, page 196. Checklist in 3rd edition, page 194.)
- ❑ Cards, each [121-12]..5.00
- ❑ Complete set of 40 cards..................................75.00

Chio (Poland)
40 numbered chip / crisp cards from Episode II: Attack of the Clones. (Images in 2nd edition, page 196. Checklist in 3rd edition, page 194.)
- ❑ Cards 1–40, each [121-13]...................................5.00
- ❑ Complete set of 40 cards..................................75.00

Confection Concepts
45 numbered Empire Strikes Back cards. Dark blue borders with puzzle scenes on back. (Images in 2nd edition, page 197. Checklist in 3rd edition, page 194.)
- ❑ Cards 1–45, each [121-14]...................................8.00
- ❑ Complete set of 45 cards..................................95.00

50 numbered Star Wars cards. Dark blue borders with puzzle scenes on back. (Images and checklist in 3rd edition, page 195.)
- ❑ Cards 1–50, each [121-15]................................10.00
- ❑ Complete set of 50 cards................................125.00

Dark Horse Comics
6 classic characters on cut-apart sheet. 2 cards per sheet. (Images and checklist in 3rd edition, page 196.)
- ❑ Cards, each..5.00
- ❑ Uncut sheet of 2, each [v1e1:115]......................35.00

Dixie / Northern Inc.
Large Cards. Set of 4 Rebel and 4 Empire. (Images and checklist in 3rd edition, page 196.)
- ❑ Empire cards, each [v1e1:115]..........................12.00
- ❑ Rebel cards, each..15.00

24 numbered story cards. Cut-apart strips of 4 cards each. (Images and checklist in 3rd edition, page 196.)
- ❑ Cards 1–24, each..5.00
- ❑ Uncut card strips, each [4:75].............................15.00

Doo Wap (France)
12 cards in 4 brochures with cut-apart strips of 3 cards. (Images and checklist in 3rd edition, page 197.)
- ❑ Brochures, each [121-16]...................................15.00
- ❑ Cards, each..10.00

Doritos
20 numbered 3D motion discs. (Images in 2nd edition, page 198. Checklist in 3rd edition, page 197.)
- ❑ Discs 1–20, each [v1e1:115].................................5.00

Doritos/Cheetos
6 numbered 3D motion cards, plus 2 bonus cards. (Images in 2nd edition, page 198. Checklist in 3rd edition, page 197.)
- ❑ Bonus cards, each...8.00
- ❑ Cards 1–6, each [v1e1:115]..................................5.00

Energizer
3 unnumbered lightsaber duels, lenticular cards. (Images in 2nd edition, page 199. Checklist in 3rd edition, page 197.)
- ❑ Cards, each [v1e1:115]..5.00

Evercrisp (Argentina)
30 numbered classic trilogy characters and ships cards. (Image and checklist in 3rd edition, page 197.)
- ❑ Cards 1–30, each..5.00
- ❑ Complete set of 30 cards..................................70.00

Fanta (Thailand)
12 unnumbered Star Wars: Special Edition scene cards. (Images and checklist in 3rd edition, page 197.)
- ❑ Cards, each [121-17]...15.00

Fernandes
Guitar pick collection checklists. 4 checklists per series. (Images and checklists in 3rd edition, page 197.)
- ❑ Series 1 classic characters, each [4:75].................8.00
- ❑ Series 2 prequel characters, each [121-18]..........8.00

Freegells (Brazil)
50 numbered plastic cards. (Images and checklist in 3rd edition, page 197.)
- ❑ Cards, each [121-19]..5.00

Fromagerie Bel (France)
10 unnumbered EPI:TPM cards. (Images in 2nd edition, page 199. Checklist in 3rd edition, page 198.)
- ❑ Cards, each [121-20]..5.00

Gummi
4 unnumbered 2" square cards from EPI:TPM.
- ❑ Cards, each [121-21]..5.00

Hollywood Chewing Gum (France)
20 numbered chewing gum box peel-away. (Images in 2nd ed., page 199. Checklist in 3rd ed., page 199.)
- ❑ Cards 1–20, each [v1e1:116].................................8.00

Kellogg's
10 numbered Stick'R Cards. Stickers are adhered to trading cards for backing. (Images and checklist in 3rd edition, page 198.)
- ❑ Cards 11–20, each [121-22]................................10.00

Kellogg's (Australia)
Ewok Adventure Collect-a-Prize game pieces. (Images and checklist in 3rd edition, page 198.)
- ❑ Cards A1–C12, each...70.00

Kellogg's (Canada)
3 oversized 3D cards.
- ❑ Cards 1–10, each..3.00

16 unnumbered cut-out cards. 4 on each of 4 different unnumbered box panels.
- ❑ Individual cards—cut apart, each........................2.00
- ❑ Uncut box panel with 4 cards, each..................14.00

10 Stick'R cards numbered 11–20. (Images in 3rd edition, page 199. Checklist in 3rd edition, page 198.)
- ❑ Cards 11–20, each [121-23]................................18.00

Kellogg's (France)
14 unnumbered Episode III: Revenge of the Sith cards.
- ❑ Cards, each [121-24]..5.00

Kent (Turkey)
27 numbered cards distributed in packets of gum. (Images and checklist in 3rd edition, page 199.)
- ❑ Cards 1–27, each [121-25]..................................12.00

121-13 Sample

121-14 Sample

121-15 Sample

121-16 Sample

121-17 Sample

121-18 Sample

121-19 Sample

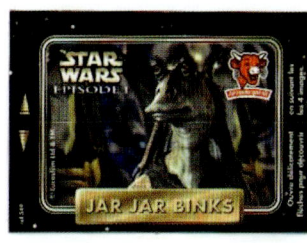
121-20 Sample

121-21 Sample

121-22 Sample

121-23 Sample

121-24 Sample

121-25 Sample

121-26 Sample

Cards: Premiums

121-27 Sample | 121-28 Sample | 121-29 Sample | 121-30 Sample | 121-31 Sample | 121-32 Sample | 121-33 Sample

121-34 Sample | 121-35 Sample | 121-36 Sample | 121-37 Sample | 121-38 Sample | 121-39 Sample | 121-40 Sample

Kraft Foods
4 unnumbered Clone Wars flip-n-fold cards. Distributed in Oscar Mayer Lunchables.
- Cards, each [v1e1:116] 4.00

La vache qui rit (France)
10 unnumbered Episode I cards. Distributed inside of Laughing Cow cheese wrappers.
- Cards, each [v1e1:116] 10.00

Masterfoods USA
4 unnumbered M&M Mpire cards. (Image in 4th edition, page 75.)
- Cards, each [121-26] 5.00

Meiji (Japan)
30 numbered EPI:TPM cards distributed in chip packets. (Images and checklist in 3rd ed., page 199.)
- Cards 1–30, each [121-27] 5.00
- Complete set of 30 cards 40.00

Myojo Foods Ltd.
30 numbered classic trilogy cards. (Images and checklist in 3rd edition, page 199.)
- Cards 1–30, each [v1e1:116] 5.00
- Complete set of 30 cards 65.00

Natur (Chile)
36 numbered cards, distributed in gum.
- Cards 1–36, each [121-28] 10.00
- Complete set of 36 cards 75.00

Nestlé
6 unnumbered lenticular scenes.
- Cards, each [121-29] 5.00

Nestlé (Chile)
5 unnumbered cards, packaged in Estrellitas and Gold candy. (Images and checklist in 3rd edition, page 200.)
- Cards, each [121-30] 8.00

Pacosa Dos / Internacional
224 numbered Droids cards.
- Cards 1–224, each 25.00

Pepsi Cola (Mexico)
24 unnumbered cards picturing Hasbro toys. (Images in 2nd edition, page 200. Checklist in 3rd edition, page 201.)
- Cards, each [121-31] 5.00
- Complete set of 24 cards 35.00

Pepsico (Argentina)
30 numbered classic trilogy characters and ships cards. (Images in 3rd edition, page 200. Checklist in 3rd edition, page 201.)
- Cards 1–30, each [121-32] 8.00

Quaker (Guatemala)
8 numbered Episode I: The Phantom Menace 3D cards. (Images and checklist in 3rd edition, page 201.)
- Cards 1–8, each [121-33] 10.00

Quality Bakers
10 unnumbered cards from classic trilogy. (Cards in 2nd edition, page 200. Checklist in 3rd edition, page 201.)
- Cards 1–10, each [121-34] 8.00

Sabritas (Mexico)
90 numbered Clone Wars cards.
- Cards 1–90, each [121-35] 4.00

Sonrics
30 numbered cards distributed by Gamesa. (Images in 2nd edition, page 200. Checklist in 3rd ed., pg. 201.)
- Cards 1–30, each [121-36] 5.00

30 numbered cards, plus 3 multipart cut-away scenes, and 10 background cards. (Images in 2nd edition, page 201. Checklist in 3rd edition, page 201.)
- Cards 1–30, each [121-37] 2.00
- Complete set of 30 base cards 50.00
- Background cards, each 5.00
- Cutaway scene cards, each [v1e1:117] 8.00

Star Wars Celebration III
21 numbered cards given away at Celebration III during collector panels. (Images in 4th ed., page 74.)
- Cards 1–21, each [v1e1:117] 5.00

Taco Bell
- Princess Leia 3D flip card [3:202] 5.00

Topps
10 numbered cards included in packages with candy head dispensers. (Images in 4th edition, page 76. Checklist in 3rd edition, page 202.)
- Cards 1–10, each [121-38] 5.00

3 unnumbered cards packed in with Hope Industries trilogy watches. One for each classic trilogy movie. (Images in 4th edition, page 76. Checklist in 3rd edition, page 202.)
- Cards, each [121-43] 8.00

Wonder Bread
16 numbered cards. Classic trilogy characters and vehicles. (Images in 2nd edition, page 201. Checklist in 3rd edition, page 202.)
- Cards 1–16, each [121-39] 10.00

York
6 unnumbered round cards, distributed under peanut butter jar caps. (Images in 2nd edition, page 201. Checklist in 3rd edition, page 202.)
- Cards, each [121-40] 12.00

Cards: Rebel Legion

Rebel Legion
- Series 1, each [v1e1:117] 1.00
- Series 2, each 1.00
- Series 3, each 1.00

Cards: Return of the Jedi

Cromy (Argentina)
- Cards 1–240, each 3.00
- Complete set of 240 cards 200.00
- Unopened card packets, each 35.00

Mello Smello
- Princess Leia lenticular promotes Vivid Vision 5.00

Monty Fabrieken Co. (Holland)
100 numbered yellow-bordered cards. (Images in 2nd edition, page 204. Checklist in 3rd edition, page 204.)
- Cards 1–100, each [122-01] 5.00
- Complete set of 100 cards 75.00
- Unopened card packets, each 80.00

O-Pee-Chee (Canada)
132 numbered red-border cards. Similar to Topps series 1. English and French text.
- Cards 1–132, each [122-02] 5.00
- Complete set of 132 cards 75.00
- Unopened card packets, each 50.00

Pacosa Dos / Internacional
200 numbered mini-cards with plain white borders and no text on the card fronts.
- Cards 1–200, each [122-03] 5.00
- Complete set of 200 cards 230.00
- Unopened card packets, each 150.00

Scanlens
132 numbered red-border cards. (Checklist in 3rd edition, page 204.)
- Cards 1–132, each [122-04] 5.00
- Complete set of 132 cards 125.00
- Unopened card packets, each 8.00

Topps
- Rack-Pack of 45 movie cards [v1e1:117] 45.00

Series 1. 132 numbered red-border cards, 33 stickers. (Images in 2nd edition, page 204. Checklist in 3rd edition, page 204.)
- Cards 1–132, each [122-05] 3.00
- Complete set of 132 cards 75.00
- Stickers 1–33, each [v1e1:117] 15.00
- Unopened card packets, each 35.00

Cards: Saga

      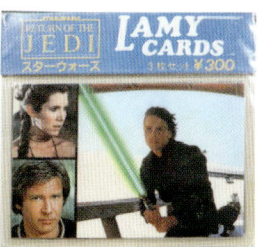

122-01 Sample | 122-02 Sample | 122-03 Sample | 122-04 Sample | 122-05 Sample | 122-06 Sample | 122-07 Sample

123-01 | 123-02 Sample | 123-03 Sample | 123-04 Sample | 123-05 Sample | 123-06 Sample

Series 2. 88 numbered blue-border cards, 22 stickers. (Images in 2nd edition, page 205. Checklist in 3rd edition, page 205.)
- Cards 133–220, each [122-06] 3.00
- Complete set of 88 cards 55.00
- Stickers 34–45, each [v1e1:117] 15.00

Yamakatsu Corporation (Japan)
Lamy cards. Return of the Jedi 3-packs. Back of package shows which cards are included.
- Luke and Leia on Sail Barge; Yoda, Chewbacca, R2-D2, and C-3PO; Princess Leia, Han Solo, Luke Skywalker [122-07] 50.00

Cards: Revenge of the Sith

Mello Smello
- Darth Vader, promotes Vivid Vision [123-01] 5.00

Safeway
16 numbered cards. Sold in pack of four cards each.
- Cards 1–16, each [123-02] 1.00

Topps
- Lenticular poster card, 10" x 8" 15.00

90 numbered cards, 6 etched foil puzzle cards, 3 lenticular morphing, 5 promotional cards.
- Cards 1–90, each [123-03] 1.00
- Complete set of 90 base cards 35.00
- Bonus cards A–F, each 5.00
- Etched foil cards 1–10, each [123-04] 5.00
- Etched foil puzzle cards F1–F6, each 5.00
- Hologram cards 1–3, each 5.00
- Lenticular morphing cards M1–M3, each 5.00
- Promotion cards P1–P5, each [123-05] 5.00
- Sticker cards 1–10, each 8.00
- Story cards 1–6, each 5.00
- Tattoo cards 1–10, each 8.00
- Tins, 3 packs, 2 exclusive bonus cards [123-06] ... 30.00
- Unopened card packets, each 10.00

Topps (UK)
68 numbered lenticular and 3D flix-pix cards.
- Cards 1–68, each [4:77] 2.00
- Complete set of 68 cards 60.00
- Unopened card packets, each 10.00

Cards: Role Playing

Scholastic
Adventures game, EPII. 3" x 3" cards. (Images in 3rd edition, page 203. Checklist in 3rd edition, page 202.)
- Cards, each [124-01] 1.00

West End Games
Distributed inside books and games. (Checklist in 3rd edition, page 203.)
- Cards, each 2.00

Cards: Saga

(Japan)
Collector cards from credit card redemption. Episodes 1–6. 10,000 produced of each. Individually numbered.
- Cards, each [125-01] 20.00

Dyna Mart (France)
200 numbered cards and 150 numbered sticker cards. Produced in the US for French market. Classic trilogy and Episode I images.
- Cards 1–200, each [125-02] 5.00
- Sticker cards s1–s150, each [125-03] 5.00

Merlin Publishing International Ltd. (France)
125 numbered cards.
- Cards 1–125, each [125-04] 3.00

Merlin Publishing International Ltd. (Germany)
125 numbered cards.
- Cards 1–125, each 3.00

Merlin Publishing International Ltd. (Italy)
125 numbered cards.
- Cards 1–125, each 3.00

Merlin Publishing International Ltd. (UK)
125 numbered cards and 3 promotional cards.
- Cards 1–125, each 3.00
- Cards P1–P3, each 5.00

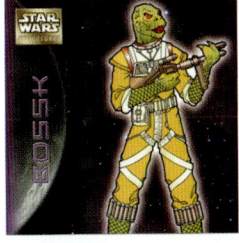    

124-01 Sample | 125-01 Sample | 125-02 Sample | 125-03 Sample | 125-04 Sample

    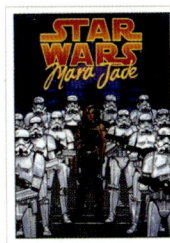 

125-05 Sample | 125-06 Sample | 126-01 Sample | 126-02 Sample | 127-01 Sample | 127-02 Sample

Cards: Saga

     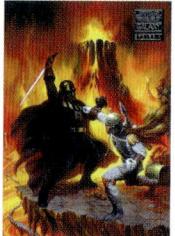  

128-01 Sample | 128-02 Sample | 129-01 Sample | 130-01 Sample | 131-01 Sample | 132-01 Sample | 133-01 Sample | 134-01 Sample

Pepsi Cola (Thailand)
Set of 4 cards. One for each classic trilogy movie, plus one Star Wears: Special Edition logo.
- ❏ A New Hope 10.00
- ❏ Empire Strikes Back 10.00
- ❏ Return of the Jedi 10.00
- ❏ Star Wars Special Edition logo 10.00

Topps
Heritage. 5 numbered promotional cards.
- ❏ Cards P1–P5, each [125-05] 6.00

Star Wars. Series 1. 24 numbered cards. Sealed package includes 1 dog tag, 1 matching trading card, 1 checklist. Value is for trading card.
- ❏ Cards 1–24, each [125-06] 3.00

Topps (Japan)
72 cards plus 6 chase cards. Scenes from all 3 classic trilogy films.
- ❏ Cards 1–72, each 2.00
- ❏ Chase cards 1–6, each 8.00

Yamakatsu Corporation (Japan)
72 cards plus 6 chase cards. Scenes from all 3 classic trilogy films.
- ❏ Card pack tied with string 140.00

Cards: Shadows of the Empire

Topps
100 numbered cards, 7 promotional cards, 1 autographed promotional card. (Images and checklist in 3rd edition, page 206.)
- ❏ Cards 1–100, each [126-01] 4.00
- ❏ Complete set of 100 base cards 50.00
- ❏ Autographed SOTE7 (redemption) [v1e1:118] 150.00
- ❏ Promotional cards SOTE1–SOTE7, each [126-02] ..10.00
- ❏ Redemption "winner" card [3:207] 45.00
- ❏ Reservation coupon [3:207] 5.00
- ❏ Unopened card packets, each 15.00

Cards: Signing

Dallas Comic-Con
- ❏ Zechariah Jensen / Kit Fisto [v1e1:118] 5.00

Dark Horse Comics
Unnumbered convention signing cards. Value for cards is unsigned. (Checklist in 3rd edition, page 208.)
- ❏ Cards unsigned, each [127-01] 10.00

Topps
- ❏ 1995 San Diego Comic-Con, limited to 5,000 [127-02] 35.00

Cards: Star Wars Finest

Topps
90 cards plus promotional, foil, matrix, and oversized chase cards. (Images in 2nd edition, page 207. Checklist in 3rd edition, page 207.)
- ❏ Cards 1–90, each [128-01] 3.00
- ❏ Complete set of 90 base cards 85.00
- ❏ Foil cards F1–F6, each [128-02] 5.00
- ❏ Matrix cards 1–4, each 10.00
- ❏ Oversized card [v1e1:118] 10.00
- ❏ Oversized refractor card 15.00
- ❏ Promo binder card 15.00

- ❏ Promo cards SWF1–SWF3 ....5.00
- ❏ Unopened card packets, each 15.00
- ❏ Refractor sheet of 90 uncut chromium cards, gold metallic print on back, limited to 250 ....250.00

Cards: Star Wars Galaxy I

Topps
140 numbered cards plus promotional, 6 foil chase cards, and promotional cards. (Images in 2nd edition, page 208. Checklist in 3rd edition, page 208.)
- ❏ Cards 1–140, each [129-01] 3.00
- ❏ Complete set of 140 base cards 60.00
- ❏ Foil cards 1–6, each 5.00
- ❏ Promo binder SWB1 card 15.00
- ❏ Promo cards, each 10.00
- ❏ Promo cards, uncut sheet 75.00
- ❏ Unopened card packets, each 15.00
- ❏ Millennium Falcon factory set, ltd. to 10,000 ....90.00

Cards: Star Wars Galaxy II

Topps
135 numbered cards, 6 foil cards, and promotional cards. (Images in 2nd edition, page 210. Checklist in 3rd edition, page 209.)
- ❏ Cards 141–275, each [130-01] 3.00
- ❏ Complete set of 135 base cards 55.00
- ❏ Foil cards 7–12, each 5.00
- ❏ Promo cards P1–P2; P4–P6, each [v1e1:118] 10.00
- ❏ Promo cards oversized, each [v1e1:118] 10.00
- ❏ Unopened card packets, each 15.00
- ❏ Deluxe Collector Set with storage tin 65.00

Cards: Star Wars Galaxy III

Topps
90 numbered cards, 6 embossed cards, 6 foil cards, 12 lenticular cards, 8 numbered promotional cards, and oversized promotional cards. (Images in 2nd edition, page 212. Checklist in 3rd edition, page 209.)
- ❏ Cards 276–365, each [131-01] 3.00
- ❏ Complete set of 90 base cards 45.00
- ❏ Embossed cards E1–E6, each 5.00
- ❏ Foil cards F13–F18, each 8.00
- ❏ Lenticular cards L1–L12 ....8.00
- ❏ Promotional cards oversized, each 10.00
- ❏ Promotional cards P1–P8, each 10.00
- ❏ Promotional cards unnumbered, each 10.00
- ❏ Unopened card packets, each 15.00

Cards: Star Wars Galaxy IV

Topps
120 numbered cards, base color printing plates, 15 bronze foil cards, 6 etched foil cards, 15 foil cards, 6 galaxy evolutions foil cards, 15 gold foil cards, 5 lost galaxy cards, 2 lost Yoda cards, 15 refractor foil cards, 3 promotional cards.
- ❏ Cards 366–486, each [132-01] 1.00
- ❏ Complete set of 120 base cards 40.00
- ❏ Base card printing plates (black, cyan, magenta, or yellow) limited to 120 of each, 1:576 packs, each 150.00
- ❏ Bronze foil cards 1–15, 1:24 packs, each 20.00
- ❏ Etched foil cards 1–6, 1:6 packs, each 10.00
- ❏ Foil cards 1–15, 1:3 packs, each 5.00
- ❏ Galaxy evolution foil cards 1–6, 1:24 packs, each ..25.00
- ❏ Gold foil cards 1–15, limited to 500 of each, 1:47 packs, each 45.00
- ❏ Lost galaxy cards 1–5, 1:24 packs, each 12.00
- ❏ Lost Yoda card, limited to 999, 1:277 packs, each 60.00
- ❏ Lost Yoda card, 1:2789 packs, each 350.00
- ❏ Promotional cards P1–P2, each 10.00

Cards: Star Wars Galaxy V

Topps
120 numbered cards, 6 etched foil cards, 15 silver foil cards, 15 copper foil cards, 15 gold foil cards.
- ❏ Cards 487–607, each [133-01] 1.00
- ❏ Complete set of 120 base cards 35.00
- ❏ Copper foil cards, each 5.00
- ❏ Etched foil cards 1–16, each 5.00
- ❏ Silver foil cards, each 15.00
- ❏ Gold foil cards, each ....OSPV

Cards: Star Wars Galaxy VI

Topps
120 numbered cards, 56 numbered continuation cards, 9 animation cels, 10 bronze foil cards, 6 etched foil cards, gold and silver foil cards.
- ❏ Cards 669–725, each 1.25
- ❏ Animation cels 1–9 ....15.00
- ❏ Bronze foil cards 1–10, each 15.00
- ❏ Gold foil cards, each ....OSPV
- ❏ Silver foil cards, each 25.00

Cards: Star Wars Galaxy Magazine

Topps
9 cards in two sets. (Checklist in 3rd edition, page 207.)
- ❏ Cards C1–C4, each 4.00
- ❏ Cards SWGM–SWGM4, each 4.00

Cards: Tarot
Fan produced artistry.
- ❏ Episode I: The Phantom Menace 45.00
- ❏ Episode III: Revenge of the Sith 45.00

Cards: The Phantom Menace
Hungary. Set of 20, unnumbered. (Images and checklist in 3rd edition, page 212.)
- ❏ Cards, each [135-01] 5.00
- ❏ Complete set of 36 cards 75.00

Japan. Set of 8 unnumbered, has Pepsi "Ask for More" logo, but not produced by Pepsi. (Images and checklist in 3rd edition, page 212.)
- ❏ Cards, each [135-02] 5.00
- ❏ Complete set of 36 cards 60.00

Prismatic Version 1. 36 unnumbered cards. (Images in 2nd edition, page 216. Checklist in 3rd edition, page 212.)
- ❏ Cards, each [135-03] 5.00
- ❏ Complete set of 36 cards 45.00

Prismatic Version II. 36 unnumbered cards. (Images in 2nd edition, page 217. Checklist in 3rd edition, page 212.)
- ❏ Cards, each [135-04] 5.00
- ❏ Complete set of 36 cards 45.00

Cards: The Phantom Menace

20th Century Fox
4 numbered cards, used to view new scenes on DVD at the store during the promotion for the release of Episode I. Walmart exclusive. (Images in 2nd edition, page 217.)
- ❏ 1 Complete Podrace Grid Sequence..........................5.00
- ❏ 2 Extended Podrace Lap Two [v1e1:120] 5.00
- ❏ 3 The Waterfall Sequence [135-05] 5.00
- ❏ 4 The Air Taxi Sequence 5.00

Bluebird
18 numbered medium cards. (Checklist in 3rd edition, page 212.)
- ❏ Cards 1–18, each 3.00
- ❏ Complete set of 18 cards..35.00

Set of 18 mini cards with numbering continued from medium-sized set. (Checklist in 3rd edition, page 213.)
- ❏ Cards 19–36, each 5.00
- ❏ Complete set of 18 mini cards 40.00

Set of 30 large cards. (Images in 2nd edition, page 216. Checklist in 3rd edition, page 213.)
- ❏ Cards 1–30, each [135-06] 4.00
- ❏ Complete set of 30 cards..45.00

Caltex (South Africa)
4 unnumbered cards. (Images and checklist in 3rd edition, page 213.)
- ❏ Cards, each [135-07] 10.00

Family Toy Warehouse
3 unnumbered lenticular cards. (Images and checklist in 3rd edition, page 213.)
- ❏ Cards, each [135-08] 10.00

Frito Lay
12 unnumbered cards. Episode I characters with an associated trait description. (Images in 2nd edition, page 218. Checklist in 3rd edition, page 213.)
- ❏ Cards, each [135-09] 2.00

Harmony (Australia)
24 numbered cards. (Images and checklist in 3rd edition, page 213.)
- ❏ Cards 1–24, each [135-10] 5.00
- ❏ Complete set of 24 cards..50.00

iKon
60 numbered cards with red and black border, plus one checklist card. (Images in 2nd edition, page 218. Checklist in 3rd edition, page 213.)
- ❏ Cards 1–61, each [135-11] 3.00
- ❏ Complete set of 61 cards..50.00

Interlace4D
6 unnumbered, oversized lenticular cards. (Checklist in 3rd edition, page 214.)
- ❏ Cards, each [135-12] 5.00

KFC
5 unnumbered character cards. (Images in 2nd edition, page 219. Checklist in 3rd edition, page 214.)
- ❏ Cards, each [135-13] 8.00

KFC (Australia)
10 numbered character cards. (Images in 2nd edition, page 219. Checklist in 3rd edition, page 214.)
- ❏ Cards 1–10, each [135-14] 8.00

KFC (Mexico)
20 numbered character cards, 1 collecting envelope. Same images as KFC, UK set. (Images in 2nd edition, page 219. Checklist in 3rd edition, page 214.)
- ❏ Cards 1–20, each [135-15] 8.00
- ❏ Complete set of 20 cards..40.00
- ❏ Collecting envelope...5.00

KFC (UK)
20 numbered character cards. Same images as KFC, Mexico set. (Images in 2nd edition, page 219. Checklist in 3rd edition, page 214.)
- ❏ Cards 1–20, each [135-16] 5.00
- ❏ Complete set of 20 cards..20.00

Meiji (Japan)
30 numbered character cards. (Images and checklist in 3rd edition, page 214.)
- ❏ Cards 1–30, each [4:79] 5.00

 135-01 Sample
 135-02 Sample
 135-03 Sample
 135-04 Sample
 135-05 Sample
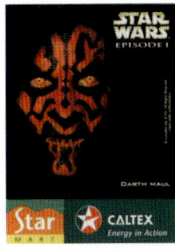 135-06 Sample
 135-07 Sample
 135-08 Sample
 135-09 Sample
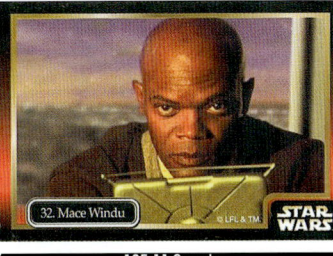 135-10 Sample
 135-11 Sample
 135-12
 135-13 Sample
 135-14 Sample
 135-15 Sample
 135-16 Sample
 135-17 Sample
 135-18 Sample
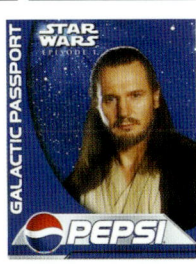 135-19 Sample
 135-20 Sample
 135-21 Sample
 135-22 Sample
 135-23 Sample
 135-24 Sample
 135-25 Sample
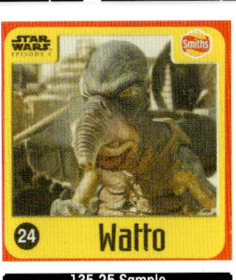 135-26 Sample
 135-27 Sample

Cards: The Phantom Menace

136-01 Sample | 137-01 Sample | 138-01 Sample | 139-01 Sample | 140-01 Sample | 141-01 Sample | 142-01 Sample | 143-01 Sample | 144-01 Sample

Pepsi Cola
24 numbered cards showing Pepsi cans with characters. Game piece attached. (Images in 2nd edition, page 219. Checklist in 3rd edition, page 215.)
- Cards 1–24, each [135-17] 1.00
- Complete set of 20 cards 25.00
- Collector Card Game Booklet 5.00

Pepsi Cola (Australia)
12 unnumbered 3" circular carton cut-out cards. (Images and checklist in 3rd edition, page 215.)
- 6-pack [135-18] 10.00
- 12-pack [v1e1-121] 10.00
- 15-pack 10.00

Pepsi Cola (Germany)
45 numbered scenes with character names. (Images in 2nd edition, page 219. Checklist in 3rd edition, page 215.)
- Cards 1–45, each [135-19] 3.00
- Complete set of 45 cards 30.00

Pepsi Cola (China)
7 unnumbered cards marked "Galactic Passport." (Images in 3rd edition, page 215. Checklist in 3rd edition, page 216.)
- Cards, each [135-20] 8.00

Pepsi Cola (Mexico)
96 unnumbered cards. (Images in 3rd edition, page 214. Checklist in 3rd edition, page 216.)
- Cards 1–96, each [135-21] 3.00
- Complete set of 96 cards 60.00

Pepsi Cola (Netherlands)
26 numbered 2" x 2" square cards featuring characters. (Images in 2nd edition, page 220. Checklist in 3rd edition, page 216.)
- Cards 1–26, each [v1e1-121] 4.00
- Complete set of 26 cards 45.00

Pepsi Cola (UK)
7 numbered pop-up cards. Perforated bottoms to form stands. (Images and checklist in 3rd edition, page 216.)
- Cards 1–7, each [135-22] 5.00

9 unnumbered character cards. Small Pepsi logo in the top left corner of image. (Images and checklist in 3rd edition, page 216.)
- Cards, each [135-23] 3.00

4 unnumbered cards. Card backs make up Darth Maul image. (Images and checklist in 3rd edition, page 216.)
- Cards, each [135-24] 5.00

Smith's Snackfood (UK)
26 numbered cards featuring characters with an associated trait description and Smiths logo in top right corner. Same images as Walkers, except for the addition of #19, Padmé. (Images in 3rd edition, page 216.)
- Cards 1–26, each [135-25] 3.00
- Complete set of 26 cards 35.00

Topps
7-packs of random movie cards in collectible tin. Includes 1 mega-size foil card. (Checklist in 3rd edition, page 216.)
- Sealed tins, each 25.00

Unif (Thailand)
6 unnumbered cards. Promotes drink products. (Images and checklist in 3rd edition, page 216.)
- Cards, each [135-26] 10.00

Walkers (UK)
25 unnumbered cards featuring characters with an associated trait description. (Images and checklist in 3rd edition, page 216.)
- Cards, each [135-27] 5.00
- Complete set of 25 cards 50.00

Cards: Tin

Metallic Images
A New Hope. 20 numbered cards inside a collector's tin. 1 Promo card. (Images in 2nd edition, page 215. Checklist in 3rd edition, page 210.)
- Set of cards plus collector's tin [136-01] 40.00
- Promo card P1 .... 15.00

Bounty Hunters. 5 scenes plus one Star Wars: Special Edition Han / Jabba scene inside a collector's tin. (Images in 2nd edition, page 215. Checklist in 3rd edition, page 211.)
- Set of cards plus collector's tin [137-01] 25.00

Dark Empire. 6 numbered cards showing covers from comics inside a collector's tin. (Images in 2nd edition, page 215. Checklist in 3rd edition, page 211.)
- Set of cards plus collector's tin [138-01] 25.00

Dark Empire II. 6 cards showing covers from comics inside a collector's tin. (Images in 2nd edition, page 215. Checklist in 3rd edition, page 211.)
- Set of cards plus collector's tin [139-01] 25.00

Empire Strikes Back. 20 numbered cards inside a collector's tin. 1 Promo card. (Images in 2nd edition, page 215. Checklist in 3rd edition, page 211.)
- Set of cards plus collector's tin [140-01] 40.00
- Promo card P2 .... 15.00

Jedi Knights. 6 scenes inside a collector's tin. (Images in 2nd edition, page 216. Checklist in 3rd edition, page 211.)
- Set of cards plus collector's tin [141-01] 25.00

Jedi Knights exclusive. 6 scenes plus bonus one Wampa scene inside a round collector's tin. Avon exclusive.
- Set of cards plus round tin 35.00

Ralph McQuarrie art. 20 numbered cards inside a collector's tin. (Images in 2nd edition, page 216. Checklist in 3rd edition, page 211.)
- Set of cards plus collector's tin [142-01] 50.00

Return of the Jedi. 20 numbered cards in a collector's tin. (Images in 2nd edition, page 216. Checklist in 3rd edition, page 211.)
- Set of cards plus collector's tin [143-01] 40.00
- Promo card P3 .... 15.00

Shadows of the Empire. 6 cards showing covers from comics inside a collector's tin. (Images in 2nd edition, page 216. Checklist in 3rd edition, page 211.)
- Set of cards plus collector's tin [144-01] 25.00

Cards: Trading-Card Game

The Trading-Card Game (TCG) play decks were built from cards purchased in random booster packs. During the years the game enjoyed a large active community. Values of individual cards varied depending on scarcity of the card and the amount of influence the card had to offer in stronger or popular play strategies.

The most desired cards used to have values of $10–$20 each, with some of the rarest cards reaching nearly $100 in value. The common cards rarely rose above $0.10 to $0.25 each. The addition of foil chase cards increased some card values.

Since the development for the Trading-Card Game has ended, the value for the cards has plunged as only a core of dedicated game players and collectors who find the card art curious have any interest.

Trading-Card Game cards are often found at auction in large quantities and without specific card listings due to the hundreds of types of cards and card variations that exist.

A brief description of each set is provided here. Complete card set listings can be found using the database at www.StarWarsDatabase.com.

Wizards of the Coast
A New Hope. 180 cards.
Cards counted by rarity:
Common: 60, Uncommon: 61, Rare: 59
Cards counter by type:
Battle: 38, Character: 63, Ground: 28, Mission: 27, Space: 24

Attack of the Clones. 180 cards.
Cards counted by rarity:
Common: 60, Uncommon: 60, Rare: 60
Cards counter by type:
Battle: 37, Character: 63, Ground: 30, Mission: 25, Space: 28

Battle of Yavin. 105 cards.
Cards counted by rarity:
Common: 34, Uncommon: 36, Rare: 35
Cards counter by type:
Battle: 19, Character: 39, Ground: 21, Mission: 7, Space: 19

Empire Strikes Back. 210 cards.
Cards counted by rarity:
Common: 70, Uncommon: 69, Rare: 71
Cards counter by type:
Battle: 38, Character: 58, Ground: 28, Location: 27, Mission: 27, Space: 32

Jedi guardians. 105 cards.
Cards counted by rarity:
Common: 34, Uncommon: 36, Rare: 35
Cards counter by type:
Battle: 13, Character: 42, Ground: 18, Mission: 15, Space: 17

Return of the Jedi. 109 cards.
Cards counted by rarity:
Common: 40, Uncommon: 29, Rare: 40
Cards counter by type:
Battle: 15, Character: 41, Ground: 19, Location: 15, Mission: 4, Space: 15

Cards: Widevision

145-01 Sample Front and Back   146-01 Sample   146-02 Sample   146-03   146-04

Revenge of the Sith. 110 cards.
Cards counted by rarity:
Common: 40, Uncommon: 30, Rare: 40
Cards counter by type:
Battle: 17, Character: 35, Equipment: 8, Ground: 13,
Location: 7, Mission: 9, Space: 21

Rogues and Scoundrels. 105 cards.
Cards counted by rarity:
Common: 35, Uncommon: 35, Rare: 35
Cards counter by type:
Battle: 11, Character: 45, Ground: 11, Mission: 12,
Space: 20

Sith Rising. 90 cards.
Cards counted by rarity:
Common: 29, Uncommon: 30, Rare: 31
Cards counter by type:
Battle: 14, Character: 36, Ground: 17, Mission: 9,
Space: 14

The Phantom Menace. 90 cards.
Cards counted by rarity:
Common: 30, Uncommon: 30, Rare: 30
Cards counter by type:
Battle: 7, Character: 31, Ground: 20, Location: 12,
Mission: 6, Space: 14

Cards: Trading-Card Game, Pocketmodels

WizKids
Game packs, 4–8 Pocketmodels and 6 game cards.
❏ Base set, Han Solo package 20.00
❏ Ground Assault, Darth Vader package 15.00
❏ Ground Assault, Obi-Wan Kenobi package 15.00
❏ Order 66, Anakin Skywalker package 15.00
❏ Order 66, Commander Cody package 15.00
❏ Promo pack 1 ship model sheet, 1 info page, and 2 cards 25.00
❏ Yoda package 15.00

Power-Up packs, Imperial.
❏ Bullseye Squadron, Target exclusive 25.00
❏ Razor Squadron, exclusive to Walmart 25.00

Base set. 120 cards plus 6 specials. Cards 1–40 common, 41–80 uncommon, 81–120 rare.
❏ Cards 1–40, each 2.00
❏ Cards 41–80, each 6.00
❏ Cards 81–120, each 8.00
❏ Complete set of 120 .... 175.00
❏ Special cards s1–s6, each 10.00

Base set, ships.
Ship cards, each 2.00
❏ #9 Screamer Squadron, Taanab Yellow Aces, Storm Leader, Darth Vader's Tie Advanced x1 .... 12.50
❏ #18 Obi-Wan Kenobi's Jedi Interceptor, Anakin Skywalker's Jedi Interceptor, Picador Group, Confessor Group 11.00
❏ #23 Millennium Falcon 20.00

Clone Wars. Cards 1–40 common, 41–80 uncommon, 81–120 rare.
❏ Cards 1–40, each 2.00
❏ Cards 41–80, each 6.00
❏ Cards 81–120, each 8.00
❏ Complete set of 120 .... 150.00

Clone Wars, ships.
Ship cards, each 6.00

Ground Assault. Cards 1–40 common, 41–80 uncommon, 81–120 rare, 1 special.
❏ Cards 1–40, each 2.00
❏ Cards 41–80, each 4.00
❏ Cards 81–120, each 8.00
❏ Complete set of 120 .... 35.00
❏ s7 Echo Base 6.00

Ground Assault, ships.
❏ Ship cards, each 6.00

Order 66. Cards 1–20 common, 21–40 uncommon, 41–60 rare.
❏ Cards 1–20, each 2.00
❏ Cards 21–40, each 4.00
❏ Cards 41–60, each 8.00
❏ Complete set of 60 .... 15.00

Order 66, ships.
Ship cards, each 8.00

Scum and Villainy. Cards 1–20 common, 21–40 uncommon, 41–60 rare.
❏ Cards 1–20, each 2.00
❏ Cards 21–40, each 4.00
❏ Cards 41–60, each 8.00
❏ Complete set of 60 .... 75.00

Scum and Villainy, ships.
❏ Ship cards, each 6.00

Tins.
❏ Battle of Hoth 20.00
❏ Includes exclusive Millennium Falcon, exclusive to Star Wars Celebration IV 35.00
❏ The Force Unleashed 20.00

Cards: TV Week

TV Week
Set of 4 cards advertising Special Edition videos. Back advertises Special Edition videos. Gold-colored borders. (Images in 2nd edition, page 222. Checklist in 3rd edition, page 216.)
❏ Cards 1–4, each [145-01] 5.00

Cards: Vehicle

Topps
72 numbered cards, 6 promotional cards, 4 chase cards, 1 redemption card, 1 redeemed card. (Images in 2nd edition, page 223. Checklist in 3rd edition, page 217.)
❏ Cards 1–72, each [146-1] 2.00
❏ Complete set of 72 cards 85.00
❏ Chase cards C1–C4, each [146-2] 8.00
❏ Promo card P1 limited to 3,200 [v1e1:122] 85.00
❏ Promo card P1 refractor limited to 350 .... 250.00
❏ Promo card P2 limited to 1,600 [146-3] 125.00
❏ Promo card P2 refractor limited to 175 .... 350.00
❏ Redeemed card, oversized 3D 45.00
❏ Redemption card [146-4] 25.00
❏ Redemption card bonus envelope [v1e1:122] 5.00

Cards: Wallet

Antioch
8 unnumbered classic trilogy cards.
❏ Cards, each [v1e1:122] 5.00

5 unnumbered Episode I: The Phantom Menace cards.
❏ Cards, each [v1e1:122] 5.00

Paizo Publishing / Fan Club
Fan Club Membership cards.
❏ 2003 [v1e1:122] 10.00
❏ 2004 [v1e1:122] 10.00
❏ 2005 .... 10.00

Star Wars Insider
Space battle images.
❏ Tatooine [v1e1:122] 10.00
❏ Death Star II [v1e1:122] 10.00

Cards: Widevision

Topps
A New Hope. 120 numbered cards, 10 chase cards, 4 Kenner cards, 7 promotional cards. (Images in 2nd edition, page 224. Checklist in 3rd edition, page 218.)
❏ Cards 1–120, each [147-1] 1.00
❏ Complete set of 120 base cards 35.00
❏ Chase cards C1–C10, each 5.00
❏ Kenner cards K1–K4, each 10.00
❏ Promo cards P0–P6, each 6.00
❏ Promo binder card #00 .... 15.00
❏ Promo card 5" x 7" 8.00
❏ Unopened card packets, each 5.00

Attack of the Clones. 80 numbered cards, 23 hand signed autograph cards, 1 hand signed chase card, 2 promo cards. (Checklist in 3rd edition, page 219.)
❏ Cards 1–80, each 1.00
❏ Complete set of 80 base cards 45.00
❏ Promo cards P1 and S1, each [148-02] 5.00
❏ Unopened card packets, each 10.00
❏ Ahmed Best, Jar Jar Binks voice 55.00
❏ Alethea McGrath, Jocasta Nu 25.00
❏ Amy Allen, Aayla Secura 25.00
❏ Andrew Secombe, Watto voice 25.00
❏ Ayesha Dharker, Queen Jamillia 25.00
❏ Bodie Taylor, Clone trooper autographed 45.00
❏ Bonnie Piesse, Beru Whitesun 75.00
❏ Daniel Logan, Boba Fett [v1e1:123] 85.00
❏ David Bowers, Mas Amedda 25.00
❏ Frank Oz, Yoda 120.00
❏ Jay Laga'aia, Captain Typho 25.00
❏ Jesse Jensen, Saesee Tiin 65.00
❏ Joel Edgerton, Owen Lars [148-03] 50.00
❏ Kenny Baker, R2-D2 .... 130.00
❏ Leeanna Walsman, Zam Wesell 30.00
❏ Mary Oyaya, Luminara Unduli 25.00
❏ Matt Doran, Elan Sleazebaggano 25.00
❏ Matt Sloan, Plo Koon 25.00
❏ Nalini Krishan, Barriss Offee 25.00
❏ Rena Owen, Taun We voice 25.00
❏ Ronald Falk, Dexter Jettster 25.00
❏ Silas Carson, Ki Adi Mundi 45.00
❏ Silas Carson, Nute Gunray 80.00
❏ Zachariah Jensen, Kit Fisto 65.00

Clone Wars. 80 numbered cards, 13 autograph, 20 foil, 10 animation clear cel, and 8 season two preview cards. Complete card set listings can be found using the database at www.StarWarsDatabase.com.
Cards 1–80, each [149-01] 1.00
Complete set of 80 base cards 35.00
Autograph cards A1–A13, each [149-02] 35.00

Cards: Widevision

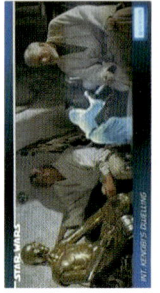       

147-01 | 148-01 | 148-02 | 148-03 | 149-01 | 149-02 | 149-03 | 150-01

150-02 | 151-01 | 151-02 | 152-01 | 152-02 | 153-01 | 154-01 | 155-01

❑ Clear animation cards C1–C10, each [149-03] 12.00
❑ Foil cards F1–F20, each 8.00
❑ Preview cards PV1–PV8, each 5.00
❑ Unopened card packets, each 6.00

Empire Strikes Back. 144 numbered cards, 10 chase cards, 8 promotional cards. (Images in 2nd edition, page 226. Checklist in 3rd edition, page 219.)
❑ Cards 1–144, each [150-01] 1.00
❑ Complete set of 144 base cards 45.00
❑ Chase cards C1–C10, each 15.00
❑ Promo cards P1–P6, each [150-02] 10.00
❑ Promo card #0 ....15.00
❑ Promo card 5" x 7" 10.00
❑ Unopened card packets, each 15.00

Return of the Jedi. 144 numbered cards, 9 promotional cards, 10 chase cards, 1 redemption card, 1 redeemed card. (Images in 2nd edition, page 228. Checklist in 3rd edition, page 220.)
❑ Cards 1–144, each [151-01] 1.00
❑ Complete set of 144 base cards 35.00
❑ Chase cards C1–C10, each [151-02] 15.00
❑ Promo cards P1–P6, each 10.00
❑ Promo card #0 ....15.00
❑ Promo card 5" x 7" 10.00
❑ Promo card DIII 15.00
❑ Redemption card 3-D offer 35.00
❑ Unopened card packets, each 15.00

Revenge of the Sith. 80 numbered cards, 10 chrome art cards (hobby), 10 chrome art cards (retail), 10 flix-pix cards, 5 autograph cards.
❑ Cards 1–80, each [152-01] 1.00
❑ Complete set of 80 base cards 20.00
❑ Chrome cards (hobby) H1–H10, each 15.00
❑ Chrome cards (retail) R1–R10, each 10.00
❑ Flix-pix cards 1–10, each 12.00
❑ Unopened card packets, each 15.00
❑ Amy Allen (Aayla Secura) 35.00
❑ Matthew Wood (General Grievous) [v1e1-123] ...125.00
❑ Michael Kingma (Tarrful) 45.00
❑ Peter Mayhew (Chewbacca) 65.00
❑ Samuel L. Jackson (Mace Windu) [152-02] 550.00

Star Wars: Special Edition, hobby set. 72 numbered cards, 2 holographic cards, 6 laser-cut cards. (Checklist in 3rd edition, page 221.)
❑ Cards 1–72, each 1.00
❑ Complete set of 80 base cards 20.00
❑ Holographic cards H1–H2, each 15.00
❑ Laser cut chrome cards C1–C6, each 10.00
❑ Unopened card packets, each 15.00

Special Edition retail set. 72 cards plus 5 Galoob chase, 4 Kenner chase, 6 laser cut, 8 promo cards. (Images in 2nd edition, page 230. Checklist in 3rd edition, page 221.)
❑ Cards 1–72, each [153-01] 1.00
❑ Complete set of 72 base cards 30.00
❑ Galoob chase cards G1–G5, each 10.00
❑ Kenner chase cards H1–H4, each 10.00
❑ Laser-cut cards C1–C6, each 15.00
❑ Promo cards P1–P8, each 12.00

The Phantom Menace series 1. 80 numbered cards. (Images in 2nd edition, page 232. Checklist in 3rd edition, page 222.)
❑ Cards 1–80, each [154-01] 1.00
❑ Complete set of 80 cards 30.00

Hobby special sets: 40 numbered bonus cards, 8 chrome cards.
❑ Bonus cards X1–X40, each 5.00
❑ Complete set of 40 bonus cards 35.00
❑ Chrome cards C1–C8, each 10.00

Retail special sets: 10 mirror cards, 5 unnumbered oversized cards, 16 stickers, 3 trivia cards, 2 promo cards.
❑ Mirror cards F1–F10, each 10.00
❑ Oversized cards, each 8.00
❑ Promo cards 0–000, each 15.00
❑ Promo cards SW1–SW9, each 10.00
❑ Sticker cards S1–S16, each 12.00
❑ Trivia cards H1–H3, each 8.00

The Phantom Menace series 2. 80 numbered cards. (Images in 2nd edition, page 234. Checklist in 3rd edition, page 223.)
❑ Cards 1–80, each [155-01] 1.00
❑ Cards 1–80, set 25.00

Hobby special sets: 4 chrome cards, 6 foil cards, 3 oversized box cards.
❑ Chrome cards HC1–HC4, each 15.00
❑ Foil embossed cards HE1–HE6, each 18.00
❑ Oversized cards, each 8.00

Retail special sets: 4 chrome cards, 6 foil cards.
❑ Chrome cards C1–C4, each 10.00
❑ Foil embossed cards E1–E6, each 15.00

CCG (Customized Card Game)

Customized card game decks were built from cards blindly purchased in random booster packs. During the years the game had a large active play group, values of individual cards varied depending on the scarcity of the card and amount of influence the card had to offer in stronger or popular play strategies.

Most of most desired cards had values of $10–$20 each, with some of the rarest cards reaching nearly $100 in value. The most common of the cards rarely exceeded $0.10 to $0.25 in value, each. The addition of foil highlights to chase cards increased card value in proportion to the value of the non-foil version of the card. The cards also enjoyed international release, allowing collectors to locate and treasure foreign cards for their set.

Since the development for the customized card game ended, the value of the cards has dropped to only a fraction of the amount they used to command. Only a smaller core of gamers and collectors who find the cards to be curious have interest.

CCG cards are often found at auction in large quantities and without specific card listings due to the hundreds of cards and card variations that exist.

Collectors may pick up inexpensive cards as novelties. Gamers usually are willing to pay more, but only for specific cards they desire to complete a specific strategy for play.

A complete checklist for the CCG cards may be found in the second edition from page 135 to page 161. Complete card set listings can be found using the database at www.StarWarsDatabase.com.

Decipher.
Young Jedi, Battle of Naboo. 158 cards.
Cards counted by rarity.
C (61), R (30), SS (10), SRF (6), URF (4), U (39), VRF (8)
Cards counted by type.
- Dark Side: Battle (11), Characters (38), Effects (5), Foil (9), Locations (3), Starships (4), Weapons (9)
- Light Side: Battle (15), Characters (33), Effects (5), Foil (9), Locations (3), Starships (4), Weapons (10)

Young Jedi, Battle of Naboo Enhanced. 12 cards.
Cards counted by rarity.
PM (12)
Cards counted by type.
Dark Side Character (6), Light Side Character (6)

CCG: Customized Card Game

Young Jedi, Boonta Eve Podrace. 60 cards.
Cards counted by rarity.
C (18), R (18), UR (2), U (22)
Cards counted by type.
- Dark Side: Battle (4), Characters (17), Effects (3), Objective (1), Starship (1), Weapons (4)
- Light Side: Battle (4), Characters (15), Effects (3), Objective (1), Starship (1), Weapons (6)

Young Jedi, Duel of Fates. 60 cards.
Cards counted by rarity.
C (19), R (18), UR (2), U (21)
Cards counted by type.
- Dark Side: Battle (11), Characters (10), Effects (5), Starships (1), Weapons (3)
- Light Side: Battle (9), Characters (11), Effects (7), Starships (1), Weapons (2)

Young Jedi, Jedi Council. 158 cards.
Cards counted by rarity.
C (60), R (30), SS (10), SRF (6), URF (4), U (40), VRF (8)
Cards counted by type.
- Dark Side: Battle (15), Characters (35), Foil (9), Locations (3), Starships (3), Weapons (14)
- Light Side: Battle (13), Characters (39), Foil (9), Locations (3), Starships (3), Weapons (12)

Young Jedi, Menace of Maul. 158 cards.
Cards counted by rarity.
C (60), CF (8), R (30), RF (4), SS (10), U (40), UF (6)
Cards counted by type.
- Dark Side: Battle (14), Characters (36), Foil (9), Locations (3), Starships (3), Weapons (14)
- Light Side: Battle (18), Characters (33), Foil (9), Locations (3), Starships (3), Weapons (13)

Young Jedi, Menace of Maul Enhanced. 6 cards.
Cards counted by rarity.
PM (6)
Cards counted by type.
Dark Side: Characters (3), Light Side: Characters (3)

Young Jedi, Reflections. 101 cards.
Cards counted by set.
Battle of Naboo Enhanced (12), Battle of Naboo (7), Boonta Eve Pod Race (12), Duel of Fates (10), Jedi Council (6), Menace of Maul Enhanced (6), Menace of Maul (6), Premium (1), Reflections (41)
Cards counted by type.
- Dark Side: Armed and Dangerous (6), Combo Battle (7), Double Impact (7), Foil (30)
- Light Side: Armed and Dangerous (7), Combo Battle (7), Double Impact (7), Foil (30)

1st Anthology. 6 cards total.
Cards counted by rarity.
Preview (6)
Cards counted by type.
Character (2), Effect (2), Starship (2)

2nd Anthology. 6 cards.
Cards counted by rarity.
Preview (6)
Cards counted by type.
Character (2), Location (2), Starship (2)

3rd Anthology. 6 cards.
Cards counted by rarity.
Preview (6)
Cards counted by type.
Character (1), Effect (2), Objective (2), Starship (1)

A New Hope. 162 cards.
Cards counted by rarity.
C1 (10), C2 (42), C3 (2), R1 (30), R2 (24), U1 (30), U2 (24)
Cards counted by type.
Automated Weapon (2), Character Weapon (5), Character: Alien (24), Character: Alien/Rebel (1), Character: Droid (10), Character: Imperial (10), Character: Rebel (7), Creature Vehicle (1), Death Star Weapon (1), Device (10), Effect (19), Epic Event (2), Immediate Effect (4), Location (17), Lost Interrupt (13), Shuttle Vehicle (2), Starship Weapon (2), Starship (11), Swamp Creature (1), Transport Vehicle (1), Used Interrupt (11), Used or Lost Interrupt (5), Utinni Effect (3)

Cloud City. 180 cards.
Cards counted by rarity.
C (50), R (80), U (50)
Cards counted by type.
Character: Alien (15), Character: Droid (1), Character: Imperial (6), Character: Rebel (2), Character Weapon (4), Combat Vehicle (2), Device (7), Effect (27), Epic Event (1), Immediate Effect (5), Location Sector (4), Location: Site (15), Location: System (2), Lost Interrupt (38), Starship (5), Used Interrupt (21), Used or Lost Interrupt (20), Utinni Effect (3)

Coruscant. 189 cards.
Cards counted by rarity.
C (60), R (69), U (60)
Cards counted by type.
Character: Alien (13), Character: Darth Maul (2), Character: Droid (5), Character: Jedi Master (8), Character: Republic (38), Character Weapon (6), Effect (24), Immediate Effect (2), Location: Site (22), Location: System (8), Lost Interrupt (10), Objective (4), Political Effect (8), Starship: Capital (2), Starship: Starfighter (7), Starship Weapon (1), Used Interrupt (19), Used or Lost Interrupt (1), Used or Lost Interrupt (7), Used or Starting Interrupt (2)

Dagobah. 180 cards.
Cards counted by rarity.
C (50), R (80), U (50)
Cards counted by type.
Character: Alien (3), Character: Droid (2), Character: Imperial (12), Character: Jedi Master (1), Character: Rebel (1), Character Weapon (6), Creature (11), Device (8), Effect (40), Immediate Effect (3), Jedi Test (5), Location: Sector (4), Location: Site (14), Location: System (5), Lost Interrupt (21), Mobile Effect (3), Starship Weapon (1), Starship (8), Used Interrupt (15), Used Interrupt (12), Utinni Effect (5)

Death Star II. 182 cards.
Cards counted by rarity.
C (50), R (78), U (50), UR (2), XR (2)
Cards counted by type.
Admiral's Orders (10), Characters: Imperial (23), Characters: Jedi Master / Imperial (1), Characters: Rebel (26), Effects (16), Epic Events (1), Events (14), Interrupts (13), Jedi Tests (1), Locations: Sector (3), Locations: Site (4), Locations: System (7), Objectives (2), Starships (49), Weapons (12)

Empire Strikes Back. 60 cards.
Cards counted by rarity.
C (54), PM (6)
Cards counted by type.
Auto. Weapon (4), Character Weapon (3), Character: Alien (2), Character: Droid (4), Character: Imperial (9), Character: Rebel (8), Device (3), Effect (2), Location (10), Lost Interrupt (10), Used Interrupt (3), Vehicle (2)

Endor. 180 cards.
Cards counted by rarity.
C (50), R (80), U (50)
Cards counted by type.
Artillery Weapon (1), Automated Weapon (1), Character: Imperial (1), Character: Alien (14), Character: Droid (1), Character: Imperial (24), Character: Rebel (18), Character Weapon (6), Combat Vehicle (11), Effect (27), Epic Event (1), Location: Site (18), Location: System (4), Lost Interrupt (12), Objective (2), Starship: Starfighter (3), Transport Vehicle (1), Used Interrupt (20), Used Interrupt (11), Used or Starting Interrupt (2), Vehicle Weapon (2)

Hoth. 162 cards.
Cards counted by rarity.
C1 (10), C2 (42), C3 (2), R1 (30), R2 (24), U1 (30), U2 (24)
Cards counted by type.
Artillery Weapon (5), Automated Weapon (4), Character Weapon (3), Character: Droid (9), Character: Imperial (9), Character: Rebel (20), Combat Vehicle (8), Creature Vehicle (1), Device (8), Effect (12), Epic Event (1), Immediate Effect (5), Location (19), Lost Interrupt (15), Mobile Effect (2), Snow Creature (1), Starship Weapon (1), Starship (3), Used Interrupt (20), Used or Lost Interrupt (7), Utinni Effect (6), Vehicle Weapon (3)

Jabba's Palace. 180 cards.
Cards counted by rarity.
C (50), R (80), U (50)
Cards counted by type.
Character-Alien (69), Character: Droid (3), Character: Rebel (1), Character: Alien (19), Character Weapon (7), Creature (3), Device (4), Effect (14), Immediate Effect (2), Location-Site (7), Location: System (4), Location: Site (6), Lost Interrupt (10), Mobile Effect (2), Transport Vehicle (3), Used Interrupt (15), Used or Lost Interrupt (5), Used or Starting Interrupt (2), Vehicle Weapon (2)

Jabba's Palace sealed deck. 20 cards.
Cards counted by rarity.
PR(20)
Cards counted by type.
Characters: Alien (4), Effects (6), Locations: Site (4), Objectives (2), Vehicles: Transport (2), Weapons: Character (2)

Jedi Knights. 173 cards.
Cards counted by rarity.
C (40), F (32), PL (6), PR (4), P (1), RS (50), US (1), U (39)
Cards counted by type.
Character: Alliance Hero (8), Character: Alliance (16), Character: Empire Hero (8), Character: Empire (22), Character: Independent (18), Event (36), Force (10), Location (8), Starship (15), Theme (8), Weapon (24)

Jedi Knights, Master of the Force. 140 cards.
Cards counted by rarity.
C (40), R (39), RS (21), U (40)
Cards counted by type.
Character: Alliance Hero (2), Character: Alliance (19), Character: Empire Dark Hero (2), Character: Empire (15), Character: Independent (7), Event (30), Force: Black (4), Force: Blue (14), Force: Green (2), Force: Orange (2), Jedi Power (10), Sith Power (6), Starship (15), Theme (8), Weapon (4)

Jedi Knights, Master of the Force. 140 cards.
Cards counted by rarity.
C (40), R (39), RS (21), U (40)
Cards counted by type.
Character: Alliance Hero (2), Character: Alliance (19), Character: Empire Dark Hero (2), Character: Empire (15), Character-Independent (7), Event (30), Force: Black (4), Force: Blue (14), Force: Green (2), Force: Orange (2), Jedi Power (10), Sith Power (6), Starship (15), Theme (8), Weapon (4)

Jedi Knights, Scum and Villainy. 140 cards.
Cards counted by rarity.
C (40), R (30), RS (30), U (40)
Cards counted by type.
Character: Alliance Hero (4), Character: Alliance (7), Character: Empire Dark Hero (4), Character: Empire (17), Character: Independent (6), Event (27), Force (18), Jedi Power (11), Sith Power (9), Starship (15), Theme (8), Weapon (14)

Jedi Pack. 11 cards.
Cards counted by rarity.
PR (11)
Cards counted by type.
Aliens (2), Effects (2), Game Aids (1), Imperials (2), Interrupts (1), Locations (1), Vehicles (2)

Official Sealed Deck Premiums. 18 cards.
Cards counted by rarity.
PM (18)
Cards counted by type.
Character: Alien (2), Character: Imperial (1), Character: Rebel (1), Effect (2), Location: Site (2), Location: System (2), Starship (6), Used or Lost Interrupt (2)

CCG: Customized Card Game

156-01

156-02

156-03

156-04 Front and Back

156-05

156-06

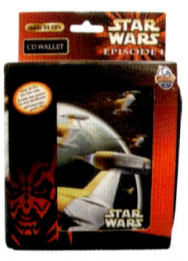
156-07

156-08

156-09

Premiere Enhanced. 6 cards.
Cards counted by rarity.
PM (6)
Cards counted by type.
Character: Imperial (2), Character: Rebel (4)

Premiere Two-Player Into Set Premiums. 6 cards.
Cards counted by rarity.
PM (6)
Cards counted by type.
Location: Site (2), Character: Imperial (1), Character: Rebel (1), Effect (2)

Premiere Limited. 324 cards. Black-border images.
Cards counted by rarity.
C1 (20), C2 (86), C3 (2), R1 (60), R2 (48), U1 (60), U2 (48)
Cards counted by type.
Automated Weapon (7), Character Weapon (13), Character: Alien (26), Character: Droid (14), Character: Imperial (14), Char: Rebel (15), Creature Vehicle (1), Device (17), Effect (43), Location (37), Lost Interrupt (58), Starship Weapon (5), Starship (16), Transportation Vehicle (7), Used Interrupt (40), Utinni Effect (11)

Premiere Unlimited. 324 cards. White-border images.
Cards counted by rarity.
C1 (20), C2 (86), C3 (2), R1 (60), R2 (48), U1 (60), U2 (48)
Cards counted by type.
Automated Weapon (7), Character Weapon (13), Character: Alien (26), Character: Droid (14), Character: Imperial (14), Character: Rebel (15), Creature Vehicle (1), Device (17), Effect (43), Location (37), Lost Interrupt (58), Starship Weapon (5), Starship (16), Transport Vehicle (7), Used Interrupt (40), Utinni Effect (11)

Rebel Leaders. 2 cards.
Cards counted by rarity.
PM (2)
Cards counted by type.
Character: Rebel (2)

Reflections. 114 cards.
Cards counted by rarity.
SRF (25), URF (2), VRF (87)
Cards counted by set.
A New Hope (16), Cloud City (16), Dagobah (18), Hoth (13), Jabba's Palace (10), Premiere (25), Special Edition (16)

Reflections 2. 45 cards.
Cards counted by rarity.
SRF (15), URF (10), VRF (20)
Cards counted by type.
Admiral's Order (2), Character: Alien (6), Character: Alien / Imperial (1), Character: Dark Jedi Master / Imperial (1), Character: Droid (3), Character: Imperial (3), Character: Rebel (6), Device (2), Effect (3), Lost Interrupt (3), Objective (2), Starfighter (4), Used Interrupt (3), Used or Lost Interrupt (15)

Reflections 3. 106 cards.
Cards counted by rarity.
P (100), PV/SRF (6)
Cards counted by type.
Character: Alien (4), Character: Darth Maul (1), Character: Imperial (1), Character: Jedi Master (2), Character: Rebel (3), Character: Republic (3), Character Weapon (6), Defensive Shield (34), Effect (19), Epic Event (2), Immediate Effect (5), Location: Site (5), Lost Interrupt (8), Objective (2), Starship: Starfighter (1), Used Interrupt (1), Used Interrupt (8), Vehicle-Combat (1)

Special Edition. 324 cards.
Cards counted by rarity.
C (80), F (44), R (120), U (80)
Cards counted by type.
Character: Alien (61), Character: Droid (6), Character: Imperial (9), Character: Rebel (22), Character Weapon (8), Combat Vehicle (4), Creature Vehicle (4), Creature (6), Device (4), Effect (45), Immediate Effect (6), Location: Site (41), Location: System (11), Lost Interrupt (11), Mobile Effect (1), Objective (10), Starship: Capital (6), Starship: Squadron (2), Starship: Starfighter (12), Starship Weapon (4), Starship (1), Transport Vehicle (6), Used Interrupt (31), Used or Lost Interrupt (8), Used or Starting Interrupt (2), Utinni Effect (2)

Tatooine. 99 cards.
Cards counted by rarity.
C (30), R (39), U (30)
Cards counted by type.
Character: Alien (19), Character: Darth Maul (2), Character: Droid (4), Character: Jedi Master (2), Character: Republic (4), Character Weapon (3), Creature Vehicle (1), Device (1), Effect (17), Epic Event (4), Immediate Effect (2), Location: Site (8), Lost Interrupt (10), Lost Or Starting Interrupt (2), Podracer (5), Used Interrupt (2), Used or Lost Interrupt (13)

Theed Palace. 129 cards.
Cards counted by rarity.
C (40), R (49), U (40)
Cards counted by type.
Admiral's Order (4), Character: Alien (11), Character: Dark Jedi Master (2), Character: Darth Maul (1), Character: Droid (15), Character: Jedi Master (3), Character: Republic (20), Character Weapon (3), Effect (15), Immediate Effect (2), Location: Site (6), Lost Interrupt (4), Objective (2), Starship: Capital (2), Starship: Starfighter (10), Starship Weapon (2), Used Interrupt (10), Used or Lost Interrupt (4), Vehicle: Combat (6), Vehicle: Creature (2), Vehicle: Transport (1), Vehicle Weapon (4)

CD Wallets
Continued in Volume 3, page 125

American Covers
- ❑ Darth Vader / Boba Fett [156-01] 15.00
- ❑ Episode I collage [156-02] 15.00

Animations
- ❑ Darth Vader [156-03] 20.00

Celcom (Malaysia)
- ❑ Episode II / Clone trooper [156-04] 35.00

Class of 77
- ❑ Darkside [156-05] 20.00

World Wide Licenses Ltd.
- ❑ Darth Maul [156-06] 20.00
- ❑ Space Battle [156-07] 20.00
- ❑ Star Wars logo on metal plate [156-08] 15.00
- ❑ Star Wars logo on metal plate, double wallet [156-09] ... 25.00

Cellular Phone Accessories
Continued in Volume 3, page 125

- ❑ Darth Vader phone holder [157-01] 15.00

(Japan)
- ❑ Darth Vader mobile phone seal [157-02] 5.00

(UK)
- ❑ Anakin Skywalker Clone Wars mobile sock [157-03] ... 8.00

Nokia
3220 Orange model.
- ❑ 6 Lenticular character skins [v1e1:126] 15.00
- ❑ Chewbacca fur with bandolier [157-04] 15.00
- ❑ Darth Vader light-up phone holder [157-05] ... 15.00
- ❑ Hard-side storage case, black [157-06] 20.00
- ❑ Hard-side storage case, silver [157-07] 20.00

Runa International Co., Ltd. (China)
Mascot straps.
- ❑ C-3PO 25.00
- ❑ Darth Vader 25.00
- ❑ Stormtrooper 25.00
- ❑ Yoda 25.00

Trendwerk77 (Belgium)
- ❑ Fan Box, contains charm and strap [157-08] ... 20.00
- ❑ Yoda charm strap [157-09] 10.00

Underground Toys
Earloomz bluetooth headsets. Model GL 500.
- ❑ Boba Fett [157-10] 60.00
- ❑ Darth Vader [157-11] 60.00

Cellular Phone Straps

| 157-01 | 157-02 | 157-03 Front and Back | 157-04 | 157-05 | 157-06 |

| 157-07 | 157-08 | 157-09 | 157-10 | 157-11 | 157-12 | 157-13 |

- ❏ Luke Skywalker [157-12] 60.00
- ❏ The Dark Duel [157-13] 60.00

Cellular Phone Cases and Faceplates
Continued in Volume 3, page 126

- ❏ Pod Racer / Jar Jar Binks [158-01] 16.00
- ❏ Pod Racer / R2-D2 and C-3PO [158-02] 16.00

Replacement covers for Nokia 3210 and 5100 phones.
- ❏ Darth Maul / movie poster art [158-03] 15.00
- ❏ Darth Maul / Tatooine [158-04] 15.00
- ❏ Queen Amidala [158-05] 15.00
- ❏ Queen Amidala, art [158-06] 15.00
- ❏ Yoda [158-07] 15.00

Theme stickers to cover faceplates.
- ❏ Empire / Vader Super Seal [158-08] 8.00

Creata Group
- ❏ Stormtrooper, iPhone 4 [158-09] 10.00

Dextra Accessories Ltd.
- ❏ Yoda for 3310 phone [158-10] 15.00

Image Communications, Ltd.
Episode I: The Phantom Menace.
- ❏ Anakin Skywalker 15.00
- ❏ Darth Maul 15.00

- ❏ Jar Jar Binks 15.00
- ❏ Obi-Wan Kenobi 15.00
- ❏ Queen Amidala 15.00

MPC Ltd.
Replacement covers for Nokia 3310 and 3330 phones.
- ❏ Anakin / Vader 15.00
- ❏ C-3PO [158-11] 15.00
- ❏ Clone trooper [158-12] 15.00
- ❏ Darth Vader [158-13] 15.00
- ❏ Jango Fett [158-14] 15.00
- ❏ Obi-Wan Kenobi [158-15] 15.00
- ❏ Padmé Amidala [158-16] 15.00
- ❏ R2-D2 .... 15.00
- ❏ Stormtrooper [158-17] 15.00
- ❏ The Dark Lords 15.00
- ❏ Yoda [158-18] 15.00

Nokia
Active Xpress-on Active Covers for 3510 phones.
- ❏ Anakin Skywalker [158-19] 15.00
- ❏ Jango Fett [158-20] 15.00
- ❏ Yoda [158-21] 15.00

Sony Ericsson
Episode III: Revenge of the Sith.
- ❏ Darth Vader / Epic Battle [158-22] 15.00
- ❏ General Grievous [158-23] 15.00
- ❏ Han and Chewbacca / R2-D2 and C-3PO [158-24] 15.00
- ❏ Yoda / Anakin and Obi-Wan 15.00

Cellular Phone Straps
Continued in Volume 3, Page 127

- ❏ Star Wars [159-01] 8.00
- ❏ Tennis shoe, "Dunk Low S3 Jedi" [159-02] 8.00

Bear Wars.
- ❏ Black 10.00
- ❏ Blue 10.00
- ❏ Green 10.00
- ❏ Pink [159-03] 10.00
- ❏ Red 10.00
- ❏ White 10.00

(Japan)
- ❏ Darth Maul 5.00

| 158-01 | 158-02 | 158-03 | 158-04 |

| 158-05 | 158-06 | 158-07 | 158-08 | 158-09 | 158-10 | 158-11 | 158-12 | 158-13 | 158-14 | 158-15 |

| 158-16 | 158-17 | 158-18 | 158-19 | 158-20 | 158-21 | 158-22 | 158-23 | 158-24 |

Cellular Phone Straps

159-01 | 159-02 | 159-03 | 159-04 | 159-05 | 159-06 | 159-07 | 159-08 | 159-09 | 159-10 | 159-11 | 159-12 | 159-13 | 159-14 | 159-15

159-16 | 159-17 | 159-18 | 159-19 | 159-20 | 159-21 | 159-22 | 159-23 | 159-24 | 159-25

Classic trilogy.
- Chewbacca [159-04] 15.00
- Han Solo [159-05] 15.00
- Luke Skywalker [159-06] 15.00
- Princess Leia [159-07] 15.00
- Stormtrooper [159-08] 15.00

Episode I.
- Anakin Skywalker [159-09] 15.00
- Darth Sidious [159-10] 15.00
- Jar Jar Binks [159-11] 15.00
- Ric Olié [159-12] 15.00

Episode III: Revenge of the Sith.
- Darth Vader, black strap, light-up eyes [159-13] 15.00
- Darth Vader, red strap, light-up eyes 15.00
- Lightsaber, light-up red [159-14] 12.00

(UK)
- Phone charm set, Yoda, Vader, Anakin, Star Wars logo, 4 pieces [159-15] 10.00

Spinnerz.
- Darth Vader [v1e1:127] 10.00
- Stormtrooper [v1e1:127] 10.00

1-2-Call
Episode III: Revenge of the Sith. Round medals hanging off straps.
- Anakin vs. Obi-Wan [v1e1:127] 10.00

- Clone trooper [v1e1:127] 10.00
- Darth Vader [v1e1:127] 10.00
- Yoda [v1e1:127] 10.00

Bandai (Japan)
Bell mascot.
- C-3PO [159-16] 12.00
- Darth Vader [159-17] 12.00
- R2-D2 [159-18] 12.00
- Stormtrooper [159-19] 12.00

Rubber plate collection.
- Boba Fett [159-20] 10.00
- C-3PO [159-21] 10.00
- Darth Vader [159-22] 10.00
- R2-D2 [159-23] 10.00
- Stormtrooper [159-24] 10.00
- Yoda [159-25] 10.00

Strap collection.
- Anakin Skywalker [159-26] 10.00
- Clone trooper [159-27] 10.00
- Obi-Wan Kenobi [159-28] 10.00
- R2-D2 [159-29] 10.00
- Yoda [159-30] 10.00

Color Bear (Japan)
- Boba Fett [159-31] 15.00
- Darth Vader [159-32] 15.00

Dracco Company Ltd. (Germany)
Collect all 12 Mobile Tags. Chocolate egg premiums.
- Ahsoka Tano 10.00
- Anakin Skywalker 10.00
- Anakin Skywalker with lightsaber 10.00
- Asajj Ventress 10.00
- C-3PO 10.00
- Clone Captain Rex 10.00
- General Grievous 10.00
- Obi-Wan orange background 10.00
- Obi-Wan with blue background 10.00
- Obi-Wan with lightsaber 10.00
- R2-D2 .... 10.00
- Yoda 10.00

Heart Art Collection, Ltd. (Japan)
- Darth Vader sound strap [159-33] 15.00
- R2-D2 LED strap [159-34] 15.00

Episode III: Revenge of the Sith. Mobile Cleaners.
- Darth Vader [159-35] 10.00
- R2-D2 and C-3PO [159-36] 10.00
- Yoda [159-37] 10.00

Iwaya (Japan)
2" PEZ nondispensing charm straps.
- Boba Fett [159-38] 12.00
- C-3PO [159-39] 12.00
- Chewbacca [159-40] 12.00

159-26 | 159-27 | 159-28 | 159-29 | 159-30 | 159-31 | 159-32 | 159-33

159-34 | 159-35 | 159-36 | 159-37 | 159-38 | 159-39 | 159-40 | 159-41 | 159-42 | 159-43 | 159-44 | 159-45

Chalkboards

 159-46
 159-47
 159-48
 159-49
 159-50
 159-51
 159-52
 159-53

 159-54
 159-55
 159-56
 159-57
 159-58
 159-59

 159-60
 159-61
 159-62
 159-63
 159-64
 159-65
 159-66

- ❏ Darth Vader [159-41] 12.00
- ❏ R2-D2 [159-42] 12.00
- ❏ Stormtrooper [159-43] 12.00
- ❏ Wicket [159-44] 12.00
- ❏ Yoda [159-45] 12.00

Just Toys International
Angry Birds phone danglers. Set of 10, unnumbered. Distributed by UCC Distributing Inc. Contains 1 dangler, 2 stickers, 1 collector sheet.
- ❏ Chewbacca bird 10.00
- ❏ Darth Vader pig 10.00
- ❏ Death Star 10.00
- ❏ Han bird 10.00
- ❏ Luke Skywalker bird 10.00
- ❏ Obi-Wan bird [159-46] 10.00
- ❏ Princess Leia bird 10.00
- ❏ R2-D2 egg 10.00
- ❏ Stormtrooper pig 10.00
- ❏ Wedge bird 10.00

Mafuyu
- ❏ Chewbacca [v1e1:127] 18.00
- ❏ Princess Leia [v1e1:127] 18.00

Medicom (Japan)
Be@rbrick straps for Suntory.
- ❏ Battle Droid [159-47] 15.00
- ❏ C-3PO [159-48] 15.00
- ❏ Darth Maul 15.00

- ❏ Darth Vader [159-49] 15.00
- ❏ Jar Jar Binks [159-50] 15.00
- ❏ R2-D2 [159-51] 15.00
- ❏ Star Wars 15.00
- ❏ Yoda [159-52] 15.00

Meiji (Japan)
- ❏ Qui-Gon Jinn [159-53] 15.00

PansonWorks (Japan)
PepsiNex Star Wars 3D characters.
- ❏ Anakin Skywalker [159-54] 20.00
- ❏ Battle Droid [159-55] 20.00
- ❏ C-3PO [159-56] 20.00
- ❏ Darth Maul [159-57] 20.00
- ❏ Darth Sidious [159-58] 20.00
- ❏ Darth Vader [159-59] 20.00
- ❏ Jabba the Hutt 20.00
- ❏ Jar Jar Binks [159-60] 20.00
- ❏ Obi-Wan Kenobi [159-61] 20.00
- ❏ Queen Amidala [159-62] 20.00
- ❏ R2-D2 [159-63] 20.00
- ❏ Yoda [159-64] 20.00

Showa Note (Japan)
- ❏ Watto [159-65] 12.00

Sony Ericsson
- ❏ Darth Vader helmet in crystal [v1e1:127] 15.00
- ❏ Darth Vader helmet, metal [159-66] 15.00

Cellular Phones
Continued in Volume 3, page 127

Mobistar
- ❏ Samsung 450 Star Wars tempo [160-01] 150.00

Nokia (France)
- ❏ Episode I, boxed [160-02] 175.00

Certificates

LEGO / Walmart
- ❏ Jedi Challenge Certificate of Achievement [161-01] 15.00
- ❏ Jedi Lightsaber Building Contest [v1e1:128] 15.00

Toys R Us
- ❏ Episode I Toy Premiere, May 3, 1999 [161-02] 20.00

Union Underwear Co.
- ❏ Honorary Jedi Knight, Underoos premium [161-03] 50.00

Chalkboards
Continued in Volume 3, page 127

Manton
- ❏ R2-D2 and Wicket the Ewok [v1e1:128] 95.00

 160-01
 160-02
 161-01
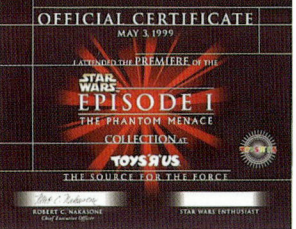 161-02
 161-03

Champagne and Wine

| 162-01 | 162-02 | 162-03 | 162-04 | 162-05 |

163-01	163-02	163-03	163-04	163-05
163-06	163-07	163-08	163-09	163-10
163-11	163-12	163-13	163-14	163-15

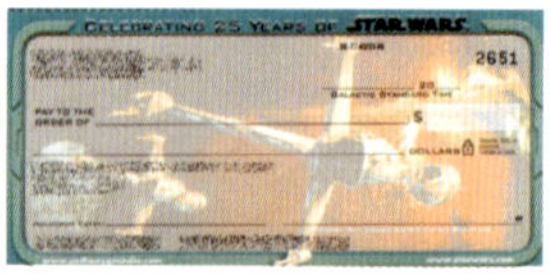

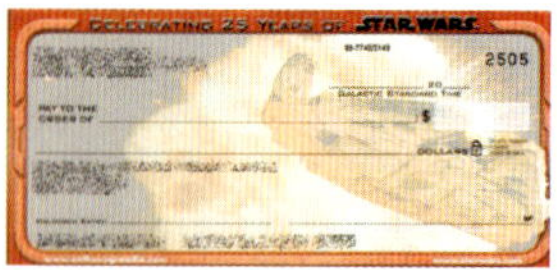

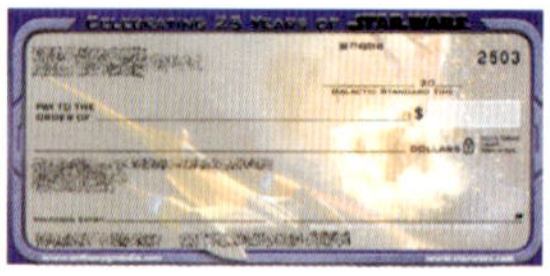

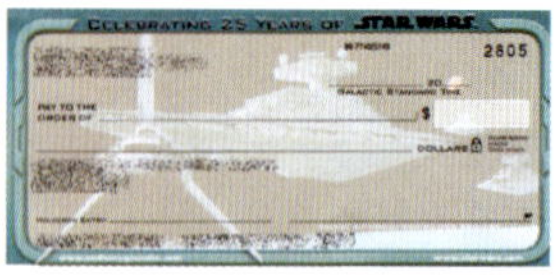

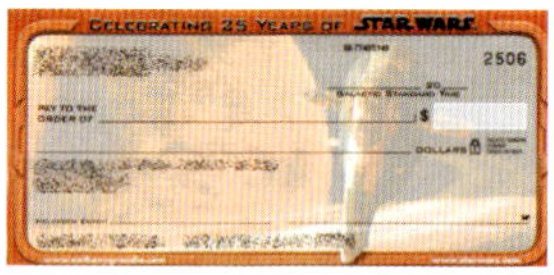

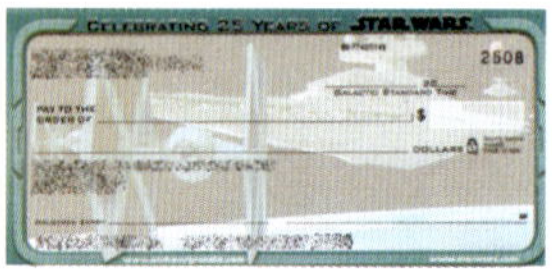

Champagne and Wine

Veuve Clicquot Ponsardin
- ❑ La Grande Dame 1990 [v1e1:128] 800.00

Viandante del Cielo
- ❑ 2003 Lucas Skywalker Ranch chardonnay [v1e1:128] ... 300.00

Checkbook Covers

- ❑ Darth Vader tooled into leather [162-01] 25.00
- ❑ Darth Vader tooled into vinyl [v1e1:129] 20.00
- ❑ Star Wars logo set against starfield on blue vinyl [162-02] 15.00

Clone Wars.
- ❑ Yoda, leather [162-03] 35.00

The Anthony Grandio Company
- ❑ 25th Anniversary, vinyl [162-04] 25.00
- ❑ 30th Anniversary printed leather, 250 produced 50.00
- ❑ Imperial logo, leather [v1e1:129] 25.00
- ❑ Rebellion logo, leather [v1e1:129] 25.00
- ❑ Star Wars Celebration IV foil on vinyl, 500 produced ..45.00
- ❑ Star Wars Celebration IV printed leather, 250 produced [162-05] 65.00
- ❑ Star Wars vinyl with gold lettering 25.00

Celebration 3 exclusives.
- ❑ Darth Vader, leather [v1e1:129] 45.00
- ❑ Darth Vader, vinyl 30.00

Clone Wars.
- ❑ Heroes [v1e1:129] 25.00
- ❑ Villains [v1e1:129] 25.00

Checks

Kenner
- ❑ Refund for out-of-stock action figure poster 50.00

Pepsi
- ❑ Prize check for finding Gold Yoda can 75.00

The Anthony Grandio Company
25th anniversary, 24 designs.
- ❑ A-Wing Fighters [163-01] 3.00
- ❑ B-Wing fighters [163-02] 3.00
- ❑ Darth Vader's TIE Fighter [163-03] 3.00
- ❑ Jedi Starfighter [v1e1:129] 3.00
- ❑ Medical Frigate [v1e1:129] 3.00
- ❑ Millennium Falcon [163-04] 3.00
- ❑ Millennium Falcon escapes the Death Star [163-05] .. 3.00
- ❑ Millennium Falcon evades TIE Fighters [163-06] 3.00
- ❑ Naboo Fighter [163-07] 3.00
- ❑ Naboo Royal Starship [163-08] 3.00
- ❑ Naboo Starship [v1e1:129] 3.00
- ❑ Shuttle Tydirium [163-09] 3.00
- ❑ Sith Infiltrator [v1e1:129] 3.00
- ❑ Slave I [163-10] 3.00
- ❑ Slave I—Jango boarding [v1e1:129] 3.00
- ❑ Solar Sailer [v1e1:129] 3.00
- ❑ Star Destroyer [163-11] 3.00
- ❑ Super Star Destroyer [v1e1:129] 3.00
- ❑ TIE Bomber [163-12] 3.00
- ❑ Trade Federation Fighter [163-13] 3.00
- ❑ Trade Federation Landing Ship [163-14] 3.00
- ❑ X-Wing squadron [163-15] 3.00
- ❑ X-Wings attack Death Star [v1e1:129] 3.00
- ❑ Y-Wing Fighter [v1e1:129] 3.00

2nd series; 9 characters.
- ❑ C-3PO 5.00
- ❑ Chewbacca 5.00
- ❑ Darth Vader 5.00
- ❑ Han Solo 5.00
- ❑ Luke Skywalker 5.00
- ❑ Obi-Wan Kenobi 5.00
- ❑ Princess Leia 5.00
- ❑ R2-D2 .... 5.00
- ❑ Yoda 5.00

Collector Sets
- ❑ Path to the Dark Side, 8 checks stamped "commemorative document non negotiable." Unreleased 9th check (Anakin Member of Toydarian Junk Dealer Association) in its own folder, 2,005 produced, individually numbered 175.00

First 100 collector sets.
- ❑ Power of the Dark Side, includes uncut sheets 150.00
- ❑ Star Wars Armada, includes uncut sheets 150.00

Path to the Dark Side, 8 designs.
- ❑ A Jedi's Sacrifice, (Anakin Jedi Council representative) 3.00
- ❑ Bitter Betrayal, (Anakin Jedi Council representative) 3.00
- ❑ Consequences of Loss, (Anakin Jedi Council representative) 3.00
- ❑ Dark Transformation, (Anakin Jedi Council representative) 3.00
- ❑ Forbidden Love, (Anakin Padawan) 3.00
- ❑ Moment of Decision, (young Anakin) 3.00
- ❑ Restoration, (The One who has brought balance to the Force) 3.00
- ❑ Ultimate Battle, (Darth Vader Sith apprentice) 3.00

Cigar Bands

G. Gezelle (Belgium)
Episode I characters produced with different background colors.
- ❑ 1 Qui-Gon Jinn [164-01] 3.00
- ❑ 2 Queen Amidala [164-02] 3.00
- ❑ 3 Rodian [164-03] 3.00
- ❑ 4 Senator Palpatine [164-04] 3.00
- ❑ 5 Anakin Skywalker [164-05] 3.00
- ❑ 6 Handmaiden [164-06] 3.00
- ❑ 7 Shmi Skywalker [164-07] 3.00
- ❑ 8 Obi-Wan Kenobi [164-08] 3.00
- ❑ 9 Padmé [164-09] 3.00
- ❑ 10 Sio Babble [164-10] 3.00
- ❑ 11 Queen Amidala [164-11] 3.00
- ❑ 12 Mace Windu [164-12] 3.00
- ❑ 13 Jar Jar Binks [164-13] 3.00
- ❑ 14 Twi'lek [164-14] 3.00
- ❑ 15 Captain Panaka [164-15] 3.00
- ❑ 16 Darth Maul [164-16] 3.00
- ❑ 17 Neimoidian [164-17] 3.00
- ❑ 18 Senate guard [164-18] 3.00
- ❑ 19 Neimoidian [164-19] 3.00
- ❑ 20 Chancellor Valorum [164-20] 3.00

Morrita
Sets produced with 5 different background colors: blue, gray, purple, red, or white.
- ❑ 1 Han Solo [164-21] 3.00
- ❑ 2 Obi-Wan Kenobi [164-22] 3.00
- ❑ 3 Darth Vader [164-23] 3.00
- ❑ 4 Han Solo [164-24] 3.00
- ❑ 5 Luke Skywalker [164-25] 3.00
- ❑ 6 C-3PO [164-26] 3.00
- ❑ 7 Yoda [164-27] 3.00
- ❑ 8 Obi-Wan Kenobi [164-28] 3.00
- ❑ 9 R2-D2 C-3PO [164-29] 3.00
- ❑ 10 Boba Fett [164-30] 3.00
- ❑ 11 R2-D2 C-3PO [164-31] 3.00
- ❑ 12 Luke Skywalker [164-32] 3.00
- ❑ 13 R2-D2 [v1e1:130] 3.00
- ❑ 14 Ewok [v1e1:130] 3.00
- ❑ 15 Jawa [v1e1:130] 3.00
- ❑ 16 Emperor [v1e1:130] 3.00
- ❑ 17 Luke Skywalker [v1e1:130] 3.00

Cigar Bands

- ❏ 18 Chewbacca [v1e1:130]..................3.00
- ❏ 19 Star Wars [v1e1:130]..................3.00
- ❏ 20 Han / Leia [v1e1:130]..................3.00
- ❏ 21 Lando Calrissian [v1e1:130]..................3.00
- ❏ 22 Yoda [v1e1:130]..................3.00
- ❏ 23 C-3PO [v1e1:130]..................3.00
- ❏ 24 Leia Organa [v1e1:130]..................3.00

Sets produced with gold design and 5 different background colors: blue, gray, purple, red, or white.
- ❏ 1 Han Solo [v1e1:130]..................3.00
- ❏ 2 Obi-Wan Kenobi [v1e1:130]..................3.00
- ❏ 3 Darth Vader [v1e1:130]..................3.00
- ❏ 4 Han Solo [v1e1:130]..................3.00
- ❏ 5 Luke Skywalker [v1e1:130]..................3.00
- ❏ 6 C-3PO [v1e1:130]..................3.00
- ❏ 7 Yoda [v1e1:130]..................3.00

- ❏ 8 Obi-Wan Kenobi [v1e1:130]..................3.00
- ❏ 9 R2-D2 C-3PO [v1e1:130]..................3.00
- ❏ 10 Boba Fett [v1e1:130]..................3.00
- ❏ 11 R2-D2 C-3PO [v1e1:130]..................3.00
- ❏ 12 Luke Skywalker [v1e1:130]..................3.00
- ❏ 13 R2-D2 [164-33]..................3.00
- ❏ 14 Ewok [164-34]..................3.00
- ❏ 15 Jawa [164-35]..................3.00
- ❏ 16 Emperor [164-36]..................3.00
- ❏ 17 Luke Skywalker [164-37]..................3.00
- ❏ 18 Chewbacca [164-38]..................3.00
- ❏ 19 Star Wars [164-39]..................3.00
- ❏ 20 Han / Leia [164-40]..................3.00
- ❏ 21 Lando Calrissian [164-41]..................3.00
- ❏ 22 Yoda [164-42]..................3.00
- ❏ 23 C-3PO [164-43]..................3.00
- ❏ 24 Leia Organa [164-44]..................3.00

Murillo

Episode I sets produced with 5 different background colors: blue, white, red, yellow, or green.
- ❏ 1 Heroes (art) [164-45]..................3.00
- ❏ 2 Royal Starship in the Tatooine desert (cartoon) [164-46]..................3.00
- ❏ 3 Darth Maul (cartoon) [164-47]..................3.00
- ❏ 4 Queen Amidala (art) [164-48]..................3.00
- ❏ 5 Trade Federation Battleship (cartoon) [164-49]..................3.00
- ❏ 6 Qui-Gon and Obi-Wan with lightsabers (cartoon) [164-50]..................3.00
- ❏ 7 Heroes in Shmi's home (cartoon) [164-51]..................3.00
- ❏ 8 Jabba the Hutt (cartoon) [164-52]..................3.00
- ❏ 9 Watto in the pod race hangar (cartoon) [164-53]..................3.00
- ❏ 10 Darth Maul releases probe droids (cartoon) [164-54]..................3.00

Clipboards

165-01

166-01

166-02

167-01

166-03

166-04

167-02

- ❏ C-3PO 8.00
- ❏ Chewbacca [167-01] 8.00
- ❏ Darth Vader [167-02] 8.00
- ❏ Jango Fett 8.00
- ❏ R2-D2 ....8.00
- ❏ Stormtrooper 8.00
- ❏ Yoda 8.00

Sculpted character clips.
- ❏ Anakin Skywalker [167-03] 16.00
- ❏ C-3PO [167-04] 16.00
- ❏ Chewbacca [167-05] 16.00
- ❏ Darth Vader [167-06] 16.00
- ❏ Jango Fett [167-07] 16.00
- ❏ R2-D2 [167-08] 16.00
- ❏ Stormtrooper [167-09] 16.00
- ❏ Yoda [167-10] 16.00

Clipboards
Reding Stationary (Australia)
- ❏ Empire Strikes Back, R2-D2 [165-01] 95.00

Clippos
Cadbury
- ❏ Anakin Skywalker [166-01] 5.00
- ❏ Darth Maul [166-02] 5.00
- ❏ Jar Jar Binks [166-03] 5.00
- ❏ Queen Amidala [166-04] 5.00

Clips, Snack Chip
Continued in Volume 3, Page 128

Pepsi Cola (Japan)
Concealment bags.
- ❏ Anakin Skywalker 8.00

Clocks
Continued in Volume 3, Page 129

- ❏ C-3PO and R2-D2 [168-01] 20.00
- ❏ C-3PO and R2-D2 portable clock radio, Return of the Jedi 35.00
- ❏ Darth Maul alarm clock, round, face lights up when touched [168-02] 25.00
- ❏ Darth Maul vs. Qui-Gon Jinn alarm [168-03] ...50.00
- ❏ Darth Maul with lightsaber pendulum, plays Star Wars Main Theme [168-04] 30.00
- ❏ Darth Vader led alarm clock, color night light [168-05] 35.00

167-03

167-04

167-05

167-06

167-07

167-08

167-09

167-10

168-01

168-02

168-03

168-04

168-05

168-06

168-07

168-08

168-09

168-10

168-11

168-12

Clocks

9" x 11" battery powered.
- ❏ Empire Strikes Back Special Edition 35.00
- ❏ Return of the Jedi Special Edition 35.00
- ❏ Star Wars Special Edition 35.00

Projection alarm clocks.
- ❏ Darth Vader 50.00
- ❏ Mpire, 2,400 produced 125.00
- ❏ Space Battle 65.00

(Australia)
- ❏ Darth Vader twin bell alarm [168-06] 40.00

(Belgium)
Episode III: Revenge of the Sith.
- ❏ Darth Vader, approximately 30cm 25.00
- ❏ Darth Vader alarm [168-07] 45.00

(France)
- ❏ Captain Rex 55.00

(Japan)
- ❏ Imperial logo, lights up 80.00

Episode III: Revenge of the Sith. Wall clocks.
- ❏ Darth Vader [168-08] 45.00
- ❏ Sith [168-09] 45.00

(UK)
- ❏ Clone Wars lenticular alarm clock [168-10] 40.00
- ❏ Episode III epic duel 35.00

Bradley Time
- ❏ 3-way "Anywhere" clock, C-3PO and R2-D2 [168-11] 350.00
- ❏ C-3PO and R2-D2 battery-operated [168-12] 265.00
- ❏ C-3PO and R2-D2 cube clock radio [168-13] 100.00
- ❏ C-3PO and R2-D2 wind-up talking alarm clock, Empire Strikes Back 265.00
- ❏ C-3PO and R2-D2 wind-up talking alarm clock, Star Wars 225.00
- ❏ Droids and TIE Fighter battery-operated [168-14] 175.00
- ❏ Droids and TIE Fighter battery-operated, exclusive to KB Toys [168-15] 175.00
- ❏ Space Battle Scene and 2nd Death Star, black frame under glass 100.00
- ❏ Super Live Adventure Clock, digital tabletop clock [168-16] 475.00

Clicks
Retro alarm clocks.
- ❏ Darth Vader [168-17] 35.00
- ❏ Darth Vader, brown clock face and hands [168-18] 35.00

168-13

168-14

168-15

168-16

168-17

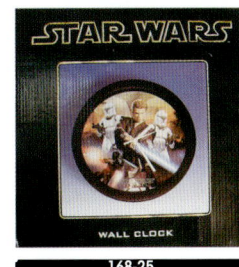
168-18 168-19

168-20

168-21

168-22

168-23

168-24

168-25

168-26 168-27 168-28 168-29 168-30 168-31 168-32

168-33

168-34

168-35

168-36

168-37

168-38

168-39

168-40

168-41

168-42

168-43

168-44

Clocks

    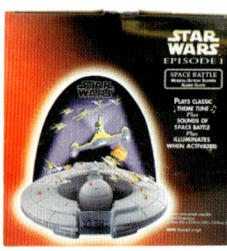 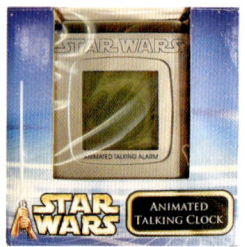

168-45 | 168-46 | 168-47 | 168-48 | 168-49 | 168-50

   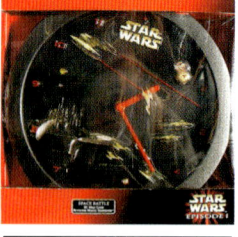 

168-51 | 168-52 | 168-53 | 168-54 | 168-55 | 168-56

Clock-Wise
- ☐ Death Star battle (Return of the Jedi) artwork 45.00

Disney / MGM
- ☐ Star Wars wall clock [168-19] 25.00

FAB (Fashion Accessory Bazaar) Starpoint
- ☐ iConnect MP3 Speaker alarm clock [168-20] 35.00

Humbrol (UK)
- ☐ Mold and Paint (Glow), Jango Fett [168-21] 45.00

IMC Toys (UK)
- ☐ Darth Vader, clock radio [168-22] 50.00
- ☐ Darth Vader, clock radio [168-23] 50.00

JazWares, Inc
- ☐ R2-D2 projection alarm clock 45.00
- ☐ R2-D2 projection alarm clock, white mail order box 35.00

Micro Games of America
- ☐ Darth Vader AM / FM clock radio [168-24] 65.00

NECA
- ☐ Attack of the Clones wall clock [168-25] 35.00

Nelsonic
Mini-clocks.
- ☐ Darth Maul on Sith Speeder [168-26] 50.00
- ☐ Jar Jar Binks [168-27] 50.00
- ☐ Naboo Fighter [168-28] 50.00
- ☐ Queen Amidala [168-29] 50.00
- ☐ Qui-Gon Jinn [168-30] 50.00

Pepsi Cola (Thailand)
- ☐ Boba Fett 30.00

Pepsi Cola (UK)
- ☐ R2-D2 Alarm Clock (Pepsi promotion) [168-31] 130.00

Sakar International
Clone Wars alarm clock radios. Exclusive to Toys R Us.
- ☐ Anakin [168-32] 50.00
- ☐ Obi-Wan [168-33] 50.00
- ☐ Rex [168-34] 50.00

Spearmark International (UK)
- ☐ Darth Vader digital alarm [168-35] 75.00

Taito (Japan)
- ☐ Darth Vader, EP5 version [168-36] 135.00
- ☐ Darth Vader alarm clock, "Last Happy Prize" [168-37] 125.00
- ☐ Darth Vader bust [168-38] 135.00
- ☐ Darth Vader pointing [168-39] 140.00
- ☐ Darth Vader, Episode 3 ....125.00
- ☐ Darth Vader, Episode 5 ....125.00
- ☐ Stormtrooper [168-40] 150.00

Episode III: Revenge of the Sith. Travel alarm clocks.
- ☐ Darth Vader [168-41] 35.00
- ☐ Yoda [168-42] 35.00

The LEGO Group
Features light and snooze. Additional LEGO blocks included.
- ☐ Chewbacca vs. Stormtrooper [168-43] 70.00

Thinkway
- ☐ Anakin's podracer [168-44] 45.00
- ☐ Jar Jar Binks, includes pit droid [168-45] 50.00
- ☐ Naboo Fighter [168-46] 50.00

Tomy
- ☐ R2-D2 alarm clock and LCD game, Myojo Foods premium 200.00

Welby Elgin
Battery-operated wall clocks, Empire Strikes Back.
- ☐ C-3PO and R2-D2 ....140.00
- ☐ Darth Vader and Stormtroopers [168-47] 145.00

Wesco Limited (UK)
- ☐ Clone Wars wall clock [v1e1-132] 35.00
- ☐ Darth Vader 3D wall clock with red glow [168-48] 35.00
- ☐ Darth Vader radio alarm clock 50.00
- ☐ Darth Vader topper alarm clock 40.00

Zeon
- ☐ Episode I Battleship alarm clock, sculpted Naboo Fighter flies over, digital display [168-49] 65.00

Alarm clocks.
- ☐ Animated talking clock [168-50] 35.00
- ☐ Jar Jar travel alarm [168-51] 25.00
- ☐ Pod race viewscreen [168-52] 45.00
- ☐ R2-D2 travel alarm [168-53] 25.00

Wall clocks.
- ☐ Jedi / Sith [168-54] 35.00
- ☐ Space Battle [168-55] 35.00

Zeon (UK)
- ☐ Jedi Training wall clock [168-56] 75.00

Clothing: Aprons
Continued in Volume 3, page 129

Barco
Pizza Hut Episode I employee aprons.
- ☐ Anakin [169-01] 125.00
- ☐ Dark Maul 125.00
- ☐ Queen Amidala [169-02] 125.00

Star Wars Celebration VI
- ☐ Bantha Meat diagram BBQ Apron, convention exclusive [169-03] 50.00

Star Wars Shop
- ☐ Darth Vader [169-04] 35.00
- ☐ Princess Leia [169-05] 35.00

Taito (Japan)
Craft aprons with helmet shaped storage containers.
- ☐ Darth Vader [169-06] 50.00
- ☐ Stormtrooper [169-07] 50.00

Williams-Sonoma
- ☐ Kids character apron [169-08] 45.00

Clothing: Baby
Continued in Volume 3, page 130

- ☐ Stormtrooper, infant jumper [v1e1-145] 15.00

169-01 | 169-02 | 169-03 | 169-04 | 169-05 | 169-06 | 169-07 | 169-08

Clothing: Caps

172-01

172-02 Front and Bottom

172-03

172-04 Image 1 and Image 2

170-01

171-01

172-05

172-06

172-07

172-08

Giant Manufacturing
- Darth Vader, Star Wars Celebration III [170-01] 15.00

Hot Topic
Infant body suits.
- Darth Vader, "Who's Your Daddy?" 18.00
- Yoda, "Size Matters Not" 18.00

Star Wars Celebration VI
- R2-D2 Baby Body Suit and Cap Set 25.00

Clothing: Bibs, Baby
Continued in Volume 3, page 130

Hot Topic
- Yoda: Good Food, Hmm? [171-01] 10.00

Small Planet Co. Ltd. (Japan)
- Darth Vader 15.00
- R2-D2 .... 15.00

Star Wars Celebration V
- Ugnaughty or Ugnice? [v1e1:133] 30.00

Star Wars Celebration VI
- Bib Fortuna "Baby Bib" 25.00

Clothing: Boots
Continued in Volume 3, page 130

- Anakin Skywalker [172-01] 25.00
- Darth Maul, attacking [172-02] 25.00
- Darth Maul, face [172-03] 20.00
- Darth Vader / Luke Skywalker, lenticular [172-04] 25.00
- Ewoks, vinyl [172-05] 65.00
- Podracing [172-06] 20.00
- Stormtrooper / Star Wars [172-07] 40.00
- Yoda, Clone Wars, rubber [172-08] 25.00

Clothing: Caps
Continued in Volume 3, page 131

- 20th Anniversary [173-01] 35.00
- Celebration III Logo (Fiber Optic Lights), black cap with Velcro strap [173-02] 50.00
- Clone Wars, Captain Rex and Anakin [173-03] 15.00
- Commander Fox, exclusive to Target 15.00
- Commander Fox helmet [173-04] 15.00
- Jedi white front with blue bill 12.00

173-01

173-02

173-03

173-04

173-05

173-06

173-07

173-08

173-09

173-10

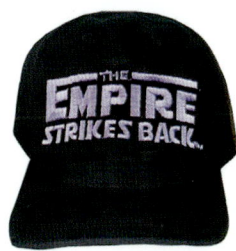
173-11

173-12

173-13

173-14

173-15

173-16

173-17

173-18

Clothing: Caps

173-19 | 173-20 | 173-21 | 173-22 | 173-23 | 173-24 | 173-25

173-26 | 173-27 | 173-28 | 173-29 | 173-30

- ❏ "Jedi," Yoda [173-05] 10.00
- ❏ LEGO Darth Vader, "I Am Your Father" [173-06] 10.00
- ❏ R2-D2 and C-3PO [173-07] 10.00
- ❏ Star Wars Celebration IV 18.00
- ❏ Star Wars clone logo [173-08] 14.00
- ❏ Star Wars early logo, gray with Vader and Stormtrooper 14.00
- ❏ Star Wars logo with trimmed bill [173-09] 18.00
- ❏ Ten-year anniversary, black with gold [v1e1:134] 25.00
- ❏ Ten-year anniversary, black with silver [173-10] 20.00
- ❏ The Empire Strikes Back [173-11] 10.00
- ❏ Vader helmet and flames [173-12] 10.00
- ❏ "Vader," Darth Vader caricature [173-13] 10.00

Episode I: The Phantom Menace.
- ❏ Anakin Skywalker [173-14] 10.00
- ❏ Darth Maul [173-15] 10.00
- ❏ Naboo Bravo Squadron [173-16] 10.00

Star Wars Special Edition.
- ❏ Silver logo on black cap [v1e1:134] 10.00
- ❏ Star Wars Trilogy, silver and red thread on black cap [173-17] 10.00

501st Legion
- ❏ Imperial emblem, TK ID embroidered on back [173-18] ...20.00

Applause
- ❏ Logo on tan cap with black-trimmed bill [173-19] 10.00

Baseball caps, Episode I.
- ❏ Darth Maul [173-20] 10.00
- ❏ Jar Jar Binks [173-21] 10.00
- ❏ Pod Race, Anakin Skywalker, black with red bill [4:88] 10.00
- ❏ Pod Race, Anakin Skywalker, sky blue [173-22] 10.00
- ❏ R2-D2 [4:88] 10.00
- ❏ Star Wars Episode I, silver logo on black cap [173-23] 10.00
- ❏ Star Wars logo strip down front, "Pod Racer" embroidered [4:88] 10.00
- ❏ Star Wars: Episode I blue bill with lightsaber [173-24] 10.00
- ❏ Star Wars: Episode I blue cap, silver threading [173-25] ..10.00
- ❏ The Dark Side, Darth Maul's red face on black cap, red and white text on yellow bill [173-26] 10.00

Bucket hats, Episode I.
- ❏ Darth Maul with red band [173-27] 10.00
- ❏ Star Wars logo, Episode I [173-28] 10.00

B/W Character Merchandising
- ❏ Empire Strikes Back black and silver 18.00

Bossini
Attack of the Clones.
- ❏ Black [173-29] 10.00
- ❏ White [173-30] 10.00

173-31 | 173-32 | 173-33 | 173-34 | 173-35

173-36 | 173-37 | 173-38 | 173-39 | 173-40 | 173-41 | 173-42

173-43 | 173-44 | 173-45 | 173-46 | 173-47 | 173-48

Clothing: Caps

173-49 173-50 173-51 173-52 173-53 173-54

173-55 173-56 173-57 173-58 173-59 173-60 173-61

Burger King (Argentina)
Character caps.
- ❏ Chewbacca [173-31] 150.00
- ❏ R2-D2 [173-32] 150.00
- ❏ Yoda [173-33] 150.00

Chase Authentics
- ❏ M&M Dale Jerrett with Mpire Anakin and Padmé [173-34] 25.00
- ❏ Nascar Jeff Gordon, Space Battle [4:88] 25.00

DeAgostini
- ❏ Twenty-fifth anniversary logo on black cap, Star Wars Fact File premium [173-35] 35.00

Disney / MGM
- ❏ Fitted cap, black with gold stitch logo 25.00
- ❏ Star Wars weekends 25.00

Star Wars Weekends.
- ❏ 2001 R2-D2 projecting hologram Mickey [v1e1:135] 40.00
- ❏ 2003 Star Wars Weekends, leather logo 35.00
- ❏ 2005 Darth Vader / Mickey 25.00
- ❏ 2006 Darth Vader, embroidered 25.00
- ❏ 2006 Imperial emblem, embroidered 25.00

Dixie / Northern Inc.
- ❏ Mesh with characters and Empire Strikes Back logo ... 50.00

Drew Pearson Marketing
- ❏ Boba Fett [173-36] 25.00
- ❏ C-3PO [173-37] 25.00
- ❏ Chewbacca [v1e1:135] 25.00
- ❏ Clone trooper, orange on blue [173-38] 25.00
- ❏ Darth Vader [173-39] 25.00
- ❏ Darth Vader, mesh [173-40] 25.00
- ❏ Jabba the Hutt [4:89] 25.00
- ❏ Obi-Wan Kenobi [173-41] 25.00
- ❏ R2-D2 [173-42] 25.00
- ❏ Sith, black letters on red [173-43] 25.00
- ❏ Star Wars red logo with silver lightsaber [173-44] 25.00
- ❏ Star Wars, black and blue [173-45] 20.00
- ❏ Star Wars, blue and gold [173-46] 20.00
- ❏ Star Wars, orange and black [173-47] 20.00

Episode III: Revenge of the Sith.
- ❏ Sith [173-48] 20.00
- ❏ Star Wars logo blue [173-49] 20.00
- ❏ Star Wars logo yellow [173-50] 20.00

Factors, Etc.
- ❏ Embroidered logo, stars on bill [173-51] 70.00

Falcon Headwear
- ❏ Plus 8 Digital with Star Wars Logo on back 65.00

    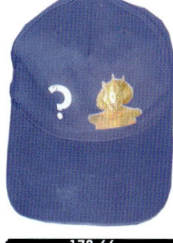  

173-62 173-63 173-64 173-65 173-66 173-67 173-68

173-69 173-70 173-71 173-72 173-73 173-74

173-75 173-76 173-77 173-78 173-79

Clothing: Caps

174-01 | 174-02 | 174-03 | 174-04 | 174-05 Front and Back of Pair One | 174-05 Front and Back of Pair Two

174-06 | 174-07 | 174-08 | 174-09 | 174-10 | 174-11 | 174-12 | 174-13 | 174-14

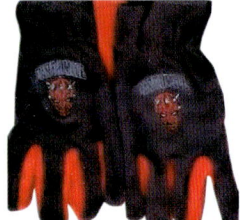       

174-15 | 174-16 | 174-17 | 174-18 | 174-19 | 174-20 | 174-21 | 174-22

Fan Club
- Attack of the Clones [173-52] 35.00
- Episode I black cap with silver embroidered logo and elastic strap [173-53] 25.00
- Episode I bucket hat with embroidered silver logo 25.00
- Star Wars Fan Club 30.00
- SW Fan Club, black with embroidered logo patch 30.00

Fresh Caps Ltd.
- 3D plastic Vader head on cap bill 15.00
- Boba Fett [173-54] 15.00
- Darth Maul name and face with slide buckle 15.00
- Darth Vader [v1e1:135] 15.00
- Glitter X-Wing 20.00
- Podrace [173-55] 15.00
- Return of the Jedi [173-56] 15.00
- "Star Wars Celebration" embroidered 50.00
- Stormtrooper [173-57] 10.00
- Stormtrooper, "Freeze you Rebel scum" black cap with THX-style character on front, quotation on back 20.00
- Stormtrooper, "Freeze you Rebel scum" black cap with THX-style character on front, quotation on front 20.00
- SW Episode I logo, dark green cap, slide buckle 15.00
- SW Episode I logo, olive green cap, slide buckle 15.00
- Vader, "Never underestimate the darkside" black cap with THX-style character on front, quotation on back [173-58] 15.00
- Vader, "Never underestimate the darkside" black cap with THX-style character on front, quotation on front 15.00
- X-Wing / Star Wars [173-59] 15.00
- Yoda, "May the Force be with you" black cap with THX-style character on front, quotation on back 15.00
- Yoda, "May the Force be with you" black cap with THX-style character on front, quotation on front 15.00

Frito Lay
- Episode II logo [173-60] 20.00

General Mills
- Mesh w/ battle scene and Star Wars logo [v1e1:135] ... 135.00
- Mesh with Empire Strikes Back logo and characters [v1e1:135] 150.00

Headmaster Inc.
- Star Wars Celebration II with Velcro strap 45.00

Home Game Inc.
- Queen Amidala [173-61] 40.00

Jedicon
- 1997 Jedicon, black with silver text [173-62] 50.00

Kellogg's
- Kellogg's "C-3PO's The Force" [173-63] 150.00

KFC (Australia)
Employee mystery caps, Episode I prerelease. Blue cap with a question mark and character face.
- C-3PO [173-64] 150.00
- Jar Jar Binks [173-65] 150.00
- Queen Amidala [173-66] 150.00
- Sebulba [v1e1:135] 150.00
- Watto [v1e1:135] 150.00

LucasArts
- Jedi Academy logo 30.00
- Star Wars Galaxies 50.00
- X-Wing embroidered logo, knit 35.00

M&M World
- Dark Side lineup adult hat 40.00
- Jedi lineup adult hat 40.00

Marlin Tease
- Star Wars logo embroidered, black with white 20.00

Mexico Collector Convention
2003. Power of the Force style logo.
- Embroidered / crew 150.00
- Patch 55.00

Millennium Collection
- Rebel Alliance Logo / May the Force be with you [173-67] 20.00

Otto
- Celebration III logo, blue and white 50.00

Pepsi Cola
- Episode I logo [173-68] 15.00
- Nascar #24 with Episode I logo [173-69] 15.00

Pizza Hut (Australia)
Employee mystery caps, Episode I prerelease. Red cap with a question mark and character face.
- C-3PO [v1e1:135] 150.00
- Jar Jar Binks [v1e1:135] 150.00
- Queen Amidala [v1e1:135] 150.00
- Sebulba [173-70] 150.00
- Watto [173-71] 150.00

Sales Corp. of America
- Admiral Ackbar [173-72] 100.00
- Darth Vader and Royal Guards [173-73] 120.00
- Darth Vader and Royal Guards, blue [173-74] 115.00
- Gamorrean Guard [4:90] 120.00
- Jabba the Hutt [v1e1:136] 100.00
- "JEDI" corduroy with stars on bill 100.00
- Luke and Darth Vader [173-75] 100.00
- Luke and Darth Vader duel [173-76] 100.00
- Return of the Jedi Hi-C premium cap [173-77] 175.00
- Return of the Jedi logo [173-78] 100.00

Star Wars Celebration VI
- Blue Harvest Logo Cap 65.00

Sunrise Identity
Star Wars Celebration III exclusives. City and date on back with slide buckle.
- Celebration III, black cap 65.00
- Celebration III, red cap 65.00

Super Live Adventure (Japan)
- Star Wars [173-79] 150.00

Thinking Cap
- Empire Strikes Back logo 80.00
- Imperial with metal rank insignia [4:90] 95.00
- Star Wars Rebel Forces 75.00
- Yoda ears [v1e1:136] 80.00

Clothing: Earmuffs

Rayman/Ridless Products Group
- Return of the Jedi Earmuffs 160.00

Clothing: Hats

 175-01
 175-02
 175-03
 175-04
 175-05
 175-06
 175-07
 175-08
 175-09
 175-10

Clothing: Gloves and Mittens
Continued in Volume 3, page 135

- Darth Vader, grip palms [174-01] 15.00

Lenticular.
- Darth Vader vs. Luke Skywalker, blue [174-02] 20.00
- Darth Vader vs. Luke Skywalker, gray 20.00
- Darth Vader vs. Luke Skywalker, red 20.00

(Japan)
Riding gloves.
- Darth Vader [174-03] 130.00
- Stormtrooper [174-04] 130.00

ABG Accessories
- LEGO Star Wars mix and match, 2 pair [174-05] 25.00

Character gloves, without fingers.
- Chewbacca [174-06] 30.00
- Yoda [174-07] 30.00

Fingerless gloves with button flap
- Star Wars logo, black with white [174-08] 12.00

Magic stretch gloves.
- Darth Vader, red / gray [174-09] 20.00
- Darth Vader Sith Lord [174-10] 15.00
- LEGO Star Wars 15.00
- Stormtrooper [174-11] 20.00

Drew Pearson Marketing
- Darth Vader, black and red 15.00
- Darth Vader, blue [174-12] 15.00
- Star Wars, flame in palm [174-13] 15.00
- Vader [174-14] 15.00

Handcraft Mfg. Corp.
- Darth Maul, fleece [174-15] 15.00
- Star Wars logo, fleece [174-16] 15.00

Rubies
Revenge of the Sith.
- Darth Vader gauntlets [174-17] 20.00

Sales Corp. of America
Gloves.
- C-3PO [174-18] 100.00
- Chewbacca [174-19] 100.00
- Darth Vader [174-20] 100.00
- R2-D2 [174-21] 100.00

Mittens.
- C-3PO 125.00
- Chewbacca 125.00
- Darth Vader, blue [174-22] 125.00
- Paploo 125.00
- R2-D2 ....125.00
- Wicket 125.00

Tomokuni
- X-Wing 65.00

Clothing: Hats
Continued in Volume 3, page 136

- Clone Wars [175-01] 15.00
- Star Wars jester hat [175-02] 25.00
- Star Wars stocking cap [175-03] 20.00

2-Piece sets, hat and gloves.
- Captain Rex [175-04] 25.00
- Captain Rex, black and red with gloves [175-05] 25.00
- Captain Rex, blue with Captain Rex gloves [175-06] 25.00
- Clone Wars with Anakin Skywalker gloves [175-07] 25.00
- Clones, blue with blue Republic cog gloves [175-08] 25.00
- Clones, red with red Republic cog gloves [175-09] 25.00
- Darth Vader, black with Vader / flame gloves [175-10] 25.00
- Darth Vader, dark blue with gloves [175-11] 25.00
- Darth Vader, light blue with gloves [175-12] 25.00

Boxed sets.
- Darth Vader hat / mittens, button-back fingers [175-13] 45.00

Classic trilogy knit hats.
- Darth Vader patch on purple knit [175-14] 20.00

ABG Accessories
- Chewy fur hat [175-15] 35.00
- Chewy fur hat with mitten scarf [175-16] 40.00
- Darth Maul Peruvian hat [175-17] 25.00
- Darth Vader, black and silver [175-18] 25.00

 175-11
 175-12
 175-13
 175-14
 175-15
 175-16
 175-17
 175-18
 175-19
 175-20
 175-21
 175-22
 175-23

Clothing: Hats

 175-24
 175-25
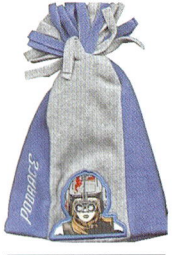 175-26
 175-27
 175-28
 175-29
 175-30
 175-31
 175-32
 175-33
 175-34
 175-35
 175-36
 175-37
 175-38
 175-39
 175-40
 175-41

- ❏ Darth Vader knit visor hat, red / gray [175-19] 15.00
- ❏ Darth Vader Peruvian hat 25.00
- ❏ Darth Vader Peruvian hat, black and silver [175-20].......25.00
- ❏ Darth Vader Peruvian mohawk hat [175-21]..................30.00
- ❏ Ewok [175-22]...30.00
- ❏ Jedi Master LEGO Star Wars, exclusive to Target 15.00
- ❏ Wampa fur hat 30.00

2-Piece sets, hat and shirt.
- ❏ Darth Vader, "Vader," red on black 18.00

3-Piece sets, hat, gloves, and scarf.
- ❏ Darth Vader, red and black 25.00

Comic Images
- ❏ Classic Yoda retro ears cap, exclusive to Star Wars Celebration V 50.00
- ❏ Yoda head and ears 30.00

Disney Theme Park Merchandise
- ❏ R2-D2 ears hat..40.00

Drew Pearson Marketing
- ❏ Darth Vader, blue [175-23] 10.00
- ❏ Sith Lord [175-24]..10.00
- ❏ Vader, eyes [175-25]...10.00

Fresh Caps Ltd.
- ❏ Anakin Skywalker, Pod Race [175-26] 15.00
- ❏ Episode I, black with stripes, round logo.....................15.00
- ❏ Episode I, black with stripes, round logo, no cuff [175-27]...15.00
- ❏ Episode I, blue with stripes, round logo [4:90] 15.00
- ❏ Jar Jar [175-28] 15.00
- ❏ Pod Racing crew cap [175-29].......................................15.00
- ❏ Star Wars [175-30]...15.00
- ❏ Star Wars crew cap [175-31]..15.00
- ❏ Star Wars Episode I crew cap [175-32]..........................15.00

Grossman
- ❏ C-3PO, knit [175-33] 80.00
- ❏ Chewbacca, knit [175-34]..80.00
- ❏ Gamorrean Guard, knit [175-35]....................................80.00
- ❏ Paploo (Ewok), knit [4:90] 80.00
- ❏ R2-D2, knit [175-36] 80.00

- ❏ Return of the Jedi logo, knit..80.00
- ❏ Wicket (Ewok), knit [175-37]...80.00

Marks and Spencer (UK)
- ❏ Darth Maul [v1e1:137]...20.00

Sales Corp. of America
Return of the Jedi cuffed knit hats.
- ❏ Black with red text [175-38]...65.00
- ❏ Patch logo [175-39]..65.00
- ❏ Red with black text [175-40]..65.00
- ❏ White with red text [175-41]..65.00

Star Wars Celebration VI
- ❏ Celebration VI, logo 50.00
- ❏ Jabba the Hutt, knit 45.00

Clothing: Hoodies
Continued in Volume 3, page 140

- ❏ Comic art hoodie and T-shirt 2-pack, toddler sizes 20.00
- ❏ Darth Vader, red, blue and black striped [176-01] 15.00

Celebration IV
- ❏ Chewbacca, fur-lined hood 150.00

Mad Engine
- ❏ Chewbacca, zip-up [176-02] 75.00

Star Wars Celebration Japan (Japan)
- ❏ Boba Fett 200.00
- ❏ Stormtrooper...200.00

Star Wars Celebration VI
- ❏ Darth Vader...60.00
- ❏ R2-D2 pullover 60.00

Clothing: Jackets
Continued in Volume 3, page 142

- ❏ X-Wing Fighter [177-01]...275.00
- ❏ X-Wing Rogue Squadron, leather bomber [177-02]......350.00

Rain jackets..
- ❏ Anakin Skywalker..25.00
- ❏ Darth Maul [177-03]...25.00
- ❏ Darth Vader, black vinyl [177-04]..................................25.00
- ❏ Jar Jar Binks [177-05]..30.00
- ❏ Sith Lord [177-06] 25.00
- ❏ Star Wars Episode I [177-07]...35.00

ABG Accessories
- ❏ Vader rain slicker..25.00

Adam Joseph Industries
Rain jackets.
- ❏ C-3PO and R2-D2, blue..50.00
- ❏ Darth Vader and Royal Guards, silver 50.00
- ❏ Darth Vader and Royal Guards, yellow [177-08]............50.00

Adidas
- ❏ Death Star letterman jacket [177-09] 650.00

Baltro Italiana
- ❏ Star Wars, wool..85.00

Bright Red Group
- ❏ "Darth Vadar Lives" *[sic]* patch, black with white trim, unlined [177-10]..150.00
- ❏ "Darth Vadar Lives" *[sic]* patch, red with white trim, quilted 150.00
- ❏ "MTFBWY" patch, white with black trim, quilted 150.00
- ❏ Star Wars logo patch, blue with white trim, quilted....130.00
- ❏ Star Wars logo patch, blue with white trim, unlined [3:279] 125.00

Celebration IV
- ❏ AT-AT driver, fleece zip-up, red [177-11] 45.00

Disney / MGM
- ❏ Star Tours crew member jacket [177-12] 300.00

Star Wars Weekends.
- ❏ 2006 Poster art applique 75.00

Fan Club
- ❏ 10th Anniversary [177-13]...275.00
- ❏ Boba Fett embroidered on denim [4:91] 175.00

Clothing: Leg Warmers

176-01

176-02

177-01

177-02

177-03

177-04

177-05

177-06

177-07

177-08

177-09

- Darth Vader's Helmet embroidered on denim 135.00
- Han Solo's vest [177-14] 125.00
- Luke Skywalker's fatigue jacket [177-15] 150.00
- Podracing jacket.......................................85.00

Galoob
- 1999 Toy Design Team [177-16] 575.00

Home Game Inc.
- Battle Above Death Star II rain jacket [177-17]............80.00

Hot Topic
- Stormtrooper skull and crossbones [177-18]..........45.00

Lucasfilm
Cast and Crew.
- Episode I, 75 produced [v1e1:138]............345.00
- The Phantom Menace [177-19]..................225.00

North End
- Celebration III rubber patch on front [4:91] 225.00

Star Wars Celebration II
- Darth Maul embroidered [177-20] 400.00

Star Wars Celebration V
- Rain jacket with logo 25.00

Taira Racing
Leather racing jackets.
- Boba Fett [177-21] 1,800.00
- Darth Vader 1,800.00
- Stormtrooper [177-22] 1,800.00

Tiger Electronics
- Electronic Toy Design Team, Maul art [4:91]................285.00

Y.Y. Boueki (Japan)
- Staff jacket, red [177-23] 95.00

Clothing: Leg Warmers
Continued in Volume 3, page 143

Sales Corp. of America
- C-3PO...130.00
- Chewbacca..130.00
- Darth Vader..130.00
- Ewok, blue and white...............................130.00
- Ewok, pink and white...............................130.00
- "Jedi," black and red [178-01]....................130.00
- "Jedi," black, red, and white.....................130.00
- R2-D2..130.00
- Return of the Jedi logo, applique.................130.00

177-10

177-11

177-12

177-13

177-14

177-15

177-16

177-17

177-18

177-19

177-20

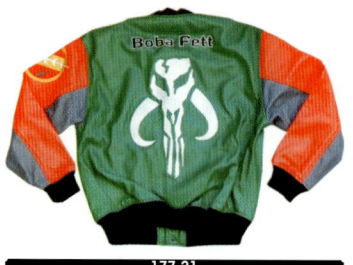
177-21

177-22

177-23

178-01

Clothing: Neckties

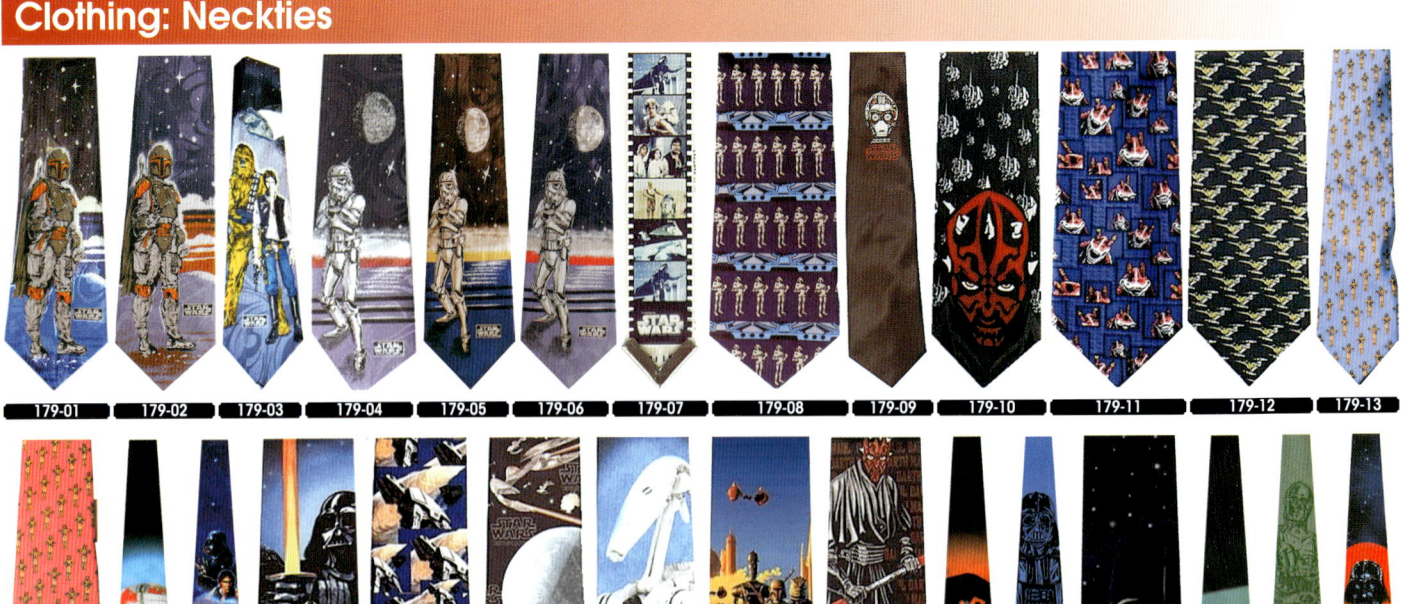

Clothing: Neckties
Continued in Volume 3, Page 143

Star Wars Galaxy style artwork.
- ❏ Boba Fett, blue planet [179-01] 30.00
- ❏ Boba Fett, red planet [179-02] 30.00
- ❏ Han Solo and Chewbacca [179-03] 30.00
- ❏ Stormtrooper, black tie with red surface [179-04] 30.00
- ❏ Stormtrooper, black tie with yellow surface [179-05] 30.00
- ❏ Stormtrooper, blue tie with red surface [179-06] 30.00

Fan Club
- ❏ 15th anniversary, scenes from trilogy, 35mm plastic film [179-07] 35.00

Marks and Spencer (UK)
Episode I: The Phantom Menace.
- ❏ Battle Droids repeating [179-08] 40.00
- ❏ C-3PO [179-09] 40.00
- ❏ Darth Maul icons repeating [v1e1:139] 40.00
- ❏ Darth Maul in front of repeating pattern of probe droids [179-10] 40.00
- ❏ Jar Jar Binks making faces, square icons [179-11] 40.00
- ❏ Jedi icon between crossed sabers [v1e1:139] ... 40.00
- ❏ Naboo Fighter icons repeating [179-12] 40.00
- ❏ R2-D2 icons repeating [v1e1:139] 40.00

Pizza Hut (Canada)
- ❏ Episode I employee perk 35.00

Psycho Bunny
- ❏ C-3PO, light blue [179-13] 45.00
- ❏ C-3PO, pink [179-14] 45.00
- ❏ Ewoks 45.00

Ralph Marlin and Co.
Polyester/blend.
- ❏ Anakin Skywalker in podracer 25.00
- ❏ Anakin Skywalker in podracer gear [179-15] 25.00
- ❏ A New Hope 1995 international video artwork [179-16] 25.00
- ❏ A New Hope style "A" poster art (Vader's lightsaber extends along length of tie) [179-17] 25.00
- ❏ AT-AT McQuarrie art [179-18] 25.00
- ❏ Battle Above Naboo [179-19] 25.00
- ❏ Battle Droid art over Federation tank [179-20] 25.00
- ❏ Bounty hunters artwork [179-21] 25.00
- ❏ Darth Maul (name and drawings) [179-22] 25.00
- ❏ Darth Maul line-art bust over repeating name [v1e1:140] 25.00
- ❏ Darth Maul photo over Tatooine duel scene [179-23] .. 25.00
- ❏ Darth Vader line art [179-24] 25.00
- ❏ Darth Vader video art (same as 1995 A New Hope video release) [179-25] 25.00
- ❏ Death Star Assault (McQuarrie art of TIE chasing X-Wing) [179-26] 25.00
- ❏ Death Star Rising (X-Wings attack Death Star) 25.00
- ❏ Droids line art and square photo on sage green [179-27] 25.00
- ❏ Empire Strikes Back 1995 international video artwork [179-28] 25.00
- ❏ Gold and black Darth Vader helmet repeating pattern 25.00
- ❏ Han and Chewbacca line art and square photo on navy [179-29] 25.00
- ❏ Invasion Army, battle droids on STAPs and tanks [179-30] 25.00
- ❏ Jar Jar Binks over bubble pattern on blue background [179-31] 25.00
- ❏ Jar Jar Binks above Anakin's pod racer [179-32] 25.00
- ❏ Jar Jar posed over repeating name [179-33] 25.00
- ❏ Jedi Obi-Wan Kenobi [179-34] 25.00
- ❏ Jedi Obi-Wan Kenobi Jedi Master [179-35] 25.00
- ❏ Jedi Qui-Gon Jinn [179-36] 25.00
- ❏ Qui-Gon Jinn [179-37] 25.00
- ❏ Qui-Gon Jinn Jedi Master [179-38] 25.00
- ❏ Race to Freedom [179-39] 25.00
- ❏ Return of the Jedi 1995 international video artwork [179-40] 25.00
- ❏ Sith Darth Maul (photos of character) [179-41] ... 25.00
- ❏ Sith Lord [179-42] 25.00
- ❏ Sith, The Dark Side [179-43] 25.00
- ❏ Space Battle (Naboo fighters) [179-44] 25.00
- ❏ Starfighters (The Phantom Menace) [179-45] 25.00
- ❏ Stormtrooper video art (same as 1995 Empire Strikes Back video release) [179-46] 25.00
- ❏ Star Wars characters (character photos and Star Wars logo at bottom) [179-47] 25.00
- ❏ Star Wars Characters II (from top to bottom: Han, Ben, Leia, Luke, Vader) [179-48] 25.00
- ❏ Star Wars original illustration [179-49] 25.00
- ❏ T.I.E. tie (3 TIE Fighters in trench) [179-50] 25.00
- ❏ The Phantom Menace characters [179-51] 25.00

146

Clothing: Pants and Shorts

- ❑ Yoda line art and square Luke/Yoda photo on emerald [179-52] 25.00
- ❑ Yoda video art (same as 1995 Return of the Jedi video release) [179-53] 25.00
- ❑ Young Skywalker [179-54] 25.00

Silk.
- ❑ All Character Icons (character vignettes repeating pattern in green, orange, red, black, and blue) [179-55] 35.00
- ❑ Anakin Skywalker icons repeating [179-56] 35.00
- ❑ Battle Droid icons repeating [179-57] 35.00
- ❑ Cantina (on orange tie) 35.00
- ❑ Darth Maul face repeating, silk [179-58] 35.00
- ❑ Darth Vader from Star Wars novel cover artwork repeating pattern, limited edition in tin [v1e1:141] 35.00
- ❑ Imperial vehicles "blueprints" [179-59] 35.00
- ❑ Jar Jar Binks icons repeating—black [179-60] 35.00
- ❑ Jar Jar Binks icons repeating—navy [179-61] 35.00
- ❑ Jedi icons repeating—black [v1e1:141] 35.00
- ❑ Jedi icons repeating—navy [179-62] 35.00
- ❑ Jedi vs. Sith pattern repeating [179-63] 35.00
- ❑ Jung poster art [179-64] 35.00
- ❑ Rebel Alliance Blueprint [179-65] 35.00
- ❑ Silver-and-black Darth Vader helmet, repeating 35.00
- ❑ Sith, The Dark Side pattern repeating [179-66] 35.00
- ❑ Starfighter blueprints, black [v1e1:141] 35.00
- ❑ Starfighter blueprints, navy [179-67] 35.00
- ❑ Starfighter blueprints, olive [v1e1:141] 35.00
- ❑ Star Wars Vehicles, black [179-68] 35.00
- ❑ Star Wars Vehicles, multicolor line drawings [179-69] 35.00
- ❑ The Phantom Menace Ships repeating [179-70] 35.00
- ❑ Yoda artwork 35.00

Tie Mart
- ❑ Episode I logos on space background [179-71] 20.00

Clothing: Outfits, 2-Piece
Continued in Volume 3, Page 144

Giant Manufacturing
- ❑ Anakin Skywalker [v1e1:141] 18.00
- ❑ Clone trooper No. 214736184505196 [v1e1:141] 18.00
- ❑ Droids [v1e1:141] 18.00
- ❑ Jango Fett Dangerous Bounty Hunter [v1e1:141] 18.00
- ❑ Jedi Knight Yoda [v1e1:141] 18.00
- ❑ R2-D2 [v1e1:141] 18.00
- ❑ Yoda [v1e1:141] 18.00

Kids Headquarters
Shirt-and-pants sets.
- ❑ Bravo Squadron polyester black / black 18.00
- ❑ Bravo Squadron polyester blue / blue 18.00
- ❑ Darth Maul black polyester / white nylon 18.00
- ❑ Droids sweats, gray and blue / blue 18.00
- ❑ Jar Jar nylon jogger, green / blue 18.00
- ❑ Jar Jar sweats, gray and blue / blue 18.00
- ❑ Naboo starfighter, white polyester / black nylon 18.00
- ❑ R2-D2, Pit Droid, C-3PO knit shirt and sweat pants 18.00

Shirt-and-shorts sets.
- ❑ Anakin Skywalker, dark blue / gray 15.00
- ❑ Darth Maul, gray / black 15.00
- ❑ Darth Maul, white / black 15.00
- ❑ Droids, yellow with dark blue 15.00
- ❑ Jar Jar (4 faces), blue / gray 15.00
- ❑ Jar Jar, light blue / dark blue 15.00
- ❑ Jedi duel, black / gray 15.00
- ❑ Jedi vs. Sith, gray / blue / dark blue 15.00
- ❑ Jedi vs. Sith, red / gray 15.00
- ❑ Naboo starfighter embroidered on knit polo shirt 15.00
- ❑ Naboo starfighter, dark blue / gray 15.00
- ❑ Pit droid, yellow with dark blue 15.00
- ❑ Pit droids, blue shirt, red shorts [v1e1:141] 15.00
- ❑ Podracing, gray / red 15.00

Clothing: Overalls

Bibb Co.
- ❑ Toddler suit 15.00

Kids Headquarters
- ❑ Jar Jar overalls and long sleeve shirt set 24.00
- ❑ Pit Droid [180-01] 24.00

Liberty Trouser Co.
- ❑ Short pants sun suit 20.00
- ❑ Star Wars overalls 20.00

Clothing: Pants and Shorts
Continued in Volume 3, Page 144

- ❑ Luke "Use the Force" / Droids "We're Doomed" shorts [v1e1:143] 10.00

Bibb Co.
Star Wars jeans.
- ❑ Chambray 20.00
- ❑ Corduroy 20.00

Gans Enterprises
Denim jeans.
- ❑ Darth Vader and droids [181-01] 20.00
- ❑ Darth Vader, Ewok, Jedi logo 20.00

Giant Manufacturing
- ❑ Sport shorts, black with red piping [181-02] 16.00

Harley, Inc.
Variety, any style.
- ❑ Pants 20.00
- ❑ Shorts 18.00

Clothing: Pants and Shorts

Liberty Trouser Co.
Jeans, Star Wars with over-all pattern.
- ❏ Brown 24.00
- ❏ Navy blue 24.00
- ❏ Royal blue 24.00

Shorts with Return of the Jedi logo.
- ❏ Fleece 18.00
- ❏ Gym 18.00

Shorts, Star Wars with over-all pattern.
- ❏ Navy blue 18.00
- ❏ Royal blue 18.00

Mr. Seb Sportswear
- ❏ Shorts, athletic with Jedi logo 30.00

Reknown
- ❏ Short pants 18.00

Sales Corp. of America
- ❏ Shorts, gym 65.00

Clothing: Ponchos
Continued in Volume 3, Page 148

Rain ponchos.
- ❏ Darth Vader [182-01] 25.00
- ❏ Star Wars black, adult-sized, yellow logo [182-02] 125.00

Adam Joseph Industries
Rain ponchos.
- ❏ C-3PO and R2-D2, blue [182-03] 85.00
- ❏ Darth Vader and Royal Guards, silver [182-04] 85.00

B/W Character Merchandising
- ❏ Rain cape, plastic Empire Strikes Back 140.00

Ben Cooper
- ❏ C-3PO [182-05] 55.00
- ❏ Darth Vader [182-06] 55.00
- ❏ Darth Vader, red package [182-07] 85.00
- ❏ Yoda [182-08] 65.00

Pyramid
- ❏ Darth Maul rain poncho 15.00
- ❏ Jedi vs. Sith rain poncho [182-09] 15.00

Star Wars Celebration V
- ❏ Celebration V logo rain poncho 25.00

Clothing: Robes
Continued in Volume 3, Page 148

- ❏ Clone Wars [183-01] 35.00
- ❏ Darth Vader [183-02] 20.00
- ❏ LEGO Star Wars [183-03] 20.00
- ❏ Star Wars, black with blue trim [183-04] 35.00

Vintage.
- ❏ Empire Strikes Back [183-05] 60.00
- ❏ Return of the Jedi [183-06] 60.00

501st Legion (Japan)
- ❏ Garrison happy jacket 150.00

Mr. Australia Garments
- ❏ C-3PO 34.00
- ❏ C-3PO's head 34.00
- ❏ Darth Vader and Stormtroopers 34.00
- ❏ Han and Chewbacca 34.00
- ❏ Luke on Tauntaun 34.00
- ❏ R2-D2, gray 34.00
- ❏ R2-D2, red 34.00
- ❏ Yoda 34.00

Wilker Bros.
- ❏ Darth Vader 30.00
- ❏ "May the Force be with you" 20.00

Clothing: Scarves
Continued in Volume 3, Page 148

Boy Scouts of America
Mid-America Council.
- ❏ 1978 Scout-O-Rama [184-01] 50.00

Grossman
- ❏ C-3PO 75.00
- ❏ Chewbacca 75.00
- ❏ Darth Vader 75.00
- ❏ R2-D2 ....75.00
- ❏ Return of the Jedi logo 75.00
- ❏ Wicket 75.00

Psycho Bunny
Cashmere.
- ❏ Darth Vader 85.00
- ❏ R2-D2 ....135.00
- ❏ Stormtrooper 135.00

Silk fashion.
- ❏ C-3PO and R2-D2 [184-02] 45.00
- ❏ Millennium Falcon [184-03] 45.00
- ❏ Stormtroopers [184-04] 45.00

Ralph Marlin and Co.
- ❏ Queen Amidala, 22" x 22" silk fashion [184-05] 35.00

Clothing: Shirts
Continued in Volume 3, Page 149

- ❏ 2-piece: Star Wars comic art jacket and vehicles art shirt, youth sizes [185-01] 25.00
- ❏ 2012 Save Lars Expedition [185-02] 35.00
- ❏ Admit One—Return of the Jedi Opening Day [185-03] ..45.00
- ❏ "All I Need To Know About Life I Learned From Star Wars" [185-04] 24.00
- ❏ Anakin / Podracer line drawing polo [185-05] 15.00
- ❏ Anakin, "Don't Look Back" 15.00
- ❏ AT-AT Xing, gray 12.00
- ❏ @@ (AT-AT) [v1e1:144] 25.00
- ❏ Bart Wars [v1e1:144] 15.00
- ❏ Boba Fett [185-06] 15.00
- ❏ Brisk - Darth Maul and Yoda, Episode I in 3D promotional tie-in [185-07] 40.00
- ❏ C-3PO, Star Wars Celebration IV logo 30.00
- ❏ C-3PO and R2-D2, navy, toddler sizes [185-08] 12.00
- ❏ C-3PO and R2-D2 on black shirt with red sleeves [185-09] 15.00

 182-01
 182-02
 182-03
 182-04
 182-05
 182-06
 182-07

 182-08
 182-09
 183-01
 183-02
 183-03
 183-04
 183-05

 183-06
184-01
184-02
184-03
184-04
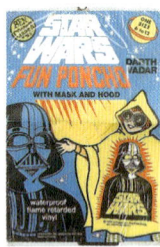
 184-05

Clothing: Shirts

 185-01
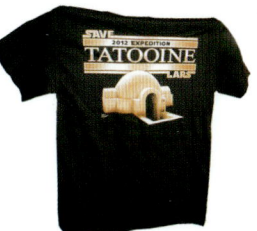 185-02
 185-03
 185-04
 185-05
 185-06
 185-07
 185-08
 185-09
 185-10

- C-3PO and R2-D2, shadowed [185-10] 15.00
- Captain Rex [185-11] 15.00
- Cast and Crew, exclusive to Star Wars Celebration Europe 35.00
- Celebration IV fleece pullover 30.00
- Celebration IV logo, date on back 20.00
- Character icons 3x3 [185-12] 15.00
- Chewbacca—brown photo booth style images [185-13] 15.00
- Clone Wars characters, Star Wars Celebration III [v1e1:144] 15.00
- Clone Wars children's sports jersey [185-14] 20.00
- Dark Side / Revenge [v1e1:144] 15.00
- Darth Maul sweatshirt, black with red stripes circling sleeves [185-15] 25.00
- Darth Maul, Sith 15.00
- Darth Vader, icons, gray [185-16] 25.00
- Darth Vader—Who's Your Daddy?, black shirt, adult sizes [185-17] 15.00
- Darth Vader / Space Battle over Death Star II long sleeves [4:95] 15.00
- Darth Vader / Space Battle over Death Star II short sleeves [185-18] 15.00
- Darth Vader helmet, black shirt with gold silk screen, exclusive to KMart [185-19] 20.00
- Darth Vader helmet sketch art [185-20] 15.00
- Darth Vader hooded sweatshirt, black, exclusive to Star Wars Celebration IV 35.00
- Darth Vader sweatshirt, blue with gray sleeves, blue cuffs [185-21] 15.00
- Darth Vader with lightsaber [185-22] 15.00
- Darth Vader, "Come to the Dark Side. We Have Cookies" 20.00
- Darth Vader, "Crushin' Fools. Like a Boss" 20.00
- Darth Vader, lightsaber, Death Star, neon colors [185-23] 15.00
- Darth Vader, Star Wars 30 Years, tan, exclusive to Star Wars Celebration IV 20.00
- Darth, purple and silver [185-24] 20.00
- Empire Line-Up 20.00
- Episode I characters / Pepsi logo on sleeve 18.00
- Family Guy: Blue Harvest......................................20.00
- Han Solo, orange on black with Star Wars Celebration IV logo 40.00
- Jeff Gordon 24, Pepsi / Lays / Episode I [185-25] 24.00
- Join the Celebration, Star Wars: Special Edition with release dates 45.00
- Luke, Vader, X-Wings sampled from a Dave Dorman painting, olive green long sleeve 15.00
- May the Forks be With You, black [185-26] 15.00
- Millennium Falcon blueprints, red shirt, adult sizes 15.00
- Podracing on Tatooine, blue and red [4:95] 15.00
- R2-D2, blue, exclusive to Star Wars Celebration IV 40.00
- R2-D2 / C-3PO / Pit Droids [185-27] 15.00
- R2-D2 / C-3PO / Star Wars [4:95] 15.00
- Red Leader (fox) 15.00
- Sith Happens, Vader's chest box [185-28] 18.00
- Sith Lord 15.00
- Size Matters Not, Yoda art 20.00
- Something Something, Something Darkside 20.00
- Star Destroyer [185-29] 15.00
- Star Wars—Luke, Leia, starships, brown shirt, adult sizes, features Dave Dorman artwork 15.00
- Star Wars clone trooper [185-30] 15.00
- Star Wars is Forever, character icons, black, exclusive to Star Wars Celebration IV 40.00
- Star Wars reveals Darth Vader, Star Wars Celebration IV logo 40.00
- Star Wars the Saga Continues [185-31] 20.00
- Star Wars, battle above Death Star silver on black, women's [185-32] 20.00
- Stormtrooper [4:95] 15.00
- Stormtrooper armor, exclusive to Star Wars Celebration Europe [185-33] 35.00
- Stormtrooper, toddler size [185-34] 15.00
- Support Our Troops, Darth Vader and Stormtroopers [185-35] 30.00
- Support Our Troops, Stormtroopers [185-36] 30.00
- The Force Unleashed [185-37] 18.00
- The Star Wars Trilogy Special Edition [185-38] 18.00
- Trade Federation Fighters attacking Naboo Fighters [185-39] 18.00
- Trust Me—A Jedi I Am, green, adult sizes [185-40] 15.00
- Vader is Coming! Look Busy..................................15.00
- Vader, Sith Lord [185-41] 15.00
- Yoda wearing Santa hat, "An Elf I Am Not" [185-42] 15.00

Angry Birds.
- May the BIRDS be with you! 20.00
- Six shot..20.00
- Use the Force..20.00

Black character drawing on white t-shirt.
- Princess Leia [185-43] 20.00
- Stormtrooper 20.00

Clone Wars.
- Anakin, Obi-Wan, Captain Rex, Ahsoka [185-44] 15.00
- Anakin, Obi-Wan, Captain Rex, Yoda [185-45] 15.00

 185-11
 185-12
 185-13
 185-14
 185-15

185-16
 185-17
 185-18
185-19
 185-20

149

Clothing: Shirts

 185-21
 185-22
 185-23
 185-24
 185-25

 185-26
 185-27
 185-28
 185-29
 185-30

❏ Anakin, Obi-Wan, Yoda, background icons [185-46] 15.00
❏ Commander Fox, Captain Rex, Anakin, Obi-Wan, Yoda, Jabba [185-47] 15.00
❏ Yoda [185-48] 15.00
❏ Yoda, Obi-Wan, Anakin, Ahsoka, Clone troopers, Captain Rex [185-49] 15.00

Episode II: Attack of the Clones.
❏ C-3PO R2-D2, droids background [185-50] 15.00
❏ Droid Army [v1e1:145] 15.00
❏ Yoda, Anakin / Padmé / movie logo [185-51] 20.00

Episode III: Revenge of the Sith.
❏ ARC-170s, Darth Vader, Yoda, Clones, R2-D2, C-3PO [185-52] 15.00
❏ Darth Vader, Jedi Star Fighters, Yoda [185-53] 15.00
❏ Darth Vader, Yoda, General Grievous, Chewbacca, Clone trooper, C-3PO, R2-D2 [185-54] 15.00
❏ R2-D2 blue sleeveless [185-55] 15.00

LEGO characters.
❏ Jedi Knight, long sleeve 20.00
❏ LEGO Vader Rules!, blue long sleeve youth shirt 20.00
❏ Pilot Luke Skywalker, "Use the Force!", blue 20.00
❏ Vader, Stormtrooper, Chewbacca, Yoda, Boba Fett in trapezoidal frame, brown, youth-sized 20.00

May the Forest Be With You.
❏ Washington 25.00

Return of the Jedi yellow T-shirt with appliqué.
❏ Admiral Ackbar [185-56] 15.00
❏ R2-D2 and Wicket [185-57] 15.00

Revenge of the Sith.
❏ Anakin vs. Obi-Wan—epic duel, navy [185-58] 15.00
❏ Anakin vs. Obi-Wan—epic duel yellow shirt [185-59] 15.00
❏ Darth Vader silhouette art [185-60] 15.00
❏ Imperial Domination with cog [185-61] 15.00
❏ Jedi starfighter and ARC-170's [185-62] 15.00
❏ Star Wars logo (clones) 15.00
❏ Star Wars Tri-Fighters attacking starfighter [185-63] 15.00
❏ Star Wars Vader black and white [185-64] 15.00
❏ Stormtrooper skull and crossbones [185-65] 15.00
❏ Vader overlooking lava [185-66] 15.00
❏ Yoda—Justice [185-67] 15.00
❏ Yoda—lightsaber action [v1e1:146] 15.00

Star Wars Uncut. Exclusive to Star Wars Celebration VI.
❏ Death Star 25.00
❏ R2-D2 ....25.00

Star Wars, rebel alliance print.
❏ Blue [4:96] 15.00
❏ Purple [4:96] 15.00

Sweatshirts, children's with caricature characters.
❏ Darth Vader [185-68] 18.00
❏ Grievous [185-69] 18.00
❏ Star Wars: Darth Vader, Luke, Yoda [185-70] 18.00

Sweatshirts, children's with LEGO characters.
❏ Darth Vader [185-71] 20.00
❏ Death Star / TIE Fighters [185-72] 25.00
❏ General Grievous [v1e1:147] 20.00
❏ Millennium Falcon, hooded [v1e1:147] 25.00
❏ Republic Clone trooper, hooded [v1e1:147] 25.00

Tank tops, adult sizes. Exclusive to Star Wars Celebration VI.
❏ Slave Leia, green 30.00

Tank tops, youth sizes.
❏ Jar Jar green on black 15.00

All Out Fan
❏ A Jedi's Strength Flows From the Force [185-73] 20.00
❏ Boba Fett [185-74] 20.00
❏ Empire Strikes Back, vintage fan club logo [185-75] 20.00
❏ Powrot JEDI [v1e1:147] 20.00
❏ Stormtrooper [185-76] 20.00

Amate Textile
El Regreso del Jedi.
❏ Baby Ewoks 20.00
❏ Biker Scouts 20.00
❏ Darth Vader and Luke 20.00
❏ Darth Vader and Luke duel 20.00
❏ Han, Luke, and Leia 20.00
❏ Vader's Helmet, Star Wars logo, dogfight 24.00

American Marketing Enterprises, Inc.
❏ Boba Fett, artwork 15.00
❏ Bounty Hunters, artwork 15.00
❏ Chewbacca, artwork 15.00
❏ Droids and red sky, artwork 15.00
❏ Emperor 15.00
❏ Empire Villains, artwork 15.00
❏ Empire Strikes Back Vader with crossed lightsabers, artwork 15.00
❏ Han Solo, artwork 15.00

 185-31
 185-32
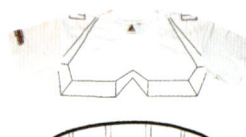
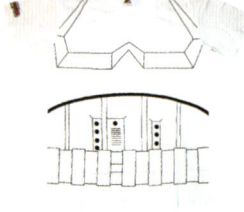 185-33
 185-34
 185-35

 185-36
 185-37
 185-38
 185-39
 185-40

Clothing: Shirts

 185-41
 185-42
 185-43
 185-44
 185-45

185-46
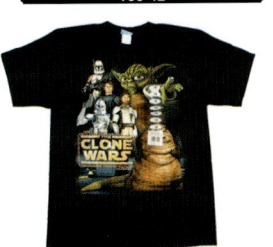 185-47
 185-48
 185-49
 185-50

- ❏ Jawa with big wrench, artwork 15.00
- ❏ Luke and Leia swinging, artwork 15.00
- ❏ Movie Poster 'A', artwork 15.00
- ❏ Rancor 15.00
- ❏ Vader, artwork 15.00
- ❏ Yoda, artwork 15.00

Barrett Sportswear
- ❏ Star Wars trilogy for Musicland, Sci-Fi Channel and Suncoast Video 45.00

Big Dog
- ❏ Attack of the Bones [185-77] 20.00
- ❏ Dog Wars, polo [v1e1:147] 20.00
- ❏ Dog Wars, sweatshirt [185-78] 30.00
- ❏ Grrrl Power [185-79] 20.00
- ❏ Return of the Dogi [4:96] 20.00
- ❏ South Bark Wars, "Oh my Gawd, he killed Kenny!" [4:96] 20.00
- ❏ Southbark Wars, gray or white shirt [4:96] 20.00
- ❏ The Empire Bites Back [185-80] 20.00
- ❏ The Panting Menace, Bark Maul [185-81] 15.00
- ❏ Yo Quiero nar un Jadog mastor [4:96] 20.00
- ❏ Yodog: It's not the size of the dog in the fight... [185-82] 20.00

Bing Harris Sargood
- ❏ Return of the Jedi 15.00

Bossini
- ❏ Darth Vader / Star Destroyer [185-83] 15.00
- ❏ Luke / Hoth [185-84] 15.00
- ❏ Luke and Leia / Anakin and Padmé [185-85] ...15.00

- ❏ R2-D2 and C-3PO [185-86] 15.00
- ❏ Stormtrooper [185-87] 15.00
- ❏ Super Battle Droid [v1e1:148] 15.00

Burger King
Episode III: Revenge of the Sith.
- ❏ Darth Vader [185-88] 35.00

Changes
- ❏ Han Solo blasting stormtroopers [185-89] 15.00
- ❏ Hildebrant brothers poster art, white shirt with blue collar 15.00

Episode I: The Phantom Menace images on black T-shirt, 2-sided.
- ❏ Darth Maul, The Darkside [185-90] 15.00
- ❏ Jar Jar Binks [185-91] 15.00
- ❏ Jedi vs. Sith [185-92] 15.00
- ❏ Naboo space battle [185-93] 15.00
- ❏ Sebulba / STAP [185-94] 15.00

Chunk (UK)
- ❏ Dark Side High 1980 Darth Vader lavender 30.00
- ❏ Dark Side High 1980 Darth Vader pink 30.00
- ❏ Dark Side High 1980 Stormtrooper blue 30.00
- ❏ Dark Side High 1980 Stormtrooper green 30.00
- ❏ Darth Vader Metal with guitar 30.00
- ❏ Leia, "Tatooine—A Chunk Resort 1983" blue ...30.00
- ❏ Leia, "Tatooine—A Chunk Resort 1983" yellow ..30.00
- ❏ Stormtrooper Metal with guitar 30.00
- ❏ Stormtrooper Surfing 30.00
- ❏ Yoda Disco, "Can You Feel The Force?" 30.00

Coca-Cola (China)
Episode III: Revenge of the Sith.
- ❏ Anakin Skywalker [v1e1:148] 35.00
- ❏ Anakin vs. Obi-Wan tank top [185-95] 35.00
- ❏ Darth Vader [185-96] 35.00

Creative Conventions
- ❏ 10th anniversary Star Wars Convention 65.00

Disney / MGM
- ❏ Clone trooper, orange 2-sided [185-97] 15.00
- ❏ Star Tours [185-98] 15.00
- ❏ Star Tours, Now the adventure is real [185-99] ...15.00
- ❏ Star Wars lightsaber, 2-sided [v1e1:148] 15.00
- ❏ Stormtrooper punching through Imperial logo [v1e1:148] 25.00

Star Wars Weekends.
- ❏ 2003 Star Wars Weekends, Mickey and Yoda [185-100] ..25.00
- ❏ 2004 Mickey / A New Hope poster 25.00
- ❏ 2004 Mickey and Minnie / A New Hope poster [185-101] 25.00
- ❏ 2005 Darth Vader / Mickey 25.00
- ❏ 2005 Darth Vader / Mickey baby doll b/w [185-102] ..25.00
- ❏ 2006 Vader / Yoda glittered T-shirt 25.00
- ❏ 2006 Vader / Yoda polo 25.00
- ❏ 2006 Vader / Yoda T-shirt 25.00

Disney Theme Park Merchandise
- ❏ Darth Maul, exclusive pass holder shirt 50.00
- ❏ Donald as Darth Maul, 2012 Star Wars Weekends logo 50.00

 185-51
 185-52
 185-53
 185-54
 185-55

 185-56
 185-57
 185-58
 185-59
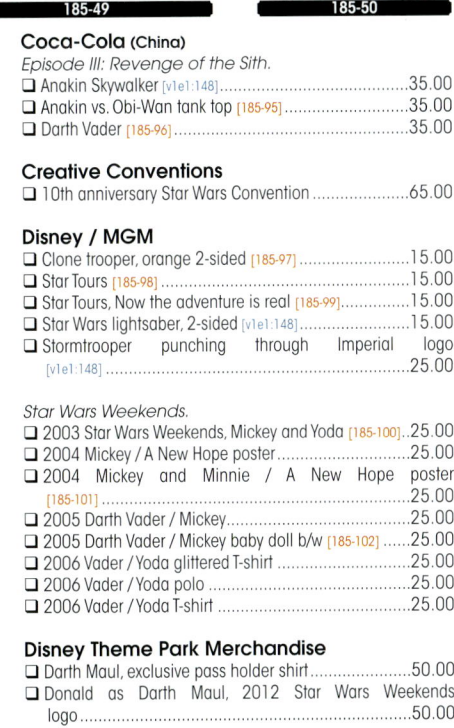 185-60

Clothing: Shirts

- ❑ Last Tour to Endor 25.00
- ❑ Obi-Wan Mickey vs. Darth Maul Donald, exclusive pass holder shirt 50.00
- ❑ Star Tours Opening Day 2011 [185-103] 30.00

Drew Pearson Marketing
Classic Trilogy Collection sports jerseys.
- ❑ Baseball: Vader 77 .... 125.00
- ❑ Baseball: Yoda 80 .... 125.00
- ❑ Basketball: Fett 80 .... 100.00
- ❑ Basketball: Vader 77 .... 100.00
- ❑ Football: Fett 80 .... 125.00
- ❑ Football: Vader 77 .... 125.00
- ❑ Football: Yoda 80 .... 125.00

Ecko Unlimited
- ❑ I (Heart) Star Wars, black and pink glitter design [185-104] 25.00

ELMS Marketing
- ❑ Star Wars Episode I, Battle Droid [v1e1:148] 18.00

Factors, Etc.
- ❑ C-3PO 20.00
- ❑ C-3PO and R2-D2 .... 20.00
- ❑ C-3PO and R2-D2 on sand 20.00
- ❑ C-3PO, glitter 20.00
- ❑ Chewbacca 20.00
- ❑ Chewbacca, glitter 20.00
- ❑ Darth Vader 20.00
- ❑ Darth Vader and Obi-Wan Kenobi 20.00
- ❑ Darth Vader and X-Wing Fighter 20.00
- ❑ "Darth Vader Lives" 20.00
- ❑ Darth Vader, glitter 20.00
- ❑ Han Solo 20.00
- ❑ Han Solo and Chewbacca 20.00
- ❑ Jawas 20.00
- ❑ Jawas, glitter 20.00
- ❑ Luke Skywalker 20.00
- ❑ Luke Skywalker, glitter 20.00
- ❑ "May the Force be with you" 20.00
- ❑ Millennium Falcon, glitter [4:97] 20.00
- ❑ Princess Leia 20.00
- ❑ Princess Leia, glitter 20.00
- ❑ R2-D2 .... 20.00
- ❑ R2-D2, glitter [4:97] 20.00
- ❑ Star Wars logo 20.00
- ❑ Star Wars logo, glitter 20.00
- ❑ Stormtrooper on Dewback 20.00
- ❑ Stormtrooper, glitter 20.00
- ❑ X-Wing and TIE Fighter Dogfight 20.00

Fan Club
- ❑ 1987 "First Ten Years" [4:97] 35.00
- ❑ Episode II: Attack of the Clones, clone design 20.00
- ❑ Episode I, 100% cotton, long sleeve, black with white logo embroidered 25.00
- ❑ Episode I, 100% cotton, short sleeve, black or white with logo embroidered across chest 25.00
- ❑ Episode I, 3-button polo, tan 45.00
- ❑ Episode I, denim, long sleeve 50.00
- ❑ Official Star Wars Fan Club Member [185-105] 35.00

Fifth Sun
- ❑ Angry Birds—The Force is Awesome!, girls' black-and-pink long-sleeve shirt 15.00
- ❑ Angry Birds—Those Guys, navy with white long sleeves 15.00

Angry Birds.
- ❑ May the Birds Be With You, girls' purple-and-white long-sleeve shirt 15.00

Freeze
- ❑ Boba Fett and Darth Vader on black shirt 15.00
- ❑ Darth Vader and small red plasticized square on black shirt 15.00
- ❑ Darth Vader on gray shirt [v1e1:148] 15.00
- ❑ Droids and green framing on black shirt 15.00
- ❑ Droids and small blue plasticized square on black shirt 15.00
- ❑ Droids, reflective silver / gold on black shirt 15.00
- ❑ "Lord Vader" and blueprints of his TIE fighter on black shirt 15.00
- ❑ "Star Wars, May the Force be with you" silver and black on black shirt 15.00

Giant Manufacturing
- ❑ 3D Jar Jar Binks head 15.00
- ❑ Anakin with lightsaber [185-106] 20.00
- ❑ Anakin Skywalker [185-107] 15.00
- ❑ Anakin Skywalker, "Anakin's Destiny" [185-108] 15.00
- ❑ Anakin Skywalker running on half brown, half black shirt 15.00
- ❑ Anakin Skywalker's destiny [185-109] 15.00
- ❑ Asteroid chase, superimposed on Jango's helmet [185-110] 15.00
- ❑ Bantha Skull [v1e1:149] 20.00
- ❑ Boba Fett 3D 24.00

185-61	185-62	185-63	185-64	185-65
185-66	185-67	185-68	185-69	185-70
185-71	185-72	185-73	185-74	185-75
185-76	185-77	185-78	185-79	185-80

Clothing: Shirts

- Boba Fett applique 15.00
- Boba Fett zippered hooded jerseys, applique (front) with mask and motto (back) 25.00
- Boba Fett, "Let the Hunt Begin" 18.00
- Bounty Hunter, baseball jersey [185-111] 15.00
- C-3PO and R2-D2 [185-112] 15.00
- C-3PO and R2-D2, green neon border [185-113] 15.00
- Celebration III Darth Vader, black [v1e1:149] 30.00
- Celebration III Darth Vader, red [185-114] 30.00
- Chewbacca camouflage 24.00
- Chewbacca, Mommy's Little Monster [v1e1:149] ... 15.00
- Darth Maul "Sith" on green shirt 15.00
- Darth Maul action pose in green glowing ink on black shirt 15.00
- Darth Maul and horizontal pattern stripe on white shirt 15.00
- Darth Maul black spiral tie-dye on red shirt 15.00
- Darth Maul face and horizontal flames 15.00
- Darth Maul green lettering, tattoo pattern all over 15.00
- Darth Maul on black and red diagonal tie-dye 15.00
- Darth Star (crossed sabers Vader and Death Star) on black shirt 15.00
- Darth Vader [v1e1:149] 15.00
- Darth Vader / Anakin Skywalker, baseball jersey [185-115] 15.00
- Darth Vader Anakin Skywalker on dark blue shirt 15.00
- Darth Vader mask above two lighted lightsabers, black shirt 15.00
- Darth Vader mask with metal flames 15.00
- Darth Vader silver helmet, "Darth Vader" on sleeve [185-116] 15.00
- Darth Vader with ignited lightsaber, bursting through shirt 15.00
- Darth Vader with ignited lightsaber, inside hinged collector's tin, exclusive to Kohl's 25.00
- Darth Vader, "Don't push my buttons" [185-117] 15.00
- Darth Vader, "Embrace the Dark Side" 18.00
- Darth Vader, "Menace to Society," kids' sizes only [v1e1:149] 15.00
- Darth Vader, "Never Underestimate the Dark Side" [185-118] 15.00
- Darth Vader, "Revenge" 15.00
- Darth Vader, "Sith" with "Sith" on back 15.00
- Darth Vader, "Your Empire Needs You" [185-119] 20.00
- Darth Vader, classic art, helmet [v1e1:149] 15.00
- Darth Vader, gray with movie scenes [185-120] 15.00
- Death Star Battle art [185-121] 20.00
- Droids, baseball jersey [185-122] 15.00
- Emperor Palpatine [v1e1:150] 20.00
- Empire Strikes Back "The Saga Continues" 20.00
- Empire Strikes Back poster art [v1e1:150] 20.00
- Episode I "line up" 15.00
- Episode I "the Emperor" 15.00
- Episode II with clone trooper [185-123] 15.00
- Episode II with gunship [v1e1:150] 15.00
- Executive Order Sixty-Six [4:98] 20.00
- Imperial cog, white logo on black shirt 15.00
- Jango Fett [185-124] 15.00
- Jango Fett in front of clone trooper army, baseball jersey [185-125] 15.00
- Jango Fett with scene of Jango vs. Obi-Wan [185-126] .. 15.00
- Jar Jar Binks with long tongue on green and blue tie-dye shirt 15.00
- Jedi Starfighter [185-127] 15.00
- Jedi starfighter with picture of Obi-Wan [185-128] ... 15.00
- Jedi, Anakin's Speeder [185-129] 15.00
- Jedi, Yoda, Obi-Wan and Anakin, baseball jersey [185-130] 15.00
- Luke Skywalker Jedi, anime [185-131] 15.00
- Mos Eisley Cantina [185-132] 15.00
- Obi-Wan vs. Jango with movie scenes on back [v1e1:150] 15.00
- Pod race scene in large Star Wars logo on red tie-dye shirt 15.00
- Pod racer on blue and brown tie-dye shirt 15.00
- Princess Leia, "Princess," kids' sizes only [v1e1:150] 15.00
- Queen Amidala on dark blue tie-dye 15.00
- Queen Amidala on pink and red tie-dye 15.00
- R2-D2 and C-3PO caricature art [4:98] 20.00
- Rebel Alliance logo, red on black shirt 15.00
- Return of the Jedi poster art 15.00
- Revenge of the Sith logo 15.00
- Revenge of the Sith movie poster art 15.00
- Sith Happens [185-133] 20.00
- Sith Lord photo on dark blue shirt 15.00
- Sith, Darth Maul on black and red V-neck tie-dye 15.00
- Slave I vs. Jedi Starfighter, cross-fire [185-134] 15.00
- Slave I vs. Jedi Starfighter, pursuit [v1e1:150] 15.00
- Star Wars Death Star Attack [v1e1:151] 15.00
- Star Wars Death Star Trench orange, anime [185-135] .. 15.00
- Star Wars Episode III: Revenge of the Sith Vader lava art [185-136] 15.00
- Star Wars logo on starfield [4:99] 20.00
- Star Wars poster art [185-137] 20.00
- Star Wars, Darth Vader on back [185-138] 18.00
- Star Wars, Luke as X-wing pilot, anime style [185-139] ... 15.00
- Star Wars orange oval on horizontal double-sided lightsaber 15.00
- Star Wars yellow oval 15.00

185-81	185-82	185-83	185-84	185-85
185-86	185-87	185-88	185-89	185-90
185-91	185-92	185-93	185-94	185-95	185-96
185-97	185-98	185-99	185-100	185-101	185-102

Clothing: Shirts

- ❏ The Phantom Menace "Jedi shadow" tie-dye..............15.00
- ❏ The Phantom Menace "new band" on black shirt........15.00
- ❏ The Phantom Menace lightsaber duel in large Star Wars logo 15.00
- ❏ The Phantom Menace space battle in horizontal strip on white shirt 15.00
- ❏ The Phantom Menace space battle in large Star Wars logo on slate shirt 15.00
- ❏ Vader was Framed 15.00
- ❏ Vader's chest box 15.00
- ❏ Wicket, Daddy's Little Ewok [185-140]..............15.00
- ❏ X-Wing battles TIE Fighter above Death Star 15.00
- ❏ X-Wing and TIE Fighters, "Star Wars" on sleeve [185-141]..............15.00
- ❏ X-Wings escape the Death Star, "Star Wars" on sleeve [185-142]..............15.00
- ❏ Yoda block letters, Yoda art in oval, "JEDI MASTER" on dark green shirt..............18.00
- ❏ Yoda, "Meditate On THIS"..............15.00
- ❏ Young Vader, two-tone dyed 15.00

Baby one-piece.
- ❏ Chewbacca, Mommy's Little Monster [v1e1:151]..............15.00
- ❏ Princess Leia [v1e1:151]..............15.00

Revenge of the Sith.
- ❏ Vader helmet in flames b/w [185-143]..............15.00

Tank tops, youth sizes.
- ❏ R2-D2 [185-144]..............15.00

Thin polyester. Front and back printed identically.
- ❏ Droids in front of starfield [185-145] 18.00
- ❏ Jango Fett [185-146] 18.00
- ❏ Naboo starfighters [185-147] 18.00
- ❏ Villains in front of starfield [185-148] 18.00

Hanes
- ❏ 20th Anniversary logo on black sweatshirt 28.00
- ❏ Darth Vader and "Join the Dark Side"..............18.00
- ❏ Darth Vader, "The Empire wants you" on blue shirt..............18.00
- ❏ Darth Vader's head with glow-in-the-dark "X-ray" features on black shirt 18.00
- ❏ "JEDI" in huge lettering with scenes in the letters, on brick red shirt 18.00
- ❏ Rancor on white shirt..............18.00
- ❏ Space battle on black shirt [185-149]..............18.00
- ❏ "Star Wars" metalized oval logo 18.00
- ❏ "Star Wars," Darth Vader, and lightsaber battle on black shirt 18.00

Harley, Inc.
Star Wars designs.
- ❏ Polo shirts 25.00
- ❏ T-shirts 20.00
- ❏ Tank tops 25.00

Hasbro
- ❏ Star Wars Episode III, prerelease convention 65.00

Hi-C
- ❏ Return of the Jedi: T-Shirt premium from Hi-C 45.00

Hot Topic
- ❏ Chewie [v1e1:151]..............18.00
- ❏ I (heart) Darth Vader..............18.00
- ❏ Jabba the Hutt, "Original Gangsta" [185-150]..............18.00
- ❏ Princess Leia caricature [185-151]..............20.00
- ❏ Princess Leia pink toddler long-sleeve [185-152]..............15.00
- ❏ Size Matters Not, toddler size 18.00
- ❏ Speak softly, but carry a big blaster 18.00
- ❏ Star Wars logo x 4 ....18.00
- ❏ Stormtrooper / Jolly Roger [185-153]..............18.00
- ❏ The Force is strong in this one..............18.00
- ❏ Who's Your Daddy, toddler size 18.00
- ❏ Yoda [v1e1:152]..............18.00
- ❏ Yoda, "Judge Me by My Size Do You?"..............18.00
- ❏ Yoda, "Pull My Finger" [185-154]..............18.00

Baby doll style.
- ❏ Artoo, silver trim and highlights [185-155]..............15.00
- ❏ Chewbacca, "I'd Just As Soon Kiss A Wookiee" [185-156]..............20.00
- ❏ Ewok [185-157]..............20.00
- ❏ Luke [185-158]..............20.00
- ❏ Princess Leia, "Somebody Has To Save Our Skins" [185-159]..............20.00
- ❏ Solo [v1e1:152]..............20.00
- ❏ Wicket [185-160]..............20.00

Ringer style t-shirt.
- ❏ Boba Fett 18.00
- ❏ Boba Fett caricature [185-161]..............18.00
- ❏ Chewbacca, "Let the wookiee win" [185-162]..............18.00

 185-103
 185-104
 185-105
 185-106
 185-107
 185-108

 185-109
 185-110
 185-111
 185-112
 185-113

 185-114
 185-115
 185-116
 185-117
 185-118

 185-119
 185-120
 185-121
 185-122
 185-123

Clothing: Shirts

- ❑ Darth Vader classic [185-163] 18.00
- ❑ Imperial AT-AT Walker [v1e1:152] 18.00
- ❑ Stormtrooper caricature [185-164]..........18.00
- ❑ Yoda, "There is no try ... Only do" [185-165]..........18.00
- ❑ Yoda, "Y'all Better Recognize!" [185-166]..........18.00

ILM
Pre-Episode I production crew only, "ILM Dept. of Defense"
- ❑ "Loose Lips Sink Starships" [185-167]..........45.00
- ❑ The Empire is Watching 45.00

In Advance
- ❑ A New Hope style "C" poster art on black shirt [185-168] 15.00
- ❑ Blue Darth Vader helmet and Luke on black shirt, blue Vader and crossed lightsabers on back 15.00
- ❑ C-3PO head fills up orange shirt..........15.00
- ❑ Darth Vader / Funeral Pyre 20.00
- ❑ Darth Vader and "The Galactic Empire Wants You" on gray shirt 15.00
- ❑ Darth Vader and "The Galactic Empire Wants You" on white shirt 15.00
- ❑ Darth Vader and saber and blue window on black shirt 15.00
- ❑ Darth Vader and saber and blue window on gray shirt, long sleeve with Star Wars logo on sleeve 15.00
- ❑ Darth Vader and saber and blue window on white shirt, long sleeve with Star Wars logo on sleeve 15.00
- ❑ Darth Vader and star destroyer and "Join the Empire and See the Universe" on black shirt 15.00
- ❑ Darth Vader helmet fills up black shirt 15.00
- ❑ Darth Vader, 2 stormtroopers, blueprint on black shirt, short sleeve with Imperial emblem on sleeve [185-169] 15.00
- ❑ Darth Vader, Death Star II, Falcon [185-170] 15.00
- ❑ Darth Vader, Death Star II, Falcon, long sleeve 15.00
- ❑ Darth Vader, Death Star II, star destroyer, yellow sun on black shirt (long sleeve) 15.00
- ❑ Darth Vader, fighters, and exploding TIE on black shirt, blue Vader and crossed lightsabers on back..........15.00
- ❑ Darth Vader, fighters, and exploding TIE on black shirt (nothing on back) 15.00
- ❑ Darth Vader, star destroyer, and 2 stormtroopers on dark blue shirt 15.00
- ❑ Droids and twin suns on white shirt..........15.00
- ❑ Droids in orange glow, yellow Star Wars logo on back 15.00
- ❑ Fett head fills up brown shirt 15.00
- ❑ Luke and Yoda and Return of the Jedi logo on gray shirt 15.00
- ❑ Stormtrooper head fills up green shirt 15.00
- ❑ TIEs and X-Wing in trench, XRS logo on back..........15.00
- ❑ TIEs shooting an X-Wing over the Death Star surface on black shirt 15.00
- ❑ Yoda head fills up black shirt..........15.00

Isaac Morris Ltd.
- ❑ Darth Vader hooded sweatshirt, resembles Darth Vader's suit with mesh mask attached to hood..........20.00
- ❑ Death Star surrounded by character faces, navy with white long sleeves 15.00

J E M Sportswear
- ❑ Anakin Skywalker on gray shirt 15.00
- ❑ Darth Maul's eyes / "At last..." 2-sided black shirt 15.00
- ❑ Droid fighters on tie-dyed dark gray shirt..........15.00
- ❑ Jar Jar's head on blue shirt..........15.00
- ❑ Jedi vs. Sith on tie-dyed dark gray shirt 15.00
- ❑ Lightsaber battle on black shirt 15.00
- ❑ Naboo space battle on tie-dyed dark blue shirt 15.00
- ❑ "Star Wars Darth / Maul" 2-sided black shirt 15.00
- ❑ "Star Wars Episode I" Darth Maul eyes on black shirt ..15.00
- ❑ The Phantom Menace characters on black shirt 15.00
- ❑ The Phantom Menace villains on black shirt 15.00

KFC
Episode I: The Phantom Menace.
- ❑ Defeat the Dark Side, green crew shirt [185-171] 15.00

KFC (Australia)
Employee mystery caps, Episode I prerelease. Blue shirt with a question mark and character face.
- ❑ C-3PO [185-172]..........50.00
- ❑ Jar Jar Binks 50.00
- ❑ Queen Amidala 50.00
- ❑ Sebulba [185-173]..........50.00
- ❑ Watto..........50.00

Kids Headquarters
- ❑ Anakin blue knit shirt, short sleeves 15.00
- ❑ Darth Maul button front red with short black sleeves [185-174] 15.00
- ❑ Jedi vs. Sith red [185-175]..........15.00

Clothing: Shirts

- Jedi vs. Sith white with short black sleeves 15.00
- Sith Lord black knit shirt, short sleeves 15.00

Knitwear, Inc.
- Black shirt with Star Wars diagonal gray, Episode I red; Star Wars white embroidered on sleeves 15.00
- Darth Maul "The Darkside" 15.00
- "Episode I Darth Maul The Dark Side" with rubber oval logo on sleeve 15.00
- "Sith Lord" all-over print 15.00

Kortex
- Darth Vader, "May the Force be with you" 25.00

Return of the Jedi designs.
- Baby Ewoks and Wicket, white sleeveless 25.00
- Baby Ewoks, blue sleeveless 25.00
- Baby Ewoks, white tank top 25.00
- Han Solo and Millennium Falcon 25.00
- Luke Skywalker and Stormtrooper 25.00
- R2-D2 and C-3PO 25.00
- Return of the Jedi, white on blue 25.00
- Speeder bike, white with red sleeves 25.00
- Wicket and R2-D2, blue sleeveless 25.00
- Wicket, blue tank top 25.00
- Wicket, white sleeveless 25.00

Lee Sportswear
- Darth Maul black baseball jersey with red striped sleeves [4:100] 15.00
- Darth Maul button-up baseball style [185-176] 15.00
- Darth Maul red baseball jersey with black striped sleeves [185-177] 15.00

- Darth Maul with Sith probe droids 15.00
- Denim, long sleeves, Star Wars over pocket, Qui-Gon, Obi-Wan, and Darth Maul embroidered on back [4:101] 24.00
- Episode I logo, white shirt 15.00
- Episode I, long sleeves, Fan Club exclusive [4:101] 30.00
- Jedi / Sith button-up baseball style [185-178] 15.00
- Jedi vs. Sith, black shirt 15.00
- Star Wars logo (with pictures inside) 15.00
- Star Wars, Qui-Gon, Darth Maul, Obi-Wan [4:101] 15.00

Liquid Blue
- Anakin's Pod Racer [2:382] 18.00
- Asteroid Field, 2-sided [2:382] 18.00
- Boba Fett [2:382] 18.00
- Chewbacca [2:382] 18.00
- Darth Maul 18.00
- Darth Maul Silhouette, 2-sided [2:382] 18.00
- Death Star Battle [2:382] 18.00
- Death Star II [2:382] 18.00
- Droids [2:382] 18.00
- Droids on Tatooine [2:382] 18.00
- Episode I Teaser [2:382] 18.00
- Heroes [2:382] 18.00
- Jabba's Palace [2:382] 18.00
- Jar Jar Binks [2:382] 18.00
- Jedi Council [2:382] 18.00
- Jedi Master [2:382] 18.00
- Lightsaber Duel, 2-sided [2:382] 18.00
- Millennium Falcon [2:382] 18.00
- Mos Espa, 2-sided [2:382] 18.00
- Planet Hoth, 2-sided [2:382] 18.00
- Podracer 18.00

- Podracer canyon 18.00
- Pod Racer with logo [2:382] 18.00
- Queen Amidala [2:382] 18.00
- Sand People [2:382] 18.00
- Sebulba's Pod Racer [2:383] 18.00
- Slave I [2:382] 18.00
- Space Battle, 2-sided [2:382] 18.00
- STAP with Battle Droid [2:382] 18.00
- Star Wars Poster, 2-sided [2:382] 18.00
- Star Wars Space Battle, 2-sided [2:382] 18.00
- Stormtroopers [2:382] 18.00
- Submarine Chase, 2-sided 18.00
- TIE Fighters [2:382] 18.00
- Watto [2:382] 18.00
- Yoda 18.00

LucasArts
- AT-AT blueprint, Rebel Strike 20.00
- Bantha skull sweatshirt, Bounty Hunter 30.00
- Jedi Starfighter, puck wrapped [185-179] 20.00
- Knights of the Old Republic zippered sweatshirt 40.00
- TIE Fighter [185-180] 20.00
- X-Wing polo 35.00

Star Wars Galaxies.
- Concept art 20.00
- Wookiee raging 25.00

Lucasfilm
- Revenge of the Sith hooded sweatshirt 45.00
- Revenge of the Sith T-shirt 20.00
- Revenge of the Sith T-shirt, Hyperspace logo sleeve [185-181] 45.00

185-144   185-145   185-146   185-147   185-148

185-149   185-150   185-151   185-152   185-153

185-154   185-155   185-156   185-157   185-158   185-159

185-160   185-161   185-162   185-163   185-164

Clothing: Shirts

M&M World
- Dark Side character lineup 25.00
- Jedi character lineup 25.00
- Join me and together we can rule the Mpire 25.00
- Storm trooper character lineup 25.00

Mad Engine
- Biker Vader [185-182] 15.00
- Graph Paper Art, white shirt featuring Darth Vader, Boba Fett, R2-D2, youth sizes [185-183] 15.00
- R2-D2 retro study 15.00
- Star Wars distressed logo with X-Wing Fighter 15.00
- Star Wars: The Empire Strikes Back, black art on red shirt, featuring Boba Fett, AT-ATs, Cloud City, youth sizes ... 15.00
- Star Wars: War of Wars all-over print blue 20.00
- Wish You Were Here troopers [185-184] 15.00

Melanie Taylor Kent Ltd.
- Hollywood Blvd. Artwork 15.00

Mexico Collector Convention
2003. Power of the Force style logo.
- Polo 35.00
- T-shirt 25.00
- T-shirt, staff 95.00

Mighty Fine
8-bit / pixel.
- Characters, long-sleeve charcoal gray shirt featuring Darth Vader, Boba Fett, and Stormtrooper 15.00
- Classic logo 15.00
- Death Star 15.00
- Millennium Falcon, black [185-185] 15.00

Mondragon
Die Ruckkehr der Jedi-Ritter.
- C-3PO, R2-D2, Wicket with star background 25.00
- Vader's helmet and the duel 25.00
- Woklings 25.00

MSD International
L'Empire Contre-Attaque.
- C-3PO and R2-D2 .... 30.00
- Yoda 30.00

Le Retour Du Jedi.
- Red letters on cream 20.00
- Red letters on white 20.00

Star Wars.
- Star Wars gray letters with red outline 15.00
- Star Wars logo with red and silver letters 15.00

Nick Jr.
- Clone Wars [185-186] 25.00

NTD Apparel Inc. (UK)
- Jabba the Hutt Presents: Podracing [185-187] 15.00

Patty Marsh Productions
- Ewoks "Color-Me" 25.00

Pepsi Cola
- Episode I, polo [185-188] 25.00

Perfect Fit
- C-3PO, Empire Strikes Back 25.00

Pizza Hut (Australia)
Employee mystery caps, Episode I prerelease. Red shirt with a question mark and character face.
- C-3PO [185-189] 50.00
- Jar Jar Binks 50.00
- Queen Amidala 50.00
- Sebulba [185-190] 50.00
- Watto 50.00

Playthings
- Han, Chewbacca, Luke, Leia 15.00

Primal Wear
Cycling jerseys.
- A New Hope 80.00
- Empire Strikes Back 80.00
- Return of the Jedi 80.00
- Star Wars Logo 80.00
- Star Wars Stormtrooper 80.00

Reknown
- C-3PO and R2-D2, angled background 15.00
- C-3PO and R2-D2, round background 15.00
- Hildebrandt Bros. Art 15.00
- Star Wars logo 15.00

Royal Prints
- Ironed-on decal on 100% cotton shirt, sealed in poly bag with header [185-191] 35.00

Seio Insatsu Co.
- Return of the Jedi designs 20.00

157

Clothing: Shirts

 185-184
 185-185
 185-186
 185-187
 185-188

 185-189
 185-190
 185-191
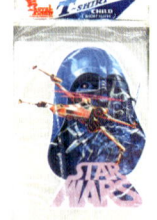 185-191
 185-192
 185-193

 185-194
 185-195
 185-196
 185-197
 185-198
 185-199

Shirt.Woot
- ❏ Tin Man and C-3PO 25.00

Star Wars Celebration IV
- ❏ Volunteer, orange 35.00
- ❏ Yoda, "Do or Do Not, There is No Try" 15.00

Star Wars Celebration V
- ❏ Boba Fett jet ski, women's 25.00
- ❏ Dark Side Lanes bowling shirt 60.00
- ❏ Darth Vader aloha shirt 80.00
- ❏ Han, "I know," men's 25.00

- ❏ I (heart) Scoundrels, women's 25.00
- ❏ I am not a committee, women's 25.00
- ❏ Leia, "I love you," women's 25.00
- ❏ Tauntaun logo, polo 40.00

Star Wars Celebration VI
- ❏ Admiral Ackbar 2012 Election T-shirt [185-192] 30.00
- ❏ Biker Scout Polo Shirt 30.00
- ❏ Bossk Bail Bonds T-shirt 30.00
- ❏ Celebration VI Logo Shirt 30.00
- ❏ Crew, blue 35.00
- ❏ Crew, lime green 35.00

- ❏ Cup O' Jawa T-shirt 30.00
- ❏ Darth Maul Tiki T-shirt 30.00
- ❏ Darth Vader Celebration VI Logo T-shirt 30.00
- ❏ Galactic Games T-shirt 30.00
- ❏ How to Draw R2-D2 T-shirt 30.00
- ❏ Jabba's Palace Maintenance Workman Shirt 60.00
- ❏ Jedi Knight badge exclusive 20.00
- ❏ Join the Party T-shirt 30.00
- ❏ Kids' Chewbacca "Laugh It Up, Fuzzball" T-shirt 20.00
- ❏ Kids' Star Wars Alphabet T-shirt Bounty Hunters 20.00
- ❏ Kids' Star Wars Alphabet T-shirt Princess Leia 20.00
- ❏ Lightsaber Dueling Association 30.00

 186-01
 186-02
 186-03
 186-04
 186-05

186-06 186-07 186-08 186-09 186-10 186-11 186-12

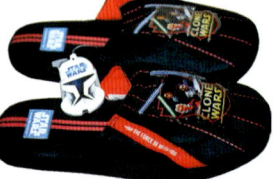

186-13 186-14 186-15 186-16 186-17 186-18

Clothing: Shoes, Sandals, and Slippers

- ❏ Luke Skywalker Celebration VI Logo T-shirt 30.00
- ❏ Mace Windu Celebration VI Logo T-shirt 30.00
- ❏ Men's "I Love You" T-shirt................................30.00
- ❏ Men's and Women's' "I Love You" T-shirt pair 50.00
- ❏ Mos Eisley Spaceport T-shirt.............................30.00
- ❏ Palpatine / Vader 2012 Election T-shirt..................30.00
- ❏ Retro Female Stormtrooper................................30.00
- ❏ Return of the Jedi Concept Art T-shirt...................30.00
- ❏ Star Wars Tiki Hawaiian shirt............................60.00
- ❏ Star Wars Tiki kids' T-shirt.............................20.00
- ❏ Tatooine Stamp Art T-shirt...............................30.00
- ❏ The Droids You're Looking For T-shirt....................30.00
- ❏ TIE Fighter tie-dye T-shirt..............................30.00
- ❏ Toddler Star Wars Alphabet T-shirt.......................20.00
- ❏ VaderAde T-shirt...30.00
- ❏ Women's "I Know" T-shirt.................................30.00
- ❏ Women's Alderaan Stamp Art...............................30.00
- ❏ Women's Galactic Princess T-shirt........................30.00
- ❏ Women's Hula Leia Tiki T-shirt...........................30.00
- ❏ Women's Retro Han Solo T-shirt...........................30.00
- ❏ Women's Star Wars Alphabet T-shirt.......................30.00

Sunrise Identity
Exclusive to Star Wars Celebration III.
- ❏ Epic duel, green with orange trim........................25.00
- ❏ Vader image and Celebration III on back 65.00
- ❏ Yoda, Jedi Master, silhouette hooded jersey 65.00

Taco Bell
- ❏ "Play The Feel The Force Game" 35.00

Tee Fury
- ❏ Kessel Fun-Run [185-193] 15.00

The Duck Co.
Atlanta Aquarium
- ❏ "Luke, I am Your Otter!" 25.00

The LEGO Group
- ❏ "Don't get cocky," Han Solo..............................25.00
- ❏ Episode II mini figures on black [185-194]...............35.00
- ❏ Episode II: Attack of the Clones, Republic gunship 26.00
- ❏ "Let the Wookiee Win" 25.00
- ❏ "Now I Am The Master," Obi-Wan and Darth Vader 25.00
- ❏ Yoda, Celebration II exhibitor [185-195].................75.00

LEGO Star Wars characters.
- ❏ Chewbacca, "Let the Wookiee Win!"........................25.00
- ❏ Han Solo, "Don't get cocky" 25.00
- ❏ Luke Skywalker, "I am a Jedi"............................25.00
- ❏ Obi-Wan and Vader, "Now I am the Master" 25.00

Thunder Creek
- ❏ I did it all for the Wookiee 15.00
- ❏ Sith Happens 15.00

Thyrring Agency
- ❏ Return of the Jedi designs 18.00

Top Textiles Ltd.
Tank tops, youth sizes.
- ❏ Mos Espa Arena [v1e1:153]................................15.00

Tour Champ
- ❏ Jawas, Star Wars Galaxy art [185-196] 15.00

Tsurumoto Room Co.
- ❏ Star Wars designs, silk screened.........................35.00

Union Underwear Co.
Return of the Jedi.
- ❏ Darth Vader & Luke Skywalker, The Knits tag [185-197]...25.00
- ❏ Han and Leia on Endor, Screen Stars tag [185-198] 25.00
- ❏ Princess Leia, Han Solo, Luke Skywalker, Screen Stars tag [185-199]...25.00

Uniprints
- ❏ Chewbacca 15.00
- ❏ Darth Vader 15.00
- ❏ Empire Strikes Back: Logo 15.00
- ❏ Empire Strikes Back: Probe Droid 15.00
- ❏ Empire Strikes Back: Tauntaun 15.00
- ❏ Empire Strikes Back: X-Wing Fighter 15.00
- ❏ Empire Strikes Back: Yoda 15.00
- ❏ Ewoks with Return of the Jedi logo 15.00
- ❏ Han Solo 15.00
- ❏ Luke Skywalker 15.00
- ❏ Millennium Falcon 15.00
- ❏ Return of the Jedi: C-3PO and R2-D2 ....15.00
- ❏ Return of the Jedi: Stormtrooper and AT-ST Vehicle 15.00
- ❏ Star Wars Cast, main characters 15.00
- ❏ Star Wars: Logo 15.00
- ❏ Star Wars: TIE Fighter 15.00
- ❏ Star Wars: X-Wing Fighter 15.00
- ❏ Wicket on Vine 15.00
- ❏ Wicket the Ewok 15.00
- ❏ Wicket W. Warrick 15.00

We Love Fine
Tank tops, adult sizes.
- ❏ Chewbacca 30.00
- ❏ R2-D2 ....30.00

Wonder Works
- ❏ Imperial Forces—Japanese Style Darth Vader and Stormtroopers 30.00

Wright and Co.
Return of the Jedi designs.
- ❏ Black logo on white 20.00
- ❏ Ewoks 20.00
- ❏ Logo, Darth Vader, and red circle on white 20.00
- ❏ Speeder bike 20.00
- ❏ Stormtrooper 20.00
- ❏ Yoda 20.00

Yagi Shoten Co.
- ❏ Darth Vader 25.00
- ❏ Empire Strikes Back logo 25.00
- ❏ Millennium Falcon 25.00

Clothing: Shoes, Sandals, and Slippers
Continued in Volume 3, Page 156

Flip flops.
- ❏ Anakin Skywalker [186-01]................................20.00
- ❏ X-Wing / TIE Fighter, vintage [186-02]...................95.00

Slippers.
- ❏ Anakin Skywalker and Sebulba [186-03] 20.00
- ❏ Darth Maul [186-04] 20.00
- ❏ Darth Maul, Tatooine [186-05] 20.00

(Australia)
- ❏ Yoda slippers [186-06]...................................20.00

(Japan)
- ❏ Star Wars slippers [186-07] 150.00

(UK)
- ❏ Vader with Velcro and buckles, sandals [186-08] 20.00

Slippers.
- ❏ Darth Vader, gray and black [v1e1:154] 20.00
- ❏ Darth Vader, pink and black [186-09] 20.00
- ❏ R2-D2 [186-10] 20.00

Slippers. Clone Wars.
- ❏ Anakin Skywalker [186-11] 15.00
- ❏ Anakin, Obi-Wan, Yoda [186-12] 15.00
- ❏ Anakin, Obi-Wan, Yoda, "May the Force be with you" [186-13] 15.00

186-19

186-20

186-21

186-22

186-23

186-24

186-25

186-26

186-27

186-28

186-29

186-30

Clothing: Shoes, Sandals, and Slippers

186-31   186-32   186-33   186-34   186-35   186-36

❑ Master Yoda [186-14]......................................15.00
❑ Obi-Wan Kenobi [186-15].............................15.00
❑ Red and black flat [186-16].........................20.00
❑ Red and black with heel [186-17].................20.00

Buster Brown and Co.
❑ Anakin Skywalker / Darth Vader, black and blue, lace-less elastic [186-18]................................20.00
❑ Anakin Skywalker / Darth Vader, white and blue, Velcro fasteners [186-19]................................20.00
❑ Anakin Skywalker open heel [186-20]..............20.00
❑ Anakin Skywalker, destiny black-and-silver [186-21].......15.00
❑ Anakin Skywalker, destiny white [186-22].........20.00
❑ Clone trooper [186-23]................................15.00
❑ Clone trooper foil [186-24]..........................15.00
❑ Darth Vader with lightsaber [186-25]..............15.00
❑ Darth Vader with lightsaber [186-26]..............15.00
❑ Darth Vader, helmet only, Velcro [v1e1-154].....15.00
❑ Darth Vader, helmet with flames, white [186-27]....20.00
❑ Droids: C-3PO and R2-D2, flashes [186-28]......15.00
❑ Yoda, saber flashes [186-29]........................15.00

Sandals.
❑ Anakin Skywalker / Darth Vader [186-30].......20.00
❑ Darth Vader, flames art [186-31].................20.00
❑ Darth Vader, helmet art [186-32]................20.00
❑ Droids sandals, blue..................................20.00
❑ Jedi Starfighter [186-33]............................20.00
❑ Star Wars logo with Imperial logo on strap [186-34]......20.00

Slippers.
❑ Anakin's Destiny [186-35]...........................20.00
❑ Darth Vader with lightsaber, black and red....20.00
❑ Jango Fett, flashing red LEDs [186-36].........20.00
❑ Vader, gray..20.00

Clarks of England (UK)
❑ C-3PO..110.00
❑ Chewbacca..110.00
❑ Darth Vader [186-37]...............................110.00
❑ Darth Vader Lives....................................110.00
❑ Luke Skywalker.......................................110.00
❑ "May the Force be with you"....................110.00
❑ Princess Leia..125.00
❑ R2-D2..110.00
❑ Reflective [186-38]...................................100.00
❑ Reflective with b/w stripes [186-39]............100.00
❑ Stormtrooper..125.00
❑ TIE Fighter..110.00
❑ Tusken Raider..150.00

Sandals.
❑ Cosmic Rambler......................................100.00
❑ Landspeeder..120.00
❑ Solar Racer..100.00
❑ Star Rider..100.00

Slippers.
❑ Star Wars logo..120.00

Comic Images
Slippers with sculpted head on toe of slippers.
❑ Chewbacca..35.00
❑ Darth Vader [186-40]................................20.00
❑ Yoda..20.00

Step-in slippers.
❑ Boba Fett [186-41]...................................20.00
❑ Darth Vader [186-42]................................20.00
❑ Yoda [186-43]...20.00

Toddler slippers.
❑ Chewbacca [186-44].................................15.00
❑ Darth Vader [186-45]................................15.00
❑ Yoda [186-46]...15.00

Converse
❑ Stormtrooper punch-out flip-flops [186-47]....75.00

Footzee
❑ C-3PO and R2-D2 slippers [186-48]..............35.00

Handcraft Mfg. Corp.
Slipper socks.
❑ Darth Vader mukluks................................45.00

Kid Nation
❑ Anakin Skywalker pod racing white x-trainer......20.00
❑ Anakin Skywalker pod racing white, Velcro........20.00

186-37   186-38   186-39   186-40   186-41   186-42

186-43   186-44   186-45   186-46   186-47   186-48   186-49

186-50   186-51   186-52   186-53

     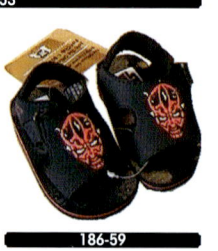

186-54   186-55   186-56   186-57   186-58   186-59

Clothing: Sleepwear

186-60

186-61

186-62

186-63

186-64

186-65

186-66   186-67   186-68

186-69

186-70

186-71

186-72

- Anakin Skywalker water shoes 20.00
- Anakin Skywalker water shoes red/blue/black [186-49]..20.00
- Bespin gantry multi-motion image, black 2-strap Velcro, court shoes 20.00
- Darth Maul "The Dark Side" athletic, black with white strings 20.00
- Darth Maul athletic black/silver/blue 20.00
- Darth Maul black hiker with blue trim [186-50] 20.00
- Darth Maul black x-trainer with white and silver trim [186-51] 20.00
- Darth Maul black/silver/blue 20.00
- Darth Maul tennis with black and red sole and red design inside [186-52] 20.00
- Darth Vader and his TIE Fighter, white/blue/black high tops, Velcro [186-53] 20.00
- Darth Vader repeating pattern, black upper / white under, slip-on shoes 20.00
- Darth Vader with Imperial cog hiking boot, black 20.00
- Darth Vader with Imperial cog on toe, black shoes, Velcro 20.00
- Darth Vader, black shoes, Velcro [186-54] 20.00
- Episode I logo on black-and-gray suede court shoe ...20.00
- Pod Racing, white/blue/green 20.00
- Star Wars canvas sneakers, black/white 20.00
- Stormtrooper, black below trooper, white shoes, Velcro 20.00
- Stormtrooper, white shoes, strings [v1e1:155] 20.00
- Stormtrooper, white shoes, Velcro 20.00

Sandals.
- Anakin Skywalker heavy sandals, dark tan 15.00
- Anakin Skywalker sandals, blue [186-55] 15.00
- Anakin Skywalker, slip-ons [186-56] 15.00
- Darth Maul black sport sandal [186-57] 15.00
- Darth Maul face-bottom sandals [186-58] 15.00
- Darth Maul flip-flops, black 15.00
- Darth Maul heavy sandals, black/red [186-59] 15.00
- Darth Vader, Death Star [186-60] 15.00
- Droids sandals, blue and silver, elastic back [186-61] 15.00
- Podracing black sport sandal 15.00

Slippers with sculpted head on toe of slippers.
- Chewbacca [186-62] 40.00
- Darth Maul [186-63] 25.00
- Jar Jar Binks [186-64] 35.00

Slippers.
- Darth Vader, gray 15.00
- Naboo fighter [186-65] 15.00
- Pod Racing gray, Velcro 15.00
- R2-D2 [186-66] 15.00

Marks and Spencer (UK)
Slippers, adult sizes.
- C-3PO / R2-D2 lenticular [186-67] 45.00

Stride Rite
- Captain Rex (side) 30.00
- Darth Maul sandals 30.00
- R2-D2 / Star Wars slip-ons, toddler sizes [186-68] 30.00

Slipper socks.
- C-3PO and R2-D2 [186-69] 35.00
- Darth Vader [186-70] 35.00
- Wicket the Ewok [186-71] 35.00
- Yoda [186-72] 35.00

Vintage slippers.
- Darth Vader 75.00
- Ewoks 75.00

Vintage.
- C-3PO and R2-D2 ....50.00
- Darth Vader 50.00
- Ewoks [4:103] 50.00
- Millennium Falcon 65.00
- X-Wing Fighter [4:103] 65.00

Clothing: Sleepwear
Continued in Volume 3, Page 144

- C-3PO with droids background and pants [187-01] 20.00
- Darth Vader, Snow troopers, AT-AT's, 2-piece red with black [187-02] 20.00
- Jar Jar Binks [187-03] 20.00
- Jar Jar Binks in Naboo swamp [v1e1:142] 20.00
- Jar Jar, 1-piece sleeper [187-04] 20.00
- Jedi, 2-piece [v1e1:142] 20.00

Clone Wars.
- Anakin, Obi-Wan, Yoda, Clones [187-05] 20.00
- Anakin, Obi-Wan, Yoda, Jedi [187-06] 20.00
- Obi-Wan, Anakin, Yoda, long sleeves, black and blue [187-07] 20.00
- Obi-Wan, Anakin, Yoda, Clones, "Force, Power, Strength," green and black [187-08] 20.00
- Obi-Wan, Rex, Yoda, Anakin [187-09] 20.00

Episode III: Revenge of the Sith.
- Darth Vader / Revenge [187-10] 25.00
- Star Wars Jedi [187-11] 25.00
- Star Wars Revenge of the Sith [187-12] 25.00

LEGO Star Wars.
- Anakin Skywalker [187-13] 25.00

187-01

187-02

187-03

187-04

187-05

187-06

187-07

187-08

187-09

187-10

187-11

187-12

187-13

187-14

Clothing: Sleepwear

187-15 187-16 187-17 187-18 187-19 187-20

187-21 187-22 187-23 187-24 187-25 187-26 187-27 187-28

187-29 187-30 187-31 187-32 187-33 187-34 187-35 187-36

- ❏ Anakin Skywalker, Clone Wars / Darth Vader, Star Wars; red and black 15.00
- ❏ Classic characters sleep pants [187-14] 15.00
- ❏ Clone Wars, gray flannel with Anakin, Yoda, and R2-D2 [187-15] 18.00
- ❏ Darth Vader and Stormtroopers pajama pants, black fleece, exclusive to Target 18.00
- ❏ Darth Vader and TIE Advanced [187-16] 15.00
- ❏ Darth Vader, Han Solo, Luke Skywalker [187-17] 18.00
- ❏ Luke, Darth Vader, Millennium Falcon [187-18] 18.00
- ❏ Sleep set, 2-piece, Darth Vader red shirt, gray pants, exclusive to Target [187-19] 17.00

(Germany)
Pyjamas.
- ❏ Savage [187-20] 24.00

(UK)
- ❏ Clone Wars, 2-piece, blue [187-21] 20.00
- ❏ Clone Wars, gray character top with black sleeves 15.00

American Marketing Enterprises, Inc.
- ❏ Anakin Skywalker with Vader background, includes cape [187-22] 18.00
- ❏ Jango Fett [187-23] 18.00
- ❏ Jedi Starfighter [187-24] 18.00
- ❏ LEGO Star Wars [187-25] 15.00
- ❏ LEGO Star Wars, Rebel Alliance 15.00

2-piece sleep wear sets.
- ❏ Darth Vader and "Vader" 25.00
- ❏ "May the Force be with you" 15.00

LEGO Star Wars.
- ❏ A Long Time Ago, Stormtrooper, Darth Vader, Emperor, Death Star, TIE Fighters 15.00
- ❏ Classic heroes, sky blue [187-26] 15.00

Big Dog
- ❏ Empire Bites Back [4-93] 20.00
- ❏ Return of the Dogi [4-93] 20.00

Bing Harris Sargood
- ❏ Return of the Jedi 20.00

Briefly Stated
Lounge pants.
- ❏ Something, Something, Something, Dark Side [187-27] ...18.00
- ❏ Star Wars [187-28] 18.00
- ❏ Star Wars / Darth Vader, black plush with white Star Wars logo and Vader helmets [187-29] 18.00

Harley, Inc.
- ❏ Star Wars 20.00

Jumpin Jammerz
Adult footed pajamas.
- ❏ Dark Side 65.00
- ❏ Good Guys 65.00
- ❏ Space Ships 65.00

Long Eddies
- ❏ Anakin Skywalker, long sleeves and legs [187-30] 20.00
- ❏ Darth Vader and Luke Skywalker [4-93] 20.00
- ❏ Jedi vs. Sith, long sleeves and legs [187-31] 20.00

Marks and Spencer (UK)
- ❏ Star Wars 20.00

PCA Apparel
- ❏ Darth Vader with Velcro-attaching cape 20.00
- ❏ Jedi vs. Sith white T-shirt tops with blue shorts 20.00
- ❏ Lightsaber duel T-shirt tops with black shorts 20.00
- ❏ STAPs and battle droids button front 20.00

Penshiel
Empire Strikes Back designs.
- ❏ Darth Vader and Luke 20.00
- ❏ Image collage 20.00

Return of the Jedi designs.
- ❏ Darth Vader, Jabba the Hutt, and Luke 20.00
- ❏ Image Collage 20.00

Penshield Ltd.
- ❏ Empire Strikes Back, nightgown 35.00

Reknown
- ❏ Star Wars 20.00

Webundies
Lounge pants.
- ❏ Darth Vader / Death Star [187-32] 25.00
- ❏ LEGO Star Wars [187-33] 25.00

Wilker Bros.
- ❏ Admiral Ackbar 45.00
- ❏ Baby Ewoks 45.00
- ❏ Biker Scouts 45.00
- ❏ Boba Fett 45.00
- ❏ Boba Fett and Darth Vader 45.00
- ❏ Boba Fett, C-3PO, Chewbacca, and R2-D2 ....45.00
- ❏ C-3PO and Darth Vader 45.00
- ❏ C-3PO and Ewoks 45.00
- ❏ C-3PO and Luke Skywalker 45.00
- ❏ C-3PO and R2-D2 ....45.00
- ❏ C-3PO, R2-D2, and X-Wing 45.00
- ❏ C-3PO, R2-D2, and Chewbacca [187-34] 45.00
- ❏ C-3PO, R2-D2, and Emperor's guards 45.00
- ❏ Cantina Band 45.00
- ❏ Chewbacca 45.00
- ❏ Chewbacca and Millennium Falcon 45.00
- ❏ Darth Vader 45.00
- ❏ Darth Vader and Death Star 45.00
- ❏ Darth Vader and Emperor's guards 45.00
- ❏ Darth Vader and Luke Skywalker 45.00
- ❏ "Darth Vader Lives" 45.00
- ❏ Droopy McCool 45.00
- ❏ Ewoks in Village 45.00
- ❏ Gamorrean Guards 45.00
- ❏ Han Solo and Chewbacca [187-35] 45.00
- ❏ Han Solo and Darth Vader 45.00
- ❏ Jabba the Hutt 45.00
- ❏ Jabba the Hutt and Bib Fortuna 45.00
- ❏ Jabba the Hutt and Boba Fett 45.00
- ❏ Latara 45.00
- ❏ Luke Skywalker and Princess Leia 45.00
- ❏ Luke Skywalker on Tauntaun [187-36] 45.00
- ❏ Max Rebo 45.00
- ❏ Paploo on Speeder Bike 45.00
- ❏ Princess Kneesaa 45.00
- ❏ Princess Kneesaa on swing 45.00
- ❏ Princess Kneesaa skipping rope 45.00
- ❏ Stormtrooper 45.00
- ❏ Stormtrooper and R2-D2 ....45.00

Clothing: Socks and Tights

- Wicket and Princess Kneesaa in bush 45.00
- Wicket and Princess Kneesaa on skateboard 45.00
- Wicket and Princess Kneesaa on teeter-totter 45.00
- Wicket and Princess Kneesaa on vine 45.00
- Wicket and Princess Kneesaa playing instruments 45.00
- Wicket and Princess Kneesaa tug-of-war 45.00
- Wicket and Princess Kneesaa with flowers 45.00
- Wicket and R2-D2 .... 45.00
- Wicket in basket 45.00
- Wicket on vine 45.00
- Wicket the Ewok 45.00
- Wicket with balloons 45.00
- Wicket with butterfly net 45.00
- Wicket with walking stick 45.00
- Wiley the Ewok 45.00
- Yoda 45.00
- Yoda and Luke Skywalker 45.00

Nightgowns.
- Darth Vader 50.00
- Darth Vader and Death Star 50.00
- Darth Vader and Luke Skywalker 50.00
- Luke Skywalker and Princess Leia 50.00
- Luke Skywalker and Yoda 50.00
- Princess Kneesaa 50.00
- R2-D2 and C-3PO 50.00
- R2-D2, C-3PO and Starfield 50.00
- Yoda 50.00

Clothing: Socks and Tights
Continued in Volume 3, Page 159

- R2-D2 [188-01] 10.00
- R2-D2 [188-02] 10.00

Darth Vader header card.
- Darth Vader [188-03] 10.00

Darth Vader Spanish header card. Star Wars.
- Darth Vader [188-04] 10.00
- Darth Vader, color [188-05] 10.00
- X-Wings [188-06] 12.00

Episode III: Revenge of the Sith, ankle length.
- Epic duel [188-07] 10.00

Episode I header card.
- The Dark Side, Darth Maul [188-08] 15.00

(Japan)
- R2-D2 character socks, image split between socks 10.00

163

Clothing: Socks and Tights

(UK)
- ❏ Vader [188-09] 10.00

Clone header card.
- ❏ 2-pack: Yoda—The Clone Wars and Anakin—Jedi [188-10] 20.00
- ❏ 2-pack: Yoda—The Clone Wars and Captain Rex—Courage 20.00
- ❏ Anakin—The Clone Wars [188-11] 10.00
- ❏ Yoda—Jedi Master [188-12] 10.00

Clone Wars 3D header card.
- ❏ 3-Pack: Darth Vader, TIE Fighter, The Force 25.00

Clone Wars header card.
- ❏ Anakin, silhouette [188-13] 12.00
- ❏ Clone Wars [188-14] 12.00
- ❏ Jedi Knight [188-15] 12.00

R2-D2 header card.
- ❏ C-3PO [188-16] 15.00
- ❏ Obi-Wan Kenobi [188-17] 15.00
- ❏ Padmé Amidala [188-18] 15.00
- ❏ Yoda [188-19] 15.00

American Supply
- ❏ Star Wars designs 15.00

British Home Stores
- ❏ Socks and Mug Set [188-20] 25.00

Charleston Hosiery
Empire Strikes Back.
- ❏ Boba Fett 45.00
- ❏ C-3PO [188-21] 45.00
- ❏ Darth Vader [188-22] 45.00
- ❏ R2-D2 [188-23] 45.00
- ❏ Snowspeeder [188-24] 45.00
- ❏ Stormtrooper [188-25] 45.00
- ❏ Yoda 45.00

Return of the Jedi.
- ❏ C-3PO and R2-D2 [188-26] 45.00
- ❏ Darth Vader 45.00
- ❏ Gamorrean Guard 45.00
- ❏ Jabba the Hutt [188-27] 45.00
- ❏ Princess Kneesaa [188-28] 45.00
- ❏ Wicket 45.00
- ❏ Wicket the Ewok swinging on vine 45.00
- ❏ Wicket the Ewok swinging on vine, long 45.00
- ❏ Wicket the Ewok, black top and yellow stripe ... 45.00
- ❏ Wicket the Ewok, green top and yellow stripe [188-29] 45.00
- ❏ Wicket the Ewok, orange top and black stripe [188-30] .. 45.00
- ❏ Wicket the Ewok, plain white 45.00
- ❏ Wicket the Ewok, red top and black stripe [188-31] 45.00

Star Wars knee socks.
- ❏ Chewbacca, 2-line logo, exclusive to KMart [188-32] 50.00
- ❏ Darth Vader, 2-line logo, exclusive to KMart [188-33] 50.00
- ❏ Space Battle [188-34] 50.00

Star Wars.
- ❏ C-3PO [188-35] 45.00
- ❏ Chewbacca [188-36] 45.00
- ❏ Darth Vader [188-37] 45.00
- ❏ R2-D2 [188-38] 45.00
- ❏ Space Battle [188-39] 45.00

Coast
- ❏ Battle Droid [188-40] 15.00
- ❏ Darth Maul [188-41] 15.00
- ❏ Obi-Wan Kenobi [188-42] 15.00
- ❏ Qui-Gon Jinn [188-43] 15.00

Doobalo S.A. de C.V. (Mexico)
- ❏ C-3PO and R2-D2 [188-44] 10.00
- ❏ Darth Vader [188-45] 10.00
- ❏ Obi-Wan Kenobi and Anakin Skywalker [188-46] 10.00
- ❏ R2-D2 [188-47] 10.00

Essentials
- ❏ Character freeze mug and sock set [188-48] 25.00
- ❏ Star Wars—X-Wing [188-49] 15.00

Essentials (UK)
- ❏ Jedi [188-50] 10.00
- ❏ R2-D2 [188-51] 10.00
- ❏ Star Wars logo [188-52] 10.00
- ❏ Vader [188-53] 10.00
- ❏ Vader (art) 10.00

George Man (UK)
- ❏ Qui-Gon Jinn [188-54] 12.00

Clothing: Socks and Tights

H and M (UK)
- R2-D2 / Star Wars [188-55] 10.00
- Yoda [188-56] 10.00

Handcraft Mfg. Corp.
- Darth Maul, Jedi duel pose [188-57] 10.00
- Darth Maul, lightsaber ignited on white background [188-58] 10.00
- Darth Maul, Sith Lord [188-59] 10.00
- Darth Maul, Tatooine pose [188-60] 10.00
- Jar Jar, face above Star Wars logo [188-61] 10.00
- Jar Jar, walking [188-62] 10.00
- Stormtrooper, "Support Our Troops" [188-63] 10.00
- Story Socks, Battle above Naboo [188-64] 10.00

High Point Knitting, Inc.
- Anakin [188-65] 10.00
- Anakin / Darth Vader [188-66] 10.00
- Darth Vader [188-67] 10.00
- Vader 10.00
- Yoda [188-68] 10.00

Clone Wars.
- Yoda, dark side 10.00
- Yoda, light side [188-69] 10.00

HYP
2-packs, crew socks.
- Darth Vader / Yoda [188-70] 15.00

2-packs, men's socks.
- Boba Fett Wanted / Mandalorian emblem [188-71] 12.00
- Darth Vader / stormtrooper helmets [188-72] 12.00
- Yoda / R2-D2 [188-73] 12.00

Junior socks.
- 2-pack: "I (heart) Star Wars" / "I (heart) Star Wars" 12.00
- 2-pack: Yoda: "Jedi Master" / "Jedi Master" [188-74] 12.00
- Artoo Detoo 12.00
- Darth Vader: "Join the Dark Side" [188-75] 10.00
- Imperial logo, silver on black [188-76] 10.00
- Rebel Alliance symbol, gold on pink [188-77] 10.00

Men's socks.
- Boba Fett top of foot [188-78] 10.00

- Darth Vader, "I Want you for the Dark Side" [188-79] 10.00
- Darth Vader, "I Want You for the Dark Side," alt [188-80] ..10.00
- Darth Vader, "World's Greatest Dad" [188-81] 10.00
- Rebel Leader [188-82] 10.00
- Stormtrooper [188-83] 10.00
- Stormtrooper skull and crossbones [188-84] 10.00
- Yoda: "Jedi Master" [188-85] 10.00

Junk Food
- 3-pack crew socks [188-86] 25.00

Ladybird (UK)
- 2-pack: Obi-Wan and Anakin Jedi Knight [188-87] 15.00

Glow-in-the-dark.
- Clone trooper [188-88] 10.00
- Darth Vader [188-89] 10.00
- Darth Vader [188-90] 10.00
- Evil Vader [188-91] 10.00
- Jedi [188-92] 10.00
- Star Wars logo [188-93] 10.00

Marks and Spencer (UK)
Classic trilogy.
- C-3PO [188-94] 10.00
- R2-D2 [188-95] 10.00

Clone Wars.
- C-3PO, R2-D2, Star Wars [188-96] 15.00

Episode I.
- 2-pack: Star Wars logo, The Dark Side [188-97] ..20.00
- Darth Maul [188-98] 10.00
- Star Wars logo [188-99] 10.00
- The Dark Side [188-100] 10.00

Master Footwear
- Ewoks designs 18.00

Next Retail Ltd. (UK)
- C-3PO and R2-D2 [188-101] 12.00

LEGO.
- 3-Pack: Luke Skywalker Jr. Jedi, Yoda Courage, Darth Vader Power of the Dark Side [188-102] 20.00

Planet Sox
Toddler and children's sizes.
- Boba Fett Bounty Hunter, exclusive to Target [188-103] ...8.00
- Chewbacca, exclusive to Target [188-104] 8.00
- Clone trooper [188-105] 8.00
- Darth Vader black and red, exclusive to Target [188-106] ..8.00
- Darth Vader cog, exclusive to Target [188-107] 8.00
- Darth Vader flames [188-108] 8.00
- Darth Vader gray, black, and red [188-109] 8.00
- Darth Vader Sith [188-110] 8.00
- Darth Vader sunrise [188-111] 8.00
- Darth Vader, helmet, exclusive to Target [188-112] 8.00
- Jedi [188-113] 8.00
- R2-D2, exclusive to Target [188-114] 8.00
- Yoda [188-115] 8.00
- Yoda Jedi Master [188-116] 8.00
- Yoda The Force [188-117] 8.00
- Yoda, white background, exclusive to Target [188-118] ...8.00

Planet Sox (UK)
- Darth Vader sunrise, children's [188-119] 8.00

Primal Wear
- Star Wars logo 15.00

Psycho Bunny
- Star Wars, gray and pink [188-120] 30.00
- Star Wars, navy and gray [188-121] 30.00

Quality Socks
- Anakin Skywalker [188-122] 10.00
- C-3PO [188-123] 10.00
- Darth Maul [188-124] 10.00
- Jar Jar Binks [188-125] 10.00
- R2-D2 [188-126] 10.00

Sainsbury (UK)
Episode I: The Phantom Menace.
- Anakin Skywalker, Podracer [188-127] 10.00

Small Planet Co. Ltd. (Japan)
- Darth Vader, on black 10.00
- Darth Vader, on white 10.00
- R2-D2 ....10.00
- R2-D2 / C-3PO 10.00

Clothing: Socks and Tights

      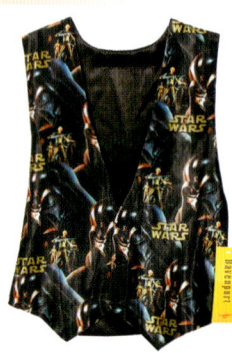

| 189-01 | 189-02 | 189-03 | 189-04 | 190-01 | 190-02 | 190-03 |

Character Socks.
- C-3PO and R2-D2 caricatures 10.00
- Darth Vader, on black...10.00
- Darth Vader with crossed lightsabers 10.00
- Ewok with spear 10.00
- Stormtrooper...10.00
- Yoda 10.00

Tesco Stores, Ltd. (UK)
- Darth Maul [188-128]..12.00

The LEGO Group
- 2-pack: LEGO Darth Vader and Stormtrooper [188-129]..15.00

Totes (UK)
- Bravo Squadron..15.00
- Darth Maul (black and white).................................15.00
- Darth Maul (color / teeth) [188-130].........................20.00
- Darth Maul (color)..20.00
- R2-D2 art [188-131]...15.00

Clothing: Suspenders

Lee Co.
Striped with badge. Cardboard hanger tab.
- C-3PO and R2-D2 die-cut badge [189-01] 65.00

- Darth Vader badge 65.00
- Yoda badge [189-02]..65.00

Striped with badge. Plastic hanger hook.
- C-3PO and R2-D2 die-cut badge [189-03] 75.00
- Darth Vader badge 75.00
- Yoda badge [189-04]..75.00

Clothing: Sweaters and Vests
Continued in Volume 3, Page 164

- Clone trooper sweater, gray [v1e1:162]....................40.00

Davenport
Vests.
- Darth Vader [190-01] 55.00
- I Want You (For The Imperial Forces) [190-02] 55.00
- Star Wars [190-03]..55.00

Clothing: Swimming Attire
Continued in Volume 3, Page 166

- Clone Wars [191-01] 10.00
- LEGO Star Wars [191-02]..15.00

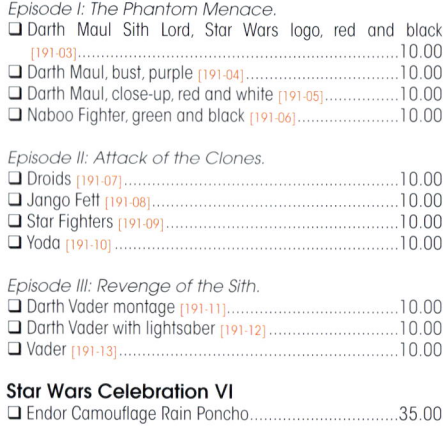

Episode I: The Phantom Menace.
- Darth Maul Sith Lord, Star Wars logo, red and black [191-03]..10.00
- Darth Maul, bust, purple [191-04].............................10.00
- Darth Maul, close-up, red and white [191-05]...........10.00
- Naboo Fighter, green and black [191-06]..................10.00

Episode II: Attack of the Clones.
- Droids [191-07]...10.00
- Jango Fett [191-08]..10.00
- Star Fighters [191-09]..10.00
- Yoda [191-10]..10.00

Episode III: Revenge of the Sith.
- Darth Vader montage [191-11].................................10.00
- Darth Vader with lightsaber [191-12].........................10.00
- Vader [191-13]...10.00

Star Wars Celebration VI
- Endor Camouflage Rain Poncho..............................35.00

Clothing: Undergarments
Continued in Volume 3, Page 167

- C-3PO boxers [192-01]..14.00
- Darth Vader / Dark Side [192-02].............................20.00
- Darth Vader, purple silk [192-03] 25.00
- Family Guy / Blue Harvest boxers [v1e1:160] 12.00
- "Feel the Force" Darth Vader [192-04] 12.00
- Hildebrandt Art [192-05] 20.00
- Star Wars Rocks boxers [192-06].............................15.00
- Vader, silk [192-07]..20.00

Clone Wars Underoos.
- Rex, Obi-Wan, and Anakin [192-08]..........................15.00

Episode I: The Phantom Menace.
- Darth Maul briefs [192-09].......................................10.00

| 191-01 | 191-02 | 191-03 |

| 191-04 | 191-05 | 191-06 | 191-07 | 191-08 |

| 191-09 | 191-10 | 191-11 | 191-12 | 191-13 |

Clothing: Undergarments

192-01

192-02

192-03

192-04

192-05

192-06

192-07

192-08

192-09

American Marketing Enterprises, Inc.
- ❏ C-3PO and R2-D2 [192-10]..................................12.00
- ❏ C-3PO pointing and R2-D2 [192-11]....................12.00
- ❏ Clone Wars, 2 knit boys' boxers [192-12]............18.00
- ❏ Clone Wars, 2 knit boys' boxers [192-13]............18.00
- ❏ Darth Vader, black [192-14].................................12.00
- ❏ Darth Vader, red [192-15]....................................12.00
- ❏ R2-D2 and C-3PO [192-16].................................12.00
- ❏ X-Wing Rogue Squadron [192-17]......................12.00

Big Dog
- ❏ Dog Wars charcoal boxers [192-18].....................25.00
- ❏ Epawsode One icons [192-19]............................25.00

Bloopers
Re-marketed irregular clothing.
- ❏ Darth Maul, boys' boxers [192-20].......................15.00

Briefly Stated
Boxer shorts.
- ❏ Darth Maul, adult [v1e1:161]...............................18.00
- ❏ Darth Maul, children's [192-21]...........................10.00
- ❏ Droids, children's...12.00
- ❏ Hoth Scene, children's..12.00
- ❏ Jar Jar pictured with patch, adult [192-22]..........12.00
- ❏ Jar Jar text, adult [v1e1:160]..............................12.00
- ❏ Naboo Space Battle, adult [192-23]....................12.00
- ❏ Naboo Space Battle, children's [192-24].............10.00
- ❏ Sebulba, adult...12.00
- ❏ Sith Lord, adult..12.00
- ❏ Space Battle, children's [v1e1:160]....................10.00
- ❏ Star Wars with drink holder [192-25]...................25.00
- ❏ Stormtroopers, children's....................................10.00

Sleep shorts.
- ❏ Darth Vader in metal collector's tin [192-26]........20.00

Fruit of the Loom
- ❏ Anakin Skywalker package, 3 boys' briefs [192-27]........10.00
- ❏ Anakin Skywalker package, "New Space Prints," 3 boys' briefs [192-28]..10.00
- ❏ C-3PO package, 3 toddler boys' briefs [192-29]...............10.00
- ❏ Darkside / Jedi vs. Sith boxers............................10.00
- ❏ Darth Maul, 3 toddler boys' boxers [192-30].......10.00
- ❏ Episode I logo package, 2 boys' briefs [192-31].10.00
- ❏ Jar Jar package, 3 toddler girls' panties [192-32]...12.00
- ❏ Lightsaber green package, 5 printed boys' briefs.......15.00
- ❏ Lightsaber red package, 5 printed boys' briefs.........15.00
- ❏ Queen Amidala package, 3 girls' panties [192-33]...12.00
- ❏ R2-D2 shaped box, 5 printed boys' briefs................15.00

Episode III: Revenge of the Sith.
- ❏ Darth Vader 2-pack boxer briefs [192-34]...........10.00
- ❏ Epic Battle 2-pack boxer briefs [192-35].............10.00
- ❏ Yoda 2-pack briefs [192-36]................................10.00

Handcraft Mfg. Corp.
- ❏ Angry Birds, 3 boys' briefs [192-38]....................10.00
- ❏ Clone Wars, 3 boys' briefs [192-39]....................10.00
- ❏ Darth Vader, boxed [192-37]...............................12.00
- ❏ LEGO Star Wars, Darth Maul pk., 3 boys' briefs [192-40]..12.00
- ❏ LEGO Star Wars, Darth Vader package, 3 boys' briefs [192-41]..15.00

192-10

192-11

192-12

192-13

192-14

192-15

192-16

192-17

192-18

192-19

192-20

192-21

192-22

192-23

Clothing: Undergarments

192-24 | 192-25 | 192-26 | 192-27 | 192-28 | 192-29 | 192-30 | 192-31 | 192-32 | 192-33

192-34 | 192-35 | 192-36 | 192-37 | 192-38 | 192-39 | 192-40 | 192-41 | 192-42

192-43 | 192-44 | 192-45 | 192-46 | 192-47 | 192-48 | 192-49 | 192-50

Hanes
- ❏ Anakin Skywalker package, 3 boys' briefs [192-43] 10.00
- ❏ Clone Wars, 3 boys' briefs [192-42] 10.00
- ❏ Yoda package, 3 boys' glow briefs [192-44] 10.00

Long Eddies
- ❏ Darth Vader and Luke children's thermal underwear...20.00
- ❏ Death Star..20.00
- ❏ Luke Skywalker..20.00

Marks and Spencer (UK)
- ❏ Darth Maul [192-45] 15.00
- ❏ Obi-Wan Kenobi [192-46] 15.00
- ❏ Sith Lord / The Dark Side [192-47] 15.00

Ralph Marlin and Co.
- ❏ Darth Vader pattern, silk [v1e1:161] 30.00
- ❏ Spaceship pattern, Star Wars logo, cotton [v1e1:161] ...25.00
- ❏ Spaceship pattern, cotton [192-48] 25.00

Short Eddies
T-shirt and boxer shorts sets, children's.
- ❏ Darth Vader..20.00
- ❏ Space Battle...20.00

Small Planet Co. Ltd. (Japan)
Boxer briefs.
- ❏ Marvel comic characters.................................20.00
- ❏ Stormtroopers..20.00

    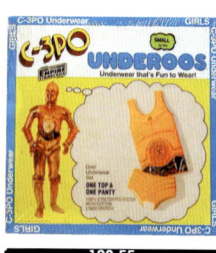 

192-51 | 192-52 | 192-53 | 192-54 | 192-55 | 192-56

192-57 | 192-58 | 192-59 | 192-60 | 192-61 | 192-62

192-63 | 192-64 | 192-65 | 192-66 | 192-67 | 192-68

Smiley 2000
☐ Darth Vader parody [v1e1:161] 20.00

Tesco Stores, Ltd. (UK)
☐ Clone Wars, 3 boys' briefs with pencil tin [192-49] 20.00

Union Underwear Co.
Underoos, thermal.
☐ Darth Vader [192-50] 100.00
☐ Han Solo, thermal [192-51] 100.00
☐ R2-D2 [192-52] 100.00
☐ Yoda [192-53] 100.00

Underoos.
☐ Boba Fett [192-54] 85.00
☐ C-3PO [192-55] 75.00
☐ Chewbacca [192-56] 85.00
☐ Darth Vader [192-57] 75.00
☐ Ewoks [192-58] 85.00
☐ Han Solo [192-59] 85.00
☐ Luke Skywalker [192-60] 85.00
☐ Luke Skywalker, flight suit [192-61] 75.00
☐ Princess Leia [192-62] 85.00
☐ Princess Leia, Return of the Jedi [192-63] 95.00
☐ R2-D2 [192-64] 75.00
☐ Wicket [192-65] 85.00
☐ Yoda [192-66] 75.00

Woolworths (UK)
3-packs of boys' slips.
☐ Clone Wars designs [192-67] 15.00
☐ Darth Vader designs [192-68] 15.00

Clothing: Visors

Drew Pearson Marketing
☐ Count Dooku [193-01] 25.00
☐ Jedi Starfighter red and black 25.00
☐ Jedi Starfighter, tan [193-02] 25.00
☐ Jedi, red [193-03] 25.00

Factors, Etc.
☐ Star Wars, May the Force be with you 45.00

Clothing: Warm-Up Suits

Sales Corp. of America
Boys: hooded with shorts.
☐ Admiral Ackbar 75.00
☐ Darth Vader 75.00
☐ Darth Vader and Royal Guards 75.00
☐ Luke and Darth Vader dueling 75.00
☐ Return of the Jedi logo 75.00

Boys: with pants.
☐ Admiral Ackbar 60.00
☐ Darth Vader 60.00

☐ Darth Vader and Royal Guards 60.00
☐ Luke and Darth Vader dueling 60.00
☐ Paploo 60.00
☐ Return of the Jedi logo 50.00

Girls.
☐ Max Rebo Band 75.00
☐ Wicket 75.00
☐ Wicket and Paploo 75.00
☐ Wicket and R2-D2 ....75.00

Toddlers: hooded fleece.
☐ Wicket and Paploo 40.00
☐ Wicket and R2-D2 ....40.00

Toddlers.
☐ Baby Ewoks 40.00
☐ Wicket and Baby Ewoks 40.00
☐ Wicket and Paploo 40.00
☐ Wicket and R2-D2 ....40.00

Clothing: Wristbands, Headbands, and Sweatbands
Continued in Volume 3, Page 171

Family Guy. Something, Something, Something, Dark Side.
☐ Boba Chicken [194-01] 10.00
☐ C-3PO Quagmire [194-02] 10.00
☐ Chewbacca Brian [v1e1:162] 10.00
☐ Darth Stewie [194-03] 10.00
☐ R2-D2 Cleveland [v1e1:162] 10.00

C and D Visionaries, Inc.
Leather.
☐ Darth Vader [v1e1:162] 15.00

Terry cloth.
☐ Anakin (logo) [v1e1:162] 8.00
☐ Boba Fett [194-04] 8.00
☐ Clone trooper [194-05] 8.00
☐ Sith [v1e1:162] 8.00
☐ Star Wars logo, black and silver 8.00
☐ Star Wars logo, on green [194-06] 8.00
☐ Vader (logo) [v1e1:162] 8.00
☐ X-Wing Squadron [194-07] 8.00
☐ Yoda, Use the Force [194-08] 8.00

Del Rey
☐ Star Wars / Read More You Must 10.00

EnSky (Japan)
☐ Star Wars, rubber wristband with sticker [194-09] 15.00

Party Express
☐ Darth Vader, 4-pack [194-10] 8.00
☐ Stormtrooper 8.00

Coasters

Coasters
Continued in Volume 3, Page 172

Black Falcon
☐ Empire Strikes Back, black print [195-01] 85.00
☐ Empire Strikes Back, blue print [195-02] 85.00

Coca-Cola (China)
Episode III: Revenge of the Sith. Round, boxed.
☐ Anakin Skywalker [v1e1:162] 18.00
☐ C-3PO and R2-D2 [195-03] 18.00
☐ Darth Vader [195-04] 18.00
☐ Yoda [v1e1:162] 18.00

Episode III: Revenge of the Sith. Square, boxed.
☐ Anakin Skywalker [195-05] 20.00
☐ Darth Vader [195-06] 20.00

Disney / MGM
☐ Cantina: Mos Eisley Tatooine, set of 12 [195-07] 35.00

iKon (Australia)
☐ 4-pack character icons [195-08] 55.00
☐ 4-pack classic characters [195-09] 55.00

Pizza Hut
Jedi Mind Tricks, 4" diameter.
☐ Levitating Straw [195-10] 10.00
☐ Mind Reading [195-11] 10.00
☐ Presidential Flip [195-12] 10.00
☐ Salt Shaker Teleportation [195-13] 10.00
☐ Straw Telekinesis [195-14] 10.00

Spearmark International (UK)
☐ Darth Vader 12.00

Star Wars Celebration III
☐ Celebration III [195-15] 25.00
☐ Celebration at Celebration III [195-16] 15.00

Star Wars Celebration VI
☐ Join the Party 2-sided, Darth Vader / Yoda 15.00
☐ Tiki art, set of 6 [195-17] 35.00

starwars.com
In 2003 the Star Wars website offered 13 themed art galleries with 12 images in each gallery. Fans could order coasters online with their choice of image. Orders came as sets of four. Each coaster is 4" square. Only the gallery themes are documented below. Value is for a set of four coasters from that gallery.
☐ Bounty Hunters gallery 20.00
☐ Clone Wars gallery 20.00
☐ Creatures gallery 20.00
☐ Droids gallery 20.00
☐ Holiday Art gallery 20.00
☐ Jedi gallery 20.00

169

Coasters

  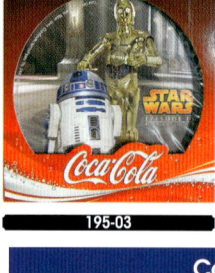 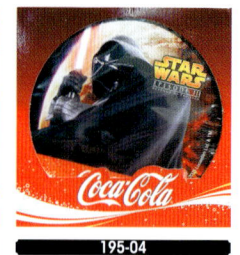  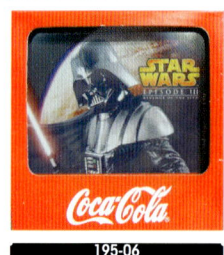

| 195-01 | 195-02 | 195-03 | 195-04 | 195-05 | 195-06 |

❏ Logo gallery 20.00
❏ Padmé gallery 20.00
❏ Poster Art gallery 20.00
❏ Princess Leia gallery 20.00
❏ Rebels gallery 20.00
❏ Sith gallery 20.00
❏ Vehicles gallery 20.00

The Encore Group
Episode III: Revenge of the Sith. 5-packs, cork backed tin.
❏ Sith [195-18] 30.00
❏ Vader [195-19] 30.00

Vandor LLC
❏ 4-pack Unleashed art [195-20] 40.00

Zak Designs
4" diameter, white plastic.
❏ Anakin Skywalker [v1e1:163] 10.00
❏ Darth Maul [v1e1:163] 10.00
❏ Jar Jar Binks [v1e1:163] 10.00
❏ Queen Amidala [v1e1:163] 10.00

Coins
Continued in Volume 3, Page 173

❏ Darth Vader challenge coin, limited to 9,999 [196-01] 45.00

20th Century Fox
❏ Star Wars Episode III, giveaway with DVD, exclusive to Target [196-02] 15.00

California Lottery
California lottery scratch-off coins.
❏ C-3PO [196-03] 8.00
❏ Darth Vader [196-04] 8.00
❏ Luke Skywalker [196-05] 8.00
❏ Princess Leia [196-06] 8.00
❏ R2-D2 [196-07] 8.00
❏ Yoda [196-08] 8.00

Cards, Inc., UK
Medalionz, bronze.
❏ Collector's set with display box, limited to 2,000 ......200.00

Medalionz, copper.
❏ 24-piece boxed collector set 120.00

Medalionz, gold.
❏ Anakin Skywalker 10.00
❏ Anakin Skywalker vs. Obi-Wan Kenobi [4:110] ...10.00
❏ ARC-170 Fighter 10.00
❏ Battle Droid 10.00
❏ C-3PO and R2-D2 ....10.00
❏ Clone trooper 10.00
❏ Count Dooku 10.00
❏ Count Dooku vs. Anakin Skywalker 10.00
❏ Darth Sidious 10.00
❏ Darth Sidious vs. Yoda 10.00
❏ Darth Vader 10.00
❏ Droid Tri-Fighter 10.00
❏ Evil Separatists 10.00
❏ Galactic Republic 10.00
❏ General Grievous 10.00
❏ General Grievous vs. Obi-Wan Kenobi 10.00
❏ Jedi Knights 10.00
❏ Jedi Starfighter 10.00
❏ Mace Windu 10.00

| 195-07 | 195-08 | 195-09 | 195-10 to 195-14 Back | 195-10 | 195-11 |

| 195-12 | 195-13 | 195-14 | 195-15 | 195-16 | 195-17 Package |

| 195-17 Open 1 of 6 | 195-17 Open 2 of 6 | 195-17 Open 3 of 6 | 195-17 Open 4 of 6 | 195-17 Open 5 of 6 | 195-17 Open 6 of 6 |

| 195-18 | 195-19 | 195-20 | 195-20 Open 1 of 4 | 195-20 Open 2 of 4 | 195-20 Open 3 of 4 | 195-20 Open 4 of 4 |

196-01

196-02

196-03

196-04

196-05

196-06

196-07

196-08

- ❑ Obi-Wan Kenobi 10.00
- ❑ Padmé Amidala...10.00
- ❑ Republic Cruiser...10.00
- ❑ Sith Lords...10.00
- ❑ Yoda...10.00

Medalionz, silver.

- ❑ Anakin Skywalker [196-09] 5.00
- ❑ Anakin Skywalker vs. Obi-Wan Kenobi [196-10]..............5.00
- ❑ ARC-170 Fighter [196-11] 5.00
- ❑ Battle Droid [196-12] 5.00
- ❑ C-3PO and R2-D2 [196-13] 5.00
- ❑ Clone trooper [196-14] 5.00
- ❑ Count Dooku [196-15] 5.00
- ❑ Count Dooku vs. Anakin Skywalker [196-16]....................5.00
- ❑ Darth Sidious [196-17]...5.00
- ❑ Darth Sidious vs. Yoda [196-18] 5.00
- ❑ Darth Vader [196-19]...5.00
- ❑ Droid Tri-Fighter [196-20]..5.00
- ❑ Evil Separatists [196-21] 5.00
- ❑ Galactic Republic [196-22]..5.00
- ❑ General Grievous [196-23]..5.00
- ❑ Grievous vs. Obi-Wan Kenobi [196-24] 5.00
- ❑ Jedi Knights [196-25]..5.00
- ❑ Jedi Starfighter [196-26] 5.00
- ❑ Mace Windu [196-27]..5.00
- ❑ Obi-Wan Kenobi [196-28]..5.00
- ❑ Padmé Amidala [196-29]...5.00
- ❑ Republic Cruiser [196-30] 5.00
- ❑ Sith Lords [196-31] 5.00
- ❑ Yoda [196-32] 5.00

Medalionz, special edition / oversized.

- ❑ Yoda, limited to 500, exclusive to TheCollectorZone.com [196-33]...90.00

Catch a Star Collectibles

- ❑ 15th Anniversary, silver, limited to 5,000 [196-34] 250.00

Celebration Europe, UK

- ❑ Darth Vader, 9 oz. gold in a lined box, limited to 30, numbered [196-35]...600.00

Disney / MGM

Star Wars Weekends. 2001 R2-D2 projecting Mickey.

- ❑ Nickel silver, limited to 1,200 [196-36]..........................75.00

Star Wars Weekends. 2003 Jedi Mickey and Yoda.

- ❑ Bronze, limited to 500...80.00
- ❑ Fine silver, limited to 500 ....95.00
- ❑ Gold, limited to 1,000 [196-37] 65.00
- ❑ Nickel silver, limited to 500 [196-38]............................80.00

Star Wars Weekends. 2004 Jedi Mickey and Leia Minnie.

- ❑ Bronze, limited to 1,000 [196-39] 65.00
- ❑ Fine silver, limited to 1,000 ....95.00
- ❑ Gold, limited to 1,000..65.00
- ❑ Nickel silver, limited to 1,000 [4:110] 75.00
- ❑ Set of 5, framed includes exclusive X-Wing coin, limited to 250 [4:110] 250.00

Star Wars Weekends. 2005 Darth Vader and Mickey.

- ❑ 1 Troy ounce, fine silver [196-40] 80.00
- ❑ Bronze, limited to 1,000..50.00
- ❑ Fine silver overlay, limited to 1,000............................55.00
- ❑ Gold, limited to 1,000 [196-41] 55.00
- ❑ Nickel silver, limited to 1,000 ....45.00
- ❑ Set of 5, framed, limited to 250 [4:110] 250.00
- ❑ Set of 6, framed includes exclusive 2000 coin, limited to 250 [4:110] 350.00

Star Wars Weekends. 2006 Darth Vader vs. Yoda.

- ❑ 1 Troy ounce, fine silver [196-42] 85.00
- ❑ Bronze, limited to 1,000 [196-43] 50.00
- ❑ Fine silver, limited to 1,000 ....55.00
- ❑ Gold, limited to 1,000..55.00
- ❑ Nickel silver, limited to 1,000 ....45.00
- ❑ Set of 5, framed [4:110]..175.00

Star Wars Weekends. 2007 Mickey, Vader, and Han.

- ❑ 1 Troy ounce, fine silver, limited to 200, numbered [196-44]...80.00
- ❑ Bronze, limited to 1,000, numbered............................45.00
- ❑ Gold, limited to 1,000, numbered...............................55.00
- ❑ Nickel silver, limited to 1,000, numbered 55.00
- ❑ Set of 5, framed, limited to 250, numbered 175.00

Star Wars Weekends. 2008 Donald and Stormtrooper.

- ❑ Antique bronze, limited to 1,000 ....45.00
- ❑ Antique copper, limited to 1,000 ....45.00
- ❑ Antique nickel, limited to 1,000 [196-45] 45.00
- ❑ Set of 6, framed, limited to 250, numbered 175.00

Star Wars Weekends. 2009 Clone Wars.

- ❑ Antique bronze, limited to 1,500 ....45.00
- ❑ Antique copper, limited to 1,500 ....45.00
- ❑ Antique silver, limited to 1,500 [196-46] 50.00

Disney Resorts

Cast coins.

- ❑ 2010 Q2 Star Performer Darth Vader [196-47]............150.00

Echo Base Toys

- ❑ Boba Fett, Hunting Season Is Now Open, limited to 250 [196-48]..50.00
- ❑ Queen Amidala, Ruler of the Naboo, limited to 250 [196-49]..50.00

Franklin Mint

- ❑ 20th Anniversary commemorative medal, 24k gold on sterling silver, limited edition [196-50]........................175.00

Goldquest

Limited to 9,999, milled edges. 2005 the government of Cook Islands.

- ❑ 1 dollar, Classic Villains, copper nickel.......................90.00
- ❑ 5 dollars, Prequel Heroes, 1 oz. silver.......................150.00
- ❑ 5 dollars, Prequel Villains, 1 oz. silver......................150.00
- ❑ 10 dollars, Classic Heroes, 1/25 oz. gold..................300.00

196-09

196-10

196-11

196-12

196-13

196-14

196-15

196-16

196-17

196-18

196-19

196-20

196-21

196-22

196-23

196-24

196-25

196-26

196-27

196-28

196-29

196-30

196-31

196-32

Coins

Hasbro
Monopoly 1000 credit coins from Star Wars worlds.
- ❏ Alderaan [196-51] 5.00
- ❏ Bespin [196-52] 5.00
- ❏ Ord Mantell [196-53] 5.00

Jupiter and Beyond
- ❏ Millennium Falcon game token [196-54] 10.00

Lucasfilm
- ❏ Darth Vader, "You Underestimate The Power Of The Dark Side" plastic, exclusive to 1996 Toy Fair [196-55] 500.00

Marti Gras Krewe Dabloons
1979 Bards of Bohemia. "Conquerors All"—features scientist on left, shield with ship in the middle, and a figure which looks like Darth Vader standing on the right.
- ❏ 10 gauge, .999 Silver 75.00
- ❏ 10 gauge, Antique Bronze [4:111] 25.00
- ❏ 10 gauge, Dual Gold & Purple 25.00
- ❏ 15 gauge, Gold Aluminum [196-56] 10.00
- ❏ 15 gauge, Purple Aluminum [3:232] 10.00
- ❏ 15 gauge, Silver Aluminum [3:232] 10.00

1979 Mystic Stripers (Mobile, AL). "Cinema Classics"—Features a ribbon with various movie names written on it and images of Mickey Mouse as "Steamboat Willie," King Kong, and an X-Wing Fighter.
- ❏ 10 gauge, .999 Silver [196-57] 75.00
- ❏ 10 gauge, Multicolored 50.00
- ❏ 10 gauge, Oxidized Silver 50.00
- ❏ 15 gauge, Silver Aluminum 25.00

1981 Confused Couples Carnival Club. "We Too R-2" "Truck No. 3"—features a robot that resembles a big-rig truck.
- ❏ 10 gauge, Antique Bronze 25.00
- ❏ 15 gauge, Gold Aluminum [196-58] 5.00
- ❏ 15 gauge, Green Aluminum [3:232] 5.00
- ❏ 15 gauge, Purple Aluminum 5.00
- ❏ 15 gauge, Silver Aluminum [3:232] 5.00

1981 Krewe of Janus New Orleans. "In the Seventies"—features a Vietnamese person with a bomb, a hippie, a football player, Richard Nixon, a gasoline pump, and R2-D2.
- ❏ 10 gauge, .999 Pure Silver 75.00
- ❏ 10 gauge, Antique Bronze 25.00
- ❏ 10 gauge, Multicolored 25.00
- ❏ 10 gauge, Oxidized Silver [4:111] 25.00
- ❏ 15 gauge, Blue Aluminum [196-59] 12.00
- ❏ 15 gauge, Gold Aluminum [3:232] 12.00

1982 Le Krewe Mystique de la Capitale. "Star Wars"—features an X-Wing Fighter firing its lasers in front of the Death Star.
- ❏ 10 gauge, .999 Silver 150.00
- ❏ 10 gauge, Antique Bronze 75.00
- ❏ 10 gauge, Multicolor "Star Wars" 75.00
- ❏ 15 gauge, Gold Aluminum [3:232] 35.00
- ❏ 15 gauge, Green Aluminum [4:111] 35.00
- ❏ 15 gauge, Purple Aluminum [3:232] 35.00
- ❏ 15 gauge, Red Aluminum 35.00
- ❏ 15 gauge, Silver Aluminum [196-60] 25.00

1983 Krewe of Carrollton. "Cinema Classics"—features images of a movie camera, an Oscar statue, and a knight's helmet with 2 tablets behind it, and 2 ribbons with various movie titles written on it. "Star Wars" appears on the rightmost ribbon.
- ❏ 10 gauge, .999 Silver [3:232] 35.00
- ❏ 10 gauge, Antique Bronze 25.00
- ❏ 10 gauge, Blue 7.00
- ❏ 10 gauge, Gold 7.00
- ❏ 10 gauge, Multicolor [196-61] 25.00
- ❏ 15 gauge, Gold [3:232] 3.00
- ❏ 15 gauge, Green [3:232] 3.00
- ❏ 15 gauge, Silver [4:111] 3.00

1986 Krewe of Houmas. "Space Fantasies"—features R2-D2 on left, Yoda in center, "V" to the right of Yoda, Enterprise on right, and Flash Gordon ship on bottom.
- ❏ 10 gauge, .999 Silver 75.00
- ❏ 10 gauge, Antique Bronze 30.00
- ❏ 10 gauge, Multicolor 30.00
- ❏ 15 gauge, Gold Aluminum [4:111] 5.00
- ❏ 15 gauge, Green Aluminum [3:233] 5.00
- ❏ 15 gauge, Purple Aluminum [196-62] 5.00

1986 Krewe of Little Rascals. "Little Rascals Salutes Space Adventures"—features "Close Encounters" ship on left, Buck Rogers in center, and R2-D2 on right.
- ❏ 15 gauge, Gold Aluminum [3:233] 8.00
- ❏ 15 gauge, Green Aluminum [196-63] 8.00
- ❏ 15 gauge, Purple Aluminum [4:111] 8.00
- ❏ 15 gauge, Silver Aluminum [3:233] 8.00

1986 Krewe of Mid-City Carnival Parade. "Space Fantasies"—features Enterprise on left, Optimus Prime in center, and Yoda on right.
- ❏ 10 gauge, .999 Silver [3:233] 75.00
- ❏ 10 gauge, Antique Bronze 20.00
- ❏ 10 gauge, Green Aluminum [3:233] 8.00
- ❏ 10 gauge, Multicolor [3:233] 20.00
- ❏ 10 gauge, Oxidized Silver [196-64] 15.00
- ❏ 10 gauge, Purple Aluminum [3:233] 8.00
- ❏ 15 gauge, Gold Aluminum [3:232] 5.00
- ❏ 15 gauge, Silver Aluminum 5.00

1992 Nereids Carnival Club. "Nereids' Cinema Classics"—features Rocky on left, Darth Vader helmet in center with Batman symbol and Enterprise behind it, and the Creature from the Black Lagoon on right.
- ❏ 15 gauge, Gold Aluminum [196-65] 10.00
- ❏ 15 gauge, Green Aluminum [4:111] 10.00
- ❏ 15 gauge, Purple Aluminum [3:233] 10.00

2002 Krewe of Aladdin. "Movies of the 20th Century"—R2-D2 on left, Scarlett O'Hara and Rhett Butler in center, Moses on bottom, Lawrence of Arabia on right.
- ❏ 10 gauge, Multicolor [3:233] 18.00
- ❏ 15 gauge, Gold Aluminum [3:233] 3.00
- ❏ 15 gauge, Silver Aluminum [196-66] 3.00

Mexico Encuentros 2004
- ❏ Darth Vader vs. Luke, blue plastic [196-67] 20.00

Museum Replicas
Exclusive to the San Diego Comic-Con.
- ❏ Imperial emblem [196-68] 20.00
- ❏ Rebel emblem [196-69] 20.00
- ❏ Republic emblem [196-70] 20.00

Paris Expo 2005
- ❏ Darth Vader [196-71] 50.00
- ❏ Yoda [196-72] 50.00

Pennsylvania Star Wars Collecting Society
- ❏ Canine Corps / Chewbacca, limited to 1,000, Celebration V exclusive 20.00
- ❏ Operation Ward57 / Obi-Wan Kenobi, limited to 1,000 [196-73] 20.00

Rarities Mint
Gold, .10oz.
- ❏ Ben Kenobi and Darth Vader 360.00
- ❏ C-3PO and R2-D2 .... 360.00
- ❏ Chewbacca and Han Solo 360.00
- ❏ Luke Skywalker and Princess Leia 360.00
- ❏ Mos Eisley Cantina Band 360.00
- ❏ Stormtroopers 360.00

Gold, .25oz.
- ❏ Ben Kenobi and Darth Vader 1,250.00

196-33  | 196-34 Display Box and Face  | 196-35 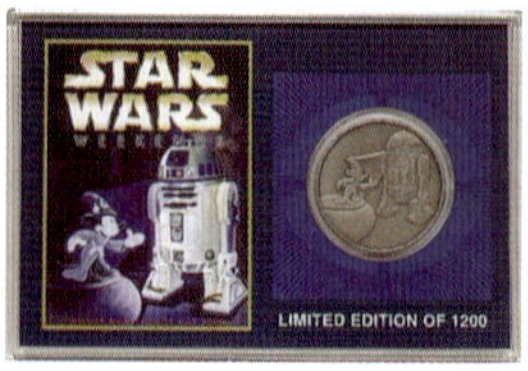 | 196-36 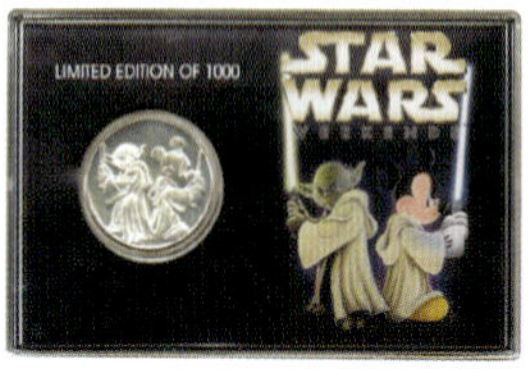 | 196-37 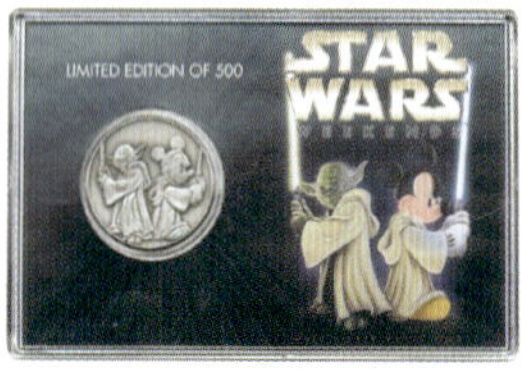 | 196-38

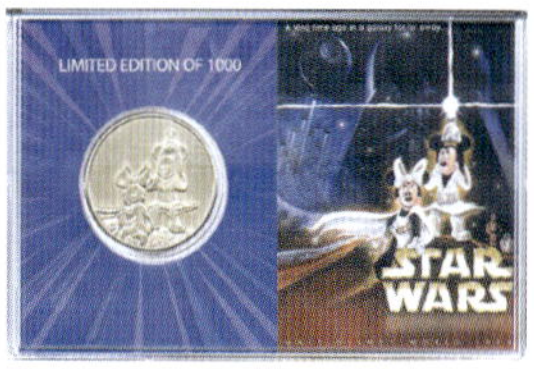

196-39  | 196-40 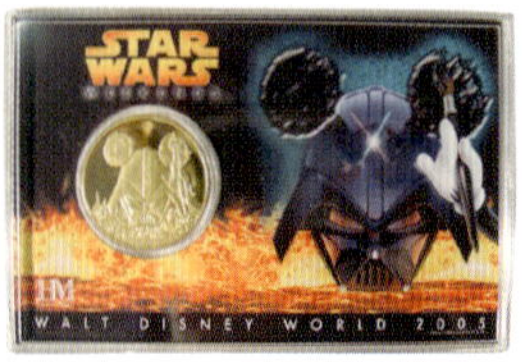 | 196-41  | 196-42  | 196-43  | 196-44  | 196-44

196-45  | 196-46  | 196-47 in Slab and Face  | 196-48  | 196-49  | 196-50 Front and Back

Coins

196-51

196-52

196-53

196-54

196-55

196-56

196-57

196-58

196-59

196-60

196-61

196-62

196-63

196-64

196-65

196-66

- ❑ C-3PO and R2-D2 ....1,250.00
- ❑ Chewbacca and Han Solo 1,250.00
- ❑ Luke Skywalker and Princess Leia 1,250.00
- ❑ Mos Eisley Cantina Band 1,250.00
- ❑ Stormtroopers 1,250.00

Gold, 1oz.

- ❑ Ben Kenobi and Darth Vader 2,300.00
- ❑ C-3PO and R2-D2 ....2,300.00
- ❑ Chewbacca and Han Solo 2,300.00
- ❑ Luke Skywalker and Princess Leia 2,300.00
- ❑ Mos Eisley Cantina Band 2,300.00
- ❑ Stormtroopers 2,300.00

Silver, 1oz.

- ❑ Ben Kenobi and Darth Vader [196-74] 165.00
- ❑ C-3PO and R2-D2 [196-75] 165.00
- ❑ Chewbacca and Han Solo [196-76] 165.00
- ❑ Luke and Princess Leia [196-77] 165.00
- ❑ Luke and Princess Leia, 15th anniversary 165.00
- ❑ Mos Eisley Cantina Band [196-78] 165.00
- ❑ Stormtroopers [196-79] 165.00

Silver, 5oz.

- ❑ Ben Kenobi and Darth Vader 300.00
- ❑ C-3PO and R2-D2 ....300.00
- ❑ Chewbacca and Han Solo 300.00
- ❑ Luke Skywalker and Princess Leia 300.00
- ❑ Mos Eisley Cantina Band 300.00
- ❑ Stormtroopers 300.00

Shochiku (Japan)

- ❑ Clone Wars [196-80] 50.00
- ❑ EPII: Young Jedi / Dark Lord of the Sith [196-81] 50.00
- ❑ EPIII: Darth Vader / Revenge of the Sith [196-82] 50.00

Singapore Mint

- ❑ Darth Vader, limited to 20,000 [196-83] 50.00

Target

- ❑ "Waiting in line is evidence of your devotion to the force, May 19, 2005," limited to 30,000 [196-84] 35.00

The Dented Helmet

- ❑ The Dented Helmet / Fett gold colored, limited to 1,000, exclusive to DragonCon [196-85] 25.00

Topps

Clone Wars 2008. Set of 12, red, exclusive to Target.

- ❑ 1 Anakin Skywalker 12.00
- ❑ 2 Ahsoka Tano 12.00
- ❑ 3 Obi-Wan Kenobi [v1e1:167] 12.00
- ❑ 4 Asajj Ventress 12.00
- ❑ 5 Yoda [v1e1:167] 12.00
- ❑ 6 Padmé Amidala 12.00
- ❑ 7 C-3PO and R2-D2 [v1e1:167] 12.00
- ❑ 8 Chancellor Palpatine 12.00
- ❑ 9 Clone Captain Rex [v1e1:167] 12.00
- ❑ 10 Count Dooku [v1e1:167] 12.00
- ❑ 11 Commander Cody [v1e1:167] 12.00
- ❑ 12 Jabba the Hutt 12.00

Clone Wars 2008. Set of 12, blue, exclusive to Walmart.

- ❑ 1 Anakin Skywalker 12.00
- ❑ 2 Ahsoka Tano [v1e1:167] 12.00
- ❑ 3 Obi-Wan Kenobi [v1e1:167] 12.00
- ❑ 4 Asajj Ventress [v1e1:167] 12.00
- ❑ 5 Yoda 12.00
- ❑ 6 Padmé Amidala 12.00
- ❑ 7 C-3PO and R2-D2 ....12.00
- ❑ 8 Chancellor Palpatine [v1e1:167] 12.00
- ❑ 9 Clone Captain Rex 12.00
- ❑ 10 Count Dooku 12.00
- ❑ 11 Commander Cody 12.00
- ❑ 12 Jabba the Hutt 12.00

Clone Wars 2008. Set of 12, yellow, exclusive to Toys R Us.

- ❑ 1 Anakin Skywalker 12.00
- ❑ 2 Ahsoka Tano 12.00
- ❑ 3 Obi-Wan Kenobi [v1e1:167] 12.00
- ❑ 4 Asajj Ventress [v1e1:167] 12.00
- ❑ 5 Yoda 12.00
- ❑ 6 Padmé Amidala 12.00
- ❑ 7 C-3PO and R2-D2 [v1e1:167] 12.00
- ❑ 8 Chancellor Palpatine [v1e1:167] 12.00
- ❑ 9 Clone Captain Rex 12.00
- ❑ 10 Count Dooku [v1e1:167] 12.00
- ❑ 11 Commander Cody [v1e1:167] 12.00
- ❑ 12 Jabba the Hutt [5:105] 12.00

196-67 Front and Back

196-68

196-69

196-70

196-71

196-72

196-73

196-74

196-75

196-76

196-77

196-78

196-79

196-80 Side 1 and Side 2

196-81 Side 1 and Side 2

196-82

196-83

196-84

196-85

Coins: Action Figure

Coins: Action Figure

Hasbro

30th anniversary exclusives.
- ☐ 30th anniversary, excl. to San Diego Comic-Con..........25.00
- ☐ 30th anniversary black box, excl. to Toy Fair [197-01].....65.00
- ☐ Celebration Europe ziplock baggie 20.00
- ☐ Celebration IV ziplock baggie [197-02] 20.00

30th anniversary.
- ☐ 4-LOM 30-41 [197-03] 5.00
- ☐ A-Wing Pilot 30-44 [197-04]......................................5.00
- ☐ Airborne trooper 30-07 [197-05] 5.00
- ☐ Anakin Skywalker 30-33 [197-06]...............................5.00
- ☐ Anakin Skywalker, Spirit 30-45 [197-07] 5.00
- ☐ Biggs Darklighter Academy Outfit 30-17 [197-08].........5.00
- ☐ Biggs Darklighter, Rebel Pilot 30-13 [197-09] 5.00
- ☐ Boba Fett, animated 30-24 [197-10] 10.00
- ☐ C-3PO 30-30 [197-11] 5.00
- ☐ Clone trooper, 7th legion 30-49 [197-12] 5.00
- ☐ Clone trooper, Hawkbat Battalion 30-50 [197-13] 5.00
- ☐ Clone trooper, training fatigues 30-55 [197-14] 5.00
- ☐ CZ-4 30-26 [197-15]..5.00
- ☐ Darth Malak 30-35 [197-16]....................................25.00
- ☐ Darth Revan 30-34 [197-17] 25.00
- ☐ Darth Vader 30-01 from binder pack [197-18]............10.00
- ☐ Darth Vader 30-16 [197-19] 5.00
- ☐ Darth Vader, holographic 30-48 [197-20].................10.00
- ☐ Death Star trooper 30-14 [197-21] 5.00
- ☐ Destroyer Droid 30-59 [197-22].................................5.00
- ☐ Elis Helrot 30-23 [197-23] 5.00
- ☐ Galactic Marine 30-02 [197-24] 5.00
- ☐ General McQuarrie 30-40 [197-25] 10.00
- ☐ Han Solo 30-11 [197-26] 5.00
- ☐ Han Solo, Bespin 30-38 [197-27] 5.00
- ☐ Hermi Odle 30-29 [197-28].......................................5.00
- ☐ Jango Fett 30-57 [197-29] 5.00
- ☐ Jawa 30-19 [197-30] 5.00
- ☐ Lando Calrissian 30-39 [197-31] 5.00
- ☐ Lava Miner 30-06 [197-32] 5.00
- ☐ Luke Skywalker 30-18 [197-33] 5.00
- ☐ Luke Skywalker, ceremony 30-12 [197-34] 5.00
- ☐ Luke Skywalker, Jedi 30-25 [197-35] 5.00
- ☐ M'iiyoom O'nith 30-22 [197-36] 5.00
- ☐ Mace Windu 30-03 [197-37] 5.00
- ☐ Naboo Soldier 30-52 [197-38] 5.00
- ☐ Obi-Wan Kenobi 30-05 [197-39] 5.00
- ☐ Padmé Amidala 30-56 [197-40] 5.00
- ☐ Pax Bonkik 30-54 [197-41] 5.00
- ☐ Qymaen jai Sheelal 30-36 [197-42] 5.00
- ☐ R2-B1 30-51 [197-43] 8.00
- ☐ R2-D2 30-04 [197-44] 5.00
- ☐ R2-D2, Endor 30-46 [197-45] 8.00

174

Coins: Action Figure

- ❏ Rebel Honor guard 30-10 [197-46] 5.00
- ❏ Rebel Vanguard 30-53 [197-47] 5.00
- ❏ Romba and Graak 30-43 [197-48] 10.00
- ❏ Roron Corobb 30-31 [197-49] 5.00
- ❏ Stormtrooper 30-20 [197-50] 8.00
- ❏ Super Battle Droid 30-08 [197-51] 5.00
- ❏ Umpass-Stay 30-27 [197-52] 5.00
- ❏ Voolvif Monn 30-58 [197-53] 10.00
- ❏ Yoda 30-32 [197-54] 5.00

30th anniversary. McQuarrie concept figures.
- ❏ Boba Fett 30-15 [197-55] 25.00
- ❏ Chewbacca 30-21 [197-56] 25.00
- ❏ Darth Vader 30-28 [197-57] 25.00
- ❏ Han Solo 30-47 [197-58] 25.00
- ❏ Luke Skywalker, exclusive to HasbroToyShop.com [197-59] 40.00
- ❏ Obi-Wan and Yoda, exclusive to HasbroToyShop.com [197-60] 40.00
- ❏ R2-D2 and C-3PO, exclusive to Star Wars Celebration IV [197-61] 45.00
- ❏ Rebel trooper 30-60 [197-62] 25.00
- ❏ Snowtrooper 30-42 [197-63] 25.00
- ❏ Starkiller Hero 30-37 [197-64] 25.00
- ❏ Stormtrooper 30-09 [197-65] 25.00

30th anniversary. Saga Legends.
- ❏ Episode I [197-66] 5.00
- ❏ Episode II [197-67] 5.00
- ❏ Episode III [197-68] 5.00
- ❏ Episode IV [197-69] 5.00
- ❏ Episode V [197-70] 5.00
- ❏ Episode VI [197-71] 5.00
- ❏ Expanded Universe [197-72] 15.00

30th anniversary. Ultimate Galactic Hunt gold coins.
- ❏ Airborne trooper [197-73] 15.00
- ❏ Biggs Darklighter [197-74] 15.00
- ❏ Boba Fett, animated debut [197-75] 30.00
- ❏ Boba Fett, McQuarrie concept [197-76] 30.00
- ❏ Chewbacca, McQuarrie concept [197-77] 30.00
- ❏ Darth Vader [197-78] 15.00
- ❏ Expanded Universe [197-79] 20.00
- ❏ Galactic Marine [197-80] 15.00
- ❏ Han Solo [197-81] 15.00
- ❏ Luke Skywalker [197-82] 15.00
- ❏ Mace Windu [197-83] 15.00
- ❏ R2-D2 [197-84] 15.00
- ❏ Stormtrooper, McQuarrie concept [197-85] .. 15.00

Galactic Hunt mail away coins.
- ❏ Bossk 10.00
- ❏ Han Solo Hoth 10.00
- ❏ IG-88 .... 10.00
- ❏ Imperial Snowtrooper 10.00
- ❏ Luke Skywalker Bespin 10.00
- ❏ Princess Leia Organa Endor 10.00
- ❏ Set of 7, boxed 45.00

JusToys
Bend-Ems premiums.
- ❏ Millennium Falcon [197-86] 10.00
- ❏ TIE Fighter [197-87] 10.00
- ❏ X-Wing Fighter [197-88] 10.00

Kenner
Droids. Gold tone.
- ❏ A-Wing Pilot [197-89] 200.00
- ❏ Boba Fett [197-90] 275.00
- ❏ C-3PO [197-91] 80.00
- ❏ Jann Tosh [197-92] 40.00
- ❏ Jord Dusat [197-93] 40.00
- ❏ Kea Moll [197-94] 30.00
- ❏ Kez-Iban [197-95] 30.00
- ❏ R2-D2 [197-96] 50.00
- ❏ Sise Fromm [197-97] 80.00
- ❏ Thall Joben [197-98] 35.00
- ❏ Tig Fromm [197-99] 80.00
- ❏ Uncle Gundy [197-100] 40.00

Ewoks. Copper tone.
- ❏ Dulok Scout [197-101] 35.00
- ❏ Dulok Shaman [197-102] 30.00
- ❏ King Gorneesh [197-103] 30.00
- ❏ Logray [197-104] 45.00
- ❏ Urgah Lady Gorneesh [197-105] 40.00
- ❏ Wicket [197-106] 50.00

Coins: Action Figure

Power of the Force 2.
- ☐ C-3PO [197-107]...15.00
- ☐ Chewbacca [197-108].....................................15.00
- ☐ Emperor Palpatine [197-109].......................10.00
- ☐ Han Solo [197-110]..10.00
- ☐ Luke Skywalker [197-111]..............................10.00
- ☐ Princess Leia [197-112].................................10.00
- ☐ Snowtrooper (Hoth Stormtrooper) [197-113]..................15.00

Power of the Force. *Author's note: These values supersede those printed in volume 2, second edition.*
- ☐ A-Wing Pilot [197-114]....................................40.00
- ☐ Amanaman [197-115]......................................50.00
- ☐ Anakin Skywalker [197-116]....................1,000.00
- ☐ AT-AT [197-117]..1,500.00
- ☐ AT-ST Driver [197-118]...................................45.00
- ☐ B-Wing Pilot [197-119]....................................60.00
- ☐ Barada [197-120]..40.00
- ☐ Bib Fortuna [197-121]....................................700.00
- ☐ Biker Scout [197-122].....................................125.00
- ☐ Boba Fett [197-123]....................................2,500.00
- ☐ C-3PO [197-124]...60.00
- ☐ Chewbacca [197-125]......................................75.00
- ☐ Chief Chirpa [197-126]..................................240.00
- ☐ Creatures [197-127].......................................300.00
- ☐ Darth Vader [197-128]....................................90.00
- ☐ Droids (R5-D4 and Power Droid) [197-129]....2,000.00
- ☐ Emperor [197-130]...90.00
- ☐ Emperor's Royal Guard [197-131]..............125.00
- ☐ EV-9D9 [197-132]...65.00
- ☐ FX-7 [197-133]...400.00
- ☐ Gamorrean Guard [197-134].......................250.00
- ☐ Greedo [197-135]...900.00
- ☐ Han Solo, Carbon Freeze [197-136]..............40.00
- ☐ Han Solo, Rebel [197-137]...........................120.00
- ☐ Han Solo, Rebel Fighter [197-138].........1,000.00
- ☐ Han Solo, Rebel Hero [197-139]..................300.00
- ☐ Hans Solo, Rebel [sic] [197-140].............1,700.00
- ☐ Hoth Stormtrooper [197-141]......................850.00
- ☐ Imperial Commander [197-142]..................330.00
- ☐ Imperial Dignitary [197-143]..........................45.00
- ☐ Imperial Gunner [197-144].............................45.00
- ☐ Jawas [197-145]..135.00
- ☐ Lando Calrissian, Rebel General (Cloud City) [197-146]..................475.00
- ☐ Lando Calrissian, Rebel General (Falcon) [197-147].......35.00
- ☐ Logray [197-148]...250.00
- ☐ Luke Skywalker, Jedi Knight [197-149].....135.00
- ☐ Luke Skywalker, Jedi Knight on Dagobah [197-150].....280.00
- ☐ Luke Skywalker, Jedi with X-Wing [197-151]..................180.00
- ☐ Luke Skywalker, Rebel Leader (Landspeeder) [197-152]..115.00
- ☐ Luke Skywalker, Rebel Leader (Scout Bike) [197-153].....35.00

Coins: Elongated

- ❏ Luke Skywalker, Rebel Leader (Stormtrooper armor, no eyes) [4:109] 1,000.00
- ❏ Luke Skywalker, Rebel Leader (Stormtrooper armor) [197-154] 70.00
- ❏ Luke Skywalker, Rebel Leader (Tauntaun) [197-155] ..2,000.00
- ❏ Lumat [197-156] 55.00
- ❏ Millenium Falcon [sic] [4:109] 450.00
- ❏ Millennium Falcon [197-157] 100.00
- ❏ Obi-Wan Kenobi [197-158] 125.00
- ❏ Paploo [197-159] 55.00
- ❏ Princess Leia, Boushh [197-160] 425.00
- ❏ Princess Leia, Rebel Leader (Endor Fatigues) [197-161] ..60.00
- ❏ Princess Leia, Rebel Leader (R2-D2) [197-162] ..2,000.00
- ❏ R2-D2 [197-163] 65.00
- ❏ Romba [197-164] 35.00
- ❏ Sail Skiff [197-165] 2,500.00
- ❏ Star Destroyer Commander [197-166] 1,800.00
- ❏ Stormtrooper [197-167] 75.00
- ❏ Teebo [197-168] 130.00
- ❏ TIE Fighter Pilot [197-169] 150.00
- ❏ Too-Onebee [197-170] 400.00
- ❏ Tusken Raider [197-171] 1,650.00
- ❏ Warok [197-172] 35.00
- ❏ Wicket [197-173] 80.00
- ❏ Yak Face [197-174] 950.00
- ❏ Yoda [197-175] 80.00
- ❏ Zuckuss [197-176] 1,650.00

Toy Fair
- ❏ Darth Vader, exclusive to 1996 Toy Fair 500.00

Coins: Elongated
Continued in Volume 3, Page 177

Dimes, Saga.
- ❏ C-3PO 5.00
- ❏ Chewbacca 5.00
- ❏ Darth Maul 5.00
- ❏ Darth Vader 5.00
- ❏ Emperor 5.00
- ❏ Millennium Falcon / scene 5.00
- ❏ Princess Leia 5.00
- ❏ Princess Leia and R2-D2 / scene 5.00
- ❏ Queen Amidala 5.00
- ❏ R2-D2 ....5.00
- ❏ Stormtrooper 5.00
- ❏ Yoda 5.00

Nickels, Saga.
- ❏ C-3PO 5.00
- ❏ Chewbacca 5.00
- ❏ Darth Maul 5.00
- ❏ Darth Vader 5.00
- ❏ Emperor 5.00
- ❏ Millennium Falcon / scene 5.00
- ❏ Princess Leia 5.00
- ❏ Princess Leia and R2-D2 / scene 5.00
- ❏ Queen Amidala 5.00
- ❏ R2-D2 ....5.00

- ❏ Stormtrooper 5.00
- ❏ Yoda 5.00

Pennies, Saga.
- ❏ C-3PO [198-01] 3.00
- ❏ Chewbacca [198-02] 3.00
- ❏ Darth Maul [198-03] 3.00
- ❏ Darth Vader [198-04] 3.00
- ❏ Emperor [198-05] 3.00
- ❏ Millennium Falcon / scene [198-06] 3.00
- ❏ Princess Leia [198-07] 3.00
- ❏ Princess Leia and R2-D2 / scene [198-08] 3.00
- ❏ Queen Amidala [198-09] 3.00
- ❏ R2-D2 [198-10] 3.00
- ❏ Stormtrooper [198-11] 3.00
- ❏ Yoda [198-12] 3.00

Pennies, Star Wars.
- ❏ C-3PO / R2-D2 / May the Force be with you [198-13] ..15.00
- ❏ Chewbacca [198-14] 15.00
- ❏ Creatures / Stormtrooper / Tusken Raiders [198-15] ..15.00
- ❏ Lord Darth Vader [198-16] 15.00

Quarters, Saga.
- ❏ C-3PO 5.00
- ❏ Chewbacca 5.00
- ❏ Darth Maul 5.00
- ❏ Darth Vader 5.00
- ❏ Emperor 5.00

Coins: Elongated

- ❏ Millennium Falcon / scene 5.00
- ❏ Princess Leia 5.00
- ❏ Princess Leia and R2-D2 / scene 5.00
- ❏ Queen Amidala 5.00
- ❏ R2-D2 .... 5.00
- ❏ Stormtrooper 5.00
- ❏ Yoda 5.00

Disney / MGM
- ❏ Death Star and Starspeeder 3000 [198-17] 10.00

Coins: Premiums
Continued in Volume 3, Page 178

Nestlé (Spain)
Cereal premiums.
- ❏ Chewbacca / 50 / Kashyyyk [199-01] 100.00
- ❏ Darth Vader / 1000 / Death Star [199-02] 100.00
- ❏ Luke Skywalker / 500 / Tatooine [199-03] 100.00
- ❏ Princess Leia / 10000 / Alderaan [199-04] 100.00

Star Wars Celebration Europe (UK)
Distributed during collecting discussion panels.
- ❏ Ben (Obi-Wan) Kenobi, Portugal [199-05] 35.00
- ❏ C-3PO, United Kingdom [199-06] 35.00
- ❏ Chewbacca, France [199-07] 35.00
- ❏ Darth Vader, Poland [199-08] 35.00
- ❏ Death Squad Commander, Belgium [199-09] 35.00
- ❏ Han Solo, Sweden [199-10] 35.00
- ❏ Jawa, Denmark [199-11] 35.00
- ❏ Luke Skywalker, Czech Republic [199-12] 35.00
- ❏ Princess Leia, Italy [199-13] 35.00

- ❏ R2-D2, Spain [199-14] 35.00
- ❏ Sand People, Finland [199-15] 35.00
- ❏ Stormtrooper, Germany [199-16] 35.00

Star Wars Celebration IV
Distributed during collecting discussion panels.
- ❏ Artoo-Detoo (R2-D2) [199-17] 50.00
- ❏ Ben (Obi-Wan) Kenobi [199-18] 50.00
- ❏ Chewbacca [199-19] 50.00
- ❏ Darth Vader [199-20] 50.00
- ❏ Death Squad Commander [199-21] 50.00
- ❏ Han Solo [199-22] 50.00
- ❏ Jawa [199-23] 50.00
- ❏ Luke Skywalker [199-24] 50.00
- ❏ Princess Leia Organa [199-25] 50.00
- ❏ Sand People [199-26] 50.00
- ❏ See-Threepio (C-3PO) [199-27] 50.00
- ❏ Stormtrooper [199-28] 50.00

Star Wars Celebration Japan (Japan)
Distributed during collecting discussion panels.
- ❏ C-3PO [199-29] 45.00
- ❏ Chewbacca [199-30] 45.00
- ❏ Darth Vader [199-31] 45.00
- ❏ Han Solo, bottle cap [199-32] 45.00
- ❏ Landspeeder [199-33] 45.00
- ❏ Luke Skywalker, plush [199-34] 45.00
- ❏ Millennium Falcon, wooden [199-35] 45.00
- ❏ R2-D2, walking [199-36] 45.00
- ❏ TIE Fighter, wooden [199-37] 45.00
- ❏ X-Wing Fighter, inflatable [199-38] 45.00
- ❏ X-Wing Fighter, transforming [199-39] 45.00
- ❏ Y-Wing Fighter [199-40] 45.00

Star Wars Reunion II (France)
- ❏ Boba Fett [199-41] 85.00

Cologne and Perfume
Continued in Volume 3, Page 179

Avon (Mexico)
Cologne for kids.
- ❏ Anakin and Amidala [200-01] 20.00
- ❏ Jedi Starfighter [200-02] 25.00
- ❏ Padmé Amidala, wrist compact [200-03] 20.00

Interparfum, S.A. (UK)
- ❏ Eau de Toilette 25.00

Star Wars Celebration V
- ❏ Eau Lando cologne 40.00
- ❏ Slave Leia perfume [200-04] 40.00

Combs

Adam Joseph Industries
Comb-n-Keepers.
- ❏ Landspeeder [201-01] 20.00
- ❏ Max Rebo Band [201-02] 25.00
- ❏ Princess Kneesaa [201-03] 30.00
- ❏ Wicket and Princess Kneesaa [201-04] 30.00

Pop-Up Combs.
- ❏ C-3PO and R2-D2 [201-05] 20.00
- ❏ Darth Vader [201-06] 20.00
- ❏ Princess Leia as Jabba's Prisoner [201-07] 26.00

199-01 Front and Back | 199-02 Front and Back | 199-03 Front and Back | 199-04 Front and Back

Comic Books

199-05	199-06	199-07	199-08	199-09	199-10	199-11	199-12
199-13	199-14	199-15	199-16	199-17	199-18	199-19	199-20
199-21	199-22	199-23	199-24	199-25	199-26	199-27	199-28
199-29	199-30	199-31	199-32	199-33	199-34	199-35	199-36

199-37

199-38

199-39

199-40

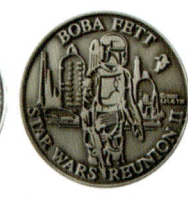
199-41

Comic Books
Continued in Volume 3, Page 180

- ❑ 2000 AD, program 166 ....15.00
- ❑ Fan Boys, exclusive to Star Wars Celebration IV 15.00
- ❑ Star Rats [v1e1:173] 10.00
- ❑ Star Wars triple comic..15.00

(France)
L'Empire Contre-Attaque
- ❑ Issues 1–2, each [v1e1:173] 15.00

La Guerre des Etoiles
- ❑ Issues 1–2, each 15.00

Le Retour du Jedi
- ❑ Issues 1–2, each 15.00

(Greece)
- ❑ Super Mttoy..45.00

(Italy)
- ❑ Guerre Stellari 45.00

(Turkey)
Milliyet Cocuk.
- ❑ 1988 001 4 Ocak..35.00
- ❑ 1989 014 3 Nisan 35.00

Tercuman Cocuk.
- ❑ 1978 048 1 Aralik 35.00
- ❑ 1982 004 22 Ocak..35.00
- ❑ 1982 023 4 Haziran 35.00
- ❑ 1982 030 23 Temmuz 35.00
- ❑ 1983 031 5 Agustos [202-01] 35.00

Blackthorne Publishing
3D Comics
- ❑ Issue 1 Star Wars [v1e1:173] 20.00
- ❑ Issue 2 Havoc on Hoth [202-02] 20.00
- ❑ Issue 3 The Dark Side of Dantooine 20.00

BlueWater Comics
- ❑ Female Force: Carrie Fisher 10.00

Bruguera
- ❑ Issue 1 [v1e1:173] 85.00
- ❑ Issues 2–6, each 35.00
- ❑ Issues 7–15, each [202-03] 25.00
- ❑ Imperio Contraataca [v1e1:173] 25.00

Especial
- ❑ Issues 1–4, each [v1e1:173] 30.00

Carlsen
- ❑ Del Af Thrawns Haevn 15.00
- ❑ Del Af Trilogy..15.00
- ❑ Der Kampf Der Droiden 15.00

Chikara Comics
- ❑ Pop Parody #1, "Episode Uno, The Parody Menace" [v1e1:173] 10.00

Comics Forum
- ❑ Issues 1–16, each [v1e1:173] 15.00
- ❑ El Retorno Del Jedi, graphic novel 25.00

Dark Horse Comics
A New Hope: Special Edition.
- ❑ Issues 1–4 [v1e1:174] 15.00

Agent of the Empire
- ❑ Issues 1–5, each 8.00

Blood Ties
- ❑ Issues 1–4, each [202-04] 15.00

Blood Ties: Boba Fett is Dead
- ❑ Issues 1–4, each 15.00

Boba Fett
- ❑ Issue 1/2 Wizard mail-away [v1e1:174] 20.00

Boba Fett Agent of Doom.
- ❑ One-shot [v1e1:174] 15.00

Boba Fett Bounty on Bar-Kooda
- ❑ One-shot [v1e1:174] 8.00

Boba Fett Enemy of the Empire
- ❑ Issues 1–4, each [202-05] 8.00

Boba Fett Murder Most Foul
- ❑ One-shot [v1e1:174] 15.00

Boba Fett Overkill
- ❑ One-shot [v1e1:174] 15.00

Boba Fett Twin Engines of Destruction
- ❑ One-shot [v1e1:174] 20.00

Boba Fett When The Fat Lady Swings
- ❑ One-shot [202-06] 10.00

Bounty Hunters
- ❑ Issues 1–2, each [v1e1:174] 8.00
- ❑ Aurra Sing 12.00

Chewbacca
- ❑ Issues 1–4, each [202-07] 5.00

Classic Star Wars
- ❑ Issues 1–20, each [202-08] 6.00

Classic Star Wars: The Early Adventures
- ❑ Issues 1–9, each [202-09] 5.00

Comic Books

Classic Star Wars: The Vandelhelm Mission
- One-shot [v1e1:174] 8.00

Clone Wars Adventures
- Trade paperback volumes 1–9, each 30.00

Crimson Empire
- Issues 1–6, each [v1e1:174] 20.00
- Trade paperback, reprints issues 1–6 with 2 Gentle Giant mini bust-ups including exclusive holo Emperor [202-10] 45.00

Crimson Empire II
- Issues 1–6, each 8.00

Dark Empire
- Issue 1 Wizard Ace edition 25.00
- Issues 1–6, each [202-11] 15.00
- Issues 1–3 2nd printing, each 10.00
- Issues 1–6 gold edition limited to 5,000 each, set 75.00
- Issues 1–6 platinum edition ltd. to 4,000 each, set ..150.00

Dark Empire II
- Issues 1–6, each [202-12] 10.00
- Issues 1–6 gold edition limited to 5,000 each, set ...120.00

Dark Force Rising
- Issues 1–6, each [202-13] 10.00

Dark Horse Classics: Dark Empire
- Issues 1–6, each 10.00

Dark Horse Comics Insider
- Volume 2, issue 7: "Beginning an All New Star Wars Adventure" [v1e1:175] 8.00
- Volume 2, issue 15, Tales of the Jedi strip part 1 ....5.00
- Volume 2, issue 16, Tales of the Jedi strip part 2 ....5.00
- Volume 2, issue 17, Tales of the Jedi strip part 3 ....5.00
- Volume 2, issue 18, Tales of the Jedi strip part 4 ....5.00
- Volume 2, issue 19, Tales of the Jedi strip part 5 ....5.00
- Volume 2, issue 20, Tales of the Jedi strip part 6 ....5.00
- Volume 2, issue 33, Tales of the Jedi: Dark Lords of the Sith sneak preview 8.00
- Volume 2, issue 34, Star Wars cover art, article on Star Wars day at San Diego Comic-Con 8.00
- Volume 2, issue 35, interview with Dark Empire team Tom Veitch and Cam Kennedy 8.00
- Volume 2, issue 43, interview with X-Wing: Rogue Squadron team Michael Stackpole and Mike Baron 8.00
- Volume 2, issue 46, Star Wars cover, Star Wars Month at Dark Horse 5.00

Dark Times
- Issue 0 ....10.00
- Issues 1–17, each [v1e1:175] 8.00

Darth Maul
- Issue 1 ....20.00
- Issue 2-4, each [v1e1:175] 15.00

Darth Maul: Death Sentence
- Issues 1-4, each [202-14] 12.00

Darth Vader and the Ghost Prison
- Issues 1-5, each [202-15] 12.00

Darth Vader and the Lost Command
- Issues 1-5, each 12.00

Dawn of the Jedi: Force Storm
- Issues 1-5, each [202-16] 15.00

Dawn of the Jedi: Prisoner of Bogan
- Issues 1-2, each 12.00

Devil Worlds
- Issues 1 and 2, each [202-17] 8.00

Droids
- Issues 1-6, [202-18] each 8.00
- Special Edition [v1e1:175] 8.00
- The Constancia Affair, exclusive to KB Toys [v1e1:175] 10.00
- The Protocol Offensive [v1e1:175] 8.00

Droids, Series 2
- Issues 1-8, each [v1e1:175] 8.00

Empire
- Issue 1 [202-19] 15.00
- Issues 2–40, each [202-20] 8.00

Empires End
- Issues 1 and 2, each [202-21] 10.00

Episode I: The Phantom Menace
- Issue 1/2 [v1e1:175] 12.00
- Issues 1–4, each [v1e1:175] 3.00

Episode I: The Phantom Menace Character One-Shots
Art covers
- Anakin Skywalker 5.00
- Obi-Wan Kenobi 5.00
- Queen Amidala 5.00
- Qui-Gon Jinn 5.00

Photo covers
- Anakin Skywalker [202-22] 8.00
- Obi-Wan Kenobi 8.00
- Queen Amidala 8.00
- Qui-Gon Jinn 8.00

Photo covers with glow-in-the-dark features, 15,000 produced
- Anakin Skywalker 25.00
- Obi-Wan Kenobi 25.00
- Queen Amidala 25.00
- Qui-Gon Jinn 30.00

Photo covers with holo foil logo, 15,000 produced
- Anakin Skywalker 25.00
- Obi-Wan Kenobi 25.00
- Queen Amidala 25.00
- Qui-Gon Jinn 25.00

Episode II Attack of the Clones
- Issues 1–4 art cover, each 5.00
- Issues 1–4 photo cover, each [202-23] 8.00

Exclusive
Exclusive to Toys R Us
- Issue 1 Full of Surprises [v1e1:175] 20.00
- Issue 2 Most Precious Weapon [v1e1:175] 22.00
- Issue 3 Practice Makes Perfect [v1e1:175] 40.00
- Issue 4 Machines of War [v1e1:175] 25.00

Free Comic Book Day
- 2002 A Jedi's Weapon 5.00
- 2004 Hide In Plain Sight (first appearance of General Grievous) ..80.00
- 2005 Brothers in Arms 15.00
- 2006 Another Day, Another Siege 15.00
- 2009 The Clone Wars: The Gauntlet of Death 18.00
- 2011 The Clone Wars: Opress Unleashed 40.00
- 2012 The Art of the Bad Deal 15.00

General Grievous
- Issues 1–4, each 15.00

Han Solo at Stars' End
- Issues 1–3, each [v1e1:175] 5.00

Handbooks
One-shots
- Crimson Empire 12.00
- Dark Empire 15.00
- Knights of the Old Republic 25.00
- X-Wing Rogue Squadron 20.00

Heir To The Empire
- Issues 1–6, each [v1e1:175] 15.00
- One-shot, San Diego Comic-Con exclusive [202-24] 25.00

Infinities A New Hope
- Issues 1–4, each [202-25] 10.00

Infinities Empire Strikes Back
- Issues 1–4, each [202-26] 15.00

Infinities Return of the Jedi
- Issues 1–4, each [202-27] 10.00

Invasion
- Issue 0 ....10.00
- Issues 1–6, each 8.00

Comic Books

Invasion: Rescues
- Issues 1–6, each [202-28] 8.00

Invasion: Revelations
- Issues 1–5, each 5.00

Jabba the Hutt
- Betrayal [202-29] 8.00
- The Dynasty Trap [v1e1:175] 10.00
- The Gaar Suppoon Hit [v1e1:175] 8.00
- The Hunger of Princess Nampi [v1e1:175] 8.00
- The Jabba Tape [v1e1:175] 10.00

Jango Fett, Open Seasons
- Issues 1–4, each [v1e1:175] 20.00

Jedi
- Aayla Secura [v1e1:175] 10.00
- Count Dooku [v1e1:175] 15.00
- Mace Windu [v1e1:175] 40.00
- Shaak Ti [202-30] 15.00
- Yoda [v1e1:175] 15.00

Jedi Academy: Leviathan
- Issues 1–4, each [v1e1:175] 10.00

Jedi Council: Acts of War
- Issues 1–4, each [202-31] 8.00

Jedi Quest
- Issues 1–4, each [v1e1:175] 5.00

Jedi The Dark Side
- Issue 1 .... 8.00
- Issues 2–5, each 5.00

Jedi vs. Sith
- Issues 1–6, each [v1e1:175] 10.00

Knight Errant
- Issue 1 .... 12.00
- Issues 2–5, each [v1e1:175] 10.00

Knight Errant: Escape
Exclusive to San Diego Comic-Con
- Issues 1–5, each [202-32] 8.00

Knights of the Old Republic
- Issue 0 .... 20.00
- Issues 1–50, each [v1e1:175] 6.00

The Last Command
- Issues 1–6, each [v1e1:175] 8.00

Legacy
- Issue 0 .... 20.00
- Issue 1/2 .... 35.00
- Issues 1–50, each [202-33] 8.00

Legacy: War
- Issues 1–6, each 10.00

Lost Tribe of the Sith - Spiral
- Issues 1–5, each 12.00

Manga: Empire Strikes Back
- Issues 1–4, each [v1e1:176] 25.00

Manga: Return of the Jedi
- Issues 1–4, each [v1e1:176] 20.00

Manga: Star Wars
- Issues 1–4, each [202-34] 25.00

Manga: The Phantom Menace
- Issues 1–2, each [v1e1:176] 15.00

Mara Jade: By The Emperor's Hand
- Issue 1 .... 35.00
- Issues 2–6, each [202-35] 15.00

Obsession
- Issues 1–5, each [v1e1:176] 15.00

Purge
- Last of the Jedi 30.00
- The Tyrant's Fist [202-36] 20.00

Qui-Gon and Obi-Wan, Last Stand on Ord Mantell
- Issues 1–3, each [v1e1:176] 5.00

Qui-Gon and Obi-Wan, The Aurorient Express
- Issues 1–2, each [202-37] 8.00

Rebellion
- Issues 1–82, each [v1e1:176] 5.00

Revenge of the Sith
- Issues 1–4, each [v1e1:176] 5.00

River of Chaos
- Issues 1–4, each [v1e1:176] 5.00

Sergio Aragonis Stomps Star Wars
- One-shot [v1e1:176] 25.00

Shadow Stalker
- One-shot [v1e1:176] 6.00

Shadows of the Empire
- Issues 1–6, each [v1e1:176] 8.00

Shadows of the Empire: Evolution
- Issues 1–5, each [202-38] 8.00

Splinter of the Mind's Eye
- Issues 1–4, each [v1e1:176] 8.00

Star Fighter Crossbones
- Issues 1–3, each [v1e1:176] 5.00

Star Wars
- Issue 0: Luke and Leia cover [v1e1:177] 25.00
- Issue 0: Princess Leia cover [v1e1:177] 15.00
- Issue 1 [v1e1:177] 15.00
- Issue 1 Foil logo, 5,000 produced 50.00
- Issues 2–45, each [202-39] 8.00

Star Wars Republic
- Issues 46–60, each [202-40] 8.00
- Issues 61–77, each [202-41] 5.00

Star Wars Tales
- Issues 1–24, each [202-42] 10.00
- Issues 5–24 photo cover, each 8.00

Star Wars: The Films and Galaxy Beyond
- Episode III DVD preorder premium [v1e1:177] 25.00

Tag and Bink Are Dead
- Issues 1–2, each [202-43] 15.00

Tag and Bink, Return of…
- Issues 1–2, each [v1e1:177] 15.00

Tales from Mos Eisley
- One-shot [202-44] 8.00

Tales of the Jedi
- Issues 1–5, each [v1e1:177] 8.00

Tales of the Jedi: Dark Lords of the Sith
- Ashcan Special Edition for Topps [v1e1:177] 25.00
- Issues 1–6, each [202-45] 8.00

Tales of the Jedi: Redemption
- Issues 1–5, each [v1e1:177] 5.00

Tales of the Jedi: The Fall of the Sith Empire
- Issue 1 Wizard exclusive signed by Kevin Anderson 70.00
- Issues 1–5, each [v1e1:177] 10.00

Tales of the Jedi: The Freedon Nadd Uprising
- Issues 1–2, each [v1e1:177] 8.00

Tales of the Jedi: The Golden Age of the Sith
- Issue 0 [202-46] 10.00
- Issues 1–5, each [v1e1:177] 8.00

Tales of the Jedi: The Sith War
- Issues 1–6, each [202-47] 8.00

The Clone Wars
- Issue 0 .... 15.00
- Issues 1–8, each 5.00

The Old Republic: The Lost Suns
- Issues 1–5, each 10.00

Underworld: The Yavin Vassilika
- Issues 1–5, each [202-48] 8.00

Union
- Issues 1–4, each [v1e1:177] 20.00

Vader's Quest
- Issues 1–4, each [202-49] 8.00

Comic Books

202-48 Sample | 202-49 Sample | 202-50 Sample | 202-51 | 202-52 | 202-53 | 202-54 Sample | 202-55

202-56 Sample | 202-57 | 202-58 Sample | 202-59 Sample | 202-60 Sample | 202-61 | 202-62 Sample | 202-63 Sample

202-64 Sample 1 and Sample 2 | 202-65 Sample | 202-66 Sample | 202-67 Sample | 202-68 Sample | 202-69 Sample | 202-70

X-Wing Rogue Leader
- Issues 1–3, each 10.00

X-Wing Rogue Squadron
- Issue 1/2 Movie Edition 18.00
- Issue 1/2 Platinum edition 15.00
- Issue 1/2 Wizard mail-away 15.00
- Issue 1 ....8.00
- Issue 2 ....8.00
- Issues 3–35, each [202-50] 5.00
- One-shot Cereal give-away 25.00

Delcourt (France)
- L'Empire Ecarlate—1 Trahison, hardcover 15.00
- L'Empire Ecarlate—2 Heritage, hardcover 15.00
- L'Ultime Commandment Vol. 1 [v1e1:174] 10.00
- L'Ultime Commandment Vol. 2 ....10.00
- Le Retour Du Jedi 10.00

Dino (Germany)
- Crimson Empire, each 20.00

Eclipse Comics
Adolescent Radioactive Black Belt Hamsters 3-D
- #2, includes 3D glasses [202-51] 10.00

Entity Comics
- Fart Wars, parody [v1e1:174] 15.00
- Return of One-Eye, parody [v1e1:174] 35.00

Epic Comics
- Samurai Cat issue 3 ....8.00

Fan Made
- The Norm, Night of the Wookiee 5.00

Feest Comics (Germany)
- Das Goldene Zeitalter Der Sith II 15.00
- Das Letzte Kommando Teil I 15.00
- Der Sith-Kreig Teil I 15.00
- Der Untergang Der Sith I-III [v1e1:174] 15.00
- Die Dunkle Seite Der Macht Teil III 15.00
- Die Lords von Sith Teil I 15.00
- Die Lords von Sith Teil II 15.00
- Die Lords von Sith Teil III 15.00
- Luke Skywalker Teil II 15.00

Classic Star Wars.
- Band 6-Band 9 [v1e1:174] 15.00

Foom
- Issue 21, Star Wars [202-52] 125.00

Hasbro
- Clone Wars Short Stories Collection [v1e1:174] 8.00

Mad House Comics
Archie series.
- 1978 February, C-3PO / R2-D2 parody cover [202-53] 35.00

Magic Press (Italy)
- Il Ritorno del lo Jedi 14.00

Mala Stripoteka (Serbia)
- Volume II: No. 1–No. 7 [202-54] 40.00

Manga
A New Hope
- Issues 1–4, each 20.00

Empire Strikes Back
- Issues 1–4, each 20.00

Return of the Jedi
- Issues 1–4, each 20.00

Star Wars Episode I: The Phantom Menace
- One-shot [v1e1:174] 25.00

Cine-Manga (Japan)
- Episode I: The Phantom Menace 25.00
- Episode II: Attack of the Clones 25.00
- Episode III: Revenge of the Sith [v1e1:174] 25.00

Marvel Comics
Howard the Duck
- Issue 22 "May the Farce be With You" 10.00
- Issue 23 "Star Waaugh!" 10.00

Marvel Age
- Issue 10 Star Wars cover 8.00

Marvel Movie Showcase
- Issue 1 Star Wars, reprints of Star Wars issues 1–3 .....35.00
- Issue 2 Star Wars, reprints of Star Wars issues 4–6 .....25.00

Marvel Super Special
- Issue 27, "Return of the Jedi" 18.00

Return of the Jedi
- Issues 1–4, direct market, each 12.00
- Issues 1–4, newsstand, each [202-56] 12.00

Multi-packs
- 2-pack 130.00
- Issues 1–4 [202-55] 50.00

Spidey Super Stories
- Issue 31, Star Jaws, parody featuring Spider-Man, Moondragon, Marvel Boy and Doctor Doom [202-57] ..135.00

Star Wars
Direct market
- Issue 1 30 cent cover 100.00
- Issue 1 35 cent cover, reprint 35.00
- Issues 2–6, each 24.00
- Issues 7–38, each [202-58] 17.00
- Issues 39–44, each 22.00
- Issues 45–67, each 16.00
- Issue 68 ....50.00
- Issues 69–80, each 15.00
- Issues 81–99, each 20.00
- Issue 100 ....40.00
- Issues 101–106, each 20.00
- Issue 107 ....45.00

Multi-packs
- Issues 7–9 diamond logo 19.00

Newsstand
- Issue 1 30 cent cover 150.00
- Issue 1 35 cent cover 1,650.00
- Issues 2–6 30 cent cover, each 24.00
- Issues 2–6 35 cent cover, each 200.00
- Issues 7–38, each [202-59] 17.00
- Issues 39–44, each 22.00
- Issues 45–67, each [202-60] 16.00
- Issue 68 ....50.00
- Issues 69–80, each 15.00
- Issues 81–99, each 20.00
- Issue 100 ....40.00
- Issues 101–106, each 20.00
- Issue 107 ....45.00
- Annual 1 ....15.00
- Annual 2 [202-61] 15.00
- Annual 3 ....15.00

Star Wars Special Edition oversized
- ❏ Issue 1: Part 1 ....15.00
- ❏ Issue 2: Part 2 ....15.00

The Mighty Avengers
- ❏ Issue 6 C-3PO hidden on cover 8.00

Marvel Comics (France)
- ❏ La Guerre Des Etoiles 35.00

Marvel Comics (Canada)
Ewoks
Newsstand
- ❏ Issues 1–6, 75 cent cover, each......................12.00
- ❏ Issues 7–8, 95 cent cover, each......................4.00

Marvel Comics (UK)
Empire Strikes Back Monthly
- ❏ Issues 140–158, each [202-62] 30.00

Empire Strikes Back Weekly
- ❏ Issues 118–139, each...................................20.00

Ewoks
- ❏ Issues 1–8, each..45.00
- ❏ Issues 9–10 Ewoks - Droids Team-Up, each [202-63] 45.00

Return of the Jedi Weekly
- ❏ Issues 1–3, each..15.00
- ❏ Issues 4–155, each [202-64] 12.00

Star Wars Monthly
- ❏ Issues 159–171, each....................................12.00

Star Wars Weekly
- ❏ Issue 1 ....175.00
- ❏ Issues 2–10, each..50.00
- ❏ Issues 11–100, each [202-65] 35.00
- ❏ Issues 101–116, each....................................20.00
- ❏ Issue 117 ....25.00

Star Wars Weekly specials
- ❏ Summer..35.00

Mundi Comics (Spain)
- ❏ Issues 1–9, each [202-66] 90.00

Parody Press
Adolescent Radioactive Black Belt Hamsters Classics
- ❏ #2, reprints Adolescent Radioactive Black Belt Hamsters 3-D #2, which also has a Star Wars parody cover 15.00

Planeta DeAgostini Comics (Mexico)
Una Nueva Esperanza
- ❏ Issues 1–4, each [202-67]..............................45.00

El Imperio Contraataca
- ❏ Issues 5–8, each..45.00

El Retorno Del Jedi
- ❏ Issues 9–12, each..35.00

Star Comics
Droids
- ❏ Issue 1...35.00
- ❏ Issues 2–8, each [202-68] 20.00

Newsstand
- ❏ Issues 1–3 75 cent cover, each......................35.00
- ❏ Issue 1–3 95 cent cover, each 20.00
- ❏ Issues 4–8, each..20.00

Ewoks
- ❏ Issue 1...25.00
- ❏ Issues 2–3, each [202-69] 15.00
- ❏ Issues 4–10, each..12.00
- ❏ Issues 11–14, each..12.00

Newsstand
- ❏ Issues 1–6, 65 cent cover, each....................20.00
- ❏ Issues 7–8, 75 cent cover, each....................15.00
- ❏ Issues 9–14, each..12.00
- ❏ Issue 12 "M" logo, Star logo in UPC box 12.00

Surco (Spain)
- ❏ Issues 1–6, each [v1e1:174] 150.00

Telecomic (Spain)
- ❏ Issue 24–27 Ewoks and Droids [v1e1:175] 40.00

YPS (Germany)
- ❏ Der Stormtrooper des Imperiums [202-70] 250.00

Computers
Continued in Volume 3, Page 187

Alienware
- ❏ Dark Side case design [203-01] 300.00
- ❏ Light Side case design [203-02] 300.00

Computers: Dust Covers
Continued in Volume 3, Page 187

World Wide Licenses Ltd.
- ❏ Darth Maul, for monitor and keyboard [203-03] 15.00

Computers: Keyboards

Sakar International
- ❏ Clone Wars [204-01] 40.00

Computers: Mice
Continued in Volume 3, Page 187

- ❏ Anakin Skywalker, sculpted [205-01] 35.00
- ❏ Episode II with Anakin / Vader mouse pad 25.00

American Covers
3D sculpted mice.
- ❏ C-3PO [205-02] 20.00
- ❏ Darth Vader [205-03] 20.00
- ❏ Stormtrooper [205-04] 20.00

JazWares, Inc
Red and black wireless.
- ❏ Darth Vader [205-05] 40.00
- ❏ Vader [205-06] 40.00

204-01

203-01 Side 1 and Side 2

203-02 Side 1 and Side 2

203-03

205-01

205-02

205-03

205-04

205-05

205-06

205-07

205-08

205-09

205-10

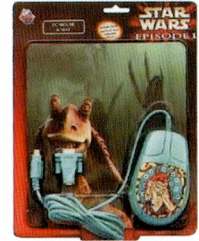
205-11

205-12

205-13

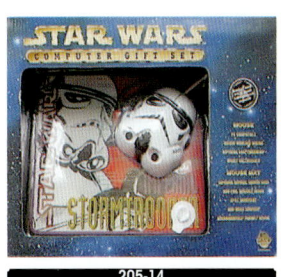
205-14

Computers: Mice

 206-01
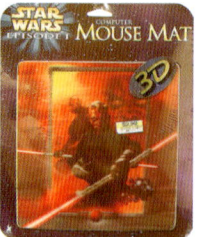 206-02
 206-03
 206-04
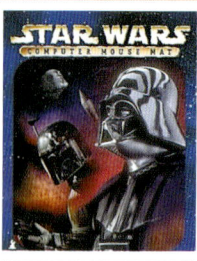 206-05
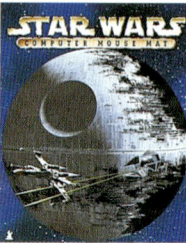 206-06
 206-07

 206-08
 206-09
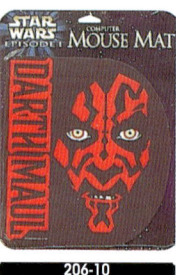 206-10
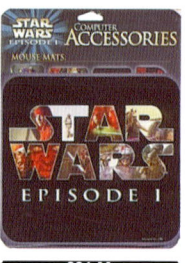 206-11
 206-12
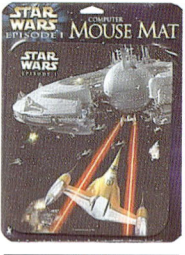 206-13
 206-14

World Wide Licenses Ltd.
❏ Anakin Skywalker [205-07] 15.00
❏ Darth Maul [205-08] 15.00
❏ Jar Jar Binks [205-09] 15.00

"Computer Gift Sets" Character mouse and mouse pad.
❏ Darth Maul [205-10] 20.00
❏ Jar Jar Binks / Naboo [205-11] 20.00

❏ C-3PO / C-3PO and R2-D2 [205-12] 35.00
❏ Darth Vader [205-13] 35.00
❏ Stormtrooper [205-14] 35.00

Computers: Mouse Pads

❏ Episode I collage with Vader in the center [4:116] 10.00

❏ Episode I collage with Yoda in the center [4:116] 10.00
❏ Episode I movie poster collage [206-01] 10.00
❏ Episode II: Attack of the Clones, heroes [206-01] 10.00

American Covers
3D lenticular.
❏ Darth Maul [206-02] 15.00
❏ Jump to light speed [206-03] 15.00
❏ Lightsaber battle [206-04] 15.00

Classic trilogy.
❏ Darth Vader / Boba Fett [206-05] 15.00
❏ Death Star [206-06] 15.00
❏ Droids [206-07] 15.00
❏ Yoda [206-08] 15.00

Episode I: The Phantom Menace.
❏ Anakin, Podracer [206-09] 10.00

❏ Darth Maul [206-10] 10.00
❏ Episode I Logo [206-11] 10.00
❏ Jedi vs. Sith [206-12] 10.00
❏ Naboo Space Battle [206-13] 10.00
❏ Queen Amidala [206-14] 10.00

Mouse Mats.
❏ Classic trilogy. [206-15] 15.00

Animations
Exclusive to Target.
❏ Chewbacca [206-16] 10.00
❏ Darth Vader [206-17] 10.00
❏ Yoda [206-18] 10.00

Entertainment Earth
❏ Clone Wars scene, exclusive to Entertainment Earth ... 15.00

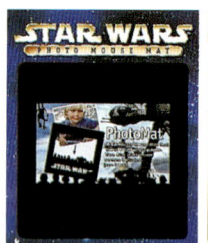 206-15
 206-16
 206-17
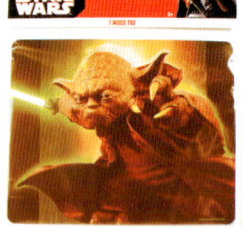 206-18
 206-19
 206-20

 206-21
 206-22
 206-23
 206-24
 206-25

 206-26 Image 1
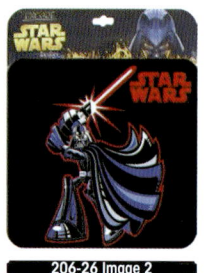 206-26 Image 2
 206-27
 206-28
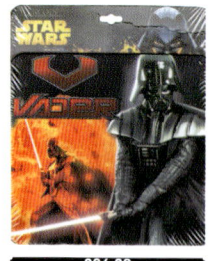 206-29
 206-30

Computers: USB Drives

207-01 207-02 207-03 207-04 207-05 207-06 207-07 207-08 207-09 207-10

Long Island Distributing Co. Ltd.
Built-in solar calculators.
- ❏ B-Wing Fighter attack [206-19] 20.00
- ❏ Bounty hunters 20.00
- ❏ Death Star trench [206-20] 20.00
- ❏ Dogfight above 2nd Death Star [206-21] 20.00
- ❏ Luke vs. Emperor [206-22] 20.00
- ❏ TIE attack [206-23] 20.00
- ❏ X-Wing Fighters [206-24] 20.00

LucasArts
- ❏ Battlefront, promo [206-25] 15.00
- ❏ Star Wars Galaxies, 8" round 20.00

Mousetrak
- ❏ Bounty hunters 15.00
- ❏ C-3PO and R2-D2 .... 15.00
- ❏ Dark Forces 15.00
- ❏ Darth Vader 15.00
- ❏ Leia and Luke on Jabba's sail barge [4:116] 15.00
- ❏ Millennium Falcon 15.00
- ❏ Rebel Assault [4:116] 15.00
- ❏ Yoda [4:116] 15.00

Pepsi Cola (Singapore)
Episode I, lenticular.
- ❏ Anakin Skywalker [4:116] 25.00
- ❏ C-3PO [4:116] 25.00
- ❏ Jar Jar Binks [4:116] 25.00
- ❏ Queen Amidala [4:116] 25.00
- ❏ Qui-Gon Jinn [4:116] 25.00

Rawcliffe
Anime style characters.
- ❏ 2-pack Darth Vader and Yoda [206-26] 20.00
- ❏ Luke and Leia [206-27] 20.00

Episode III: Revenge of the Sith.
- ❏ Darth Vader 10.00
- ❏ Yoda 10.00

The Encore Group
- ❏ Sith [206-28] 10.00
- ❏ Vader [206-29] 10.00

World Wide Licenses Ltd.
- ❏ Battle Droid with Trade Federation tank [206-30] 15.00
- ❏ Darth Maul 15.00

Computers: Software
Continued in Volume 3, Page 187

America On-Line
- ❏ Episode II CD: footage, images, sound tracks, AOL client [v1e1:181] 15.00
- ❏ Episode III CD: games, AOL client 9.0 .... 15.00

LucasArts
- ❏ Episode I Insider's Guide [v1e1:181] 15.00
- ❏ Star Wars Screen Entertainment, CD ROM 10.00
- ❏ Star Wars Screen Entertainment, floppy disk 20.00
- ❏ Star Wars: Behind the Magic for Win95/98 [v1e1:181] 35.00

Pepsi Cola
- ❏ Essential Guide to Star Wars: Episode I 20.00

Simon and Schuster Interactive
- ❏ Star Wars Trilogy Moviebook software on CD-ROM 40.00

SLC Interactive
- ❏ The Art of Drew Struzan multimedia [4:117] 45.00

Sound Source Interactive
- ❏ Star Wars Audio Clips [4:117] 15.00
- ❏ Star Wars Audio Clips (special offer) 15.00
- ❏ Star Wars Trilogy Entertainment Utility 15.00
- ❏ Star Wars Visual Clips (Macintosh Only) [v1e1:181] 15.00
- ❏ Star Wars Visual Clips add-on (special offer) 15.00

Computers: USB Drives
Continued in Volume 3, Page 187

Brushed steel. 256MB.
- ❏ C-3PO [207-01] 50.00
- ❏ Darth Vader [207-02] 50.00
- ❏ Jedi [207-03] 50.00
- ❏ R2-D2 [207-04] 50.00

Sculpted characters, soft rubber.
- ❏ Darth Vader 15.00
- ❏ R2-D2 .... 15.00
- ❏ Stormtrooper 15.00
- ❏ Yoda 15.00

 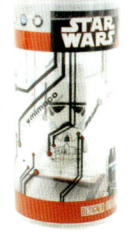    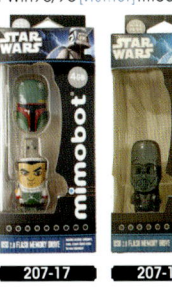    

207-11 207-12 207-13 207-14 207-15 207-16 207-17 207-18 207-19 207-20 207-21 207-22

207-23 207-24 207-25 207-26 207-27 207-28 207-29 207-30 207-31 207-32 207-33

207-34 207-35 207-36 207-37 207-38 207-39 207-40

Computers: USB Drives

208-01

209-01 Side 1 and Side 2

209-02

209-03

210-01

JazWares, Inc
2011. Sculpted characters.
- R2-D2, 2GB, exclusive to Toys R Us [207-05] 20.00

2012. Sculpted characters.
- Darth Maul, 2GB, exclusive to Toys R Us [207-06] 50.00
- R2-D2, 4GB [207-07] 20.00

Mimoco (Japan)
2008. Sculpted characters. Mimobot. Up to 2GB.
- Boba Fett, each 30.00
- C-3PO, each [207-08] 20.00
- Chewbacca, each 30.00
- Darth Sidious, each [207-09] 25.00
- Darth Vader, each 30.00
- Ewok, each 30.00
- Han Solo, each [207-10] 30.00
- Luke Skywalker, pilot, each 30.00
- Princess Leia, each [207-11] 30.00
- R2-D2, each 30.00
- Royal Guard, each 30.00
- Stormtrooper, each [207-12] 20.00

2009. Sculpted characters. Mimobot. Up to 4GB.
- C-3PO, each [207-13] 15.00
- Darth Maul, each [207-14] 15.00
- Jawa, each 25.00
- Luke Skywalker Hoth, each 25.00
- Obi-Wan Kenobi, each [207-15] 15.00
- R2-D2, each [207-16] 15.00
- Snowtrooper 20.00
- Stormtrooper 15.00
- Wampa, each 25.00
- Yoda, each 15.00

2011. Sculpted characters. Mimobot. Up to 4GB.
- Boba Fett, each [207-17] 20.00
- Bossk, each 20.00
- C-3PO, each 15.00
- Clone Captain Rex, each 40.00
- Darth Maul, each 20.00
- Darth Vader unmasked, each [207-18] 50.00
- Han Solo in Carbonite block, each 35.00
- Jawa, each 30.00
- Lobot, exclusive to San Diego Comic-Con and Star Wars Celebration, each 65.00
- Obi-Wan Kenobi, each 20.00
- R2-D2, each [207-19] 15.00
- Starkiller, The Force Unleashed II [207-20] 50.00
- Stormtrooper unmasked to Han Solo, each 45.00
- Stormtrooper unmasked to Luke Skywalker, each 45.00
- Wicket, each 30.00
- Yoda, each 15.00

2012. Sculpted characters. Mimobot. Up to 8GB.
- Admiral Ackbar, each [207-21] 30.00
- Biker Scout, each, exclusive to San Diego Comic-Con and Star Wars Celebration [207-22] 85.00
- Boba Fett, each [207-23] 30.00
- Chewbacca, exclusive to San Diego Comic-Con, limited to 1,000, individually numbered, each 85.00
- Darth Maul hooded, each 30.00
- Darth Vader unmasked, each [207-24] 65.00
- Ewok, each 30.00
- Jabba the Hutt, each [207-25] 30.00
- Jar Jar Binks, 128GB, 500 produced, individually numbered [207-26] 250.00
- Jawa, each 30.00
- Luke Skywalker Hoth, each 30.00
- Luke Skywalker Jedi, each [207-27] 30.00
- Princess Leia captive, each [207-28] 35.00
- R2-A6, limited to 1,000, individually numbered, 32GB 50.00

2013. Sculpted characters. Mimobot. To to 8GB.
- C-3PO, each [207-29] 20.00
- Darth Vader unmasked, each 25.00
- Lando Calrissian, each 20.00
- R2-D2, each 20.00
- Stormtrooper unmasked to Han Solo, each [207-30] 45.00
- Yoda, each 20.00

Tyme Machines
2009. Sculpted characters.
- Boba Fett, 4GB [207-31] 25.00
- Darth Vader, 4GB [207-32] 25.00
- Stormtrooper, 4GB [207-33] 25.00
- Yoda, 4GB [207-34] 25.00

2011. Sculpted characters.
- Boba Fett, 4GB [207-35] 20.00
- Darth Vader, 4GB [207-36] 20.00
- Darth Vader, 8GB 30.00
- Stormtrooper, 4GB [207-37] 20.00
- Stormtrooper, 8GB 30.00
- Yoda, 4GB [207-38] 20.00

2012. Sculpted characters.
- Boba Fett, 8GB 20.00
- Darth Maul, 16GB [207-39] 25.00
- Darth Vader, 8GB [207-40] 20.00
- Yoda, 4GB 20.00
- Yoda, 8GB 20.00

Computers: Wrist Rest

American Covers
- Jedi vs. Sith [v1e1:182] 10.00
- Podrace [v1e1:182] 10.00
- Scenes from Empire Strikes Back [v1e1:182] 10.00

Condoms
- Star Condoms, Star Wars parody packaging [208-01] 30.00

Confetti

Party Express
- Darth Vader, clones, Yoda [209-01] 5.00
- Star Wars generations [209-02] 5.00
- Star Wars, stars and planets [209-03] 5.00

Construction Paper

Stuart Hall
- Return of the Jedi, Biker Scout cover [210-01] 35.00

Containers, Figural
Continued in Volume 3, Page 189

Applause
- Darth Maul, PVC [211-01] 20.00
- R2-D2, PVC [211-02] 20.00

Disney Theme Park Merchandise
- R2-D2 popcorn bucket, Star Wars 3D [211-03] 35.00

Kellogg's
Mail-in "cookie jar" premiums.
- C-3PO [211-04] 25.00
- Darth Vader [211-05] 25.00
- R2-D2 [211-06] 25.00

Kellogg's (Malaysia)
- R2-D2 collectible jar [211-07] 45.00

Cookie Jars
Continued in Volume 3, Page 187

Cards, Inc. (UK)
- Boba Fett [212-01] 200.00
- C-3PO 200.00
- Clone Shock trooper [212-02] 100.00
- Clone Special Ops trooper [212-03] 100.00
- Clone trooper [212-04] 100.00
- Commander Gree [212-05] 125.00
- Darth Vader [212-06] 175.00
- General Grievous [212-07] 225.00
- R2-D2 [212-08] 125.00
- Stormtrooper [212-09] 225.00
- Yoda full [212-10] 125.00

Joy Toy (UK)
- Death Star 175.00

Roman Ceramics
- C-3PO, ceramic figure [212-11] 275.00
- R2-D2, ceramic figure [212-12] 200.00

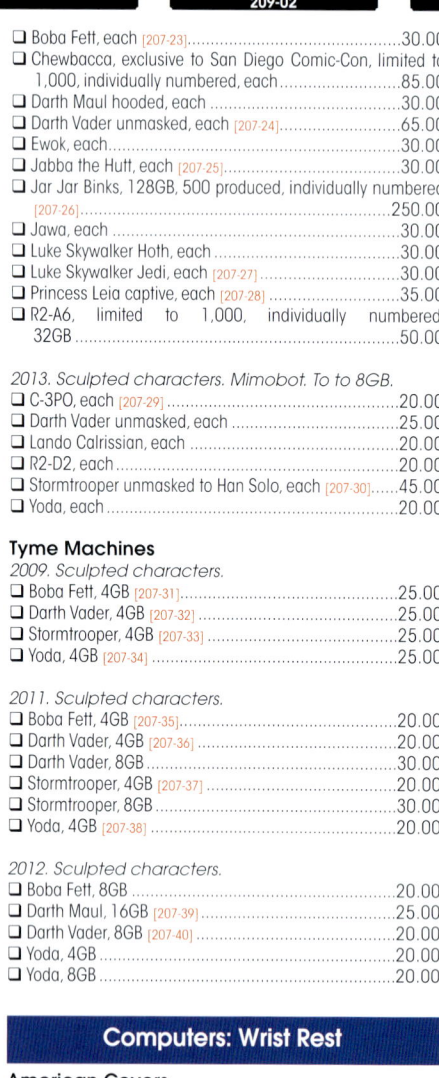

211-01

211-02

211-03

211-04

211-05

211-06

211-07

Cooking Cutters

212-01

212-02

212-03

212-04

212-05

212-06

212-07

212-08

212-09

212-10

212-11

212-12

212-12 Box

212-13 Side 1 and Side 2

212-14

212-15

212-16

212-17

212-18

Sigma
- Darth Vader and droids, ceramic 2-sided [212-13].......195.00

Star Jars
- Ben Kenobi [212-14].................................250.00
- C-3PO [212-15].....................................125.00
- Chewbacca [212-16].................................250.00
- Jabba the Hutt [212-17]............................275.00
- Princess Leia [212-18].............................250.00
- Wicket the Ewok [212-19]...........................275.00

Vandor LLC
- Darth Vader, 4,800 produced [212-20]...............125.00

Cooking Cutters
Continued in Volume 3, Page 190

Williams-Sonoma
- Sandwich cutters, limited-edition lunch box [213-01]....35.00

Cookie cutters.
- Boba Fett, Darth Vader, stormtrooper, Yoda [213-02]......25.00
- Death Star, Falcon, TIE Fighter, X-Wing [213-03]............25.00
- Jawa, R2-D2, C-3PO, Chewbacca [213-04]..................25.00

Pancake molds.
- Darth Vader, stormtrooper, Yoda [213-05] 25.00
- X-Wing Fighter, Vader's TIE Fighter, Millennium Falcon [213-06]..25.00

213-02

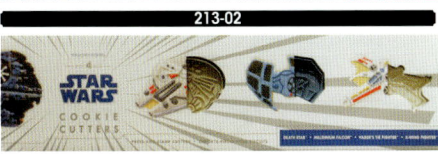
213-03

213-04

212-19

212-20

213-01

213-05

213-06

214-01

214-02

214-03

214-04

214-05

214-06

Coolers

 215-01
 215-02
 215-03
 215-04
 215-05
 215-06
 215-07
 215-08
 215-09
 215-10
 215-11
 215-12
 215-13
 215-14
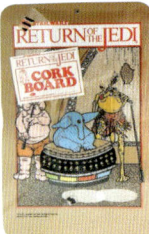 215-15
 215-16
 215-17
 215-18
 215-19
 215-20
 216-01

Coolers
Continued in Volume 3, Page 190

Bluebird Toys (UK)
Cool Bags with character art.
- ❏ Darth Vader [214-01] 35.00
- ❏ Stormtrooper [214-02] 40.00

Kooler Kraft
- ❏ R2-D2, approximately 2.5' tall, given away as Pepsi promotion [214-03] 235.00

Pepsi Cola
- ❏ MMT, holds ten 350 ml cans, comes with Battle Droid can holders [214-04] 325.00
- ❏ R2-D2 cooler [214-05] 450.00
- ❏ R2-D2 cooler [214-06] 400.00

Cork Boards
Continued in Volume 3, Page 191

Manton Cork
- ❏ AT-AT, glow-in-dark dome [v1e1:184] 75.00
- ❏ AT-AT, glow-in-dark dome round "glows" sticker [215-01] 90.00
- ❏ Boba Fett, Darth Vader, Stormtroopers [215-02] 60.00
- ❏ C-3PO and R2-D2, 2-piece set [215-03] 50.00
- ❏ C-3PO and R2-D2, glow-in-dark dome [215-04] 40.00
- ❏ C-3PO, Chewbacca, Han, Leia, Luke, R2-D2 [215-05] 130.00
- ❏ Chewbacca, glow-in-dark dome [v1e1:184] 40.00
- ❏ Chewbacca, glow-in-dark dome round "glows" sticker [215-06] 40.00
- ❏ Darth Vader [215-07] 50.00
- ❏ Darth Vader and Luke Skywalker duel [215-08] 65.00
- ❏ Darth Vader, glow-in-dark dome [215-09] 50.00
- ❏ Darth Vader, helmet and shoulders [215-10] 50.00
- ❏ Ewok hut [215-11] 75.00
- ❏ Jabba the Hutt [215-12] 60.00
- ❏ Jabba's palace [215-13] 100.00
- ❏ Luke on Tauntaun [215-14] 75.00
- ❏ Luke on Tauntaun, glow-in-dark dome [v1e1:184] 60.00
- ❏ Luke on Tauntaun, glow-in-dark dome round "glows" sticker [215-15] 60.00
- ❏ Max Rebo Band [215-16] 65.00
- ❏ Millennium Falcon "May the Force be with you" 60.00
- ❏ Paploo, Wicket, C-3PO and R2-D2 [215-17] 75.00
- ❏ Star Wars logo, Millennium Falcon, TIE Fighters, X-Wing [215-18] 75.00
- ❏ Yoda [215-19] 50.00
- ❏ Yoda, glow-in-dark 125.00
- ❏ Yoda, glow-in-dark dome [215-20] 80.00

Cosmetics
Continued in Volume 3, Page 191

Yves Saint Laurent
- ❏ One Love, Queen Amidala [216-01] 200.00

Costume Accessories
Continued in Volume 3, Page 192

Rubies
- ❏ Anakin glove [v1e1:184] 15.00
- ❏ Anakin Skywalker neck piece [217-01] 12.00
- ❏ Boba Fett inflatable jet pack [217-02] 25.00
- ❏ Darth Vader breathing device [v1e1:184] 10.00
- ❏ Jango Fett blasters and holster [217-03] 35.00
- ❏ Princess Leia headband with hair buns 25.00
- ❏ Queen Amidala super deluxe headpiece with attached wig and braids [217-04] 100.00

Clone wars.
- ❏ Ahsoka headpiece 20.00
- ❏ Anakin Skywalker gloves adult 15.00
- ❏ Anakin Skywalker gloves children's 12.00
- ❏ Obi-Wan Kenobi gloves children's [217-05] 15.00
- ❏ Pre Visla inflatable jet pack 50.00
- ❏ Pre Visla's Darksaber 35.00

Jedi braids, clip-on.
- ❏ Anakin Skywalker 10.00
- ❏ Obi-Wan Kenobi [217-06] 10.00

Rubies (Canada)
Jedi braids, clip-on.
- ❏ Anakin Skywalker [217-07] 10.00
- ❏ Obi-Wan Kenobi [v1e1:184] 10.00

 217-01
 217-02
 217-03
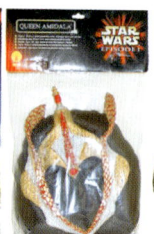 217-04
 217-05
 217-06
 217-07
 217-08

Costumes

Star Wars Celebration V
- ❏ Lando Calrissian disguise kit [217-08] 35.00

Costumes
Continued in Volume 3, Page 192

(UK)
- ❏ Clone trooper, boxed [218-01] 30.00

Acamas
- ❏ C-3PO 28.00
- ❏ Chewbacca 28.00
- ❏ Darth Vader 28.00
- ❏ Gamorrean Guard [218-02] 28.00
- ❏ Klaatu 28.00
- ❏ Luke Skywalker 28.00
- ❏ Princess Leia 28.00
- ❏ Stormtrooper 28.00
- ❏ Wicket 28.00
- ❏ Yoda 28.00

Ben Cooper
- ❏ Admiral Ackbar, Revenge 165.00
- ❏ Admiral Ackbar, Return of the Jedi [218-03] 90.00
- ❏ Boba Fett, Empire Strikes Back [218-04] 50.00
- ❏ Boba Fett, Return of the Jedi 65.00
- ❏ C-3PO (Golden Robot) 30.00
- ❏ C-3PO (Golden Robot), Empire Strikes Back 35.00
- ❏ C-3PO (Golden Robot), Star Wars [218-05] 50.00
- ❏ Chewbacca, Empire Strikes Back [218-06] 25.00
- ❏ Chewbacca, Return of the Jedi 30.00
- ❏ Chewbacca, Star Wars 50.00
- ❏ Chewbacca, Star Wars 3-piece disguise kit [218-07] 35.00
- ❏ Gamorrean Guard, Revenge 85.00
- ❏ Gamorrean Guard, Return of the Jedi [218-08] 45.00
- ❏ Klaatu, Revenge 85.00
- ❏ Klaatu, Return of the Jedi [v1e1:185] 45.00
- ❏ Lord Darth Vader, Empire Strikes Back 35.00
- ❏ Lord Darth Vader, Return of the Jedi 35.00
- ❏ Lord Darth Vader, Star Wars [218-09] 60.00
- ❏ Luke Skywalker (X-Wing Pilot), ESB [218-10] 35.00
- ❏ Luke Skywalker (X-Wing Pilot), Return of the Jedi 40.00
- ❏ Luke Skywalker (X-Wing Pilot), Star Wars 60.00
- ❏ Luke Skywalker, Empire Strikes Back 40.00
- ❏ Luke Skywalker, Return of the Jedi 40.00
- ❏ Luke Skywalker, Star Wars [218-11] 50.00
- ❏ Princess Leia, Empire Strikes Back [218-12] 45.00
- ❏ Princess Leia, Return of the Jedi 40.00
- ❏ Princess Leia, Star Wars [218-13] 50.00
- ❏ R2-D2, Empire Strikes Back [218-14] 50.00
- ❏ R2-D2, Return of the Jedi 45.00
- ❏ R2-D2, Star Wars [218-15] 65.00
- ❏ Storm trooper [sic], Empire Strikes Back [218-16] 50.00
- ❏ Storm trooper [sic], Return of the Jedi 50.00
- ❏ Storm trooper [sic], Star Wars [218-17] 65.00
- ❏ Wicket, Revenge 95.00
- ❏ Wicket, Return of the Jedi [218-18] 50.00
- ❏ Wicket, Return of the Jedi tots [218-19] 90.00
- ❏ Yoda, Empire Strikes Back [218-20] 45.00
- ❏ Yoda, Return of the Jedi 50.00

Play suits.
- ❏ Chewbacca 45.00
- ❏ Darth Vader 45.00
- ❏ Storm trooper [218-21] 45.00

Cheryl Playthings Ltd.
- ❏ C-3PO [2:257] 75.00

Croner Toys
- ❏ Stormtrooper, children's size [2:257] 75.00

Len Hunter Trading
- ❏ Darth Vader helmet, mask, vest, cape, lightsaber 35.00

Rubies
Description of contents of each set may be found in volume 1, edition 1, pages 185–187.

3D Action Suits.
- ❏ Clone trooper 25.00
- ❏ Darth Vader [218-22] 25.00

Action Suits. Clone Wars.
- ❏ Clone trooper [218-23] 15.00
- ❏ Commander Fox [218-24] 29.00

Classic trilogy.
Boba Fett
- ❏ Child, exclusive to Target 25.00

C-3PO
- ❏ Adult 65.00
- ❏ Child 30.00
- ❏ Child box set [218-25] 45.00
- ❏ Child deluxe 75.00

Chewbacca
- ❏ Adult 70.00
- ❏ Child deluxe 35.00
- ❏ Child size 15.00

Darth Vader
- ❏ Adult 75.00
- ❏ Child 20.00
- ❏ Child better 25.00
- ❏ Child better box set [4:120] 50.00
- ❏ Child box set [v1e1:185] 45.00
- ❏ Child deluxe [218-26] 100.00
- ❏ Child set 40.00

Jabba the Hutt
- ❏ Child deluxe 35.00

Luke Skywalker
- ❏ Adult 45.00
- ❏ Adult deluxe 65.00
- ❏ Child 35.00

Princess Leia
- ❏ Adult [2:257] 45.00
- ❏ Child 25.00

Stormtrooper
- ❏ Adult 55.00
- ❏ Child [2:257] 12.00
- ❏ Child boxed set [218-27] 45.00
- ❏ Child deluxe [218-28] 40.00

TaunTaun
- ❏ Adult inflatable 50.00
- ❏ Child inflatable 40.00

Tusken Raider
- ❏ Child deluxe 40.00

Yoda
- ❏ Adult 60.00
- ❏ Child deluxe 55.00

Clone Wars.
Ahsoka
- ❏ Child 35.00
- ❏ Child deluxe 65.00

Anakin Skywalker
- ❏ Adult deluxe 85.00
- ❏ Child deluxe [218-29] 65.00

Jedi
- ❏ Adult female 65.00
- ❏ Adult robe 100.00
- ❏ Child robe 50.00

Obi-Wan Kenobi
- ❏ Adult deluxe 85.00
- ❏ Child deluxe 65.00

Plo Koon
- ❏ Child 35.00
- ❏ Child deluxe 65.00

Episode I: The Phantom Menace.
Anakin Skywalker
- ❏ Action wear 25.00
- ❏ Action wear deluxe 40.00

Anakin Skywalker Jedi Apprentice
- ❏ Child 20.00

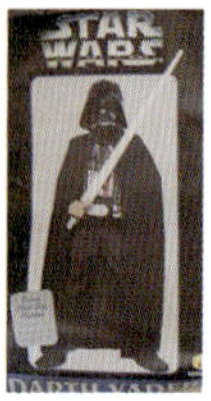

218-26

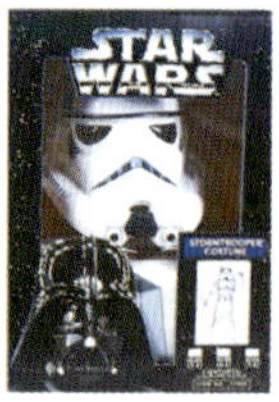

218-27

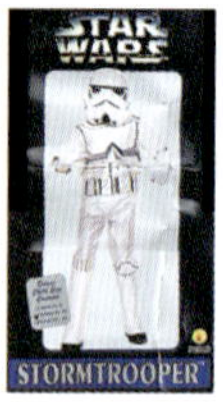

218-28

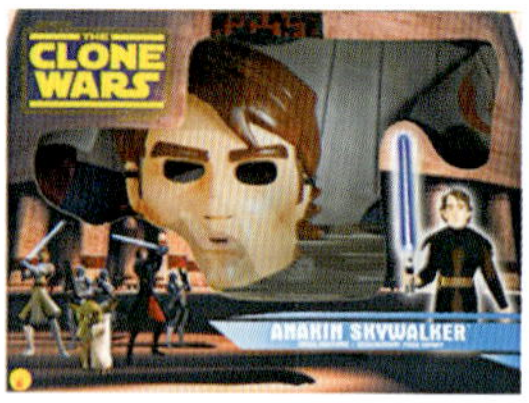

218-29

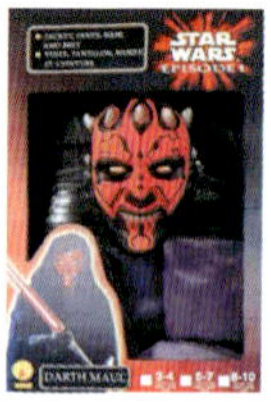

218-30

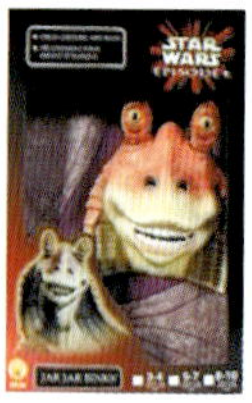

218-31

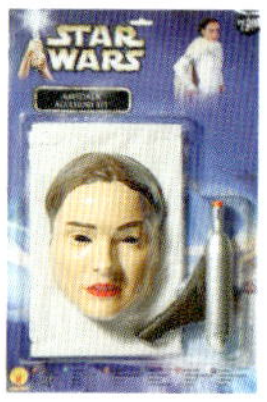

218-32

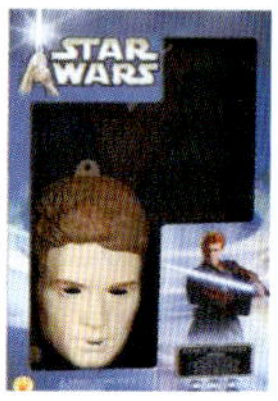

218-33

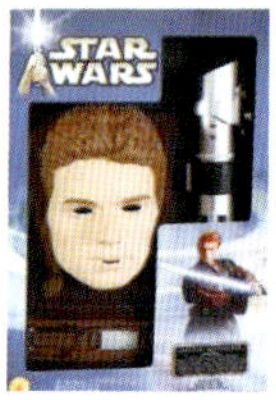

218-34

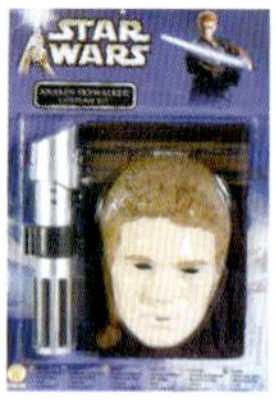

218-35

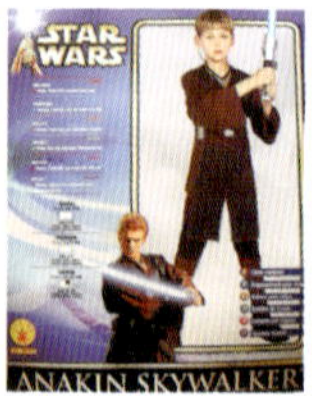

218-36

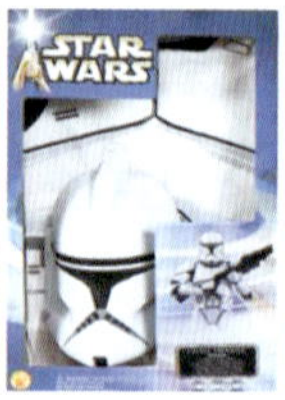

218-37

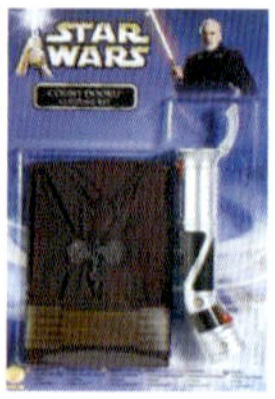

218-38

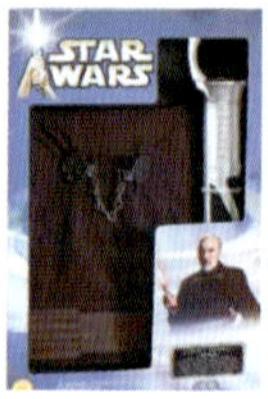

218-39

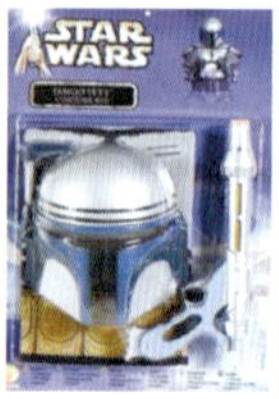

218-40

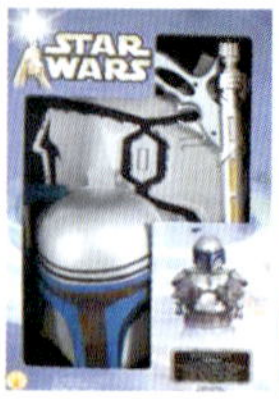

218-41

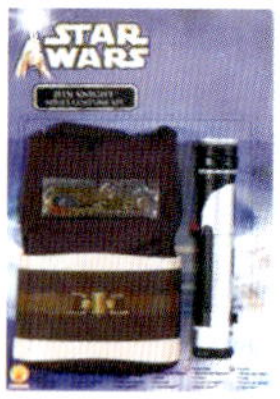

218-42

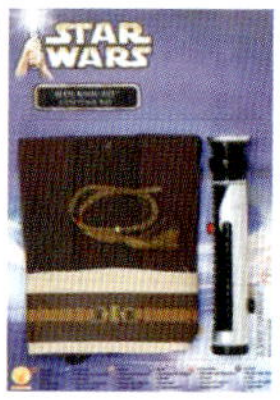

218-43

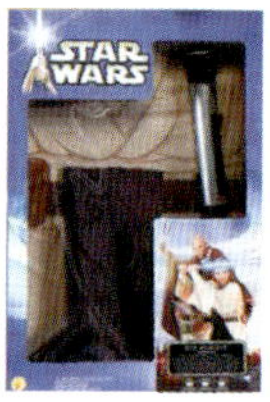

218-44

Anakin Skywalker Jedi Apprentice *continued...*
- ❑ Child deluxe....40.00
- ❑ Child super deluxe....60.00

Anakin Skywalker Pod Race
- ❑ Child....20.00
- ❑ Child deluxe....40.00
- ❑ Child super deluxe....60.00

Darth Maul
- ❑ Action wear deluxe....40.00
- ❑ Action wear....25.00
- ❑ Adult [218-30]....25.00
- ❑ Adult deluxe....50.00
- ❑ Adult super deluxe....80.00
- ❑ Child....20.00
- ❑ Child blister card....25.00
- ❑ Child boxed [v1e1:186]....25.00
- ❑ Child deluxe [2:257]....45.00
- ❑ Child super deluxe....75.00

Jar Jar Binks
- ❑ Action wear....25.00
- ❑ Action wear deluxe [218-31]....40.00
- ❑ Adult....30.00
- ❑ Adult deluxe....90.00
- ❑ Child....20.00
- ❑ Child deluxe....40.00

Jedi
- ❑ Adult robe....20.00
- ❑ Adult robe deluxe....30.00
- ❑ Child robe....20.00
- ❑ Child robe deluxe....25.00

Obi-Wan Kenobi
- ❑ Action wear....25.00
- ❑ Action wear deluxe....40.00
- ❑ Adult....35.00
- ❑ Adult deluxe....60.00
- ❑ Child blister card....15.00
- ❑ Child boxed....20.00
- ❑ Child deluxe....40.00
- ❑ Child super deluxe....60.00
- ❑ Child tunic....20.00

Queen Amidala
- ❑ Action wear....25.00
- ❑ Action wear deluxe [v1e1:186]....40.00
- ❑ Adult....20.00
- ❑ Adult deluxe....40.00
- ❑ Adult supreme....80.00
- ❑ Child....20.00
- ❑ Child deluxe [2:257]....35.00
- ❑ Child super deluxe....55.00
- ❑ Child supreme....70.00

Qui-Gon Jinn
- ❑ Action wear....25.00
- ❑ Action wear deluxe....40.00
- ❑ Adult deluxe....60.00
- ❑ Child blister card....15.00
- ❑ Child boxed....20.00
- ❑ Child deluxe....40.00
- ❑ Child super deluxe....60.00

Episode II: Attack of the Clones.

Amidala
- ❑ Child blister card [218-32]....20.00

Anakin Skywalker
- ❑ Basic....25.00
- ❑ Boxed basic [218-33]....30.00
- ❑ Boxed kit [218-34]....40.00
- ❑ Boxed set....55.00
- ❑ Costume kit [218-35]....30.00
- ❑ Costume deluxe [218-36]....35.00

Clone trooper
- ❑ Adult....70.00
- ❑ Adult deluxe....100.00
- ❑ Basic....35.00
- ❑ Boxed [218-37]....25.00
- ❑ Boxed deluxe....80.00
- ❑ Boxed large....45.00

Count Dooku
- ❑ Adult basic....85.00
- ❑ Basic [218-38]....30.00
- ❑ Boxed [218-39]....40.00

Jango Fett
- ❑ Adult deluxe....75.00
- ❑ Adult deluxe ultra....95.00
- ❑ Adult basic....70.00
- ❑ Blister card [218-40]....35.00
- ❑ Boxed [218-41]....40.00
- ❑ Boxed basic....25.00
- ❑ Boxed deluxe....95.00
- ❑ Boxed large....55.00
- ❑ Deluxe....80.00

Jedi Knight
- ❑ Adult [218-42]....45.00
- ❑ Basic [218-43]....70.00
- ❑ Boxed [218-44]....55.00
- ❑ Boxed basic....25.00
- ❑ Boxed kit....30.00

Jedi Robe
- ❑ Adult....40.00
- ❑ Adult deluxe....70.00
- ❑ Child [218-45]....25.00
- ❑ Child deluxe....45.00

Mace Windu
- ❑ Basic....25.00
- ❑ Boxed [218-46]....38.00
- ❑ Boxed large [218-47]....55.00
- ❑ Deluxe....35.00
- ❑ Blister [218-48]....30.00

Obi-Wan Kenobi
- ❑ Basic....24.00
- ❑ Boxed [218-49]....40.00
- ❑ Boxed basic....35.00
- ❑ Blister card [218-50]....30.00

Padmé Amidala
- ❑ Adult basic....70.00
- ❑ Basic....25.00
- ❑ Blister card [218-51]....30.00
- ❑ Boxed basic....25.00
- ❑ Boxed [218-52]....40.00
- ❑ Boxed deluxe....75.00
- ❑ Boxed large [218-53]....55.00

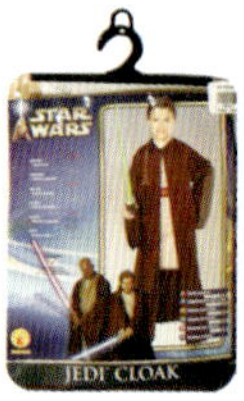

218-45

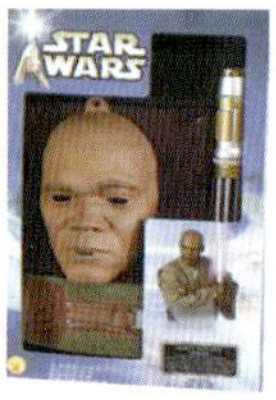

218-46

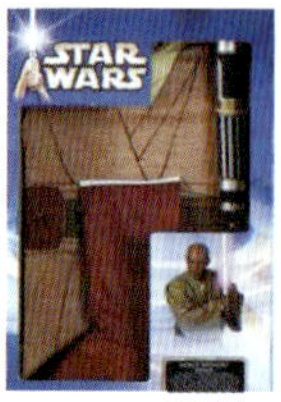

218-47

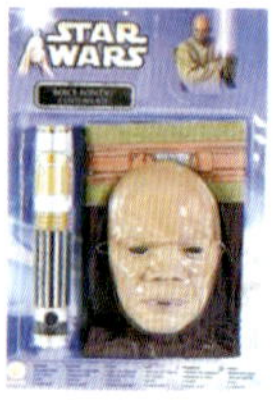

218-48

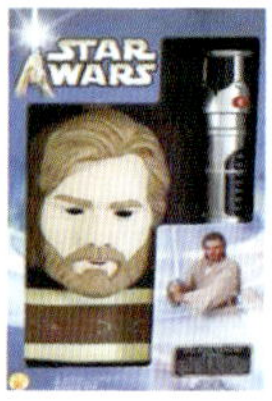

218-49

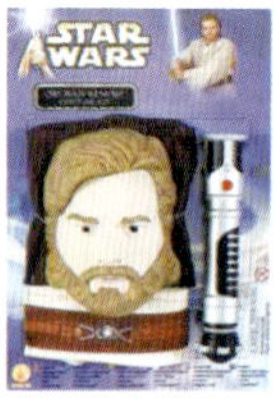

218-50

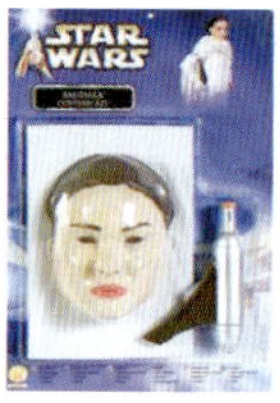

218-51

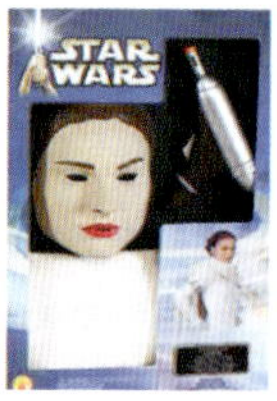

218-52

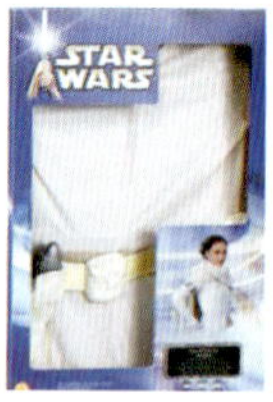

218-53

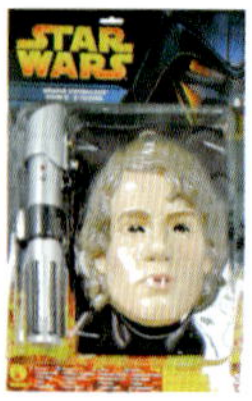

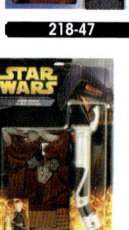

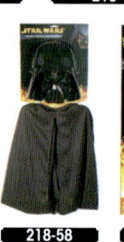

218-54

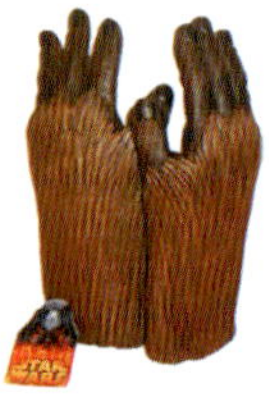
218-55

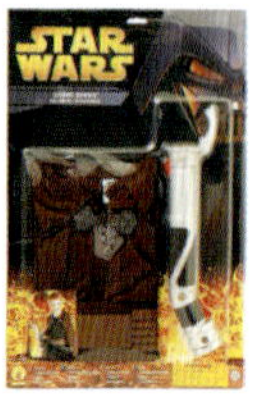

218-56

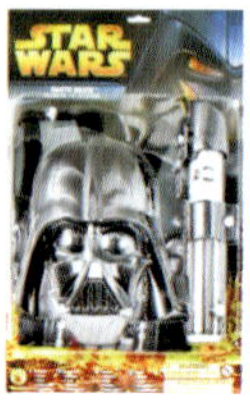

218-57

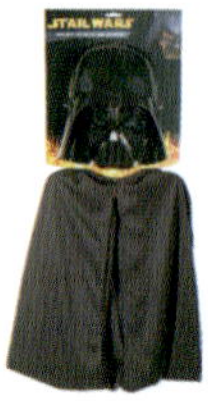
218-58

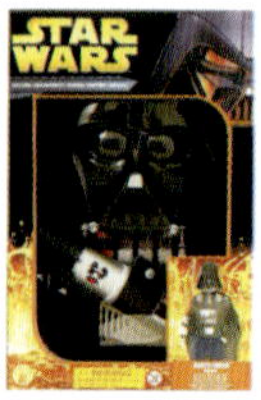

218-59

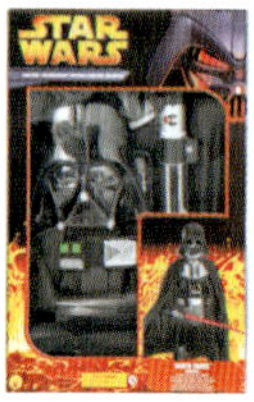

218-60

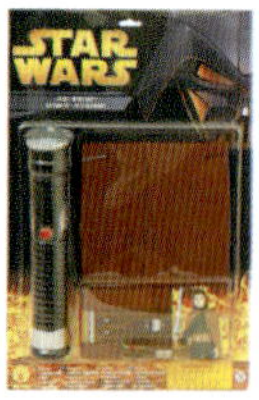

218-61

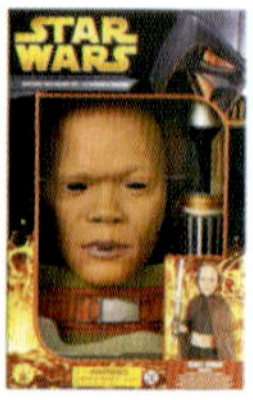

218-62

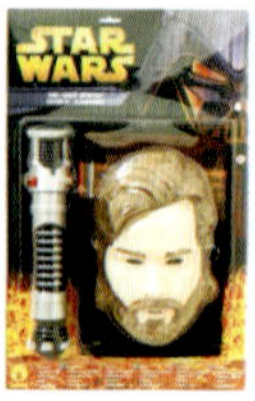

218-63

Episode III: Revenge of the Sith.

Anakin Skywalker
- ❑ Accessory kit [218-54] 15.00
- ❑ Boxed 40.00
- ❑ Deluxe 65.00

C-3PO
- ❑ Boxed 65.00
- ❑ Boxed deluxe 95.00

Chewbacca
- ❑ Accessory hands [218-55] 25.00
- ❑ Adult deluxe 100.00
- ❑ Adult supreme 650.00
- ❑ Child deluxe 70.00

Clone trooper
- ❑ Adult deluxe 75.00
- ❑ Child deluxe 75.00

Count Dooku
- ❑ Accessory kit [218-56] 25.00
- ❑ Adult robe 50.00

Darth Vader
- ❑ Accessory kit [218-57] 15.00
- ❑ Adult deluxe 80.00
- ❑ Adult supreme 1,250.00
- ❑ Child [218-58] 25.00
- ❑ Child boxed [218-59] 30.00
- ❑ Child boxed deluxe [218-60] 50.00

Jango Fett
- ❑ Adult deluxe 75.00
- ❑ Child deluxe 60.00

Jedi Knight
- ❑ Accessory kit [218-61] 25.00
- ❑ Deluxe 40.00
- ❑ Robe adult 50.00
- ❑ Robe child 35.00

Mace Windu
- ❑ Boxed [218-62] 30.00
- ❑ Boxed deluxe 40.00

Obi-Wan Kenobi
- ❑ Accessory kit [218-63] 25.00
- ❑ Boxed 30.00

Padmé Amidala
- ❑ Deluxe 30.00

Yoda
- ❑ Accessory hands [v1e1:186] 20.00
- ❑ Deluxe 50.00

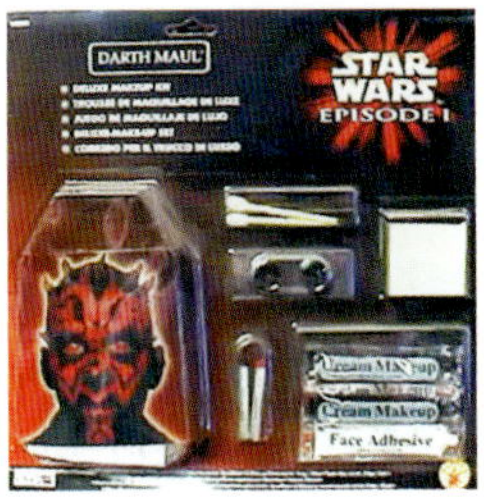

219-01

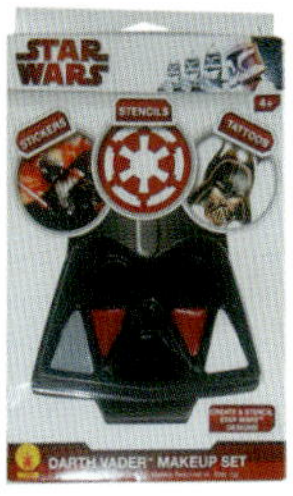

219-02

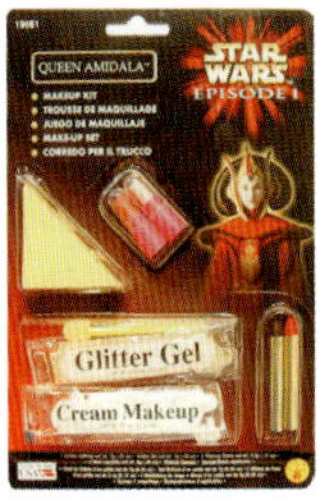

219-03

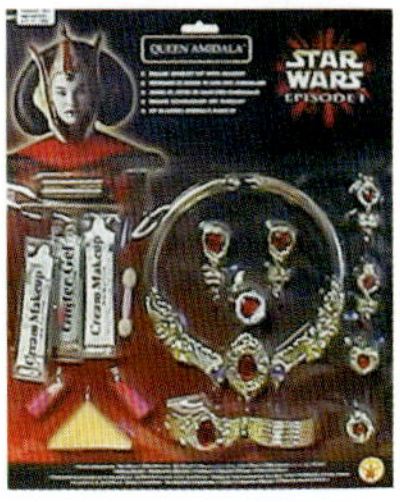

219-04

Toddler fleece costumes. Sizes: Newborn (1–6 mos.), Infant (6–12 mos.)
- ❑ Chewbacca 25.00
- ❑ Darth Vader 25.00
- ❑ Princess Leia 25.00
- ❑ Yoda 25.00

Costumes: Makeup Kits

Rubies
- ❑ Darth Maul 7.00
- ❑ Darth Maul Deluxe [219-01] 12.00
- ❑ Darth Vader with stickers, stencils, and tattoos [219-02] 15.00
- ❑ Queen Amidala [219-03] 7.00
- ❑ Queen Amidala with jewelry [219-04] 12.00

Costumes: Masks

Continued in Volume 3, Page 193

- ❑ C-3PO [220-01] 15.00
- ❑ Chewbacca [220-02] 15.00
- ❑ Darth Vader [220-03] 15.00
- ❑ Darth Vader [4:121] 20.00
- ❑ Gamorrean Guard [220-04] 25.00
- ❑ Stormtrooper [220-05] 15.00

Altmann's Armor
- ❑ AT-AT Driver [4:121] 225.00
- ❑ Boba Fett [4:121] 225.00
- ❑ Darth Vader [4:121] 300.00
- ❑ Imperial Fleet Officer [4:121] 175.00
- ❑ Imperial Gunner [4:121] 225.00

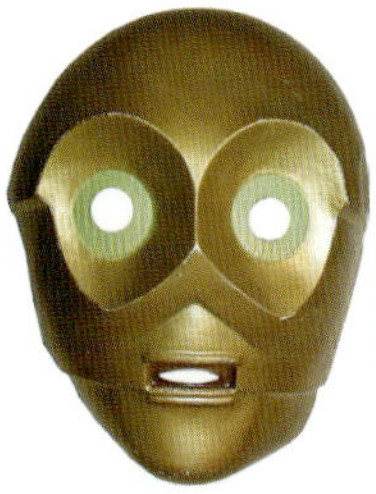
220-01

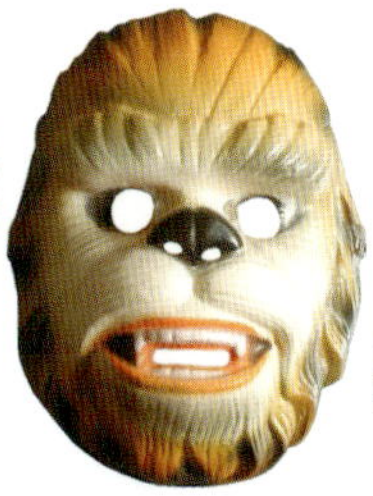
220-02

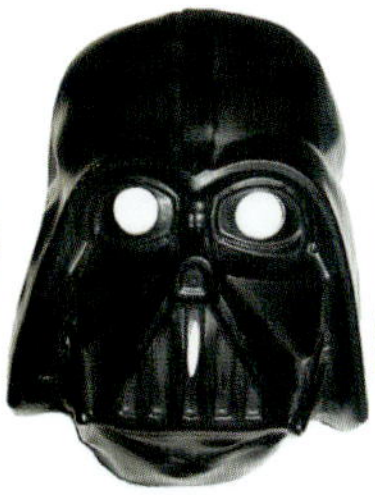
220-03

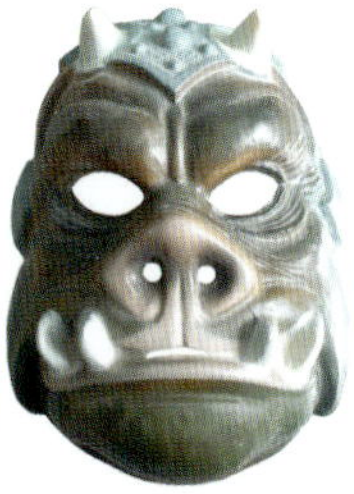
220-04

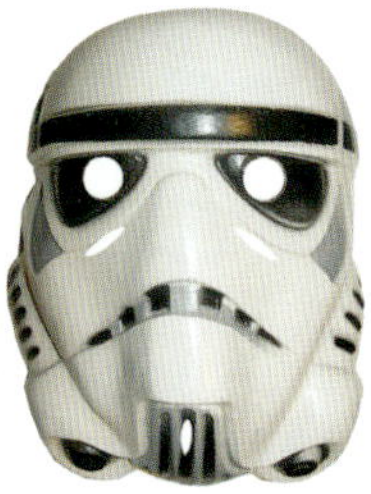
220-05

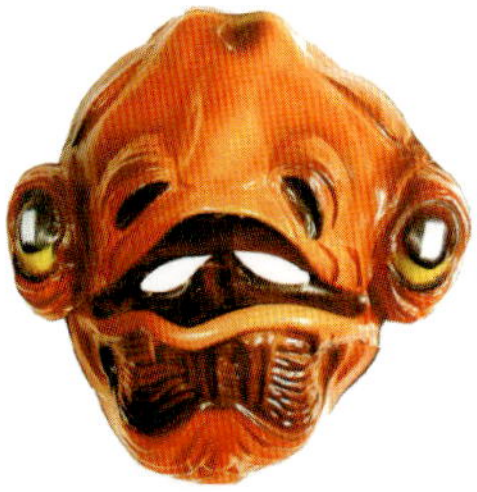
220-06

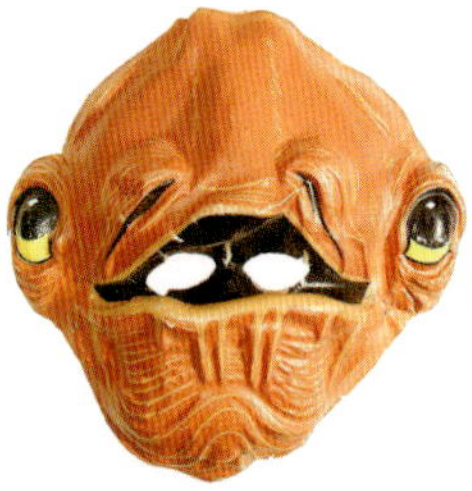
220-07

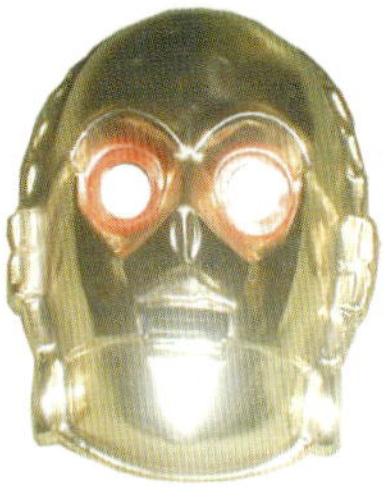
220-08

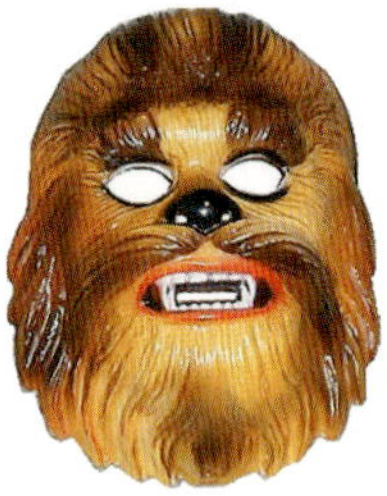
220-09

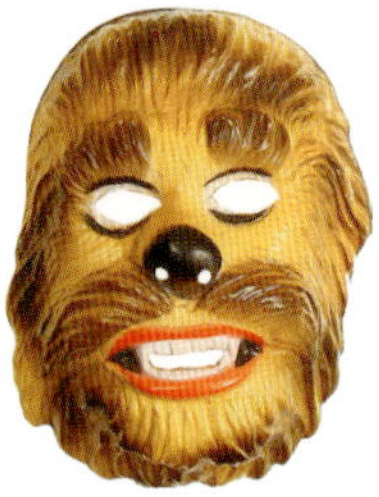
220-10

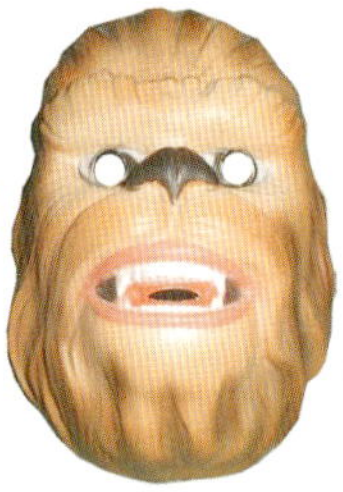
220-11

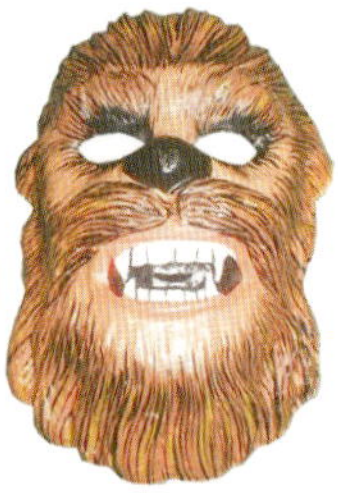
220-12

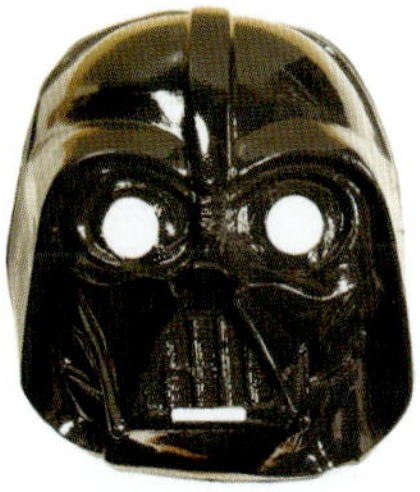
220-13

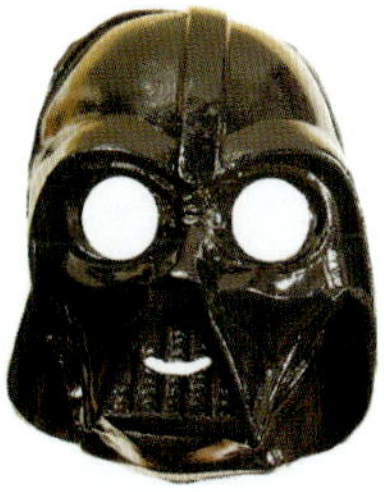
220-14

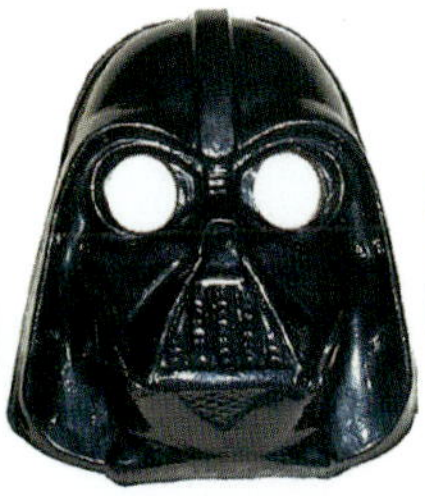
220-15

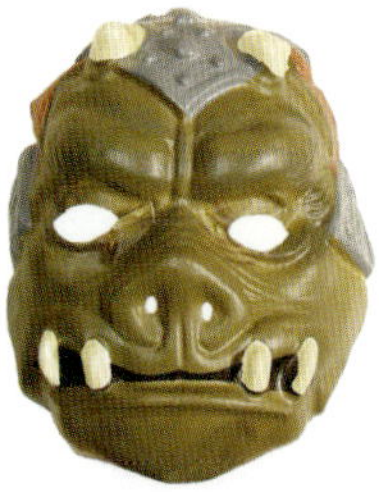
220-16

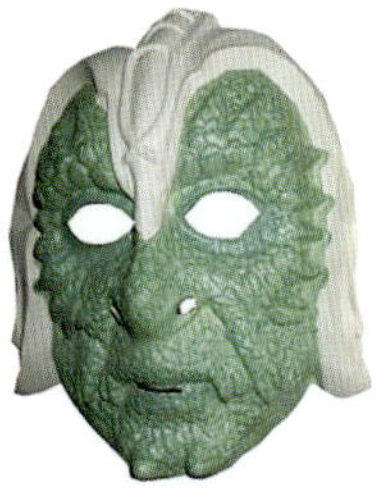
220-17

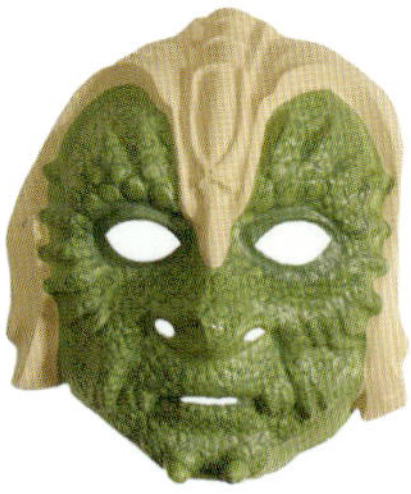
220-18

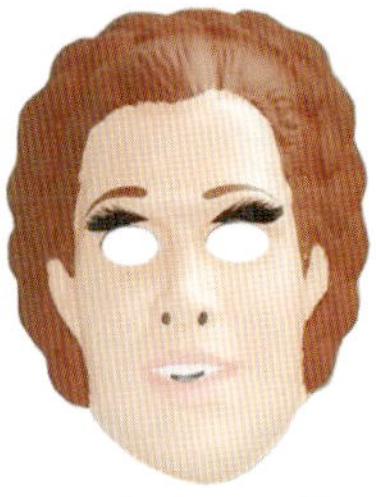
220-19

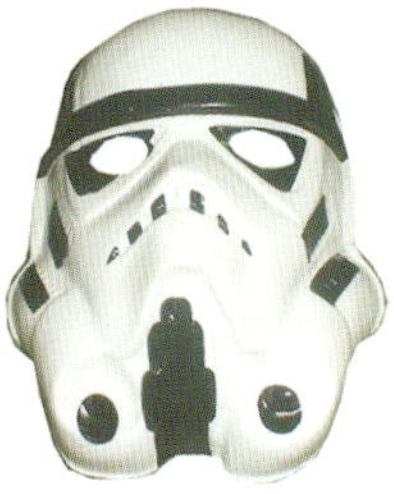
220-20

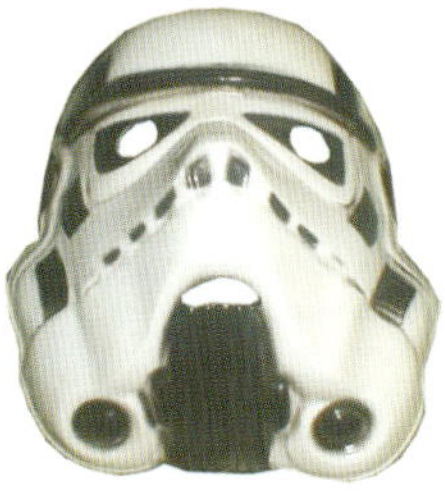
220-21

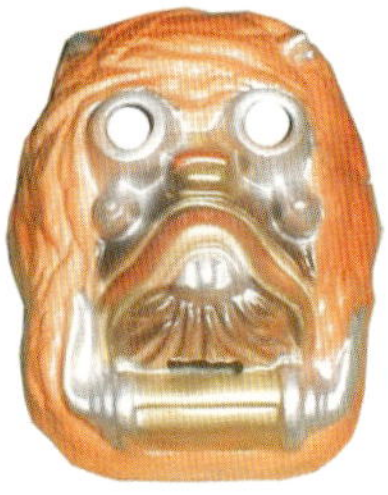
220-22

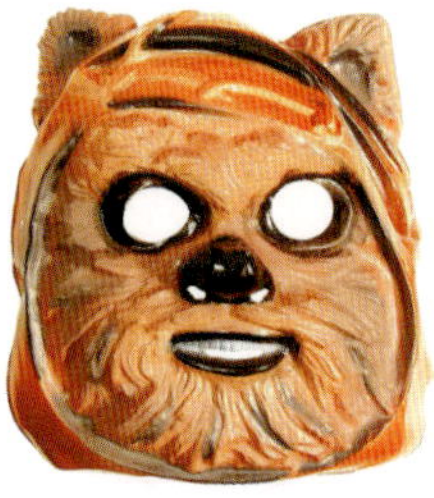
220-23

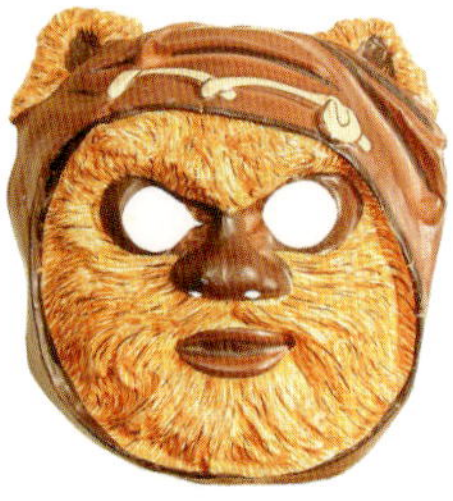
220-24

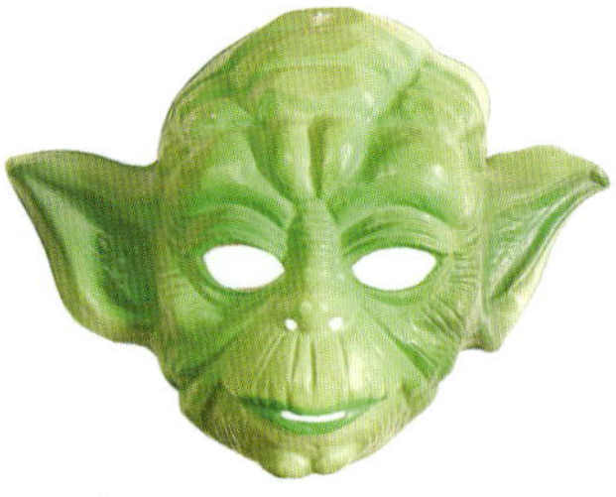
220-25

Costumes: Masks

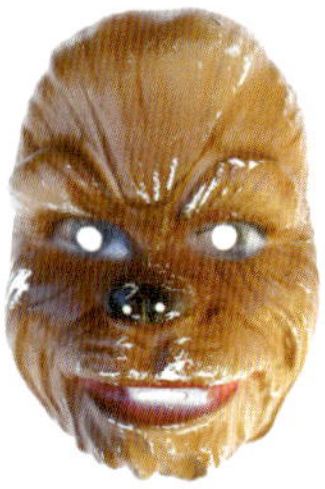

220-26

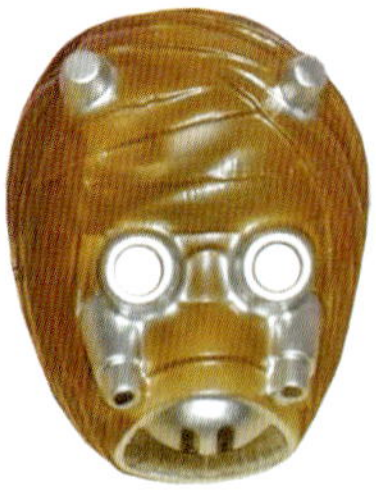

220-27

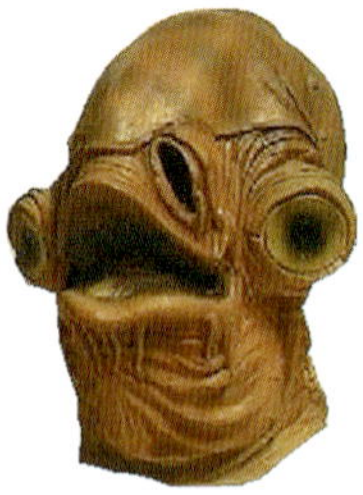

220-28

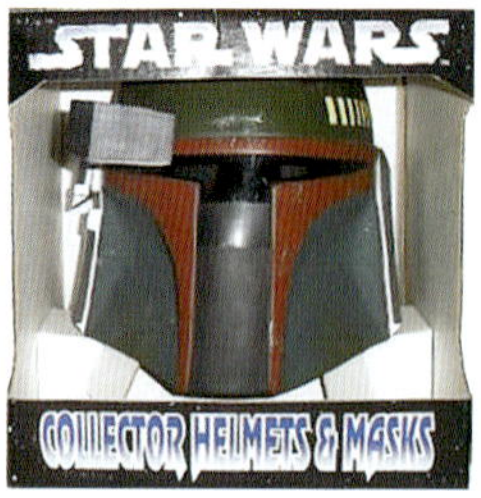

220-29

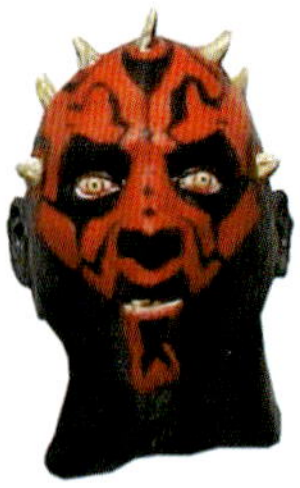

220-30

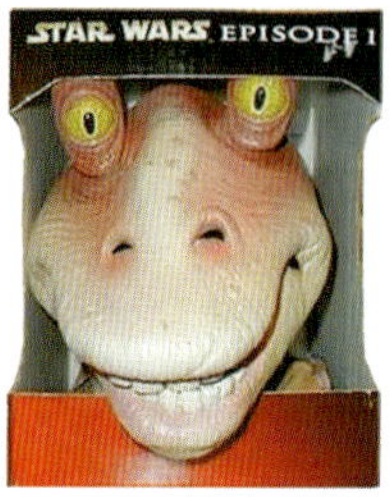

220-31

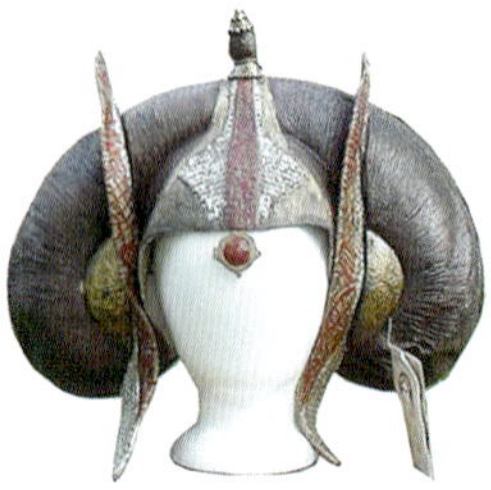

220-32

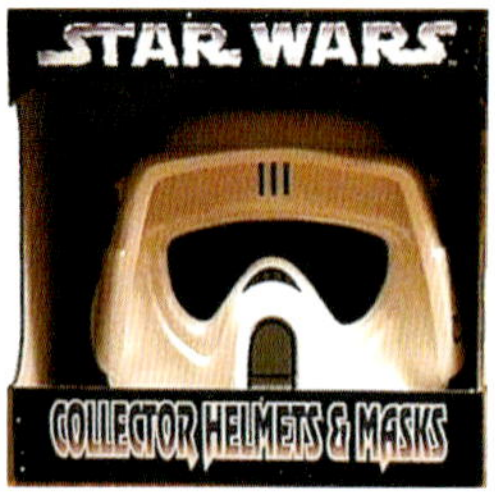

220-33

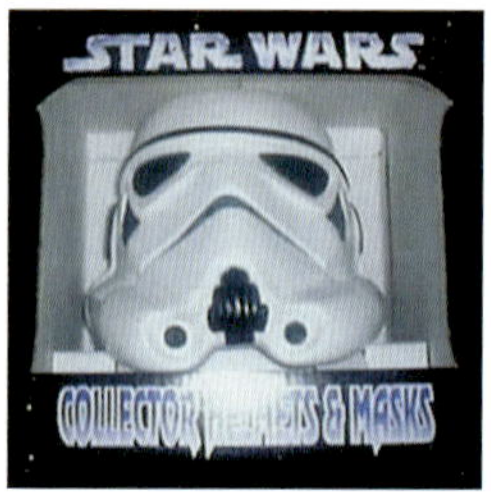

220-34

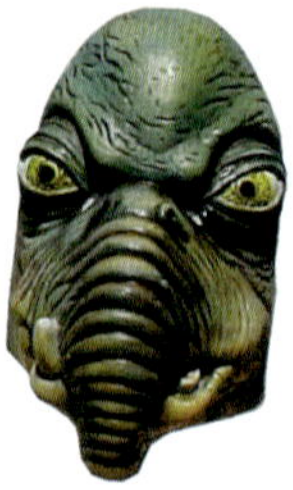

220-35

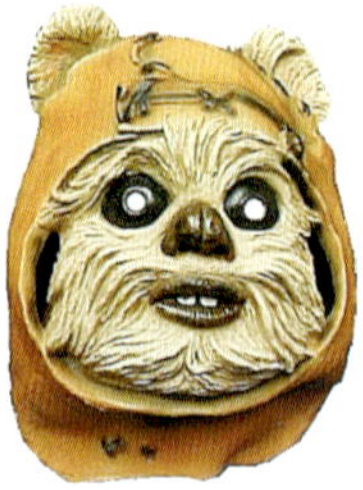

220-36

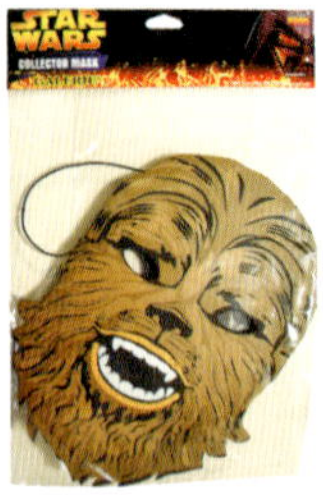

220-37

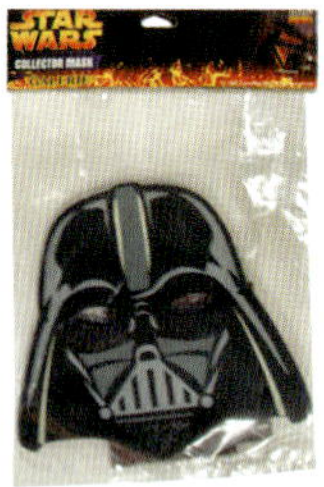

220-38

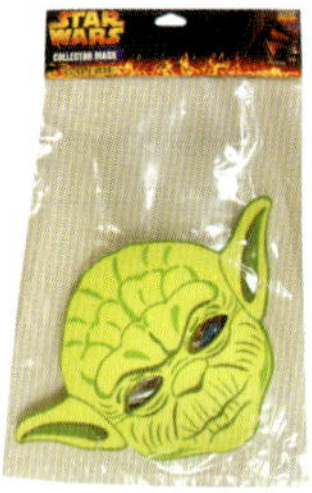

220-39

- ❑ Imperial Scout trooper *[sic]* [4:121]....250.00
- ❑ Imperial Stormtrooper [4:121]....225.00
- ❑ Rebel [4:121]....175.00
- ❑ Royal Guard [4:121]....200.00
- ❑ X-Wing Pilot [4:121]....250.00

Limited to 500, numbered.

- ❑ Stormtrooper....350.00

American Marketing Enterprises, Inc.

Limited to 500, numbered.

- ❑ Darth Vader....575.00

Ben Cooper

- ❑ Admiral Ackbar, adult [220-06]....15.00
- ❑ Admiral Ackbar, child [220-07]....15.00
- ❑ C-3PO [4:122]....15.00
- ❑ C-3PO, 1977 [220-08]....15.00
- ❑ Chewbacca, 1977 adult [220-09]....15.00
- ❑ Chewbacca, 1977 child [220-10]....15.00
- ❑ Chewbacca, adult [220-11]....15.00
- ❑ Chewbacca, children's [220-12]....15.00
- ❑ Darth Vader, mouth breather [220-13]....15.00
- ❑ Darth Vader, mouth breather smile [220-14]....20.00
- ❑ Darth Vader, nose breather [220-15]....15.00
- ❑ Gamorrean Guard [220-16]....20.00
- ❑ Klaatu, adult [220-17]....20.00
- ❑ Klaatu, child [220-18]....15.00
- ❑ Princess Leia, Hoth [220-19]....20.00
- ❑ Stormtrooper [220-20]....15.00
- ❑ Stormtrooper, 1977 [220-21]....15.00
- ❑ Tusken Raider [220-22]....30.00
- ❑ Wicket, adult [220-23]....15.00
- ❑ Wicket, child [220-24]....15.00
- ❑ Yoda [220-25]....15.00

Cesar (France)

- ❑ C-3PO....150.00
- ❑ Chewbacca, adult....150.00
- ❑ Chewbacca, child [220-26]....150.00
- ❑ Darth Vader....150.00
- ❑ Stormtrooper [4:122]....150.00
- ❑ Tusken Raider [220-27]....150.00

Don Post

- ❑ Admiral Ackbar [220-28]....55.00
- ❑ Admiral Ackbar, hands....25.00
- ❑ Anakin's Pod Helmet [2:292]....60.00
- ❑ Boba Fett....60.00
- ❑ Boba Fett, deluxe....975.00
- ❑ Boba Fett, retail [220-29]....35.00
- ❑ C-3PO, black latex; gold paint....60.00
- ❑ C-3PO, copyright by Lucas Films Ltd....50.00
- ❑ C-3PO, gold latex [v1e1:189]....195.00
- ❑ Cantina band member [v1e1:189]....45.00
- ❑ Cantina band member, hands....25.00
- ❑ Chewbacca, closed mouth....100.00
- ❑ Chewbacca, snarling....425.00
- ❑ Chewbacca, vinyl with hair....35.00
- ❑ Darth Maul [220-30]....45.00
- ❑ Darth Vader deluxe helmet, fiberglass....800.00
- ❑ Darth Vader helmet, plastic nose and respirator tips....50.00
- ❑ Darth Vader helmet, copyright by 20th Century Fox....125.00
- ❑ Darth Vader helmet, copyright by Lucasfilm Ltd.....50.00
- ❑ Darth Vader helmet, original with sticker [v1e1:189]....250.00
- ❑ Darth Vader helmet, retail distribution....35.00
- ❑ Darth Vader helmet without respirator tips....50.00
- ❑ Emperor [4:122]....125.00
- ❑ Emperor, copyright by Lucasfilm Ltd.....60.00
- ❑ Emperor's Royal Guard [v1e1:189]....95.00
- ❑ Even Piell....60.00
- ❑ Gamorrean Guard [4:122]....60.00
- ❑ Gamorrean Guard, copyright by Lucasfilm Ltd.....60.00
- ❑ Greedo [v1e1:189]....50.00
- ❑ Jar Jar Binks [220-31]....55.00
- ❑ Jar Jar Binks (deluxe) [v1e1:189]....125.00
- ❑ Jawa [4:122]....40.00
- ❑ Ki-Adi-Mundy [v1e1:189]....60.00
- ❑ Klaatu [2:293]....45.00
- ❑ Klaatu, copyright by Lucasfilm Ltd.....60.00
- ❑ Naboo starfighter helmet [2:293]....55.00
- ❑ Nien Nunb [2:293]....60.00
- ❑ Nute Gunray [4:122]....95.00
- ❑ Prince Xizor [4:122]....50.00
- ❑ Prince Xizor, hands [2:293]....25.00
- ❑ Queen Amidala—senate headpiece [220-32]....55.00
- ❑ Queen Amidala—Theed....55.00
- ❑ Rune Haako....95.00
- ❑ Scout trooper helmet, retail distribution [220-33]....55.00
- ❑ Sebulba [v1e1:189]....45.00
- ❑ Sebulba (deluxe)....75.00
- ❑ Stormtrooper helmet, copyright by Lucasfilm Ltd.....50.00
- ❑ Stormtrooper helmet, lighter eye lenses....85.00
- ❑ Stormtrooper helmet, molded band....45.00
- ❑ Stormtrooper helmet, original....100.00
- ❑ Stormtrooper helmet, painted eyes....55.00
- ❑ Stormtrooper helmet, retail....35.00
- ❑ TIE pilot helmet....110.00
- ❑ TIE pilot helmet and chest plate....1,200.00
- ❑ TIE pilot helmet, retail [v1e1:189]....40.00
- ❑ Tusken Raider [4:122]....40.00
- ❑ Tusken Raider, original....125.00
- ❑ Tusken Raider, copyright by Lucasfilm Ltd.....50.00
- ❑ Ugnaught....75.00
- ❑ Watto [220-35]....45.00
- ❑ Weequay....95.00
- ❑ Wicket, molded fur [220-36]....85.00
- ❑ Wicket, real fur....70.00
- ❑ X-Wing pilot [4:122]....110.00
- ❑ Yoda [v1e1:189]....40.00

Galerie

Collector masks.

- ❑ Chewbacca [220-37]....8.00
- ❑ Darth Vader [220-38]....8.00
- ❑ Yoda [220-39]....8.00

Gemma International (UK)

- ❑ Obi-Wan and Anakin, 6 face masks....10.00

Hallmark Party

Masks, bagged.

- ❑ Captain Rex 8-pack [220-40]....8.00
- ❑ Darth Vader 4-pack [220-41]....5.00

Kellogg's (Canada)

- ❑ Clone trooper, cereal premium....16.00

Party Express

- ❑ Captain Rex [220-42]....5.00
- ❑ Darth Vader masks, bagged pack of 4....10.00

Rubies

- ❑ Boba Fett collector edition....75.00
- ❑ Boba Fett vinyl adult [220-43]....45.00
- ❑ Boba Fett, covers head, flexible rubber....25.00
- ❑ C-3PO deluxe....60.00
- ❑ C-3PO injection molded....100.00
- ❑ C-3PO vinyl....30.00
- ❑ C-3PO, children's [220-44]....10.00
- ❑ C-3PO, covers head, flexible rubber....35.00
- ❑ C-3PO, PVC children's....10.00
- ❑ Chewbacca deluxe: sculpted latex....55.00
- ❑ Chewbacca supreme: latex, hand-layered fur....125.00
- ❑ Chewbacca, covers head, flexible rubber....25.00
- ❑ Darth Maul deluxe....20.00
- ❑ Darth Vader deluxe: two-piece mask and helmet....35.00
- ❑ Darth Vader one-sided plastic, child [220-45]....25.00
- ❑ Darth Vader super deluxe mask and helmet: injection molded ABS, cast from original Lucasfilm molds....135.00
- ❑ Darth Vader, children's PVC....10.00
- ❑ Darth Vader, covers head, 2-piece molded plastic....20.00
- ❑ Darth Vader, covers head, flexible rubber [v1e1:189]....25.00
- ❑ Emperor Palpatine deluxe....45.00
- ❑ Scout trooper [220-46]....85.00
- ❑ Stormtrooper [220-47]....15.00
- ❑ Stormtrooper collector's....95.00
- ❑ Stormtrooper covers head, flexible rubber....25.00
- ❑ Stormtrooper injection molded [220-48]....55.00
- ❑ TIE Fighter helmet collectors edition....75.00
- ❑ Tusken Raider, covers head, flexible rubber....25.00
- ❑ X-Wing Fighter helmet....75.00
- ❑ Yoda....30.00
- ❑ Yoda deluxe overhead latex, adult....60.00
- ❑ Yoda, covers head, flexible rubber....25.00

Episode I: The Phantom Menace.

- ❑ Anakin Skywalker, children's [220-49]....10.00
- ❑ Boss Nass deluxe overhead latex, adult....45.00
- ❑ Boss Nass vinyl 3/4, adult [220-50]....25.00
- ❑ Darth Maul deluxe overhead latex, adult....45.00
- ❑ Darth Maul PVC, adult....10.00
- ❑ Darth Maul PVC, children's....10.00
- ❑ Darth Maul vinyl 3/4, adult [220-51]....25.00
- ❑ Darth Maul vinyl 3/4, children's....10.00

Crackers

 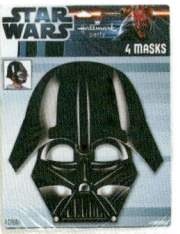     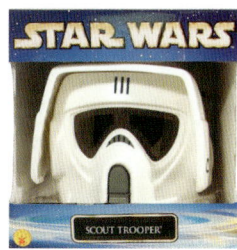

220-40　220-41　220-42　220-43　220-44　220-45　220-46

 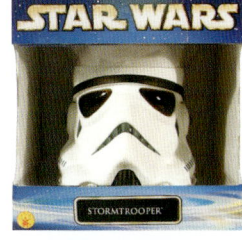     

220-47　220-48　220-49　220-50　220-51　220-52　220-53

   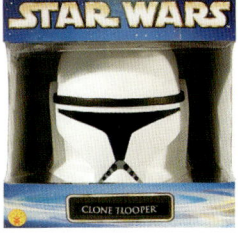   

220-54　220-55　220-56　220-57　220-58　220-59　220-60

- ❏ Jar Jar Binks deluxe overhead latex, adult 40.00
- ❏ Jar Jar Binks vinyl 3/4, adult [220-52] 20.00
- ❏ Jar Jar Binks vinyl 3/4, children's..............................10.00
- ❏ Jar Jar Binks, adult 10.00
- ❏ Jar Jar Binks, children's..10.00
- ❏ Kit Fisto latex 60.00
- ❏ Nute Gunray vinyl 3/4, adult [220-53] 45.00
- ❏ Queen Amidala, children's [220-54] 10.00
- ❏ Sebulba deluxe overhead latex, adult 45.00
- ❏ Sebulba vinyl 3/4, adult [220-55] 20.00
- ❏ Watto deluxe overhead latex, adult 40.00
- ❏ Watto vinyl 3/4, adult 20.00

Episode II: Attack of the Clones.
- ❏ Anakin Skywalker, PVC children 15.00
- ❏ Clone trooper 2-piece injection molded [220-56] 45.00
- ❏ Clone trooper 3/4 PVC [220-57] 20.00
- ❏ Clone trooper, collector 70.00
- ❏ Geonosian latex 50.00
- ❏ Jango Fett injection molded deluxe [220-58] 75.00
- ❏ Jango Fett, PVC children 15.00
- ❏ Jango Fett, PVC children 2-piece [220-59] 30.00
- ❏ Mace Windu, PVC children's 15.00
- ❏ Obi-Wan Kenobi, PVC children's 15.00
- ❏ Padmé Amidala PVC children's 15.00
- ❏ Plo Koon latex 75.00
- ❏ Saesee Tiin latex...60.00

Tapper Candies
- ❏ Party Mask 4-pack [220-60] 8.00

Walls
Paper, food premiums.
- ❏ C-3PO [v1e1:189] 20.00
- ❏ Darth Vader [v1e1:189] 20.00
- ❏ Stormtrooper [v1e1:189] 20.00

Coupons
Continued in Volume 3, Page 193

20th Century Fox
- ❏ Saving Book, distributed inside select video cassette collector editions 5.00

Cinnabon
- ❏ Princess Bunhead, free Cinnamon roll [v1e1:190]............5.00

Del Rey
- ❏ $2 rebate, Unifying Force [v1e1:190]................................2.00

Hasbro
- ❏ Clone Cash, 5 dollars off any 20-dollar purchase [v1e1:190]..20.00
- ❏ Top Trumps, buy one get one free, including Star Wars [v1e1:190]..2.00

K B Toys
- ❏ Coupon, $3 off packaged with promo TCG card [v1e1:190]..5.00

Kellogg's
- ❏ C-3PO cereal, 25 cents off [v1e1:190]..............................8.00

KFC (Canada)
- ❏ Episode I, 15-piece bucket $15.99, free 2 liter Pepsi ...5.00

Natural Balance
- ❏ $1 off vitamins [v1e1:190] 5.00

Pepsi Cola
- ❏ Call Upon Yoda, Free 2 Liter Bottle of Pepsi Lime or Diet Pepsi Lime 5.00

Pizza Hut (Australia)
- ❏ Episode I: Get Into It coupon booklet [v1e1:190].............10.00

Star Wars Celebration IV
- ❏ Friends and Family coupon 2.00

Target
- ❏ April 4th Collection Edition Darth Vader with Lava Reflection Figure line placeholder ticket 10.00
- ❏ Revenge of the Sith coupons and product catalog 5.00

Toys R Us
- ❏ Episode III: Revenge of the Sith reservation coupon 8.00

Walkers (UK)
- ❏ Free single packet of chips [v1e1:190] 8.00

Crackers

(Canada)
- ❏ Activity crackers, package of 6 [221-01] 35.00

(United Kingdom)
- ❏ The Phantom Menace , package of 6 [v1e1:190]............35.00

Boots
- ❏ The Phantom Menace, package of 6 [221-02] 35.00

Brite Sparks Ltd.
- ❏ The Phantom Menace single gift cracker, any [221-03]..20.00

Woolworths (UK)
- ❏ The Phantom Menace, package of 6 [221-04] 35.00

221-01　221-02　221-03　221-04

Crafts

222-01

222-02

222-03

222-04

222-05

222-06

223-01

223-02

223-03

223-04

223-05

223-06

Crafts
Covered in Volume 2, Second Edition, Pages 235–243

Credit and ATM Cards
Continued in Volume 3, Page 198

GE Consumer Finance
VISA cards.
- ❏ Darth Vader [222-01] 35.00
- ❏ R2-D2 and C-3PO [222-02] 35.00
- ❏ X-Wings over Yavin [222-03] 35.00

MBNA
Galactic Rewards Mastercard.
- ❏ Darth Vader [222-04] 40.00
- ❏ Logo only [222-05] 40.00
- ❏ Yoda [222-06] 40.00

Siam Commercial Bank
ATM cards, Thailand.
- ❏ Darth Vader [v1e1:195] 35.00
- ❏ Yoda [v1e1:195] 35.00

Crowns, Paper

Packed in with celebration feves.
- ❏ Original trilogy characters [223-01] 10.00
- ❏ Star Wars / Yoda / Droids [223-02] 10.00

Burger King
Episode III: Revenge of the Sith.
- ❏ Characters, original trilogy [223-03] 15.00
- ❏ Heroes [223-04] 15.00
- ❏ Heroes and Villains [223-05] 15.00
- ❏ Lightsabers [223-06] 15.00

Cup Toppers
Continued in Volume 3, Page 198

KFC
Classic trilogy characters. SW:SE promotion.
- ❏ R2-D2 [v1e1:195] 15.00
- ❏ Stormtrooper [v1e1:195] 15.00

Episode I: The Phantom Menace character topper with matching cup.
- ❏ Boss Nass [v1e1:195] 10.00
- ❏ Capt. Tarpals [v1e1:195] 10.00
- ❏ Queen Amidala [v1e1:195] 10.00
- ❏ R2-D2 [v1e1:195] 10.00

Pizza Hut
Episode I: The Phantom Menace character topper with matching cup.
- ❏ Jar Jar Binks [v1e1:195] 10.00
- ❏ Mace Windu [v1e1:195] 10.00
- ❏ Nute Gunray [v1e1:195] 10.00
- ❏ Yoda [v1e1:195] 10.00

Taco Bell
Classic trilogy characters. Star Wars: Special Edition promotion.
- ❏ C-3PO [v1e1:195] 15.00
- ❏ Darth Vader [v1e1:195] 15.00

Episode I: The Phantom Menace character topper with matching cup.
- ❏ Anakin Skywalker [v1e1:195] 10.00
- ❏ Darth Maul [v1e1:195] 10.00
- ❏ Sebulba [v1e1:195] 10.00
- ❏ Watto [v1e1:195] 10.00

Cups: Disposable
Continued in Volume 3, Page 198

(UK)
- ❏ Clone Wars, 8 pack [224-01] 15.00

Burger King
Episode III: Revenge of the Sith.
- ❏ Anakin, Obi-Wan, and Yoda plastic [224-02] 5.00
- ❏ Hot, Starships [224-03] 10.00
- ❏ King size, Chewbacca and Tarfful plastic [224-04] 5.00
- ❏ King size, Palpatine and Anakin plastic [224-05] 5.00
- ❏ Large, Obi-Wan and Anakin [224-06] 5.00
- ❏ Medium, Darth Vader [224-07] 5.00
- ❏ Small, Saga characters [224-08] 5.00

Coca-Cola
- ❏ Kenner Toys with game piece attached [224-09] 25.00

Coca-Cola / 7-11
- ❏ Darth Vader 15.00
- ❏ Stormtrooper 15.00
- ❏ Yoda 15.00

Deeko
- ❏ Illustrated Star Wars scenes, package of 8 [224-10] 20.00

Dixie / Northern Inc.
Empire Strikes Back characters.
- ❏ Artoo-Detoo [224-11] 2.00
- ❏ Boba Fett [224-12] 2.00
- ❏ Chewbacca [224-13] 2.00
- ❏ Darth Vader 2.00
- ❏ Han Solo [224-14] 2.00
- ❏ Lando Calrissian [224-15] 2.00
- ❏ Lobot 2.00
- ❏ Luke Skywalker [224-16] 2.00
- ❏ Obi-Wan Kenobi [224-17] 2.00
- ❏ Princess Leia Organa [224-18] 2.00
- ❏ See-Threepio [224-19] 2.00
- ❏ Wampa Ice Creature [224-20] 2.00
- ❏ Yoda 2.00

Empire Strikes Back scenes.
- ❏ Darth Vader assembles a group of bounty hunters on the bridge of his ship. [224-21] 2.00
- ❏ "Don't worry, they won't follow us through this asteroid field!" Han exclaimed. 2.00
- ❏ "Easy, girl, it's just another meteorite!" Luke said reassuringly. [224-22] 2.00
- ❏ Han skillfully pilots the Falcon around the huge Imperial destroyer. [224-23] 2.00
- ❏ "I must admit," C-3PO muttered, "There are times I don't understand human behavior." [224-24] 2.00
- ❏ Luke finds Cloud City suspiciously friendly ... until his fated meeting with Darth Vader. [224-25] 2.00
- ❏ "Luke, I will complete your training and we will rule the galaxy together." 2.00
- ❏ Luke's only chance against the Wampa ice creature is his lightsaber. 2.00
- ❏ Luke's tauntaun senses danger when suddenly a huge claw knocks him down. [224-26] 2.00
- ❏ "Perhaps you are not as strong as the emperor thought." [224-27] 2.00
- ❏ The crew of the Millennium Falcon was imprisoned and tortured while in Cloud City. 2.00

 224-01
 224-02
 224-03
 224-04
 224-05
 224-06
 224-07
 224-08
 224-09
 224-10

Cups: Disposable

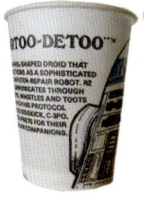         

| 224-11 | 224-12 | 224-13 | 224-14 | 224-15 | 224-16 | 224-17 | 224-18 | 224-19 | 224-20 |

       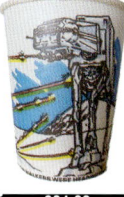  

| 224-21 | 224-22 | 224-23 | 224-24 | 224-25 | 224-26 | 224-27 | 224-28 | 224-29 | 224-30 |

- ❏ The Falcon sped through the crevice, pursued by a titanic space slug. 2.00
- ❏ The fearsome Imperial stormtroopers and their leader Darth Vader. 2.00
- ❏ The Imperial walkers were heading for the Rebel base. [224-28] 2.00
- ❏ The looming figure of Darth Vader appeared out of the darkness. 2.00
- ❏ Yoda began to teach Luke the ways of the Jedi! [224-29] ..2.00
- ❏ "You fixed us all pretty good, some friend Lando!" [224-30] 2.00

Empire Strikes Back vehicles.
- ❏ Boba Fett's ship Slave I [224-31] 2.00
- ❏ Imperial Star Destroyer [224-32] 2.00
- ❏ Imperial TIE Fighter [224-33] 2.00
- ❏ Imperial Walker 2.00
- ❏ Imperial Walker Scout 2.00
- ❏ Millennium Falcon [224-34] 2.00
- ❏ Rebel Armored Snowspeeder [224-35] 2.00
- ❏ Rebel Cruiser 2.00
- ❏ Rebel Transport 2.00
- ❏ Rebel X-Wing Fighter [224-36] 2.00

Return of the Jedi characters.
- ❏ Admiral Ackbar and the Mon Calamari [224-37] 2.00
- ❏ Bounty Hunters [224-38] 2.00
- ❏ Droopy McCool / Max Rebo / Sy Snootles [224-39] 2.00
- ❏ Emperor's Royal Guards and Darth Vader [224-40] 2.00
- ❏ Galactic Emperor 2.00
- ❏ Gamorrean Guard / Gargan / Squid Head [224-41] 2.00
- ❏ Gamorrean Guard / Hermi Odle / Salacious Crumb [224-42] 2.00
- ❏ Han Solo / Luke Skywalker / Lando Calrissian [224-43] 2.00
- ❏ Han Solo Frozen / Han Solo and Princess Leia [224-44] ..2.00
- ❏ Jabba the Hutt / Bib Fortuna / Chewbacca and Boushh [224-45] 2.00
- ❏ Kieeoo / Wicket W. Warrick / R2-D2 and Wicket [224-46] ..2.00
- ❏ Oola / Gargan / The Mole [224-47] 2.00
- ❏ Paploo / Wicket W. Warrick / R2-D2 and Wicket 2.00
- ❏ Princess Leia / Jabba the Hutt / Salacious Crumb / Bib Fortuna [224-48] 2.00
- ❏ R2-D2 / C-3PO [224-49] 2.00
- ❏ The Emperor [224-50] 2.00
- ❏ The Rancor / Luke Skywalker 2.00
- ❏ The Skiff / The Sarlacc Pit 2.00
- ❏ Yak Face / Salacious Crumb / C-3PO / ReeYees 2.00
- ❏ Yoda, The Jedi Master / Luke Skywalker [224-51] 2.00

Return of the Jedi vehicles.
- ❏ A-Wing [224-52] 2.00
- ❏ B-Wing 2.00
- ❏ Imperial Shuttle [224-53] 2.00
- ❏ The Sail Barge 2.00
- ❏ The Skiff [224-54] 2.00
- ❏ TIE Interceptor [224-55] 2.00

Saga characters.
- ❏ Ben (Obi-Wan) Kenobi 2.00
- ❏ Han Solo 2.00
- ❏ Lando Calrissian 2.00
- ❏ Yoda the Jedi master 2.00

Saga IQ tests.
- ❏ Darth Vader 5.00
- ❏ Luke Skywalker 5.00

Saga scenes.
- ❏ Darth Vader and Obi-Wan Kenobi duel to the death with their lightsabers. 2.00
- ❏ "I must admit," C-3PO muttered, "there are times I don't understand human behavior. 2.00
- ❏ Luke and C-3PO are looking for R2-D2 in the desert when the tusken raider appears. 2.00
- ❏ Lukes tauntaun senses danger and is suddenly attacked by a Hoth wampa. 2.00
- ❏ The cantina, where many space pilots often spend their leisure time. (Hammerhead / 2 Jawas) 2.00
- ❏ The cantina, where many space pilots often spend their leisure time. (Walrusman / Jawa) 2.00
- ❏ The Falcon speeds through the crevice, pursued by a titanic space slug. 2.00

Saga vehicles.
- ❏ Imperial Star Destroyer 3.00

       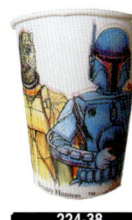 

| 224-31 | 224-32 | 224-33 | 224-34 | 224-35 | 224-36 | 224-37 | 224-38 | 224-39 |

| 224-40 | 224-41 | 224-42 | 224-43 | 224-44 | 224-45 | 224-46 | 224-47 | 224-48 | 224-49 |

  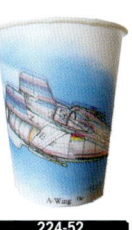     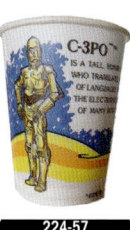 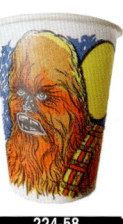 

| 224-50 | 224-51 | 224-52 | 224-53 | 224-54 | 224-55 | 224-56 | 224-57 | 224-58 | 224-59 |

Cups: Disposable

- ❏ Rebel X-Wing 3.00
- ❏ Rebel Y-Wing 3.00

Star Wars characters.
- ❏ Ben (Obi-Wan) Kenobi [224-56] 2.00
- ❏ C-3PO [224-57] 2.00
- ❏ Chewbacca [224-58] 2.00
- ❏ Death Star Droid [224-59] 2.00
- ❏ Grand Moff Tarkin [224-60] 2.00
- ❏ Greedo [224-61] 2.00
- ❏ Hammerhead [224-62] 2.00
- ❏ Han Solo [224-63] 2.00
- ❏ Lord Darth Vader [224-64] 2.00
- ❏ Luke Skywalker [224-65] 2.00
- ❏ Princess Leia Organa [224-66] 2.00
- ❏ R2-D2 [224-67] 2.00
- ❏ The Jawas [224-68] 2.00
- ❏ The Stormtrooper [224-69] 2.00
- ❏ Tusken Raiders [224-70] 2.00
- ❏ Walrus-Man [224-71] 2.00

Star Wars scenes.
- ❏ Battle above Death Star [224-72] 2.00
- ❏ C-3PO, Luke and Ben watch and listen to Princess Leia's message. [224-73] 2.00
- ❏ Darth Vader and Obi-Wan Kenobi duel to the death with their lightsabers. [224-74] 2.00
- ❏ Darth Vader orders the torture robot to commence in its prime function! [224-75] 2.00
- ❏ General Dodonna explains the Rebel strategy to destroy the Death Star. [224-76] 2.00
- ❏ Han, Ben, Luke and Chewie look in awe as their ship is dragged toward the Death Star! [224-77] 2.00
- ❏ Imperial guards fire upon the Millennium Falcon as it makes a hasty departure. [224-78] 2.00
- ❏ Luke and Ben are stopped by Imperial Soldiers at the Mos Eisley spaceport. [224-79] 2.00
- ❏ Luke and C-3PO were looking for R2-D2 in the desert when the the Tusken Raiders appeared! [224-80] 2.00
- ❏ Luke practices with the lightsaber using a small robot "seeker" for a target. [224-81] 2.00
- ❏ The cantina, where many space pilots often spend their leisure time. [224-82] 2.00
- ❏ The Jawas dragged R2-D2 back to their enormous sandcrawler. [224-83] 2.00
- ❏ The planet Alderaan is destroyed by the Death Star! [224-84] 2.00
- ❏ The Rebel Blockade Runner tries to outrun the Imperial Star Destroyer. [224-85] 2.00
- ❏ The sandcrawler is the enormous Jawa transport that scours the Tatooine deserts. [224-86] 2.00
- ❏ Trapped in the garbage compactor ... as the walls begin to move in! [224-87] 2.00

Star Wars vehicles.
- ❏ Blockade Runner [224-88] 3.00
- ❏ Imperial Star Destroyer [224-89] 3.00
- ❏ Luke's Landspeeder [224-90] 3.00
- ❏ Millennium Falcon [224-91] 3.00
- ❏ Rebel X-Wing Fighter [224-92] 3.00
- ❏ TIE Fighter [224-93] 3.00
- ❏ TIE Fighter (Vader's) [224-94] 3.00
- ❏ Y-Wing Fighter [224-95] 3.00

Drawing Board Greeting Cards, Inc.
8-packs.
- ❏ Classic Characters, dark blue 10.00
- ❏ Classic Characters, light blue [224-96] 10.00
- ❏ Cloud City [224-97] 10.00
- ❏ Darth Vader and Luke Duel [224-98] 10.00
- ❏ Ewoks Hang-Gliding [224-99] 10.00

Hallmark Party
8-packs.
- ❏ Clone Wars Opposing Forces 10.00
- ❏ LEGO Star Wars [224-100] 10.00
- ❏ Star Wars Generations [224-101] 10.00

Danglers

      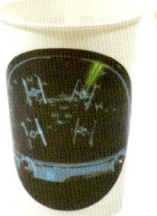  

| 224-105 | 224-106 | 224-107 | 224-108 | 224-109 | 224-110 | 224-111 | 224-112 | 224-105-112 Back |

KFC
- ❏ Boss Nass 16oz...5.00
- ❏ Boss Nass 20oz...5.00
- ❏ Boss Nass 32oz...5.00
- ❏ Jar Jar Binks 16oz...5.00
- ❏ Jar Jar Binks 20oz. [224-102].......................................5.00
- ❏ Jar Jar Binks 32oz...5.00
- ❏ Jedi 16oz...5.00
- ❏ Jedi 20oz...5.00
- ❏ Jedi 32oz...5.00
- ❏ Queen Amidala 16oz..5.00
- ❏ Queen Amidala 20oz..5.00
- ❏ Queen Amidala 32oz..5.00

KFC (Mexico)
Episode I: The Phantom Menace.
- ❏ Anakin Skywalker [224-103]......................................10.00
- ❏ Darth Maul [224-104]..10.00

Kodak (Japan)
- ❏ C-3PO and R2-D2 in Endor forest [224-105]..................35.00
- ❏ C-3PO in Jabba's throne room [224-106].....................35.00
- ❏ Imperial Star Destroyer [224-107]...............................35.00
- ❏ Jabba's throne room [224-108]...................................35.00
- ❏ Luke and Leia on Jabba's sail barge [224-109]..............35.00
- ❏ Luke and stormtroopers on Endor [224-110]................35.00
- ❏ TIE fighter attack [224-111].......................................35.00
- ❏ Yoda [224-112]..35.00

Party Express
8-packs.
- ❏ Anakin, Obi-Wan, Jango, Count Dooku.........................8.00
- ❏ Clone Wars [224-113]..8.00
- ❏ Dogfight over Death Star [224-114]..............................8.00
- ❏ Episode III [224-115]...8.00
- ❏ Qui-Gon Jinn, Obi-Wan Kenobi, Jedi vs. Sith [224-116]....8.00
- ❏ Star Wars Saga [224-117]...8.00

Pepsi Cola (Holland)
- ❏ Star Wars: Special Edition "Peel to Reveal" promotion
  [224-118]...15.00

Quela
- ❏ Vader neon, 8-pack styrofoam [224-119]....................10.00

| 224-113 | 224-114 | 224-115 | 224-116 | 224-117 | 224-118 | 224-119 |

Curtains

- ❏ Episode I Naboo space battle scenes [225-01]..............30.00

Bibb Co.
Empire Strikes Back.
- ❏ Boba Fett, exclusive to JC Penney..............................75.00
- ❏ Darth's Den..50.00
- ❏ Ice Planet..50.00
- ❏ Lord Vader...50.00
- ❏ Lord Vader's Chamber..50.00
- ❏ Spectre...50.00
- ❏ Yoda...55.00

Return of the Jedi.
- ❏ Jabba the Hutt, Ewoks, etc......................................35.00
- ❏ Logos from all 3 films...35.00
- ❏ Luke and Darth Vader Duel, AT-ST, etc......................35.00
- ❏ Star Wars Saga..35.00
- ❏ Valance..30.00

Star Wars.
- ❏ Aztec Gold..65.00
- ❏ Galaxy..65.00
- ❏ Jedi Knights...65.00
- ❏ Lord Vader..65.00
- ❏ Space Fantasy...65.00

Jay Franco and Sons
- ❏ Panels: X-Wings and Heroes [225-02]........................20.00

KIDS Home Fashions
- ❏ Lightsabers draperies [225-03].................................25.00

Westpoint Stevens
- ❏ Character study drapery with tiebacks......................45.00
- ❏ Episode I: Podracers, valance [225-04].....................30.00
- ❏ Episode II: Hangar Duel [225-05].............................35.00
- ❏ Logos and characters, 3x3 image pattern..................25.00
- ❏ Rebel and Imperial logos, valance [225-06]...............25.00

Danglers

Applause
Classic trilogy.
- ❏ Death Star [226-01]..5.00
- ❏ Millennium Falcon [226-02].......................................5.00
- ❏ Star Destroyer [226-03]...5.00
- ❏ TIE Fighter [226-04]..5.00
- ❏ X-Wing Fighter [226-05]..5.00
- ❏ Y-Wing Fighter [226-06]..5.00

Episode I: The Phantom Menace.
- ❏ Anakin's Podracer [226-07].......................................5.00
- ❏ Naboo Starfighter [226-08].......................................5.00
- ❏ Sebulba's Podracer [226-09].....................................5.00
- ❏ Sith Infiltrator [226-10]..5.00
- ❏ Trade Federation Droid Fighter [226-11]....................5.00
- ❏ Trade Federation Tank [226-12]................................5.00
- ❏ Unopened box of 12...50.00
- ❏ Unopened box of 36...85.00

   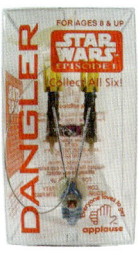 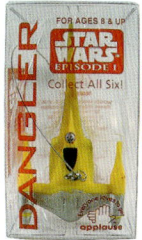    

| 225-01 | 225-02 | 225-03 | 225-04 | 225-05 | 225-06 | 226-01 | 226-02 |

| 226-03 | 226-04 | 226-05 | 226-06 | 226-07 | 226-08 | 226-09 | 226-10 | 226-11 | 226-12 |

Decals

 227-01
 227-02
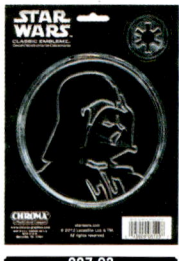 227-03
 227-04
 227-05
 227-06
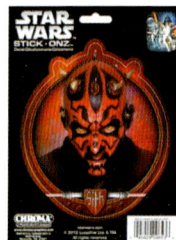 227-07

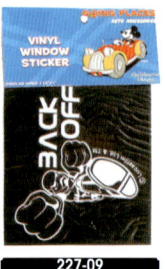 227-08
 227-09
 227-10
 227-11
 227-12
 227-13
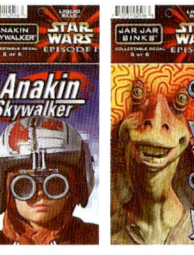 227-14 227-15 227-16

 227-17
 227-18
 227-19
 227-20
 227-21
 227-22
 227-23
 227-24
 227-25
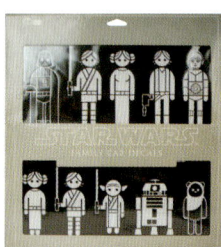 227-26

Decals
Continued in Volume 3, Page 199

C and D Visionaries, Inc.
- C-3PO and R2-D2 [v1e1:199].............................5.00
- Darth Vader 5.00
- Darth Vader, "Who's Your Daddy?" [v1e1:199]............5.00
- Darth Vader, "You Have Failed Me For The Last Time" [v1e1:199]......................................5.00
- Han Solo 5.00
- Join the Dark Side [4:128] 5.00
- Luke Skywalker...5.00
- Princess Leia, "I don't know where you get your delusions, laser brain!" [v1e1:199]..................5.00
- Star Wars, white letters on blue background...............5.00
- Yoda [v1e1:199]..5.00
- Yoda, "Do ... or do not. There is no try." [v1e1:199] 5.00

Vinyl cut.
- Boba Fett [v1e1:199].......................................10.00
- C-3PO [v1e1:199]..10.00
- Chewbacca [v1e1:199]......................................10.00
- Darth Vader [v1e1:199].....................................10.00
- Join the Dark Side [4:129]..................................10.00
- May the Force be with you ... Always [4:129]..........10.00
- My other transport is the Millennium Falcon [4:129] 10.00
- Sand People [v1e1:199].....................................10.00
- Stormtrooper [v1e1:199]....................................10.00
- Yoda [v1e1:199]..10.00
- Yoda fighting...10.00

Chroma
- My Star Wars Family [227-01] 20.00

Classic emblemz.
- Darth Vader [227-02].....................................10.00
- Darth Vader / Imperial emblem [227-03]..............10.00
- Rebel and Empire emblems [227-04] 10.00

Die Cutz.
- Darth Vader [227-05].......................................8.00
- Yoda [227-06]...8.00

Stick Onz.
- Darth Maul [227-07].......................................5.00
- Yoda [227-08]...5.00

Disney / MGM
- Jedi Training Academy 10.00
- Star Tours, glows [v1e1:199]............................25.00
- Stormtrooper, "Back Off" [227-09] 15.00

Fan Club
- Bounty Hunters...15.00
- Logo 15.00
- Star Wars [v1e1:200]......................................15.00
- The First 10 Years [v1e1:200]...........................25.00
- Yoda [v1e1:200]..15.00

Heart Art Collection, Ltd. (Japan)
- Jar Jar Binks on Kaddo [v1e1:200]....................10.00
- Star Wars with concept Boba Fett [v1e1:200] 10.00

Image Marketing
- C-3PO and R2-D2 [227-10]............................10.00
- Darth Vader [227-11].....................................10.00
- Millennium Falcon under Attack [227-12]............10.00
- Yoda [227-13]...10.00

Liquid Blue
Series 1, red header.
- #1 Queen Amidala [227-14] 5.00
- #2 Anakin Skywalker [227-15] 5.00
- #3 Jar Jar Binks [227-16] 5.00
- #4 Darth Maul [227-17] 5.00
- #5 Qui-Gon Jinn [227-18] 5.00
- #6 Obi-Wan Kenobi [227-19] 5.00

Series 2, blue header.
- #1 Jedi vs. Sith [227-20] 5.00
- #2 Jedi [227-21] 5.00
- #3 Anakin's Podracer [227-22] 5.00
- #4 Battle Droid [227-23] 5.00
- #5 Naboo Space Battle [227-24] 5.00
- #6 Federation Droid Fighter [227-25] 5.00

Star Wars Celebration V
Destinations.
- Bespin..15.00
- Dagobah..15.00
- Hoth 15.00
- The Death Star 15.00

ThinkGeek
- Star Wars Family [227-26]..............................35.00

Deodorant

Avon (Mexico)
- Heroes roll-on [228-01]..................................25.00
- Jedi 2-pack: roll-on and talc powder [228-02]..............30.00

Desktop Organizers

Grosvenor
- R2-D2 desk tidy [229-01]...............................25.00

 WET001
 228-02
 229-01
 229-02
 230-01

Dishes: Cups

231-01

231-02

231-03

231-04

231-05

231-06

231-07

231-08

231-09

231-10

231-11

Impact, Inc.
☐ Trade Federation Tank organizer [229-02] 30.00

Diaries

Antioch
☐ Queen Amidala, inset photo [v1e1:200] 12.00
☐ Queen Amidala, photo framed [v1e1:200] 12.00

Charles Letts and Co.
☐ Star Wars, 8,000 produced [v1e1:200] 50.00

Ink Group
☐ Episode I 2000 Diary [v1e1:200] 15.00

Letts
☐ Darth Vader [v1e1:200] 50.00
☐ Han Solo [v1e1:200] 50.00
☐ Millennium Falcon under attack [v1e1:200] 50.00

Q-Stat (UK)
☐ Queen Amidala diary [230-01] 15.00

Dishes: Bowls
Continued in Volume 3, Page 201

Deka
☐ Empire Strikes Back, 14 oz. [231-01] 20.00
☐ Empire Strikes Back, 20 oz. [231-02] 20.00
☐ Return of the Jedi, 14 oz. [231-03] 20.00
☐ Return of the Jedi, 20 oz. [231-04] 20.00
☐ Star Wars, 14 oz. [231-05] 25.00
☐ Star Wars, 20 oz. [231-06] 25.00

General Mills
25th anniversary, mail-in premiums.
☐ Heroes, blue-rimmed [231-07] 15.00
☐ Villains, red-rimmed [231-08] 15.00

Kellogg's
☐ R2-D2 electronic, mail-in premium [v1e1:201] 25.00

Sigma
☐ Stormtrooper sugar bowl [231-09] 250.00
☐ The World of Star Wars Fantasy [231-10] 80.00

Spearmark International (UK)
☐ Vader and Stormtroopers [231-11] 20.00

Star Wars Celebration IV
Family breakfast.
☐ Clone Wars, blue 20.00
☐ Clone Wars, green 20.00
☐ Clone Wars, pink 20.00

Trudeau
☐ Clone Wars [231-12] 15.00

Zak Designs
☐ Podracer [231-13] 10.00

Dishes: Cups
Continued in Volume 3, Page 202

☐ Episode I 3D [232-01] 5.00

Episode I.
☐ Anakin Skywalker [232-02] 5.00
☐ Qui-Gon Jinn [232-03] 5.00

Episode I. Tapered.
☐ Anakin Skywalker [232-04] 5.00

(Australia)
Lenticular cup with chocolate egg.
☐ Clone Wars Ahsoka and Commander Cody [232-05] 25.00
☐ Clone Wars Jedi [232-06] 25.00

(Germany)
☐ Clone Wars with pop-up straw [232-07] 12.00

7-Eleven Inc.
Episode III: Revenge of the Sith. Lenticular Slurpee cups with Darth Vader topper.
☐ Darth Vader [232-08] 10.00

231-12

231-13

☐ Epic Duel [232-09] 10.00
☐ Obi-Wan Kenobi 10.00
☐ Yoda [232-10] 10.00

Episode III: Revenge of the Sith. Sculpted Slurpee cups.
☐ Yoda 12.00

Applause
Classic trilogy character plastic sculpted mugs.
☐ C-3PO [232-11] 15.00
☐ Darth Vader [232-12] 15.00
☐ Stormtrooper [232-13] 15.00
☐ Wicket the Ewok [232-14] 15.00

Episode I character plastic sculpted mugs.
☐ Anakin Skywalker [232-15] 10.00
☐ C-3PO [232-16] 10.00
☐ Jar Jar Binks [232-17] 10.00
☐ Queen Amidala [232-18] 10.00

Tumbler with no-spill travel lid and handle.
☐ Darth Maul [232-19] 20.00
☐ Jar Jar [232-20] 20.00

Burger King (Argentina)
Episode III: Revenge of the Sith. Cups with sculpted character topper lid.
☐ C-3PO [232-21] 25.00
☐ Darth Vader, black [232-22] 25.00
☐ Darth Vader, red [232-23] 25.00
☐ Yoda [232-24] 25.00

232-01

232-02

232-03

232-04

232-05

232-06

232-07

232-08

232-09

232-10

Dishes: Cups

 232-11
 232-12
 232-13
 232-14
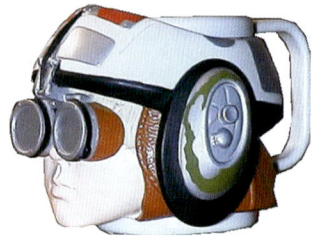 232-15

 232-16
 232-17
 232-18
 232-19
 232-20
 232-21
 232-22
 232-23

Burger King (Germany)
Episode III: Revenge of the Sith motion cups.
- #1 Anakin / Vader [232-25] 15.00
- #2 Anakin / Yoda [232-26] 15.00
- #3 Epic Duel [232-27] 15.00

Burger King (Singapore)
Episode III: Revenge of the Sith.
- Saga characters [232-28] 10.00

Cingular
- Celebration 3 [232-29] 5.00

Coca-Cola
Return of the Jedi. 7-Eleven. Canada Cup logo centered.
- Admiral Ackbar / Lando Calrissian and Nien Nunb [232-30] 20.00
- Admiral Ackbar, Lando, Luke, and Droids / Han Solo in Carbonite [232-31] 8.00
- Bib Fortuna, Gamorrean Guard, and Jabba / Max Rebo Band [232-32] 20.00
- Biker Scouts / Biker Scout and Han Solo [232-33] 20.00
- Chewbacca, Han, and Leia / C-3PO and R2-D2 [232-34] .. 20.00
- Chewbacca, Han, Lando, Luke (skiff) / Ben Kenobi and Luke [232-35] 20.00
- Darth Vader and Luke Duel / Darth Vader and Emperor [232-36] 20.00
- Emperor's Throne Room / Emperor's Royal Guards [232-37] 20.00
- Imperial Moff / Imperial Dignitaries [232-38] 20.00
- Ishi Tib, Jawas, and Klaatu / Lando Calrissian [232-39] .. 20.00
- Jabba Sail Barge / C-3PO, Ree-Yees, and Yak Face [232-40] 20.00
- Wicket / Ewok, Wicket, and AT-ST [232-41] 20.00

Return of the Jedi. 7-Eleven; Canada Cup.
- Admiral Ackbar / Lando Calrissian and Nien Nunb 20.00
- Admiral Ackbar, Lando, Luke, and Droids / Han Solo in Carbonite 20.00
- Bib Fortuna, Gamorrean Guard, and Jabba / Max Rebo Band 20.00
- Biker Scouts / Biker Scout and Han Solo 20.00
- Chewbacca, Han, and Leia / C-3PO and R2-D2 .... 20.00
- Chewbacca, Han, Lando, Luke (skiff) / Ben Kenobi and Luke 20.00
- Darth Vader and Luke Duel / Darth Vader and Emperor 20.00
- Emperor's Throne Room / Emperor's Royal Guards 20.00
- Imperial Moff / Imperial Dignitaries 20.00
- Ishi Tib, Jawas, and Klaatu / Lando Calrissian 20.00
- Jabba Sail Barge / C-3PO, Ree-Yees and Yak Face 20.00
- Wicket / Ewok, Wicket and AT-ST 20.00

 232-24
 232-25
 232-26
 232-27
 232-28
 232-29
 232-30 Side 1 and Side 2

 232-31 Side 1 and Side 2

 232-32 Side 1 and Side 2

 232-33 Side 1 and Side 2

 232-34 Side 1 and Side 2

 232-35 Side 1 and Side 2

 232-36 Side 1 and Side 2

 232-37 Side 1 and Side 2

 232-38 Side 1 and Side 2

 232-39 Side 1 and Side 2

 232-40 Side 1 and Side 2

 232-41
 232-42

Dishes: Cups

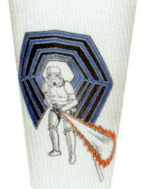         

232-43 | 232-44 | 232-45 | 232-46 | 232-47 | 232-48 | 232-49 | 232-50 | 232-51 | 232-52

232-53 | 232-54 | 232-55 | 232-56 | 232-57 | 232-58 | 232-59 | 232-60 | 232-61 | 232-62

Star Wars. Coca-Cola.
- ❑ Hammerhead, "Strange and silent Hammerhead sits motionless in the cantina—watching" [232-42] 100.00

Star Wars. Series 1. Coca-Cola / Koolee / Li'l General.
- ❑ 1 Stormtrooper 20.00
- ❑ 2 Chewbacca and Han Solo 20.00
- ❑ 3 Trash Compactor 20.00
- ❑ 4 Ben and Darth Vader Duel 20.00
- ❑ 5 Battle Above The Death Star 20.00
- ❑ 6 Luke in Falcon Gunwell 20.00
- ❑ 7 Mos Eisley 20.00
- ❑ 8 Luke Skywalker 20.00
- ❑ 9 Luke Training with Remote 20.00
- ❑ 10 Darth Vader, Leia and Tarkin 20.00
- ❑ 11 Chewbacca, Han, and Luke in Disguise 20.00
- ❑ 12 C-3PO and R2-D2 .... 20.00
- ❑ 13 Princess Leia 20.00
- ❑ 14 Tusken Raiders and Bantha 20.00
- ❑ 15 Jawas and R2-D2 .... 20.00
- ❑ 16 Tusken Raider Attacks Luke 20.00
- ❑ 17 Darth Vader Questions Rebel Soldier 20.00
- ❑ 18 Luke and Leia Swing to Safety 20.00
- ❑ 19 Han Solo, Luke and Princess Leia 20.00
- ❑ 20 Ben Shuts Down Tractor Beam 20.00

Star Wars. Series 1. Coca-Cola / Koolee / Shop & Go.
- ❑ 1 Stormtrooper 20.00
- ❑ 2 Chewbacca and Han Solo 20.00
- ❑ 3 Trash Compactor 20.00
- ❑ 4 Ben and Darth Vader Duel 20.00
- ❑ 5 Battle Above The Death Star 20.00
- ❑ 6 Luke in Falcon Gunwell 20.00
- ❑ 7 Mos Eisley 20.00
- ❑ 8 Luke Skywalker 20.00
- ❑ 9 Luke Training with Remote 20.00
- ❑ 10 Darth Vader, Leia, and Tarkin 20.00
- ❑ 11 Chewbacca, Han, and Luke in Disguise 20.00
- ❑ 12 C-3PO and R2-D2 .... 20.00
- ❑ 13 Princess Leia 20.00
- ❑ 14 Tusken Raiders and Bantha 20.00
- ❑ 15 Jawas and R2-D2 .... 20.00
- ❑ 16 Tusken Raider Attacks Luke 20.00
- ❑ 17 Darth Vader Questions Rebel Soldier 20.00
- ❑ 18 Luke and Leia Swing to Safety 20.00
- ❑ 19 Han Solo, Luke, and Princess Leia 20.00
- ❑ 20 Ben Shuts Down Tractor Beam 20.00

Star Wars. Series 1. Coca-Cola / Koolee.
- ❑ 1 Stormtrooper 15.00
- ❑ 2 Chewbacca and Han Solo 15.00

232-63 | 232-64 | 232-65 | 232-66 | 232-67 | 232-68 | 232-69 | 232-70

232-71 | 232-72 | 232-73 | 232-74 | 232-75 | 232-76 | 232-77 | 232-78 Side 1 and Side 2

232-79 Side 1 and Side 2 | 232-80 | 232-81 | 232-82 | 232-83 | 232-84 | 232-85 | 232-86 | 232-87 | 232-88 Side 1 and Side 2

Dishes: Cups

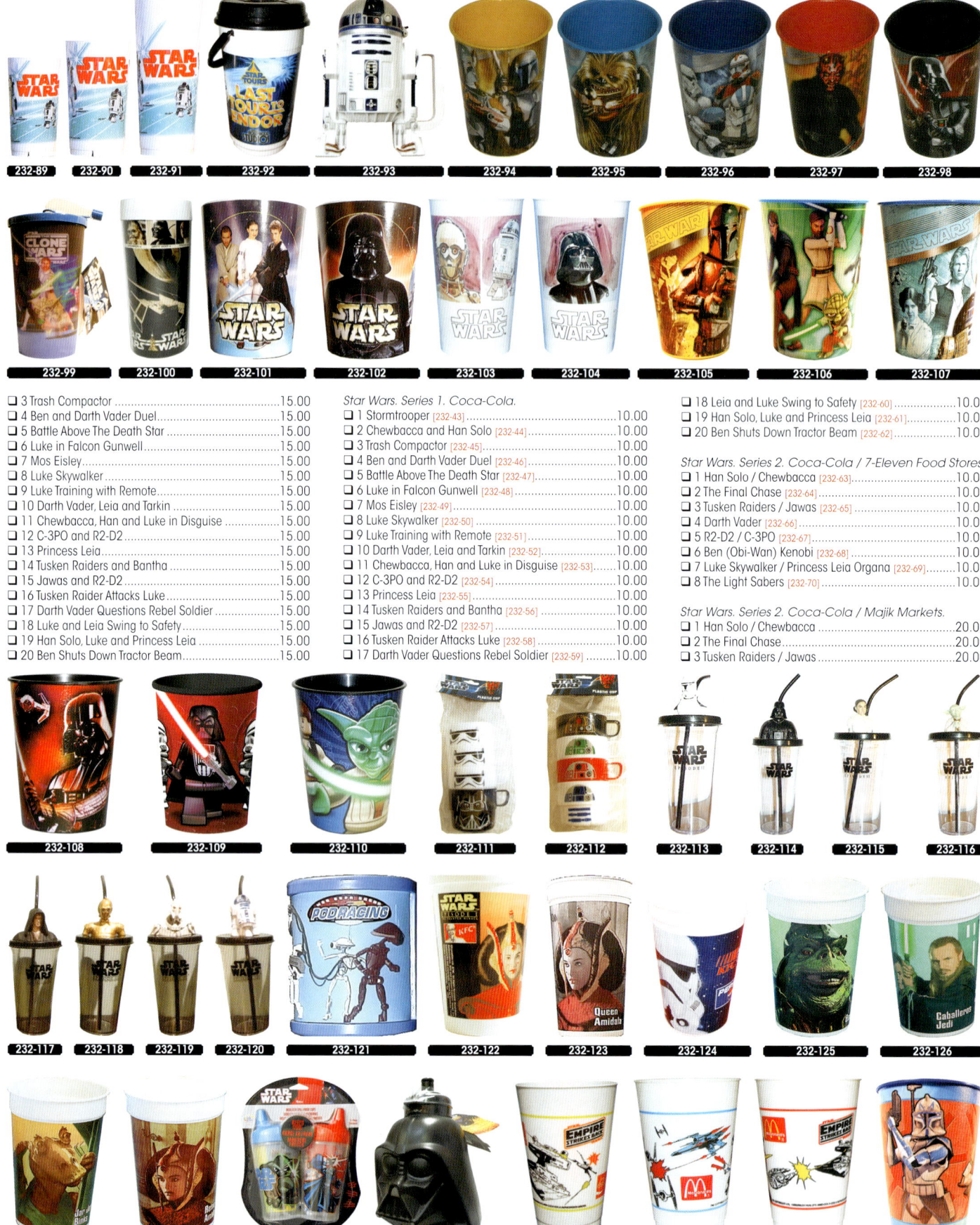

□ 3 Trash Compactor 15.00
□ 4 Ben and Darth Vader Duel.................................15.00
□ 5 Battle Above The Death Star 15.00
□ 6 Luke in Falcon Gunwell......................................15.00
□ 7 Mos Eisley..15.00
□ 8 Luke Skywalker...15.00
□ 9 Luke Training with Remote................................15.00
□ 10 Darth Vader, Leia and Tarkin 15.00
□ 11 Chewbacca, Han and Luke in Disguise 15.00
□ 12 C-3PO and R2-D2..15.00
□ 13 Princess Leia..15.00
□ 14 Tusken Raiders and Bantha 15.00
□ 15 Jawas and R2-D2...15.00
□ 16 Tusken Raider Attacks Luke 15.00
□ 17 Darth Vader Questions Rebel Soldier..............15.00
□ 18 Luke and Leia Swing to Safety 15.00
□ 19 Han Solo, Luke and Princess Leia 15.00
□ 20 Ben Shuts Down Tractor Beam........................15.00

Star Wars. Series 1. Coca-Cola.
□ 1 Stormtrooper [232-43] 10.00
□ 2 Chewbacca and Han Solo [232-44] 10.00
□ 3 Trash Compactor [232-45] 10.00
□ 4 Ben and Darth Vader Duel [232-46] 10.00
□ 5 Battle Above The Death Star [232-47] 10.00
□ 6 Luke in Falcon Gunwell [232-48] 10.00
□ 7 Mos Eisley [232-49] 10.00
□ 8 Luke Skywalker [232-50] 10.00
□ 9 Luke Training with Remote [232-51] 10.00
□ 10 Darth Vader, Leia and Tarkin [232-52] 10.00
□ 11 Chewbacca, Han and Luke in Disguise [232-53]......10.00
□ 12 C-3PO and R2-D2 [232-54] 10.00
□ 13 Princess Leia [232-55]..10.00
□ 14 Tusken Raiders and Bantha [232-56] 10.00
□ 15 Jawas and R2-D2 [232-57] 10.00
□ 16 Tusken Raider Attacks Luke [232-58] 10.00
□ 17 Darth Vader Questions Rebel Soldier [232-59] 10.00

□ 18 Leia and Luke Swing to Safety [232-60] 10.00
□ 19 Han Solo, Luke and Princess Leia [232-61].............10.00
□ 20 Ben Shuts Down Tractor Beam [232-62] 10.00

Star Wars. Series 2. Coca-Cola / 7-Eleven Food Stores.
□ 1 Han Solo / Chewbacca [232-63] 10.00
□ 2 The Final Chase [232-64] 10.00
□ 3 Tusken Raiders / Jawas [232-65] 10.00
□ 4 Darth Vader [232-66] 10.00
□ 5 R2-D2 / C-3PO [232-67] 10.00
□ 6 Ben (Obi-Wan) Kenobi [232-68] 10.00
□ 7 Luke Skywalker / Princess Leia Organa [232-69]......10.00
□ 8 The Light Sabers [232-70] 10.00

Star Wars. Series 2. Coca-Cola / Majik Markets.
□ 1 Han Solo / Chewbacca 20.00
□ 2 The Final Chase...20.00
□ 3 Tusken Raiders / Jawas 20.00

Dishes: Cups

232-135 232-136 232-137 232-138 232-139 232-140 232-141 232-142

232-143 232-144 232-145 232-146 232-147 232-148 232-149 232-150 232-151 232-152 232-153 232-154

☐ 4 Darth Vader 20.00
☐ 5 R2-D2 / C-3PO 20.00
☐ 6 Ben (Obi-Wan) Kenobi 20.00
☐ 7 Luke Skywalker / Princess Leia Organa 20.00
☐ 8 The Light Sabers 20.00

Star Wars. Series 3. Coca-Cola.
☐ Ben Kenobi [232-71] 15.00
☐ Boba Fett [232-72] 15.00
☐ C-3PO and R2-D2 [232-73] 15.00
☐ Chewbacca [232-74] 15.00
☐ Darth Vader and Grand Moff Tarkin [232-75] ...15.00
☐ Han Solo 15.00
☐ Luke Skywalker and Princess Leia [232-76] ...15.00
☐ TIE Fighter vs. X-Wing Fighter [232-77] 15.00

Theater concession promotions.
☐ Return of the Jedi, 20oz. [232-78] 20.00

☐ Star Wars / Empire Strikes Back, 20 oz. 20.00
☐ Star Wars / Empire Strikes Back, 32 oz. [232-79] ..20.00

Coca-Cola (Australia / New Zealand)
☐ Return of the Jedi [232-80] 40.00

Star Wars. Unnumbered, 12 cm tall, no descriptive text on back. "Coke is Life" embossed on bottom of cup.
☐ Darth Vader 25.00
☐ Han Solo / Chewbacca 25.00
☐ R2-D2 / C-3PO 25.00
☐ The Final Chase (X-Wing / TIE Fighter) 25.00

Coca-Cola (China)
Episode III: Revenge of the Sith. Clear colored cups with Darth Vader lid.
☐ Anakin Skywalker, red [232-81] 15.00
☐ Clone trooper, clear [232-82] 15.00

☐ Darth Vader, gray [232-83] 15.00
☐ Darth Vader, red [232-84] 15.00

Deka
☐ Empire Strikes Back 6 oz. [232-85] 20.00
☐ Empire Strikes Back 11 oz. [232-86] 20.00
☐ Empire Strikes Back 17 oz. [232-87] 20.00
☐ Return of the Jedi 6 oz. 20.00
☐ Return of the Jedi 11 oz. [232-88] 20.00
☐ Return of the Jedi 17 oz. 20.00
☐ Star Wars 6 oz. [232-89] 20.00
☐ Star Wars 11 oz. [232-90] 20.00
☐ Star Wars 17 oz. [232-91] 20.00

Disney Theme Park Merchandise
☐ Donald Duck as Darth Maul, sculpted 25.00
☐ Last Tour to Endor [232-92] 50.00
☐ R2-D2, Star Tours 3D [232-93] 25.00

232-155 232-156 232-157 232-158 232-159 232-160 232-161 232-162 232-163

232-164 232-165 232-166 232-167 232-168 232-169 232-170 232-171 232-172

232-173 232-174 232-175 232-176 232-177 232-178 232-179 232-180 232-181

Dishes: Cups

232-182

232-183

232-184

232-185

232-186

232-187

232-188

232-189

232-190

232-191

232-192

232-193

232-194

232-195

232-196

232-197

232-198

232-199

232-200

232-201

232-202

232-203

232-204

232-205

232-206

232-207

232-208

Dynamic Drinkware
❑ Bounty hunters [232-94] 5.00
❑ Chewbacca [232-95] 5.00
❑ Clone and stormtroopers [232-96] 5.00
❑ Darth Maul [232-97] 5.00
❑ Darth Vader [232-98] 5.00
❑ Yoda 5.00

Galerie
❑ The Clone Wars lenticular, cup with gum balls and straw [232-99] 4.00

General Mills
❑ Star Wars 11 oz. Cheerios mail-in premium [232-100] ...30.00

25th anniversary, mail-in premiums.
❑ Heroes, blue-rimmed [232-101] 10.00
❑ Villains, red-rimmed [232-102] 10.00

Grubee's (Canada)
❑ C-3PO / R2-D2 [232-103] 35.00
❑ Darth Vader [232-104] 35.00

Hallmark
❑ Bounty Hunters [232-105] 5.00
❑ Clone Wars—Clones and Jedi [232-106] 5.00
❑ Heroes of the rebellion, blue [232-107] 5.00
❑ Star Wars [232-108] 5.00

LEGO Star Wars.
❑ Darth Vader and Stormtroopers [232-109] 5.00
❑ Yoda, Han, and Luke [232-110] 5.00

Heart Art Collection, Ltd. (Japan)
4-packs of character cups.
❑ Darth Vader / stormtroopers [232-111] 20.00
❑ R2-D2 / R2-Q5 / R2-A6 / R2-R9 [232-112] 20.00

Hungry Jacks
Episode II: Attack of the Clones.
❑ Clone trooper [232-113] 15.00
❑ Darth Vader [232-114] 15.00
❑ Padmé Amidala [232-115] 15.00
❑ Yoda [232-116] 15.00

Episode III: Revenge of the Sith.
❑ Anakin Skywalker [232-117] 15.00
❑ C-3PO [232-118] 15.00
❑ General Grievous [232-119] 15.00
❑ R2-D2 [232-120] 15.00

Jay Franco and Sons
❑ Mos Espa arena podracing tumbler, features pit droids [232-121] 10.00

KFC
Episode I: The Phantom Menace.
❑ Heroes [232-122] 10.00

Episode I: The Phantom Menace. Characters.
❑ Boss Nass 10.00
❑ Jar Jar Binks 10.00
❑ Jedi 10.00
❑ Queen Amidala [232-123] 10.00

Special edition.
❑ Stormtrooper [232-124] 15.00

KFC (Mexico)
Episode I: The Phantom Menace.
❑ Boss Nass [232-125] 10.00
❑ Caballeros Jedi [232-126] 10.00
❑ Jar Jar Binks [232-127] 10.00
❑ Reine Amidala [232-128] 10.00

Learning Curve
❑ Insulated "sippy cup" 2-pack, 9 oz. [232-129] 15.00

Masterfoods USA
❑ Darth Vader sip cup with M&Ms inside [232-130] 10.00

McDonalds (Australia)
Empire Strikes Back. Coca Cola logo.
❑ Droids and Vehicles, yellow stripe [232-131] 35.00
❑ Heroes, blue stripe [232-132] 35.00
❑ Villains, red stripe [232-133] 35.00

McDonalds (Japan)
❑ Star Wars droids 200.00

McDonalds (New Zealand)
Empire Strikes Back. Coca Cola logo. Taller than Australian version.
❑ Droids and Vehicles, yellow stripe 25.00
❑ Heroes, blue stripe 25.00
❑ Villains, red stripe 25.00

Party Express
Plastic cups.
❑ Clone Wars: Captain Rex [232-134] 5.00
❑ Episode I Qui-Gon and Darth Maul [232-135] 5.00
❑ Episode II Anakin and Jango [232-136] 5.00
❑ Episode III Darth Vader and Yoda [232-137] 5.00

Pepperidge Farms
❑ The Creatures [232-138] 15.00
❑ The Endor Forest [232-139] 15.00
❑ The Rebels [232-140] 15.00
❑ The Vehicles [232-141] 15.00
❑ The Villains 15.00

Pepsi Cola
❑ Cantina, Las Vegas, excl. to FAO Schwarz [232-142] 30.00

Episode I: The Phantom Menace. 44oz, fluted, ridged.
❑ Battle Droid [232-143] 5.00
❑ C-3PO [232-144] 5.00
❑ Obi-Wan Kenobi [232-145] 5.00
❑ Padmé [232-146] 5.00
❑ Queen Amidala [232-147] 5.00
❑ Sebulba [232-148] 5.00

Episode I: The Phantom Menace. 44oz, smooth.
❑ C-3PO [232-149] 5.00
❑ Darth Sidious [232-150] 5.00
❑ Jar Jar Binks [232-151] 5.00
❑ Obi-Wan Kenobi [232-152] 5.00
❑ Queen Amidala [232-153] 5.00
❑ Sebulba [232-154] 5.00

Star Wars Special Edition.
❑ Darth Vader, AT-AT, Death Star QT [232-155] 15.00
❑ Darth Vader, AT-AT, Death Star [232-156] 15.00

Star Wars Special Edition. Individual characters.
❑ C-3PO [232-157] 20.00
❑ Darth Vader [232-158] 20.00
❑ R2-D2 [232-159] 20.00
❑ Stormtrooper [232-160] 20.00

Pepsi Cola (Mexico)
❑ Queen Amidala [232-161] 15.00
❑ Qui-Gon vs. Darth Maul [232-162] 15.00

Pizza Hut
Star Wars special edition take-out cups with lid.
❑ Luke and Darth Vader on Bespin gantry, 16 oz. [232-163] .10.00
❑ 'The Trilogy', 12 oz. [232-164] 10.00

Dishes: Egg Cups

233-01   233-02   233-03   233-04   233-05   233-06

233-07   233-08   233-09   233-10   233-11   233-12

Star Wars trilogy.
- ❏ C-3PO [232-165]..................15.00
- ❏ Chewbacca [232-166]............15.00
- ❏ Darth Vader [232-167]...........15.00
- ❏ R2-D2 [232-168]....................15.00

Pizza Hut (Holland)
- ❏ Star Wars: Special Edition take-out [232-169]..............15.00

Spearmark International
- ❏ Luke on Hoth, 10 oz. [232-170]..................25.00
- ❏ Luke on Hoth, 8 oz., glitter filled walls [232-171]..........25.00

Spearmark International (UK)
- ❏ Clone Wars vortex spinning tumbler [232-172]......20.00
- ❏ Death Star Battle, clear plastic [232-173].........15.00
- ❏ Episode II Flip Top Flask [232-174]................15.00
- ❏ Star Wars classic sport tumbler w/ flip-top lid [232-175]..20.00
- ❏ Vader and Stormtroopers / Luke [232-176].........15.00

Super Live Adventure (Japan)
- ❏ Characters and Falcon [232-177]..................65.00
- ❏ R2-D2 cup with coin slot in top [232-178].........75.00

Taco Bell
- ❏ Episode I characters [232-179]....................10.00

Defeat the Dark Side character cups.
- ❏ Anakin Skywalker [232-180]......................10.00
- ❏ Sebulba [232-181]..................................10.00

Episode I: The Phantom Menace.
- ❏ Darth Maul, large [232-182]......................5.00
- ❏ Jar Jar Binks, medium [232-183].................5.00
- ❏ Obi-Wan Kenobi, large [232-184]................5.00
- ❏ Queen Amidala, medium [232-185]...............5.00

Special Edition with lenticular scenes.
- ❏ A New Hope...10.00
- ❏ Empire Strikes Back [232-186]...................10.00
- ❏ Return of the Jedi [232-187]......................10.00
- ❏ Star Wars logo [232-188]..........................10.00

Star Wars Special Edition.
- ❏ C-3PO, medium [232-189]........................15.00
- ❏ Darth Vader, large................................15.00
- ❏ R2-D2, small [232-190]............................15.00

Tervis
Travel mugs. 16 oz.
- ❏ Clone Wars [232-191]...............................20.00
- ❏ Star Wars collage [232-192].......................20.00
- ❏ Yoda [232-193].......................................20.00

Texaco
- ❏ R2-D2 and C-3PO, glow-in-the-dark [232-194]......20.00

Trudeau
- ❏ Clone Wars [232-195]...............................10.00

 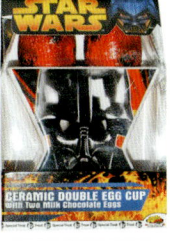 

233-13   233-14   234-01   234-02

Vandor LLC
Lenticular cups. Exclusive to Target.
- ❏ Darth Vader [232-196]..............................12.00
- ❏ R2-D2 [232-197].....................................12.00
- ❏ Stormtrooper [232-198]............................12.00
- ❏ Yoda [232-199].......................................12.00

Zak Designs
- ❏ Anakin Skywalker / Sebulba sport tumbler [v1e1-205]......10.00
- ❏ Anakin Skywalker Juice cup, blue, 8 oz. [232-200]......10.00
- ❏ Darth Maul sport tumbler with lid [v1e1-205]......10.00
- ❏ General Grievous with cover and straw [232-201]......10.00
- ❏ Podrace Juice cup, transparent blue, 8 oz. [232-202]......10.00
- ❏ Podracer half-sculpted sports bottle [v1e1-205]......10.00
- ❏ Podracer sport tumbler with lid [v1e1-205]......10.00

Episode III: Revenge of the Sith.
- ❏ Darth Vader with cover and straw [232-203]......10.00

Tumbler with no-spill travel lid.
- ❏ Darth Maul [232-204]................................15.00
- ❏ Darth Vader [232-205]...............................15.00
- ❏ Jar Jar Binks [232-206]..............................15.00
- ❏ Qui-Gon Jinn [232-207].............................15.00
- ❏ Space Battle [232-208].............................15.00

Dishes: Dish Sets
Continued in Volume 3, Page 201

(UK)
- ❏ Clone Wars 3-piece set [233-01].................25.00

Celebration V
- ❏ Mini-Cereal Collector set: tin case, bowl, spoon, milk bottle..................165.00

Deka
- ❏ Return of the Jedi: Baby's First Feeding Set.........85.00
- ❏ Return of the Jedi: Dinnerware set.................65.00

3-piece sets: plate, bowl, tumbler.
- ❏ Wicket purple box [233-02].......................175.00
- ❏ Wicket red box [233-03]...........................135.00
- ❏ Wicket white box [233-04]........................250.00

Kellogg's (Korea)
- ❏ R2-D2 breakfast droid, bagged [233-05]........35.00

Kellogg's (Malaysia)
- ❏ R2-D2 breakfast droid, boxed [233-06].........45.00

Kellogg's (Spain)
- ❏ R2-D2 breakfast droid, boxed....................65.00

Learning Curve
- ❏ Darth Vader baby 3-piece set, melamine bowl with spoon [233-07]..................18.00
- ❏ Darth Vader toddler 3-piece set, melamine plate and bowl with spoon..................20.00

Pottery Barn
- ❏ Star Wars with glass, plate, and bowl [233-08]......50.00

Sigma
- ❏ "The World of Star Wars Fantasy Childset" ceramic, boxed [233-09]..................185.00

Spearmark International (UK)
- ❏ Classic Trilogy children's set, soft sided bag [233-10]......65.00

Trudeau
3-piece sets: plate, bowl, tumbler.
- ❏ Clone Wars [233-11]................................35.00

Zak Designs
3-piece sets: plate, bowl, tumbler.
- ❏ Episode I: The Phantom Menace, boxed [233-12].........25.00
- ❏ Episode I: The Phantom Menace, clear packed [233-13]..................25.00
- ❏ Episode III: Revenge of the Sith, boxed [233-14].........25.00
- ❏ Episode III: Revenge of the Sith, clear packed.........30.00

Dishes: Egg Cups
Continued in Volume 3, Page 201

Bonbon Buddies (UK)
- ❏ Ceramic double egg cup with milk chocolate eggs [234-01]..................20.00
- ❏ R2-D2 egg cup and milk chocolate egg [234-02].........20.00

Dishes: Food Storage

235-01 | 235-02 | 236-01 | 236-02 | 236-03 | 236-04 | 236-05 | 236-06

236-07 | 236-08 | 236-09 | 236-10 | 236-11 | 236-12 | 236-13 | 236-14 | 236-15 | 236-16 | 236-17 | 236-18

Dishes: Food Storage
Continued in Volume 3, Page 208

Small Planet Co. Ltd. (Japan)
Bento boxes, stacked.
- ❏ Comic book art 65.00
- ❏ Star Wars characters 65.00

Thermos Co.
- ❏ Clone Wars [235-01] 25.00
- ❏ Darth Vader 25.00

Trudeau
- ❏ Clone Wars galaxy sandwich box [235-02] 15.00

Dishes: Glasses
Continued in Volume 3, Page 208

- ❏ Episode I icons [236-01] 15.00
- ❏ Feel the Force, Back on the Big Screen, Star Wars: Special Edition logo [236-02] 7.00

Carnival glasses.
- ❏ Star Wars, orange and yellow 95.00
- ❏ Star Wars, pink 95.00

Amora (France)
- ❏ Chewbacca and Ewok [236-03] 50.00
- ❏ Darth Vader and Stormtroopers [236-04] 50.00
- ❏ Vader and Luke duel [236-05] 50.00
- ❏ Yoda and Luke [236-06] 50.00

Burger King
Empire Strikes Back.
- ❏ C-3PO and R2-D2 [236-07] 20.00
- ❏ Darth Vader [236-08] 20.00
- ❏ Lando Calrissian [236-09] 20.00
- ❏ Luke Skywalker [236-10] 20.00

Empire Strikes Back. Thin decal, button-bottoms, exclusive to Ohio.
- ❏ C-3PO and R2-D2 [236-11] 30.00
- ❏ Darth Vader [236-12] 30.00
- ❏ Lando Calrissian [236-13] 30.00
- ❏ Luke Skywalker [236-14] 30.00

Return of the Jedi.
- ❏ Emperor's Throne Room [236-15] 15.00
- ❏ Ewok Village [236-16] 15.00
- ❏ Jabba's Palace [236-17] 15.00
- ❏ Jabba's Sail Barge [236-18] 15.00

Return of the Jedi. Plastic cups, exclusive to Massachusetts.
- ❏ Emperor's Throne Room [v1e1:207] 30.00
- ❏ Ewok Village 30.00
- ❏ Jabba's Palace [v1e1:207] 30.00
- ❏ Jabba's Sail Barge [v1e1:207] 30.00

Star Wars.
- ❏ C-3PO and R2-D2 [236-19] 30.00
- ❏ Chewbacca [236-20] 30.00

236-19 | 236-20 | 236-21 | 236-22 | 236-23 | 236-24 | 236-25

236-26 | 236-27 | 236-28 | 236-29 | 236-30 | 236-31 | 236-32 | 236-33 | 236-34 | 236-35 | 236-36

236-37 Side 1 and Side 2 | 236-38 Side 1 and Side 2 | 236-39 Side 1 and Side 2 | 236-40 Side 1 and Side 2 | 236-41 Side 1 and Side 2 | 236-42 Side 1 and Side 2

Dishes: Glasses

 236-43
 236-44
 236-45
 236-46
 236-47

 236-48
 236-49
 236-50
 236-51
 236-52

236-53
 236-54
 236-55
 236-56
 236-57

 236-58
 236-59
236-60
 236-61

❏ Darth Vader [236-21] 30.00
❏ Luke Skywalker [236-22] 30.00

Burger King (Canada)
Empire Strikes Back.
❏ C-3PO and R2-D2 ....20.00
❏ Darth Vader, Boba Fett is gray instead of blue 50.00
❏ Lando Calrissian 20.00
❏ Luke Skywalker 20.00

Crystal Craft (Australia)
❏ Anakin Skywalker [236-23] 15.00
❏ Darth Maul 15.00
❏ Droids 15.00
❏ Jar Jar Binks 15.00
❏ Jedi vs. Sith [236-24] 15.00
❏ Obi-Wan Kenobi 15.00
❏ Qui-Gon Jinn [v1e1:207] 15.00
❏ Starships [236-25] 15.00

Glazed.
❏ Artoo Detoo [236-26] 20.00
❏ C-3PO [236-27] 20.00
❏ Chewbacca [236-28] 20.00
❏ Darth Vader [236-29] 20.00
❏ Emperor's Royal Guard [236-30] 20.00
❏ Han Solo [236-31] 20.00
❏ Luke Skywalker [236-32] 20.00
❏ Obi-Wan Kenobi [236-33] 20.00
❏ Princess Leia [236-34] 20.00
❏ Stormtrooper [236-35] 20.00
❏ Yoda [236-36] 20.00

Disney / MGM
Star Wars Weekends.
❏ 2006 logo 25.00

Downpace Ltd. (UK)
Episode I.
❏ 3-pack, heroes 30.00
❏ 3-pack, villains 30.00
❏ Anakin Skywalker [236-37] 10.00
❏ Battle Droid [236-38] 10.00
❏ Darth Maul [236-39] 10.00
❏ Jar Jar [236-40] 10.00

❏ Obi-Wan [236-41] 10.00
❏ Sebulba [236-42] 10.00

Hasbro
Includes action figure. Wave 1, Target exclusives.
❏ A New Hope, Ben Kenobi [236-43] 35.00
❏ Attack of the Clones, Anakin Skywalker [236-44] 35.00
❏ Empire Strikes Back, Luke Skywalker snowspeeder pilot
   [236-45] 35.00
❏ Phantom Menace, Darth Maul [236-46] 35.00
❏ Return of the Jedi, Leia as Jabba's captive [236-47] 35.00

Includes action figure. Wave 2, not officially released.
❏ A New Hope, Han Solo [236-48] 150.00
❏ Empire Strikes Back, Yoda [236-49] 150.00
❏ Return of the Jedi, Boba Fett 150.00

Includes action figure. Wave 3, Target exclusives.
❏ Revenge of the Sith, Clone trooper [236-50] 35.00
❏ Revenge of the Sith, General Grievous [236-51] 35.00
❏ Revenge of the Sith, Obi-Wan Kenobi [236-52] 35.00

Includes action figure. Wave 4, Target exclusives.
❏ A New Hope, Han Solo [236-53] 35.00
❏ Empire Strikes Back, Yoda [236-54] 35.00
❏ Return of the Jedi, Boba Fett [236-55] 35.00

Includes action figure. Wave 5, Target exclusives.
❏ A New Hope, Princess Leia [236-56] 40.00
❏ Empire Strikes Back, Darth Vader [236-57] 30.00
❏ Return of the Jedi, Stormtrooper [236-58] 30.00

Hungry Jacks (Australia)
❏ Emperor's Throne Room [v1e1:208] 50.00
❏ Ewok Village [v1e1:208] 50.00
❏ Jabba's Palace [v1e1:208] 50.00
❏ Jabba's Sail Barge [v1e1:208] 50.00

Kotobukiya (Japan)
Kiriko etched.
❏ C-3PO, 9 oz. [236-59] 125.00
❏ R2-D2, 10 oz. [236-60] 125.00
❏ R2-P17, 10 oz. [236-61] 125.00

Pepsi Cola
Episode I: The Phantom Menace.
❏ Episode I: Anakin Skywalker [236-62] 10.00
❏ Episode I: Queen Amidala [236-63] 10.00
❏ Episode I: Qui-Gon Jinn [236-64] 10.00
❏ Episode I: R2-D2 [236-65] 10.00

Clear, etched glasses. Promotional.
❏ The Phantom Menace heroes [4:135] 40.00
❏ The Phantom Menace villains [4:135] 40.00

Pepsi Cola (Holland)
❏ C-3PO Star Wars trilogy 20.00

Pepsi Cola (China)
❏ C-3PO [v1e1:208] 25.00
❏ Darth Vader [v1e1:208] 25.00
❏ R2-D2 [v1e1:208] 25.00
❏ Stormtrooper [v1e1:208] 25.00

Dishes: Glasses

236-62   236-63   236-64   236-65   236-66   236-67 Side 1 and Side 2   236-68   236-69

236-70   236-71   236-72

236-73 Side 1 and Side 2   236-74 Side 1 and Side 2   236-75 Side 1 and Side 2   236-76 Side 1 and Side 2

Pepsi Cola (Mexico)
- ❏ C-3PO 15.00
- ❏ Darth Vader 15.00
- ❏ R2-D2 ....15.00
- ❏ Stormtrooper 15.00

Pepsi Cola (Thailand)
- ❏ C-3PO icon on blue background 20.00
- ❏ Darth Vader icon on yellow background 20.00
- ❏ R2-D2 icon on red background 20.00
- ❏ Stormtrooper icon on red background [236-66] 20.00

Pizza Hut (Australia)
- ❏ Chewbacca [236-67] 65.00
- ❏ Darth Vader [236-68] 65.00

Star Wars Celebration VI
- ❏ Mos Eisley Spaceport Pint Glass 20.00

- ❏ Tiki drinking glass, each 25.00
- ❏ Tiki drinking glass, set 95.00

Vandor LLC
2-packs.
- ❏ Clone trooper and Darth Vader, 16 oz. [236-69] 15.00

4-packs.
- ❏ Star Wars, 10 oz. [236-70] 25.00
- ❏ Star Wars, 10 oz. [236-71] 25.00
- ❏ The Empire Strikes Back, 16 oz. [236-72] 30.00

Zuko (Argentina)
Clone Wars. Character on front and back.
- ❏ Ahsoka Tano / Asajj Ventress [236-73] 20.00
- ❏ Anakin Skywalker / Anakin and Obi-Wan [236-74] 20.00
- ❏ Clone trooper / C-3PO and R2-D2 [236-75] 20.00
- ❏ Yoda / Yoda [236-76] 20.00

Dishes: Glasses, Shot
Continued in Volume 3, Page 210

Cards, Inc. (UK)
- ❏ 2-pack [237-01] 10.00
- ❏ 6-pack collector set, tin storage box 65.00
- ❏ Clone trooper, etched [v1e1:209] 15.00
- ❏ Darth Vader, etched [v1e1:209] 15.00
- ❏ Darth Vader, lava [237-02] 15.00
- ❏ Epic Duel [237-03] 15.00
- ❏ General Grievous, etched [237-04] 15.00
- ❏ Yoda [237-05] 15.00

Disney / MGM
- ❏ Jedi Academy, blue [237-06] 20.00
- ❏ Tatooine, blue [237-07] 15.00
- ❏ Tatooine, clear [237-08] 15.00

Hard Rock Cafe
- ❏ 2012 Pinsanity 8 Slave Leia [237-09] 45.00

Star Wars Celebration VI
- ❏ Darth Maul Tiki 15.00

Vandor LLC
- ❏ 4-pack, Luke, Han, Leia, Darth Vader [237-10] 30.00

Ceramic.
- ❏ Darth Vader / The Force Is Strong [237-11] 10.00
- ❏ Yoda / May the Force be with you [237-12] 10.00

237-01   237-02   237-03   237-04   237-05   237-06   237-07   237-08

237-09 Side 1 and Side 2   237-10   237-11   237-12

Dishes: Mugs

238-01 238-02 Side 1 and Side 2 238-03 238-04 238-05

 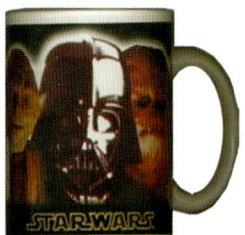    

238-06 Side 1 and Side 2 238-07 238-08 238-09 238-10

Dishes: Mugs
Continued in Volume 3, Page 210

- ☐ C-3PO ceramic [238-01] 15.00
- ☐ Darth Maul / Desert Duel [238-02] 10.00
- ☐ Darth Vader ceramic [238-03] 10.00
- ☐ Darth Vader stein [238-04] 30.00
- ☐ Jabba the Hutt [v1e1:209] 10.00
- ☐ R2-D2 ceramic hand-painted [238-05] 15.00
- ☐ Special Edition art [238-06] 15.00
- ☐ Star Wars is Forever, red ceramic, exclusive to Star Wars Celebration IV 25.00

Episode I, Tasse.
- ☐ Darth Maul with Obi-Wan and Qui-Gon [238-07] 10.00
- ☐ Naboo Fighter [238-08] 10.00

Plastic thermal mugs, Episode I: The Phantom Menace.
- ☐ Anakin Skywalker [4:135] 10.00
- ☐ Darth Maul [4:135] 10.00
- ☐ Jar Jar Binks [4:135] 10.00
- ☐ Queen Amidala [4:135] 10.00

Star Wars: Special Edition glass tankards.
- ☐ C-3PO [238-09] 20.00
- ☐ Yoda [238-10] 20.00

(Japan)
Ceramic tea mugs.
- ☐ Darth Vader 75.00
- ☐ Darth Vader and Tokyo Tower 75.00

(UK)
Ceramic mug with chocolate egg.
- ☐ Clone Wars [238-11] 15.00

Electronic talking mugs.
- ☐ Yoda [v1e1:209] 25.00

Applause
Ceramic figural mugs, Episode I.
- ☐ Darth Maul [238-12] 20.00
- ☐ Jar Jar Binks [238-13] 20.00
- ☐ R2-D2 [238-14] 20.00

Ceramic figural mugs.
- ☐ Bib Fortuna [238-15] 20.00
- ☐ Boba Fett [238-16] 20.00
- ☐ C-3PO [238-17] 20.00
- ☐ Chewbacca [238-18] 20.00
- ☐ Darth Vader [238-19] 20.00
- ☐ Darth Vader, metalized [238-20] 25.00
- ☐ Emperor Palpatine [238-21] 20.00
- ☐ Gamorrean Guard [238-22] 20.00

238-11 238-12 238-13 238-14 238-15 238-16 238-17 238-18

238-19 238-20 238-21 238-22 238-23 238-24 238-25

238-26 238-27 238-28 238-29 238-30 238-31 238-32

Dishes: Mugs

- ❏ Han Solo [238-23] 20.00
- ❏ Luke Skywalker [238-24] 20.00
- ❏ Obi-Wan Kenobi [238-25] 20.00
- ❏ Princess Leia [238-26] 20.00
- ❏ Stormtrooper [238-27] 20.00
- ❏ Tusken Raider [238-28] 20.00

Big Dog
- ❏ The Empire Bites Back [238-29] 25.00

Bonbon Buddies (UK)
Ceramic figural mugs.
- ❏ Darth Vader [238-30] 15.00

Ceramic mug with chocolate egg.
- ❏ Captain Rex [238-31] 15.00
- ❏ Darth Vader [4-136] 15.00
- ❏ Obi-Wan and Clones [238-32] 15.00

Boy Scouts of America
Mid-America Council.
- ❏ Scout-o-Rama 1978 [238-33] 65.00

California Originals
- ❏ Darth Vader, 5.5" tall, black inside 45.00
- ❏ Darth Vader, 5.5" tall, white inside 45.00
- ❏ R2-D2 stein with flip-top lid, prototype only .... OSPV

Ceramic, sculpted by Jim Rumph.
- ❏ Ben Kenobi [238-34] 125.00
- ❏ Chewbacca [238-35] 100.00
- ❏ Darth Vader [238-36] 75.00

Cards, Inc. (UK)
- ❏ Darth Vader [238-37] 15.00
- ❏ Grievous [238-38] 15.00
- ❏ Vader, Sith [238-39] 15.00
- ❏ Yoda, Jedi [238-40] 15.00
- ❏ Yoda, Jedi Master [238-41] 15.00

Episode III: Revenge of the Sith dark mugs.
- ❏ Anakin Skywalker [238-42] 15.00
- ❏ Darth Vader [4-136] 15.00
- ❏ Darth Vader "Villain" [238-43] 15.00
- ❏ Epic lightsaber duel [238-44] 15.00
- ❏ General Grievous [238-45] 15.00
- ❏ Palpatine "Evil" [238-46] 15.00
- ❏ Yoda "Justice" [238-47] 15.00

Episode III: Revenge of the Sith sculpted characters.
- ❏ Clone trooper [238-48] 20.00
- ❏ Coruscant trooper [238-49] 20.00
- ❏ Darth Vader [238-50] 20.00
- ❏ General Grievous [v1e1-209] 20.00
- ❏ Kashyyyk trooper [238-51] 20.00

 238-33
 238-34
 238-35
 238-36
 238-37

 238-38
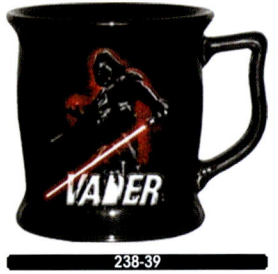 238-39
 238-40
 238-41
 238-42

 238-43
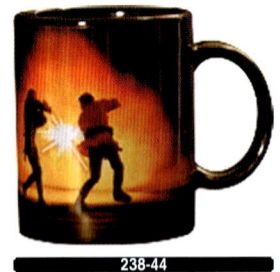 238-44
 238-45
 238-46
 238-47

 238-48
 238-49
 238-50
 238-51
 238-52

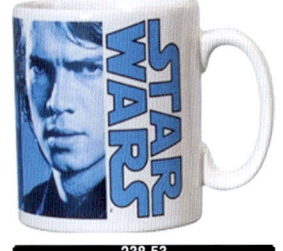 238-53
 238-54
 238-55
 238-56
 238-57

Dishes: Mugs

❏ Shock trooper [238-52] 20.00
❏ Yoda 20.00

Episode III: Revenge of the Sith white mugs with Star Wars logo.
❏ Anakin Skywalker [238-53] 20.00
❏ Clone trooper [238-54] 20.00
❏ Darth Vader [238-55] 20.00
❏ Obi-Wan Kenobi [238-56] 20.00
❏ Yoda [238-57] 20.00

Thermal, image changes.
❏ Clone trooper 15.00
❏ Darth Vader 15.00
❏ General Grievous 15.00
❏ R2-D2 ....15.00
❏ Stormtrooper 15.00
❏ Yoda 15.00

Crystal Craft (Australia)
❏ Anakin Skywalker, podracer [238-58] 15.00
❏ Darth Maul [238-59] 15.00
❏ Jar Jar [238-60] 15.00
❏ Jedi vs. Sith [238-61] 15.00
❏ Obi-Wan Kenobi [238-62] 15.00
❏ Qui-Gon Jinn [238-63] 15.00
❏ Starfighters [238-64] 15.00

Cube Works (Japan)
❏ R2-D2 travel mug [238-65] 35.00

Deka
Empire Strikes Back 10 oz.
❏ Boba Fett and Darth Vader [238-66] 15.00
❏ Chewbacca, C-3PO and R2-D2 [238-67] 15.00
❏ Han Solo, Princess Leia and Luke Skywalker [238-68] ...15.00
❏ Yoda [238-69] 15.00

Return of the Jedi 10 oz.
❏ C-3PO, R2-D2 and Wicket / Princess Leia and Ewoks [238-70] 15.00
❏ Darth Vader, Emperor's Royal Guard, Luke Skywalker, and Yoda [238-71] 15.00
❏ Wicket the Ewok [238-72] 15.00

Star Wars 10 oz.
❏ Star Wars 20.00

Disney / MGM
❏ C-3PO and Star Tours logo 30.00
❏ Galactic Empire [v1e1:209] 15.00
❏ R2-D2 and Star Tours logo 30.00
❏ Rebel Alliance [v1e1:209] 15.00
❏ Star Tours logo, silver metallic finish [238-73] 30.00
❏ Star Tours logo, silver metallic finish, tankard [238-74] 35.00
❏ Yoda, Silent Knight, Jedi Knight [238-75] 35.00

238-58

238-59

238-60

238-61

238-62

238-63

238-64

238-65

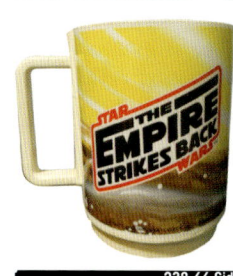

238-66 Side 1 and Side 2

238-67 Side 1 and Side 2

238-68 Side 1 and Side 2

238-69 Side 1 and Side 2

238-70 Side 1 and Side 2

238-71 Side 1 and Side 2

238-72 Side 1 and Side 2

238-73

238-74

238-75

238-76 Side 1 and Side 2

Dishes: Mugs

238-77

238-78

238-79

238-80

238-81

238-82

238-83

238-84

238-85

238-86

Star Wars Weekends.
- ❏ 2003 Mickey and Yoda 25.00
- ❏ 2004 Mickey and Minnie, A New Hope [v1e1:211] 25.00
- ❏ 2005 Darth Vader / Mickey 25.00
- ❏ 2006 Logo [238-76] 25.00
- ❏ 2007 Chrome and black 25.00

Downpace Ltd. (UK)
- ❏ Boba Fett [4:137] 15.00
- ❏ C-3PO [238-77] 15.00
- ❏ Darth Vader [238-78] 15.00
- ❏ Luke Skywalker [238-79] 15.00
- ❏ Princess Leia [238-80] 15.00
- ❏ Stormtrooper [238-81] 15.00

Fire King (Japan)
Milk glass, hand made. Exclusive to Beams.
- ❏ Chewbacca [238-82] 150.00
- ❏ Darth Vader [238-83] 150.00
- ❏ Ewok standing on Stormtrooper helmet [238-84] 150.00
- ❏ Laugh it up Fuzzball 150.00
- ❏ Yoda, "Jedi Master," green "jadite" glass [238-85] 150.00

Galerie
2 Mug gift sets with cocoa and marshmallows.
- ❏ 2010 Unleashed art [238-86] 15.00

4 or more mug gift sets with cocoa and marshmallows.
- ❏ 2007 Character art [5:131] 25.00
- ❏ 2010 Unleashed art 25.00

Candy filled ceramic mugs.
- ❏ Boba Fett [238-87] 15.00
- ❏ Darth Vader [238-88] 15.00
- ❏ Stormtrooper [238-89] 15.00
- ❏ Yoda 15.00

Ceramic mugs with cinnamon candies, excl. to Target.
- ❏ Classic trilogy [238-90] 15.00
- ❏ Episode I: The Phantom Menace [238-91] 15.00

Character mugs.
- ❏ Chewbacca 15.00
- ❏ Darth Vader 15.00
- ❏ R2-D2 [238-92] 15.00

Oversized mugs.
- ❏ Luke Skywalker vs. Darth Vader [238-93] 20.00

Half Moon Bay (UK)
Ceramic mugs with tin collector's box.
- ❏ Empire Strikes Back 25.00
- ❏ Return of the Jedi 25.00
- ❏ Star Wars 25.00
- ❏ Star Wars poster art 25.00

238-87

238-88

238-89

238-90 Side 1 and Side 2

238-91 Side 1 and Side 2

238-92

238-93

238-94

238-95

238-96

238-97

238-98

238-99

238-100

238-101

238-102

Dishes: Mugs

 238-103
 238-104 Side 1 and Side 2
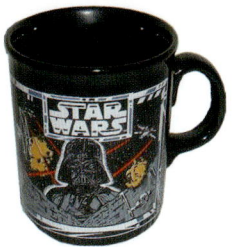
 238-105
 238-106
 238-107
 238-108
 238-109
 238-110
 238-111
 238-112

Hallmark
- Come to the Dark Side / Light Side [238-94] 25.00
- Yoda talking quote mug, "Always in motion is the Future," press button to hear Yoda quotes.............................25.00

Hamilton Collection
- Darth Vader and Luke Skywalker [238-95] 25.00
- Han Solo [238-96] 25.00
- Imperial Walkers [238-97].............25.00
- Luke Skywalker and Yoda [238-98]..............25.00
- Millennium Falcon Cockpit [238-99]............25.00
- Princess Leia [238-100] 25.00
- R2-D2 and Wicket [238-101] 25.00
- Space Battle Scene [238-102] 25.00

Houze Magic Color Inc.
- Star Wars logo [238-103] 35.00

Kiln Craft Potteries
- Return of the Jedi, colored line art [v1e1:212]............20.00

Kinnerton Confectionery (UK)
- Battle above Death Star [238-104] 15.00
- Battle above Death Star with chocolate Death Star [4:138] 15.00
- Lightsaber Duel with chocolate Death Star [238-105] 15.00

Long Island Distributing Co. Ltd.
- Darth Vader [238-106] 10.00
- Imperial Insignia [238-107] 10.00
- Rebel Insignia [238-108]................10.00
- See-Threepio [238-109] 10.00
- Stormtrooper [238-110] 10.00

Lucasfilm
- Episode III: Revenge of the Sith glass tankard [238-111] 15.00

M&M World
- Dark side character line up 20.00
- Jedi character line up 20.00

NECA
- Star Wars concept art with original logo, 5,000 produced [238-112] 25.00

Episode II: Attack of the Clones ceramic figural mugs, limited to 5,000 each.
- Clone trooper [238-113]...............15.00
- Jango Fett [238-114] 15.00

Episode II: Attack of the Clones decal mugs, limited to 10,000 each.
- Heroes [238-115]...........................10.00
- Villains [238-116]..........................10.00

Episode II: Attack of the Clones glass tankards, limited to 10,000 each.
- Droids [238-117] 15.00
- Jedi [238-118]..............................15.00
- Villains [238-119] 15.00

Noble Studios
4" pewter medallion.
- Darth Vader...45.00

Rawcliffe
- Darth Vader Manga art [238-120] 15.00
- Revenge of the Sith logo [v1e1:213]...........15.00
- Revenge of the Sith teaser art [v1e1:213] ...15.00

15 oz. mugs, 2-sided.
- Galactic Heroes [238-121] 15.00
- Princess Leia [238-122] 15.00
- Yoda [238-123]...........................15.00

Pewter logo on 12 oz. mug with curved lip and base.
- 20th Anniversary [v1e1:213].........20.00
- Bantha skull [v1e1:213]................20.00
- Boba Fett with gun 20.00
- Boba Fett's helmet [v1e1:213]........20.00
- Darth Vader 20.00
- Darth Vader with clenched fist [v1e1:213]..............20.00
- Darth Vader's lightsaber................20.00
- Imperial emblem [v1e1:213]...........20.00
- Obi-Wan Kenobi [v1e1:213] 20.00
- Princess Leia [v1e1:213]................20.00
- Rebel logo 20.00
- Star Wars Celebration II 35.00
- Star Wars logo [v1e1:213] 20.00
- The Magic of Myth [238-124].........35.00
- Yoda [v1e1:213]............................20.00

 238-113
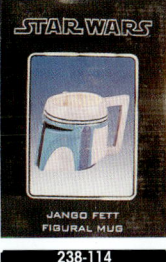 238-114
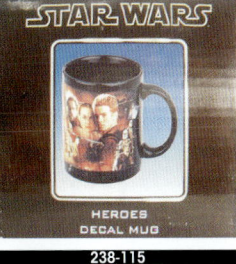 238-115
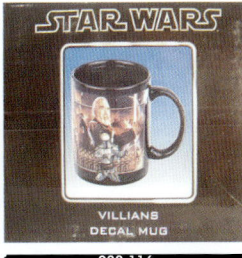 238-116
 238-117
 238-118
 238-119
 238-120
 238-121 Side 1 and Side 2

 238-122
 238-123
 238-124

Dishes: Mugs

Sigma
- 10th Anniversary 50.00
- Star Wars with thermal ink 25.00

Cartoon-style art.
- Boba Fett and Chewbacca [238-125] 30.00
- C-3PO and R2-D2 [238-126] 30.00
- Darth Vader, Princess Leia, Stormtrooper [238-127] 30.00
- Luke Skywalker and Yoda [238-128] 30.00

Sculpted figural mugs, vintage.
- Biker Scout [238-129] 35.00
- C-3PO [238-130] 35.00
- Chewbacca [238-131] 35.00
- Darth Vader [238-132] 35.00
- Gamorrean Guard [238-133] 35.00
- Han, Hoth [238-134] 35.00
- Klaatu [238-135] 35.00
- Lando, skiff guard [238-136] 35.00
- Leia [238-137] 35.00
- Luke, Pilot [238-138] 35.00
- Wicket [238-139] 35.00
- Yoda [238-140] 35.00

Skywalker Ranch
- Skywalker Ranch logo [238-141] 25.00

Spearmark International (UK)
- Vader and Stormtroopers / classic art [238-142] 15.00

Star Wars Celebration V
- Hoth Brewing glass tankard 20.00
- I *(heart)* Scoundrels 20.00
- Iggy's 88 .... 20.00

Star Wars Celebration VI
- Cup O' Jawa 25.00
- Luke and Tauntaun "Hoth Chocolate" Mug 25.00

Taito (Japan)
- Darth Vader, gaming prize [238-143] 35.00
- Jedi, gaming prize [238-144] 35.00
- Yoda, gaming prize [238-145] 35.00

Unlicensed
- Darth Vader ceramic, stars in eyes 30.00

Vandor LLC
- Mug and travel mug set 25.00
- The Empire Strikes Back mug 30.00
- The Empire Strikes Back travel mug 25.00
- Star Wars travel mug 25.00

238-129

238-125 Side 1 and Side 2

238-126 Side 1 and Side 2

238-130

238-127 Side 1 and Side 2

238-128 Side 1 and Side 2

238-131

238-132

238-133

238-134

238-135

238-136

238-137

238-138

238-139

238-140

238-141

238-142 Side 1 and Side 2

238-143

238-144

238-145

Dishes: Steins

239-01 Side 1 and Side 2

239-02 Side 1 and Side 2

239-03 Side 1 and Side 2

239-04 Side 1 and Side 2

239-05 Side 1 and Side 2

239-06

239-07

238-08

239-09

Dishes: Pitchers
Continued in Volume 3, Page 210

Coca-Cola
- ❏ Return of the Jedi [239-01] 40.00
- ❏ Star Wars / Empire Strikes Back [239-02] 45.00

Deka
- ❏ Empire Strikes Back [239-03] 45.00
- ❏ Return of the Jedi [239-04] 45.00
- ❏ Star Wars [239-05] 50.00

Disney Theme Park Merchandise
- ❏ Star Wars, glass [239-06] 40.00

Pizza Hut
Episode I: The Phantom Menace. Pepsi. 2 quart.
- ❏ Anakin Skywalker [239-07] 45.00
- ❏ Jar Jar Binks [239-08] 45.00
- ❏ Queen Amidala [239-09] 45.00

Dishes: Plates and Platters
Continued in Volume 3, Page 214

Deka
- ❏ Wicket the Ewok [240-01] 30.00

Classic trilogy compartment plates.
- ❏ Empire Strikes Back [240-02] 25.00

- ❏ Return of the Jedi [240-03] 25.00
- ❏ Star Wars [240-04] 25.00

Kellogg's
- ❏ Darth Vader / Anakin Skywalker, lenticular [240-05] 10.00

Pottery Barn
- ❏ Star Wars, 9" [240-06] 20.00

Sigma
- ❏ The World of Star Wars fantasy child set [240-07] 25.00

Spearmark International (UK)
- ❏ Star Wars classic art [240-08] 20.00

Trudeau
- ❏ Clone Wars [240-09] 10.00

Zak Designs
- ❏ Podrace, round [240-10] 10.00
- ❏ Podrace, shaped [240-11] 15.00

Dishes: Salt Shakers
Continued in Volume 3, Page 215

- ❏ Yoda salt and pepper shakers [241-01] 165.00

Sigma
- ❏ R2-D2 and R5-D4 [241-02] 325.00
- ❏ Yoda salt and pepper shakers [241-03] 450.00

Star Wars Celebration VI
- ❏ Darth Vader and Stormtrooper, printed designs on cylinder shakers [241-04] 20.00

Dishes: Steins
Continued in Volume 3, Page 215

Avon
- ❏ Star Wars: Special Edition Luke vs. Vader with hinged pewter lid [v1e1:215] 65.00

Dram Tree
Ceramic relief steins.
- ❏ Empire Strikes Back [v1e1:215] 45.00
- ❏ Return of the Jedi [v1e1:215] 45.00
- ❏ Star Wars [v1e1:215] 45.00

Hinged lid, topped with pewter figure. 3,000 produced of each.
- ❏ Boba Fett [v1e1:215] 135.00
- ❏ Darth Vader [v1e1:215] 135.00
- ❏ Yoda [v1e1:215] 135.00

Metallic Impressions
Hinged pewter lids.
- ❏ Empire Strikes Back [v1e1:215] 50.00
- ❏ Return of the Jedi [v1e1:215] 50.00
- ❏ Star Wars [v1e1:215] 50.00

240-01

240-02

240-03

240-04

240-05

240-06

240-07

240-08

240-09

240-10

240-11

Dishes: Teapots

241-01 Front | 241-01 Bottom

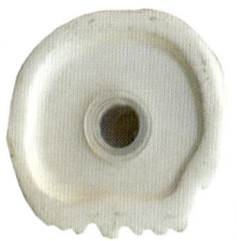
241-02

241-03 Front | 241-03 Bottom | 241-04

Dishes: Teapots
Continued in Volume 3, Page 215

Sigma
- Luke on Tauntaun [242-01] 450.00

Totally Teapots (UK)
- Darth Vader, 100 produced [242-02] 230.00

Dishes: Trays
Continued in Volume 3, Page 215

Chein Industries
- Ewoks animated scene [243-01] 200.00
- Return of the Jedi Logo and collage [243-02] 45.00

Dishes: Utensils
Continued in Volume 3, Page 215

Spoons, dated 1977 and numbered in series.
- #1 Luke Skywalker [244-01] 10.00
- #2 Princess Leia Organa [v1e1:216] 10.00
- #3 Han Solo [v1e1:216] 10.00
- #4 Chewbacca the Wookiee [v1e1:216] 10.00
- #5 See Threepio [v1e1:216] 10.00
- #6 Artoo Detoo [v1e1:216] 10.00
- #7 Darth Vader [244-02] 10.00

Birchcroft
Porcelain spoons. Episode II. Limited to 500 each.
- Clone trooper [244-03] 15.00
- Mace Windu [244-04] 15.00
- Obi-Wan Kenobi [244-05] 15.00
- Yoda [244-06] 15.00

Decopac
- Captain Rex cake topper spoon [244-07] 8.00

Kellogg's
Cereal premiums, plastic.
- Anakin Skywalker [244-08] 5.00
- C-3PO [244-09] 5.00
- Darth Maul [244-10] 5.00
- Jar Jar Binks [244-11] 5.00
- Obi-Wan Kenobi [244-12] 5.00
- Queen Amidala [244-13] 5.00

Cereal premiums, plastic. Light-up saber spoons.
- Blue 5.00
- Green 5.00
- Red [244-14] 5.00

Kellogg's (Korea)
Cereal premiums, plastic. Light-up saber spoons.
- Blue 5.00
- Green 5.00
- Red [244-15] 5.00

Kellogg's (UK)
Cereal premiums, plastic. Light-up saber spoons.
- Blue [244-16] 10.00
- Green [244-17] 10.00
- Red [244-18] 10.00
- Yellow [244-19] 10.00

Kotobukiya (Japan)
Chopsticks. Lightsaber designs. Series 1.
- 2 sets: Darth Vader and Yoda 35.00
- 2 sets: Luke Skywalker and Yoda [244-20] 35.00
- Darth Vader [244-21] 20.00
- Luke Skywalker 20.00
- Yoda, small [244-22] 20.00

Chopsticks. Lightsaber designs. Series 2.
- 2 sets: Darth Maul and Luke Skywalker 25.00
- 2 sets: Darth Maul and Mace Windu 25.00

242-01 | 242-02 | 243-01 | 243-02 | 244-01 244-02 244-03 244-04 244-05 244-06 244-07

244-08 | 244-09 | 244-10 | 244-11 | 244-12 | 244-13

244-14 | 244-15 | 244-16 | 244-17 | 244-18 | 244-19 | 244-20 | 244-21 | 244-22 | 244-23 | 244-24 | 244-25

Dispensers: Candy

 245-01
 245-02
 245-03
 245-04
 245-05
 245-06
 245-07
 245-08

 245-09
 245-10
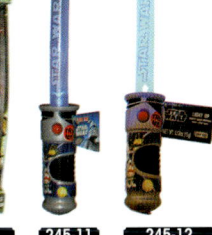 245-11 245-12
 245-13
 245-14
 245-15
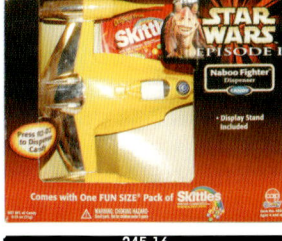 245-16
 245-17

Stor S.L. (Spain)
☐ Cutlery fork and spoon [244-23]..................12.00

Zak Designs
2-pack spoon and fork.
☐ Episode I: The Phantom Menace, Podracer [244-24]......10.00
☐ Episode III: Revenge of the Sith, Darth Vader [244-25]....10.00

Dispensers: Candy
Continued in Volume 3, Page 218

Candy Rific
Gift packs: M&M's dispenser and candy fan.
☐ Boba Fett dispenser with Darth Vader fan [245-01].........35.00
☐ Darth Vader dispenser with Darth Maul fan [245-02].....35.00
☐ Darth Vader dispenser with Obi-Wan fan [245-03]..........35.00

Gift packs. Gumball dispensers and candy fans.
☐ Darth Vader [245-04]...............35.00
☐ Yoda [245-05].................35.00

M&M dispensers with M&M character on top.
☐ Boba Fett [245-06]...............15.00
☐ Darth Vader [245-07]...............15.00
☐ Han Solo...............15.00
☐ Luke Skywalker...............15.00
☐ Obi-Wan Kenobi [245-08]...............15.00
☐ Princess Leia...............15.00

M&M dispensers with character figure top. Boxed.
☐ Darth Maul [245-09]..............20.00
☐ Darth Vader [245-10]..............20.00

M&M Minis inside light-up saber.
☐ Blue [245-11]...............5.00
☐ Blue, updated tag [245-12]...............5.00
☐ Red...............5.00
☐ Red, updated tag [245-13]...............5.00

Cap Candy
☐ Jango Fett gum dispenser [245-14]..............20.00
☐ Jar Jar Binks PEZ handler, battery operated [245-15]...........25.00
☐ Naboo Fighter dispenser with Skittles [245-16]..............20.00
☐ R2-D2 dispenser includes M&M's candies [245-17].......10.00

Galerie
Dispensers with gumballs.
☐ Darth Vader [245-18]..............20.00
☐ Yoda [245-19]..............20.00

Talking character dispensers.
☐ Clone Captain [245-20]..............5.00
☐ Clone trooper [245-21]..............5.00

 245-18
 245-19
 245-20
 245-21
 245-22
 245-23
 245-24
 245-25
 245-26 245-27

 245-28
 245-29
 245-30
 245-31
 245-32
 245-33
 245-34
 245-35
 245-36

 245-37
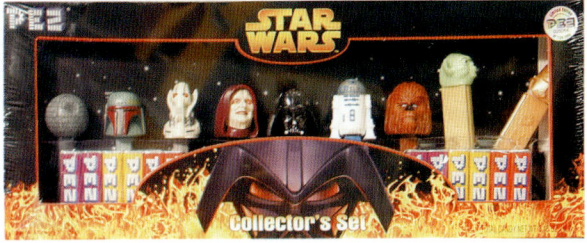 245-38
 245-39

217

Dispensers: Candy

- ❑ Darth Maul [245-22] 5.00
- ❑ Darth Vader [245-23] 5.00
- ❑ Darth Vader, red [245-24] 5.00
- ❑ Darth Vader, Santa [245-25] 5.00
- ❑ R2-D2 ....5.00

Masterfoods USA
M&M Minis inside light-up saber.
- ❑ Blue [245-26] 5.00
- ❑ Red [245-27] 5.00

Toy & Pogo mini M&M dispensers, boxed. Asia exclusive packaging.
- ❑ C-3PO [245-28] 20.00
- ❑ Death Star [245-29] 20.00
- ❑ Storm trooper [245-30] 20.00
- ❑ Yoda [245-31] 20.00

Toy & Pogo mini M&M dispensers.
- ❑ Anakin Skywalker [245-32] 15.00
- ❑ C-3PO [245-33] 15.00
- ❑ Death Star [245-34] 15.00
- ❑ Obi-Wan [245-35] 15.00
- ❑ Stormtrooper [245-36] 15.00
- ❑ Yoda [245-37] 15.00

Pez Candy, Inc.
- ❑ Star Wars Collector's Box, 250,000 produced, individually numbered [245-38] 40.00
- ❑ Star Wars Collector's Box, exclusive glow-in-the-dark Emperor figure, 250,000 produced [245-39] 45.00

Classic Interactive series.
- ❑ C-3PO, golden [245-40] 30.00
- ❑ Darth Vader, crystal [245-41] 30.00
- ❑ Yoda, crystal [245-42] 30.00

Classic trilogy. Bagged, any color package.
- ❑ Boba Fett [245-43] 5.00
- ❑ C-3PO [245-44] 5.00
- ❑ Chewbacca [245-45] 5.00
- ❑ Darth Vader [245-46] 5.00
- ❑ Luke in X-Wing Gear [245-47] 5.00
- ❑ Princess Leia [245-48] 5.00
- ❑ Stormtrooper [245-49] 5.00
- ❑ Wicket [245-50] 5.00
- ❑ Yoda [245-51] 5.00

Classic trilogy. Blue card back with Darth Vader and Stormtrooper.
- ❑ Boba Fett [245-52] 8.00
- ❑ C-3PO [245-53] 8.00
- ❑ Chewbacca [245-54] 8.00
- ❑ Darth Vader [245-55] 8.00
- ❑ Luke in X-Wing Gear [245-56] 8.00
- ❑ Princess Leia [245-57] 8.00
- ❑ Stormtrooper [245-58] 8.00
- ❑ Wicket [245-59] 8.00
- ❑ Yoda [245-60] 8.00

Classic trilogy. Green card back with C-3PO, Chewbacca, and Yoda.
- ❑ Boba Fett [245-61] 8.00
- ❑ C-3PO [245-62] 8.00
- ❑ Chewbacca [245-63] 8.00
- ❑ Yoda [245-64] 8.00

Classic trilogy. Purple card back with Darth Vader and Stormtrooper.
- ❑ Darth Vader [245-65] 8.00
- ❑ Stormtrooper [245-66] 8.00

Clone Wars. Bagged with insert.
- ❑ Ahsoka Tano 5.00
- ❑ Anakin Skywalker 5.00
- ❑ C-3PO 5.00
- ❑ Clone trooper [245-67] 5.00
- ❑ General Grievous 5.00
- ❑ Obi-Wan Kenobi 5.00

Clone Wars. Bagged.
- ❑ Ahsoka Tano [245-68] 8.00
- ❑ Anakin Skywalker [245-69] 8.00
- ❑ C-3PO [245-70] 8.00
- ❑ Clone trooper [245-71] 8.00
- ❑ General Grievous [245-72] 8.00
- ❑ Obi-Wan Kenobi [245-73] 8.00

Clone Wars. Carded.
- ❑ Ahsoka Tano [245-74] 10.00
- ❑ Anakin Skywalker [245-75] 10.00
- ❑ C-3PO [245-76] 10.00
- ❑ Clone trooper [245-77] 10.00
- ❑ General Grievous [245-78] 10.00

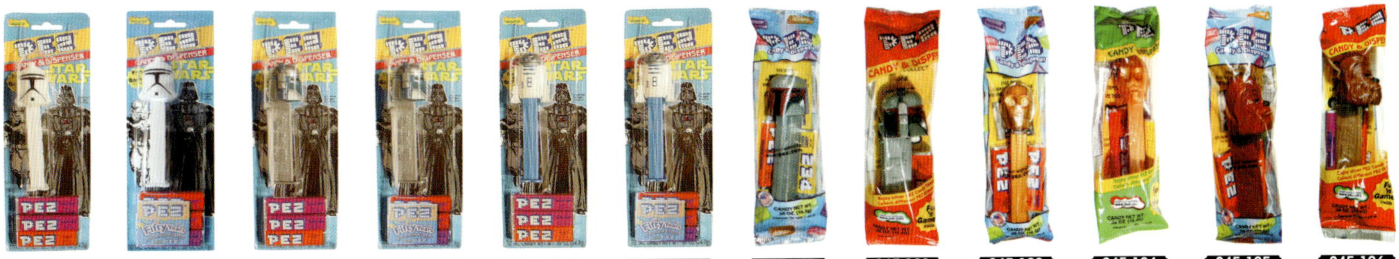

Dispensers: Candy

245-95 245-96 245-97 245-98 245-99 245-100 245-101 245-102 245-103 245-104 245-105 245-106

245-107 245-108 245-109 245-110 245-111 245-112 245-113 245-114 245-115 245-116 245-117 245-118 245-119

❏ Obi-Wan Kenobi [245-79]	10.00
❏ R2-D2 [245-80]	10.00
❏ Yoda [245-81]	10.00

Collector Series. Limited to 10,000 each. Boxed with display stand.

❏ C-3PO, golden [245-82]	35.00
❏ Darth Vader, crystal [245-83]	35.00
❏ Yoda, crystal [245-84]	35.00

Episode I. Carded.

❏ C-3PO [245-85]	12.00
❏ Darth Maul [245-86]	12.00
❏ Darth Maul [245-87]	12.00
❏ Darth Vader [245-88]	12.00
❏ General Grievous [245-89]	12.00
❏ R2-D2 [245-90]	12.00
❏ Yoda [245-91]	12.00

Episode II. Bagged, any color package.

❏ 12-pack box	28.00
❏ Clone trooper [245-92]	5.00
❏ Jango Fett [245-93]	5.00
❏ R2-D2 [245-94]	5.00

Episode II. Blue card back with Darth Vader and Stormtrooper.

❏ Clone trooper [245-95]	8.00
❏ Clone trooper [245-96]	8.00
❏ Jango Fett [245-97]	8.00
❏ Jango Fett [245-98]	8.00
❏ R2-D2 [245-99]	8.00
❏ R2-D2 [245-100]	8.00

Episode III. Bagged.

❏ Boba Fett [245-101]	5.00
❏ Boba Fett [245-102]	5.00
❏ C-3PO [245-103]	5.00
❏ C-3PO [245-104]	5.00
❏ Chewbacca [245-105]	5.00
❏ Chewbacca [245-106]	5.00
❏ Darth Vader [245-107]	5.00
❏ Darth Vader [245-108]	5.00
❏ Death Star [245-109]	8.00
❏ Death Star [245-110]	8.00
❏ Emperor Palpatine [245-111]	8.00
❏ Emperor Palpatine [245-112]	5.00
❏ General Grievous [245-113]	8.00
❏ General Grievous [245-114]	8.00
❏ R2-D2 [245-115]	5.00
❏ R2-D2 [245-116]	5.00
❏ Stormtrooper [245-117]	5.00
❏ Yoda [245-118]	5.00
❏ Yoda [245-119]	5.00

245-120 245-121 245-122 245-123 245-124 245-125 245-126 245-127 245-128 245-129 245-130 245-131 245-132

245-133 245-134 245-135 245-136 245-137 245-138 245-139 245-140 245-141 245-142 245-143 245-144

245-145 245-146 245-147 245-148 245-149 245-150 245-151 245-152 245-153 245-154 245-155

Dispensers: Candy

246-01 | 246-02 | 246-03 | 246-04 | 246-05 | 246-06 | 247-01 | 247-02 | 247-03 | 247-04

247-05 | 247-06 | 247-07 | 247-08 | 248-01 | 248-02 | 248-03 | 248-04

Episode III. Carded.
- Boba Fett [245-120] 5.00
- C-3PO [245-121] 5.00
- Chewbacca [245-122] 5.00
- Darth Vader [245-123] 5.00
- Death Star [245-124] 8.00
- Emperor Palpatine [245-125] 5.00
- Emperor Palpatine glow-in-the-dark, 50,000 produced, exclusive to Walmart [245-126] 20.00
- General Grievous [245-127] 8.00
- R2-D2 [245-128] 5.00
- Yoda [245-129] 5.00

Giant Pez dispensers. Boxed, Revenge of the Sith.
- Chewbacca [245-130] 35.00
- Clone trooper [245-131] 35.00
- Darth Vader [245-132] 35.00
- Death Star [245-133] 40.00
- Emperor Palpatine [245-134] 35.00
- General Grievous [245-135] 50.00
- R2-D2 .... 35.00
- Yoda [245-136] 35.00

Giant Pez dispensers. Carded, Revenge of the Sith.
- C-3PO [245-137] 35.00
- Chewbacca 35.00
- Darth Vader [245-138] 35.00
- R2-D2 [245-139] 35.00

Giant Pez dispensers. Crystal series.
- C-3PO [245-140] 60.00
- Darth Vader [245-141] 60.00
- Yoda [245-142] 60.00

Metallic plated. 500 produced of each. Exclusive to Toy Fair.
- C-3PO, plated gold color [245-143] ... 85.00
- Darth Vader, plated chrome color [245-144] ... 85.00

Pez Candy, Inc. (UK)
Classic trilogy. Blue card back with Darth Vader.
- C-3PO [245-145] 8.00
- Chewbacca [245-146] 8.00
- Darth Vader [245-147] 8.00

- Stormtrooper [245-148] 8.00
- Yoda [245-149] 8.00

Clone Wars, carded.
- C-3PO [245-150] 8.00
- Chewbacca [245-151] 8.00
- Darth Sidious [245-152] 8.00
- R2-D2 [245-153] 8.00
- Yoda [245-154] 8.00

Episode III. Carded.
- C-3PO [245-155] 8.00

Dispensers: Food

Heart Art Collection, Ltd. (Japan)
Pepper grinder.
- R2-D2 [246-01] 35.00
- R2-Q5 [246-02] 35.00
- R2-R9 [246-03] 35.00

Soy sauce bottles.
- R2-D2 [246-04] 35.00
- R2-Q5 [246-05] 35.00
- R2-R9 [246-06] 35.00

Dispensers: Gum

Bonbon Buddies (UK)
Gum Buddy.
- Vader above flames [247-01] 15.00
- Vader at right [247-02] 15.00
- Vader below flames [247-03] 15.00

Meiji (Japan)
Xylish 3-pack of chewing gum stick packets. Each gum holder available in blue, green, and red.
- Anakin Skywalker [247-04] 15.00
- C-3PO [247-05] 15.00
- Clone trooper [247-06] 15.00
- Jango Fett [247-07] 15.00
- R2-D2 [247-08] 15.00

Dispensers: Soap / Lotion
Continued in Volume 3, Page 220

Heart Art Collection, Ltd. (Japan)
Shampoo bottles.
- R2-D2 [248-01] 30.00
- R2-Q5 .... 30.00

Jay Franco and Sons
- Darth Maul [248-02] 20.00
- Jar Jar Binks [248-03] 20.00
- Lotion pump and fingertip towel gift set [248-04] ... 25.00

Dog Tags
Continued in Volume 3, Page 220

Applause
- Darth Maul [249-01] 10.00
- Naboo Fighter [249-02] 10.00
- Obi-Wan Kenobi [249-03] 10.00
- Trade Federation Droid Fighter [v1e1-217] ... 10.00

Celebration IV
- 30th anniversary logo 20.00

Celebration V
- Bounty Hunter 20.00
- May the Force be with you [249-04] 20.00

Courage International Inc.
- Kooky novelty mini pen [249-05] 10.00

E-MAX (Spain)
Set of 100. Numbered. 50 oval and 50 round. Value is for opened dog tag. Complete checklist and images in volume 1, first edition, pages 217–218.
- 1–50 oval, each [249-06] 5.00
- 51–100 round [249-07] 5.00
- Unopened package with 2 random tags ... 12.00

Fossil, Inc.
- Mandalorian emblem, included with watch ... 15.00

249-01 | 249-02 | 249-03 | 249-04 | 249-05 | 249-06 Sample | 249-07 Sample | 249-08 Sample | 249-09 Sample

Earphones and Headphones

Topps
Clone Wars. Series 1. Set of 24. Numbered. Sealed package includes 1 dog tag, 1 matching trading card, 1 checklist. Value is for opened dog tag.
- ☐ 1–24, each [249-08] 5.00
- ☐ Unopened Package 8.00

Star Wars. Series 1. Set of 24, numbered. Sealed package includes 1 dog tag, 1 matching trading card, 1 checklist. Chase tags have rainbow backgrounds. Value is for opened dog tag.
- ☐ 01–24, each [249-09] 5.00
- ☐ Unopened Package 8.00

Doorknob Hangers
Continued in Volume 3, Page 221

Alligator Books (UK)
- ☐ The Force is Strong here / Enter If You Dare [250-01] 5.00

Antioch
- ☐ C-3PO / You May ENTER [250-02] 10.00
- ☐ Darth Vader / ENTER [250-03] 10.00
- ☐ Jedi Welcome / Do Not Disturb [250-04] 10.00
- ☐ Sith Lord Beware / Do Not Disturb [250-05] 10.00
- ☐ Yoda / Please Enter [250-06] 10.00

Scholastic
- ☐ Endor Rebel Heroes 5.00
- ☐ Jabba the Hutt 5.00

Dry Erase Memo Boards
Continued in Volume 3, Page 222

Accessory Zone
Clone Wars. Exclusive to Target.
- ☐ Captain Rex and Clones [251-01] 10.00
- ☐ Clone trooper, Yoda, C-3PO, R2-D2 [251-02] 10.00

Animations
Dry erase boards. Exclusive to Target.
- ☐ Chewbacca [251-03] 10.00
- ☐ Darth Vader [251-04] 10.00
- ☐ Yoda [251-05] 10.00

Day Runner
Character shaped wipe-off board.
- ☐ Darth Maul 20.00
- ☐ Jar Jar Binks 20.00
- ☐ R2-D2 [251-06] 20.00
- ☐ Yoda [251-07] 20.00

Icarus (UK)
Wipe clean memo board with marker. Blue header.
- ☐ AT-ST and Speederbike [251-08] 30.00
- ☐ Chewbacca, Han Solo, and Lando Calrissian [251-09] ... 30.00
- ☐ Darth Vader and Stormtrooper 30.00
- ☐ Han Solo, Luke Skywalker, and Princess Leia [251-10] ... 30.00
- ☐ Wicket, Logray, Chief Chirpa, Baby Ewok 30.00

Wipe clean memo board with marker. White header.
- ☐ Chewbacca, Han Solo, and Lando Calrissian 35.00

- ☐ Darth Vader and Stormtrooper [251-11] 35.00
- ☐ Han Solo, Luke Skywalker, and Princess Leia [251-12] ... 35.00
- ☐ R2-D2 and C-3PO [251-13] 35.00
- ☐ Wicket, Logray, Chief Chirpa, Baby Ewok [251-14] ... 35.00

Innovative Designs
2010 Hanging dry erase boards with marker. Exclusive to Target.
- ☐ Anakin Skywalker and Count Dooku [251-15] 10.00
- ☐ Clone troopers [251-16] 10.00
- ☐ Yoda / Clone Wars [251-17] 10.00

2012 Hanging dry erase boards with marker.
- ☐ Angry Birds Tatooine, exclusive to Walmart [251-18] ... 10.00
- ☐ Boba Fett 10.00
- ☐ Yoda 10.00

Junior Achievement
- ☐ Message Center, 500 produced 175.00

Star Wars Celebration VI
- ☐ Bantha / Dune Sea [251-19] 25.00

Earphones and Headphones
Continued in Volume 3, Page 222

Coloud (UK)
- ☐ Darth Vader 65.00
- ☐ Lightspeed 65.00
- ☐ Rebel Alliance 65.00

Earphones and Headphones

252-08 252-09 252-10 252-11 252-12 252-13 252-14

      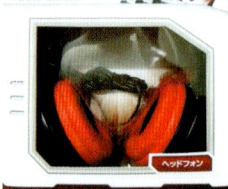

252-15 252-16 252-17 252-18 252-19 252-20 252-21

Funko
DJ headphones.
❏ Darth Vader [252-01] 50.00
❏ Stormtrooper [252-02] 50.00

Fold up headphones.
❏ 501st Clone trooper [252-03] 30.00
❏ Boba Fett [252-04] 30.00
❏ Darth Vader [252-05] 30.00
❏ Rebel Alliance [252-06] 30.00
❏ Stormtrooper [252-07] 30.00

JazWares, Inc
Earbuds.
❏ C-3PO [252-08] 15.00
❏ C-3PO, plastic clamshell packaging [252-09] 15.00
❏ Darth Maul [252-10] 15.00
❏ Darth Maul, plastic clamshell packaging [252-10] 15.00
❏ Darth Vader [252-11] 15.00
❏ Darth Vader, plastic clamshell packaging 15.00
❏ Yoda [252-12] 15.00
❏ Yoda, plastic clamshell packaging 15.00

Headphones.
❏ Darth Vader [252-13] 20.00
❏ Darth Vader, lenticular folding stereo [252-14] 20.00
❏ R2-D2 [252-15] 20.00

Philips
❏ C-3PO [252-16] 30.00
❏ Darth Vader [252-17] 30.00
❏ Luke Skywalker [252-18] 30.00

Taito (Japan)
Headphones.
❏ Artoo-Detoo [252-19] 45.00
❏ C-3PO [252-20] 45.00
❏ Darth Vader [252-21] 45.00

Erasers
Continued in Volume 3, Page 224

(Spain)
❏ Ink Eraser [253-01] 10.00

Accessory Zone
❏ 12 erasers: Darth Vader and Yoda [253-02] 5.00

Butterfly Originals
3-packs.
❏ C-3PO, Darth Vader, Millennium Falcon [253-03] 25.00
❏ C-3PO, Darth Vader, Millennium Falcon, glow [253-04] ..25.00

      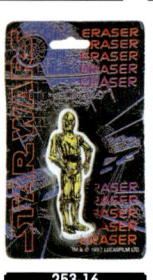  

253-01 253-02 253-03 253-04 253-05 253-06 253-07 253-08 253-09

253-10 253-11 253-12 253-13 253-14 253-15 253-16 253-17 253-18

253-19 253-20 253-21 253-22 253-23 253-24 253-25 253-26 253-27

Erasers

- Admiral Ackbar [253-05] 20.00
- Baby Ewok [253-06] 20.00
- Bib Fortuna [253-07] 20.00
- Darth Vader [253-08] 20.00
- Emperor's Royal Guard [253-09] 20.00
- Emperor's Royal Guard flat rectangular with decal.....20.00
- Gamorrean Guard [253-10] 20.00
- Jabba the Hutt [253-11] 20.00
- Max Rebo [253-12] 20.00
- R2-D2 [253-13] 20.00
- Wicket the Ewok [253-14] 20.00
- Yoda [253-15] 20.00

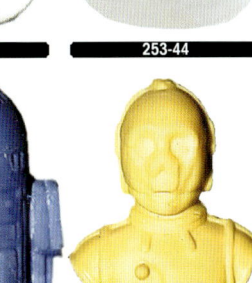

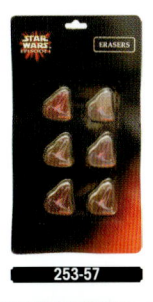
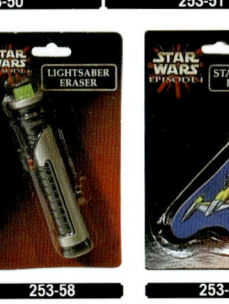
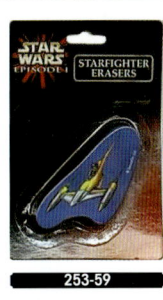

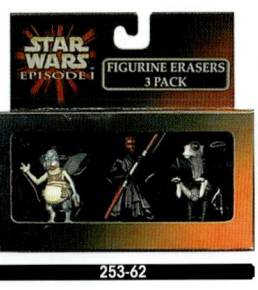

Erasers

254-01

254-02

254-03

254-04

254-05

254-06

254-07

254-08

254-09

254-10

254-11

254-12

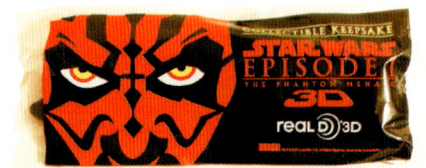
254-13

254-14

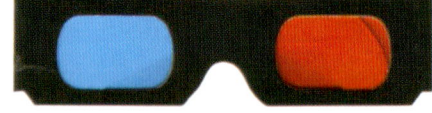
254-15 Front and Back

254-16 Front and Back

Flomo (UK)
- ❏ Death Star II scene [v1e1:220] 5.00

Funtastic Pty. Ltd. (Australia)
Death Star card back.
- ❏ C-3PO [253-16] 25.00
- ❏ Darth Vader [253-17] 25.00
- ❏ R2-D2 [253-18] 25.00

Grand Toys
- ❏ Gold Star Wars logo on black [v1e1:220] 5.00
- ❏ Queen Amidala emblem 5.00

Grosvenor
- ❏ White, in Star Wars wrap [v1e1:220] 5.00

HC Ford (UK)
Die-cut.
- ❏ Admiral Ackbar [253-19] 45.00
- ❏ Boba Fett [253-20] 30.00
- ❏ C-3PO [253-21] 30.00
- ❏ Chewbacca [253-22] 45.00
- ❏ Darth Vader [253-23] 30.00
- ❏ Gamorrean Guard [253-24] 30.00
- ❏ Jabba the Hutt [253-25] 50.00
- ❏ R2-D2 [253-26] 30.00
- ❏ Wicket the Ewok [253-27] 30.00

Perfumed, rectangular plastic case. Return of the Jedi.
- ❏ C-3PO and R2-D2, apple scent [253-28] 25.00
- ❏ Chewbacca, orange scent [253-29] 25.00
- ❏ Darth Vader, grape scent [253-30] 25.00
- ❏ Ewok, strawberry scent [253-31] 25.00
- ❏ Gamorrean Guard, mint scent [253-32] 25.00
- ❏ Han Solo, line scent [253-33] 25.00

Perfumed, rectangular plastic case. Star Wars.
- ❏ C-3PO and R2-D2, apple scent [253-34] 30.00
- ❏ Chewbacca, orange scent [253-35] 30.00
- ❏ Darth Vader, grape scent [253-36] 30.00
- ❏ Han Solo, lime scent [253-37] 30.00

- ❏ Luke Skywalker, mint scent [253-38] 30.00
- ❏ Princess Leia, strawberry scent [253-39] 30.00

Record erasers, Return of the Jedi.
- ❏ Luke and Vader on Bespin gantry [253-40] ... 20.00
- ❏ Poster art [253-41] 20.00

Helix (UK)
Pear-shaped, line art characters above name.
- ❏ Artoo Detoo [253-42] 45.00
- ❏ Chewbacca [253-43] 45.00
- ❏ Darth Vader [253-44] 45.00
- ❏ Han Solo [253-45] 45.00
- ❏ Luke Skywalker [253-46] 45.00
- ❏ Moff Tarkin [253-47] 60.00
- ❏ Princess Leia [253-48] 45.00
- ❏ See Threepio [253-49] 45.00

Sculpted busts.
- ❏ Artoo Detoo [253-50] 85.00
- ❏ C-3PO [253-51] 85.00
- ❏ Darth Vader [253-52] 85.00
- ❏ Stormtrooper [253-53] 85.00

Impact, Inc.
Multi-packs.
- ❏ 2-pack: Anakin Skywalker and Jar Jar Binks [253-54] 10.00
- ❏ 2-pack: Darth Maul and Qui-Gon Jinn [253-55] 10.00
- ❏ 6-pack: mini Anakin in Podracer [v1e1:221] 10.00
- ❏ 6-pack: mini Jedi vs. Sith [253-56] 10.00
- ❏ 6-pack: mini Space Battle [253-57] 10.00

- ❏ Lightsaber [253-58] 10.00
- ❏ Naboo Fighter [253-59] 10.00
- ❏ Trade Federation Droid Fighter [253-60] 10.00

Figurine erasers, 3-packs.
- ❏ Anakin, R2-D2, Jar Jar Binks [253-61] 25.00
- ❏ Watto, Darth Maul, Sebulba [253-62] 25.00

Figurine erasers.
- ❏ Anakin [253-63] 10.00
- ❏ Darth Maul [253-64] 10.00
- ❏ R2-D2 [253-65] 10.00
- ❏ Sebulba [253-66] 10.00
- ❏ Watto [253-67] 10.00

Innovative Designs
4-pack of shaped erasers.
- ❏ Angry Birds: Luke, Darth Vader, Stormtrooper, Yoda, exclusive to Walmart [253-68] 10.00
- ❏ Yoda, Darth Vader, Droids, Anakin 10.00

Jumbo Erasers, Angry Birds.
- ❏ Angry Birds, exclusive to Walmart [253-69] .. 5.00

Merlin
- ❏ Darth Vader image [v1e1:222] 5.00
- ❏ R2-D2 image [253-70] 5.00

Pyramid
- ❏ Star Wars logo, 1" x 1.75" [v1e1:222] 3.00

Q-Stat (UK)
- ❏ Obi-Wan eraser with Darth Maul sharpener [253-71] 12.00
- ❏ Obi-Wan Kenobi, shaped 5.00

Spin Master
Gomu erasers storage cases.
- ❏ Lightsaber with eight erasers [253-72] 15.00

Gomu erasers.
- ❏ 4-pack: Darth Vader, Millennium Falcon plus 2 secret (stormtrooper and X-Wing Fighter) [253-73] 25.00

Spin Master (UK)
- ❏ Gomu lightsaber case with eight erasers 20.00

Takara (Japan)
- ❏ R2-D2 [253-74] 60.00

Uranium (Switzerland)
Perfumed, rectangular plastic case. Star Wars.
❏ Han Solo [v1e1:222] 45.00

Eyewear: Glasses
Continued in Volume 3, Page 225

Aigan (Japan)
❏ Boba Fett 225.00
❏ Darth Vader 225.00
❏ Luke Skywalker 225.00
❏ R2-D2 ....225.00
❏ Stormtrooper 225.00

DK Publishing
❏ "Read More You Must" sunglasses 25.00

Hot Topic
❏ Let the Wookiee Win sunglasses [254-01] 18.00

IMT Accessories
Clone Wars light-up sunglasses.
❏ Black [254-02] 12.00
❏ Blue light-up [254-03] 12.00
❏ White light-up [254-04] 21.00

Episode III: Revenge of the Sith sunglasses.
❏ Anakin Skywalker, silver frames [254-05] 10.00
❏ Chewbacca, green frames 10.00
❏ Chewbacca, orange frames [254-06] 10.00
❏ Darth Vader (left), red frames [254-07] 10.00
❏ Darth Vader (right), red frames 10.00
❏ Darth Vader, blue frames [254-08] 10.00
❏ General Grievous, orange frames 10.00
❏ Star Wars (C-3PO and R2-D2), black frames [254-09] 10.00
❏ Star Wars (C-3PO and R2-D2), blue frames [254-10] 10.00
❏ Yoda, orange frames..10.00

IMT Accessories (UK)
❏ Clone Wars sunglasses, white [254-11] 12.00

Look3D Eyewear (Australia)
❏ Anakin Skywalker podracer 3D glasses [254-12] 25.00

Real 3D
❏ Star Wars, exclusive to Star Wars Celebration VI [254-13] 20.00

3D premiere of The Phantom Menace.
❏ Anakin Skywalker..25.00
❏ Darth Maul [254-14] 35.00

Scholastic
❏ Jedi Apprentice [254-15] 10.00

Wizards of the Coast
❏ 3D Star Wars miniatures promotion [254-16] 10.00

Fabrics
Continued in Volume 3, Page 227

Springs Industries, Inc.
Textiles by the yard.
❏ C-3PO and R2-D2 [v1e1:222] 15.00
❏ Darth Vader [v1e1:222] 15.00
❏ Jedi justice pattern [v1e1:222] 15.00
❏ Princess Leia [v1e1:222] 15.00
❏ Revenge orange fleece [v1e1:222] 15.00
❏ Revenge Vader pattern [v1e1:222] 15.00
❏ Star Wars / Darth Vader [v1e1:222] 15.00
❏ Starfighters pattern (classic trilogy) [v1e1:222] 15.00
❏ Starfighters pattern (EPIII) [v1e1:222] 15.00
❏ Vader looks over Epic Duel wall panel [v1e1:222] 15.00
❏ Yoda and Darth Vader panels [v1e1:222] 15.00
❏ Yoda pattern [v1e1:222] 15.00

Fans
Continued in Volume 3, Page 230

Candy Rific
Battery operated with M&Ms.
❏ Boba Fett [255-01] 15.00
❏ Darth Maul [255-02] 15.00
❏ Darth Vader [255-03] 15.00
❏ Obi-Wan Kenobi [255-04] 15.00
❏ Princess Leia [255-05] 15.00

Fans, Hand
Continued in Volume 3, Page 230

Baleno (China)
Limited edition.
❏ Clone troopers 20.00
❏ Darth Vader and Clone trooper 20.00

EnSky (Japan)
Limited edition.
❏ Episode I: The Phantom Menace [256-01] 15.00
❏ Episode II: Attack of the Clones [256-02] 15.00
❏ Saga [256-03] 15.00

Star Wars Celebration Japan (Japan)
❏ Star Wars Celebration Japan [256-04] 25.00

Star Wars Celebration V
❏ Death Star, orange [256-05] 20.00

Taito (Japan)
Paper and bamboo fans, plastic lightsaber handles.
❏ Darth Vader [256-06] 30.00
❏ R2-D2 and C-3PO [256-07] 30.00
❏ Yoda [256-08] 30.00

255-01 | 255-02 | 255-03 | 255-04 | 255-05 | 256-01 | 256-02 | 256-03 | 256-04 Side 1 and Side 2 | 256-05

256-06 | 256-07 | 256-08 | 256-09

256-10 | 256-11 | 256-12 | 256-13

256-14 Front and Back | 256-15 | 256-16

Fans, Hand

257-01

257-02

257-03

257-04

257-05

257-06

257-07

257-08

257-09

257-10

257-11

257-12

Paper and bamboo fans. Lightsaber handle. Darth Vader.
- ❏ Flaming helmet [256-09] 25.00
- ❏ Oval on white fan [256-10] 25.00
- ❏ Silhouetted in red [256-11] 25.00
- ❏ Vader [256-12] 25.00

Paper and bamboo fans. Lightsaber handle. Episode III.
- ❏ Anakin and Obi-Wan (Jedi) [256-13] 100.00
- ❏ Darth Vader A [256-14] 100.00
- ❏ Darth Vader B [256-15] 100.00
- ❏ Yoda [256-16] 100.00

Figures: Ceramic

Sigma
- ❏ Bib Fortuna [257-01] 30.00
- ❏ Boba Fett [257-02] 75.00
- ❏ C-3PO and R2-D2 [257-03] 45.00
- ❏ Darth Vader [257-04] 45.00
- ❏ Emperor Palpatine [257-05] 30.00
- ❏ Gamorrean Guard [257-06] 35.00
- ❏ Han Solo [257-07] 40.00
- ❏ Klaatu [257-08] 30.00
- ❏ Lando Calrissian [257-09] 35.00
- ❏ Luke Skywalker [257-10] 40.00
- ❏ Princess Leia Boushh Disguise [257-11] ... 35.00
- ❏ Wicket the Ewok [257-12] 40.00

Figurines: Galactic Village Collection

Hawthorne Village
Environment with character figure. Individually numbered.
- ❏ AT-ST with Ewok 75.00
- ❏ AT-AT with Princess Leia [258-01] 100.00
- ❏ Dagobah swamp with Luke Skywalker [258-02] ... 75.00
- ❏ Endor Bunker with Han Solo [258-03] ... 75.00
- ❏ Ewok Village with Wicket [258-04] 100.00
- ❏ Hoth Rebel Base with Darth Vader [258-05] ... 75.00
- ❏ Jabba's Palace with Jabba the Hutt [258-06] ... 75.00
- ❏ Jabba's Sail Barge with Princess Leia [258-07] ... 100.00
- ❏ Jawa Sand Crawler with C-3PO [258-08] ... 75.00
- ❏ Mos Eisley Cantina with Han Solo 75.00
- ❏ Wampa Cave with Luke Skywalker [258-09] ... 75.00
- ❏ Yoda's Hut with Yoda [258-10] 75.00

Figurines: Porcelain

Alcara, SAS (France)
1st series feves. Hand-painted porcelain or ceramic figurines.
- ❏ A-Wing fighter [v1e1:224] 8.00
- ❏ AT-AT [v1e1:224] 8.00
- ❏ C-3PO [v1e1:224] 8.00
- ❏ Darth Vader [v1e1:224] 8.00
- ❏ Darth Vader's TIE Fighter [v1e1:224] ... 8.00
- ❏ Imperial Star Destroyer [v1e1:224] 8.00
- ❏ Millennium Falcon [v1e1:224] 8.00
- ❏ R2-D2 [v1e1:224] 8.00
- ❏ Sand Crawler [v1e1:224] 8.00
- ❏ Slave I [v1e1:224] 8.00
- ❏ Snowspeeder [v1e1:224] 8.00
- ❏ Star Wars classic logo [v1e1:224] 8.00
- ❏ X-Wing Fighter [v1e1:224] 8.00

2nd series feves. Hand painted porcelain or ceramic figurines.
- ❏ C-3PO [v1e1:224] 8.00
- ❏ Chewbacca [v1e1:224] 8.00
- ❏ Darth Maul [v1e1:224] 8.00
- ❏ Darth Vader [v1e1:224] 8.00
- ❏ Jango Fett [v1e1:224] 8.00
- ❏ Queen Amidala [v1e1:224] 8.00
- ❏ R2-D2 [v1e1:224] 8.00
- ❏ Star Wars classic logo [v1e1:224] 8.00
- ❏ Stormtrooper [v1e1:224] 8.00
- ❏ Yoda [v1e1:224] 8.00

258-01

258-02

258-03

258-04

258-05

258-06

258-07

258-08

258-09

258-10

259-01

259-02

259-03

259-04

226

Flashlights and Lanterns

260-01 | 261-01 Sample | 263-01 | 263-06

3rd series feves. 10 packs.
- ☐ Darth Vader [259-01] 45.00
- ☐ Master Yoda [259-02] 45.00

M&M World
Approximately 6" tall. 2,500 produced of each.
- ☐ Boba Fett [259-03] 55.00
- ☐ Darth Maul 55.00
- ☐ Darth Vader 55.00
- ☐ Luke Skywalker 55.00
- ☐ Princess Leia [259-03] 55.00

Film

Agfa
- ☐ 3-pack with free flying disc [v1e1:224] 80.00
- ☐ 3-pack with free yo-yo [260-01] 80.00

Film Frames

20th Century Fox
70 mm frame, any.
- ☐ A New Hope 25.00
- ☐ Empire Strikes Back 25.00
- ☐ Revenge of the Jedi, title frame 65.00
- ☐ Return of the Jedi 25.00

Willitts Designs
Collector's Box Sets. Four frames included.
- ☐ Empire Strikes Back, first edition 125.00
- ☐ Empire Strikes Back, second edition 125.00
- ☐ Return of the Jedi 145.00

70 mm film frame mounted in a 7.5" x 2.75" acrylic holder with conceptual artwork or movie scenes. Complete checklist and images in volume 1, first edition pages 224-225.
- ☐ A New Hope, each [261-1] 25.00
- ☐ Empire Strikes Back, each 25.00
- ☐ Return of the Jedi, each 25.00

Fish Tanks

Planet Pets Inc.
- ☐ R2-D2, exclusive to Petco [262-01] 230.00

Fishing Accessories
Continued in Volume 3, Page 231

Bimini Bay Outfitters Ltd.
- ☐ Tackle box, Clone Wars, exclusive to Target [263-01] 15.00

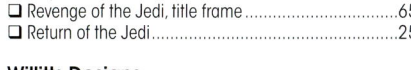

262-01 | 263-02 | 263-03 | 263-04 | 263-05 | 263-07 | 263-08

Fun casting combos. Rod, reel, tackle box, and casting plug.
- ☐ Clone Wars [263-02] 15.00
- ☐ Clone Wars, Captain Fox package, exclusive to Target [263-03] 25.00
- ☐ Darth Vader [263-04] 25.00
- ☐ Darth Vader, lightsaber handle [263-05] 20.00

IMT Accessories
- ☐ Star Wars rod, reel, tackle box, and casting plug 25.00

Shakespeare
- ☐ Clone Wars tackle box [263-06] 20.00

Clone Wars fishing kits.
- ☐ Rod with reel, practice casting targets [263-07] 25.00
- ☐ Rod with reel, tackle box and casting plug [263-08] 25.00

Flags
Continued in Volume 3, Page 231

Great Scott
- ☐ Darth Vader 28" x 40" [264-01] 20.00
- ☐ Darth Vader, Star Wars Trilogy art 20" x 36" [264-02] ...20.00
- ☐ Stormtrooper, Empire Strikes Back Trilogy Art, 20" x 36" [264-03] 20.00
- ☐ X-Wing Fighter 28" x 40" [264-04] 20.00
- ☐ Yoda, Return of the Jedi Trilogy art 20" x 36" [264-05] ...20.00

Lucasfilm
- ☐ Stormtrooper skull and crossbones, 3' x 5' 1 sided 25.00

Flashlights and Lanterns
Continued in Volume 3, Page 231

Candy Rific
Mpire characters.
- ☐ Darth Maul [265-01] 10.00
- ☐ Darth Vader [265-02] 10.00
- ☐ Stormtrooper [265-03] 10.00

Digital Blue, Inc.
Lightsaber flashlights.
- ☐ Anakin [265-04] 20.00
- ☐ Darth Maul [265-05] 25.00
- ☐ Yoda [265-06] 20.00

M&M World
- ☐ Mpire promotional [265-07] 30.00

Master Replicas
LED flashlights. Handle is mini-replica lightsaber.
- ☐ Darth Vader [265-08] 25.00
- ☐ Luke Skywalker [265-09] 25.00
- ☐ Yoda [265-10] 25.00

Sakar International
- ☐ Jedi, white [265-11] 15.00
- ☐ Rebels, black [265-12] 15.00

Santoki LLC
- ☐ Darth Maul [265-13] 15.00
- ☐ Darth Vader [265-14] 15.00
- ☐ Stormtrooper [265-15] 15.00

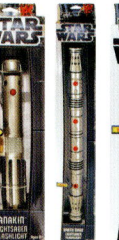

264-01 | 264-02 | 264-03 | 264-04 | 264-05 | 265-01 | 265-02 | 265-03 | 265-04 | 265-05 | 265-06

Flashlights and Lanterns

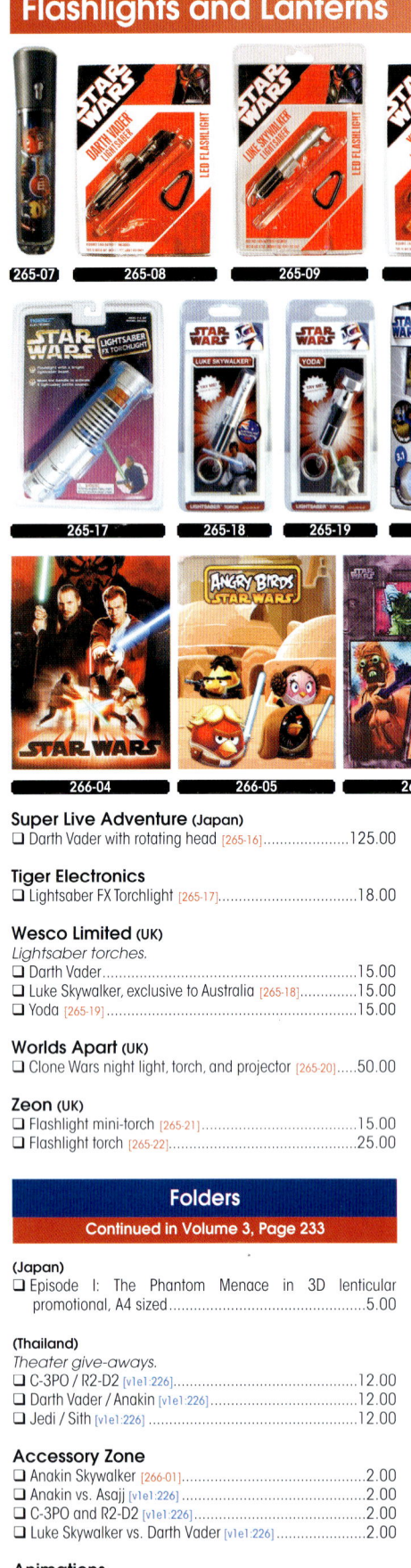

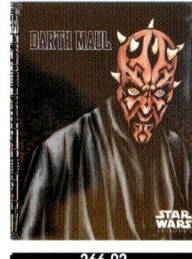

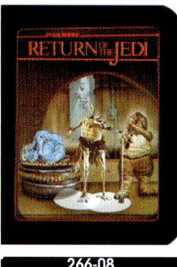

Super Live Adventure (Japan)
- Darth Vader with rotating head [265-16] 125.00

Tiger Electronics
- Lightsaber FX Torchlight [265-17] 18.00

Wesco Limited (UK)
Lightsaber torches.
- Darth Vader 15.00
- Luke Skywalker, exclusive to Australia [265-18] 15.00
- Yoda [265-19] 15.00

Worlds Apart (UK)
- Clone Wars night light, torch, and projector [265-20] 50.00

Zeon (UK)
- Flashlight mini-torch [265-21] 15.00
- Flashlight torch [265-22] 25.00

Folders
Continued in Volume 3, Page 233

(Japan)
- Episode I: The Phantom Menace in 3D lenticular promotional, A4 sized 5.00

(Thailand)
Theater give-aways.
- C-3PO / R2-D2 [v1e1:226] 12.00
- Darth Vader / Anakin [v1e1:226] 12.00
- Jedi / Sith [v1e1:226] 12.00

Accessory Zone
- Anakin Skywalker [266-01] 2.00
- Anakin vs. Asajj [v1e1:226] 2.00
- C-3PO and R2-D2 [v1e1:226] 2.00
- Luke Skywalker vs. Darth Vader [v1e1:226] 2.00

Animations
Clone Wars.
- Jedi and Clones 15.00
- Obi-Wan Kenobi 15.00
- Yoda 15.00

Episode III: Revenge of the Sith.
- Darth Vader 2.00
- Darth Vader helmet [v1e1:226] 2.00
- Darth Vader lightsaber down [v1e1:226] 2.00
- Darth Vader lightsaber up [v1e1:226] 2.00

Impact, Inc.
- Anakin Skywalker [v1e1:226] 2.00
- Darth Maul / Darth Sidious [266-02] 2.00
- Jar Jar Binks [v1e1:226] 2.00
- Jedi vs. Sith [v1e1:226] 3.00
- Podrace [v1e1:226] 3.00
- Queen Amidala [v1e1:226] 2.00
- Qui-Gon Jinn [v1e1:226] 2.00
- R2-D2 / C-3PO [v1e1:227] 2.00
- Space Battle [v1e1:227] 3.00

Innovative Designs
- Anakin / Captain Rex 2.00
- Captain Rex and clones 2.00
- Captain Rex, Clones / Captain Rex 2.00
- Darth Maul, Tatooine Duel / Darth Maul 2.00
- Darth Vader [266-03] 2.00
- Jedi vs. Sith / Obi-Wan vs. Darth Maul [266-04] 2.00
- Obi-Wan and clones 2.00
- Obi-Wan, Anakin, Yoda, Clone trooper / Jedi 2.00

Angry Birds.
- Chewbacca, Han Solo, Luke Skywalker, Obi-Wan Kenobi, Princess Leia, in front of Darth Vader 2.00
- Chewbacca, Obi-Wan Kenobi, Princess Leia, Han Solo, Luke, Darth Vader, and various fighters 2.00
- Death Star 9.00
- Tatooine [266-05] 2.00

Mead
- B-Wing Attack [v1e1:227] 4.00
- Bounty Hunters neon [v1e1:227] 6.00
- C-3PO 4.00
- C-3PO R2-D2 neon [v1e1:227] 6.00
- C-3PO / phrases [v1e1:227] 3.00
- Darth Vader, Dark Lord of the Sith [v1e1:227] 3.00
- "Freeze You Rebel Scum" [v1e1:227] 3.00
- Han / Millennium Falcon [v1e1:227] 3.00
- Han Solo 4.00
- He's No Good To Me Dead neon [v1e1:227] 6.00
- Jabba's Palace neon [v1e1:227] 6.00
- Luke Skywalker [v1e1:227] 3.00
- "May the Force be with you" [4:145] 3.00
- "May the Force be with you" [v1e1:227] 4.00
- "Never Under Estimate The Power of ..." [v1e1:227] 3.00
- Opening Crawl / Stormtrooper / Tantive IV [v1e1:227] 3.00
- Princess Leia [4:146] 3.00
- Princess Leia [v1e1:227] 4.00
- Princess Leia's plea / R2-D2 [v1e1:227] 3.00
- R2-D2 .... 4.00
- Space Ships 4.00
- Starfighters [v1e1:227] 3.00
- Tatooine neon [266-06] 6.00
- Title Crawl 4.00
- Yoda 4.00
- Yoda / phrases [v1e1:227] 3.00

Vintage.
- Ben Kenobi / Stormtroopers [v1e1:227] 11.00
- C-3PO and R2-D2 [v1e1:227] 10.00
- Chewbacca, Han, and Luke [v1e1:227] 11.00
- Darth Vader and Stormtroopers 10.00
- Leia and Luke [v1e1:227] 10.00
- X-Wing and Tie Fighter [v1e1:227] 11.00

Pyramid
Episode II: Attack of the Clones.
- Anakin vs. Obi-Wan 2.00
- Sith Lords [v1e1:227] 2.00
- Villains 2.00

Stuart Hall
Empire Strikes Back.
- Bounty Hunters 11.00
- C-3PO and R2-D2 [266-07] 8.00
- Character collage [v1e1:227] 11.00
- Chewbacca 11.00
- Darth Vader 11.00
- Darth Vader and Stormtroopers [v1e1:227] 8.00
- Luke on Dagobah [v1e1:227] 11.00
- Yoda on Dagobah [v1e1:227] 11.00

Return of the Jedi.
- B-Wing, and Tie Interceptor [v1e1:227] 8.00
- C-3PO, R2-D2, and Wicket the Ewok [v1e1:227] 8.00
- Emperor's throne room 8.00
- Jabba the Hutt and Salacious Crumb [v1e1:227] 8.00
- Max Rebo Band [266-08] 8.00
- Speeder Bikes [v1e1:227] 8.00

Taito (Japan)
Clear files sets of 3.
- C-3PO and R2-D2, Darth Vader, Obi-Wan Kenobi 15.00
- Darth Vader, Boba Fett, Luke Skywalker 15.00
- Darth Vader, Yoda, Han, and Chewbacca 15.00
- Stormtrooper, R2-D2, Princess Leia 15.00
- Yoda, Darth Maul, Anakin Skywalker 15.00

Furniture: Chairs and Sofas

267-01 Packaged and Inflated

267-02 Packaged and Inflated

267-03

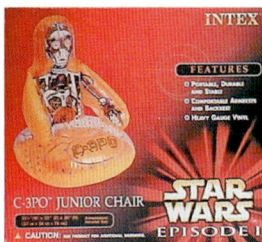
267-04

267-05

267-06

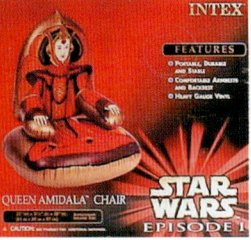
267-07

267-08

267-09

267-10

Furniture: Inflatable

Baleno (China)
- ❏ Darth Vader [267-01] 45.00
- ❏ Yoda [267-02] 45.00

Hedstrom
- ❏ Clone Wars inflatable chair [267-03] 30.00

Intex Recreation Corp.
- ❏ C-3PO junior chair [267-04] 25.00
- ❏ Darth Maul chair [267-05] 25.00
- ❏ Jar Jar chair [267-06] 20.00
- ❏ Queen Amidala chair [267-07] 20.00
- ❏ R2-D2 Junior chair [267-08] 20.00

Kellytoy
- ❏ Sith Lord [267-09] 20.00
- ❏ Yoda 20.00

Toy Quest
- ❏ Plush inflatable lounge [267-10] 50.00

Furniture: Beds
Continued in Volume 3, Page 234

Kidnap Furniture Ltd. (Ireland)
Headboards.
- ❏ R2-D2 and C-3PO [268-01] 1,250.00
- ❏ Vader, Luke, Stormtrooper [268-02] 1,750.00

Monkey Business
- ❏ Darth Vader, toddler [268-03] 100.00

Toy Quest
- ❏ Jedi Starfighter, inflatable [268-04] 150.00

Worlds Apart (UK)
- ❏ Clone Wars ready bed [268-05] 85.00

Furniture: Bookcases
Continued in Volume 3, Page 234

American Toy and Furniture Co.
- ❏ Return of the Jedi [269-01] 200.00

Furniture: Chairs and Sofas
Continued in Volume 3, Page 234

- ❏ Darth Vader, beanbag [270-01] 25.00

Episode III: Revenge of the Sith folding camp-style chairs.
- ❏ Clone [270-02] 35.00
- ❏ Darth Vader [270-03] 35.00
- ❏ Darth Vader eyes [270-04] 35.00
- ❏ Darth Vader, children's [270-05] 35.00
- ❏ Epic duel, children's [270-06] 35.00
- ❏ Jedi [270-07] 35.00

Folding saucer camp-style chairs.
- ❏ Darth Vader [270-08] 40.00

Episode III: Revenge of the Sith.
- ❏ Darth Vader, children's folding [270-09] 30.00

American Toy and Furniture Co.
- ❏ Wicket the Ewok rocker [v1e1:229] 450.00

Return of the Jedi. Blue wood with white logo.
- ❏ Banner back [270-10] 100.00
- ❏ Full back [270-11] 100.00

Brava Soft Furnishings (Australia)
- ❏ Wicket beanbag [270-12] 75.00

Camp Planner International Co., Ltd.
Camp chairs, children's sizes.
- ❏ Captain Rex [270-13] 35.00
- ❏ Darth Maul [270-14] 35.00
- ❏ R2-D2 [270-15] 35.00

Character World Ltd. (UK)
- ❏ Anakin and Sebulba podracer, beanbag [270-16] 50.00

Idea Nuova
- ❏ Darth Vader stadium chair 40.00
- ❏ Jedi stadium chair 40.00

Littens Co. (UK)
- ❏ Clone Wars, beanbag [v1e1:229] 35.00

268-01

268-02

268-03

268-04

268-05

269-01

270-01

270-02 Chair and Case

270-03 Chair and Case

270-04 Chair and Case

Furniture: Chairs and Sofas

| 270-05 Chair and Case | 270-06 Chair and Case | 270-07 Chair and Case | 270-08 | 270-09 Chair and Case |

| 270-10 | 270-11 | 270-12 | 270-13 Chair and Case | 270-14 Chair and Case | 270-15 Chair and Case |

| 270-16 | 270-17 | 270-18 | 270-19 | 270-20 | 270-21 | 270-22 | 270-23 |

270-24

270-25 Chair and Case

270-26

Martin Yaffe
Episode I: The Phantom Menace rocking chairs.
❏ Anakin Skywalker [270-17] 275.00
❏ Queen Amidala [270-18] 275.00

Pipsqueaks
Episode I: The Phantom Menace. Hardwood.
❏ Anakin [270-19] 250.00
❏ Jar Jar [270-20] 250.00
❏ Sebulba [270-21] 250.00
❏ Watto [270-22] 250.00

Pottery Barn
❏ R2-D2 Anywhere Chair [270-23] 100.00
❏ R2-D2 Anywhere Chair, cover only 40.00

Skywalker Ranch
❏ Picnic chair [v1e1:229] 90.00

SlumberTrek (Australia)
❏ Darth Vader beanbag [270-24] 35.00

ThinkGeek
❏ R2-D2 camp chair [270-25] 50.00

Worlds Apart (UK)
❏ Clone Wars flip out sofa [270-26] 75.00

Furniture: Clothes Racks

Adam Joseph Industries
❏ C-3PO and R2-D2 .... 650.00

American Toy and Furniture Co.
❏ Ewoks [271-01] 500.00
❏ Luke and Darth Vader Dueling [271-01] 175.00

Furniture: Desks
Continued in Volume 3, Page 235

American Toy and Furniture Co.
❏ Ewoks 2-sided desk with benches 1,375.00
❏ Return of the Jedi student desk and chair [272-01] 450.00
❏ Wicket activity desk and bench [272-02] 575.00

Born to Play
❏ Episode I desk and stool [272-03] 300.00

Furniture: Nightstands

American Toy and Furniture Co.
❏ Return of the Jedi [273-01] 365.00

271-01

271-02

| 272-01 | 272-02 | 272-03 | 273-01 |

Game Pieces, Promotional

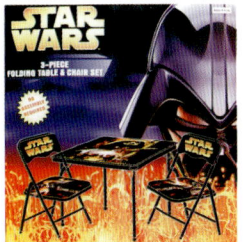 274-01
 274-02
 274-03
 274-04
 274-05

 275-01
 275-02
 275-03
 275-04
 275-05
 275-06

Furniture: Tables
Continued in Volume 3, Page 236

Episode III: Revenge of the Sith.
- ❑ Darth Vader card table, 2 children's folding chairs [274-01] 165.00
- ❑ Darth Vader, round hardwood with 2 matching chairs [274-02] 140.00

Outdoor patio sets. Round table with umbrella, 2 children's folding chairs.
- ❑ Revenge of the Sith [274-03] 175.00

American Toy and Furniture Co.
- ❑ Ewoks picnic table 1,500.00
- ❑ Return of the Jedi table with 2 chairs [274-04] 650.00

Pipsqueaks
- ❑ Episode I: Podracer Table, hardwood [274-05] 245.00

Furniture: Toy Chests and Storage
Continued in Volume 3, Page 236

American Toy and Furniture Co.
- ❑ Ewoks storage bench [275-01] 2,500.00
- ❑ Ewoks toy chest [275-02] 465.00
- ❑ R2-D2 toy chest [275-03] 185.00
- ❑ Wicket the Ewok and friends roll around [275-04] ... 2,500.00

Born to Play
- ❑ Episode I [v1e1:230] 120.00

Monkey Business
- ❑ 9-bin toy organizer, epic duel art [275-05] 75.00
- ❑ Darth Vader, Episode III [275-06] 95.00

Game Pieces, Promotional
Continued in Volume 3, Page 236

(New Zealand)
- ❑ Count Dooku token [4:148] 5.00

Burger King
- ❑ Everybody Wins, scratch-off, Coca-Cola [4:148] 45.00

Burger King (UK)
Choose Your Destiny scratch-off cards.
- ❑ Anakin Skywalker [276-01] 5.00
- ❑ Bail Organa [276-02] 5.00
- ❑ C-3PO [276-03] 5.00
- ❑ Chancellor Palpatine [276-04] 5.00
- ❑ Chewbacca [276-05] 5.00
- ❑ Clone trooper [276-06] 5.00
- ❑ Count Dooku [276-07] 5.00
- ❑ Darth Sidious [276-08] 5.00
- ❑ Darth Vader [276-09] 5.00
- ❑ General Grievous [276-10] 5.00
- ❑ Mace Windu [276-11] 5.00
- ❑ Obi-Wan Kenobi [276-12] 5.00
- ❑ Padmé Amidala [276-13] 5.00
- ❑ R2-D2 [276-14] 5.00
- ❑ Tarfful [276-15] 5.00
- ❑ Yoda [276-16] 5.00

Cheesestrings (Canada)
12 different Saga Secrets game pieces.
- ❑ Anakin Skywalker [276-17] 5.00
- ❑ Boba Fett [276-18] 5.00
- ❑ Darth Maul [276-19] 5.00
- ❑ Darth Vader [276-20] 5.00
- ❑ Luke and Leia [276-21] 5.00
- ❑ Luke and Yoda [276-22] 5.00
- ❑ Obi-Wan Kenobi [276-23] 5.00
- ❑ Princess Leia [276-24] 5.00
- ❑ Qui-Gon Jinn [276-25] 5.00
- ❑ R2-D2 and C-3PO [276-26] 5.00
- ❑ Stormtroopers [276-27] 5.00
- ❑ Yoda [276-28] 5.00

Coca-Cola (Canada)
Vinyl inserts under bottle caps.
- ❑ A Luc Skywalker [276-29] 35.00
- ❑ B Leia Organa [276-30] 250.00
- ❑ C Ben (Obi-Wan) Kenobi [276-31] 35.00
- ❑ D Dark Vador [276-32] 250.00
- ❑ E Yan Solo [276-33] 35.00
- ❑ F Chiquetaba [276-34] 250.00
- ❑ G Z6PO [276-35] 35.00
- ❑ H R2-D2 [276-36] 250.00

 276-01
 276-02
 276-03
 276-04
 276-05
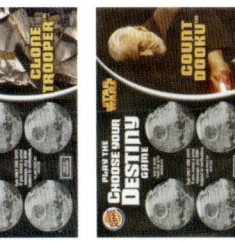 276-06
 276-07
276-08

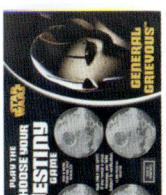 276-09
 276-10
 276-11
 276-12
 276-13
 276-14
276-15
 276-16

Game Pieces, Promotional

276-17 | 276-18 | 276-19 | 276-20 | 276-21 | 276-22 | 276-23

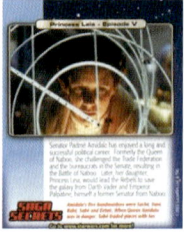      

276-24 | 276-25 | 276-26 | 276-27 | 276-28 | 276-29 | 276-30

   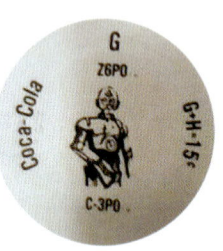 

276-31 | 276-32 | 276-33 | 276-34 | 276-35 | 276-36

Coca-Cola (Singapore)
Sprite Lucky Empire. Vinyl inserts under bottle caps.
- Boba Fett 150.00
- C-3PO 150.00
- Chewbacca 150.00
- Darth Vader 150.00
- Darth Vader and Boba Fett 150.00
- Darth Vader Hoth 150.00
- Han Solo 150.00
- Han Solo and Tauntaun 150.00
- Han Solo Hoth 150.00
- Lando Calrissian 150.00
- Luke Skywalker 150.00
- Millennium Falcon Spaceship 150.00
- Princess Leia 150.00
- Princess Leia and Chewbacca 150.00
- Slave I 150.00
- Snow Speeder 150.00

Frito Lay
- Can You Resist framed game cards, promotional 100.00

"...Can´t Resist" peel-to-win game pieces.
- Anakin / Helping [276-37] 5.00
- Darth Maul / Pursuit [276-38] 5.00
- Darth Sidious / Domination [276-39] 5.00
- Jar Jar / Appetite [276-40] 5.00
- Mace Windu / Inquiry [276-41] 5.00
- Nute and Rune / Cowardice [276-42] 5.00
- Obi-Wan / Honor [276-43] 5.00
- Padmé / Curiosity [276-44] 5.00
- Queen Amidala / Duty [276-45] 5.00
- Qui-Gon / Instincts [276-46] 5.00
- R2-D2 / Bravery [276-47] 5.00
- Sebulba / Cheating [276-48] 5.00
- Watto / Chance [276-49] 5.00

Kellogg's (Australia)
- Ewok Adventure Collect-a-Prize piece, any [4:149] 150.00

Picture Name Decoder Discs.
- #1: Princess Leia is cared for by Ewoks [276-50] 45.00
- #2: Ewoks on the forest moon of Endor [276-51] 45.00
- #3: Han Solo and C-3PO hatch a plan [276-52] 45.00
- #4: Max Rebo plays keyboards [276-53] 45.00
- #5: Gamorrean Guard on Jabba's sail barge [276-54] 45.00
- #6: Heroes held captive on moon of Endor [276-55] 45.00
- #7: C-3PO and Logray the Ewok [276-56] 45.00
- #8: Luke Skywalker rescues Princess Leia [276-57] 45.00
- #9: Jabba the Hutt with Bib Fortuna [276-58] 45.00
- #10: Squidhead in Jabba the Hutt's palace [276-59] 45.00
- #11: Darth Vader awaits the Emperor [276-60] 45.00
- #12: Lando Calrissian and Nien Nunb [276-61] 45.00
- #13: Chewbacca captures AT-ST Walker [276-62] 45.00
- #14: Salacious Crumb in Jabba's court [276-63] 45.00
- #15: Luke Skywalker fights Gamorrean Guards [276-64] 45.00
- #16: Jabba turns Leia into dancing girl [276-65] 45.00

Pepsi Cola (UK)
- Find the Rebel Alliance to Win bottle label [4:150] 10.00

Star Wars Trilogy Trivia
Scratch Off: A New Hope
- Another name for Ben Kenobi is: [276-66] 5.00
- Luke's uncle is named: [276-67] 5.00
- Princess Leia claims she was on a diplomatic mission from: [276-68] 5.00
- The Death Star's vulnerable point is: [276-69] 5.00

276-37 | 276-38 | 276-39 | 276-40 | 276-41

 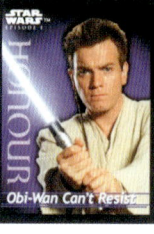      

276-42 | 276-43 | 276-44 | 276-45 | 276-46 | 276-47 | 276-48 | 276-49

Game Pieces, Promotional

276-50   276-51   276-52   276-53   276-54

276-55   276-56   276-57   276-58   276-59   276-60

276-61   276-62   276-63   276-64   276-65 Front and Back

Scratch Off: Empire Strikes Back
- During their duel, Darth Vader cuts off Luke's: [276-70] ..5.00
- In what substance is Han frozen? [276-71] 5.00
- Who does Luke encounter in a cave during his Jedi training? [276-72] 5.00
- Who fixes the Falcon's hyper drive motivator? [276-73] ..5.00

Scratch Off: Return of the Jedi
- Leia kills Jabba the Hutt with her: [276-74] 5.00
- The Ewoks live on the forest moon of: [276-75] 5.00
- Who falls in love with Princess Leia? [276-76] 5.00
- Who kills the Emperor? [276-77] 5.00

Taco Bell
Feel the Force peel-off game.
- 1 Luke Skywalker [276-78] 5.00
- 2 Princess Leia [276-79] 5.00
- 3 Han Solo ($100,000 prize winner) ....OSPV
- 4 Obi-Wan Kenobi [276-80] 5.00
- 5 Lando Calrissian [276-81] 5.00
- 6 C-3PO [276-82] 5.00
- 7 Emperor Palpatine [276-83] 5.00
- 8 Darth Vader ($10,000 prize winner) ....OSPV
- 9 Yoda ($1,000 prize winner) ....OSPV
- 10 Chewbacca [276-84] 5.00
- 11 R2-D2 [276-85] 5.00

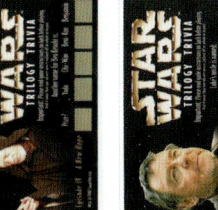    

276-66   276-67   276-68   276-69   276-70   276-71

276-72   276-73   276-74   276-75   276-76   276-77   276-78 Back and Front

276-79   276-80   276-81   276-82   276-83   276-84   276-85   276-86   276-87

Game Pieces, Promotional

- ☐ 12 (instant winner) 25.00
- ☐ 13 (instant winner) 25.00
- ☐ 14 (instant winner) 25.00
- ☐ 15 (instant winner) 25.00
- ☐ 16 (instant winner) 25.00
- ☐ 17 (instant winner) 25.00
- ☐ 18 (instant winner) 25.00
- ☐ 19 (instant winner) 25.00
- ☐ 20 (wristwatch instant winner) 25.00
- ☐ 21 Nien Nunb (food winner) [276-86] 25.00
- ☐ 22 Rancor monster (food winner) 25.00
- ☐ 23 Salacious Crumb (food winner) [276-87] .. 25.00
- ☐ 24 Tusken Raider (food winner) 25.00

Toys R Us
- ☐ Destroy The Death Star scratch off [v1e1-233] 15.00

Tricon Global Restaurants, Inc.
Defeat the Dark Side instant winners.
- ☐ $10,000 VISA shopping spree .... OSPV
- ☐ 2-piece chicken meal at KFC or combo meal at Taco Bell [276-88] 10.00
- ☐ 3-piece chicken snack at KFC or nachos supreme at Taco Bell 10.00
- ☐ Apple Imac computer 10.00
- ☐ Bread sticks at Pizza Hut, regular nachos at Taco Bell .. 10.00
- ☐ Crispy strips at KFC or taco at Taco Bell [276-89] .. 10.00
- ☐ Crispy strips at KFC or soft taco at Taco Bell 10.00
- ☐ Darth Maul CD-player .... OSPV
- ☐ Individual side item at KFC or regular nachos at Taco Bell [276-89] 10.00
- ☐ Individual side item at KFC or Pepsi 2 liter / 2 dine-in beverages at Pizza Hut 10.00
- ☐ Individual dessert at KFC or cinnamon twists at Taco Bell [276-90] 10.00
- ☐ Lincoln Navigator .... OSPV
- ☐ Lucas Learning Episode I PC/Mac game ..... OSPV
- ☐ LucasArt Entertainment Episode I CD-ROM game ...... OSPV
- ☐ Meade refracting telescope .... OSPV
- ☐ Medium 3-topping pizza at Pizza Hut or 8-piece chicken meal at KFC 10.00
- ☐ Nintendo 64 with Episode I Racer cartridge .... OSPV
- ☐ Official Star Wars Fan Club membership 25.00
- ☐ Pepsi 2 liter / 2 dine-in beverages at Pizza Hut or original taco at Taco Bell 10.00
- ☐ Pepsi 2 liter / 2 dine-in beverages at Pizza Hut or regular nachos at Taco Bell 10.00
- ☐ Seneca Sports wheeled sports package ..... OSPV
- ☐ Star Wars Speeder .... OSPV
- ☐ THX home entertainment system .... OSPV
- ☐ Trip for 2 around the world .... OSPV

Defeat the Dark Side.
- ☐ #1 Ric Olié, $10,000 winner [276-91] 3.00
- ☐ #2 Daultay Dofine, $10,000 winner [276-92] .... OSPV
- ☐ #3 R2-D2, $10,000 winner [276-93] 3.00
- ☐ #4 Yoda, $1,000 winner [276-94] 0.00
- ☐ #5 Mace Windu, $1,000 winner [276-95] 3.00
- ☐ #6 Sebulba, $1,000,000 winner [276-96] 3.00
- ☐ #7 Anakin Skywalker, $1,000,000 winner [276-97] 3.00
- ☐ #8 Watto, $1,000,000 winner [276-98] 3.00
- ☐ #9 C-3PO, $1,000,000 winner [276-99] 3.00
- ☐ #10 Shmi Skywalker, $1,000,000 winner, only 1 produced—not redeemed [276-100] .... OSPV
- ☐ #11 Darth Maul, $1,000,000 winner [276-101] 3.00
- ☐ #12 Qui-Gon Jinn, $1,000,000 winner [276-102] 3.00
- ☐ #13 Battle Droid, $1,000,000 winner, only 1 produced—not redeemed [276-103] .... OSPV
- ☐ #14 Jar Jar Binks, $1,000,000 winner [276-104] 3.00
- ☐ #15 Boss Nass, $1,000,000 winner [276-105] 3.00
- ☐ #16 Queen Amidala, $1,000,000 winner [276-106] 3.00
- ☐ #17 Senator Palpatine, $1,000,000 winner [276-107] ... 3.00
- ☐ #18 Obi-Wan Kenobi, $1,000,000 winner [276-108] 3.00
- ☐ #19 Darth Sidious, $1,000,000 winner [276-109] 3.00
- ☐ #20 Chancellor Velorum, $1,000,000 winner, only 1 produced—not redeemed [276-110] .... OSPV
- ☐ Unopened 2-pack 10.00
- ☐ Unopened pack of 50 .... 150.00
- ☐ Unopened single 5.00

Walkers (UK)
"Can You Resist?" scratch off game. Episode I characters.
- ☐ Any character [276-111] 15.00

Geocaching Coins and Path Tags
Continued in Volume 3, Page 236

Astromech (dome).
- ☐ Black detail 50.00
- ☐ Red detail [v1e1-172] 50.00

234

Gift Cards

 277-01
 277-02
 277-03
 277-04
 277-05
 277-06
 277-07
 277-08

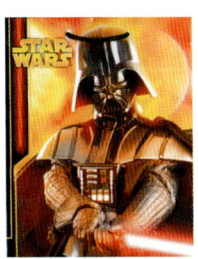 277-09
 277-10
 277-11
 277-12
 277-13
 277-14
 278-01

Cache Wars.
- ❏ Logo, brass colored [v1e1:172] 30.00
- ❏ Logo, silver colored 35.00

GeoSmurfs.
- ❏ Blue smurf, brown garb, blue lightsaber [v1e1:172] 25.00
- ❏ Red smurf, black garb, red sparkle lightsaber 25.00

Gift Bags
Continued in Volume 3, Page 236

- ❏ B-Wing Fighter attack..............................15.00
- ❏ Empire Strikes Back 26.00
- ❏ Return of the Jedi SE [277-01] 26.00
- ❏ Space battle above second Death Star 10.00
- ❏ X-Wings 10.00

Die-cut top.
- ❏ Chewbacca [277-02] 10.00
- ❏ Darth Vader.......................................10.00
- ❏ Darth Vader with stormtroopers [277-03] 10.00
- ❏ R2-D2 [277-04] 10.00

Shopping-style.
- ❏ Droids, R2-D2 and C-3PO 35.00

Animations.
- ❏ Darth Vader, exclusive to Target..................5.00
- ❏ Yoda, exclusive to Target 5.00

Cleo
- ❏ Episode I...10.00

Expressions
Gift bags.
- ❏ Clone Wars Jedi / Clone Wars Villains [277-05]............10.00
- ❏ LEGO Star Wars [277-06] 10.00
- ❏ LEGO Star Wars [277-07] 10.00
- ❏ Luke and Alliance heroes / Darth Vader and Imperials ..10.00

Fan Club
- ❏ Star Wars Celebration.............................20.00

Hallmark
Classic trilogy.
- ❏ Join the Dark Side 12.00

Clone Wars.
- ❏ Ahsoka, Obi-Wan, Anakin, Yoda 12.00
- ❏ Captain Rex / Yoda [277-08] 12.00
- ❏ Clones / Captain Rex 12.00
- ❏ Jedi / Sith 12.00
- ❏ Yoda, Captain Rex, Anakin, Obi-Wan................12.00

Revenge of the Sith.
- ❏ Darth Vader [277-09] 12.00
- ❏ Yoda / Darth Vader [277-10] 12.00

LEGO Star Wars.
- ❏ Darth Vader and stormtroopers [277-11]............12.00

Hallmark / Expressions
- ❏ Darth Vader [277-12] 12.00

LEGO characters.
- ❏ Han, Luke, Chewbacca, Yoda, Birthday in a Bag. Gift bag, birthday card, tissue sheets.. Card: "It's Your Destiny" / "... to have a Happy Birthday!" [277-13] 12.00
- ❏ Han, Luke, Leia, Yoda / Darth Vader and Stormtroopers, Death Star gift card attached [277-14] 12.00

Hallmark / Presentations
Gift bags with tag and tissue.
- ❏ Anakin, Captain Rex, Commander Cody 15.00

Gift Boxes
Continued in Volume 3, Page 237

Expressions
- ❏ Yoda / Darth Vader................................20.00

Hallmark / Presentations
- ❏ Clone Wars [278-01] 20.00

Gift Cards
Continued in Volume 3, Page 237

Barnes and Noble
- ❏ Clone Wars [279-01] 10.00

 279-01 Front and Sleeve Side 1 and Sleeve Side 2

 279-02
 279-03
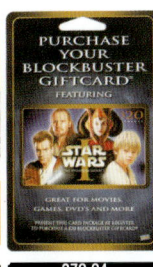 279-04
 279-05

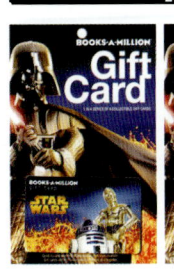 279-06
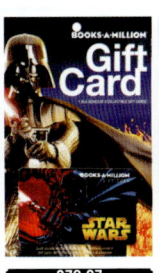 279-07
 279-08
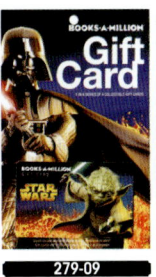 279-09
 279-10
 279-11

 279-12 Front and Sleeve
 279-13

Gift Cards

   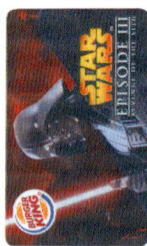 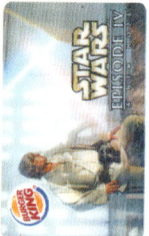    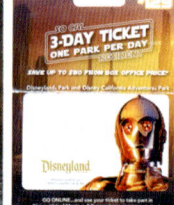

279-14 Image 1 and Image 2 | 279-15 | 279-16 | 279-17 | 279-18 Image 1 and Image 2 | 279-19 | 279-20

279-21 | 279-22 | 279-23 | 279-24 | 279-25 | 279-26 | 279-27 | 279-28

BioWare
☐ 2400 cartel Coins—Star Wars the Old Republic [279-02]..5.00

Blockbuster Video
☐ Battlefront $15 [279-03] 20.00
☐ Episode I: The Phantom Menace $20 [279-04]..............20.00
☐ Star Wars Trilogy 7 Week Rental Card [v1e1 234].........20.00
☐ Yoda $10 [279-05]......................................20.00

Books-a-Million
Episode III: Revenge of the Sith.
☐ C-3PO and R2-D2 [279-06]...............................10.00
☐ Darth Vader [279-07]...................................10.00
☐ Epic Duel [279-08].....................................10.00
☐ Master Yoda [279-09]...................................10.00

Borders, Inc.
☐ Anakin in podracer helmet, $25 gift card [279-10].......10.00
☐ Darth Maul, $50 gift card [279-11].....................10.00

Episode III: Revenge of the Sith.
☐ Darth Vader [279-12]...................................10.00

Burger King
☐ Episode III characters [279-13]........................10.00

Lenticular scenes from each movie.
☐ EP1: Darth Maul / Darth Maul vs. Obi-Wan Kenobi [279-14]...............................15.00
☐ EP2: Yoda vs. Count Dooku [279-15].....................15.00
☐ EP3: Anakin Skywalker / Darth Vader [279-16]...........15.00
☐ EP4: Luke Skywalker / Darth Vader vs. Obi-Wan Kenobi [279-17]..........................15.00
☐ EP5: Boba Fett / Han Solo [279-18].....................15.00
☐ EP6: Jabba the Hutt / Captive Princess Leia [279-19]...15.00

Disneyland Resorts
☐ Southern California 3-Day Ticket [279-20]..............25.00

Hot Topic
☐ Movie poster art on C-3PO and R2-D2 hanger card [279-21]...10.00

K-Mart
☐ Anakin in podracer helmet, $50 cash card, May 1999 [279-22]..25.00
☐ Darth Maul, $50 cash card, September 1999.............25.00
☐ Jar Jar Binks, $50 cash card, June 1999................25.00
☐ Queen Amidala, $50 cash card, August 1999.............25.00
☐ Qui-Gon Jinn, $50 cash card, July 1999 [279-23]........25.00

LucasArts
60 day prepaid game cards.
☐ Boba Fett [279-24].....................................10.00
☐ Darth Vader [279-25]...................................10.00
☐ Human [279-26]...10.00
☐ Mos Eisley [279-27]....................................10.00
☐ Wookiee [279-28].......................................10.00

Sideshow Collectibles
☐ 30th anniversary, exclusive to Star Wars Celebration IV [279-29]....................................5.00

Sony Online Entertainment
☐ Captain Argyus station cash [279-30]..................10.00

Suncoast
☐ Anakin Skywalker......................................15.00
☐ Darth Maul [279-31]...................................15.00

Target
☐ Darth Vader, lights up and breaths [279-32]...........15.00

Tower Records
☐ Anakin and Padmé [279-33].............................25.00
☐ Jango [279-34]..25.00
☐ Movie poster art [279-35].............................25.00
☐ Yoda [279-36]...25.00

Toys R Us
☐ Battlefront $10 gift card [279-37]....................15.00
☐ Captain Rex / Clones [279-38].........................15.00
☐ Clone Wars [279-39]...................................15.00
☐ Darth Vader [279-40]..................................15.00
☐ Darth Vader, close-up [279-41]........................15.00

Toys R Us (Canada)
☐ LEGO TIE Interceptor [279-42].........................20.00

Toys R Us (UK)
☐ Anakin Skywalker and Obi-Wan Kenobi, 10£ [279-43].....20.00

Walmart
☐ Six episode saga [279-44].............................10.00

        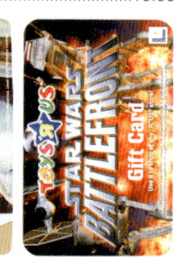

279-29 | 279-30 | 279-31 | 279-32 | 279-33 | 279-34 | 279-35 | 279-36 | 279-37

279-38 | 279-39 | 279-40 | 279-41 | 279-42 | 279-43 | 279-44 | 279-45

Gift Wrap

    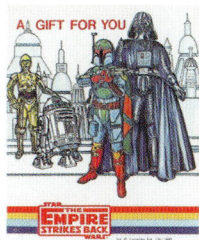  

280-01 280-02 280-03 280-04 280-05 280-06 280-07

 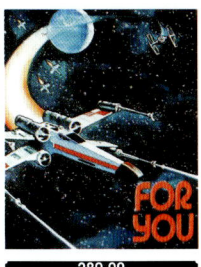     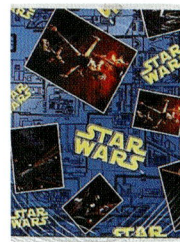

280-08 280-09 280-10 280-11 280-12 280-13 281-01

Episode III: Revenge of the Sith video game.
- ❏ PlayStation2...5.00
- ❏ Xbox..5.00

Reflective; combine to make one image.
- ❏ Anakin Skywalker, C-3PO, and R2-D2.................5.00
- ❏ General Grievous and Darth Sidious...................5.00
- ❏ Obi-Wan Kenobi..5.00
- ❏ Tri Fighters and Jedi Starfighter.......................5.00
- ❏ Yoda and Clone trooper..................................5.00

Woolworths (UK)
- ❏ Darth Vader [279-45]......................................10.00

Gift Certificates

Clarks of England (UK)
- ❏ Star Wars with original art [4:153]....................25.00

Gift Tags
Continued in Volume 3, Page 238

- ❏ 10-pack, R2-D2 and Jar Jar Binks [280-01].............8.00

Cleo
- ❏ 30 Foil-leaf gift tags, Episode I [280-02]...............10.00
- ❏ 30 Foil-leaf gift tags, Episode I, exclusive to Walmart [280-03]..12.00

Drawing Board Greeting Cards, Inc.
- ❏ C-3PO and R2-D2, card art...............................10.00
- ❏ C-3PO and R2-D2, card photo..........................10.00
- ❏ C-3PO and R2-D2, tag self-adhesive 5-pack [280-04]....20.00
- ❏ Cloud City, card [280-05]................................10.00
- ❏ Darth Vader and Luke Duel, card [280-06]...........10.00
- ❏ Ewoks Hang-Gliding, tag [280-07]....................12.00
- ❏ Leia, Luke, and Han, card...............................12.00
- ❏ R2-D2, stick-on decoration [280-08]..................15.00
- ❏ X-Wing Fighter, card [280-09].........................10.00
- ❏ Yoda, stick-on decoration [280-10]...................12.00

Hallmark
- ❏ Classic Neon...5.00
- ❏ Darth Vader..5.00
- ❏ LEGO Star Wars, 3 sheets of 6 [280-11]...............8.00
- ❏ R2-D2, die-cut [280-12]..................................5.00
- ❏ The Phantom Menace C-3PO and R2-D2 [280-13]......5.00

Gift Wrap
Continued in Volume 3, Page 238

Ambassador
- ❏ Attack of the Clones characters and vehicles against blue star field [4:154]....................................10.00
- ❏ Clone Wars characters [4:153].........................10.00
- ❏ Star Wars classic trilogy, blue starfield background [4:153]..10.00
- ❏ Star Wars classic trilogy, starship battles on blue technical background, folded [281-01]..........10.00

Cleo
- ❏ Clone Wars characters, exclusive to Target.........10.00
- ❏ Podracer, red sparkled...................................12.00
- ❏ Space Battle, black sparkled............................12.00

Danilo Promotions Ltd. (UK)
- ❏ Darth Maul [281-02].......................................10.00

Drawing Board Greeting Cards, Inc.
- ❏ C-3PO, R2-D2, Darth Vader, and battle scene, 12 foot roll [v1e1:235]..................................20.00
- ❏ C-3PO, R2-D2, Darth Vader, and battle scene, 5 ft roll..15.00
- ❏ C-3PO, R2-D2, Darth Vader, and battle scene, folded [281-03]..15.00
- ❏ Characters Empire Strikes Back, folded [281-04]....15.00
- ❏ Characters Star Wars, folded [281-05]...............15.00
- ❏ Cloud City, folded..15.00
- ❏ Cloud City, roll..20.00
- ❏ Darth Vader and Luke Duel, folded [281-06]........15.00
- ❏ Darth Vader and Luke Duel, roll........................20.00
- ❏ Dogfight, folded [281-07]................................15.00
- ❏ Dogfight, roll [v1e1:235].................................30.00
- ❏ Ewoks Hang-Gliding, folded [281-08]................20.00
- ❏ Ewoks Hang-Gliding, roll.................................25.00
- ❏ "Happy Birthday" with photos, folded [281-09]....15.00
- ❏ "Happy Birthday" with photos, roll [v1e1:235]....20.00

Gemma International (UK)
2 Sheets, 2 tags.
- ❏ Clone Wars [281-10].......................................15.00
- ❏ Star Wars [281-11]...15.00

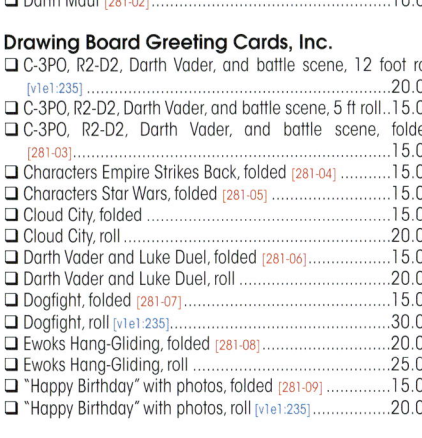

   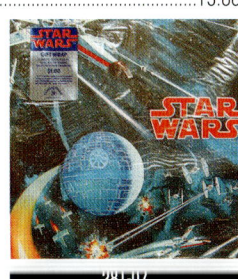

281-02 281-03 281-04 281-05 281-06 281-07

    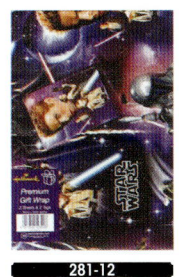  

281-08 281-09 281-10 281-11 281-12 281-13 281-14

237

Gift Wrap

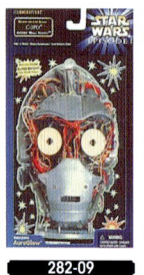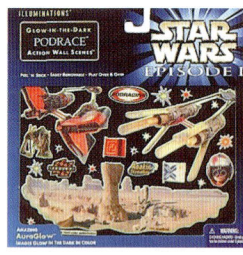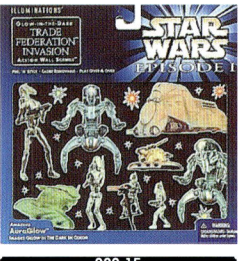

Hallmark
15 square foot rolls.
- ❏ Clone Wars heroes 15.00
- ❏ Yoda and Darth Vader, X-Wings and TIE Fighters 15.00

20 square foot rolls.
- ❏ Clone Wars characters on blue background, ARC troopers and Savage Opress, individually numbered 15.00
- ❏ Saga Characters on blue background........................15.00

70 square foot rolls.
- ❏ LEGO Star Wars 20.00

Hallmark (UK)
Episode II, folded.
- ❏ Characters [281-12] 10.00
- ❏ Characters and Vehicles, blue foil [281-13] 10.00

Marks and Spencer (UK)
2 Sheets, 2 tags.
- ❏ Episode I: The Phantom Menace [281-14].....................15.00

Glow In The Dark Decorations

Glow Zone
- ❏ Anakin Skywalker wall plaque [282-01].....................15.00
- ❏ Darth Maul wall plaque [282-02].................................15.00

8 Glow-in-the-dark decorations.
- ❏ Classic trilogy [282-03]..25.00
- ❏ The Phantom Menace [282-04]....................................20.00

Illuminations
- ❏ Queen Amidala [282-05] 12.00

Action Wall Scenes.
- ❏ Battle Zone [282-06] 20.00
- ❏ Characters [282-07] 20.00
- ❏ Heroes, Villains, and Droids [282-08] 20.00

Action Wall Scenes. 36 pieces in plastic envelope.
- ❏ Droids [v1e1:236]..10.00
- ❏ Jedi vs. Sith [v1e1:236] 10.00
- ❏ Land Battle [v1e1:236] 10.00
- ❏ Space Battle [v1e1:236]...10.00

Box of approximately 40 pieces.
- ❏ Characters [v1e1:236]..20.00
- ❏ Land Battle [v1e1:236] 20.00
- ❏ Podrace [v1e1:236]..20.00
- ❏ Space Battle [v1e1:236]...20.00

Decals, character's head.
- ❏ C-3PO [282-09] 10.00
- ❏ Darth Maul [282-10] 10.00
- ❏ Jar Jar Binks [282-11] 10.00
- ❏ Obi-Wan Kenobi [282-12] 10.00

Decals, flat 10" x 9.5" Action Wall Scenes.
- ❏ Droids [282-13] 15.00
- ❏ Gungan Adventure [v1e1:236]....................................15.00
- ❏ Jedi vs. Sith 15.00
- ❏ Podrace [282-14]...15.00
- ❏ Space Battle [v1e1:236]...15.00
- ❏ Trade Federation Invasion [282-15] 15.00

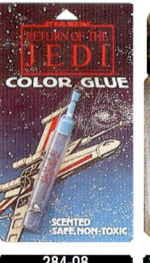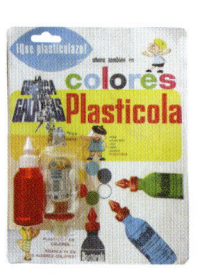

Greeting Cards

285-01

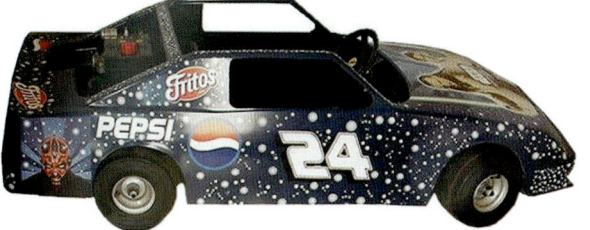
285-02

286-01

286-02

Golf Club Covers

Bridgestone Sports (Japan)
- ☐ Darth Vader...45.00
- ☐ Stormtrooper..45.00
- ☐ TIE Fighter..45.00

Comic Images
- ☐ Chewbacca...25.00
- ☐ Darth Vader...25.00
- ☐ Stormtrooper..25.00
- ☐ Yoda..20.00

287-01

287-02 Front and Back

287-03

287-04

287-05

Decals, flat 13" x 10.5" Action Wall Scenes.
- ☐ Battle Droids [v1e1:237]..................................15.00
- ☐ Jedi [282-16]...15.00

Joker Ltd. (Switzerland)
Power Glow medallions.
- ☐ 3-piece Queen Amidala [282-17]........................15.00
- ☐ 3-piece Starships, hero [282-18].......................15.00
- ☐ 3-piece Starships, villain [282-19].....................15.00
- ☐ 3-piece Villains [282-20].................................15.00
- ☐ 5-piece Starship battles [282-21].......................15.00
- ☐ 10-piece Heroes [v1e1:237]..............................25.00
- ☐ 10-piece Villains [v1e1:237].............................25.00

Glowsticks
Continued in Volume 3, Page 238

Gemma International (UK)
Approximately 12".
- ☐ Blue..8.00
- ☐ Green [283-01]..8.00
- ☐ Red..8.00

Glue

Beecham Italia S.p.A. (Italy)
UHU glue pads Clone Wars.
- ☐ 40-pack [284-01]..15.00
- ☐ 40-pack with free second sheet [284-02]..............20.00

UHU glue stick with Kenner Ewok figure. Some figures additionally in baggie inside the plastic bubble.
- ☐ Logray [284-03]..500.00
- ☐ Lumat...500.00
- ☐ Paploo..500.00
- ☐ Teebo [284-04]..500.00
- ☐ Warok..500.00

UHU glue stick. Clone Wars. Any of 8 random characters on glue barrels.
- ☐ 2-pack, Ahsoka / Yoda, 21 g glue sticks [284-05]......40.00
- ☐ 2-pack, Anakin / Ahsoka, 8 g glue sticks [284-06].....40.00
- ☐ 4-pack, Ahsoka / R2-D2, 1 free glue stick [284-07]...75.00

Butterfly Originals
- ☐ Color glue, Return of the Jedi [284-08]................15.00

Flomo (UK)
- ☐ Star Wars logo on prismatic background [284-09]......8.00

Impact, Inc.
- ☐ R2-D2 glue stick [284-10]................................10.00

Plasticola (Argentina)
Colored glue with R2-D2 pencil sharpener. The pencil sharpener differs from the vintage action figure in construction. It is smaller and the dome does not turn.
- ☐ Bottled glue, any color [284-11].........................800.00

Rose Art Industries
- ☐ Lightsaber glue stick [284-12]...........................10.00

Episode III: Revenge of the Sith
- ☐ Darth Vader light-up glue bottle.........................20.00
- ☐ Lightsaber glue stick [284-13]...........................10.00

Go Carts
- ☐ Darth Vader [285-01]....................................375.00
- ☐ Darth Vader go kart, 6v rechargeable..................500.00
- ☐ Darth Vader motorbike, 12v rechargeable.............325.00

Manco Productions
- ☐ Episode I, motorized [285-02].........................1,500.00

Golf Bags

Bridgestone Sports (Japan)
- ☐ Darth Vader [286-01]....................................850.00
- ☐ Stormtrooper [286-02]...................................850.00

Golf Ball Markers

Bridgestone Sports (Japan)
- ☐ Star Wars themes..35.00

Goodie Bags
Continued in Volume 3, Page 239

Look-o-Look
- ☐ Chupa Chups sucker, sticker, and Chewbacca head sucker holder [287-01]..10.00

Party Express
- ☐ Darth Vader / Saga, activity card, whistle, sticker, maze, ring [287-02]..10.00
- ☐ Episode III: Revenge of the Sith, activity card, sticker, thumb wrestler, and 2 suckers [287-03]...................10.00

Tapper Candies
Episode I: The Phantom Menace: Character mask, Darth Maul sticker, Smarties candy, Chupa-Chups lollipop, Jedi vs. Sith coin battle game.
- ☐ Anakin, lightsaber yo-yo [v1e1:237]...................10.00
- ☐ Anakin, slap band..10.00
- ☐ Darth Maul, lightsaber yo-yo [287-04].................10.00
- ☐ Darth Maul, slap band [v1e1:237].....................10.00

Episode II: Attack of the Clones.
- ☐ Activity card, sticker, party favor, and candy [287-05].....10.00

Greeting Cards
Continued in Volume 3, Page 239

- ☐ "A long, long, long time ago ..." / "You were born.", oversized [288-01]...10.00
- ☐ Darth Vader, "5"..10.00
- ☐ Darth's nephew ... Bruce Vader [288-02].............10.00
- ☐ R2-D2, "Beep-beep! Fweep! Weeeoooo!" [288-03]...10.00
- ☐ Yoda delivering presents using the force, 10 cards with envelopes...25.00
- ☐ Yoda, Episode II,...10.00

288-01

288-02

288-03

288-04

288-05

288-06

288-07

288-08

288-09

Greeting Cards

Episode II. Approximately 8" x 5"
- Heroes / Celebrate [288-04] 10.00
- Jango Fett / Happy Birthday [288-05] 10.00
- Obi-Wan Kenobi / Have a Great Day [288-06] 10.00
- Padmé Amidala / Enjoy Your Birthday [288-07] 10.00

(France)
Tous ensemble pour le le meilleur et pour l'empire.
- Classic book cover art [288-08] 10.00
- Heroes on Hoth [288-09] 10.00
- Leia / Jabba [288-10] 10.00
- Luke [288-11] 10.00
- Movie poster cover art [288-12] 10.00
- Novel cover art [288-13] 10.00
- R2-D2 / C-3PO [288-14] 10.00

Un anniversaire intergalactique
- Chewbacca [288-15] 10.00
- Darth Vader [288-16] 10.00
- Leia [288-17] 10.00
- Yoda [288-18] 10.00

501st Legion
- Rudolph / Hoth, "Happy Holidays from the 501st Legion," art by Matt Busch [288-19] 25.00

98% Funny
- Revenge of the Rabbi [v1e1:238] 10.00

Danilo Promotions Ltd. (UK)
- C-3PO / R2-D2, "By my calculations, Artoo ..." [288-20] ...10.00
- Captain Rex/Anakin/Obi-Wan, "Birthday Boy" [288-21] ...10.00
- Chewbacca and Tarful, "Go wild this birthday and talk nonsense ..." [288-22] 10.00
- Darth Vader, "I know what you've got for your birthday ..." [288-23] 10.00
- Princess Leia, "Princess for a Day" [288-24] 10.00
- Space, "A long time ago in a galaxy far far away ..." [v1e1:238] 10.00
- Yoda, "Use the force this Birthday ..." (blue) [288-25] ...10.00
- Yoda, "Use the force this Birthday ..." (green) [288-26] ...10.00

Episode I: The Phantom Menace.
- Anakin, "Stay away from those energy binders ..." [288-27] 10.00
- Battle Droid, "Droids to Battle Stations!" [288-28] ...10.00
- Darth Maul [4:155] 10.00
- Darth Maul, "At last we will have revenge ..." [288-29] ...10.00
- Darth Maul, "You're another year older ..." [288-30] ...10.00
- Jedi Council [4:155] 10.00
- Jedi vs. Sith, "May the Force be with you ..." [288-31] ...10.00
- Obi-Wan vs. Darth Maul [v1e1:238] 10.00
- Obi-Wan, padawan [4:155] 10.00
- Qui-Gon Jinn [4:155] 10.00
- Qui-Gon Jinn with glittered border, blank 10.00
- Qui-Gon Jinn, "You May Be Another year Older ..." ...10.00
- Yoda, "Time for Reflection on your Birthday" [288-32] ...10.00

Episode I: The Phantom Menace. Mini standees.
- Obi-Wan Kenobi, "May the Force be with you On Your Birthday!" 12.00

For a relative.
- Anakin / Obi-Wan / Yoda / Ahsoka, "Happy Birthday Son" [288-33] 10.00
- Anakin / Yoda, "Happy Birthday Nephew" [288-34] ...10.00

For a relative. Includes a button.
- Anakin Skywalker, "Happy Birthday Nephew" [288-35] ...12.00
- Darth Vader, "Happy birthday Dad" [288-36] 12.00
- Darth Vader, "Happy birthday Son. You may be another year older..." [288-37] 12.00
- Obi-Wan / Anakin / Clones, "Brother—Today is a special day" [288-38] 12.00
- Vader, "Happy birthday Brother." [288-39] 12.00
- Yoda, "Happy Birthday Grandson—Another year older you are ..." [288-40] 12.00
- Yoda, "Son. Special you are..." [288-41] 12.00

Includes a button.
- Anakin, "On this birthday..." [288-42] 12.00
- Darth Vader, "Birthday Greetings..." [288-43] 12.00
- Episode III, "Happy Birthday Grandson" [288-44] ...12.00
- Obi-Wan / Clones / Anakin / Yoda, "The day has come... We must join forces..." [288-45] 12.00
- Yoda, "Happy Birthday Jedi" [288-46] 12.00
- Yoda, "Your special day it is" [288-47] 12.00

Specific birthday. Includes a button.
- "10 Today" / "Jedi" [288-48] 12.00
- "10 Today" / "10 Today" [288-49] 12.00
- "10 Today" / "Obey Your Master" [288-50] 12.00
- "11 Today" / "Use the Force" [288-51] 12.00
- " 6 Today" / "6 Today" [288-52] 12.00
- " 6 Today" / "6 Today" [288-53] 12.00
- " 7 Today" / "7 Today" [288-54] 12.00
- " 7 Today" / "7 Today" [288-55] 12.00
- " 8 Today" / "8 Today" [288-56] 12.00
- " 8 Today" / "8 Today" [288-57] 12.00
- " 9 Today—Let's Celebrate!" [288-58] 12.00
- " 9 Today" / "Jedi Starfighter" [288-59] 12.00
- " 9 Today" / "Use the Force" [288-60] 12.00

Talking cards.
- Darth Vader, "Birthday Greetings..." [288-61] 15.00
- Obi-Wan Kenobi, "A special birthday message to you Son" [288-62] 15.00
- Yoda, "21 Today" [288-63] 15.00
- Yoda, "A special day this is ..." [288-64] 15.00
- Yoda, "Another year older you may be ..." [288-65] ...15.00
- Yoda, "Be Mindful and Use the Force" [288-66] ..15.00

DCI Studios
Tomato Cards.
- A Long, long, long time ago in a galaxy not too far away ... you were born. Happy Birthday [288-67] 8.00
- Far away in a galaxy, a long, long, long time ago ... You were born [v1e1:239] 8.00

Drawing Board Greeting Cards, Inc.
- C-3PO and R2-D2 floating away with balloons ...15.00
- C-3PO and R2-D2, "For A Fine Boy" [288-68] 15.00
- C-3PO sitting and thinking, embossed 15.00
- C-3PO, R2-D2, Aliens, Gamorrean Guard 15.00
- Chewbacca, "Do Not Fear" 15.00
- Chewbacca, Han, Leia, R2-D2, C-3PO, Jabba the Hutt, Wicket 15.00
- Darth Vader, "Space Bulletin for Grandson" 15.00
- Ewok and Princess Leia [288-69] 15.00
- Ewoks: Archery Range 15.00
- Ewoks: Baby Ewoks 15.00
- Ewoks: Ewok in Glider 15.00
- Ewoks: Fishing 15.00
- Ewoks: Nature Study 15.00
- Ewoks: Playing Music 15.00
- Ewoks: Princess Kneesaa and Baga 15.00
- Ewoks: Swimming 15.00
- Female Ewok, "For A Very Special Girl" [288-70] ...15.00

288-37 288-38 288-39 288-40 288-41 288-42 288-43 288-44 288-45 288-46

288-47 288-48 288-49 288-50 288-51 288-52 288-53 288-54 288-55 288-56 288-57

288-58 288-59 288-60 288-61 288-62 288-63 288-64 288-65 288-66

288-67 288-68 288-69 288-70 288-71 288-72 288-73 288-74 288-75

288-76 288-77 288-78 288-79 288-80 288-81 288-82 288-83 288-84

288-85 288-86 288-87 288-88 288-89 288-90 288-91 288-92 288-93

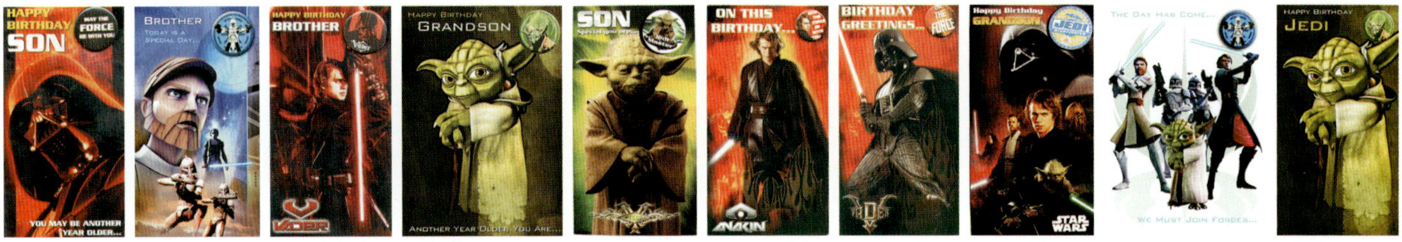

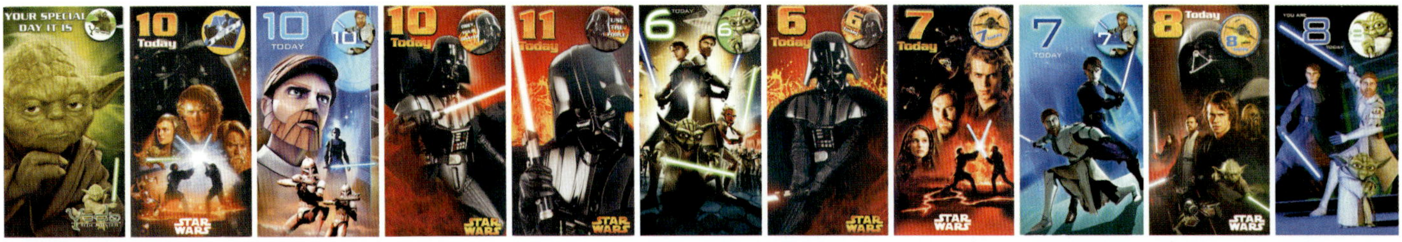

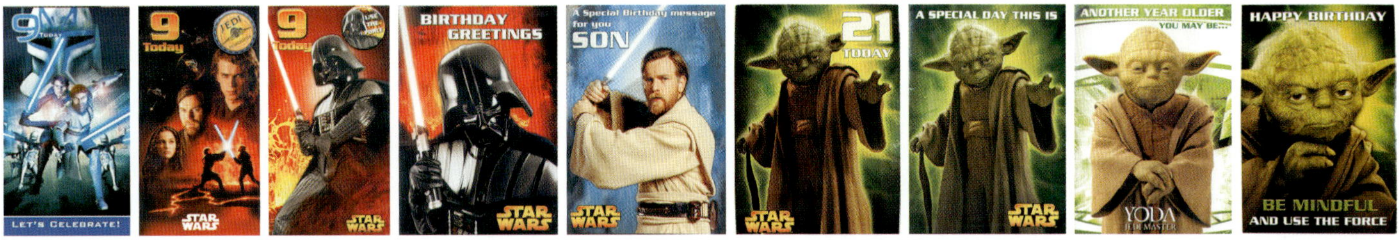

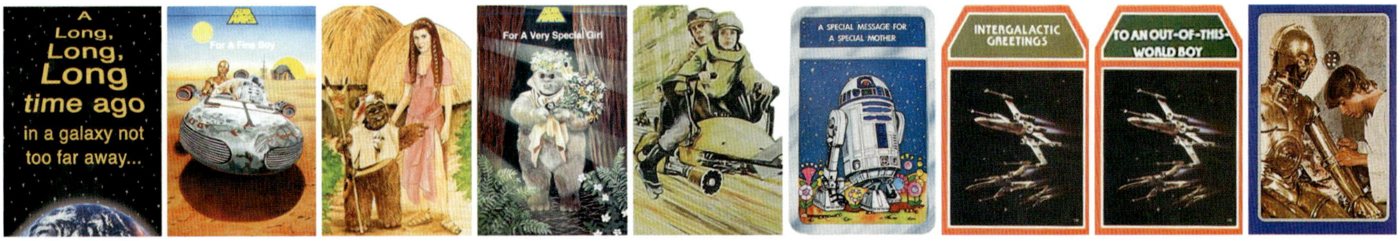

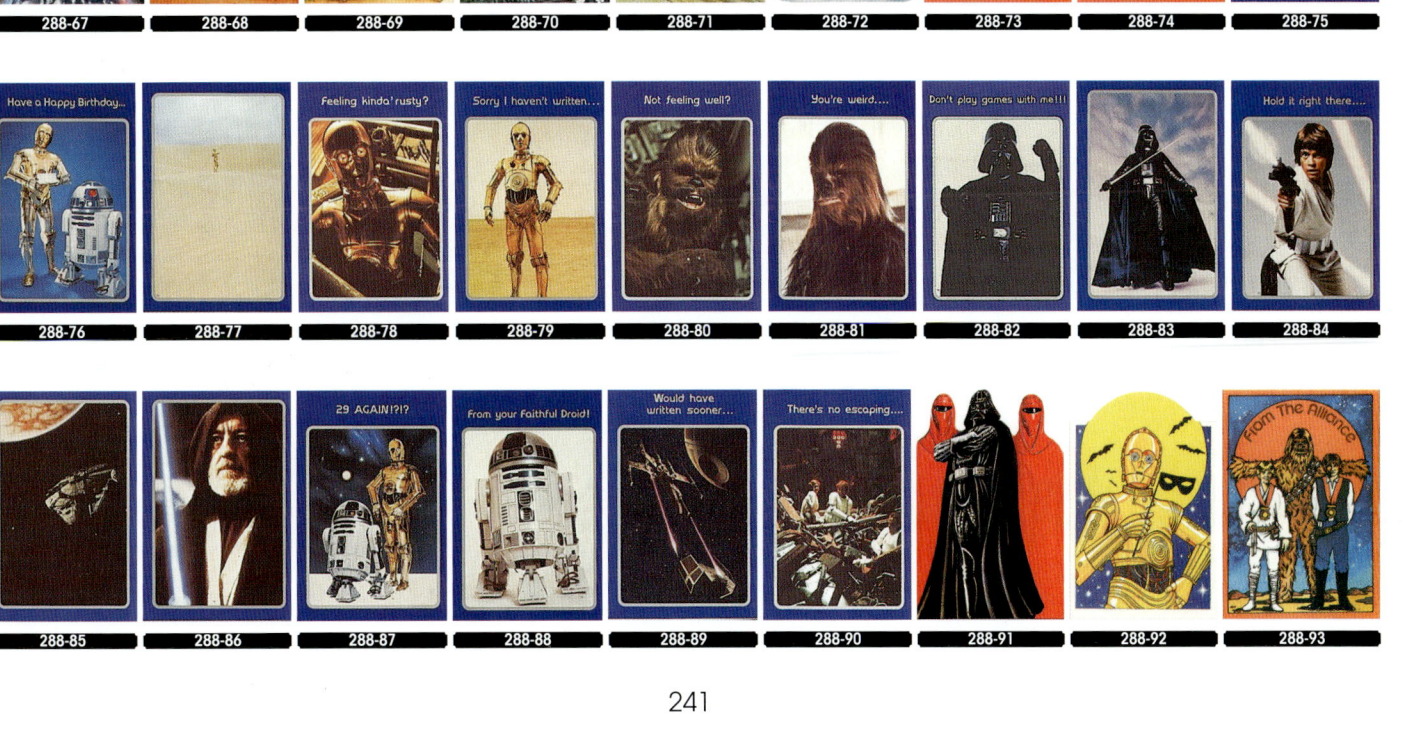

Greeting Cards

 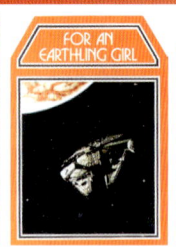  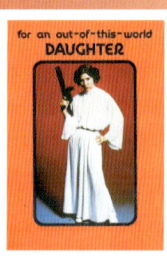 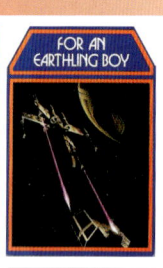     

288-94 | 288-95 | 288-96 | 288-97 | 288-98 | 288-99 | 288-100 | 288-101 | 288-102 | 288-103

     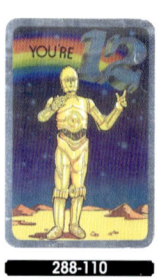    

288-104 | 288-105 | 288-106 | 288-107 | 288-108 | 288-109 | 288-110 | 288-111 | 288-112 | 288-113

288-114 | 288-115 | 288-116 | 288-117 | 288-118 | 288-119 | 288-120 | 288-121 | 288-122

288-123 | 288-124 | 288-125 | 288-126 | 288-127 | 288-128 | 288-129 | 288-130 | 288-131

  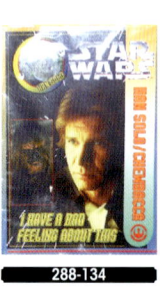 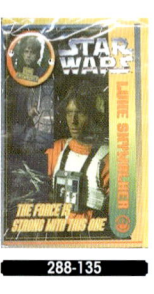    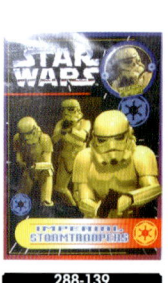

288-132 | 288-133 | 288-134 | 288-135 | 288-136 | 288-137 | 288-138 | 288-139

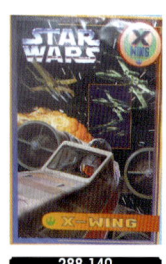       

288-140 | 288-141 | 288-142 | 288-143 | 288-144 | 288-145 | 288-146 | 288-147

Greeting Cards

❏ Han, Leia, and Luke [4:156] 15.00
❏ Hoojibs and R2-D2 ....15.00
❏ Leia and Luke on Speederbike [288-71] 15.00
❏ R2-D2, "A Special Message for a Special Mother" [288-72] 15.00
❏ X-Wing Fighters, "Intergalactic Greetings" [288-73] ...15.00
❏ X-Wing Fighters, "To An Out-Of-This-World Boy" [288-74] 15.00

Blue border design.
❏ C-3PO and Luke Skywalker in Ben's Hut [288-75] 15.00
❏ C-3PO holding birthday cake, and R2-D2 [288-76] 15.00
❏ C-3PO Lost on Tatooine [288-77] 15.00
❏ C-3PO, "Feeling Kinda Rusty" [288-78] 15.00
❏ C-3PO, "Sorry haven't written" [288-79] 15.00
❏ Chewbacca, "Not feeling well?" [288-80] 15.00
❏ Chewbacca, "You're Weird" [288-81] 15.00
❏ Darth Vader, "Don't Play Games With Me!!!" [288-82] ...15.00
❏ Darth Vader, "Happy Birthday, Earthling!" [288-83] ...15.00
❏ Luke Skywalker, "Hold it right there ..." [288-84] 15.00
❏ Millennium Falcon [288-85] 15.00
❏ Obi-Wan, "May the Force be with you" [288-86] 15.00
❏ R2-D2 and C-3PO, "29 Again!?!?" [288-87] 15.00
❏ R2-D2, "From Your Faithful Droid" [288-88] 15.00
❏ Space Dogfight, "Would have written sooner..." [288-89] 15.00
❏ Trash Compactor, "There's no escaping..." [288-90] ...15.00

Friendship, die-cut.
❏ Darth Vader and Emperor's Royal Guards [288-91] 20.00

Halloween.
❏ C-3PO with Mask [288-92] 20.00

❏ Chewbacca, Han, and Luke, "From The Alliance" [288-93] 20.00
❏ Darth Vader with bats 20.00
❏ Luke Skywalker, "For An Out-Of-This-World Son" [288-94] 20.00
❏ Millennium Falcon, "For An Earthling Girl" [288-95] ...20.00
❏ Obi-Wan Kenobi, "Happy Halloween" [288-96] 20.00
❏ Princess Leia, "For An Out-Of-This-World Daughter" [288-97] 20.00
❏ Space Dogfight, "For An Earthling Boy" [288-98] 20.00

Happy Birthday, die-cut, large.
❏ Boba Fett 20.00
❏ C-3PO holding cake [288-99] 20.00
❏ Chewbacca [288-100] 20.00
❏ Darth Vader lightsaber drawn [288-101] 20.00
❏ Han, Leia, and Luke [288-102] 20.00
❏ Luke on Tauntaun [288-103] 20.00
❏ Obi-Wan Kenobi [288-104] 20.00
❏ R2-D2 and C-3PO [288-105] 20.00
❏ R2-D2, "Puh-Wheet! Puh-Wheet!" [288-106] 20.00
❏ Stormtrooper [288-107] 20.00
❏ Yoda [288-108] 20.00

Happy Birthday.
❏ C-3PO and Ewoks [288-109] 20.00
❏ C-3PO and R2-D2, "Happy Birthday" 20.00
❏ C-3PO and R2-D2, "Have a Happy Birthday" 20.00
❏ C-3PO, "You're 12 ..." [288-110] 20.00
❏ Chewbacca, "Now that you're 7 ..." [288-111] 20.00
❏ Chewbacca, Han, and Leia, "Happy Birthday" [288-112] ...20.00
❏ Darth Vader pointing [288-113] 20.00
❏ Darth Vader, 11th birthday [288-114] 20.00

❏ Darth Vader, fold-out game card, birthday 20.00
❏ Ewoks: Kenner Preschool Birthday Club Card 20.00
❏ Max Rebo Band [288-115] 20.00
❏ Obi-Wan Kenobi, "Honored one, now that you're 10 ..." [288-116] 20.00
❏ R2-D2 and Wicket [288-117] 20.00
❏ R2-D2, "Earthling, my calculations confirm that you are 9." [288-118] 20.00
❏ Stormtrooper, 8th birthday 20.00
❏ Wicket with woklings [288-119] 20.00
❏ Yoda, "A Birthday Puzzle for You" [288-120] 20.00

Holidays.
❏ C-3PO and R2-D2, "Enjoy the Holidays" [288-121] ...20.00
❏ C-3PO and R2-D2, "For An Earthling Girl" [288-122] ...20.00
❏ C-3PO and R2-D2, "Peace and Goodwill " 20.00
❏ C-3PO, "For An Out-Of-This-World Grandson" [288-123] ...20.00
❏ Chewbacca, "Happy Holidays" [288-124] 20.00
❏ Obi-Wan Kenobi, "Happy Holidays" [288-125] 20.00
❏ Princess Leia and R2-D2, "For An Out-Of-This-World Granddaughter" [288-126] 20.00
❏ R2-D2 with wreath 20.00

Valentine's Day.
❏ C-3PO and R2-D2, "To Son On Valentine's Day" 20.00
❏ C-3PO, "Valentine Greetings" 20.00
❏ Chewbacca, "To You on Valentine's Day" [288-127] ...20.00
❏ R2-D2, "A Valentine Message for You" 20.00

Fan Club
❏ Reproduction of Christmas in the Stars album cover [v1e1:241] 10.00
❏ Jawa Christmas [v1e1:241] 10.00

288-148 | 288-149 | 288-150 | 288-151 | 288-152 | 288-153 | 288-154 | 288-155

288-156 | 288-157 | 288-158 | 288-159 | 288-160 | 288-161 | 288-162

288-163 | 288-164 | 288-165 | 288-166 | 288-167 | 288-168 | 288-169 | 288-170

288-171 | 288-172 | 288-173 | 288-174 | 288-175 | 288-176 | 288-177

243

Greeting Cards

 288-178
 288-179
 288-180
 288-181
 288-182
 288-183
 288-184
 288-185

 288-186
 288-187
 288-188
 288-189
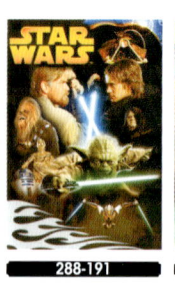 288-190
 288-191
288-192
 288-193

 288-194
 288-195
 288-196
 288-197
 288-198
 288-199
 288-200
 288-201

 288-202
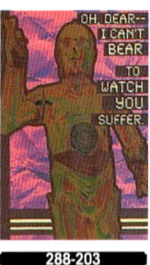 288-203
 288-204
 288-205
 288-206
 288-207
 288-208
 288-209
 288-210

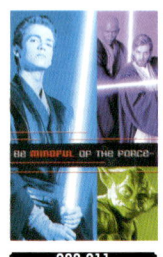 288-211
 288-212
 288-213
 288-214
 288-215
 288-216
 288-217

 288-218
 288-219
 288-220
 288-221
 288-222
 288-223
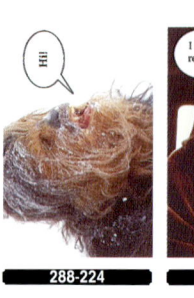 288-224
 288-225

Greeting Cards

Gamma International Ltd.
- Darth Vader children's mask card [288-128] 12.00

Character standee.
- C-3PO and R2-D2, Droid Duo [288-129] 15.00
- Darth Vader, "The Force is Strong with this one..." [288-130] 15.00
- TIE Fighter, "Happy Birthday" [288-131] 15.00

Classic trilogy cards with button included.
- Darth Vader [288-132] 15.00
- Han Leia and Luke [288-133] 15.00
- Han Solo [288-134] 15.00
- Luke Skywalker [288-135] 15.00
- Millennium Falcon [288-136] 15.00
- Obi-Wan [288-137] 15.00
- Princess Leia [288-138] 15.00
- Stormtroopers [288-139] 15.00
- X-Wing Fighter [288-140] 15.00
- Yoda [288-141] 15.00

Hallmark
- "Birthday Greetings ... from the Bark Side!" [288-142] 10.00
- Darth Vader, "C'mon. You're a cool dude ..." [288-143]....10.00
- Darth Vader, "Feel the Power of the Force." [288-144] 12.00
- Darth Vader, "For the last time, I get to put the Death Star on top of the tree!" [288-145] 12.00
- Darth Vader, "It is your destiny to have an unforgettable birthday!" 12.00
- Darth Vader, "The Death Star Will Be Completed on Schedule. And NO, I Don't Need To Read the Instructions!" [288-146]..12.00
- "Happy 6th Birthday Young Jedi" [288-147] 12.00
- If Yoda Were a Dad, "Reckless, you are. Borrow the car, you may not." [288-148] 12.00
- Jedi and Clones, "Happy Birthday, Young Jedi" [288-149] 12.00
- Leia, "It's Your Day so You decide: ..." [288-150] 12.00
- Nephew—Happy Valentine's Day to the neatest nephew in the galaxy! [288-151] 12.00
- Roller Coaster, "Oh My. I think I just oiled Myself!" [288-152] 12.00
- Yoda dog, "Party, you will." [288-153] 10.00
- Yoda, "Joy, celebration, life I feel." [288-154] 12.00

Cards that play sounds from films.
- A long time ago 20.00
- Darth Vader 20.00
- Darth Vader, "I have you now!" [288-155] 20.00
- Do, or do not. 20.00
- Obi-Wan Kenobi, "The Force Must Be Strong With You ..." [288-156] 20.00
- Princess Leia and R2-D2, "My only hope ..." [288-157] ...20.00
- Yoda, "Trying to use the Force to blow out your birthday candles?" [288-158] 20.00

Cards that play video.
- The Force is Strong with This one [288-159] 25.00

Create a custom printed card online from templates.
- Anakin, "You're one year braver, one year stronger..." [288-160] 14.00

Hallmark (Australia)
- Anakin and Padmé, "Be Mine! It is your destiny!" [288-161] 15.00
- Anakin, "It is your destiny! It is ..." [288-162] 15.00
- Heroes, "May the Force be with you ..." [288-163] 15.00
- Jango, "Adventure awaits you!" [288-164] 15.00
- Mace Windu, "The Force will guide you" [288-165] 15.00
- Obi-Wan and Anakin, "The day has come ..." 15.00
- Obi-Wan, Anakin, and Jango, "Be mindful of the Force..." 15.00
- Obi-Wan, "To the wise one ..." [288-166] 15.00
- Padmé, "It is time for you to have a great birthday!" [288-167] 15.00
- R2-D2 and C-3PO, "Never underestimate the power of a great friend" [288-168] 15.00

3D image card attached to blank greeting card.
- Anakin Skywalker [288-169] 15.00
- Battle Droids [288-170] 15.00
- Darth Maul [288-171] 15.00
- Jedi vs. Sith [288-172] 15.00
- Obi-Wan Kenobi [288-173] 15.00
- Queen Amidala [288-174] 15.00
- Qui-Gon Jinn [288-175] 15.00
- R2-D2 / C-3PO [288-176] 15.00

6" x 6".
- Anakin [288-177] 8.00
- Padmé [288-178] 8.00

Holofoil covers.
- Be Mindful of the Force [v1e1:242] 8.00
- The Day has Come... [v1e1:242] 8.00

Hallmark (UK)
- Anakin Skywalker 10.00

245

Greeting Cards

- ❏ Be Mindful of the Force..10.00
- ❏ Birthday wishes from the dark side 10.00
- ❏ Padmé Amidala..10.00
- ❏ The day has come ... /to celebrate your birthday 10.00

Hallmark / Connections
- ❏ "5" / "Today, your birthday ... Tomorrow, the Galaxy!"' with sheet of 9 stickers [288-179] 8.00
- ❏ Anakin, "Happy Birthday..." [288-180] 8.00
- ❏ Anakin, C-3PO, Obi-Wan, R2-D2, Yoda, "Another Birthday..." [288-181] 8.00
- ❏ "Another Year Older ..." [288-182]...............................8.00
- ❏ "Be mindful of the Force—"..8.00
- ❏ Captain Rex, "Happy Birthday! You're as loyal and highly skilled as Captain Rex!" Double-sided glow-in-the-dark poster of Captain Rex [288-183]..............................8.00
- ❏ Concentrate ... / Use the Force ... Fulfill your birthday destiny! [288-184] 8.00
- ❏ Darth Vader and Yoda, "Another year older ..." [288-185]..8.00
- ❏ Darth Vader, "As long as you live in my fully operational battle station, you'll obey my rules." [288-186] 8.00
- ❏ Darth Vader, "I have you now, young Jedi" [288-187]..8.00
- ❏ Darth Vader, "It is your destiny to have an unforgettable birthday!" [288-188]...8.00
- ❏ Epic Duel, "It's your time to rule!" [288-189] 8.00
- ❏ Jedi and Clones, "Happy Birthday Young Jedi" [288-190]..8.00
- ❏ Star Wars characters, "Wishing you an adventure-filled birthday!" [288-191] 8.00
- ❏ Yoda, "Grandson" [288-192] 8.00
- ❏ Yoda, "Smarty-pants, you are." [288-193]....................8.00
- ❏ Yoda, "Birthday adventure awaits! ..." [288-194] 8.00
- ❏ Yoda, "Master Yoda predicts ..." [288-195].................8.00
- ❏ Yoda, "Reckless, you are. Borrow the car, you may not." [288-196]..8.00
- ❏ Yoda, "Strong with you the Force is ..." [288-197].......8.00
- ❏ Yoda, "Strong you are with the Force ..." [288-198]....8.00

Button cards.
- ❏ Darth Vader, "I have you now ..." [288-199] 10.00
- ❏ Yoda (LEGO), "Strong in the Force you have become..." [288-200]..10.00

Dog Cards.
- ❏ Darth Vader, "You will have a happy Halloween." [288-201]..8.00
- ❏ Yoda, "Drop the treats you will." [288-202] 8.00

Hallmark / Expressions
- ❏ C-3PO, "Oh, dear—I can't bear to watch you suffer." [288-203]..10.00
- ❏ C-3PO, "That's funny, the damage doesn't look as bad from out here." [288-204] 10.00
- ❏ "Damn! Where's the Force when you need it?"...........10.00
- ❏ Darth Vader, "It is useless to resist. There is no escape. It is your destiny. It is ..." [288-205] 10.00
- ❏ Darth Vader, "Valentine, there's a disturbance in the Force" [288-206]..10.00
- ❏ "Have a speed-chasing, podracing ..." [288-207] 10.00
- ❏ LEGO Luke Skywalker / Death Star, "It's your destiny..." [288-208]..10.00
- ❏ Leia, "Me? Forget Your Birthday?" [288-209] 10.00
- ❏ "May the Force be with you / Mighty Blasters / At Last We Will Have Revenge" [288-210]..10.00

Episode II: Attack of the Clones.
- ❏ Anakin, "You Have Completed Your Course of Knowledge.."...10.00
- ❏ Be Mindful of the Force ... [288-211]...........................10.00
- ❏ Mace Windu and Obi-Wan, "Your Task of Obtaining A High School Diploma is Complete ..." 10.00

Hallmark / Innovations
Cards that play sound.
- ❏ 7 Darth Maul and Darth Vader/ "7 years brave, 7 years smart, 7 years strong ..." [288-212]....................................15.00
- ❏ C-3PO and R2-D2, "In a galaxy far, far away..." [288-213]..15.00
- ❏ Chewbacca, "Here's a little birthday advice from the rebel alliance ..." [288-214] 15.00
- ❏ Darth Vader, "Across the centuries and the galaxies, one question has plagued mankind—"Why?" And dads have the answer ..." [288-215] 15.00
- ❏ Darth Vader, "Feel the Power of the Force" 15.00
- ❏ Han and Chewbacca, "Jump into Hyperspace!" [288-216]..15.00
- ❏ Lightsaber, "May The Fun Be With You Today. Happy Birthday," motion sensor and LEDs [288-217] 15.00
- ❏ "Use the Force. Trust your feelings. Believe in yourself."..15.00
- ❏ Yoda and Anakin, "A true Jedi lets nothing stand in the way of Birthday fun." [288-218]..15.00
- ❏ Yoda, "Strong, clever, and Brave You Are ..." [288-219]......15.00

Hallmark / Shoebox Greetings
- ❏ (Artoo-Detoo with a heart) [288-220].........................15.00
- ❏ (Chewbacca) [288-221]...15.00
- ❏ "Dang! There it goes again" [288-222].......................15.00
- ❏ "Got It!" [288-223] 15.00
- ❏ "Hi!" [288-224] 15.00
- ❏ "I am ready." [288-225] 15.00
- ❏ "I'm the luckiest girl in the galaxy" [288-226].............15.00
- ❏ "Intergalactic PMS hits Princess Leia" [288-227].........15.00
- ❏ "It's your birthday ... party like Chewbacca" 15.00
- ❏ "Like it?" [288-228] 15.00
- ❏ "Luke learns that true friends put up with a lot" [288-229]..15.00
- ❏ (Luke Smiling) [288-230]...15.00
- ❏ "Party" [288-231]..15.00
- ❏ "Think about a flowing cape. Seriously." [288-232]....15.00
- ❏ "True friends never let each other get cut in half by a lightsaber" [288-233] 15.00
- ❏ "Vader, get away from my office, now!" [288-234]......15.00
- ❏ (Yoda Standing) [288-235] 15.00
- ❏ "You want to know where your destiny lies, Luke?" [288-236]..15.00
- ❏ "You will regret this rash assault, Luke!" [288-237] 15.00
- ❏ "You! See a stylist!" [288-238] 15.00

Hasbro
Packaged with Holiday Edition action figures.
- ❏ 2002 Santa C-3PO and Reindeer R2 [288-239] 15.00
- ❏ 2003 Santa Yoda [288-240].......................................15.00
- ❏ 2004 Jawas with gifts 15.00
- ❏ 2005 Darth Vader building stormtrooper snowman 15.00

Lucas Companies
- ❏ 1983 Ewok Santa, Lucasfilm [288-241] 85.00
- ❏ 1999 "Happy Holidays," Lucas Digital........................25.00
- ❏ 1999 Jawas catching toys from the sky, Lucas Learning [288-242]..25.00
- ❏ 1999 Podracer pilots caroling, Lucasfilm [288-243] 25.00
- ❏ 2000 "Happy Holidays," LucasArts [288-244] 25.00
- ❏ 2000 "May all of your dreams come true in the New Year," Lucasfilm [288-245] 25.00
- ❏ 2000 Christmas stars, Lucas Digital..........................25.00
- ❏ 2001 "Seasons Greetings" / "From all your friends at Lucas Digital Ltd." 25.00
- ❏ 2001 "Wishing you Peace ..." / "From Our Worlds to Yours," Lucasfilm [288-246] 25.00
- ❏ 2001 Snow angel / "Wanna Play?", LucasArts...........25.00
- ❏ 2002 Game figures on motorcycle / "Oh what fun it is to ride!!", LucasArts [288-247] 25.00
- ❏ 2002 Yoda "Exactly alike, no two are ..." / "Beautiful all," Lucasfilm [288-248] 25.00
- ❏ 2002 Yoda with candle / "May the Magic of this Holiday Season light up your year," Lucas Digital [288-249]........25.00
- ❏ 2003 Yoda stellar horizon / "Envisioning unlimited possibilities for the New Year" [288-250].................25.00
- ❏ 2004 Snowflake 25.00
- ❏ 2007 Caroling Stormtroopers....................................25.00

Our Town
- ❏ Los Angeles City Council, "May The Farce Be With You" [4:158] 10.00

Portal
- ❏ "May the Force be with you on your Birthday" [288-251]..10.00

Skywalkers
- ❏ "Happy Birthday" [v1e1:243]......................................35.00
- ❏ "Season's Greetings" [288-252].................................35.00

Greeting Cards: Valentines, Boxed
Continued in Volume 3, Page 242

Drawing Board Greeting Cards, Inc.
Classroom valentines, packages of 32.
- ❏ C-3PO and R2-D2 [289-01]..45.00
- ❏ Ewok [289-02]..35.00
- ❏ Return of the Jedi [289-03]..30.00
- ❏ Wicket the Ewok [289-04] 35.00

Hallmark
- ❏ 32 Metallic Valentines, Episode I [289-05] 10.00
- ❏ 32 Valentines with 48 fun stickers, Episode II 10.00

| 289-01 | 289-02 | 289-03 | 289-04 | 289-05 | 289-06 | 289-07 | 289-08 |

| 289-09 | 289-10 | 289-11 | 289-12 | 289-13 | 289-14 | 289-15 | 289-16 | 289-17 |

Hallmark (Canada)
Episode II: Attack of the Clones, French packaging.
- ❏ 32 Valentines with 48 fun stickers [289-06] 8.00

Hallmark Party
- ❏ 32 LEGO Star Wars Valentines, exclusive to Target 8.00
- ❏ 32 LEGO Star Wars Valentines, bonus poster [289-07] ...10.00

Paper Magic Group
Classic trilogy.
- ❏ 30 Stand-Up Valentines; 10 different designs [289-08] ..10.00
- ❏ 30 Valentines; 10 different designs [289-09] 10.00
- ❏ 32 Holofoil Valentines; 10 different designs and 48 "seals" [289-10] 10.00
- ❏ 40-Card Valentine Kit; 10 different designs, 48 "seals", 2 bookmarks, window cling [289-11] 10.00
- ❏ Deluxe Valentine Kit: Over 80 pieces: Window Cling, 3D Display, 40 Valentines, 45 Stickers [289-12] 10.00
- ❏ Deluxe Valentine Kit: Window Cling, 3D Display, 40 Valentines, 45 Stickers [289-13] 10.00
- ❏ Holographic Valentines: 30 stand-up Valentines with envelopes [289-14] 10.00

Clone Wars.
- ❏ 27 Lenticular Valentines [289-15] 12.00
- ❏ 27 Lenticular Valentines [289-16] 12.00
- ❏ 27 Lenticular Valentines, exclusive to Target 12.00
- ❏ 34 Valentines with poster [289-17] 12.00
- ❏ 34 Valentines with poster [289-18] 12.00

Episode I: The Phantom Menace.
- ❏ 28 Deluxe Fold and Seal cards with seals [289-19] 10.00
- ❏ 32 Fold and Seal cards with seals [289-20] 10.00

Episode II: Attack of the Clones.
- ❏ 30 Foil Valentines, Anakin box [289-21] 10.00
- ❏ 30 Foil Valentines, Anakin box, punch-out hanger 10.00
- ❏ 30 Foil Valentines, window box [289-22] 10.00
- ❏ 30 Foil Valentines, Yoda box [289-23] 10.00
- ❏ 32 Valentines with seals 10.00
- ❏ 32 Valentines with seals, punch-out hanger [289-24] 10.00

Episode III: Revenge of the Sith.
- ❏ 32 Foil Valentines, Flashy Foil. Includes 32 fold-and-seal cards with seals 10.00
- ❏ 32 Valentines, includes 32 fold-and-seal cards with seals 10.00
- ❏ 32 Valentines with poster and tattoos, 15" x 19" poster inside 10.00
- ❏ 34 Valentines, flashy foil. Contains 34 fold-and-seal cards with seals [289-25] 10.00
- ❏ 34 Valentines, flashy foil. Includes 34 fold-and-seal valentines with seals [289-26] 10.00

Saga.
- ❏ 32 Valentines, 8 designs with seals [289-27] 12.00
- ❏ 32 Valentines and tattoos with Yoda poster, 7 designs with 20 tattoo designs, exclusive to Target [289-28] 12.00

Star Wars. Exclusive to Target.
- ❏ 16 Valentines with magnets [289-29] 10.00
- ❏ 16 Valentines with pencils [289-30] 10.00
- ❏ 16 Valentines with pencils [289-31] 10.00
- ❏ 27 Lenticular Valentines [289-32] 10.00

Valentines mailboxes. Exclusive to Target.
- ❏ 32 Star Wars valentines, Darth Vader [289-33] 15.00
- ❏ 32 Star Wars valentines, Yoda [289-34] 15.00

Growth and Height Charts
Continued in Volume 3, Page 243

Random House
- ❏ Star Wars "Grow" chart [290-01] 65.00

Ready Roll (UK)
- ❏ Height chart, The Phantom Menace [290-02] 75.00

Guide Maps
Continued in Volume 3, Page 243

Disney / MGM
Star Wars Weekends, 2000.
- ❏ May 19–21 [v1e1:244] 15.00

Star Wars Weekends, 2001.
- ❏ May 11–13 ....10.00
- ❏ May 18–20 ....10.00
- ❏ May 25–27 ....10.00

Star Wars Weekends, 2011.
- ❏ May 20 [291-01] 10.00

Guitar Cases

Fernandes
- ❏ Star Wars logo, hard-sided [2:261] 270.00
- ❏ Star Wars logo, soft-sided 250.00

Guitar Picks
Continued in Volume 3, Page 243

Fernandes
Classic Trilogy, 2002.
- ❏ 1 Darth Vader [v1e1:245] 10.00
- ❏ 2 Stormtrooper [v1e1:245] 10.00
- ❏ 3 R2-D2 [v1e1:245] 10.00
- ❏ 4 C-3PO [v1e1:245] 10.00
- ❏ 5 Boba Fett [v1e1:245] 10.00
- ❏ 6 Luke Skywalker [v1e1:245] 10.00
- ❏ 7 Princess Leia [v1e1:245] 10.00
- ❏ 8 Han Solo [v1e1:245] 10.00
- ❏ 9 Yoda [v1e1:245] 10.00
- ❏ 10 Chewbacca [v1e1:245] 10.00
- ❏ 11 Jabba the Hutt [v1e1:245] 10.00
- ❏ 12 Jawa [v1e1:245] 10.00
- ❏ 13 Ewok [v1e1:245] 10.00
- ❏ 14 Tusken Raider [v1e1:245] 10.00
- ❏ 15 TIE Fighter Pilot [v1e1:245] 10.00
- ❏ 16 Rebel Alliance [v1e1:245] 10.00
- ❏ 17 Galactic Empire, holographic [v1e1:245] 24.00
- ❏ 18 Darth Vader, holographic [v1e1:245] 24.00
- ❏ 19 Stormtrooper, holographic [v1e1:245] 24.00
- ❏ 20 Boba Fett, holographic [v1e1:245] 24.00
- ❏ Counter display box, empty 10.00
- ❏ Unopened package contains 1 random pick and checklist card 15.00

Episode II: Attack of the Clones 2003.
- ❏ 1 Anakin Skywalker [v1e1:245] 10.00
- ❏ 2 Padmé Amidala [v1e1:245] 10.00
- ❏ 3 Obi-Wan Kenobi [v1e1:245] 10.00
- ❏ 4 Yoda [v1e1:245] 10.00
- ❏ 5 Mace Windu [v1e1:245] 10.00
- ❏ 6 Clone trooper [v1e1:245] 10.00
- ❏ 7 Jango Fett [v1e1:245] 10.00
- ❏ 8 Count Dooku [v1e1:245] 10.00
- ❏ 9 Zam Wesell [v1e1:245] 10.00
- ❏ 10 Super Battle Droid [v1e1:245] 10.00
- ❏ 11 Count Dooku Icon [v1e1:245] 10.00
- ❏ 12 R2-D2 [v1e1:245] 10.00
- ❏ 13 C-3PO [v1e1:245] 10.00
- ❏ 14 Clone trooper [v1e1:245] 10.00
- ❏ 15 Jedi Starfighter [v1e1:245] 10.00
- ❏ 16 Anakin Skywalker / Darth Vader [v1e1:245] 10.00
- ❏ 17 Jango Fett, hologram [v1e1:245] 24.00
- ❏ 18 Anakin Skywalker, hologram [v1e1:245] 24.00
- ❏ 19 Yoda, hologram [v1e1:245] 24.00
- ❏ 20 Clone trooper, hologram [v1e1:245] 24.00
- ❏ 21 Secret, hologram (Jango Fett) 24.00
- ❏ 22 Clone trooper Red, hologram mail-away 35.00
- ❏ 23 Clone trooper Yellow, hologram mail-away 35.00
- ❏ Counter display box, empty 10.00
- ❏ Unopened package contains 1 random pick and checklist card 15.00

247

Guitar Straps

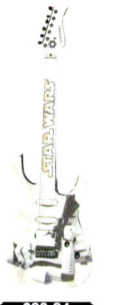

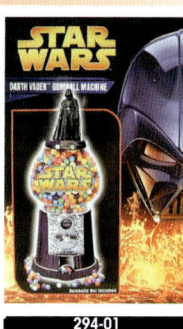

292-01 | 292-02 | 292-03 | 293-01 | 293-02 | 293-03 | 293-04 | 293-05 | 294-01 | 294-02

Guitar Straps
Continued in Volume 3, Page 244

Fernandes
- Darth Vader [292-01] 50.00
- Star Wars logo [292-02] 50.00
- Vader and Stormtrooper [292-03] 50.00

Guitars
Continued in Volume 3, Page 244

Fernandes
Nomad models.
- Boba Fett [293-01] 750.00
- Darth Vader 750.00
- Stormtrooper [293-02] 750.00

Nomad models. Series 2, limited to 75.
- Boba Fett 3,500.00

Retrorocket models, series 1, hard case, limited to 250.
- Darth Vader [293-03] 1,250.00
- Stormtrooper [293-04] 1,250.00

Retrorocket models, series 2, hard case, limited to 75.
- Boba Fett [293-05] 5,000.00
- Yoda 5,000.00

Gumball Machines

Comic Images
- Darth Vader [294-01] 50.00
- Yoda [294-02] 50.00

Gym Sets

Gym Dandy
- Scout Walker Command Tower with 7 ft. slide 5,000.00
- Scout Walker Command Tower with Speederbike .. 3,500.00
- Speederbike swing add-on [295-01] 600.00

Hair Gel
Continued in Volume 3, Page 244

Avon (Mexico)
- Anakin and Clones [296-01] 25.00

Hairbrushes
Continued in Volume 3, Page 244

Avon (Mexico)
- Padmé Amidala [297-01] 30.00

Handbills

Imax
- Episode II: Size Matters Not, November 1st 5.00

Major Cineplex
- Anakin Skywalker 5.00
- Count Dooku 5.00
- Geonosis 5.00
- Jango Fett 5.00
- Mace Windu 5.00
- Movie Poster art 5.00
- Obi-Wan Kenobi 5.00
- Padmé Amidala 5.00
- Zam Wesell 5.00

Handkerchiefs
Continued in Volume 3, Page 244

Iwamota (Japan)
- C-3PO and R2-D2, Empire Strikes Back movie credits .. 120.00
- Luke on Dagobah, Empire Strikes Back The Saga Continues 120.00

Marubeni (Japan)
- Darth Vader, Bespin gantry 130.00
- R2-D2 and Wicket 130.00

Mitsubishi (Japan)
- Star Cars, C-3PO and R2-D2 [4:161] 150.00

Psycho Bunny
- C-3PO and R2-D2, blue background 45.00
- C-3PO and R2-D2, purple background 45.00
- C-3PO and R2-D2, red background [298-01] 45.00
- C-3PO and R2-D2, white background 45.00
- Millennium Falcon, blue background [298-02] 45.00
- Millennium Falcon, gray background 45.00
- Millennium Falcon, pink background 45.00
- Stormtroopers, blue background [298-03] 45.00
- Stormtroopers, purple background 45.00

Helmets, Miniature

Gentle Giant Studios
- Darth Vader 65.00
- TIE Pilot 65.00
- X-Wing Pilot 65.00

Riddell
- Boba Fett [299-01] 175.00
- C-3PO [299-02] 95.00
- Darth Vader [299-03] 100.00
- Stormtrooper [299-04] 150.00
- X-Wing Pilot [299-05] 125.00

Tomy (Japan)
- AT-AT Driver [299-06] 35.00
- Biker Scout [299-07] 35.00
- Boba Fett [299-08] 35.00
- Boushh [299-09] 35.00
- C-3PO [299-10] 35.00

295-01

296-01

297-01 Open and Boxed

298-01

298-02

298-03

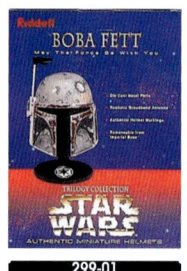
299-01

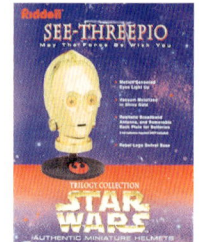
299-02

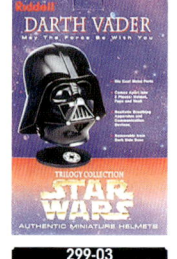
299-03

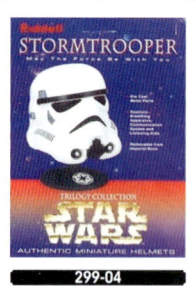
299-04

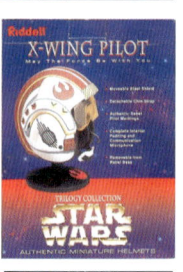
299-05

Holiday Containers

299-06 | 299-07 | 299-08 | 299-09 | 299-10 | 299-11 Helmet On and Helmet Off | 299-12

299-13 | 299-14 | 299-15 | 299-16 | 299-17 | 299-18 | 299-19 | 299-20

300-01 | 300-02 | 300-03 | 300-04

- ❏ Darth Vader [299-11] 35.00
- ❏ Imperial Gunner [299-12] 35.00
- ❏ Jango Fett / chase [299-13] 50.00
- ❏ Kashyyyk trooper / chase [299-14] 50.00
- ❏ Rebel trooper [299-15] 35.00
- ❏ Skiff guard [299-16] 35.00
- ❏ Stormtrooper [299-17] 35.00
- ❏ TIE Pilot [299-18] 35.00
- ❏ X-Wing Pilot [299-19] 35.00
- ❏ X-Wing Pilot Biggs Darklighter / chase [299-20] 50.00

300-05 | 300-06 | 300-07

Helmets, Sports
Continued in Volume 3, Page 245

(UK)
- ❏ Clone Wars [300-01] 35.00

Dynacraft
- ❏ Darth Maul multi-sport, children's 25.00
- ❏ Queen Amidala multi-sport, children's [300-02] 25.00

M.V. Sports and Leisure Ltd.
- ❏ Darth Maul [300-03] 35.00
- ❏ Death Star Attack [300-04] 35.00
- ❏ Jar Jar Binks [300-05] 35.00
- ❏ Sith Probe Droids, "Darth Maul Sith Lord" [300-06] 30.00

Shoei (Japan)
- ❏ Stormtrooper motorcycle helmet [300-07] 1,275.00

Holiday Containers
Continued in Volume 3, Page 245

(UK)
- ❏ Clone Wars, Easter pail [301-01] 20.00

Her Universe
Trick-or-treat sacks.
- ❏ Star Wars [301-02] 20.00

PTI Group Inc.
Easter pails, plush. Exclusive to Target.
- ❏ Captain Rex [301-03] 25.00
- ❏ Clone trooper [301-04] 25.00
- ❏ Yoda [301-05] 30.00

Easter pails.
- ❏ Clone Wars, 4-sided [301-06] 15.00

Rubies
Candy bowl holders.
- ❏ Boba Fett [301-07] 50.00
- ❏ Darth Maul [301-08] 50.00
- ❏ Darth Vader [301-09] 50.00
- ❏ Jawa 50.00
- ❏ Stormtrooper 50.00
- ❏ Yoda [301-10] 50.00

Pails: trick-or-treat.
- ❏ Clone Wars [301-11] 20.00
- ❏ Darth Vader [301-12] 25.00
- ❏ Darth Vader [301-13] 15.00
- ❏ Darth Vader 10.00

301-01 | 301-02 | 301-03 | 301-04 | 301-05 | 301-06

Holiday Containers

| 301-07 | 301-08 | 301-09 | 301-10 | 301-11 | 301-12 | 301-13 | 301-14 | 301-15 |

Trick-or-treat sacks. Exclusive to Target.
- Anakin, Rex, Obi-Wan, Yoda [301-14] 10.00
- Luke Skywalker vs. Darth Vader [301-15] 10.00
- Star Wars 10.00

Holiday Decoration Crafts
Continued in Volume 3, Page 247

Paper Magic Group
Pumpkin carving kits. Exclusive to Target.
- 2007 [302-01] 15.00
- 2009 .... 10.00
- 2011 .... 10.00
- 2012 [302-02] 10.00

Pumpkin push-ins. Exclusive to Target.
- 2011 Yoda [302-03] 15.00
- 2012 Darth Vader [302-04] 15.00
- 2012 Yoda [302-05] 15.00

Holiday Easter Egg Coloring Kits
Continued in Volume 3, Page 223

Dudley Eggs
- 2006 Star Wars, exclusive to Target [303-01] 10.00
- 2007 30th anniversary, exclusive to Target [303-02] 15.00
- 2008 Star Wars, exclusive to Target [303-03] 10.00
- 2009 Clone Wars, exclusive to KMart [303-04] 15.00
- 2009 Clone Wars, glow-in-the-dark poster, exclusive to Target 15.00
- 2009 Star Wars, exclusive to Target [303-05] 10.00
- 2010 Clone Wars [303-06] 15.00
- 2011 Clone Wars 3D, exclusive to Target [303-07] 15.00

Holiday Easter Eggs
Continued in Volume 3, Page 223

Galerie
Hide an Egg.
- Anakin, Obi-Wan, and Yoda eggs, 22 pack [304-01] 25.00
- Clone Wars eggs [304-02] 25.00

Plastic eggs with stickers, candy ring, and candy stars.
- Darth Vader / red [304-03] 5.00
- R2-D2 / blue [304-04] 5.00
- Yoda / yellow [304-05] 5.00

Mello Smello
- Sticker sheet [304-06] 10.00
- Tattoos [304-07] 10.00

    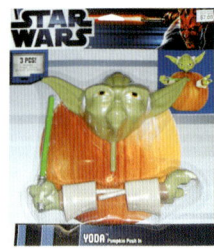 

| 302-01 | 302-02 | 302-03 | 302-04 | 302-05 | 303-01 |

  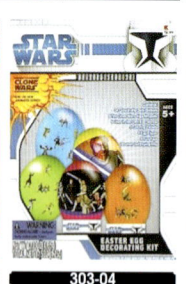     

| 303-02 | 303-03 | 303-04 | 303-05 | 303-06 | 303-07 | 304-01 | 304-02 |

| 304-03 | 304-04 | 304-05 | 304-06 | 304-07 | 304-08 | 304-09 | 305-01 |

    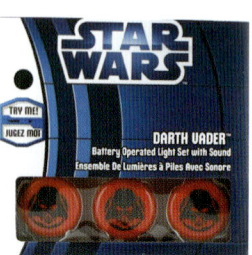

| 306-01 | 306-02 | 306-03 | 306-04 | 306-05 | 306-06 |

Holiday Ornaments

Paper Magic Group
40 tattoos in plastic eggs.
- ☐ Characters / blue [304-08].................................5.00
- ☐ Emblems / red [304-09].....................................5.00

Holiday Easter Grass

Dudley Eggs
- ☐ Clone Wars, exclusive to Target [305-01].............10.00

Holiday Lighting
Continued in Volume 3, Page 247

Kurt S. Adler, Inc.
- ☐ C-3PO [306-01]..25.00
- ☐ Clone trooper [306-02]......................................25.00
- ☐ R2-D2 [306-03]...25.00
- ☐ Yoda [306-04]..25.00
- ☐ Yoda, Clone Wars [306-05]................................25.00

Nonfigural light sets.
- ☐ Darth Vader, round [306-06].............................25.00

Holiday Ornaments
Continued in Volume 3, Page 247

4" resin nutcracker ornaments.
- ☐ C-3PO...10.00
- ☐ Darth Vader [307-01].......................................10.00
- ☐ Stormtrooper..10.00
- ☐ Yoda [307-02]...10.00

501st Legion
Ball ornaments with 501st art, dated.
- ☐ 2007 Red [307-03]...35.00
- ☐ 2008 Green [307-04]...35.00
- ☐ 2009 Purple [307-05]...35.00
- ☐ 2010 Gold [307-06]...35.00
- ☐ 2011 White [307-07]..35.00
- ☐ 2012 Black [307-08]...35.00

Christopher Radko
Individually mouth-blown glass ornaments.
- ☐ C-3PO [307-09]...75.00
- ☐ C-3PO and R2-D2 [307-10]...............................150.00
- ☐ Chewbacca [307-11]..75.00
- ☐ Darth Vader [307-12]...75.00
- ☐ Darth Vader on second Death Star [307-13]...130.00
- ☐ Darth Vader, lightsaber drawn [307-14]..........200.00
- ☐ Ewoks [307-15]...150.00

Holiday Ornaments

- ❏ Stormtrooper [307-16] 75.00
- ❏ Yoda [307-17] 75.00

Hallmark

1996.
- ❏ Millennium Falcon [307-18] 30.00
- ❏ Vehicles: AT-AT, TIE Fighter, X-Wing Fighter [307-19] 30.00

1997.
- ❏ C-3PO and R2-D2 [307-20] 30.00
- ❏ Darth Vader [307-21] 35.00
- ❏ Luke Skywalker, Bespin (Classic series #1) [307-22] 25.00
- ❏ Yoda [307-23] 30.00

1998.
- ❏ Boba Fett [307-24] 35.00
- ❏ Ewoks, set of 3 [307-25] 35.00
- ❏ Princess Leia (Classic series #2) [307-26] 25.00
- ❏ Star Wars lunch box [307-27] 15.00
- ❏ X-Wing Fighter [307-28] 35.00

1999.
- ❏ Chewbacca [307-29] 35.00
- ❏ Darth Vader's TIE Fighter [307-30] 35.00
- ❏ Han Solo (Classic series #3) [307-31] 25.00
- ❏ Max Rebo Band, set of 3 [307-32] 25.00
- ❏ Naboo Fighter [307-33] 25.00
- ❏ Queen Amidala [307-34] 25.00

2000.
- ❏ Darth Maul [307-35] 25.00
- ❏ Gungan Sub [307-36] 20.00
- ❏ Jedi Council [307-37] 25.00
- ❏ Obi-Wan Kenobi (Classic series #4) [307-38] 25.00
- ❏ Qui-Gon Jinn [307-39] 25.00
- ❏ Stormtrooper [307-40] 25.00

2001.
- ❏ Anakin Skywalker [307-41] 25.00
- ❏ Battle of Naboo, set of 3 [307-42] 20.00
- ❏ Empire Strikes Back Lunchbox [307-43] 25.00
- ❏ Jar Jar Binks [307-44] 25.00
- ❏ Naboo Royal Starship [307-45] 30.00
- ❏ R2-D2 (Classic series #5) [307-46] 25.00

2002.
- ❏ Darth Vader, Final Duel (Classic series #6) [307-47] 25.00
- ❏ Death Star II [307-48] 35.00
- ❏ Jango Fett [307-49] 35.00
- ❏ Luke Skywalker, Final Duel [307-50] 25.00
- ❏ Obi-Wan Kenobi [307-51] 25.00
- ❏ Slave I [307-52] 25.00

2003.
- ❏ C-3PO (Classic series #7) [307-53] 25.00
- ❏ Clone troopers [307-54] 25.00
- ❏ Padmé Amidala [307-55] 25.00
- ❏ TIE Fighter [307-56] 40.00
- ❏ Yoda, Jedi Master [307-57] 25.00

2004.
- ❏ Anakin Skywalker [307-58] 30.00
- ❏ Chewbacca and C-3PO [307-59] 25.00
- ❏ Star Destroyer and Blockade Runner [307-60] 50.00
- ❏ Star Wars: A New Hope poster [307-61] 20.00

2005.
- ❏ Clone trooper Lieutenant [307-62] 30.00
- ❏ Darth Vader Bespin gantry [307-63] 30.00
- ❏ Jedi Starfighter [307-64] 30.00
- ❏ Princess Leia captive [307-65] 25.00
- ❏ TIE Advanced X1 and Millennium Falcon miniatures [307-66] 30.00

2006.
- ❏ Anakin Skywalker and Obi-Wan Kenobi [307-67] 60.00
- ❏ Asajj Ventress, Anakin Skywalker, and Yoda, Clone Wars miniatures [307-68] 25.00
- ❏ Imperial AT-AT and Rebel Snowspeeder [307-69] 80.00
- ❏ Luke Skywalker and Yoda [307-70] 30.00

2007.
- ❏ A Jedi Legacy Revealed [307-71] 50.00
- ❏ R2-D2 and Jawa [307-72] 45.00
- ❏ The Adventure Begins [307-73] 40.00
- ❏ Tusken Raider [307-74] 130.00

2008.
- ❏ Death Star and Star Destroyer [307-75] 35.00
- ❏ Emperor Palpatine [307-76] 25.00
- ❏ Emperor's Royal Guard [307-77] 35.00
- ❏ Imperial Shuttle [307-78] 60.00
- ❏ The Final Confrontation [307-79] 45.00

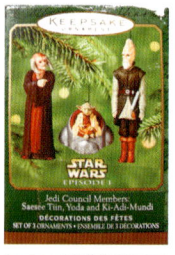 307-37
 307-38
 307-39
 307-40
 307-41
 307-42
 307-43
 307-44
 307-45
 307-46
 307-47
 307-48
 307-49
 307-50
 307-51
 307-52
 307-53
 307-54
 307-55
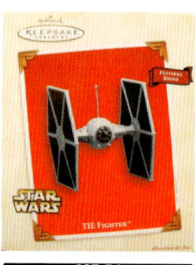 307-56
 307-57
 307-58
 307-59
 307-60
 307-61
 307-62
 307-63
 307-64
 307-65
 307-66

Holiday Ornaments

2009.
- ☐ A Deadly Duel, Jedi vs. Sith [307-80].............................50.00
- ☐ Anakin Skywalker and Ahsoka Tano [307-81]...............75.00
- ☐ Greedo [307-82]...80.00
- ☐ Han Solo, stormtrooper disguise [307-83].....................30.00
- ☐ Luke's Landspeeder [307-84]...45.00
- ☐ Shock trooper and Shadow trooper, 700 produced, individually numbered, exclusive to San Diego Comic-Con [307-85]...1,250.00

2010.
- ☐ Boba Fett and Han Solo [307-86]...................................45.00
- ☐ Boba Fett and Yoda, 500 produced, exclusive to Star Wars Celebration V [307-87]..300.00
- ☐ Captain Rex and Yoda [307-88].....................................50.00
- ☐ His Masters Bidding [307-89]...35.00
- ☐ K-3PO and R-3PO, San Diego Comic-Con [307-90]......600.00
- ☐ Lando Calrissian, exclusive to Keepsake Ornament Premiere [307-91]..75.00
- ☐ Luke Skywalker, snowspeeder pilot [307-92].................35.00
- ☐ Rebel Snowspeeder [307-93]...40.00

2011.
- ☐ Bossk [307-94]...45.00
- ☐ Dengar and IG-88, exclusive to San Diego Comic-Con [307-95]..1,350.00
- ☐ Jedi Master Yoda [307-96]...30.00
- ☐ R2-Q5 and R2-A3, exclusive to New York Comic-Con [307-97]...800.00
- ☐ Showdown at the Cantina [307-98]................................40.00
- ☐ Slave I [307-99]..50.00

2012.
- ☐ 4-LOM and Zuckuss, San Diego Comic-Con [307-100]..200.00
- ☐ Darth Vader—Peek Buster [307-101].............................25.00
- ☐ General Grievous [307-102]...45.00
- ☐ Han Solo - the Rescue [307-103]...................................35.00
- ☐ Momaw Nadon [307-104]...45.00
- ☐ Obi-Wan Kenobi and Ponda Baba, 2,000 produced, exclusive to Star Wars Celebration VI [307-105].............300.00
- ☐ Sith Apprentice Darth Maul [307-106]............................40.00
- ☐ TIE Interceptor [307-107]...50.00

LEGO Star Wars characters.
- ☐ 2011 Darth Vader [307-108]...25.00
- ☐ 2012 Stormtrooper [307-109]...25.00

Seasons.
- ☐ Clones [307-110]...25.00
- ☐ R2-D2 [307-111]...20.00
- ☐ Yoda [307-112]...20.00

307-67

307-68

307-69

307-70

307-71

307-72

307-73

307-74

307-75

307-76

307-77

307-78

307-79

307-80

307-81

307-82

307-83

307-84

307-85

307-86

307-87

307-88

307-89

Holiday Ornaments

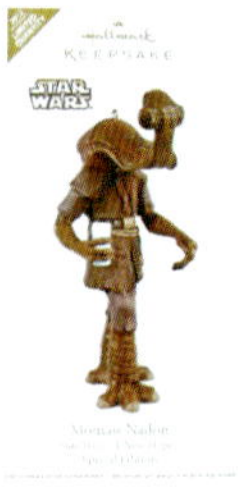

307-104

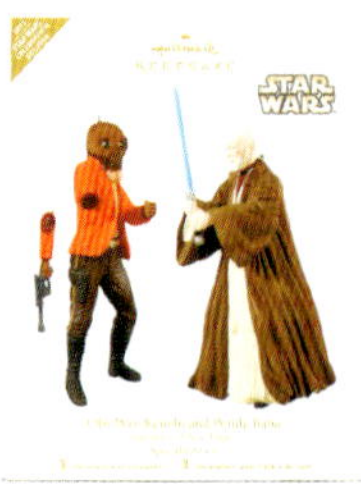

307-105

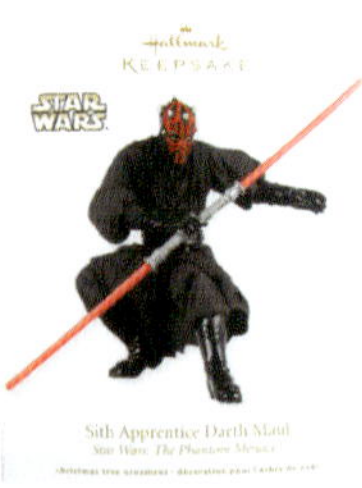

307-106

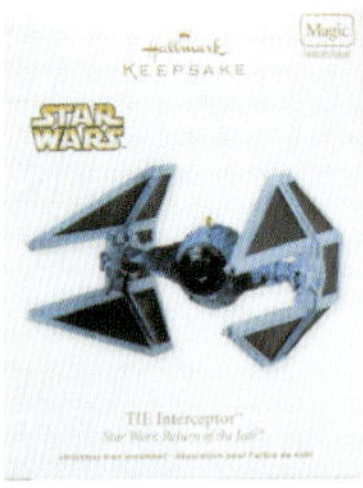

307-107

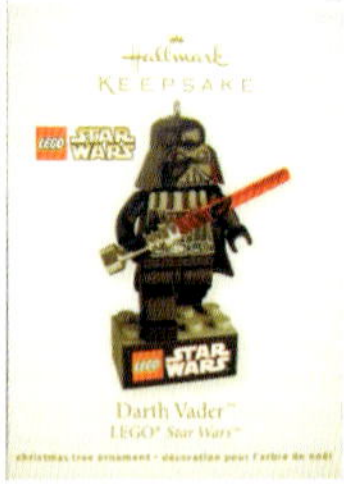

307-108

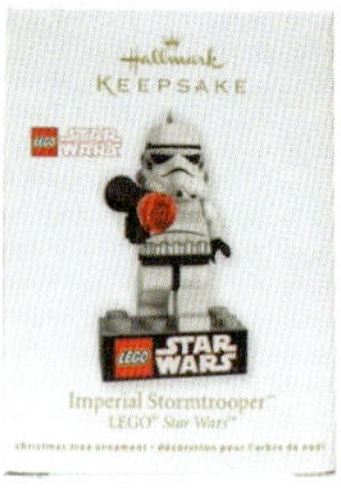

307-109

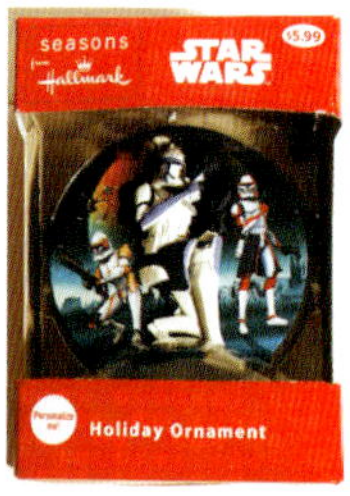

307-110

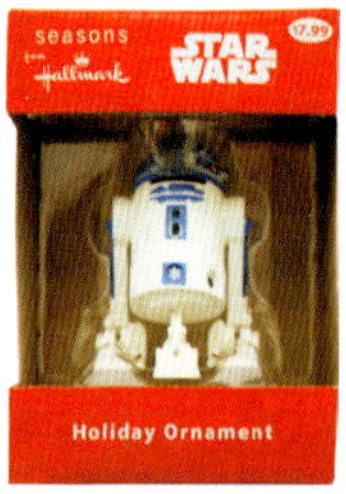

307-111

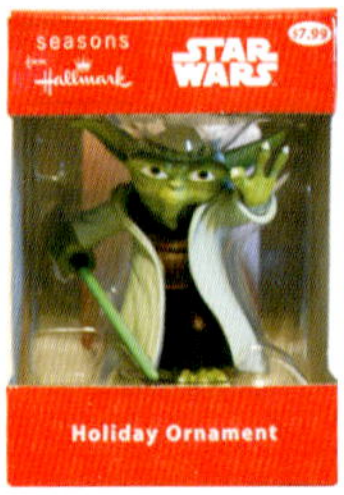

307-112

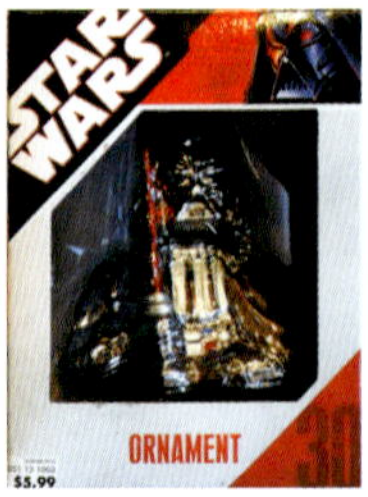

307-113

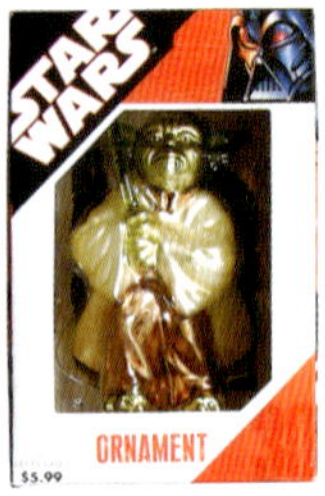

307-114

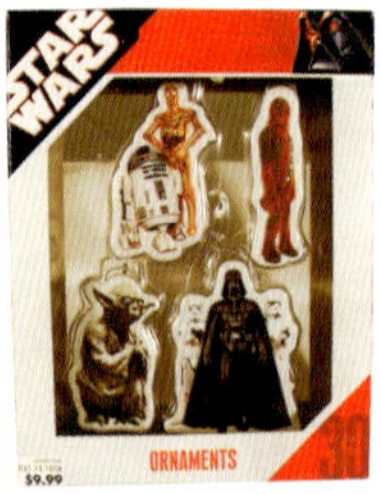

307-115

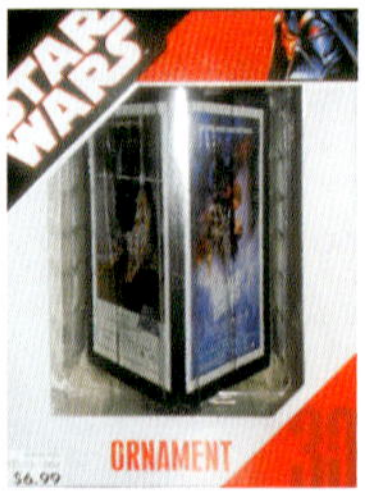

307-116

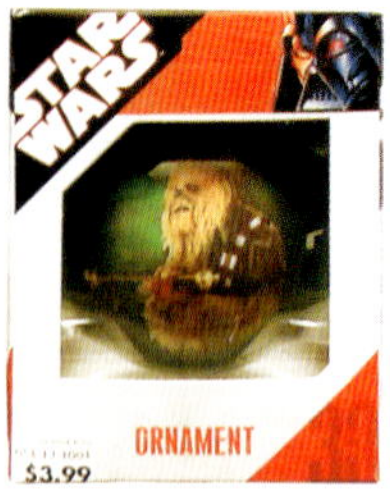

307-117

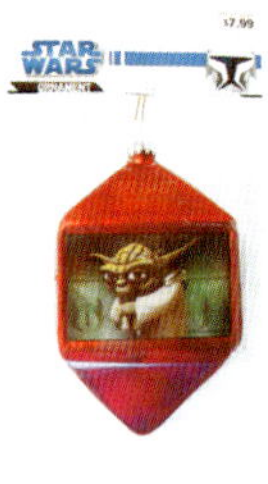

307-118

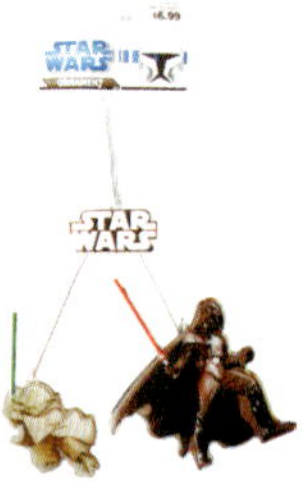

307-119

HHK Trading Co. Ltd.

- ❑ Blown glass Darth Vader [307-113] 20.00
- ❑ Blown glass Yoda [307-114] 15.00
- ❑ Characters, shaped, package of 4, C-3PO and R2-D2, Chewbacca, Yoda, Darth Vader and Stormtroopers [307-115] 12.00
- ❑ Movie Posters [307-116] 15.00
- ❑ Ornamental ball, green, Chewbacca and Yoda [307-117] .. 12.00
- ❑ Ornamental ball, red, Anakin vs. Obi-Wan and Darth Vader vs. Obi-Wan 12.00

Hmk Custom Manufacturing

2008. Exclusive to Target.

- ❑ Clone Wars, 3-sided, Yoda, Jedi, Clones [307-118] 12.00
- ❑ Yoda and Darth Vader, dangling [307-119] 10.00

2008. Blown glass. Exclusive to Target.

- ❑ Chewbacca [307-120] 25.00
- ❑ Darth Vader [307-121] 20.00
- ❑ R2-D2 [307-122] 25.00
- ❑ Yoda [307-123] 20.00

2009. Exclusive to Target.

- ❑ Clone Wars [307-124] 20.00
- ❑ Clone Wars ball 15.00

2009. Blown glass. Exclusive to Target.

- ❑ Chewbacca [307-125] 25.00
- ❑ Darth Vader [307-126] 25.00
- ❑ R2-D2 [307-127] 25.00
- ❑ Yoda [307-128] 25.00

2010.

- ❑ Yoda, exclusive to Star Wars Celebration V 160.00

2010. Blown glass. Exclusive to Target.

- ❑ Captain Rex helmet [307-129] 8.00
- ❑ Darth Vader [307-130] 8.00
- ❑ R2-D2 [307-131] 8.00
- ❑ Yoda [307-132] 8.00

2011. Exclusive to Target.

- ❑ Yoda with light-up lightsaber [307-133] 12.00

2011. Blown glass. Exclusive to Target.

- ❑ Captain Rex helmet [307-134] 15.00
- ❑ Darth Vader 15.00
- ❑ R2-D2 [307-135] 15.00
- ❑ Yoda [307-136] 15.00

2011. Boxed.

- ❑ Yoda, Clone Wars [307-137] 25.00

2011. Carded. Exclusive to Target.

- ❑ 5-pack [307-138] 15.00

2012. Blown glass. Exclusive to Target.

- ❑ C-3PO [307-139] 20.00
- ❑ Darth Maul [307-140] 25.00
- ❑ Darth Vader figural [307-141] 15.00
- ❑ Darth Vader helmet [307-142] 35.00
- ❑ R2-D2 [307-143] 25.00
- ❑ Yoda [307-144] 20.00

2012. Carded. Exclusive to Target.

- ❑ Clone Wars set of 5 [307-145] 20.00

Kurt S. Adler, Inc.

2-piece hand-crafted glass ornament sets. 2006.

- ❑ Boba Fett and Darth Vader [307-146] 20.00
- ❑ Yoda and C-3PO [307-147] 20.00

2-piece holiday ornament sets. 2005.

- ❑ Boba Fett / Episode IV [307-148] 20.00
- ❑ C-3PO / Episode I: The Phantom Menace [307-149] 20.00
- ❑ Darth Vader / Episode III: Revenge of the Sith [307-150] .. 20.00
- ❑ Yoda / Episode II: AOTC [307-151] 20.00

2-piece holiday ornament sets. 2006.

- ❑ Darth Vader / Episode IV: A New Hope [307-152] 20.00
- ❑ R2-D2 / EPV: Empire Strikes Back [307-153] 20.00
- ❑ Stormtrooper / Episode III: Revenge of the Sith [307-154] .. 20.00
- ❑ Yoda / EPVI: Return of the Jedi [307-155] 20.00

Ceramic holiday ornaments. 2005.

- ❑ Boba Fett [307-156] 15.00
- ❑ C-3PO [307-157] 15.00
- ❑ Chewbacca [307-158] 15.00
- ❑ Darth Vader [307-159] 15.00
- ❑ Luke Skywalker, X-Wing Pilot [307-160] 15.00
- ❑ R2-D2 [307-161] 15.00
- ❑ Yoda [307-162] 15.00

Ceramic holiday ornaments. 2006.

- ❑ Boba Fett [307-163] 15.00

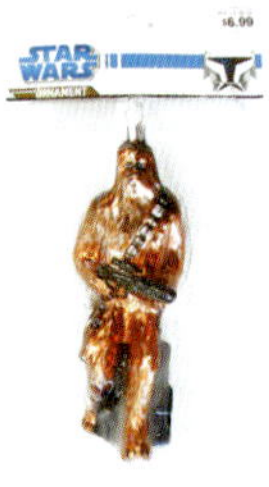

307-120

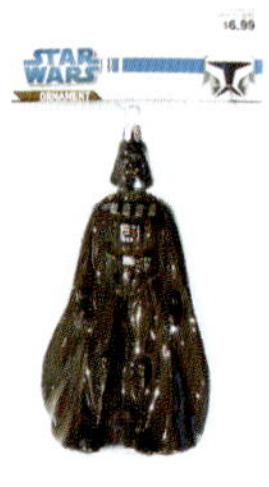

307-121

307-122

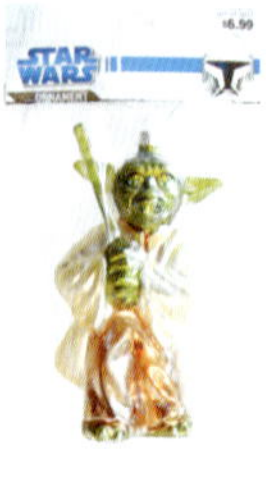

307-123

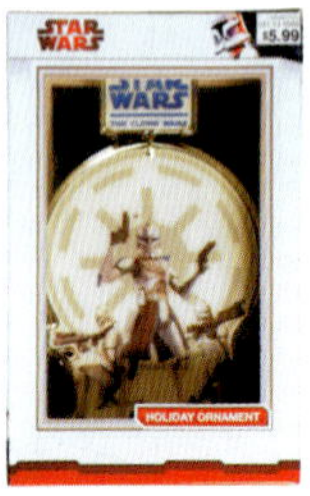

307-124

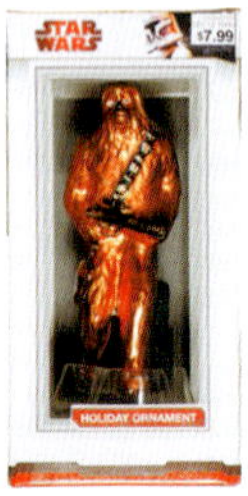

307-125

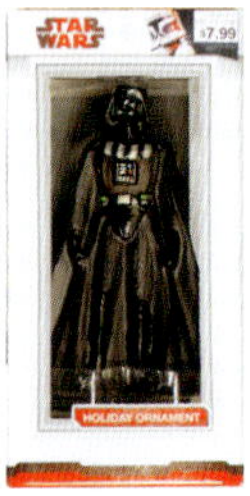

307-126

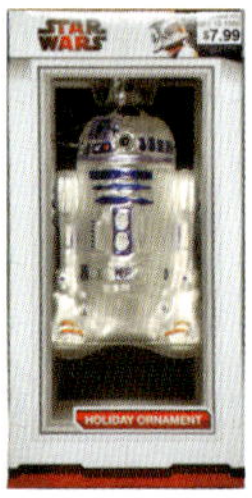

307-127

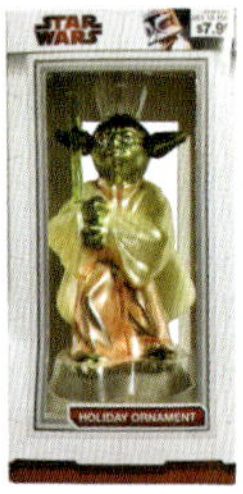

307-128

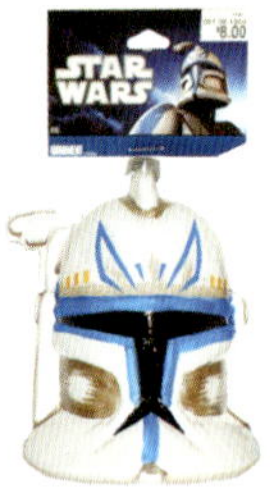

307-129

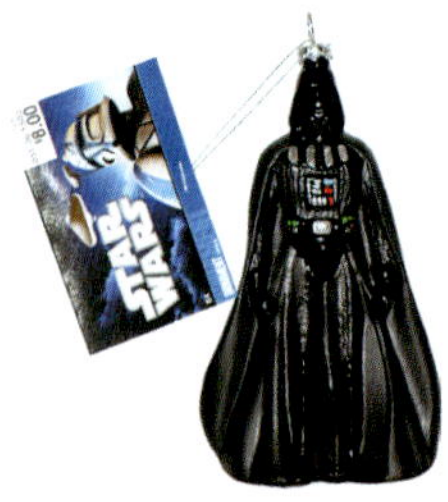

307-130

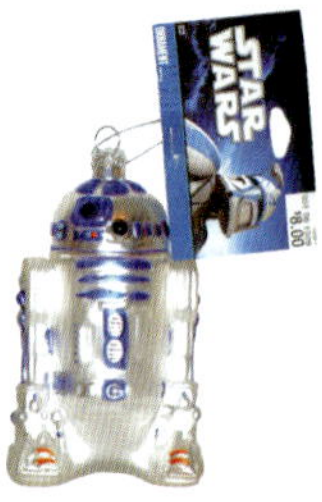

307-131

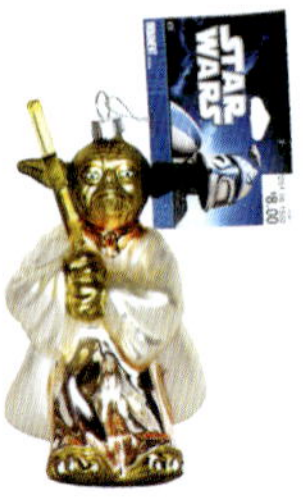

307-132

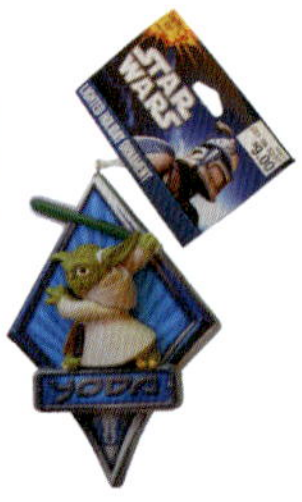

307-133

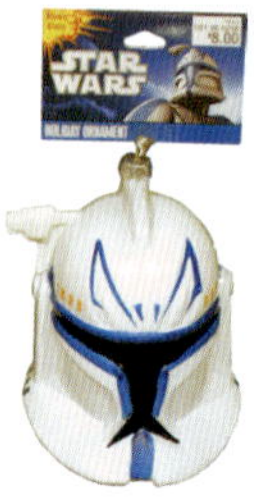

307-134

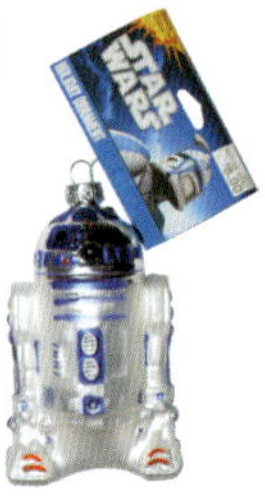

307-135

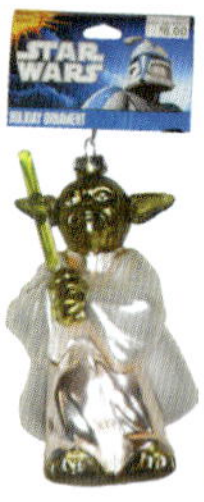

307-136

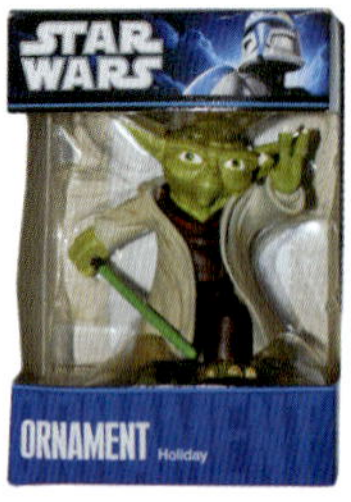

307-137

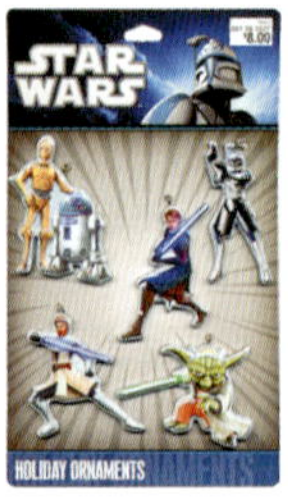

307-138

Holiday Ornaments

| 307-139 | 307-140 | 307-141 | 307-142 | 307-143 | 307-144 | 307-145 | 307-146 | 307-147 | 307-148 |

  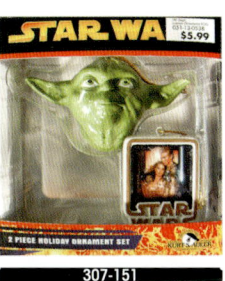 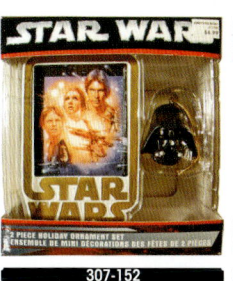  

| 307-149 | 307-150 | 307-151 | 307-152 | 307-153 | 307-154 |

| 307-155 | 307-156 | 307-157 | 307-158 | 307-159 | 307-160 | 307-161 | 307-162 |

- ☐ C-3PO [307-164]……………………………15.00
- ☐ Chewbacca [307-165]……………………15.00
- ☐ Darth Vader [307-166]……………………15.00
- ☐ Emperor Palpatine [307-167]……………15.00
- ☐ Luke Skywalker, X-Wing Pilot [307-168]…15.00
- ☐ Princess Leia [307-169]……………………15.00
- ☐ Queen Amidala [307-170]…………………15.00
- ☐ R2-D2 [307-171]……………………………15.00
- ☐ Stormtrooper [307-172]……………………15.00
- ☐ Yoda, classic [307-173]……………………15.00
- ☐ Yoda, prequel [307-174]……………………15.00

Hand crafted glass ornaments. 4" helmets. 2005.
- ☐ Boba Fett [307-175]…………………………20.00
- ☐ C-3PO [307-176]……………………………20.00
- ☐ Darth Vader [307-177]………………………20.00

Hand-crafted glass holiday ornaments. 5". 2005.
- ☐ Boba Fett [307-178]…………………………25.00
- ☐ C-3PO and R2-D2 [307-179]………………50.00
- ☐ Darth Vader [307-180]………………………25.00
- ☐ Star Wars logo [307-181]……………………20.00
- ☐ Yoda [307-182]………………………………20.00

Hand-crafted glass holiday ornaments. 5". 2006.
- ☐ C-3PO and R2-D2 [307-183]………………35.00
- ☐ Darth Vader [307-184]………………………25.00
- ☐ Yoda [307-185]………………………………25.00

Holiday ornament gift set in tin storage box. One full-figure plus two heads. 2005.
- ☐ Darth Vader / Yoda and C-3PO [307-186]…30.00
- ☐ Yoda / Darth Vader and Boba Fett [307-187]…30.00

Holiday ornament gift set. Figure plus two heads. 2005.
- ☐ Darth Vader / Yoda and C-3PO [307-188]…30.00
- ☐ Yoda / Darth Vader and Boba Fett [307-189]…30.00

M&M full round resin ornaments. 2005.
- ☐ Clone trooper and Boba Fett………………25.00
- ☐ Droids [307-190]……………………………25.00
- ☐ Emperor and Vader [307-191]……………25.00
- ☐ Luke vs. Vader [307-192]…………………25.00
- ☐ Movie Poster pose [307-193]………………25.00

M&M Mpire characters. Sold boxed. 2005.
- ☐ Boba Fett [307-194]…………………………20.00
- ☐ Bobba Fett [sic] [307-195]…………………20.00
- ☐ C-3PO [307-196]……………………………20.00
- ☐ Chewbacca [307-197]………………………20.00

| 307-163 | 307-164 | 307-165 | 307-166 | 307-167 | 307-168 | 307-169 | 307-170 |

 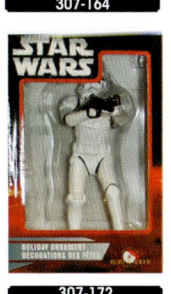  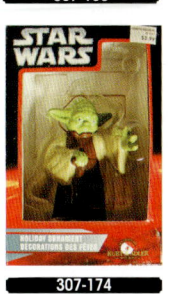    

| 307-171 | 307-172 | 307-173 | 307-174 | 307-175 | 307-176 | 307-177 | 307-178 |

Holiday Ornaments

| 307-179 | 307-180 | 307-181 | 307-182 | 307-183 | 307-184 | 307-185 | 307-186 |

| 307-187 | 307-188 | 307-189 | 307-190 | 307-191 |

❑ Clone trooper [307-198].....................20.00
❑ Darth Maul [307-199].........................20.00
❑ Darth Vader [307-200].......................20.00
❑ Han Solo [307-201]............................20.00
❑ Luke Skywalker [307-202]..................20.00
❑ Princess Leia [307-203].....................20.00
❑ Queen Amidala [307-204]...................20.00
❑ R2-D2 [307-205].................................20.00

M&M Mpire characters. Sold boxed. 2006.
❑ Boba Fett [v1e1:251]..........................20.00
❑ C-3PO [v1e1:251]...............................20.00
❑ Clone trooper [v1e1:251]....................20.00
❑ Darth Maul [v1e1:251].........................20.00
❑ Darth Vader [v1e1:251]......................20.00
❑ Princess Leia [v1e1:251]....................20.00
❑ R2-D2 [v1e1:251].................................20.00

M&M Mpire characters. Sold loose with tags. 2005.
❑ Anakin Skywalker [v1e1:251]...............15.00
❑ Boba Fett [v1e1:251]..........................15.00
❑ C-3PO [v1e1:251]...............................15.00
❑ Chewbacca [v1e1:251]......................15.00
❑ Clone trooper [v1e1:251]....................15.00
❑ Darth Vader [v1e1:251]......................15.00
❑ General Grievous [v1e1:251]..............15.00
❑ Han Solo [v1e1:251]...........................15.00
❑ Luke Skywalker [v1e1:251].................15.00
❑ Princess Leia [v1e1:251]....................15.00
❑ Queen Amidala [v1e1:251].................15.00
❑ R2-D2 [v1e1:251]................................15.00

Mini holiday ornament sets. 2005.
❑ 5-piece: vehicles [307-206]................15.00
❑ 5-piece: Mpire characters [307-207]...15.00

Mini holiday ornament sets. 2006.
❑ 5-piece: classic characters [307-208]..15.00
❑ 5-piece: vehicles [307-209]................15.00
❑ 5-piece: the Dark Side [307-210]........15.00
❑ 5-piece: the Force [307-211]..............15.00
❑ 7-piece: the Dark Side [307-212]........30.00
❑ 7-piece: the Force [307-213]..............30.00

Plush ornaments. 2005.
❑ Chewbacca [307-214]........................10.00
❑ Darth Vader [307-215].......................10.00
❑ R2-D2 [307-216].................................10.00
❑ Yoda [307-217]...................................10.00

Polonaise.
❑ Darth Vader [307-218].......................80.00
❑ Yoda and Darth Vader [307-219]........65.00

| 307-192 | 307-193 | 307-194 | 307-195 | 307-196 | 307-197 | 307-198 | 307-199 |

| 307-200 | 307-201 | 307-202 | 307-203 | 307-204 | 307-205 | 307-206 | 307-207 | 307-208 |

| 307-209 | 307-210 | 307-211 | 307-212 | 307-213 | 307-214 | 307-215 |

256

Holiday Ornaments

307-216 307-217 307-218 307-219 Side 1 and Side 2 307-220

307-221 307-222 307-223 307-224 307-225 307-226 307-227

Porcelain holiday ornaments. 2006. No package.
- Jabba the Hutt [307-220] 35.00

Spinner (head/helmet). 2005.
- Boba Fett [307-221] 12.00
- C-3PO [307-222] 12.00
- Darth Vader [307-223] 12.00
- Yoda [307-224] 12.00

Tree Toppers.
- Santa Yoda, figural [307-225] 75.00
- Yoda, lights up [307-226] 65.00
- Yoda, figural with light-up lightsaber [307-227] 50.00
- Yoda, figural with light-up lightsaber [307-228] 50.00

Lucasfilm
- Star Wars II: AOTC, Video / DVD preorder [v1e1:252] 25.00

Rawcliffe
- Royal Starship, satin finished pewter, 4.5" x 1.75" [v1e1:252] 30.00

Pewter danglers.
- Boba Fett [307-229] 15.00
- C-3PO [307-230] 15.00
- Chewbacca [307-231] 15.00
- Clone trooper [307-232] 15.00
- Darth Vader [307-233] 15.00
- Death Star [307-234] 15.00
- Jedi starfighter [307-235] 15.00
- Millennium Falcon [307-236] 15.00
- R2-D2 [307-237] 15.00
- Slave I [307-238] 15.00
- Wicket the Ewok [307-239] 15.00
- Yoda [307-240] 15.00

Pewter, stamped, 2-sided.
- C-3PO levitating [307-241] 40.00
- Jar Jar Binks in junk shop [307-242] 40.00
- Queen Amidala [307-243] 40.00
- Saber battle [307-244] 40.00
- Space battle [307-245] 40.00
- X-Wing Fighter [307-246] 40.00
- Yoda with X-Wing Fighter [307-247] 40.00

The Encore Group
Figure dangling inside of glass water globe.
- C-3PO [307-248] 25.00
- Chewbacca [307-249] 25.00
- Darth Vader [307-250] 25.00
- Millennium Falcon [307-251] 25.00
- R2-D2 [307-252] 25.00
- Yoda [307-253] 25.00

307-228 307-229 307-230 307-231 307-232 307-233 307-234 307-235 307-236 307-237 307-238 307-239 307-240

  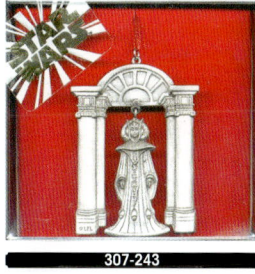 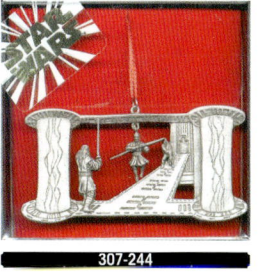 

307-241 307-242 307-243 307-244 307-245

307-246 307-247 307-248 307-249 307-250 307-251 307-252 307-253

Holiday Stockings

308-01 • 308-02 • 308-03 • 308-04 • 308-05 • 308-06 • 308-07 • 308-08 • 308-09 • 308-10

308-11 • 308-12 • 308-13 • 308-14 • 308-15 • 308-16 • 308-17 • 308-18 • 308-19 • 308-20 • 308-21

Holiday Stockings
Continued in Volume 3, Page 251

Kurt S. Adler, Inc.
Caricature art.
- Darth Vader [308-01] 30.00
- Yoda [308-02] 30.00

Cuff with art and figure head.
- Captain Rex, Clone Wars [308-03] 35.00
- Darth Vader, black with red line art [308-04] 35.00
- Yoda, Clone Wars [308-05] 35.00

Cuffed with art.
- Darth Vader [308-06] 30.00
- Darth Vader, Sith [308-07] 25.00
- Vader (helmet) [308-08] 25.00
- Yoda [308-09] 25.00
- Yoda, Jedi [308-10] 25.00

Felt with vinyl treatment.
- Vader [308-11] 20.00
- Yoda, Jedi Master [308-12] 20.00

Plush.
- Darth Vader [308-13] 15.00
- Yoda [308-14] 15.00

Quilted, Clone Wars.
- Anakin [308-15] 25.00

- Captain Rex [308-16] 25.00
- Yoda, May the Force be with you [308-17] 25.00
- Yoda [308-18] 25.00

Talking cuff with art and resin figure head.
- Darth Vader [308-19] 20.00
- Darth Vader [308-20] 25.00
- Yoda [308-21] 20.00
- Yoda 25.00

Holograms

3D Arts
- C-3PO and R2-D2, 2" x 2" in acrylic stand 15.00
- Darth Vader 4" x 6" in matted frame 30.00
- Darth Vader, 2" x 2" in acrylic stand 15.00
- Millennium Falcon 4" x 6" in matted frame 30.00
- Millennium Falcon, 3" x 2" in acrylic stand 20.00
- X-Wing Fighter, 2" x 2" in acrylic stand 15.00

A.H. Prismatic
- Darth Vader, 3" x 4.5" hologram, 8" x 10" matted ... 50.00
- Millennium Falcon, 3.5" x 2'75" in 5" x 3.75" acrylic stand 75.00
- Millennium Falcon, 3" x 4.5" hologram, 5" x 7" matted . 40.00

Fantasma
8" x 10" matted.
- Darth Vader 50.00
- Space Battle [309-01] 40.00

Inflatables

Burger King
- Darth Vader 9' x 12' includes inflater fan [310-01] ... 1,250.00

Pepsi Cola
- Anakin Skywalker's Jedi Starfighter [310-02] 50.00

The Phantom Menace inflatable display cans.
- Pepsi [310-03] 35.00
- Pepsi, gold Yoda [310-04] 50.00

Pizza Hut
- Royal Starship, 12' cold-air inflatable [310-05] 4,500.00

Instrument Knobs

Fernandes
English packaging.
- Boba Fett [311-01] 25.00
- C-3PO [311-02] 25.00
- Darth Vader [311-03] 25.00
- Stormtrooper [311-04] 25.00

Fernandes (Japan)
- Boba Fett [311-05] 30.00
- C-3PO [311-06] 30.00
- Darth Vader [311-07] 30.00
- Stormtrooper [311-08] 30.00

309-01 • 310-01 • 310-02 • 310-03 • 310-04 • 310-05

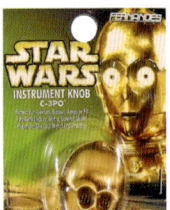      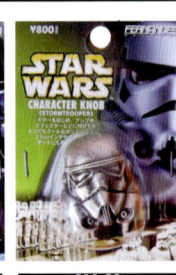

311-01 • 311-02 • 311-03 • 311-04 • 311-05 Close-Up • 311-06 • 311-07 • 311-08

Jewelry: Earrings

312-01 312-02 312-03 313-01 313-02 313-03

314-01 314-02 314-03 314-04 314-05 315-01 315-02

Iron-On Transfers
Continued in Volume 3, Page 253

Code 3 Collectibles
- Darth Vader 10.00

Factors, Etc.
- Boba Fett 25.00
- C-3PO [2:283] 25.00
- C-3PO and R2-D2, blue background 25.00
- Chewbacca [2:283] 25.00
- Darth Vadar Lives [sic] [2:283] 25.00
- Darth Vader helmet and ships [2:283] 25.00
- "Darth Vader Lives" [2:283] 25.00
- Darth Vader, glitter [2:283] 25.00
- Empire Strikes Back logo [2:283] 25.00
- Empire Strikes Back poster art 25.00
- Han Solo and Chewbacca [2:283] 25.00
- Jawa, glitter [2:283] 25.00
- Lando Calrissian 25.00
- Luke and Yoda 25.00
- Luke on Tauntaun 25.00
- Luke with X-Wing 25.00
- May the Force be with you 25.00
- "May the Force be with you" [2:283] 25.00
- Millennium Falcon 25.00
- Princess Leia 25.00
- R2-D2 .... 25.00
- Star Destroyer 25.00
- Star Wars Hildebrandt poster art 25.00

- Star Was logo, glitter 30.00
- TIE Fighter 25.00
- X-Wing Fighter 25.00
- Yoda, glitter 30.00

Flex-print (Australia)
- C-3PO [312-01] 12.00
- Darth Vader [312-02] 12.00
- Han Solo / Chewbacca 12.00
- R2-D2 [312-03] 12.00

Jewelry: Bracelets
Continued in Volume 3, Page 254

Disney / MGM
- Star Tours admission band [3:150] 20.00

Walt Disney Weekends. Rubber bracelets.
- Imperial logo 20.00
- Rebel Alliance logo 20.00

Factors, Etc.
- C-3PO, gold-finished head 40.00
- Darth Vader, black-painted head 40.00
- R2-D2, unfinished metal 40.00
- Stormtrooper, white-painted head 40.00
- X-Wing, unfinished metal 40.00

Fan Made Artistry
- Darth Maul [3:150] 10.00

Jewelry: Bracelets, Charm
Continued in Volume 3, Page 255

Bioworld Merchandising
- Star Wars charms [313-01] 25.00

Factors, Etc.
- C-3PO, Darth Vader, R2-D2 [313-02] 45.00
- Chewbacca, Stormtrooper, X-Wing [313-03] .. 75.00

Jewelry: Cufflinks
Continued in Volume 3, Page 256

- C-3PO and R2-D2, lenticular [314-01] 20.00
- Darth Maul [314-02] 20.00
- Darth Maul, lenticular [314-03] 20.00
- Jar Jar Binks [314-04] 20.00
- R2-D2 [314-05] 20.00

Jewelry: Earrings
Continued in Volume 3, Page 257

Factors, Etc.
Clip-on.
- C-3PO [315-01] 35.00
- Darth Vader [315-02] 35.00
- R2-D2 .... 35.00

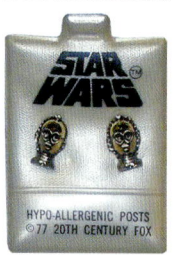 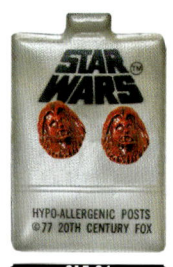   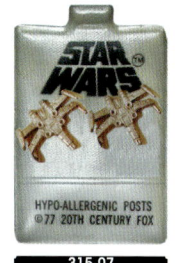  

315-03 315-04 315-05 315-06 315-07 315-08

315-09 315-10 316-01 316-02 316-03 316-04

Jewelry: Earrings

317-01 | 317-02 | 317-03 | 317-04 | 317-05 | 317-06 | 317-07 | 317-08 | 317-09

317-10 | 317-11 | 317-12 | 317-13 | 317-14 | 317-15 | 317-16 | 317-17

317-18 | 317-19 | 317-20 | 317-21 | 317-22 | 317-23 | 317-24 | 317-25 | 317-26 | 317-27 | 317-28 | 317-29

Round trademark. Trapezoid logo.
- C-3PO [315-03] 25.00
- Chewbacca [315-04] 35.00
- Darth Vader [315-05] 25.00
- R2-D2 [315-06] 25.00
- Stormtrooper 25.00
- X-Wing [315-07] 35.00

Small trademark. Rectangular logo.
- C-3PO [315-08] 30.00
- Chewbacca 35.00
- Darth Vader [315-09] 30.00
- R2-D2 .... 30.00
- Stormtrooper [315-10] 30.00
- X-Wing 35.00

Jewelry: Hair Barrettes
Continued in Volume 3, Page 259

Factors, Etc.
- C-3PO [316-01] 35.00
- Darth Vader [316-02] 35.00
- R2-D2 [316-03] 35.00

Silver hang card with earrings.
- C-3PO 75.00
- Darth Vader [316-04] 75.00
- R2-D2 .... 75.00

Jewelry: Necklaces
Continued in Volume 3, Page 259

Adam Joseph Industries
Charms, gold-colored blister packed to red card backs.
- C-3PO [317-01] 50.00
- Emperor's Royal Guard [317-02] 50.00
- Ewok [317-03] 50.00
- R2-D2 [4:163] 50.00
- Salacious Crumb [317-04] 50.00

Charms, gold colored on black plastic hang cards.
- C-3PO [317-05] 25.00

- Emperor's Royal Guard [317-06] 25.00
- Ewok [317-07] 25.00
- May the Force be with you [317-08] 25.00
- R2-D2 [317-09] 25.00
- Rebel Alliance logo [317-10] 25.00
- Return of the Jedi logo [317-11] 25.00
- Salacious Crumb [317-12] 25.00
- X-Wing Fighter Pilot [317-13] 25.00
- Yoda [317-14] 25.00

Die-cast pendants, painted.
- Darth Vader [317-15] 20.00
- R2-D2 [317-16] 20.00
- Yoda [317-17] 20.00

Creative Conventions
10th anniversary McQuarrie art.
- A New Hope 40.00
- Darth Vader in Flames 40.00
- Yoda 40.00

Factors, Etc.
C-3PO, brass colored, articulated.
- Bagged 25.00
- Boxed [317-18] 35.00
- Carded [317-19] 35.00
- Loose [4:163] 15.00

Chewbacca, painted, articulated.
- Bagged 35.00
- Boxed [317-20] 45.00
- Carded [317-21] 40.00
- Loose 20.00

Darth Vader helmet, painted.
- Bagged 25.00
- Boxed [317-22] 35.00
- Carded [317-23] 35.00
- Loose 15.00

R2-D2, steel colored, articulated.
- Bagged 25.00
- Boxed [317-24] 40.00
- Carded [317-25] 35.00
- Loose 15.00

Stormtrooper helmet, painted.
- Bagged 25.00
- Boxed [317-26] 35.00
- Carded [317-27] 35.00
- Loose [4:163] 15.00

X-Wing Fighter, steel colored.
- Bagged 30.00
- Boxed [317-28] 45.00
- Carded [317-29] 35.00
- Loose [4:163] 15.00

Jap Industries (Japan)
Sterling silver, sculpted.
- Han Solo in Carbonite 200.00

Noble Design
Lightsaber platinum electroplated pendants.
- Darth Vader 200.00
- Luke Skywalker [317-30] 200.00
- Mace Windu 200.00
- Yoda 200.00

Rock Rebel
- Imperial cog [317-31] 18.00
- Jedi [317-32] 18.00
- Rebel Alliance emblem [317-33] 18.00
- Sith [317-34] 18.00
- Star Wars logo [317-35] 18.00

Takara (Japan)
Star Wars logo.
- Gold, small [317-36] 100.00
- Silver, large [v1e1:255] 100.00
- Silver, small [v1e1:255] 100.00

Tomy (Japan)
Light-Up necklaces.
- Boba Fett [317-37] 25.00
- Darth Vader [317-38] 25.00
- R2-D2 [317-39] 25.00
- Star Wars logo [317-40] 25.00
- Yoda [317-41] 25.00

Wallace Berrie and Co.
- C-3PO and R2-D2 [317-42] 35.00

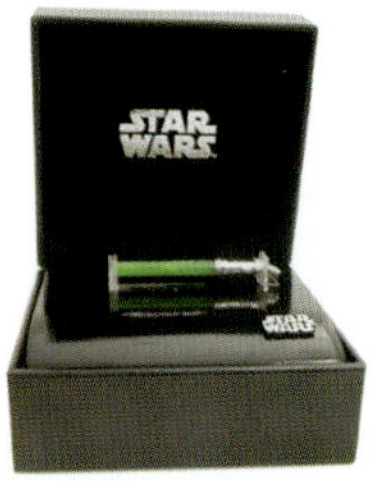

317-30

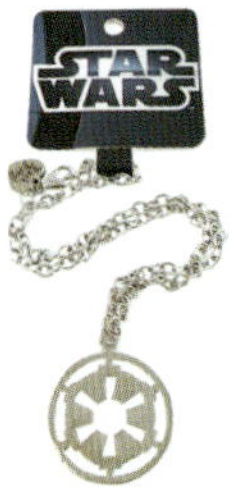

317-31

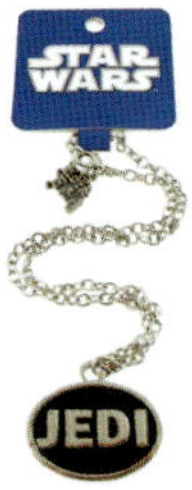

317-32

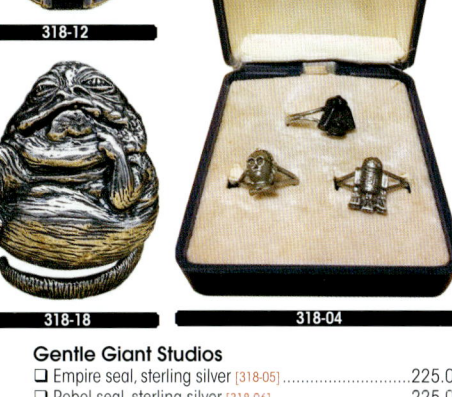

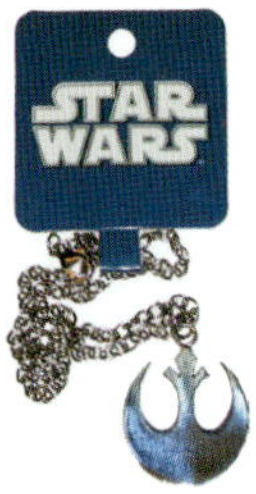

317-33

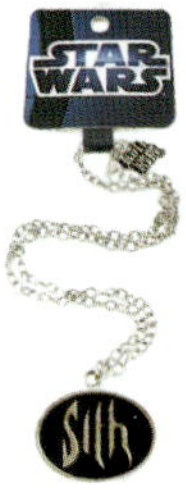

317-34

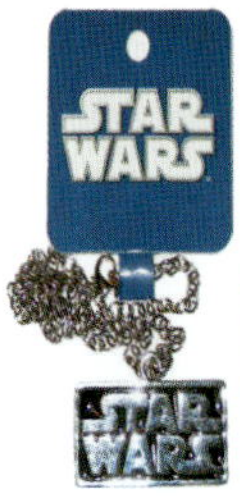

317-35

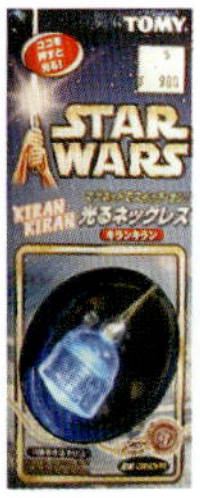

317-37

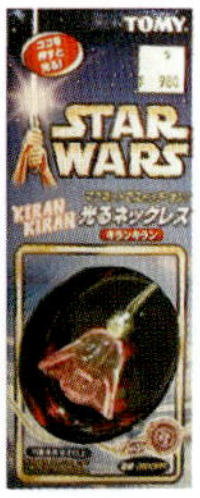

317-38

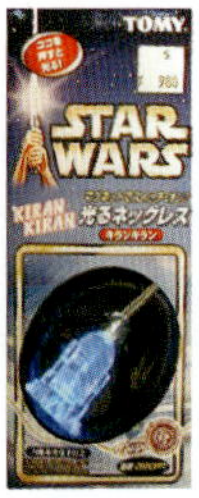

317-39

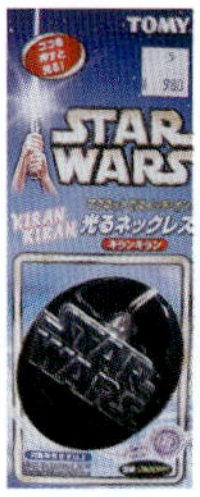

317-40

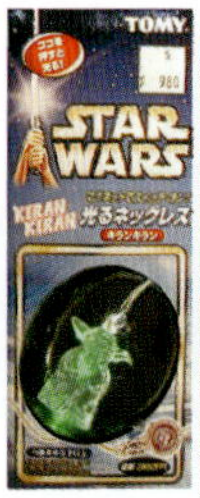

317-41

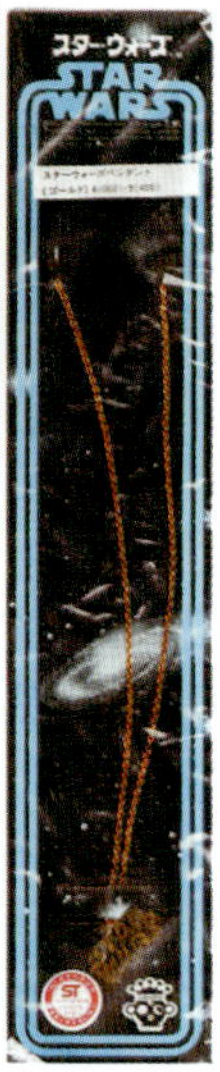

317-36

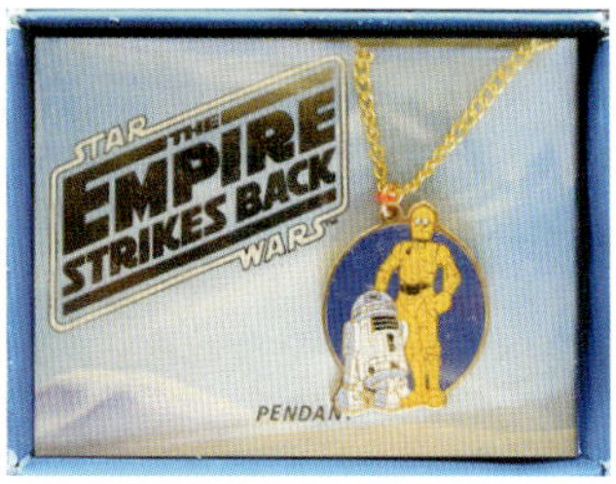

317-42

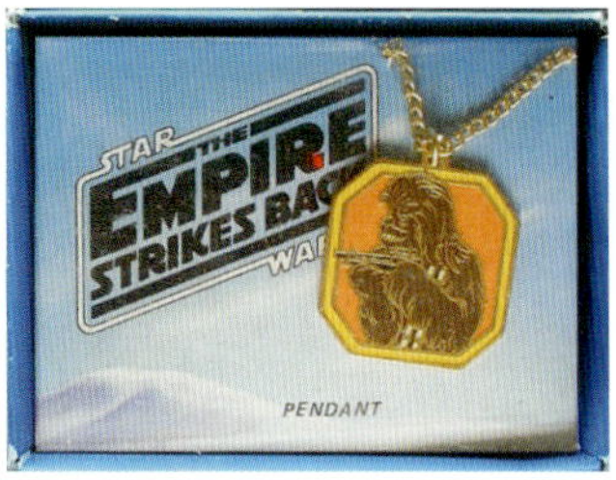

317-43

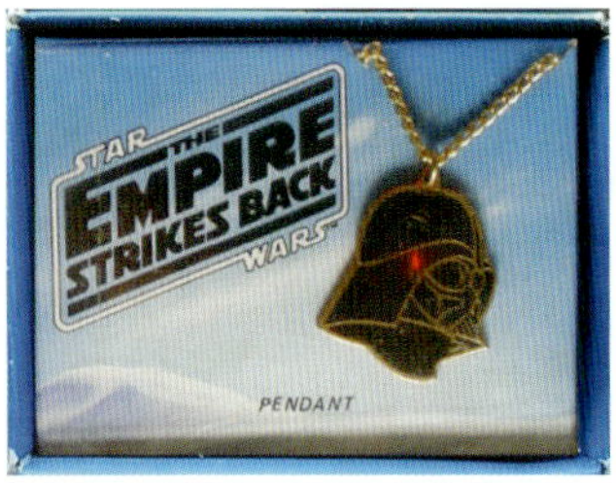

317-44

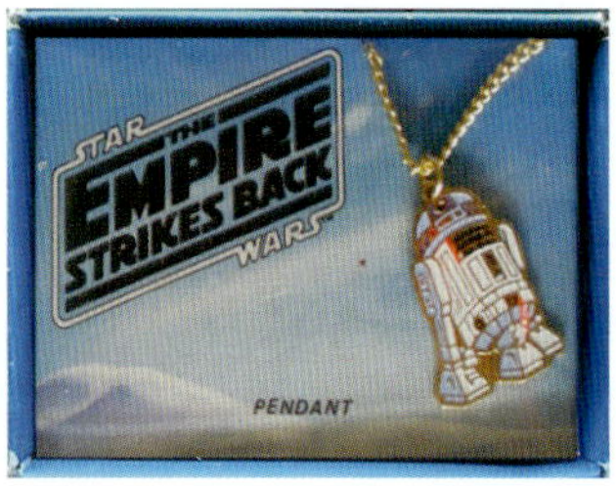

317-45

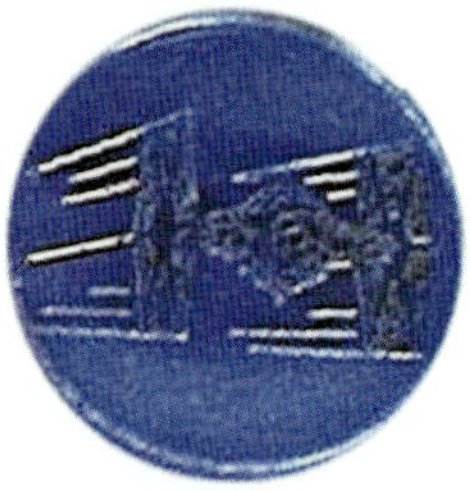
318-01

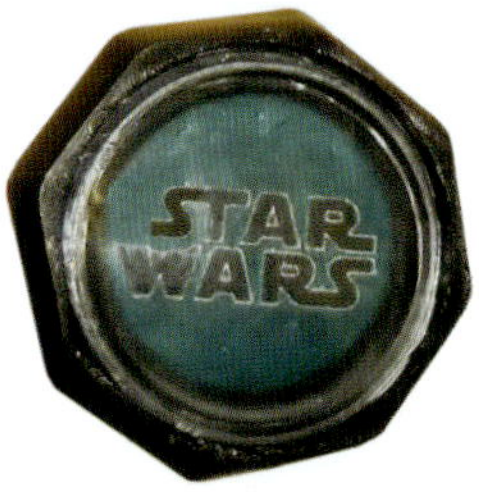

318-02

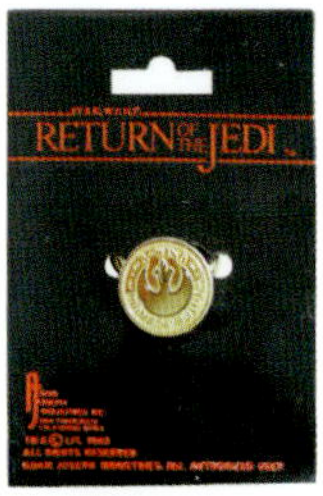

318-03

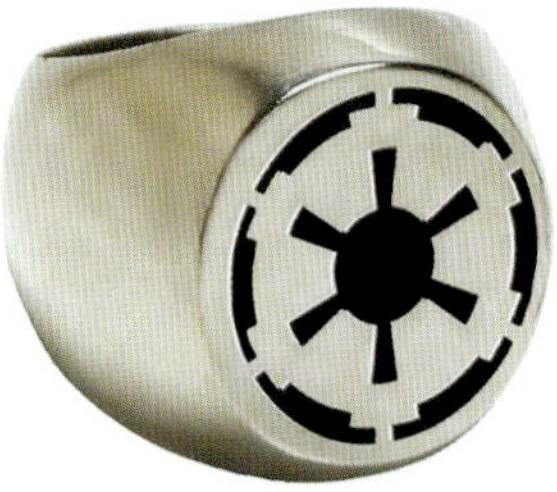
318-05

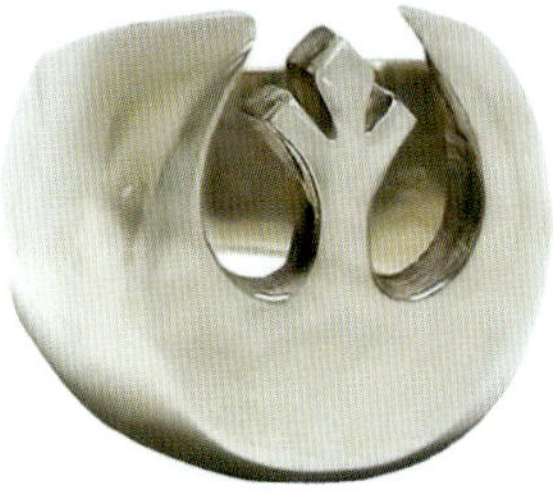
318-06

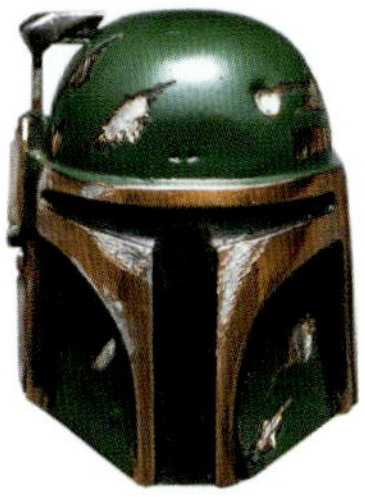
318-07

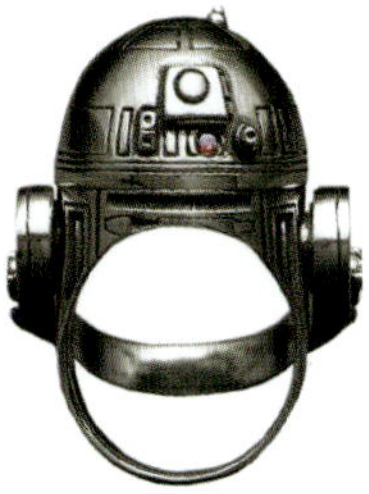
318-08

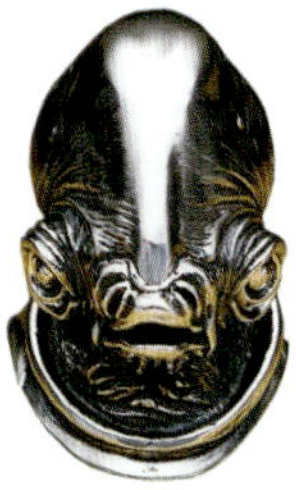
318-09

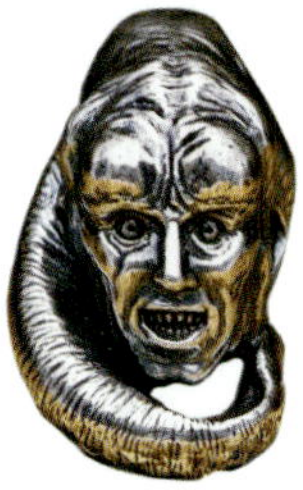
318-10

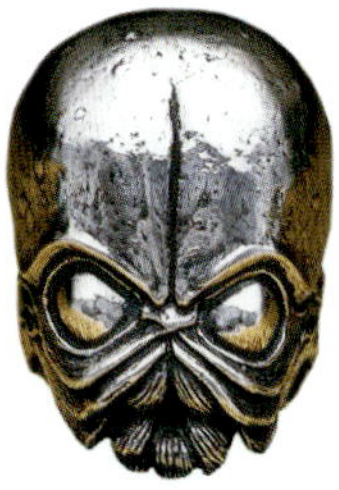
318-11

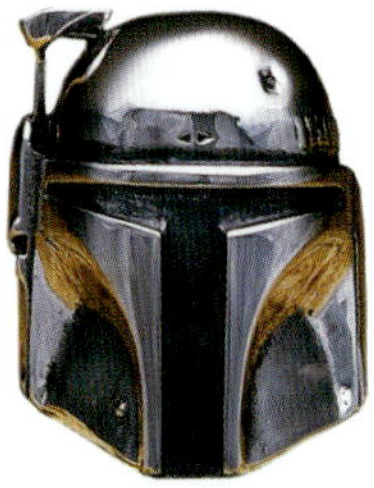
318-12

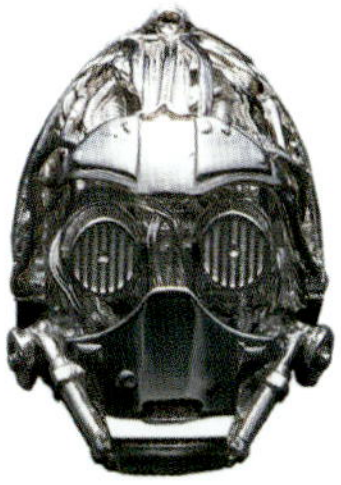
318-13

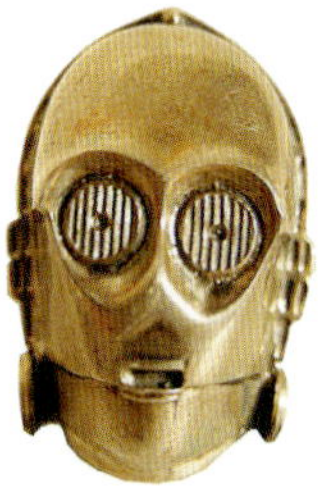
318-14

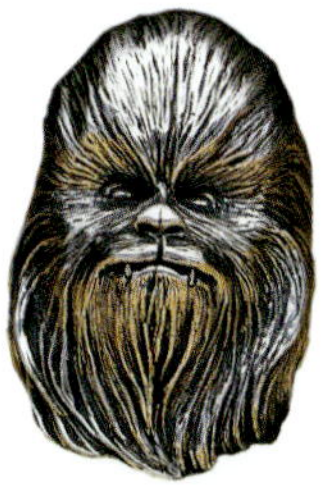
318-15

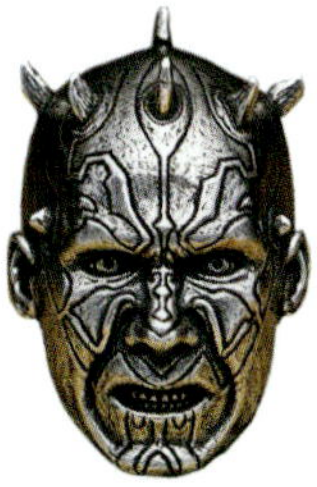
318-16

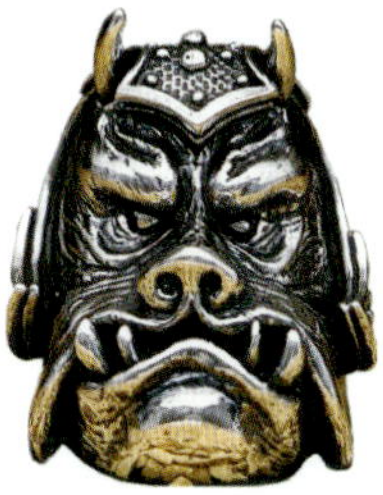
318-17

318-18

318-04

❑ Chewbacca [317-43] 35.00
❑ Darth Vader [317-44] 35.00
❑ R2-D2 [317-45] 35.00

Jewelry: Rings

Continued in Volume 3, Page 261

Fan made, sterling silver, sculpted.
❑ Boba Fett [v1e1:256] 60.00
❑ C-3PO 75.00
❑ Chewbacca [v1e1:256] 75.00
❑ Darth Maul [v1e1:256] 60.00
❑ Darth Vader 60.00

Gumball machine trinkets.
❑ Stormtrooper red or blue [4:164] 50.00
❑ "The Force" 50.00
❑ TIE Fighter red or blue [318-01] 50.00

(Argentina)
❑ Star Wars, octagon gumball machine trinket [318-02] 50.00

Adam Joseph Industries
❑ X-Wing Fighter Pilot [318-03] 50.00

Factors, Etc.
❑ C-3PO 15.00
❑ Chewbacca 15.00
❑ Darth Vader 15.00
❑ R2-D2 .....15.00
❑ Stormtrooper 15.00
❑ X-Wing 15.00
❑ Set 1: C-3PO, Chewbacca, R2-D2 [318-04] 80.00
❑ Set 2: Darth Vader, Stormtrooper, X-Wing fighter 90.00

Gentle Giant Studios
❑ Empire seal, sterling silver [318-05] 225.00
❑ Rebel seal, sterling silver [318-06] 225.00

Jap Industries (Japan)
Imperial set.
❑ 3-piece boxed set: Darth Vader, Boba Fett, Stormtrooper, 300 produced 800.00
❑ Boba Fett [318-07] 250.00
❑ Darth Vader 250.00
❑ Stormtrooper 250.00

Rebel set.
❑ 3-piece boxed set: C-3PO, R2-D2, Chewbacca, 300 produced 800.00
❑ C-3PO 250.00
❑ Chewbacca 250.00
❑ R2-D2 [318-08] 250.00

Jewelry: Rings

318-19   318-20   318-21   318-22   318-23 Image 1 and Image 2

    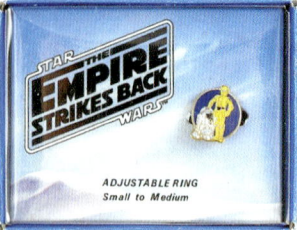 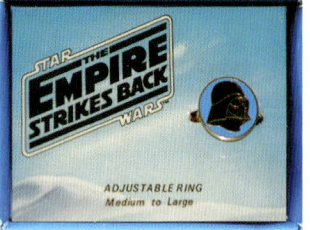

318-24   318-25   318-26   318-27   318-28   318-29

   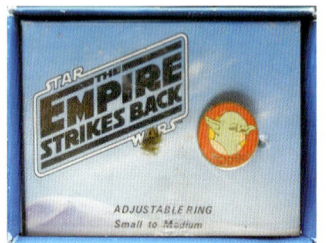

318-30   318-31   318-32   318-33

319-01   319-02   319-03   319-04   319-05   319-06   319-07   319-08

 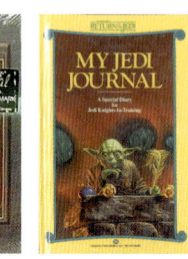   

319-09   319-10   319-11   319-12   319-13   319-14   319-15   319-16

Sterling silver, sculpted.
- ❏ Admiral Ackbar [318-09] 175.00
- ❏ Bib Fortuna [318-10] 175.00
- ❏ Biker Scout [v1e1:256] 175.00
- ❏ Bith [318-11] 175.00
- ❏ Boba Fett [318-12] 175.00
- ❏ C-3PO [318-13] 175.00
- ❏ C-3PO [318-14] 175.00
- ❏ Chewbacca [318-15] 175.00
- ❏ Darth Maul [318-16] 175.00
- ❏ Darth Vader 175.00
- ❏ Gamorrean Guard [318-17] 175.00
- ❏ Jabba the Hutt [318-18] 175.00
- ❏ Jar Jar Binks [v1e1:256] 175.00
- ❏ Jawa [318-19] 350.00
- ❏ R2-D2 [v1e1:256] 175.00
- ❏ Rancor [v1e1:256] 175.00
- ❏ Sebulba [v1e1:256] 175.00

- ❏ Stormtrooper [318-20] 175.00
- ❏ Tusken Raider [v1e1:256] 175.00
- ❏ Wicket [318-21] 175.00
- ❏ Yoda [318-22] 175.00

Party Express
- ❏ Darth Vader / Star Wars lenticular [318-23] 5.00

Clone Wars.
- ❏ Anakin Skywalker [318-24] 3.00
- ❏ Captain Rex [318-25] 3.00
- ❏ Obi-Wan Kenobi [318-26] 3.00
- ❏ Yoda [318-27] 3.00

Wallace Berrie and Co.
- ❏ C-3PO and R2-D2 [318-28] 40.00
- ❏ Darth Vader [318-29] 40.00
- ❏ "May the Force be with you" [318-30] 40.00

- ❏ R2-D2 [318-31] 40.00
- ❏ X-Wing Fighter [318-32] 40.00
- ❏ Yoda [318-33] 40.00

Journals, Blank
Continued in Volume 3, Page 262

120 pages.
- ❏ Darth Maul / Jedi vs. Sith [319-01] 10.00
- ❏ Star Wars [319-02] 10.00
- ❏ Star Wars 10.00
- ❏ Yoda / Dagobah 10.00

Antioch
- ❏ 20th Anniversary with Rystall bookmark and 2 wallet cards [319-03] 30.00

Keychains

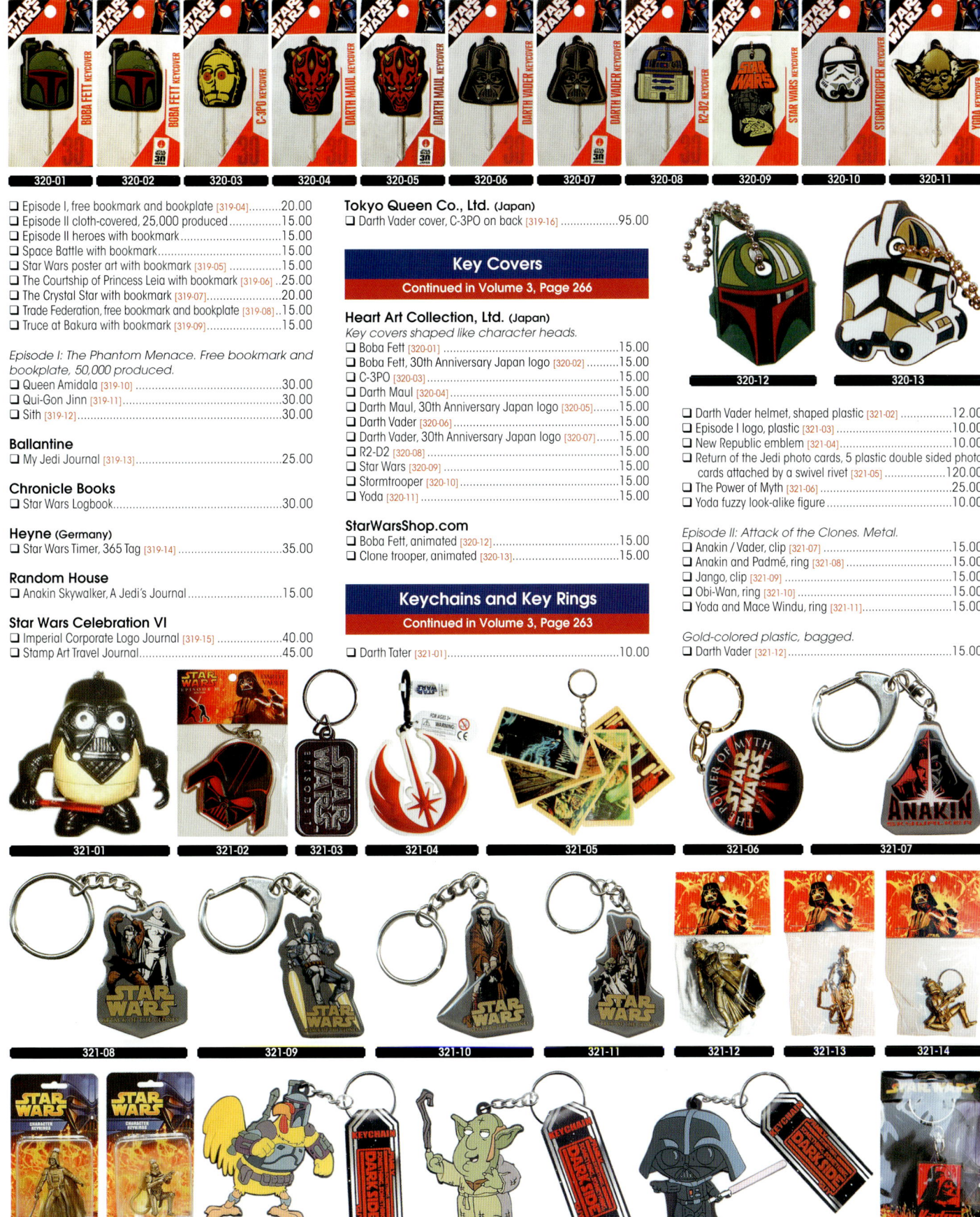

- Episode I, free bookmark and bookplate [319-04]..........20.00
- Episode II cloth-covered, 25,000 produced 15.00
- Episode II heroes with bookmark 15.00
- Space Battle with bookmark....................................15.00
- Star Wars poster art with bookmark [319-05] 15.00
- The Courtship of Princess Leia with bookmark [319-06]..25.00
- The Crystal Star with bookmark [319-07]......................20.00
- Trade Federation, free bookmark and bookplate [319-08]..15.00
- Truce at Bakura with bookmark [319-09]......................15.00

Episode I: The Phantom Menace. Free bookmark and bookplate, 50,000 produced.
- Queen Amidala [319-10]...30.00
- Qui-Gon Jinn [319-11]..30.00
- Sith [319-12]...30.00

Ballantine
- My Jedi Journal [319-13]...25.00

Chronicle Books
- Star Wars Logbook..30.00

Heyne (Germany)
- Star Wars Timer, 365 Tag [319-14] 35.00

Random House
- Anakin Skywalker, A Jedi's Journal 15.00

Star Wars Celebration VI
- Imperial Corporate Logo Journal [319-15] 40.00
- Stamp Art Travel Journal..45.00

Tokyo Queen Co., Ltd. (Japan)
- Darth Vader cover, C-3PO on back [319-16] 95.00

Key Covers
Continued in Volume 3, Page 266

Heart Art Collection, Ltd. (Japan)
Key covers shaped like character heads.
- Boba Fett [320-01]...15.00
- Boba Fett, 30th Anniversary Japan logo [320-02] 15.00
- C-3PO [320-03]...15.00
- Darth Maul [320-04]...15.00
- Darth Maul, 30th Anniversary Japan logo [320-05].......15.00
- Darth Vader [320-06]...15.00
- Darth Vader, 30th Anniversary Japan logo [320-07].....15.00
- R2-D2 [320-08]...15.00
- Star Wars [320-09]...15.00
- Stormtrooper [320-10]..15.00
- Yoda [320-11]..15.00

StarWarsShop.com
- Boba Fett, animated [320-12]...................................15.00
- Clone trooper, animated [320-13].............................15.00

Keychains and Key Rings
Continued in Volume 3, Page 263

- Darth Tater [321-01]..10.00

- Darth Vader helmet, shaped plastic [321-02] 12.00
- Episode I logo, plastic [321-03]................................10.00
- New Republic emblem [321-04]...............................10.00
- Return of the Jedi photo cards, 5 plastic double sided photo cards attached by a swivel rivet [321-05] 120.00
- The Power of Myth [321-06] 25.00
- Yoda fuzzy look-alike figure 10.00

Episode II: Attack of the Clones. Metal.
- Anakin / Vader, clip [321-07]...................................15.00
- Anakin and Padmé, ring [321-08]..............................15.00
- Jango, clip [321-09]...15.00
- Obi-Wan, ring [321-10]...15.00
- Yoda and Mace Windu, ring [321-11]........................15.00

Gold-colored plastic, bagged.
- Darth Vader [321-12]...15.00

263

Keychains

321-21 | 321-22 | 321-23 | 321-24 | 321-25 | 321-26 | 321-27 | 321-28 | 321-29

321-30 | 321-31 | 321-32 | 321-33 | 321-34 | 321-35 | 321-36

- ❑ General Grievous [321-13].................................15.00
- ❑ Stormtrooper [321-14]......................................15.00

Gold-colored plastic, carded.
- ❑ Darth Vader [321-15]..20.00
- ❑ General Grievous 20.00
- ❑ Stormtrooper [321-16]......................................20.00

Something Something Something Dark Side.
- ❑ Boba Chicken [321-17]......................................15.00
- ❑ Carl Yoda [321-18]...15.00
- ❑ Darth Stewie [321-19].....................................15.00

(Belgium)
Rubber.
- ❑ Vader [321-20]..10.00
- ❑ Yoda [v1e1:258]..10.00

(Japan)
- ❑ R2-D2 etched with padded case [321-21].............40.00

(UK)
Lightsaber torches with glowing LED.
- ❑ Darth Vader [321-22].......................................10.00

3D Arts
Square lasergram keychains.
- ❑ C-3PO and R2-D2 ....30.00
- ❑ Darth Vader 30.00
- ❑ X-Wing Fighter 30.00
- ❑ Yoda 30.00

A.H. Prismatic
Hologram in 2" plastic square.
- ❑ AT-AT [321-23]...30.00
- ❑ C-3PO and R2-D2 [321-24].................................30.00
- ❑ Darth Vader [321-25].......................................30.00
- ❑ Millennium Falcon 30.00
- ❑ TIE Fighter 30.00
- ❑ X-Wing Fighter [321-26]...................................30.00
- ❑ X-Wing vs. TIE Fighter, Star Wars logo [321-27] 30.00

Adam Joseph Industries
Ewoks. Plastic.
- ❑ Princess Kneesaa [321-28].................................25.00
- ❑ Wicket [321-29]..25.00

Return of the Jedi. Brass.
- ❑ Darth Vader [321-30].......................................25.00
- ❑ Millennium Falcon [321-31]................................25.00
- ❑ R2-D2 [321-32]...25.00
- ❑ Yoda [321-33]..25.00

321-37 | 321-38 | 321-39 | 321-40 | 321-41 | 321-42 | 321-43 | 321-44 | 321-45

321-46 | 321-47 | 321-48 | 321-49 | 321-50 | 321-51 | 321-52

321-53 | 321-54 | 321-55 | 321-56 | 321-57 | 321-58 | 321-59

Keychains

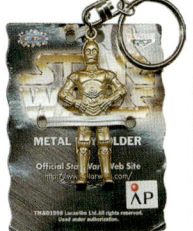  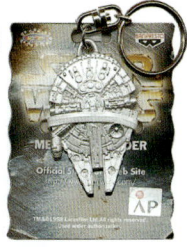  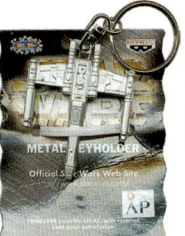   

321-60 | 321-61 | 321-62 | 321-63 | 321-64 | 321-65 | 321-66 | 321-67

321-68 | 321-69 | 321-70 | 321-71 | 321-72 | 321-73

321-74 | 321-75 | 321-76 | 321-77 | 321-78 | 321-79 | 321-80

Applause
- ❏ Jedi vs. Sith on blue oval [321-34] 10.00
- ❏ Jedi vs. Sith round [321-35] 10.00
- ❏ Podracing [321-36] 10.00

3D metal, articulated.
- ❏ Jar Jar Binks [321-37] 12.00
- ❏ Jar Jar Binks, carded [321-38] 20.00
- ❏ Jar Jar Binks, hang tag [v1e1:258] 15.00
- ❏ Pit Droid [v1e1:258] 15.00
- ❏ Pit Droid, carded [321-39] 30.00
- ❏ Pit Droid, hang tag [321-40] 20.00
- ❏ Watto [321-41] 12.00
- ❏ Watto, carded 20.00
- ❏ Watto, hang tag [321-42] 15.00
- ❏ Watto, Pit Droid, Jar Jar, carded [321-43] 45.00

Flat vinyl.
- ❏ Boba Fett [321-44] 10.00
- ❏ Darth Maul [321-45] 8.00
- ❏ Darth Vader [321-46] 10.00
- ❏ Greedo [321-47] 10.00
- ❏ Jar Jar Binks [321-48] 8.00
- ❏ Stormtrooper [321-49] 10.00

PVC figures on card backs.
- ❏ Anakin Skywalker [321-50] 10.00
- ❏ Darth Maul [321-51] 10.00
- ❏ Destroyer Droid 10.00
- ❏ Jar Jar Binks 10.00
- ❏ Obi-Wan Kenobi 10.00
- ❏ Pit Droid 10.00
- ❏ Queen Amidala [321-52] 10.00
- ❏ Qui-Gon Jinn 10.00

PVC figures.
- ❏ Anakin Skywalker [321-53] 8.00
- ❏ Darth Maul [321-54] 8.00
- ❏ Destroyer Droid [321-55] 8.00
- ❏ Jar Jar Binks 8.00
- ❏ Obi-Wan Kenobi [321-56] 8.00
- ❏ Pit Droid [321-57] 8.00
- ❏ Queen Amidala [321-58] 8.00
- ❏ Qui-Gon Jinn [321-59] 8.00

Avon
Gold colored. Same style as Playco Toys. Sold in brown boxes without graphics.
- ❏ Artoo Detoo 20.00
- ❏ Darth Vader 20.00
- ❏ Luke Skywalker 20.00
- ❏ Stormtrooper 20.00

321-81 | 321-82 | 321-83 | 321-84 | 321-85 | 321-86 | 321-87 | 321-88

321-89 | 321-90 | 321-91 | 321-92 | 321-93 | 321-94 | 321-95 | 321-96 | 321-97

Keychains

| 321-98 | 321-99 | 321-100 | 321-101 | 321-102 | 321-103 | 321-104 | 321-105 | 321-106 | 321-107 |

| 321-108 | 321-109 | 321-110 | 321-111 | 321-112 | 321-113 | 321-114 | 321-115 | 321-116 |

Banpresto (Japan)
Sculpted metal figures.
- C-3PO [321-60] 35.00
- Darth Vader [321-61] 35.00
- Millennium Falcon [321-62] 35.00
- R2-D2 [321-63] 35.00
- X-Wing Fighter [321-64] 35.00

Basic Fun
2-Packs.
- Darth Maul / Qui-Gon Jinn [321-65] 25.00
- Darth Vader / Boba Fett [321-66] 25.00
- Luke Skywalker / Yoda 25.00
- Princess Leia / R2-D2 [321-67] 25.00

Clone Wars.
- 25-pack [321-68] 65.00

Clone Wars. Boxed set keychains in oval packaging.
- Set 1, Ahsoka Tano, Assassin Droid, Commander Cody, Gha Nachkt, Kit Fisto, Luminara, Obi-Wan Kenobi, R2-D2, Rotta the Huttlet [321-69] 50.00
- Set 2, Anakin Skywalker, Asajj Ventress, C-3PO, Cad Bane, Commander Fox, Plo Kloon, General Whorm, Yoda 50.00
- Set 3, Aayla Secura, Mace Windu, Count Dooku, Captain Rex, Magna guard, General Grievous, Nahdar Vebb, R2-KT 50.00

Clone Wars. Series 1, individually carded.
- Ahsoka Tano 10.00
- Assassin Droid 10.00
- Commander Cody 10.00
- Gha Nachkt 10.00
- Kit Fisto 10.00
- Luminara Unduli 10.00
- Obi-Wan Kenobi 10.00
- R2-D2 .... 10.00

Clone Wars. Series 2, individually carded.
- Anakin Skywalker 10.00
- Asajj Ventress 10.00
- C3-PO 10.00
- Cad Bane 10.00
- Commander Fox 10.00
- General Whorm 10.00
- Plo Kloon 10.00
- Yoda 10.00

Clone Wars. Series 3, individually carded.
- Aayla Secura 10.00
- Captain Rex 10.00

| 321-117 | 321-118 | 321-119 | 321-120 | 321-121 | 321-122 | 321-123 | 321-124 | 321-125 |

| 321-126 | 321-127 | 321-128 | 321-129 | 321-130 | 321-131 | 321-132 | 321-133 | 321-134 | 321-135 | 321-136 |

| 321-137 | 321-138 | 321-139 | 321-140 | 321-141 | 321-142 | 321-143 | 321-144 | 321-145 | 321-146 | 321-147 |

Keychains

- ❑ Count Dooku 10.00
- ❑ General Grievous 10.00
- ❑ Mace Windu 10.00
- ❑ Magna guard 10.00
- ❑ Nahdar Vebb 10.00
- ❑ R2-KT 10.00

Figural, Clone Wars-style packaging.
- ❑ Anakin Skywalker [321-70] 10.00
- ❑ C-3PO [321-71] 10.00
- ❑ Clone Captain Rex [321-72] 10.00
- ❑ Clone Commander Cody [321-73] 10.00
- ❑ Darth Vader [321-74] 10.00
- ❑ General Grievous [321-75] 10.00
- ❑ Obi-Wan Kenobi [321-76] 10.00
- ❑ Stormtrooper [321-77] 10.00
- ❑ Yoda 10.00

Individually packaged, blue.
- ❑ Biker Scout 10.00
- ❑ Boba Fett [321-78] 10.00
- ❑ Chewbacca [321-79] 10.00
- ❑ Death Star 10.00
- ❑ Han Solo 10.00
- ❑ Millennium Falcon [321-80] 10.00

Individually packaged.
- ❑ Boba Fett [321-81] 10.00
- ❑ C-3PO [321-82] 10.00
- ❑ Darth Maul [321-83] 10.00
- ❑ Darth Vader [321-84] 10.00
- ❑ Princess Leia [321-85] 10.00
- ❑ Qui-Gon Jinn [321-86] 10.00
- ❑ R2-D2 [321-87] 10.00
- ❑ Stormtrooper [321-88] 10.00

Sold loose with tag.
- ❑ Anakin Skywalker [321-89] 8.00
- ❑ Boba Fett [321-90] 8.00
- ❑ C-3PO [321-91] 8.00
- ❑ Chewbacca [321-92] 8.00
- ❑ Clone trooper [321-93] 8.00
- ❑ Count Dooku [321-94] 8.00
- ❑ Count Dooku, holographic [321-95] 8.00
- ❑ Darth Maul 8.00
- ❑ Darth Vader [321-96] 8.00
- ❑ Darth Vader, holographic [321-97] 8.00
- ❑ Emperor Palpatine [321-98] 8.00
- ❑ Emperor Palpatine, holographic [321-99] .. 8.00
- ❑ General Grievous [321-100] 8.00
- ❑ Jabba the Hutt 8.00
- ❑ Jango Fett [321-101] 8.00
- ❑ Jango Fett, holographic 8.00

267

Keychains

- ❏ Luke Skywalker [321-102].................................8.00
- ❏ Mace Windu [321-103].....................................8.00
- ❏ Obi-Wan Kenobi [321-104]................................8.00
- ❏ Princess Leia [321-105]....................................8.00
- ❏ Queen Amidala [321-106].................................8.00
- ❏ Queen Amidala, holographic [321-107]................8.00
- ❏ Qui-Gon Jinn [321-108]....................................8.00
- ❏ R2-D2 [321-109]...8.00
- ❏ Stormtrooper [321-110]....................................8.00
- ❏ Stormtrooper, holographic [321-111]...................8.00
- ❏ Super Battle Droid [321-112].............................8.00
- ❏ Wicket [321-113]...8.00
- ❏ Yoda [321-114]..8.00

Stack-Ems.
- ❏ Boba Fett [321-115]...15.00
- ❏ C-3PO..15.00
- ❏ Captain Rex [321-116].....................................20.00

- ❏ Chewbacca [321-117].......................................15.00
- ❏ Commander Cody [321-118]..............................20.00
- ❏ Commander Fox [321-119]................................20.00
- ❏ Darth Vader [321-120]......................................15.00
- ❏ R2-D2 [321-121]..15.00
- ❏ Stormtrooper [321-122]....................................15.00

Basic Fun (Australia)
- ❏ 25-pack, includes special edition gold Darth Vader....50.00

Basic Fun (Canada)
- ❏ 25-pack, includes special edition Hologram Darth Vader, exclusive to Walmart [321-123]....................50.00

Be@rbrick (Japan)
Teddy Bears.
- ❏ Chewbacca [321-124].......................................25.00
- ❏ Darth Maul [321-125].......................................25.00

C and D Visionaries, Inc.
- ❏ Anakin collage [321-126]..................................5.00
- ❏ A New Hope Movie Poster [321-127]...................5.00
- ❏ Boba Fett [321-128]...5.00
- ❏ Chewbacca and Han [321-129]..........................5.00
- ❏ Darth Vader [321-130]......................................5.00
- ❏ Darth Vader flaming helmet [321-131].................5.00
- ❏ Darth Vader on Bespin [321-132]........................5.00
- ❏ Darth Vader with Emperor [321-133]....................5.00
- ❏ Darth Vader's TIE Fighter [321-134].....................5.00
- ❏ Droids on Endor [321-135]................................5.00
- ❏ Evil—Darth Vader [321-136]...............................5.00
- ❏ General Grievous [321-137]...............................5.00
- ❏ General Grievous—close-up [321-138]................5.00
- ❏ Han in Carbonite [321-139]...............................5.00
- ❏ Lightsaber fight [321-140].................................5.00
- ❏ My other transport is the Millennium Falcon [321-141]....5.00
- ❏ Obi-Wan Kenobi [321-142]................................5.00

Keychains

- Princess Leia [321-143] 5.00
- Princess Leia captive [321-144] 5.00
- Princess Leia captive close-up [321-145] 5.00
- Return of the Jedi logo [321-146] 5.00
- Sith / Darth Vader [321-147] 5.00
- Sith Lord [321-148] 5.00
- Star Wars logo [321-149] 5.00
- Who's Your Daddy? [321-150] 5.00
- Wicket [321-151] 5.00
- Yoda (concentrating) [321-152] 5.00
- Yoda and Luke [321-153] 5.00
- Yoda collage [321-154] 5.00
- Yoda sitting [321-155] 5.00
- Yoda standing [321-156] 5.00
- Yoda with lightsaber [321-157] 5.00
- Yoda, "Do ... or do not. There is no try." [321-158] 5.00

Cards, Inc. (UK)
- Darth Vader [321-159] 10.00
- Darth Vader eyes [321-160] 10.00
- Epic Duel [321-161] 10.00
- Jedi [321-162] 10.00
- Sith Lord [321-163] 10.00
- Yoda eyes [321-164] 10.00

Etched metal.
- Clone trooper [321-165] 15.00
- Darth Vader [321-166] 15.00
- Grievous [321-167] 15.00
- Jedi [321-168] 15.00

Hedz, sculpted.
- Boba Fett [321-169] 20.00
- C-3PO [321-170] 20.00
- Chewbacca [321-171] 20.00
- Clone trooper [321-172] 20.00
- Darth Maul [321-173] 20.00
- Darth Vader [321-174] 20.00
- Jango Fett [321-175] 20.00
- R2-D2 [321-176] 20.00
- Stormtrooper [321-177] 20.00
- Yoda [321-178] 20.00

Manga style, die-cut rubber.
- Boba Fett [321-179] 25.00

- Darth Vader [321-180] 25.00
- Droids [321-181] 25.00
- Han Solo and Chewbacca [321-182] 25.00
- Luke and Leia [321-183] 25.00
- Yoda vs. Darth Sidious [321-184] 25.00

Cingular
- Star Wars Vader Viper, exclusive to Star Wars Celebration III [321-185] 15.00

Classico
3D laser engraved glass cube keychains with illumination.
- Darth Vader, illuminated red 30.00

Coca-Cola
- R2-D2 Co-bot miniature 75.00

Creative Conventions
1.5" x 2" white background.
- Darth Vader in Flames 10.00
- Luke Skywalker, "A New Hope" triangular logo 10.00
- Yoda in circle 10.00

Crystal Craft (Australia)
- Bravo Squadron [321-186] 15.00
- JEDI [321-187] 15.00
- Naboo Royal Starship [321-188] 15.00
- Podracing [321-189] 15.00
- Star Wars Episode I logo [321-190] 15.00
- The Dark Side [321-191] 15.00

Disney / MGM
- Empire / Rebellion, spinning [321-192] 20.00
- Jedi Training Academy [321-193] 20.00
- Triangular design with Star Tours logo [321-194] 30.00

Characters.
- Boba Fett [321-195] 20.00
- Stormtrooper [321-196] 20.00

Flashing lightsaber keychains.
- Blue 20.00
- Purple 20.00
- Red 20.00

Star Wars Weekends.
- 2001 R2-D2 projecting hologram Mickey [321-197] 30.00
- 2003 Logo spinner [321-198] 30.00
- 2004 Mickey and Minnie poster art [321-199] 20.00
- 2005 Darth Vader / Mickey 20.00
- 2006 Star Wars Weekends logo 20.00
- "Yoda," lightsaber shape, flashes green 20.00

Disney Theme Park Merchandise
- Star Tours [321-200] 35.00
- Star Wars Weekends 2011, Jedi Mickey vs. Darth Vader [321-201] 20.00

Downpace Ltd. (UK)
Classic trilogy characters.
- Boba Fett [321-202] 25.00
- Boba Fett with gun [321-203] 25.00
- C-3PO [321-204] 25.00
- Darth Vader helmet [321-205] 25.00
- Darth Vader profile [321-206] 25.00
- Darth Vader reaching [321-207] 25.00
- Princess Leia [321-208] 25.00
- R2-D2 [321-209] 25.00
- Stormtrooper [321-210] 25.00
- Yoda [321-211] 25.00

Episode I characters.
- Anakin Skywalker [321-212] 15.00
- Battle Droid [321-213] 15.00
- Darth Maul [321-214] 15.00
- Jar Jar Binks [321-215] 15.00
- Obi-Wan Kenobi [321-216] 15.00
- Qui-Gon Jinn [321-217] 15.00

Factors, Etc.
- C-3PO 25.00
- Chewbacca 25.00
- Darth Vader helmet, 1.25" painted black 25.00
- R2-D2 1" unpainted metal 25.00
- Stormtrooper helmet, 1" painted white 25.00
- X-Wing Fighter, 2" unpainted 25.00

Fan Club
- 10th Anniversary 1.5" square plastic 30.00
- Official Star Wars Fan Club, 1977 [321-218] 50.00

269

Keychains

    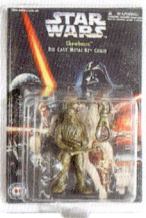 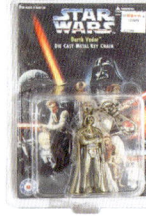  

321-278 | 321-279 | 321-280 | 321-281 | 321-282 | 321-283 | 321-284 | 321-285

 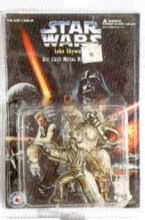   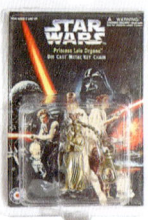 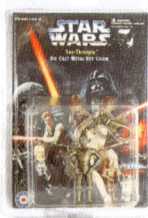  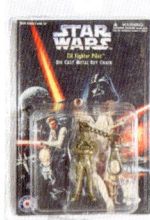

321-286 | 321-287 | 321-288 | 321-289 | 321-290 | 321-291 | 321-292 | 321-293

Granmark (Mexico)
- ❏ El Regreso Del Jedi [321-219] 35.00

Hallmark Party
- ❏ Yoda disc on clip ring, from 48-pack of party favors [321-220] 5.00

Happinet (Japan)
Lucite with caricatures.
- ❏ Anakin Skywalker [321-221] 15.00
- ❏ Boba Fett [321-222] 15.00
- ❏ C-3PO [321-223] 15.00
- ❏ Chewbacca [321-224] 15.00
- ❏ Darth Maul [321-225] 15.00
- ❏ Darth Vader [321-226] 15.00
- ❏ Grievous [321-227] 15.00
- ❏ Han Solo [321-228] 15.00
- ❏ Jabba the Hutt [321-229] 15.00
- ❏ Leia Organa [321-230] 15.00
- ❏ Luke Skywalker [321-231] 15.00
- ❏ Obi-Wan Kenobi [321-232] 15.00
- ❏ R2-D2 [321-233] 15.00
- ❏ Stormtrooper [321-234] 15.00
- ❏ Wicket [321-235] 15.00
- ❏ Yoda [321-236] 15.00

Hasbro (Japan)
US release with marketing sticker.
- ❏ Death Star, recorder [321-237] 20.00
- ❏ Stormtrooper, speaks one phrase [321-238] 20.00

Hickock (Mexico)
- ❏ Admiral Ackbar 25.00
- ❏ Bib Fortuna [321-239] 25.00
- ❏ C-3PO 25.00
- ❏ Chewbacca 25.00
- ❏ Darth Vader 25.00
- ❏ Emperor Palpatine 25.00
- ❏ Han Solo 25.00
- ❏ Lando Calrissian 25.00
- ❏ Luke Skywalker 25.00
- ❏ Princess Leia 25.00
- ❏ R2-D2 .... 25.00
- ❏ Stormtrooper 25.00

Hollywood Pins
- ❏ "20-Years 1977–1997" [321-240] 30.00
- ❏ Darth Vader, mask [321-241] 20.00
- ❏ Darth Vader, mask (small) [321-242] 20.00
- ❏ Darth Vader, portrait [321-243] 25.00
- ❏ Millennium Falcon [321-244] 20.00
- ❏ New Republic 25.00
- ❏ New Republic, antique finish [321-245] 25.00
- ❏ "Power of the Dark Side" [321-246] 20.00

    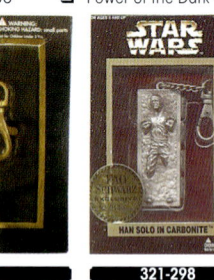 

321-294 | 321-295 | 321-296 | 321-297 | 321-298 | 321-299

 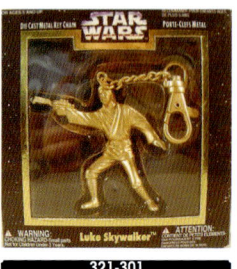     

321-300 | 321-301 | 321-302 | 321-303 | 321-304 | 321-305 | 321-306 | 321-307

321-308 | 321-309 | 321-310 | 321-311 | 321-312 | 321-313 | 321-314 | 321-315 | 321-316 | 321-317 | 321-318

270

Keychains

- ❏ R2-D2 [321-247].....................................20.00
- ❏ Rebel Forces [321-248]...........................20.00
- ❏ Rebel Forces, antique finish [321-249].....20.00
- ❏ Yoda..20.00

International Gaming Technology
- ❏ Star Wars video slots [321-250]...............25.00

LucasArts
- ❏ Lightsaber, blinks, Jedi Outcast Collector's Edition premium [321-251].......................20.00

Lucasfilm
- ❏ Skywalker Ranch screwdriver keyring......30.00

M&M World
- ❏ M&M Anakin [321-252].........................20.00
- ❏ M&M Boba Fett [321-253].....................20.00
- ❏ M&M Clone trooper [321-254]................20.00
- ❏ M&M Darth Vader [321-255]..................20.00

Movistar (Argentina)
Nokia 1100 set of 4 with tin.
- ❏ Clone trooper [321-256].........................15.00
- ❏ Darth Vader [321-257]...........................15.00
- ❏ Epic Duel [321-258]...............................15.00
- ❏ Yoda [321-259]......................................15.00

Pepsi Cola
- ❏ Star Wars Trilogy, presented to Taco Bell managers [321-260]......................................50.00

Pepsi Cola (Netherlands)
Episode I promotional flashlights.
- ❏ Jar Jar Binks [321-261]...........................65.00
- ❏ Queen Amidala......................................65.00

Pet Bear (Japan)
Blister and card back package.
- ❏ Darth Vader [321-262]...........................15.00
- ❏ Stormtrooper [321-263].........................15.00
- ❏ Yoda [321-264].....................................15.00

Color bear package.
- ❏ Boba Fett [321-265].............................25.00
- ❏ Darth Vader..25.00
- ❏ Stormtrooper......................................25.00

Crawl babies. Wind-up.
- ❏ Darth Vader..30.00
- ❏ Stormtrooper [321-266].........................30.00

Vibration figures.
- ❏ Darth Vader [321-267]..........................30.00

Pin USA
- ❏ Clone trooper [321-268].......................15.00
- ❏ Darth Vader [321-269].........................15.00
- ❏ Sith [321-270].....................................15.00
- ❏ Vader helmet, flames [321-271]............15.00

PlastiColor
- ❏ Boba Fett [321-272]............................12.00

- ❏ Darth Vader [321-273].........................12.00
- ❏ Death Star [321-274]...........................12.00
- ❏ Imperial emblem [321-275]...................12.00
- ❏ Rebel emblem [321-276].......................12.00
- ❏ Stormtrooper [321-277].......................12.00

Playco Toys
- ❏ Admiral Ackbar [321-278]....................20.00
- ❏ Artoo-Detoo [321-279]........................15.00
- ❏ Boba Fett [321-280]............................15.00
- ❏ Boba Fett, KMart price tag printed on backer card [321-281]...............................25.00
- ❏ Chewbacca [321-282].........................15.00
- ❏ Darth Vader [321-283].........................15.00
- ❏ Emperor Palpatine [321-284]................20.00
- ❏ Greedo [321-285]................................20.00
- ❏ Han Solo [321-286].............................15.00
- ❏ Luke Skywalker [321-287]....................15.00
- ❏ Luke Skywalker in X-Wing Gear [321-288]...15.00
- ❏ Obi-Wan Kenobi [321-289]...................15.00
- ❏ Princess Leia [321-290].......................16.00
- ❏ See Threepio [321-291]........................15.00
- ❏ Stormtrooper [321-292].......................15.00
- ❏ TIE Fighter Pilot [321-293]...................20.00
- ❏ Yoda [321-294]...................................15.00

Boxed.
- ❏ 4-pack: Artoo Detoo, Darth Vader, Luke Skywalker, See Threepio [321-295]...........35.00
- ❏ 4-pack: Boba Fett, Han Solo, Obi-Wan Kenobi, Yoda [321-296]...........................35.00

271

Keychains

   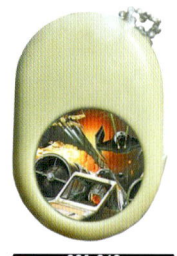   

321-359   321-360   321-361   321-362   321-363   321-364   321-365

321-366   321-367   321-368   321-369   321-370   321-371   321-372   321-373   321-374

- ❏ C-3PO, individually numbered [321-297] 25.00
- ❏ Han Solo in Carbonite, 10,000 produced, individually numbered, exclusive to FAO Schwarz [321-298] 40.00

Playco Toys (Canada)
Figures are gold painted and packaged in square window boxes.
- ❏ Artoo-Detoo [321-299] 25.00
- ❏ Darth Vader [321-300] 25.00
- ❏ Luke Skywalker [321-301] 25.00
- ❏ See Threepio [321-302] 25.00

Rawcliffe
Pewter based keychains and keyrings. Flat or sculpted. Finished, enamel painted, or raw.
- ❏ 20-Year Anniversary brushed finish [321-303] 35.00
- ❏ 20-Year Anniversary enamel finish [321-304] 35.00
- ❏ Anakin's lightsaber [321-305] 20.00
- ❏ Bantha skull 20.00
- ❏ Blaster pistol [321-306] 20.00
- ❏ Blaster rifle 20.00
- ❏ Boba Fett [321-307] 20.00
- ❏ Boba Fett BlasTech EE-3 rifle [321-308] 20.00
- ❏ Boba Fett icon 20.00
- ❏ Boba Fett's helmet [321-309] 20.00
- ❏ Chewbacca's head 20.00
- ❏ Darth Vader [321-311] 20.00
- ❏ Darth Vader, crossed lightsabers 20.00
- ❏ Darth Vader, fist 20.00
- ❏ Darth Vader, lightsaber 20.00
- ❏ Darth Vader, "Never Underestimate the Dark Side." 20.00
- ❏ Death Star [321-310] 20.00
- ❏ Imperial emblem 20.00
- ❏ Jango Fett's blaster [321-312] 20.00
- ❏ Lightsaber, Qui-Gon's, part of Jedi Power Battle for Playstation promotion 30.00
- ❏ Mandalorian emblem 20.00
- ❏ Millennium Falcon [321-313] 20.00
- ❏ Millennium Falcon, CompUSA promotion, boxed 30.00
- ❏ Obi-Wan Kenobi [321-314] 20.00
- ❏ Obi-Wan Kenobi with lightsaber [321-315] 20.00
- ❏ Obi-Wan's lightsaber 20.00
- ❏ Princess Leia 20.00
- ❏ Princess Leia with blaster on square background 20.00
- ❏ R2-D2 [321-316] 20.00
- ❏ Rebel Alliance emblem 20.00
- ❏ Slave I 20.00
- ❏ Star Wars Episode I logo [321-317] 20.00
- ❏ Stormtrooper [321-318] 20.00
- ❏ Stormtrooper helmet, flat 20.00
- ❏ Stormtrooper helmet, sculpted [321-319] 20.00
- ❏ Stormtrooper rifle (E-11) [321-320] 20.00
- ❏ TIE Squadron [321-321] 20.00
- ❏ Wookiee blaster [321-322] 20.00
- ❏ Yoda, "Try not. Do. Or do not. There is no try." (chain) 20.00
- ❏ Yoda, "Try not. Do. Or do not. There is no try." (ring) [321-323] 20.00
- ❏ Yoda, standing on rock 20.00

Blister card. Blue rebel alliance.
- ❏ Millennium Falcon [321-324] 30.00
- ❏ R2-D2 [321-325] 30.00

Blister card. Red galactic empire.
- ❏ Boba Fett helmet [321-326] 30.00
- ❏ Darth Vader helmet [321-327] 30.00
- ❏ Death Star [321-328] 30.00

Classic vehicles series.
- ❏ AT-AT [321-329] 25.00
- ❏ AT-ST [321-330] 25.00
- ❏ Sand Skiff [321-331] 25.00
- ❏ Shuttle Tydirium [321-332] 25.00
- ❏ TIE Fighter [321-333] 25.00

Episode I The Phantom Menace.
- ❏ Anakin Skywalker emblem 20.00
- ❏ Battle Droid blaster [321-334] 20.00
- ❏ Darth Maul, "At last we will have revenge!" 20.00
- ❏ Gungan Sub 20.00
- ❏ Jar Jar Binks 20.00
- ❏ Pit Droid 20.00
- ❏ Podracing 20.00
- ❏ Queen Amidala's gun [321-335] 20.00
- ❏ Royal Starship 20.00
- ❏ Trade Federation Starfighter badge 20.00

Episode II: Attack of the Clones.
- ❏ Anakin Lightsaber [321-336] 20.00
- ❏ Clone trooper Helmet [321-337] 20.00
- ❏ Jango Pistol [321-338] 20.00
- ❏ Jedi Starfighter [321-339] 20.00
- ❏ Slave I [321-340] 20.00

321-375   321-376   321-377   321-378   321-379   321-380

321-381   321-382   321-383   321-384   321-385   321-386   321-387   321-388

Keychains

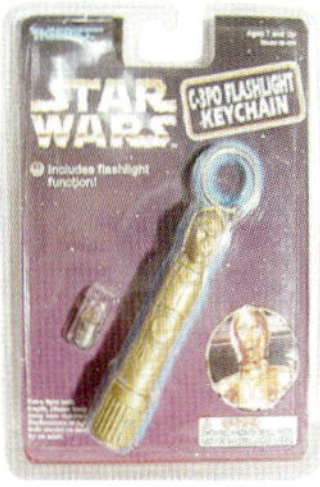
321-389

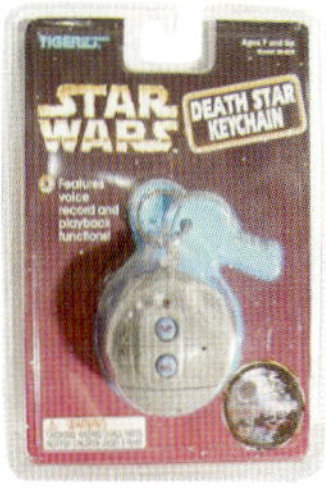
321-390

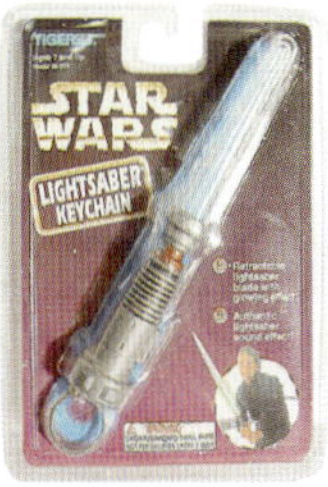
321-391

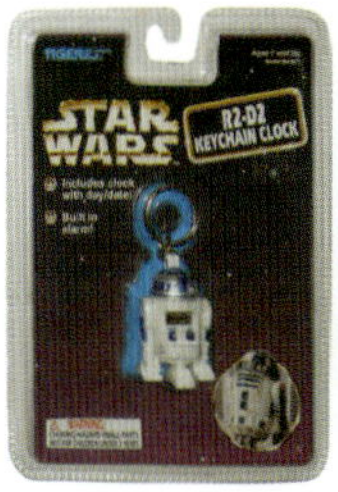
321-392

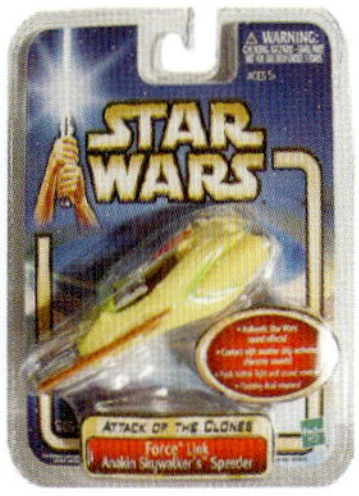
321-393

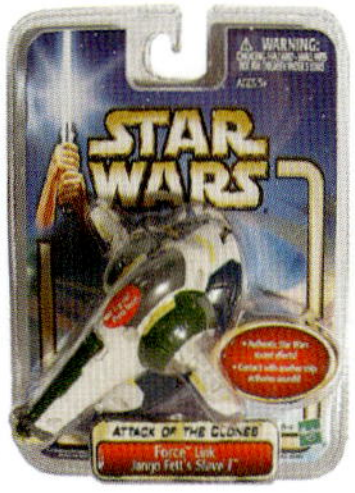
321-394

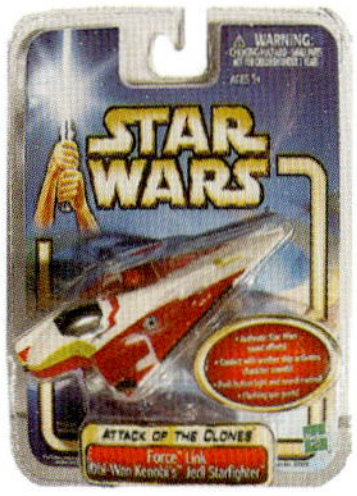
321-395

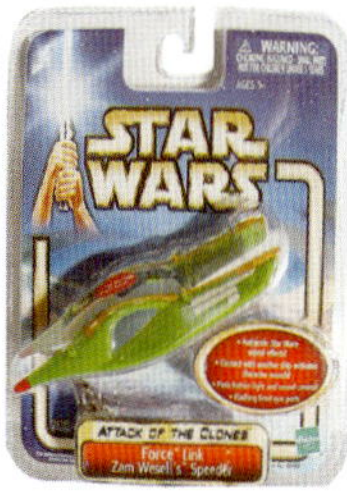
321-396

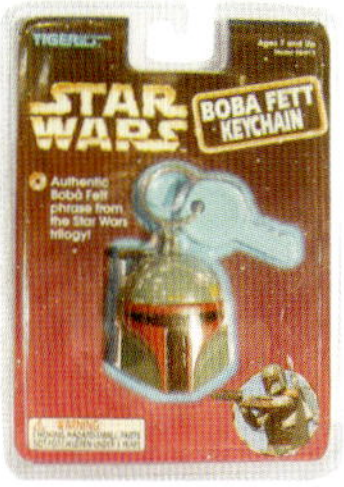
321-397

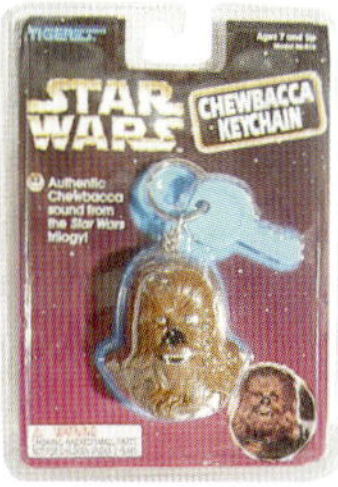
321-398

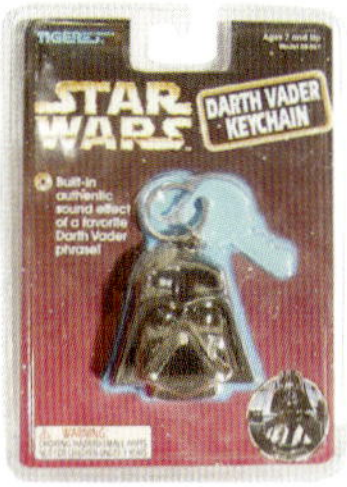
321-399

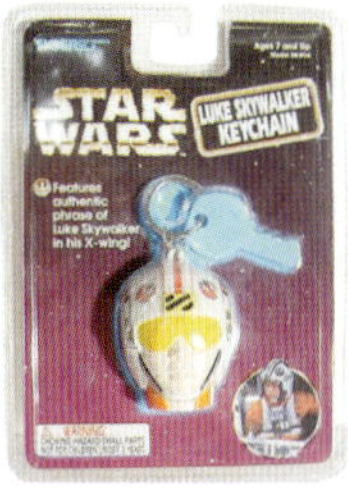
321-400

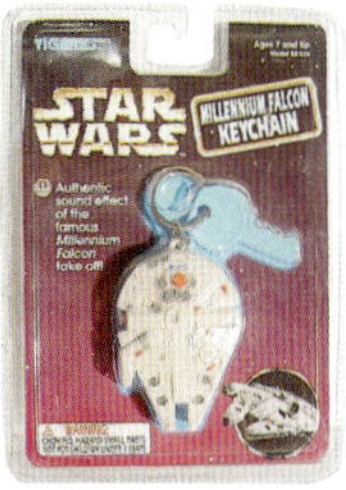
321-401

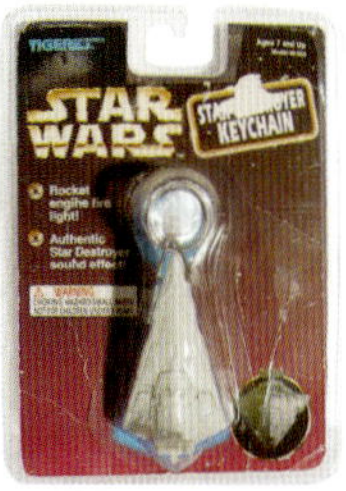
321-402

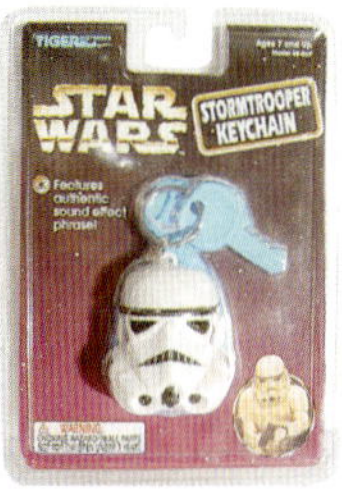
321-403

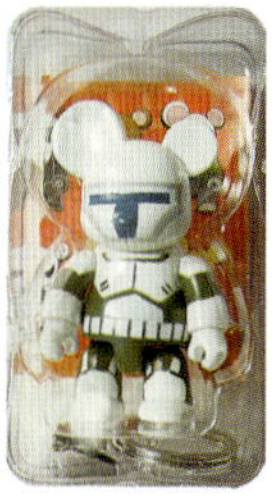
321-404

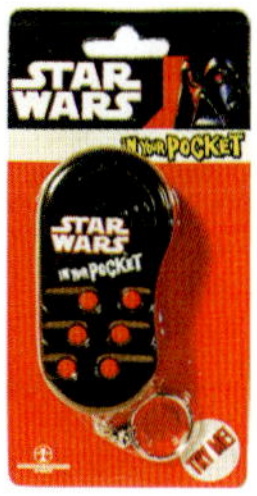
321-405

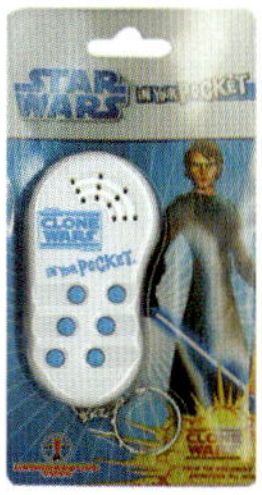
321-406

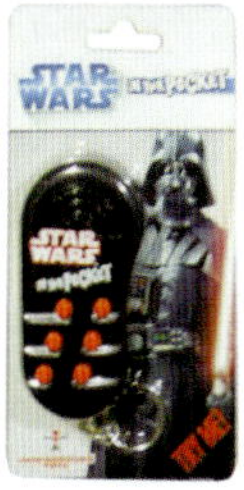
321-407

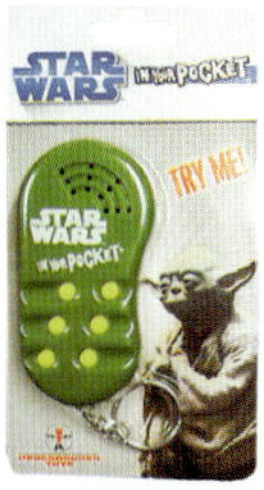
321-408

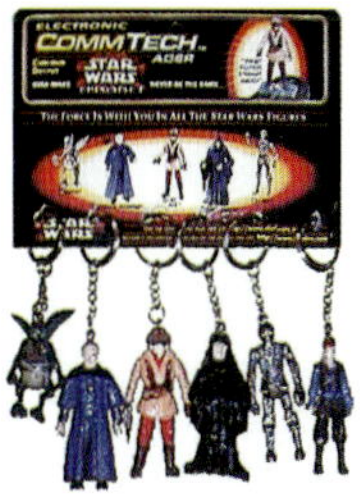
321-409 Set A

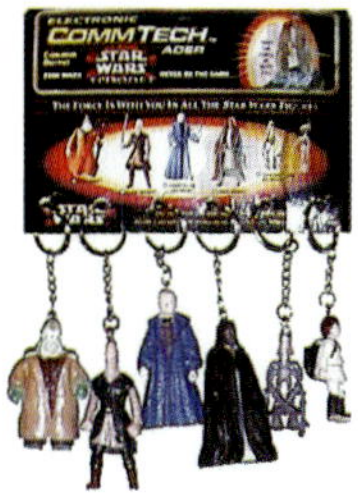
321-409 Set B

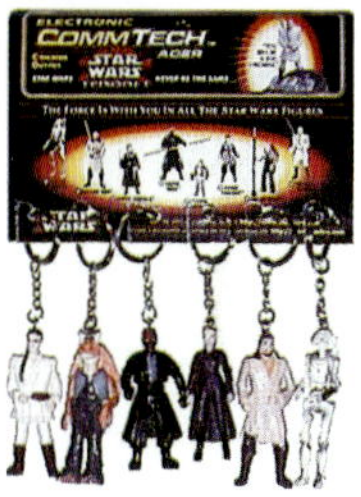
321-409 Set C

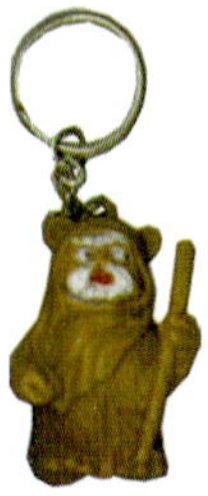
321-410

Logo series.
- ❑ Celebration II [321-341] 35.00
- ❑ Empire Strikes Back [321-342] 20.00
- ❑ Episode I [321-343] 20.00
- ❑ Magic of Myth 35.00
- ❑ Return of the Jedi [321-344] 20.00
- ❑ Shadows of the Empire [321-345] 20.00
- ❑ Star Wars [321-346] 20.00

Rock Rebel
- ❑ Imperial cog [321-347] 15.00
- ❑ Jedi [321-348] 15.00
- ❑ Rebel Alliance emblem [321-349] 15.00
- ❑ Sith [321-350] 15.00
- ❑ Star Wars logo [321-351] 15.00

Helmets.
- ❑ Boba Fett [321-352] 15.00
- ❑ Darth Vader [321-353] 15.00
- ❑ Stormtrooper [321-354] 15.00

Showa Note
Episode II: Attack of the Clones. Metal.
- ❑ Jango Fett [321-355] 10.00
- ❑ R2-D2 [321-356] 10.00

Simba (Germany)
Clone Wars dome packaging.
- ❑ Chewbacca [321-357] 25.00
- ❑ Stormtrooper [321-358] 25.00

Small Planet Co. Ltd. (Japan)
- ❑ Key Case, stormtrooper print [321-359] 30.00

Star Wars Celebration IV
- ❑ Celebration IV, stainless steel [321-360] 35.00

Star Wars Celebration V
Laser cut emblems.
- ❑ Imperial 30.00
- ❑ Rebel Alliance 30.00

Star Wars Celebration VI
- ❑ Darth Vader's lightsaber 30.00
- ❑ Luke Skywalker's lightsaber 30.00

Stiefelmayer-Contento
3D laser-engraved glass cube with illumination.
- ❑ AT-RT, illuminates red 30.00
- ❑ C-3PO, illuminates blue 30.00
- ❑ Clone trooper, illuminates red 30.00
- ❑ Emperor (lightning), illuminates blue 30.00
- ❑ Emperor (lightsaber), illuminates red 30.00
- ❑ Han Solo, illuminates blue 30.00
- ❑ R2-D2, illuminates blue 30.00
- ❑ Star Wars logo, illuminates red 30.00
- ❑ Yoda, illuminates blue 30.00

Takara (Japan)
- ❑ R2-D2 inflatable [321-361] 200.00

Takara TOMY A.R.T.S. (Japan)
Sound eggs.
- ❑ Chewbacca, "Rrooaarrgghh!" 10.00
- ❑ Darth Vader, "Hooooo-pah" 10.00
- ❑ Death Star battle, "Whoosh! Boom!" [321-362] 10.00
- ❑ Han Solo, "I've got a bad feeling about this." 10.00
- ❑ Luke vs. Vader, "Buzzzzz. Clash!" 10.00
- ❑ Yoda, "May the Force be with you" 10.00

The LEGO Group
Clone Wars.
- ❑ Ahsoka Tano 20.00
- ❑ Anakin Skywalker 20.00
- ❑ Asajj Ventress 20.00
- ❑ Commander Cody 20.00
- ❑ Obi-Wan Kenobi [321-363] 20.00
- ❑ Plo Koon [321-364] 20.00

Episode III: Revenge of the Sith
- ❑ Anakin Skywalker 20.00
- ❑ Chewbacca [321-365] 20.00
- ❑ Darth Vader [321-366] 20.00
- ❑ R2-D2 [321-367] 20.00
- ❑ Yoda [321-368] 20.00

LEGO mini-figures.
- ❑ Boba Fett 25.00
- ❑ C-3PO 15.00
- ❑ Chewbacca 15.00
- ❑ Clone trooper Pilot [321-369] 25.00
- ❑ Darth Maul 20.00
- ❑ Darth Maul bagged 25.00
- ❑ Darth Vader [321-370] 15.00
- ❑ Darth Vader bagged 20.00
- ❑ Emperor 15.00
- ❑ Emperor's Royal Guard 25.00
- ❑ Luke, X-Wing pilot [321-371] 15.00
- ❑ Obi-Wan Kenobi 15.00
- ❑ Princess Leia slave outfit 20.00
- ❑ Princess Leia, captive 20.00
- ❑ R2-D2 ....15.00
- ❑ R2-D2 hang tag [321-372] 15.00
- ❑ R2-Q5 [321-373] 20.00
- ❑ R2-Q5 hang tag 20.00
- ❑ Snowtrooper 25.00
- ❑ Stormtrooper bagged 25.00
- ❑ Stormtrooper hang tag 15.00
- ❑ Yoda bagged [321-374] 20.00
- ❑ Yoda hang tag 15.00

LEGO mini-vehicles.
- ❑ Darth Vader's TIE Advanced 25.00
- ❑ Millennium Falcon 25.00
- ❑ Y-Wing Starfighter 25.00

The Promotions Factory (Canada)
8-packs.
- ❑ Series 1 [321-375] 35.00
- ❑ Series 2 [321-376] 35.00
- ❑ Series 3 [321-377] 35.00

8-packs with storage tin. Exclusive to Walmart.
- ❑ C-3PO tin, heroes [321-378] 24.00
- ❑ Darth Vader tin, villains [321-379] 24.00
- ❑ Plain tin, assorted [321-380] 35.00

Individual carded. Clone Wars dome packaging.
- ❑ Princess Leia [321-381] 25.00

Individual carded. Series 1. Exclusive to Walmart.
- ❑ Princess Leia [321-382] 25.00
- ❑ Queen Amidala [321-383] 25.00

Individual carded. Series 2. Exclusive to Walmart.
- ❑ Darth Vader [321-384] 25.00

Keychains

322-01 | 322-02 | 322-03 | 322-04 | 323-01 | 324-01 | 324-02 | 324-03

324-04 | 324-05 Side 1 and Side 2 and Side 3 | 324-06 | 324-07 | 324-08 | 324-09 | 324-10 | 324-11

- ❑ Han Solo [321-385].................................25.00
- ❑ Jango Fett [321-386]................................25.00
- ❑ Mace Windu [321-387].............................25.00

Individual carded. Series 3. Exclusive to Walmart.
- ❑ Clone trooper [321-388].........................25.00

Tiger Electronics
- ❑ C-3PO, flashlight [321-389]....................15.00
- ❑ Death Star, records and plays back [321-390] 15.00
- ❑ Lightsaber, lights and sound [321-391] 15.00
- ❑ R2-D2, digital clock, cardboard hang card.............15.00
- ❑ R2-D2, digital clock, plastic hang card [321-392]......15.00

Episode II: Attack of the Clones Force Link.
- ❑ Anakin Skywalker's Speeder [321-393].........15.00
- ❑ Jango Fett's Slave I [321-394]...................15.00
- ❑ Obi-Wan Kenobi's Jedi Starfighter [321-395]......15.00
- ❑ Zam Wesell's Speeder [321-396]................15.00

Plays one phrase or sound.
- ❑ Boba Fett [321-397]..................................15.00
- ❑ Chewbacca [321-398]...............................15.00
- ❑ Darth Vader [321-399]..............................15.00
- ❑ Jabba the Hutt..15.00
- ❑ Luke Skywalker [321-400].........................15.00
- ❑ Millennium Falcon [321-401]......................15.00
- ❑ Star Destroyer [321-402]..........................15.00
- ❑ Stormtrooper [321-403]............................15.00

Tomy (Japan)
Miniature weapons with light-up features.
- ❑ Blaster, Han Solo [322-01].......................20.00
- ❑ Lightsaber, Darth Vader..........................20.00
- ❑ Lightsaber, Luke Skywalker A New Hope......20.00
- ❑ Lightsaber, Luke Skywalker Return of the Jedi........20.00
- ❑ Lightsaber, Obi-Wan Kenobi....................20.00

UA Movie Theaters (China)
- ❑ Qee, black..30.00
- ❑ Qee, white [321-404]..............................30.00

Underground Toys
Star Wars In Your Pocket.
- ❑ Classic trilogy, six movie selections; voices and effects [321-405]......20.00
- ❑ Clone Wars [321-406]..............................20.00
- ❑ Darth Vader [321-407].............................20.00
- ❑ Yoda [321-408]......................................20.00

Unlicensed
- ❑ 6-pack, any 6 hanging off header copied from Hasbro header [321-409]......35.00

PVC mini figures hanging from ring and chain.
- ❑ Anakin Skywalker......................................5.00
- ❑ Battle Droid...5.00
- ❑ Boss Nass..5.00
- ❑ C-3PO...5.00
- ❑ Chancellor Velorum..................................5.00
- ❑ Darth Maul...5.00
- ❑ Darth Sidious..5.00
- ❑ Gasgano...5.00
- ❑ Jar Jar Binks..5.00
- ❑ Ki-Adi-Mundi..5.00
- ❑ Mace Windu...5.00
- ❑ Obi-Wan Kenobi......................................5.00
- ❑ Padmé..5.00
- ❑ Queen Amidala.......................................5.00
- ❑ Qui-Gon Jinn..5.00
- ❑ Ric Olié...5.00
- ❑ Senator Palpatine...................................5.00
- ❑ Watto..5.00

Vintage
- ❑ Wicket, hollow [321-410].........................25.00

Williams
- ❑ C-3PO, Star Wars Episode I Pinball [2-287].....20.00
- ❑ Darth Maul, Star Wars Episode I Pin 2000 [2-287]......20.00
- ❑ R2-D2 [2-287]..20.00
- ❑ Trade Federation Droid Starfighter [2-287]......20.00
- ❑ Wrench, Official pinball pit droid [2-287]......30.00

Keys, Hotel
Continued in Volume 3, Page 267

Celebration 3. Sponsored by Target.
- ❑ Darth Vader [322-01]..............................15.00
- ❑ Darth Vader with lightsaber down [322-02].....15.00
- ❑ Darth Vader with lightsaber up [322-03].......15.00
- ❑ Epic Duel [322-04].................................15.00

Lampshades

- ❑ Star Wars, B/W scenes..........................100.00

Hay Jax Manufacturing
- ❑ Return of the Jedi characters on brown background...50.00

Scanlite
- ❑ Empire Strikes Back kit form with free poster [323-01]...40.00

Lamps and Lights
Continued in Volume 3, Page 267

- ❑ Darth Vader lava lamp [324-01]................75.00
- ❑ R2-D2 character lamp [324-02]................75.00

(France)
- ❑ Plasma ball lamp [324-03].......................75.00

(UK)
- ❑ Clone Wars, children's pendant................30.00
- ❑ Clone Wars, glow-in-dark children's lamp......35.00

Episode I, ceramic with shade.
- ❑ Podrace [324-04]....................................50.00
- ❑ Space battle [324-05]..............................50.00

Wall lights.
- ❑ Darth Maul..35.00
- ❑ Jar Jar Binks...35.00

Funko
Character lamps with built-in alarm clocks.
- ❑ 501st Clone trooper, exclusive to Star Wars Celebration V [324-06]......65.00

Idea Nuova
- ❑ EVA lamp [324-07].................................50.00

Museum Replicas
Lightsaber with shade and pull.
- ❑ Anakin / Republic...................................75.00
- ❑ Darth Vader / Empire [324-08]..................75.00
- ❑ Yoda / Republic.....................................75.00

Sid Cadeaux (Australia)
- ❑ Magma Lamp [324-09]............................65.00

Taito (Japan)
Lightsabers.
- ❑ Darth Vader lightsaber, red [324-10]..........30.00
- ❑ Luke Skywalker lightsaber, green [324-11].....30.00

Windmill Ceramics
- ❑ Chewbacca 9.5" tall, unlicensed.............130.00
- ❑ Darth Vader 12" tall, unlicensed..............90.00
- ❑ R2-D2 8.5" tall, unlicensed....................85.00

Lamps and Lights: Night and Reading Lights
Continued in Volume 3, Page 268

Adam Joseph Industries
- ❑ C-3PO disc-cut [325-01].........................30.00
- ❑ C-3PO sculpted [325-02].........................35.00
- ❑ Darth Vader sculpted [325-03]..................35.00
- ❑ Princess Kneesaa sculpted [325-04].........35.00
- ❑ R2-D2 die-cut [325-05]...........................30.00
- ❑ Wicket sculpted [325-06].........................35.00
- ❑ Yoda die-cut [325-07].............................30.00
- ❑ Yoda sculpted [325-08]...........................35.00

Idea Nuova
- ❑ Darth Vader...20.00
- ❑ Darth Vader lava night light [325-10]..........25.00

Laundry Bags and Hampers

 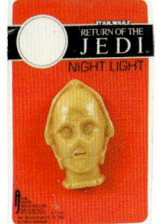     

Northlight Productions, Ltd. (UK)
- R2-D2 .... 450.00

Lanyards
Continued in Volume 3, Page 269

501st Legion
- www.501st.com [326-01] 5.00

C and D Visionaries, Inc.
- Darth Vader, "Join the Darkside" 5.00
- Darth Vader, "Star Wars" [326-02] 5.00
- Star Wars logo [326-03] 5.00
- Yoda [326-04] 5.00
- Yoda, "There is no Try" [326-05] 5.00

Disney Theme Park Merchandise
- Empires Strikes back 30th anniversary with 9 pins ... 125.00
- Pin trader with four pins 55.00
- Star Wars Weekends 2012 .... 45.00
- Wookiee Bandolier with pin 60.00

Mexico Collector Convention (Mexico)
- Star Wars Encuentros [326-06] 20.00

Official Pix
- Fan Days 5.00

Promotions Factory (Australia)
- Clip and Carry lanyard with bonus ID card [326-07] 15.00

Rebel Legion
- Rebel Legion [326-08] 5.00

Star Wars Celebration II
- Celebration II, exclusive to Fan Club 20.00

Star Wars Celebration III
- Celebration III, exclusive to Fan Club [326-09] 20.00

Star Wars Celebration IV
- Celebration IV 20.00

Star Wars Celebration V
- Celebration V 20.00
- Celebration V, hyperspace [v1e1:269] 25.00
- Celebration V, VIP [v1e1:269] 50.00

Star Wars Celebration VI
- Dave School 5.00
- Star Wars Celebration VI [326-11] 20.00

Star Wars Celebration Europe (UK)
- Celebration Europe 20.00
- Hyperspace, blue 25.00

Star Wars Celebration Japan (Japan)
- Celebration Japan [326-10] 20.00

Laser Light Spinners
Fantasma
- Star Wars logo and ships [327-01] 65.00

Laser Pointers
(Japan)
- Lightsaber hilt design 65.00

LucasArts
- Star Wars: Lethal Alliance, promo 45.00

Master Replicas
- Darth Maul lightsaber [328-01] 40.00

Star Wars Celebration IV
- Star Wars Celebration IV [328-02] 35.00

Laundry Bags and Hampers

Adam Joseph Industries
- C-3PO and R2-D2 [329-01] 50.00
- Darth Vader and Emperor's Royal Guards [329-02] 50.00
- Princess Kneesaa and Wicket [329-03] 50.00
- Wicket the Ewok [329-04] 50.00
- Wicket the Ewok (and Bagga) [329-05] 50.00

Boy Scouts of America
- Mid-America Council, Scout-o-Rama 1978, canvas laundry sack with drawstring [329-06] 130.00

Taito (Japan)
Pop-up astromech, mesh.
- Blue 40.00
- Red 40.00

License Plates

330-01 330-02 330-03 330-04

330-05 330-06 330-07 330-08 330-09 330-10 330-11 330-12

330-13 330-14 330-15 330-16 330-17 330-18 330-19

330-20 330-21 330-22 330-23 330-24 330-25 330-26

330-27 330-28 330-29 330-30 330-31 330-32 330-33 330-34

License Plates

Continued in Volume 3, Page 270

Disney / MGM

- ❑ Boba Fett [330-01] 25.00
- ❑ Darth Vader [330-02] 25.00
- ❑ Jedi Training Academy [330-03] 30.00
- ❑ Stormtrooper [330-04] 25.00

Topps

Mini license plates. Set of 30. Magnet on back.

- ❑ C3PO, Protocol Droid [330-05] 10.00
- ❑ DBL BLDED, Sith Apprentice [330-06] 10.00
- ❑ DSNGRTNS, Bounty Hunter [330-07] 10.00
- ❑ FEARED, In Search of Skywalker [330-08] 10.00
- ❑ FRMBOY, Outer Rim [330-09] 10.00
- ❑ GAMBLER, Bespin Mining Colony [330-10] 10.00
- ❑ GLD LDR, Sullustan Pilot [330-11] 10.00
- ❑ GNGSTR, Tatooine Kingpin [330-12] 10.00
- ❑ GRIEVOUS, Separatist [330-13] 10.00
- ❑ HATRED, Dark Side [330-14] 10.00
- ❑ HERO, Chosen One [330-15] 10.00
- ❑ HIGHNESS, Rebel Leader [330-16] 10.00
- ❑ ITSATRAP, Naval Commander [330-17] 10.00
- ❑ JEDIMSTR, Jedi Master [330-18] 10.00
- ❑ LEGEND, Jedi Warrior [330-19] 10.00
- ❑ LUMINOUS, Dagobah [330-20] 10.00
- ❑ MNDLRN, Bounty Hunter [330-21] 10.00
- ❑ NOEWOKS, Endor Patrol [330-22] 10.00
- ❑ PRTYSOVR, Jedi Defender [330-23] 10.00
- ❑ R2D2, Astromech Droid [330-24] 10.00
- ❑ RED 5, Rogue Squadron [330-25] 10.00
- ❑ ROUGE2, Rebel Alliance [330-26] 10.00
- ❑ RRRRUGH!, Wookiee Co-Pilot [330-27] 10.00
- ❑ SITHLORD, Empire State [330-28] 10.00
- ❑ SITHMSTR, Galactic Tyrant [330-29] 10.00
- ❑ SLVGRL, Rescue Mission [330-30] 10.00
- ❑ SPIRITUAL, Jedi Order [330-31] 10.00
- ❑ TRIPPED, Hoth Patrol [330-32] 10.00
- ❑ USETHE4S, Jedi Knight [330-33] 10.00
- ❑ YT1300, Scoundrel [330-34] 10.00

Lip Balm

Continued in Volume 3, Page 271

Added Extras, LLC

Lightsaber case lights up. Includes bonus clip.

- ❑ Anakin Skywalker [331-01] 15.00
- ❑ Darth Vader [331-02] 15.00
- ❑ Yoda [331-03] 15.00

Lightsaber case lights up. Includes bonus clip. Dome package.

- ❑ Anakin Skywalker [331-04] 15.00
- ❑ Darth Vader [331-05] 15.00
- ❑ Yoda [331-06] 15.00

Avon (Mexico)

- ❑ Episode II: Anakin and Padmé label 20.00

Minnetonka

Picture of character on barrel.

- ❑ Anakin Skywalker [331-07] 10.00
- ❑ Darth Maul [331-08] 10.00
- ❑ Darth Vader [331-09] 10.00
- ❑ Jar Jar Binks [331-10] 10.00
- ❑ Queen Amidala [331-11] 10.00

Sculpt of character for cap.

- ❑ Anakin Skywalker [331-12] 15.00
- ❑ Darth Maul [331-13] 15.00
- ❑ Darth Vader [331-14] 15.00
- ❑ Jar Jar Binks [331-15] 15.00
- ❑ Queen Amidala [331-16] 15.00

331-01 331-02 331-03 331-04 331-05 331-06

331-07 331-08 331-09 331-10 331-11 331-12 331-13 331-14 331-15 331-16 332-01 332-02

Lottery Scratch-Off Tickets

Lotion

Avon (Mexico)
- ❏ Queen Amidala hand cream [332-01] 20.00

Minnetonka
- ❏ Queen Amidala bottle with sculpted character cap [332-02] 15.00

Lottery Scratch-Off Tickets

Episode III: Revenge of the Sith.
- ❏ Retailer exclusive card [333-01] 60.00

Episode III: Revenge of the Sith. California.
- ❏ A New Hope: C-3PO and R2-D2 [333-02] 12.00
- ❏ A New Hope: Heroes [333-03] 12.00
- ❏ Attack of the Clones: poster art [333-04] 12.00
- ❏ Attack of the Clones: Yoda [333-05] 12.00
- ❏ Empire Strikes Back: Falcon cockpit [333-06] 12.00
- ❏ Empire Strikes Back: Yoda, Lando, Vader, Boba Fett [333-07] 12.00
- ❏ Return of the Jedi: Emperor and Darth Vader [333-08] ...12.00
- ❏ Return of the Jedi: Emperor, Luke, Vader, Yoda [333-09] ...12.00
- ❏ Revenge of the Sith: Epic Duel [333-10] 12.00
- ❏ Revenge of the Sith: Vader art logo [333-11] 12.00
- ❏ The Phantom Menace: Darth Maul [333-12] 12.00
- ❏ The Phantom Menace: poster art [333-13] 12.00

Episode III: Revenge of the Sith. Montana.
- ❏ Anakin Skywalker [333-14] 12.00
- ❏ C-3PO and R2-D2 [333-15] 12.00
- ❏ Chewbacca [333-16] 12.00
- ❏ Darth Sidious [333-17] 12.00
- ❏ Darth Vader [333-18] 12.00
- ❏ General Grievous [333-19] 12.00
- ❏ Obi-Wan Kenobi [333-20] 12.00
- ❏ Yoda [333-21] 12.00

Star Wars Saga.
- ❏ A New Hope: C-3PO and R2-D2 ....12.00
- ❏ A New Hope: Darth Vader vs. Obi-Wan Kenobi 12.00
- ❏ A New Hope: Luke, Leia, Han, Obi-Wan 12.00
- ❏ Attack of the Clones: Padmé, Anakin, Obi-Wan, Jango Fett 12.00
- ❏ AOTC: Yoda 12.00
- ❏ Empire Strikes Back: Chewbacca, Han, Leia, C-3PO 12.00
- ❏ Empire Strikes Back: Yoda, Lando, Darth Vader 12.00
- ❏ Return of the Jedi: Emperor, Luke, Darth Vader 12.00
- ❏ Return of the Jedi: Millennium Falcon and Death Star II 12.00
- ❏ Return of the Jedi: Wicket the Ewok 12.00
- ❏ Revenge of the Sith: Anakin vs. Obi-Wan 12.00
- ❏ Revenge of the Sith: Darth Vader's helmet..................12.00
- ❏ Revenge of the Sith: Padmé, Anakin, Obi-Wan 12.00
- ❏ The Phantom Menace: Darth Maul 12.00
- ❏ The Phantom Menace: Naboo Palace 12.00
- ❏ The Phantom Menace: Qui-Gon Jinn, Anakin, Queen Amidala 12.00

(Australia)
- ❏ C-3PO [333-22] 15.00
- ❏ C-3PO and R2-D2 ....15.00
- ❏ Clone trooper 15.00
- ❏ Darth Vader [333-23] 15.00
- ❏ Emperor 15.00
- ❏ General Grievous 15.00
- ❏ Obi-Wan Kenobi 15.00
- ❏ R2-D2 [333-24] 15.00
- ❏ Yoda [333-25] 15.00

(Belgium)
- ❏ C-3PO [333-26] 15.00
- ❏ Darth Vader [333-27] 15.00
- ❏ Obi-Wan Kenobi [333-28] 15.00
- ❏ Yoda [333-29] 15.00

(France)
- ❏ Anakin Skywalker [333-30] 15.00
- ❏ Chewbacca [333-31] 15.00
- ❏ Darth Vader [333-32] 15.00
- ❏ General Grievous [333-33] 15.00
- ❏ Han Solo [333-34] 15.00
- ❏ Jango Fett [333-35] 15.00
- ❏ Luke Skywalker [333-36] 15.00
- ❏ Obi-Wan Kenobi [333-37] 15.00
- ❏ Princess Leia [333-38] 15.00
- ❏ R2-D2 and C-3PO [333-39] 15.00
- ❏ Reine Amidala [333-40] 15.00
- ❏ Yoda [333-41] 15.00

Lottery Scratch-Off Tickets

(Mexico)
- ❏ Anakin and Padmé [333-42] 15.00
- ❏ Anakin Skywalker podracing [333-43] 15.00
- ❏ Attack of the Clones movie poster art [333-44] 15.00
- ❏ C-3PO and R2-D2 [333-45] 15.00
- ❏ C-3PO, Jabba, Princess Leia [333-46] 15.00
- ❏ Chewbacca, Han, C-3PO, Princess Leia [333-47] 15.00
- ❏ Clone troopers [333-48] 15.00
- ❏ Darth Maul [333-49] 15.00
- ❏ Darth Vader and Boba Fett [333-50] 15.00
- ❏ Darth Vader, Revenge of the Sith art [333-51] 15.00
- ❏ Emperor, Luke, Darth Vader, Yoda [333-52] 15.00

Lottery Scratch-Off Tickets

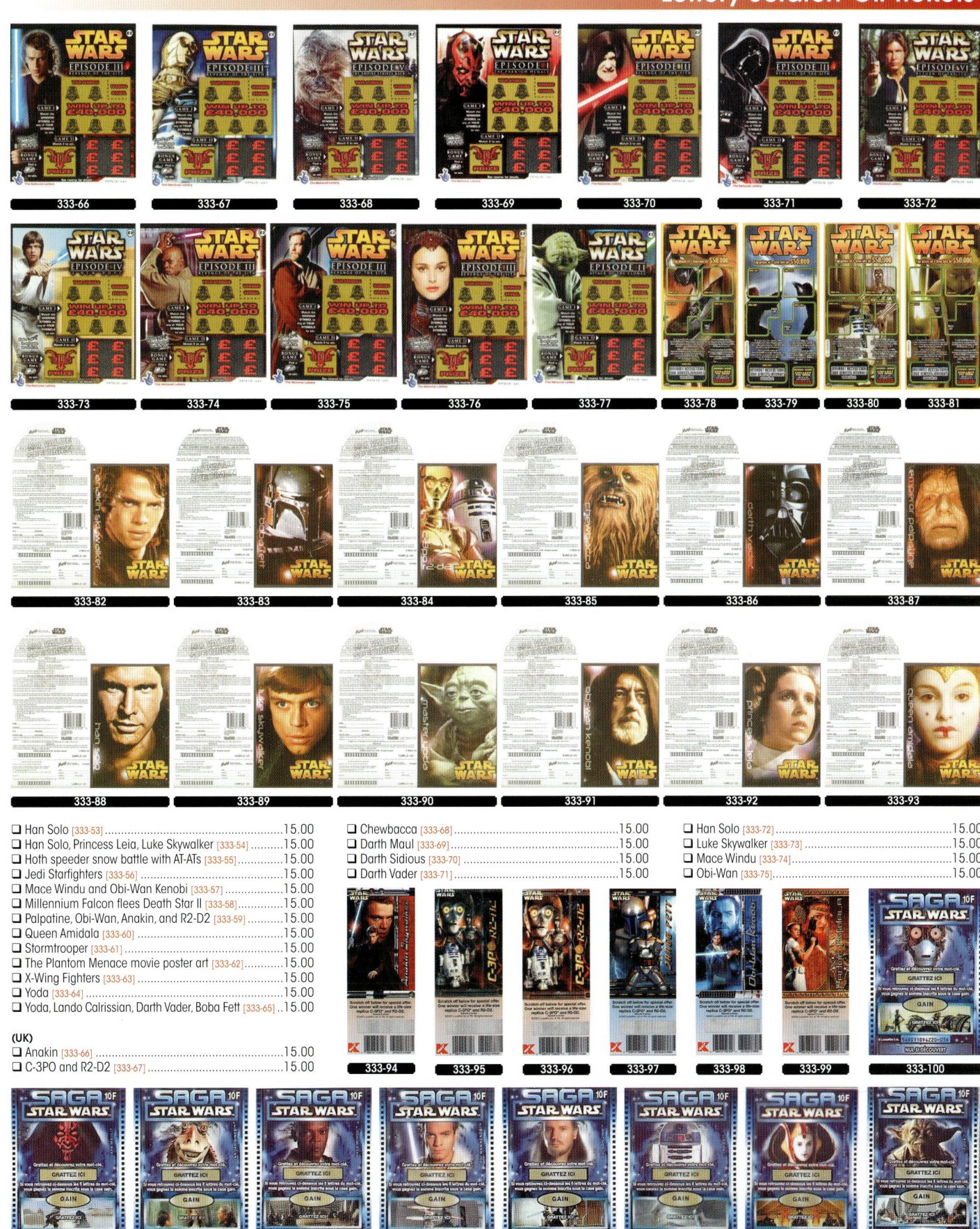

- ❑ Han Solo [333-53] 15.00
- ❑ Han Solo, Princess Leia, Luke Skywalker [333-54] 15.00
- ❑ Hoth speeder snow battle with AT-ATs [333-55] 15.00
- ❑ Jedi Starfighters [333-56] 15.00
- ❑ Mace Windu and Obi-Wan Kenobi [333-57] 15.00
- ❑ Millennium Falcon flees Death Star II [333-58] 15.00
- ❑ Palpatine, Obi-Wan, Anakin, and R2-D2 [333-59] 15.00
- ❑ Queen Amidala [333-60] 15.00
- ❑ Stormtrooper [333-61] 15.00
- ❑ The Phantom Menace movie poster art [333-62] 15.00
- ❑ X-Wing Fighters [333-63] 15.00
- ❑ Yoda [333-64] 15.00
- ❑ Yoda, Lando Calrissian, Darth Vader, Boba Fett [333-65] ..15.00

(UK)
- ❑ Anakin [333-66] 15.00
- ❑ C-3PO and R2-D2 [333-67] 15.00

- ❑ Chewbacca [333-68] 15.00
- ❑ Darth Maul [333-69] 15.00
- ❑ Darth Sidious [333-70] 15.00
- ❑ Darth Vader [333-71] 15.00

- ❑ Han Solo [333-72] 15.00
- ❑ Luke Skywalker [333-73] 15.00
- ❑ Mace Windu [333-74] 15.00
- ❑ Obi-Wan [333-75] 15.00

Lottery Scratch-Off Tickets

 334-01
 334-02
 334-03
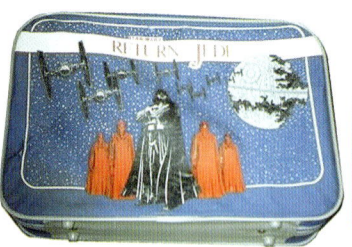 334-04
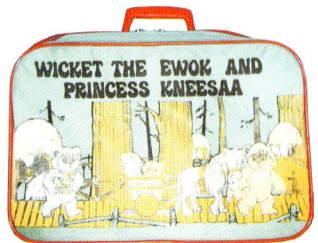 334-05
 334-06

 334-07
 334-08 Side 1 and Side 2
 334-09
 334-10
 334-11

 335-01
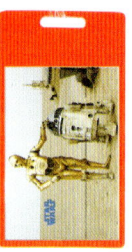 335-02
 335-03
 335-04
 335-05
 335-06

- ❏ Queen Amidala [333-76] 15.00
- ❏ Yoda [333-77] 15.00

Atlantic Lottery Corporation Inc. (Canada)
Episode III: Revenge of the Sith.
- ❏ Darth Vader [333-78] 10.00
- ❏ Epic Duel [333-79] 10.00
- ❏ R2-D2 and C-3PO [333-80] 10.00
- ❏ Yoda [333-81] 10.00

British Columbia Lottery Corp. (Canada)
Sample tickets. No play value.
- ❏ Anakin Skywalker [333-82] 45.00
- ❏ Boba Fett [333-83] 45.00
- ❏ C-3PO and R2-D2 [333-84] 45.00
- ❏ Chewbacca [333-85] 45.00
- ❏ Darth Vader [333-86] 45.00
- ❏ Emperor Palpatine [333-87] 45.00
- ❏ Han Solo [333-88] 45.00
- ❏ Luke Skywalker [333-89] 45.00
- ❏ Master Yoda [333-90] 45.00
- ❏ Obi-Wan Kenobi [333-91] 45.00
- ❏ Princess Leia [333-92] 45.00
- ❏ Queen Amidala [333-93] 45.00

KMart
Promotional game ticket.
- ❏ Anakin Skywalker [333-94] 25.00
- ❏ C-3PO, blue tint to face [333-95] 25.00
- ❏ C-3PO, brown tint to face [333-96] 25.00
- ❏ Jango Fett [333-97] 25.00

- ❏ Obi-Wan Kenobi [333-98] 25.00
- ❏ Padmé Amidala [333-99] 25.00

La Francaise des Jeux (France)
Instant lottery ticket.
- ❏ C-3PO [333-100] 15.00
- ❏ Dark Maul [333-101] 15.00
- ❏ Jar Jar Binks [333-102] 15.00
- ❏ Mace Windu [333-103] 15.00
- ❏ Obi-Wan Kenobi [333-104] 15.00
- ❏ Qui-Gon Jinn [333-105] 15.00
- ❏ R2-D2 [333-106] 15.00
- ❏ Reine Amidala [333-107] 15.00
- ❏ Yoda [333-108] 15.00

Luggage
Continued in Volume 3, Page 271

- ❏ Darth Vader above epic duel [334-01] 35.00
- ❏ Vader vs. Skywalker, set of 4 .... 150.00

Accessory Network
- ❏ Darth Vader [334-02] 35.00
- ❏ Darth Vader, Boba Fett, Stormtroopers [334-03] 45.00

Adam Joseph Industries
- ❏ Darth Vader and Emperor's Royal Guards [334-04] 150.00
- ❏ Princess Kneesaa and Wicket, 17" x 10.25" 175.00
- ❏ Princess Kneesaa and Wicket, 18" x 11.5" [334-05] 175.00

Pottery Barn
- ❏ Darth Vader 18" [334-06] 100.00
- ❏ Darth Vader 22" [334-07] 120.00

Premier Luggage
- ❏ Empire Strikes Back, 2 sided [334-08] 300.00

Pyramid
Pilot style carry on.
- ❏ Anakin / Podracing 35.00
- ❏ Jedi 35.00
- ❏ Podracing with Anakin and Sebulba [334-09] 35.00
- ❏ Sith [334-10] 35.00

Wheeled carry on with pull-up handles.
- ❏ Boba Fett 40.00
- ❏ Darth Vader 40.00
- ❏ Luke Skywalker 40.00
- ❏ Stormtrooper [334-11] 40.00

Luggage Tags
Continued in Volume 3, Page 272

Animations
- ❏ Angry Birds Darth Vader pig, Target exclusive [335-01] ...10.00

Get Solo LLC
- ❏ C-3PO and R2-D2 [335-02] 10.00
- ❏ Darth Vader [335-03] 10.00
- ❏ Jedi Starfighter 10.00
- ❏ Luke, Han, Leia [335-04] 10.00
- ❏ Stormtrooper 10.00
- ❏ Wicket 10.00
- ❏ Yoda [335-05] 10.00

Star Wars Celebration IV
- ❏ Celebration IV [335-06] 20.00

Lunch Boxes
Continued in Volume 3, Page 272

- ❏ Podrace, plastic with thermos [4:173] 30.00

 336-01
 336-02
 336-03
 336-04
 336-05
 336-06
 336-07

Lunch Boxes

 336-08
 336-09
 336-10
 336-11
 336-12

 336-13
 336-14
 336-15
 336-16
 336-17

Clone Wars, zippered.
- Captain Rex and Jedi heroes 20.00
- Yoda [v1e1:273] 20.00

Episode I: The Phantom Menace. Shaped with bottle.
- Anakin Skywalker, wrench-shaped ice block [336-01] 30.00
- Darth Maul with sandwich case [4:173] 25.00

(Germany)
- Obi-Wan, Ahsoka, and Anakin, zippered [336-02] 20.00

Animations
Exclusive to Target.
- Chewbacca [336-03] 15.00
- Darth Vader [336-04] 15.00
- Yoda [336-05] 15.00

AZ Designz (Australia)
- Darth Maul [336-06] 20.00
- Jar Jar [336-07] 20.00

Big Dog
- The Empire Bites Back [336-08] 50.00

Calego International
- Queen Amidala [336-09] 50.00
- Starfighters [336-10] 25.00
- Starfighters, dome [336-11] 25.00

Canadian Thermos Products
- A New Hope: movie art, blue [336-12] 100.00
- A New Hope: movie art, red [336-13] 150.00
- Dogfight over Death Star [336-14] 125.00
- Empire Strikes Back: movie art [336-15] 100.00
- Return of the Jedi: movie art [336-16] 90.00

Cinemax
- Star Wars, promotional, "Coming in November..." [v1e1:273] 35.00

Disney / MGM
- Jedi Training Academy [336-17] 25.00

Galerie
- Darth Vader, shaped tin [336-18] 15.00

Sold filled with popcorn.
- Clone Wars, heroes [336-19] 15.00
- Clone Wars, Jedi [336-20] 15.00

Half Moon Bay (UK)
- Star Wars tin tote [336-21] 10.00

Hallmark
- Return of the Jedi replica, tin, mini-size collectible 15.00

Jollibee
- R2-D2 lunch accessory kit [336-22] 65.00

Kellogg's (Korea)
- R2-D2 lunch accessory kit 65.00

King Seeley-Thermos
- Droids: cartoon C-3PO and R2-D2 on lid; thermos with cartoon droids [336-23] 160.00
- Empire Strikes Back: Dagobah swamp and Hoth battle; thermos with Yoda [336-24] 100.00
- Empire Strikes Back: Millennium Falcon and Luke, R2-D2 and Yoda; thermos with Yoda [336-25] 100.00
- Empire Strikes Back: Chewbacca, Han, Leia, and Luke on lid; thermos with Yoda. [336-26] 100.00
- Empire Strikes Back: logo with photo inserts; thermos with Yoda. [336-27] 100.00
- Ewoks: Ewoks on lid, thermos with Ewok [336-28] 100.00
- Return of the Jedi: Jabba's palace and space battle; thermos with Ewok [336-29] 90.00
- Return of the Jedi: Luke and Jabba's palace creatures; plain thermos 90.00
- Return of the Jedi: R2-D2 and Wicket on lid; thermos with Ewok [336-30] 90.00
- Star Wars: space battle and Mos Eisley, no art on top, bottom, or sides 175.00
- Star Wars: Space Battle and Mos Eisley; thermos with C-3PO and R2-D2 [336-31] 100.00
- Star Wars: Darth Vader and stormtroopers on paper decal [336-32] 150.00
- Star Wars: Darth Vader, C-3PO, and R2-D2 on paper decal; thermos with C-3PO and R2-D2 [336-33] 135.00
- Wicket the Ewok, thermos with Ewok [336-34] 200.00

Pottery Barn
- Darth Vader 45.00
- X-Wings [336-35] 45.00

 336-18
 336-19
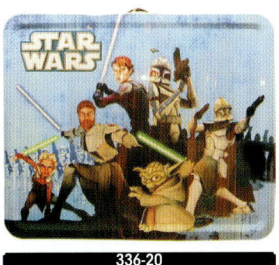 336-20
 336-21
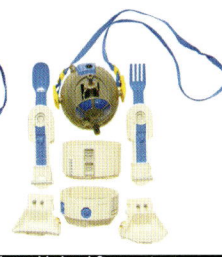 336-22 Assembled and Open

 336-23
 336-24 Side 1 and Side 2

 336-25 Side 1 and Side 2

Lunch Boxes

336-26

336-27

336-28

336-29 Side 1 and Side 2

336-30

336-31 Side 1 and Side 2

336-32

336-33

Pyramid
- Anakin Skywalker podracer, includes bottle [336-365]....15.00
- Darth Maul bust, includes bottle [336-37]................15.00
- Darth Maul full-body, includes bottle [336-38]..........15.00
- Darth Maul, style A [336-39]............................15.00
- Darth Maul, style B [336-40]............................20.00
- Darth Maul, style C [336-41]............................25.00
- Jar Jar, style A [336-42]...............................15.00
- Jar Jar, style B [336-43]...............................20.00
- Jar Jar, style C..25.00
- Jedi vs. Sith, style A [336-44].........................15.00
- Jedi vs. Sith, style B [336-45].........................20.00
- Jedi vs. Sith, style C..................................25.00
- Jedi, style A [336-46]..................................15.00
- Jedi, style B...20.00
- Jedi, style C...25.00
- Podracing: Anakin and Sebulba, style A [336-47].........15.00
- Podracing: Anakin and Sebulba, style B..................20.00
- Podracing: Anakin and Sebulba, style C..................25.00
- Podracing, style A [336-48].............................15.00
- Podracing, style B......................................20.00
- Podracing, style C [336-49].............................25.00
- Queen Amidala, style A..................................15.00
- Queen Amidala, style B [336-50].........................20.00
- Queen Amidala, style C..................................25.00

Episode II: Attack of the Clones.
- Anakin Skywalker [336-51]...............................20.00
- Clone trooper [336-52]..................................20.00
- Heroes [336-53]...20.00
- Heroes with water bottle attached [336-54]..............15.00
- Jedi Training Academy [336-55]..........................20.00

Spearmark International (UK)
- Clone Wars: Anakin, Yoda, clone troopers [336-56].......20.00
- Episode II cool bag, sandwich box, and sports bottle ..20.00

Plastic, classic art decal featuring Luke and Leia, Vader and Stormtrooper.
- Double thermos [336-57].................................45.00
- Rectangular [336-58]....................................45.00

The LEGO Group
- LEGO Star Wars [336-59]................................20.00

Thermos Co.
- Captain Rex, shaped [336-60]...........................20.00
- Darth Vader sculpted [336-61]..........................40.00
- R2-D2 canister [336-62]................................30.00
- Something, Something, Darkside, Family Guy (parody), Blu-ray exclusive premium, exclusive to Best Buy [336-63] 25.00

Clone Wars 3D.
- Anakin and Obi-Wan [336-64]............................25.00
- Anakin, Rex, Obi-Wan [336-65]..........................20.00

336-34

336-35

336-36

336-37

336-38

336-39

336-40

336-41

336-42

336-43

336-44

336-45

336-46

336-47

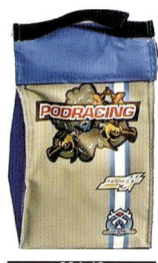
336-48

336-49

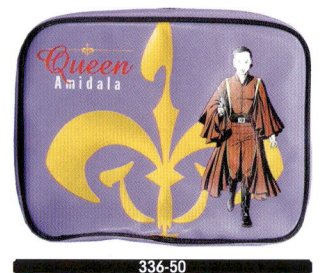
336-50

336-51

Lunch Boxes

336-52 Side 1 and Side 2

336-53

336-54

336-55

336-56

336-57

336-58

336-59

336-60

❏ Captain Rex [336-66] 20.00
❏ Heroes [336-67] 15.00

Episode III: Revenge of the Sith.
❏ Darth Vader [336-68] 20.00

❏ Darth Vader, dual compartment 25.00
❏ Epic Duel [336-69] 15.00

Hard plastic with graphic thermos.
❏ Jango Fett with Slave I thermos [336-70] 25.00

❏ Jedi battles with duel graphics on thermos [336-71] 20.00
❏ R2-D2 and C-3PO 3D sculpted front with droids thermos [336-72] 25.00
❏ Yoda [336-73] 20.00

336-61

336-62

336-63

336-64

336-65

336-66

336-67

336-68

336-69

336-70

336-71

336-72

336-73

336-74

336-75

336-76

336-77

336-78

336-79

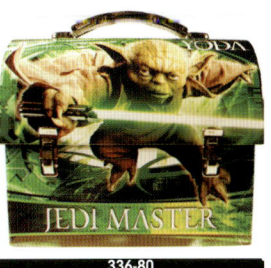
336-80

Lunch Boxes

336-81

336-82

336-83 Side 1 and Side 2

336-84

336-85

336-86

336-87

336-88

Metal lunchboxes with plain white thermos.
- ❏ Episode II Heroes and Villains [336-74] 30.00
- ❏ Movie poster art / Soundtrack poster art [336-75] 30.00

Tin Box Company
- ❏ Darth Vader [336-76] 15.00
- ❏ Empire Strikes Back 15.00
- ❏ Epic Duel [336-77] 20.00
- ❏ Return of the Jedi [336-78] 15.00
- ❏ Star Wars [336-79] 15.00
- ❏ Yoda, Jedi Master [336-80] 15.00

Square.
- ❏ Empire [336-81] 15.00
- ❏ Hildebrandt art [336-82] 15.00
- ❏ Jedi / Sith [336-83] 15.00
- ❏ Poster Art [336-84] 15.00
- ❏ Yoda [336-85] 15.00

Vandor LLC
Movie art.
- ❏ A New Hope 15.00
- ❏ Empire Strikes Back 15.00
- ❏ Return of the Jedi 15.00

Zak Designs
Episode III: Revenge of the Sith.
- ❏ Darth Vader hard plastic [336-86] 20.00
- ❏ Darth Vader sandwich carrier [336-87] 15.00
- ❏ Darth Vader soft vinyl [336-88] 15.00

Magnets
Continued in Volume 3, Page 274

- ❏ Episode I: The Phantom Menace Car #24 ....10.00
- ❏ Family Guy / Blue Harvest [337-01] 15.00

1970s monster magnet series.
- ❏ Mono, Darth Vader likeness [337-02] 10.00

3.5" x 5" movie image inside border trim.
- ❏ Anakin Skywalker [337-03] 5.00
- ❏ Darth Maul [337-04] 5.00
- ❏ Jar Jar [337-05] 5.00
- ❏ Naboo Space Battle [337-06] 5.00
- ❏ Obi-Wan Kenobi [337-07] 5.00
- ❏ Queen Amidala [337-08] 5.00

Mpire, approximately 2" round.
- ❏ Anakin 5.00
- ❏ C-3PO 5.00
- ❏ Chewbacca 5.00
- ❏ Clone trooper 5.00
- ❏ Count Dooku 5.00
- ❏ Darth Maul 5.00
- ❏ Darth Vader 5.00
- ❏ Emperor 5.00
- ❏ Han 5.00
- ❏ Luke 5.00
- ❏ Obi-Wan 5.00
- ❏ Princess Leia 5.00
- ❏ Queen Amidala 5.00

(Thailand)
Episode III: Revenge of the Sith. 2" x 3".
- ❏ Anakin Skywalker attacking [337-09] 5.00
- ❏ Anakin Skywalker standing [337-10] 5.00
- ❏ C-3PO [337-11] 5.00
- ❏ Darth Sidious [337-12] 5.00
- ❏ Darth Vader [337-13] 5.00
- ❏ General Grievous [337-14] 5.00
- ❏ Obi-Wan Kenobi [337-15] 5.00
- ❏ Padmé [337-16] 5.00

337-01

337-02

337-03

337-04

337-05

337-06

337-07

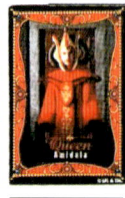
337-08

337-09

337-10

337-11

337-12

337-13

337-14

337-15

337-16

337-17

337-18

337-19

337-20

337-21

337-22

337-23

337-24

337-25

337-26

337-27

337-28

337-29

337-30

337-31

337-32

337-33

337-34

Magnets

□ R2-D2 [337-17].....................................5.00
□ Yoda [337-18].......................................5.00

20th Century Fox (Thailand)
Episode II movie promotion, 1.75" x 2.75".
□ Anakin Skywalker................................4.00
□ Padmé Amidala....................................4.00

A.H. Prismatic
□ AT-AT [337-19].....................................15.00
□ Darth Vader [337-20]............................15.00
□ Darth Vader with lightsaber [337-21]....15.00
□ Dogfight in Space [337-22]...................15.00
□ Imperial Star Destroyer [337-23]...........15.00
□ Millennium Falcon in asteroid field [337-24]...15.00

□ Millennium Falcon over Death Star [337-25]..........15.00
□ TIE Interceptor [337-26].......................15.00
□ X-Wing Fighter flying [337-27]..............15.00
□ X-Wing Fighter in combat [337-28].......15.00

Accessory Zone
□ 9 magnets, Clone Wars, exclusive to Target [337-29].....10.00

Magnets

337-95

337-96

337-97

❑ Sheet of 6, exclusive to Target [337-30]........................10.00

Adam Joseph Industries

❑ Chewbacca [337-31]..20.00
❑ Chewbacca, Darth Vader, R2-D2, and Yoda [337-32]......30.00
❑ Wicket and Kneesaa [337-33]....................................20.00

Animations

❑ Saga Magnets, sheet of 10 [337-34]............................8.00

Applause

3D sculpted magnets.
❑ 4-pack boxed [337-35]..25.00
❑ Battle Droid [337-36]..10.00
❑ Jar Jar Binks [337-37]...10.00
❑ Naboo fighter [337-38]..10.00
❑ Watto [337-39]..10.00

Die-cut magnets with stamped detailing.
❑ AT-AT [337-40]..5.00
❑ Millennium Falcon...5.00
❑ Snowspeeder [337-41]..5.00
❑ TIE Fighter [337-42]...5.00
❑ X-Wing Fighter [337-43]..5.00

Episode I die-cut magnets with stamped detailing.
❑ Naboo starfighter [337-44]...5.00
❑ Trade Federation Droid fighter [337-45].........................5.00

artbox

Series 1.
❑ Admiral Ackbar [337-46]..15.00
❑ AT-AT Driver...15.00
❑ Bith (Figrin D'an) [337-47]...15.00
❑ Darth Vader..15.00
❑ IG-88 [337-48]..15.00
❑ Luke Skywalker [337-49]..15.00
❑ Nien Nunb [337-50]...15.00
❑ Zuckuss [337-51]...15.00

At-A-Boy

❑ A New Hope Falcon cockpit...5.00
❑ B-Wings in battle..5.00
❑ Ben holding lightsaber...5.00
❑ Ben Kenobi 5.00
❑ Ben Kenobi portrait...5.00
❑ Boba Fett in Cloud City corridor......................................5.00
❑ Bounty hunter line-up..5.00
❑ C-3PO portrait..5.00
❑ Chewbacca, snow covered..5.00
❑ Darth Vader flanked by two stormtroopers........................5.00
❑ Darth Vader portrait..5.00
❑ Darth Vader portrait (shuttle ramp in background) [337-52]..5.00
❑ Darth Vader reaches out on Cloud City gantry....................5.00
❑ Darth Vader silhouetted in Empire Strikes Back freeze chamber 5.00
❑ Darth Vader with beige background 5.00
❑ Droids in Blockade Runner corridor [337-53]......................5.00
❑ Droids in Hoth base corridor 5.00
❑ Emperor Palpatine portrait..5.00
❑ Empire Strikes Back 'A' poster with credits........................5.00
❑ Empire Strikes Back Luke in the tree 5.00

337-98 337-99 337-100 337-101 337-102 337-103 337-104 337-105 337-106 337-107

337-108 337-109 337-110 337-111 337-112 337-113 337-114 337-115 337-116

337-117 337-118 337-119 337-120 337-121 337-122 337-123 337-124 337-125 337-126 337-127

337-128 337-129 337-130 337-131 337-132 337-133 337-134 337-135 337-136 337-137 337-138 337-139

337-140 337-141 337-142 337-143 337-144 337-145 337-146 337-147 337-148 337-149

Magnets

- Falcon in flight 5.00
- Han and Chewbacca blasting (publicity shot) 5.00
- Han and Leia kiss (Empire Strikes Back) 5.00
- Han blasting 5.00
- Han in gunner chair... 5.00
- Han on tauntaun 5.00
- Han portrait 5.00
- Han Solo 5.00
- Holochess aboard the Falcon.................................. 5.00
- Interior of Ben's house... 5.00
- Leia consoles Luke 5.00
- Leia hand on hip, gun up...................................... 5.00
- Leia on Falcon 5.00
- Leia programming R2-D2....................................... 5.00
- Luke and Leia Return of the Jedi swing [337-54] 5.00
- Luke and X-Wing in swamp..................................... 5.00
- Luke looking at the sunsets................................... 5.00
- Luke playing with T-16 .... 5.00
- Luke portrait [337-55] 5.00
- Luke sees charred relatives.................................... 5.00
- Luke, Leia, and Han in Death Star [337-56].................. 5.00
- R2-D2 .... 5.00
- Return of the Jedi 'A' poster with credits [337-57] 5.00
- Sandtrooper on dewback 5.00

337-150	337-151	337-152	337-153	337-154	337-155	337-156	337-157	337-158	337-159
337-160	337-161	337-162	337-163	337-164	337-165	337-166	337-167	337-168	337-169
337-170	337-171	337-172	337-173	337-174	337-175	337-176	337-177	337-178	337-179
337-180	337-181	337-182	337-183	337-184	337-185	337-186	337-187	337-188	337-189
337-190	337-191	337-192	337-193	337-194	337-195	337-196	337-197	337-198	337-199
337-200	337-201	337-202	337-203	337-204	337-205	337-206	337-207	337-208	337-209
337-210	337-211	337-212	337-213	337-214	337-215	337-216	337-217	337-218	337-219
337-220	337-221	337-222	337-223	337-224	337-225	337-226	337-227	337-228	337-229
337-230	337-231	337-232	337-233	337-234	337-235	337-236	337-237	337-238	337-239

Magnets

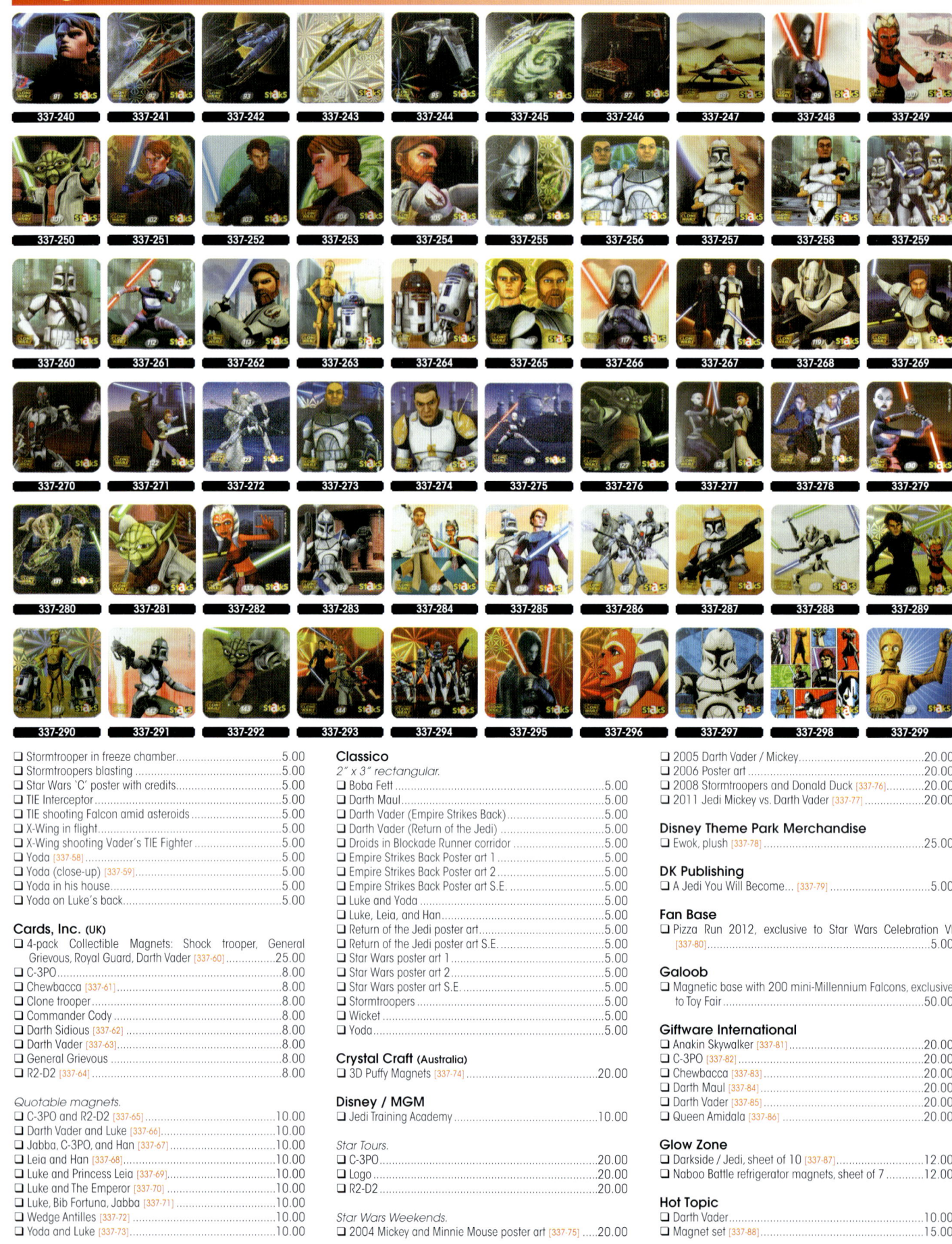

❏ Stormtrooper in freeze chamber.....................................5.00
❏ Stormtroopers blasting 5.00
❏ Star Wars 'C' poster with credits......................................5.00
❏ TIE Interceptor..5.00
❏ TIE shooting Falcon amid asteroids 5.00
❏ X-Wing in flight...5.00
❏ X-Wing shooting Vader's TIE Fighter 5.00
❏ Yoda [337-58]...5.00
❏ Yoda (close-up) [337-59]..5.00
❏ Yoda in his house...5.00
❏ Yoda on Luke's back...5.00

Cards, Inc. (UK)
❏ 4-pack Collectible Magnets: Shock trooper, General Grievous, Royal Guard, Darth Vader [337-60]........25.00
❏ C-3PO..8.00
❏ Chewbacca [337-61]..8.00
❏ Clone trooper...8.00
❏ Commander Cody 8.00
❏ Darth Sidious [337-62]...8.00
❏ Darth Vader [337-63]..8.00
❏ General Grievous 8.00
❏ R2-D2 [337-64]...8.00

Quotable magnets.
❏ C-3PO and R2-D2 [337-65]...10.00
❏ Darth Vader and Luke [337-66]...10.00
❏ Jabba, C-3PO, and Han [337-67]...10.00
❏ Leia and Han [337-68]..10.00
❏ Luke and Princess Leia [337-69]...10.00
❏ Luke and The Emperor [337-70]..10.00
❏ Luke, Bib Fortuna, Jabba [337-71]..10.00
❏ Wedge Antilles [337-72]..10.00
❏ Yoda and Luke [337-73]...10.00

Classico
2" x 3" rectangular.
❏ Boba Fett 5.00
❏ Darth Maul 5.00
❏ Darth Vader (Empire Strikes Back)....................................5.00
❏ Darth Vader (Return of the Jedi).......................................5.00
❏ Droids in Blockade Runner corridor 5.00
❏ Empire Strikes Back Poster art 1 ....5.00
❏ Empire Strikes Back Poster art 2 ....5.00
❏ Empire Strikes Back Poster art S.E. 5.00
❏ Luke and Yoda 5.00
❏ Luke, Leia, and Han...5.00
❏ Return of the Jedi poster art..5.00
❏ Return of the Jedi poster art S.E. 5.00
❏ Star Wars poster art 1 ....5.00
❏ Star Wars poster art 2 ....5.00
❏ Star Wars poster art S.E. 5.00
❏ Stormtroopers 5.00
❏ Wicket...5.00
❏ Yoda..5.00

Crystal Craft (Australia)
❏ 3D Puffy Magnets [337-74] 20.00

Disney / MGM
❏ Jedi Training Academy 10.00

Star Tours.
❏ C-3PO..20.00
❏ Logo 20.00
❏ R2-D2...20.00

Star Wars Weekends.
❏ 2004 Mickey and Minnie Mouse poster art [337-75] 20.00
❏ 2005 Darth Vader / Mickey..20.00
❏ 2006 Poster art 20.00
❏ 2008 Stormtroopers and Donald Duck [337-76]..............20.00
❏ 2011 Jedi Mickey vs. Darth Vader [337-77] 20.00

Disney Theme Park Merchandise
❏ Ewok, plush [337-78] 25.00

DK Publishing
❏ A Jedi You Will Become... [337-79] 5.00

Fan Base
❏ Pizza Run 2012, exclusive to Star Wars Celebration VI [337-80] 5.00

Galoob
❏ Magnetic base with 200 mini-Millennium Falcons, exclusive to Toy Fair 50.00

Giftware International
❏ Anakin Skywalker [337-81]...20.00
❏ C-3PO [337-82]...20.00
❏ Chewbacca [337-83]...20.00
❏ Darth Maul [337-84]...20.00
❏ Darth Vader [337-85]..20.00
❏ Queen Amidala [337-86]..20.00

Glow Zone
❏ Darkside / Jedi, sheet of 10 [337-87].................................12.00
❏ Naboo Battle refrigerator magnets, sheet of 7 ....12.00

Hot Topic
❏ Darth Vader..10.00
❏ Magnet set [337-88]...15.00

337-300

337-301

337-302

337-303

337-304

337-305

337-306

337-307

337-308

337-309

337-310

337-311

337-312

337-313

337-314

337-315

Movie poster art.
- ❑ A New Hope 5.00
- ❑ Empire Strikes Back 5.00

Howard Eldon
- ❑ A New Hope, triangular logo....................................20.00
- ❑ Return of the Jedi, Yoda in circle...............................20.00
- ❑ The Empire Strikes Back, Darth Vader in flames 20.00

Innovative Designs
Clone Wars 12-packs. Exclusive to Target.
- ❑ Anakin, Ahsoka, logo, General Grievous, R2-D2, C-3PO, Obi-Wan art, Republic emblem, Anakin art, clone trooper, Yoda, Obi-Wan [337-89] 15.00
- ❑ Mace Windu, clone, super battle droid, Anakin, General Grievous, Ahsoka, Yoda, Obi-Wan, Jabba, C-3PO, battle droid, Captain Rex [337-90] 15.00

KFC
- ❑ Anakin Skywalker [337-91] 15.00
- ❑ Darth Maul [337-92] 15.00
- ❑ Jar Jar Binks [337-93]...15.00
- ❑ Queen Amidala [337-94] 15.00

Kotobukiya (Japan)
- ❑ R2 Magnet Collection, exclusive to Star Wars Celebration Japan [337-95] 75.00
- ❑ R2 Magnet Collection [337-96] 50.00
- ❑ Real Masks Magnet Collection [337-97] 50.00

Series 1.
- ❑ Boba Fett (mystery / chase piece) [337-98] 35.00
- ❑ C-3PO [337-99] 15.00
- ❑ Darth Vader [337-100]...15.00
- ❑ Jawa [337-101] 15.00
- ❑ R2-D2 [337-102]...15.00
- ❑ Stormtrooper [337-103]..15.00
- ❑ TIE Fighter pilot [337-104] 15.00
- ❑ Tusken Raider [337-105]..15.00

Series 2.
- ❑ Biker scout [337-106] 15.00
- ❑ Boushh (mystery / chase piece)....................................40.00
- ❑ Chewbacca [337-107]...15.00
- ❑ Clone trooper [337-108]..15.00
- ❑ Darth Maul [337-109]..15.00
- ❑ Greedo [337-110] 15.00
- ❑ Royal Guard [337-111] 15.00
- ❑ Yoda [337-112]...15.00

Series 3.
- ❑ Clone trooper [337-113]..15.00
- ❑ Commander Cody [337-114] 15.00
- ❑ Gamorrean Guard [337-115] 15.00
- ❑ General Grievous [337-116] 15.00
- ❑ General Grievous Bodyguard [337-117] 15.00
- ❑ Jango Fett [337-118] 15.00
- ❑ *(Mystery)* 40.00
- ❑ The Emperor [337-119] 15.00

Series 4.
- ❑ AT-AT driver...15.00
- ❑ Bith..15.00
- ❑ Darth Vader (removable helmet) 40.00
- ❑ IG-88 ....15.00
- ❑ Luke Skywalker (X-Wing pilot)......................................15.00
- ❑ (Mystery) 15.00
- ❑ Nien Nunb 15.00
- ❑ Zuckuss 15.00

Le Gaulois
Set of 28. Food premiums.
- ❑ 1 Anakin Skywalker [337-120] 5.00
- ❑ 2 Qui-Gon Jinn [337-121] 5.00
- ❑ 3 Darth Maul [337-122]...5.00
- ❑ 4 Jar Jar Binks [337-123] 5.00
- ❑ 5 Comte Dooku [337-124]..5.00
- ❑ 6 Clone trooper [337-125]..5.00
- ❑ 7 Jango Fett [337-126] 5.00
- ❑ 8 Jabba le Hutt [337-127] 5.00
- ❑ 9 Dark Vador [337-128]...5.00
- ❑ 10 Anakin Skywalker [337-129] 5.00
- ❑ 11 Obi-Wan Kenobi [337-130] 5.00
- ❑ 12 L'Emereur [337-131] 5.00
- ❑ 13 Yoda [337-132]...5.00
- ❑ 14 Chancellor Palpatine [337-133]..5.00
- ❑ 15 General Grievous [337-134] 5.00
- ❑ 16 Chewbacca [337-135]...5.00
- ❑ 17 Tarfful [337-136]..5.00
- ❑ 18 Mace Windu [337-137] 5.00
- ❑ 19 Padmé Amidala [337-138] 5.00
- ❑ 20 Bail Organa [337-139] 5.00
- ❑ 21 R2-D2 [337-140]..5.00
- ❑ 22 C-3PO [337-141]..5.00
- ❑ 23 Luke Skywalker [337-142]...5.00
- ❑ 24 Obi-Wan Kenobi [337-143]..5.00
- ❑ 25 Princess Leia [337-144] 5.00
- ❑ 26 Yan Solo [337-145] 5.00
- ❑ 27 Lando Calrissian [337-146] 5.00
- ❑ 28 Boba Fett [337-147] 5.00

Mega-Mags
Giant Magnets.
- ❑ Darth Vader [337-148]...15.00
- ❑ Millennium Falcon [337-149] 15.00

Panini (UK)
Clone Wars Staks. Square magnets. Set of 150. Numbered.
- ❑ Magnets 1–150, each [337-150] through [337-299] 5.00

Pepsi Cola
Hologram magnets, gold background.
- ❑ Anakin Skywalker [337-300]..10.00
- ❑ Battle droid [337-301] 10.00
- ❑ Boss Nass [337-302] 10.00
- ❑ C-3PO [337-303]...10.00
- ❑ Captain Tarpals [337-304] 10.00
- ❑ Darth Maul [337-305]...10.00
- ❑ Darth Vader [337-306]..10.00
- ❑ Episode I Logo [337-307] 10.00
- ❑ Jar Jar Binks [337-308] 10.00
- ❑ Mace Windu [337-309] 10.00
- ❑ Nute Gunray [337-310] 10.00
- ❑ Queen Amidala [337-311] 10.00
- ❑ R2-D2 [337-312]...10.00
- ❑ Sebulba [337-313] 10.00
- ❑ Watto [337-314] 10.00
- ❑ Yoda [337-315]...10.00

Pizza Hut
- ❑ Anakin Skywalker [337-317]...15.00

337-317

337-318

337-319

337-320

337-321

337-322

337-323

337-324

337-325

337-326

337-327

337-328

337-329

337-330

337-331

337-332

Magnets

| 337-336 | 337-337 | 337-338 | 337-339 | 337-340 | 337-341 | 337-342 | 337-343 | 337-344 | 337-345 | 337-346 | 337-347 |

  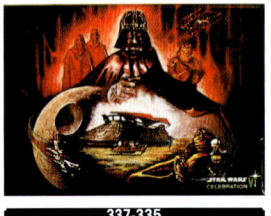    

| 337-333 | 337-334 | 337-335 | 337-348 | 337-349 | 337-350 | 337-351 |

❏ Darth Maul [337-318] 15.00
❏ Jar Jar Binks [337-319] 15.00
❏ Queen Amidala [337-320] 15.00

Die-cut with phone number for delivery.
❏ Darth Maul [337-321] 20.00

Pizza Hut (France)
❏ Darth Vader [337-322] 20.00
❏ R2-D2 and C-3PO [337-323] 20.00
❏ Yoda [337-324] 20.00

Pizza Hut (Mexico)
❏ Jar Jar Binks [337-325] 25.00

Scholastic
❏ Episode III: Revenge of the Sith cover art 5.00

Star Wars Celebration
❏ Anakin Skywalker 10.00

Star Wars Celebration Europe (UK)
❏ Logo refrigerator magnet [337-326] 20.00

Star Wars Celebration III
❏ Clone trooper [337-327] 20.00
❏ Darth Vader [337-328] 20.00
❏ General Grievous [337-329] 20.00
❏ Royal Guard [337-330] 20.00

Star Wars Celebration IV
❏ C-3PO 20.00
❏ Chewbacca 20.00
❏ Darth Vader [337-331] 20.00
❏ Princess Leia 20.00
❏ Yoda [337-332] 20.00

Star Wars Celebration V
❏ Boba Fett 20.00
❏ O Lando! 20.00
❏ Star Wars phrase magnet set 20.00

Star Wars Celebration VI
❏ "Join the Party" [337-333] 20.00
❏ Return of the Jedi heroes [337-334] 20.00
❏ Return of the Jedi villains [337-335] 20.00
❏ Stamp art set 20.00

The LEGO Group
❏ ARF trooper, Embo, Aurra Sing [337-336] 35.00
❏ Boba Fett, Princess Leia, Royal Guard [337-337] 40.00
❏ Chewbacca, Darth Vader, Obi-Wan Kenobi [337-338] .. 35.00
❏ Chewbacca, Darth Vader, Obi-Wan Kenobi [337-339] .. 35.00
❏ Darth Vader, Snowtrooper, shadow trooper [337-340] .. 35.00
❏ Han Solo, Paploo, scout trooper [337-341] 35.00
❏ Stormtrooper, Y-Wing pilot, AT-ST driver [337-342] 35.00
❏ Yoda, Anakin, clone trooper [337-343] 35.00
❏ Yoda, Count Dooku, Mace Windu [337-344] ... 35.00

3-packs. 30th anniversary collection.
❏ Boba Fett, Princess Leia, Royal Guard [337-345] 40.00
❏ Stormtrooper, X-Wing pilot, AT-ST driver [337-346] ... 35.00

| 338-01 | 338-02 | 338-03 |

 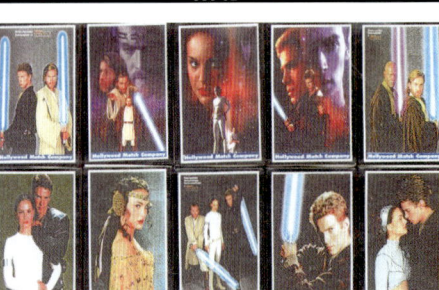 

| 338-04 | 338-05 | 338-06 |

Media Players: Digital

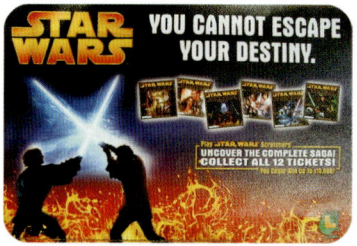 339-01
 339-02
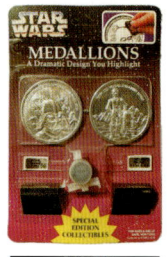 340-01
 340-02
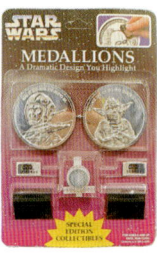 340-03

 340-04
 340-05
 340-06
 341-01
 341-02
 341-03

Anniversary edition.
❏ Stormtrooper, silver [337-347] 75.00

World Wide Licenses Ltd.
❏ Darth Maul—the Dark Side [337-348] 10.00
❏ Episode I logo [337-349] 10.00
❏ Jar Jar Binks [337-350] 10.00
❏ Jedi [HOX351] 10.00

Matchboxes

Hollywood Match Company
10 packs of wooden stick matches.
❏ Characters [338-01] 35.00
❏ Movie posters [338-02] 35.00
❏ Episode I [338-03] 35.00
❏ Episode I characters [338-04] 35.00
❏ Episode I previews 35.00
❏ Episode II characters [338-05] 35.00
❏ Episode II promotions [338-06] 35.00

Mats

California Lottery
❏ Change mat [339-01] 30.00

Recticel Sutcliffe Ltd. (UK)
❏ Play mat, artwork from all 3 movies, 39" x 24" [339-02] 160.00

Medallions

Craft House
Paintable / weathering craft.
❏ C-3PO and R2-D2 / Darth Vader [340-01] 25.00
❏ Han Solo / Princess Leia [340-02] 25.00
❏ Luke Skywalker / Yoda [340-03] 25.00

Noble Studios
4" pewter medallions.
❏ Darth Vader [340-04] 95.00
❏ Obi-Wan Kenobi [340-05] 95.00
❏ Yoda [340-06] 130.00

Medals
Continued in Volume 3, Page 276

Disney Hollywood Studios
❏ Star Tours 3D, "Join the Rebellion" 150.00

Media Player Accessories
Continued in Volume 3, Page 276

Skins for iPod Touch 2G.
❏ Darth Vader [341-01] 15.00
❏ Stormtrooper [341-02] 15.00
❏ Stormtrooper helmet [341-03] 15.00

Media Players: CD
Continued in Volume 3, Page 277

JazWares, Inc
❏ Darth Vader helmet, radio CD player [342-01] 75.00

Sakar International
❏ CD boombox [342-02] 50.00
❏ Obi-Wan Kenobi, Clone Wars [342-03] 40.00

Tiger Electronics
❏ Darth Maul [342-04] 65.00

Media Players: Digital
Continued in Volume 3, Page 277

(UK)
❏ Darth Vader MP3 player with radio, 512 MB 75.00

 342-01
 342-02
 342-03
 342-04
 343-01
 343-02

 343-03
 344-01
 344-02
 344-03
 344-04
 344-05
 344-06

Media Players: Digital

Sakar International
- Digital MP3 player, changeable face plates [343-01].....45.00

Taito (Japan)
MP3 players shaped as lightsabers.
- Darth Vader [343-02]..35.00
- Luke Skywalker [343-03]..35.00

Media Players: Radio, Cassette

Kenner
- Artoo-Detoo (R2-D2) radio [344-01]......................225.00
- Luke Skywalker AM headset radio [344-02]...........525.00

Micro Games of America
- C-3PO AM/FM radio...35.00
- Darth Vader AM/FM radio [344-03].........................30.00
- Millennium Falcon cassette player............................40.00

Takara (Japan)
- R2-D2, "Drink Coca-Cola" [344-04]........................550.00

Tiger Electronics
- R2-D2 Data droid [344-05]..40.00
- R2-D2, flat with belt clip [344-06]............................35.00

Media, Audio: Cassettes
Continued in Volume 3, Page 277

- An Hour of Superthemes [345-01]...........................10.00
- Cinema Gala [345-02]..10.00
- Galactic Funk by Mecco [345-03]............................10.00
- Return of the Jedi / Empire Strikes Back / Star Wars, Chromium Dioxide [345-04].....................................10.00
- Return of the Jedi / Empire Strikes Back / Star Wars, full cover [345-05]..10.00
- Return of the Jedi / Empire Strikes Back / Star Wars, white border [345-06]..10.00
- Return of the Jedi / Empire Strikes Back / Star Wars, white border with text [345-06]..10.00
- Return of the Jedi, movie poster cover [345-07]............10.00
- Return of the Jedi soundtrack, movie poster cover, red and black text on white bottom third [345-08].................10.00
- Return of the Jedi soundtrack, National Philharmonic Orchestra [345-09]...10.00
- Return of the Jedi soundtrack, National Philharmonic Orchestra, saber cover [345-10]..............................10.00
- Star Wars in High Fidelity [345-11].........................10.00
- Star Wars, A Stereo Space Odyssey [345-12].........10.00
- Star Wars, the original motion picture soundtrack [345-13]..10.00
- Star Wars, white banner above and below [345-14].......10.00
- Story of Star Wars, white banner above and below [345-15]..10.00
- The Empire Strikes Back, Luke / Hoth cover [345-16]......10.00

Seven Star Chrome Series.
- 30 The Empire Strikes Back [345-17].....................10.00
- 65 Return of the Jedi [345-18].................................10.00

(Germany)
- Kreig der Sterne [345-19]..10.00

(Norway)
- Stjerne krigen [345-20]..24.00

20th Century Fox
- Star Wars Twin Pack, set of 2 [345-21]...................10.00
- Star Wars, Vader cover [345-22].............................10.00
- Story of Star Wars [345-23].....................................11.00
- Story of Star Wars, Parts 1 and 2 [345-24].............10.00

BMG Entertainment
- Star Wars soundtrack, 2 cassettes............................8.00

Buena Vista Records
Read-along stories.
- 3-pack: Star Wars, Empire Strikes Back, Return of the Jedi Children's Library [345-25]....................................18.00
- 3-pack: Star Wars Trilogy [345-26].........................12.00
- Adventures in ABC [345-27]....................................10.00
- Adventures in Colors and Shapes............................10.00
- Droid World [345-28]..10.00
- Empire Strikes Back...10.00
- Ewoks Join the Fight..10.00
- Ewoks: The Battle for Endor [345-29].....................10.00
- Planet of the Hoojibs...10.00
- Rebel Mission to Ord Mantell..................................10.00
- Return of the Jedi [345-30]......................................10.00
- Star Wars [345-31]...10.00

The Story of ... Read-along stories.
- Empire Strikes Back [345-32]..................................12.00
- Return of the Jedi...12.00
- Star Wars [345-33]...12.00

German Releases
24-page book with read-along tape.
- Das Imperium Schlagt Zuruck [345-34]..................20.00
- Jedi Ritter [345-35]...20.00

Highbridge Company
Full-cast Audio Drama, 2 cassettes.
- Dark Empire [345-36]...18.00
- Dark Empire II [345-37]..18.00
- Dark Forces: Soldier for the Empire [345-38]........18.00

Original Radio Drama as heard on National Public Radio, original music/effects.
- Empire Strikes Back: 10 episodes, 5 cassettes [345-39]..35.00
- Return of the Jedi: 6 episodes, 3 cassettes [345-40]....25.00
- Star Wars: 13 episodes, 6 cassettes [345-41]........35.00
- Trilogy gift pack, 14 cassettes................................85.00

Pickwick
- Sounds of Star Wars [345-42]..................................10.00

Polygram Records
- Christmas in the Stars [345-43]...............................26.00

Media, Audio: CDs

   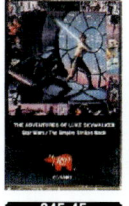       

345-42   345-43   345-44   345-45   345-46   345-47   345-48   345-49   345-50   345-51   345-52

345-53   345-54   345-55   345-56   345-57   345-58   345-59   345-60   345-61   345-62   345-63

345-64   345-65   345-66   345-67   345-68   345-69   345-70   345-71   345-72   345-73

- ❏ Star Wars Soundtrack [345-44]..........................15.00
- ❏ The Adventures of Luke Skywalker, Star Wars/Empire Strikes Back [345-45]..........................10.00
- ❏ The Empire Strikes Back, Vader starfield cover [345-46] .10.00
- ❏ The Empire Strikes Back, Vader starfield full cover [345-47]..........................10.00

Movie soundtracks.
- ❏ Empire Strikes Back, Vader starfield cover with lower third red and black text [345-48]..........................35.00

Rainbow
Read-along cassettes.
- ❏ Droid World [345-49]..........................20.00
- ❏ Planet of the Hoojibs [345-50]..........................20.00
- ❏ Star Wars [345-51]..........................20.00
- ❏ The Empire Strikes Back [345-52]..........................20.00

Rhino
Star Wars Episode I 24-page book and tape read-along with Micro Machine vehicle pack-in.
- ❏ (No pack-in) [345-53]..........................15.00
- ❏ Anakin's Podracer [345-54]..........................25.00
- ❏ Flash Speeder [345-55]..........................25.00
- ❏ Sith Infiltrator [345-56]..........................25.00

RSO Records
- ❏ Empire Strikes Back, music from [345-57]..........................10.00

Skywalkers
- ❏ A Wind to Shake The Stars [345-58]..........................20.00

Sony Classical
- ❏ Star Wars Trilogy, the Skywalker Symphony [345-59]......10.00

Spelto (Sweden)
- ❏ Irymd-Imperiet Slar Tillbaka (Empire Strikes Back) [345-60]..........................25.00
- ❏ Jedins Aterkomst (Return of the Jedi) [345-61]..........25.00
- ❏ Stjarnornas Krig (Star Wars) [345-62]..........................25.00

Stage and Screen Productions
- ❏ A Saga in Outer Space [345-63]..........................10.00

TW Kids
- ❏ The Mixed-Up Droid [345-64]..........................25.00

Read-along cassettes with bonus toy included.
- ❏ Empire Strikes Back, Snowspeeder Micromachine [345-65]..........................20.00
- ❏ Return of the Jedi, Millennium Falcon Micromachine [345-66]..........................20.00
- ❏ Star Wars, five stickers [345-67]..........................20.00

Walt Disney Records
Read-along cassettes with 3 mini-figures.
- ❏ A New Hope [345-68]..........................25.00
- ❏ Empire Strikes Back [345-69]..........................25.00
- ❏ Return of the Jedi [345-70]..........................25.00

Read-along cassettes.
- ❏ A New Hope [345-71]..........................10.00
- ❏ Empire Strikes Back [345-72]..........................10.00
- ❏ Return of the Jedi [345-73]..........................10.00

Media, Audio: CDs
Continued in Volume 3, Page 277

- ❏ Battle of the Heroes from Revenge of the Sith [346-01] ...18.00
- ❏ Duel of the Fates radio edit single [346-02] 10.00
- ❏ Empire Strikes Back soundtrack, National Philharmonic Orchestra [346-03]..........................10.00
- ❏ Figrin D'an and the Modal Nodes [346-04] 12.00
- ❏ Max Reebo Band..........................12.00
- ❏ Space Themes [v1e1:283]..........................10.00
- ❏ Space Trax Commemorative Edition by Starlight Orchestra, includes 3 St. Vincent postage stamps. [346-05]............10.00
- ❏ Space Trax: The best of Science Fiction Movies and TV, 3 bonus collectible Star Wars stamps 25.00
- ❏ The Phantom Menace Ultimate Edition 2 CD set [346-06]..........................50.00

Rebel Force Band.
- ❏ Living in these Star Wars..........................15.00

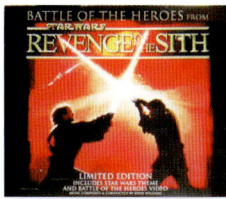 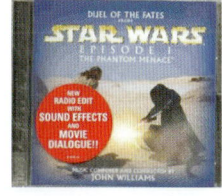 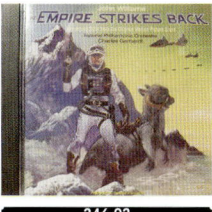   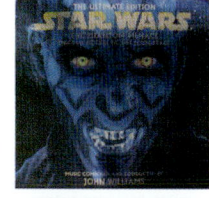

346-01   346-02   346-03   346-04   346-05   346-06

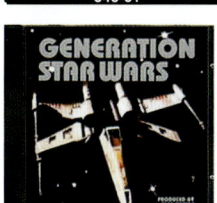  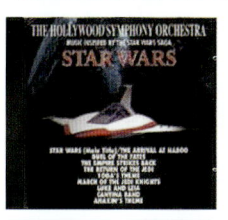   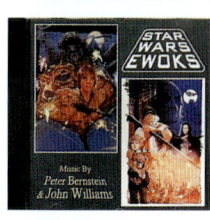

346-07   346-08   346-09   346-10   346-11   346-12

Media, Audio: CDs

Alec Empire
- Generation Star Wars, music [346-07] 15.00

Arista Records
- Star Wars Trilogy: The Original Soundtrack Anthology 4 CD set 25.00

BCI Music
- A Tribute to the Music of Star Wars [346-08] 10.00

Big Ear Music
- Music inspired by the Star Wars Saga by Hollywood Symphony Orchestra [346-09] 10.00

BMG Entertainment
- Max Rebo band: Jedi Rocks, selected from the Original Motion Picture Soundtrack Return of the Jedi:SE [346-10] 10.00

CBS Records
- John Williams, The Star Wars Trilogy 35.00

Delta
- Music of the Star Wars Saga by Bruno Bertone Orchestra [v1e1:283] 15.00

Fan Club (UK)
- Galactic Uplink, November 2001 [v1e1:283] 15.00

Film Orchestra
- A Tribute to the Music of Star Wars [346-11] 10.00

Force Records
- Soundtrack from Caravan of Courage and Ewok Adventure [346-12] 10.00

Highbridge Company
- Crimson Empire, 2 CDs, Abridged 20.00
- Empire Strikes Back: 5 CDs [346-13] 55.00
- Return of the Jedi: 3 CDs 35.00
- Star Wars: 7 CDs 60.00
- Tales of the Jedi, 3 CDs, Abridged 30.00
- Tales of the Jedi: Dark Lords of the Sith, 2 CDs 35.00
- Trilogy radio drama CD set, 15 CDs [346-14] 110.00
- Trilogy radio drama deluxe CD set; 15 CDs [v1e1:283]..160.00

K R B Music Company
- Music from the Star Wars Trilogy performed by the New World Orchestra 10.00

Kid Rhino
- Junior Jedi Training Manual read-along [346-15] 25.00

Lake Shore Records
- Synthesized Star Wars [346-16] 10.00

Laserlight
- Music of the Star Wars Saga by Bruno Bertone Orchestra volumes 1 and 2 [346-17] 25.00

Madacy Entertainment Group, Inc. (Canada)
- Space Wars volume 2, by the Starlite Orchestra 10.00

Mecoman Productions
- Star Wars Party [346-18] 15.00

Mercury Records
- Star Wars and Other Galactic Funk, by Meco 20.00
- The Best of Meco 10.00

Oglio Entertainment Group
- Cocktails in the Cantina music [346-19] 15.00

Polygram Records
- The Empire Strikes Back soundtrack 15.00

RCA Victor
- A New Hope Special Edition 20.00
- A New Hope Special Edition, deluxe 25.00
- Cantina Band picture disc CD single 15.00
- Darth Vader helmet-shaped CD single 20.00
- Empire Strikes Back Special Edition 20.00
- Empire Strikes Back Special Edition, deluxe [346-20] 30.00
- Rebo band picture disc CD single 20.00
- Return of the Jedi music [346-21] 15.00
- Return of the Jedi Special Edition 20.00
- Return of the Jedi Special Edition, deluxe edition 30.00

Rhino
- Christmas in the Stars [346-22] 16.00

Star Wars Episode I 24-page book and read-along CD with MicroMachine pack-in.
- (No pack in) [346-23] 15.00
- Anakin's Podracer 30.00
- Gungan Sub 30.00
- Sith Infiltrator MicroMachine 30.00

Score
- Star Wars: The Corellian Edition [346-24] 20.00
- The Music of Star Wars: 30th Anniversary [346-25] 45.00

Sony Classical
- A New Hope special 2 CD set 25.00

- Empire Strikes Back special 2 CD set 25.00
- Episode 3 Revenge of the Sith with bonus DVD 30.00
- John Williams conducts John Williams [346-26] 15.00
- Return of the Jedi special 2 CD set 25.00
- Star Wars Trilogy Collector's Edition soundtracks 50.00
- The Star Wars Trilogy 15.00

Episode II: Attack of the Clones movie soundtracks.
- Anakin and Padmé cover 15.00
- Jango Fett cover 15.00
- Movie poster art cover [346-27] 15.00
- Yoda cover 15.00

Episode II: Attack of the Clones movie soundtracks. Limited edition includes bonus track.
- Anakin and Padmé cover [346-28] 20.00
- Jango Fett cover [346-29] 20.00
- Yoda cover [346-30] 20.00

Sony Music Soundtrax
- The Phantom Menace Ultimate Edition 2 CD set 30.00
- The Phantom Menace with fold-out poster 10.00

Style Wars
- Style Wars, Free The Funk, music [346-31] 25.00

Varese Sarabande Records
- Shadows of the Empire 35.00

Wasabees
- Duel of the Fates dance remixes [346-32] 10.00

Media, Audio: Records
Continued in Volume 3, Page 277

- Christmas in the Stars [347-01] 65.00
- Empire Strikes Back soundtrack, National Philharmonic Orchestra [347-02] 25.00
- Ewok Celebration / Lapti Nek by Meco, 45rpm 10.00
- Meco plays music from Empire Strikes Back [347-03] 15.00
- Music from Star Wars performed by The Electric Moog Orchestra [347-04] 15.00
- Star Sounds [347-05] 10.00
- Star Wars and other Space Movie Themes by Geoff Love and His Orchestra [347-06] 35.00
- Star Wars Episode I soundtrack [347-07] 45.00
- Star Wars Theme / Cantina Band by Meco, 45rpm 15.00
- Star Wars, also a Space Odyssey by the London Philharmonic Orchestra [347-08] 10.00

Media, Audio: Records

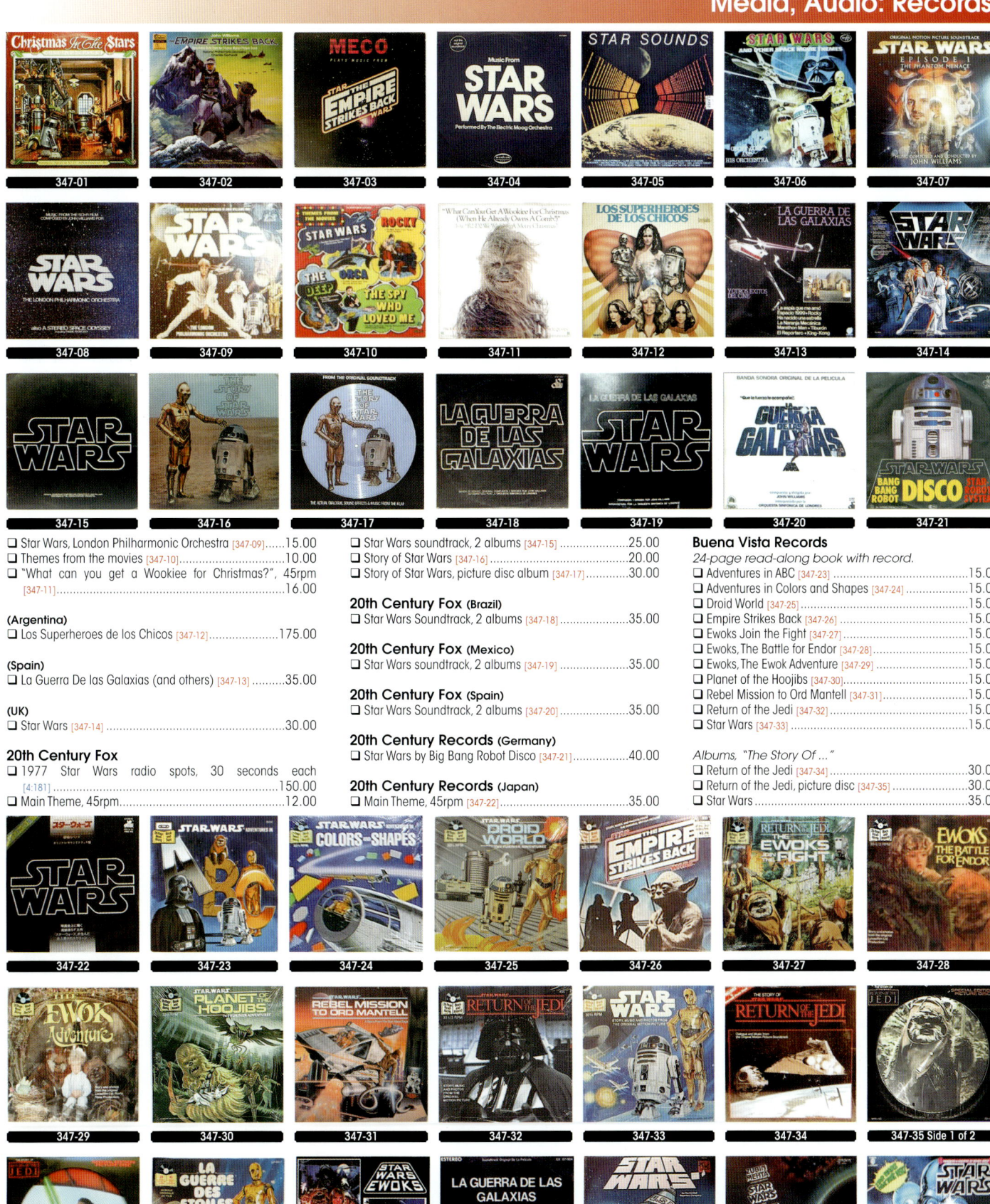

- ❏ Star Wars, London Philharmonic Orchestra [347-09] 15.00
- ❏ Themes from the movies [347-10] 10.00
- ❏ "What can you get a Wookiee for Christmas?", 45rpm [347-11] 16.00

(Argentina)
- ❏ Los Superheroes de los Chicos [347-12] 175.00

(Spain)
- ❏ La Guerra De las Galaxias (and others) [347-13] 35.00

(UK)
- ❏ Star Wars [347-14] 30.00

20th Century Fox
- ❏ 1977 Star Wars radio spots, 30 seconds each [4:181] 150.00
- ❏ Main Theme, 45rpm 12.00

- ❏ Star Wars soundtrack, 2 albums [347-15] 25.00
- ❏ Story of Star Wars [347-16] 20.00
- ❏ Story of Star Wars, picture disc album [347-17] 30.00

20th Century Fox (Brazil)
- ❏ Star Wars Soundtrack, 2 albums [347-18] 35.00

20th Century Fox (Mexico)
- ❏ Star Wars soundtrack, 2 albums [347-19] 35.00

20th Century Fox (Spain)
- ❏ Star Wars Soundtrack, 2 albums [347-20] 35.00

20th Century Records (Germany)
- ❏ Star Wars by Big Bang Robot Disco [347-21] 40.00

20th Century Records (Japan)
- ❏ Main Theme, 45rpm [347-22] 35.00

Buena Vista Records
24-page read-along book with record.
- ❏ Adventures in ABC [347-23] 15.00
- ❏ Adventures in Colors and Shapes [347-24] 15.00
- ❏ Droid World [347-25] 15.00
- ❏ Empire Strikes Back [347-26] 15.00
- ❏ Ewoks Join the Fight [347-27] 15.00
- ❏ Ewoks, The Battle for Endor [347-28] 15.00
- ❏ Ewoks, The Ewok Adventure [347-29] 15.00
- ❏ Planet of the Hoojibs [347-30] 15.00
- ❏ Rebel Mission to Ord Mantell [347-31] 15.00
- ❏ Return of the Jedi [347-32] 15.00
- ❏ Star Wars [347-33] 15.00

Albums, "The Story Of ..."
- ❏ Return of the Jedi [347-34] 30.00
- ❏ Return of the Jedi, picture disc [347-35] 30.00
- ❏ Star Wars 35.00

Media, Audio: Records

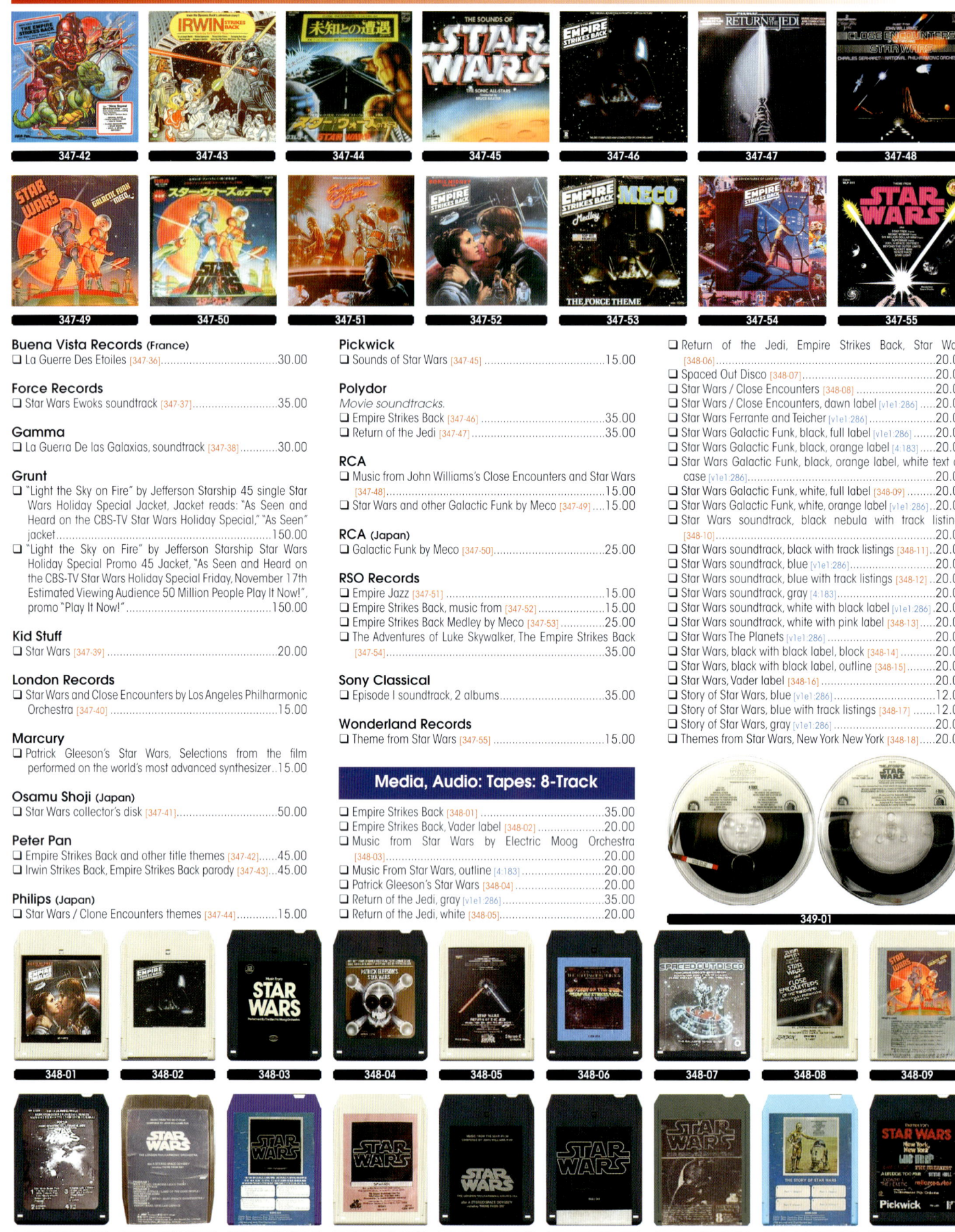

Buena Vista Records (France)
- La Guerre Des Etoiles [347-36]................30.00

Force Records
- Star Wars Ewoks soundtrack [347-37]..........35.00

Gamma
- La Guerra De las Galaxias, soundtrack [347-38]............30.00

Grunt
- "Light the Sky on Fire" by Jefferson Starship 45 single Star Wars Holiday Special Jacket, Jacket reads: "As Seen and Heard on the CBS-TV Star Wars Holiday Special," "As Seen" jacket................150.00
- "Light the Sky on Fire" by Jefferson Starship Star Wars Holiday Special Promo 45 Jacket, "As Seen and Heard on the CBS-TV Star Wars Holiday Special Friday, November 17th Estimated Viewing Audience 50 Million People Play It Now!", promo "Play It Now!"................150.00

Kid Stuff
- Star Wars [347-39]................20.00

London Records
- Star Wars and Close Encounters by Los Angeles Philharmonic Orchestra [347-40]................15.00

Marcury
- Patrick Gleeson's Star Wars, Selections from the film performed on the world's most advanced synthesizer..15.00

Osamu Shoji (Japan)
- Star Wars collector's disk [347-41]................50.00

Peter Pan
- Empire Strikes Back and other title themes [347-42]......45.00
- Irwin Strikes Back, Empire Strikes Back parody [347-43]...45.00

Philips (Japan)
- Star Wars / Clone Encounters themes [347-44]............15.00

Pickwick
- Sounds of Star Wars [347-45]................15.00

Polydor
Movie soundtracks.
- Empire Strikes Back [347-46]................35.00
- Return of the Jedi [347-47]................35.00

RCA
- Music from John Williams's Close Encounters and Star Wars [347-48]................15.00
- Star Wars and other Galactic Funk by Meco [347-49]....15.00

RCA (Japan)
- Galactic Funk by Meco [347-50]................25.00

RSO Records
- Empire Jazz [347-51]................15.00
- Empire Strikes Back, music from [347-52]................15.00
- Empire Strikes Back Medley by Meco [347-53]...........25.00
- The Adventures of Luke Skywalker, The Empire Strikes Back [347-54]................35.00

Sony Classical
- Episode I soundtrack, 2 albums................35.00

Wonderland Records
- Theme from Star Wars [347-55]................15.00

Media, Audio: Tapes: 8-Track

- Empire Strikes Back [348-01]................35.00
- Empire Strikes Back, Vader label [348-02]................20.00
- Music from Star Wars by Electric Moog Orchestra [348-03]................20.00
- Music From Star Wars, outline [4:183]................20.00
- Patrick Gleeson's Star Wars [348-04]................20.00
- Return of the Jedi, gray [v1e1:286]................35.00
- Return of the Jedi, white [348-05]................20.00
- Return of the Jedi, Empire Strikes Back, Star Wars [348-06]................20.00
- Spaced Out Disco [348-07]................20.00
- Star Wars / Close Encounters [348-08]................20.00
- Star Wars / Close Encounters, dawn label [v1e1:286]......20.00
- Star Wars Ferrante and Teicher [v1e1:286]................20.00
- Star Wars Galactic Funk, black, full label [v1e1:286]........20.00
- Star Wars Galactic Funk, black, orange label [4:183]........20.00
- Star Wars Galactic Funk, black, orange label, white text on case [v1e1:286]................20.00
- Star Wars Galactic Funk, white, full label [348-09].........20.00
- Star Wars Galactic Funk, white, orange label [v1e1:286]...20.00
- Star Wars soundtrack, black nebula with track listings [348-10]................20.00
- Star Wars soundtrack, black with track listings [348-11]..20.00
- Star Wars soundtrack, blue [v1e1:286]................20.00
- Star Wars soundtrack, blue with track listings [348-12]..20.00
- Star Wars soundtrack, gray [4:183]................20.00
- Star Wars soundtrack, white with black label [v1e1:286]..20.00
- Star Wars soundtrack, white with pink label [348-13]......20.00
- Star Wars The Planets [v1e1:286]................20.00
- Star Wars, black with black label, block [348-14]..........20.00
- Star Wars, black with black label, outline [348-15].........20.00
- Star Wars, Vader label [348-16]................20.00
- Story of Star Wars, blue [v1e1:286]................12.00
- Story of Star Wars, blue with track listings [348-17] 12.00
- Story of Star Wars, gray [v1e1:286]................20.00
- Themes from Star Wars, New York New York [348-18]......20.00

Media, Audio: Tapes: Reel-to-Reel

20th Century Fox
- Star Wars Soundtrack 165.00
- Star Wars Soundtrack and Story of Star Wars, boxed set [349-01] 375.00
- Story of Star Wars 150.00

Media, Movies: Discs: DVDs, Blu-ray, 3D, 4K

Continued in Volume 3, Page 278
- A Galaxy Far Far Away [350-01] 20.00
- Droids [350-02] 15.00
- Episode 4: The New Hope 60.00
- Episode 5: The Empire Strikes Back 60.00
- Episode 6: Return of the Jedi 60.00
- Ewoks [350-03] 15.00
- Star Wars vs. Star Trek, The Rivalry Continues [350-04] ...15.00
- Thumbwars: The Phantom Cuticle [350-05] 15.00

Five Star Collection.
- Star Wars Special Edition [350-06] 15.00

20th Century Fox
- Bart Wars: The Simpsons Strike Back 30.00
- Caravan of Courage / The Battle for Endor 15.00
- Classic trilogy collection 60.00
- Classic trilogy collection widescreen 75.00
- Clone Wars, volume 1 [350-07] 15.00
- Clone Wars, vol. 1 wholesale club packaging [350-08] ..15.00
- Clone Wars, volume 2 [350-09] 15.00
- Clone Wars, volume 2 wholesale club packaging 15.00
- Complete Original Trilogy, bonus theatrical version, exclusive tin, exclusive to Best Buy 95.00
- Episode I: Phantom Menace [350-10] 25.00
- Episode I: Phantom Menace widescreen [350-11] 25.00
- Episode I: Phantom Menace, limited edition [350-12] ...45.00
- Episode I: Phantom Menace, wholesale pkg. [350-13] ...45.00
- Episode II: Attack of the Clones [350-14] 30.00
- Episode II: Attack of the Clones, widescreen [350-15] ...25.00
- Episode II: Attack of the Clones, widescreen wholesale [350-16] 30.00
- Episode III: Revenge of the Sith [350-17] 40.00
- Episode III: Revenge of the Sith widescreen [350-18] ..40.00
- Family Guy Presents Blue Harvest, DVD [350-19] 10.00
- Family Guy: It's A Trap, DVD [350-20] 10.00
- Family Guy: Something, Something, Something Darkside, Blu-ray 10.00
- Family Guy: Something, Something, Something Darkside, DVD [350-21] 10.00
- Laugh It Up, Fuzzball: The Family Guy Trilogy, Blu-ray disc, 2010, 3-disc Set [350-22] 30.00
- Laugh It Up, Fuzzball: The Family Guy Trilogy, DVD, 2010, 3-disc Set [350-23] 30.00
- Laugh It Up, Fuzzball: The Family Guy Trilogy, multi-format 30.00
- R2-D2: Beneath the Dome [350-24] 15.00
- Return of the Jedi, bonus theatrical version, exclusive artwork, exclusive to Target 45.00
- Return of the Jedi, bonus theatrical version, exclusive graphic novel, exclusive to Walmart [350-25] 45.00
- Return of the Jedi, bonus theatrical version, full screen [350-26] 45.00
- Saga boxed set: 2002 Episode I and Episode II [350-27] 40.00
- Star Wars A New Hope, bonus theatrical version, exclusive artwork, exclusive to Target 45.00
- Star Wars A New Hope, bonus theatrical version, exclusive graphic novel, exclusive to Walmart [350-28] ...45.00
- Star Wars Classic Trilogy full-frame 3-disc set 35.00
- Star Wars Classic Trilogy full-frame 4-disc set 50.00
- Star Wars Classic Trilogy widescreen 50.00
- Star Wars Classic Trilogy widescreen 3-disc set 35.00
- Star Wars Classic Trilogy widescreen 6-disc set [350-29] 65.00
- Story of Star Wars bonus dvd, exclusive to Walmart [350-30] 15.00
- The Empire Strikes Back, bonus theatrical version, exclusive artwork, exclusive to Target 45.00
- The Empire Strikes Back, bonus theatrical version, exclusive graphic novel, exclusive to Walmart [350-31] ...45.00
- The Empire Strikes Back, bonus theatrical version, full screen [350-32] 45.00

Media, Movies: Discs

 351-01
 351-02
 351-03
 351-04
 351-05
 351-06

 351-07
 351-08
 351-09
 351-10
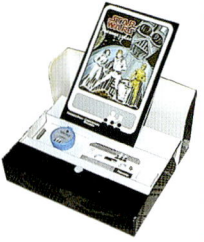 351-11
 351-12

20th Century Fox (Canada)
- Clone Wars, volume 1 .... 35.00

A&E
- Star Wars Empire of Dreams for Emmy consideration, not for resale [350-33] 200.00

DK Publishing
- You Can Draw Star Wars, exclusive to Star Wars Celebration IV 25.00
- You Can Draw Star Wars 15.00

Film Threat
- Starwoids [350-34] 20.00
- Starwoids Ultimate Fan Celebration special edition, 2 discs 20.00

History Channel
- Star Wars Tech [350-35] 35.00

InterActual
- THX Ultimate Demo Disc, Star Wars scenes 35.00

Jim Henson Home Entertainment
- Muppet Show, Best of, includes Mark Hamill / Luke Skywalker [350-36] 35.00

Macht Movie Productions
- The Force Amoung Us, DVD [350-37] 20.00

Magna (Turkey)
- Dunyayi Kurtaran Adam [v1e1 286] 65.00

Media Trip
- George Lucas in Love 20.00

Michael Wiese Productions
- Hardware Wars Special Edition 15.00

MMG
- Star Ballz, adult parody [350-38] 45.00

Passport Video
- Stars of Star Wars: Interviews with the Cast 15.00

Sideshow Collectibles
- The Virtual Experience v5.2, exclusive to Star Wars Celebration IV 15.00

Synapse Films
- Star Warped 15.00

The Dave School
- DROIDS: The Jawa Adventure [350-39] 20.00

The Sun / World News
- Heroes and Villains [350-40] 15.00

Turner Home Entertainment
- Star Wars Robot Chicken [350-41] 30.00

Unicorn Video
- Star Wait [350-42] 15.00

Warner Home Video
Clone Wars.
- A Galaxy Divided 25.00
- A Galaxy Divided, bonus 5th episode, exclusive to Walmart [350-43] 25.00
- Clone Wars movie DVD 2-pack, includes "The Battle Begins" picture book, exclusive to Walmart [350-44] 30.00
- The Clone Wars Movie [350-45] 40.00

Media, Movies: Films

- La Guerre des Etoiles [351-01] 75.00

(France)
- El Imperio Contraactaca [351-02] 85.00

Ken Films
Star Wars, selected scenes, 8mm.
- B/W, silent, 42.5m [351-03] 35.00
- Color, silent, 42.5m [351-04] 40.00
- Color, sound, 42.5m [351-05] 80.00
- Color, sound, 91m [351-06] 95.00
- Color, sound, plastic case (Han/Chewbacca) [351-07] 85.00
- Color, sound, plastic case (movie art) [351-08] 75.00

The Empire Strikes Back, selected scenes, 8mm.
- Color, 17 minutes, part 1 [351-09] 95.00
- Color, 17 minutes, part 2 [351-10] 95.00

Pendulum Press
- Filmstrip with audio cassette and workbook [351-11] .. 850.00

Toei Co. (Japan)
- Star Wars [351-12] 75.00

Media, Movies: Laser Discs and CEDs

20th Century Fox
- Making of Star Wars / Empire Strikes Back Special Effects [352-01] 85.00

Capacitance Electronic Disc System (CEDs).
- Star Wars [352-02] 25.00

 352-01
 352-02
 352-03
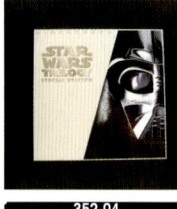 352-04
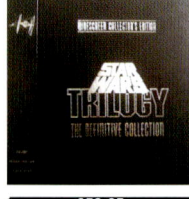 352-05
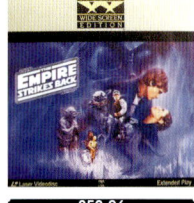 352-06
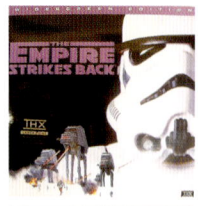 352-07

 352-08
 352-09
 352-10
 352-11
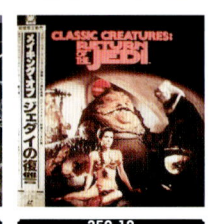 352-12
 352-13
 352-14

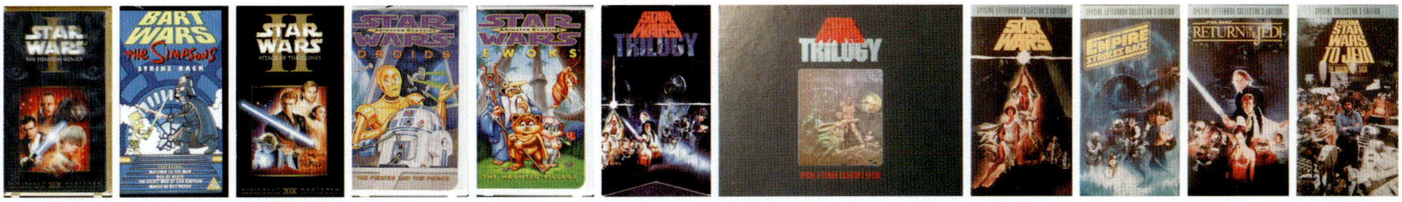

Media, Movies: Video Cassettes

353-01 | 354-01 | 354-02 | 354-03 | 354-04 | 354-05 | 354-06 Collector Box | 354-06 Tape 1, Tape 2, Tape 3, and Tape 4

     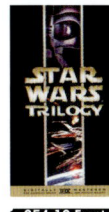   

354-07 | 354-08 | 354-09 | 354-10 | 354-11 | 354-12 Front | 354-12 Side 1 and Side 2 | 354-13

       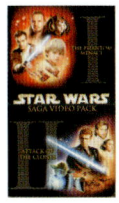  

354-14 | 354-15 | 354-16 | 354-17 | 354-18 | 354-19 | 354-20 | 354-21 | 354-22 | 354-23

❑ The Making of Star Wars / Special FX: Empire Strikes Back [352-03] 25.00

Classic Trilogy boxed sets.
❑ 1997 Special Edition widescreen [352-04] 180.00
❑ Definitive Collection [352-05] 250.00

Empire Strikes Back.
❑ 1984 Extended play [v1e1:287] 40.00
❑ 1985 Standard play 65.00
❑ 1989 Widescreen [352-06] 45.00
❑ 1992 Extended play [v1e1:287] 50.00
❑ 1995 THX widescreen [352-07] 65.00

Return of the Jedi.
❑ 1986 Extended play [v1e1:287] 70.00
❑ 1990 Widescreen [352-08] 70.00
❑ 1992 Extended play [v1e1:287] 70.00
❑ 1995 THX widescreen [352-09] 65.00

Star Wars.
❑ 1982 [v1e1:288] 50.00
❑ 1983 Extended Play 40.00
❑ 1985 Standard play [v1e1:288] 115.00
❑ 1989 Widescreen [352-10] 65.00
❑ 1992 Extended Play [4:191] 115.00
❑ 1992 Widevision 35.00
❑ 1995 THX widescreen [352-11] 65.00

20th Century Fox (Japan)
English with Japanese subtitles.
❑ Classic Creatures: Return of the Jedi [352-12] 65.00
❑ SP FX: The Empire Strikes Back [352-13] 65.00
❑ The Making of Star Wars as told by C-3PO and R2-D2 [352-14] 65.00
❑ The Making of Star Wars as told by C-3PO and R2-D2 / SP FX: The Empire Strikes Back [352-15] 85.00

The Phantom Menace.
❑ 1999 [352-16] 115.00

CBS / Fox Video
❑ Guerre Etoiles [352-17] 50.00
❑ L'Empire Contre-Attaque [352-18] 50.00

Capacitance Electronic Disc System (CEDs).
❑ Empire Strikes Back [352-19] 35.00
❑ Return of the Jedi, blue, part 1 [352-20] 20.00
❑ Return of the Jedi, blue, part 2 ....20.00
❑ Return of the Jedi, white, part 1 [352-21] 20.00
❑ Return of the Jedi, white, part 2 ....20.00
❑ Star Wars [352-22] 25.00

CBS / Fox Video (Japan)
❑ Ewok Adventure [352-23] 90.00

International Video Co. Ltd.
❑ A New Hope 75.00

❑ Empire Strikes Back [352-24] 75.00
❑ Return of the Jedi [352-25] 75.00

Lightning (UK)
❑ The Empire Strikes Back [352-26] 35.00

MGM / United Artists
Ewoks, live action.
❑ 1990 The Ewok Adventure [352-27] 45.00
❑ 1991 The Battle for Endor [352-28] 45.00

Skywalker Sound
❑ THX WOW, includes scenes from classic trilogy [4:191] ..35.00

Media, Movies: Video Cassette Storage Cases

20th Century Fox
❑ Episode I plastic case with lenticular cover, preordering video premium, exclusive to Toys R Us [353-01] 15.00

Media, Movies: Video Cassettes
❑ Star Wars Definitive Collection (PAL only) 185.00

20th Century Fox
❑ Bart Wars: The Simpsons Strike Back [354-01] 25.00

352-15 | 352-16 | 352-17 | 352-18 | 352-19 | 352-20 | 352-21

   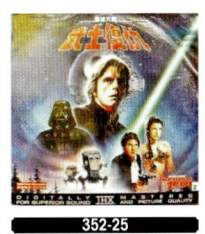  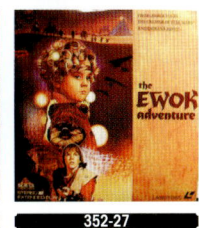 

352-22 | 352-23 | 352-24 | 352-25 | 352-26 | 352-27 | 352-28

Media, Movies: Video Cassettes

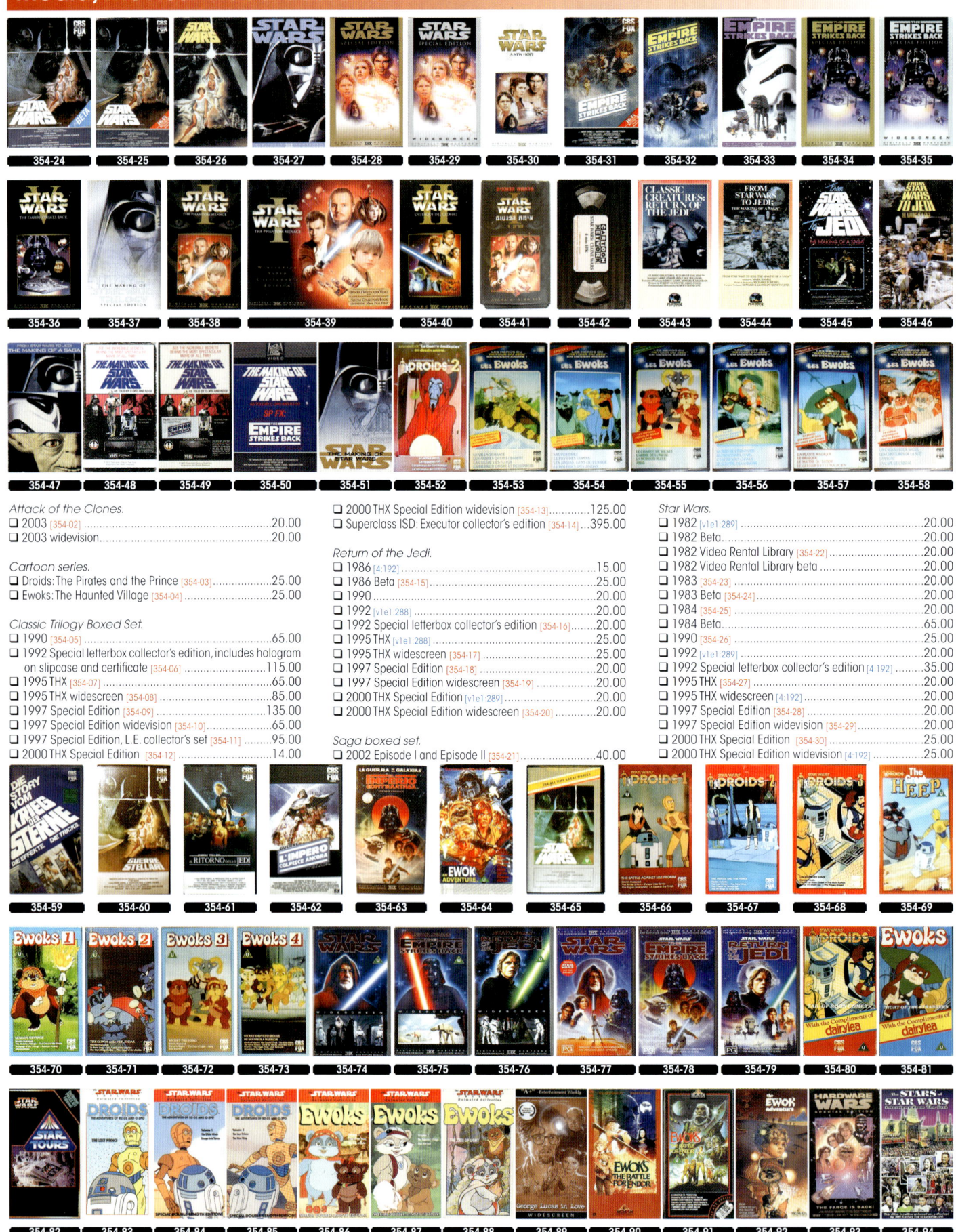

Attack of the Clones.
- ❏ 2003 [354-02] 20.00
- ❏ 2003 widevision 20.00

Cartoon series.
- ❏ Droids: The Pirates and the Prince [354-03] 25.00
- ❏ Ewoks: The Haunted Village [354-04] 25.00

Classic Trilogy Boxed Set.
- ❏ 1990 [354-05] 65.00
- ❏ 1992 Special letterbox collector's edition, includes hologram on slipcase and certificate [354-06] 115.00
- ❏ 1995 THX [354-07] 65.00
- ❏ 1995 THX widevision [354-08] 85.00
- ❏ 1997 Special Edition [354-09] 135.00
- ❏ 1997 Special Edition widevision [354-10] 65.00
- ❏ 1997 Special Edition, L.E. collector's set [354-11] 95.00
- ❏ 2000 THX Special Edition [354-12] 14.00
- ❏ 2000 THX Special Edition widevision [354-13] ... 125.00
- ❏ Superclass ISD: Executor collector's edition [354-14] ...395.00

Return of the Jedi.
- ❏ 1986 [4:192] 15.00
- ❏ 1986 Beta [354-15] 25.00
- ❏ 1990 .... 20.00
- ❏ 1992 [v1e1:288] 20.00
- ❏ 1992 Special letterbox collector's edition [354-16] 20.00
- ❏ 1995 THX [v1e1:288] 25.00
- ❏ 1995 THX widescreen [354-17] 25.00
- ❏ 1997 Special Edition [354-18] 20.00
- ❏ 1997 Special Edition widescreen [354-19] 20.00
- ❏ 2000 THX Special Edition [v1e1:289] 20.00
- ❏ 2000 THX Special Edition widescreen [354-20] ... 20.00

Saga boxed set.
- ❏ 2002 Episode I and Episode II [354-21] 40.00

Star Wars.
- ❏ 1982 [v1e1:289] 20.00
- ❏ 1982 Beta 20.00
- ❏ 1982 Video Rental Library [354-22] 20.00
- ❏ 1982 Video Rental Library beta 20.00
- ❏ 1983 [354-23] 20.00
- ❏ 1983 Beta [354-24] 20.00
- ❏ 1984 [354-25] 20.00
- ❏ 1984 Beta 65.00
- ❏ 1990 [354-26] 25.00
- ❏ 1992 [v1e1:289] 20.00
- ❏ 1992 Special letterbox collector's edition [4:192] ... 35.00
- ❏ 1995 THX [354-27] 20.00
- ❏ 1995 THX widescreen [4:192] 20.00
- ❏ 1997 Special Edition [354-28] 20.00
- ❏ 1997 Special Edition widevision [354-29] 20.00
- ❏ 2000 THX Special Edition [354-30] 25.00
- ❏ 2000 THX Special Edition widevision [4:192] ... 25.00

Mirrors

The Empire Strikes Back.
- ☐ 1984 [354-31] 30.00
- ☐ 1984 Beta [v1e1:289] 20.00
- ☐ 1990 [354-32] 25.00
- ☐ 1992 .... 25.00
- ☐ 1992 special letterbox collector's edition [4:192] ... 35.00
- ☐ 1995 THX [354-33] 20.00
- ☐ 1995 THX widescreen [4:192] 25.00
- ☐ 1997 Special Edition [354-34] 20.00
- ☐ 1997 Special Edition widescreen [354-35] 25.00
- ☐ 2000 THX Special Edition [354-36] 20.00
- ☐ 2000 THX Special Edition widescreen [4:192] 20.00

The Making of Star Wars Trilogy Special Edition.
- ☐ 1997 [354-37] 20.00

The Phantom Menace.
- ☐ 2000 [354-38] 20.00
- ☐ 2000 Widescreen [v1e1:289] 30.00
- ☐ 2000 Widescreen video collector's edition [354-39] ... 40.00

20th Century Fox (France)
- ☐ Attack of the Clones [354-40] 20.00

20th Century Fox (Germany)
- ☐ Bart Wars: The Simpsons Strike Back 35.00

20th Century Fox (Israel)
- ☐ The Phantom Menace [354-41] 20.00

Cartoon Network
- ☐ Clone Wars 4 min. screening preview [354-42] 25.00

CBS / Fox Video
Classic Creatures: Return of the Jedi.
- ☐ 1985 [354-43] 30.00

From Star Wars to Jedi: The Making of a Saga.
- ☐ 1986 [354-44] 25.00
- ☐ 1986 Beta 25.00
- ☐ 1989 [354-45] 25.00
- ☐ 1992 [354-46] 25.00
- ☐ 1992 Special Collector's Edition [4:193] 25.00
- ☐ 1995 [354-47] 25.00

The Making of Star Wars.
- ☐ 1979 [354-48] 35.00
- ☐ 1980 [354-49] 25.00
- ☐ 1980 Beta 35.00
- ☐ 1982 Special FX: Empire Strikes Back 15.00
- ☐ 1983 Special FX: Empire Strikes Back Beta [354-50] ... 20.00
- ☐ 1995 Cereal mail-in premium [354-51] 35.00
- ☐ 1997 Special FX: Empire Strikes Back VHS 30.00

CBS / Fox Video (France)
Cartoon: Droids.
- ☐ Droids 1 .... 35.00
- ☐ Droids 2 [354-52] 40.00

Les Ewoks
- ☐ Episode 1 [354-53] 35.00
- ☐ Episode 2 [354-54] 35.00
- ☐ Episode 3 [354-55] 35.00
- ☐ Episode 4 [354-56] 35.00
- ☐ Episode 5 [354-57] 35.00
- ☐ Episode 6 [354-58] 35.00

CBS / Fox Video (Germany)
- ☐ Die Story vom Krieg der Sterna [354-59] 25.00

CBS / Fox Video (Italy)
- ☐ Guerre Stellari [354-60] 20.00
- ☐ Il Retorno Dello Jedi [354-61] 20.00
- ☐ L'Impero Colpisce Ancora [354-62] 20.00

CBS / Fox Video (Spain)
- ☐ El Imperio Contraataca [354-63] 30.00

CBS / Fox Video (UK)
- ☐ Caravan of Courage, An Ewok Adventure [354-64] ... 50.00

All-time greatest movies series.
- ☐ Star Wars [354-65] 35.00

Cartoon: Droids.
- ☐ 1 The Battle Against Sise Fromm [354-66] 35.00
- ☐ 2: The Pirate and the Prince [354-67] 35.00
- ☐ 3: Uncharted Space [354-68] 35.00
- ☐ The Great Heep [354-69] 75.00

Cartoon: Ewoks.
- ☐ 1: Morag's Revenge [354-70] 35.00
- ☐ 2: The Gupins [354-71] 35.00
- ☐ 3: Wicket the Hero [354-72] 35.00
- ☐ 4: Wicket's Adventures [354-73] 35.00

Classic trilogy, THX releases, widescreen.
- ☐ A New Hope [354-74] 35.00
- ☐ Empire Strikes Back [354-75] 35.00
- ☐ Return of the Jedi [354-76] 35.00

Classic trilogy, THX releases.
- ☐ A New Hope [354-77] 20.00
- ☐ Empire Strikes Back [354-78] 20.00
- ☐ Return of the Jedi [354-79] 20.00

Dairylea promotions.
- ☐ Droids: Tale of Roon Comets [354-80] 75.00
- ☐ Ewoks: Night of the Strangers [354-81] 75.00

Disney / MGM
- ☐ Star Tours, press kit edition [354-82] 125.00

J2 Communications
Droids, 1990.
- ☐ The Lost Prince [354-83] 20.00
- ☐ Vol. 1: The White Witch / Escape into Terror [354-84] ... 20.00
- ☐ Vol. 2: The Lost Prince / The New King [354-85] ... 20.00

Ewoks, 1990.
- ☐ Cries of the Trees / The Tree of Light [354-86] ... 20.00
- ☐ The Haunted Village / Blue Harvest [354-87] 20.00
- ☐ The Tree of Light [354-88] 20.00

Mediatrip.com
- ☐ George Lucas in Love [354-89] 20.00

MGM / UA
- ☐ Ewoks—The Battle for Endor [354-90] 45.00
- ☐ Ewoks—The Battle for Endor [354-91] 45.00
- ☐ The Ewok Adventure [354-92] 45.00

Michael Weise Productions
- ☐ Hardware Wars, parody [354-93] 20.00

MMG
- ☐ Star Ballz, adult parody 45.00

Passport Video
- ☐ "Stars of Star Wars: Interviews with the Cast" unauthorized video [354-94] 20.00

Milk Caps

Stanpac
- ☐ Darth Vader, "The Force is With You" [2:305] ... 20.00

Mirrors
Continued in Volume 3, Page 279

- ☐ C-3PO and R2-D2, 8" x 10" [355-01] 35.00
- ☐ Darth Vader over logo, prismatic foil , 6" x 8" [355-02] ... 30.00
- ☐ Darth Vader, Obi-Wan Kenobi (art) [355-03] 50.00
- ☐ Darth Vader, prismatic frame, 3.75" x 4.5" [355-04] ... 40.00
- ☐ Darth Vader, Star Wars, 8" x 10", red [355-05] ... 50.00
- ☐ Darth Vader, The Empire Strikes Back, 12" x 12" foil reflection [355-06] ... 60.00
- ☐ Darth Vader, The Empire Strikes Back, 12" x 12" glass painted 50.00
- ☐ Darth Vader, The Empire Strikes Back, 12" x 12" glass reflection [355-07] ... 50.00
- ☐ Luke (pilot), C-3PO, R2-D2 [355-08] 50.00
- ☐ Luke, C-3PO, R2-D2 (art) [355-09] 65.00
- ☐ Star Wars, Luke and Leia logo, pink [355-10] 50.00
- ☐ Star Wars, poster art 12" x 18" 35.00
- ☐ Star Wars, poster art 24" x 36" 225.00
- ☐ Star Wars logo and X-Wing, red and blue [355-11] ... 50.00
- ☐ Star Wars logo and X-Wing, red and yellow [355-12] ... 50.00
- ☐ Star Wars, X-Wing over planet. blue, background painted black [355-13] ... 50.00
- ☐ Star Wars, X-Wing over planet, blue, background unpainted [355-14] ... 50.00
- ☐ Star Wars, X-Wing over planet, red [355-15] ... 50.00

355-01 | 355-02 | 355-03 | 355-04 | 355-05 | 355-06

355-07 | 355-08 | 355-09 | 355-10 | 355-11

Mirrors

355-12　　　　355-13　　　　355-14　　　　355-15

355-16　355-17　355-18　355-19　355-20　355-21

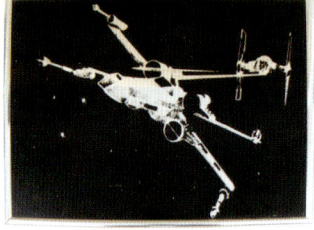   
355-22　　355-23　　355-24　　355-25　355-26

Cosalt Exporters Ltd.
- ❑ Death Star Battle [355-16] 150.00

Disney Theme Park Merchandise (Japan)
- ❑ Star Tours pocket mirror [355-17]...............100.00
- ❑ Star Tours round mirror with handle [355-18] 130.00

Factors, Etc.
3" round, mirrored back.
- ❑ Darth Vadar Lives [sic] [355-19] 30.00

Lightline Industries
Chrome frame 10" x 15"
- ❑ C-3PO and R2-D2 [355-20] 300.00
- ❑ Darth Vader [355-21] 300.00
- ❑ Darth Vader vs. Obi-Wan Kenobi [355-22] 375.00
- ❑ Dogfight [355-23] 350.00
- ❑ Han Solo and Chewbacca [355-24] 250.00

Chrome frame 20" x 30"
- ❑ Dogfight...2,500.00
- ❑ Obi-Wan, Leia, and Luke [355-25]............2,500.00

Sigma
- ❑ Darth Vader [355-26] 95.00

Mobiles

Fan Club
- ❑ Revenge of the Sith, "Welcome to the Star Wars Fan Club"..25.00

Glow Zone
- ❑ Episode I glow-in-the-dark [356-01]..............25.00

KFC
- ❑ The Phantom Menace cup topper mobile 85.00

Circle danglers, Naboo fighter on back.
- ❑ Anakin Skywalker..40.00
- ❑ Boss Nass 40.00
- ❑ Jar Jar Binks 40.00
- ❑ Obi-Wan Kenobi 40.00
- ❑ Queen Amidala 40.00
- ❑ Qui-Gon Jinn 40.00

Pepsi Cola
- ❑ Mobile: X-Wings vs. TIEs, Star Wars SE Trilogy [4-184] ...160.00

Molds, Candy and Food
Continued in Volume 3, Page 285

Wilton
- ❑ Boba Fett, Darth Vader, stormtrooper [357-01] 25.00
- ❑ C-3PO, Chewbacca, Darth Vader, R2-D2, stormtrooper, Ewok, Yoda suckers [357-02] 25.00
- ❑ C-3PO, Chewbacca, R2-D2, Yoda candy, C-3PO and Chewbacca suckers [357-03] 25.00
- ❑ Chewbacca, C-3PO, R2-D2, Yoda 25.00
- ❑ R2-D2, large [357-04] 25.00
- ❑ Two mold sheets featuring Darth Vader, R2-D2, Chewbacca, C-3PO, Yoda, stormtrooper [357-05] 45.00

Movie Cash Certificates

The Properties Group
Cereal premiums during Episode II: Attack of the Clones.
- ❑ Anakin Skywalker [358-01] 10.00
- ❑ Jango Fett [358-02] 10.00
- ❑ Obi-Wan Kenobi [358-03] 10.00
- ❑ Padmé Amidala [358-04] 10.00

Music Boxes

Sigma
- ❑ Ion Turret with C-3PO [359-01] 450.00
- ❑ Max Rebo band [359-02] 400.00
- ❑ Wicket and Princess Kneesaa [359-03] 250.00

358-01　358-02　358-03　358-04

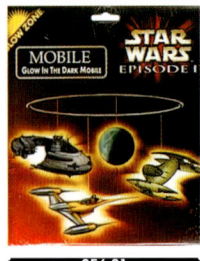    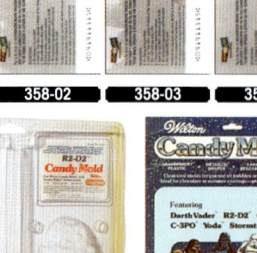 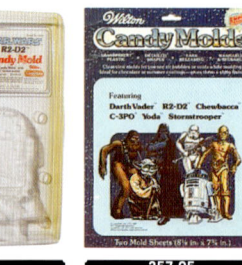
356-01　357-01　357-02　357-03　357-04　357-05

Notebooks, Tablets, Memo Pads

359-01

359-02

359-03

360-01

360-02

360-03

360-04

360-05

360-06

360-07

360-08

360-09

Name Badges
Continued in Volume 3, Page 285

20th Century Fox
- ❑ Star Wars early bird-style logo, self-stick [360-01] 80.00

Disney / MGM
- ❑ Star Wars weekends cast member [360-02] 65.00

Drawing Board Greeting Cards, Inc.
- ❑ Darth Vader, 16-pack [360-03] 20.00
- ❑ Star Wars logo, 16-pack [360-04] 20.00

KFC
Employee name badges, "Welcome to Naboo."
- ❑ Anakin Skywalker [360-05] 35.00
- ❑ Darth Maul 35.00
- ❑ Jar Jar Binks [360-06] 35.00
- ❑ Obi-Wan Kenobi [360-07] 35.00
- ❑ Queen Amidala 35.00

Star Wars Celebration
2007 Los Angeles. Collector Social, medallion image.
- ❑ Artoo-Detoo (R2-D2) 5.00
- ❑ Ben (Obi-Wan) Kenobi 5.00
- ❑ Chewbacca 5.00
- ❑ Darth Vader [360-08] 5.00
- ❑ Death Squad Commander 5.00
- ❑ Han Solo 5.00
- ❑ Jawa 5.00
- ❑ Luke Skywalker 5.00
- ❑ Princess Leia Organa 5.00
- ❑ Sand People 5.00
- ❑ See-Threepio (C-3PO) 5.00
- ❑ Stormtrooper 5.00

2010 Orlando. Collector Social name tag with medallion image.
- ❑ Collector Social name tag [360-09] 5.00

Star Wars Celebration (UK)
2007 London. Collector Social, medallion image.
- ❑ Ben (Obi-Wan) Kenobi, Portugal 5.00
- ❑ C-3PO, United Kingdom 5.00
- ❑ Chewbacca, France 5.00
- ❑ Darth Vader, Poland 5.00
- ❑ Death Squad Commander, Belgium 5.00
- ❑ Han Solo, Sweden 5.00
- ❑ Jawa, Denmark 5.00
- ❑ Luke Skywalker, Czech Republic 5.00
- ❑ Princess Leia, Italy 5.00
- ❑ R2-D2, Spain 5.00
- ❑ Sand People, Finland 5.00
- ❑ Stormtrooper, Germany 5.00

Starlog
- ❑ Starlog salutes Star Wars 25.00

Newspaper Strips
- ❑ B/W, any day, trimmed 5.00
- ❑ Color, any day, trimmed 10.00

Note Cubes

Impact, Inc.
- ❑ Darth Maul 15.00

Notebooks, Tablets, and Memo Pads
Continued in Volume 3, Page 286

- ❑ 10th Anniversary notepads [361-01] 25.00
- ❑ Collector tin set with light-up pen [361-02] 15.00

Accessory Zone
- ❑ 12-pack spiral mini-notebooks [361-03] 15.00
- ❑ Captain Rex and clones, composition 10.00

Pocket memo pads, lenticular, 50 sheets. Exclusive to Target.
- ❑ Captain Rex [361-04] 8.00
- ❑ Darth Vader [361-05] 8.00

Spiral.
- ❑ Anakin and Obi-Wan [361-06] 10.00

Spiral. 50 sheets.
- ❑ Clone Wars, exclusive to Target [361-07] 8.00
- ❑ Han and Chewbacca, exclusive to Target [361-08] 8.00

Animations
Episode III: Revenge of the Sith.
- ❑ Darth Vader helmet 10.00

361-01

361-02

361-03

361-04

361-05

361-06

361-07

361-08

361-09

361-10

361-11

361-12

361-13

361-14

361-15

361-16

361-17

Notebooks, Tablets, Memo Pads

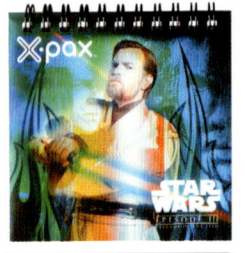      

361-18 • 361-19 • 361-20 • 361-21 • 361-22 • 361-23 • 361-24

361-25 • 361-26 • 361-27 • 361-28 • 361-29 • 361-30 • 361-31 • 361-32

Magnetic notepads, 60 sheets. Exclusive to Target.
- ❏ Chewbacca [361-09] 10.00
- ❏ Darth Vader [361-10] 10.00
- ❏ Yoda [361-11] 10.00

Spiral. 50 sheets. Revenge of the Sith. Exclusive to Target.
- ❏ Boba Fett art [361-12] 8.00
- ❏ Darth Vader [361-13] 8.00
- ❏ Darth Vader art [361-14] 8.00
- ❏ Yoda [361-15] 8.00
- ❏ Yoda art [361-16] 8.00

Spiral. 80 sheets. Wide ruled. Revenge of the Sith.
- ❏ Darth Vader art 10.00
- ❏ Darth Vader helmet 10.00
- ❏ Darth Vader lightsaber down 10.00
- ❏ Darth Vader lightsaber up 10.00

Antioch
- ❏ Mini-Notebook with "Lost City of the Jedi" cover art [361-17] 10.00

Celcom (Malaysia)
Episode III: Revenge of the Sith.
- ❏ Obi-Wan top spiral for X-Pax with storage tin [361-18] ...25.00

Cosmos Tablet Company, Inc.
10.5 x 8" tablets. 40 sheets. Blue line art covers.
- ❏ Battle over Death Star [361-19] 30.00
- ❏ C-3PO and R2-D2 [361-20] 30.00
- ❏ Han Solo [361-21] 30.00
- ❏ Jawas [361-22] 30.00
- ❏ Obi-Wan shutting off tractor beam [361-23] 30.00
- ❏ Princess Leia [361-24] 30.00
- ❏ Stormtrooper blasted [361-25] 30.00
- ❏ Stormtroopers [361-26] 30.00

Dalmatian Press
- ❏ Artist pad with crayons and stickers [361-27] 12.00

Drawing Board Greeting Cards, Inc.
- ❏ Darth Vader, Death Star, and TIE Fighters [361-28] 20.00
- ❏ Darth Vader Official Duty Roster [361-29] 20.00
- ❏ Ewok with horn, "Notes" [361-30] 20.00
- ❏ Ewoks, "Droppin' a Line" [361-31] 20.00
- ❏ Wookiee Doodle Pad [361-32] 20.00

Grosvenor
- ❏ Episode II heroes, spiral, A4 [361-33] 10.00

HC Ford (UK)
- ❏ Darth Vader, memo [361-34] 25.00
- ❏ Gamorrean Guard / Han Solo, memo [361-35] 30.00
- ❏ R2-D2, C-3PO / Darth Vader / Luke Skywalker, memo [361-36] 30.00

    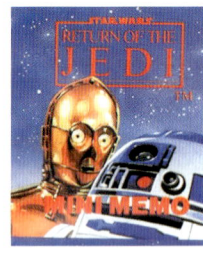 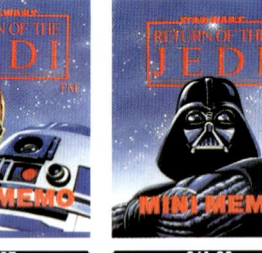 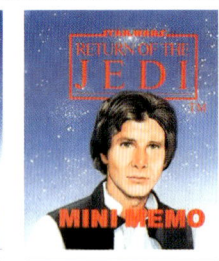

361-33 • 361-34 • 361-35 • 361-36 • 361-37 • 361-38 • 361-39

   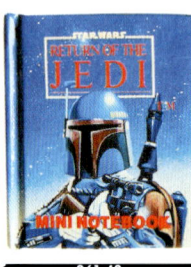  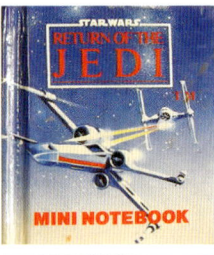 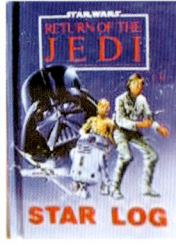

361-40 • 361-41 • 361-42 • 361-43 • 361-44 • 361-45 • 361-46

 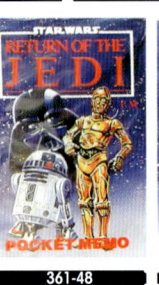      

361-47 • 361-48 • 361-49 • 361-50 • 361-51 • 361-52 • 361-53 • 361-54

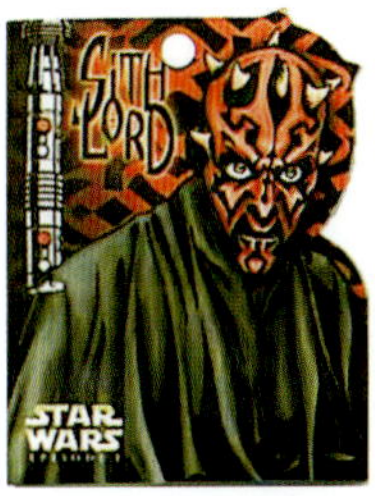

361-55

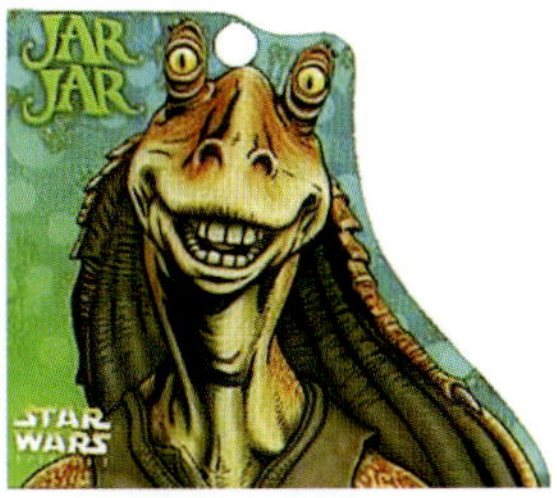

361-56

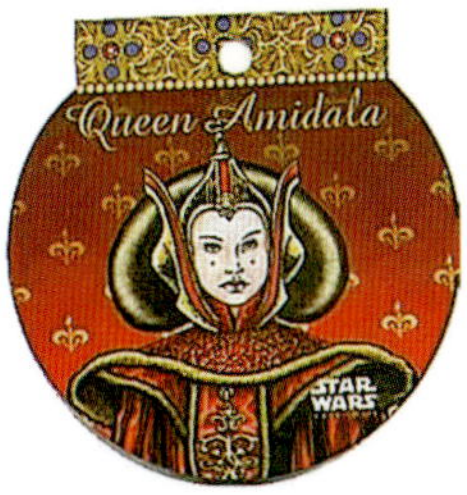

361-57

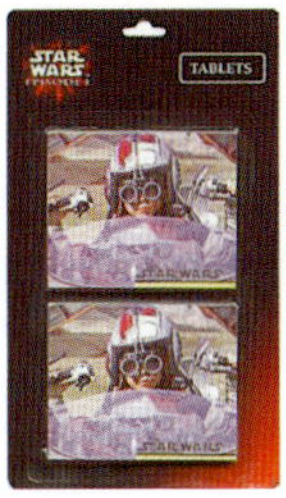

361-58

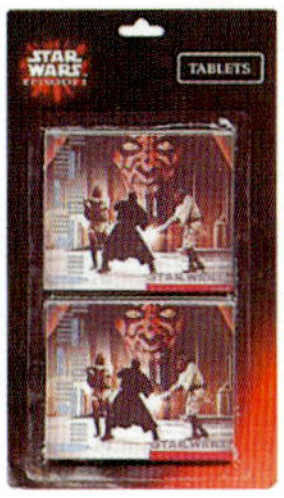

361-59

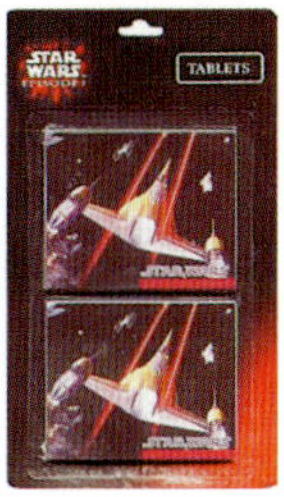

361-60

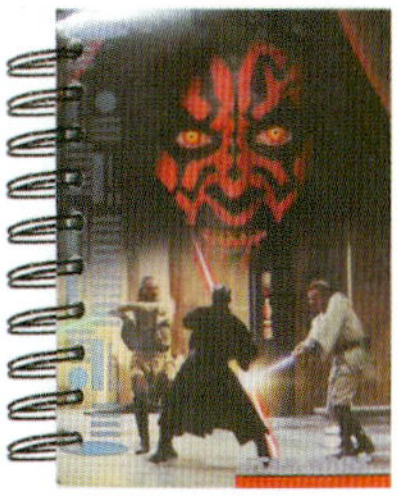
361-61

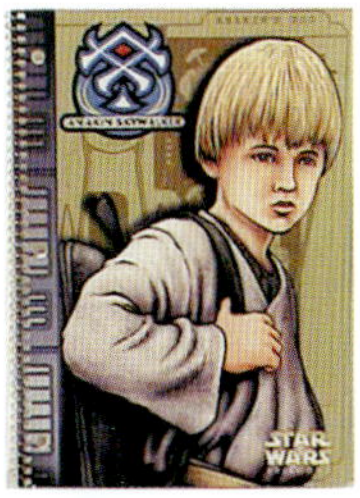
361-62

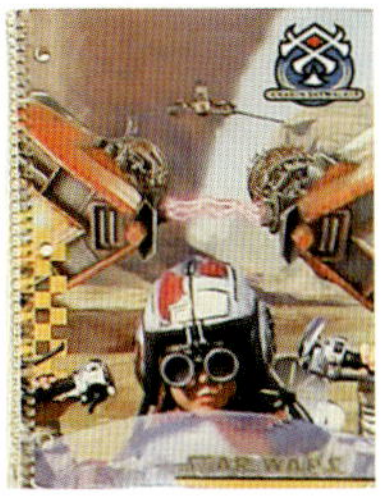
361-63

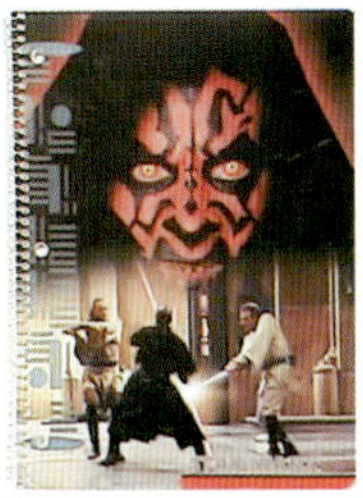
361-64

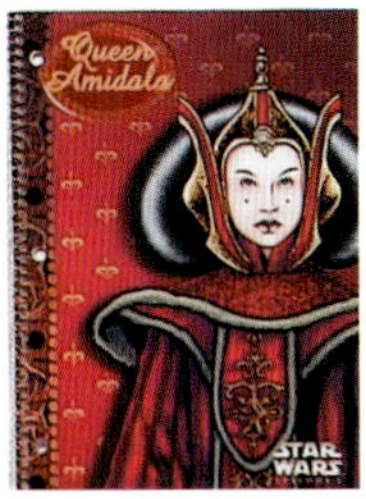

361-65

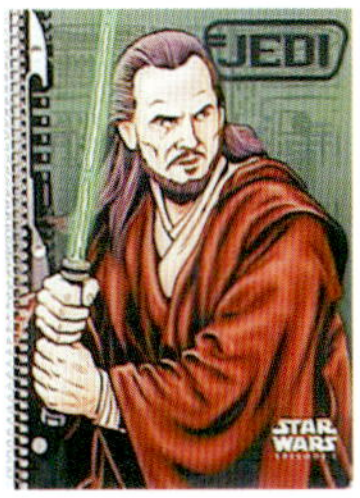

361-66

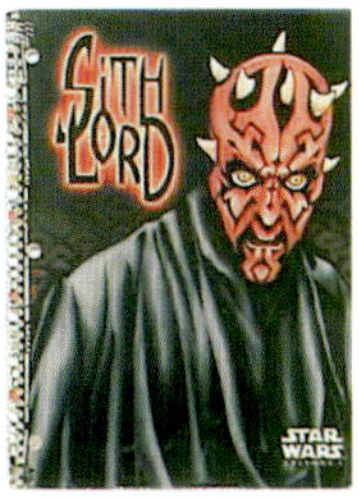

361-67

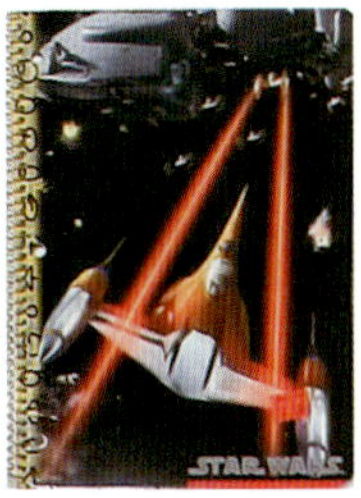

361-68

Mini memo pads.

- ❑ C-3PO and R2-D2 [361-37] 20.00
- ❑ Darth Vader [361-38] 20.00
- ❑ Han Solo [361-39] 20.00
- ❑ Luke Skywalker [361-40] 20.00
- ❑ Princess Leia [361-41] 20.00
- ❑ Yoda [361-42] 20.00

Mini-Notebooks, hardcover.

- ❑ Boba Fett [361-43] 25.00
- ❑ Obi-Wan Kenobi [361-44] 25.00
- ❑ Space battle [361-45] 25.00

Notebooks, hardcover.

- ❑ Star Log [361-46] 35.00

Pocket memo pads.

- ❑ 3-pack [361-47] 50.00

- ❑ C-3PO and R2-D2 [361-48] 20.00
- ❑ Han and Chewbacca [361-49] 20.00
- ❑ Luke and Yoda [361-50] 20.00

Sketchpad.

- ❑ Collage of character photos 45.00

Impact, Inc.

3″ x 5″, 60 sheets.

- ❑ Anakin [361-51] 10.00
- ❑ Darth Maul [361-52] 10.00
- ❑ Jar Jar [361-53] 10.00
- ❑ Obi-Wan [361-54] 10.00

50 sheets, die-cut.

- ❑ Darth Maul [361-55] 10.00
- ❑ Jar Jar [361-56] 10.00
- ❑ Queen Amidala [361-57] 10.00

Packages of 2.

- ❑ Anakin Skywalker podracer [361-58] 15.00
- ❑ Jedi vs. Sith [361-59] 15.00
- ❑ Space battle [361-60] 15.00

Spiral. 180 sheets. 5″ x 7″ wide ruled.

- ❑ Jedi vs. Sith [361-61] 10.00

Spiral. 50 sheets. 8″ x 10.5″ wide ruled.

- ❑ Anakin Skywalker [361-62] 10.00
- ❑ Anakin Skywalker, podracer [361-63] 10.00
- ❑ Jar Jar 10.00
- ❑ Jedi vs. Sith [361-64] 10.00
- ❑ Queen Amidala [361-65] 10.00
- ❑ Qui-Gon Jinn [361-66] 10.00
- ❑ R2-D2 / C-3PO 10.00
- ❑ Sith Lord [361-67] 10.00
- ❑ Space battle over Naboo [361-68] 10.00

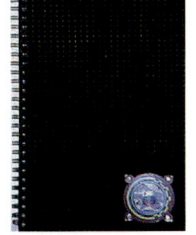

361-69

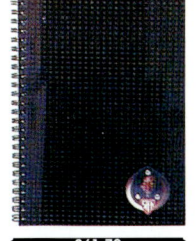

361-70

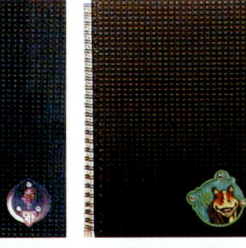

361-71

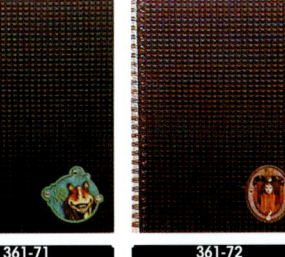

361-72

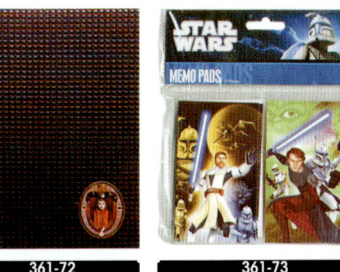

361-73

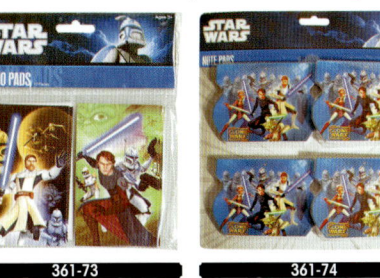

361-74

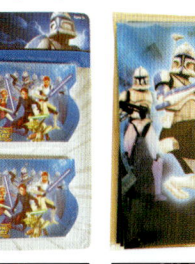

361-75

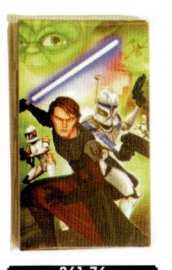

361-76

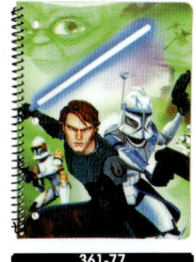

361-77

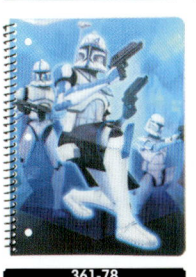

361-78

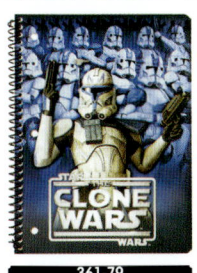

361-79

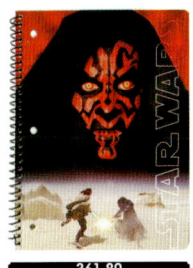

361-80

361-81

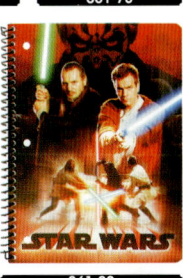

361-82

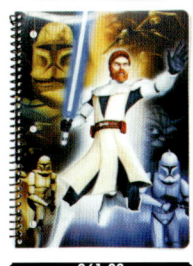

361-83

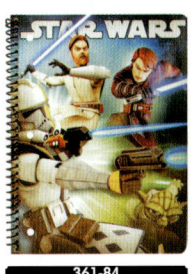

361-84

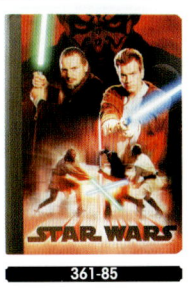

361-85

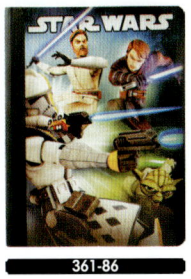

361-86

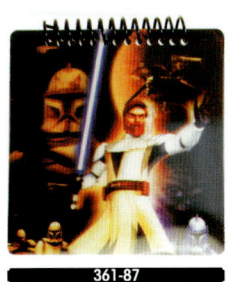

361-87

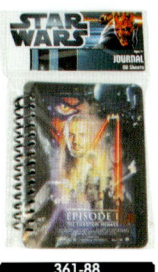

361-88

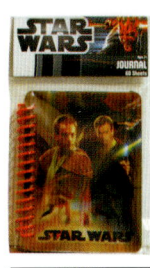

361-89

Notebooks, Tablets, Memo Pads

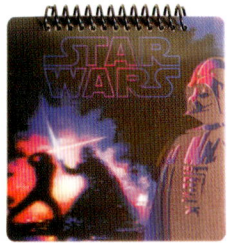 361-90
 361-91
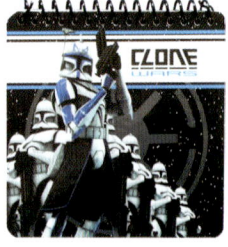 361-92
 361-93
 361-94
 361-95

 361-96
 361-97
 361-98
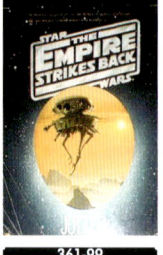 361-99
 361-100
 361-101
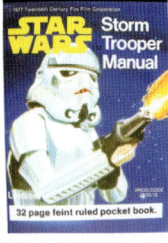 361-102
 361-103

Spiral. 90 sheets. 6" x 9" wide ruled. Black rubber cover with riveted character icon.
- Anakin Skywalker [361-69] 10.00
- Darth Maul [361-70] 10.00
- Jar Jar Binks [361-71] 10.00
- Queen Amidala [361-72] 10.00

Innovative Designs
- 12-pack: mini memo pads [361-73] 10.00
- 4-pack: Clone Wars [361-74] 10.00
- Clones and Captain Rex, 20 sheets [361-75] 10.00
- Yoda, Cody, Anakin, Rex, 20 sheets [361-76] ... 10.00

1 subject notebooks. 70 wide-rule sheets.
- Anakin / Captain Rex [361-77] 10.00
- Captain Rex and clones [361-78] 10.00
- Captain Rex, clones / Captain Rex [361-79] 10.00
- Darth Maul, Tatooine Duel / Darth Maul [361-80] 10.00
- Darth Vader [361-81] 10.00
- Jedi Duel / Obi-Wan vs. Darth Maul [361-82] 10.00
- Obi-Wan and clones [361-83] 10.00
- Obi-Wan, Anakin, Yoda, clone trooper, and Jedi [361-84] 10.00

Composition notebook. 100 wide-rule sheets.
- Captain Rex, clones / Captain Rex 12.00
- Darth Maul, Tatooine Duel / Darth Maul 12.00
- Jedi vs. Sith / Obi-Wan vs. Darth Maul [361-85] 12.00
- Obi-Wan, Anakin, Yoda, clone trooper, and Jedi [361-86] 12.00

Pocket memo pads, lenticular. Exclusive to Target.
- Clone Wars [361-87] 10.00
- Episode I poster / Battle Above Naboo [361-88] 10.00
- Qui-Gon and Obi-Wan / Jedi vs. Sith [361-89] 10.00
- Star Wars [361-90] 10.00

Pocket memo pads. Exclusive to Target.
- Battle Above Naboo [361-91] 8.00
- Clone Wars / Captain Rex [361-92] 8.00
- Darth Maul vs. Obi-Wan [361-93] 8.00
- Darth Vader [361-94] 8.00
- Jedi [361-95] 8.00

Jollibee
- C-3PO paper dispenser 20.00

Letraset
- C-3PO and R2-D2, For Intergalactic Messages [361-96] ... 35.00
- C-3PO's Exercise Book [361-97] 35.00
- Chewbacca's Space Notes [361-98] 35.00
- Empire Strikes Back jotter, probe droid cover [361-99] ... 50.00
- Princess Leia's Rebel Jotter [361-100] 35.00
- R2-D2's Memory Bank [361-101] 35.00
- Stormtrooper Manual [361-102] 35.00

 361-104
 361-105
 361-106
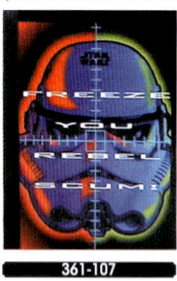 361-107
 361-108
 361-109
 361-110

 361-111
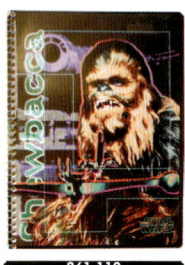 361-112
 361-113
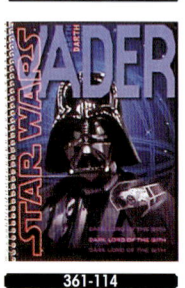 361-114
 361-115
 361-116
 361-117

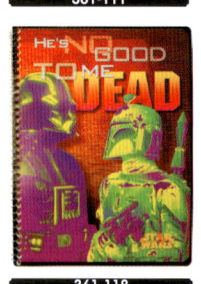 361-118
 361-119
 361-120
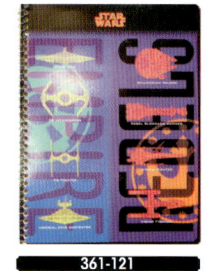 361-121
 361-122
 361-123
 361-124

Notebooks, Tablets, Memo Pads

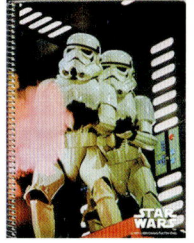 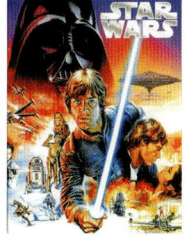     

361-125 361-126 361-127 361-128 361-129 361-130 361-131

     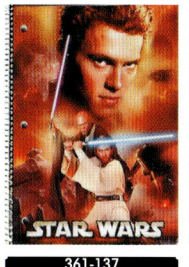  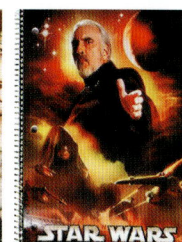

361-132 361-133 361-134 361-135 361-136 361-137 361-138 361-139

Magic World
50 pages, graph paper.
- ARC-170s [361-103] 12.00
- Darth Vader [361-104] 12.00
- Jedi Starfighter, ground [361-105] 12.00
- Jedi Starfighter, space [361-106] 12.00

Mead
Composition. Small 5.5" x 3.5".
- "Freeze You Rebel Scum!" [361-107] 10.00
- "May the Force be with you" [361-108] 10.00
- "Never Underestimate the Dark Side" [361-109] ...10.00
- Star Wars Star Fighters [361-110] 10.00

Spiral.
- C-3PO 10.00
- C-3PO / R2-D2 [361-111] 15.00
- Chewbacca [361-112] 15.00

- Darth Vader [361-113] 15.00
- Darth Vader, Dark Lord of Sith [361-114] 10.00
- "Freeze You Rebel Scum" [361-115] 10.00
- Han and Millennium Falcon [361-116] 10.00
- "May the Force be with you" 10.00
- Neon: bounty hunters [361-117] 20.00
- Neon: he's no good to me dead [361-118] ...20.00
- Neon: I've got a bad feeling about this [361-119] ...20.00
- "Never Under Estimate the Dark Side" [361-120] ...10.00
- Starships [361-121] 10.00
- Stormtroopers 10.00

Spiral. Vintage.
- Ben, Han, Leia, and Luke [361-122] 20.00
- C-3PO and R2-D2 [361-123] 20.00
- Chewbacca and Han [361-124] 20.00
- Darth Vader 20.00
- Stormtroopers [361-125] 20.00

Merlin
- Empire Strikes Back cover [361-126] 15.00
- Luke / X-Wing Fighter [361-127] 15.00
- Vader / TIE Fighter [361-128] 15.00

Shaped
- C-3PO [361-129] 10.00
- Chewbacca [361-130] 10.00
- Darth Vader [361-131] 10.00
- Stormtrooper [361-132] 10.00

Spiral.
- Boba Fett [361-133] 10.00
- Darth Vader 10.00

Pyramid
- Anakin Skywalker 8.00
- Mace Windu 8.00

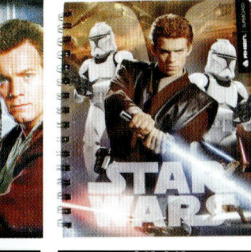  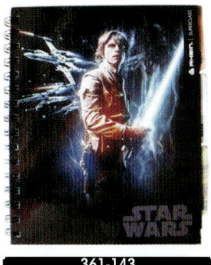  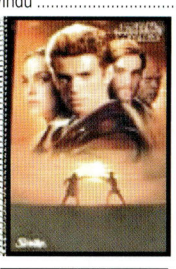 

361-140 361-141 361-142 361-143 361-144 361-145 361-146

361-147 361-148 361-149 361-150 361-151 361-152 361-153 361-154

361-155 361-156 361-157 361-158 361-159 361-160 361-161

307

Notebooks, Tablets, Memo Pads

 361-162
 361-163
 361-164
 361-165
 361-166

 361-167
 361-168
 361-169
 361-170
 361-171

 361-172
 361-173
 361-174
 361-175
 361-176
 361-177
 361-178
 361-179

 361-180
 361-181
 361-182
 361-183
 361-184
 361-185
 361-186

Episode II: Attack of the Clones pocket notebooks.
- Anakin Skywalker [361-134] 5.00
- Mace Windu [361-135] 5.00

Spiral. Episode II: Attack of the Clones.
- C-3PO / R2-D2 [361-136] 5.00
- Heroes [361-137] 5.00
- Jango Fett [361-138] 5.00
- Villains [361-139] 5.00

Q-Stat (UK)
- Obi-Wan Kenobi [361-140] 8.00

Rhein
- Anakin Skywalker and clone troopers [361-141] 5.00
- Darth Vader [361-142] 5.00
- Luke Skywalker and X-Wing Fighters [361-143] 5.00

Scribe (Mexico)
Spiral. Episode II: Attack of the Clones.
- C-3PO / R2-D2 [361-144] 10.00
- Heroes [361-145] 10.00
- Jango Fett [361-146] 10.00
- Padmé / space [361-147] 10.00
- Padmé Amidala [361-148] 10.00
- Zam Wesell [361-149] 10.00

Spiral. Return of the Jedi.
- AT-ST [361-150] 20.00
- Lightsaber [361-151] 20.00
- Millennium Falcon [361-152] 20.00

- Princess Leia, Jabba's Prisoner [361-153] 20.00
- Yoda [361-154] 20.00

Star Wars Celebration Japan (Japan)
- Episode 1: The Phantom Menace [361-155] 25.00
- Episode 2: Attack of the Clones [361-156] 25.00
- Episode 3: Revenge of the Sith [361-157] 25.00
- Episode 4: A New Hope [361-158] 25.00
- Episode 5: The Empire Strikes Back [361-159] 25.00
- Episode 6: Return of the Jedi [361-160] 25.00

Stuart Hall
- Aliens [361-161] 20.00
- Boba Fett 20.00
- C-3PO and R2-D2 [361-162] 20.00
- Darth Vader and stormtroopers 20.00
- Doodle Pad: Max Rebo band [361-163] 20.00
- Luke Skywalker in Bepin fatigues 20.00
- Millennium Falcon Escapes a Star Destroyer [361-164]...20.00
- Pencil Tablet: R2-D2 and Wicket the Ewok [361-165] 30.00
- Yoda 20.00

Learn to Letter and Write series.
- Boba Fett [361-166] 25.00
- Darth Vader / stormtroopers [361-167] 25.00
- Ewok hang gliding [361-168] 20.00
- Luke Skywalker [361-169] 25.00
- Yoda 25.00

Pocket memo pads, 3" x 5" vertical.
- Aliens [361-170] 20.00

- Boba Fett 20.00
- C-3PO and R2-D2 [361-171] 20.00
- Darth Vader and stormtroopers 20.00
- Luke Skywalker [361-172] 20.00
- Yoda [361-173] 20.00

Pocket memo pads.
- Biker scouts 10.00
- C-3PO, R2-D2, and Wicket 10.00
- Darth Vader and Luke Skywalker 10.00
- Jabba the Hutt 10.00
- Max Rebo band 10.00
- Space battle scene 10.00

Scribble pads.
- R2-D2 and C-3PO [361-174] 30.00

Spiral. Empire Strikes Back.
- 2-1B, aliens, bounty hunters, probot, and ugnaught [361-175] 15.00
- Boba Fett [361-176] 15.00
- Darth Vader and stormtroopers [361-177] 15.00
- Darth Vader on Bespin [361-178] 15.00
- Darth Vader, Han, Lando, Leia, and Luke 15.00
- Han, Leia, and Luke on Hoth [361-179] 15.00
- Leia and Luke on Bespin, Hoth snowtroopers [361-180] ..15.00
- Luke and stormtroopers on Bespin 15.00
- Luke on Dagobah 15.00
- Millennium Falcon and Star Destroyer [361-181] 15.00
- Vader Silhouette 15.00
- Yoda [361-182] 15.00

Oven Mitts

  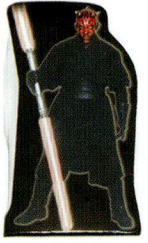      

361-187 | 361-188 | 361-189 | 361-190 | 361-191 | 361-192 | 361-193 | 361-194 | 361-195

361-196 | 361-197 | 361-198 | 361-199 | 361-200 | 361-201 | 361-202 | 361-203

Spiral. Return of the Jedi.
- ❏ B-Wing and TIE Fighter [361-183]..................10.00
- ❏ C-3PO, R2-D2, and Wicket [361-184]..................10.00
- ❏ Darth Vader, Emperor Palpatine, Luke Skywalker [361-185]..................10.00
- ❏ Jabba and Salacious Crumb..................10.00
- ❏ Max Rebo band [361-186]..................10.00
- ❏ R2-D2 and Wicket the Ewok..................10.00
- ❏ Speeder Bikers [361-187]..................10.00

Spiral. Star Wars.
- ❏ C-3PO and R2-D2..................20.00
- ❏ Princess Leia, Luke, Ben, Han [361-188]..................20.00

Taito (Japan)
Memo pads.
- ❏ C-3PO..................15.00
- ❏ Darth Maul [361-189]..................15.00
- ❏ Darth Vader [361-190]..................15.00
- ❏ R2-D2 [361-191]..................15.00
- ❏ Yoda..................15.00

Tokyo Queen Co., Ltd. (Japan)
- ❏ Darth Vader / Rebel base [361-192]..................25.00
- ❏ Death Star battle / droid [361-193]..................25.00
- ❏ Droids / Death Star corridor [361-194]..................25.00
- ❏ Escape Pod [361-195]..................25.00
- ❏ Luke / R2-D2 / Death Star battle [361-196]..................25.00
- ❏ Star Wars—shows sandtrooper, Luke / C-3PO, Han / Chewbacca [361-197]..................25.00

Union
Plastic pocket for paper and pen, magnetic back.
- ❏ 10th anniversary, blue [361-198]..................45.00
- ❏ 10th anniversary, pink [361-199]..................45.00

Vandor LLC
40 sheets of sticky notes, set of 2. Exclusive to Target.
- ❏ Darth Vader and stormtrooper [361-200]..................10.00
- ❏ R2-D2 and C-3PO [361-201]..................10.00

Magnetic list pads.
- ❏ R2-D2 [361-202]..................10.00
- ❏ Stormtrooper [361-203]..................10.00

Note Cards
Continued in Volume 3, Page 288

Drawing Board Greeting Cards, Inc.
- ❏ C-3PO and R2-D2 [362-01]..................30.00
- ❏ C-3PO, Chewbacca, and Darth Vader [362-02]..................35.00
- ❏ Ewoks [362-03]..................25.00
- ❏ Hildebrandt art [362-04]..................30.00
- ❏ R2-D2 [362-05]..................30.00

Nutcrackers
Continued in Volume 3, Page 288

Kurt S. Adler, Inc.
2007.
- ❏ Artoo-Detoo, 7" [363-01]..................35.00

- ❏ Darth Vader [363-02]..................35.00
- ❏ Stormtrooper..................35.00
- ❏ Yoda [363-03]..................35.00

2010.
- ❏ Captain Rex [363-04]..................50.00
- ❏ Darth Vader [363-05]..................35.00
- ❏ R2-D2 [363-06]..................35.00
- ❏ Stormtrooper [363-07]..................40.00
- ❏ Yoda, Clone Wars [363-08]..................35.00

Steinbach (Germany)
- ❏ Darth Vader, 2,000 produced [v1e1:305]..................375.00
- ❏ Darth Vader, 7,500 produced [v1e1:305]..................250.00
- ❏ Yoda, 7,500 produced [v1e1:305]..................250.00

Oil Lamps

Lamplight Farms Inc.
- ❏ Star Wars oil lamp, base shows drawings of Darth Vader, R2-D2, C-3PO; originally shipped with fuel, wick, and wax seal [364-01]..................85.00

Oven Mitts
Continued in Volume 3, Page 289

Star Wars Shop
- ❏ Space slug [365-01]..................35.00

 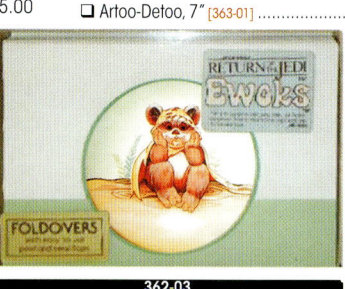 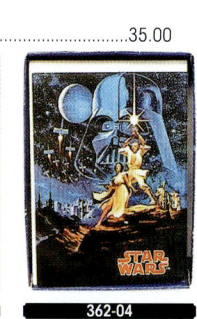 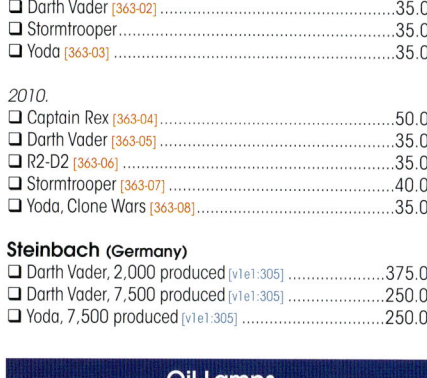  

362-01 | 362-02 | 362-03 | 362-04 | 362-05 | 363-01

363-02 | 363-03 | 363-04 | 363-05 | 363-06 | 363-07 | 363-08 | 364-01 All 3 Sides | 365-01

Packaging: Bags and Boxes

366-01   366-02   366-003   366-004   366-005   366-06

Packaging: Bags and Boxes

KFC
- Anakin Skywalker..5.00
- Darth Maul, large [366-01]......................................5.00
- Darth Maul, small..5.00
- Queen Amidala [366-02]...5.00

Taco Bell
Star Wars Special Edition paper bags.
- C-3PO, medium [366-03]...5.00
- Darth Vader, large [366-04].....................................5.00
- R2-D2, small [366-05]...5.00

Episode I plastic bags.
- Darth Maul, large..5.00
- Jar Jar Binks, medium..5.00
- Pit droid, small [366-06]...5.00

Packaging: Beverage
Continued in Volume 3, Page 289

BelaVista (Brazil)
Brin-Q powdered drink mix with Star Wars scenes. 60 numbered scenes in set.
Framboesa.
- Chewbacca on Hoth, framboesa #32 [367-01]...............10.00
- Falcon escapes Star Destroyer #40 [367-02]................10.00
- Gamorrean Guard #28 [367-03]..................................10.00
- Leia during Yavin battle #24 [367-04].........................10.00
- Luke in Dagobah cave #12 [367-05]............................10.00
- Yoda trains Luke #08 [367-06]...................................10.00

Laranja.
- C-3PO on Tatooine #11 [367-07]................................10.00
- Han attacks on Cloud City #07 [367-08]......................10.00
- Han Solo in carbonite #27 [367-09]............................10.00
- Luke and Leia escape sail barge #35 [367-10]............10.00
- Luke in Ben's hut #15 [367-11]..................................10.00
- Medical frigate #55 [367-12].....................................10.00
- Rancor #51 [367-13]..10.00
- X-Wing approaching Dagobah #03 [367-14]................10.00
- X-Wing leaving Dagobah #59 [367-15].......................10.00

Morango.
- Bib Fortuna #22 [367-16]..10.00
- Han and Leia, "The Kiss" #30 [367-17].......................10.00
- Luke on sail barge #34 [367-18]................................10.00
- Return of the Jedi poster art #58 [367-19]..................10.00
- Return of the Jedi poster lightsaber #14 [367-20]........10.00
- Tusken on Bantha #50 [367-21].................................10.00

Uva.
- AT-ATs attacking #49 [367-22]..................................10.00
- Droids on blockade runner #37 [367-23]....................10.00
- Lando in Falcon cockpit #45 [367-24].........................10.00
- Luke and Leia at Death Star chasm #53 [367-25].......10.00
- Vader confronts Leia #13 [367-26].............................10.00
- X-Wings coming around Yavin #33 [367-27]...............10.00
- Stormtrooper on Cloud City #41 [367-28]...................10.00

Coca-Cola (China)
Episode III: Revenge of the Sith. Soda cans.
- Boxed collector's set of six, 310 produced [367-29].....210.00
- Coca-Cola, Anakin [367-30].......................................20.00
- Coca-Cola, Darth Vader [367-31]................................20.00
- Coca-Cola, R2-D2 and C-3PO [367-32].......................20.00

       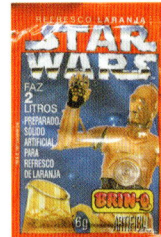

367-01-367-06 Front   367-01   367-02   367-03   367-04   367-05   367-06   367-07-367-15 Front

367-07   367-08   367-09   367-10   367-11   367-12   367-13   367-14

367-15   367-16-367-21 Front   367-16   367-17   367-18   367-19   367-20   367-21

367-22-367-28 Front   367-22   367-23   367-24   367-25   367-26   367-27   367-28

Packaging: Beverage

367-29 367-30 367-31 367-32 367-33 367-34 367-35 367-36 367-37 367-38 367-39 367-40 367-41

367-42 367-43 367-44 367-45 367-46 367-47 367-48 367-49 367-50 367-51 367-52 367-53 367-54

367-55 367-56 367-57 367-58 367-59 367-60 367-61 367-62 367-63 367-64 367-65 367-66 367-67 367-68

❑ Sprite Ice, clone trooper [367-33]....................20.00
❑ Sprite, Obi-Wan Kenobi [367-34]....................20.00
❑ Vanilla Coke, Yoda [367-35]....................20.00

Coca-Cola (China)

Episode III: Revenge of the Sith cans.
❑ Anakin Skywalker [367-36]....................20.00
❑ C-3PO and R2-D2 [367-37]....................20.00
❑ Darth Vader [367-38]....................20.00

Fan Club

❑ Episode I soda pop storage case, two-door front, Naboo fighter handles, Fan Club exclusive [367-39]....................35.00

Hi-C

❑ Hi-C can label droids shown, T-shirt and cap offer [2:317]....................30.00
❑ Hi-C cans droids shown, T-shirt and cap offer [2:317]....35.00

Nestlé

❑ Nestlé Quik can with pendant offer on label....................30.00

Pepsi Cola

Episode I: Production samples. Classic characters.
❑ Mountain Dew, C-3PO color [367-40]....................250.00
❑ Pepsi One, Han Solo [367-41]....................175.00
❑ Pepsi, Luke Skywalker [367-42]....................175.00

Episode I: The Phantom Menace production samples.
❑ 4-pack, color box [2:317]....................250.00
❑ Anakin Skywalker [367-43]....................40.00
❑ Chancellor Valorum [367-44]....................40.00
❑ Obi-Wan Kenobi [367-45]....................40.00
❑ Padmé Naberrie [367-46]....................40.00

Episode I: The Phantom Menace. 1 liter bottles.
❑ Diet Pepsi, Queen Amidala....................10.00
❑ Mountain Dew, Darth Maul....................10.00
❑ Pepsi One, Episode I C-3PO....................10.00
❑ Pepsi, Anakin Skywalker....................10.00
❑ Storm, battle droid....................10.00

Episode I: The Phantom Menace. 2 liter bottles.
❑ Diet Pepsi, Queen Amidala....................10.00
❑ Mountain Dew, Darth Maul....................10.00
❑ Pepsi One, C-3PO....................10.00
❑ Pepsi, Anakin Skywalker....................10.00
❑ Storm, battle droid....................10.00

Episode I: The Phantom Menace. 12 oz. cans.
❑ 12-pack of Diet Pepsi, Queen Amidala [367-47]....................5.00
❑ 12-pack of Mountain Dew, Darth Maul [2:317]....................5.00
❑ 12-pack of Pepsi One, C-3PO [2:317]....................5.00
❑ 12-pack of Pepsi, Anakin Skywalker [2:318]....................5.00
❑ 12-pack of Storm, Jar Jar Binks....................5.00

367-69 367-70 367-71 367-72 367-73 367-74 367-75 367-76 367-77 367-78 367-79 367-80 367-81 367-82 367-83 367-84

367-85 367-86 367-87 367-88 367-89 367-90 367-91 367-92 367-93 367-94 367-95 367-96 367-97

367-98 367-99 367-100 367-101 367-102 367-103 367-104 367-105

Packaging: Beverage

- 24-pack of Diet Pepsi, Padmé 8.00
- 24-pack of Mountain Dew, Darth Maul [2:317] 8.00
- 24-pack of Pepsi One, C-3PO [2:317] 8.00
- 24-pack of Pepsi, Anakin Skywalker [2:318] 8.00
- 24-pack of Storm, Jar Jar Binks [2:318] 8.00

- #1 Pepsi, Anakin Skywalker [367-48] 5.00
- #2 Pepsi, Sebulba [367-49] 5.00
- #3 Pepsi, Qui-Gon Jinn [367-50] 5.00
- #4 Pepsi, Watto [367-51] 5.00
- #5 Pepsi, Jabba the Hutt [367-52] 5.00
- #6 Pepsi, Senator Palpatine [367-53] 5.00
- #7 Pepsi, R2-D2 [367-54] 5.00
- #8 Pepsi, Darth Sidious [367-55] 5.00
- #9 Mountain Dew, Darth Maul [367-56] 5.00
- #10 Mountain Dew, Jar Jar [367-57] 5.00
- #11 Mountain Dew, Mace Windu [367-58] 5.00
- #12 Mountain Dew, Obi-Wan Kenobi [367-59] 5.00
- #13 Mountain Dew, Captain Panaka [367-60] 5.00
- #14 Mountain Dew, Rune Haako [367-61] 5.00
- #15 Mountain Dew, Ric Olié [367-62] 5.00
- #16 Mountain Dew, Destroyer droid [367-63] 5.00
- #17 Diet Pepsi, Queen Amidala [367-64] 5.00
- #18 Diet Pepsi, Padmé [367-65] 5.00
- #19 Diet Pepsi, Shmi Skywalker [367-66] 5.00
- #20 Diet Pepsi, battle droid [367-67] 5.00
- #21 Pepsi One, Chancellor Valorum [367-68] 5.00
- #22 Pepsi One, C-3PO [367-69] 5.00
- #23 Pepsi One, Nute Gunray [367-70] 5.00
- #24 Pepsi One, Boss Nass [367-71] 5.00
- Mountain Dew, "Gold Yoda" [367-72] 90.00
- Pepsi One, "Gold Yoda" [367-73] 35.00
- Pepsi, "Destiny", limited to 1:900 cases [367-74] .. 125.00
- Pepsi, "Gold Yoda" [367-75] 35.00
- Storm, Jar Jar Binks [367-76] 5.00
- Storm, Qui-Con Jinn [367-77] 5.00

Episode I: The Phantom Menace. 12 oz. cans. New York.
- #1 Pepsi, Anakin Skywalker [367-78] 5.00
- #2 Pepsi, Sebulba 5.00
- #3 Pepsi, Qui-Gon Jinn 5.00
- #4 Pepsi, Watto 5.00
- #5 Pepsi, Jabba the Hutt 5.00
- #6 Pepsi, Senator Palpatine 5.00
- #7 Pepsi, R2-D2 .... 5.00
- #8 Pepsi, Darth Sidious 5.00
- #9 Mountain Dew, Darth Maul 5.00
- #10 Mountain Dew, Jar Jar 5.00
- #11 Mountain Dew, Mace Windu 5.00
- #12 Mountain Dew, Obi-Wan Kenobi 5.00
- #13 Mountain Dew, Captain Panaka 5.00
- #14 Mountain Dew, Rune Haako 5.00
- #15 Mountain Dew, Ric Olié 5.00
- #16 Mountain Dew, Destroyer droid 5.00
- #17 Diet Pepsi, Queen Amidala 5.00
- #18 Diet Pepsi, Padmé 5.00
- #19 Diet Pepsi, Shmi Skywalker 5.00
- #20 Diet Pepsi, battle droid 5.00
- #21 Pepsi One, Chancellor Valorum 5.00
- #22 Pepsi One, C-3PO 5.00
- #23 Pepsi One, Nute Gunray 5.00
- #24 Pepsi One, Boss Nass 5.00

Episode I: The Phantom Menace. 16 oz. bottles.
- Lipton Tea, Natural Lemon, Obi-Wan Kenobi [367-79] 5.00
- Lipton Tea, Obi-Wan Kenobi [367-80] 5.00
- Lipton Tea, Raspberry, Obi-Wan Kenobi [367-81] 5.00
- Lipton Tea, Raspberry, Watto 5.00
- Lipton Tea, Sweetened w/Lemon, Obi-Wan Kenobi .. 5.00
- Lipton Tea, Sweetened, Watto [367-82] 5.00

Episode I: The Phantom Menace. 20 oz. bottles.
- Diet Mountain Dew, Padmé [367-83] 5.00
- Diet Pepsi, Queen Amidala [367-84] 5.00
- Lipton Tea, Brisk Lemon, Obi-Wan Kenobi 5.00
- Lipton Tea, Brisk, Obi-Wan Kenobi [367-85] 5.00
- Lipton Tea, Sweetened, Watto [367-86] 5.00
- Mountain Dew, Darth Maul [367-87] 5.00
- Mug Root Beer, Sebulba [367-88] 5.00
- Orange Slice, Jar Jar Binks [367-89] 5.00
- Pepsi One, C-3PO [367-90] 5.00
- Pepsi, Anakin Skywalker [367-91] 5.00
- Storm, battle droid [367-92] 5.00
- Wild Cherry Pepsi, Captain Panaka [367-93] 5.00

Episode III: Revenge of the Sith. 2 liter bottles.
- Caffeine-free Diet Pepsi, R2-D2 and C-3PO 5.00
- Diet Mountain Dew, clone trooper 5.00
- Diet Pepsi, Chewbacca 5.00
- Mountain Dew, General Grievous [367-94] 5.00
- Pepsi, Darth Vader 5.00

Episode III: Revenge of the Sith. 12 oz. cans.
- 12-pack of caffeine-free Diet Pepsi, Yoda [367-95] .. 5.00
- 12-pack of Diet Mountain Dew, Yoda [367-96] 5.00
- 12-pack of Diet Pepsi, Yoda [367-97] 5.00
- 12-pack of Mountain Dew, Yoda [367-98] 5.00
- 12-pack of Pepsi, Yoda [367-99] 5.00
- 12-pack of Sierra Mist, Yoda 5.00
- 24-pack of Diet Pepsi, Yoda [367-100] 5.00
- 24-pack of Mountain Dew, Yoda [367-101] 5.00
- 24-pack of Sierra Mist, Yoda [367-102] 5.00

Star Wars Special Edition. 1 liter bottles.
- Pepsi, Darth Vader 5.00

Star Wars Special Edition. 2 liter bottles.
- Caffeine-free Diet Pepsi, stormtrooper [4:202] 10.00
- Caffeine-free Pepsi, Darth Vader 10.00
- Diet Mountain Dew, AT-AT 10.00
- Diet Pepsi, stormtrooper 10.00
- Mountain Dew, Millennium Falcon [4:202] 10.00
- Pepsi, Darth Vader [4:202] 10.00
- Pepsi, stormtrooper 10.00

Star Wars Special Edition. 3 liter bottles.
- Diet Pepsi, stormtrooper 15.00
- Pepsi, Darth Vader 15.00

Star Wars Special Edition. 12 oz. cans.
- 12-pack of caffeine-free Diet Pepsi, stormtrooper 5.00
- 12-pack of Diet Mountain Dew, Speederbikes [2:318] .. 5.00
- 12-pack of Diet Pepsi, stormtrooper [2:318] 5.00
- 12-pack of Mountain Dew, Luke 5.00
- 12-pack of Mountain Dew, X-Wings [2:318] 5.00
- 12-pack of Pepsi, Darth Vader 5.00
- 12-pack of Pepsi, stormtrooper 5.00
- 12-pack of Pepsi, Yoda 5.00
- 24-pack of caffeine-free Diet Pepsi, stormtrooper ... 5.00
- 24-pack of caffeine-free Pepsi, Darth Vader 5.00
- 24-pack of Diet Pepsi, stormtrooper [2:318] 5.00
- 24-pack of Mountain Dew, X-Wings [2:318] 5.00
- 24-pack of Pepsi, C-3PO [2:318] 5.00
- 24-pack of Pepsi, Darth Vader [2:318] 5.00
- 24-pack of Pepsi, Yoda [2:318] 5.00
- Diet Pepsi, "Gold Yoda" [367-103] 35.00
- Diet Pepsi, R2-D2 [367-104] 5.00
- Diet Pepsi, stormtrooper [367-105] 5.00
- Pepsi, Darth Vader [367-106] 5.00
- Pepsi, Star Wars: Special Edition logo [367-107] 5.00
- Pepsi, Vader's TIE Fighter, production sample [367-108] .. 340.00
- Pepsi, Vader's TIE Fighter, production sample Death Star background [367-109] 340.00
- Winner gold Yoda can, factory sealed empty [367-110] .. 65.00

Star Wars Special Edition. 20 oz. bottles.
- Caffeine-free Diet Pepsi, stormtrooper 10.00
- Caffeine-free Pepsi, Darth Vader 10.00
- Diet Pepsi, stormtrooper [4:203] 10.00
- Pepsi, Darth Vader [4:203] 10.00

Pepsi Cola (Argentina)
Episode I: The Phantom Menace 354 cc cans.
- Anakin Skywalker [367-111] 5.00
- Darth Maul [367-112] 5.00
- Jar Jar Binks [367-113] 5.00
- Obi-Wan Kenobi [367-114] 5.00
- Queen Amidala [367-115] 5.00
- Qui-Gon Jinn [367-116] 5.00

Packaging: Beverage

Episode I: The Phantom Menace 354 cc cans.
- ❏ Anakin Skywalker [367-117] 5.00
- ❏ Darth Maul [367-118] 5.00
- ❏ Jar Jar Binks [367-119] 5.00
- ❏ Obi-Wan Kenobi [367-120] 5.00
- ❏ Queen Amidala [367-121] 5.00
- ❏ Qui-Gon Jinn [367-122] 5.00

Pepsi Cola (Australia)
- ❏ Anakin Skywalker, Pepsi [367-123] 4.00
- ❏ C-3PO, 7-Up [367-124] 4.00
- ❏ Darth Maul, Pepsi [367-125] 4.00
- ❏ Jar Jar Binks, Pepsi Max [367-126] 4.00
- ❏ Obi-Wan Kenobi, Pepsi [367-127] 4.00
- ❏ Queen Amidala, Diet Pepsi [367-128] 4.00
- ❏ Qui-Gon Jinn, Pepsi [367-129] 4.00
- ❏ Watto, Mountain Dew [367-130] 4.00

Pepsi Cola (Austria)
- ❏ Anakin Skywalker, Pepsi [367-131] 5.00
- ❏ Jar Jar Binks, Pepsi Max [367-132] 5.00
- ❏ Queen Amidala, Diet Pepsi [367-133] 5.00
- ❏ Qui-Gon Jinn, Pepsi [367-134] 5.00
- ❏ Yoda, 7-Up [367-135] 5.00

Pepsi Cola (Brazil)
- ❏ Anakin Skywalker, Pepsi [367-136] 5.00
- ❏ Darth Maul, Pepsi [367-137] 5.00
- ❏ Jar Jar Binks, Pepsi [367-138] 5.00
- ❏ Obi-Wan Kenobi, Pepsi [367-139] 5.00
- ❏ Qui-Gon Jinn, Pepsi [367-140] 5.00
- ❏ Rainha Amidala, Diet Pepsi [367-141] 5.00
- ❏ Rainha Amidala, Pepsi [4:203] 5.00
- ❏ Yoda, 7-Up [367-142] 5.00

Pepsi Cola (Canada)
- ❏ #1 Anakin Skywalker, Pepsi [367-143] 5.00
- ❏ #2 Sebulba, Pepsi [367-144] 5.00
- ❏ #3 Qui-Gon Jinn, Pepsi [367-145] 5.00
- ❏ #4 Watto, Pepsi [367-146] 5.00
- ❏ #5 Jabba, Pepsi [367-147] 5.00
- ❏ #6 Senator Palpatine, Pepsi [367-148] 5.00
- ❏ #7 R2-D2, Pepsi [367-149] 5.00
- ❏ #8 Darth Sidious, Pepsi [367-150] 5.00
- ❏ #9 Darth Maul, Mountain Dew [367-151] .. 5.00
- ❏ #10 Jar Jar Binks, Mountain Dew [367-152] ... 5.00
- ❏ #11 Mace Windu, Mountain Dew [367-153] ... 5.00
- ❏ #12 Obi-Wan Kenobi, Mountain Dew [367-154] ... 5.00
- ❏ #13 Queen Amidala, Diet Pepsi [367-155] 5.00
- ❏ #14 Padmé, Diet Pepsi [367-156] 5.00
- ❏ #15 Shmi Skywalker, Diet Pepsi [367-157] ... 5.00
- ❏ #16 Battle droid, Diet Pepsi [367-158] 5.00
- ❏ #17 Chancellor Valorum, 7-Up [367-159] 5.00
- ❏ #18 C-3PO, 7-Up [367-160] 5.00
- ❏ #19 Nute Gunray, 7-Up [367-161] 5.00
- ❏ #20 Boss Nass, 7-Up [367-162] 5.00

Pepsi Cola (France)
Episode I: The Phantom Menace 330 ml cans.
- ❏ Anakin Skywalker [367-163] 5.00
- ❏ Darth Maul [367-164] 5.00
- ❏ Queen Amidala [367-165] 5.00

Pepsi Cola (Germany)
Episode I: The Phantom Menace 1.5 L bottles.
- ❏ Anakin Skywalker, Pepsi [367-166] 5.00

Episode I: The Phantom Menace 1 L bottles.
- ❏ Darth Maul, Pepsi [367-167] 5.00
- ❏ Qui-Gon Jinn, Pepsi [367-168] 5.00

Episode I: The Phantom Menace 2 L bottles.
- ❏ Anakin Skywalker, Pepsi [367-169] 5.00

Episode I: The Phantom Menace 330 ml cans.
- ❏ Jar Jar Binks, Pepsi Boom [4:203] 5.00
- ❏ Qui-Gon Jinn, Pepsi [367-170] 5.00
- ❏ Rainha Amidala, Pepsi Light [367-171] 5.00
- ❏ Watto, Mirando [367-172] 5.00
- ❏ Yoda, 7-Up [367-173] 5.00

Episode I: The Phantom Menace 500 ml cans.
- ❏ Darth Maul, Pepsi [367-174] 5.00
- ❏ R2-D2, Pepsi Max [367-175] 5.00

Star Wars Special Edition cans.
- ❏ Darth Vader [367-176] 10.00

Pepsi Cola (Greece)
Episode I: The Phantom Menace bottles.
- ❏ 4-pack Darth Maul Pepsi [367-177] 25.00
- ❏ 6-pack Jar Jar Binks orange [367-178] ... 35.00

Episode I: The Phantom Menace cans.
- ❏ 4-pack Qui-Gon Jinn orange [367-179] ... 35.00
- ❏ 6-pack Anakin Skywalker Pepsi [367-180] ... 25.00
- ❏ 6-pack Queen Amidala orange [367-181] 35.00
- ❏ Anakin Skywalker [367-182] 8.00
- ❏ C-3PO [367-183] 8.00
- ❏ Jar Jar Binks [367-184] 8.00
- ❏ Obi-Wan Kenobi [367-185] 8.00
- ❏ Queen Amidala [367-186] 8.00
- ❏ Qui-Gon Jinn [367-187] 8.00
- ❏ R2-D2 [367-188] 8.00
- ❏ Watto [367-189] 8.00
- ❏ Yoda [367-190] 8.00

Pepsi Cola (Holland)
Episode I: The Phantom Menace cans.
- ❏ Anakin Skywalker, Pepsi [367-191] 5.00
- ❏ Jar Jar Binks, Pepsi Max [367-192] 5.00
- ❏ Qui-Gon Jinn, Pepsi [367-193] 5.00
- ❏ R2-D2, Pepsi Max [367-194] 5.00
- ❏ Watto, Sisi [367-195] 5.00
- ❏ Yoda, 7-Up [367-196] 5.00

Star Wars Special Edition cans.
- ❏ 7-Up 10.00
- ❏ Pepsi 10.00
- ❏ Pepsi Max [367-198] 10.00
- ❏ Slice, prizes [367-199] 10.00
- ❏ Slice, tickets [367-200] 10.00

Pepsi Cola (Italy)
Episode I: The Phantom Menace 330 ml cans.
- ❏ Anakin Skywalker, Pepsi [367-201] 5.00
- ❏ C-3PO, 7-Up [367-202] 5.00
- ❏ Darth Maul, Pepsi [367-203] 5.00
- ❏ Qui-Gon Jinn, Pepsi [367-204] 5.00
- ❏ R2-D2, Pepsi Max [367-205] 5.00

Star Wars Special Edition cans.
- ❏ Darth Vader [367-206] 10.00
- ❏ Millennium Falcon [367-207] 10.00
- ❏ Stormtrooper [367-208] 10.00

Pepsi Cola (Japan)
- ❏ Darth Maul, full-body top [367-209] 10.00
- ❏ Darth Maul, full-body bottom [367-209] ... 10.00
- ❏ Nute Gunray, full-body top [367-210] 10.00
- ❏ Nute Gunray, full-body bottom [367-210] ... 10.00
- ❏ Obi-Wan Kenobi, full-body bottom [367-211] ... 10.00
- ❏ Obi-Wan Kenodi, full-body top [367-211] .. 10.00
- ❏ Queen Amidala, full-body top [367-212] .. 10.00
- ❏ Queen Amidala, full-body bottom [367-212] .. 10.00
- ❏ R2-D2, full-body top [367-213] 10.00
- ❏ R2-D2, full-body bottom [367-213] 10.00
- ❏ Watto, full-body top [367-214] 10.00
- ❏ Watto, full-body bottom [367-214] 10.00

Energy Cola.
- ❏ Darth Vader, "Give Yourself to the Dark Side." [367-215] .. 20.00

Episode I: The Phantom Menace 350 ml cans.
- ❏ Anakin Skywalker [367-216] 5.00
- ❏ C-3PO, gold rim [367-217] 5.00
- ❏ C-3PO, gold rim, celebration 2000 [367-218] .. 8.00
- ❏ Darth Maul [367-219] 5.00
- ❏ Jar Jar Binks [367-220] 5.00
- ❏ Obi-Wan Kenobi [367-221] 5.00

Packaging: Beverage

❏ Queen Amidala [367-222] 5.00
❏ R2-D2 [367-223] 5.00
❏ R2-D2, gold rim [367-224] 5.00

Episode I: The Phantom Menace 500 ml cans.
❏ Anakin Skywalker [367-225] 5.00
❏ C-3PO, gold rim [367-226] 5.00
❏ C-3PO, gold rim, celebration 2000 [367-227] .. 8.00
❏ Darth Maul [367-228] 5.00
❏ Queen Amidala [367-229] 5.00
❏ R2-D2, gold rim [367-230] 5.00

Episode II: Attack of the Clones cans.
❏ Anakin Skywalker [367-231] 5.00
❏ Clone troopers [367-232] 5.00
❏ Jango Fett [367-233] 5.00
❏ Jedi [367-234] 5.00

Pepsi Twist 300 ml cone-topped cans. Episode III, color.
❏ Anakin Skywalker 8.00

❏ Queen Amidala [367-235] 8.00
❏ R2-D2 and C-3PO [367-236] 8.00
❏ Yoda [367-237] 8.00

Pepsi Twist 350 ml cans. Episode III, color.
❏ Chancellor Palpatine [367-238] 5.00
❏ Darth Vader [367-239] 5.00
❏ General Grievous [367-240] 5.00
❏ Han Solo and Chewbacca [367-241] 5.00
❏ Luke Skywalker [367-242] 5.00
❏ Obi-Wan Kenobi [367-243] 5.00
❏ Princess Leia [367-244] 5.00
❏ Stormtrooper [367-245] 5.00

Pepsi Cola (Korea)
Episode I: The Phantom Menace 250 ml cans.
❏ Darth Maul [367-246] 5.00
❏ Jar Jar Binks [367-247] 5.00
❏ Queen Amidala [367-248] 5.00
❏ Qui-Gon Jinn [367-249] 5.00

Pepsi Cola (Malaysia)
Episode I: The Phantom Menace 325 ml cans.
❏ Anakin Skywalker [367-250] 5.00
❏ Darth Maul [367-251] 5.00
❏ Jar Jar Binks [367-252] 5.00
❏ Queen Amidala [367-253] 5.00

Pepsi Cola (Mexico)
❏ Anakin Skywalker [367-254] 5.00
❏ Darth Maul [367-255] 5.00
❏ Jar Jar Binks [367-256] 5.00
❏ Queen Amidala [367-257] 5.00

Star Wars Special Edition cans.
❏ Darth Vader, Pepsi [367-258] 12.00
❏ Millennium Falcon, 7-Up [367-259] 12.00
❏ Stormtrooper, KAS [367-260] 12.00
❏ Stormtrooper, Orange [367-261] 12.00
❏ Stormtrooper, Pepsi Light [367-262] 12.00
❏ Stormtrooper, Pepsi Max [367-263] 12.00

Packaging: Beverage

Star Wars Special Edition.
- ❏ Darth Vader, Pepsi 1/2 liter bottle [367-264].....................12.00

Pepsi Cola (New Zealand)
- ❏ Anakin Skywalker, Pepsi [367-265].....................5.00
- ❏ Jar Jar Binks, Pepsi Max [367-266].....................5.00
- ❏ Queen Amidala, Diet Pepsi [367-267].....................5.00
- ❏ Sebulba, Miranda [v1e1:309].....................5.00
- ❏ Watto, Mountain Dew [367-268].....................5.00
- ❏ Yoda, 7-Up [367-269].....................5.00

Pepsi Cola (Poland)
Star Wars Special Edition cans.
- ❏ Darth Vader, Pepsi [367-270].....................15.00

Pepsi Cola (Portugal)
- ❏ Anakin Skywalker, Pepsi [367-271].....................5.00
- ❏ C3-PO, 7-Up [367-272].....................5.00
- ❏ Qui-Gon Jinn, Pepsi [367-273].....................5.00
- ❏ Yoda, 7-Up [367-274].....................5.00

Pepsi Cola (Puerto Rico)
Star Wars Special Edition cans.
- ❏ R2-D2 [367-275].....................10.00
- ❏ Stormtrooper [367-276].....................10.00

Pepsi Cola (Singapore)
- ❏ Anakin Skywalker podrace [367-277].....................64.00
- ❏ Darth Maul [367-278].....................5.00
- ❏ Jar Jar Binks [367-279].....................5.00
- ❏ Qui-Gon Jinn [367-280].....................5.00

Star Wars Special Edition cans.
- ❏ Darth Vader, Pepsi 10.00
- ❏ Millennium Falcon, 7-Up [367-281].....................10.00
- ❏ Stormtrooper, Pepsi 10.00

Pepsi Cola (South Africa)
Star Wars Special Edition cans.
- ❏ Darth Vader, Pepsi [367-282].....................15.00

Pepsi Cola (Spain)
- ❏ #1 Anakin Skywalker, Pepsi [367-283].....................5.00
- ❏ #2 Qui-Gon Jinn, Pepsi [367-284].....................5.00
- ❏ #3 Reina Amidala, Diet Pepsi [367-285].....................5.00
- ❏ #4 R2-D2, Pepsi Max [367-286].....................5.00
- ❏ #5 Darth Maul, Kas Limon [367-287].....................5.00
- ❏ #6 Obi-Wan Kenobi, Kas Narania [367-288].....................5.00
- ❏ #7 Yoda, 7-Up [367-289].....................5.00
- ❏ #8 Jar Jar Binks, Pepsi Boom [367-290].....................5.00

Star Wars Special Edition cans.
- ❏ Darth Vader, Pepsi (large helmet) [367-291].....................10.00
- ❏ Darth Vader, Pepsi (small helmet) [367-292].....................10.00
- ❏ Millennium Falcon, Pepsi [367-293].....................10.00
- ❏ Stormtrooper, Pepsi (large helmet) [367-294].....................10.00
- ❏ Stormtrooper, Pepsi (small helmet) [367-295].....................10.00
- ❏ Stormtrooper, Pepsi Boom 10.00
- ❏ Stormtrooper, Pepsi Free [367-296].....................10.00
- ❏ Stormtrooper, Pepsi Light (large helmet) [367-297].....................10.00
- ❏ Stormtrooper, Pepsi Light (small helmet) [367-298].....................10.00
- ❏ Stormtrooper, Pepsi Max (large flash) [367-299].....................10.00
- ❏ Stormtrooper, Pepsi Max (small flash) [367-300].....................10.00

Pepsi Cola (Thailand)
Star Wars Special Edition cans.
- ❏ Darth Vader, Pepsi [367-301].....................12.00
- ❏ Millennium Falcon, Orange Slice [367-302].....................12.00
- ❏ Millennium Falcon, Strawberry Slice [367-303].....................12.00
- ❏ Stormtrooper, Pepsi [367-304].....................12.00

Pepsi Cola (Turkey)
Episode I: The Phantom Menace 350 ml cans.
- ❏ Anakin Skywalker [367-305].....................5.00
- ❏ C-3PO [367-306].....................5.00
- ❏ Darth Maul [367-307].....................5.00
- ❏ Jar Jar Binks [367-308].....................5.00
- ❏ Kralice Amidala [367-309].....................5.00

Pepsi Cola (UK)
Episode I: The Phantom Menace 150 ml cans.
- ❏ Anakin Skywalker, Pepsi [367-310].....................5.00
- ❏ Jar Jar Binks, Pepsi Max [367-311].....................5.00
- ❏ Obi-Wan Kenobi, Diet Pepsi [367-312].....................5.00
- ❏ Queen Amidala, Diet Pepsi [367-313].....................5.00
- ❏ Qui-Gon Jinn, Pepsi [367-314].....................5.00
- ❏ R2-D2, Pepsi Max [367-315].....................5.00

Episode I: The Phantom Menace cans.
- ❏ Anakin Skywalker, Pepsi [367-316].....................5.00
- ❏ C-3PO, 7-Up [367-317].....................5.00
- ❏ C-3PO, 7-Up Lite [367-318].....................5.00
- ❏ Jar Jar Binks, Pepsi Max [367-319].....................5.00
- ❏ Obi-Wan Kenobi, Diet Pepsi [367-320].....................5.00
- ❏ Queen Amidala, Diet Pepsi [367-321].....................5.00

315

Packaging: Beverage

- ❏ Qui-Gon Jinn, Pepsi [367-322] 5.00
- ❏ R2-D2, Pepsi Max [367-323] 5.00
- ❏ Yoda, 7-Up [367-324] 5.00
- ❏ Yoda, 7-Up Lite [367-325] 5.00

Star Wars Special Edition bottles.
- ❏ Pepsi Max 1.5 L 12.00

Star Wars Special Edition cans.
- ❏ Darth Vader, Pepsi [4-205] 10.00
- ❏ Millennium Falcon, 7-Up [367-326] 10.00
- ❏ Stormtrooper, Diet Pepsi [367-327] 10.00
- ❏ Stormtrooper, Pepsi [367-328] 10.00

Star Wars Special Edition.
- ❏ 8-pack of cans 15.00
- ❏ 12-pack of cans 15.00

Red Bull (Thailand)
- ❏ Anakin Skywalker 15.00
- ❏ Anakin Skywalker (lightsaber high) 15.00
- ❏ Anakin Skywalker (lightsaber low) 15.00
- ❏ Clone Commander 15.00
- ❏ Clone trooper 15.00
- ❏ Clone trooper (running) 15.00
- ❏ Darth Sidious 15.00
- ❏ Darth Vader 15.00
- ❏ Darth Vader (facing left) 15.00
- ❏ Darth Vader (facing right) 15.00
- ❏ General Grievous (2 lightsabers) 15.00
- ❏ General Grievous (walking) 15.00
- ❏ General Grievous's mask 15.00
- ❏ Grievous's Bodyguard 15.00
- ❏ Jedi Starfighter and ARC-170s 15.00
- ❏ Jedi Starfighter under attack 15.00
- ❏ Jedi Starfighters 15.00
- ❏ Obi-Wan (starship corridor) 15.00
- ❏ Obi-Wan Kenobi 15.00
- ❏ Obi-Wan vs. Anakin 15.00
- ❏ R2-D2 and C-3PO 15.00
- ❏ Tri-Fighters 15.00
- ❏ Yoda (leaping) 15.00
- ❏ Yoda (lightsaber high) 15.00
- ❏ Yoda (lightsaber left) 15.00

Ting Hsin Intl. Group
- ❏ Ice Tea—Star Wars Episode III 340ml [367-329] 15.00

Ty-Phoo (UK)
- ❏ 80 Teabags with Merlin sticker premium 45.00

Unilever
Brisk products. 1l bottles. C-3PO and R2-D2 promoting 'Feel the Force—Star Wars Kinect'.
- ❏ Lemon Iced Tea [367-330] 10.00

Brisk products. 1 L bottles. Episode I in 3D—Uncap the App promotion.
- ❏ Fruit Punch [367-331] 5.00
- ❏ Iced Tea with Lemonade [367-332] 5.00
- ❏ Lemonade [367-333] 5.00
- ❏ No Calorie Lemon Iced Tea [367-334] 5.00
- ❏ Peach Iced Green Tea 5.00
- ❏ Pink Lemonade [367-335] 5.00
- ❏ Raspberry Iced Tea [367-336] 5.00
- ❏ Strawberry Melon [367-337] 5.00
- ❏ Sweet Tea [367-338] 5.00

Brisk products. 24 fluid ounce cans.
- ❏ Raspberry Darth Maul 15.00

Zuko (Argentina)
- ❏ Clone Wars 15.00

368-01

368-02

368-03

368-04

368-05

368-06

368-07

368-08

368-09

368-10

368-11

368-15

368-16

368-17 Side 1 and Side 2

368-12

368-18 Side 1 and Side 2

368-19 Side 1 and Side 2

368-20 Side 1

368-13

368-20 Side 2

368-21 Side 1 and Side 2 (blue)

368-21 Side 1 and Side 2 (white)

368-14

Packaging: Candy

 368-22
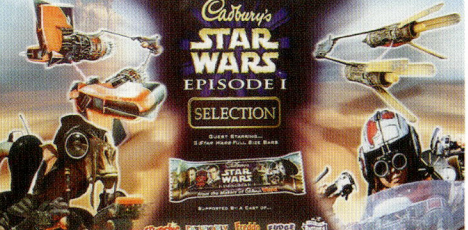 368-23
 368-24 Wrapper and Individual Chocolate Bar Patterns

 368-25 368-26
 368-27
 368-28
 368-29
 368-30
 368-31

Packaging: Candy
Continued in Volume 3, Page 291

☐ Darth Vader and Death Star on blue background........10.00
☐ TV 20-pack Episodio I [v1e1:310] 25.00

(Japan)
Astromech gum pots.
☐ Green [368-01]................................10.00
☐ R2-D2 [368-02]................................10.00
☐ Red [368-03]..................................10.00

(Spain)
Gummy-style candy.
☐ 8-pack with Jar Jar header 20.00
☐ Anakin [v1e1:310] 8.00

☐ Darth Maul [v1e1:310]..........................8.00
☐ Jar Jar [v1e1:310].............................8.00
☐ R2-D2 [v1e1:310]...............................8.00

(UK)
Episode III: Revenge of the Sith.
☐ Jam-filled mallow, Darth Vader package [368-04]..........10.00

Bazooka Bubblegum
☐ Darth Vader counter display dispenser [368-05].............25.00

Bimbo (Mexico)
Bimbo Cao 3-pack, free sticker inside.
☐ Anakin Skywalker [368-06] 15.00
☐ Battle droid, 4-pack [368-07].......................20.00
☐ Darth Maul [368-08]................................15.00
☐ Darth Maul, 4-pack [368-09].........................20.00
☐ Queen Amidala [368-10].............................15.00

Bimbo Cao Tubo, free sticker inside.
☐ Queen Amidala [368-11].............................15.00
☐ Qui-Gon Jinn [368-12].............................15.00

Mi Merienda, free sticker inside.
☐ Darth Maul [368-13]................................15.00
☐ Queen Amidala [368-14].............................15.00

Bonbon Buddies (UK)
Milk chocolate eggs packaged with toys.
☐ Christophsis battle fun activity [368-15]...........15.00
☐ Mini travel game [368-16].........................15.00

Bondy Fiesta (Mexico)
Surprise eggs. Each contains 1 lollipop, memory cards, a medallion, and a sticker. Eggs may be blue or white.
☐ 12-pack, unopened display 60.00
☐ Ahsoka [368-17]...................................10.00

 368-32
 368-33 Package and Wrapper

 368-34
 368-35
 368-36
 368-37
 368-38
 368-39
 368-40
 368-41

 368-42
 368-43
 368-44
 368-45
 368-46
 368-47
 368-48
 368-49

 368-50
 368-51
 368-52
 368-53
 368-54
 368-55
 368-56
 368-57

Packaging: Candy

- ❏ Anakin [368-18] 10.00
- ❏ Mace Windu [368-19] 10.00
- ❏ Obi-Wan Kenobi [368-20] 10.00
- ❏ Yoda [368-21] 10.00

Cadbury
Episode I: The Phantom Menace.
- ❏ Chocolate egg and 2 chocolate bars [368-22] 10.00
- ❏ Selection 8-pack with masks on back [368-23] 10.00
- ❏ Textured milk chocolate bar [368-24] 5.00

Episode I 6 textured milk chocolate bars in cardboard lightsaber tube.
- ❏ Blue 15.00
- ❏ Green 15.00
- ❏ Red, double 20.00

Treat-size crunchies in plastic character container.
- ❏ Darth Maul [368-25] 25.00
- ❏ R2-D2 [368-26] 25.00

Cadbury (UK)
- ❏ Fingers 150 g, Episode I, Clippo promotion [368-27] 15.00

Candy Max (Mexico)
Duncan gum wrappers. Foil The Phantom Menace wrappers inside each wrapper.
- ❏ Anakin Skywalker [368-28] 5.00
- ❏ Darth Maul [368-29] 5.00
- ❏ Jar Jar Binks [368-30] 5.00
- ❏ Queen Amidala [368-31] 5.00

Candy Rific
Real sound talkers. Talking bobble head candy containers 0.53 oz.
- ❏ Darth Vader [368-32] 5.00
- ❏ Yoda [368-33] 5.00

Cap Candy
Episode I. Battle pop with push button battle action.
- ❏ Darth Maul [368-34] 5.00
- ❏ Obi-Wan Kenobi [368-35] 5.00
- ❏ Qui-Gon Jinn [368-36] 5.00

Episode I: The Phantom Menace.
- ❏ Darth Maul saber stick [368-37] 5.00
- ❏ Jar Jar Binks monster mouth candy [368-38] 20.00
- ❏ Obi-Wan Kenobi lightsaber pop candy [368-39] 5.00

Spin pops with motorized dueling action.
- ❏ Darth Maul [368-40] 8.00
- ❏ Qui-Gon Jinn [368-41] 8.00

Episode II: Attack of the Clones lollipop holders.
- ❏ Anakin Skywalker [368-42] 10.00
- ❏ Clone trooper [368-43] 10.00
- ❏ Darth Vader [368-44] 10.00
- ❏ Jango Fett [368-45] 10.00
- ❏ Stormtrooper [368-46] 10.00

Episode II: Attack of the Clones.
- ❏ Count Dooku lightsaber candy [368-47] 5.00
- ❏ R2-D2 galaxy dipper [368-48] 5.00

Episode III: Revenge of the Sith lollipop holders.
- ❏ Chewbacca [368-49] 10.00
- ❏ Darth Vader [368-50] 10.00
- ❏ Yoda [368-51] 10.00

Episode III: Revenge of the Sith Spliquid, light-up sabers.
- ❏ Blue [368-52] 3.00
- ❏ Red [368-53] 3.00

Episode III: Revenge of the Sith. Spin pops.
- ❏ Chewbacca [368-54] 8.00
- ❏ Darth Vader [368-55] 8.00

Film action containers filled with Tart n'Tinys.
- ❏ Anakin Skywalker [368-56] 5.00
- ❏ Darth Sidious 5.00
- ❏ Jar Jar Binks 5.00
- ❏ Queen Amidala 5.00
- ❏ R2-D2 [368-57] 5.00

Chupa Chups
Classic trilogy character on lollipop wrapper.
- ❏ C-3PO [368-58] 10.00
- ❏ Darth Vader [368-59] 10.00
- ❏ Emperor [368-60] 10.00
- ❏ Han [368-61] 10.00
- ❏ Luke [368-62] 10.00
- ❏ Princess Leia [368-63] 10.00
- ❏ R2-D2 [368-64] 10.00
- ❏ Stormtrooper [368-65] 10.00
- ❏ Yoda [368-66] 10.00

Packaging: Candy

 368-88
 368-89
 368-90
 368-91
 368-92

 368-93
 368-94
 368-95
 368-96
 368-97
 368-98
 368-99
 368-100

 368-101
 368-102
 368-103 368-104 368-105 368-106
 368-107
 368-108
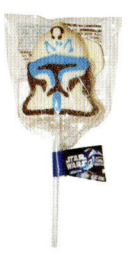 368-109
 368-110
 368-111

Episode I character on lollipop wrapper.
- Anakin Skywalker [368-67] 10.00
- Battle droid [368-68] 10.00
- Darth Maul [368-69] 10.00
- Jar Jar Binks [368-70] 10.00
- Obi-Wan Kenobi [368-71] 10.00
- Queen Amidala [368-72] 10.00
- Qui-Gon Jinn [368-73] 10.00
- Watto [368-74] 10.00

Episode I: The Phantom Menace. Tin canisters.
- Anakin Skywalker [368-75] 5.00
- Jedi Heroes [368-76] 5.00
- Queen Amidala [368-77] 5.00
- Sith Villains [368-78] 5.00

Pop Machines.
- C-3PO and stormtrooper 5.00
- Darth Vader [368-79] 5.00
- Darth Vader and Luke 5.00
- Han and Chewbacca 5.00

Space Box Port-A-Chups. Lollipop w/ character cover.
- C-3PO [368-80] 10.00
- Stormtrooper [368-81] 10.00

Crazy Planet
Episode I: 4 mega stickers, 2 gum, 1 sticker.
- Anakin Skywalker 10.00
- Battle droid 10.00
- Darth Maul 10.00
- Jar Jar Binks 10.00
- Obi-Wan Kenobi [368-82] 10.00
- Queen Amidala 10.00
- Qui-Gon Jinn 10.00
- Watto 10.00

Dracco Company Ltd. (Germany)
- Lightsaber candy 5.00

Frito Lay
- Anakin Skywalker Cracker Jack tin [368-83] 10.00

Galerie
- Clone Wars lollipops, 26 count [368-84] 10.00
- Darth Vader / Yoda egg-shaped candy case [368-85] 5.00

- Darth Vader and Yoda gummy candy, 60 ct. [368-86] 10.00
- Star Wars candy coins [368-87] 10.00

Candy canes. 12-packs.
- Cherry [368-88] 10.00
- Sour raspberry and sour cherry [368-89] 10.00

Darth Vader eggs with candy, plastic.
- 25 trick-or-treat favors [368-90] 15.00

Darth Vader's helmet filled with candy.
- Black [368-91] 5.00
- Blue 5.00
- Red [368-92] 5.00

Embossed tin boxes.
- Darth Vader, silver, exclusive to Target [368-93] 5.00

Hard candy lollipops.
- Darth Vader, black cherry [368-94] 5.00
- Darth Vader, grape [368-95] 5.00
- Darth Vader, strawberry [368-96] 5.00

Hero lollipops with removable lenticular stickers.
- Blue raspberry / Anakin [368-97] 5.00
- Green apple / Yoda [368-98] 5.00
- Strawberry / Yoda [368-99] 5.00

Hide an Egg.
- 16 candy-filled eggs [368-100] 12.00

Light-up Jedi starfighters.
- Red [368-101] 10.00
- Yellow [368-102] 10.00

Light-up lightsaber lollipops.
- Blue [368-103] 5.00
- Green [368-104] 5.00
- Green, Easter eggs on wrapper, exclusive to Target 5.00
- Red [368-105] 5.00
- Red, Easter eggs on wrapper, exclusive to Target [368-106] 5.00

Lollipops included.
- 32 lollipop valentines, lollipop swap, exclusive to Target [368-107] 10.00

Marshmallow lollipops.
- Captain Rex [368-108] 10.00
- Captain Rex, flag label [368-109] 10.00
- Yoda [368-110] 10.00
- Yoda, flag label [368-111] 10.00

Valentine hearts with box of Darth Vader gummies. Exclusive to Target.
- Classic trilogy [368-112] 15.00
- Darth Vader, "You Will Be My Valentine" [368-113] 15.00

Valentine's Day boxes, heart-shaped tins.
- Darth Maul, exclusive to Target [368-114] 15.00
- Darth Vader, exclusive to Target [368-115] 15.00
- Darth Vader 3D glasses [368-116] 15.00
- Yoda, cherry lollipops, exclusive to Target [368-117] 15.00
- Yoda 3D glasses [368-118] 15.00

Valentine's Day boxes, heart-shaped. Exclusive to Target.
- Darth Maul, red [368-119] 15.00
- Darth Vader / Anakin Skywalker [368-120] 15.00
- Darth Vader, black [368-121] 15.00
- Darth Vader, red [368-122] 15.00
- Yoda, black [368-123] 15.00

Harmony Foods
Jelly tins.
- Darth Vader [368-124] 6.00
- The droids [368-125] 6.00

Hersheys
Empire Strikes Back Photo on 6-pack of candy.
- Kit Kat (Luke on Tauntaun) [368-126] 150.00
- Milk chocolate (C-3PO and R2-D2) [368-127] 150.00
- Milk chocolate with almonds (Chewbacca) [368-128] ..150.00
- Mr. Goodbar (Darth Vader) [368-129] 150.00
- Reese's crunchy peanut butter cups (Darth Vader) [368-130] 150.00
- Reese's peanut butter cups (Boba Fett) [368-131] 150.00
- Rollo (Luke on Tauntaun) [368-132] 150.00
- Whatchamacallit (Darth Vader) [368-133] 150.00

Hollywood Chewing Gum (France)
- Blanchur [4:208] 8.00
- Green fresh [4:208] 8.00

Packaging: Candy

 368-112
 368-113
 368-114
 368-115
 368-116
 368-117
 368-118
 368-119
 368-120
 368-120
 368-121
 368-122
 368-123
 368-124
 368-125

- Ice Fresh [v1e1:313] 8.00
- Parfum [4:208] 8.00
- Power Mint [4:208] 8.00

Kinnerton Confectionery (UK)
- Box of 9 chocolate shapes [368-134] 15.00
- Darth Vader milk chocolate lollipop [368-135] 10.00
- R2-D2 shaped tin for jellies [4:208] 10.00

Fruit-flavoured shaped jellies in cardboard Episode I character package.
- Darth Maul [368-136] 10.00
- Jar Jar Binks [368-137] 10.00

Hexagon tin containers.
- Anakin Skywalker in podracer gear [368-138] 15.00
- Darth Maul [368-139] 15.00

Hollow chocolate eggs with Star Wars jelly shapes.
- Cut-out bookmark on box [368-140] 15.00
- Darth Vader folded container [368-141] 10.00
- Death Star trench 15.00
- Stormtrooper folded container 10.00

Jelly Shapes in folded cardboard container with collectible badge premium.
- R2-D2 [368-142] 10.00
- Stormtrooper [368-143] 10.00

Jelly Shapes in tin with decorative character bust.
- Anakin [368-144] 15.00
- Darth Maul [368-145] 15.00
- Darth Vader [368-146] 15.00
- Jar Jar Binks [368-147] 15.00
- R2-D2 [368-148] 15.00

Marks and Spencer (UK)
Chunky 'Stardust' bars.
- 5-pack [368-149] 15.00
- Clone trooper wrapper [368-150] 10.00
- Darth Vader wrapper [368-151] 10.00
- Obi-Wan wrapper [368-152] 10.00
- Yoda wrapper [368-153] 10.00

Masterfoods USA
3 Musketeers with glow-in-the-dark wrappers.
- 11.00 oz. (contains individual packets.) [368-154] 15.00
- "What is Anakin's secret?" 2.00
- "What is Chancellor Palpatine's secret?" 2.00
- "Who is a Sith Lord?" 2.00
- "Who is R2-D2's master?" 2.00
- "Who was Anakin's Jedi mentor?" 2.00
- "Who was Count Dooku's Jedi mentor?" 2.00
- "Who's home planet is Kashyyyk?" 2.00

 368-126
 368-127
 368-128
 368-129

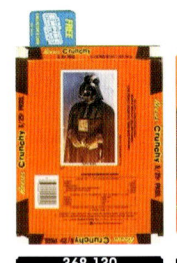 368-130
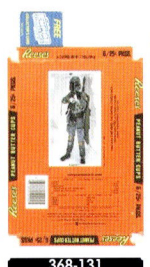 368-131
 368-132
 368-133
 368-134
 368-135
 368-136
 368-137

Packaging: Candy

 368-138
 368-139
 368-140
 368-141
 368-142
 368-143
 368-144

 368-145
 368-146
 368-147
 368-148
 368-149
 368-150
 368-151
 368-152
 368-153

 368-154
 368-155
 368-156
 368-157

 368-158
 368-159
 368-160
 368-161
 368-162 368-163

Lucas Crazy Hair.
- ☐ Anakin Skywalker 8.00
- ☐ Darth Vader Lava Berry [368-155] 8.00
- ☐ R2D-Goo [368-156] 8.00
- ☐ Wookiee Kiss [368-157] 8.00

M-azing crunchy with glow-in-the-dark wrappers.
- ☐ 11.10 oz. (contains individual packets.) [368-158] 10.00
- ☐ "What is Anakin's secret?" 2.00
- ☐ "Who is a Sith Lord?" 2.00
- ☐ "Who is R2-D2's master?" 2.00
- ☐ "Who was Anakin's Jedi mentor?" 2.00

M-azing peanut butter with glow-in-the-dark wrappers.
- ☐ 11.10 oz. (contains individual packets.) 10.00
- ☐ "Who is a Sith Lord?" 2.00
- ☐ "Who is R2-D2's master?" 2.00
- ☐ "Who was Anakin's Jedi mentor?" 2.00

M&M Minis.
- ☐ 1.08 oz. black tube [368-159] 3.00
- ☐ 1.94 oz. black tube 3.00
- ☐ 1.94 oz. gold tube 3.00
- ☐ 1.94 oz. green tube 3.00
- ☐ 1.08 oz. green tube, Chewbacca topped [368-160] 5.00
- ☐ 1.08 oz. green tube, Darth Vader topped [368-161] 5.00
- ☐ 1.08 oz. green tube, General Grievous topped [368-162] 5.00
- ☐ 1.08 oz. green tube, R2-D2 topped [368-163] 5.00

M&M Peanut with glow-in-the-dark wrappers.
- ☐ 11.23 oz. (contains individual packets.) 10.00
- ☐ "What is Anakin's secret?" 2.00
- ☐ "Who is a Sith Lord?" 2.00
- ☐ "Who is R2-D2's master?" 2.00
- ☐ "Who was Anakin's Jedi mentor?" 2.00
- ☐ "Who was Count Dooku's Jedi mentor?" 2.00
- ☐ "Who's home planet is Kashyyyk?" 2.00

M&M Plain with glow-in-the-dark wrappers.
- ☐ 11.17 oz. (contains individual packets.) 10.00
- ☐ "What is Anakin's secret?" 2.00
- ☐ "Who is a Sith Lord?" 2.00
- ☐ "Who is R2-D2's master?" 2.00
- ☐ "Who was Anakin's Jedi mentor?" 2.00
- ☐ "Who was Count Dooku's Jedi mentor?" 2.00
- ☐ "Who's home planet is Kashyyyk?" 2.00

M&Ms collectible packaging. Jedi mix, 3.14 oz.
- ☐ 11.17 oz. (contains individual packets.) 10.00
- ☐ 1: Anakin Skywalker 2.00
- ☐ 2: C-3PO and R2-D2 ....2.00
- ☐ 3: Obi-Wan Kenobi 2.00
- ☐ 4: Han Solo 2.00
- ☐ 5: Queen Amidala 2.00
- ☐ 6: Mace Windu 2.00

 368-164
 368-164 Inside of Wrapper
 368-165

 368-166
 368-167
 368-168
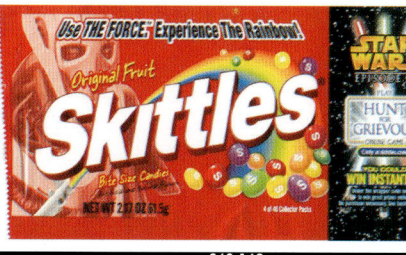 368-169

Packaging: Candy

368-170

368-171

368-172

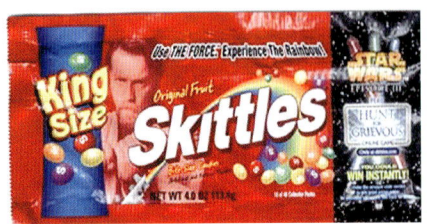
368-173

368-174

368-175

368-176

368-177

368-178

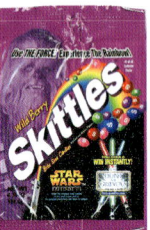
368-179

368-180

M&Ms collectible packaging. Jedi peanut mix, 3.27 oz.
- ❏ 7: Anakin Skywalker 2.00
- ❏ 8: C-3PO and R2-D2 .... 2.00
- ❏ 9: Obi-Wan Kenobi 2.00
- ❏ 10: Luke Skywalker 2.00
- ❏ 11: Chewbacca 2.00
- ❏ 12: Princess Leia 2.00

M&Ms collectible packaging. Darth mix, 3.14 oz.
- ❏ 13: Darth Vader 2.00
- ❏ 14: Darth Sidious 2.00
- ❏ 15: General Grievous 2.00
- ❏ 16: Darth Maul 2.00
- ❏ 17: Boba Fett 2.00
- ❏ 18: Clone trooper 2.00

M&Ms collectible packaging. Peanut Darth mix, 3.27 oz.
- ❏ 19: Darth Vader 2.00
- ❏ 20: Darth Sidious 2.00
- ❏ 21: General Grievous 2.00

- ❏ 22: Darth Maul 2.00
- ❏ 23: Boba Fett 2.00
- ❏ 24: Count Dooku 2.00

M&Ms collectible packaging. Milk chocolate Jedi mix, 14 oz.
- ❏ 25: Princess Leia [v1e1:314] 2.00
- ❏ 26: Obi-Wan Kenobi [v1e1:314] 2.00
- ❏ 27: C-3PO [368-164] 2.00
- ❏ 28: Luke Skywalker [v1e1:314] 2.00

M&Ms collectible packaging. Peanut Jedi mix, 14 oz.
- ❏ 29: Queen Amidala 2.00
- ❏ 30: Chewbacca 2.00
- ❏ 31: Han Solo 2.00
- ❏ 32: Anakin Skywalker 2.00

M&Ms collectible packaging. Dark chocolate Darth mix, 14 oz.
- ❏ 33: Clone trooper [v1e1:314] 2.00

- ❏ 34: Darth Maul [368-165] 2.00
- ❏ 35: Darth Vader [v1e1:314] 2.00
- ❏ 36: Darth Tyrannus [v1e1:314] 2.00

M&Ms collectible packaging. Dark chocolate peanut Darth mix, 14 oz.
- ❏ 37: Darth Vader 2.00
- ❏ 38: Darth Tyrannus 2.00
- ❏ 39: General Grievous 2.00
- ❏ 40: Boba Fett [368-166] 2.00

M&Ms collectible packaging. Milk chocolate Jedi mix, 21.3 oz.
- ❏ 41: Princess Leia 2.00
- ❏ 42: Obi-Wan Kenobi 2.00
- ❏ 43: C-3PO 2.00
- ❏ 44: Luke Skywalker 2.00

M&Ms collectible packaging. Peanut Jedi mix, 21.3 oz.
- ❏ 45: Queen Amidala 2.00

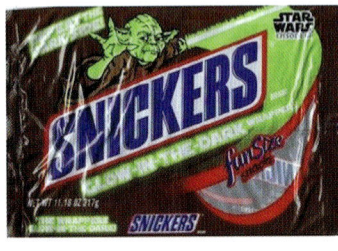
368-181

368-182

368-183

368-184

368-185

368-186

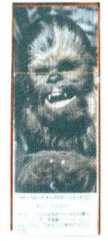
368-187

368-188

368-189

368-190

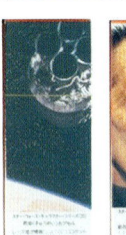
368-191

368-192

368-193

368-194

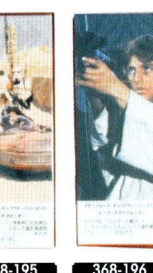
368-195

368-196

368-197

368-198

368-199

368-200

368-201

368-202

368-203

Packaging: Candy

 368-204
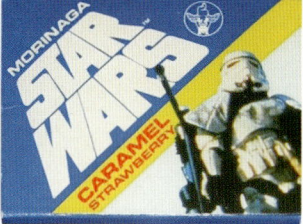 368-205
 368-206
 368-207
 368-208
 368-209
 368-210
 368-211
 368-212 368-213

 368-214
 368-215
 368-216
 368-217
 368-218
 368-219
 368-220

- ❏ 46: Chewbacca 2.00
- ❏ 47: Han Solo 2.00
- ❏ 48: Anakin Skywalker 2.00
- ❏ 49: Clone trooper 2.00
- ❏ 50: Darth Maul 2.00
- ❏ 51: Darth Vader 2.00
- ❏ 52: Darth Tyrannus 2.00

M&Ms collectible packaging. Peanut Darth mix, 21.3 oz.
- ❏ 53: Darth Vader 2.00
- ❏ 54: Darth Tyrannus 2.00
- ❏ 55: General Grievous 2.00
- ❏ 56: Boba Fett 2.00

M&Ms collectible packaging. Milk chocolate Jedi mix, 5.3 oz.
- ❏ 57: Princess Leia [v1e1:314] 2.00
- ❏ 58: Obi-Wan Kenobi [368-167] 2.00
- ❏ 59: C-3PO [v1e1:314] 2.00
- ❏ 60: Luke Skywalker [v1e1:314] 2.00

M&Ms collectible packaging. Peanut Jedi mix, 5.3 oz.
- ❏ 61: Queen Amidala 2.00
- ❏ 62: Chewbacca 2.00
- ❏ 63: Han Solo 2.00
- ❏ 64: Anakin Skywalker 2.00

M&Ms collectible packaging. Dark chocolate Darth mix, 5.3 oz.
- ❏ 65: Clone trooper 2.00
- ❏ 66: Darth Maul 2.00
- ❏ 67: Darth Vader 2.00
- ❏ 68: Darth Tyrannus 2.00

M&Ms collectible packaging. Dark chocolate peanut Darth mix, 5.3 oz.
- ❏ 69: Darth Vader 2.00
- ❏ 70: Darth Tyrannus 2.00
- ❏ 71: General Grievous 2.00
- ❏ 72: Boba Fett 2.00

Milky Way with glow-in-the-dark wrappers.
- ❏ 11.24 oz (contains individual packets.) [368-168] 15.00
- ❏ "What is Anakin's secret?" 2.00
- ❏ "Who is R2-D2's master?" 2.00
- ❏ "Who loses the battle on Mustafar?" 2.00
- ❏ "Whose home planet is Dagobah?" 2.00

Skittles collectible packaging. 2.17 oz.
- ❏ 1: Anakin Skywalker [v1e1:315] 2.00
- ❏ 2: Obi-Wan Kenobi [v1e1:315] 2.00
- ❏ 3: Darth Vader [v1e1:315] 2.00
- ❏ 4: General Grievous [368-169] 2.00

Skittles collectible packaging. 2.17 oz. Tropical.
- ❏ 5: Darth Maul [v1e1:315] 2.00
- ❏ 6: Darth Sidious [v1e1:315] 2.00
- ❏ 7: Jabba the Hutt [v1e1:315] 2.00
- ❏ 8: Queen Amidala [368-170] 2.00

Skittles collectible packaging. 2.17 oz. Wild berry.
- ❏ 9: Chewbacca [v1e1:315] 2.00

 368-221
 368-222
 368-223
 368-224
 368-225
 368-226
 368-227

 368-228
 368-229
 368-230
 368-231
 368-232
 368-233
 368-234
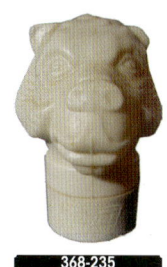 368-235

 368-236
 368-237
 368-238
 368-239
 368-240
 368-241
 368-242

Packaging: Candy

- 10: Yoda [v1e1:315] 2.00
- 11: Boba Fett [v1e1:315] 2.00
- 12: C-3PO and R2-D2 [368-171] 2.00

Skittles collectible packaging. 1.8 oz. Sour.
- 13: Han Solo [368-172] 2.00
- 14: Princess Leia [v1e1:315] 2.00
- 15: Luke Skywalker [v1e1:315] 2.00
- 16: Darth Vader [v1e1:315] 2.00

Skittles collectible packaging. 4 oz.
- 17: Anakin Skywalker [4:209] 2.00
- 18: Obi-Wan Kenobi [368-173] 2.00
- 19: Darth Vader [4:209] 2.00
- 20: General Grievous [4:209] 2.00

Skittles collectible packaging. 3.3 oz. Sour.
- 21: Han Solo [4:209] 2.00
- 22: Princess Leia [4:209] 2.00
- 23: Luke Skywalker [4:209] 2.00
- 24: Darth Vader [368-174] 2.00

Skittles collectible packaging. 16 oz.
- 25: Anakin Skywalker [368-175] 2.00
- 26: Obi-Wan Kenobi [4:209] 2.00
- 27: Darth Vader [4:209] 2.00
- 28: General Grievous [4:209] 2.00

Skittles collectible packaging. 16 oz. Wild berry.
- 29: Chewbacca [4:209] 2.00
- 30: Yoda [4:210] 2.00

- 31: Boba Fett [368-176] 2.00
- 32: C-3PO and R2-D2 [4:210] 2.00

Skittles collectible packaging. 13.3 oz. Sour.
- 33: Han Solo [4:210] 2.00
- 34: Princess Leia [4:210] 2.00
- 35: Luke Skywalker [368-177] 2.00
- 36: Darth Vader [4:210] 2.00

Skittles collectible packaging. 6.75 oz.
- 37: Anakin Skywalker [368-178] 2.00
- 38: Obi-Wan Kenobi [v1e1:316] 2.00
- 39: Darth Vader [v1e1:316] 2.00
- 40: General Grievous [v1e1:316] 2.00

Skittles collectible packaging. 6.75 oz. Wild berry.
- 41: Chewbacca [368-179] 2.00
- 42: Yoda [v1e1:316] 2.00
- 43: Boba Fett [v1e1:316] 2.00
- 44: C-3PO and R2-D2 [v1e1:316] 2.00

Skittles collectible packaging. 5.35 oz. Sour.
- 45: Han Solo [v1e1:316] 2.00
- 46: Princess Leia [368-180] 2.00
- 47: Luke Skywalker [v1e1:316] 2.00
- 48: Darth Vader [v1e1:316] 2.00

Skittles with glow-in-the-dark wrappers.
- "What is Anakin's secret?" 2.00
- "Who is a Sith Lord?" 2.00
- "Who is R2-D2's master?" 2.00

- "Who was Anakin's Jedi mentor?" 2.00
- "Who was Count Dooku's Jedi mentor?" ... 2.00
- "Who's home planet is Kashyyyk?" 2.00

Snickers with glow-in-the-dark wrappers.
- 11.18 oz. (contains individual packets.) [368-181] 15.00
- "What is Anakin's secret?" 2.00
- "Who is a Sith Lord?" 2.00
- "Who is R2-D2's master?" 2.00
- "Who loses the battle on Mustafar?" 2.00
- "Who was Count Dooku's Jedi mentor?" ... 2.00
- "Who's home planet is Kashyyyk?" 2.00
- "Who's home planet is Dagobah?" 2.00

Starburst with glow-in-the-dark wrappers.
- "What is Anakin's secret?" 2.00
- "Who is a Sith Lord?" 2.00
- "Who is R2-D2's master?" 2.00

Twix with glow-in-the-dark wrappers.
- 11.24 oz. (contains individual packets.) ...15.00
- "Who is a Sith Lord?" 2.00
- "Who is R2-D2's master?" 2.00
- "Who was Anakin's Jedi mentor?" 2.00

Meiji (Japan)
- The Phantom Menace, bonus trading card [368-182] 20.00

Star Wars movie candy.
- Chocolate tube [368-183] 85.00
- Large box [368-184] 85.00

368-243

368-244

368-245

368-246

368-247

368-248

368-249

368-250

368-251

368-252

368-253

368-254

368-255

368-256

368-257

368-258

368-259

368-260

368-261

368-262 368-263

368-264

368-265

368-266

368-267

368-268

368-269

368-270

Packaging: Cards

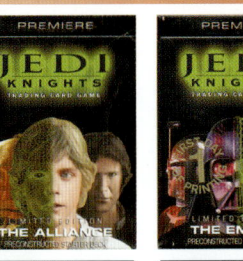

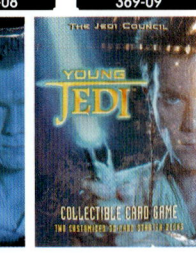

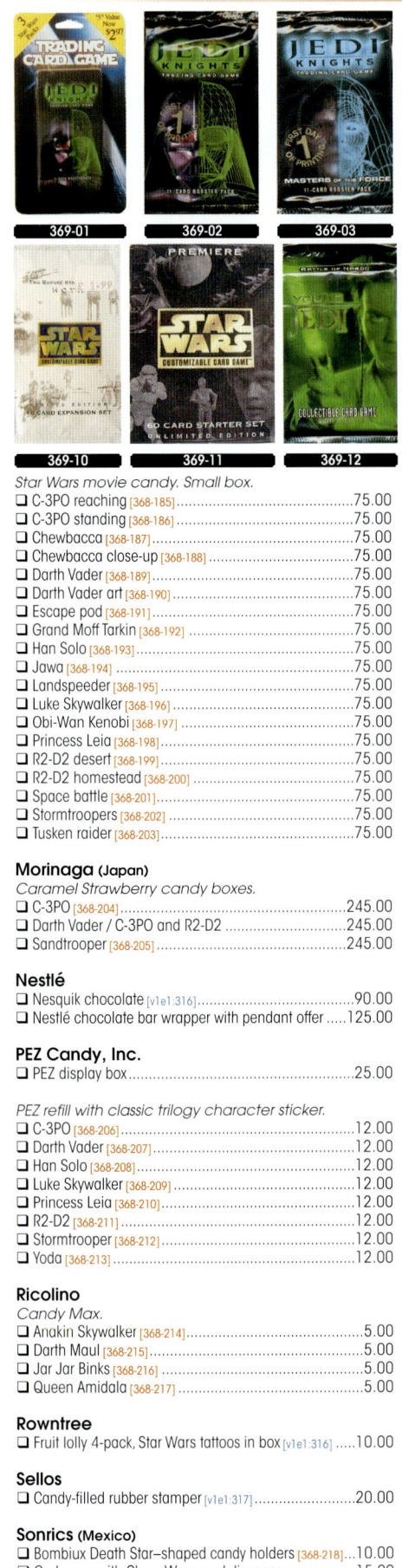

Star Wars movie candy. Small box.
- ❏ C-3PO reaching [368-185]..........................75.00
- ❏ C-3PO standing [368-186]...........................75.00
- ❏ Chewbacca [368-187]..................................75.00
- ❏ Chewbacca close-up [368-188]...................75.00
- ❏ Darth Vader [368-189].................................75.00
- ❏ Darth Vader art [368-190]............................75.00
- ❏ Escape pod [368-191].................................75.00
- ❏ Grand Moff Tarkin [368-192].........................75.00
- ❏ Han Solo [368-193]......................................75.00
- ❏ Jawa [368-194]..75.00
- ❏ Landspeeder [368-195]................................75.00
- ❏ Luke Skywalker [368-196]............................75.00
- ❏ Obi-Wan Kenobi [368-197]...........................75.00
- ❏ Princess Leia [368-198]................................75.00
- ❏ R2-D2 desert [368-199]................................75.00
- ❏ R2-D2 homestead [368-200].........................75.00
- ❏ Space battle [368-201]................................75.00
- ❏ Stormtroopers [368-202]..............................75.00
- ❏ Tusken raider [368-203]...............................75.00

Morinaga (Japan)
Caramel Strawberry candy boxes.
- ❏ C-3PO [368-204]..245.00
- ❏ Darth Vader / C-3PO and R2-D2................245.00
- ❏ Sandtrooper [368-205]...............................245.00

Nestlé
- ❏ Nesquik chocolate [v1e1:316]......................90.00
- ❏ Nestlé chocolate bar wrapper with pendant offer.....125.00

PEZ Candy, Inc.
- ❏ PEZ display box...25.00

PEZ refill with classic trilogy character sticker.
- ❏ C-3PO [368-206]..12.00
- ❏ Darth Vader [368-207].................................12.00
- ❏ Han Solo [368-208]......................................12.00
- ❏ Luke Skywalker [368-209]............................12.00
- ❏ Princess Leia [368-210]................................12.00
- ❏ R2-D2 [368-211]...12.00
- ❏ Stormtrooper [368-212]...............................12.00
- ❏ Yoda [368-213]...12.00

Ricolino
Candy Max.
- ❏ Anakin Skywalker [368-214]...........................5.00
- ❏ Darth Maul [368-215].....................................5.00
- ❏ Jar Jar Binks [368-216]...................................5.00
- ❏ Queen Amidala [368-217]..............................5.00

Rowntree
- ❏ Fruit lolly 4-pack, Star Wars tattoos in box [v1e1:316].....10.00

Sellos
- ❏ Candy-filled rubber stamper [v1e1:317].........20.00

Sonrics (Mexico)
- ❏ Bombiux Death Star–shaped candy holders [368-218]...10.00
- ❏ Gudu pop with Clone Wars card dispenser [368-219]....15.00

Landia. Star Wars Special Edition.
- ❏ Bespin #1...10.00
- ❏ Bespin #2...10.00
- ❏ Death Star #1...10.00
- ❏ Death Star #2...10.00
- ❏ Hoth #1..10.00
- ❏ Hoth #2..10.00
- ❏ Sarlacc #1..10.00
- ❏ Sarlacc #2..10.00
- ❏ Tatooine #1..10.00
- ❏ Tatooine #2..10.00

Star Wars Celebration VI
- ❏ Minti-chlorians breath mints........................15.00

Tombola
- ❏ Chocolate egg wrapper, X-Wing Fighter [368-220].....10.00

Topps
Boxes, empty.
- ❏ ESB sculpted candy dispensers [368-221].....35.00
- ❏ ESB II: sculpted candy dispensers................35.00
- ❏ ESB wax packs, series 1..............................75.00
- ❏ ESB wax packs, series 2 [368-222]..............75.00
- ❏ ESB wax packs, series 3 [368-223]..............75.00
- ❏ ROTJ wax packs, series 1............................75.00
- ❏ ROTJ wax packs, series 2............................75.00
- ❏ ROTJ sculpted candy dispensers [368-224]..35.00
- ❏ Star Wars wax packs, series 1...................150.00
- ❏ Star Wars wax packs, series 2 [368-225]....150.00
- ❏ Star Wars wax packs, series 3 [368-226]....125.00
- ❏ Star Wars wax packs, series 4...................125.00
- ❏ Star Wars wax packs, series 5 [368-227]....125.00

Dispenser, sculpted Empire Strikes Back.
- ❏ Boba Fett [368-228].....................................10.00
- ❏ C-3PO [368-229]..10.00
- ❏ Chewbacca [368-230]..................................10.00
- ❏ Darth Vader [368-231].................................10.00
- ❏ Stormtrooper [368-232]...............................10.00

Dispenser, sculpted Empire Strikes Back series 2.
- ❏ 2-1B [368-233]...10.00
- ❏ Bossk [368-234]...10.00
- ❏ Tauntaun [368-235]......................................10.00
- ❏ Yoda [368-236]...10.00

Dispenser, sculpted Return of the Jedi.
- ❏ Admiral Ackbar [368-237]............................10.00
- ❏ Baby Ewok [368-238]...................................10.00
- ❏ Darth Vader [368-239].................................10.00
- ❏ Ewok [368-240]..10.00
- ❏ Jabba the Hutt [368-241].............................10.00
- ❏ Sy Snootles [368-242]..................................10.00

- ❏ Sugar free gum, box only [368-243]............50.00

Wax wrappers.
- ❏ Empire Strikes Back series 1 [368-244].......40.00
- ❏ Empire Strikes Back series 2 [368-245].......40.00
- ❏ Empire Strikes Back series 3......................40.00
- ❏ Return of the Jedi series 1: Darth Vader [368-246].....35.00
- ❏ Return of the Jedi series 1: Jabba the Hutt [368-247]...35.00
- ❏ Return of the Jedi series 1: Luke Skywalker [368-248]..35.00
- ❏ Return of the Jedi series 1: Wicket the Ewok [368-249]..35.00
- ❏ Return of the Jedi series 2: Baby Ewok [368-250].....35.00
- ❏ Return of the Jedi series 2: C-3PO [368-251]...35.00
- ❏ Return of the Jedi series 2: Lando skiff guard [368-252]..35.00
- ❏ Return of the Jedi series 2: Princess Leia [368-253]....35.00
- ❏ Star Wars series 1 [368-254].......................45.00
- ❏ Star Wars series 2 [368-255].......................45.00
- ❏ Star Wars series 3 [368-256].......................45.00
- ❏ Star Wars series 4 [368-257].......................40.00
- ❏ Star Wars series 5 [368-258].......................40.00

Sculpted character head candy dispensers.
- ❏ 4-pack on header card plus 10 collector cards, Yoda, Chewbacca, C-3PO, Darth Vader [368-259]..........25.00

Topps (Ireland)
Sculpted character head candy dispensers.
- ❏ 4-pack on header card plus 10 collector cards, Yoda, Chewbacca, C-3PO, Darth Vader [368-260]..........25.00

Vadeboncocur (Germany)
- ❏ Chocolate Jar Jar Binks [368-261]................20.00

Winterito (Peru)
Tableta Sabor a Chocolate.
- ❏ Ahsoka Tano [368-262]................................10.00
- ❏ Anakin Skywalker [368-263]........................10.00
- ❏ Asajj Ventress [368-264].............................10.00
- ❏ Captain Rex [368-265]................................10.00
- ❏ Obi-Wan Kenobi [368-266]..........................10.00
- ❏ Yoda [368-267]...10.00

Zeon (UK)
Tinned mints.
- ❏ Darth Vader [368-268].................................10.00
- ❏ Death Star [368-269]...................................10.00
- ❏ Stormtrooper [368-270]...............................10.00

Packaging: Cards

Beckett Associates
- ❏ Trading card game (3 random packs) [369-01]...15.00

Decipher
Jedi Knights CCG. Base set. 11 card booster.
- ❏ Darth Vader [v1e1:317]................................10.00
- ❏ Darth Vader, 1st day [369-02].....................10.00
- ❏ Darth Vader, 1st day, wrapper only..............5.00
- ❏ Darth Vader, wrapper only...........................5.00

Jedi Knights CCG. Masters of the Force. 11 card booster.
- ❏ Palpatine [4:211]..10.00
- ❏ Palpatine, 1st day [369-03]..........................10.00
- ❏ Palpatine, 1st day, wrapper only...................5.00
- ❏ Palpatine, wrapper only................................5.00

Packaging: Cards

369-19   369-20   369-21   369-22   369-23   369-24   369-25   369-26   369-27

   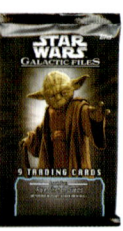   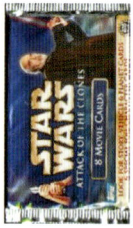   

369-28   369-29   369-30   369-31   369-32   369-33   369-34   369-35   369-36   369-37

Jedi Knights CCG. Premiere limited edition starter decks.
- The Alliance [369-04] 15.00
- The Alliance, 1st day 18.00
- The Alliance, 1st day, box only 5.00
- The Alliance, box only 3.00
- The Empire [4:211] 15.00
- The Empire, 1st day [369-05] 18.00
- The Empire, 1st day, box only 5.00
- The Empire, box only 3.00

Jedi Knights CCG. Scum and Villainy. 11-card booster.
- Boba Fett [369-06] 4.00
- Boba Fett, 1st day 7.00
- Boba Fett, 1st day, wrapper only 2.00
- Boba Fett, wrapper only 1.00

Star Wars CCG.
- A New Hope, 5-card expansion 3.00
- Boba Fett, 11-card booster [369-07] 4.00
- Dagobah, 9-card expansion, limited [369-08] 3.00
- Han Solo, 11-card booster [369-09] 4.00
- Hoth, 15-card expansion, limited [369-10] 3.00
- Premiere 60-card starter set [369-11] 15.00

Star Wars CCG. Premiere Enhanced. 15-card booster.
- Unlimited retail display box 5.00
- Unlimited with Boba Fett premium card [v1e1:318] 16.00
- Unlimited with Darth Vader premium card [v1e1:318] 16.00
- Unlimited with Han premium card 16.00
- Unlimited with Leia premium card 16.00
- Unlimited with Luke premium card [v1e1:318] 16.00
- Unlimited with Obi-Wan premium card [v1e1:318] 16.00

Young Jedi CCG.
- Battle of Naboo, 11-card booster [369-12] 5.00
- Battle of Naboo, two customized starter decks [369-13] 10.00
- Duel of Fates, two 30-card customized starter decks [4:211] 10.00
- Duel of the Fates, 11-card booster [369-14] 5.00
- Menace of Darth Maul, 11-card booster [369-15] 5.00
- Menace of Darth Maul, two 30-card customized starter decks [369-16] 10.00
- The Jedi Council, 11-card booster [369-17] 5.00
- The Jedi Council, two 30-card customized starter decks [369-18] 10.00

Young Jedi CCG. Premiere Enhanced. Four 15-card boosters.
- Darth Maul premium card [v1e1:318] 15.00
- Mace Windu premium card 15.00
- Queen Amidala premium card 15.00
- Qui-Gon Jinn premium card 15.00
- Sebulba premium card 15.00
- Trade Federation Tank premium card 15.00

Hallmark / Expressions
- Episode I trivia trading cards, Topps widevision [369-19] .. 10.00

Panini (UK)
- Staks [369-20] 1.00

370-01   370-02   370-03   370-04   370-05   370-06   370-07   370-08

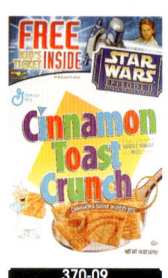  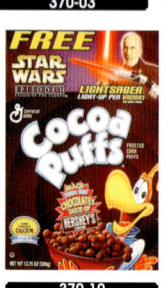  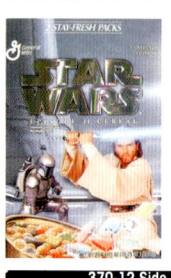   

370-09   370-09 Inside Box   370-10   370-11   370-12 Side 1 and Side 2   370-13   370-14

370-15   370-16   370-17   370-18   370-19   370-20   370-21   370-22

Packaging: Cereal

370-23 | 370-24 | 370-25 | 370-26 | 370-27 | 370-28 | 370-29 | 370-30

370-31 | 370-32 | 370-33 | 370-34 | 370-35 | 370-36 | 370-37 | 370-38

Topps
- 30th anniversary 1-pack hanging card back [369-21] 2.00
- 30th anniversary 24-pack box 2.00
- Clone Wars 24-pack box 60.00
- Clone Wars Adventures 24-pack box 50.00
- Clone Wars bonus box, exclusive to Walmart [369-22] .. 15.00
- Clone Wars bonus box, exclusive to Target 15.00
- Clone Wars bonus box, exclusive to Toys R Us 15.00
- Clone Wars, 7 trading cards [369-23] 5.00
- Episode I widevision trading card box, empty 5.00
- Episode I, 6 widevision cards [369-24] 5.00
- Rise of the Bounty Hunters 24-pack box, season 2 ... 80.00
- Rise of the Bounty Hunters 8-pack tin box [369-25] ... 25.00
- Star Wars Galaxy retail display box 5.00
- Star Wars Galaxy 7 empty wrapper [369-26] 3.00

Empire Strikes Back Illustrated.
- Trading card box, empty [369-27] 5.00

Galactic Files.
- 12-pack, Anakin Skywalker [369-28] 5.00
- 12-pack, Luke Skywalker [369-29] 5.00
- 12-pack, Princess Leia [369-30] 5.00
- Jumbo Pack, double pack containing 16 cards 10.00
- Retail pack: Yoda [369-31] 5.00
- Trading card box 175.00

Tin collector box of 35.
- Anakin and Ahsoka [369-32] 25.00
- Yoda [369-33] 25.00

Topps (Ireland)
Empire Strikes Back initial stickers [2:324] 145.00

Topps (UK)
Episode II: Attack of the Clones, wrapper only.
- Count Dooku [369-34] 3.00

- Jango Fett [369-35] 3.00
- Obi-Wan Kenobi [369-36] 3.00
- Padmé Amidala [369-37] 3.00

Packaging: Cereal
Continued in Volume 3, Page 296

General Mills
Blu-ray promotion boxes, empty.
- Cinnamon Toast Crunch 21.25 oz. [370-01] 15.00
- Honey Nut Cheerios 21.6 oz. 15.00
- Lucky Charms 20.5 oz. [370-02] 15.00

Episode I 3D. Character pen premium.
- Cheerios, 14 oz. 15.00
- Cookie Crisp, 11.25 oz. [370-03] 15.00
- Reese's Puffs, 13 oz. 15.00

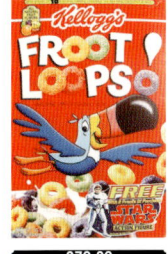    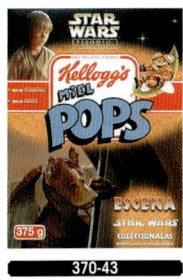 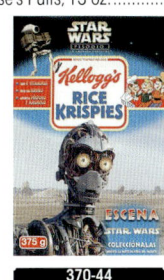 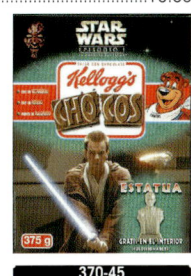

370-39 | 370-40 | 370-41 | 370-42 | 370-43 | 370-44 | 370-45

 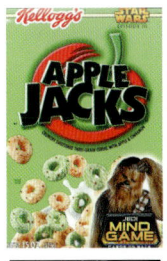  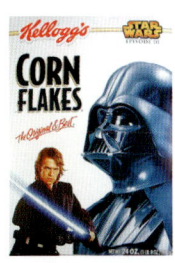  

370-46 | 370-47 | 370-48 | 370-49 | 370-50 | 370-51

 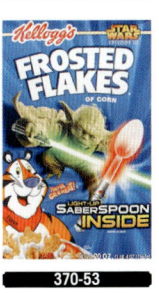    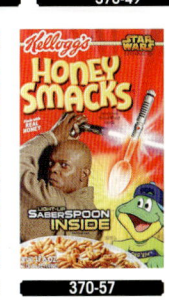  

370-52 | 370-53 | 370-54 | 370-55 | 370-56 | 370-57 | 370-58 | 370-59

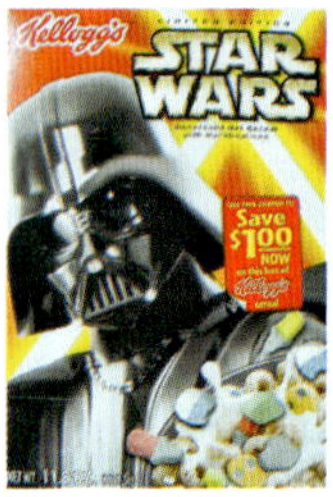

Packaging: Cereal

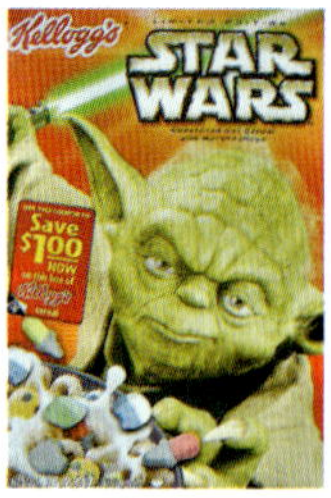

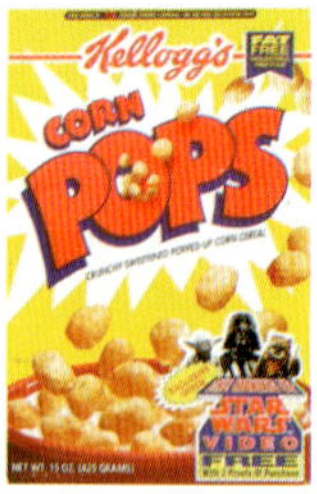

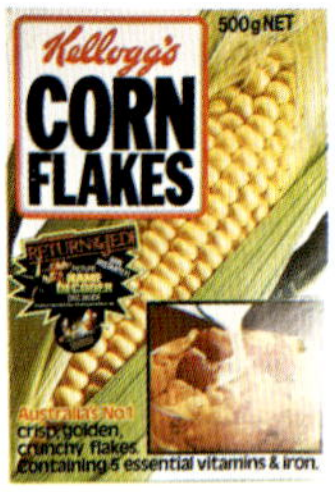

Episode I The Phantom Menace 3D movie poster.
- ❏ Honey Nut Cheerios 21.6 oz 20.00
- ❏ Lucky Charms 20.5 oz. 20.00

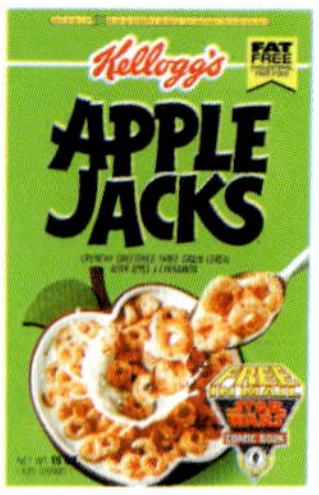

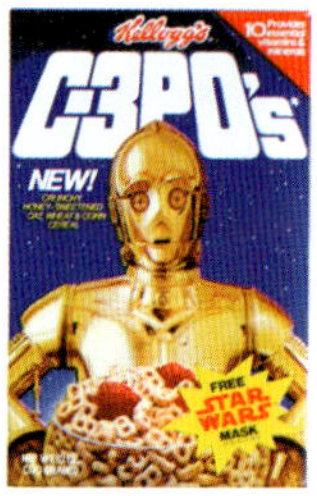

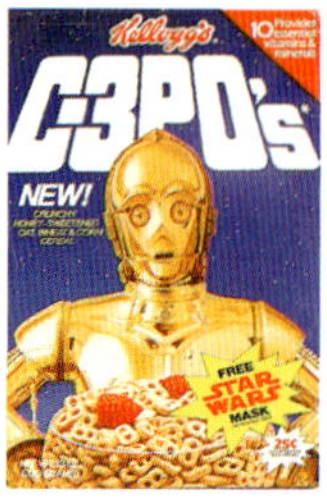

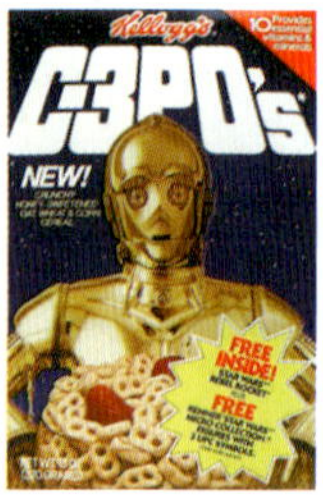

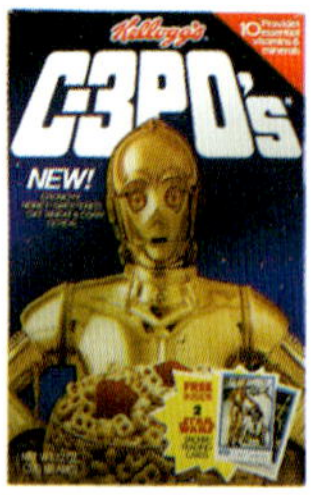

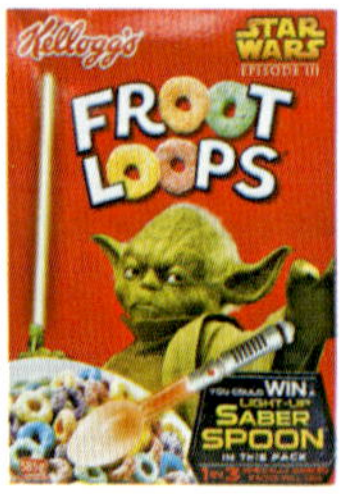

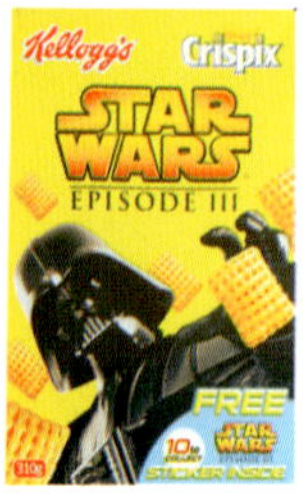

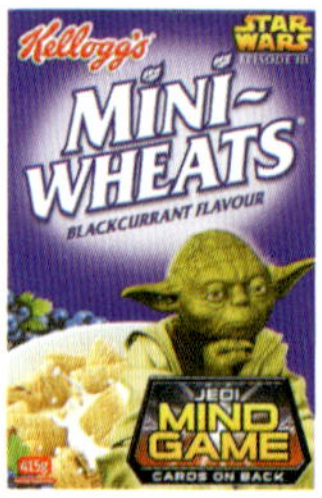

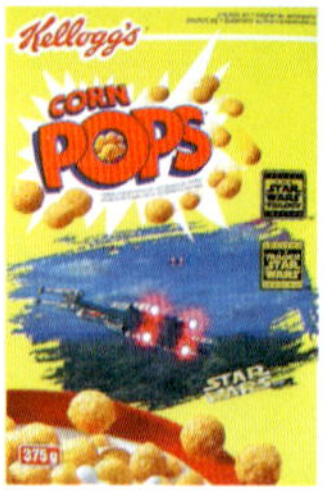

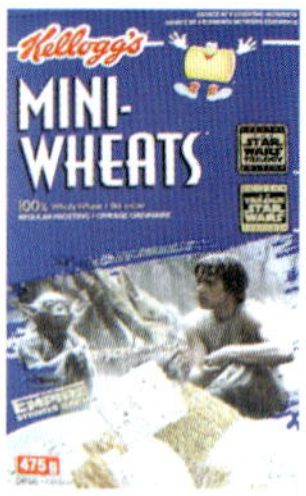

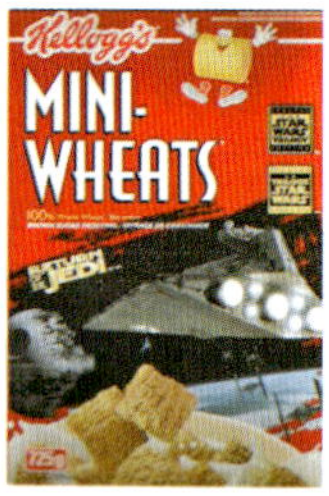

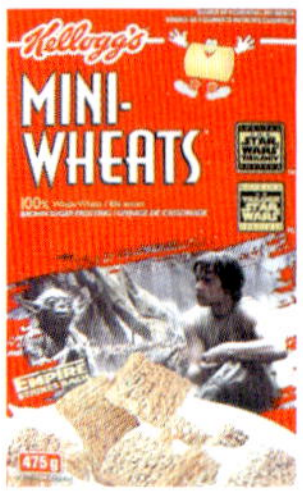

Episode II, empty.
- ❏ Cheerios, collectible cup and bowl offer [370-04] 10.00
- ❏ Cheerios, free toy car offer [370-05] 15.00
- ❏ Chex Corn, temporary tattoos and clone crunch recipe [370-06] 12.00
- ❏ Chex Rice, temporary tattoos and clone crunch recipe [370-07] 12.00
- ❏ Cinnamon Toast Crunch, lightsaber light-up pen inside [370-08] 10.00
- ❏ Cinnamon Toast Crunch, Movie Cash inside [370-09] 15.00
- ❏ Cocoa Puffs, lightsaber light-up pen inside [370-10] 12.00
- ❏ Cookie Crisp, collectible cup and bowl offer [370-11] 10.00
- ❏ Episode II cereal 2-pack [370-12] 18.00
- ❏ Episode II Cereal, Collector's Edition #1 [370-13] 15.00
- ❏ Episode II Cereal, Collector's Edition #2 [370-14] 15.00
- ❏ Golden Grahams, free toy car offer [370-15] 15.00
- ❏ Golden Grahams, Movie Cash inside [370-16] 15.00
- ❏ Honey Nut Cheerios, free toy car offer [370-17] 15.00
- ❏ Honey Nut Cheerios, lightsaber light-up pen inside [370-18] 12.00
- ❏ Honey Nut Cheerios, lightsaber light-up pen inside, 2-pack 12.00
- ❏ Honey Nut Chex, collectible cup and bowl offer [370-19] . 10.00
- ❏ Honey Nut Chex, free toy car offer [370-20] 15.00
- ❏ Lucky Charms, Movie Cash inside [370-21] 15.00
- ❏ Reeses Puffs, lightsaber light-up pen inside [370-22] 12.00
- ❏ Trix, Movie Cash inside [370-23] 15.00

Vintage, empty.
- ❏ Boo Berry, Star Wars Collector Cards [370-24] 140.00
- ❏ Boo Berry, Star Wars Stick-Ons 150.00
- ❏ Cheerios with 16 oz. Tumbler mail-in offer [370-25] 65.00
- ❏ Cheerios, Star Wars Mini-Poster, 10 oz. 35.00
- ❏ Cheerios, Star Wars Mini-Poster, 7 oz. [370-26] 65.00
- ❏ Cocoa Puffs, Star Wars Collector Cards [370-27] 145.00
- ❏ Cocoa Puffs, Star Wars Stick-Ons [370-28] 145.00
- ❏ Count Chocula, Star Wars Stick-Ons [370-29] 165.00
- ❏ Crazy Cow Chocolate, Star Wars Collector Cards, Darth Vader inset [370-30] 400.00
- ❏ Crazy Cow Chocolate, Star Wars Collector Cards, Tusken Raider inset [370-31] 250.00
- ❏ Crazy Cow Strawberry, Star Wars Collector Cards, Darth Vader inset [370-32] 250.00
- ❏ Crazy Cow Strawberry, Star Wars Collector Cards, Tusken Raider inset [370-33] 240.00
- ❏ Franken Berry, Star Wars Collector Cards [370-34] 180.00
- ❏ Franken Berry, Star Wars Stick-Ons 165.00
- ❏ Lucky Charms with mobiles offer [370-35] 150.00
- ❏ Lucky Charms, Star Wars Stick-Ons, 14 oz. 175.00
- ❏ Lucky Charms, Star Wars Stick-Ons, 9 oz. [370-36] 175.00

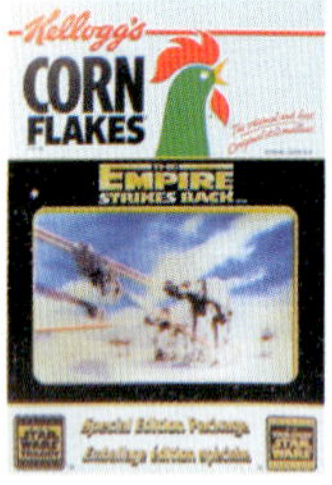

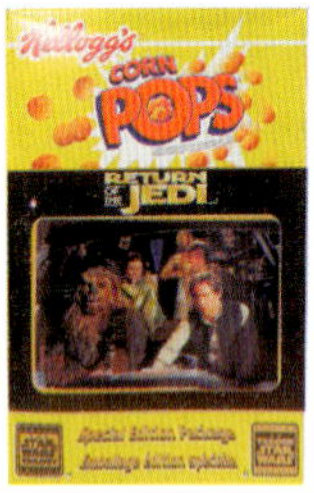

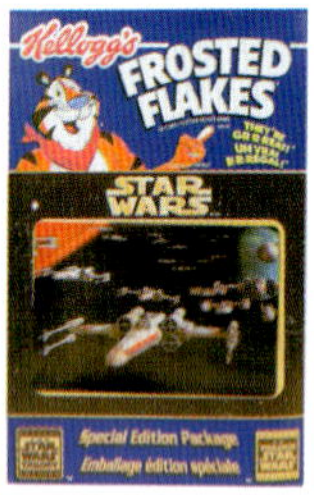

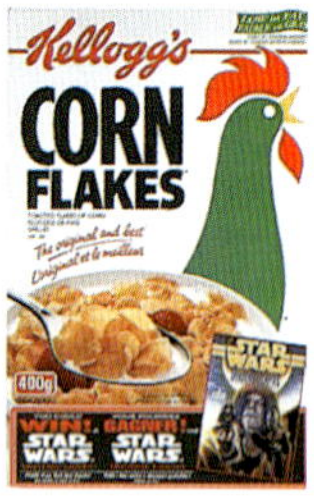

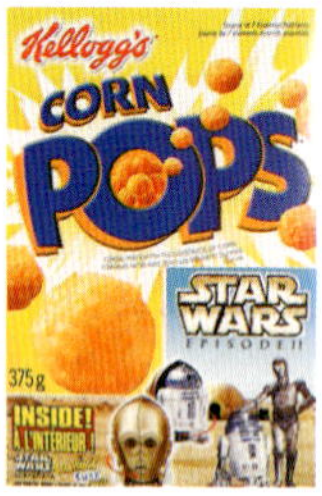

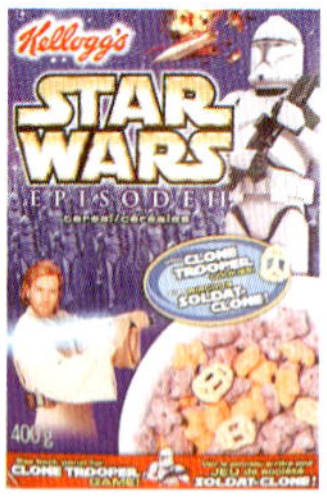

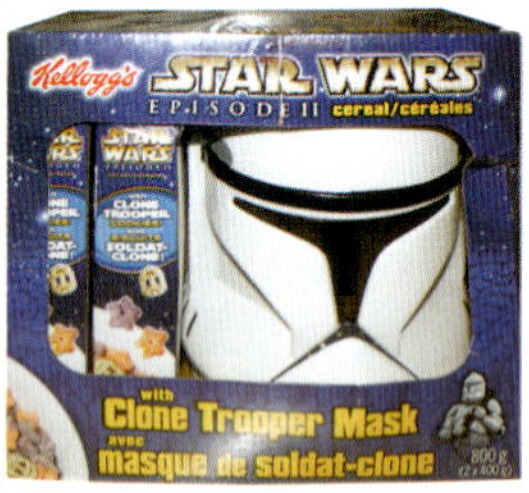

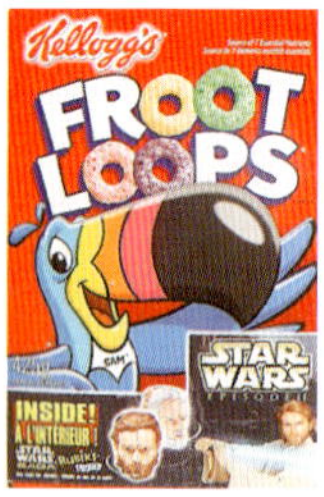

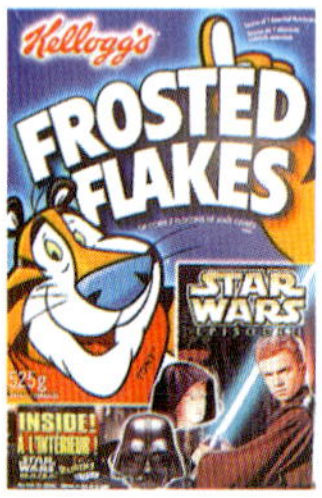

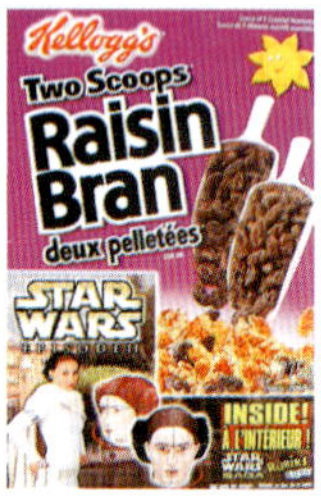

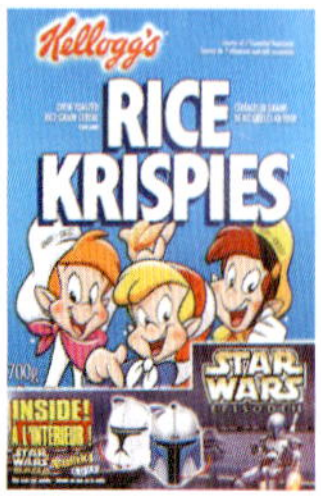

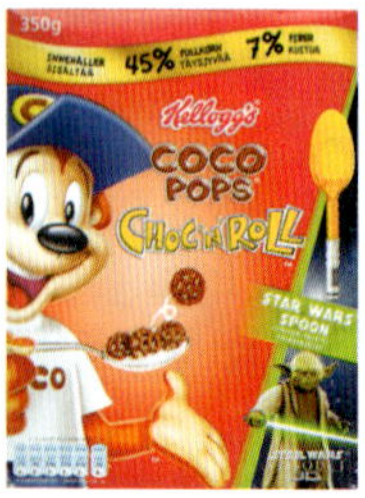

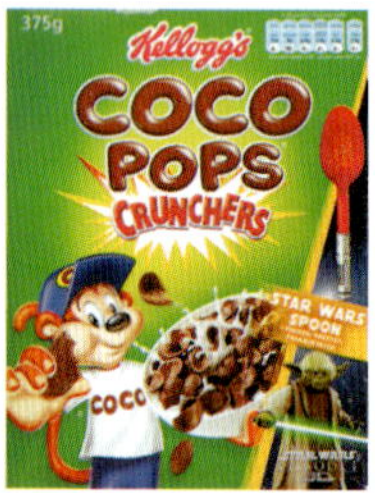

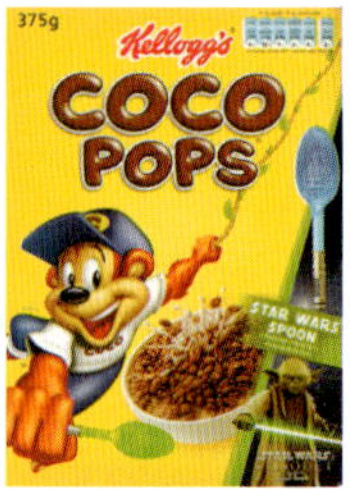

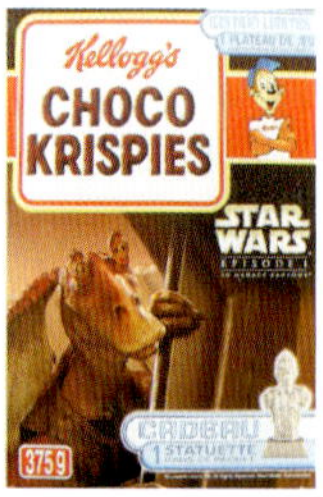

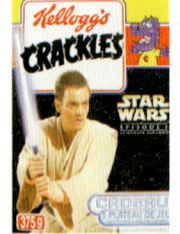
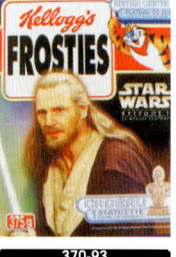

Packaging: Cereal

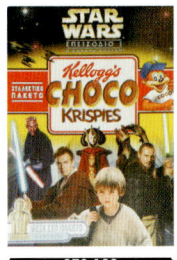 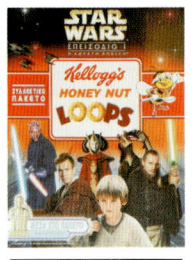 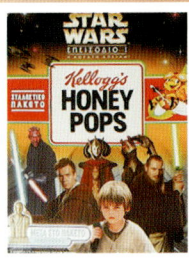  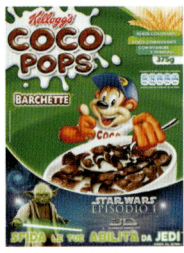  

370-100 | 370-101 | 370-102 | 370-103 | 370-104 | 370-105 | 370-106

   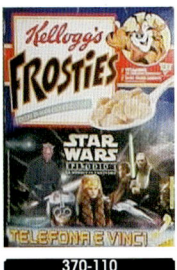     

370-107 | 370-108 | 370-109 | 370-110 | 370-111 | 370-112 | 370-113 | 370-114 | 370-115

❏ Trix with mobiles offer [370-37] 150.00
❏ Trix, Star Wars Stick-Ons [370-38] 160.00

Kellogg's

Empty.
❏ Froot Loops for Han Solo figure mail-in [370-39] 50.00
❏ Raisin Bran, videos: Experience the Force [370-40] 35.00
❏ Raisin Bran, videos: Save up to $7.00 [370-41] 45.00

Episode I. Free poster on back, empty.
❏ Honey Loops, Padmé [370-42] 30.00
❏ Miel Pops, Jar Jar [370-43] 30.00
❏ Miel Pops, Jar Jar on Kaadu 30.00
❏ Rice Krispies, R2-D2 repairing podracer [370-44] 30.00
❏ Rice Krispies, R2-D2 repairing royal starship.................30.00

Episode I, empty.
❏ Chocos with free mini statue [370-45] 30.00

Episode III, empty.
❏ 8-pack 8.56 oz. [370-46] 50.00
❏ Apple Jacks 15 oz, Jedi mind game [370-47]................25.00
❏ Corn Flakes, 18 oz., Anakin Skywalker, Episode III information 25.00
❏ Corn Flakes, 18 oz., C-3PO and R2-D2, Episode III information [370-48] 25.00
❏ Corn Flakes, 24 oz., Anakin Skywalker, Episode III information [370-49] 25.00
❏ Corn Flakes, 24 oz., C-3PO and R2-D2, Episode III information 25.00
❏ Corn Pops 15 oz., Jedi mind game [370-50] 25.00
❏ Corn Pops 19.5 oz. with free SaberSpoon [370-51] 25.00
❏ Crispix 12 oz., R2-D2 snack bowl offer [370-52] 30.00
❏ Froot Loops 15 oz. with free SaberSpoon 25.00
❏ Froot Loops 18 oz. with free SaberSpoon 25.00
❏ Frosted Flakes 20 oz. with free SaberSpoon [370-53].....25.00
❏ Frosted Mini-Wheats 24.3 oz., free DVD offer [370-54] ...20.00
❏ Frosted Mini-Wheats big bite 20.4 oz., free DVD offer [370-55] 20.00
❏ Frosted Mini-Wheats maple and brown sugar, 16.5 oz., free DVD offer [370-56] 20.00
❏ Honey Smacks 17.6 oz. w/ free Saber Spoon [370-57]...25.00
❏ Raisin Bran Crunch 18.2 oz., Jedi mind game [370-58]...25.00
❏ Smorz 10.5 oz., Jedi mind game [370-59] 30.00
❏ Star Wars 11.8 oz., Darth Vader box 35.00
❏ Star Wars 11.8 oz., Darth Vader box, $1.00 off coupon [370-60] 30.00
❏ Star Wars 11.8 oz., Yoda box 35.00
❏ Star Wars 11.8 oz., Yoda box, $1.00 coupon [370-61] 30.00

Vintage, empty.
❏ Any box with video tape mail-in [370-62] 100.00
❏ Any with Return of the Jedi Decoder Game Piece inside [370-63] 200.00
❏ Apple Jacks, for comic book mail-in [370-64] 120.00

 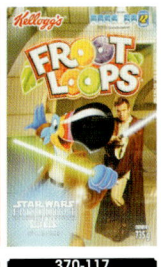     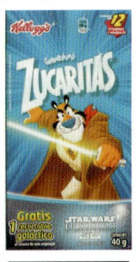   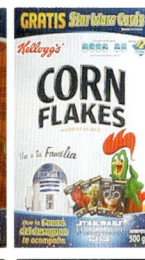

370-116 | 370-117 | 370-118 | 370-119 | 370-120 | 370-121 | 370-122 | 370-123 | 370-124 | 370-125

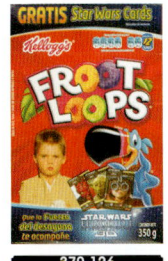       

370-126 | 370-127 | 370-128 | 370-129 | 370-130 | 370-131 | 370-132 | 370-133

      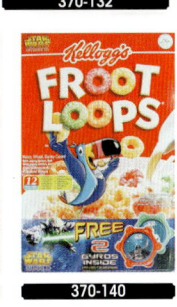 

370-134 | 370-135 | 370-136 | 370-137 | 370-138 | 370-139 | 370-140 | 370-141

Packaging: Cereal

Vintage, empty. C-3PO's.
- ❏ Cut-out C-3PO mask [370-65].................................75.00
- ❏ Cut-out C-3PO mask and 25 cent coupon [370-66] 75.00
- ❏ Cut-out Chewbacca mask 75.00
- ❏ Cut-out Darth Vader mask 75.00
- ❏ Cut-out Darth Vader mask and 25 cent coupon..........75.00
- ❏ Cut-out Luke Skywalker mask 75.00
- ❏ Cut-out Luke Skywalker mask and 25 cent coupon.....75.00
- ❏ Cut-out stormtrooper mask 75.00
- ❏ Cut-out stormtrooper mask and 25 cent coupon 75.00
- ❏ Cut-out Yoda mask..75.00
- ❏ Plastic rebel-rocket premium [370-67] 135.00
- ❏ Stick'R trading cards premium [370-68] 100.00

Kellogg's (Australia)
Episode III, empty.
- ❏ Coco Pops, Jedi mind game....................................35.00
- ❏ Froot Loops 585 g with free SaberSpoon [370-69].........35.00
- ❏ Frosties, Jedi mind game 35.00
- ❏ Honey Crispix, 310 g, sticker inside [370-70]...............35.00
- ❏ Mini-Wheats Blackcurrant flavour, 415 g, Jedi mind game [370-71] 35.00

Kellogg's (Canada)
Star Wars "magic eye" back, empty.
- ❏ Corn Pops [370-72]...25.00
- ❏ Frosted Mini-Wheats [370-73] 25.00
- ❏ Mini-Wheats, Imperial Cruiser [370-74] 25.00
- ❏ Mini-Wheats, Luke / Yoda [370-75] 25.00

Star Wars Special Edition trilogy lenticular image, empty.
- ❏ 3-pack, Special Edition 75.00
- ❏ Corn Flakes, Empire Strikes Back [370-76]..................20.00
- ❏ Corn Pops, Return of the Jedi [370-77].......................20.00
- ❏ Frosted Flakes, Star Wars [370-78] 20.00

Empty.
- ❏ Any, Shadows of the Empire cut-out cards [370-79] 50.00

Episode II, empty.
- ❏ Corn Pops, Rubik's Cube premium [370-80]..................35.00
- ❏ Episode II cereal [370-81]..30.00
- ❏ Episode II cereal 2-pack with clone trooper mask [370-82]...40.00
- ❏ Froot Loops, Rubik's Cube premium [370-83]...............35.00
- ❏ Frosted Flakes, Rubik's Cube premium [370-84] 35.00
- ❏ Raisin Bran, Rubik's Cube premium [370-85] 35.00
- ❏ Rice Krispies, Rubik's Cube premium [370-86] 35.00

Kellogg's (Denmark)
Episode I 3D, empty. Lightsaber spoon premium.
- ❏ Coco Pops Choc 'n' Roll, 375 g [370-87] 40.00
- ❏ Coco Pops Crunchers, 375 g [370-88] 40.00
- ❏ Coco Pops, 375 g [370-89].......................................40.00
- ❏ Rice Krispies, 375 g [370-90] 40.00

Kellogg's (France)
Episode I, empty.
- ❏ Choco Krispies with free mini statue [370-91] 35.00

- ❏ Crackles [370-92] 35.00
- ❏ Frosties with free mini statue [370-93].......................35.00
- ❏ Miel Pops with free breakfast spoon [370-94]...............40.00
- ❏ Smacks with free breakfast spoon [370-95].................40.00

Kellogg's (Germany)
Episode I, empty.
- ❏ Chocos with free crystal scene [370-96] 45.00
- ❏ Frosties with free crystal scene [370-98] 45.00

Episode II, empty.
- ❏ Froot Loops with free mini statue [370-97] 35.00
- ❏ Smacks with free mini statue [370-99] 35.00

Kellogg's (Greece)
Episode I, empty.
- ❏ Choco Krispies 375 g with free mini statue [370-100] 45.00
- ❏ Honey Nut Loops 375 g with free mini statue [370-101] ..45.00
- ❏ Honey Pops with free mini statue [370-102] 45.00

Kellogg's (Israel)
Clone Wars, empty.
- ❏ Coco Pops Chocos 375 g [370-103] 45.00

Kellogg's (Italy)
Episode I 3D, empty.
- ❏ Coco Pops Barchette, 375 g [370-104].........................40.00
- ❏ Coco Pops Palline, 375 g [370-105] 40.00
- ❏ Coco Pops Rotelle, 350 g [370-106] 40.00

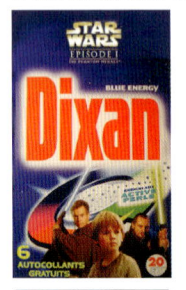        

       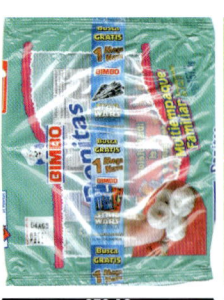 

330

Packaging: Cookies

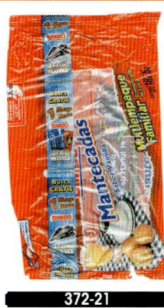

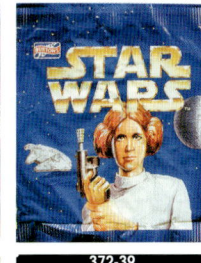

Episode I 3D, empty. Lightsaber spoon premium.
- ❏ Coco Pops Palline, 375 g [370-107] 35.00
- ❏ Coco Pops Riso Ciok, 375 g [370-108] 35.00

Episode I, empty.
- ❏ Chocos [370-109] 30.00
- ❏ Frosties [370-110] 30.00

Kellogg's (Mexico)
- ❏ Episode III: Revenge of the Sith [370-111] 30.00
- ❏ Honey Nut, videos: Making of Star Wars $5.99 .... 35.00

Episode I 3D, empty.
- ❏ Choco Krispis, 30 g [370-112] 25.00
- ❏ Choco Krispis, 180 g [370-113] 25.00
- ❏ Choco Krispis, 40 g [370-114] 25.00
- ❏ Corn Pops, 590 g [370-115] 25.00
- ❏ Froot Loops, 25 g [370-116] 25.00
- ❏ Froot Loops, 735 g [370-117] 25.00
- ❏ Froot Loops, 120 g [370-118] 25.00
- ❏ Froot Loops, 25 g [370-119] 25.00
- ❏ Froot Loops, 25 g 25.00
- ❏ Krave, 300 g [370-120] 25.00
- ❏ Zucaritas, 195 g [370-121] 25.00
- ❏ Zucaritas, 40 g [370-122] 25.00
- ❏ Zucaritas, 35 g [370-123] 25.00

Episode I 3D, empty. Free cards premium.
- ❏ Choco Krispis, 530 g [370-124] 30.00
- ❏ Corn Flakes, 500 g [370-125] 30.00
- ❏ Froot Loops, 350 g [370-126] 30.00
- ❏ Zucaritas, 730 g [370-127] 30.00

Episode I 3D, empty. Lightsaber spoon premium.
- ❏ Choco Krispis, 750 g [370-128] 25.00
- ❏ Corn Flakes, 660 g [370-129] 25.00
- ❏ Froot Loops, 520 g [370-130] 25.00
- ❏ Zucaritas, 950 g [370-131] 25.00

Kellogg's (Spain)
Episode I with free poster on back, empty.
- ❏ Choco Krispies, Anakin's podracer [370-132] 30.00
- ❏ Choco Krispies, Sebulba 30.00
- ❏ Smacks, Darth Maul Naboo [370-133] 30.00
- ❏ Smacks, Darth Maul Tatooine 30.00

Kellogg's (Sweden)
Episode I, empty.
- ❏ Choco Krispies with free mini statue [370-134] ... 30.00
- ❏ Smacks [370-135] 30.00

Kellogg's (Thailand)
Episode III, empty. 2 free gyros promotion.
- ❏ Chocos Chex [370-136] 40.00
- ❏ Coacoa Frosties [370-137] 40.00
- ❏ Cocoa Krispies [370-138] 40.00
- ❏ Corn Flakes [370-139] 40.00
- ❏ Froot Loops [370-140] 40.00
- ❏ Frosties [370-141] 40.00

Kellogg's (UK)
- ❏ 8-pack, variety [370-142] 80.00

Nestlé
Empty.
- ❏ Estrellitas with free coin [370-143] 75.00
- ❏ Nesquik [370-144] 35.00

Nestlé (Argentina)
Episode II, empty.
- ❏ Nesquik 210g [370-145] 30.00

Nestlé (Czechoslovakia)
Episode II, empty. Lenticular card premium.
- ❏ Chocapic [370-146] 30.00
- ❏ Nesquick [370-147] 30.00

Nestlé (Mexico)
Episode II, empty.
- ❏ Cheerios 375 g [370-148] 30.00
- ❏ Chocapic 550 g [370-149] 30.00
- ❏ Crunch 580 g [370-150] 30.00
- ❏ La Lechera Flakes 440 g 30.00
- ❏ La Lechera Flakes 630 g [370-151] 30.00
- ❏ Nesquick 380 g 30.00
- ❏ Nesquick 560 g [370-152] 30.00
- ❏ Nesquik 750 g 30.00
- ❏ Trix 340 g 30.00
- ❏ Trix 480 g [370-153] 30.00
- ❏ Zucosos 660 g [370-154] 30.00

Packaging: Cleaners

Dixan (Belgium)
- ❏ Episode I, Dixan Blue Energy with Active Perls [371-01] .. 50.00

Pine-Sol
- ❏ Pine-Sol bottle with Star Wars Label, 15 oz. [371-02] ... 125.00
- ❏ Pine-Sol bottle with Star Wars Label, 28 oz. [371-03] ... 170.00
- ❏ Pine-Sol bottle with Star Wars Label, 40 oz. [371-04] ... 200.00

Packaging: Cookies
Continued in Volume 3, Page 299

Bimbo (Mexico)
- ❏ Conchas 120 g chocolate [372-01] 10.00
- ❏ Conchas 120 g vanilla [372-02] 10.00
- ❏ Donas 105 g baseball bag [372-03] 10.00
- ❏ Donas 105 g dressed bag [372-04] 10.00
- ❏ Donas 105 g headphones bag [372-05] 10.00
- ❏ Donas 105 g jogging bag [372-06] 10.00
- ❏ Donas 105 g karate bag [372-07] 10.00
- ❏ Donas 105 g soccer bag narrow [372-08] 10.00
- ❏ Donas 105 g soccer bag wide [372-09] 10.00
- ❏ Donitas 105 g dressed bag [372-10] 10.00
- ❏ Donitas 105 g football bag [372-11] 10.00
- ❏ Donitas 105 g headphones bag [372-12] 10.00
- ❏ Donitas 157.5 g blue bag [372-13] 10.00
- ❏ Donitas 157.5 g green bag [372-14] 10.00
- ❏ Madelenas 78 g baseball bag [372-15] 10.00
- ❏ Madelenas 78 g football bag [372-16] 10.00
- ❏ Madelenas 78 g karate bag [372-17] 10.00
- ❏ Madelenas 78 g soccer bag [372-18] 10.00
- ❏ Mantecadas 125 g baseball bag [372-19] 10.00
- ❏ Mantecadas 125 g soccer bag [372-20] 10.00
- ❏ Mantecadas Sabor 187.5 g Vainilla [372-21] 10.00

Packaging: Cookies

372-42

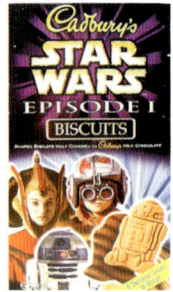
372-43

372-44

372-45

372-46

372-47

372-48

372-49

372-50

372-51

372-52

372-53

❏ Panque con Nueces 270 g [372-22] 10.00
❏ Panque con Pasas 285 g [372-23] 10.00
❏ Panquecitos 140 g [372-24] 10.00
❏ Roles de Canela 385 g [372-25] 10.00

Negrito. Mini figure premium.
❏ Anakin Skywalker [372-26] 15.00
❏ Clone trooper [372-27] 15.00
❏ Darth Vader [372-28] 15.00
❏ General Grievous [372-29] 15.00

❏ Obi-Wan Kenobi [372-30] 15.00
❏ Yoda [372-31] 15.00

Negrito. Star card premium.
❏ Dressed bag, 62 g [372-32] 10.00
❏ Football bag, 62 g [372-33] 10.00
❏ Headphones bag, 62 g [372-34] 10.00

Burtons
❏ Star Wars Biscuits [372-35] 25.00

❏ C-3PO [372-36] 10.00
❏ Darth Vader [372-37] 10.00
❏ Luke Skywalker [372-38] 10.00
❏ Princess Leia [372-39] 10.00
❏ R2-D2 [372-40] 10.00
❏ Yoda [372-41] 10.00
❏ Retail Package [372-42] 20.00

Cadbury
❏ Biscuits, Episode I [372-43] 20.00

372-54

372-55

372-56

372-57

372-58

372-59

372-60

372-61

372-62

Packaging: Cookies

372-63

372-64

372-65

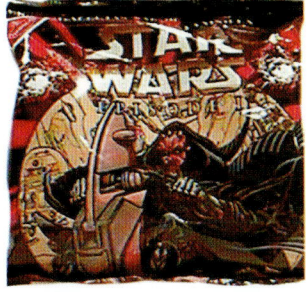
372-66

372-67

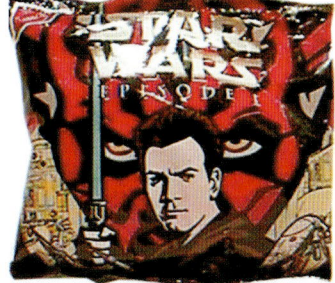
372-68

372-69

372-70

372-71

372-72

372-73

373-04 Side 1 and Side 2

373-05 Side 1 and Side 2

373-06 Side 1 and Side 2

373-07 Side 1 and Side 2

Gamesa
Arcoiris.
- R2-D2 [372-44] 15.00

Chocolate Chokis.
- Episode I: Anakin [372-45] 10.00
- Episode I: Jar Jar [372-46] 10.00
- Episode I: Padmé [372-47] 10.00
- Luke Skywalker [372-48] 12.00

Emperador.
- C-3PO 75 g [372-49] 12.00
- Darth Vader 75 g [372-50] 12.00
- Darth Vader 825 g [372-51] 15.00

Flups.
- Darth Maul [372-52] 10.00
- Obi-Wan [372-53] 10.00
- Queen Amidala 10.00

Merengue.
- Luke Skywalker [372-54] 15.00

Piruetas.
- Darth Vader 15.00
- R2-D2 [372-55] 15.00

Keebler
Cookie jar mail-in premium.
- Chips Deluxe chocolate lovers 15 oz. [372-56] 10.00
- Chips Deluxe original 18 oz. [372-57] 10.00
- ELFudge double stuffed 12 oz. [372-58] 10.00
- ELFudge original 15 oz. [372-59] 10.00
- Fudge Shoppe deluxe grahams 12.5 oz. [372-60] 10.00
- Fudge Shoppe grasshopper 10 oz. [372-61] 10.00
- Fudge Shoppe Lava stripes 11.5 oz. [372-62] 10.00
- Fudge sticks 8.5 oz. [372-63] 10.00
- Grahams cinnamon crisp 14 oz. [372-64] 10.00

373-01 Side 1 and Side 2

373-02 Side 1 and Side 2

373-03 Side 1 and Side 2

373-08 Side 1 and Side 2

373-09 Side 1 and Side 2

Nabisco
- Anakin in podrace helmet 12.00
- C-3PO and R2-D2 [372-65] 12.00
- Darth Maul on Sith speeder [372-66] 12.00
- Jedi vs. Jedi [372-67] 12.00
- Obi-Wan with Maul background [372-68] 12.00
- Trade Federation Battleship [372-69] 12.00

Pepperidge Farms
- Rebel Alliance I, vanilla [372-70] 25.00
- Rebel Alliance II, peanut butter [372-71] 25.00
- The Imperial Forces, chocolate [372-72] 25.00

Williams-Sonoma
- Mini-iced cookies 8.46 oz. [372-73] 5.00

Packaging: Facial Tissues

 374-01
 375-01
 375-02
 375-03
 375-04
 375-05
 375-06

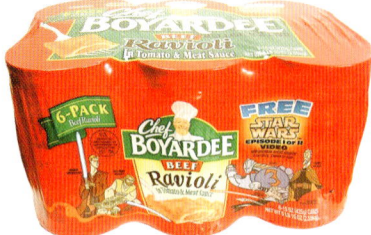 375-07
 375-08
 375-09
 375-10
 375-11

 375-12
 375-13
 375-14
 375-15
 375-16
 375-17
 375-18

Packaging: Facial Tissue
Continued in Volume 3, Page 300

Puffs
Character art on bottom of the box.
- ❏ Bespin, Darth Vader [373-01] 65.00
- ❏ Bespin, Luke Skywalker 65.00
- ❏ Dagobah, R2-D2 [373-02] 65.00
- ❏ Dagobah, Yoda 65.00
- ❏ Hoth, Han Solo [373-03] 65.00
- ❏ Hoth, Princess Leia 65.00

Zewa (Belgium)
Softis.
- ❏ Anakin Skywalker [373-04] 12.00
- ❏ C-3PO [373-05] 12.00
- ❏ Chewbacca [373-06] 12.00
- ❏ Luke Skywalker [373-07] 12.00

- ❏ Qui-Gon Jinn [373-08] 12.00
- ❏ Yoda [373-09] 12.00

Packaging: Food Trays

20th Century Fox
- ❏ Popcorn fold-out Star Wars: Special Edition, Three Reasons Why They Build Movie Theaters [374-01] 25.00

Packaging: Food Wrappers
Continued in Volume 3, Page 301

Burger King
Episode III: Revenge of the Sith. Choose you Destiny game.
- ❏ Fry wrapper, king size [375-01] 8.00
- ❏ Fry wrapper, large [375-02] 8.00
- ❏ Fry wrapper, medium [375-03] 5.00
- ❏ Fry wrapper, small [375-04] 5.00

Episode III: Revenge of the Sith. Paper bags.
- ❏ 17 New Toys to add to your collection [375-05] 15.00
- ❏ Choose Your Destiny Game [375-06] 20.00

ConAgra Foods
Chef Boyardee pasta. Clone Wars promotion. Canned pasta. Beef Ravioli. Padmé Amidala, Yoda, and Count Dooku. 15 oz. Character inside label.
- ❏ 6-pack [375-07] 45.00
- ❏ 8-pack [375-08] 50.00
- ❏ Anakin Skywalker 10.00
- ❏ Asajj Ventress [375-09] 10.00
- ❏ Count Dooku 10.00
- ❏ Obi-Wan Kenobi 10.00
- ❏ Yoda 10.00

 375-19
 375-20
 375-21
 375-22
 375-23
 375-24

 375-25
 375-26
 375-27
 375-28

334

Packaging: Food Wrappers

375-29

375-30

375-31

375-32

375-33

375-34

Beefaroni. Mace Windu and battle droids. 15 oz. Character inside label.
- ❑ Anakin Skywalker [375-10] 10.00
- ❑ Asajj Ventress 10.00
- ❑ Count Dooku 10.00
- ❑ Mace Windu 10.00
- ❑ Obi-Wan Kenobi 10.00
- ❑ Yoda 10.00

Mini Beef Ravioli. C-3PO, R2-D2, and battle droids. 15 oz. Character inside label.
- ❑ Anakin Skywalker [375-11] 10.00
- ❑ Asajj Ventress 10.00
- ❑ Count Dooku 10.00
- ❑ Mace Windu 10.00
- ❑ Obi-Wan Kenobi 10.00
- ❑ Yoda 10.00

Overstuffed Beef Ravioli. Obi-Wan Kenobi and Durge. 15 oz. Character inside label.
- ❑ Anakin Skywalker [375-12] 10.00
- ❑ Asajj Ventress 10.00
- ❑ Count Dooku 10.00
- ❑ Mace Windu 10.00
- ❑ Obi-Wan Kenobi 10.00
- ❑ Yoda 10.00

Spaghetti and Meatballs. Anakin Skywalker and Asajj Ventress. 15 oz. Character inside label.
- ❑ Anakin Skywalker [375-13] 10.00
- ❑ Asajj Ventress 10.00
- ❑ Count Dooku 10.00
- ❑ Mace Windu 10.00
- ❑ Obi-Wan Kenobi 10.00
- ❑ Yoda 10.00

Chef Boyardee pasta. Deep dish meals.
- ❑ Cheese Lover's Lasagna. Padmé Amidala, Yoda, and Count Dooku [375-14]..15.00
- ❑ Cheese Pizza Kit. Anakin Skywalker, and Asajj Ventress [375-15] 15.00
- ❑ Cheesy Burger Macaroni. Durge and Obi-Wan Kenobi [375-16] 15.00
- ❑ Pepperoni and Sausage Rotini. Mace Windu and battle droids. Asajj Ventress [375-17] 15.00

ConAgra Foods (Peru)
- ❑ Act II popcorn 3-pack. Sabor mantequilla., Episode I in 3D—Tazo promotion [375-18]..8.00

Frigo
- ❑ La Guerra de las Galaxias [375-19] 75.00
- ❑ La Guerra de las Galaxias, individual [375-20] 20.00

375-35

375-36

375-37

375-38

375-39

375-40

375-41

375-42

375-43

375-44

375-45

375-46

375-47

375-48

375-49

Packaging: Food Wrappers

375-50 375-51 375-52 375-53 375-54 375-55 375-56 375-57

375-58 375-59 375-60 375-61 375-62 375-63

375-64 375-65 375-66 375-67 375-68 375-69

Heinz (UK)
Star Wars pasta shapes in tomato sauce.
- Darth Maul hologram, 400 g [375-21] 20.00
- Darth Maul, 400 g [375-22] 20.00
- Jar Jar Binks, 205 g [375-23] 20.00
- Starfighters hologram, 205 g [375-24] 20.00

Kellogg's
- Rice Krispies Treats 8-pack, cookie jar offer [375-25] 10.00

Cereal and milk bars 6-pack, cookie jar offer.
- Cocoa Krispies [375-26] 10.00
- Froot Loops [375-27] 10.00
- Frosted Flakes [375-28] 10.00

Eggo. Mail-in plate premium.
- Cinnamon toast 10 sets of 4 [375-29] 10.00
- French toaster sticks 32 sticks [375-30] 10.00

- Homestyle 16-pack [375-31] 10.00
- Minis 10 sets of 4 [375-32] 10.00
- Waf-fulls strawberry 6-pack [375-33] 10.00
- Waffles chocolate chip, 10-pack [375-34] 10.00

LEGO Star Wars II Video Game Promotion.
- Eggo waffles, 8-pack [375-35] 10.00

Pop-Tarts 12-pack, "Listen for Vader Music."
- Brown Sugar Cinnamon [375-36] 10.00
- Chocolate chip [375-37] 10.00
- Frosted blueberry [375-38] 10.00
- Frosted cherry [375-39] 10.00
- Frosted Chocolate Fudge [375-40] 10.00
- Frosted strawberry [375-41] 10.00
- Smores [375-42] 10.00
- Strawberry [375-43] 10.00
- Wild Berry [375-44] 10.00

Pop-Tarts 12-pack.
- Star Wars lava berry [375-45] 10.00

Kellogg's (Australia)
LCMs. 8 bars, 176 g.
- Coco Pops / Kaleidos [375-46] 15.00
- Corn Flakes / Honey [375-47] 15.00
- Rice Bubbles [375-48] 15.00
- Rice Bubbles / Choc Chip [375-49] 15.00

Muesli Bars. 8 bars, 250 g.
- Choc Honeycomb [375-50] 15.00
- Choc Malt [375-51] 15.00
- Choc Vanilla Malt [375-52] 15.00

Individual wrappers.
- Choc Honeycomb [375-53] 5.00
- Choc Malt [375-54] 5.00
- Choc Vanilla Malt [375-55] 5.00

375-70 375-71 375-72 375-73

375-74 375-75 375-76 375-77

Packaging: Food Wrappers

375-78

375-79

375-80

375-81

375-82

375-83

375-84

375-85

Kellogg's (UK)
Cereal and milk bars 6-pack, Episode III sticker dispenser offer.
- Coco Pops [375-56] 10.00
- Frosties [375-57] 10.00
- Rice Krispies [375-58] 10.00

KFC
Carry-out food bags, Defeat the Dark Side.
- Queen Amidala, large 10.00

Paper barrels, Episode I.
- Battle Above Naboo. Large [375-59] 12.00
- Battle Above Naboo. Medium [375-60] 12.00
- Defenders of Naboo. Large [375-61] 12.00
- Defenders of Naboo. Medium [375-62] 12.00
- Ground Assault. Large [375-63] 12.00
- Ground Assault. Medium [375-64] 12.00

- Invasion of Theed. Large [375-65] 12.00
- Invasion of Theed. Medium [375-66] 12.00
- Star Wars Special Edition. Medium [375-67] 20.00

KFC (Australia)
Carryout food packaging.
- Fries box, Jar Jar Binks [375-68] 8.00
- Nugget box, Jar Jar Binks [375-69] 8.00

Kraft Foods
Oscar Mayer Lunchables. Clone Wars Conquest collectible card games.
- Chicken Dunks [375-70] 10.00
- Cracker Stackers, Turkey and American [375-71] ..10.00
- Mini Hot Dogs [375-72] 10.00
- Nachos [375-73] 10.00
- Pizza, Extra Cheesy [375-74] 10.00
- Pizza, Pepperoni [375-75] 10.00

Oscar Mayer Lunchables. Free Clone Wars flip-n-fold card.
- Chicken Dunks [375-76] 10.00
- Cracker Stackers, Ham and American [375-77] 10.00
- Cracker Stackers, Turkey and American [375-78] .10.00
- Mini Hot Dogs [375-79] 10.00
- Nachos [375-80] 10.00
- Pizza, Extra Cheesy [375-81] 10.00
- Pizza, Pepperoni [375-82] 10.00

Oscar Mayer Lunchables. Clone Wars poster on box.
- Chicken Shake-Ups, BBQ [375-83] 10.00
- Cracker Stackers, Bologna and American [375-84]...10.00
- Cracker Stackers, Turkey and Cheddar [375-85] ...10.00
- Mini Bugers [375-86] 10.00
- Pizza and Treatza [375-87] 10.00
- Wrapz, Beef Taco 10.00
- Wrapz, Grilled Chicken [375-88] 10.00

375-86

375-87

375-88

375-89

375-90

375-91 Side 1 and Side 2

375-92 Side 1 and Side 2

375-93 Side 1 and Side 2

375-94 Side 1 and Side 2

375-95 Side 1 and Side 2

375-96 Side 1 and Side 2

375-97 Side 1 and Side 2

Packaging: Food Wrappers

Oscar Mayer Lunchables. Maxed Out. "Get Cloned" promotion.
- ☐ Chicken Strips [375-89].................................10.00
- ☐ Cracker Combo [375-90].................................10.00
- ☐ Deep-dish pizza 10.00
- ☐ Ultimate nachos 10.00

La Serenisima (Argentina)
Serenito 117 g dessert cups. Red or blue lid; any character.
- ☐ Anakin / Benico [375-91].................................15.00
- ☐ Battle droid / Maoui [375-92].................................15.00
- ☐ Darth Maul / Genio [375-93].................................15.00
- ☐ Darth Sidious / Bruno [375-94].................................15.00
- ☐ Jar Jar Binks / Bruno [375-95].................................15.00
- ☐ Maescro Yoda / Chapi [375-96].................................15.00
- ☐ Nute Gunray / Chapi [375-97].................................15.00
- ☐ Obi-Wan Kenobi / Genio [375-98].................................15.00
- ☐ Qui-Gon Jinn / Maoui [375-99].................................15.00
- ☐ Reina Amidala / Maoui [375-100].................................15.00
- ☐ Sebulba / Benito [375-101].................................15.00
- ☐ Watto / Bruno [375-102].................................15.00

Serenito 125 g dessert cups. Glow-in-the-dark.
- ☐ Anakin / Maoui [375-103].................................15.00
- ☐ Baccle droid / Bruno 15.00

La vache qui rit (France)
- ☐ Contains one Episode 1 trading card.................................15.00

Masterfoods USA
Kudos 10-packs.
- ☐ Episode I, variety [375-104].................................10.00
- ☐ Episode II, variety [375-105].................................10.00
- ☐ Episode III, M&Ms Darth Vader, Obi-Wan, Anakin with Anakin card on back [375-106].................................10.00
- ☐ Episode III, M&Ms Yoda, Chewbacca, Obi-Wan [375-107]..10.00
- ☐ Episode IV, Snickers [375-108].................................10.00
- ☐ EPV [375-109].................................10.00
- ☐ EPVI, Peanut butter [375-110].................................10.00

Kudos 40-packs.
- ☐ Episode III, Variety [375-111].................................15.00

Meiji (Japan)
- ☐ Seasoning packets with bonus trading card.................................20.00

Nagatanien
- ☐ Anakin Skywalker—salmon [375-112].................................5.00
- ☐ Battle droid—salmon [375-113].................................5.00
- ☐ C-3PO—salmon [375-114].................................5.00
- ☐ Curry Box, contains individual packets [375-115].................................25.00
- ☐ Darth Maul—okaka [375-116].................................5.00
- ☐ Darth Maul—salmon [375-117].................................5.00

375-98 Side 1 and Side 2 | 375-99 Side 1 and Side 2 | 375-100 Side 1 and Side 2 | 375-101 Side 1 and Side 2

375-102 Side 1 and Side 2 | 375-103 Side 1 and Side 2 | 375-104 | 375-105 | 375-106 | 375-107

375-108 | 375-109 | 375-110 | 375-111 | 375-112 Side 1 and Side 2

375-113 Side 1 and Side 2 | 375-114 Side 1 and Side 2 | 375-115 | 375-116 | 375-117

      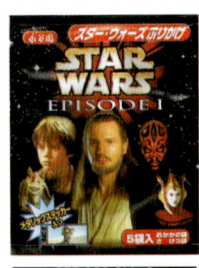

375-118 Side 1 and Side 2 | 375-119 Side 1 and Side 2 | 375-120 Side 1 and Side 2 | 375-121 Side 1

Packaging: Food Wrappers

 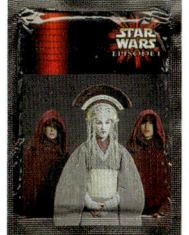     

375-121 Side 2   375-122 Side 1 and Side 2   375-123 Side 1 and Side 2   375-124 Side 1 and Side 2

375-125 Side 1 and Side 2   375-126 Side 1 and Side 2   375-127 Side 1 and Side 2   375-128

- ❑ Darth Sidious—salmon [375-118] 5.00
- ❑ Obi-Wan Kenobi—okaka [375-119] 5.00
- ❑ Obi-Wan Kenobi—salmon [375-120] 5.00
- ❑ Packet, contains food and Episode I sticker [375-121] 15.00
- ❑ Queen Amidala—okaka [375-122] 5.00
- ❑ Queen Amidala (Senate)—salmon [375-123] 5.00
- ❑ Qui-Gon Jinn—okaka [375-124] 5.00
- ❑ R2-D2—salmon [375-125] 5.00
- ❑ Sebulba—salmon [375-126] 5.00
- ❑ Shmi Skywalker—salmon [375-127] 5.00
- ❑ Yoda—okaka [375-128] 5.00

Nestlé
- ❑ Nesquik chocolate milk powder [375-129] 30.00

Nestlé (Philippines)
- ❑ 2-pack Wonder Cup Trilogy Treats with Gentxt download links..15.00

Nicholas and Harris (UK)
- ❑ R2-D2 / X-Wing Fighter cake box [375-130] 15.00

Orchard Hill Farms.
Frozen entrees.
- ❑ Safari Supper, Star Wars offer 50.00
- ❑ Sundown Supper, 9 oz., Star Wars offer......................50.00

Parmalat Food, Inc.
Cheestrings, Episode II Connector Card inside.
- ❑ Cheddar flavor [375-131] 10.00
- ❑ Pizza flavor [375-132] 10.00

Pizza Hut
- ❑ Anakin Skywalker [375-133] 15.00
- ❑ C-3PO 15.00
- ❑ Darth Maul [375-134] 15.00
- ❑ Jar Jar Binks [375-135] 15.00
- ❑ Nute Gunray, New Yorker size [375-136] 15.00
- ❑ Queen Amidala [375-137] 15.00
- ❑ Qui-Gon Jinn..15.00
- ❑ R2-D2, personal size [375-138] 15.00

Episode I: The Phantom Menace. Large—collect all 4 to make mural.
- ❑ Darth Maul [375-139] 20.00
- ❑ Darth Sidious [375-140] 20.00
- ❑ Obi-Wan Kenobi [375-141] 20.00
- ❑ Qui-Gon Jinn [375-142] 20.00

Episode I: The Phantom Menace. Medium—collect all 4 to make mural.
- ❑ Anakin Skywalker [375-143] 20.00
- ❑ C-3PO [375-144] 20.00
- ❑ Jar Jar Binks [375-145] 20.00
- ❑ Queen Amidala [375-146] 20.00

  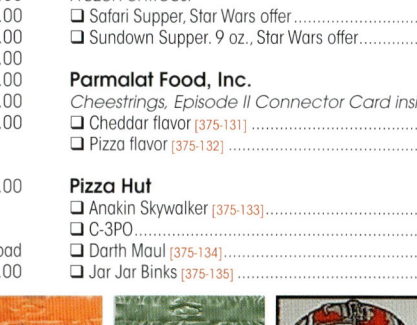   

375-129   375-130   375-131   375-132   375-133   375-134   375-135

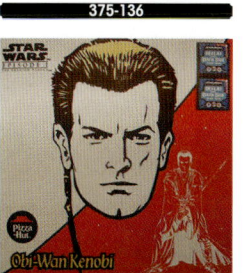 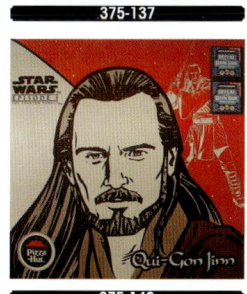   

375-136   375-137   375-138   375-139   375-140

 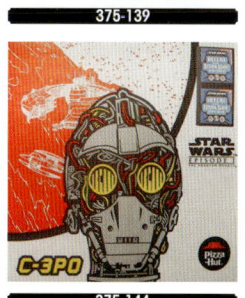 

375-141   375-142   375-143   375-144   375-145

Packaging: Food Wrappers

375-146   375-147   375-148   375-149   375-150   375-151

375-152   375-153   375-154   375-155   375-156   375-157

Star Wars: Special Edition pizza boxes.
- ❏ C-3PO and Millennium Falcon [375-147]........................25.00
- ❏ Darth Vader and Star Destroyer [375-148].....................25.00
- ❏ R2-D2 and X-Wing Fighter [375-149]............................25.00
- ❏ Stormtrooper [375-150]..25.00

Pizza Hut (Australia)
Episode I: The Phantom Menace pizza boxes.
- ❏ Anakin Skywalker [375-151]..15.00
- ❏ Jar Jar Binks [375-152]...15.00
- ❏ Queen Amidala [375-153]...15.00

Star Wars: Special Edition pizza boxes.
- ❏ Bespin Duel [375-154]...15.00
- ❏ Bespin Duel, personal size [375-155]..........................15.00

Pizza Hut (UK)
- ❏ Anakin Skywalker large [375-156]..............................15.00
- ❏ Queen Amidala small [375-157]..................................15.00

ThinkGeek
- ❏ Coffee: Dark Side roast..20.00

Wonder Bread
- ❏ Wonder Bread wrapper with Star Wars trading card premium...50.00

Packaging: Fruit Snacks
Continued in Volume 3, Page 304

Wrappers.
- ❏ .9 oz. blue and white [376-01]....................................1.00
- ❏ .9 oz. red and white [376-02].....................................1.00
- ❏ Erupters, 1.2 oz. green and silver [376-03]..................1.00

ALDI Inc,
- ❏ Lunch Buddies. Six pouches, 5.4 oz. [376-04]............10.00

Associated Wholesale Grocers, Inc.
- ❏ Best Choice. Six pouches, 5.4 oz. [376-05]................10.00

Betty Crocker
- ❏ Jedi Berry Blast, six rolls, magic motion sticker [376-06]..10.00

Backpack tag premium.
- ❏ Fruit By The Foot, Anakin Skywalker [376-07]..............12.00
- ❏ Fruit By The Foot, Mace Windu [4-218]......................12.00
- ❏ Fruit By The Foot, Obi-Wan Kenobi [4-218]................12.00
- ❏ Fruit By The Foot, Yoda [4-218].................................12.00
- ❏ Fruit Roll-Ups, Anakin Skywalker [4-218]...................12.00
- ❏ Fruit Roll-Ups, Mace Windu [376-08].........................12.00
- ❏ Fruit Roll-Ups, Obi-Wan Kenobi [4-218].....................12.00
- ❏ Fruit Roll-Ups, Yoda [v1e1:328]................................12.00

Star Wars Blu-ray promotion.
- ❏ Fruit By The Foot, six 0.75 oz. rolls [376-09]..............10.00
- ❏ Fruit Roll-Ups, 18 0.37 oz. rolls [376-10]...................10.00

     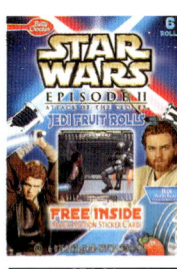 

376-01   376-02   376-03   376-04   376-05   376-06   376-07

       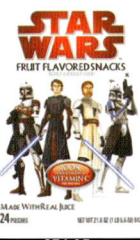

376-08   376-09   376-10 Side 1 and Side 2   376-11   376-12   376-13   376-14   376-15

376-16   376-17   376-18   376-19   376-20   376-21   376-22   376-23

Packaging: Fruit Snacks

376-24 | 376-25 | 376-26 Box | 376-26 Pouch | 376-27 | 376-28 | 376-29

  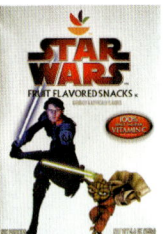     

376-30 | 376-31 | 376-32 | 376-33 | 376-34 | 376-35 | 376-36 | 376-37

Empty wrappers.
- Anakin Skywalker [v1e1:328] 3.00
- Barriss Offee [v1e1:328] 3.00
- Luke Skywalker [376-11] 3.00
- Luminara Unduli [v1e1:328] 3.00
- Mace Windu [376-12] 3.00
- Obi-Wan Kenobi [v1e1:328] 3.00
- Stass Allie [v1e1:328] 3.00
- Yoda [376-13] 3.00

Fruit By The Foot. Fruit strip backing. Jedi trivia / facts.
- Are You A Star Wars Star? 3.00
- Asteroid Evasion 3.00
- Build Your Own Lightsaber 3.00
- Droid Match 3.00
- Name the Alien 3.00
- Who Said it? (classic trilogy) 3.00
- Who Said It? (prequel) 3.00

Jedi Berry Blast. Fruit strip backing. Jedi trivia / facts.
- Jango Fett [4:219] 3.00
- Jango Fett's Gun 3.00
- Jedi Starfighter [4:219] 3.00
- Mace Windu's Lightsaber [4:219] 3.00

Big Y
- Six pouches, 5.4 oz., box only 10.00

ConAgra Foods
- Classic trilogy, single pouch, 4.5 oz [376-14] 10.00
- Clone Wars, 24 pouches, 21.6 oz. [376-15] 15.00
- Episode I, single pouch, 4.5 oz [376-16] 10.00
- Episode I, 24 pouches, 21.6 oz. [376-17] 15.00
- Kids Classics. Five pouches, 4.0 oz. 10.00
- Kids Classics. Five pouches, 4.5 oz. [376-18] 10.00
- Kids Classics. Six pouches, 4.8 oz. 10.00
- Kids Classics. Six pouches, 5.4 oz. 10.00

Dolgencorp, LLC
Clover Valley.
- Five pouches, 4 oz 10.00
- Five pouches, 4 oz., Star Wars [376-19] 10.00
- Five pouches, 4.5 oz., box only [376-20] 10.00

Favorite Brands International, Inc.
Farley's.
- Fruit Snacks, 0.9 oz. single pouch 1.00
- Fruit Snacks, box 10 pouches 9 oz. [376-21] 10.00
- Fruit Snacks, box 36 pouches 32.4 oz. [376-22] 15.00
- Fruit Snacks, Fruit Punch flavor, bag 2.25 oz. [376-23] 3.00
- Fruit Snacks, Tropical Fruit flavor, bag 2.25 oz. [376-24] 3.00
- Glitter Roll, Galactic Watermelon flavor, 8 pouches 5 oz. [376-25] 10.00
- Mega-duals, 1.1 oz. single pouch 1.00
- Mega-duals, box 8 pouches 8.8 oz. [376-26] 10.00

  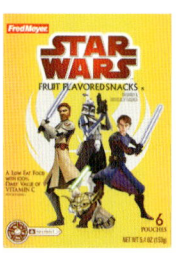     

376-38 | 376-39 | 376-40 | 376-41 | 376-42 Side 1 and Side 2 | 376-43 Side 1 and Side 2

     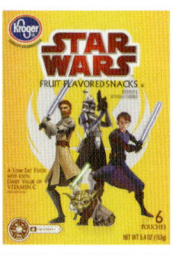  

376-44 Side 1 and Side 2 | 376-45 | 376-46 | 376-47 | 376-48 | 376-49 | 376-50

      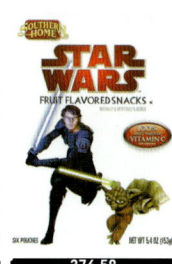

376-51 | 376-52 | 376-53 | 376-54 | 376-55 | 376-56 | 376-57 | 376-58

Packaging: Fruit Snacks

 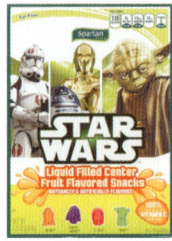      

376-59 | 376-60 | 376-61 | 376-62 | 376-63 | 376-64 | 376-65 | 376-66

 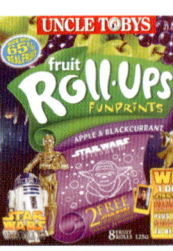  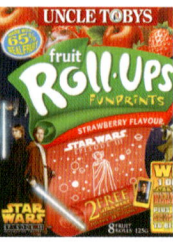    

376-67 | 376-68 | 376-69 | 376-70 | 376-71 | 376-72 | 376-73 | 376-74

Farley's. Sales samples with "Top Secret" art removed from package.
- Fruit Snacks, box 10 pouches 9 oz. [376-27] 50.00
- Glitter Roll, Galactic Watermelon flavor, box 8 pouches 5 oz. [376-28] 50.00
- Mega-duals, box 8 pouches 8.8 oz. [376-29] 50.00

Federated Group Inc.
- Hy-Top. Six pouches, 4.8 oz. [376-30] 10.00
- Hy-Top. Six pouches, 5.4 oz. 10.00

Food Lion
- Food Lion. Six pouches, 4.8 oz. [376-31] 10.00
- Food Lion. Six pouches, 5.4 oz. 10.00

Foodhold USA LLC
- Giant / Stop N Shop. Six pouches, 5.4 oz. [376-32] 10.00
- Giant / Stop N Shop. Six pouches, 5.4 oz. [376-33] 10.00

Giant
- Carlisle. Six pouches, 5.4 oz. 10.00
- Landover. Six pouches, 4.8 oz. 10.00
- Landover. Twenty pouches, 16 oz. 10.00

Giant Eagle, Inc.
- Giant Eagle. Six pouches, 5.4 oz. [376-34] 10.00

H-E-B
- Hill County Fare. Six pouches, 5.4 oz. [376-35] 10.00

Harris Teeter
- Six pouches, 4.8 oz. [376-36] 10.00

Hy-Vee
- Hy-Vee. Six pouches, 5.4 oz. [376-37] 10.00

IGA, inc.
- IGA. Six pouches, 4.8 oz. [376-38] 10.00

Ingles Markets, Inc.
- Laura Lynn. Six pouches, 4.8 oz. [376-39] 10.00

Inter-American Products
- Fred Meyer. Six pouches, 5.4 oz. [376-40] 10.00
- Ralph's. Six pouches, 5.4 oz. [376-41] 10.00

Kellogg's
Fruit Snacks, 10 0.9 oz. packets.
- Darth Vader and Anakin Skywalker [376-42] 15.00
- Darth Vader and droids [376-43] 15.00
- Darth Vader and droids, print sample [376-44] 35.00
- Packet, empty [376-45] 1.00

Kroger
- Fred Meyer. Six pouches, 4.8 oz. [376-46] 10.00
- Kroger. Six pouches, 4.8 oz. 10.00
- Kroger. Six pouches, 4.8 oz., blue background featuring A New Hope art and The Phantom Menace art [376-47] 10.00
- Kroger. Six pouches, 5.4 oz. [376-48] 10.00

Meijer Distribution Inc.
- Meijer. Six pouches, 5.4 oz. [376-49] 10.00

Nash Finch Company
- Our Family. Six pouches, 5.4 oz. [376-50] 10.00

Onpoint Inc.
- America's Choice. Six pouches, 5.4 oz. [376-51] 10.00

Price Chopper Inc.
- Price Chopper. Six pouches, 4.8 oz. [376-52] 10.00
- Price Chopper. Six pouches, 5.4 oz. 10.00

Publix Super Markets
- Publix. Six pouches, 5.4 oz. [376-53] 10.00

Roundy's Supermarkets Inc.
- Roundy's. Six pouches, 5.4 oz. [376-54] 10.00

Safeway
- Ten pouches, 8 oz. 10.00
- Twenty pouches, 16 oz. [376-55] 15.00

Save-A-Lot Food Stores, Ltd.
- Market Selections Erupters, 6 pouches, 7.2 oz. [376-56] ..15.00

Schnuck Markets Inc.
- Schnucks. Six pouches, 5.4 oz. [376-57] 10.00

Southern Home
- Six pouches, 5.4 oz. [376-58] 10.00

Spartan Stores Distribution LLC
- Spartan. Six pouches, 4.8 oz. 10.00
- Spartan. Six pouches, 5.4 oz. [376-59] 10.00
- Star Wars Erupters. Six pouches, 7.2 oz. [376-60] 10.00

Stater Bros
- Stater. Six pouches, 4.8 oz. [376-61] 10.00
- Stater. Six pouches, 5.4 oz. 10.00

SuperValu Inc.
- Acme. Six pouches, 5.4 oz. [376-62] 10.00
- Albertsons. Six pouches, 5.4 oz. [376-63] 10.00
- Essential Everyday. Six pouches, 4.8 oz. 10.00
- Essential Everyday. Six pouches, 5.4 oz. [376-64] 10.00
- Flavorite. Six pouches, 5.4 oz. [376-65] 10.00
- Jewel. Six pouches, 5.4 oz. [376-66] 10.00
- Shop 'n Save. Six pouches, 5.4 oz. [376-67] 10.00
- Six pouches, 5.4 oz. 10.00

The Uncle Toby's Company (Australia)
Fruit Roll-Ups Fun Prints.
- Apple and Black Currant, 8-pack [376-68] 15.00
- Strawberry, 20-pack [376-69] 15.00
- Strawberry, 8-pack [376-70] 15.00

Topco Associates LLC
- Food Club. Six pouches, 4.8 oz. [376-71] 10.00
- Food Club. Six pouches, 5.4 oz. 10.00
- Shur Fine. Six pouches, 5.4 oz. [376-72] 10.00

Western Family Foods, Inc.
- Shur Fine. Six pouches, 4.8 oz. 10.00
- Shur Fine. Six pouches, 5.4 oz. [376-73] 10.00

Winn-Dixie Stores. Inc.
- Winn Dixie. Six pouches, 5.4 oz. [376-74] 10.00

Packaging: Gum
Continued in Volume 3, Page 306

Bondy Fiesta (Mexico)
80-piece retail box; sticker premiums.
- Captain Rex 65.00
- Yoda [377-01] 65.00

377-01 | 377-02 | 377-03 Sample 1 (#14) | 377-04 Sample 2 (#21) | 377-05 All Four Wrappers Shown

Packaging: Kids Meals

378-01 | 378-02 | 378-03 | 378-04 | 378-05 | 378-06 | 378-07 | 378-08

378-09 | 378-10 | 378-11 | 378-12 | 378-13 | 378-14 | 378-15 | 378-16 | 378-17 | 378-18 | 378-19 | 378-20 | 378-21

378-22 | 378-23 | 378-24 | 378-25 | 378-26 and Treat Reference

Kent (Turkey)
- ❏ Super bubble gum [377-02] 8.00

Topps
Mini poster wrapped inside gum package. Set of 56. Numbered. Full set with images in 4th edition, page 219.
- ❏ Mini posters 1–56, each [377-03] 10.00
- ❏ Unopened package, any of 4 wrappers: Han Solo, Darth Vader, Luke Skywalker, Princess Leia, each [377-04] 30.00

Packaging: Ice Cream
Continued in Volume 3, Page 306

Akagi (Japan)
Episode I 3D promotion.
- ❏ Darth Maul [378-01] 12.00
- ❏ Obi-Wan Kenobi [378-02] 12.00
- ❏ R2-D2 [378-03] 12.00

Blue Bunny
- ❏ Darth Vader frozen confection with gumball eyes box [378-04] 20.00
- ❏ Darth Vader frozen confection with gumball eyes wrapper [378-05] 5.00
- ❏ Star Wars bomb pop individual wrapper [378-06] 5.00
- ❏ Star Wars bomb pop package [378-07] 20.00

Campina Ijsfabbrieken
- ❏ Return of the Jedi promotion on wrapper [378-08] 10.00

Lyons Maid (UK)
- ❏ FAB 8-pack with Star Wars tattoo inside [378-09] 25.00

Ice Lolly wrappers, Star Wars.
- ❏ Artoo-Detoo R2-D2 [378-10] 45.00
- ❏ Chewbacca [378-11] 45.00
- ❏ Darth Vader [378-12] 45.00
- ❏ See-Threepio C-3PO [378-13] 45.00
- ❏ Stormtroopers [378-14] 45.00
- ❏ Tusken Raiders [378-15] 45.00

Ice Lolly wrappers, The Empire Strikes Back.
- ❏ Boba Fett [378-16] 45.00
- ❏ Darth Vader [378-17] 45.00
- ❏ Lando Calrissian [378-18] 45.00
- ❏ Princess Leia Organa [378-19] 45.00
- ❏ Tauntaun [378-20] 45.00
- ❏ Yoda [378-21] 45.00

Masterfoods USA
- ❏ M&M's cookie ice cream sandwiches 6-pack [378-22] ..10.00
- ❏ M&M's ice cream cones 6-pack [378-23] 10.00

Pauls
- ❏ Return of the Jedi with Jedi Jelly [378-24] 125.00
- ❏ Star Wars popsicle 10-pack [378-25] 150.00

Wells (UK)
- ❏ Battle droid Ice package [378-26] 60.00

Packaging: Kids Meals
Continued in Volume 3, Page 306

Burger Chef
Funmeal trays.
- ❏ C-3PO droid puppet [379-01] 150.00
- ❏ Darth Vader card game [379-02] 350.00
- ❏ Flight game with spinner [379-03] 250.00
- ❏ Landspeeder [379-04] 200.00
- ❏ R2-D2 droid puppet [379-05] 150.00
- ❏ TIE Fighter [379-06] 200.00
- ❏ X-Wing Fighter [379-07] 200.00

Burger King
Episode III: Revenge of the Sith.
- ❏ Anakin Skywalker [379-08] 45.00
- ❏ Darth Vader [379-09] 45.00
- ❏ General Grievous [379-10] 60.00
- ❏ Yoda [379-11] 45.00

Burger King (Argentina)
Episode III: Revenge of the Sith.
- ❏ Darth Vader / Yoda [379-12] 30.00

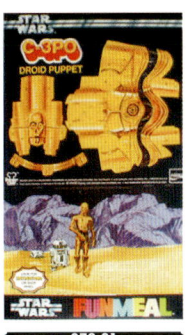  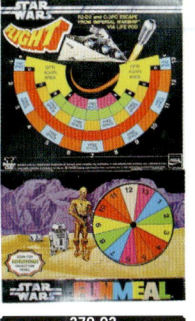 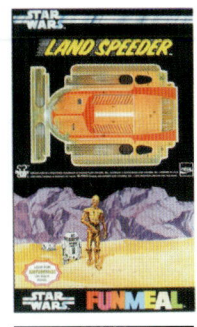   

379-01 | 379-02 | 379-03 | 379-04 | 379-05 | 379-06 | 379-07

343

Packaging: Kids Meals

379-08 | 379-09 | 379-10 | 379-11

379-12 Side 1 | 379-12 Side 2 | 379-13 | 379-14 | 379-15

379-16 | 379-17 Side 1 | 379-17 Side 2 | 379-18 Side 1 | 379-18 Side 2

KFC
- Tatooine, Coruscant & Naboo on box 15.00

KFC (Australia)
- Star Wars: Special Edition 40.00
- Star Wars: Special Edition, toy inside [379-13] 45.00

- Star Wars: The Phantom Menace 20.00
- Star Wars: The Phantom Menace, toy inside 25.00

KFC (Mexico)
- Star Wars: The Phantom Menace [379-14] 15.00
- Star Wars: The Phantom Menace, bucket style [379-15] ..15.00

McDonald's
- Clone Wars 2011 [379-16] 15.00
- Episode I 3D 2012 [379-17] 15.00

Clone Wars.
- C-3PO [379-18] 15.00
- Captain Rex [379-19] 15.00
- Darth Vader [379-20] 15.00
- Yoda [379-21] 15.00

McDonald's (Canada)
- Clone Wars 15.00

McDonald's (Israel)
- Clone Wars [379-22] 25.00

McDonald's (Mexico)
- Clone Wars [379-23] 15.00

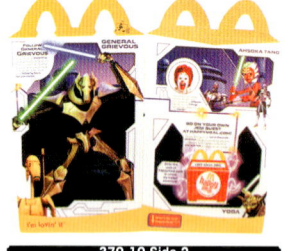  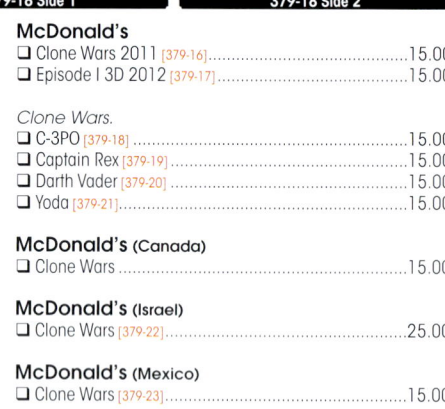

379-19 Side 1 | 379-19 Side 2 | 379-20 Side 1

379-20 Side 2 | 379-21 Side 1 | 379-21 Side 2 | 379-22 Side 1 | 379-22 Side 2

379-23 Side 1 | 379-23 Side 2 | 379-24 Side 1 | 379-24 Side 2 | 379-25

380-01 | 380-02 | 380-03 | 380-04 | 381-01 | 381-02 | 381-03 | 381-04 | 381-05

McDonald's (UK)
❑ 2009 Explore the Galaxy..25.00
❑ 2011 Clone Wars..20.00

Quick Restaurants (France)
❑ Star Wars Magic Box package [379-24]........................30.00

Taco Bell
Fun Meal boxes.
❑ Empire Strikes Back..20.00
❑ Return of the Jedi [379-25]..20.00
❑ Star Wars..20.00

Packaging: Margarine

Doriana (Argentina)
El Regreso del Jedi character cutout lids.
❑ C-3PO [380-01]..45.00
❑ R2-D2 [380-02]..45.00
❑ Wicket the Ewok [380-03]..45.00
❑ Yoda [380-04]..45.00

Packaging: Nuts

Sabritas (Mexico)
Star Wars Special Edition / Feel the Force.
❑ Cacahuates, Bontana Surtida [381-01]........................12.00
❑ Cacahuates, con Limon [381-02]..12.00
❑ Cacahuates, Enchilados [381-03]..12.00
❑ Cacahuates, Estilo Japones [381-04]........................12.00
❑ Pepitas [381-05]..12.00

Packaging: Paper Cups
Continued in Volume 3, Page 306

Dixie / Northern Inc.
Empire Strikes Back.
❑ AT-AT and Snowspeeder [382-01]........................50.00
❑ Darth Vader [382-02]..50.00
❑ Luke on Tauntaun [382-03]..50.00
❑ Millennium Falcon [382-04]..50.00
❑ Star Destroyer [382-05]..50.00
❑ Twin-pod Cloud Car [382-06]..50.00
❑ X-Wing in Swamp [382-07]..50.00
❑ Yoda [382-08]..50.00

Empire Strikes Back. $1.00 cash refund offer.
❑ AT-AT and Snowspeeder [382-09]........................60.00
❑ Darth Vader [382-10]..60.00
❑ Luke on Tauntaun..60.00
❑ Millennium Falcon..60.00
❑ Star Destroyer..60.00
❑ Twin-pod Cloud Car..60.00
❑ X-Wing in Swamp [382-11]..60.00
❑ Yoda [382-12]..60.00

Non-Star Wars. Empire Strikes Back story cards.
❑ Beverage flavor collection, 40 9 oz. cups. Eight total non-Star Wars cup designs..40.00
❑ Beverage flavor collection, 80 9 oz. cups. Eight total non-Star Wars cup designs [382-13]..35.00
❑ Floral collection. Beige color theme, 100 3oz. cups....40.00
❑ Floral collection. Beige color theme, 200 3oz. cups....40.00
❑ Floral collection. Blue, yellow, pink color theme, 100 3 oz. cups..40.00
❑ Floral collection. Blue, yellow, pink color theme, 200 3 oz. cups..40.00
❑ Floral collection. Yellow and orange theme., 100 3 oz. cups..40.00
❑ Floral collection. Yellow and orange theme., 200 3 oz. cups [382-14]..35.00
❑ Fresh Herbs Designer Collection, 100 5 oz. cups [382-15]..35.00
❑ Fresh Herbs Designer Collection, 50 5 oz. cups [382-16]..35.00
❑ Plant collection, 100 3 oz. cups..40.00
❑ Plant collection, 200 3 oz. cups..40.00

Return of the Jedi.
❑ B-Wing, Luke Skywalker and Yoda [382-17]....................45.00
❑ Darth Vader, Emperor, Emperor's Royal Guard [382-18]..45.00
❑ Ewoks [382-19]..45.00
❑ Jabba the Hutt and Princess Leia [382-20]....................45.00

Return of the Jedi. Bilingual Canadian packaging.
❑ B-Wing, Luke Skywalker and Yoda..50.00
❑ Darth Vader, Emperor, Emperor's Royal Guard [382-21]..50.00
❑ Ewoks..50.00
❑ Jabba the Hutt and Princess Leia [382-22]....................50.00

382-01 | 382-02 | 382-03 | 382-04 | 382-05 | 382-06 | 382-07 | 382-08 | 382-09 | 382-10 | 382-11 | 382-12

382-13 | 382-14 | 382-15 | 382-16 | 382-17 | 382-18 | 382-19 | 382-20 | 382-21 | 382-22 | 382-23 | 382-24 | 382-25

382-26 | 382-27 | 382-28 | 382-29 | 382-30 | 382-31 | 382-32 | 382-33 | 382-34 | 382-35 | 382-36 | 382-37 | 382-38

Packaging: Kids Meals

383-03

383-01

383-02

383-04

383-05

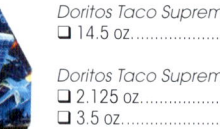
383-06

383-07

383-08

383-09

Star Wars Saga.
- ❑ C-3PO and R2-D2 [382-23] 70.00
- ❑ Darth Vader [382-24] 70.00
- ❑ Han Solo, Princess Leia and stormtroopers [382-25] 70.00
- ❑ Luke Skywalker and Yoda [382-26] 70.00

Star Wars Saga. Win a Movie Party with Darth Vader.
- ❑ C-3PO and R2-D2 [382-27] 85.00
- ❑ Darth Vader [382-28] 85.00
- ❑ Han Solo, Princess Leia and stormtroopers [382-29] 80.00
- ❑ Luke Skywalker and Yoda [382-30] 80.00

Star Wars.
- ❑ Chewbacca and Han Solo [382-31] 100.00
- ❑ Darth Vader [382-32] 100.00
- ❑ Death Star, TIE Fighter and X-Wing Fighter [382-33] 100.00
- ❑ Droids [382-34] 100.00
- ❑ Luke Skywalker [382-35] 100.00
- ❑ Obi-Wan Kenobi [382-36] 100.00
- ❑ Princess Leia [382-37] 100.00
- ❑ Stormtrooper [382-38] 100.00

Packaging: Shoes
Continued in Volume 3, Page 307

Buster Brown and Co.
Shoeboxes.
- ❑ Episode II [383-01] 10.00
- ❑ Episode II with free sunglasses 15.00
- ❑ Episode III toddler 10.00
- ❑ Episode III youth 10.00
- ❑ Episode III, Saga design 10.00

Kid Nation
- ❑ Darth Vader [383-02] 25.00
- ❑ Episode I shoebox [383-03] 15.00
- ❑ Stormtrooper [383-04] 20.00

Stride Rite
Shoe bag.
- ❑ Clarks shoes [383-05] 50.00

Shoeboxes.
- ❑ Return of the Jedi images [383-06] 35.00
- ❑ Star Wars MTFBWY 30.00
- ❑ X-Wings, Empire Strikes Back [383-07] 70.00
- ❑ X-Wings, Star Wars [383-08] 65.00

Vans
- ❑ Poster Art show box [383-09] 25.00

Packaging: Snack Chips
Continued in Volume 3, Page 307

Chiro (Hungary)
Master Croc. Episode II trading card inside. Blue strip.
- ❑ Foldimogyoros 10.00
- ❑ Grill 10.00
- ❑ Pizza 10.00
- ❑ Pizza [384-01] 10.00
- ❑ Sajtos 10.00

Master Croc. Episode II trading card inside. Gold strip.
- ❑ Foldimogyoros [384-02] 10.00
- ❑ Pizza 10.00
- ❑ Sajtos 10.00

Frito Lay
Cheetos with one 3D motion card free inside.
- ❑ 13.5 oz. 10.00
- ❑ 15.5 oz. 10.00

Doritos Cooler Ranch with one 3D motion card inside.
- ❑ 14.5 oz. 10.00

Doritos Nacho Cheesier 3Ds with game card inside.
- ❑ 10 oz. 10.00
- ❑ 2.5 oz. 10.00
- ❑ 6 oz. 10.00

Doritos Nacho Cheesier R2-D2 with game card inside.
- ❑ 14.5 oz. 10.00
- ❑ 25 oz. 10.00
- ❑ 3.5 oz. 10.00

Doritos Nacho Cheesier with 3D motion card inside.
- ❑ 14.5 oz. 10.00

Doritos Nacho Cheesier with one motion disc inside.
- ❑ 2.125 oz. [384-03] 10.00
- ❑ 3.5 oz. 10.00

Doritos Pizza Cravers with one 3D motion card inside.
- ❑ 14.5 oz. 10.00

Doritos Pizza Cravers with one motion disc inside.
- ❑ 2.125 oz. 10.00
- ❑ 3.5 oz. 10.00

Doritos Smokey Red BBQ Qui-Gon Jinn graphic.
- ❑ 14.5 oz. with game card inside 10.00
- ❑ 3.5 oz. 10.00

Doritos Taco Supreme with 3D motion card inside.
- ❑ 14.5 oz. 10.00

Doritos Taco Supreme with one motion disc inside.
- ❑ 2.125 oz. 10.00
- ❑ 3.5 oz. 10.00

Episode II: Attack of the Clones with character pictures on package.
- ❑ Doritos Cooler Ranch 13.5 oz., Mace Windu and Jango [384-04] 10.00
- ❑ Doritos Nacho Cheese 13.5 oz., Anakin and Padmé [384-05] 10.00
- ❑ Doritos Spicier Nacho 13.5 oz., clone trooper [384-06] ..10.00
- ❑ Lays Classic 12.25 oz., Anakin and Padmé [384-07] 10.00
- ❑ Lays Classic 5.5 oz., Anakin and Padmé 10.00
- ❑ Lays KC Masterpiece Barbecue 12.25 oz., Obi-Wan and Jango [384-08] 10.00
- ❑ Lays Sour Cream and Onion 12.25 oz., Yoda and Obi-Wan [384-09] 10.00
- ❑ Lays Sour Cream and Onion 5.5 oz., Yoda and Obi-Wan 10.00
- ❑ Lays Wavy 12.25 oz., C-3PO and R2-D2 [384-10] 10.00
- ❑ Ruffles BBQ Blast 7 oz., Jango Fett [384-11] ..10.00
- ❑ Ruffles Cheddar Sour Cream 7 oz., Yoda [384-12] 10.00
- ❑ Ruffles Original 12.25 oz., Anakin and Obi-Wan [384-13] .10.00

Episode II: Attack of the Clones. 3D Star Pic premium in package.
- ❑ 3D's Doritos Jalipino Cheddar 7 oz. [384-14] ...10.00
- ❑ 3D's Doritos Nacho Cheesier 7 oz. [384-15] 10.00
- ❑ 3D's Doritos Zesty Ranch 7 oz. [384-16] 10.00
- ❑ 3D's Ruffles BBQ Blast 7 oz. [384-17] 10.00
- ❑ 3D's Ruffles Maximum Cheddar 7 oz. [384-18] ...10.00
- ❑ 3D's Ruffles Supreme Sour Cream and Onion 7 oz. 10.00
- ❑ Cheetos Crunchy 12-pack [384-19] 10.00
- ❑ Cheetos Crunchy 9.5 oz. [384-20] 10.00
- ❑ Cheetos Flamin' Hot 9.5 oz. [384-21] 10.00
- ❑ Cheetos Puffs 11 oz. [384-22] 10.00
- ❑ Cheetos Puffs 12-pack 10.00
- ❑ Cheetos X's and O's 10.00
- ❑ Cracker Jack [384-23] 10.00
- ❑ Doritos Cooler Ranch 12-pack [384-24] 10.00
- ❑ Doritos Nacho Cheesier 12-pack [384-25] 10.00
- ❑ Funyuns 12-pack [384-26] 10.00
- ❑ Lay's Planet Lunch 24-pack box with two premiums ...10.00

Episode III: Revenge of the Sith with character pictures on package.
- ❑ Assortment bag 24-pack, Darth Vader graphic [384-27] ..15.00
- ❑ Assortment bag 24-pack, TIE Fighter graphic [384-28] ...15.00
- ❑ Assortment bag 24-pack, X-Wing Fighter graphic [384-29] 15.00
- ❑ Cheetos crunchy 1 oz., C-3PO 10.00
- ❑ Cheetos crunchy 1 oz., General Grievous 10.00
- ❑ Cheetos crunchy 1 oz., Wicket 10.00
- ❑ Cheetos twisted 2 5/8 oz., Darth Vader and Yoda 10.00
- ❑ Cheetos twisted 9.5 oz., Darth Vader and Yoda 10.00
- ❑ Doritos cooler ranch 1 oz., Han Solo 15.00
- ❑ Doritos cooler ranch 1 oz., Princess Leia 10.00
- ❑ Doritos cooler ranch 1 oz., R2-D2 [384-30] 10.00
- ❑ Fritos original 1 oz., Luke 10.00
- ❑ Fritos original 1 oz., Obi-Wan 10.00
- ❑ Fritos original 1 oz., Yoda 10.00
- ❑ Lay's classic 11.5 oz., Star Wars sticker premium [384-31] 10.00
- ❑ Lay's classic 1 oz., Anakin Skywalker (young) ...10.00
- ❑ Lay's classic 1 oz., Chewbacca [384-32] 10.00
- ❑ Lay's classic 1 oz., Padmé 10.00
- ❑ Lay's wavy 11.5 oz., Star Wars sticker premium [384-33] ..10.00

Lay's Classic Potato Chips Anakin Skywalker photo
- ❑ 12.25 oz. 10.00
- ❑ 13.25 oz. with game card inside 10.00

Packaging: Snack Chips

    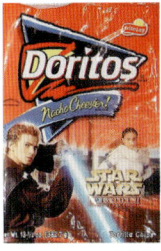    

384-01　384-02　384-03　384-04　384-05　384-06　384-07　384-08　384-09

384-10　384-11　384-12　384-13　384-14　384-15　384-16　384-17　384-18

❏ 3 oz. 10.00
❏ 5.5 oz. 10.00
❏ 5.5 oz. with game card inside 10.00
❏ 7.5 oz. 10.00

Lay's Ketchup-flavored chips with Episode I card offer.
❏ 70 g [384-34] 10.00

Lay's Pizza Flavored Potato Chips with Obi-Wan Kenobi action figure offer.
❏ 1.75 oz. 15.00
❏ 14 oz. 15.00
❏ 3.25 oz. 15.00
❏ 6 oz. 15.00
❏ 9 oz. 15.00

Lay's Potato Chips with Obi-Wan Kenobi action figure offer
❏ 1.75 oz. 15.00
❏ 14 oz. 15.00

❏ 3.25 oz. 15.00
❏ 6 oz. 15.00
❏ 9 oz. 15.00

Lay's Salt and Vinegar Potato Chips Jar Jar Binks photo.
❏ 13.5 oz. with game card inside 10.00
❏ 5.5 oz. with game card inside 10.00
❏ 7.5 oz. 10.00

Lay's Salt and Vinegar Potato Chips R2-D2 photo.
❏ 50 g with game card inside [384-35] 10.00

Lay's Sour Cream & Onion Chips Queen Amidala photo.
❏ 13.5 oz. with game card inside 10.00
❏ 3 oz. 10.00
❏ 5.5 oz. with game card inside 10.00
❏ 7.5 oz. 10.00

Lay's Stax.
❏ Cheddar, 5.75 oz. [384-36] 10.00

❏ Dill Pickle, 5.75 oz. [384-37] 10.00
❏ Original, 6 oz. [384-38] 10.00

Lay's Toasted Onion & Cheese Chips Obi-Wan photo.
❏ 13.5 oz. with game card inside 10.00
❏ 3 oz. 10.00
❏ 5.5 oz. with game card inside 10.00

Multi-pack boxes with adventure game printed inside box with cut-out game pieces on insert card.
❏ A New Hope 15.00
❏ Empire Strikes Back 15.00
❏ Return of the Jedi 15.00

Frito Lay (Thailand)
❏ Cheetos, Star Wars Special Edition [384-39] 15.00

Matutano Snack Ventures (Spain)
Boca bits. Queen Amidala package.
❏ 15 g with Jar Jar toy offer on back 10.00

    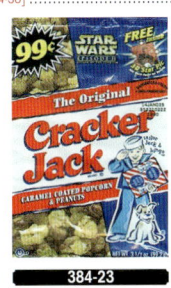   

384-19　384-20　384-21　384-22　384-23　384-24　384-25　384-26

  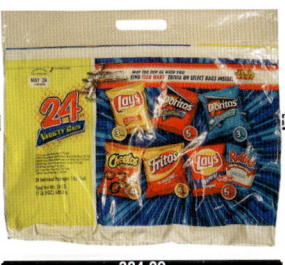   

384-27　384-28　384-29　384-30　384-31　384-32

384-33　384-34　384-35　384-36 Sides 1 and 2　384-37 Sides 1 and 2　384-38 Sides 1 and 2　384-39　384-40　384-41

Packaging: Snack Chips

❑ 27 g [384-40] 10.00
❑ 50 g 10.00
Bugles 3-D's with Jar Jar Binks package.
❑ 36 g [384-41] 10.00
❑ 65 g 10.00
❑ 85 g 10.00
Cheetos Pandilla with Anakin Skywalker package.
❑ 14 g with Jar Jar toy offer on back 10.00
❑ 31 g [384-42] 10.00
❑ 75 g 10.00
Cheetos Pelotazos.
❑ 22 g with Jar Jar toy offer on back 10.00
Cheetos Rizos with Anakin Skywalker package.
❑ 14 g with Jar Jar toy offer on back 10.00
❑ 27 g [384-43] 10.00
❑ 57 g 10.00
Cheetos Sticks with Anakin Skywalker package.
❑ 18 g with Jar Jar toy offer on back 10.00
❑ 36 g [384-44] 10.00
❑ 70 g 10.00

❑ Churreria Santa Ana, 120 g with Qui-Gon photo 10.00
❑ Churreria Santa Ana, 170 g with Qui-Gon photo 10.00
❑ Churreria Santa Ana, 41 g with Qui-Gon photo [384-45] .10.00
❑ Doritos Rock and Cream, 110 g with Darth Maul photo.10.00
❑ Doritos Rock and Cream, 80 g with Darth Maul photo [384-46] 10.00
❑ Doritos Tex-Mex, 110 g with Darth Maul photo 10.00
❑ Doritos Tex-Mex, 30 g with Darth Maul photo [384-47] ...10.00
❑ Doritos Tex-Mex, 44 g with Darth Maul photo 10.00
❑ Doritos Tex-Mex, 80 g with Darth Maul photo 10.00
❑ Fritos Matutano Barbacoa, 130 g with Jar Jar photo...10.00
❑ Fritos Matutano Barbacoa, 50 g with Jar Jar photo [384-48] 10.00
❑ Fritos Matutano Barbacoa, 95 g with Jar Jar photo.....10.00
❑ Fritos Matutano Ketchup, 25 g with Jar Jar toy offer on back 10.00
❑ Lay's a la Vinagreta, 110 g with Qui-Gon photo [384-49] 10.00
❑ Lay's a la Vinagreta, 160 g with Qui-Gon photo 10.00
❑ Lay's Doradas con Cebolleta, 110 g with Qui-Gon photo [384-50] 10.00

❑ Lay's Doradas con Cebolleta, 160 g with Qui-Gon photo 10.00
❑ Lay's Doradas con Cebolleta, 44 g with Qui-Gon photo 10.00
❑ Lay's Ligeras 33% Menos Grasa, 140 g with Qui-Gon photo 10.00
❑ Lay's Ligeras 33% Menos Grasa, 30 g with Qui-Gon photo [384-51] 10.00
❑ Lay's Ligeras 33% Menos Grasa, 44 g with Qui-Gon photo 10.00
❑ Lay's Receta Campesina, 110 g with Qui-Gon photo [384-52] 10.00
❑ Lay's Receta Campesina, 160 g with Qui-Gon photo ..10.00
❑ Lay's, 125 g with Qui-Gon photo...............................10.00
❑ Lay's, 170 g with Qui-Gon photo...............................10.00
❑ Lay's, 30 g with Qui-Gon photo.................................10.00
❑ Lay's, 44 g with Qui-Gon photo [384-53] 10.00
❑ Ruffles Alioli ole, 110 g with Obi-Wan photo...............10.00
❑ Ruffles Alioli ole, 160 g with Obi-Wan photo...............10.00
❑ Ruffles Alioli ole, 44 g with Obi-Wan photo.................10.00
❑ Ruffles Jamon Jamon, 110 g with Obi-Wan photo......10.00

Packaging: Snack Chips

| 384-87 | 384-88 | 384-89 | 384-90 | 384-91 | 384-92 | 384-93 | 384-94 | 384-95 |

   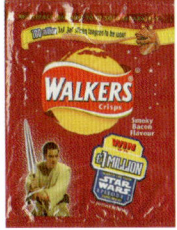  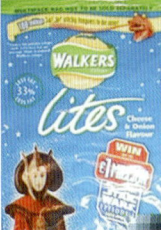 

| 384-96 | 384-97 | 384-98 | 384-99 | 384-100 | 384-101 | 384-102 | 384-103 |

- ❏ Ruffles Jamon Jamon, 30 g with Obi-Wan photo 10.00
- ❏ Ruffles Jamon Jamon, 44 g Obi-Wan photo [384-54] 10.00
- ❏ Ruffles Onduladas, 125 g with Obi-Wan photo 10.00
- ❏ Ruffles Onduladas, 170 g with Obi-Wan photo 10.00
- ❏ Ruffles Onduladas, 44 g with Obi-Wan photo [384-55]... 10.00
- ❏ Ruffles Pimenton Molon, 110 g with Obi-Wan photo ... 10.00
- ❏ Ruffles Pimenton Molon, 160 g with Obi-Wan photo ... 10.00
- ❏ Ruffles Pimenton Molon, 44 g with Obi-Wan photo [384-56] . 10.00
- ❏ Ruffles Queso y eso, 110 g with Obi-Wan photo 10.00
- ❏ Ruffles Queso y eso, 160 g with Obi-Wan photo 10.00
- ❏ Ruffles Queso y eso, 44 g with Obi-Wan photo [384-57] 10.00

Proctor and Gamble
Blu-ray promotion. Pringles, 6.38 oz. canisters.
- ❏ BBQ, Boba Fett [384-58] 10.00
- ❏ Cheddar Cheese, Chewbacca [384-59] 10.00
- ❏ Original, Darth Vader [384-60] 10.00
- ❏ Pizza, Princess Leia [384-61] 10.00
- ❏ Salt and Vinegar, Han Solo [384-62] 10.00
- ❏ Sour Cream and Onion, Luke Skywalker [384-63] 10.00

Episode III: Revenge of the Sith. Pringles, 200 g canisters.
- ❏ Hot and Spicy [384-64] 10.00
- ❏ Original [384-65] 10.00
- ❏ Paprika [384-66] 10.00
- ❏ Sour Cream and Onion [384-67] 10.00

Sabritas (Mexico)
Episode I: The Phantom Menace.
- ❏ Ruffles, Anakin [384-68] 10.00
- ❏ Ruffles, Jar Jar [384-69] 10.00
- ❏ Ruffles, Queen Amidala [384-70] 10.00
- ❏ Sabritas, Anakin [384-71] 10.00
- ❏ Sabritas, Darth Maul [384-72] 10.00
- ❏ Sabritas, Obi-Wan [384-73] 10.00
- ❏ Sabritas, Queen Amidala [384-74] 10.00

Free Clone Wars card inside.
- ❏ Casera Jalapeno 10.00
- ❏ Cronchos 10.00
- ❏ Doritos Diablo 10.00

- ❏ Doritos Flamin Hot 10.00
- ❏ Doritos Incognita 10.00
- ❏ Doritos Nachos 10.00
- ❏ Doritos Pizzerolas 10.00
- ❏ Doritos Toro 10.00
- ❏ Ruffles Cremay Especias 10.00
- ❏ Ruffles Picante 10.00
- ❏ Ruffles Queso [384-75] 10.00
- ❏ Ruffles Saladas 10.00
- ❏ Sabritas Adobadas 10.00
- ❏ Sabritas Caseras 10.00
- ❏ Sabritas Limon 10.00
- ❏ Tostitos 10.00
- ❏ Tostitos Flamin Hot 10.00

Star Wars Special Edition / Feel the Force.
- ❏ Cacahuates Enchilados [384-76] 15.00
- ❏ Cheetos [384-77] 15.00
- ❏ Cheetos, colmulos pico [384-78] 15.00
- ❏ Quesosabritas [384-79] 15.00

| 384-104 | 384-105 | 384-106 | 384-107 | 384-108 | 384-109 | 384-110 | 384-111 | 384-112 | 384-113 |

    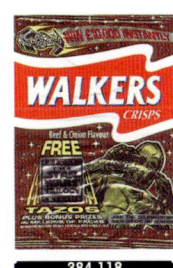   

| 384-114 | 384-115 | 384-116 | 384-117 | 384-118 | 384-119 | 384-120 | 384-121 |

   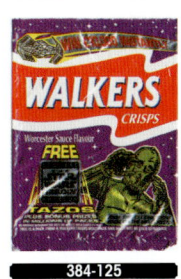    

| 384-122 | 384-123 | 384-124 | 384-125 | 384-126 | 384-127 | 384-128 | 384-129 |

Packaging: Snack Chips

     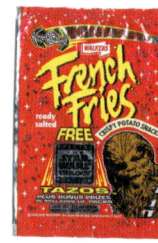  

384-130   384-131   384-132   384-133   384-134   384-135   384-136   384-137

    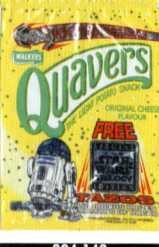 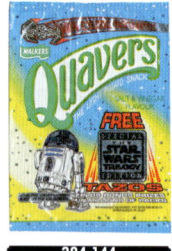 

384-138   384-139   384-140   384-141   384-142   384-143   384-144   384-145

Star Wars Special Edition.
- C-3PO, Cheetos [384-80] 15.00
- C-3PO, Cheetos colmulos pico [384-81] 15.00
- C-3PO, Poffets chile-limon [384-82] 15.00
- Darth Vader, Poffets caramelo [384-83] 15.00
- Darth Vader, Vive La Aventura [384-84] 15.00
- R2-D2, Cheetos torciditos [384-85] 15.00
- R2-D2, Poffets queso [384-86] 15.00
- R2-D2, Vive La Aventura [384-87] 15.00

Smith's Snackfood
Episode I: The Phantom Menace. Doritos Corn Chips.
- Cheese supreme with Yoda packaging, 230 g [384-88] ..10.00
- Cheese supreme with Yoda packaging, 50 g 10.00
- Cool Tang with C-3PO packaging, 230 g [384-89] 10.00
- Cool Tang with C-3PO packaging, 50 g 10.00
- Nacho cheese with Qui-Gon packaging, 230 g 10.00
- Nacho cheese with Qui-Gon packaging, 50 g [384-90]..10.00
- Original with Queen Amidala packaging, 230 g 10.00

Lay's multi-packs.
- 12-pack, flavour mix, C-3PO package 10.00
- 12-pack original, Anakin package 10.00
- 12-pack Texas BBQ, Jar Jar package 10.00
- 18-pack, flavour mix, Yoda package 10.00

Lay's cheddar cheese and onion.
- Amidala packaging, 100 g 10.00
- Amidala packaging, 200 g 10.00
- Amidala packaging, 50 g 10.00

Lay's original.
- Anakin packaging, 100 g 10.00
- Anakin packaging, 50 g 10.00

Lay's roast chicken.
- Obi-Wan packaging, 100 g 10.00
- Obi-Wan packaging, 250 g 10.00
- Obi-Wan packaging, 50 g 10.00
- Lay's, salt and vinegar with R2-D2 packaging, 250 g ..10.00
- Lay's, salt and vinegar with R2-D2 packaging, 550 g ..10.00
- Lay's, Texas BBQ with Jar Jar packaging, 100 g 10.00
- Lay's, Texas BBQ with Jar Jar packaging, 200 g [384-91]..10.00
- Lay's, Texas BBQ with Jar Jar packaging, 50 g 10.00

Sunshine Biscuits L.L.C.
Episode III: Revenge of the Sith. Cheez-It Crackers.
- C-3PO 16 oz. [384-92] 15.00
- Chewbacca Twisterz 13 oz. [384-93] 15.00
- Darth Vader 16 oz. [384-94] 15.00
- R2-D2 10 oz. [384-95] 15.00

UFO
- Empire Strikes Back promotion, sticker premiums 20.00

Walkers (UK)
Episode I: The Phantom Menace.
- Cheetos, Jar Jar package 10.00
- Crisps, Obi-Wan Kenobi pkg. barbecue [384-96] 10.00
- Crisps, Obi-Wan Kenobi pkg. beef and onion [384-97]....10.00
- Crisps, Obi-Wan Kenobi package cheese and onion [384-98] 10.00
- Crisps, Obi-Wan Kenobi package cheese and onion, multi-pack 10.00
- Crisps, Obi-Wan Kenobi package prawn cocktail, multi-pack [384-99] 10.00
- Crisps, Obi-Wan Kenobi package smoky bacon, multi-pack [384-100] 10.00
- Doritos, Darth Maul pkg. tangy cheese [384-101] 10.00
- French Fries, Jar Jar pkg. ready salted 10.00
- Lites, Queen Amidala package cheese and onion, multi-pack [384-102] 10.00
- Lites, Queen Amidala pkg. salted, multi-pack [384-103] ..10.00
- MAX, Qui-Gon Jinn pkg. hard cheese and onion [384-104] 10.00
- MAX, Qui-Gon Jinn pkg. salt and vinegar 10.00
- Monster Munch, Jar Jar pkg. pickled onion [384-105] ..10.00
- Sundog popcorn, Jar Jar package [384-106] 10.00

Star Wars Special Edition.
- Crinkles, C-3PO pkg. cream cheese and chive [384-107]..10.00
- Crinkles, C-3PO package cream cheese and chive, 175g [384-108]
- Crisps, C-3PO pkg. 6-pack barbecue [384-109] 10.00
- Crisps, C-3PO pkg. 6-pack cheese and onion [384-110]..10.00
- Crisps, C-3PO pkg. 6-pack mixed flavors [384-111] 10.00
- Crisps, C-3PO pkg. 6-pack mixed flavors lites [384-112]..10.00
- Crisps, C-3PO pkg. 6-pack mixed flavors savoury 10.00
- Crisps, C-3PO pkg. 6-pack salt and vinegar [384-113] 10.00
- Crisps, C-3PO pkg. 6-pack salted lites [384-114] 10.00
- Crisps, C-3PO pkg. 10-pack mixed flavors [384-115] 10.00
- Crisps, C-3PO pkg. 15-pack mixed flavors [384-116] 10.00
- Crisps, C-3PO pkg. barbecue [384-117] 10.00
- Crisps, C-3PO pkg. beef and onion [384-118] 10.00
- Crisps, C-3PO pkg. cheese and onion [384-119] 10.00
- Crisps, C-3PO pkg. prawn cocktail [384-120] 10.00
- Crisps, C-3PO pkg. roast chicken [384-121] 10.00

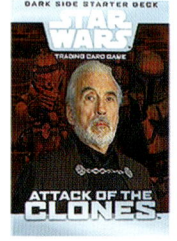  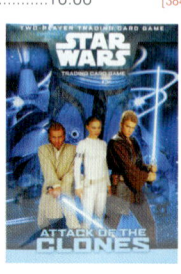  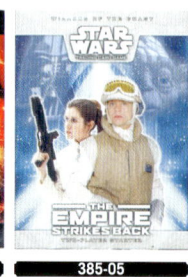    

385-01   385-02   385-03   385-04   385-05   385-06   385-07   385-08   385-09

385-10   385-11   385-12   385-13   385-14   385-15   385-16   385-17   385-18   385-19   385-20

386-01 Front and Back

386-02 Front and Back

386-03 Front and Back

386-04 Front

386-04 Back

386-05 Front and Back

386-06 Front and Back

386-07 Front and Back

- ❑ Crisps, C-3PO pkg. salt and vinegar 10.00
- ❑ Crisps, C-3PO pkg. salt and vinegar, 175 g [384-122] 10.00
- ❑ Crisps, C-3PO pkg. salted 10.00
- ❑ Crisps, C-3PO pkg. salted, 175 g [384-123] 10.00
- ❑ Crisps, C-3PO pkg. smoky bacon....10.00
- ❑ Crisps, C-3PO pkg. tomato ketchup [384-124] 10.00
- ❑ Crisps, C-3PO pkg. worcester sauce [384-125] 10.00
- ❑ Doritos, Darth Vader pkg. 6-pack mixed flavors [384-126]..10.00
- ❑ Doritos, Darth Vader pkg. 6-pack tangy cheese [384-127]..10.00
- ❑ Doritos, Darth Vader pkg. cool original [384-128] 10.00
- ❑ Doritos, Darth Vader package cool original, movie bag [384-129] 10.00
- ❑ Doritos, Darth Vader pkg. sizzlin' barbeque [384-130] 10.00
- ❑ Doritos, Darth Vader pkg. tangy cheese [384-131] 10.00
- ❑ Doritos, Darth Vader pkg. tangy cheese, movie bag....10.00
- ❑ Double Crunch, C-3PO package 5-pack mixed flavors [384-132] 10.00
- ❑ Double Crunch, C-3PO pkg. chargrilled steak 10.00
- ❑ Double Crunch, C-3PO pkg. original salted....10.00
- ❑ Double Crunch, C-3PO pkg. smoked cheddar....10.00
- ❑ French Fries, Chewbacca pkg. 6-pack mixed [384-133] ..10.00
- ❑ French Fries, Chewbacca pkg. salt and vinegar [384-134]..10.00
- ❑ French Fries, Chewbacca pkg. salted [384-135] 10.00
- ❑ French Fries, Chewbacca pkg. worcester [384-136] 10.00
- ❑ Lites, C-3PO pkg. cheese and onion [384-137]....10.00
- ❑ Lites, C-3PO pkg. salt and vinegar [384-138]....10.00
- ❑ Lites, C-3PO pkg. salted [384-139]....10.00
- ❑ Monster Munch, stormtrooper package pickled onion [384-140] 10.00
- ❑ Quavers, R2-D2 pkg. 6-pack mixed flavors [384-141]....10.00
- ❑ Quavers, R2-D2 pkg. 6-pack original cheese [384-142] ..10.00
- ❑ Quavers, R2-D2 pkg. cheese [384-143]....10.00
- ❑ Quavers, R2-D2 pkg. salt and vinegar [384-144]....10.00
- ❑ Quavers, R2-D2 pkg. tangy tomato [384-145]....10.00

Packaging: TCG

Wizards of the Coast

2-Player Trading Card Game.

- ❑ Advanced Starter Deck, dark side [385-01]....10.00
- ❑ Advanced Starter Deck, light side [385-02]....10.00
- ❑ Attack of the Clones [385-03]....10.00
- ❑ Revenge of the Sith [385-04]....15.00
- ❑ The Empire Strikes Back [385-05] 15.00

A New Hope. 11 additional game cards.

- ❑ Luke Skywalker [385-06] 10.00
- ❑ Princess Leia [385-07]....10.00
- ❑ Stormtroopers [385-08]....10.00

Attack of the Clones.

- ❑ Game cards, packet of 5 random cards [385-09]....10.00
- ❑ Game cards, packet of 5 random cards [385-10]....10.00

Battle of Yavin. 11 additional game cards.

- ❑ Grand Moff Tarkin [385-11]....10.00
- ❑ Han and Chewbacca [385-12]....10.00
- ❑ Luke Skywalker, pilot [385-13]....10.00

Return of the Jedi. 11 additional game cards.

- ❑ Jabba the Hutt [385-14]....10.00
- ❑ Luke Skywalker [385-15] 10.00
- ❑ Princess Leia [385-16]....10.00

Revenge of the Sith. 11 additional game cards.

- ❑ Anakin Skywalker [385-17] 10.00
- ❑ Darth Vader [385-18]....10.00
- ❑ Obi-Wan Kenobi [385-19]....10.00

Sith Rising.

- ❑ Game cards, 2 packets of 5 random cards [385-20] 12.00

Packaging: Yogurt

Continued in Volume 3, Page 308

Bridge Farm Dairies (UK)

Dairy Time.

- ❑ Admiral Ackbar, pineapple....25.00
- ❑ Chewbacca, fudge [386-01]....25.00
- ❑ Darth Vader, black cherry [386-02]....25.00
- ❑ Ewoks, banana [386-03]....25.00
- ❑ Jabba the Hutt, peach melba [386-04]....25.00
- ❑ Luke Skywalker, rapsberry [386-05]....25.00
- ❑ Princess Leia, strawberry [386-06] 25.00
- ❑ Yoda, gooseberry [386-07] 25.00

La Serenisima (Argentina)

Clone Wars Yogurisimo, 175 g cups.

- ❑ Anakin [386-08]....15.00
- ❑ Clone trooper [386-09] 15.00
- ❑ Obi-Wan [386-10]....15.00
- ❑ Yoda [386-11]....15.00

Clone Wars Yogurisimo, 190 g bottles.

- ❑ Ahsoka / vanilla [386-12] 10.00
- ❑ Anakin / vanilla [386-13]....10.00
- ❑ Asajj Ventress / Frutilla [386-14] 10.00
- ❑ Battle droid / Frutilla [386-15]....10.00
- ❑ C-3PO / vanilla [386-16]....10.00
- ❑ Clone trooper / Frutilla [386-17] 10.00
- ❑ General Grievous / vanilla [386-18] 10.00
- ❑ Obi-Wan / Frutilla [386-19]....10.00
- ❑ R2-D2 / vanilla [386-20]....10.00
- ❑ Yoda / Frutilla [386-21]....10.00

Yoplait

16-pack box featuring glow-in-the-dark lightsaber tubes. Episode I 3D promotion.

- ❑ Strawberry banana burst / blue raspberry ice [386-22]....10.00
- ❑ Strawberry watermelon / peach [386-23]....10.00

24-pack box featuring glow-in-the-dark lightsaber tubes.

- ❑ Strawberry splash and berry blue blast [386-24]....10.00

8-pack box featuring glow-in-the-dark lightsaber tubes.

- ❑ Burstin' melon berry and cool cotton candy [386-25]....10.00
- ❑ Red raspberry and paradise punch [386-26] 10.00
- ❑ Rootbeer float and banana split [386-27]....10.00
- ❑ Strawberry kiwi kick and chill out cherry....10.00
- ❑ Strawberry splash and berry blue blast 10.00
- ❑ Watermelon meltdown and strawberry banana burst [386-28]....10.00

8-pack box featuring glow-in-the-dark lightsaber tubes. Episode I 3D promotion.

- ❑ Chill out cherry and strawberry kiwi kick [386-29]....10.00
- ❑ Cool cotton candy and burstin' melon berry [386-30] 10.00
- ❑ Strawberry milkshake and banana split 10.00
- ❑ Strawberry splash and berry blue blast [386-31]....10.00
- ❑ Watermelon meltdown and strawberry banana burst..10.00

Individual tubes. Glow-in-the-dark lightsaber tubes.

- ❑ Anakin Skywalker, cool cotton candy [386-32] 5.00
- ❑ Barriss Offee, burstin' melon berry [386-33]....5.00

386-08

386-09

386-10

386-11 Front and Back

386-12 Front and Back

386-13 Front and Back

386-14 Front and Back

Packaging: Yogurt

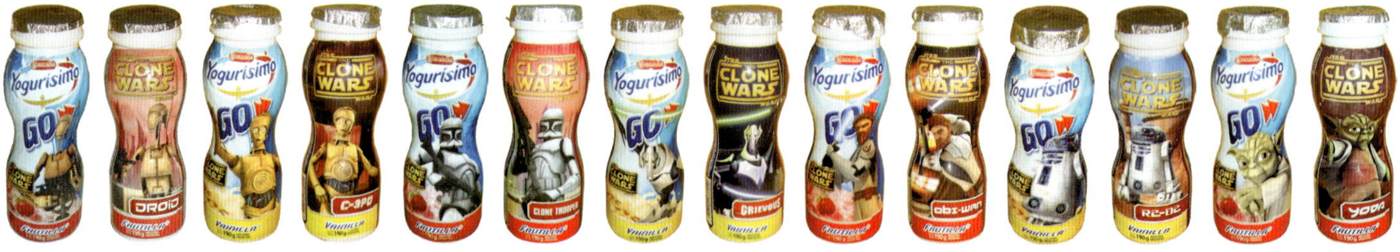

386-15 Front and Back | 386-16 Front and Back | 386-17 Front and Back | 386-18 Front and Back | 386-19 Front and Back | 386-20 Front and Back | 386-21 Front and Back

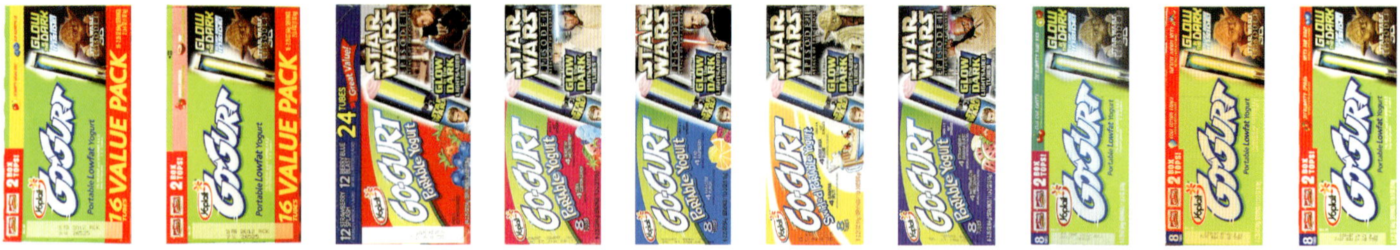

386-22 | 386-23 | 386-24 | 386-25 | 386-26 | 386-27 | 386-28 | 386-29 | 386-30 | 386-31

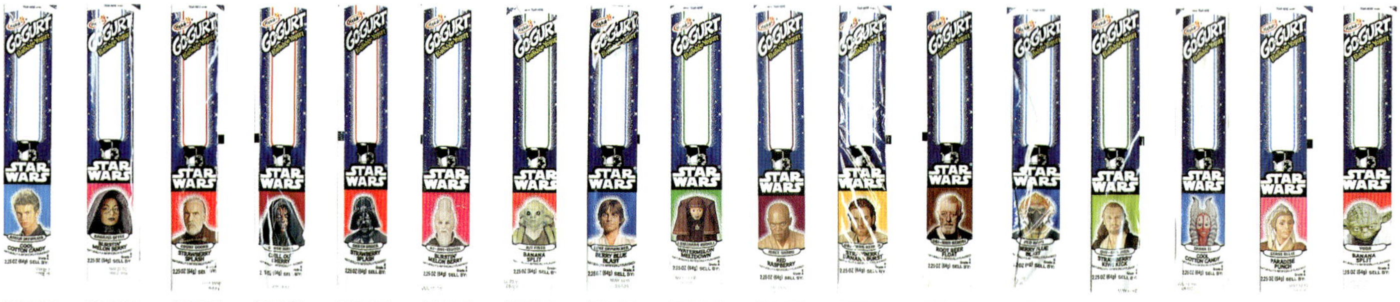

386-32 | 386-33 | 386-34 | 386-35 | 386-36 | 386-37 | 386-38 | 386-39 | 386-40 | 386-41 | 386-42 | 386-43 | 386-44 | 386-45 | 386-46 | 386-47 | 386-48

- ❑ Count Dooku, strawberry splash [386-34] 5.00
- ❑ Darth Maul, chill out cherry [386-35] 5.00
- ❑ Darth Vader, strawberry splash [386-36] 5.00
- ❑ Ki-Adi Mundi, burstin' melon berry [386-37] 5.00
- ❑ Kit Fisto, banana split [386-38] 5.00
- ❑ Luke Skywalker, berry blue blast [386-39] 5.00
- ❑ Luminara Unduli, watermelon meltdown [386-40] 5.00
- ❑ Mace Windu, red raspberry [386-41] 5.00
- ❑ Obi-Wan (EP II), strawberry banana burst [386-42] 5.00
- ❑ Obi-Wan (EP IV), rootbeer float [386-43] 5.00
- ❑ Plo Koon, berry blue blast [386-44] 5.00
- ❑ Qui Gon Jinn, strawberry kiwi kick [386-45] 5.00
- ❑ Shaak Ti, cool cotton candy [386-46] 5.00
- ❑ Stass Allie, paradise punch [386-47] 5.00
- ❑ Yoda, banana split [386-48] 5.00

Pads: Sports

Continued in Volume 3, Page 309

- ❑ Knee and elbow pad set [387-01] 20.00
- ❑ Knee and elbow pads in Darth Maul case [387-02] 25.00

Dynacraft

Episode I glove, knee, and elbow pad set.

- ❑ Darth Maul [387-03] 20.00
- ❑ Queen Amidala [387-04] 20.00

M.V. Sports and Leisure Ltd.

- ❑ Darth Maul knee and elbow pads [387-05] 25.00

Seneca Sports Inc.

Protective gear backpack: knee pads and water bottle.

- ❑ Imperial Assault [387-06] 30.00
- ❑ R2-D2 [387-07] 30.00

Pails: Tin

Continued in Volume 3, Page 309

Playworks International (Australia)

- ❑ Clone Wars: Yoda and Obi-Wan [388-01] 15.00

Tin Box Company

Exclusive to Target.

- ❑ Return of the Jedi [388-02] 10.00
- ❑ Yoda [388-03] 10.00

Paint

Continued in Volume 3, Page 309

St. Majewski (Poland)

- ❑ 12 Farby Akwarelowe [389-01] 15.00
- ❑ 12 Farby Plakatowe [389-02] 30.00

Testers

- ❑ Detail paints for vinyl kits [389-03] 25.00

Paper

Reding Stationary (Australia)

- ❑ Empire Strikes Back loose leaf refill [390-01] 40.00

Paper Clips and Note Tabs

Flomo (UK)

- ❑ Star Wars prism sticker, spring operated [4:225] 5.00

Paper Reinforcements

Butterfly Originals

- ❑ Return of the Jedi foil, 48-pack [v1e1:335] 15.00

Individual, distributed in vending machine capsules.

- ❑ C-3PO 5.00
- ❑ Darth Vader [v1e1:335] 5.00
- ❑ Darth's TIE Fighter 5.00
- ❑ Han Solo 5.00
- ❑ Jabba the Hutt [v1e1:335] 5.00
- ❑ Luke Skywalker 5.00

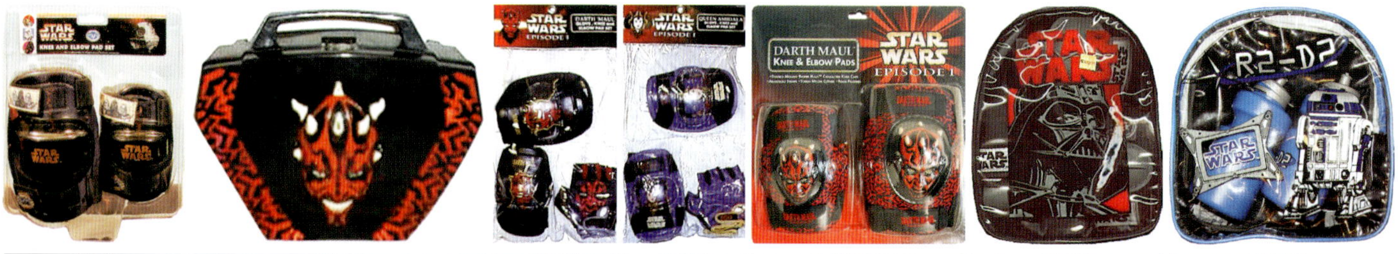

387-01 | 387-02 | 387-03 | 387-04 | 387-05 | 387-06 | 387-07

Party Bags and Treat Boxes

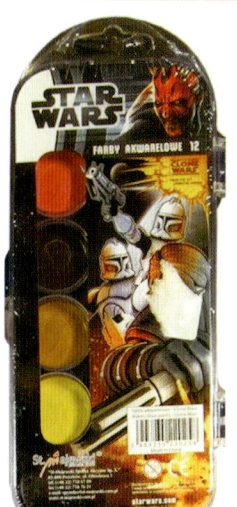
389-01

388-01 Side 1 and Side 2

388-02

388-03

389-02

389-03

- ☐ Millennium Falcon..5.00
- ☐ R2-D2 [v1e1:335]..5.00
- ☐ Shuttle Tydirium 5.00
- ☐ TIE Fighter 5.00

Paper Toweling

Zewa (Belgium)
- ☐ Softis, Episode III [390-02]........................85.00

Paper Weights

3D Arts
Classic trilogy character holograms.
- ☐ Darth Vader...20.00
- ☐ Yoda 20.00

Fossil, Inc.
- ☐ 25th anniversary, included with watch [391-01] 35.00

Party Bags and Treat Boxes
Continued in Volume 3, Page 310

(UK)
- ☐ Clone Wars loot bags, 6-pack [392-01] 10.00

Drawing Board Greeting Cards, Inc.
- ☐ Darth Vader and Luke duel, 8-pack [392-02].................25.00
- ☐ Ewoks, 8-pack [392-03]................................25.00

Gemma International (UK)
Bags are valued in original 8-packs.
- ☐ Anakin, Obi-Wan, Yoda, clones [392-04] 10.00
- ☐ Captain Rex and clones / Obi-Wan and Anakin............10.00
- ☐ Darth Sidious, epic duel 10.00

Hallmark Party
- ☐ Star Wars generations [392-05]................10.00
- ☐ Yoda, from 48-pack of party favors [392-06] 5.00

Bags are valued in original 8-packs.
- ☐ Clone Wars opposing forces [392-07]................10.00
- ☐ LEGO Star Wars [392-08] 10.00

Hunter Leisure, Ltd. (Australia)
- ☐ Episode III: Vader / Jedi [392-09] 10.00

MT Creations (France)
- ☐ Revenge of the Sith / epic battle..............................12.00

Paper Magic Group
- ☐ R2-D2 and C-3PO treat sacks, 24-count [392-10] 15.00

 390-01    390-02    391-01    392-01    392-02    392-03    392-04   392-05

 392-06    392-07    392-08    392-09    392-10    392-11    392-12    392-13

 392-14    392-15    392-16    392-17    392-18    392-19    392-20    392-21    392-22

Party Bags and Treat Boxes

393-01 | 393-02 | 393-03 | 393-04 | 393-05 | 393-06 | 393-07

 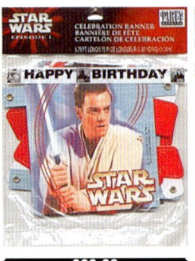      

393-08 | 393-09 | 393-10 | 393-11 | 393-12 | 393-13 | 393-14 | 394-01

Bags are valued in original 8-packs.
- Classic, Millennium Falcon flees Death Star [392-11] 10.00
- Classic, neon [392-12] 10.00
- Clone Wars [392-13] 10.00
- EPI Darth Maul with Jedi vs. Sith scene [392-14] 10.00
- EPII Jango and Jedi [392-15] 10.00
- Star Wars saga [392-16] 10.00
- Yoda [392-17] 10.00

Treat boxes.
- Classic trilogy, 3D effect [392-18] 15.00
- Clone Wars [392-19] 15.00
- Episode III: Revenge of the Sith Darth Vader [392-20] 15.00

Quela
- Darth Vader neon, 8-pack [392-21] 15.00

Unique (Canada)
- Episode I: Jedi vs. Sith [392-22] 15.00

Party Banners
Continued in Volume 3, Page 311

- Yoda, "Happy Birthday" [393-01] 10.00

Drawing Board Greeting Cards, Inc.
- Empire Strikes Back birthday [393-02] 12.00

Gemma International (UK)
- Captain Rex, Anakin Skywalker, Obi-Wan Kenobi 15.00

Hallmark Party
- Clone Wars opposing Forces [393-03] 10.00
- "Happy Birthday," Yoda, Jedi, Captain Rex [393-04] 10.00
- Jumbo birthday banner kit [393-05] 15.00
- Star Wars generations [393-06] 10.00

Party Express
Celebration, Happy Birthday.
- Clone Wars [393-07] 10.00
- Darth Vader / Yoda / stormtroopers [393-08] 10.00
- Episode I: The Phantom Menace [393-09] 10.00
- Episode II: Attack of the Clones [393-10] 10.00
- Episode III: Revenge of the Sith [393-11] 10.00
- Star Wars saga [393-12] 10.00

Unique (Canada)
- Jedi vs. Sith [393-13] 15.00
- Darth Maul door sign, 27" x 60" [393-14] 18.00

Party Blowouts
Continued in Volume 3, Page 311

Drawing Board Greeting Cards, Inc.
4-packs.
- Empire Strikes Back: Darth Vader [394-01] 30.00
- Ewoks [394-02] 30.00
- Return of the Jedi: Darth Vader [394-03] 25.00

Hallmark Party
- Clone Wars opposing forces [394-04] 10.00

- LEGO Star Wars [394-05] 10.00
- Star Wars generations [394-06] 10.00

Hunter Leisure, Ltd. (Australia)
- Jedi, 8-pack 12.00

MT Creations (France)
- Jedi and Sith, 10-pack 10.00

Party Express
8-packs.
- Classic trilogy. X-Wing vs. TIE Fighter [394-07] 10.00
- Clone Wars [394-08] 10.00
- EPI: TPM. Jedi and Sith silhouettes [394-09] 10.00
- EPII: AOTC. Jedi silhouettes [394-10] 10.00
- EPIII: ROTS. Darth Vader [394-11] 10.00
- Saga: starships [394-12] 10.00
- Star Wars. Darth Vader and stormtroopers 10.00

Unique (Canada)
8-packs.
- Darth Maul vs. Jedi [394-13] 15.00

Party Centerpieces
Continued in Volume 3, Page 311

Drawing Board Greeting Cards, Inc.
- Cloud City [395-01] 50.00
- Darth Vader and Luke Duel [395-02] 40.00
- Ewoks in Forest [395-03] 75.00

394-02 | 394-03 | 394-04 | 394-05 | 394-06 | 394-07 | 394-08

   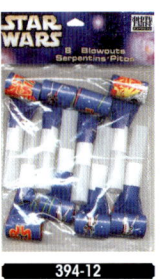 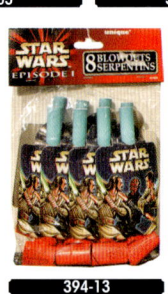 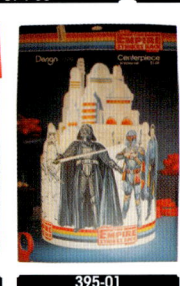  

394-09 | 394-10 | 394-11 | 394-12 | 394-13 | 395-01 | 395-02 | 395-03

Party Decorations

 395-04
 395-05
 395-06
 395-07
 395-08
 395-09
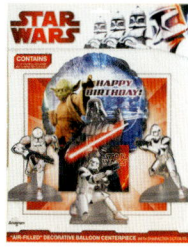 396-01

 396-02
 396-03
 396-04
 396-05
 396-06
 396-07

Party Express
- ❏ Classic trilogy [395-04] 12.00
- ❏ Classic, neon [395-05] 15.00
- ❏ Clone Wars [395-06] 12.00
- ❏ Darth Vader, 2-sided 10.00
- ❏ Darth Vader [395-07] 10.00
- ❏ Darth Vader [395-08] 10.00
- ❏ EPI: TPM party table centerpiece [395-09] 10.00

Unique (Canada)
- ❏ Episode I: The Phantom Menace..............................12.00

Party Decorations
Continued in Volume 3, Page 311

Anagram International
- ❏ Decorative balloon centerpiece [396-01] 15.00

Gemma International (UK)
- ❏ Clone Wars party pack, plates, cups, napkins, table cover [396-02] 20.00

Hallmark Party
- ❏ 5-piece party backdrop [396-03] 15.00

Licensia
- ❏ Ewoks party pack, mask, paper plates, coasters, hat [396-04] 65.00

MT Creations (France)
- ❏ Darth Vader hanging decoration.........................10.00

Party Express
Crepe paper streamers with character silhouettes.
- ❏ Cone Wars [396-05]...10.00
- ❏ Darth Vader [396-06] 10.00

- ❏ Jedi and Sith [396-07] 10.00
- ❏ Jedi duel [396-08] 10.00
- ❏ Starfighters 10.00

Hanging decorations 3-packs.
- ❏ Darth Vader, Yoda, epic duel [396-09]...............10.00
- ❏ Yoda, Darth Vader, Death Star attack [396-10] ...10.00

Honeycomb party decorations.
- ❏ Darth Vader [396-11] 10.00

Wall hangings, set of 3.
- ❏ Classic trilogy starships [396-12] 20.00
- ❏ Jedi vs. Sith [396-13] 10.00

Star Wars Celebration VI
Paper lanterns.
- ❏ Death Star [396-14] 25.00

 396-08
 396-09
 396-10
 396-11
 396-12
 396-13

 396-14
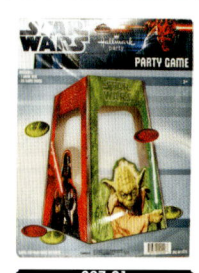 397-01
 397-02
 397-03
 397-04
 397-05
 397-06

 398-01
 398-02
 398-03
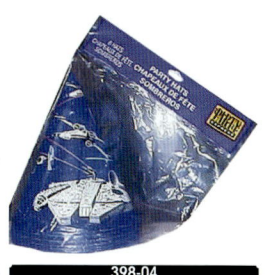 398-04
 398-05
 398-06
 398-07

Party Games

399-01 399-02 399-03 399-04 399-05 399-06 399-07 399-08 399-09

  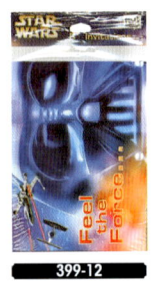     

399-10 399-11 399-12 399-13 399-14 399-15 399-16 399-17

Party Games
Continued in Volume 3, Page 312

Hallmark Party
- Disc toss [397-01] 12.00

Licensia
- Ewoks amazing maze game [397-02] 80.00

Party Express
- Help restore order to the galaxy [397-03] 10.00
- Party activity kit, Darth Vader 4-pack 10.00
- Pin Vader [397-04] 10.00
- Space battle [397-05] 15.00

Unique (Canada)
- Star Wars lightsaber game [397-06] 15.00

Party Hats
Continued in Volume 3, Page 312

(UK)
- Clone Wars, Captain Rex 10.00

501st Legion
- 501st Legion Imperial Bash, "Party Like a Hutt," exclusive to Star Wars Celebration VI [398-01] 10.00

Drawing Board Greeting Cards, Inc.
- Star Wars punch-out, 8-pack [v1e1:337] 35.00

Vintage. 8-pack of cone hats.
- Cloud City [398-02] 20.00
- Darth Vader and Luke Duel 20.00
- Ewok glider [398-03] 25.00

Party Express
8-pack of cone hats.
- Battle above Death Star [398-04] 10.00
- Droids with Star Wars logo, neon 10.00
- Episode I: The Phantom Menace, Jar Jar Binks [398-05] 10.00
- Episode II: Attack of the Clones, Jedi duel [398-06] 10.00
- Star Wars saga [398-07] 10.00

Party Invitations
Continued in Volume 3, Page 312

- C-3PO, R2-D2, Naboo Fighter: Invitaciones te Invito a mi Fiesta 15.00
- Darth Vader, "Attention! A Birthday Party," 8-pack 15.00

(UK)
- Clone Wars, "You are invited ..." [399-01] 10.00

Drawing Board Greeting Cards, Inc.
8-packs.
- C-3PO and R2-D2 .... 15.00
- C-3PO and R2-D2, postcards 15.00
- Cloud City [399-02] 20.00
- Darth Vader and Luke Duel [399-03] 20.00
- Ewok glider [399-04] 25.00
- Heroes and villains 15.00
- R2-D2 [399-05] 25.00

Gemma International (UK)
- Clone Wars, "Join the Force ..." [399-06] 10.00

Hallmark Party
8-sets: invitations and thank you cards.
- Clone Wars opposing forces, "Forces are gathering ..." [399-07] 15.00

8-packs.
- LEGO Star Wars, "It is your Destiny ..." [399-08] 10.00
- Yoda, "A birthday party, it is!" / "Invited you are!" with envelopes, seals, save-the-date stickers [399-09] 10.00

MT Creations (France)
- Clone trooper, die-cut with envelope 10.00

Party Express
8-packs.
- "Be Mindful of the Force ..." [399-10] 10.00
- Clone Wars, "Invited you are ..." [399-11] 10.00
- Darth Vader, "Feel the Force ..." [399-12] 15.00
- Darth Vader, "It is your destiny ..." 10.00
- Darth Vader, "Nothing can stop us ..." [399-13] 10.00
- Droids with Star Wars logo, neon [399-14] 15.00

400-01 400-02 400-03 401-01 401-02 401-03 401-04

401-05 401-06 401-07 401-08 401-09 401-10 Design 1

356

Party Decorations

 401-10 Design 2
 401-11
 401-12
 401-13
 401-14
 401-15
 401-16
 401-17
 401-18
 401-19
 401-20
 401-21

❏ Obi-Wan, Qui-Gon, "Nothing can stop us..." [399-15] 10.00
❏ R2-D2 [399-16] 10.00

Unique (Canada)
❏ Qui-Gon vs. Maul art, 8-pack [399-17] 15.00

Party Mazes
Continued in Volume 3, Page 312

Hallmark Party
❏ 4x6 sheet, "Help Chewbacca avoid the bounty hunters and find the droids!" 5.00

MT Creations (France)
❏ 501st clone trooper 5.00
❏ Epic battle 5.00
❏ Jedi vs. Sith 5.00
❏ The Sith 5.00
❏ Yoda 5.00

Party Express
❏ 4x6 sheet, "Let the Force Guide You" 5.00
❏ Darth Vader and Yoda, 4-pack [400-01] 10.00

Tapper Candies
6-pack party fun games.
❏ Anakin, Padmé, Obi-Wan, Jango Fett [400-02] 10.00
❏ Anakin, Padmé, Obi-Wan, Jango Fett, alternate assortment [400-03] 10.00

Party Napkins
Continued in Volume 3, Page 313

Deeko
❏ Star Wars [401-01] 25.00

Drawing Board Greeting Cards, Inc.
❏ C-3PO and R2-D2, any size (beverage or dinner) [401-02] 20.00
❏ Cloud City, any size (beverage or dinner) [401-03] 20.00
❏ Darth Vader and Luke duel, beverage [401-04] 15.00
❏ Darth Vader and Luke duel, dinner [401-05] 15.00
❏ Ewok glider, beverage [401-06] 15.00
❏ Ewok glider, dinner [401-07] 15.00

Drawing Board Greeting Cards, Inc. (Canada)
❏ Darth Vader and Luke duel, beverage 20.00
❏ Darth Vader and Luke duel, dinner [401-08] 20.00

Hallmark Party
Clone Wars opposing forces.
❏ ARC trooper [401-09] 10.00

LEGO Star Wars.
❏ Hoth heroes, Darth Vader, Boba Fett, dinner [401-10] 10.00

Star Wars generations.
❏ Darth Vader, beverage 10.00
❏ Darth Vader, dinner [401-11] 10.00

Hunter Leisure, Ltd. (Australia)
Episode III: Revenge of the Sith.
❏ Jedi / Vader [401-12] 15.00

Party Express
Classic trilogy.
❏ Dogfight over Death Star, dinner [401-13] 10.00
❏ Ships in neon colors, dinner [401-14] 15.00
❏ Star Wars saga, beverage [401-15] 10.00
❏ Star Wars saga, dinner 10.00

Clone Wars.
❏ Captain Rex, beverage [401-16] 8.00
❏ Jedi, dinner [401-17] 8.00
❏ Yoda, amazing 3D [401-18] 8.00

Episode I: The Phantom Menace.
❏ Obi-Wan Kenobi, Jedi vs. Sith, beverage [401-19] 8.00
❏ Qui-Gon Jinn, Jedi vs. Sith, dinner [401-20] 8.00

Episode II: Attack of the Clones.
❏ Anakin, Mace Windu, Padmé, Obi-Wan, dinner [401-21] 10.00
❏ Jango, Obi-Wan and Anakin, beverage [401-22] 10.00

Episode III: Revenge of the Sith.
❏ Darth Vader, dinner [401-23] 8.00
❏ Yoda, beverage [401-24] 8.00

Quela
❏ Vader / Imperial logo, 8-pack [401-25] 15.00

 401-22
 401-23
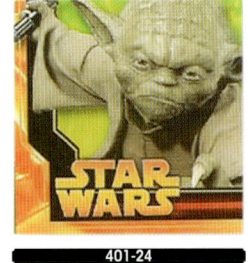 401-24
 401-25
 402-01
 403-01
 403-02
 403-03
 403-04
 403-05
 403-06
 403-07

Party Place Cards

Party Place Cards
Continued in Volume 3, Page 313

Drawing Board Greeting Cards, Inc.
- C-3PO and R2-D2, 8-pack [402-01] 25.00

MT Creations (France)
- Jedi starfighter, 6" x 8.25" cardboard 10.00

Party Plates
Continued in Volume 3, Page 313

(UK)
- Clone Wars, Anakin, Obi-Wan, Yoda, 6-pack [403-01] 10.00

Deeko
8-packs of plates.
- Star Wars, 7" [403-02] 20.00
- Star Wars, 9" 20.00

Drawing Board Greeting Cards, Inc.
- Empire Strikes Back: Cloud City, 7" pack [403-03] 20.00
- Empire Strikes Back: Cloud City, 9" pack [403-04] 20.00
- Ewoks, 7" pack [403-05] 20.00
- Ewoks, 9" pack [403-06] 20.00
- Return of the Jedi: Darth Vader and Luke duel, 7" pack 15.00
- Return of the Jedi: Darth Vader and Luke duel, 9" pack [403-07] 15.00
- Star Wars: C-3PO, R2-D2, and X-Wing Fighters, 9" pack .. 35.00
- Star Wars: Darth Vader, Death Star and TIE Fighters, 7" pack [403-08] 25.00

Drawing Board Greeting Cards, Inc. (Canada)
- Return of the Jedi, 9", 8-pack 20.00

Gemma International (UK)
- Captain Rex and Anakin, 9", 8-pack [403-09] 10.00

Hallmark
8-packs of plates.
- Clone Wars / customizable [403-10] 10.00
- Darth Vader / customizable [403-11] 10.00
- Star Wars generations, 7", 4 designs [403-12] 10.00
- Star Wars generations, 9", 2 designs [403-13] 10.00

Hallmark Party
8-packs of plates.
- Clone Wars opposing forces, 7", 3 designs [403-14] 10.00
- Clone Wars opposing forces, 9", 2 designs [403-15] 10.00

403-08 | 403-09 | 403-10 | 403-11 | 403-12 Design 1 and Design 2

403-13 Design 1 and Design 2 | 403-14 Design 1 and Design 2 | 403-15 Design 1 and Design 2

403-16 | 403-17 | 403-18 Design 1 and Design 2 | 403-19 Design 1 and Design 2

403-20 | 403-21 | 403-22 | 403-23 | 403-24 | 403-25

403-26 | 403-27 | 403-28 Design 1 and Design 2 | 403-29 | 403-30

Party Table Covers

404-01 | 404-02 | 404-03 | 405-01 | 405-02 | 405-03 | 406-01 | 406-02 | 406-03

406-04 | 406-05 | 406-06 | 406-07 | 406-08 | 406-09 | 406-10 | 406-11 | 406-12 | 406-13 | 406-14

- ❏ LEGO Star Wars, 7" [403-16] 10.00
- ❏ LEGO Star Wars, 9" [403-17] 10.00

Party Express
8-packs of plates.
- ❏ Clone Wars, 7", 3 designs [403-18] 10.00
- ❏ Clone Wars, 9", 2 designs [403-19] 10.00
- ❏ Darth Vader, shaped [403-20] 12.00
- ❏ Dogfight over Death Star, 7" [403-21] 15.00
- ❏ Dogfight over Death Star, 9" 15.00
- ❏ EPII: AOTC Anakin / heroes, 9" [403-22] 10.00
- ❏ EPII: AOTC Jango / heroes, 9" [403-23] 10.00
- ❏ EPIII: Revenge of the Sith Darth Vader and Yoda, 9" 10.00
- ❏ EPIII: Revenge of the Sith Darth Vader, 7" [403-24] 10.00
- ❏ Obi-Wan Kenobi, Jedi vs. Sith scene, 7" [403-25] 10.00
- ❏ Qui-Gon Jinn, Jedi vs. Sith scene, 9" [403-26] 10.00
- ❏ Star Wars Saga, 7" 10.00
- ❏ Star Wars Saga, 9" [403-27] 10.00
- ❏ Yoda and Darth Vader, 7", 2 designs [403-28] 10.00
- ❏ Yoda and Darth Vader, 9", amazing 3D effect [403-29] ...10.00

Unique (Canada)
- ❏ Darth Maul vs. Jedi, 8-pack [403-30] 20.00

Party Ribbons
Continued in Volume 3, Page 314

Hallmark Party
- ❏ Yoda, Jedi Master guest of honor [404-01] 8.00

Party Express
- ❏ Birthday Jedi Knight guest of honor [404-02] 8.00

Tapper Candies
- ❏ Attack of the Clones, guest of honor, lights up [404-03] ..10.00

Party Supplies
Continued in Volume 3, Page 314

Hallmark Party
48 piece Party Favor Packs. 40 fun favors and 8 treat sacks.
- ❏ Star Wars generations [405-01] 20.00

MT Creations (France)
- ❏ Coffret Festif, (de 50 accessories inclus dans ce set) [405-02] 35.00

Party Express
48 piece Party Favor Packs. 40 fun favors and 8 treat sacks.
- ❏ Yoda and Darth Vader [405-03] 20.00

Party Table Covers
Continued in Volume 3, Page 314

Deeko
- ❏ Space battle design, 35" x 35", 3-pack [406-01] 25.00

Drawing Board Greeting Cards, Inc.
- ❏ C-3PO, R2-D2, and Star Wars logo, 60" x 96" [406-02] ...25.00
- ❏ Cloud City and characters, 60" x 96" [406-03] 25.00
- ❏ Darth Vader and Luke dueling, 54" x 96" [406-04] 25.00
- ❏ Ewok gliders, 54" x 96" [406-05] 25.00

Drawing Board Greeting Cards, Inc. (Canada)
- ❏ Darth Vader and Luke dueling, 54" x 96" 25.00

Gemma International (UK)
- ❏ Clone Wars [406-06] 10.00

Hallmark Party
Covers are 54" x 102".
- ❏ Clone Wars opposing forces [406-07] 10.00
- ❏ LEGO Star Wars [406-08] 10.00
- ❏ Star Wars generations, design in corner [406-09] 10.00
- ❏ Star Wars generations, design covers front 10.00

Party Express
Covers are 54" x 102".
- ❏ Clone Wars [406-10] 10.00
- ❏ Episode III: Revenge of the Sith [406-11] 10.00
- ❏ Yoda and Darth Vader, X-Wings and TIE Fighters 3D ...12.00

Covers are 54" x 90".
- ❏ Classic trilogy, spaceship art [406-12] 10.00
- ❏ Episode I: The Phantom Menace, tech design with Jedi and Sith silouette border [406-13] 10.00
- ❏ Episode II: Attack of the Clones, Jedi duel 10.00
- ❏ Star Wars saga [406-14] 10.00

406-15 | 406-16 | 407-01 | 407-02 | 407-03 | 407-04 | 407-05 | 407-06 | 407-07

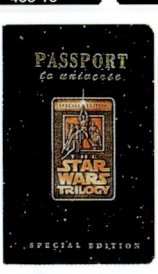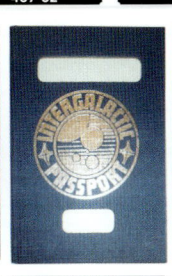

407-08 | 408-01 | 408-02 | 408-03 | 408-04 | 408-05 | 408-06 | 408-07

Party Table Covers

Quela
- Classic trilogy characters 15.00
- Darth Vader neon [406-15] 15.00
- Starfighter battle 15.00

Unique (Canada)
- Jedi vs. Sith, graphic [406-16] 20.00

Party Thank You Cards
Continued in Volume 3, Page 315

- C-3PO: "Thanks," 8-pack 10.00

Drawing Board Greeting Cards, Inc.
- R2-D2 Thank you cards, 8-pack [407-01] 12.00

Hallmark Party
8-packs.
- Clone Wars opposing forces, "Thanks!" [407-02] 10.00
- Darth Vader, "Thanks!" / "This will be a birthday long remembered!" with envelopes, seals [407-03] 10.00
- LEGO Star Wars, "Thanks!" [407-04] 10.00

Heartline
- Darth Vader, thank you 10.00
- Yoda, Thank you, I do! 10.00

Party Express
8-packs.
- Attack of the Clones heroes [407-05] 10.00
- Captain Rex [407-06] 10.00
- Darth Vader [407-07] 10.00
- Jar Jar Binks [407-08] 10.00

Passports
Continued in Volume 3, Page 315

- Passport to universe, Star Wars Special Edition [408-01] .. 20.00

Ballantine
- The Star Wars intergalactic passport [408-02] 35.00

Cast and Crew
- Intergalactic passport [408-03] 2,400.00

Pepsi Cola
- Anakin [408-04] 10.00
- Qui-Gon Jinn [408-05] 10.00
- Watto [408-06] 10.00

Star Wars Celebration VI
- Galactic passport [408-07] 6.00

Patches

- Celebration Europe logo [409-01] 25.00
- Colorado Wildfires 2012 .... 15.00
- Empire Strikes Back logo [4.226] 20.00
- Star Wars Special Edition [409-02] 25.00

Celebration III logo.
- Cloth [409-03] 25.00
- Rubber [v1e1-338] 25.00

Sewing On Patches.
- Darth Maul [409-04] 10.00
- Imperial cog [409-05] 10.00

- Separatists [409-06] 10.00
- Star Wars [409-07] 10.00

(Japan)
- Anakin [409-08] 15.00
- Clone trooper (helmet) [409-09] 15.00
- Darth Vader [409-10] 15.00
- Darth Vader (flaming helmet) [409-11] 15.00
- Darth Vader (helmet) [409-12] 15.00
- Darth Vader (imperial cog) [409-13] 15.00
- Darth Vader (sunrise) [409-14] 15.00
- Darth Vader oval [409-15] 15.00
- Darth Vader shield [409-16] 15.00
- Grievous [409-17] 15.00
- Jedi [409-18] 15.00
- Jedi Starfighter [409-19] 15.00
- Revenge of the Sith logo [409-20] 15.00
- Sith [409-21] 15.00
- Sith Lord [409-22] 15.00
- Star Wars logo [409-23] 15.00
- Vader [409-24] 15.00
- Yoda [409-25] 15.00

20th Century Fox
- Episode III: Revenge of the Sith DVD release promotional 20.00

Boy Scouts of America
- 1997 Fall Fellowship [4.226] 25.00
- 1997 Olde Mill Star Wars Adventure [409-26] 25.00
- 1998 GFRC Day Camp [409-27] 20.00
- Cub Scout Winter Event [409-28] 35.00
- Mid-Valley Spring-78 Camporee [409-29] 25.00
- Pack 659 Halloween Carnival 2008 .... 20.00
- Scout Wars Fall Round Up 80 [409-30] 20.00

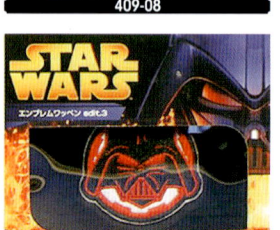
409-01

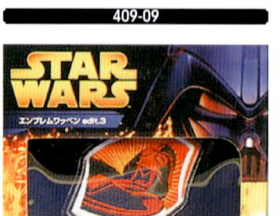
409-02

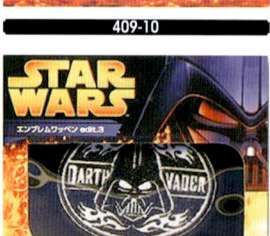
409-03

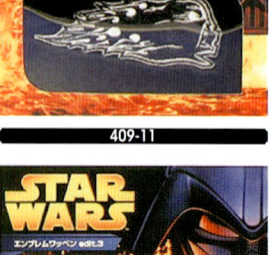
409-04

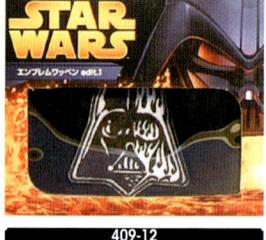
409-05

409-06

409-07

409-08

409-09

409-10

409-11

409-12

409-13

409-14

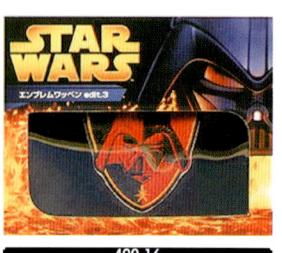
409-15

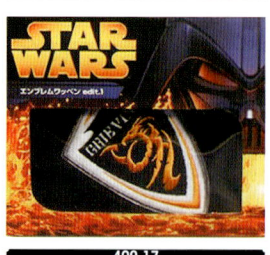
409-16

409-17

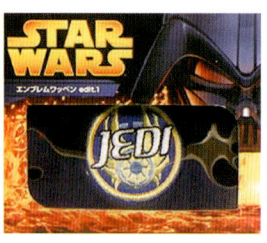
409-18

409-19

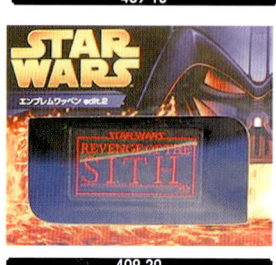
409-20

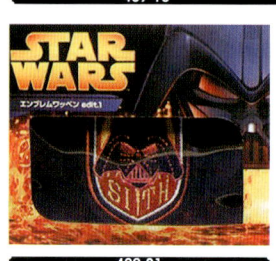
409-21

409-22

Patches

 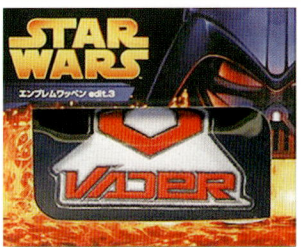   

409-23   409-24   409-25   409-26   409-27

- ❏ Scout Wars Round Up 80, rectangular, features Luke, Leia, Vader, TIE Fighter, X-Wing...20.00
- ❏ Tu Cubin Noonie Lodge, The Lodge Strikes Back, 2011 Teepee Week 25.00

Catalina Council.
- ❏ 1978 D2 Roundup [409-31] 35.00

Catawba Lodge 459 NOAC.
- ❏ 1994 [4:227] 40.00

Central Okanagan.
- ❏ 1998 Cuboree Camp Dunlop [4:227] 35.00

Chicago.
- ❏ 1982 Camporall [409-32] 25.00

Chickasaw.
- ❏ 1978 Cub Day Camp [4:227] 25.00

Colonial Virginia Council.
- ❏ CVC 2005 Star Wars Cub Parent Weekend 20.00

Eastern Okla Council.
- ❏ 1978 Scout Regatta [409-33] 35.00

Eluwak.
- ❏ 1997 Eluwak Strikes Back Camporee [409-34] 20.00

FCC Powahay District.
- ❏ 1995 Spring Camporee [4:227] 35.00

- ❏ Battle of the Ice Planet Hoyt, AT-AT, Luke on tauntaun. For event at Hoyt Scout Reservation 20.00

Fort A.P. Hill National Jamboree.
- ❏ 2001 Sith Park Empire Council, red border [4:227] 20.00
- ❏ 2001 Sith Park Empire Council, silver border [4:227] 20.00

Grand River Cubs.
- ❏ 1978 Canadian Star War-EE [4:227] 25.00

Great Salt Lake Council.
- ❏ Jedi Training Camp [409-35] 25.00

Illiniwek.
- ❏ 1978 Webelos Camporee [409-36] 35.00

Jamboree Staff.
- ❏ 2001 blue border [4:227] 20.00
- ❏ 2001 pink border [4:227] 20.00
- ❏ 2001 white border [4:227] 20.00
- ❏ 2001 yellow border [4:227] 20.00

Kiowa District.
- ❏ 1981 Camporee [409-37] 35.00

Lake Huron Area Council.
- ❏ 1982 Day Camp [409-38] 30.00

Lincoln Heritage Council.
- ❏ 2012 Pleasant Valley Camporee—Southern Indiana, features green alien with Yoda ears wearing scout uniform 35.00

Los Angeles Area Council NOAC.
- ❏ 2000 3-part set, black border [4:227] 50.00
- ❏ 2000 3-part set, light blue border [4:227] 50.00
- ❏ 2000 3-part set, silver mylar border [4:227] 150.00

Los Angeles Area Council Pow Wow.
- ❏ 1997 Red border, staff issue [4:227] 50.00
- ❏ 1997 Yellow border, participant issue [4:227] 50.00

Marin Council.
- ❏ 1993 [409-39] 60.00
- ❏ 1997 Yoda brown border [4:227] 85.00
- ❏ 1997 Yoda gold mylar border [4:227] 250.00
- ❏ 1997 Yoda green border [4:227] 55.00
- ❏ 1997 Yoda yellow border [409-40] 40.00
- ❏ 2001 Gold mylar border, Donor issue [409-41] 125.00
- ❏ 2001 Green border, Jamboree Trader issue [4:227] 35.00
- ❏ 2001 Red border, Special Recognition issue [4:227] ...150.00
- ❏ 2001 Silver border, Troop Leadership issue [4:227] 250.00
- ❏ 2005 Eagle Scout—Yoda 75.00
- ❏ 2005 Friendship / Scout Spirit—Yoda, blue border 25.00
- ❏ 2005 Friendship / Scout Spirit—Yoda, green border ...25.00
- ❏ 2005 Friendship / Scout Spirit—Yoda, red border 25.00
- ❏ 2007 Friendship / Scout Spirit—Yoda, gray border, World Jamboree 25.00
- ❏ 2007 World Citizenship—Darth Vader, maroon border, World Jamboree 25.00
- ❏ 2010 Clean / Reverent—Captain Rex 35.00
- ❏ 2010 Courage / Confidence—Jabba the Hutt 35.00
- ❏ 2010 Courage / Confidence—Jabba the Hutt, standard elongated shoulder patch shape 35.00

409-28   409-29   409-30   409-31   409-32   409-33

409-34   409-35   409-36   409-37   409-38

409-39   409-40   409-41

Patches

409-42   409-43   409-44   409-45   409-46   409-47   409-48

- ☐ 2010 Courteous / Kind—Republic Fleet 35.00
- ☐ 2010 Discovery / Exploration—Anakin, Obi-Wan, Captain Rex 35.00
- ☐ 2010 Friendship / Scout Spirit—Anakin Skywalker 35.00
- ☐ 2010 Friendship / Scout Spirit—Anakin Skywalker, standard elongated shoulder patch shape 35.00
- ☐ 2010 Helpful / Friendly—Y-Wing Starfighters 35.00
- ☐ 2010 Leadership / Citizenship—Anakin and Obi-Wan 35.00
- ☐ 2010 Obedient / Cheerful—General Grievous 35.00
- ☐ 2010 Respect / Understanding—Yoda, Obi-Wan, Anakin 35.00
- ☐ 2010 Thrifty / Brave—Commander Cody and clone troopers 35.00
- ☐ 2010 Trustworthy / Loyal—Jedi Starfighters 35.00
- ☐ 2010 Vision / Wisdom—Yoda 35.00
- ☐ 2010 Vision / Wisdom—Yoda, standard elongated shoulder patch shape 35.00

Menawa.
- ☐ 1999 Camporee, ghost issue [4:228] 20.00

Mid-America Council.
- ☐ 1978 Scout-O-Rama [409-42] 35.00

Middle Tennessee Council.
- ☐ Join the Force [4:228] 20.00

Northern New Jersey Council.
- ☐ No Be Bo Sco—Episode 73—Summer Camp 1999, features Rebel logo and Star Wars style text 20.00

Occoneechee Council.
- ☐ 2005 Sea Scout Ship inner Obi-Wan and Anakin........20.00
- ☐ 2005 Sea Scout Ship outer Anakin 20.00
- ☐ 2005 Sea Scout Ship outer C-3PO and R2-D2............20.00
- ☐ 2005 Sea Scout Ship outer Darth Vader 20.00
- ☐ 2005 Sea Scout Ship outer Obi-Wan 20.00
- ☐ 2005 Sea Scout Ship outer Yoda 20.00
- ☐ 2005 Sea Scout Ship outer Yoda / Force 20.00
- ☐ Sea Scout Ship 762 uncut Jacket Patch 50.00

Pioneer Valley Council.
- ☐ 1997 Cub Day Camp [4:228] 20.00

Ridgewood / Glen Rock Council.
- ☐ 1997 Jamboree [4:228] 55.00

Rockland County Council.
- ☐ 1979 Star War Fall Camporee [409-43] 25.00

Shelter Rock.
- ☐ 1994 [4:228] 15.00

Tah Heetch Lodge NOAC.
- ☐ 2000 silver mylar border, regular issue [4:228] 75.00
- ☐ 2000 yellow border, contingent issue [4:228] 175.00
- ☐ 2002 silver mylar border, regular issue [4:228] 75.00
- ☐ 2002 yellow border, Contingent issue 150.00
- ☐ 2004 [4:228] 60.00

Tecumseh District.
- ☐ 1977 Star Wars Camporee [409-44] 25.00

Valley Trails District.
- ☐ 1981 Space O Ree [4:228] 25.00

West Scarborough.
- ☐ 1999 Katimavih [4:228] 20.00

Western Star.
- ☐ Spring Camporee [4:228] 25.00

Yosemite Area Council.
- ☐ 1978 Cub Day Camp [4:228] 35.00

C and D Visionaries, Inc.
- ☐ Bantha Skull / Mandalorian 10.00
- ☐ Clone trooper [409-45] 10.00
- ☐ Leia, round [409-46] 10.00
- ☐ New Republic Special Forces [409-47] 10.00
- ☐ R2-D2 [409-48] 10.00
- ☐ Rebel Insignia [409-49] 10.00
- ☐ Revenge of the Jedi [409-50] 10.00
- ☐ Revenge of the Sith [409-51] 10.00
- ☐ Star Wars—Han, Luke, Leia [409-52] 10.00
- ☐ The Empire Strikes Back [409-53] 10.00

Back patches.
- ☐ Clone trooper [409-54] 20.00
- ☐ Imperial cog [409-55] 20.00

Cards, Inc. (UK)
- ☐ Collector's Embroidered Emblems, 6-patch set, 8,000 produced, individually numbered 45.00

  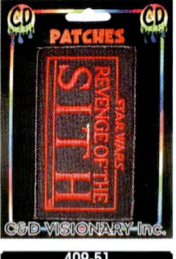 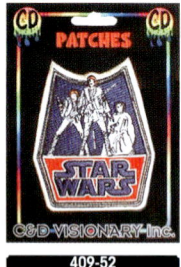   

409-49   409-50   409-51   409-52   409-53   409-54   409-55

  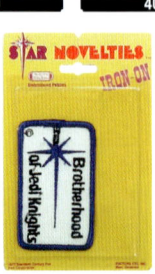     

409-56   409-57   409-58   409-59   409-60   409-61   409-62   409-63

409-64   409-65   409-66   409-67   409-68   409-69   409-70   409-71

Patches

409-72

409-73

409-74

409-75

409-76

409-77

409-78

Cast and Crew
- ☐ A New Hope, no TM [4:228]..................................OSPV
- ☐ Blue Harvest, embroidered hat patch [4:228].........OSPV
- ☐ Blue Harvest, silk-screened hat patch [4:228]........OSPV
- ☐ Empire Strikes Back, Vader in Flames [409-56]......OSPV
- ☐ ILM [4:228]..OSPV
- ☐ ILM VFX 02, Attack Gunship [4:228]......................OSPV
- ☐ Norwegian Unit / Star Wars set of 2 [4:228]...........OSPV
- ☐ Revenge of the Sith hat patch [4:228]....................OSPV
- ☐ Skywalker Ranch [v1e1:340]..................................OSPV
- ☐ Star Wars, early lettering style [4:228]....................OSPV
- ☐ The Star Wars [4:228]..OSPV
- ☐ Yoda, Revenge of the Jedi, 5" x 3" [4:228].............OSPV
- ☐ Yoda, Revenge screenwriter [4:228].......................OSPV

ILM VFX Crew 99.
- ☐ Battle droid Tank [v1e1:341]......................................25.00
- ☐ Boss Nass [v1e1:341]..25.00
- ☐ Darth Maul [v1e1:341]..25.00
- ☐ Jar Jar [v1e1:341]..25.00
- ☐ Naboo Fighter [v1e1:341]..25.00
- ☐ Podracer [v1e1:341]..25.00
- ☐ Queen Amidala [v1e1:341]..25.00
- ☐ SW I [v1e1:341]...25.00
- ☐ Watto [v1e1:341]...25.00

The Phantom Menace. Animation Unit.
- ☐ Animation Unit [4:229]...25.00
- ☐ BNS [4:229]..25.00
- ☐ DRD [4:229]..25.00
- ☐ JJB [4:229]..25.00
- ☐ WTO [4:229]..25.00

The Phantom Menace. Knoll Unit.
- ☐ CLP [4:229]..25.00
- ☐ FBB [4:229]..25.00
- ☐ Knoll Unit [4:229]..25.00
- ☐ PRS [4:229]..25.00
- ☐ SPB [4:229]..25.00

The Phantom Menace. Muren Unit.
- ☐ GGB [4:229]...25.00
- ☐ Muren Unit [4:229]..25.00
- ☐ NSP [4:229]..25.00
- ☐ OGB [4:229]...25.00
- ☐ UWS [4:229]...25.00

The Phantom Menace. Production Unit.
- ☐ ACT [4:229]..25.00
- ☐ ART [4:229]..25.00
- ☐ CGS [4:229]..25.00
- ☐ EDL [4:229]..25.00
- ☐ PRO [4:229]..25.00
- ☐ Production Unit [4:229]..25.00
- ☐ SCN [4:229]..25.00
- ☐ TEC [4:229]..25.00

The Phantom Menace. Squires Unit.
- ☐ GSR [4:229]..25.00
- ☐ JDB [4:229]..25.00
- ☐ QNB [4:229]...25.00
- ☐ Squires Unit [4:229]...25.00
- ☐ THD [4:229]..25.00

The Phantom Menace. Stage Unit.
- ☐ CAM [4:229]...25.00
- ☐ MDL [4:229]...25.00
- ☐ PYR [4:229]..25.00
- ☐ Stage Unit [4:229]..25.00
- ☐ STG [4:229]..25.00

Code 3 Collectibles
Insignia patches Included with replica vehicle.
- ☐ 501st / TIE Fighter...20.00
- ☐ Clone trooper / Republic Gunship.............................20.00
- ☐ Imperial / AT-ST..20.00
- ☐ Mandalorian / Slave I..20.00
- ☐ Rebel / Millennium Falcon..20.00
- ☐ Rebel / X-Wing Fighter...20.00
- ☐ Skywalker Fire Dept. [4:229]....................................50.00

Dark Horse Comics
- ☐ Dawn of the Jedi, excl. to Star Wars Celebration VI.....10.00

Data East
- ☐ Star Wars Pinball [409-57].......................................75.00

DC Metro Area SW Collecting Club
- ☐ 30 Years of the Force, exclusive to Star Wars Celebration IV..30.00
- ☐ Sixth Anniversary—Holiday Special Boba Fett—Washington Monument rocket pack 30.00

Dixie / Northern Inc.
- ☐ 4th Place Prize, Darth Vader Appearance sweepstakes [4:229]..200.00

409-79

409-80

409-81

409-82

409-83

409-84

409-85

409-86

409-87

409-88

409-89

409-90

409-91

409-92

409-93

409-94

Patches

409-95 | 409-96 | 409-97 | 409-98 | 409-99

409-100 | 409-101 | 409-102

Factors, Etc.
- ❏ Brotherhood of Jedi Knights 3.5" second issue [4:229] ...25.00
- ❏ Brotherhood of Jedi Knights 3" original [409-58] ...25.00
- ❏ Darth Vadar Lives (misspelled), iron-on [409-59] ...25.00
- ❏ Darth Vader, clenched fist [4:230] ...25.00
- ❏ May the Force be with You [409-60] ...25.00
- ❏ Rebel Forces, green accents [4:230] ...25.00
- ❏ Rebel Forces, tan accents [4:230] ...25.00
- ❏ Star Wars 3.5" original [4:230] ...25.00
- ❏ Star Wars 4" [4:230] ...25.00
- ❏ Star Wars pyramid logo [409-61] ...25.00
- ❏ Star Wars pyramid logo without trademark [4:230] ...25.00

Fan Club
- ❏ A New Hope [v1e1:341] ...20.00
- ❏ Empire Strikes Back 10th Anniversary [409-62] ...40.00
- ❏ Empire Strikes Back First 10 Years [409-63] ...50.00
- ❏ Empire Strikes Back logo, red outline [4:230] ...25.00
- ❏ Empire Strikes Back logo, white outline [4:230] ...25.00
- ❏ Official Fan Club [4:230] ...20.00
- ❏ Official Fan Club, 2nd issue [409-64] ...15.00
- ❏ Return of the Jedi logo [4:230] ...10.00
- ❏ Revenge of the Jedi logo [4:230] ...15.00
- ❏ Rogue trooper 1977–2007 ...15.00
- ❏ Vader in Flames [v1e1:341] ...15.00
- ❏ Yoda / Return of the Jedi [v1e1:341] ...15.00
- ❏ Yoda / Revenge of the Jedi [4:230] ...30.00

Fan Based
501st Legion, events.
- ❏ 2009 ALL-CON Dallas [409-65] ...15.00

Girl Scouts USA
Pioneer Girl Scout Council.
- ❏ Blue detail [409-66] ...40.00
- ❏ Pink detail [4:232] ...40.00

H and M (Sweden)
Iron-on.
- ❏ Darth Vader, Yoda, "Jedi" [409-67] ...25.00

Heart Art Collection, Ltd. (Japan)
- ❏ Boba Fett [409-68] ...15.00
- ❏ C-3PO [409-69] ...15.00
- ❏ C-3PO and R2-D2 [409-70] ...15.00
- ❏ Darth Vader [409-71] ...15.00
- ❏ Empire Strikes Back [409-72] ...15.00
- ❏ Star Wars [409-73] ...15.00
- ❏ Stormtrooper [409-74] ...15.00
- ❏ Yoda [409-75] ...15.00

Kellogg's
- ❏ C-3PO's "The Force" premium cap [409-76] ...75.00

Kenner
- ❏ Hat patch [4:232] ...OSPV
- ❏ Return of the Jedi, internal [v1e1:343] ...OSPV
- ❏ Sculpting smock patch [4:232] ...OSPV
- ❏ Star Wars / ESB sweepstakes 3rd prize ...400.00

Kid Rhino
- ❏ Official Jedi Knight [4:232] ...10.00

LucasArts
- ❏ Republic Commando [409-77] ...15.00
- ❏ Star Wars Battlefront Renegade Squadron, 3" diameter, exclusive to Star Wars Celebration IV ...15.00
- ❏ Star Wars Battlefront Renegade Squadron, 3" diameter, exclusive to Star Wars Celebration V ...15.00
- ❏ Star Wars Galaxies [4:232] ...20.00

Lucasfilm Fan Club
- ❏ Logo, red on black [4:232] ...20.00
- ❏ Logo, silver on black [4:232] ...20.00
- ❏ Lucasfilm, Ltd. [4:232] ...20.00
- ❏ Star Wars [409-78] ...20.00

Media Play
- ❏ Darth Vader, Revenge of the Sith soundtrack [4:232] ...20.00

Paizo Publishing / Fan Club
Bantha Tracks. Included with Fan Club membership kit.
- ❏ 2003 [409-79] ...25.00
- ❏ 2007 ...25.00

Pepsi
- ❏ Bravo Squadron [4:232] ...20.00
- ❏ Bravo Squadron, diamond [4:232] ...20.00
- ❏ Naboo Starfighter [4:232] ...20.00

Leather jacket patches, promotional.
- ❏ Naboo Bravo Squadron [4:232] ...75.00
- ❏ Trade Federation Starfighter [4:232] ...75.00

R2-KT Fan Club
- ❏ Fan Club 'Patch 5', 300 produced [409-80] ...15.00
- ❏ Halloween, 300 produced [409-81] ...15.00
- ❏ Valentines, cupid ...15.00
- ❏ Valentines, heart ...15.00

Droids Need Hugs Too.
- ❏ Chibi Leia, 300 produced [409-82] ...15.00
- ❏ Jawa, 300 produced [409-83] ...15.00
- ❏ WALL-E, 300 produced [409-84] ...15.00

Rancho Obi-Wan
- ❏ Obi-Wan Charter Member [409-85] ...50.00
- ❏ Orange border [409-86] ...30.00
- ❏ Rancho Obi-Wan Grand Reopening Patch [409-87] ...35.00
- ❏ Rancho Obi-Wan World Record Night Patch [409-88] ...35.00
- ❏ Yoda, exclusive to Star Wars Celebration VI [409-89] ...25.00

Rebel Legion
- ❏ 2011 Rebel Legion Patch Collectors [409-90] ...OSPV

RebelScum.com
- ❏ Rebelscum, Celebration III [409-91] ...30.00

Sales Corp. of America
Scarf and hat patches.
- ❏ C-3PO [4:233] ...25.00
- ❏ Chewbacca [4:233] ...25.00
- ❏ Darth Vader [4:233] ...25.00
- ❏ Darth Vader [4:233] ...25.00
- ❏ Ewok [4:233] ...25.00
- ❏ Gamorrean Guard [4:233] ...25.00
- ❏ R2-D2 [4:233] ...25.00

Scholastic
- ❏ May the Force be with you, iron-on [4:233] ...8.00

Star Tours
- ❏ Endor Express, shoulder patch [4:233] ...100.00
- ❏ Euro Disneyland—Rex [4:233] ...40.00
- ❏ Galactic Empire [4:233] ...15.00
- ❏ Logo [4:233] ...25.00
- ❏ Logo on blue triangle [4:233] ...35.00
- ❏ Logo on gray triangle [4:233] ...100.00
- ❏ Logo on white triangle [4:233] ...40.00
- ❏ Rebel Alliance [4:233] ...15.00
- ❏ Tour Director [4:233] ...25.00

Star Wars Celebration V
- ❏ 2010 World Championship Trivia Contest, Bossk, 200 produced [409-92] ...200.00
- ❏ Boba Fett, Celebration V [409-93] ...35.00

Star Wars Celebration VI
- ❏ 2012 World Championship Trivia Contest, icons [409-94] ...100.00
- ❏ Blue Harvest logo ...15.00
- ❏ Bossk Bail Bonds [409-95] ...15.00
- ❏ Celebration VI logo [409-96] ...15.00
- ❏ Galactic Games "There Is No Try" Patch ...15.00
- ❏ Imperial Corporate logo ...15.00
- ❏ Jabba's Palace Maintenance—Rancor Level ...15.00
- ❏ Mos Eisley Space Port [409-97] ...15.00

Thinking Cap
- ❏ Empire Strikes Back hat patch [4:233] ...50.00
- ❏ Yoda Hat Patch [4:233] ...50.00

Unlicensed
- ❏ 25th Anniversary [409-98] ...25.00

Walt Disney Resorts
- ❏ STAR WARS [409-99] ...8.00

Wizards of the Coast
- ❏ Star Wars Celebration II [409-100] ...35.00

Yodaholonet.com
- ❏ Luke and Yoda, exclusive to Star Wars Celebration V [409-101] ...15.00
- ❏ Yoda, graphic [409-102] ...15.00

Pencil and Pen Toppers

410-01 | 410-02 | 410-03 | 410-04 | 410-05 | 410-06 | 410-07 | 410-08

Patterns

Butterick
- Darth Vader (5186) [410-01] 25.00
- Luke and Leia (5175) [410-02] 25.00

McCall's
- Ewok Costume [410-03] 25.00
- Five Patterns, Empire Strikes Back [410-04] 35.00
- Night Wear, Return of the Jedi [410-05] 40.00
- Robes and Cloaks [410-06] 15.00
- Shirt, Return of the Jedi 15.00

Simplicity Pattern Co.
Episode III: Revenge of the Sith.
- 0577 Padmé and Leia [410-07] 20.00
- 0579 Anakin, Utapau administrator, Obi-Wan [410-08] .. 20.00

Pencil and Pen Toppers
Continued in Volume 3, Page 315

Star Wars Celebration III.
- Clone Lieutenant 10.00
- General Grievous 10.00
- Royal Guard 10.00

Squeeze Meez Clone Helmets from Set 1 and Set 2

Squeeze Meez Clone Helmets from Set 3 and Set 4

411-01 | 411-03 | 411-04 | 411-05 | 411-06 | 411-07 | 411-08 | 411-09 | 411-10

411-11 | 411-12 | 411-13 | 411-14 | 411-15 | 411-16 | 411-17 | 411-18 | 411-19 | 411-20 | 411-21 | 411-22

411-23 | 411-24 | 411-25 | 411-26 | 411-27 | 411-28 | 411-29 | 411-30 | 411-33

Pencil and Pen Toppers

412-1 412-2 412-3 412-4 412-5 412-6 412-7 412-8 412-9 412-10 412-11 412-12

   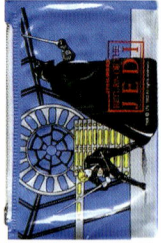    

412-13 412-14 412-15 412-16 412-17 412-18 412-19 412-20 Side 1 and Side 2

Bulls i Toy
Squeeze Meez pen toppers.
- ☐ Set 1: clone trooper, ARF trooper Boil, ARF trooper, Mystery topper [411-01] 12.00
- ☐ Set 2: Commander Gree, Commander Fox, clone trooper Niner, Mystery topper [411-02] 12.00
- ☐ Set 3: clone trooper Blaster, clone Commander Cody, Commander Wolffe, Mystery topper 12.00
- ☐ Set 4: ARC trooper Fives, clone pilot Warthog, clone trooper pilot, Mystery topper [411-03] 12.00

Butterfly Originals
- ☐ C-3PO [411-03] 10.00
- ☐ Darth Vader [411-04] 10.00
- ☐ Emperor's Royal Guard [411-05] 10.00
- ☐ Wicket [411-06] 10.00

Foamheads, Inc.
- ☐ Darth Vader, antenna, pencil, keychain topper, exclusive to Star Wars Celebration III [411-07] 15.00

HC Ford (UK)
- ☐ Admiral Ackbar [411-08] 12.00
- ☐ Bib Fortuna [411-09] 12.00
- ☐ Chewbacca [411-10] 12.00
- ☐ Darth Vader, short [411-11] 12.00
- ☐ Darth Vader, tall [411-12] 12.00
- ☐ Gamorrean Guard [411-13] 12.00
- ☐ Han Solo [411-14] 12.00
- ☐ Imperial guard [411-15] 12.00
- ☐ Luke Skywalker [411-16] 12.00

- ☐ R2-D2 [411-17] 12.00
- ☐ Wicket [411-18] 12.00
- ☐ Yoda [411-19] 12.00

Hard plastic cylinders.
- ☐ Darth Vader and stormtrooper [411-20] 15.00
- ☐ Luke Skywalker and R2-D2 ....15.00

Kellogg's (Singapore)
Cereal premiums, Episode II: Attack of the Clones.
- ☐ Anakin [411-21] 8.00
- ☐ C-3PO [411-22] 8.00
- ☐ Clone trooper [411-23] 8.00
- ☐ Darth Vader [411-24] 8.00
- ☐ Jango Fett [411-25] 8.00
- ☐ R2-D2 [411-26] 8.00
- ☐ Yoda 8.00

Nestlé (Philippines)
Episode III: Revenge of the Sith. Gold chase figures. Wonder Cup premiums.
- ☐ Anakin Skywalker 10.00
- ☐ C-3PO 10.00
- ☐ Clone trooper 10.00
- ☐ Darth Vader 10.00
- ☐ Obi-Wan Kenobi 10.00
- ☐ Yoda [411-27] 10.00

Episode III: Revenge of the Sith. Wonder Cup premiums.
- ☐ Anakin Skywalker 10.00

- ☐ C-3PO 10.00
- ☐ Clone trooper 10.00
- ☐ Darth Vader 10.00
- ☐ Obi-Wan Kenobi 10.00
- ☐ Yoda 10.00

Vending Supply
Star Wars character look-alikes. Rubbery. Available from vending machines in multiple colors.
- ☐ Darth Vader [411-28] 15.00
- ☐ Greedo [411-29] 15.00
- ☐ R2-D2 [411-30] 15.00
- ☐ R5-D4 [411-31] 15.00
- ☐ Robot [411-32] 15.00
- ☐ Stormtrooper [411-33] 15.00

Pencil Cases and Boxes
Continued in Volume 3, Page 315

- ☐ Darth Maul tin [412-1] 5.00
- ☐ Darth Maul tin, shaped [412-2] 8.00
- ☐ Jedi vs. Sith, zippered [412-3] 5.00
- ☐ Queen Amidala tin [412-4] 5.00
- ☐ Star Wars, dog fight scene, magnetic clasp, cast and staff listings [412-5] 65.00

(Australia)
- ☐ Queen Amidala, zippered [412-6] 10.00
- ☐ Queen Amidala, zippered narrow [412-7] 10.00

    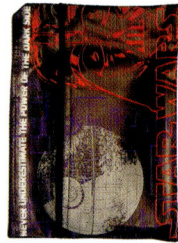

412-21 Side 1 and Side 2   412-22 Side 1 and Side 2   412-23

412-24 Side 1 and Side 2   412-25 Side 1 and Side 2   412-26 412-27 412-28 412-29 412-30

Pencil Cases and Boxes

412-31 | 412-32 | 412-33 | 412-34 | 412-35 | 412-36 | 412-37 | 412-38 | 412-39

412-40 | 412-41 | 412-42 | 412-43 | 412-44 | 412-45 | 412-46 | 412-47 Side 1 and Side 2 | 412-48 | 412-49

(Germany)
- ❏ Clone Wars, Commander Fox, Captain Rex, Anakin, Yoda, Obi-Wan, Ahsoka [412-8] 10.00

A.H. Prismatic
Holographic sticker affixed to lid of black metal boxes.
- ❏ B-Wing Starfighter / Millennium Falcon / X-Wing Fighter [412-9] 25.00
- ❏ Darth Vader / X-Wing Fighter / C-3PO and R2-D2 [412-10] 25.00
- ❏ Death Star Battle / Imperial Cruiser / AT-AT [412-11] 25.00
- ❏ Millennium Falcon / Darth Vader / TIE Interceptor [412-12] 25.00
- ❏ X-Wing Fighter / Millennium Falcon / Darth Vader [412-13] 25.00

Animations
- ❏ Sith Lord [412-14] 8.00

Ars Una Studio
- ❏ Yoda, Clone Wars, vertical zippered [412-15] 15.00

Butterfly Originals
- ❏ Darth Vader and Luke Skywalker duel, zippered pouch [412-16] 20.00

Creata Promotions
- ❏ C-3PO and R2-D2, Darth Vader and Empire Strikes Back logo on reverse side [412-17] 20.00

Flomo (UK)
- ❏ Darth Vader / Luke, Death Star attack [412-18] 50.00
- ❏ Vader / Star Destroyer / Death Star II, prism [412-19] 15.00

Frankel N Roth (UK)
Bags of Character, Return of the Jedi zipper pouches.
- ❏ Luke Skywalker / Darth Vader, zippered, silver [412-20] ... 50.00
- ❏ Luke in Jabba's Palace [412-21] 35.00
- ❏ Rebel Hangar [412-22] 35.00

Funtastic Pty. Ltd.
Double pouch, zippered, 9" x 12".
- ❏ C-3PO and R2-D2 .... 15.00
- ❏ Darth Vader [412-23] 15.00

Galerie
Electronic game cases with M&Ms inside.
- ❏ Darth Vader / Epic Duel [412-24] 10.00
- ❏ Yoda / R2-D2 and C-3PO [412-25] 10.00

Grand Toys
- ❏ Darth Maul character shaped, zippered [412-26] 12.00

Zippered pencil bags.
- ❏ Darth Maul 8.00

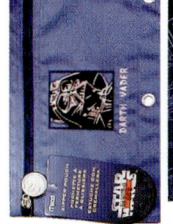  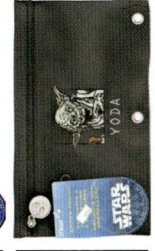        

412-50 | 412-50 | 412-52 | 412-53 | 412-54 | 412-55 | 412-56 | 412-57 | 412-58 | 412-59 | 412-60

      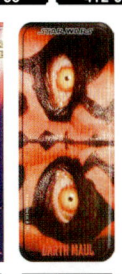    

412-61 | 412-62 | 412-63 | 412-64 | 412-65 | 412-66 | 412-67 | 412-68 | 412-69 | 412-70 | 412-71 | 412-72

       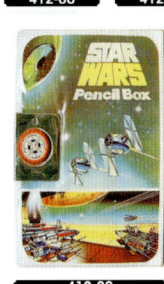  

412-73 | 412-74 | 412-75 | 412-76 | 412-77 | 412-78 | 412-79 | 412-80 | 412-81 | 412-82

Pencil and Pen Toppers

- ❑ Destroyer droid...10.00
- ❑ Queen Amidala, art [412-27].............................10.00
- ❑ Queen Amidala, photos [412-28]......................10.00

Grosvenor
- ❑ Jango Fett, zippered [412-29]...........................10.00
- ❑ Star Wars logo on black starfield, tin................10.00

HC Ford (UK)
- ❑ Darth Vader, spaceships, and Return of the Jedi logo, plastic box with metal clasp [412-30]..........75.00

Helix (UK)
- ❑ C-3PO and R2-D2 on drawing instruments tin............50.00
- ❑ "May The Force be With You" [412-31]..............60.00

Zippered, plastic.
- ❑ Ben Kenobi, white [412-32]..............................40.00
- ❑ C-3PO [412-33]..40.00
- ❑ Darth Vader [412-34].......................................40.00
- ❑ Han Solo, white [412-35].................................40.00
- ❑ Luke Skywalker, white [412-36].......................40.00
- ❑ Princess Leia, white [412-37]...........................40.00
- ❑ R2-D2 [412-38]..40.00
- ❑ Stormtrooper, red [412-39].............................40.00

Impact, Inc.
- ❑ Anakin Skywalker podracing, zippered [412-40]..............10.00
- ❑ Darth Maul with lightsaber tin, shaped [412-41]..............10.00
- ❑ Darth Maul, zippered [412-42].........................10.00
- ❑ Jar Jar transformable pencil case [412-43].......20.00
- ❑ "Jedi vs. Sith" Qui-Gon Jinn, Obi-Wan, Darth Sidious, Darth Maul, tin box [412-44]..............8.00
- ❑ Podracer pencil pouch [412-45]......................10.00
- ❑ "Tatooine," tin box [412-45].............................8.00

Innovative Designs
Pencil bags.
- ❑ Angry Birds characters, Chewbacca, Han Solo, Luke Skywalker, Obi-Wan Kenobi, Princess Leia [412-46]..........10.00
- ❑ Darth Vader / Anakin Skywalker.....................10.00
- ❑ Darth Vader / Yoda..10.00

Magic World
- ❑ General Grievous / Yoda [412-47]....................15.00

Mead
Zipper pouches with grommets for binder storage.
- ❑ Darth Vader, black [412-48]............................10.00
- ❑ Darth Vader, blue [412-49].............................10.00
- ❑ Darth Vader, patch [412-50]...........................10.00
- ❑ Star Wars patch, blueprint design [412-51]....10.00
- ❑ Yoda, patch [412-52].......................................10.00

Merlin
- ❑ Boba Fett, tin [412-53]....................................15.00
- ❑ Stormtroopers / dogfight, tin [412-54]............15.00

Metal Box Ltd.
Tin boxes.
- ❑ C-3PO [412-55]..20.00
- ❑ Chewbacca [412-56]..20.00
- ❑ Darth Vader [412-57].......................................20.00
- ❑ R2-D2 [412-56]..20.00
- ❑ Yoda..20.00

Nestlé (Philippines)
Episode III: Revenge of the Sith.
- ❑ Darth Vader [412-58].......................................20.00
- ❑ Darth Vader attacking [412-59]......................20.00

Pyramid
- ❑ Episode II heroes, zippered [412-60]...............10.00

Q-Stat (UK)
- ❑ Episode I Podracing, mechanical compartments [412-61]..........20.00

Pencil tins.
- ❑ Anakin Skywalker [412-62]..............................8.00
- ❑ Darth Maul [412-63]..8.00
- ❑ Queen Amidala [412-64].................................8.00

Zippered pencil bags.
- ❑ Destroyer droid [412-65].................................10.00

Rapport
- ❑ Return of the Jedi, blue [412-66].....................35.00

Rose Art Industries
- ❑ Lightsaber pencil case [412-67].......................15.00

Sunburst Merchandising
Episode I, tin.
- ❑ Darth Maul [412-68]..10.00
- ❑ Jar Jar Binks [412-69]......................................10.00
- ❑ Podracing [412-70]..10.00
- ❑ Queen Amidala [412-71]..................................10.00

Tin Box Company
Pencil boxes.
- ❑ C-3PO and R2-D2 [412-72]..............................8.00
- ❑ Darth Vader [412-73].......................................8.00
- ❑ Empire, exclusive to Target [412-74]..............8.00
- ❑ Hildebrant art, exclusive to Target [412-75]....8.00
- ❑ Sith Lord, exclusive to Target [412-76]............8.00
- ❑ Yoda, lightsaber left, exclusive to Target [412-77]..........8.00
- ❑ Yoda, lightsaber right [412-78]........................8.00
- ❑ Yoda, Obi-Wan, Anakin, exclusive to Target [412-79]..........8.00

YAM
Combination lock.
- ❑ Death Star / Rebel Base [412-80]...................45.00
- ❑ Han and Chewbacca / Millennium Falcon [412-81]..........45.00
- ❑ Stormtroopers / Tatooine [412-82].................45.00

Pencil Cups

HC Ford (UK)
- ❑ Artwork of characters, 4" high metal [413-01]..........175.00

Sigma
- ❑ Yoda [413-02]..85.00

Pencil Sharpeners
Continued in Volume 3, Page 315

(Asia)
Keychains.
- ❑ AT-ST..50.00
- ❑ Han and Chewbacca......................................50.00
- ❑ Jabba and captive Leia...................................50.00
- ❑ Stormtrooper and Luke..................................50.00
- ❑ R2-D2 and C-3PO..50.00
- ❑ Yoda...50.00

414-01   414-02   414-03

414-04   414-05   414-06

414-07

414-08

414-09   414-10   414-11

414-12   414-13

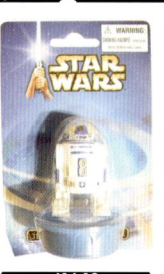

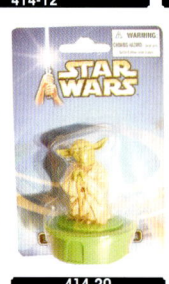

414-14   414-15   414-16

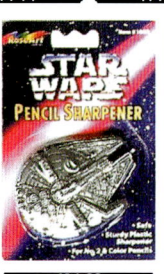
414-17   414-18   414-19   414-20

414-21   414-22   414-23

Pencils

Accessory Zone
❏ Darth Vader and Yoda 12-pack [414-01]..........................8.00

Animations
❏ Darth Vader [414-02]..2.00

Butterfly Originals
❏ Darth Vader, sculpted [414-03].................................15.00
❏ Wicket sharpener with eraser [414-04]..........................20.00

Figural characters.
❏ R2-D2 [414-05]...25.00
❏ Yoda [414-06]..25.00

Crystal Craft (Australia)
❏ R2-D2 sharpener with Jabba the Hutt eraser [414-07]...120.00

Flomo (UK)
❏ Star Wars, round prism [414-08]................................10.00

Grand Toys
❏ Queen Amidala emblem, round [4:236]............................10.00
❏ Queen Amidala, round [4:236]...................................10.00

Grosvenor
❏ Star Wars logo, round [4:236]..................................10.00

HC Ford (UK)
Line drawing on dome-shaped sharpener.
❏ C-3PO and R2-D2..45.00
❏ Darth Vader and stormtrooper [414-09]..........................45.00
❏ Han Solo and Chewbacca...45.00
❏ Luke and Leia..45.00

Oval-shaped sharpener with image.
❏ Darth Vader and X-Wing Fighter, blue [414-10].................35.00
❏ Darth Vader and X-Wing Fighter, red [414-11]..................35.00

Square sharpener with image.
❏ Darth Vader and X-Wing Fighter [414-12].......................25.00

Helix (UK)
❏ Death Star shaped [414-13]....................................85.00

Impact, Inc.
❏ Destroyer droid sharpener / eraser combo [414-14]........15.00
❏ Federation Tank sculpted [414-15].............................15.00

Innovative Designs
❏ Clone Wars 12-pack [414-16]...................................10.00

Jollibee
❏ Obi-Wan Kenobi..14.00

Merlin
❏ Darth Vader, round [414-17]...................................10.00

Pyramid
❏ Jango Fett, round [414-18]....................................5.00
❏ R2-D2, figural [414-19].......................................12.00
❏ Yoda, figural [414-20]..12.00

Q-Stat (UK)
❏ Darth Maul, round [414-21]....................................10.00

Rose Art Industries
❏ Millennium Falcon sculpted [414-22]...........................15.00

Takara (Japan)
❏ R2-D2 [414-23]..125.00

Pencil Trays

Sigma
❏ C-3PO [415-01]..130.00

Pencils
Continued in Volume 3, Page 318

❏ 12 colored pencils in clear Star Wars tube case with R2-D2 figural top [416-01]..........................15.00

(UK)
❏ 2-pack, push point, 1 black, 1 colors [416-02]................10.00
❏ Lightsaber pencil set...15.00

Accessory Zone
❏ Lightsaber 16" pencil with micro notebook [416-03]............5.00

6-packs. Push pencils. Exclusive to Target.
❏ Asajj Ventress / Anakin Skywalker.............................12.00
❏ Asajj Ventress / Captain Rex [416-04].........................12.00
❏ Clone trooper / Obi-Wan and Yoda [416-05].....................12.00

Animations
❏ 12-pack Darth Vader [416-06]..................................8.00
❏ 6-pack Darth Vader theme [416-07].............................8.00
❏ 8-pack Darth Vader theme with sharpener [416-08]..............10.00
❏ Pencil, Darth Vader...2.00

6-packs. Push pencils. Exclusive to Target.
❏ Boba Fett [416-09]..10.00
❏ Darth Vader [416-10]..10.00
❏ Yoda [416-11]...10.00

369

Pencils

8-pack, colored pencils. Exclusive to Target.
- ❏ Darth Vader [416-12] 10.00
- ❏ Yoda 10.00

Mechanical pencils.
- ❏ Darth Vader 4-pack [416-13] 12.00

Butterfly Originals
4-packs. Blister packed on Darth Vader header card with Return of the Jedi logo.
- ❏ C-3PO [416-14] 20.00
- ❏ Darth Vader [416-15] 20.00
- ❏ Return of the Jedi logo [416-16] 20.00

Character-topped Return of the Jedi pencils.
- ❏ C-3PO [416-17] 12.00
- ❏ Darth Vader [416-18] 12.00
- ❏ Emperor's Royal Guard [416-19] 12.00
- ❏ Wicket the Ewok [416-20] 12.00

Pop-a-Point. Embossed with "May the Force be with you."
- ❏ 2-pack [416-21] 15.00
- ❏ 6-pack, colored [416-22] 25.00

Disney / MGM
- ❏ Star Tours, reflective with logo and droids [416-23] 8.00

Fan Club
- ❏ Empire Strikes Back logo and character strip [416-24] 8.00
- ❏ Star Wars logo and Character strip 8.00

Fantasma
- ❏ Star Wars logo and art on foil [416-25] 8.00
- ❏ Star Wars logo and art on foil, fringe topped [416-26] ... 10.00

Flomo (UK)
Classic trilogy starship silhouettes with Star Wars logo.
- ❏ Blue [416-27] 5.00
- ❏ Gray [416-28] 5.00
- ❏ Red [416-29] 5.00

Funtastic Pty. Ltd.
- ❏ C-3PO / R2-D2 [416-30] 5.00
- ❏ C-3PO / R2-D2 3-pack [416-31] 15.00

Grand Toys
Episode I pencil with character topper.
- ❏ 2-pack with lightsaber handle toppers [416-32] 8.00
- ❏ Anakin Skywalker [416-33] 5.00
- ❏ Darth Maul [416-34] 5.00
- ❏ Jar Jar Binks [416-35] 5.00

Grosvenor
- ❏ 10-pack, C-3PO, R2-D2, Star Wars logo [416-36] 10.00
- ❏ C-3PO, Lando, R2-D2, Boba Fett, logo [416-37] 8.00

HC Ford (UK)
- ❏ C-3PO and R2-D2 [416-38] 8.00
- ❏ C-3PO and R2-D2 [416-39] 8.00
- ❏ Chewbacca and Han Solo [416-40] 8.00
- ❏ Darth Vader and stormtroopers [416-41] 8.00
- ❏ Darth Vader and X-Wing Fighter [416-42] 8.00
- ❏ Luke Skywalker and Princess Leia [416-43] 8.00

Colored pencils.
- ❏ C-3PO and R2-D2, tri-colored pencil lead [416-44] 10.00

Mechanical pencils.
- ❏ Droids, Luke, Leia, Darth Vader [416-45] 15.00

Pencil set.
- ❏ Return of the Jedi [416-46] 25.00

416-47

416-48

416-49

416-50

416-51

416-52

Pennants

416-53 | 416-54 | 416-55 | 416-56 | 416-57 | 416-58 | 416-59 | 416-60 | 416-61 | 416-62 | 416-63 | 416-64 | 416-65 | 416-66

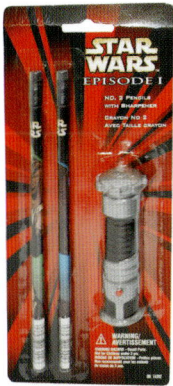

416-67 | 416-68 | 416-69 | 416-70 | 416-71 | 416-72 | 416-73 | 416-74 | 416-75 | 416-76 | 416-77

Pencils with puffed dangle toppers.
- Luke Skywalker and Princess Leia [416-47] 15.00

Helix (UK)
- "May the Force be with you" in gold on blue pencil....10.00
- Stormtrooper packaging, 12 colored pencils [416-48].....30.00

Character-topped pencils.
- C-3PO..10.00
- Darth Vader...10.00
- R2-D2..10.00
- Stormtrooper...10.00

Hunter Leisure, Ltd. (Australia)
- 6-pack, Revenge of the Sith [416-49]...........................8.00

Innovative Designs
12-packs.
- Generations. Darth Maul, Boba Fett, Anakin Skywalker, Yoda, Luke, Darth Vader [416-50] 5.00

4-packs of pencils with erasers.
- Angry Birds, exclusive to Walmart [416-51]..............10.00
- Clone Wars [416-52]...12.00
- Darth Vader and Yoda 12.00

Individuals. Pop-a-Point.
- Clones and Yoda [416-53]...5.00
- Cody, Anakin, Obi-Wan, Rex [416-54] 5.00

Magic World
- 6-pack, colored [416-55] 10.00

Mead
3 characters, art.
- 4-pack [416-56]..10.00

- 72-pack [416-57]..45.00
- C-3PO, Chewbacca, R2-D2 [416-58].........................3.00
- Darth Vader, Luke, Leia [416-59]................................3.00
- Darth Vader, stormtrooper, Boba Fett [416-60]..........3.00
- Luke, Leia, Han [416-61]..3.00

Merlin
- Star Wars Darth Vader [416-62]..................................4.00
- Star Wars TIE Fighters [416-63]..................................4.00
- X-Wings and Alliance logo [416-64]............................4.00

Pentech
Episode I character pencils.
- 2-pack w/ Anakin and Amidala pencil toppers [416-65] ...8.00
- 2-pack with Darth Maul and Jar Jar pencil toppers [416-66]..8.00
- 2-pack with lightsaber pencil sharpener [416-67]..........12.00
- 8-pack [416-68]...8.00

Pyramid
- 6-pack, Attack of the Clones characters [416-69] 8.00
- 10-pack, pens and pencils, AOTC [416-70] 10.00
- Star Wars logo and starfield, gold on black [416-71].......3.00

Q-Stat (UK)
Colored pencils. Black barrel with gold Star Wars logo. Part of the Jar Jar Binks art kit.
- Any of 6 colors, each [416-72].....................................2.00

Pencil sets. 2 pencils, pencil pouch, sharpener, eraser.
- Jedi vs. Sith..10.00
- Podrace 10.00

Rose Art Industries
Episode III: Revenge of the Sith.
- 4-pack, 1 of each design [416-73]................................8.00

- 8-pack, 2 of each design 10.00
- Clone troopers 3.00
- General Grievous 3.00
- Star Wars 3.00
- Vader 3.00

Episode III: Revenge of the Sith.
- Mechanical, 4-pack [416-74].......................................8.00

Episode III: Revenge of the Sith. Pencils with toppers.
- 2-pack "E-Racer" toppers...8.00
- 3-pack 8.00

Foil.
- 3-pack [416-75]...5.00
- 6-pack [416-76]...8.00

Star Wars Kids
- StarWarsKids.com [416-77].......................................5.00

Pennants

- 10th Anniversary [417-01]..45.00

Disney / MGM
- Jedi Training Academy [417-02].................................20.00

Ice Capades
Ice Capades and Ewoks.
- Flag [417-03] 150.00
- Princess Kneesaa [417-04].......................................250.00
- Wicket [417-05]...250.00

Mexico Collector Convention
- Power of the Force style logo, felt 25.00

417-01 | 417-02 | 417-03

Pennants

417-04 417-05

Star Tours
☐ C-3PO, R2-D2, and Rex, red tail [417-06] 85.00

Super Live Adventure (Japan)
☐ Feature graphic [417-07] 175.00

Pens and Markers
Continued in Volume 3, Page 319

Lightsaber pen in tin collector case.
☐ Darth Vader, red [418-01] 35.00
☐ Yoda, green [418-02] 35.00

(Japan)
Sculpted character pen top with art print on barrel.
☐ C-3PO / R2-D2 ....30.00

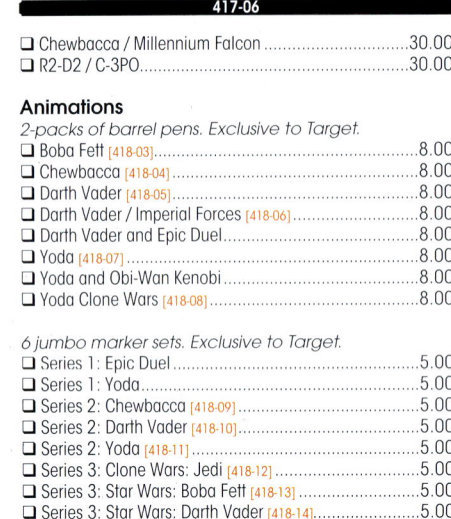

417-06

☐ Chewbacca / Millennium Falcon 30.00
☐ R2-D2 / C-3PO 30.00

Animations
2-packs of barrel pens. Exclusive to Target.
☐ Boba Fett [418-03] 8.00
☐ Chewbacca [418-04] 8.00
☐ Darth Vader [418-05] 8.00
☐ Darth Vader / Imperial Forces [418-06] 8.00
☐ Darth Vader and Epic Duel 8.00
☐ Yoda [418-07] 8.00
☐ Yoda and Obi-Wan Kenobi 8.00
☐ Yoda Clone Wars [418-08] 8.00

6 jumbo marker sets. Exclusive to Target.
☐ Series 1: Epic Duel 5.00
☐ Series 1: Yoda 5.00
☐ Series 2: Chewbacca [418-09] 5.00
☐ Series 2: Darth Vader [418-10] 5.00
☐ Series 2: Yoda [418-11] 5.00
☐ Series 3: Clone Wars: Jedi [418-12] 5.00
☐ Series 3: Star Wars: Boba Fett [418-13] 5.00
☐ Series 3: Star Wars: Darth Vader [418-14] 5.00

Butterfly Originals
☐ C-3PO card with markers [418-15] 18.00
☐ Darth Vader helmet on clip (any color) [418-16] 5.00
☐ Return of the Jedi, 2-pack [418-17] 18.00

417-07

Felt-tip markers.
☐ Darth Vader, black [418-18] 20.00
☐ Darth Vader, red 20.00

Chupa Chups
Sculpted character pens with concealed lollipops.
☐ Darth Vader [418-19] 10.00
☐ Stormtrooper [418-20] 10.00

Comic Images
Bobble pens.
☐ Darth Vader [418-21] 10.00
☐ Yoda [418-22] 10.00

Courage International Inc.
Kooky Klickers.
☐ Boba Fett art #17 [418-23] 8.00
☐ C-3PO art #15 [418-24] 8.00
☐ Darth Vader, individually numbered [418-25] 15.00
☐ Darth Vader art #19 [418-26] 8.00
☐ General Grievous art #20 [418-27] 8.00
☐ Luke Skywalker art [418-28] 8.00
☐ Princess Leia [418-29] 8.00
☐ Stormtrooper [418-30] 8.00
☐ Stormtrooper art [418-31] 8.00

Kooky Klickers. Clone Wars.
☐ Ahsoka Tano #2 [418-32] 8.00

      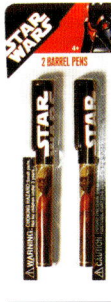  

418-01 418-02 418-03 418-04 418-05 418-06 418-07 418-08 418-09

418-10 418-11 418-12 418-13 418-14

418-15 418-16 418-17 418-18 418-19 418-20 418-21 418-22 418-23 418-24 418-25

Pens and Markers

| 418-26 | 418-27 | 418-28 | 418-29 | 418-30 | 418-31 | 418-32 | 418-33 | 418-34 | 418-35 | 418-36 |

 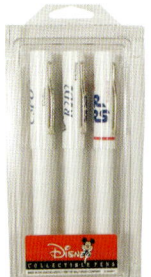   

| 418-37 | 418-38 | 418-39 | 418-40 | 418-41 |

❑ Anakin Skywalker #1 [418-33] 8.00
❑ Captain Rex #3 [418-34] 8.00
❑ General Grievous #4 [418-35] 8.00
❑ Obi-Wan Kenobi #5 [418-36] 8.00

Kooky Klickers. Sets of 4.
❑ C-3PO, Luke Skywalker, Boba Fett, Darth Vader with stand, large backer card [418-37] 40.00

Disney / MGM
❑ Set of 3: Star Tours logo, C-3PO, R2-D2 [418-38] 35.00

Disney Theme Park Merchandise
Kooky pens.
❑ Heroes, Mickey, Stitch, Minnie [418-39] 40.00
❑ Villains, Stitch, Goofy, Donald [418-40] 40.00
❑ Villains, Daisy, Donald, Stitch [418-41] 40.00

Fan Club
❑ Floaty Pen, Star Wars Insider renewal premium [418-42] 30.00

Fan Club (UK)
Black-ink revealing logo and character.
❑ C-3PO [418-43] 35.00
❑ Darth Vader [418-44] 35.00
❑ R2-D2 [418-45] 35.00

Fantasma
❑ Star Wars logo and line art on foil background 25.00

Fisher
❑ Rebel Fighter pen, black rubberized grip, "Star Wars" on clip, and Rebel emblem on end [418-46] 40.00
❑ Titanium space pen, "Star Wars" and "May the Force be with you" imprinted on barrel 50.00
❑ Titanium space pen, "Star Wars" and "May the Force be with you" imprinted on barrel, Dave Prowse autographed, 200 produced, individually numbered [418-47] 100.00

Funtastic Pty. Ltd.
❑ Star Wars logo on technical background. Included in art kits. Valued each. [418-48] 5.00

General Mills
Episode I 3D character pens. Cereal premiums.
❑ Anakin Skywalker [418-49] 10.00
❑ C-3PO 10.00
❑ Darth Maul 10.00
❑ Jar Jar Binks 10.00
❑ Obi-Wan Kenobi [418-50] 10.00
❑ Queen Amidala 10.00
❑ R2-D2 ....10.00
❑ Yoda [418-51] 10.00

Episode II lightsaber light-up pens. Cereal premiums.
❑ Anakin Skywalker, blue blade [418-52] 5.00
❑ Count Dooku, red blade [418-53] 5.00
❑ Darth Vader, red blade [418-54] 5.00
❑ Luke Skywalker, green blade [418-55] 5.00
❑ Mace Windu, purple blade [418-56] 5.00

Grosvenor (UK)
Star Wars Saga, package of 3.
❑ C-3PO, R2-D2 and logo on each [418-57] 8.00

| 418-42 | 418-43 | 418-44 | 418-45 | 418-46 | 418-47 | 418-48 | 418-49 | 418-50 | 418-51 | 418-52 | 418-53 |

| 418-54 | 418-55 | 418-56 | 418-57 | 418-58 | 418-59 | 418-60 | 418-61 | 418-62 | 418-63 | 418-64 | 418-65 |

373

Pens and Markers

| 418-66 | 418-67 Side 1 | 418-67 Side 2 | 418-68 | 418-69 | 418-70 | 418-71 | 418-72 | 418-73 |

   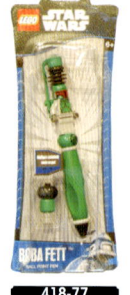    

| 418-74 | 418-75 | 418-76 | 418-77 | 418-78 | 418-79 | 418-80 | 418-81 |

Helix (UK)
Colored felt tips, boxed set.
- Set of five [418-58] 50.00
- Set of ten 65.00

Innovative Designs
- 2-pack Angry Birds pens, exclusive to Walmart [418-59] .. 8.00
- 2-pack Angry Birds pens [418-60] 8.00

2010. 2-packs of quotable pens. Exclusive to Target.
- Anakin and Ahsoka [418-61] 8.00
- Count Dooku and C-3PO [418-62] 8.00
- Yoda and Obi-Wan [418-63] 8.00

2011. 2-packs of quotable pens. Exclusive to Target.
- Anakin and Ahsoka [418-64] 10.00
- Yoda and Obi-Wan [418-65] 10.00

8-packs with roller stamps.
- Clone Wars [418-66] 10.00

Jumbo pens. 11" long.
- Angry Birds, exclusive to Walmart [418-67] 5.00

Markers with characters on barrels. 8-packs.
- Angry Birds, exclusive to Walmart [418-68] 10.00
- Saga 10.00

Jollibee
- Darth Vader with light-up lightsaber 10.00

Mead
- 8-pack, Royal Guard, jawa, C-3PO, Yoda, R2-D2, Boba Fett, Chewbacca, Darth Vader [418-69] 10.00
- C-3PO [418-70] 5.00
- Darth Vader [418-71] 5.00
- Princess Leia and R2-D2 [418-72] 5.00
- Stormtroopers "Freeze You Rebel Scum" [418-73] 5.00

Merlin
- X-Wing Squadron Incom T-65 [418-74] 5.00

MZB Imagination LLC
Connect and build pens.
- 4-pack: series 1 [418-75] 25.00
- 4-pack: series 2 [418-76] 25.00
- Boba Fett [418-77] 10.00
- Darth Vader [418-78] 10.00

Connect and build pens. Includes additional mini-figure.
- C-3PO / Jango Fett [418-79] 15.00
- Darth Vader / Luke Skywalker pilot [418-80] 15.00
- Jango Fett / C-3PO [418-81] 15.00
- Luke Skywalker X-Wing pilot / Darth Vader [418-82] ... 15.00
- R2-D2 / Chewbacca [418-83] 15.00
- Stormtrooper / tusken raider [418-84] 15.00

Penline
Characters printed on pen barrels and caps.
- Darth Vader [418-85] 10.00
- Han Solo [418-86] 10.00
- Luke Skywalker [418-87] 10.00
- R2-D2 [418-88] 10.00

Pentech
- 3-pack of ballpoint pens, sculpted as lightsabers, Episode I [418-89] 8.00
- 6-pack of character ballpoint pens, Episode I [418-90] 8.00
- Darth Maul ballpoint, includes collectors tin [418-91] .. 12.00
- Darth Maul highlight marker [418-92] 10.00

 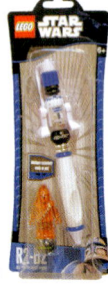 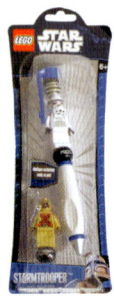        

| 418-82 | 418-83 | 418-84 | 418-85 | 418-86 | 418-87 | 418-88 | 418-89 | 418-90 | 418-91 | 418-92 |

   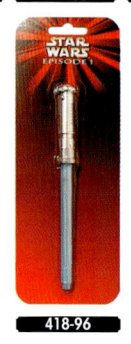    

| 418-93 | 418-94 | 418-95 | 418-96 | 418-97 | 418-98 | 418-99 | 418-100 |

Pens and Markers

 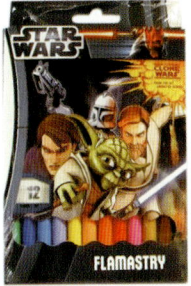      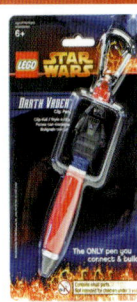 

418-101 | 418-102 | 418-103 | 418-104 | 418-105 | 418-106 | 418-107 | 418-108 | 418-109 | 418-110

6-pack. Each marker has character on barrel.
- ❏ Darth Maul cap, plus battle droid, Sebulba, Watto, Rune Haako, Nute Gunray [418-93] 25.00
- ❏ Jar Jar Binks cap, plus Anakin Skywalker, Obi-Wan Kenobi, Qui-Gon Jinn, R2-D2, Queen Amidala [418-94] 25.00

Q-Stat (UK)
Colored markers from Jar Jar Binks art kit. Colored barrel with gold Star Wars logo.
- ❏ Any of 6 colors, each [418-95] 3.00

Episode I: The Phantom Menace.
- ❏ Blue barrel pen with lightsaber handle [418-96] 8.00

Rose Art Industries
- ❏ Set of 3, Vader in Flames [418-97] 5.00
- ❏ Super Stamper washable markers: rebel emblem, Boba Fett, R2-D2, Yoda, Darth Vader, Imperial emblem, X-Wing Fighter, TIE Fighter [418-98] 15.00

Episode III: Revenge of the Sith.
- ❏ 2-pack Anakin and Darth Vader [418-99] 10.00

Star Wars washable markers
- ❏ Set of 5, thin [418-100] 5.00
- ❏ Set of 8, character, Han Solo, Luke Skywalker, Darth Vader, Chewbacca, Boba Fett, C-3PO, Princess Leia, Obi-Wan Kenobi [418-101] 10.00

Space World (Japan)
- ❏ Star Wars Exhibition 75.00

St. Majewski (Poland)
- ❏ 12 Clone Wars flamastry markers [418-102] 20.00

Star-light
Glowing pens with elliptical case.
- ❏ Blue, exclusive to Star Wars Celebration II [418-103] 25.00
- ❏ Red, exclusive to Star Wars Celebration II [418-104] 25.00
- ❏ Red, Star Wars Trading Card Game 20.00

Super Live Adventure (Japan)
- ❏ 3-pen set, Indiana Jones, Star Wars, Super Live Adventure [418-105] 95.00

Taito (Japan)
Lightsaber pens, light-up.
- ❏ Darth Vader, red [418-106] 15.00
- ❏ Luke, blue [418-107] 15.00
- ❏ Obi-Wan, green [418-108] 15.00

The CDM Company
- ❏ Darth Vader clip pen [418-109] 15.00
- ❏ Star Wars POD pen, exclusive to Comic-Con [418-110] ... 45.00

Writing System Connect and Build Pens.
- ❏ Anakin Skywalker [418-111] 25.00
- ❏ C-3PO [418-112] 25.00
- ❏ Chewbacca [418-113] 25.00
- ❏ Clone trooper [418-114] 25.00
- ❏ Darth Maul [418-115] 25.00
- ❏ Darth Vader [418-116] 25.00
- ❏ Jango Fett [418-117] 25.00
- ❏ Luke Skywalker [418-118] 25.00
- ❏ Obi-Wan Kenobi [418-119] 25.00
- ❏ Paploo [418-120] 25.00
- ❏ R2-D2 [418-121] 25.00
- ❏ Stormtrooper [418-122] 25.00
- ❏ Tusken Raider [418-123] 25.00
- ❏ Yoda [418-124] 25.00

Writing System Connect and Build Pens. Episode III Revenge of the Sith
- ❏ Chewbacca [418-125] 20.00
- ❏ Darth Vader [418-126] 20.00
- ❏ R2-D2 [418-127] 20.00
- ❏ Yoda [418-128] 20.00

Writing System Connect and Build Pens. Red packages.
- ❏ Chewbacca [418-129] 20.00
- ❏ Darth Vader [418-130] 20.00

418-111 | 418-112 | 418-113 | 418-114 | 418-115 | 418-116 | 418-117

418-118 | 418-119 | 418-120 | 418-121 | 418-122 | 418-123 | 418-124 | 418-125 | 418-126 | 418-127 | 418-128

418-129 | 418-130 | 418-131 | 418-132 | 418-133 | 418-134 | 418-135 | 418-136 | 418-137

375

Pens and Markers

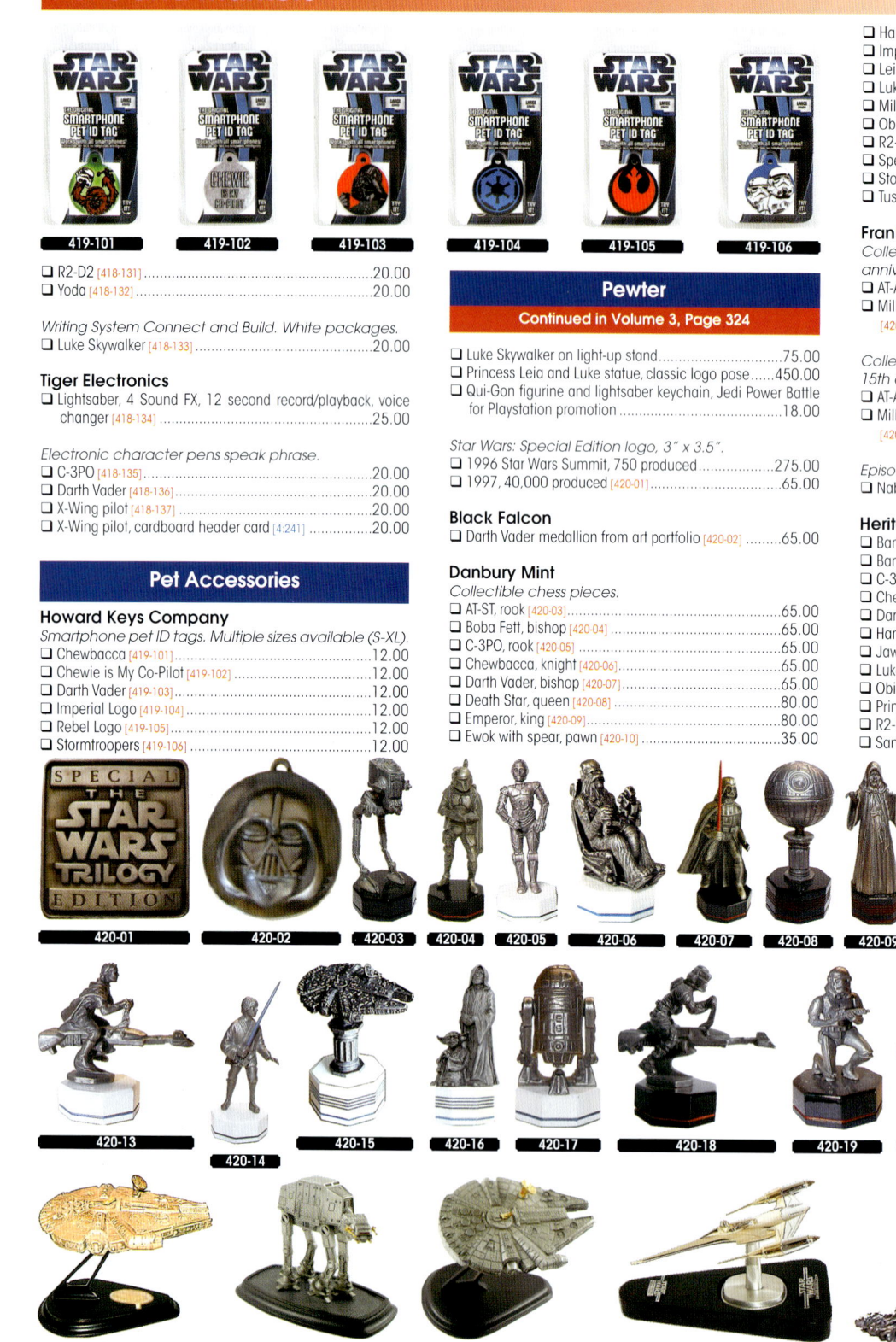

□ R2-D2 [418-131]......20.00
□ Yoda [418-132]......20.00

Writing System Connect and Build. White packages.
□ Luke Skywalker [418-133]......20.00

Tiger Electronics
□ Lightsaber, 4 Sound FX, 12 second record/playback, voice changer [418-134]......25.00

Electronic character pens speak phrase.
□ C-3PO [418-135]......20.00
□ Darth Vader [418-136]......20.00
□ X-Wing pilot [418-137]......20.00
□ X-Wing pilot, cardboard header card [4:241]......20.00

Pet Accessories

Howard Keys Company
Smartphone pet ID tags. Multiple sizes available (S-XL).
□ Chewbacca [419-101]......12.00
□ Chewie is My Co-Pilot [419-102]......12.00
□ Darth Vader [419-103]......12.00
□ Imperial Logo [419-104]......12.00
□ Rebel Logo [419-105]......12.00
□ Stormtroopers [419-106]......12.00

Pewter
Continued in Volume 3, Page 324

□ Luke Skywalker on light-up stand......75.00
□ Princess Leia and Luke statue, classic logo pose......450.00
□ Qui-Gon figurine and lightsaber keychain, Jedi Power Battle for Playstation promotion......18.00

Star Wars: Special Edition logo, 3" x 3.5".
□ 1996 Star Wars Summit, 750 produced......275.00
□ 1997, 40,000 produced [420-01]......65.00

Black Falcon
□ Darth Vader medallion from art portfolio [420-02]......65.00

Danbury Mint
Collectible chess pieces.
□ AT-ST, rook [420-03]......65.00
□ Boba Fett, bishop [420-04]......65.00
□ C-3PO, rook [420-05]......65.00
□ Chewbacca, knight [420-06]......65.00
□ Darth Vader, bishop [420-07]......65.00
□ Death Star, queen [420-08]......80.00
□ Emperor, king [420-09]......80.00
□ Ewok with spear, pawn [420-10]......35.00
□ Han, bishop [420-11]......65.00
□ Imperial Probot, rook [420-12]......65.00
□ Leia, knight [420-13]......65.00
□ Luke, bishop [420-14]......65.00
□ Millennium Falcon, queen [420-15]......85.00
□ Obi-Wan and Yoda, king [420-16]......80.00
□ R2-D2, rook [420-17]......65.00
□ Speeder Bike trooper, knight [420-18]......65.00
□ Stormtrooper, pawn [420-19]......35.00
□ Tusken Raider on Bantha, knight [420-20]......65.00

Franklin Mint
Collector's edition in gold for Star Wars 20th anniversary.
□ AT-AT [420-21]......450.00
□ Millennium Falcon, 7" x 5" with black plastic base [420-22]......450.00

Collector's edition in pewter and gold for Star Wars 15th anniversary.
□ AT-AT [420-23]......500.00
□ Millennium Falcon, 7" x 5" with black plastic base [420-24]......500.00

Episode I: The Phantom Menace. Vehicles.
□ Naboo Starfighter, deluxe [420-25]......250.00

Heritage / Star Trek Galore
□ Bantha, no riders or saddle [420-26]......45.00
□ Bantha with two Sand People riders [420-27]......65.00
□ C-3PO [420-28]......45.00
□ Chewbacca [420-29]......45.00
□ Darth Vader......45.00
□ Han Solo......50.00
□ Jawa [420-30]......45.00
□ Luke Skywalker [420-31]......45.00
□ Obi-Wan Kenobi [420-32]......45.00
□ Princess Leia [420-33]......45.00
□ R2-D2 [420-34]......50.00
□ Sand Person, standing [420-35]......45.00

Pewter

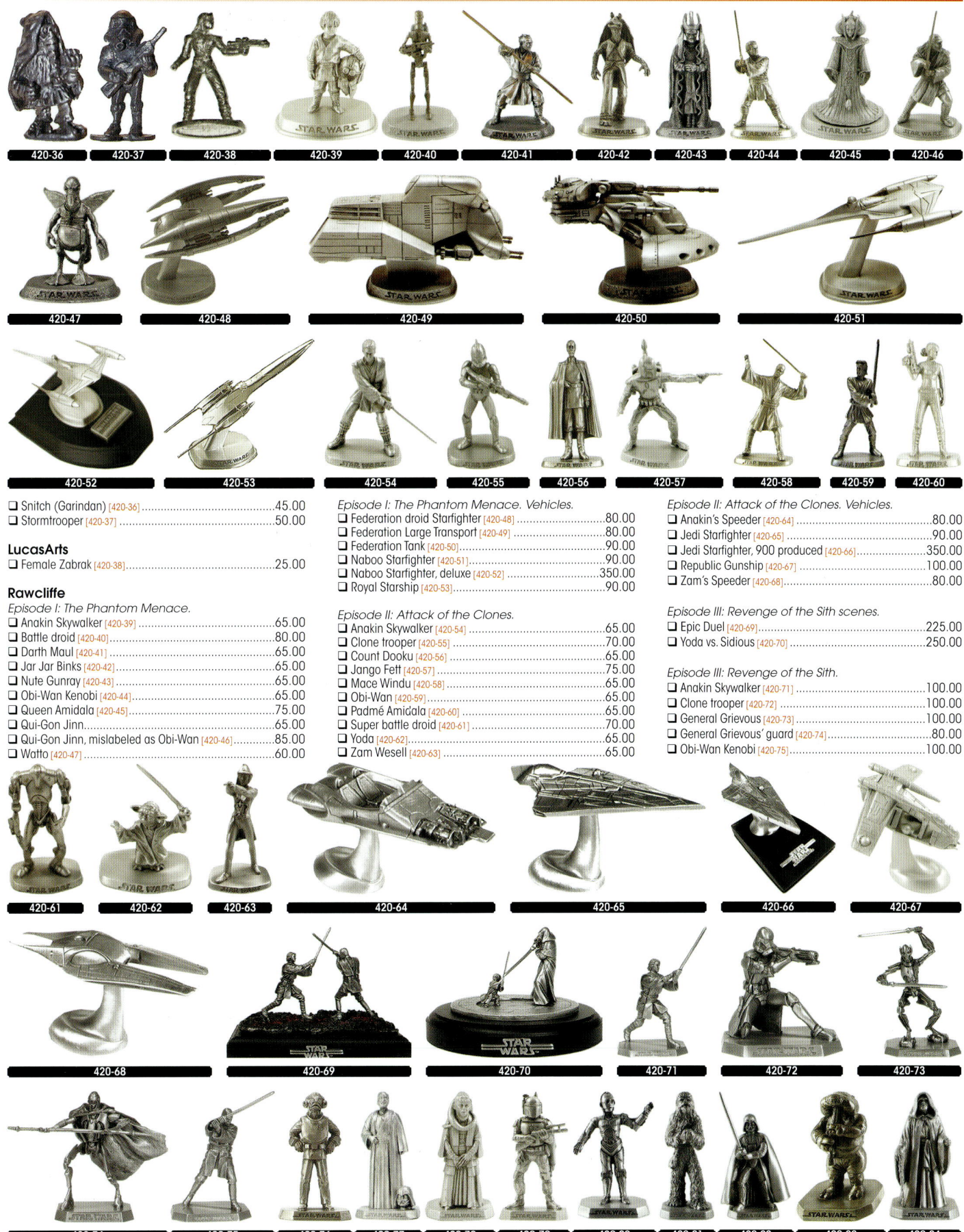

❏ Snitch (Garindan) [420-36] 45.00
❏ Stormtrooper [420-37] 50.00

LucasArts
❏ Female Zabrak [420-38] 25.00

Rawcliffe
Episode I: The Phantom Menace.
❏ Anakin Skywalker [420-39] 65.00
❏ Battle droid [420-40] 80.00
❏ Darth Maul [420-41] 65.00
❏ Jar Jar Binks [420-42] 65.00
❏ Nute Gunray [420-43] 65.00
❏ Obi-Wan Kenobi [420-44] 65.00
❏ Queen Amidala [420-45] 75.00
❏ Qui-Gon Jinn 65.00
❏ Qui-Gon Jinn, mislabeled as Obi-Wan [420-46] 85.00
❏ Watto [420-47] 60.00

Episode I: The Phantom Menace. Vehicles.
❏ Federation droid Starfighter [420-48] 80.00
❏ Federation Large Transport [420-49] 80.00
❏ Federation Tank [420-50] 90.00
❏ Naboo Starfighter [420-51] 90.00
❏ Naboo Starfighter, deluxe [420-52] 350.00
❏ Royal Starship [420-53] 90.00

Episode II: Attack of the Clones.
❏ Anakin Skywalker [420-54] 65.00
❏ Clone trooper [420-55] 70.00
❏ Count Dooku [420-56] 65.00
❏ Jango Fett [420-57] 75.00
❏ Mace Windu [420-58] 65.00
❏ Obi-Wan [420-59] 65.00
❏ Padmé Amidala [420-60] 65.00
❏ Super battle droid [420-61] 70.00
❏ Yoda [420-62] 65.00
❏ Zam Wesell [420-63] 65.00

Episode II: Attack of the Clones. Vehicles.
❏ Anakin's Speeder [420-64] 80.00
❏ Jedi Starfighter [420-65] 90.00
❏ Jedi Starfighter, 900 produced [420-66] 350.00
❏ Republic Gunship [420-67] 100.00
❏ Zam's Speeder [420-68] 80.00

Episode III: Revenge of the Sith scenes.
❏ Epic Duel [420-69] 225.00
❏ Yoda vs. Sidious [420-70] 250.00

Episode III: Revenge of the Sith.
❏ Anakin Skywalker [420-71] 100.00
❏ Clone trooper [420-72] 100.00
❏ General Grievous [420-73] 100.00
❏ General Grievous' guard [420-74] 80.00
❏ Obi-Wan Kenobi [420-75] 100.00

377

Pewter

Original trilogy.
- Admiral Ackbar [420-76] 30.00
- Anakin Skywalker (Boxed with Hasbro's Deluxe Monopoly CD Game) [420-77] 20.00
- Bib Fortuna [420-78] 30.00
- Boba Fett [420-79] 45.00
- C-3PO [420-80] 35.00
- Chewbacca [420-81] 35.00
- Darth Vader [420-82] 40.00
- Droopy McCool [420-83] 30.00
- Emperor [420-84] 35.00
- Ewok [420-85] 35.00
- Gamorrean Guard [420-86] 35.00
- Han Solo [420-87] 40.00
- Jabba and Leia, 2,005 produced [420-88] 400.00
- Jabba the Hutt [420-89] 75.00
- Lando Calrissian [420-90] 30.00
- Luke Skywalker [420-91] 40.00
- Max Rebo [420-92] 30.00
- Obi-Wan Kenobi [420-93] 40.00
- Princess Leia [420-94] 40.00
- Princess Leia as Jabba's prisoner [420-95] 45.00
- Princess Leia as Jabba's prisoner promotion (round base) [420-96] 35.00
- R2-D2 [420-97] 35.00
- Stormtrooper [420-98] 40.00
- Stormtrooper Dark Forces promotion [420-99] .. 75.00
- Sy Snootles [420-100] 30.00
- Yoda [420-101] 40.00

Original trilogy. Vehicles.
- A-Wing Fighter [420-102] 65.00
- B-Wing Fighter [420-103] 65.00
- Darth Vader's TIE Fighter, 15,000 produced [420-104] .. 225.00
- Death Star II, 4,500 produced [420-105] 60.00
- Imperial Star Destroyer [420-106] 75.00
- Millennium Falcon [420-107] 75.00
- Millennium Falcon, 15,000 produced [420-108] .. 260.00
- Outrider [420-109] 50.00
- Sail Barge [420-110] 70.00
- Shuttle Tydirium [420-111] 65.00
- Slave I [420-112] 75.00
- Snowspeeder [420-113] 65.00
- Speeder Bike [420-114] 60.00
- TIE Bomber [420-115] 65.00
- TIE Fighter [420-116] 65.00
- TIE Interceptor, deluxe, 7,500 produced [420-117] .. 265.00
- X-Wing Fighter [420-118] 75.00
- X-Wing Fighter, deluxe, 15,000 produced [420-119] .. 235.00
- Y-Wing Fighter [420-120] 75.00

Show West March 5, 1996.
- X-Wing Fighter deluxe, 4,500 produced [420-121] ... 1,400.00

Photo Albums

Robert Frederick
- The Empire Strikes Back photograph album [421-01] 25.00

Photo Frames

Continued in Volume 3, Page 325

Disney Theme Park Merchandise
- Hyperspace, for 5" x 7" [422-01] 40.00
- Obi-Wan Mickey vs. Darth Maul Donald 45.00
- Princess, magnetic back for 2" x 3" [422-02] .. 25.00

Sigma
- C-3PO [422-03] 65.00
- Darth Vader [422-04] 85.00
- R2-D2 [422-05] 80.00

Piano Rolls, Player

Play-Rite Music Rolls
- Star Wars 88 note [423-01] 45.00

Piñatas

Continued in Volume 3, Page 325

Hallmark
- Darth Vader ribbon, 3D [424-01] 30.00
- Darth Vader ribbon, round [424-02] 25.00
- Millennium Falcon 40.00

Pins

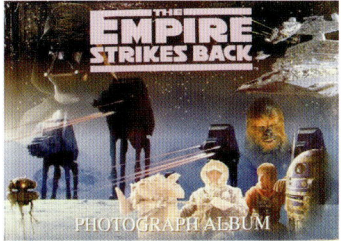
421-01

422-01

422-02

422-03

422-04

Pins
Continued in Volume 3, Page 324

- ☐ C-3PO and R2-D2 on square blue background with white logo [425-01] 10.00
- ☐ Darth Vader look-alike [425-02] 12.00
- ☐ Episode I logo, ellipse 10.00
- ☐ Star Wars Episode I logo 10.00
- ☐ The Power of Myth [425-03] 25.00

Art of Star Wars, Kyoto Museum, Japan, sets of 3.
- ☐ Clone trooper, Jedi Academy, Jango Fett [425-04] 30.00
- ☐ Darth Vader, R2-D2, stormtrooper [425-05] 30.00
- ☐ Millennium Falcon, X-Wing, Death Star II [425-06] 30.00

Gold background with full-color character.
- ☐ C-3PO and R2-D2 [425-07] 18.00
- ☐ Clone trooper 18.00
- ☐ Darth Sidious [425-08] 18.00
- ☐ Darth Vader [425-09] 18.00
- ☐ Yoda [425-10] 18.00

3D Arts
Square lasergram.
- ☐ C-3PO and R2-D2 ....20.00
- ☐ Darth Vader 20.00
- ☐ Millennium Falcon 20.00
- ☐ X-Wing Fighter 20.00

Activa Consumer Promotions Corp. (Canada)
Winnipeg Free Press.
- ☐ Anakin Skywalker [425-11] 10.00
- ☐ Bail Organa [425-12] 10.00
- ☐ Boba Fett [425-13] 10.00
- ☐ C-3PO [425-14] 10.00
- ☐ Chewbacca [425-15] 10.00

422-05

423-01

424-01

424-02

- ☐ Count Dooku [425-16] 10.00
- ☐ Darth Maul [425-17] 10.00
- ☐ Darth Sidious [425-18] 10.00
- ☐ Darth Vader [425-19] 10.00
- ☐ General Grievous [425-20] 10.00
- ☐ Han Solo [425-21] 10.00
- ☐ Jabba the Hutt [425-22] 10.00
- ☐ Luke Skywalker [425-23] 10.00
- ☐ Mace Windu [425-24] 10.00
- ☐ Obi-Wan Kenobi [425-25] 10.00
- ☐ Padmé Amidala [425-26] 10.00
- ☐ Princess Leia [425-27] 10.00
- ☐ R2-D2 [425-28] 10.00
- ☐ Stormtrooper [425-29] 10.00
- ☐ Yoda [425-30] 10.00

Adam Joseph Industries
Brass colored, sculpted, blister packed to red card.
- ☐ C-3PO [425-31] 40.00
- ☐ Emperor's Royal Guard [425-32] 40.00

Brass, sculpted.
- ☐ C-3PO [425-33] 30.00
- ☐ Emperor's Royal Guard [425-34] 30.00

- ☐ "May the Force be with you" [425-35] 30.00
- ☐ R2-D2 [425-36] 30.00
- ☐ Return of the Jedi logo [425-37] 30.00
- ☐ Salacious Crumb [425-38] 30.00
- ☐ Star Wars logo [425-39] 30.00
- ☐ The Force [425-40] 30.00
- ☐ Wicket the Ewok [425-41] 30.00
- ☐ X-Wing pilot [425-42] 30.00
- ☐ Yoda [425-43] 30.00

Plastic, sculpted.
- ☐ Princess Kneesaa [425-44] 25.00
- ☐ Wicket the Ewok [425-45] 25.00

Applause
- ☐ Anakin Skywalker [425-46] 12.00
- ☐ Battle droid [425-47] 12.00
- ☐ C-3PO [425-48] 12.00
- ☐ Darth Maul [425-49] 12.00
- ☐ Darth Sidious 12.00
- ☐ Episode I: The Phantom Menace logo [425-50] 12.00
- ☐ Jar Jar Binks [425-51] 12.00
- ☐ Naboo Starfighter [425-52] 12.00
- ☐ Obi-Wan Kenobi [425-53] 12.00

425-01

425-02

425-03

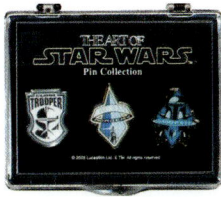
425-04

425-05

425-06

425-07

425-08

425-09

425-10

425-11

425-12

425-13

425-14

425-15

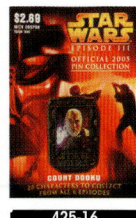
425-16

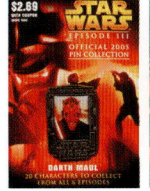
425-17

425-18

425-19

425-20

425-21

425-22

425-23

425-24

425-25

425-26

Pins

❏ Queen Amidala [425-54]	12.00	
❏ Qui-Gon Jinn [425-55]	12.00	
❏ R2-D2 [425-56]	12.00	
❏ Trade Federation droid Fighter [425-57]	12.00	

Framed Collections.
❏ Dark Side: Darth Maul, Darth Sidious, battle droid, droid Starship, Episode I Logo [425-58] 40.00

Pin and keychain sets.
❏ Darth Maul with Watto keychain [425-59] 30.00
❏ Jar Jar Binks with Jar Jar keychain [425-60] 30.00

Atari
Black and silver, promotional.
❏ C-3PO 50.00
❏ Darth Vader 50.00
❏ R2-D2 .... 50.00

Boston Science Museum
❏ Millennium Falcon, "I made the jump!" 50.00

C2 Ventures
❏ Star Wars Celebration II VIP [425-61] 130.00

Cards, Inc. (UK)
Enamel.
❏ General Grievous [425-62] 10.00
❏ Jedi [425-63] 10.00
❏ Lightsaber [425-64] 10.00
❏ Sith 10.00

Etched metal.
❏ Clone trooper [425-65] 10.00
❏ Darth Vader [425-66] 10.00
❏ General Grievous [425-67] 10.00
❏ Jedi emblem [425-68] 10.00
❏ Lightsaber [425-69] 10.00
❏ Republic emblem [425-70] 10.00

Castoline
❏ Chewbacca [425-71] 12.00
❏ Darth Vader [425-72] 12.00
❏ Logo, Star Wars [425-73] 12.00
❏ Logo, Star Wars: Special Edition [425-74] .. 12.00
❏ Logo, Twenty Years 1977–1997 [425-75] ... 12.00
❏ Luke Skywalker [425-76] 12.00
❏ Millennium Falcon [425-77] 12.00
❏ Princess Leia and R2-D2 [425-78] 12.00
❏ R2-D2 [425-79] 12.00
❏ Stormtrooper [425-80] 12.00

Completist Publications
❏ Gus and Duncan's Guide To Star Wars Prototypes 5.00
❏ Logo 5.00

Pins

425-82   425-83   425-84   425-85   425-86

  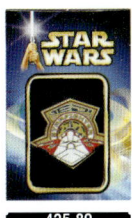   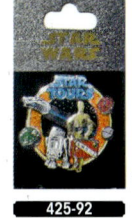 

425-87   425-88   425-89   425-90   425-91   425-92   425-93

425-94   425-95   425-96   425-97   425-98

Crystal Craft (Australia)
- Darth Vader 20.00
- Rebel alliance 20.00
- Star Wars 20.00
- Yoda [425-81] 20.00

DC Metro Area SW Collecting Club
- 2004 Yoda with Washington Monument lightsaber, for charity, 500 produced [425-82] 25.00
- 2006 Chewbacca on Washington Monument, for charity, 500 produced [425-83] 25.00
- 2008 Boba Fett with Washington monument jet pack, individually numbered [425-84] 25.00
- 2010 Luke on tauntaun with Washington monument background, individually numbered 25.00
- 2012 R2-D2 with hologram Washington Monument, for charity, individually numbered [425-85] 15.00
- Yoda with Monument lightsaber 5.00

Disney / MGM
- C-3PO / Disneyland 35 year anniversary [425-86] 25.00
- Chewbacca 15.00
- Chip and Dale with lightsaber [425-87] 75.00
- Darth Tater [425-88] 15.00
- Darth Vader 15.00
- Jedi Starfighter, Episode II opening night premium [425-89] 50.00
- R2-D2 .... 15.00
- Star Tours 15th anniversary [425-90] 50.00
- Star Tours 1987 [425-91] 65.00
- Star Tours Endor, C-3PO and R2-D2 [425-92] 35.00
- Star Tours logo [425-93] 40.00
- Star Tours Paris logo [425-94] 45.00
- Star Tours Tatooine Express [425-95] 40.00
- Star Tours The Leader In Galactic Sightseeing [425-96] 45.00
- Star Tours Tokyo, opening day [425-97] 180.00
- Star Tours with REX 40.00
- Star Tours, hidden Mickey 35.00
- Star Tours, press and preview [425-98] 65.00
- Stormtrooper 15.00
- Year of a Million Dreams, Mickey [425-99] 45.00
- Yoda, Silent Knight, Jedi Knight [425-100] 40.00

Disney Weekends 2000 May, dangler pin limited to 3,000.
- Anakin [425-101] 25.00
- Boba Fett [425-102] 25.00
- Chewbacca [425-103] 25.00
- Chewbacca, autographed by designer [425-104] 25.00
- Darth Vader [425-105] 25.00
- Princess Leia [425-106] 25.00
- R2-D2 [425-107] 25.00

Disney Weekends 2000 May, limited to 7,500.
- Mickey head with laser light [425-108] 30.00

425-99   425-100   425-101   425-102   425-103   425-104   425-105   425-106   425-107

      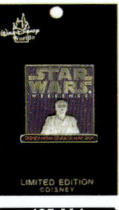    

425-108   425-109   425-110   425-111   425-112   425-113   425-114   425-115   425-116   425-117   425-118

 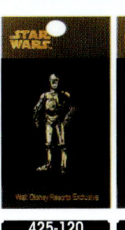   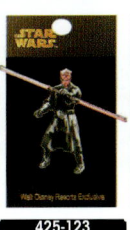       

425-119   425-120   425-121   425-122   425-123   425-124   425-125   425-126   425-127   425-128   425-129   425-130

Pins

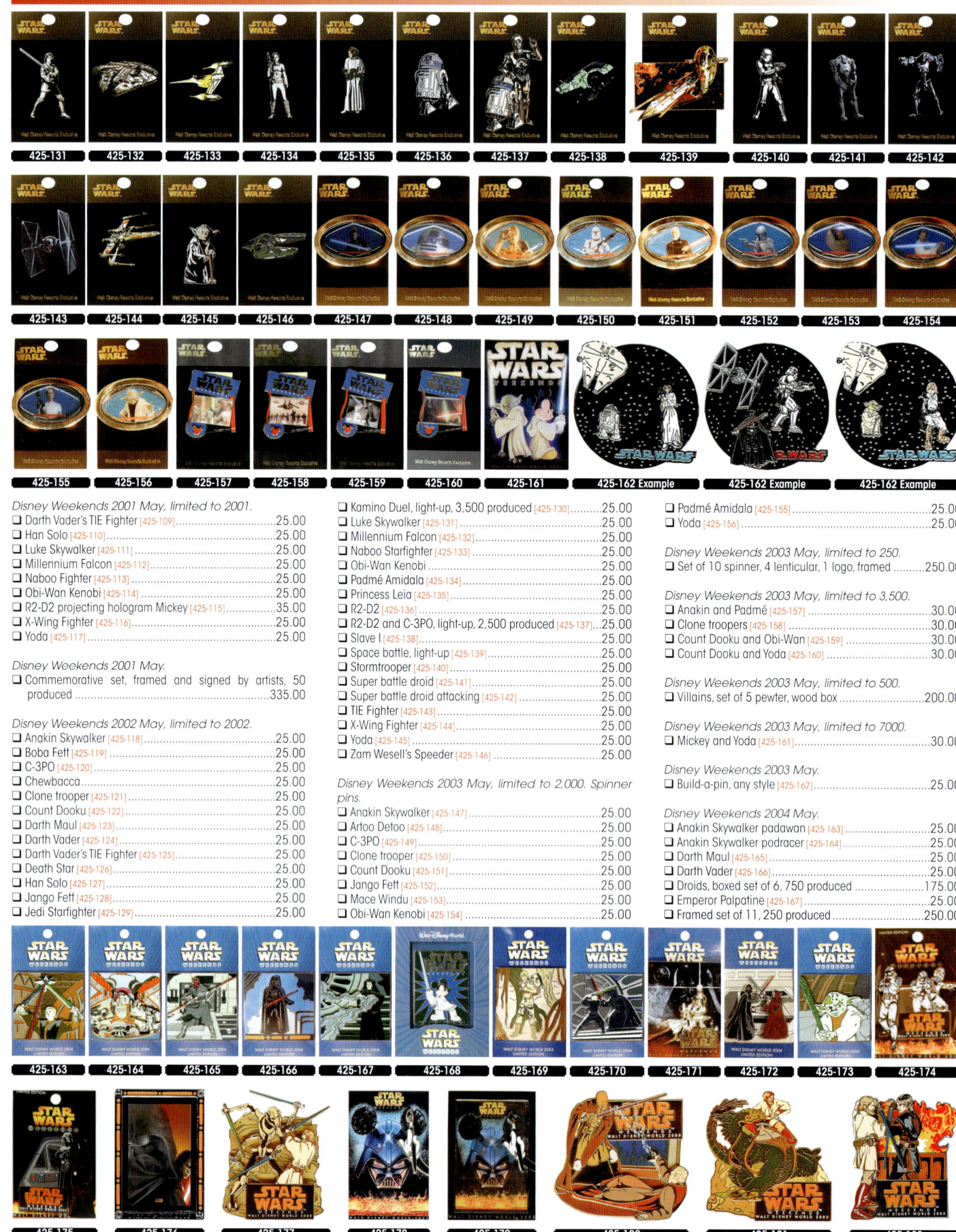

Disney Weekends 2001 May, limited to 2001.
- Darth Vader's TIE Fighter [425-109].................................25.00
- Han Solo [425-110]..25.00
- Luke Skywalker [425-111]...25.00
- Millennium Falcon [425-112]...25.00
- Naboo Fighter [425-113]...25.00
- Obi-Wan Kenobi [425-114]...25.00
- R2-D2 projecting hologram Mickey [425-115]..................35.00
- X-Wing Fighter [425-116]...25.00
- Yoda [425-117]..25.00

Disney Weekends 2001 May.
- Commemorative set, framed and signed by artists, 50 produced 335.00

Disney Weekends 2002 May, limited to 2002.
- Anakin Skywalker [425-118]..25.00
- Boba Fett [425-119]...25.00
- C-3PO [425-120]..25.00
- Chewbacca..25.00
- Clone trooper [425-121]...25.00
- Count Dooku [425-122]..25.00
- Darth Maul [425-123]...25.00
- Darth Vader [425-124]..25.00
- Darth Vader's TIE Fighter [425-125].................................25.00
- Death Star [425-126]..25.00
- Han Solo [425-127]..25.00
- Jango Fett [425-128]...25.00
- Jedi Starfighter [425-129]..25.00

- Kamino Duel, light-up, 3,500 produced [425-130]...........25.00
- Luke Skywalker [425-131]...25.00
- Millennium Falcon [425-132]...25.00
- Naboo Starfighter [425-133]..25.00
- Obi-Wan Kenobi..25.00
- Padmé Amidala [425-134]...25.00
- Princess Leia [425-135]..25.00
- R2-D2 [425-136]...25.00
- R2-D2 and C-3PO, light-up, 2,500 produced [425-137]...25.00
- Slave I [425-138]...25.00
- Space battle, light-up [425-139]..25.00
- Stormtrooper [425-140]...25.00
- Super battle droid [425-141]...25.00
- Super battle droid attacking [425-142]..............................25.00
- TIE Fighter [425-143]..25.00
- X-Wing Fighter [425-144]..25.00
- Yoda [425-145]...25.00
- Zam Wesell's Speeder [425-146]......................................25.00

Disney Weekends 2003 May, limited to 2,000. Spinner pins.
- Anakin Skywalker [425-147]..25.00
- Artoo Detoo [425-148]..25.00
- C-3PO [425-149]..25.00
- Clone trooper [425-150]...25.00
- Count Dooku [425-151]...25.00
- Jango Fett [425-152]...25.00
- Mace Windu [425-153]...25.00
- Obi-Wan Kenobi [425-154]...25.00

- Padmé Amidala [425-155]..25.00
- Yoda [425-156]...25.00

Disney Weekends 2003 May, limited to 250.
- Set of 10 spinner, 4 lenticular, 1 logo, framed..........250.00

Disney Weekends 2003 May, limited to 3,500.
- Anakin and Padmé [425-157]..30.00
- Clone troopers [425-158]..30.00
- Count Dooku and Obi-Wan [425-159]...............................30.00
- Count Dooku and Yoda [425-160].....................................30.00

Disney Weekends 2003 May, limited to 500.
- Villains, set of 5 pewter, wood box...............................200.00

Disney Weekends 2003 May, limited to 7000.
- Mickey and Yoda [425-161]..30.00

Disney Weekends 2003 May.
- Build-a-pin, any style [425-162].......................................25.00

Disney Weekends 2004 May.
- Anakin Skywalker padawan [425-163]..............................25.00
- Anakin Skywalker podracer [425-164]..............................25.00
- Darth Maul [425-165]...25.00
- Darth Vader [425-166]...25.00
- Droids, boxed set of 6, 750 produced......................175.00
- Emperor Palpatine [425-167]...25.00
- Framed set of 11, 250 produced..............................250.00

Pins

 425-183
 425-184
 425-185
 425-186
 425-187

 425-188
 425-189
 425-190
 425-191
 425-192
 425-193

- ❑ Jedi Mickey, 3", 500 produced [425-168] 35.00
- ❑ Luke and Yoda [425-169] 25.00
- ❑ Luke vs. Darth Vader [425-170] 25.00
- ❑ Mickey and Minnie / movie poster [425-171] 30.00
- ❑ Obi-Wan vs. Darth Vader [425-172] 25.00
- ❑ Yoda, Episode II [425-173] 25.00

Disney Weekends 2005 May.
- ❑ Chewbacca and Tarfful 25.00
- ❑ Clone troopers [425-174] 25.00
- ❑ Darth Vader and Darth Sidious [425-175] 25.00
- ❑ Episode III: Revenge of the Sith Opening Day [425-176] .. 50.00
- ❑ Grievous vs. Obi-Wan [425-177] 25.00
- ❑ Logo [425-178] 25.00
- ❑ Logo, jumbo [425-179] 25.00
- ❑ Mace Windu vs. Darth Sidious [425-180] 25.00
- ❑ Obi-Wan and Boga [425-181] 25.00
- ❑ Obi-Wan vs. Anakin [425-182] 25.00
- ❑ Set of 3 Anakin's Transformation pins, boxed [425-183] ..50.00
- ❑ Set of 4 Sith Lord pins, boxed 75.00
- ❑ Set of 5 WDW logo pins, boxed, 500 produced 165.00
- ❑ Set of 9 pins framed, 100 produced 250.00
- ❑ Yoda vs. Darth Sidious [425-184] 25.00

Disney Weekends 2006 May.
- ❑ Darth Vader confronts Luke [425-185] 25.00
- ❑ Darth Vader destroys Emperor [425-186] 25.00
- ❑ Defend-ears of the Kingdom, only available with purchase of hand painted cel [425-187] 90.00
- ❑ Han Solo fights stormtroopers [425-188] 25.00
- ❑ Jabba the Hutt and Leia [425-189] 25.00
- ❑ Jedi, guests that purchased a build-your-own light saber at the Once Upon a Toy Store, downtown Disney received this pin [425-190] 45.00
- ❑ Jumbo logo pin, ltd. to 750 [425-191] 150.00
- ❑ Obi-Wan detains Jango Fett [425-192] 25.00
- ❑ Qui-Gon Jinn challenges Darth Maul [425-193] 25.00
- ❑ R2-D2 and C-3PO [425-194] 25.00
- ❑ Set of 8 boxed, Hero / Villain with lightsaber, 500 produced 250.00
- ❑ Set of 9 framed, all eight saga scene pins plus Yoda vs. Vader, ltd. to 100 .... 250.00
- ❑ Yoda Confronts Darth Sidious [425-195] 25.00
- ❑ Yoda vs. Vader logo [425-196] 35.00

Disney Weekends 2007 June.
- ❑ 2007 logo, 5,500 produced 12.00

Disney Weekends 2007 June. Boxed sets.
- ❑ Bounty Hunters, IG-88, Bossk, Boba Fett, Dengar, 500 produced 85.00
- ❑ Jumbo pins (vehicles), TIE Fighter, TIE X1 advanced, Death Star, X-Wing Fighter, Y-Wing Fighter, 500 produced ... 175.00
- ❑ Movie Posters, Star Wars, Empire Strikes Back, Return of the Jedi, 500 produced 60.00

Disney Weekends 2007 June. Cartoon Characters.
- ❑ Darth Goofy 30.00
- ❑ Emperor Stitch 30.00
- ❑ Mickey Mouse as Luke Skywalker 30.00
- ❑ Mickey, X-Wing pilot 30.00
- ❑ Princess Minnie 30.00

Disney Weekends 2007 June. Characters.
- ❑ Darth Vader 30.00
- ❑ Han Solo and Chewbacca [425-197] 30.00
- ❑ Luke Skywalker [425-198] 30.00
- ❑ Obi-Wan Kenobi [425-199] 30.00
- ❑ Princess Leia [425-200] 30.00
- ❑ R2-D2 and C-3PO [425-201] 30.00
- ❑ Stormtrooper [425-202] 30.00
- ❑ TIE Fighter pilot [425-203] 30.00

Disney Weekends 2007 June. Framed set.
- ❑ Characters with completer pin, 100 produced 275.00

Disney Weekends 2007 June. Jumbo pins.
- ❑ 30th anniversary, 500 produced 100.00

Disney Weekends 2007 June. Potatohead Characters.
- ❑ Artoo Potatoo 25.00
- ❑ Darth Tater 25.00
- ❑ Spudtrooper 25.00

Disney Weekends 2008 June.
- ❑ Boxed set of 4 jumbo clone pins, Jango Fett, clone commander, shock trooper, stormtrooper, 500 produced 125.00

 425-194 425-195 425-196

 425-197
 425-198
 425-199
 425-200
 425-201
 425-202
 425-203

 425-204
 425-205
 425-206
 425-207
 425-208
 425-209
 425-210
 425-211

 425-212
 425-213
 425-214
 425-215
 425-216
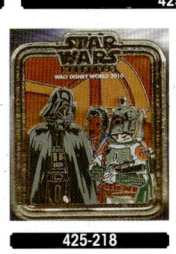 425-217
 425-218 425-219

Pins

- Boxed set of 6 jumbo helmet pins, Darth Vader, stormtrooper, TIE pilot, clone trooper Imperial guard, Boba Fett, 500 produced 125.00
- Jumbo pin, clones, Jango Fett plus 4 clones, 500 produced 95.00
- Star Wars Weekends 2008 logo, 7,000 produced 50.00

Disney Weekends 2008 June. Characters.
- 10 pins in framed set, 100 produced 275.00
- Anakin Skywalker and clone commander Appo 25.00
- Darth Vader and TIE Fighter pilot 25.00
- Han Solo and Boba Fett completer pin, 100 prod......150.00
- Jango Fett and Count Dooku 25.00
- Kit Fisto and clone commander 25.00
- Luke and Han as stormtroopers 25.00
- Obi-Wan Kenobi and clone commander Cody 25.00
- Princess Leia and stormtrooper 25.00
- Yoda and clone commander Gree 25.00

Disney Weekends 2009, spinner / characters.
- Anakin Skywalker and Obi-Wan Kenobi [425-204] 25.00
- Darth Maul and Darth Sidious [425-205] 25.00
- Darth Sidious and Darth Vader [425-206] 25.00
- General Grievous and Asajj Ventress [425-207] 25.00
- Queen Amidala and Senator Palpatine [425-208] 25.00
- Qui-Gon Jinn and Mace Windu [425-209] 25.00

Disney Weekends 2009.
- Mickey and Yoda [425-210] 35.00

Disney Weekends 2010 June.
- Empire Strikes Back anniversary, 250 prod. [425-211] ..175.00
- AT-ST and snowtroopers 30.00
- Boba Fett loading Han onto Slave I 30.00
- Darth Vader vs. Luke Skywalker [425-212] 30.00
- Darth Vader, Lando Calrissian, Boba Fett [425-213] 30.00
- Donald Duck in Carbonite, spinner 35.00
- Mickey Mouse vs. Boba Fett, 2010 logo [425-214] 30.00
- Wampa, exclusive to Vacation Club 90.00

Disney Weekends 2010 June. 3D.
- Boba Fett [425-215] 30.00
- Chewbacca and C-3PO [425-216] 30.00
- Darth Vader [425-217] 30.00
- Darth Vader, Lando, and Boba Fett [425-218] 30.00
- Hoth battle [425-219] 30.00
- Interrupted kiss [425-220] 30.00
- Jedi training [425-221] 30.00
- Lightsaber duel [425-222] 30.00

Disney weekends 2011. Framed sets.
- 11-pin galaxy, 9 passport, logo, and Star Tours, 200 produced 350.00
- 9-pin passports 300.00

384

Pins

Disney Theme Park Merchandise

- ❏ 7-pack, mini pins, emblems [425-223] 14.00
- ❏ "Artoo, Is That You?", Fastpass [425-224] 45.00
- ❏ Chip and Dale Adventure 8-pack 165.00
- ❏ Han Solo in Carbonite pass holder pin, 4,000 produced [425-225] 30.00
- ❏ "I Am Your Father," Father's Day 2010 [425-226] ...25.00
- ❏ Jedi Training Academy logo [425-227] 10.00
- ❏ Mickey and Donald on tauntauns, Disney vacation club exclusive [425-228] 40.00
- ❏ R2-MK [425-229] 20.00
- ❏ R2-MK, Jedi Mickey, and Celebration V logo [425-230] ...25.00
- ❏ Snowspeeder with pilot, 500 produced 20.00
- ❏ Star Tours Boarding Party, exclusive to Star Wars Celebration V [425-231] 35.00
- ❏ Star Tours Launching 2011 [425-232] 35.00
- ❏ Stormtrooper w/ Mickey Mouse ice cream bar [425-233] ...25.00
- ❏ Yoda Height Requirement 15.00

10-pin collection, muppets. 1 box contains 2 random character pins on a special background card.
- ❏ Animal as a Tusken Raider [425-235] 45.00
- ❏ Beaker as C-3PO [425-236] 35.00
- ❏ Dr. Honeydew as R2-D2 [425-237] 40.00
- ❏ Fozzie as Chewbacca [425-238] 35.00
- ❏ Gonzo as Darth Vader [425-239] 45.00
- ❏ Kermit as Luke Skywalker [425-240] 40.00
- ❏ Link Hogthrob as Han Solo [425-241] 35.00
- ❏ Miss Piggy as Princess Leia [425-242] 40.00
- ❏ Rizzo as Yoda [425-243] 35.00
- ❏ Sam the American Eagle as Obi-Wan Kenobi [425-244] ...35.00
- ❏ Unopened box [425-245] 50.00

10-pin collection, quotable. 1 box contains 2 random character pins on a special background card.
- ❏ Donald Duck as Darth Maul 10.00
- ❏ Donald Duck as Han Solo: "I know" 10.00
- ❏ Goofy as C-3PO: "I have a bad feeling about this"....10.00
- ❏ Goofy as Darth Vader: "I am your father" 10.00
- ❏ Mickey Mouse as Anakin Skywalker: "I am a Jedi" ...10.00
- ❏ Mickey Mouse as Luke Skywalker: "No!" 10.00
- ❏ Minnie Mouse as Princess Leia: "I love you" 10.00
- ❏ Pete as Boba Fett: "He's no good to me dead" 10.00
- ❏ Stitch as General Grievous: "You Jedi scum" 10.00
- ❏ Stitch as Yoda: "May the Force be with you" 10.00
- ❏ Unopened box [425-246] 20.00

10-pin collection. 1 box contains 2 random character pins on a special background card.
- ❏ Chip and Dale as Ewoks 15.00
- ❏ Daisy Duck as Aurra Sing [425-247] 15.00
- ❏ Donald Duck as Darth Maul [425-248] 15.00
- ❏ Donald Duck as Han Solo [425-249] 15.00
- ❏ Goofy as Chewbacca [425-250] 15.00
- ❏ Mickey Mouse as Anakin Skywalker [425-251] 15.00

Pins

- ❏ Minnie Mouse as Princess Leia [425-252] 15.00
- ❏ Pete as Boba Fett [425-253] 50.00
- ❏ Stitch as the emperor [425-254] 35.00
- ❏ Stitch as Yoda [425-255] 35.00
- ❏ Unopened box [425-256] 30.00

Celebration V.
- ❏ Last Tour to Endor 15.00
- ❏ R2-MK, Mickey Mouse, Celebration V logo 20.00

Featured Attraction collection.
- ❏ Star Tours, Mickey Mouse and AT-AT, 3,000 produced .. 40.00

Magazine Reveal Conceal series. 4,000 produced of each.
- ❏ Assassin, Jango Fett [425-257] 30.00
- ❏ Bad, Count Dooku [425-258] 30.00
- ❏ Bounty Hunter, Boba Fett [425-259] 30.00
- ❏ Clone, Clone trooper [425-260] 30.00
- ❏ Droid, C-3PO and R2-D2 [425-261] 30.00
- ❏ Empire, Emperor's Royal Guard [425-262] 30.00
- ❏ Force, Yoda [425-263] 30.00
- ❏ Hero, Kit Fisto [425-264] 30.00
- ❏ Hotpod, Sebulba [425-265] 30.00
- ❏ Jedi, Luke Skywalker [425-266] 30.00
- ❏ Lightspeed, Millennium Falcon [425-267] 30.00
- ❏ Modern Wookiee, Chewbacca [425-268] 30.00
- ❏ Rogue, Han Solo [425-269] 30.00
- ❏ Royal Rebel, Luke Skywalker [425-270] 30.00
- ❏ Saber, Obi-Wan Kenobi [425-271] 30.00
- ❏ Separatist, General Grievous [425-272] 30.00
- ❏ Sith, Darth Maul [425-273] 30.00
- ❏ Slime, Jabba the Hutt [425-274] 30.00
- ❏ Stick and Stone, Wicket [425-275] 30.00

Mickey Mouse icon.
- ❏ Imperial seal [425-276] 8.00
- ❏ Imperial seal, pre-production, back is stamped "PP", sold through Disney Expedition auction 250.00
- ❏ Rebel Alliance seal [425-277] 8.00

Piece of Disney History.
- ❏ Star Tours, 3,500 produced [425-278] 26.00

Star Tours.
- ❏ The Adventures Continue - Darth Vader with skytrooper, open edition pin features Darth Vader with his red lightsaber, a skytrooper, and includes the Star Tours logo as a dangle element [425-279] 10.00

Star Wars Weekends, 2010.
- ❏ Boba Fett and Han Solo in Carbonite [425-280] 15.00
- ❏ Han Solo in Carbonite, Passholder [425-281] 15.00

Star Wars Weekends, 2011.
- ❏ Aly San San and Starspeeder 1000 [425-282] 15.00
- ❏ Aly San San Close-Up and Starspeeder 1000 [425-283] .. 30.00
- ❏ Darth Maul, Passholder exclusive [425-284] 15.00
- ❏ Darth Vader and skytrooper [425-285] 15.00
- ❏ I am the rebel spy [425-286] 15.00
- ❏ Logo, Mickey vs. Darth Vader [425-287] 20.00
- ❏ Star Tours grand opening, Disneyland Resort Passholder exclusive [425-288] 15.00
- ❏ Star Tours grand opening, Walt Disney World Passholder exclusive [425-289] 15.00
- ❏ Star Tours logo [425-290] 15.00
- ❏ Starspeeder 1000, C-3PO, R2-D2 member exclusive, Disney Vacation Club [425-291] 45.00

Star Wars Weekends, 2011. Passport pins.
- ❏ Chewbacca 20.00
- ❏ Darth Vader 20.00
- ❏ Han Solo 20.00
- ❏ Lando Calrissian 20.00
- ❏ Luke Skywalker 20.00
- ❏ Obi-Wan Kenobi 20.00
- ❏ Princess Leia 20.00
- ❏ Yoda 20.00

Star Wars Weekends, 2012.
- ❏ 10 Pin framed set, 500 produced 500.00
- ❏ 2012 logo Donald Duck as Darth Maul, 6,800 produced 30.00
- ❏ Booster pin set: Yoda, Han and Leia, Darth Vader and Obi-Wan Kenobi, stormtroopers 50.00
- ❏ Darth Maul, vacation club exclusive, 2,000 produced 40.00

425-375

425-376

425-377

425-378

425-379

425-380

425-381

425-382

425-383

425-384

425-385

425-386

425-387

425-388

425-389

- ❑ Darth Maul in Mickey Mouse icon pin........................20.00
- ❑ Darth Maul spinner pin..30.00
- ❑ Darth Vader sliding door pin......................................30.00
- ❑ Donald, "Join the Duck Side" [425-292] 20.00
- ❑ Droids and Landspeeder, annual Passholder, 5,000 produced 50.00
- ❑ Easel box pin set, 300 produced 220.00
- ❑ Jumbo pin: Darth Vader Through the Years, 500 produced 150.00
- ❑ Lightsaber boxed set, Darth Maul, Darth Vader, Darth Sidious, Yoda, Jedi Mickey, 550 produced...........................200.00
- ❑ Luke Skywalker, "Own a Piece of the Death Star" 35.00

Star Wars Weekends, 2012. Sculpted lightsaber pins.

- ❑ Darth Maul, "Fear is my Ally".......................................30.00
- ❑ Darth Sidious, "You will be Destroyed"........................30.00
- ❑ Darth Vader, "Join the Dark Side"................................30.00
- ❑ Yoda, "Destroy the Sith, We Must" 30.00

Vinylmation.

- ❑ 3D pin set 1: Mickey Luke, Minnie Leia, Stitch Yoda 90.00
- ❑ 3D pin set 2: Goody Darth Vader, Donald stormtrooper, Pete Boba Fett 90.00
- ❑ Boba Fett, Darth Vader, and mystery pin 140.00

Vinylmation mystery pins set.

- ❑ 6-pack of starter trading pins plus mystery pin: stormtrooper, Darth Vader, Han Solo, Chewbacca, R2-D2, C-3PO ...200.00
- ❑ Boba Fett [425-293] 25.00
- ❑ Lando Calrissian [425-294]..25.00
- ❑ Luke Skywalker [425-295] 25.00
- ❑ Princess Leia [425-296]..25.00
- ❑ Yoda [425-297] 25.00

Disneyland Resort Paris (France)

- ❑ 4-pin booster set, Minnie as Leia, Goofy as Vader, Mickey as Luke, Stitch as Yoda [425-298]......................................75.00

DK Publishing

- ❑ Yoda, "Read You Will" 8.00

Downpace Ltd. (UK)

Character pin badges.

- ❑ Boba Fett [425-299] 15.00
- ❑ Boba Fett with gun [425-300]..15.00
- ❑ C-3PO [425-301]..15.00
- ❑ Darth Vader helmet [425-302] 15.00
- ❑ Darth Vader profile [425-303]...15.00
- ❑ Darth Vader reaching [425-304]...15.00
- ❑ Princess Leia [425-305]...15.00
- ❑ R2-D2 [425-306] 15.00
- ❑ Stormtrooper [425-307]...15.00
- ❑ Yoda [425-308] 15.00

Factors, Etc.

Scatter pins.

- ❑ Darth Vader, C-3PO, R2-D2, original logo [425-309] 45.00
- ❑ Darth Vader, C-3PO, R2-D2, revised logo [425-310].........35.00
- ❑ Stormtrooper, X-Wing, Chewbacca [425-311] 40.00

Fan Club

- ❑ Star Wars Celebration, Denver Colorado [425-312] 40.00

Fan Made

- ❑ Thank the Maker www.ThankYouGeorge.com [425-313] ..5.00
- ❑ TK-0076, fight against kidney cancer [425-314]............10.00

Fox Studios

DVD classic trilogy promotion.

- ❑ A New Hope [425-315] 10.00
- ❑ Empire Strikes Back [425-316] 10.00
- ❑ Return of the Jedi [425-317]...10.00

GB eye (UK)

- ❑ Trooper [425-318] 12.00

Hard Rock Cafe

300 produced of each.

- ❑ 2005 Luke and Leia, Indianapolis [425-319]................175.00
- ❑ 2012 Crossed Guitars, Orlando [425-320] 100.00
- ❑ 2012 Falcon Guitar, Orlando [425-321] 100.00

2012 Pinsanity 8. Las Vegas. 300 produced of each.

- ❑ Boba Fett [425-322] 75.00
- ❑ Darth Vader [425-323]...75.00
- ❑ Death Star [425-324]..75.00
- ❑ Princess Leia [425-325]..75.00
- ❑ X-Wing [425-326]..75.00

Hasbro

Power of the Jedi 2001 Tour.

- ❑ Amanaman [425-327] 50.00
- ❑ Boba Fett [425-328] 50.00
- ❑ Ellors Madak [425-329] 50.00

Her Universe

Characters dressed as Santa. Includes autographed COA.

- ❑ Chewbacca, individually numbered [425-330] 25.00
- ❑ R2-D2, 500 produced [425-331] 35.00
- ❑ Yoda, 500 produced, individually numbered..............35.00

Hollywood Pins

- ❑ Admiral Ackbar [425-332] 15.00
- ❑ AT-AT [425-333] 15.00
- ❑ Ben Kenobi [425-334] 15.00
- ❑ Black Sun logo 15.00
- ❑ Boba Fett [425-335] 20.00
- ❑ Boba Fett Insignia (Round) 15.00
- ❑ Boba Fett, "He's No Good To Me Dead" [425-336] 15.00
- ❑ C-3PO [425-337]...15.00
- ❑ C-3PO, "We're Doomed ..." [425-338] 15.00
- ❑ Chewbacca [425-339]...15.00
- ❑ Darth Vader [425-340]..15.00
- ❑ Darth Vader helmet [425-341] 20.00
- ❑ Darth Vader helmet, sculpted [v1e1:364] 10.00
- ❑ Darth Vader, "Power of the Dark Side ..." [425-342]........15.00
- ❑ Emperor [425-343]...15.00
- ❑ Emperor's Royal Guard 20.00
- ❑ Far Star...15.00
- ❑ "Freeze You Rebel Scum!" [425-344]..............................20.00
- ❑ Gamorrean Guard [425-345] 15.00

425-390

425-391

425-392

425-393

425-394

425-395

425-396

425-397

425-398

425-399

425-400

425-401

425-402

425-403

425-404

425-405

Pins

- ❏ Imperial Emblem...10.00
- ❏ Jabba the Hutt [425-346].................................10.00
- ❏ Lando Calrissian [425-347]..............................10.00
- ❏ Lightsabers crossed over Star Wars logo........10.00
- ❏ Luke on tauntaun [425-348].............................12.00
- ❏ Max Rebo band [425-349]................................12.00
- ❏ "May The Force Be With You" [425-350].........20.00
- ❏ Millennium Falcon [425-351]............................15.00
- ❏ Millennium Falcon, round [425-352].................15.00
- ❏ Princess Leia [425-353]....................................15.00
- ❏ R2-D2 [425-354]..15.00
- ❏ Rebel Alliance logo, large [425-355]................15.00
- ❏ Rebel Alliance logo, large gold [425-356].......15.00
- ❏ Rebel Alliance logo, mini..................................10.00
- ❏ Rebel Alliance logo, small................................10.00
- ❏ Rebel Alliance logo, small gold [425-357].......10.00
- ❏ Rebel Alliance logo, small red [425-358].........10.00
- ❏ Rebel forces...15.00
- ❏ Return of the Jedi [425-359].............................20.00
- ❏ Slave I...15.00
- ❏ Star Wars [425-360]..20.00
- ❏ Star Wars 20th anniversary [425-361].............25.00
- ❏ Star Wars trilogy special edition, antique finish [425-362]...10.00
- ❏ Stormtrooper [425-363]....................................15.00
- ❏ "Taking the Galaxy by Storm," Star Wars Summit exclusive..65.00
- ❏ The Empire Strikes Back [425-364]..................20.00
- ❏ TIE Fighter [425-365]...15.00
- ❏ TIE Fighter squadron [425-366].......................15.00
- ❏ TIE Fighter, round [425-367].............................15.00
- ❏ Wicket the Ewok [425-368]..............................15.00
- ❏ X-Wing Fighter [425-369].................................15.00
- ❏ X-Wing Fighter, round [425-370]......................20.00
- ❏ X-Wing Fighter, sculpted [425-371].................10.00
- ❏ Yoda [425-372]...15.00
- ❏ Yoda, "Try Not ..."..15.00

Howard Eldon
10th anniversary, enameled.
- ❏ C-3PO...20.00
- ❏ Darth Vader...20.00
- ❏ Empire Strikes Back logo..................................20.00
- ❏ R2-D2...10.00
- ❏ Return of the Jedi logo......................................10.00
- ❏ Star Wars logo, "The First Ten Years" [425-373]......50.00

Jaycees of New Hampshire
1983 convention.
- ❏ Darth Vader, Luke, Leia, "We Are Family" [425-374].......35.00
- ❏ Jabba the Hutt, "New Hampshire Jaycees" [425-375]....35.00
- ❏ Princess Leia, "New Hampshire Jaycee Women" [425-376]..35.00
- ❏ Yoda, "New Hampshire Senate" [425-377].....35.00

Jedicon
- ❏ 1997 Jedi Con [425-378]...................................15.00

KFC
- ❏ Queen Amidala EPI, employee pin [425-379]........25.00

Lions Club
District 4L2 of Southern California.
- ❏ Thats Entertainment [425-380].........................30.00

Little League Baseball
Division 1 umpire.
- ❏ Darth Vader, "Come over to the blue side," blue..........50.00
- ❏ Darth Vader, "Come over to the blue side," cyan.........50.00
- ❏ Darth Vader, "Come over to the blue side," purple......50.00
- ❏ Darth Vader, "Come over to the blue side," red...........50.00
- ❏ Darth Vader, "Come over to the blue side," white........50.00

Maryland District 4, Galactic All-Star.
- ❏ Darth Vader [425-381].......................................35.00
- ❏ Yoda [425-382]...35.00

South Carolina Division 1.
- ❏ C-3PO [425-383]...35.00
- ❏ Luke Skywalker [425-384].................................35.00
- ❏ Princess Leia [425-385]....................................35.00

LucasArts
- ❏ Star Wars Galaxies, 3,000 produced [425-386]......30.00

Lucasfilm
- ❏ Framed set of 16, CIII badge art, 275 produced........200.00

388

Pins

M&M World
Characters, flat painted brass.
- Anakin Skywalker [425-387] 10.00
- Darth Vader [425-388] 10.00
- The Emperor 10.00

Characters, sculpted.
- Anakin Skywalker [425-389] 20.00
- Boba Fett [425-390] 20.00
- C-3PO and R2-D2 [425-391] 20.00
- Chewbacca and Han Solo [425-392] 20.00
- Darth Maul [425-393] 20.00
- Darth Vader [425-394] 20.00
- General Grievous [425-395] 20.00
- Luke Skywalker [425-396] 20.00
- Obi-Wan Kenobi [425-397] 20.00
- Princess Leia [425-398] 20.00
- Stormtrooper [425-399] 20.00
- The Emperor [425-400] 20.00

Master Replicas
Legacy Collector Pin series. 500 produced of each.
- 2002 Han Solo blaster [425-401] 25.00
- 2003 Darth Vader lightsaber [425-402] 25.00
- 2004 All Terrain Armored Transport [425-403] 25.00
- 2005 Luke Skywalker lightsaber [425-404] 25.00
- 2006 Millennium Falcon [425-405] 25.00

McDonald's
- May The Fries Be With You, "what famous people say about McDonald's Fries" series, 500 produced [425-406] 100.00

NiubNiubsUniverse.com
- Ewok Landscaping, 2007 diorama workshop, exclusive to Star Wars Celebration IV 20.00

Pin USA
- 10 pin set, Attack of the Clones framed, 2,002 produced 115.00
- 10 pin set, silver anniversary framed 110.00
- Anakin Skywalker portrait [425-407] 15.00
- Anakin Skywalker torso [425-408] 15.00
- Anakin / Vader logo [425-409] 15.00
- Attack of the Clones logo [425-410] 15.00
- Boba Fett logo [425-411] 15.00
- Clone trooper logo [425-412] 15.00
- Count Dooku portrait [425-413] 15.00
- Droid Army logo [425-414] 15.00
- Imperial logo [425-415] 15.00
- Jango Fett portrait [425-416] 15.00
- Jango Fett torso [425-417] 15.00
- Jedi Academy logo [425-418] 15.00
- Jedi Starfighter 3 logo [425-419] 15.00
- Jedi Starfighter logo [425-420] 15.00
- Jedi Training Academy logo [425-421] 15.00
- Mace Windu portrait [425-422] 15.00
- Mace Windu torso [425-423] 15.00
- Obi Wan Kenobi torso [425-424] 15.00
- Obi Wan Kenobi portrait [425-425] 15.00
- Padmé Amidala portrait [425-426] 15.00
- Padmé Amidala torso [425-427] 15.00
- Rebel Logo [425-428] 15.00
- Zam Wessell portrait [425-429] 15.00
- Zam Wessell torso [425-430] 15.00

Celebration III.
- Logo [425-431] 30.00

Clone Wars.
- Boxed set of 6 .... 75.00

Episode III: Revenge of the Sith.
- Darth Vader emblems 30.00
- Emblem: 'Jedi' rank 15.00
- Emblem: Jedi Starfighter 15.00
- Emblem: Vader helmet in flames 15.00
- Jedi emblems 30.00
- Obi-Wan Kenobi 15.00
- Yoda 15.00

Revenge of the Sith.
- Anakin Skywalker [425-432] 15.00
- Boba Fett [425-433] 15.00
- C-3PO and R2-D2 [425-434] 15.00
- Chewbacca [425-435] 15.00
- Clone trooper [425-436] 15.00
- Clone trooper helmet [425-437] 15.00
- Darth Vader [425-438] 15.00
- Darth Vader helmet [425-439] 15.00
- General Grievous [425-440] 15.00
- General Grievous helmet [425-441] 15.00
- General Grievous helmet 15.00
- Han Solo [425-442] 15.00
- 'HERO' [425-443] 15.00
- Jedi Starfighter creed [425-444] 15.00
- Jedi starship on shield [425-445] 15.00
- Jedi wings on shield [425-446] 15.00
- Jedi, round, blue and gold [425-447] 15.00
- Jedi, round, blue and silver [425-448] 15.00
- Lightsaber raised [425-449] 15.00
- Luke Skywalker [425-450] 15.00
- Princess Leia [425-451] 15.00
- Sith [425-452] 15.00
- Vader helmet between flames [425-453] 15.00
- Vader's helmet / flames [425-454] 15.00
- Yoda [425-455] 15.00

Revenge of the Sith. Framed set.
- Darth Vader 150.00
- Yoda 140.00

Revenge of the Sith. Pewter.
- General Grievous [425-456] 40.00
- Grievous [425-457] 40.00
- 'Jedi Starfighter', 'Loyalty, honor, valor' [425-458] .. 40.00
- Lightsaber raised [425-459] 40.00
- 'Sith Lord' 40.00

Set of 3 to celebrate Classic Trilogy DVD release.
- A New Hope [425-460] 10.00
- Empire Strikes Back [425-461] 10.00
- Return of the Jedi [425-462] 10.00

RebelScum.com
- RebelScum [425-463] 20.00
- RebelScum.com blue 20.00
- RebelScum.com red [425-464] 20.00
- Star Wars is Forever, Celebration 3 [425-465] 25.00

Rose Parade 2007
- George Lucas, "Grand Marshal" [425-466] 70.00
- Stormtrooper, "Star Wars Spectacular" [425-467] . 50.00

Scholastic
- Yoda, "Read, You Will." [425-468] 10.00

Seattle Area Lucasfilm Artifact Collector Club (SARLACC)
- 2009 Millennium Falcon at Cloud City with Space Needle, for charity, individually numbered 20.00

Skywalker Ranch
- "Taking the Galaxy by Force", November 3 and 4, 1994 [425-469] 175.00

Star Wars Celebration V
- Logo / Boba Fett 40.00

Boxed deluxe pin. 100 produced of each.
- Boba Fett [425-470] 50.00

425-458

425-459

425-460

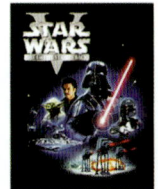
425-461

425-462

425-463

425-464

425-465

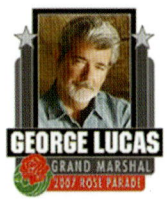
425-466

425-467

425-468

425-469

425-470

425-471

425-472

425-473

Pins

425-474   425-475   425-476   425-477   425-478   425-479   425-480   425-481   425-482   425-483

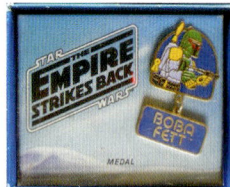     

425-484   425-485   425-486   425-487   425-488   425-489

425-490   425-491   425-492   425-493   425-494

☐ Slave I space shuttle [425-471] 65.00
☐ Yoda [425-472] 50.00

Star Wars Celebration VI
☐ Logo, blue [425-473] 30.00
☐ Logo, green 30.00
☐ Logo, purple 30.00
☐ Logo, red 30.00

Sunburst Merchandising
☐ Bravo Squadron [425-474] 12.00
☐ Episode I logo [425-475] 12.00
☐ The Dark Side [425-476] 12.00
☐ Trade Federation Starfighter [425-477] 12.00

Sunkus (Japan)
☐ Box set: Episode III: Revenge of the Sith [425-478] 120.00

12 pins, individually blind-packed, exclusive to Circle-K.
☐ Anakin Skywalker, square 15.00

☐ C-3PO, square 15.00
☐ Chewbacca, square 15.00
☐ Clone trooper 501st 15.00
☐ Count Dooku, square 15.00
☐ Darth Sidious, square 15.00
☐ Darth Vader, shaped 15.00
☐ Mace Windu, square 15.00
☐ Obi-Wan Kenobi, shaped 15.00
☐ Padmé, square 15.00
☐ R2-D2, shaped 15.00
☐ Yoda, square 15.00

SWChicks.com
☐ Female Jedi, "Fight for the Cure of breast cancer" [425-479] 35.00

Takara (Japan)
☐ C-3PO [425-480] 80.00
☐ R2-D2 [425-481] 80.00
☐ X-Wing Starfighter [425-482] 95.00

United States Postal Service
☐ Commemorative stamp set of 15 .... 75.00

Variety Children's Charity
Golden Heart.
☐ C-3PO and R2-D2 [425-483] 20.00

Wallace Berrie and Co.
Medals.
☐ Boba Fett [425-484] 35.00
☐ Chewbacca [425-485] 30.00
☐ Darth Vader with Empire Strikes Back logo [425-486] 30.00
☐ Millennium Falcon Pilot [425-487] 35.00
☐ X-Wing Fighter Pilot [425-488] 25.00
☐ Yoda, May The Force Be With You [425-489] 30.00

Walt Disney Resorts
☐ C-3PO and R2-D2 ride Space Mountain, 750 produced, exclusive to Where Dreams HapPin [425-490] 40.00

Wizards of the Coast
☐ Star Wars Celebration II, May 3–5, 2002 [425-491] 18.00
☐ Star Wars Celebration II, pewter [425-492] 10.00
☐ Star Wars Trading Card Game [425-493] 5.00

YodasHolonet.com
☐ Yoda, for Rady Children's Hospital, 300 produced, individually numbered [425-494] 30.00

Pins, Stick and Lapel
Continued in Volume 3, Page 329

Factors, Etc.
☐ C-3PO [426-01] 25.00

 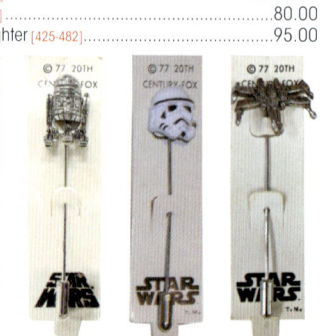 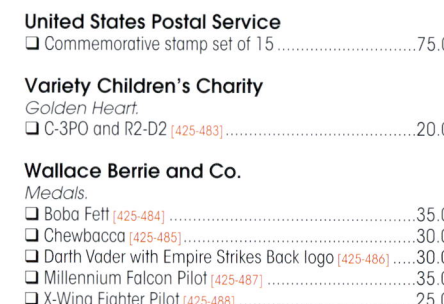 

426-01   426-01   426-02   426-03   426-03   426-04   426-05   426-06   426-07

426-08   427-01   427-02   427-03

Placemats

 427-04
 427-05
 427-06
 427-07
 427-08

 427-09
 427-10
 427-11
 427-12
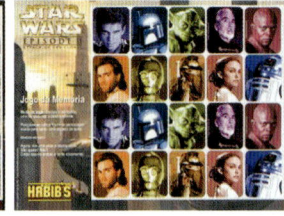 427-13

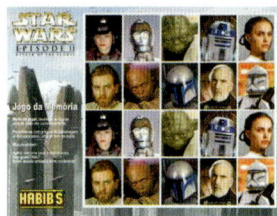 427-14
 427-15
 427-16
 427-17
 427-18

❑ Chewbacca [426-02] 25.00
❑ Darth Vader, square logo [426-03] 25.00
❑ Darth Vader, trapazoid logo 25.00
❑ R2-D2, square logo [426-04] 25.00
❑ R2-D2, trapazoid logo [426-05] 25.00
❑ Stormtrooper [426-06] 25.00
❑ X-Wing [426-07] 25.00

Pin USA
❑ Imperial logo [426-08] 10.00
❑ Rebel phoenix 10.00

Placemats
Continued in Volume 3, Page 329

Barcel (Mexico)
❑ Vader and General Grievous on wheel bike [427-01] 20.00
❑ Vader and General Grievous, lava [427-02] 20.00
❑ Vader, General Grievous, Commander Cody [427-03] 20.00

Burger King
❑ Empire Strikes Back glasses, promotional [427-04] 95.00

❑ Everybody Wins game, Empire Strikes Back promotional [427-05] 80.00
❑ Play the Choose Your Destiny Game [427-06] 15.00

Dixie
Empire Strikes Back.
❑ AT-ATs [427-07] 30.00
❑ Galaxy scene [427-08] 30.00
❑ Luke and Darth Vader [427-09] 30.00
❑ Yoda and Luke [427-10] 30.00

 427-19
 427-20
 427-21
 427-22
 427-23

 427-24 Side 1 and Side 2
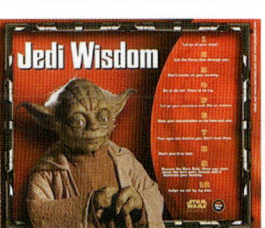
 427-25
 427-26
 427-27

 427-28
 427-28
 427-28
 427-28

Placemats

Drawing Board Greeting Cards, Inc.
- ☐ Maze, 8-pack [427-11] 50.00

Habib's Restaurant (Brazil)
Episode II: Attack of the Clones character memory games.
- ☐ Action [427-12] 25.00
- ☐ Art [427-13] 25.00
- ☐ Close-ups [427-14] 25.00

Icarus (UK)
- ☐ Darth Vader, Luke, Imperial Guards, and speeder bikes [v1e1:370] 40.00
- ☐ Jabba the Hutt, Princess Leia, Lando Calrissian, and Wicket [v1e1:370] 40.00

Return of the Jedi logo, 9" x 11".
- ☐ Bounty hunters [427-15] 40.00
- ☐ C-3PO and R2-D2 [427-16] 40.00
- ☐ Ewoks [427-17] 40.00
- ☐ Luke on tauntaun [427-18] 40.00

Star Wars logo, 9" x 11".
- ☐ C-3PO and R2-D2 [427-19] 50.00
- ☐ Chewbacca, Han, and Lando [427-20] 50.00
- ☐ Darth Vader and stormtroopers [427-21] 50.00
- ☐ Yoda [427-22] 50.00

Pizza Hut
- ☐ Don't Leave Coruscant Without Them [427-23] 10.00
- ☐ Jedi Trivia / Jedi Wisdom [427-24] 10.00
- ☐ Kids Pack with mini transforming play sets ad [427-25] .. 10.00

RLC Imports (Australia)
The Empire Strikes Back.
- ☐ Boba Fett, Darth Vader, stormtroopers [427-26] 50.00
- ☐ C-3PO, R2-D2, Millennium Falcon 50.00
- ☐ Han Solo and Chewbacca in Falcon cockpit 50.00
- ☐ Luke, Leia, snowspeeder, Millennium Falcon [427-27] ... 50.00

Sigma
- ☐ Empire Strikes Back 4-pack: Luke and Yoda, C-3PO and R2-D2, Darth Vader and Leia, Chewbacca and Boba Fett [427-28] 120.00

Plate Racks

Hamilton Collection
- ☐ 15th anniversary, hangs on wall [428-01] 150.00

Plates: Collector

Cards, Inc. (UK)
4" mini plates with display stand.
- ☐ Darth Vader [429-01] 15.00
- ☐ General Grievous [429-02] 15.00
- ☐ Jedi duel [429-03] 15.00
- ☐ Lord Vader [429-04] 15.00
- ☐ The droids [429-05] 15.00
- ☐ Yoda [429-06] 15.00

8". 3,000 produced of each.
- ☐ Anakin Skywalker, series II [429-07] 50.00
- ☐ Battle droids, series IV [429-08] 50.00
- ☐ Boba Fett and Jango Fett, Forbidden Planet exclusive, 999 produced [429-09] 80.00
- ☐ Boba Fett, series III [429-10] 50.00
- ☐ C-3PO, series III [429-11] 50.00
- ☐ Clone trooper, series II [429-12] 50.00
- ☐ Darth Maul, series IV [429-13] 50.00
- ☐ Darth Vader, series I [429-14] 50.00
- ☐ General Grievous, series II [429-15] 50.00
- ☐ Han Solo, series III [429-16] 50.00
- ☐ Heroes and villains, series V [429-17] 50.00

Play Houses

- ❑ Jedi, series V [429-18] 50.00
- ❑ Lando Calrissian, series III [429-19] 50.00
- ❑ Luke Skywalker, series I [429-20] 50.00
- ❑ Obi-Wan Kenobi, series II [429-21] 50.00
- ❑ Padmé Amidala, series IV [429-22] 50.00
- ❑ Qui-Gon Jinn, series IV [429-23] 50.00
- ❑ R2-D2, series I [429-24] 50.00
- ❑ Sith, series V [429-25] 50.00
- ❑ Stormtrooper, series I [429-26] 50.00
- ❑ The duel, series V [429-27] 50.00

Hamilton Collection
Character Scenes.
- ❑ 1 Han Solo [429-28] 35.00
- ❑ 2 Darth Vader and Luke Skywalker [429-29] 35.00
- ❑ 3 Princess Leia [429-30] 35.00
- ❑ 4 Imperial Walkers [429-31] 35.00
- ❑ 5 Luke and Yoda [429-32] 35.00
- ❑ 6 Space Battle [429-33] 30.00
- ❑ 7 R2-D2 and Wicket [429-34] 35.00
- ❑ 8 Millennium Falcon Cockpit [429-35] 35.00

Heroes and Villains.
- ❑ 1 Luke Skywalker [429-36] 35.00
- ❑ 2 Han Solo [429-37] 35.00
- ❑ 3 Darth Vader [429-38] 35.00
- ❑ 4 Princess Leia [429-39] 35.00
- ❑ 5 Obi-Wan Kenobi [429-40] 35.00
- ❑ 6 Emperor Palpatine [429-41] 35.00
- ❑ 7 Yoda [429-42] 35.00
- ❑ 8 Boba Fett [429-43] 45.00
- ❑ 9 Chewbacca [429-44] 35.00
- ❑ 10 Jabba The Hutt [429-45] 50.00
- ❑ 11 Lando Calrissian [429-46] 35.00
- ❑ 12 R2-D2 [429-47] 35.00

Space Vehicles.
- ❑ 1 Millennium Falcon [429-48] 35.00
- ❑ 2 TIE Fighter [429-49] 25.00
- ❑ 3 Red Five [429-50] 25.00
- ❑ 4 Imperial shuttle [429-51] 25.00
- ❑ 5 Star Destroyer [429-52] 25.00
- ❑ 6 Snowspeeders [429-53] 25.00
- ❑ 7 B-Wing Fighter [429-54] 25.00
- ❑ 8 Slave I [429-55] 50.00
- ❑ 9 Medical frigate [429-56] 25.00
- ❑ 10 Jabba's sail barge [429-57] 30.00
- ❑ 11 Y-Wing Fighter [429-58] 25.00
- ❑ 12 Death Star [429-59] 25.00

Tenth Anniversary.
- ❑ Trilogy scenes [429-60] 65.00

Trilogy series.
- ❑ 1 Star Wars [429-61] 35.00
- ❑ 2 Empire Strikes Back [429-62] 35.00
- ❑ 3 Return of the Jedi [429-63] 35.00

Play Houses
Continued in Volume 3, Page 329

ERO Industries
- ❑ Episode I: The Phantom Menace [430-01] 35.00

(UK)
- ❑ Magic pop-up tent [430-02] 45.00

430-01

430-02   430-03   430-04   430-05   430-06

429-37   429-38   429-39   429-40   429-41   429-42

429-43   429-44   429-45   429-46   429-47   429-48   429-49

429-50   429-51   429-52   429-53   429-54   429-55   429-56

429-57   429-58   429-59   429-60   429-61   429-62   429-63

Play Houses

430-07 430-08 430-09 430-10 430-11

431-01 431-02 431-03 431-04 431-05 431-06 431-07 431-08

Playhut
Clone Wars.
- 2-in-1 bed topper and tent; bed tent also functions as stand-alone play hut [430-03] 50.00
- Adventure hut [430-04] 45.00
- AT-TE Hide 'N Fun [430-05] 45.00
- Classic hideaway [430-06] 35.00
- Control center [430-07] 35.00
- Hide 'N Fun elite [430-08] 30.00
- Hideaway [430-09] 30.00

Worlds Apart (UK)
Pop'n'Fun.
- Pop-out play tunnel with Episode I space battle scenes [430-10] 35.00
- Pop-up Naboo Fighter [430-11] 60.00

Playing Cards
Continued in Volume 3, Page 330
- Episode I perforated sheets with bits of gum 15.00
- Episode III: Revenge of the Sith [431-01] 10.00
- Family Guy, Blue Harvest [431-02] 12.00
- Star Wars classic trilogy [431-03] 10.00
- Star Wars prelude [431-04] 10.00

(Russia)
Deck of 36 cards (4 suits, 6-A).
- Episode II: Attack of the Clones [431-05] 15.00
- Episode III: Revenge of the Sith [431-06] 15.00

Cartamundi
- 3D playing cards with collectible tin [431-07] 10.00
- Classic trilogy [431-08] 10.00
- Clone Wars, Captain Rex [431-09] 12.00
- Clone Wars, red Clone troopers, exclusive to Target [431-10] 12.00
- Famous quotes [431-11] 12.00
- Heroes [431-12] 12.00
- Heroes and Villains playing cards [431-13] 10.00
- Heroes and Villains, 2 decks [431-14] 12.00
- Heroes and Villains, 2 decks [431-15] 12.00
- Heroes and Villains, 2 decks, characters [431-16] 12.00
- Heroes and Villains, 2 decks, characters [431-17] 12.00
- Heroes and Villains, Clone Wars, 2 decks [431-18] 35.00
- Heroes and Villains, Clone Wars, 2 decks [431-19] 35.00
- Ladies of Star Wars [431-20] 15.00
- Prequel trilogy [431-21] 12.00
- Star Wars 30th anniversary, 2 decks [431-22] 50.00
- Star Wars posters [431-23] 15.00
- The Empire Strikes Back 30th anniversary, 2 decks [431-24] 12.00

    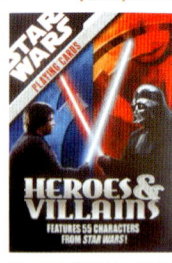 

431-09 431-10 431-11 431-12 431-13 431-14

   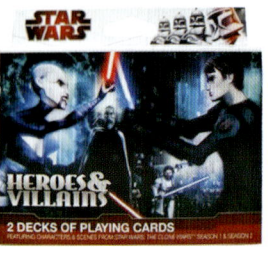 

431-15 431-16 431-17 431-18 431-19

 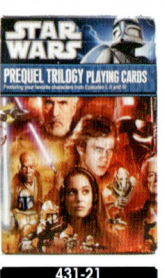     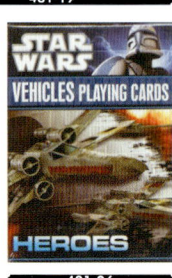

431-20 431-21 431-22 431-23 431-24 431-25 431-26

Pogs

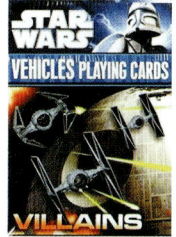 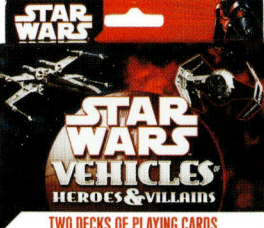   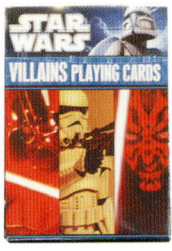 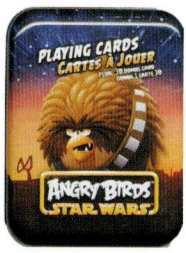

431-27 431-28 431-29 431-30 431-31 431-32

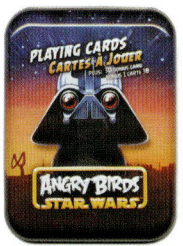     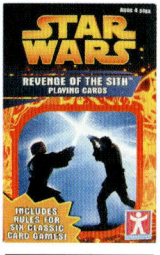  

431-33 431-34 431-35 431-36 431-37 431-38 431-39

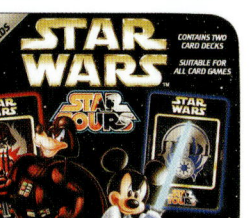     

431-40 431-41 431-42 431-43 431-44 431-45

- ❏ The Phantom Menace 3D [431-25].................10.00
- ❏ Vehicles / Heroes [431-26] 10.00
- ❏ Vehicles / Villains [431-27] 10.00
- ❏ Vehicles of Heroes and Villains, 2 decks [431-28] 12.00
- ❏ Vehicles of Heroes and Villains, 2 decks [431-29] 12.00
- ❏ Vehicles, 2 decks [431-30] 25.00
- ❏ Villains [431-31] 15.00

Angry Birds in collector tin with matching 3D card.
- ❏ Chewbacca [431-32] 15.00
- ❏ Darth Vader [431-33] 15.00
- ❏ Han [431-34] 15.00
- ❏ Luke [431-35] 15.00

Limited edition, exclusive to Star Wars Celebration IV.
- ❏ 1-pack, 5,000 produced, individually numbered........30.00
- ❏ 3-pack, 5,000 produced, individually numbered........30.00

Promotion Cards, exclusive to Star Wars Celebration VI.
- ❏ Ace of Hearts, Qui-Gon Jinn 5.00
- ❏ Jack of Hearts, Darth Maul 5.00
- ❏ King of Hearts, Obi-Wan Kenobi 5.00
- ❏ Queen of Hearts, Padmé Amidala 5.00
- ❏ Ten of Hearts, Anakin Skywalker 5.00

Character Games, Ltd. (UK)
- ❏ Attack of the Clones [431-36] 10.00
- ❏ Classic Star Wars [431-37] 10.00
- ❏ Revenge of the Sith [431-38] 15.00

Disney / MGM
- ❏ Rebel Alliance / Galactic Empire [431-39] 15.00
- ❏ Star Tours, Sith / Jedi, tin storage box [431-40] 20.00

EnSky (Japan)
- ❏ R2-D2 die-cut playing cards [431-41] 25.00

Glow Zone
- ❏ Glow-in-the-Dark [431-42] 20.00

International Playing Card Company
- ❏ 2 decks (Heros / Villains) in collector tin [431-43]..........18.00
- ❏ Heros deck [431-44] 10.00
- ❏ Villains deck [431-45] 10.00

Pog Slammers

Canada Games (Canada)
- ❏ 1 Star Wars [432-01] 12.00

- ❏ 2 Empire Strikes Back [432-02] 12.00
- ❏ 3 Return of the Jedi [432-03] 12.00
- ❏ 4 Luke [432-04] 12.00
- ❏ 5 Leia [432-05] 12.00
- ❏ 6 Han [432-06] 12.00
- ❏ 7 Darth Vader [432-07] 12.00
- ❏ 8 Jabba the Hutt [432-08] 12.00

Topps
Available in black, gold, and silver.
- ❏ Ben Kenobi [432-09] 10.00
- ❏ Boba Fett [432-10] 10.00
- ❏ Darth Vader [432-11] 10.00
- ❏ Emperor Palpatine [432-12] 10.00
- ❏ Han Solo [432-13] 10.00
- ❏ Luke Skywalker [432-14] 10.00
- ❏ Princess Leia [432-15] 10.00
- ❏ Stormtrooper [432-16] 10.00

Pogs

Sheets of 6, unpunched.
- ❏ Darkness [5:247] 15.00
- ❏ Heroes [1:293] 15.00

432-01 432-02 432-03 432-04 432-05 432-06 432-07 432-08

432-09 432-10 432-11 432-12 432-13 432-14 432-15 432-16

Pogs

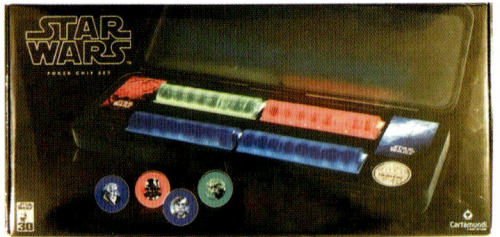
433-01

434-01

434-02

434-03

434-04

434-05

434-06

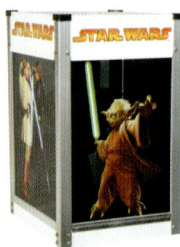
434-07 Side 1 and Side 2

434-08

434-09

434-10

(Peru)
Images from all six movies plus Expanded Universe art. Backgrounds of random color. Set of 48, unnumbered.
- ❏ Pogs, any of 48, each [v1e1:374] 1.00
- ❏ Set of 48 .... 50.00

Canada Games (Canada)
Set of 70 numbered 9–78. (Numbers 1–8 are the slammers.) Images in the 2nd edition, page 351. Checklist in 3rd edition, page 348.
- ❏ Pogs 9–78, each [v1e1:374] 2.00
- ❏ Pog checklist: Boba Fett 5.00
- ❏ Pog checklist: Darth Vader 5.00
- ❏ Pog checklist: Han Solo 5.00
- ❏ Pog checklist: Luke Skywalker 5.00
- ❏ Set of 70 .... 80.00

Kent (Turkey)
"Floppies" distributed in packets of gum. Set of 40, numbered. Images and checklist in the 3rd edition, page 349.
- ❏ Pogs 1–40, each [v1e1:374] 2.00
- ❏ Set of 40 .... 75.00

Nagatanien (Japan)
2.5" round. Set of 20, numbered. Images in the 2nd edition, page 349. Checklist in 3rd edition, page 350.
- ❏ Pogs 1–20, each [v1e1:374] 2.00
- ❏ Set of 20 .... 50.00

Schmidt (Germany)
Set of 70, numbered. Images in the 3rd edition, page 349. Checklist in 3rd edition, page 350.
- ❏ Pogs 1–70, each [v1e1:374] 2.00
- ❏ Set of 70 .... 65.00

Tomy (Japan)
Advertising—In Store Now!!
- ❏ Clone trooper [v1e1:374] 8.00
- ❏ Yoda [3:350] 8.00

Topps
Set of 70, numbered, plus two "00" pogs. Images in the 2nd edition, page 353. Checklist in 3rd edition, page 350.
- ❏ 00-A C-3PO and R2-D2 .... 6.00
- ❏ 00-B Darth Vader (promo) 6.00

- ❏ Pogs 1–70, each [v1e1:374] 2.00
- ❏ Set of 70 .... 75.00

Galaxy art, foil. Set of 10, numbered. Images in the 2nd edition, page 353. Checklist in 3rd edition, page 350.
- ❏ Pogs 1–10, each [v1e1:374] 2.00
- ❏ Set of 10 .... 25.00

Poker Chips
Continued in Volume 3, Page 330

Cartamundi
- ❏ Original Trilogy, 200 chips, 2 card decks, dealer button, case with light-up holders, 20,000 produced, exclusive to The Sharper Image [433-01] 165.00

Popcorn Poppers
Continued in Volume 3, Page 331

Snappy Popcorn
Popcorn poppers with cart.
- ❏ Droids 4 oz. [434-01] 1,200.00
- ❏ Jedi 4 oz. [434-02] 1,200.00
- ❏ Revenge of the Sith 6 oz. [434-03] 1,400.00
- ❏ Vader 4 oz. [434-04] 1,200.00
- ❏ Vader 6- oz. [434-05] 1,400.00

Popcorn poppers.
- ❏ Droids 4 oz. 16" x 14" x 24" [434-06] 650.00
- ❏ Jedi 4 oz. 16" x 14" x 24" [434-07] 650.00
- ❏ Revenge of the Sith 6 oz. 20" x 14" x 26" [434-08] 850.00
- ❏ Vader 4 oz. 16" x 14" x 24" [434-09] 650.00
- ❏ Vader 6 oz. 20" x 14" x 26" [434-10] 650.00

Postcards
Continued in Volume 3, Page 331

- ❏ R2-D2 and C-3PO, rebel blockage runner [v1e1:376] ... 5.00
- ❏ The First Ten Years, Star Wars [435-01] 10.00
- ❏ Yoda clay sculpture 5.00

Art of Star Wars, Kyoto Museum 2003.
- ❏ C-3PO and R2-D2 [v1e1:376] 8.00
- ❏ Clone trooper [v1e1:376] 8.00
- ❏ Darth Vader's mask [v1e1:376] 8.00
- ❏ Jango Fett [v1e1:376] 8.00
- ❏ The Art of Star Wars [435-02] 8.00

(Japan)
- ❏ Clone Wars 8.23 [435-03] 8.00

(UK)
28 full-color postcard packs.
- ❏ Revenge of the Sith [435-04] 35.00
- ❏ Revenge of the Sith—characters [435-05] 35.00
- ❏ Revenge of the Sith—iconic [435-06] 35.00

20th Century Fox
- ❏ A New Hope [435-07] 10.00
- ❏ Empire Strikes Back [4:256] 10.00
- ❏ Return of the Jedi [435-08] 10.00
- ❏ Star Wars: Special Edition logo [435-09] 10.00
- ❏ The Phantom Menace promotional [435-10] 10.00

3D Arts
Lasergrams.
- ❏ C-3PO and R2-D2 [4:256] 12.00
- ❏ Darth Vader [435-11] 12.00
- ❏ Millennium Falcon [435-12] 12.00
- ❏ X-Wing Fighter [435-13] 12.00

A.H. Prismatic (UK)
Holographic foil images.
- ❏ Darth Vader 15.00
- ❏ Millennium Falcon and TIE Fighters 15.00
- ❏ Millennium Falcon in Asteroid Field 15.00

ArtCard
Episode II: Attack of the Clones promotional cards.
- ❏ Anakin Skywalker [435-14] 8.00
- ❏ Count Dooku [435-15] 8.00
- ❏ Geonosian [435-16] 8.00
- ❏ Jango Fett [435-17] 8.00
- ❏ Mace Windu [435-18] 8.00
- ❏ Padmé Amidala [435-19] 8.00
- ❏ Yoda 8.00
- ❏ Zam Wesell [435-20] 8.00

435-01

435-02

435-03

435-04

435-05

435-06

435-07

435-08

435-09

Postcards

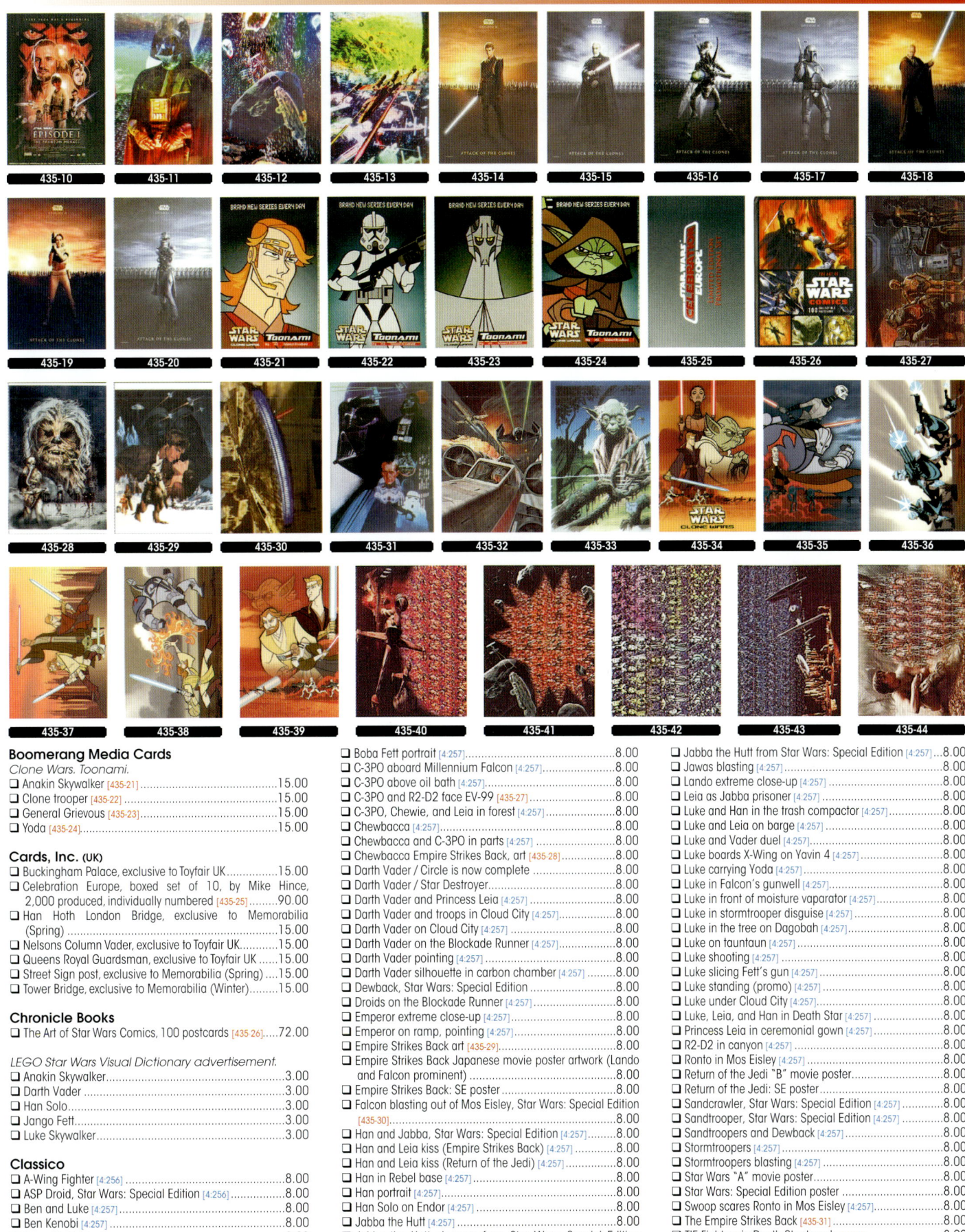

Boomerang Media Cards
Clone Wars. Toonami.
- Anakin Skywalker [435-21] 15.00
- Clone trooper [435-22] 15.00
- General Grievous [435-23] 15.00
- Yoda [435-24] 15.00

Cards, Inc. (UK)
- Buckingham Palace, exclusive to Toyfair UK 15.00
- Celebration Europe, boxed set of 10, by Mike Hince, 2,000 produced, individually numbered [435-25] 90.00
- Han Hoth London Bridge, exclusive to Memorabilia (Spring) 15.00
- Nelsons Column Vader, exclusive to Toyfair UK 15.00
- Queens Royal Guardsman, exclusive to Toyfair UK ... 15.00
- Street Sign post, exclusive to Memorabilia (Spring) 15.00
- Tower Bridge, exclusive to Memorabilia (Winter) 15.00

Chronicle Books
- The Art of Star Wars Comics, 100 postcards [435-26] 72.00

LEGO Star Wars Visual Dictionary advertisement.
- Anakin Skywalker 3.00
- Darth Vader 3.00
- Han Solo 3.00
- Jango Fett 3.00
- Luke Skywalker 3.00

Classico
- A-Wing Fighter [4:256] 8.00
- ASP Droid, Star Wars: Special Edition [4:256] 8.00
- Ben and Luke [4:257] 8.00
- Ben Kenobi [4:257] 8.00
- Ben with lightsaber [4:257] 8.00
- Ben, Luke, and C-3PO view Mos Eisley [4:257] 8.00
- Boba Fett portrait [4:257] 8.00
- C-3PO aboard Millennium Falcon [4:257] 8.00
- C-3PO above oil bath [4:257] 8.00
- C-3PO and R2-D2 face EV-99 [435-27] 8.00
- C-3PO, Chewie, and Leia in forest [4:257] 8.00
- Chewbacca [4:257] 8.00
- Chewbacca and C-3PO in parts [4:257] 8.00
- Chewbacca Empire Strikes Back, art [435-28] 8.00
- Darth Vader / Circle is now complete 8.00
- Darth Vader / Star Destroyer 8.00
- Darth Vader and Princess Leia [4:257] 8.00
- Darth Vader and troops in Cloud City [4:257] 8.00
- Darth Vader on Cloud City [4:257] 8.00
- Darth Vader on the Blockade Runner [4:257] 8.00
- Darth Vader pointing [4:257] 8.00
- Darth Vader silhouette in carbon chamber [4:257] 8.00
- Dewback, Star Wars: Special Edition 8.00
- Droids on the Blockade Runner [4:257] 8.00
- Emperor extreme close-up [4:257] 8.00
- Emperor on ramp, pointing [4:257] 8.00
- Empire Strikes Back art [435-29] 8.00
- Empire Strikes Back Japanese movie poster artwork (Lando and Falcon prominent) 8.00
- Empire Strikes Back: SE poster 8.00
- Falcon blasting out of Mos Eisley, Star Wars: Special Edition [435-30] 8.00
- Han and Jabba, Star Wars: Special Edition [4:257] 8.00
- Han and Leia kiss (Empire Strikes Back) [4:257] 8.00
- Han and Leia kiss (Return of the Jedi) [4:257] 8.00
- Han in Rebel base [4:257] 8.00
- Han portrait [4:257] 8.00
- Han Solo on Endor [4:257] 8.00
- Jabba the Hutt [4:257] 8.00
- Jabba the Hutt close-up from Star Wars: Special Edition [4:257] 8.00
- Jabba the Hutt from Star Wars: Special Edition [4:257] ... 8.00
- Jawas blasting [4:257] 8.00
- Lando extreme close-up [4:257] 8.00
- Leia as Jabba prisoner [4:257] 8.00
- Luke and Han in the trash compactor [4:257] 8.00
- Luke and Leia on barge [4:257] 8.00
- Luke and Vader duel [4:257] 8.00
- Luke boards X-Wing on Yavin 4 [4:257] 8.00
- Luke carrying Yoda [4:257] 8.00
- Luke in Falcon's gunwell [4:257] 8.00
- Luke in front of moisture vaparator [4:257] 8.00
- Luke in stormtrooper disguise [4:257] 8.00
- Luke in the tree on Dagobah [4:257] 8.00
- Luke on tauntaun [4:257] 8.00
- Luke pointing [4:257] 8.00
- Luke shooting [4:257] 8.00
- Luke slicing Fett's gun [4:257] 8.00
- Luke standing (promo) [4:257] 8.00
- Luke under Cloud City [4:257] 8.00
- Luke, Leia, and Han in Death Star [4:257] 8.00
- Princess Leia in ceremonial gown [4:257] 8.00
- R2-D2 in canyon [4:257] 8.00
- Ronto in Mos Eisley [4:257] 8.00
- Return of the Jedi "B" movie poster 8.00
- Return of the Jedi: SE poster 8.00
- Sandcrawler, Star Wars: Special Edition [4:257] 8.00
- Sandtrooper, Star Wars: Special Edition [4:257] 8.00
- Sandtroopers and Dewback [4:257] 8.00
- Stormtroopers [4:257] 8.00
- Stormtroopers blasting [4:257] 8.00
- Star Wars "A" movie poster 8.00
- Star Wars: Special Edition poster 8.00
- Swoop scares Ronto in Mos Eisley [4:257] 8.00
- The Empire Strikes Back [435-31] 8.00
- TIE Fighters in Death Star trench [4:257] 8.00
- Tusken Raider [4:257] 8.00

Postcards

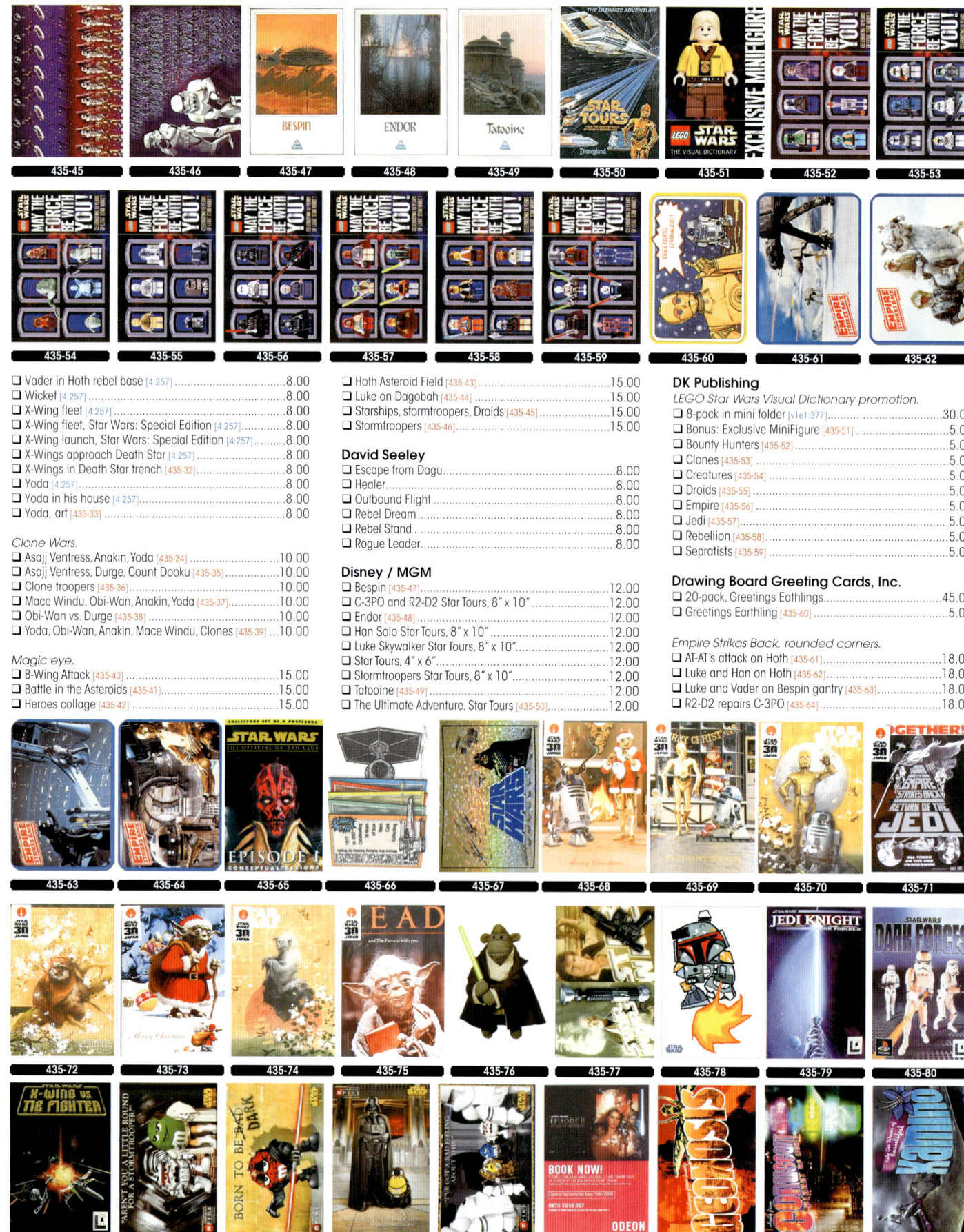

- ❏ Vader in Hoth rebel base [4:257] 8.00
- ❏ Wicket [4:257] 8.00
- ❏ X-Wing fleet [4:257] 8.00
- ❏ X-Wing fleet, Star Wars: Special Edition [4:257] 8.00
- ❏ X-Wing launch, Star Wars: Special Edition [4:257] 8.00
- ❏ X-Wings approach Death Star [4:257] 8.00
- ❏ X-Wings in Death Star trench [435-32] 8.00
- ❏ Yoda [4:257] 8.00
- ❏ Yoda in his house [4:257] 8.00
- ❏ Yoda, art [435-33] 8.00

Clone Wars.
- ❏ Asajj Ventress, Anakin, Yoda [435-34] 10.00
- ❏ Asajj Ventress, Durge, Count Dooku [435-35] 10.00
- ❏ Clone troopers [435-36] 10.00
- ❏ Mace Windu, Obi-Wan, Anakin, Yoda [435-37] 10.00
- ❏ Obi-Wan vs. Durge [435-38] 10.00
- ❏ Yoda, Obi-Wan, Anakin, Mace Windu, Clones [435-39] ...10.00

Magic eye.
- ❏ B-Wing Attack [435-40] 15.00
- ❏ Battle in the Asteroids [435-41] 15.00
- ❏ Heroes collage [435-42] 15.00

- ❏ Hoth Asteroid Field [435-43] 15.00
- ❏ Luke on Dagobah [435-44] 15.00
- ❏ Starships, stormtroopers, Droids [435-45] 15.00
- ❏ Stormtroopers [435-46] 15.00

David Seeley
- ❏ Escape from Dagu 8.00
- ❏ Healer 8.00
- ❏ Outbound Flight 8.00
- ❏ Rebel Dream 8.00
- ❏ Rebel Stand 8.00
- ❏ Rogue Leader 8.00

Disney / MGM
- ❏ Bespin [435-47] 12.00
- ❏ C-3PO and R2-D2 Star Tours, 8" x 10" 12.00
- ❏ Endor [435-48] 12.00
- ❏ Han Solo Star Tours, 8" x 10" 12.00
- ❏ Luke Skywalker Star Tours, 8" x 10" 12.00
- ❏ Star Tours, 4" x 6" 12.00
- ❏ Stormtroopers Star Tours, 8" x 10" 12.00
- ❏ Tatooine [435-49] 12.00
- ❏ The Ultimate Adventure, Star Tours [435-50] 12.00

DK Publishing
LEGO Star Wars Visual Dictionary promotion.
- ❏ 8-pack in mini folder [v1e1-377] 30.00
- ❏ Bonus: Exclusive MiniFigure [435-51] 5.00
- ❏ Bounty Hunters [435-52] 5.00
- ❏ Clones [435-53] 5.00
- ❏ Creatures [435-54] 5.00
- ❏ Droids [435-55] 5.00
- ❏ Empire [435-56] 5.00
- ❏ Jedi [435-57] 5.00
- ❏ Rebellion [435-58] 5.00
- ❏ Sepratists [435-59] 5.00

Drawing Board Greeting Cards, Inc.
- ❏ 20-pack, Greetings Eathlings 45.00
- ❏ Greetings Earthling [435-60] 5.00

Empire Strikes Back, rounded corners.
- ❏ AT-AT's attack on Hoth [435-61] 18.00
- ❏ Luke and Han on Hoth [435-62] 18.00
- ❏ Luke and Vader on Bespin gantry [435-63] 18.00
- ❏ R2-D2 repairs C-3PO [435-64] 18.00

Postcards

 435-90
 435-91
 435-92
 435-93
 435-94
 435-95

 435-96
 435-97
 435-98
 435-99
 435-100
 435-101
 435-102

Fan Club (UK)
❏ Collector's set of 9 postcards, Maul cover [435-65] 25.00

Fan Made
StarWarsCards.net.
❏ 2003 1 of 3—Leia and R2, 250 produced 6.00
❏ 2003 2 of 3—Luke and Yoda, 250 produced 6.00
❏ 2003 3 of 3—Jabba's throne room, 250 produced 6.00
❏ 2004 / 2005 sketch by Dale Smith III 6.00
❏ 2007 artwork by Duncan Irvine [435-66] 6.00

Fantasma
❏ Star Wars, holofoil [435-67] 15.00

Filmwert Berlin (Germany)
Christmas theme.
❏ C-3PO and R2-D2 in Santa's workshop 10.00
❏ C-3PO and R2-D2 shopping 10.00
❏ Santa C-3PO and reindeer R2-D2 .... 10.00
❏ Santa Yoda 10.00

GB Posters (UK)
❏ Attack of the Clones poster art 10.00
❏ Yoda Montage 10.00

Gentle Giant Studios
❏ Clone Commanders 10.00
❏ Sy Snootles, Max Rebo on Tour 10.00

Heart Art Collection, Ltd. (Japan)
❏ C-3PO and R2-D2, Christmas [435-68] 10.00
❏ C-3PO and R2-D2, Christmas shopping [435-69] 10.00
❏ C-3PO and R2-D2, floral [435-70] 10.00
❏ "Together!" [435-71] 10.00
❏ Wicket, floral [435-72] 10.00

❏ Yoda, Christmas [435-73] 10.00
❏ Yoda, floral [435-74] 10.00
❏ Yoda: Read [435-75] 10.00

I T V Digital
❏ Obi-Wan sock monkey [435-76] 12.00

Icons Authentic Replicas
❏ Advertisement for Ben's lightsaber and Han's blaster [435-77] 10.00

JAKe
❏ Boba Fett, exclusive to Star Wars Celebration IV [435-78] 8.00

Living Waters Publications
Unique Tracts—Pro-Christian message with scripture references on the back of cards with Episode I scenes.
❏ Darth Maul 10.00
❏ Jedi vs. Sith 10.00
❏ Obi-Wan Kenobi 10.00
❏ Queen Amidala 10.00

LucasArts
❏ Dark Forces II promotional [435-79] 8.00
❏ Dark Forces promotional [435-80] 8.00
❏ X-Wing vs. TIE Fighter [435-81] 8.00

M&M World
Episode III: Revenge of the Sith.
❏ "Aren't you a little round for a stormtrooper?" [435-82] .. 10.00
❏ "Born to be dark" [435-83] 10.00
❏ "Dare to go to the Dark Side" [435-84] 10.00
❏ "I've got a bad feeling about this!" [435-85] 10.00

Odeon
❏ Episode II:AOTC "Book Now" movie premiere [435-86] ... 12.00

Oral-B
Dental check-up reminders.
❏ 25-packs, dentist stock unopened 190.00
❏ C-3PO and R2-D2 [4:258] 20.00
❏ Chewbacca, Han, Leia, Luke, C-3PO [v1e1:378] 20.00
❏ Ewoks 20.00
❏ Jabba the Hutt and Bib Fortuna [4:258] 20.00
❏ Luke and Darth Vader [4:258] 20.00

Paizo Publishing / Fan Club
❏ Greetings from lovely Geonosis [435-87] 10.00
❏ Hello from Coruscant [435-88] 10.00
❏ Rides the waves of beautiful Kamino [435-89] 10.00

Pop-Shots
❏ Birthday Greetings from Mos Eisley [435-90] 20.00
❏ C-3PO and Ewoks, Happy Birthday, They Think You're Some Sort of God [435-91] 20.00
❏ C-3PO and R2-D2, We've Been Through A Lot Together [435-92] 20.00
❏ C-3PO and R2-D2, You Artoo Older Then Me, Happy Birthday [435-93] 20.00
❏ Falcon Cockpit, It Seems Like A Millennium Since Your Last Birthday 20.00
❏ Leia and Han, Help Me Obi-Wan Kenobi, I Think I'm Falling In Love [435-94] 20.00
❏ The Duel, You Have Learned Much, Young One, Happy Birthday [435-95] 20.00
❏ Yoda, When 900 Years Old You Reach ..., Happy Birthday [435-96] 20.00

Powerhouse Museum
❏ Star Wars The Magic of Myth [435-97] 15.00

 435-103
 435-104
 435-105
 435-106
 435-107
 435-108
 435-109
 435-110
 435-111

 435-112
 435-113
 435-114
 435-115
 435-116
 435-117
 435-118
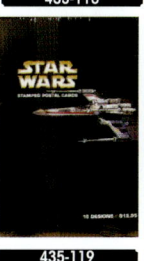 435-119
 435-120

Postcards

Randy Martinez
- ❏ The Art of Randy Martinez [435-98] 5.00

Reedpop
- ❏ Celebration VI "Coming Soon to a Galaxy Near You." ... 10.00
- ❏ Celebration VI "Tickets On Sale Now." [435-99] 10.00

Star Wars Celebration V advertising postcards.
- ❏ AT-AT [435-100] 10.00
- ❏ Roller Coaster [435-101] 10.00
- ❏ Swamp Gators [435-102] 10.00

Robert Hendrickson
Promotes RobertHendrickson.net.
- ❏ Yoda with lightsaber 5.00

San Diego Comic-Con
2003. San Diego Comic-Con.
- ❏ 1 of 4 Boba Fett [435-103] 10.00
- ❏ 2 of 4 Yoda [435-104] 10.00
- ❏ 3 of 4 Asajj Ventress [435-105] 10.00
- ❏ 4 of 4 Clone troopers [435-106] 10.00

Sankyo Co., Ltd. (Japan)
Exclusive to Star Wars Celebration Japan.
- ❏ Darth Vader advancing, red background [435-107] 15.00
- ❏ Darth Vader, red horizon art [435-108] 15.00

Sony Ericsson
Episode III: Revenge of the Sith.
- ❏ Anakin Skywalker [435-109] 5.00
- ❏ Emperor Palpatine [435-110] 5.00
- ❏ General Grievous [435-111] 5.00
- ❏ Obi-Wan Kenobi [435-112] 5.00
- ❏ Yoda [435-113] 5.00

Star Wars Celebration V
- ❏ Set of 12 [435-114] 25.00

Star Wars Celebration VI
- ❏ Celebration VI postcard set [435-115] 20.00

Suncoast
- ❏ Advertises Celebration II, May 3–5, 2002, 6" x 9" 10.00

The LEGO Group
- ❏ Anakin / Darth Vader [4:259] 5.00
- ❏ AT-TE [4:259] 5.00
- ❏ Cloud Car [v1e1:378] 5.00
- ❏ Cloud City [4:259] 5.00
- ❏ Episode I Speeder Chase [4:259] 5.00
- ❏ Jango Fett [4:259] 5.00
- ❏ Jango Fett's Slave I vs. Obi-Wan's Jedi Starfighter [4:259] 5.00
- ❏ Just Imagine ... Speeder Bikes [435-116] 5.00
- ❏ Just Imagine ... X-Wing Fighter [v1e1:378] 5.00
- ❏ Republic Gunship [v1e1:378] 5.00
- ❏ Super Battle Droid [4:259] 5.00
- ❏ Use The Force, shows Darth Vader [435-117] 5.00

ThinkGeek
- ❏ Greeting from Orlando, exclusive to Star Wars Celebration VI 5.00

Topps
- ❏ B-Wing / Slave 1 Vehicles card set promo [435-118] ... 8.00

United States Postal Service
- ❏ Star Wars 15 designs stamped [435-119] 25.00

First day, hand canceled in Los Angeles.
- ❏ Anakin and Obi-Wan 15.00
- ❏ Boba Fett [435-120] 15.00
- ❏ C-3PO 15.00
- ❏ Chewbacca and Han Solo 15.00
- ❏ Darth Maul 15.00
- ❏ Darth Vader 15.00
- ❏ Emperor Palpatine 15.00
- ❏ Luke Skywalker 15.00
- ❏ Millennium Falcon 15.00
- ❏ Obi-Wan Kenobi 15.00
- ❏ Princess Leia and R2-D2 .... 15.00
- ❏ Queen Amidala 15.00
- ❏ Stormtroopers 15.00
- ❏ X-Wing Starfighter 15.00
- ❏ Yoda 15.00

Zigzag (Germany)
- ❏ Episode III: Revenge of the Sith teaser art 10.00

Posters

- ❏ A Long Time Ago In A Galaxy Far, Far Away, 17" x 22" [436-01] 10.00
- ❏ "All I needed to know about life I learned from Star Wars" [436-02] 15.00
- ❏ American one-sheet poster checklist revised, 27" x 40" rolled [436-03] 20.00
- ❏ American one-sheet poster checklist [2:357] 95.00
- ❏ Are Your Children Fully Immunized?, 14" x 22" [436-04] .. 85.00
- ❏ Battle Above Death Star II [436-05] 20.00
- ❏ Boba Fett [436-06] 20.00
- ❏ C-3PO and R2-D2, red background, 18.5" x 23" [436-07] 12.00
- ❏ Celebration Japan 30.00
- ❏ Chewbacca, Hoth, 12" x 17" [436-08] 25.00
- ❏ Clone Wars, "May 27, 2007," 11" x 17" exclusive to Star Wars Celebration IV 15.00
- ❏ Collect Medallions, exclusive to Star Wars Celebration Japan 25.00
- ❏ Empire Strikes Back radio broadcast, 27" x 40" 50.00
- ❏ Empire Strikes Back radio broadcast, 27" x 40" reprint [436-09] 16.00
- ❏ Empire Strikes Back, 24" x 36" Collector's Edition, similar to style "A" [436-10] 10.00
- ❏ Empire Strikes Back, 24" x 36", similar to advance style [v1e1:379] 10.00
- ❏ Episode III DVD: Own it on DVD November 1 [436-11] 15.00
- ❏ Empire Strikes Back 25th anniversary [436-12] 45.00
- ❏ Heir to the Empire, 28" x 22" [2:357] 20.00
- ❏ Revenge of the Sith Soundtrack, 24" x 24", "includes exclusive bonus DVD" 20.00
- ❏ Star Wars Celebration VI, orange art [436-13] 15.00
- ❏ Star Wars in Concert, 27" x 40" [436-14] 50.00
- ❏ Star Wars in Concert, 27" x 40" reprint 20.00
- ❏ Star Wars, concept concession poster [436-16] 450.00
- ❏ Star Wars, concept concession, reprint, 27" x 40" 20.00
- ❏ The Art of Star Wars, 28" x 20", Japanese 70.00
- ❏ Unleashed art, 23" x 34" [v1e1:380] 35.00
- ❏ X-Wing and TIE Fighter, cutaway view [436-15] 30.00

Mobile posters. Star Wars Special Edition KMart ads.
- ❏ Darth Vader 20.00
- ❏ Luke Skywalker 20.00
- ❏ Yoda, Star Wars 20.00

Posters

(Mexico)
Episode I: The Phantom Menace.
- ❑ Anakin podracer [436-17] 15.00
- ❑ Darth Maul [436-18] 15.00
- ❑ Obi-Wan Kenobi [436-19] 15.00

Episode II: Attack of the Clones.
- ❑ Anakin's Destiny [436-20] 10.00
- ❑ Clone trooper [436-21] 15.00
- ❑ Droideka [436-22] 17.00

20th Century Fox
- ❑ DVD Releases [436-23] 35.00
- ❑ Episode II: AOTC. Theatrical release [436-24] 45.00
- ❑ Episode II: AOTC. Theatrical teaser [436-25] 30.00
- ❑ MTFBWY: One Year Old Today [436-26] 350.00
- ❑ Star Wars: Special Edition Join the Celebration [2:357] ..65.00
- ❑ THX Video Poster, 27" x 40" [436-27] 50.00
- ❑ Yoda, "May The Forth be With You" [436-28] 65.00

Bus stop posters.
- ❑ Episode I—3D, mylar, printed one-sided [436-29] 75.00

Episode I: The Phantom Menace advertising.
- ❑ One businessman, One gambler, Watto [436-30] 145.00
- ❑ One hero, One destiny, Anakin Skywalker [436-31] 145.00
- ❑ One love, One quest, Queen Amidala [436-32] 165.00
- ❑ One mind, One mission, Battle Droid [436-33] 165.00

Episode III: Revenge of the Sith.
- ❑ Darth Vader, "Who's Your Daddy" 11" x 17" [436-34] 10.00
- ❑ Theater 2 sided [436-35] 45.00
- ❑ Theater advance 45.00

20th Century Fox (Canada)
- ❑ Episode I: The Phantom Menace Be The First To Own On Video April 4, 27" x 40" [436-36] 20.00

20th Century Fox (Iceland)
- ❑ Episode II: AOTC. Theatrical release 75.00

20th Century Fox (Thailand)
Episode II: Attack of the Clones.
- ❑ Heroes, theater [436-37] 125.00
- ❑ Villains, theater [436-38] 125.00

Aquaris
- ❑ Family Guy Blue Harvest [436-39] 10.00

At-A-Glance
- ❑ Anakin [436-40] 6.00
- ❑ Darth Maul 6.00
- ❑ Jar Jar 6.00
- ❑ Jedi Battle 6.00
- ❑ Podrace 6.00
- ❑ Queen Amidala 6.00
- ❑ Space Battle 6.00

Bantha Tracks
- ❑ Star Wars First Ten Years 1977–1987 Poster 34.00

Burger King
Empire Strikes Back Poster, 18" x 24".
- ❑ Bespin [436-41] 14.00
- ❑ Dagobah [436-42] 14.00
- ❑ Hoth [436-43] 14.00

C and D Visionaries, Inc.
- ❑ Darth Vader, epic duel 12.00
- ❑ Darth Vader, Sith 12.00

Classic trilogy.
- ❑ Heroes 12.00
- ❑ Villains 12.00

Cartamundi
Playing card proof posters. 2007 produced, individually numbered, exclusive to Star Wars Celebration IV.
- ❑ Heroes 15.00
- ❑ Posters 15.00
- ❑ Villains 15.00

CBS / Fox Video
- ❑ Star Wars Trilogy, 25" x 38" [2:357] 85.00

Celebration I
- ❑ Star Wars Celebration, Obi-Wan and Qui-Gon Jinn with insets at the bottom 5.00

Celebration III
- ❑ Epic Duel, 24" x 36" 35.00

- ❑ Revenge of the Sith characters, 24" x 34", by Joe Corroney and Jeff Carlisle 45.00

Coca-Cola
Distributed in 1977 through fast food restaurants.
- ❑ Chewbacca [436-44] 16.00
- ❑ Darth Vader [436-45] 16.00
- ❑ Luke Skywalker [436-46] 16.00
- ❑ R2-D2 and C-3PO [436-47] 16.00

Code 3 Collectibles
3D mini-posters.
- ❑ 1976–style Star Wars convention poster, individually numbered, exclusive to San Diego Comic-Con 45.00
- ❑ A New Hope, 3,000 produced [436-48] 80.00
- ❑ A New Hope style D, 3,000 produced [436-49] 80.00
- ❑ Empire Strikes Back [436-50] 80.00
- ❑ Empire Strikes Back, excl. to Star Wars Celebration III ..120.00
- ❑ Return of the Jedi [436-51] 80.00
- ❑ Return of the Jedi, 10th Anniversary 35.00
- ❑ Revenge of the Jedi 80.00
- ❑ Revenge of the Sith, 5,000 produced, individually numbered, exclusive to Best Buy 80.00
- ❑ Revenge of the Sith, Darth Vader [436-52] 35.00

Dark Horse Comics
- ❑ Episode II: AOTC, 2 sided with Lucas Books 10.00
- ❑ Graphic Novel Chronology, 2 sided 10.00
- ❑ Star Wars Timeline (color) 10.00
- ❑ Vader's Quest 4 page pull-out 10.00

Decipher
CCG posters.
- ❑ Cloud City, "As you wish", 25.5" x 33.5" 10.00
- ❑ Darth Vader, "You have only begun to discover your power," 22" x 28" 10.00
- ❑ Jabba's Palace, "Soon you will learn to appreciate me," 25.5" x 33.5" 10.00
- ❑ Star Wars Special Edition limited edition 9-card expansion set, 10.5" x 33" 10.00

Disney / MGM
Destinations, set of 8, exclusive to Disneyland.
- ❑ Bespin 45.00
- ❑ Dagobah 45.00

Posters

436-50　　436-51　　436-52　　436-53　　436-54　　436-55　　436-56　　436-57

    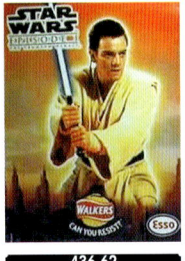  

436-58　　436-59　　436-60　　436-61　　436-62　　436-63　　436-64

- ❏ Endor—Celebration 45.00
- ❏ Endor—Moon 45.00
- ❏ Hoth 45.00
- ❏ Star Tours 60.00
- ❏ Tatooine 45.00
- ❏ Yavin 45.00

Star Wars Weekends.
- ❏ 2003 Mickey and Yoda 35.00
- ❏ 2005 Darth Vader / Mickey 35.00
- ❏ 2007 X-Wing Mickey 35.00
- ❏ 2012 Donald Duck as Savage Opress 50.00

Dixie / Northern Inc.
- ❏ Storycard poster, mail-in premium [436-53] 50.00

Duncan Heinz
Mail-in poster premiums.
- ❏ C-3PO and R2-D2 [436-54] 25.00
- ❏ Darth Vader [436-55] 25.00
- ❏ Han and Leia [436-56] 25.00
- ❏ Luke Skywalker [436-57] 25.00

Encuentros
- ❏ 2004 Encuentros [436-58] 45.00

Esso
Co-produced with Pepsi.
- ❏ Anakin Skywalker [436-59] 15.00
- ❏ Darth Maul [436-60] 15.00

Co-produced with Walkers.
- ❏ Jar Jar Binks [436-61] 15.00
- ❏ Obi-Wan Kenobi [436-62] 15.00

Fan Club
- ❏ Star Wars Celebration [436-63] 25.00

Fine Molds (Japan)
- ❏ Models featuring Slave I [v1e1:380] 15.00

Fox Video
- ❏ 27" x 40" DVD art, Darth Vader 25.00

Freegells (Brazil)
- ❏ Giant poster to attach set of 50 plastic cards [436-64] ... 20.00

Frito Lay
11" x 17" Find the Hero Inside, Publix exclusives.
- ❏ Dark Destiny 20.00
- ❏ Fett Family 20.00
- ❏ Jedi Justice 20.00
- ❏ Skywalker Saga 20.00

GB Eye
- ❏ Star Wars Episode 4 A New Hope—China, reprint [436-65] ... 10.00

Gentle Giant Studios
- ❏ Max Rebo Band, designed for blacklight, exclusive to Premiere Guild 75.00

Hasbro
- ❏ 1995–1997 Figure Collection [436-66] 30.00
- ❏ 2002 Figure Collection, exclusive to Star Wars Celebration II [436-67] 20.00
- ❏ 2008 Figure Collection, excl. to Toys R Us [436-68] ... 25.00
- ❏ 2009 Figure Collection, exclusive to San Diego Comic-Con 25.00
- ❏ 30th Anniversary figure collection, exclusive to Star Wars Celebration Europe [436-69] 20.00
- ❏ Clone Wars, action figures [436-70] 20.00
- ❏ Clones on battlefield, exclusive poster from Entertainment Earth 4 figure set 15.00
- ❏ Jedi and Heores, Wizardcon 2002 exclusive [436-71] ... 15.00
- ❏ OTC Classic Scene with action figures, 2004 Comic-Con exclusive [436-72] 15.00
- ❏ Revenge of the Sith—56 action figures 15.00

Hasbro (Australia)
- ❏ 2002 figure collection, exclusive to Toys R Us [436-73] ... 35.00

Hi-C
- ❏ Return of the Jedi, 2 sided mail-in premium [436-74] ... 45.00

Highbridge Company
- ❏ Star Wars NPR broadcast, "Now Available on Cassette and Compact Discs" [436-75] 25.00

Hollywood Heroes
- ❏ Droids, Ewoks, Power of the Force, exclusive to Star Wars Celebration IV, 16" x 18" 35.00

436-65　　　　436-66　　　　　436-67　　　　　436-68

  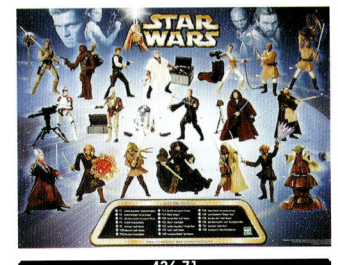 

436-69　　　　436-70　　　　　436-71　　　　　436-72

Posters

ILM
- Yoda and the Hulk [436-76] 45.00

John Alvin
- Celebration IV 350.00

Kellogg's
- Celebrate the Saga, 32" x 15" 20.00

Kellogg's (Singapore)
Episode III: Revenge of the Sith. 15" x 20".
- Anakin Skywalker [436-77] 15.00
- C-3PO and R2-D2 [436-78] 15.00
- Clone trooper [436-79] 15.00
- Darth Vader [436-80] 15.00
- Emperor Palpatine [436-81] 15.00
- General Grievous [436-82] 15.00
- Mace Windu [436-83] 15.00
- Obi-Wan Kenobi [436-84] 15.00
- Yoda [436-85] 15.00

Kenner
Planetary maps.
- Death Star 11.00
- Endor 8.00
- Tatooine 8.00

Lucasfilm
- Clone Wars [436-86] 20.00
- Clone Wars season 1 [436-87] 20.00
- Clone Wars volume II [436-88] 20.00
- Primera Star Wars Convencion, 17–19 Marzo ... 25.00
- Size Matters Not, IMAX, Insider exclusive [436-89] ... 45.00

M&M World
- The Dark Side of Chocolate [436-90] 20.00

Mello Smello
12" x 18" lenticular.
- Anakin Skywalker / Darth Vader [436-91] 20.00
- Darth Vader [436-92] 20.00
- Darth Vader [436-93] 20.00
- Darth Vader and Palpatine [436-94] 20.00
- General Grievous [436-95] 20.00
- Jedi Master Yoda [436-96] 20.00

12" x 18" lenticular. Classic trilogy.
- Heroes [436-97] 20.00

26" x 18" lenticular, VividVision. Limited to 500 of each. Individually numbered, exclusive to Star Wars Celebration IV.
- Boba Fett 35.00
- Leia Slave 35.00
- Sith Rising 35.00
- Star Wars 35.00

8" x 10" lenticular.
- Darth Vader 15.00
- General Grievous 15.00
- Han Solo 15.00
- Jedi Master Yoda 15.00
- Jedi Starfighters 15.00
- Luke Skywalker 15.00
- R2-D2 .... 15.00
- R2D2 and C3PO 15.00

Revenge of the Sith DVD release promotions. Limited to 5,000 of each with COA, 8" x 10".
- Anakin and Obi-Wan 20.00
- Boba Fett 20.00
- Clone troopers 20.00
- Darth Vader 20.00

Revenge of the Sith DVD release promotions. Limited to 5,000 of each with COA, 12" x 18".
- Jedi Knights 25.00

Revenge of the Sith lenticular 3D.
- R2-D2 [436-98] 25.00
- Starfighters [436-99] 25.00

Mexico Collector Convention
- 2003 July 12 and 13, rolled 85.00

Mondo
24" x 35" movie posters.
- Empire Strikes Back [436-100] 50.00
- Return of the Jedi [436-101] 50.00
- Star Wars [436-102] 50.00

24" x 35".
- Chewbacca 50.00
- Dawn on Tatooine, 410 produced, individually numbered [v1e1:382] 50.00
- R2-D2 exploded 50.00
- Sanctuary Moon 50.00
- Ten Banthas 50.00

N.S.W. Building Society Ltd. (Australia)
Premiums for Star Wars savings accounts.
- Ewoks poster 300.00
- Return of the Jedi poster 300.00

Official Pix
- Fan Days II, 27" x 40", October 25–26 [436-103] ... 10.00

Orquesta Pops De Mexico
- 2004 Julio Star Wars en Concierto [436-104] 75.00

Paizo Publishing / Fan Club
- Return of the Jedi 20th Anniversary, folded [436-105] ... 25.00

Pepsi Cola
Exclusive to Pizza Hut. Special Edition (SE).
- 1997 Empire Strikes Back [436-106] 20.00
- 1997 Return of the Jedi 20.00
- 1997 Star Wars [436-107] 20.00

Pepsi Cola / Frito Lay
11" x 17", free with Pepsi or Lays purchase.
- 1 Queen Amidala 15.00
- 2 Anakin Skywalker 15.00
- 3 Darth Maul [436-108] 15.00
- 4 Jar Jar Binks 15.00

Photomosaics
- Darth Vader [436-109] 35.00
- Darth Vader helmet [436-110] 35.00
- Jedi Master Yoda [436-111] 35.00

Portal
- At Last We will Have Revenge [436-112] 25.00
- Star Wars Episode I: The Phantom Menace [436-113] ... 25.00
- The Art of Ralph McQuarrie (Empire Strikes Back), 24" x 36" 30.00

Posters

436-94 | 436-95 | 436-96 | 436-97 | 436-98

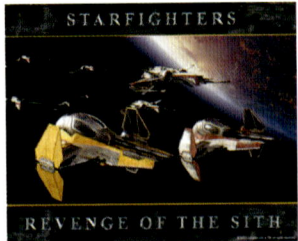     

436-99 | 436-100 | 436-101 | 436-102 | 436-103 | 436-104

Proctor and Gamble
Mail-in poster premiums.
- Droids [436-114] 30.00
- Heroes Battle [436-115] 30.00
- Lightsaber Duel [436-116] 30.00

Randy Martinez
- O Lando, exclusive to Star Wars Celebration V 15.00

Rolling Thunder Graphics
- Darth Vader, signed by Dave Dorman 85.00

Russell Walks
- Boba Fett, official Celebration V 20.00

Sales Corp. of America
11" x 14" sold flat.
- Battle 25.00
- Darth [436-117] 25.00
- Emperor 25.00
- Ewoks 25.00
- Jabba 25.00
- Jedi Cast 25.00
- Jedi Poster 25.00
- Lightsaber 25.00
- Saber Duel 25.00
- Speeder 25.00

Scholastic
- Anakin, "The Force runs strong in those who read" Episode I 10.00

Episode II Adventures, 14" x 17".
- Anakin Skywalker 5.00
- Arena Battle [436-118] 5.00
- Boba Fett (young) 5.00
- Clone Army 5.00
- Count Dooku 5.00
- Dexter Jettster 5.00
- Jango Fett 5.00
- Kamino 5.00
- Mace Windu 5.00
- Obi-Wan Kenobi 5.00
- Padmé Amidala 5.00
- Yoda 5.00

SciPubTech
Cutaway view posters, 36" x 24".
- AT-AT and snowspeeder, deluxe 40.00
- AT-AT and snowspeeder, regular [436-119] 25.00
- Millennium Falcon, deluxe 40.00
- Millennium Falcon, regular [436-120] 25.00
- X-Wing Fighter, deluxe 40.00
- X-Wing Fighter, regular [436-121] 25.00

Skywalkers
- The Empire Strikes Back [436-122] 30.00
- Your pictorial guide to the major characters [4:262] 25.00

Smithsonian Institute
- The Magic of Myth, Oct. 1997–Oct. 1998 [436-123] 40.00

Sony Classical
- Attack of the Clones soundtrack release [4:262] 25.00

Star Wars Celebration Europe
- The Next 30 Years 50.00

Star Wars Celebration VI
- "Join the Party" 20.00
- Star Wars Alphabet 20.00
- Star Wars TRI Art Poster 20.00

Star Wars Insider
- 136 Vintage Action Figures with common variations .. 25.00
- Galaxy Poster Map 25.00

Sunshine Biscuits L.L.C.
- Darth Vader, mail-in premium 30.00

Taco Bell
Episode I: The Phantom Menace premiums, 17" x 22".
- No. 1 Anakin Skywalker 12.00
- No. 2 Qui-Gon Jinn 12.00
- No. 3 Watto 12.00
- No. 4 Darth Maul [436-124] 12.00

The LEGO Group
- 10th anniversary Star Wars mini-figures, 15,000 produced, individually numbered [v1e1:383] 65.00
- Asteroid Ambush / Clone troopers 10.00
- Republic Gunship / Republic Gunship 10.00
- Speeder Chase / Republic Gunships 10.00
- Tusken Attack / Arena Droids 10.00
- X-Wing and Falcon flee the Death Star with Imperial fighters in pursuit, 17" x 22" 10.00

    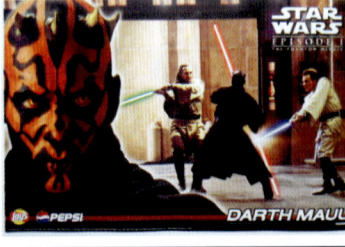  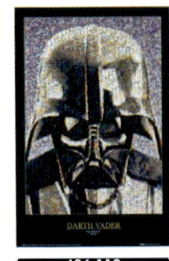

436-105 | 436-106 | 436-107 | 436-108 | 436-109 | 436-110

     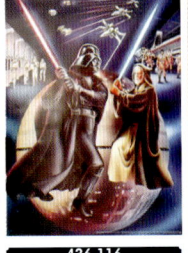 

436-111 | 436-112 | 436-113 | 436-114 | 436-115 | 436-116 | 436-117

Posters

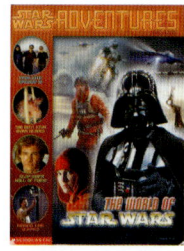
436-118

436-119

436-120

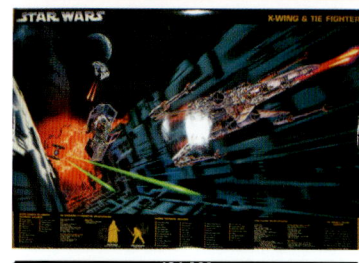
436-121

436-122

436-123

436-124

436-125

436-126

436-127

436-128

Theatrical

Attack of the Clones, advance.
- ❏ 108" x 60" [436-125] 340.00
- ❏ 27" x 40", rolled [2:359] 50.00
- ❏ 27" x 40", rolled, double-sided [2:359] 100.00

Attack of the Clones.
- ❏ 27" x 40", rolled [2:359] 40.00
- ❏ 27" x 40", rolled, double-sided [436-126] 60.00

Caravan of Courage, style "A".
- ❏ 27" x 41" folded 50.00
- ❏ 27" x 41" rolled [436-127] 85.00

Caravan of Courage, style "B".
- ❏ 27" x 41" folded 50.00
- ❏ 27" x 41" rolled [436-128] 85.00

Empire Strikes Back 10th anniversary.
- ❏ 27" x 41" art [436-129] 125.00
- ❏ 27" x 41" gold mylar [436-130] 350.00
- ❏ 27" x 41" silver mylar [2:359] 300.00

Empire Strikes Back advance, style "A".
- ❏ 27" x 41" folded [2:358] 450.00
- ❏ 27" x 41" rolled [436-131] 500.00
- ❏ 41" x 81" folded [2:358] 2,000.00
- ❏ Reprint 27" x 40" rolled 16.00

Empire Strikes Back rerelease 1981.
- ❏ 14" x 36" [2:358] 75.00

- ❏ 27" x 41" folded [436-132] 75.00
- ❏ 27" x 41" rolled [2:358] 100.00
- ❏ 28" x 22" folded 75.00
- ❏ 28" x 22" rolled 100.00
- ❏ 30" x 41" 100.00
- ❏ 40" x 60" 450.00

Empire Strikes Back rerelease 1982.
- ❏ 14" x 36" [2:358] 75.00
- ❏ 27" x 41" folded [436-133] 70.00
- ❏ 27" x 41" rolled [2:358] 75.00
- ❏ 28" x 22" folded 75.00
- ❏ 28" x 22" rolled 100.00
- ❏ 30" x 41" 80.00
- ❏ 40" x 60" 100.00

Empire Strikes Back, style "A".
- ❏ 14" x 36" [2:358] 175.00
- ❏ 27" x 41" folded [436-134] 400.00
- ❏ 27" x 41" rolled [v1e1:383] 465.00
- ❏ 28" x 22" folded 450.00
- ❏ 28" x 22" rolled 525.00
- ❏ 30" x 41" 485.00
- ❏ 40" x 60" 875.00
- ❏ Reprint 27" x 40" 25.00

Empire Strikes Back, style "B".
- ❏ 14" x 36" [2:358] 100.00
- ❏ 27" x 41" folded [v1e1:383] 125.00
- ❏ 27" x 41" rolled [436-135] 155.00
- ❏ 28" x 22" folded 100.00

- ❏ 28" x 22" rolled 125.00
- ❏ 30" x 41" 175.00
- ❏ 40" x 60" 175.00
- ❏ Reprint 27" x 40" 25.00

Empire Strikes Back, style "C".
- ❏ 27" x 41" rolled 125.00
- ❏ Reprint 27" x 40" [436-136] 25.00

Empire Strikes Back, style "D".
- ❏ 27" x 41" rolled [436-137] 100.00
- ❏ Reprint 27" x 40" 25.00

Return of the Jedi 10th anniversary advance.
- ❏ 27" x 41" rolled [436-138] 240.00
- ❏ Reprint 27" x 40" [436-139] 25.00

Return of the Jedi 10th anniversary.
- ❏ 27" x 41" rolled [2:359] 100.00

Return of the Jedi rerelease 1985.
- ❏ 14" x 36" [2:359] 60.00
- ❏ 27" x 41" folded [436-140] 50.00
- ❏ 27" x 41" rolled [2:359] 75.00
- ❏ 28" x 22" folded 100.00
- ❏ 28" x 22" rolled 160.00
- ❏ 30" x 41" 75.00
- ❏ 40" x 60" 150.00

Return of the Jedi, style "A".
- ❏ 14" x 36" [2:359] 125.00

436-129

436-130

436-131

436-132

436-133

436-134

436-135

436-136

436-137

436-138

436-139

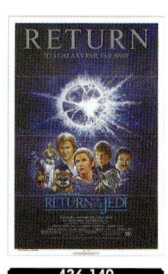
436-140

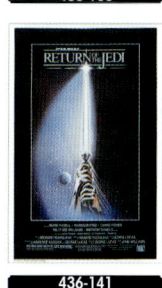
436-141

436-142

436-143

436-144

Posters

436-145 | 436-146 | 436-147 | 436-148 | 436-149 | 436-150 | 436-151 | 436-152

- ❏ 27" x 41" folded [2:359] 125.00
- ❏ 27" x 41" rolled [436-141] 175.00
- ❏ 28" x 22" folded 100.00
- ❏ 28" x 22" rolled 150.00
- ❏ 30" x 41" 125.00
- ❏ 40" x 60" 325.00
- ❏ Reprint 27" x 40" 25.00

Return of the Jedi, style "B".
- ❏ 14" x 36" [2:359] 125.00
- ❏ 27" x 41" folded [2:359] 125.00
- ❏ 27" x 41" rolled [436-142] 195.00
- ❏ 28" x 22" folded 100.00
- ❏ 28" x 22" rolled 150.00
- ❏ 30" x 41" 125.00
- ❏ 40" x 60" 425.00
- ❏ Reprint 27" x 40" 25.00

Revenge of the Jedi first advance, second version.
- ❏ 27" x 41" folded 375.00
- ❏ 27" x 41" rolled [436-143] 525.00

Revenge of the Jedi first advance.
- ❏ 27" x 41" folded 550.00
- ❏ 27" x 41" rolled 775.00

Star Wars "Happy Birthday".
- ❏ 27" x 41" rolled [v1e1:384] 2,000.00

Star Wars 10th Anniversary.
- ❏ 27" x 41" mylar [2:358] 150.00
- ❏ 27" x 41" rolled, Struzan [2:358] 300.00

Star Wars advance, style "B".
- ❏ 27" x 41" folded [2:358] 200.00
- ❏ 27" x 41" rolled [2:358] 350.00

Star Wars first advance.
- ❏ 27" x 41" folded 350.00
- ❏ 27" x 41" rolled [436-144] 400.00

Star Wars reissue 1979.
- ❏ 27" x 41" folded 140.00
- ❏ 27" x 41" rolled [436-145] 185.00

Star Wars reissue 1981.
- ❏ 14" x 36" 75.00
- ❏ 27" x 41" folded [2:358] 200.00
- ❏ 27" x 41" rolled [436-146] 250.00
- ❏ 28" x 22" folded 100.00
- ❏ 28" x 22" rolled [2:358] 140.00
- ❏ 30" x 41" 75.00
- ❏ 40" x 60" 100.00

Star Wars reissue 1982.
- ❏ 14" x 36" 75.00
- ❏ 27" x 41" folded [2:358] 200.00
- ❏ 27" x 41" rolled [436-147] 225.00
- ❏ 28" x 22" folded 140.00
- ❏ 28" x 22" rolled 180.00
- ❏ 30" x 41" 165.00
- ❏ 40" x 60" 325.00

Star Wars Special Edition.
- ❏ Advance, 24" x 36" soundtrack promo [2:359] 20.00
- ❏ Advance, 27" x 40" (Return of the Jedi March 14) [436-148] 40.00
- ❏ Advance, 27" x 40" (Return of the Jedi March 7) [2:359] 50.00
- ❏ Empire Strikes Back 27" x 40" [436-149] 50.00
- ❏ Empire Strikes Back, 40" x 30" rolled, double-sided 30.00
- ❏ Reprint Return of the Jedi, 27" x 40" [436-150] 25.00
- ❏ Reprint Star Wars, 27" x 40" [2:359] 25.00
- ❏ Return of the Jedi 27" x 40" [2:359] 40.00
- ❏ Return of the Jedi 27" x 40", double-sided [2:359] 65.00
- ❏ Return of the Jedi, 27" x 40" (Return of the Jedi March 7) [2:359] 50.00
- ❏ Return of the Jedi, 27" x 40", double-sided (Return of the Jedi March 14) [2:359] 40.00
- ❏ Return of the Jedi, 40" x 30" rolled, double-sided [2:359] 30.00
- ❏ Star Wars, 27" x 40" [2:359] 50.00
- ❏ Star Wars, 27" x 40", double-sided [436-151] 65.00
- ❏ Star Wars, 40" x 30" rolled, double-sided 40.00

Star Wars style "A".
- ❏ 14" x 36" [2:358] 125.00
- ❏ 27" x 41" folded [2:358] 300.00
- ❏ 27" x 41" rolled [436-152] 395.00
- ❏ 28" x 22" folded 300.00
- ❏ 28" x 22" rolled [436-153] 395.00

- ❏ 30" x 41" 775.00
- ❏ 40" x 60" rolled 700.00
- ❏ 41" x 81" folded [2:358] 750.00
- ❏ 81" x 81" [2:358] 525.00
- ❏ Reprint 27" x 40" 25.00
- ❏ Reprint, 38" x 27" 25.00

Star Wars style "C".
- ❏ 27" x 41" folded [2:358] 350.00
- ❏ 27" x 41" rolled [436-154] 450.00
- ❏ Reprint, 26.5" x 40" 25.00

Star Wars style "D".
- ❏ 27" x 41" folded [2:358] 400.00
- ❏ 27" x 41" rolled [436-155] 450.00
- ❏ 30" x 41" 795.00
- ❏ 40" x 60" 775.00
- ❏ Reprint, 27" x 40" 25.00

The Phantom Menace.
- ❏ 27" x 40" advance, rolled [436-156] 40.00
- ❏ 27" x 40" advance, rolled, double-sided [2:359] 120.00
- ❏ 27" x 40", rolled [v1e1:384] 20.00

Theatrical, Foreign (Argentina)
- ❏ Star Wars style "C", 29" x 43" [436-157] 150.00

Theatrical, Foreign (Australia)
- ❏ 3 In One Programme [436-158] 375.00
- ❏ 3 In One Programme, 27" x 39" reprint 25.00
- ❏ All Three on One Programme, 13" x 30" [436-159] 150.00
- ❏ Star Wars style "C", 13" x 30" [436-160] 175.00

Theatrical, Foreign (Belgium)
- ❏ Star Wars style "A", 14" x 22" [436-161] 150.00

Theatrical, Foreign (France)
- ❏ Empire Strikes Back similar to style "B", 47" x 63" folded [436-162] 225.00
- ❏ Star Wars similar to style "A", 47" x 63" folded [436-163] 300.00

Theatrical, Foreign (Germany)
- ❏ Episode I: The Phantom Menace 23" x 32" [2:359] 40.00
- ❏ Kampf um Endor (Ewoks: The Battle for Endor), 23" x 33" [436-164] 35.00

436-153 | 436-154 | 436-155 | 436-156 | 436-157 | 436-158

     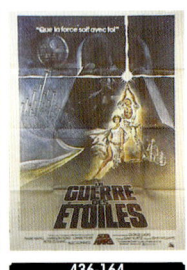   

436-159 | 436-160 | 436-161 | 436-162 | 436-163 | 436-164 | 436-165 | 436-166 | 436-167

Posters

Theatrical, Foreign (India)
- ☐ Empire Strikes Back, 27" x 41", character frames across top [436-165] 100.00

Theatrical, Foreign (Italy)
- ☐ Empire Strikes Back similar to style "B", 13" x 27" 80.00
- ☐ Empire Strikes Back, 39" x 55", similar to style "B" [436-166] 250.00
- ☐ Star Wars style "A", 13" x 27" [436-167] 100.00
- ☐ Star Wars style "A", 55" x 79" 300.00
- ☐ Star Wars, 39" x 55" [436-168] 250.00
- ☐ Star Wars, 40" x 28" [436-169] 175.00

Theatrical, Foreign (Japan)
- ☐ Return of the Jedi, 20" x 30", Japan style "B" [436-170] .50.00
- ☐ Return of the Jedi, 20" x 30", similar to style "A" [436-171] 50.00

20" x 29".
- ☐ Star Wars 350.00
- ☐ Star Wars advance 300.00
- ☐ Star Wars advance 1982 [436-172] 275.00
- ☐ Star Wars style "A", 1982 [436-173] 250.00

Theatrical, Foreign (Poland)
- ☐ Star Wars, 27" x 39" [436-174] 750.00

Theatrical, Foreign (Spain)
- ☐ Episode I: The Phantom Menace 27" x 40", double-sided [2:360] 20.00
- ☐ Episode I: The Phantom Menace advance, 27" x 40", double-sided [2:360] 95.00

TITAN Magazines
- ☐ Star Wars Insider / Clone Wars Magazine, 11" x 17" ... 10.00

Tommy Lee Edwards
- ☐ Scout Racers, 300 produced, individually numbered .. 75.00

Topps
- ☐ 18" x 22" Star Wars Galaxy Deluxe Trading Cards from Topps on sale here 20.00
- ☐ 25 Years, 12" x 18" [v1e1:384] 15.00
- ☐ Attack of the Clones movie cards, 2 sided Celebration II giveaway 15.00
- ☐ Empire Strikes Back press sheet, mail-in premium 45.00
- ☐ Star Wars Galaxy Series 7 on sale here [436-175] 15.00

Episode II: Attack of the Clones.
- ☐ Move cards poster, tri-folded, 2 sides 20.00

Trends International Corp.
- ☐ Cape 10.00
- ☐ Chewie 25.00
- ☐ Empire 10.00
- ☐ Episode I: The Phantom Menace, 24" x 36" one-sheet 15.00
- ☐ Episode I: The Phantom Menace, 24" x 36" 3D [436-176] 10.00
- ☐ George Lucas Episode II Selects, exclusive to Star Wars Celebration II [2:360] 25.00
- ☐ Princess Leia 15.00
- ☐ Star Wars Episode III: Revenge of the Sith [436-177] .. 10.00
- ☐ Star Wars Episode III: Revenge of the Sith, teaser [436-178] 10.00
- ☐ Star Wars saga 20.00
- ☐ Star Wars saga collage [436-179] 12.00
- ☐ Stormtroopers [436-180] 10.00
- ☐ The Force Unleashed 2 .... 20.00
- ☐ Unleashed 15.00

Angry Birds Star Wars.
- ☐ Epic [436-181] 10.00
- ☐ One sheet [436-182] 10.00

Clone Wars.
- ☐ Anakin 15.00
- ☐ Close-ups 15.00
- ☐ Group 15.00
- ☐ The Clone Wars movie poster [436-183] 20.00

Episode I: The Phantom Menace, 24" x 36".
- ☐ Advance design [436-184] 10.00
- ☐ Episode I: The Phantom Menace [436-185] 10.00
- ☐ Heroes 10.00
- ☐ Heroes, foil [436-186] 30.00
- ☐ Jar Jar [436-187] 10.00
- ☐ Jedi vs. Sith [4:263] 10.00
- ☐ Queen Amidala [436-188] 10.00
- ☐ Queen Amidala, foil [436-189] 20.00
- ☐ Space Battle, foil [v1e1:384] 20.00
- ☐ Villains [436-190] 10.00
- ☐ Villains, foil 30.00

Episode II: Attack of the Clones, 22" x 34".
- ☐ Anakin 2570 [436-191] 10.00
- ☐ Darkside 2585 [436-192] 10.00

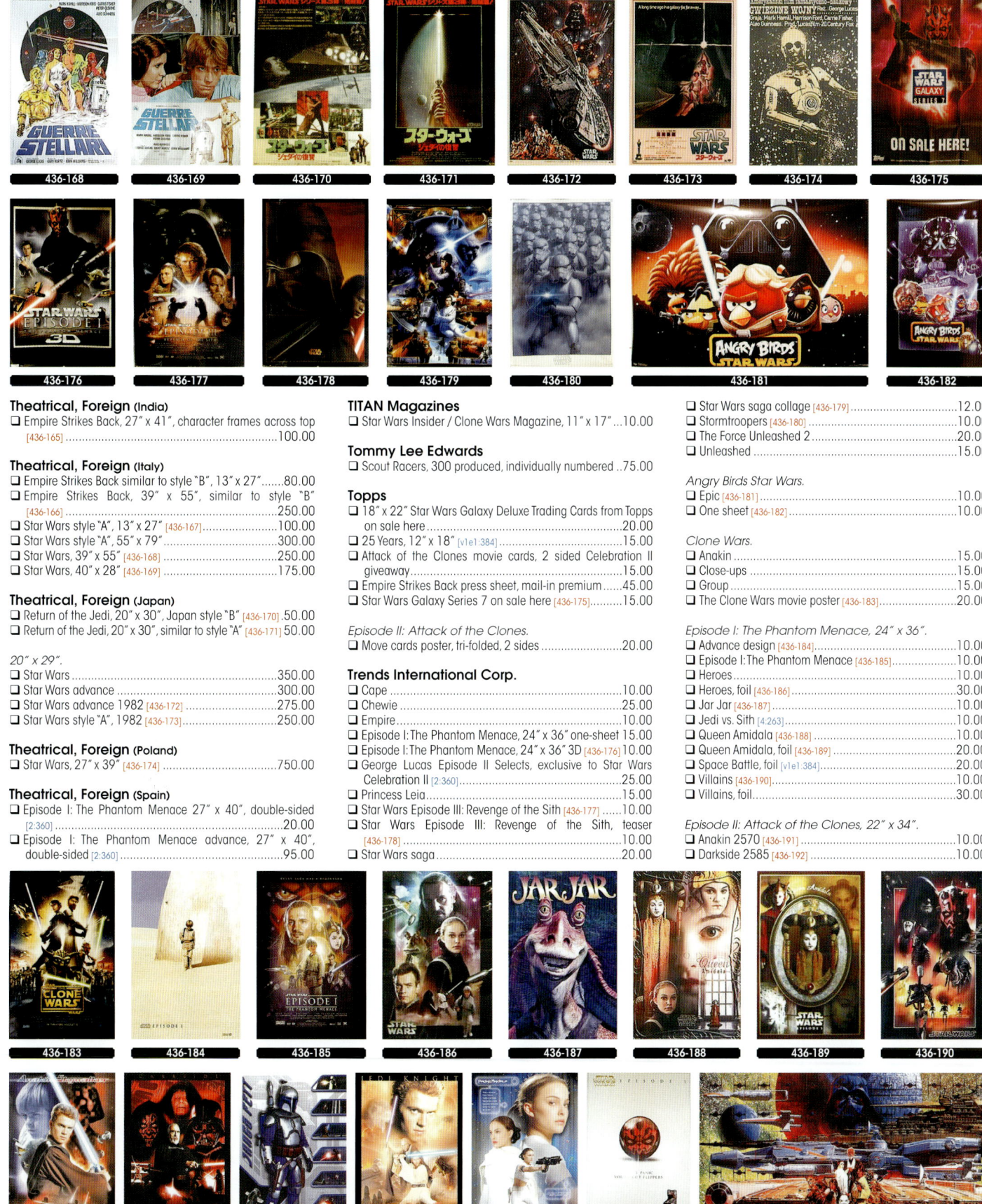

Posters

- Jango Fett 2590 [436-193] 10.00
- Jedi knight 2580 [436-194] 10.00
- Padmé 2575 [436-195] 10.00
- Space battle 2595 ....10.00

Episode II: Attack of the Clones.
- Star Wars One-Sheet 2560, 25" x 35" [2-360] 25.00

Episode III: Revenge of the Sith, 23" x 33".
- Walks 8450 ....15.00

Episode III: Revenge of the Sith, 24" x 36".
- Battle 8479 ....10.00
- Jedi 8481 ....10.00
- Sith 8483 ....10.00
- Vader 8477 ....10.00
- Yoda Jedi Master 8599 ....10.00

Tsuneo Sanda
- Celebration, 27" x 40" 175.00

Vanity Fair
- February 1999 Cover, 23.5c [2-360] 35.00

Western Graphics Corp.
- Empire Strikes Back [v1e1-384] 35.00
- Trench 1356 ....35.00

Williams
- Don't Panic—You've Got Flippers [436-196] 25.00

Wizards of the Coast
- Empire Strikes Back TCG promo, 25" x 22" 15.00

Zigzag (Germany)
- Fleets, 22" x 39" [436-197] 25.00

Posters: Mini
Continued in Volume 3, Page 333

- Episode I: 3D [437-01] 5.00

20th Century Fox
- Clone Wars in theaters August 15 [437-02] 5.00

20th Century Fox (Japan)
7.25"x10.25", 1-sheet flyers in the style of vintage movie posters. 25th anniversary premiums.
- Empire Strikes Back [437-03] 10.00
- Empire Strikes Back [437-04] 10.00
- Return of the Jedi, advance [437-05] 10.00
- Star Wars [437-06] 10.00

Blockbuster Video (Mexico)
Episode II DVD pre-order premium.
- Anakin and Padmé [437-07] 10.00
- Blockbuster envelope to store 3 mini-posters [437-08] ...10.00
- Jango Fett [437-09] 10.00
- Yoda [437-10] 10.00

General Mills
Cereal premiums. Mini-poster with scene to color.
- Dogfight Over Death Star 25.00
- Hildebrandt Art [437-11] 25.00
- Imperial Cruiser [437-12] 25.00
- Yavin Celebration (Droids) [437-13] 25.00

Lucas Arts
- Darth Vader 20.00

Nabisco (Australia)
Wheaties premiums.
- An Imperial stormtrooper [437-14] 25.00
- An X-Wing Fighter [437-15] 25.00
- Ben Kenobi [437-16] 25.00
- Han and Chewbacca [437-17] 25.00
- Imperial stormtroopers [437-18] 25.00
- Luke Skywalker [437-19] 25.00
- Luke Skywalker and his Uncle [437-20] 25.00
- On board the Millennium Falcon [437-21] 25.00
- Tuskrn raiders [437-22] 25.00

The LEGO Group
- Snowspeeders attacking AT-STs, 10.5" x 17" 10.00

Topps
Empire Strikes Back widevision mini-posters.
- 1 Advance one-sheet 10.00
- 2 Domestic one-sheet 10.00
- 3 Style B 10.00
- 4 Australian one-sheet 10.00
- 5 German one-sheet 10.00
- 6 Radio Show 10.00

Return of the Jedi widevision mini-posters.
- 1 Advance one-sheet 10.00
- 2 One-sheet style B 10.00
- 3 Rerelease one-sheet 10.00
- 4 Japanese 10.00
- 5 Japanese 10.00
- 6 Polish 10.00

408

Press Kits
Continued in Volume 3, Page 333

Category with images covered in volume 1, first edition, page 386.

Publications

Category with images covered in 5th edition, pages 257–264.

Pucks

- Darth Maul, Tampa Bay Lightning, February 16, 2012 [438-01] 100.00

In Glas Co.
- Yoda playing goalie with a lightsaber, Colorado Avalanche at Los Angeles Kings, March 22, 2010, 500 produced, exclusive to Staples Center [438-02] 100.00

Punch-Out Activities
Continued in Volume 3, Page 333

Clarks of England (UK)
- Helmet and Space Ship, Custom Concepts Incorporated [439-01] 85.00

Frito Lay
Build-a-droids.
- C-3PO [439-02] 15.00
- R2-D2 [439-03] 15.00

General Mills
Punch-out spaceships, cereal premiums.
- Landspeeder [439-04] 80.00
- Millennium Falcon [439-05] 80.00
- TIE Fighter [439-06] 80.00
- X-Wing Fighter [439-07] 80.00

Paizo Publishing / Fan Club
- Fan Club 2003 membership mini-standee [439-08] 10.00

Purses / Carry Bags
Continued in Volume 3, Page 333

Accessory Network
- A New Hope art / Darth Vader reversible 35.00
- Darth Vader [440-01] 35.00
- Darth Vader / Revenge [440-02] 35.00

Adam Joseph Industries
- Ewoks 150.00
- Princess Kneesaa, shaped [440-03] 135.00
- Wicket and Kneesaa [440-04] 120.00
- Wicket the Ewok 120.00
- Wicket the Ewok, shaped 135.00

Bioworld Merchandising
Satchels.
- Icons, blue [440-05] 45.00
- Icons, pink [440-06] 45.00
- Movie art, blue 45.00
- Movie art, pink [440-07] 45.00

Giftware International
- Chewbacca [440-08] 30.00
- Darth Vader [440-09] 30.00
- Jar Jar Binks [440-10] 35.00
- R2-D2 [440-11] 30.00

Kathrine Baumann Design
- Queen Amidala mini audiere, 75 produced [440-12] ... 475.00

Small Planet Co. Ltd. (Japan)
Stormtrooper print.
- Hip bag 45.00
- Shoulder bag 90.00
- Transit pass case [440-13] 40.00
- Zipper pouch 40.00

Purses, Coin
Continued in Volume 3, Page 335

- Queen Amidala treasure keeper look-alike [441-01] 10.00

(UK)
- Clone Wars [441-02] 10.00

438-01

438-02 Top and Bottom

439-01

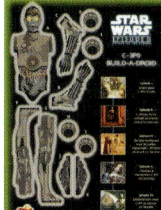
439-02

439-03

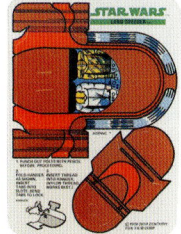
439-04

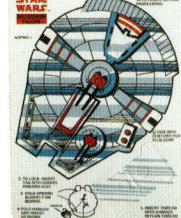
439-05

439-06

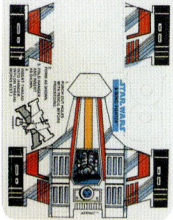
439-07

439-08

440-01

440-02

440-03

440-04

440-05

440-06

440-07

440-08

440-09

440-10

440-11

440-12

440-13

Purses, Coin

441-01 | 441-02 | 441-03 | 441-04 | 441-05 | 441-06

    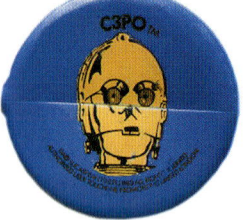 

441-07 | 441-08 | 441-09 | 441-10 | 441-11 | 441-12

441-13 | 441-14 | 441-15 | 441-16 | 441-17

Applause
Treasure Keepers.
- Jar Jar Binks [441-03]..................................10.00
- Queen Amidala [441-04]..............................10.00
- R2-D2 [441-05]...10.00
- Yoda [441-06]..10.00

Pyramid
- Anakin Skywalker, canvas [441-07]..............15.00

Taito (Japan)
Lightsaber coin holders with belt hooks.
- Darth Vader [441-08]...................................25.00
- Luke Skywalker [441-09].............................25.00

Touchline (UK)
3" round with split, any color. Sold loose.
- Admiral Ackbar [441-10]..............................25.00
- C-3PO [441-11]..25.00
- Chewbacca [441-12]...................................25.00
- Darth Vader [441-13]...................................25.00
- Ewok [441-14]..25.00
- Jabba the Hutt [441-15]..............................25.00
- R2-D2 [441-16]..25.00
- Stormtrooper [441-17]................................25.00

Push Pins

Rose Art Industries
- Star Wars collector set, 12-pieces [442-01]..................30.00

Refrigerators
Continued in Volume 3, Page 336

7-Eleven Inc. (Japan)
Lucky draw lottery.
- R2-D2 [443-01]... 1,150.00

Pepsi Cola (Japan)
Lucky draw lottery.
- R2-D2 32" x 20" x 14", 2,000 produced [443-02]....2,100.00

Remote Controls
Continued in Volume 3, Page 336

Kash 'N' Gold
- Lightsaber Universal Remote Control with sound effects [444-01]..35.00

Taito (Japan)
Lightsaber universal remote controls.
- Darth Vader [444-02]...................................30.00
- Luke Skywalker [444-03].............................30.00

Telemania (UK)
- Darth Maul's Sith Infiltrator universal remote [444-04]..40.00

Replicas
Continued in Volume 3, Page 336

Code 3 Collectibles
- AT-ST vehicle [445-01]................................400.00
- Darth Vader's TIE Fighter, 5,000 produced, individually numbered..365.00
- Darth Vader's TIE Fighter Signature Series, 500 produced, individually numbered [445-02]..................500.00
- Millennium Falcon......................................300.00
- Republic Gunship [4:271]...........................315.00
- Skywalker Ranch Engine 1589 with replica patch, 7,500 produced, individually numbered................300.00
- Slave I, 5,000 prod., individually numbered [445-03]...300.00
- Slave I, signature series, 500 produced, individually numbered...500.00
- X-Wing Fighter, Red Five, 5,000 produced, individually numbered [v1e1:387]...................................300.00
- X-Wing Fighter, Red Five, signature series, individually numbered...500.00

Corgi
- Merger premium, scaled replica lightsaber, Medalionz coin, scaled car, exclusive to Toy Fair..................135.00

Don Post
Life-size, cast from original props.
- Boba Fett [v1e1:387]................................ 6,000.00

    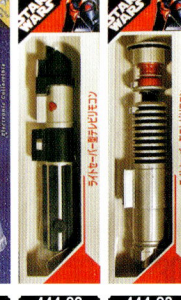  

442-01 | 443-01 | 443-02 | 444-01 | 444-02 | 444-03 | 444-04

Replicas

 445-01  445-02  445-03  445-04  445-05 445-06

 445-07 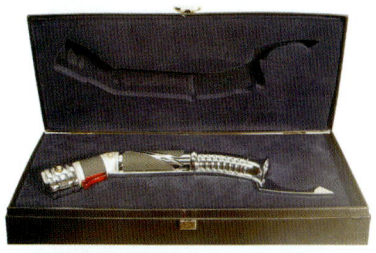 445-08  445-09 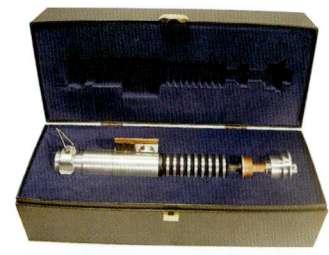 445-10

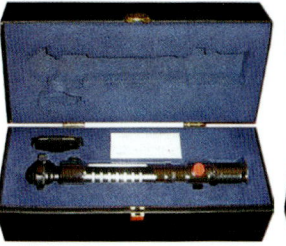 445-11 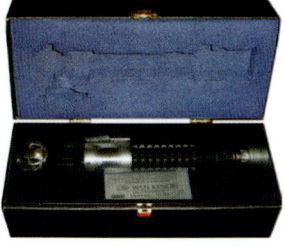 445-12 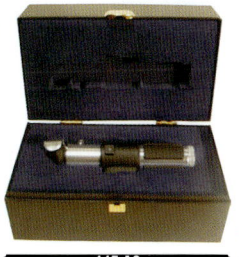 445-13  445-14  445-15  445-16

- ❏ See Threepio 15,000.00
- ❏ Stormtrooper, 500 produced, individually numbered [3:369] 4,500.00

eFX Inc.
- ❏ TIE Fighter, A New Hope, 657 produced, individually numbered 1,650.00
- ❏ X-Wing Fighter, signed by Mark Hamill, 833 produced, individually numbered 1,500.00

1:1 helmets.
- ❏ Clone trooper, exclusive to StarWarsShop.com..........725.00
- ❏ Clone trooper captain, 400 produced, exclusive to StarWarsShop.com 725.00
- ❏ Stormtrooper, Episode IV, released 07/08/08, 500 produced 725.00

Lightsabers, reveal.
- ❏ Luke Skywalker, Return of the Jedi, 1,000 produced, individually numbered 600.00

Lightsabers.
- ❏ Ahsoka Tano, individually numbered 400.00
- ❏ Master Orgus, The Old Republic, exclusive to Bioware employees 800.00

Gentle Giant Studios
.45 scale helmets.
- ❏ Darth Vader, gold colored...80.00

Hasbro
1:1 lightsabers. FX edition.
- ❏ Anakin Skywalker..125.00
- ❏ Darth Maul..150.00
- ❏ Darth Vader..125.00
- ❏ Darth Vader's...120.00
- ❏ Luke Skywalker A New Hope..................................120.00
- ❏ Luke Skywalker Return of the Jedi............................125.00
- ❏ Obi-Wan Kenobi 125.00
- ❏ Yoda 125.00

Icons Authentic Replicas
Replicas in Plexiglas display cases.
- ❏ Lightsaber, Darth Vader's, 10,000 prod. [v1e1:387] 350.00
- ❏ Lightsaber, Luke Skywalker's, 10,000 produced 350.00
- ❏ Lightsaber, Obi-Wan Kenobi's, 10,000 produced 350.00
- ❏ TIE Fighter.. 1,500.00
- ❏ X-Wing Fighter [445-04] 1,950.00

Illusive Originals
- ❏ Han Solo in Carbonite prop, 2,500 produced, individually numbered [v1e1:387] 2,800.00

Master Replicas
- ❏ AT-AT [445-05]..400.00
- ❏ AT-AT signature edition 1,700.00
- ❏ Y-Wing Studio Scale D 1,575.00

1:1 accessories.
- ❏ Emperor's cane [445-06]...225.00
- ❏ Jedi Training Remote, 2,500 produced [445-07]..........250.00
- ❏ Medal of Yavin 200.00
- ❏ Medal of Yavin, 2,500 produced, exclusive to Star Wars Celebration IV..45.00

1:1 helmets.
- ❏ 212th Attack Battalion trooper, individually numbered 400.00
- ❏ 501st Legion trooper helmet, 750 produced, individually numbered 400.00
- ❏ Boba Fett, signature edition, 750 produced, individually numbered 600.00
- ❏ Clone Commander Gree, 500 produced, individ. numbered, exclusive to Master Replicas Collector Society..........400.00
- ❏ Clone trooper Episode III, 2,500 produced, individually numbered 350.00
- ❏ Darth Vader, using original studio molds.............. 1,000.00
- ❏ Darth Vader, using original studio molds, signature edition (Hayden Christensen), 500 produced 1,600.00
- ❏ Shadow stormtrooper, 500 produced, individually numbered, exclusive to Master Replicas Collector Society..........600.00
- ❏ Shock trooper Episode III, 750 produced, individually numbered 450.00

1:1 lightsabers.
- ❏ Anakin Skywalker LE 360.00
- ❏ Anakin Skywalker Revenge of the Sith....................500.00
- ❏ Count Dooku, 3,500 produced [445-08]......................300.00
- ❏ Darth Maul battle damaged 350.00
- ❏ Darth Maul's, 2,500 produced 450.00
- ❏ Darth Maul's, signature series 560.00
- ❏ Darth Vader's, 7,500 produced [445-09] 350.00
- ❏ Darth Vader's Empire Strikes Back, 2,000 produced..350.00
- ❏ Darth Vader's, signature series 1,200.00
- ❏ Luke Skywalker's, 3,500 produced [445-10]................350.00
- ❏ Luke Skywalker's, signature series, 500 produced, individually numbered 750.00
- ❏ Mace Windu's..450.00
- ❏ Mara Jade, signature edition, 750 produced, individually numbered 300.00
- ❏ Obi-Wan Kenobi's, 3,500 produced [445-11]................350.00
- ❏ Obi-Wan Kenobi's (Phantom Menace) Elite edition....650.00
- ❏ Obi-Wan Kenobi's, weathered [445-12] 500.00
- ❏ Qui-Gon Jinn CE..130.00
- ❏ Qui-Gon Jinn LE..370.00
- ❏ Yoda's [445-13] 300.00
- ❏ Yoda's Revenge of the Sith limited edition...............250.00

1:1 lightsabers. FX edition.
- ❏ Anakin Skywalker..130.00
- ❏ Darth Maul, dual bladed 250.00
- ❏ Darth Maul, single blade 175.00
- ❏ Darth Vader's..130.00
- ❏ Luke Skywalker's...130.00
- ❏ Mace Windu's 130.00
- ❏ Obi-Wan Kenobi's..125.00
- ❏ Yoda's..125.00

1:1 weapons.
- ❏ Boba Fett's blaster, limited edition 580.00
- ❏ Boba Fett's blaster, signature edition 680.00
- ❏ Han Solo's blaster 725.00
- ❏ Han Solo's blaster 650.00
- ❏ Jango Fett blaster set [445-14]....................................475.00
- ❏ Princess Leia blaster 400.00
- ❏ Rebel blaster 400.00
- ❏ Stormtrooper blaster 400.00
- ❏ Thermal Detonator [445-15].......................................225.00
- ❏ Thermal Detonator, 'as built by' edition, 750 produced 265.00
- ❏ Thermal Detonator, signature edition, 750 produced 335.00

.33 scale weapons.
- ❏ Boba Fett's blaster 50.00

Replicas

445-17 445-18 445-19 445-20 445-21

   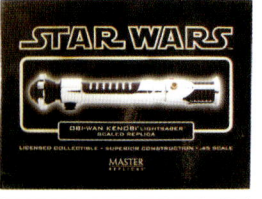 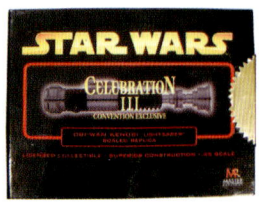
445-22 445-23 445-24 445-25 445-26

   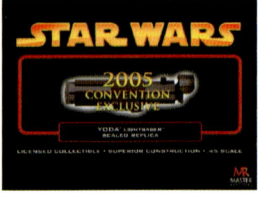 
445-27 445-28 445-29 445-30 445-31

- ❏ Han Solo's blaster 50.00
- ❏ Han Solo's blaster, black chrome, 3,000 produced, exclusive to San Diego Comic-Con 50.00
- ❏ Stormtrooper blaster 55.00
- ❏ Stormtrooper blaster, gold scope 95.00

.45 scale helmets.
- ❏ Boba Fett 50.00
- ❏ Darth Vader [445-16] 100.00
- ❏ Shadow stormtrooper, exclusive to San Diego Comic-Con 90.00
- ❏ Stormtrooper 60.00
- ❏ X-Wing pilot, Luke Skywalker 50.00
- ❏ X-Wing pilot, Wedge Antilles, exclusive to Star Wars Celebration IV 75.00

.45 scale lightsabers.
- ❏ Anakin Skywalker, AOTC 45.00
- ❏ Anakin Skywalker, black chrome, exclusive to StarWarsShop.com [445-17] 200.00
- ❏ Anakin Skywalker, Revenge of the Sith 45.00
- ❏ Count Dooku 45.00
- ❏ Count Dooku, 18k gold, 250 produced 150.00
- ❏ Darth Maul battle damaged, single blade [445-18] 45.00
- ❏ Darth Maul dual bladed, exclusive to MR Collectors' Society 65.00
- ❏ Darth Sidious, exclusive to Best Buy [445-19] 65.00
- ❏ Darth Sidious, chrome European exclusive, 5,000 produced 75.00
- ❏ Darth Tyranus Revenge of the Sith 45.00
- ❏ Darth Vader [445-20] 45.00
- ❏ Darth Vader, Revenge of the Sith [445-21] 50.00
- ❏ Luke Skywalker [445-22] 45.00
- ❏ Luke Skywalker, A New Hope 45.00
- ❏ Luke Skywalker, Return of the Jedi, exclusive to eBay.com [445-23] 65.00
- ❏ Mace Windu [445-24] 45.00
- ❏ Mace Windu with Millennium Falcon pin, exclusive to MR Collectors' Society 75.00
- ❏ Mace Windu, 18k gold, 250 produced 175.00
- ❏ Obi-Wan Kenobi [445-25] 45.00
- ❏ Obi-Wan Kenobi, exclusive to Celebration III [445-26] ... 45.00
- ❏ Obi-Wan Kenobi 18k gold, 150 produced, exclusive to Star Wars Celebration III 375.00
- ❏ Obi-Wan Kenobi A New Hope, as first built, 18k gold, Collector Society exclusive [445-27] 125.00
- ❏ Obi-Wan Kenobi A New Hope, weathered, 500 produced, exclusive to Walmart [445-28] 45.00
- ❏ Obi-Wan Kenobi prequel, as first built, 18k gold, 2004 convention exclusive, 250 produced 175.00
- ❏ Obi-Wan Kenobi prequel, as first built, 2004 convention exclusive [445-29] 45.00
- ❏ Obi-Wan Kenobi Revenge of the Sith 45.00
- ❏ Qui-Gon Jinn with 30th anniversary pin, exclusive to MR Collectors' Society 75.00
- ❏ Yoda 50.00
- ❏ Yoda, black chrome, 2005 Comic-con exclusive [445-30] 65.00
- ❏ Yoda, chrome European exclusive, 5,000 produced 75.00

Collector's Society membership kit.
- ❏ Card, Darth Maul .45 saber, Darth Vader patch, report [v1e1:389] 75.00

Collectors accessories.
- ❏ .45 scale lightsaber display case 75.00

Rubies
- ❏ Darth Vader Life-size display figure 4,500.00

Shepperton Design Studios
- ❏ Stormtrooper A New Hope Stunt Helmets from original molds 850.00

Sideshow Collectibles
Life-sized character statues.
- ❏ C-3PO 5,950.00
- ❏ R2-D2 .... 5,450.00

Star Wars Celebration Japan (Japan)
- ❏ Ewok Fur [445-31] 130.00

Tomy (Japan)
Lightsabers.
- ❏ Darth Vader 325.00
- ❏ Luke Skywalker 325.00

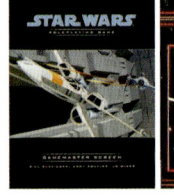         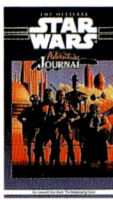 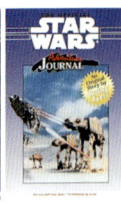
446-01 446-02 446-03 446-04 446-05 446-06 446-07 446-08 446-09 446-10 446-11

    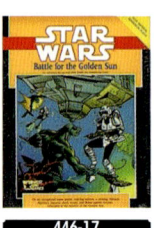  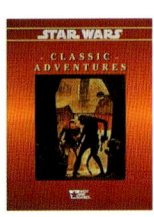  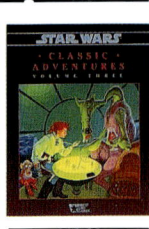
446-12 446-13 446-14 446-15 446-16 446-17 446-18 446-19 446-20 446-21

Role-Playing Game

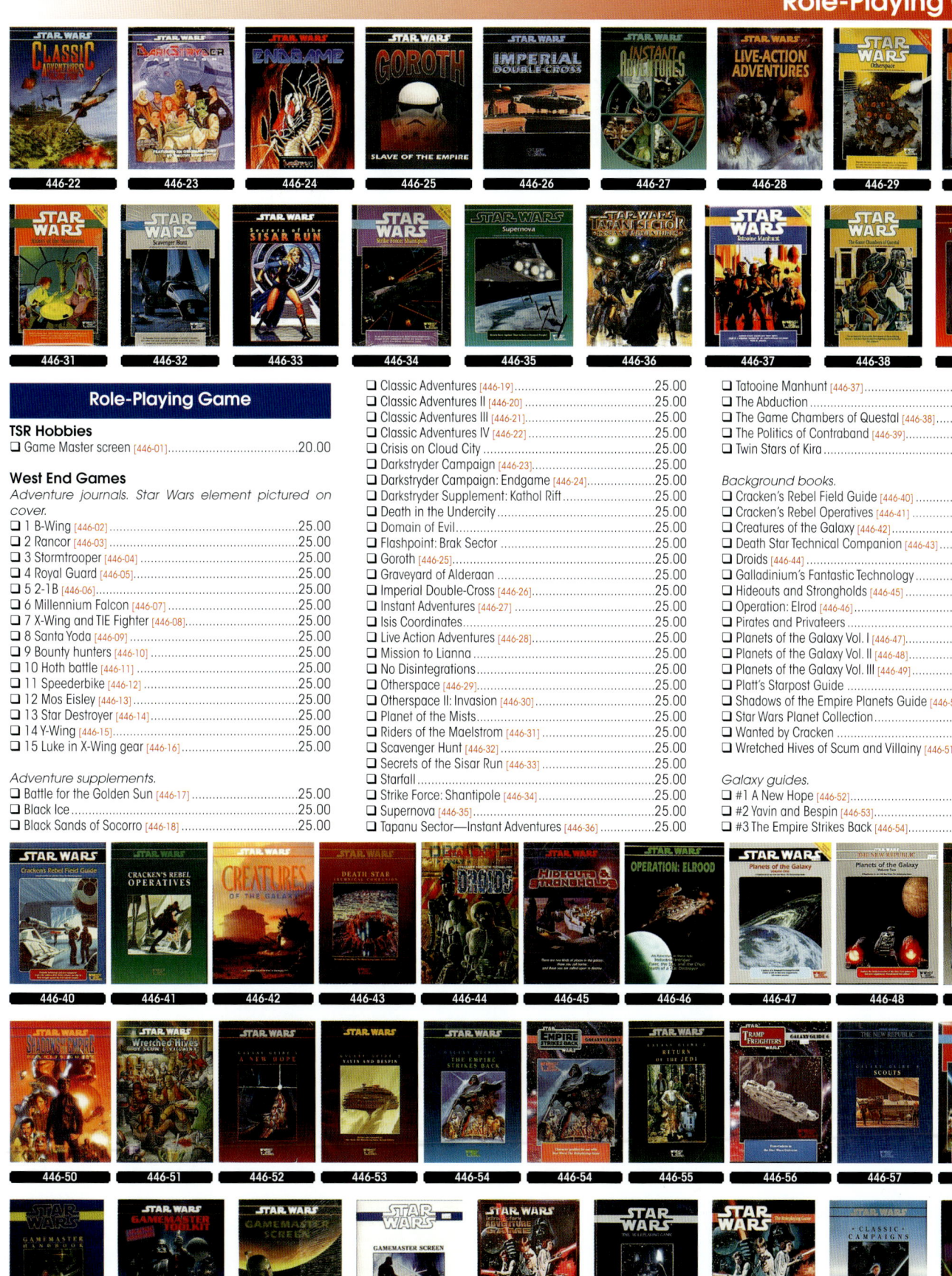

Role-Playing Game

TSR Hobbies
- ❏ Game Master screen [446-01].........................$20.00

West End Games
Adventure journals. Star Wars element pictured on cover.
- ❏ 1 B-Wing [446-02]...$25.00
- ❏ 2 Rancor [446-03]..$25.00
- ❏ 3 Stormtrooper [446-04]..................................$25.00
- ❏ 4 Royal Guard [446-05]...................................$25.00
- ❏ 5 2-1B [446-06]..$25.00
- ❏ 6 Millennium Falcon [446-07]..........................$25.00
- ❏ 7 X-Wing and TIE Fighter [446-08]..................$25.00
- ❏ 8 Santa Yoda [446-09].....................................$25.00
- ❏ 9 Bounty hunters [446-10]...............................$25.00
- ❏ 10 Hoth battle [446-11]....................................$25.00
- ❏ 11 Speederbike [446-12].................................$25.00
- ❏ 12 Mos Eisley [446-13]....................................$25.00
- ❏ 13 Star Destroyer [446-14]..............................$25.00
- ❏ 14 Y-Wing [446-15]..$25.00
- ❏ 15 Luke in X-Wing gear [446-16]....................$25.00

Adventure supplements.
- ❏ Battle for the Golden Sun [446-17]..................$25.00
- ❏ Black Ice...$25.00
- ❏ Black Sands of Socorro [446-18].....................$25.00
- ❏ Classic Adventures [446-19]............................$25.00
- ❏ Classic Adventures II [446-20].........................$25.00
- ❏ Classic Adventures III [446-21].......................$25.00
- ❏ Classic Adventures IV [446-22].......................$25.00
- ❏ Crisis on Cloud City..$25.00
- ❏ Darkstryder Campaign [446-23].......................$25.00
- ❏ Darkstryder Campaign: Endgame [446-24].....$25.00
- ❏ Darkstryder Supplement: Kathol Rift...............$25.00
- ❏ Death in the Undercity.....................................$25.00
- ❏ Domain of Evil..$25.00
- ❏ Flashpoint: Brak Sector...................................$25.00
- ❏ Goroth [446-25]..$25.00
- ❏ Graveyard of Alderaan.....................................$25.00
- ❏ Imperial Double-Cross [446-26].......................$25.00
- ❏ Instant Adventures [446-27].............................$25.00
- ❏ Isis Coordinates..$25.00
- ❏ Live Action Adventures [446-28]......................$25.00
- ❏ Mission to Lianna...$25.00
- ❏ No Disintegrations..$25.00
- ❏ Otherspace [446-29]...$25.00
- ❏ Otherspace II: Invasion [446-30].....................$25.00
- ❏ Planet of the Mists...$25.00
- ❏ Riders of the Maelstrom [446-31].....................$25.00
- ❏ Scavenger Hunt [446-32].................................$25.00
- ❏ Secrets of the Sisar Run [446-33]....................$25.00
- ❏ Starfall..$25.00
- ❏ Strike Force: Shantipole [446-34]....................$25.00
- ❏ Supernova [446-35]..$25.00
- ❏ Tapanu Sector—Instant Adventures [446-36]...$25.00
- ❏ Tatooine Manhunt [446-37]..............................$25.00
- ❏ The Abduction..$25.00
- ❏ The Game Chambers of Questal [446-38].......$25.00
- ❏ The Politics of Contraband [446-39]................$25.00
- ❏ Twin Stars of Kira...$25.00

Background books.
- ❏ Cracken's Rebel Field Guide [446-40].............$30.00
- ❏ Cracken's Rebel Operatives [446-41]..............$30.00
- ❏ Creatures of the Galaxy [446-42].....................$30.00
- ❏ Death Star Technical Companion [446-43]......$30.00
- ❏ Droids [446-44]...$30.00
- ❏ Galladinium's Fantastic Technology.................$30.00
- ❏ Hideouts and Strongholds [446-45]..................$30.00
- ❏ Operation: Elrod [446-46].................................$30.00
- ❏ Pirates and Privateers......................................$30.00
- ❏ Planets of the Galaxy Vol. I [446-47]................$30.00
- ❏ Planets of the Galaxy Vol. II [446-48]...............$30.00
- ❏ Planets of the Galaxy Vol. III [446-49]..............$30.00
- ❏ Platt's Starpost Guide.......................................$30.00
- ❏ Shadows of the Empire Planets Guide [446-50]...$30.00
- ❏ Star Wars Planet Collection..............................$30.00
- ❏ Wanted by Cracken..$30.00
- ❏ Wretched Hives of Scum and Villainy [446-51]...$30.00

Galaxy guides.
- ❏ #1 A New Hope [446-52]..................................$20.00
- ❏ #2 Yavin and Bespin [446-53]..........................$20.00
- ❏ #3 The Empire Strikes Back [446-54]..............$20.00

413

Role-Playing Game

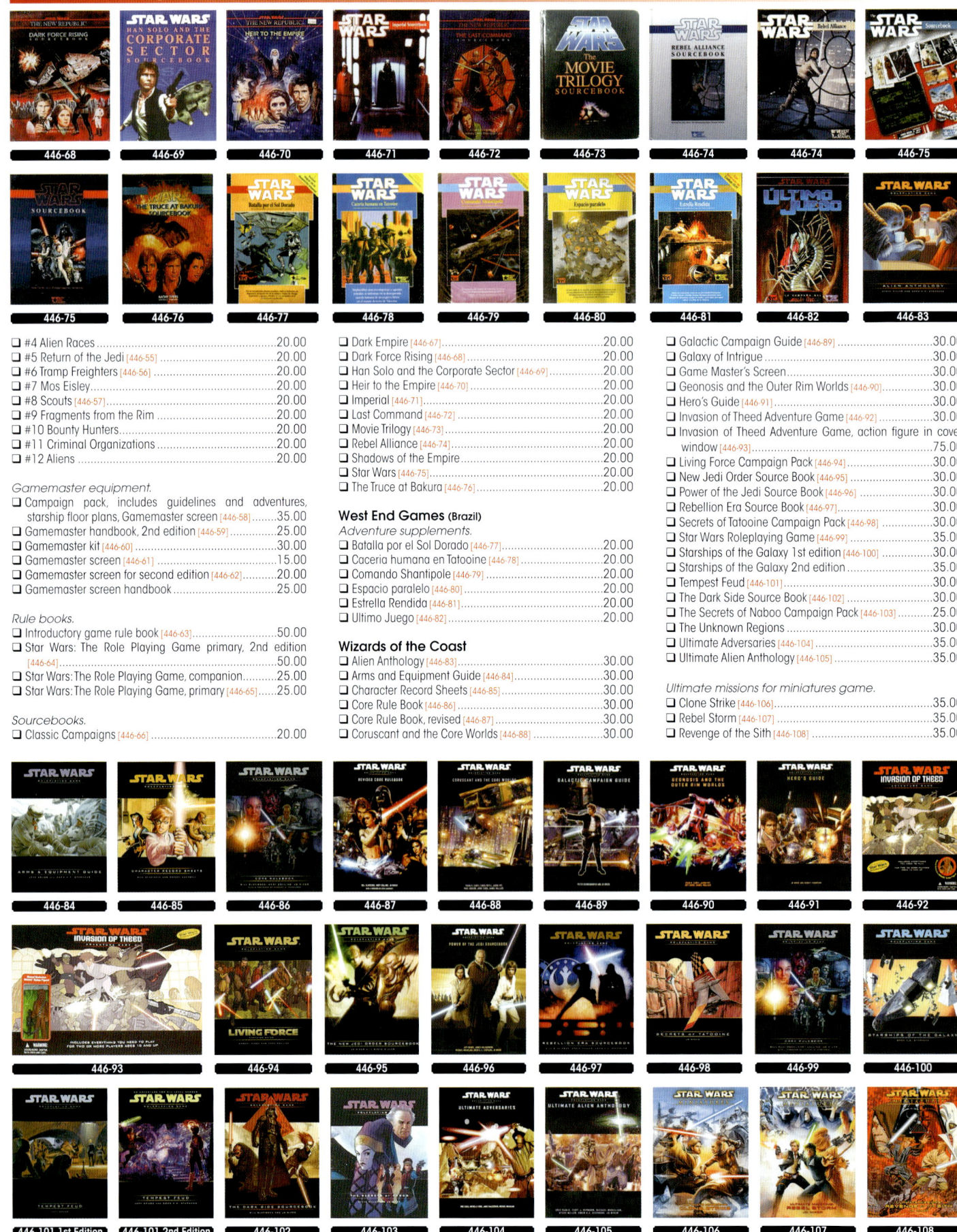

- ☐ #4 Alien Races 20.00
- ☐ #5 Return of the Jedi [446-55] 20.00
- ☐ #6 Tramp Freighters [446-56] 20.00
- ☐ #7 Mos Eisley 20.00
- ☐ #8 Scouts [446-57] 20.00
- ☐ #9 Fragments from the Rim 20.00
- ☐ #10 Bounty Hunters 20.00
- ☐ #11 Criminal Organizations 20.00
- ☐ #12 Aliens 20.00

Gamemaster equipment.
- ☐ Campaign pack, includes guidelines and adventures, starship floor plans, Gamemaster screen [446-58] 35.00
- ☐ Gamemaster handbook, 2nd edition [446-59] 25.00
- ☐ Gamemaster kit [446-60] 30.00
- ☐ Gamemaster screen [446-61] 15.00
- ☐ Gamemaster screen for second edition [446-62]..........20.00
- ☐ Gamemaster screen handbook 25.00

Rule books.
- ☐ Introductory game rule book [446-63] 50.00
- ☐ Star Wars: The Role Playing Game primary, 2nd edition [446-64] 50.00
- ☐ Star Wars: The Role Playing Game, companion 25.00
- ☐ Star Wars: The Role Playing Game, primary [446-65] 25.00

Sourcebooks.
- ☐ Classic Campaigns [446-66] 20.00
- ☐ Dark Empire [446-67] 20.00
- ☐ Dark Force Rising [446-68] 20.00
- ☐ Han Solo and the Corporate Sector [446-69] 20.00
- ☐ Heir to the Empire [446-70] 20.00
- ☐ Imperial [446-71] 20.00
- ☐ Last Command [446-72] 20.00
- ☐ Movie Trilogy [446-73] 20.00
- ☐ Rebel Alliance [446-74] 20.00
- ☐ Shadows of the Empire 20.00
- ☐ Star Wars [446-75] 20.00
- ☐ The Truce at Bakura [446-76] 20.00

West End Games (Brazil)
Adventure supplements.
- ☐ Batalla por el Sol Dorado [446-77] 20.00
- ☐ Caceria humana en Tatooine [446-78] 20.00
- ☐ Comando Shantipole [446-79] 20.00
- ☐ Espacio paralelo [446-80] 20.00
- ☐ Estrella Rendida [446-81] 20.00
- ☐ Ultimo Juego [446-82] 20.00

Wizards of the Coast
- ☐ Alien Anthology [446-83] 30.00
- ☐ Arms and Equipment Guide [446-84] 30.00
- ☐ Character Record Sheets [446-85] 30.00
- ☐ Core Rule Book [446-86] 30.00
- ☐ Core Rule Book, revised [446-87] 30.00
- ☐ Coruscant and the Core Worlds [446-88] 30.00
- ☐ Galactic Campaign Guide [446-89] 30.00
- ☐ Galaxy of Intrigue 30.00
- ☐ Game Master's Screen 30.00
- ☐ Geonosis and the Outer Rim Worlds [446-90] 30.00
- ☐ Hero's Guide [446-91] 30.00
- ☐ Invasion of Theed Adventure Game [446-92] 30.00
- ☐ Invasion of Theed Adventure Game, action figure in cover window [446-93] 75.00
- ☐ Living Force Campaign Pack [446-94] 30.00
- ☐ New Jedi Order Source Book [446-95] 30.00
- ☐ Power of the Jedi Source Book [446-96] 30.00
- ☐ Rebellion Era Source Book [446-97] 30.00
- ☐ Secrets of Tatooine Campaign Pack [446-98] 30.00
- ☐ Star Wars Roleplaying Game [446-99] 35.00
- ☐ Starships of the Galaxy 1st edition [446-100] 30.00
- ☐ Starships of the Galaxy 2nd edition 35.00
- ☐ Tempest Feud [446-101] 30.00
- ☐ The Dark Side Source Book [446-102] 30.00
- ☐ The Secrets of Naboo Campaign Pack [446-103] 25.00
- ☐ The Unknown Regions 30.00
- ☐ Ultimate Adversaries [446-104] 35.00
- ☐ Ultimate Alien Anthology [446-105] 35.00

Ultimate missions for miniatures game.
- ☐ Clone Strike [446-106] 35.00
- ☐ Rebel Storm [446-107] 35.00
- ☐ Revenge of the Sith [446-108] 35.00

414

Role-Playing Miniatures

West End Games

Blister packed figures and vehicles.

- Aliens of the Galaxy [447-01] 20.00
- Aliens of the Galaxy #2 [447-02] 20.00
- Aliens of the Galaxy #3 ....20.00
- AT-AT 35.00
- AT-PT 35.00
- Bantha and Rider 20.00
- Bounty Hunters #1 [447-03] 20.00
- Bounty Hunters #2 ....20.00
- Bounty Hunters #3 [447-04] 20.00
- Darkstryder #1 ....35.00
- Darkstryder #2 [447-05] 35.00
- Darkstryder #3 ....35.00
- Darth Vader, Leia, and Luke 20.00
- Denizens of Cloud City [447-06] 20.00
- Denizens of Tatooine [447-07] 20.00
- Droids [447-08] 20.00
- Emperor 20.00
- Encounter on Hoth [447-09] 35.00
- Ewoks 20.00
- Gamorrean Guards [447-10] 35.00
- Heir to the Empire Villains 20.00
- Heroes #1: Luke, C-3PO, R2-D2 [447-11] 20.00
- Heroes #2: Chewbacca, Han, Leia [447-12] 20.00
- Hoth Rebels [447-13] 20.00
- Imperial Army troopers #1 ....20.00
- Imperial Army troopers #2 ....20.00
- Imperial Crew with Heavy Blaster 20.00
- Imperial Navy troopers #1 ....20.00
- Imperial Navy troopers #2 ....20.00
- Imperial Officers [447-14] 20.00
- Imperial Speederbikes [447-15] 35.00
- Imperial Troop Pack 35.00
- Jabba the Hutt 35.00
- Jabba's Servants 35.00
- Jedi Knights 20.00
- Landspeeder [447-16] 35.00
- Mon Calamari [447-17] 20.00
- Mos Eisley Cantina [447-18] 35.00
- Mos Eisley Cantina Aliens #1 ....20.00
- Mos Eisley Cantina Aliens #2 ....20.00
- Mos Eisley Space Station 35.00
- Nogri [447-19] 20.00
- Pilots and Gunners 20.00
- Pirates [447-20] 35.00
- Rebel Commanders #1 ....20.00
- Rebel Commanders #2 ....20.00
- Rebel Commandos #1 ....20.00
- Rebel Commandos #2 ....20.00
- Rebel Operatives [447-21] 20.00
- Rebel Speeder Bikes 35.00
- Rebel Troop Pack 35.00
- Rebel troopers #1 [447-22] 20.00
- Rebel troopers #2 [447-23] 20.00
- Rebel troopers #3 ....20.00
- Rebel troopers #4 ....20.00
- Sandtroopers 20.00
- Scout troopers 20.00
- Skywalkers [447-24] 20.00
- Snowspeeder 35.00
- Snowtroopers 20.00
- Storm Skimmers [447-25] 35.00
- Stormtroopers #1 ....20.00
- Stormtroopers #2 ....20.00
- Stormtroopers #3 ....20.00
- Stormtroopers #4 ....20.00
- Tauntaun and Rider 20.00
- Users of the Force 20.00
- Wookiees [447-26] 20.00
- Zero G troopers [447-27] 20.00

Boxed figures.

- A New Hope [447-28] 50.00
- Bounty Hunters [447-29] 50.00
- Empire Strikes Back [447-30] 50.00
- Heroes of the Rebellion [447-31] 50.00
- Imperial Forces [447-32] 50.00
- Imperial troopers [447-33] 50.00
- Jabba's Palace [447-34] 50.00
- Mos Eisley Cantina [447-35] 50.00
- Rancor Pit [447-36] 50.00
- Rebel Characters [447-37] 50.00
- Rebel troopers [447-38] 50.00
- Return of the Jedi [447-39] 50.00
- Stormtroopers [447-40] 50.00
- Zero G Assault troopers [447-41] 50.00

Guide books.

- Star Wars Miniatures Battles [447-42] 30.00
- Star Wars Miniatures Battles Companion [447-43] .30.00

Starter sets.

- Miniature Battles 65.00
- Mos Eisley 65.00
- Vehicles [447-44] 65.00

Wizards of the Coast

- Cerean Jedi [447-45] 15.00
- Cerean Noble [447-46] 15.00
- Female Human Fringer [447-47] 15.00
- Female Human Handmaiden 15.00
- Female Human Scoundrel 15.00
- Female Human Scout [447-48] 15.00
- Female Human Soldier 15.00
- Female Twi'lek Jedi 15.00
- Gungan Scout 15.00
- Male Human Fringer 15.00
- Male Human Jedi 15.00
- Male Human Scout 15.00
- Male Human Soundrel [447-49] 15.00
- Male Twi'lek Scoundrel [447-50] 15.00
- Roadian Soldier 15.00
- Rodian Scout [447-51] 15.00
- Wookiee Scout 15.00

Convention exclusives.

- Snowtrooper with E-Web blaster, square base and embossed Star Wars logo, exclusive to Star Wars Celebration IV ..50.00

Map packs.

- The Attack on Teth [447-52] 20.00
- The Crystal Caves of Ilum, contains Coruscant Streets and Crystal Caves of Ilum maps [447-53] 20.00

Miniatures Game.

- AT-AT Imperial Walker Colossal Pack [447-54] ...85.00
- Attack on Endor. Includes an AT-ST, 3 stormtroopers, 4 maps, abbreviated scenario book [447-55] 80.00
- Battle of Hoth scenario pack, exclusive to Target ..60.00
- Galaxy Tiles, customizable terrain [447-56] 25.00
- Rancor Attack! 35.00

Miniatures Game. Alliance and Empire.

- Admiral Piett #24 (R) 4.00
- Advance Agent, Officer #58 (UC) 2.50
- Advance Scout #59 (C) 2.00
- Aurra Sing, Jedi Hunter #2 (VR) 20.00
- Biggs Darklighter #3 (VR) 6.00
- Boba Fett, Enforcer #38 (VR) 25.00
- C-3PO and R2-D2 #5 (R) 5.00
- Chadra-Fan Pickpocket #39 (UC) 2.50
- Chewbacca, Enraged Wookiee #4 (R) 5.00
- Darth Vader, Imperial Commander #25 (VR) 8.00
- Death Star Gunner #26 (UC) 2.50
- Death Star Trooper #27 (C) 2.00
- Duro Explorer #40 (C) 2.00
- Elite Hoth Trooper #6 (C) 2.00
- Ephant Mon #41 (VR) 8.00
- Ewok Hang Glider #42 (R) 5.00
- Ewok Warrior #43 (C) 2.00
- Gamorrean Guard #44 (C) 2.00
- Han Solo in stormtrooper Armor #8 (R) 5.00
- Han Solo on Tauntaun #9 (VR) 8.00
- Han Solo, Rogue #7 (R) 5.00
- Heavy stormtrooper #28 (UC) 2.50
- Human Force Adept #45 (C) 2.00
- Imperial Governor Tarkin #29 (R) 5.00
- Imperial Officer #30 (UC) 2.50

 447-01
 447-02
 447-03
 447-04
 447-05
 447-06
 447-07
 447-08
 447-09
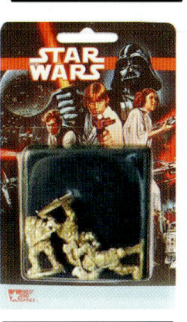 447-10
 447-11
 447-12
 447-13
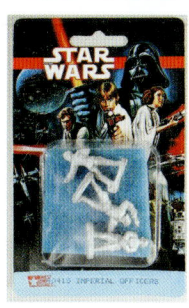 447-14

Role-Playing Miniatures

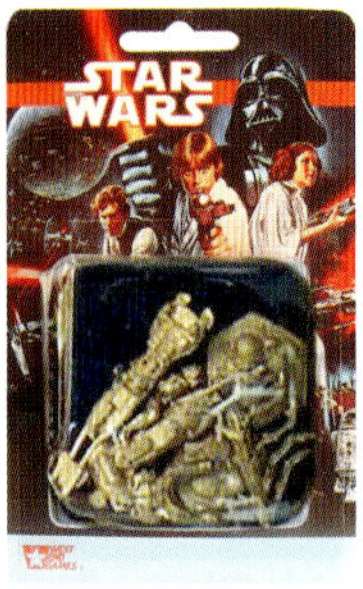

447-15

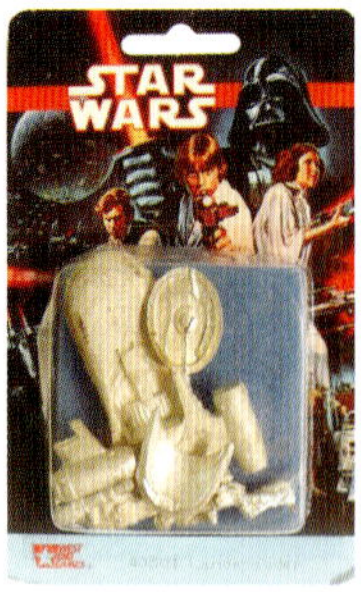

447-16

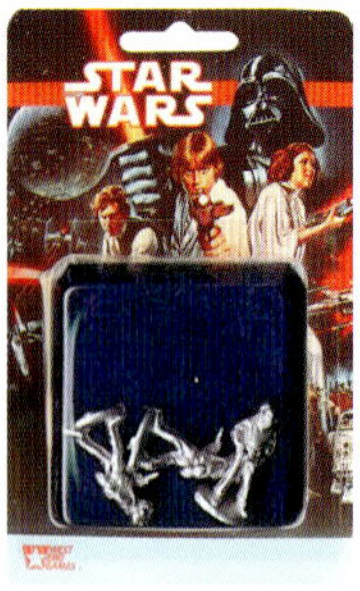

447-17

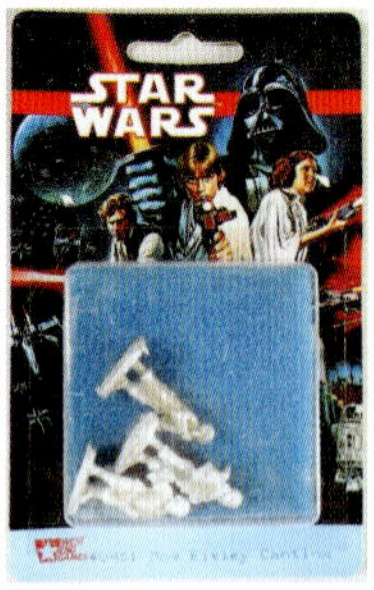

447-18

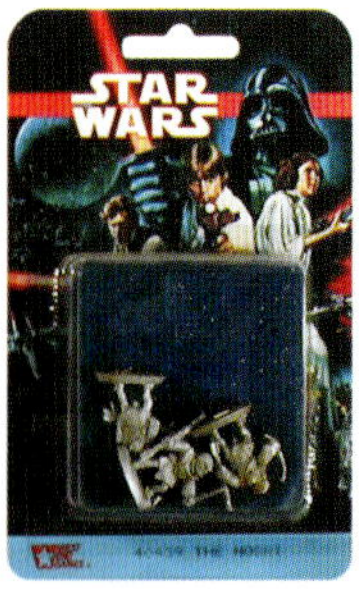

447-19

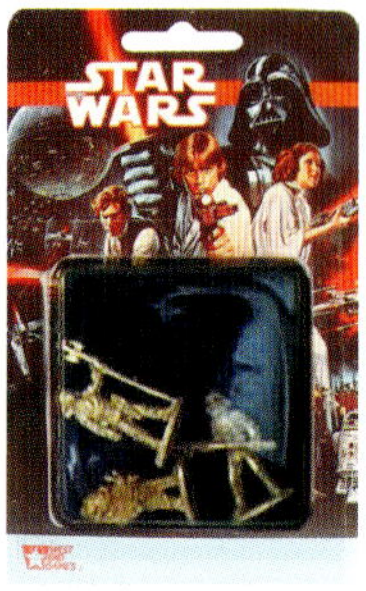

447-20

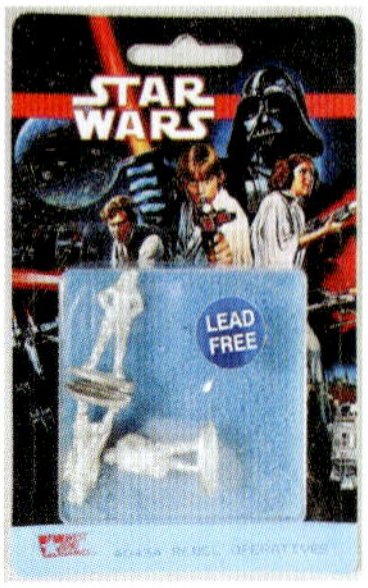

447-21

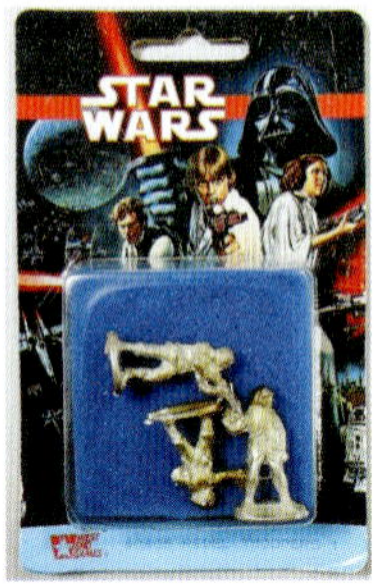

447-22

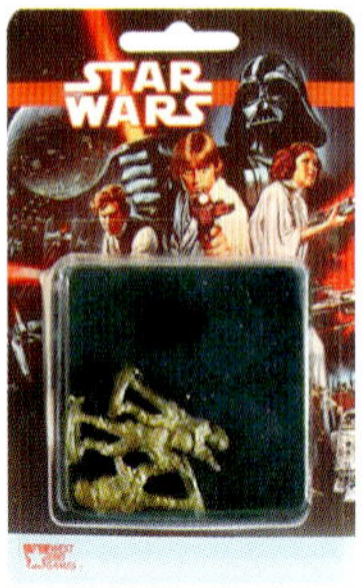

447-23

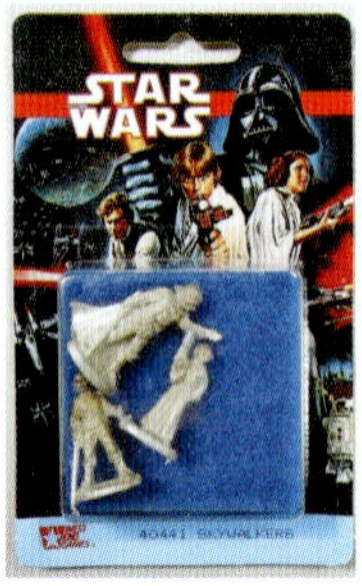

447-24

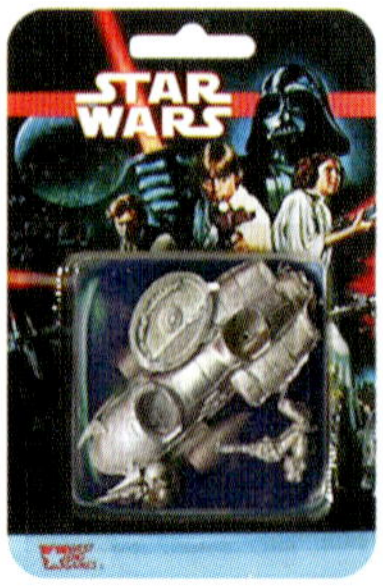

447-25

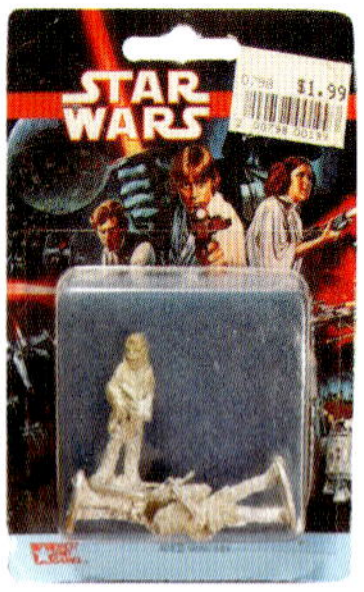

447-26

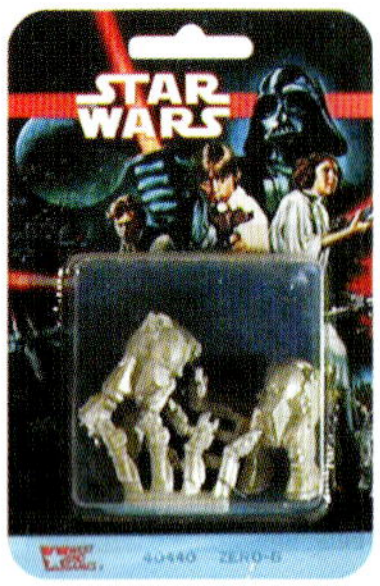

447-27

- ❑ Ithorian Commander #10 (UC) 2.50
- ❑ Jabba, Crime Lord #46 (VR) 25.00
- ❑ Jawa on Ronto #47 (VR) 12.00
- ❑ Jawa Trader #48 (UC) 2.50
- ❑ Lando Calrissian, Dashing Scoundrel #49 (R) 5.00
- ❑ Luke Skywalker, Champion of the Force #11 (VR) 25.00
- ❑ Luke Skywalker, Hero of Yavin #12 (R) 5.00
- ❑ Luke's Landspeeder #13 (VR) 18.00
- ❑ Mara Jade, Jedi #37 (R) 10.00
- ❑ Mon Calamari Tech Specialist #14 (C) 2.00
- ❑ Nikto Soldier #50 (C) 2.00
- ❑ Obi-Wan Kenobi, Force Spirit #15 (VR) 18.00
- ❑ Princess Leia #16 (R) 5.00
- ❑ Quinlan Vos, Infiltrator #1 (VR) 20.00
- ❑ Rampaging Wampa #51 (VR) 18.00
- ❑ Rebel Commando #17 (C) 2.00
- ❑ Rebel Commando Strike Leader #18 (UC) 2.50
- ❑ Rebel Leader #19 (UC) 2.50
- ❑ Rebel Pilot #20 (C) 2.00
- ❑ Rebel Trooper #21 (UC) 2.50
- ❑ Rodian Scoundrel #52 (UC) 2.50
- ❑ Scout Trooper #31 (UC) 2.50
- ❑ Snivvian Fringer #53 (C) 2.00
- ❑ Snowtrooper #32 (C) 2.00
- ❑ Storm Commando #33 (R) 18.00
- ❑ Stormtrooper #34 (C) 2.00
- ❑ Stormtrooper Officer #35 (UC) 2.50
- ❑ Stormtrooper on Repulser Sled #36 (VR) 20.00
- ❑ Talz Spy #54 (UC) 2.50
- ❑ Transdoshan Mercenary #55 (UC) 2.50
- ❑ Tusken Raider #56 (C) 2.00
- ❑ Twi'lek Rebel Agent #22 (UC) 2.50
- ❑ Wicket #57 (R) 6.00
- ❑ Wookiee Freedom Fighter #23 (C) 2.00
- ❑ Yomin Carr #60 (R) 5.00

Miniatures Game. Bounty Hunters.

- ❑ 4-LOM, Bounty Hunter #32 (R) 7.00
- ❑ Aqualish Assassin #15 (C) 2.00
- ❑ Ayy Vida #16 (R) 5.00
- ❑ Basilisk War Droid #54 (UC) 6.00
- ❑ Bib Fortuna #17 (R) 5.00
- ❑ Bith Black Sun Vigo #18 (UC) 2.00
- ❑ Boba Fett, Bounty Hunter #19 (VR) 45.00
- ❑ Boshek #20 (R) 5.00
- ❑ Bossk, Bounty Hunter #21 (R) 7.00
- ❑ Boushh #22 (R) 7.00
- ❑ Calo Nord #23 (R) 7.00
- ❑ Chewbacca with C-3PO #6 (VR) 15.00
- ❑ Commerce Guild Homing Spider Droid #2 (UC) 5.00
- ❑ Corellian Pirate #24 (UC) 2.50
- ❑ Corporate Alliance Tank Droid #3 (UC) 4.00
- ❑ Dannik Jerriko #25 (VR) 11.00
- ❑ Dark Hellion Marauder on Swoop Bike #26 (UC) 2.50
- ❑ Dark Hellion Swoop Gang Member #27 (C) 2.00
- ❑ Defel Spy #28 (C) 2.00
- ❑ Dengar Bounty Hunter #29 (R) 5.00
- ❑ Djas Puhr #30 (R) 4.00
- ❑ Droid Starfighter in Walking Mode #4 (R) 8.00
- ❑ E522 Assassin Droid #31 (UC) 2.50
- ❑ Gamorrean Thug #33 (C) 2.00
- ❑ Garindan #34 (R) 10.00
- ❑ Han Solo Scoundrel #7 (VR) 18.00
- ❑ Huge Crab Droid #5 (UC) 3.00
- ❑ Human Blaster-for-Hire #35 (C) 2.00
- ❑ IG-88, Bounty Hunter #36 (VR) 22.50
- ❑ ISP Speeder #1 (R) 6.00
- ❑ Jango Fett, Bounty Hunter #37 (VR) 34.00
- ❑ Klatooinian Hunter #38 (C) 2.00
- ❑ Komari Vosa #39 (R) 10.00
- ❑ Lord Vader #13 (UC) 25.00
- ❑ Luke Skywalker of Dagobah #8 (R) 13.00
- ❑ Mandalore the Indomitable #55 (VR) 32.00
- ❑ Mandalorian Blademaster #56 (UC) 2.00
- ❑ Mandalorian Commander #57 (UC) 2.00
- ❑ Mandalorian Soldier #58 (C) 2.50
- ❑ Mandalorian Supercommando #59 (UC) 2.00
- ❑ Mandalorian Warrior #60 (C) 2.50
- ❑ Mistryl Shadow Guard #40 (UC) 2.00
- ❑ Mustafarian Flea Rider #41 (R) 5.00
- ❑ Mustafarian Soldier #42 (C) 2.50
- ❑ Nikto Gunner on Desert Skiff #43 (VR) 30.00
- ❑ Nym #44 (VR) 15.00
- ❑ Princess Leia Hoth Commander #9 (R) 12.50
- ❑ Quarren Bounty Hunter #45 (C) 2.00
- ❑ Rebel Captain #10 (UC) 2.50
- ❑ Rebel Heavy Trooper #11 (UC) 2.00
- ❑ Rebel Snowspeeder #12 (UC) 8.00
- ❑ Rodian Hunt Master #46 (UC) 2.50
- ❑ Talon Karrde #14 (VR) 13.00
- ❑ Tamtel Skreej (Lando Calrissian) #47 (VR) 18.00
- ❑ Tusken Raider Sniper #48 (C) 2.00
- ❑ Utapaun on Dactillion #49 (R) 4.00
- ❑ Weequay Leader #50 (UC) 2.50
- ❑ Weequay Thug #51 (C) 2.00
- ❑ Young Krayt Dragon #52 (VR) 30.00
- ❑ Zuckuss #53 (R) 8.00

Miniatures Game. Champions of the Force miniatures.

- ❑ Arcona Smuggler #55 (C) 2.00
- ❑ Barriss Offee #20 (R) 10.00
- ❑ Bastila Shan #1 (VR) 18.00
- ❑ Clone Commander Bacara #21 (R) 6.00
- ❑ Clone Commander Cody #22 (R) 8.00
- ❑ Clone Commander Gree #23 (R) 8.00
- ❑ Corran Horn #52 (R) 8.00
- ❑ Coruscant Guard #46 (C) 2.00
- ❑ Crab Droid #39 (UC) 4.00
- ❑ Dark Jedi #7 (UC) 2.50
- ❑ Dark Jedi Master #8 (UC) 2.50
- ❑ Dark Side Enforcer #9 (UC) 2.50
- ❑ Dark Trooper Phase I #47 (C) 2.00
- ❑ Dark Trooper Phase II #48 (UC) 2.50
- ❑ Darth Bane #10 (VR) 23.00
- ❑ Darth Malak #11 (VR) 20.00
- ❑ Darth Maul, Champion of the Sith #40 (R) 16.00
- ❑ Darth Nihilus #12 (VR) 24.00
- ❑ Darth Sidious, Dark Lord of the Sith #41 (R) 12.00
- ❑ Darth Vader, Champion of the Sith #49 (VR) 20.00
- ❑ Depa Billaba #24 (R) 9.00
- ❑ Even Piell #25 (R) 8.00
- ❑ Exar Kun #13 (VR) 24.00
- ❑ General Windu #26 (R) 12.00
- ❑ Gundark #56 (UC) 2.00
- ❑ HK-47 #57 (VR) 20.00
- ❑ Hoth Trooper with ATGAR Cannon #43 (R) 14.00
- ❑ Jacen Solo #53 (VR) 16.00
- ❑ Jaina Solo #54 (VR) 22.50
- ❑ Jedi Consular #2 (UC) 2.50
- ❑ Jedi Guardian #3 (UC) 2.50
- ❑ Jedi Padawan #27 (UC) 2.00
- ❑ Jedi Sentinel #4 (UC) 2.50
- ❑ Jedi Weapon Master #28 (UC) 2.00
- ❑ Kashyyyk Trooper #29 (C) 2.00
- ❑ Luke Skywalker, Young Jedi #44 (VR) 18.00
- ❑ Mas Amedda #30 (R) 8.00
- ❑ Massassi Sith Mutant #14 (UC) 2.00
- ❑ Octuptarra Droid #42 (R) 9.00
- ❑ Old Republic Commander #5 (UC) 2.50
- ❑ Old Republic Soldier #6 (C) 2.00
- ❑ Queen Amidala #31 (R) 10.00
- ❑ Qui-Gon Jinn, Jedi Master #32 (R) 9.00
- ❑ R5 Astromech Droid #58 (C) 2.00
- ❑ Republic Commando—Boss #33 (UC) 2.00
- ❑ Republic Commando—Fixer #34 (C) 2.00
- ❑ Republic Commando—Scorch #35 (C) 2.00
- ❑ Republic Commando—Sev #36 (C) 2.00
- ❑ Saleucami Trooper #37 (C) 2.00
- ❑ Sandtrooper 50 (C) 2.00
- ❑ Sith Assault Droid #15 (UC) 2.00
- ❑ Sith Trooper #16 (C) 2.00
- ❑ Sith Trooper #17 (C) 2.00
- ❑ Sith Trooper Commander #18 (UC) 2.00
- ❑ Snowtrooper with E-Web Blaster #51 (R) 12.00
- ❑ Ugnaught Demolitionist #59 (C) 2.00
- ❑ Ulic Qel-Droma #19 (VR) 16.00
- ❑ Utapau Trooper #38 (C) 2.00
- ❑ Varactyl Wrangler #60 (C) 2.00
- ❑ Yoda of Dagobah #45 (VR) 18.00

Miniatures Game. Clone Strike Game.

- ❑ Booster Pack: Clone trooper graphic [447-57] 12.00

Role-Playing Miniatures

- ❏ Booster Pack: Mace Windu graphic [447-58] 12.00
- ❏ Booster Pack: Super Battle Droid graphic [447-59] 12.00
- ❏ Starter Set [447-60] 20.00

Miniatures Game. Clone Strike miniatures.
- ❏ Aayla Secura (VR) 20.00
- ❏ Aerial Clone Trooper Captain (R) 17.00
- ❏ Agen Kolar (R) 6.00
- ❏ Anakin Skywalker (VR) 20.00
- ❏ Aqualish Spy (C) 2.00
- ❏ ARC Trooper (UC) 5.00
- ❏ Asajj Ventress (R) 16.00
- ❏ Aurra Sing (VR) 54.00
- ❏ Battle Droid (C) 2.00
- ❏ Battle Droid Officer (UC) 2.00
- ❏ Battle Droid on STAP (R) 10.00
- ❏ Captain Typho (R) 10.00
- ❏ Clone Trooper (C) 2.00
- ❏ Clone Trooper Commander (UC) 2.00
- ❏ Clone Trooper Grenadier (C) 2.00
- ❏ Clone Trooper Sergeant (C) 2.00
- ❏ Count Dooku (VR) 26.00
- ❏ Dark Side Acolyte (UC) 7.00
- ❏ Darth Maul (VR) 44.00
- ❏ Darth Sidious (VR) 26.00
- ❏ Destroyer Droid (R) 24.00
- ❏ Devaronian Bounty Hunter (C) 2.00
- ❏ Durge (R) 14.00
- ❏ Dwarf Spider Droid (R) 12.00
- ❏ General Grievous (VR) 18.00
- ❏ General Kenobi (R) 8.00
- ❏ Geonosian Drone (C) 2.00
- ❏ Geonosian Overseer (UC) 2.50
- ❏ Geonosian Picador on Orray (R) 16.00
- ❏ Geonosian Soldier (UC) 2.50
- ❏ Gran Raider (C) 2.00
- ❏ Gungan Cavalry on Kaadu (R) 7.00
- ❏ Gungan Infantry (C) 2.00
- ❏ Ishi Tib Scout (UC) 2.50
- ❏ Jango Fett (R) 14.00
- ❏ Jedi Guardian (UC) 2.50
- ❏ Ki-Adi-Mundi (R) 15.00
- ❏ Kit Fisto (R) 14.00
- ❏ Klatooinian Enforcer (C) 2.00
- ❏ Luminara Unduli (R) 12.00
- ❏ Mace Windu (VR) 27.00
- ❏ Naboo Soldier (C) 2.50
- ❏ Nikto Soldier (C) 2.00
- ❏ Padmé Amidala (VR) 22.00
- ❏ Plo Koon (R) 12.00
- ❏ Quarren Raider (C) 2.50
- ❏ Qui-Gon Jinn (VR) 24.00
- ❏ Quinlan Vos (VR) 26.00
- ❏ Rodian Mercenary (UC) 2.50
- ❏ Saesee Tiin (R) 15.00
- ❏ Security Battle Droid (C) 2.00
- ❏ Super Battle Droid (UC) 2.50
- ❏ Weequay Mercenary (C) 2.00
- ❏ Wookiee Commando (UC) 2.50
- ❏ Yoda (VR) 27.00
- ❏ Zam Wesell (R) 15.00

Miniatures Game. Clone Wars.
- ❏ Ahsoka Tano / Republic (VR) 20.00
- ❏ Anakin Skywalker on STAP / Republic (VR) 12.00
- ❏ Anakin Skywalker, Champion of Nelvaan / Republic (R) 3.00
- ❏ Anakin Skywalker, Jedi / Republic (R) 5.00
- ❏ Aqualish Warrior / Fringe (C) 2.00
- ❏ ARC Trooper Sniper / Republic (UC) 2.00
- ❏ Asajj Ventress, Separatist Assassin / Separatists (R) 5.00
- ❏ Barriss Offee, Jedi Knight / Republic (R) 4.00
- ❏ Battle Droid / Separatists (C) 2.00
- ❏ Battle Droid / Separatists (C) 2.00
- ❏ Battle Droid Sniper / Separatists (UC) 2.00
- ❏ Booster Pack: Anakin and Ahsoka graphic 12.00
- ❏ Booster Pack: Clone trooper graphic 12.00
- ❏ Booster Pack: Padmé graphic 12.00
- ❏ Captain Rex / Republic (VR) 27.00
- ❏ Chameleon Droid / Separatists (R) 7.00
- ❏ Clone Trooper on Gelagrub / Republic (R) 4.00
- ❏ Commander Gree / Republic (R) 3.00
- ❏ Count Dooku of Serenno / Separatists (R) 5.00
- ❏ Darth Sidious Hologram / Sith (VR) 18.00
- ❏ Durge, Jedi Hunter / Separatists (VR) 20.00
- ❏ Elite Clone Trooper Commander / Republic (UC) 2.50
- ❏ Elite Clone Trooper Grenadier / Republic (C) 2.50
- ❏ Galactic Marine / Republic (UC) 4.00
- ❏ General Aayla Secura / Republic (R) 5.00
- ❏ General Grievous, Droid Army Commander / Separatists (VR) 30.00
- ❏ General Obi-Wan Kenobi / Republic (R) 5.00
- ❏ Gha Nachkt / Fringe (R) 2.00
- ❏ Heavy Clone Trooper / Republic (C) 2.00
- ❏ Heavy Super Battle Droid / Separatists (C) 2.00
- ❏ Human Soldier of Fortune / Fringe (C) 2.00
- ❏ IG-100 MagnaGuard / Separatists (UC) 2.50
- ❏ IG-86 Assassin Droid / Fringe (UC) 2.00
- ❏ Luminara Unduli, Jedi Master / Republic (R) 5.00
- ❏ Mon Calamari Knight / Republic (UC) 2.00
- ❏ Neimoidian Warrior / Separatists (C) 2.00
- ❏ Nelvaanian Warrior / Fringe (UC) 2.00
- ❏ Odd Ball / Republic (R) 2.00
- ❏ Padmé Amidala, Senator / Republic (VR) 12.50
- ❏ Quarren Isolationist / Separatists (UC) 2.00
- ❏ Rocket Battle Droid / Separatists (UC) 2.00
- ❏ Star Corps Trooper / Republic (UC) 5.00
- ❏ Starter set 20.00
- ❏ Super Battle Droid / Separatists (C) 2.00
- ❏ Techno Union Warrior / Separatists (C) 2.00
- ❏ Trandoshan Scavenger / Fringe (UC) 2.50
- ❏ Utapaun Warrior / Fringe (C) 2.00
- ❏ Wookiee Scoundrel / Republic (C) 2.00
- ❏ Yoda on Kybuck / Republic (VR) 15.00

447-28	447-29	447-30	447-31	447-32	447-33	447-34	447-35	447-36

447-137	447-38	447-39	447-40	447-41	447-42	447-43	447-44

447-45	447-46	447-47	447-48	447-49	447-50	447-51

Role-Playing Miniatures

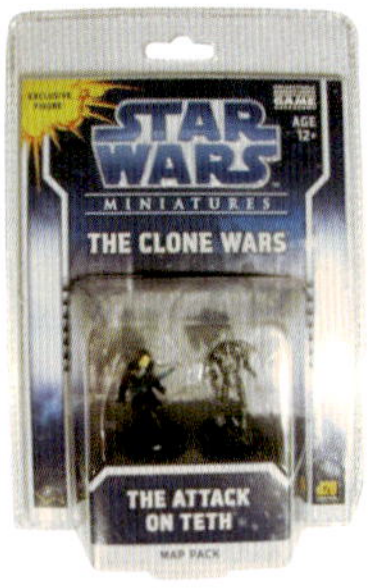

447-52

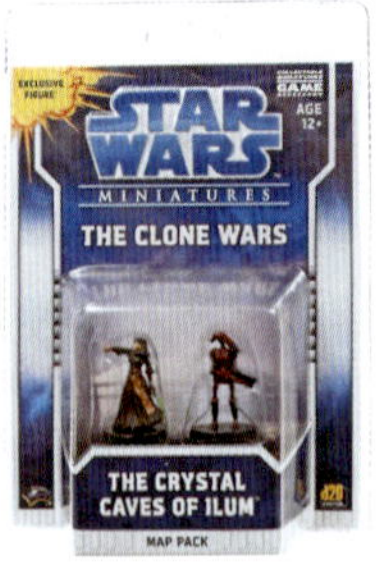

447-53

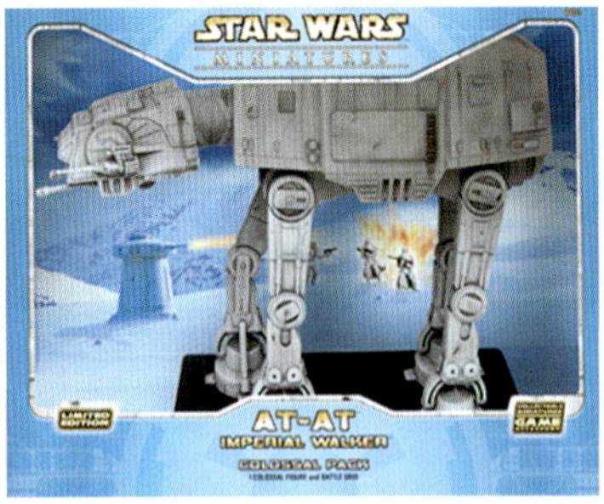

447-54

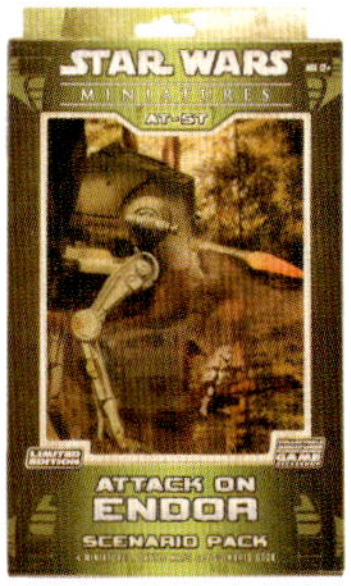

447-55

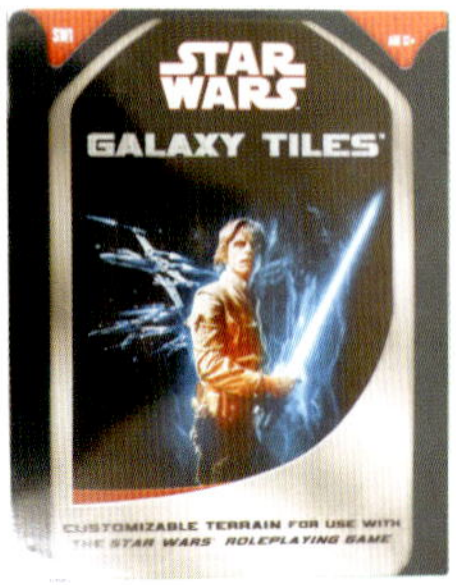

447-56

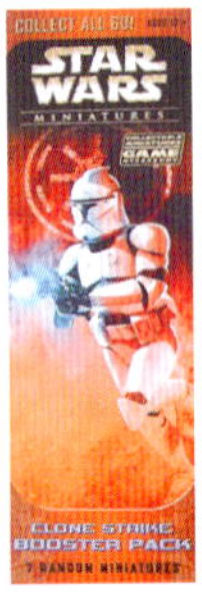

447-57

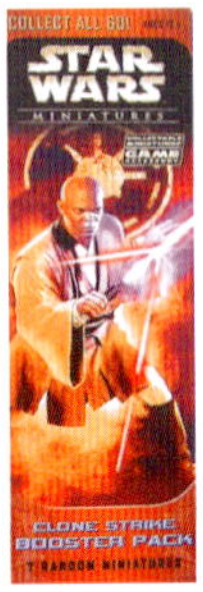

447-58

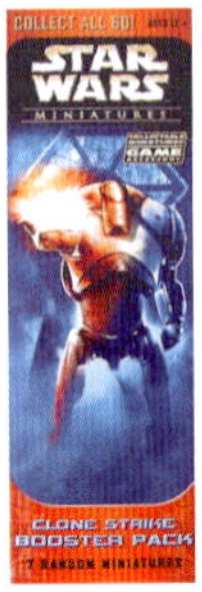

447-59

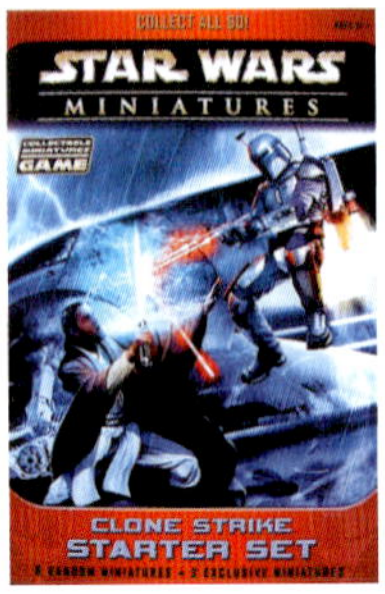

447-60

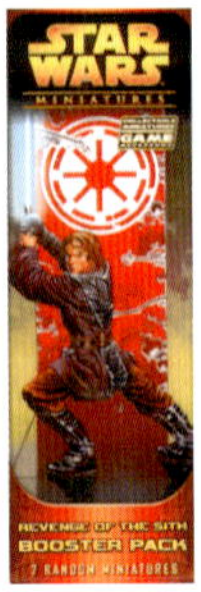

447-61

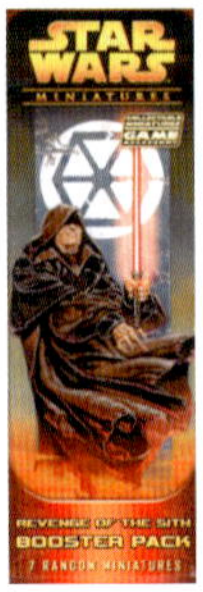

447-62

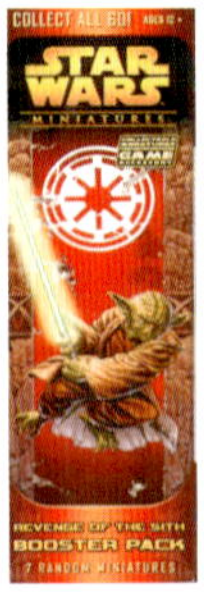

447-63

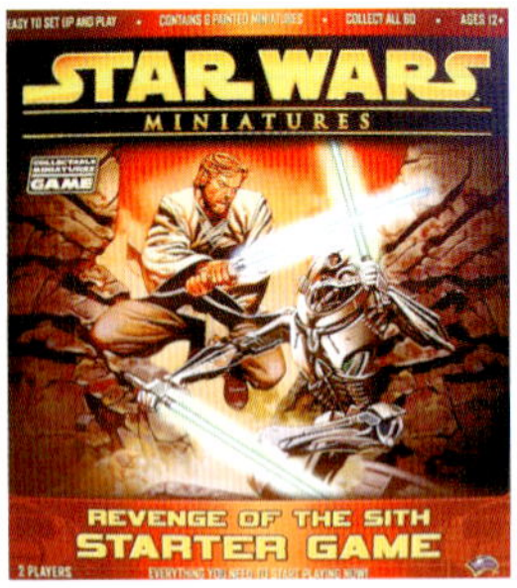

447-64

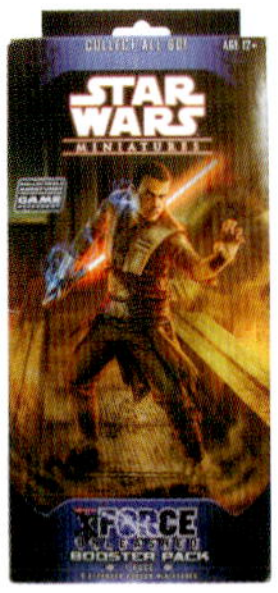

447-65

Miniatures Game. Force Unleashed.

❑ 2-1B / Rebels (R) 5.00
❑ Admiral Ozzel / Imperial (R) 4.00
❑ Amanin Scout / Fringe (UC) 2.00
❑ AT-AT Driver / Imperial (UC) 2.00
❑ Boba Fett, Mercenary / Fringe (VR) 30.00
❑ Caamasi Noble / Fringe (C) 2.00
❑ Chewbacca of Hoth / Rebels (VR) 5.00
❑ Cloud Car Pilot / Fringe (C) 2.00
❑ Dark Trooper / Imperial (UC) 3.00
❑ Darth Revan / Sith (VR) 50.00
❑ Darth Vader, Unleashed / Imperial (VR) 15.00
❑ Elite Hoth Trooper / Rebels (C) 2.00
❑ Emperor's Shadow Guard / Imperial (UC) 3.00
❑ Evo Trooper / Imperial (UC) 2.00
❑ Felucian stormtrooper Officer / Imperial (UC) 2.00
❑ Felucian Warrior on Rancor / Fringe (VR) 35.00
❑ Garm Bel Iblis (R) 6.00
❑ Golan Arms DF.9 Anti-Infantry Battery / Rebels (UC) 5.00
❑ Gotal Imperial Assassin / Imperial (C) 2.00
❑ Han Solo in Carbonite / Rebels (VR) 8.00
❑ Han Solo of Hoth / Rebels (VR) 8.00
❑ Hoth Trooper Officer / Rebels (UC) 2.00
❑ Hoth Trooper with Repeating Blaster Cannon / Rebels (UC) 3.00
❑ Imperial Navy Trooper / Imperial (C) 2.00
❑ Junk Golem / Fringe (UC) 2.00
❑ Juno Eclipse / Rebels (R) 6.00
❑ K-3PO / Rebels (R) 7.00
❑ Kazdan Paratus / Republic (R) 9.00
❑ Knobby White Spider / Fringe (UC) 2.00
❑ Luke Skywalker and Yoda / Rebels (VR) 20.00
❑ Luke Skywalker, Hoth Pilot Unleashed / Rebels (R) 12.50
❑ Luke's Snowspeeder / Rebels (VR) 10.00
❑ Maris Brood / Fringe (VR) 20.00
❑ Master Kota / Rebels (R) 12.00
❑ Mon Calamari Medic / Rebels (C) 2.00
❑ Muun Tactics Broker / Fringe (C) 2.00
❑ Mynock / Fringe (UC) 2.50
❑ Obi-Wan Kenobi, Unleashed / Rebels (R) 8.00
❑ Princess Leia of Cloud City / Rebels (R) 3.00
❑ PROXY / Fringe (R) 6.00
❑ Raxus Prime Trooper / Imperial (C) 2.50
❑ Rebel Marksman / Rebels (UC) 2.00
❑ Rebel Troop Cart / Rebels (UC) 4.00
❑ Rebel Trooper on Tauntaun / Rebels (R) 10.00
❑ Rebel Vanguard / Rebels (UC) 3.00
❑ Shaak Ti, Jedi Master / Republic (VR) 22.00
❑ Snowtrooper / Imperial (C) 2.00
❑ Star Destroyer Officer / Imperial (UC) 2.00
❑ Stormtrooper / Imperial (UC) 2.00
❑ Telosian Tank Droid / Fringe (UC) 3.00
❑ TIE Crawler / Imperial (UC) 2.00
❑ Uggernaut / Fringe (R) 5.00
❑ Ugnaught Boss / Fringe (UC) 2.00
❑ Ugnaught Tech / Fringe (C) 2.00
❑ Vader's Apprentice, Redeemed / Rebels (R) 22.00
❑ Vader's Apprentice, Unleashed / Imperial (VR) 30.00
❑ Verpine Tech / Rebels (C) 2.00
❑ Wedge Antilles, Red Two / Rebels (R) 2.00
❑ Wookiee Hunter AT-ST / Imperial (R) 9.00
❑ Wookiee Warrior / Rebels (C) 2.00

Miniatures Game. Imperial Entanglements.

❑ 181st Imperial Pilot / Imperial (UC) 2.00
❑ Arica / Imperial (R) 5.00
❑ Bacta Tank / Fringe (UC) 3.00
❑ Bespin Guard / Fringe (C) 2.00
❑ Bothan Commando / Rebels (C) 2.00
❑ C-3PO, Ewok Diety / Rebels (VR) 13.00
❑ Chiss Mercenary / Fringe (C) 2.00
❑ Darth Vader, Legacy of the Force / Imperial (VR) 24.00
❑ Dash Rendar, Renegade Smuggler / Fringe (VR) 18.00
❑ Duros Scout / Fringe (C) 2.00
❑ Emperor Palpatine on Throne / Imperial (VR) 26.00
❑ Ewok Scout / Fringe (C) 2.00
❑ General Crix Madine / Rebels (R) 5.00
❑ General Rieekan / Rebels (VR) 22.00
❑ Imperial Dignitary / Imperial (UC) 2.50
❑ Jawa Scavenger / Fringe (C) 2.00
❑ Kyp Durron / New Republic (R) 5.00
❑ Leia, Bounty Hunter / Rebels (VR) 15.00
❑ Lobot, Computer Liaison Officer / Fringe (R) 4.00
❑ Logray, Ewok Shaman / Fringe (R) 4.00
❑ Luke Skywalker, Rebel Commando / Rebels (VR) 20.00
❑ Mercenary Commander / Fringe (UC) 2.00
❑ Moff Jerjerrod / Imperial (R) 3.00
❑ Mouse Droid / Fringe (UC) 4.00
❑ R2-D2 with Extended Sensor / Rebels (R) 5.00
❑ Rebel Commando Pathfinder / Rebels (UC) 2.00
❑ Rebel Trooper / Rebels (C) 2.00
❑ Sandtrooper / Imperial (C) 2.50
❑ Sandtrooper Officer / Imperial (UC) 2.50
❑ Scout Trooper / Imperial (C) 2.00
❑ Shock Trooper / Imperial (UC) 2.00
❑ Snowtrooper / Imperial (C) 2.00
❑ Snowtrooper Commander / Imperial (UC) 2.50
❑ Stormtrooper / Imperial (C) 2.50
❑ Thrawn (Mitth'raw'nuruodo) / Imperial (R) 7.00
❑ Twi'lek Black Sun Vigo / Fringe (UC) 2.50
❑ Ugnaught Droid Destroyer / Fringe (UC) 2.50
❑ Veteran Rebel Commando / Rebels (C) 2.00
❑ Whiphid Tracker / Fringe (UC) 2.00
❑ Xizor / Fringe (VR) 20.00

Miniatures Game. Jedi Academy.

❑ Anakin Solo (R) 4.00
❑ Antarian Ranger (C) 2.00
❑ Cade Skywalker, Padawan (R) 3.00
❑ Crimson Nova Bounty Hunter (UC) 2.50
❑ Darth Maul Sith Apprentice (VR) 26.00
❑ Darth Plagueis (VR) 30.00
❑ Darth Sidious, Sith Master (R) 13.00
❑ Death Watch Raider (C) 2.00
❑ Disciple Of Ragnos (C) 2.00
❑ Exceptional Jedi Apprentice (UC) 2.50
❑ Felucian (UC) 4.00
❑ Grand Master Luke Skywalker (R) 18.00
❑ Grand Master Yoda (R) 4.00
❑ Heavy Clone Trooper (C) 2.00
❑ HK-50 Assassin Droid (UC) 2.00
❑ Imperial Sentinel (UC) 2.50
❑ Jedi Battle Master (UC) 2.00
❑ Jedi Crusader (UC) 2.50
❑ Jensaarai Defender (UC) 2.50
❑ Kol Skywalker (VR) 25.00
❑ Krath War Droid (C) 2.00
❑ Kyle Katarn, Combat Instructor (R) 3.00
❑ Leia Skywalker, Jedi Knight (R) 4.00
❑ Master K'Kruhk (VR) 18.00
❑ Naga Sadow (VR) 30.00
❑ Peace Brigade Thug (C) 2.00
❑ Praetorite Vong Priest (UC) 2.50
❑ Praetorite Vong Warrior (C) 2.00
❑ Qui-Gon Jinn, Jedi Trainer (R) 2.00
❑ R4 Astromech Droid (C) 2.00
❑ Reborn (C) 2.00
❑ Rocket Battle Droid (C) 2.00
❑ Sith Apprentice (UC) 2.50
❑ Sith Lord (UC) 2.50
❑ Stormtrooper (C) 2.00
❑ The Dark Woman (VR) 25.00
❑ The Jedi Exile (VR) 3.00
❑ Vodo-Siosk Baas (VR) 30.00
❑ Youngling (C) 2.00
❑ Yuuzhan Ossus Guardian (UC) 2.50

Miniatures Game. Knights of the Old Republic.

❑ ASN Assassin Droid (UC) 2.50
❑ Atton Rand (VR) 12.00
❑ Bao-Dur (R) 3.00
❑ Boma (UC) 2.00
❑ Captain Panaka (R) 3.00
❑ Captain Tarpals (R) 4.00
❑ Carth Onasi (VR) 20.00
❑ Czerka Scientist (C) 2.00
❑ Darth Malak, Dark Lord of the Sith (VR) 29.00
❑ Darth Sion (VR) 35.00
❑ Darth Vader, Scourge of the Jedi (R) 6.00
❑ Echani Handmaiden (C) 2.00
❑ Elite Sith Trooper (UC) 2.00
❑ General Wedge Antilles (R) 5.00

Role-Playing Miniatures

❑ GenoHaradan Assassin (C) 2.00
❑ Gungan Artillerist (C) 2.00
❑ Gungan Shieldbearer (UC) 4.00
❑ Gungan Soldier (C) 2.00
❑ Han Solo, Smuggler (R) 4.00
❑ Jar Jar Binks (VR) 18.00
❑ Jarael (R) 9.00
❑ Jawa Scout (C) 2.00
❑ Jolee Bindo (VR) 12.00
❑ Juggernaut War Droid (C) 2.00
❑ Juhani (VR) 22.00
❑ Kreia (VR) 28.00
❑ Leia Organa, Senator (VR) 13.00
❑ Luke Skywalker, Jedi (R) 5.00
❑ Mandalore the Ultimate (VR) 40.00
❑ Mandalorian Captain (UC) 2.00
❑ Mandalorian Commando (C) 2.00
❑ Mandalorian Marauder (C) 2.00
❑ Mandalorian Quartermaster (UC) 2.00
❑ Mandalorian Scout (C) 2.00
❑ Massiff (UC) 2.50
❑ Master Lucien Draay (VR) 22.00
❑ Mira (VR) 20.00
❑ Mission Vao (R) 3.00
❑ Obi-Wan Kenobi, Padawan (VR) 18.00
❑ Old Republic Captain (UC) 2.00
❑ Old Republic Guard (C) 2.00
❑ RA-7 Death Star Protocol Droid (UC) 2.50
❑ Rakghoul (UC) 3.00
❑ Shyrack (UC) 2.00
❑ Sith Assassin (UC) 2.00
❑ Sith Guard (C) 2.00
❑ Sith Heavy Assault Droid (UC) 2.00
❑ Sith Marauder (UC) 2.00
❑ Sith Scoundrel Operative (C) 2.00
❑ Sith Trooper Captain (UC) 2.00
❑ Squint (VR) 13.00
❑ Supreme Chancellor Palpatine (R) 3.00
❑ T1 Series Bulk Loader Droid (UC) 2.00
❑ T3-M4 (R) 6.00
❑ Tusken Raider Scout (C) 2.00
❑ Visas Marr (R) 4.00
❑ Wookiee Elite Warrior (C) 2.00
❑ Wookiee Trooper (C) 2.00
❑ Zaalbar (R) 3.00
❑ Zayne Carrick (R) 5.00

Miniatures Game. Legacy of the Force.

❑ Antares Draco / Imperial (R) 3.00
❑ Boba Fett, Mercenary Commander/Mandalorian (VR)..5.00
❑ Bothan Noble / Rebel (UC) 2.50
❑ Cade Skywalker, Bounty Hunter / Fringe (VR) 5.00
❑ Canderous Ordo / Mandalorian (R) 3.00
❑ Corellian Security Officer / New Republic (UC) 2.50
❑ Darth Cadeus / Sith (VR) 5.00
❑ Darth Krayt / Sith (VR) 5.00
❑ Darth Nihl / Sith (VR) 5.00
❑ Darth Talon / Sith (VR) 5.00
❑ Darth Tyranus, Legacy of the Dark Side / Separatist (R)...3.00
❑ Deena Shan / Rebel (R) 3.00
❑ Deliah Blue / Fringe (R) 3.00
❑ Dug Fringer / Fringe (UC) 2.50
❑ Duros Scoundrel / Fringe (C) 2.00
❑ Elite Rebel Commando / Rebel (UC) 2.50
❑ Emperor Roan Fel / Imperial (VR) 5.00
❑ Galactic Alliance Scout / New Republic (C) 2.00
❑ Galactic Alliance Trooper / New Republic (C) 2.00
❑ General Dodonna / Rebel (R) 3.00
❑ Gotal Mercenary / Fringe (C) 2.00
❑ Guard Droid / Fringe (C) 2.00
❑ Han Solo, Galactic Hero / New Republic (R) 3.00
❑ Human Bodyguard / Fringe (C) 2.00
❑ Human Scoundrel / Fringe (C) 2.00
❑ Human Scout / Fringe (C) 2.00
❑ Imperial Knight / Imperial (UC) 2.50
❑ Imperial Knight / Imperial (UC) 2.50
❑ Imperial Pilot / Imperial (C) 2.00
❑ Imperial Security Officer / Imperial (UC) 2.50
❑ Jagged Fel / Imperial (R) 3.00
❑ Jariah Syn / Fringe (R) 3.00
❑ Kel Dor Bounty Hunter / Fringe (C) 2.00
❑ Kyle Katarn, Jedi Battlemaster / New Republic (VR) 5.00
❑ Leia Organa Solo, Jedi Knight / New Republic (VR) 5.00
❑ Luke Skywalker, Force Spirit / New Republic (VR) 5.00
❑ Luke Skywalker, Legacy of the Light Side / Rebel (R) 3.00
❑ Lumiya, the Dark Lady / Sith (R) 3.00
❑ Mandalorian Gunslinger / Mandalorian (UC) 2.50
❑ Mandalorian Trooper / Mandalorian (UC) 2.50
❑ Mara Jade Skywalker / New Republic (VR) 5.00
❑ Marasiah Fel / Imperial (R) 3.00
❑ Moff Morlish Veed / Imperial (VR) 5.00
❑ Moff Nyna Calixte / Imperial (R) 3.00
❑ Noghri Commando Imperial / Imperial (UC) 2.50
❑ Nomi Sunrider / Old Republic (VR) 5.00
❑ Old Republic Recruit / Old Republic (C) 2.00
❑ Old Republic Scout / Old Republic (C) 2.00
❑ Rebel Honor Guard / Rebel (C) 2.00
❑ Republic Commando Training Sergeant / Republic (UC) 2.50
❑ Rodian Blaster-for-Hire / Fringe (UC) 2.50
❑ Shado Vao / New Republic (R) 3.00
❑ Shadow stormtrooper / Imperial (UC) 2.50
❑ Trandoshan Mercenary / Fringe (C) 2.00
❑ Twi'lek Scout / Rebel (C) 2.00
❑ Wolf Sazen / New Republic (VR) 5.00
❑ Yuuzhan Vong Elite Warrior / Yuuzhan Vong (UC) 2.50
❑ Yuuzhan Vong Jedi Hunter / Yuuzhan Vong (UC) 2.50
❑ Yuuzhan Vong Shaper / Yuuzhan Vong (UC) 2.50
❑ Yuuzhan Vong Warrior / Yuuzhan Vong (C) 2.00

Miniatures Game. Rebel Storm Game.

❑ Booster Pack: Boba Fett graphic 12.00
❑ Booster Pack: Han Solo graphic 12.00
❑ Booster Pack: stormtrooper graphic 12.00
❑ Starter Set 20.00

Miniatures Game. Rebel Storm miniatures promotional pieces.

❑ Elite stormtrooper (P), Comic-Con 2004 exclusive 15.00
❑ MonCalimari Officer (P), Origins exclusive 15.00

Miniatures Game. Rebel Storm miniatures.

❑ 4-LOM (R) 8.00
❑ Bespin Guard (C) 2.00
❑ Boba Fett (VR) 35.00
❑ Bossk (R) 5.00
❑ Bothan Spy (UC) 2.50
❑ C-3PO (R) 6.00
❑ Chewbacca (R) 6.00
❑ Commando on Speeder Bike (VR) 18.00
❑ Darth Vader, Dark Jedi (R) 8.00
❑ Darth Vader, Sith Lord (VR) 13.00
❑ Dengar (R) 6.00
❑ Duros Mercenary (UC) 2.50
❑ Elite Hoth Trooper (UC) 2.50
❑ Elite Rebel Trooper (C) 2.00
❑ Elite Snowtrooper (UC) 2.50
❑ Elite stormtrooper (UC) 2.50
❑ Emperor Palpatine (VR) 20.00
❑ Ewok (C) 2.00
❑ Gamorrean Guard (UC) 2.50
❑ General Veers (R) 5.00
❑ Grand Moff Tarkin (R) 5.00
❑ Greedo (R) 5.00
❑ Han Solo (R) 12.50
❑ Heavy stormtrooper (UC) 2.50
❑ Hoth Trooper (C) 2.00
❑ IG-88 (R) 7.00
❑ Imperial Officer (UC) 2.50
❑ Ithorian Scout (UC) 2.50
❑ Jabba the Hutt (VR) 18.00
❑ Jawa (C) 2.00
❑ Lando Calrissian (R) 8.00
❑ Luke Skywalker, Jedi Knight (VR) 16.00
❑ Luke Skywalker, Rebel (R) 18.00
❑ Mara Jade, Emperor's Hand (R) 12.00
❑ Mon Calamari Mercenary (C) 2.00
❑ Obi-Wan Kenobi (VR) 19.00
❑ Princess Leia, Captive (VR) 12.00
❑ Princess Leia, Senator (R) 7.00
❑ Probe Droid (VR) 18.00
❑ Quarren Assassin (UC) 2.50
❑ R2-D2 (R) 12.00
❑ Rebel Commando (UC) 2.50
❑ Rebel Officer (UC) 2.50
❑ Rebel Pilot (C) 2.00
❑ Rebel Trooper (C) 2.00
❑ Rebel Trooper (C) 2.00
❑ Royal Guard (UC) 2.50
❑ Sandtrooper on Dewback (VR) 20.00
❑ Scout Trooper (UC) 2.50
❑ Scout Trooper on Speeder Bike (VR) 20.00
❑ Snowtrooper (C) 2.00
❑ Stormtrooper (C) 2.00
❑ Stormtrooper (C) 2.00
❑ Stormtrooper (C) 2.00
❑ Stormtrooper Officer (UC) 2.50
❑ Tusken Raider (C) 2.00
❑ Tusken Raider (P) 5.00
❑ Twi'lek Bodyguard (UC) 2.50
❑ Twi'lek Scoundrel (C) 2.00
❑ Wampa (VR) 20.00
❑ Wookiee Soldier (C) 2.00
❑ Wookiee Soldier (P) 5.00

Miniatures Game. Revenge of the Sith Game.

❑ Booster Pack: Anakin Skywalker [447-61] 10.00
❑ Booster Pack: Darth Sidious [447-62] 10.00
❑ Booster Pack: Yoda [447-63] 10.00
❑ Starter Set [447-64] 20.00

Miniatures Game. Revenge of the Sith miniatures.

❑ Agen Kolar, Jedi Master #1 (R) 8.00
❑ Alderaan Trooper #2 (UC) 2.50
❑ Anakin Skywalker, Jedi Knight #3 (R) 12.00
❑ Anakin Skywalker, Sith Apprentice #56 (VR) 25.00
❑ AT-RT #4 (VR) 22.00
❑ Bail Organa #5 (VR) 9.00
❑ Battle Droid #25 (C) 2.00
❑ Battle Droid #26 (C) 2.00
❑ Boba Fett, Young Mercenary #42 (R) 8.00
❑ Bodyguard Droid #27 (UC) 2.50
❑ Bodyguard Droid #28 (UC) 2.50
❑ Captain Antilles #6 (R) 5.00
❑ Chagrian Mercenary Commander #43 (UC) 2.50
❑ Chewbacca of Kashyyyk #7 (VR) 12.00
❑ Clone Trooper #8 (C) 2.00
❑ Clone Trooper #9 (C) 2.00
❑ Clone Trooper Commander #10 (UC) 2.50
❑ Clone Trooper Gunner #11 (C) 2.00
❑ Dark Side Adept #57 (UC) 2.50
❑ Darth Tyranus #29 (R) 12.00
❑ Darth Vader #58 (VR) 20.00
❑ Destroyer Droid #30 (R) 14.00
❑ Devaronian Soldier #44 (C) 2.00
❑ Emperor Palpatine, Sith Lord #59 (VR) 28.00
❑ General Grievous, Jedi Hunter #31 (VR) 28.00
❑ General Grievous, Supreme Commander #32 (R) 6.00
❑ Gotal Fringer #45 (UC) 2.50
❑ Grievous's Wheel Bike #33 (VR) 17.00
❑ Human Mercenary #46 (UC) 2.50
❑ Iktotchi Tech Specialist #47 (UC) 2.50
❑ Jedi Knight #12 (UC) 2.50
❑ Mace Windu, Jedi Master #13 (VR) 22.00
❑ Medical Droid #48 (R) 7.00
❑ Mon Mothma #14 (VR) 9.00
❑ Muun Guard #34 (UC) 2.50
❑ Nautolan Soldier #49 (C) 2.00
❑ Neimoidian Solder #36 (UC) 2.50
❑ Neimoidian Soldier #35 (UC) 2.50
❑ Obi-Wan Kenobi #15 (R) 10.00
❑ Polis Massa Medic #16 (C) 2.00
❑ R2-D2, Astromech Droid #17 (VR) 18.00
❑ Royal Guard #60 (UC) 2.50
❑ San Hill #37 (R) 4.00
❑ Senate Guard #18 (UC) 2.50
❑ Separatist Commando #38 (C) 2.00
❑ Shaak Ti #19 (R) 12.00
❑ Sly Moore #50 (R) 5.00
❑ Stass Allie #20 (R) 8.00
❑ Super Battle Droid #39 (C) 2.00
❑ Super Battle Droid #40 (C) 2.00
❑ Tarfful #21 (R) 5.00
❑ Tion Medon #51 (R) 7.00
❑ Utapaun Soldier #52 (C) 2.00
❑ Utapaun Soldier #53 (C) 2.00
❑ Wat Tambor #41 (R) 5.00
❑ Wookiee Berserker #22 (C) 2.00
❑ Wookiee Scout #23 (UC) 2.50
❑ Yoda, Jedi Master #24 (R) 20.00
❑ Yuzzem #54 (C) 2.00
❑ Zabrak Fringer #55 (C) 2.00

Miniatures Game. Star Wars: Universe.

❑ 57/60 Nom Anor #57 (R) 9.00
❑ Abyssin Black Sun Thug #12 (C) 2.00

Role-Playing Miniatures

- Acklay #13 (Huge U) 12.00
- Admiral Ackbar #43 (VR) 12.00
- ASP-7 #14 (UC) 4.00
- AT-ST #33 (HUGE R) 14.00
- B'omarr Monk #15 (R) 7.00
- Baron Fel #34 (VR) 10.00
- Battle Droid #6 (UC) 2.50
- Bith Rebel #44 (C) 2.00
- Chewbacca, Rebel Hero #45 (R) 10.00
- Clone Trooper #1 (C) 2.00
- Clone Trooper on BARC Speeder #2 (HUGE R) 14.00
- Dark Side Marauder #35 (UC) 6.00
- Dark Trooper Phase III #36 (UC) 4.00
- Darth Maul on Sith Speeder #7 (VR) 19.00
- Darth Vader, Jedi Hunter #37 (R) 20.00
- Dash Rendar #16 (R) 8.00
- Dr. Evazan #17 (VR) 8.00
- Dresselian Commando #46 (C) 2.00
- Elite Clone Trooper #3 (UC) 2.50
- Flash Speeder #4 (UC) 8.00
- Gonk Power Droid #18 (C) 2.00
- Grand Admiral Thrawn #38 (VR) 24.00
- Guri #19 (R) 2.50
- Hailfire Droid #8 (HUGE U) 12.00
- Han Solo, Rebel Hero #47 (R) 12.50
- Kaminoan Ascetic #20 (C) 2.00
- Kyle Katarn #52 (VR) 12.00
- Lando Calrissian, Hero of Tanaab #21 (R) 6.00
- Lobot #22 (R) 7.00
- Luke Skywalker on Tauntaun #48 (R) 12.00
- Luke Skywalker, Jedi Master #53 (VR) 25.00
- New Republic Commander #54 (C) 2.00
- New Republic Trooper #55 (C) 2.00
- Nexu #23 (UC) 4.00
- Nien Nunb #49 (R) 6.00
- Nightsister Sith Witch #39 (UC) 5.00
- Noghri #40 (UC) 6.00
- Nute Gunray #9 (R) 6.00
- Obi-Wan Kenobi on Boga #5 (HUGE VR) 23.00
- Ponda Baba #24 (R) 6.00
- Prince Xizor #25 (VR) 16.00
- Princess Leia, Rebel Hero #50 (R) 12.00
- Rancor #26 (HUGE VR) 32.50
- Reek #27 (HUGE U) 12.00
- Rodian Black Sun Vigo #28 (UC) 2.00
- Shistavanen Pilot #29 (UC) 2.50
- Stormtrooper #41 (C) 2.00
- Stormtrooper Commander #42 (UC) 2.50
- Super Battle Droid #10 (C) 2.00
- Super Battle Droid Commander #11 (UC) 4.00
- Tusken Raider on Bantha #30 (HUGE U) 9.00
- Vornskr #31 (C) 2.00
- Warmaster Tsavong Lah #58 (VR) 14.00
- Wedge Antilles #51 (R) 8.00
- X-1 Viper Droid #32 (HUGE U) 8.00
- Young Jedi Knight #56 (C) 2.00
- Yuuzhan Vong Subaltern #59 (UC) 2.00
- Yuuzhan Vong Warrior #60 (C) 2.00

Miniatures Game. The Force Unleashed.
- Booster Pack: Huge, 6 random figures [447-65] 22.00

Starship Battles game.
- Huge booster 15.00
- Starter Set 40.00

Role-Playing Miniatures: Starship Battles

Wizards of the Coast
- Booster Pack, 7 randomized, prepainted, fully assembled, durable plastic starships 22.00
- Starter Set 40.00

Dark Side
- Asajj Ventress's Starfighter 20.00
- Banking Clan Frigate 15.00
- Cloak Shape Fighter 4.00
- Commerce Guild Destroyer 5.00
- Darth Vader's TIE Advanced x1 ....20.00
- Droid Trifighter 6.00
- General Grievous's Starfighter 20.00
- Geonosian Starfighter 2.00
- Geonosian Starfighter Ace 2.00
- Imperial Interdictor Cruiser 15.00
- Imperial Shuttle 3.00
- Imperial Star Destroyer 5.00
- Invisible Hand 15.00
- Palpatine's Shuttle 20.00
- Scarab Droid Starfighter 2.00
- Sith Infiltrator 3.00
- Slave 1 (Boba Fett) 20.00
- Slave 1 (Jango Fett) 20.00
- Super Star Destroyer Executor 20.00
- Techno Union Starfighter 2.00
- TIE Bomber 2.00
- TIE Fighter 2.00
- TIE Fighter Ace 3.00
- TIE Interceptor 3.00
- TIE Interceptor Ace 3.00
- Trade Federation Battleship 10.00
- Trade Federation Droid Control Ship 15.00
- Virago 15.00
- Vulture Droid Starfighter 2.00
- Vulture Droid Starfighter Advanced 2.00

Light Side
- A-Wing Starfighter 2.00
- A-Wing Starfighter Ace 4.00
- Anakin Skywalker's Jedi Interceptor 15.00
- ARC-170 Starfighter 15.00
- B-Wing Starfighter Ace 4.00
- Jedi Starfighter 2.00
- Luke Skywalker's X-Wing 15.00
- Millennium Falcon 15.00
- Mon Calamari Cruiser Home One 15.00
- Mon Calamari MC80 ....5.00
- Mon Calamari Star Defender Viscount 15.00
- Naboo Starfighter 2.00
- Obi-Wan's Jedi Interceptor 15.00
- Outrider 5.00
- Rebel Assault Frigate 5.00
- Rebel Cruiser 5.00
- Rebel Transport 5.00
- Republic Assault Ship 15.00
- Republic Cruiser 5.00
- Rogue Squadron X-Wing 20.00
- SoroSuub Patrol Fighter 2.00
- Tantive IV 15.00
- Utapaun P-38 Starfighter 5.00
- V-Wing Starfighter 2.00
- Venator-class Star Destroyer 5.00
- Wild Karrde 13.00
- X-Wing Starfighter 2.00
- X-Wing Starfighter Ace 3.00
- Y-Wing Starfighter 2.00
- Y-Wing Starfighter Ace 3.00

Rubber Bands
Continued in Volume 3, Page 336

ABG Accessories
- Star Wars 5.00

Dizzy Heights Entertainment, Inc.
- Series 1 [448-01] 5.00
- Series 2 [448-02] 5.00

Rubber Stamps
Continued in Volume 3, Page 336

Adam Joseph Industries
- 24-count display box, full 500.00
- Admiral Ackbar [449-01] 20.00
- Biker scout [449-02] 20.00
- C-3PO [449-03] 20.00
- Chewbacca [449-04] 20.00
- Darth Vader [449-05] 20.00
- Emperor's Royal Guard [449-06] 20.00
- Gamorrean Guard [449-07] 20.00
- Millennium Falcon [449-08] 20.00
- TIE Fighter [449-09] 20.00
- Wicket [449-10] 20.00
- X-Wing pilot [449-11] 20.00
- Yoda [449-12] 20.00

Ewok 3 in 1.
- Princess Kneesaa [449-13] 25.00
- Wicket [449-14] 25.00

448-01

448-02

449-01

449-02

449-03

449-04

449-05

449-06

449-07

449-08

449-09

449-10

449-11

449-12

449-13

449-14

Rulers

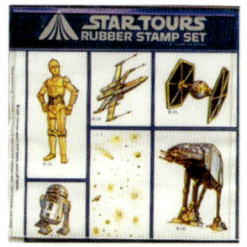
449-15

449-16

449-17

449-18

449-19

449-20

449-21

449-22

449-23

449-24

449-25

449-26

450-01

All Night Media Inc.
- Star Tours, plastic case and stamp artwork [449-15] 24.00

Innovative Designs
- 3 stamps with ink pad 15.00

Pyramid
- R2-D2 [449-16] 10.00
- Yoda [449-17] 10.00

Rose Art Industries
- Sticker and Stamper Studio, over 175 pieces in vinyl carry case [449-18] 40.00

Episode III: Revenge of the Sith. 2-pack of roller stampers.
- Clone trooper and C-3PO & R2-D2 .... 20.00
- Yoda and Darth Vader [449-19] 20.00

Gift sets.
- 4-piece: R2-D2, C-3PO, Darth Vader, stormtrooper [449-20] 40.00
- 5-piece: R2-D2, C-3PO, Darth Vader, stormtrooper, Yoda [449-21] 50.00

Individual stampers.
- C-3PO [449-22] 10.00
- Darth Vader [449-23] 10.00
- R2-D2 [449-24] 10.00
- Stormtrooper [449-25] 10.00
- Yoda [449-26] 10.00

Rugs
Continued in Volume 3, Page 337

- C-3PO and R2-D2 area rug [450-01] 150.00
- Podracing, 26" x 43" [450-02] 25.00
- Stormtrooper, helmet [450-03] 25.00

Jay Franco and Sons
- Angry Birds Chewbacca [450-04] 25.00
- Darth Vader, helmet [450-05] 25.00
- TIE Fighters [450-06] 30.00

Skywalker Ranch
- Skywalker Ranch 195.00

Taito (Japan)
- Boba Fett [450-07] 45.00
- Darth Vader [450-08] 45.00
- Stormtrooper [450-09] 45.00

ThinkGeek
- Wampa [450-10] 200.00

Rulers
Continued in Volume 3, Page 337

- Return of the Jedi, box of 12 .... 144.00

Butterfly Originals
- Return of the Jedi logo and battle scenes, 6" 10.00
- Return of the Jedi logo and characters on glossy label, 12" [451-01] 15.00
- Star Wars logo and Return of the Jedi vehicles and characters, 12" 15.00

DK Publishing
- Blueprints, 6", exclusive to Fan Club [451-02] 10.00

Flomo (UK)
- Hoth scene, lenticular, 18 cm [451-03] 10.00

Grand Toys
6" rulers.
- Battle Droids [451-04] 5.00
- Darth Maul [451-05] 5.00
- Queen Amidala, art [451-06] 5.00
- Queen Amidala, jewelry [451-07] 5.00

Grosvenor
- Clone trooper, 6" [451-08] 8.00

HC Ford (UK)
- Return of the Jedi, 6" [451-09] 20.00

Helix (UK)
- Stormtroopers pressed on back, 12" [451-10] 18.00

Impact, Inc.
- The Phantom Menace, stencil, 12" [451-11] 8.00

450-02

450-03

450-07

450-08

450-09

450-10

450-04

450-05

450-06

Rulers

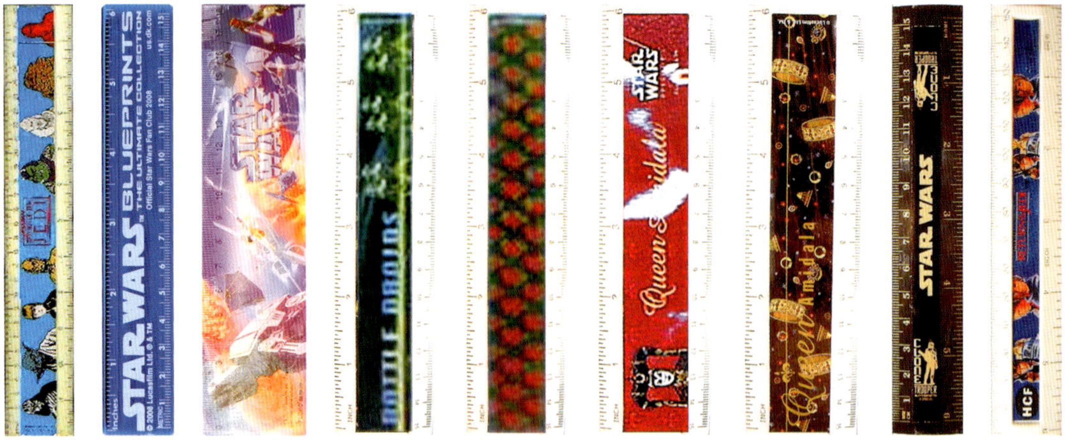

451-01 451-02 451-03 451-04 451-05 451-06 451-07 451-08 451-09

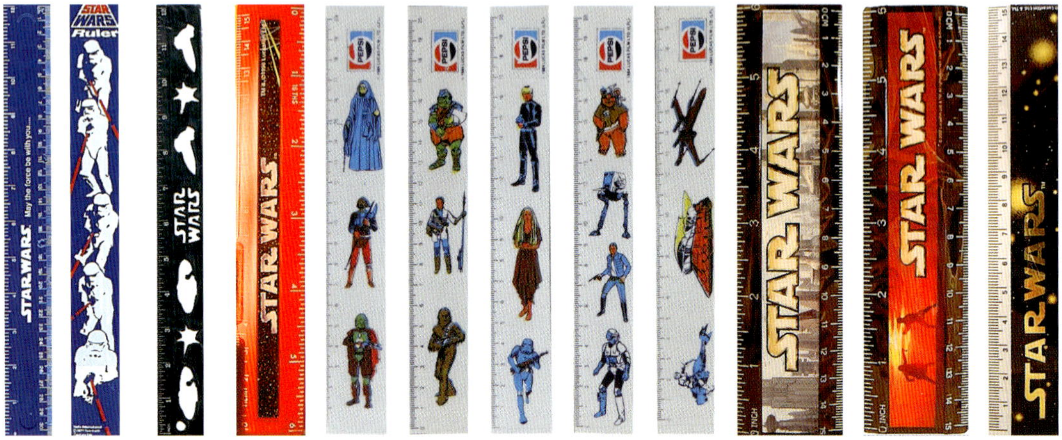

451-10 451-11 451-12 451-13 451-14 451-15 451-16 451-17 451-23 451-24 451-25

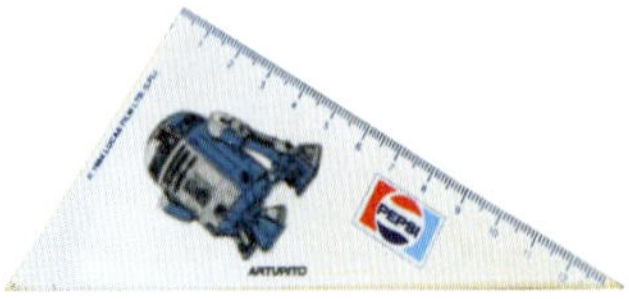

451-18

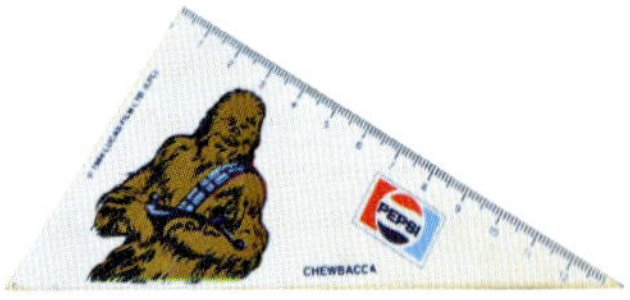

451-19

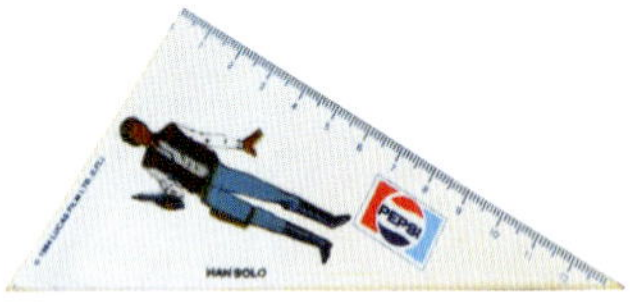

451-20

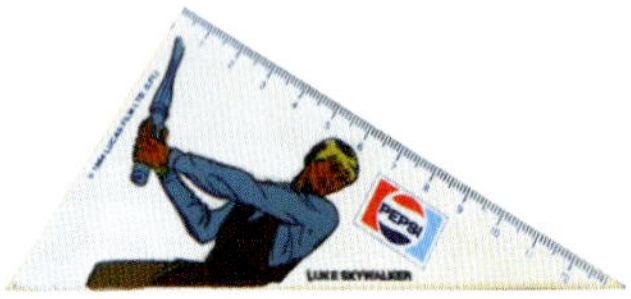

451-21

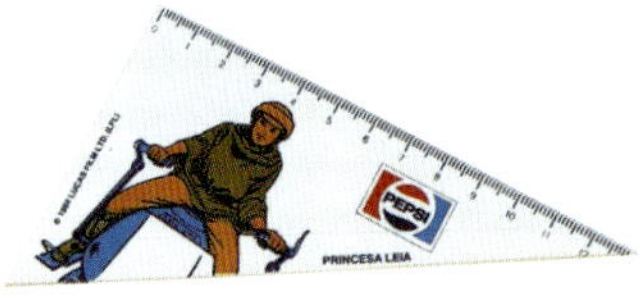

451-22

Innovative Designs
- ❑ Star Wars, 12" 5.00

Jollibee
- ❑ Yoda tape measure 20.00

Merlin
- ❑ Star Wars logo on red ruler [451-12]............................15.00

Pepsi Cola (Argentina)
- ❑ Emperor, Lando, Boba Fett [451-13] 45.00
- ❑ Gamorrean Guard, Boushh, Chewbacca [451-14] 45.00
- ❑ Luke, Leia, stormtrooper [451-15]................................45.00
- ❑ Paploo, AT-ST, Han, Biker Scout [451-16] 45.00
- ❑ Speeder Bike, Sail Barge, X-Wing [451-17]......................45.00

Rulers, triangle.
- ❑ Arturito (R2-D2) [451-18] 60.00
- ❑ Chewbacca [451-19] 60.00
- ❑ Han Solo [451-20] 60.00
- ❑ Luke Skywalker [451-21] 60.00
- ❑ Princess Leia [451-22] 60.00

Pyramid
- ❑ 6" Coruscant [451-23] 5.00
- ❑ 6" Duel [451-24] 5.00

Q-Stat (UK)
- ❑ Star Wars logo in space [451-25] 5.00

School Boxes

Continued in Volume 3, Page 316

Impact, Inc.
- ❑ Jar Jar Binks, sculpted [452-01].................................15.00
- ❑ "Jedi vs. Sith" Qui-Gon Jinn, Obi-Wan, Darth Sidious, Darth Maul [452-02]...5.00
- ❑ Watto, Sebulba, Anakin, and Jar Jar [452-03]..................5.00

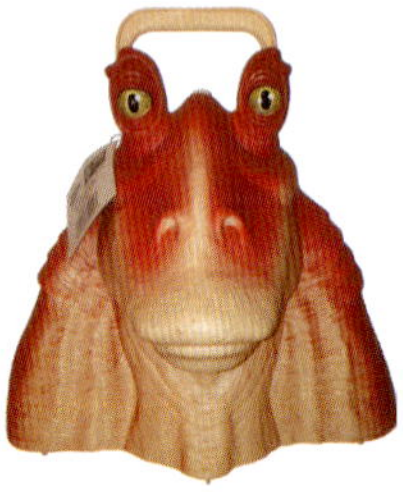

452-01

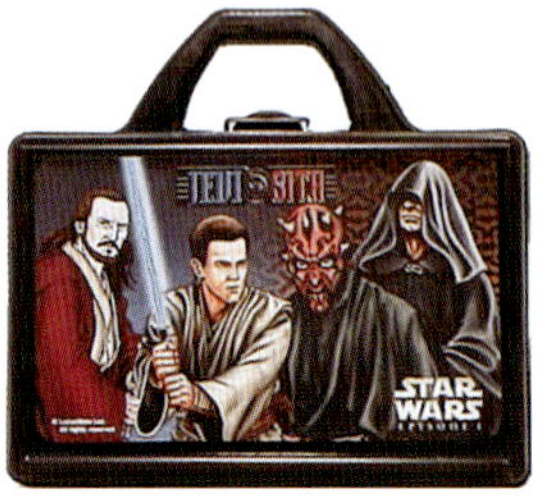

452-02

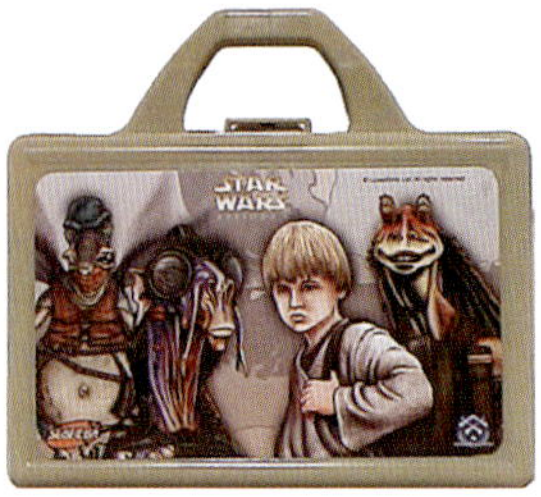

452-03

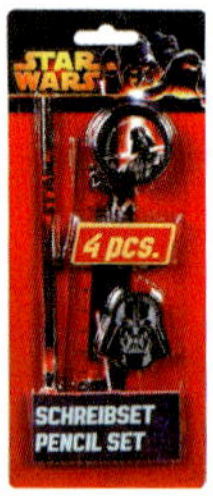

453-01

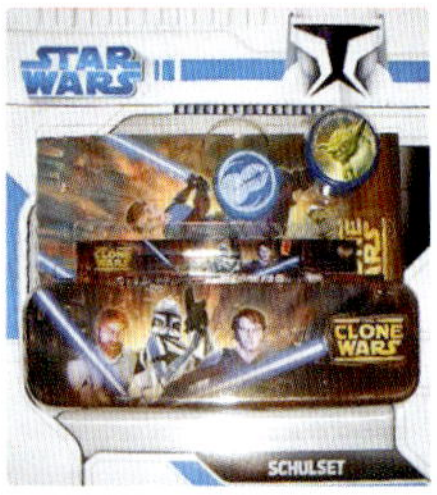

453-02

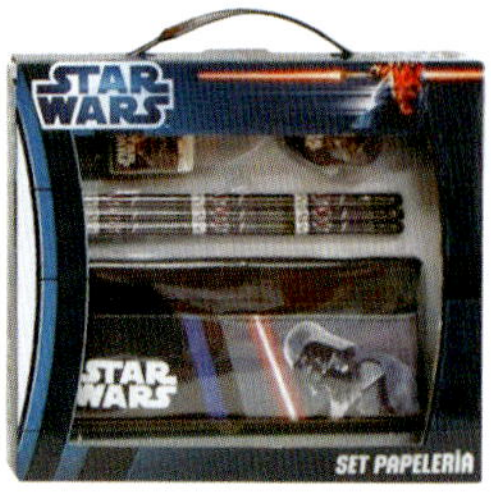

453-03

453-04

453-05

453-06

453-07

453-08

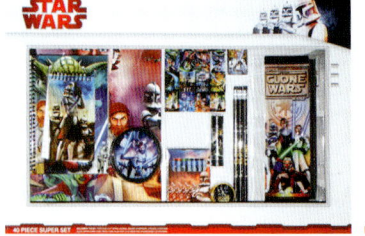

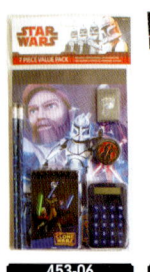

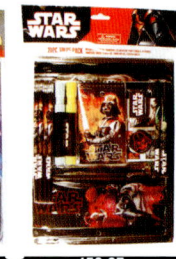

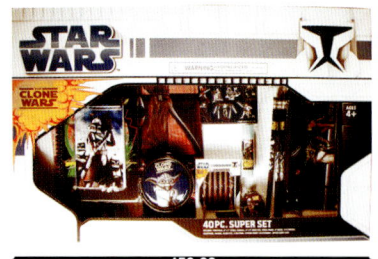

School Kits

453-09 | 453-10 | 453-11 | 453-12 | 453-13 | 453-14 | 453-15

453-16 | 453-17 | 453-18 | 453-19 | 453-20 | 453-21

School Kits
Continued in Volume 3, Page 337

(Germany)
- 4-piece Darth Vader Schreibset Pencil Set [453-01] 12.00
- Clone Wars schulset [453-02] 15.00

(Spain)
- Star Wars / Darth Vader set [453-03] 20.00

Accessory Zone
40-piece super sets.
- Clone Wars, portfolio, spiral journal, memo pad, pencil pouch, ruler, pencils, sharpener, eraser, glue stick, crayons, stickers, zipper carry case [453-04] 20.00
- Star Wars, portfolio, spiral journal, memo pad, pencil pouch, ruler, pencils, sharpener, eraser, glue stick, crayons, stickers, zipper carry case [453-05] 20.00

7-piece value packs.
- Clone Wars, notepad, memo pad, calculator, pencils, sharpener, eraser [453-06] 12.00

Animations
- Revenge of the Sith 15.00

20-piece super set.
- Darth Vader, portfolios, themebook, memo pad, pencil pouch, pencils, pencil sharpener, eraser, pens, highlighters, sticker sheets [453-07] 15.00

40-piece super sets.
- Clone Wars, portfolio, spiral journal, memo pad, pencil pouch, ruler, pencils, sharpener, eraser, glue stick, crayons, stickers, zipper carry case [453-08] 25.00
- Star Wars, portfolio, spiral journal, memo pad, pencil pouch, ruler, pencils, sharpener, eraser, glue stick, crayons, stickers, zipper carry case [453-09] 25.00

Butterfly Originals
- Return of the Jedi school kit with ruler, pencil, pencil bag, sharpener, and eraser [453-10] 30.00

Flomo (UK)
Prismatic designs.
- 2 pencils, clip, eraser, sharpener, pencil box [453-11] 25.00
- 2 pencils, clip, eraser, sharpener, pencil box, ruler, glue [453-12] 25.00
- 2 pencils, clip, eraser, sharpener, scissors, sticker [453-13] 20.00

Funtastic Pty. Ltd.
- School kit with ruler, pencil, pencil bag, sharpener, and eraser [453-14] 20.00

Grand Toys
- Darth Maul art, zippered pouch, ruler, sharpener, eraser [453-15] 15.00
- Destroyer droid, zippered pouch, ruler, sharpener, eraser [453-16] 15.00
- Queen Amidala art, zippered pouch, ruler, sharpener, eraser [453-17] 15.00
- Queen Amidala photo, zippered pouch, ruler, sharpener, eraser [453-18] 15.00

Grosvenor
- School stationery set: pencil case, sharpener, eraser, pencil, ruler [453-19] 15.00

Helix (UK)
- Chewbacca and Han padded front, assorted school supplies, large [v1e1:391] 60.00
- Pencil box, pencils, eraser, and sharpener 70.00
- Star Destroyer padded front, assorted school supplies, small [453-20] 90.00

Hunter Leisure, Ltd. (Australia)
- Fun Pack, Revenge of the Sith: color-your-own puzzle, scribbler, sticker book, sticker sheet, crayons [453-21] ... 20.00

Impact, Inc.
- Carry-along school set, carry case, pencil pouch, 2 pencils, memo pad, pencil sharpener, eraser, glue stick, 12" ruler [453-22] 20.00
- Study kit, "Jedi vs. Sith" eraser, ruler, pencil sharpener, vinyl zippered pencil case [453-23] 10.00
- Study kit, "Tatooine" eraser, ruler, pencil sharpener, vinyl zippered pencil case [453-24] 10.00
- Value pack, "Anakin's Pod" portfolio, theme book, memo pad, pencil, zippered pencil case, sharpener, eraser, ruler 15.00
- Value pack, "Jedi vs. Sith" portfolio, theme book, memo pad, pencil, zippered pencil case, sharpener, eraser, ruler 15.00

453-22 | 453-23 | 453-24 | 453-25 | 453-26 | 453-27 | 453-28 | 453-29 | 453-30 | 453-31

453-32 | 453-33 | 453-34 | 453-35 | 453-36 | 453-37 | 453-38 | 453-39

School Kits

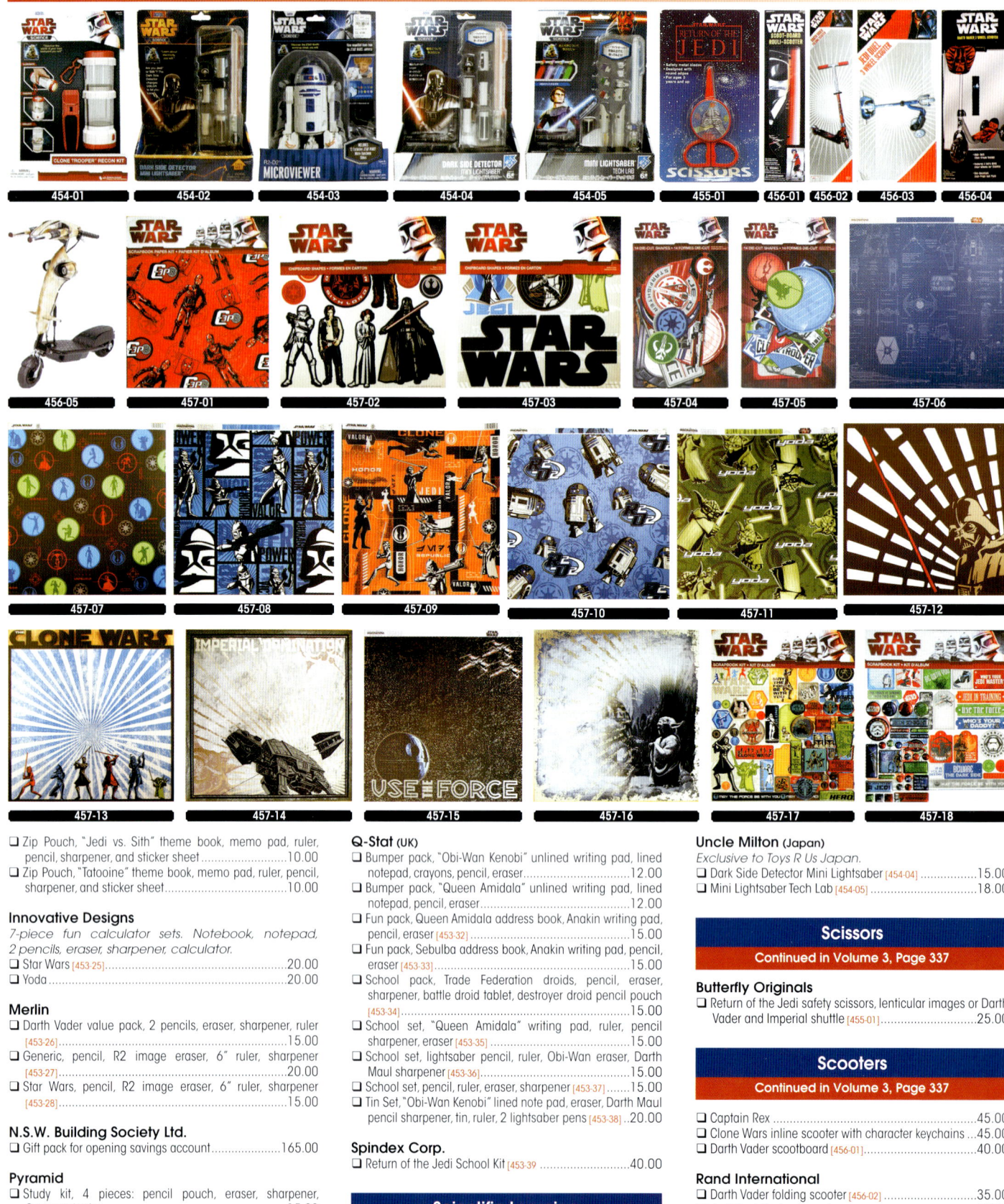

☐ Zip Pouch, "Jedi vs. Sith" theme book, memo pad, ruler, pencil, sharpener, and sticker sheet 10.00
☐ Zip Pouch, "Tatooine" theme book, memo pad, ruler, pencil, sharpener, and sticker sheet.....................................10.00

Innovative Designs
7-piece fun calculator sets. Notebook, notepad, 2 pencils, eraser, sharpener, calculator.
☐ Star Wars [453-25]..20.00
☐ Yoda 20.00

Merlin
☐ Darth Vader value pack, 2 pencils, eraser, sharpener, ruler [453-26]..15.00
☐ Generic, pencil, R2 image eraser, 6" ruler, sharpener [453-27]..20.00
☐ Star Wars, pencil, R2 image eraser, 6" ruler, sharpener [453-28]..15.00

N.S.W. Building Society Ltd.
☐ Gift pack for opening savings account......................165.00

Pyramid
☐ Study kit, 4 pieces: pencil pouch, eraser, sharpener, Coruscant ruler..15.00
☐ Study kit, 4 pieces: pencil pouch, eraser, sharpener, Kamino ruler [453-29]...15.00

Value packs, 11 pieces. Character themes.
☐ Anakin Skywalker [453-30] 20.00
☐ Count Dooku [453-31] 20.00

Q-Stat (UK)
☐ Bumper pack, "Obi-Wan Kenobi" unlined writing pad, lined notepad, crayons, pencil, eraser........................12.00
☐ Bumper pack, "Queen Amidala" unlined writing pad, lined notepad, pencil, eraser...12.00
☐ Fun pack, Queen Amidala address book, Anakin writing pad, pencil, eraser [453-32] 15.00
☐ Fun pack, Sebulba address book, Anakin writing pad, pencil, eraser [453-33] 15.00
☐ School pack, Trade Federation droids, pencil, eraser, sharpener, battle droid tablet, destroyer droid pencil pouch [453-34]..15.00
☐ School set, "Queen Amidala" writing pad, ruler, pencil sharpener, eraser [453-35]...15.00
☐ School set, lightsaber pencil, ruler, Obi-Wan eraser, Darth Maul sharpener [453-36]..15.00
☐ School set, pencil, ruler, eraser, sharpener [453-37] 15.00
☐ Tin Set, "Obi-Wan Kenobi" lined note pad, eraser, Darth Maul pencil sharpener, tin, ruler, 2 lightsaber pens [453-38] ..20.00

Spindex Corp.
☐ Return of the Jedi School Kit [453-39] 40.00

Scientific Learning
Continued in Volume 3, Page 337

Uncle Milton
☐ Clone trooper Recon Kit [454-01]................................20.00
☐ Dark Side Detector Mini Lightsaber [454-02] 15.00
☐ R2-D2 Microviewer [454-03]..45.00

Uncle Milton (Japan)
Exclusive to Toys R Us Japan.
☐ Dark Side Detector Mini Lightsaber [454-04] 15.00
☐ Mini Lightsaber Tech Lab [454-05] 18.00

Scissors
Continued in Volume 3, Page 337

Butterfly Originals
☐ Return of the Jedi safety scissors, lenticular images or Darth Vader and Imperial shuttle [455-01]............................25.00

Scooters
Continued in Volume 3, Page 337

☐ Captain Rex 45.00
☐ Clone Wars inline scooter with character keychains ...45.00
☐ Darth Vader scootboard [456-01]...............................40.00

Rand International
☐ Darth Vader folding scooter [456-02] 35.00
☐ Jedi Duel 3-wheel scooter [456-03]............................50.00

Sport Fun, Inc.
☐ Darth Vader 3-wheel scooter [456-04] 50.00

Zap World
☐ STAP scooter, motorized [456-05] 950.00

ShoeLaces

 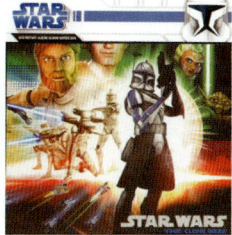  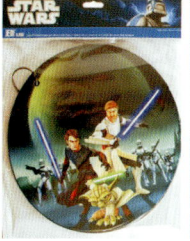    

458-01 | 458-02 | 458-03 | 458-04 | 458-05 | 458-06 | 458-07 | 458-08

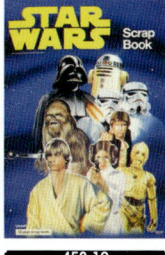 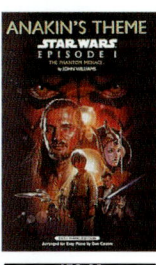   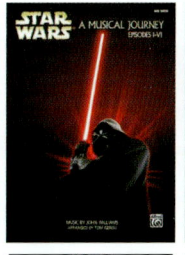 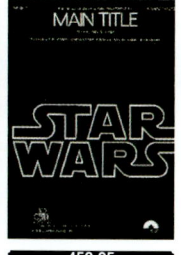 

458-09 | 458-10 | 459-01 | 459-02 | 459-03 | 459-04 | 459-05 | 459-06

Scrapbooking Supplies
Continued in Volume 3, Page 337

Creative Imaginations, LLC
- Scrapbook Paper Kit, 4 double-sided papers, 4 specialty foil papers [457-01] 18.00

Chipboard shapes. 2 sheets, 23 pieces.
- Classic Trilogy [457-02] 10.00
- Clone Wars [457-03] 10.00

Die-cut shapes, 14 pieces.
- Star Wars [457-04] 10.00
- The Clone Wars [457-05] 10.00

Paper, 2 sided, 12" x 12".
- Blueprints [457-06] 10.00
- C-3PO 10.00
- Clone Wars icons [457-07] 10.00
- Clones [457-08] 10.00
- Darth Vader 10.00
- Honor valor [457-09] 10.00
- R2-D2 [457-10] 10.00
- Yoda [457-11] 10.00

Paper, die-cut, 12" x 12".
- Black Armor [457-12] 10.00
- Stormtrooper 10.00
- The Clone Wars [457-13] 10.00

Paper, specialty foil.
- 30th Anniversary 5.00
- Clones 5.00
- Darth Vader 5.00
- Empire Strikes Back Crawl 5.00
- Honor Valor 5.00
- Hoth [457-14] 5.00
- Millennium Falcon 5.00
- Star Wars Logo 5.00
- Target 5.00
- Use The Force [457-15] 5.00

- Yoda [457-16] 5.00
- Yoda Rocks! 5.00

Scrapbook kits.
- Clone Wars, 8 double-sided papers, 12" x 12" cardboard sticker, epoxy sticker [457-17] 40.00
- Star Wars, 8 double-sided papers, 12" x 12" cardboard sticker, epoxy sticker [457-18] 40.00

Scrapbooks
Continued in Volume 3, Page 339

Creative Imaginations, LLC
8" x 8" instant album. 20 pre-designed scrapbook pages.
- Classic [458-01] 25.00
- Clone Wars [458-02] 25.00

Chipboard albums.
- Death Star [458-03] 15.00
- Jedi [458-04] 15.00

Mini book kit.
- Clone Wars, 1 mini book, 8 papers, 1 chipboard sticker, 1 cardstock sticker, 1 epoxy sticker [458-05] 20.00
- Star Wars, 1 mini book, 8 papers, 1 chipboard sticker, 1 cardstock sticker, 1 epoxy sticker [458-06] 20.00

Souvenir albums.
- Darth Vader [458-07] 20.00
- Yoda [458-08] 20.00

HC Ford (UK)
- Collage of character photos [458-09] 50.00

Letraset
- Collage of character photos [458-10] 60.00

Sheet Music
- Anakin's Theme, easy piano [459-01] 10.00

- Ewok Celebration [459-02] 10.00
- Star Wars Main Theme, easy piano [459-03] 10.00

Alfred Publishing
- A Musical Journey: Music from Episodes I–VI, big note piano [459-04] 15.00
- A Musical Journey: Music from Episodes I–VI, five finger piano 15.00
- The Clone Wars: Easy Piano 20.00

Fox Fanfare Music
- Cantina Band Dan Coates Easy Piano Solo 15.00
- Empire Strikes Back Han Solo and the Princess 15.00
- Empire Strikes Back Medley 15.00
- Star Wars Princess Leia's Theme 15.00
- Star Wars (Main Title) Dan Coates Piano Solo 15.00
- Star Wars (Main Title) Original Piano Solo [459-05] 15.00

Schaum
- Star Wars (Main Title) [459-06] 20.00

Shoe Charms
Continued in Volume 3, Page 339

Jibbitz / Crocs
Sound, light-up, and limited edition charms.
- Han Solo in Carbonite, limited edition [460-01] 15.00
- Obi-Wan, light-up, lightsaber flashes [460-02] 15.00

Shoelaces

C and D Visionaries, Inc.
- Star Wars, glow-in the-dark [461-01] 10.00

Stride Rite
- Ewoks and Return of the Jedi logo, 27" [4:277] 25.00
- Ewoks and Return of the Jedi logo, 36" [461-02] 25.00
- Return of the Jedi Logo, 27" [4:277] 25.00
- Return of the Jedi Logo, 36" [461-03] 25.00
- Star War Logo with Darth Vader helmet, 27" [461-04] 25.00

460-01 | 460-02 | 461-01 | 461-02 | 461-03 | 461-04 | 461-05 | 461-06 | 462-01

Shoelaces

- ☐ Star War Logo with Darth Vader helmet, 36" [4-277] 25.00
- ☐ Star War Logo, 27" [4-277] 25.00
- ☐ Star War Logo, 36" [4-277] 25.00
- ☐ Star Wars Logo with Droids, 27" [4-277] 25.00
- ☐ Star Wars Logo with Droids, 36" [461-05] 25.00
- ☐ Star Wars Logo with Spaceships, 27" 25.00
- ☐ Star Wars Logo with Spaceships, 36" [461-06] 25.00

Shower Curtains
Continued in Volume 3, Page 340

Jay Franco and Sons
- ☐ TPM: Space Battle, 70" x 72", vinyl [462-01] 20.00

Signs
Continued in Volume 3, Page 340

C and D Visionaries, Inc.
- ☐ My other transport is the Millennium Falcon [463-01] 25.00

Norben
7" x 9.5".
- ☐ Anakin Skywalker Podracer [463-02] 5.00
- ☐ Jedi vs. Sith [463-03] 5.00

Star Wars Celebration V
Retro tin signs.
- ☐ Hoth Blue Milk Brewing 25.00

- ☐ Iggy's Eighty-Eight 25.00
- ☐ Vader's Fist Orange Juice 25.00

TinSigns International
Movie poster artwork, 15" x 24" tin.
- ☐ Empire Strikes Back 20.00
- ☐ Star Wars 20.00

Skateboards
Continued in Volume 3, Page 340

- ☐ Star Wars [464-01] 25.00

Episode III: Revenge of the Sith.
- ☐ Darth Vader small 20.00
- ☐ Millennium Falcon (poster art) 25.00

Bravo Sports
21-inch skateboards.
- ☐ Clone Wars—Anakin [464-02] 30.00
- ☐ Clone Wars—Heroes [464-03] 30.00

Brookfield Athletic
- ☐ Darth Vader and Luke Skywalker Duel [464-04] 45.00

M.V. Sports and Leisure Ltd.
- ☐ Darth Maul 8" x 31" 35.00
- ☐ Jar Jar Binks 8" x 28" [464-05] 35.00

Plan B
- ☐ Boba Fett 50.00
- ☐ Darth Vader 50.00
- ☐ Yoda 50.00

Seneca Sports Inc.
- ☐ C-3PO and R2-D2 [464-06] 35.00
- ☐ Darth Maul / Sith double-sided decal [464-07] 35.00
- ☐ Darth Vader [464-08] 35.00
- ☐ Death Star trench battle (McQuarrie art) 35.00
- ☐ Podracing / Anakin double-sided decal [4-278] 35.00
- ☐ Yoda (McQuarrie art) [464-09] 35.00

Sport Fun, Inc.
- ☐ Anakin Skywalker / Clone trooper [464-10] 35.00
- ☐ Jango Fett / Slave I [464-11] 35.00

Episode III: Revenge of the Sith.
- ☐ Darth Vader [464-12] 35.00

Skates: Ice, Roller, and Inline

- ☐ Anakin Skywalker, podracer accents [465-01] 35.00
- ☐ Learn to skate combo [465-02] 45.00

Brookfield Athletic
- ☐ Darth Vader ice skates [465-03] 250.00
- ☐ Darth Vader roller skates [465-04] 250.00
- ☐ Wicket the Ewok ice skates [465-05] 250.00
- ☐ Wicket the Ewok roller skates [465-06] 250.00

426

Snow Globes

    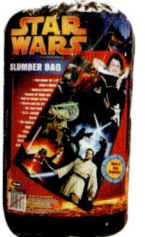    

466-13 | 467-01 Outside and Inside | 467-02 | 467-03 | 467-04 | 467-05 | 467-06 | 467-07

467-08 | 467-09 | 467-10 | 467-11 | 467-12 | 467-13 | 467-14 | 467-15 | 467-16

Seneca Sports Inc.
- Darth Maul inline skates, gray with red accents [465-07] 40.00
- Imperial Runner Quad Skates, black with TIE fighter accents [465-08] 40.00
- R2-D2 inline youth adjustable skates [465-09] 45.00
- Rogue Squadron inline skates, black with red accents [465-10] 45.00

Slap Bands
Continued in Volume 3, Page 340

Bulls i Toy
Clone Wars characters.
- Ahsoka Tano [466-01] 5.00
- Anakin Skywalker [466-02] 5.00
- General Grievous [466-03] 5.00
- Obi-Wan Kenobi [466-04] 5.00
- Savage Opress [466-05] 5.00
- Yoda [466-06] 5.00

Saga characters.
- Anakin Skywalker [466-07] 5.00
- Boba Fett [466-08] 5.00
- Darth Maul [466-09] 5.00
- Darth Vader [466-10] 5.00
- Stormtrooper [466-11] 5.00
- Yoda [466-12] 5.00

Tapper Candies
- Slap Bands, Jedi and Sith, 4-pack [466-13] 5.00

Sleeping Bags
Continued in Volume 3, Page 340

- Royal Guard, stormtrooper, Darth Vader [467-01] 50.00

Episode I: The Phantom Menace.
- Podracing, Anakin Skywalker and Sebulba [467-02] 65.00

Episode III: Revenge of the Sith.
- Heroes and Villains [467-03] 50.00

Bibb Co.
- Empire Strikes Back: Boba Fett, exclusive to JCPenney 175.00
- Empire Strikes Back: Lord Vader's Chamber 150.00
- Empire Strikes Back: Spectre [467-04] 150.00
- Empire Strikes Back: Yoda [467-05] 150.00
- Return of the Jedi: Jabba the Hutt, Ewoks, etc. 150.00
- Return of the Jedi: logos from all 3 films 150.00
- Return of the Jedi: Star Wars Adventure [467-06] 150.00
- Return of the Jedi: Star Wars Saga [467-07] 150.00
- Star Wars: Galaxy [v1e1:393] 150.00

ERO Industries
- Anakin Skywalker, podracer [467-08] 35.00
- Luke and Darth Vader, exclusive to Toys R Us [467-09] 60.00
- R2-D2 with metallic accents, The Phantom Menace, 54" long [467-10] 45.00
- Space Battle, The Phantom Menace [467-11] 35.00

Idea Nuova
- Darth Vader slumber sack / backpack, 27" x 70" [467-12] 30.00

Monkey Business
Episode III: Revenge of the Sith. 29" x 60".
- Darth Vader [467-13] 35.00
- Epic duel [467-14] 35.00

Rose Art Industries
Episode III: Revenge of the Sith. 30" x 57"
- Epic duel under Vader's helmet [467-15] 35.00

SlumberTrek (Australia)
- Darth Vader 70 cm x 160 cm 45.00

ThinkGeek
- TaunTaun with COA, exclusive to www.ThinkGeek.com [467-16] 250.00

Snow Tubes and Sleds

Dynalech Action Inc.
- Captain Rex, foam [468-01] 40.00
- Millennium Falcon, foam [468-02] 50.00
- X-Wing, inflatable [468-03] 75.00
- Yoda, foam [468-04] 40.00

Intex Recreation Corp.
- Darth Maul Sno-Tube 39" [468-05] 50.00

Snow Globes, Water Globes, and Globes
Continued in Volume 3, Page 341

Department 56
- Snowspeeder attacking AT-AT on Hoth, fan club exclusive [469-01] 95.00

Kurt S. Adler, Inc.
Musical holiday waterballs.
- Darth Vader building Death Star in the snow [469-02] ...35.00
- Darth Vader checking Naughty and Nice list [469-03] ...35.00
- Santa Yoda [469-04] 35.00
- Santa Yoda [469-05] 35.00
- Santa Yoda with Christmas tree base [469-06] 35.00
- Santa Yoda with sleigh base [469-07] 35.00

NECA
- Episode II Asteroid Battle, 5,000 produced [469-08] 75.00

Rawcliffe
Mini water globes.
- R2-D2, Christmas 20.00

Snow globes.
- Hoth Battle [469-09] 60.00
- Yoda vs. Darth Sidious [469-10] 95.00

Water globes.
- Anakin Skywalker vs. Obi-Wan Kenobi duel [469-11] 75.00
- C-3PO and R2-D2 [469-12] 15.00
- Darth Vader [469-13] 15.00
- Movie poster style "A" artwork [469-14] 120.00
- Yoda [469-15] 15.00

  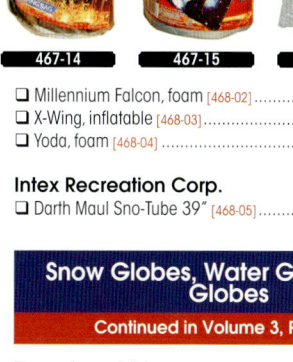  

468-01 | 468-02 | 468-03 | 468-04 | 468-05

Soap Dishes

469-01 | 469-02 | 469-03 | 469-04 | 469-05 | 469-06 | 469-07 | 469-08

469-09 | 469-10 | 469-11 | 469-12 | 469-13 | 469-14 | 469-15

470-01 | 470-02 | 470-03

Soap Dishes
Continued in Volume 3, Page 341

Jay Franco and Sons
- Anakin seated in podracer, sculpted [470-01] 20.00
- Star Wars decal, starfighters [470-02] 12.00

Sigma
- Landspeeder soap dish [470-03] 250.00

Soap, Sanitizer, and Body Wash
Continued in Volume 3, Page 341

Added Extras, LLC
- 3-pack: Yoda, Rex, Obi-Wan [471-01] 20.00
- Savage Opress red bath foam with Anakin Skywalker blue bath foam bonus refill [471-02] 15.00

Antiseptic hand-cleansing gel with bonus holder.
- Anakin Skywalker [471-03] 5.00
- Clone Wars 2-pack [471-04] 10.00

Addis (UK)
2-packs. Character soaps.
- Baby Ewoks and Wicket [471-05] 50.00
- C-3PO and R2-D2 [471-06] 50.00
- Darth Vader and Luke Skywalker [471-07] 50.00

3-packs. Foam bath and soaps.
- Baby Ewoks and Wicket [471-08] 75.00
- C-3PO and R2-D2 [471-09] 75.00
- Darth Vader and Luke Skywalker 75.00

4-packs. Shower gel, sponge, and soaps.
- Baby Ewoks and Wicket 95.00
- C-3PO and R2-D2 .... 95.00
- Darth Vader and Luke Skywalker [471-10] 95.00

Individual bars.
- C-3PO [4:379] 20.00
- Darth Vader 20.00
- Luke Skywalker 20.00
- R2-D2 [4:379] 20.00
- Wicket W. Warrick [4:379] 20.00
- Woklings [4:379] 20.00

Cliro (UK)
- Starships, from bubble bath 2-pack [471-11] 125.00

Sculpted "Soap Models."
- C-3PO [471-12] 40.00
- R2-D2 [471-13] 40.00

Cliro (Germany)
Sculpted "Soap Models."
- C-3PO 50.00
- R2-D2 [v1e1:394] 50.00

Grosvenor
- Podracer game on container [471-14] 20.00

Minnetonka
Bottled with sculpted character cap.
- Darth Maul [471-15] 15.00
- Darth Vader [471-16] 15.00
- Stormtrooper [471-17] 15.00

Galactic glycerin soap, 3.5 oz., gift inside: character figure.
- Anakin Skywalker 10.00
- C-3PO [471-18] 10.00
- Chewbacca [471-19] 10.00
- Darth Maul [471-20] 10.00
- Darth Vader [471-21] 10.00
- Jar Jar Binks [471-22] 10.00
- Queen Amidala [471-23] 10.00
- R2-D2 [471-24] 10.00
- Yoda [471-25] 10.00

     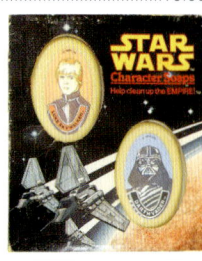 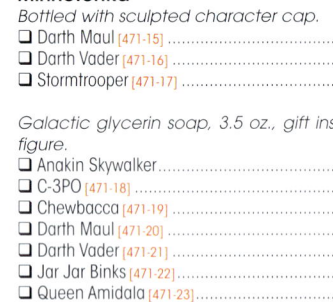

471-01 | 471-02 | 471-03 | 471-04 | 471-05 | 471-06 | 471-07

471-08 | 471-09 | 471-10 | 471-11 Can 1 / Can 2 | 471-12 Boxed / Open | 471-13 Boxed / Open

Soap: Bubble Bath

   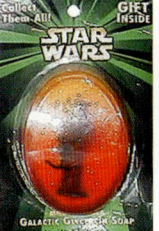   

471-14 · 471-15 · 471-16 · 471-17 · 471-18 · 471-19 · 471-20 · 471-21 · 471-22

471-23 · 471-24 · 471-25 · 471-26 · 471-27 · 471-28

Minnetonka (Canada)
Galactic Glycerin Soap, 3.5 oz., bi-language. Gift Inside: character figure.
- ☐ Anakin Skywalker [471-26] 10.00
- ☐ C-3PO 10.00
- ☐ Chewbacca 10.00
- ☐ Darth Maul [471-27] 10.00
- ☐ Darth Vader 10.00
- ☐ Jar Jar Binks 10.00
- ☐ Queen Amidala 10.00
- ☐ R2-D2 .... 10.00
- ☐ Yoda 10.00

Omni Cosmetics (UK)
1 oz. bars, sculpted character images. 4-packs.
- ☐ C-3PO, R2-D2, C-3PO, Darth Vader, and Lando Calrissian [471-28] 50.00
- ☐ Leia, Luke, Yoda, and Chewbacca [471-29] 50.00

4 oz. bars, sculpted character image, tri-logo packaging.
- ☐ Luke Skywalker 25.00
- ☐ Princess Leia 25.00

4 oz. bars, sculpted character images.
- ☐ C-3PO [471-30] 20.00
- ☐ Darth Vader [471-31] 20.00
- ☐ Gamorrean Guard [471-32] 20.00
- ☐ Luke Skywalker [471-33] 20.00
- ☐ Princess Leia [471-34] 20.00
- ☐ Wicket the Ewok [471-35] 20.00
- ☐ Yoda [471-36] 20.00

Rose Art Industries
Bottled with sculpted character cap.
- ☐ Darth Vader Fun Suds Spray Soap [471-37] 15.00

Style International (Mexico)
Episode III: Revenge of the Sith.
- ☐ Anakin Skywalker [471-38] 35.00
- ☐ C-3PO [471-39] 35.00
- ☐ Chewbacca [471-40] 35.00
- ☐ Clone trooper [471-41] 35.00
- ☐ Darth Vader [471-42] 35.00
- ☐ General Grievous [471-43] 35.00
- ☐ Obi-Wan [471-44] 35.00
- ☐ R2-D2 [471-45] 35.00
- ☐ Yoda [471-46] 35.00

Soap: Bubble Bath
Continued in Volume 3, Page 342

Added Extras, LLC
- ☐ Clone Wars [472-01] 8.00

Addis (UK)
- ☐ Ben Kenobi [472-02] 45.00
- ☐ C-3PO [472-03] 45.00
- ☐ Chewbacca [472-04] 45.00
- ☐ Darth Vader [472-05] 45.00
- ☐ Han Solo [472-06] 45.00
- ☐ Luke Skywalker [472-07] 45.00
- ☐ Princess Leia [472-08] 45.00
- ☐ R2-D2 [472-09] 45.00
- ☐ Wicket the Ewok [472-10] 45.00

Foam Bath
- ☐ Princess Kneesaa [472-11] 50.00

Cliro (UK)
Bubble bath in character labeled cans.
- ☐ 2-pack Imperial Cruiser with foam shampoo [472-12] .. 125.00
- ☐ Artoo Detoo [472-13] 50.00
- ☐ Chewbacca [472-14] 50.00
- ☐ Darth Vader [472-15] 50.00
- ☐ See Threepio [472-16] 50.00
- ☐ Starships [472-17] 50.00

Sculpted character bottles.
- ☐ Darth Vader [472-18] 150.00
- ☐ R2-D2 [472-19] 125.00

Cosrich Group, Inc.
Sculpted character cap.
- ☐ R2-D2 [472-20] 25.00
- ☐ Yoda [472-21] 25.00

Grosvenor
- ☐ Darth Vader [472-22] 25.00
- ☐ Galactic Bath Foam [472-23] 25.00
- ☐ Gungan Bongo [472-24] 30.00
- ☐ Jango Fett [472-25] 35.00
- ☐ R2-D2, non-electronic [472-26] 20.00

471-29 · 471-30 · 471-31 · 471-32 · 471-33 · 471-34 · 471-35 · 471-36 · 471-37

471-38 · 471-39 · 471-40 · 471-41 · 471-42 · 471-43 · 471-44 · 471-45 · 471-46

Soap: Bubble Bath

Minnetonka
- Darth Vader with foil label [472-27] 10.00
- Gungan Sub with tub fizzers [472-28] 15.00
- Jar Jar Binks bottle w/ sculpted character cap [472-29]..15.00
- Jar Jar Binks with foil label [472-30] 10.00
- Yoda bottle with sculpted character cap [472-31] 15.00

Omni Cosmetics
- Battle Scene "refuling station" [472-32] 40.00
- Luke Skywalker, 2 oz. from travel kit [472-33] 25.00

Figure-shaped bottles.
- Chewbacca [472-34] 30.00
- Darth Vader [472-35] 30.00
- Jabba the Hutt [472-36] 35.00
- Luke Skywalker [472-37] 35.00
- Princess Leia [472-38] 35.00
- R2-D2 [472-39] 30.00
- Wicket the Ewok [472-40] 35.00
- Yoda [472-41] 30.00

Soap: Shampoo
Continued in Volume 3, Page 343

Added Extras, LLC
- Clone Wars 3-in-1, body wash, shampoo, conditioner [473-01] 8.00

Cliro
- Starships, can [473-02] 80.00

474-01 474-02 474-03 474-04 475-01 476-01

Consumer Products
- Empire Strikes Back foam bath and shampoo set [473-03] 75.00

Grosvenor
- Darth Maul figural bottle [473-04] 20.00
- R2-D2 bath and shower foam, electronic [473-05] 25.00

Minnetonka
- Anakin Skywalker bottle with sculpted character cap [473-06] 10.00
- Anakin Skywalker galactic shampoo [473-07] 10.00
- C-3PO bottle with sculpted character cap [473-08] 10.00

Omni Cosmetics
- Battle Scene "refuelling station" [473-09] 40.00
- Luke Skywalker, 2 oz. from travel kit [473-10] 25.00
- Princess Leia cream rinse, 2 oz. from travel kit [473-11] 30.00
- Princess Leia, 2 oz. from travel kit [473-12] 30.00

Figural bottles inside Sears mailer packaging.
- Darth Vader 85.00
- Jabba the Hutt 85.00
- Luke Skywalker 85.00
- R2-D2 ....85.00
- Wicket the Ewok 85.00
- Yoda 85.00

Figural bottles.
- Darth Vader 30.00
- Jabba the Hutt 35.00
- Luke Skywalker 35.00
- R2-D2 ....30.00
- Wicket the Ewok 35.00
- Yoda 30.00

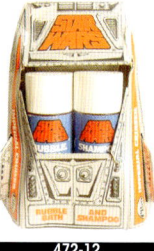

472-01 472-02 472-03 472-04 472-05 472-06 472-07 472-08 472-09 472-10 472-11 472-12 472-13 472-14 472-15 472-16 472-17 Sides 1 & 2

472-18 472-19 472-20 472-21 472-22 472-23 472-24 472-25 472-26 472-27 472-28

472-29 472-30 472-31 472-32 472-33 472-34 472-35 472-36 472-37 472-38 472-39 472-40 472-41 473-01

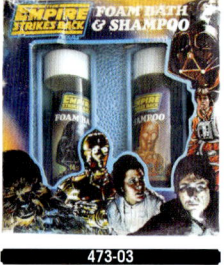

473-02 Sides 1 & 2   473-03   473-04   473-05   473-06   473-07   473-08   473-09   473-10   473-11   473-12

Stamps

477-01   478-01   478-02   478-03   478-04

478-05   478-06   478-07   478-08

Speakers
Continued in Volume 3, Page 343

Digital Blue
- R2-D2 speaker dock [474-01] 40.00

Funko
- Darth Vader lamp / clock / speaker 85.00

Sakar International
- Clone Wars for MP3 players [474-02] 25.00

Taito (Japan)
- R2-D1 (red), 12 cm [474-03] 35.00
- R2-D2 (blue), 12 cm [474-04] 35.00

Spinners
Continued in Volume 3, Page 343

Fantasma
- Laser light spinner, logo and ships on refractive foil, covering 3.75" metal disc [475-01] 65.00

Sponges

Addis (UK)
- Darth Vader pictured on one side [476-01] 20.00

Sprinklers
Continued in Volume 3, Page 343

Sport Fun, Inc.
- Vader Force sprinkler [477-01] 30.00

Stamp Collecting Kits

H.E. Harris and Company
- Star Wars postage stamp collecting kit, bagged [478-01] 30.00
- Star Wars postage stamp collecting kit, boxed [478-02] ..35.00

6 Star Wars seals, 10 genuine stamps, 300 hinges.
- Cantina Scenes [478-03] 75.00
- Death Star [478-04] 75.00
- Escape from Death Star [478-05] 75.00
- Space Ships [478-06] 75.00
- Tatooine [478-07] 75.00
- Tatooine Residents [478-08] 75.00

Stamps
Continued in Volume 3, Page 343

Episode II sheet of 1 stamp 25,00. Limited to 2,000.
- Naboo Fighter [3:382] 18.00
- STAP [3:382] 18.00

Episode II sheet of 9 stamps 5,00 each. Ltd. to 2,000.
- Blue [3:382] 18.00
- Brown [3:382] 18.00
- Light blue [3:382] 18.00

(Chechenia)
- Episode I plus classic trilogy sheet of 9 [2:387] 10.00

(Republique Centrafricaine)
- Star Wars 3 sheet 600f [2:387] 12.00

(Republique Du Mali)
- Empire Strikes Back sheet of 32 [2:387] 10.00
- Return of the Jedi sheet of 18 [2:387] 10.00
- Star Wars sheet of 31 [2:387] 10.00

(Republique Togolaise)
- Empire Strikes Back sheet of 9, 350f [2:387] 10.00
- Star Wars 2000f Star Wars stamp [2:387] 10.00
- Return of the Jedi sheet of 9, 190f [2:387] 10.00

(Tatarstan)
- Empire Strikes Back 5.00 .... 10.00
- Phantom Menace 5.00 .... 10.00
- Return of the Jedi 5.00 .... 10.00
- Star Wars 5.00 .... 10.00
- Sheet of 12 classic movies 15.00

Australia Post (Australia)
- 25th anniversary stamp kit 35.00
- 25th anniversary stamp sheet [479-01] 20.00

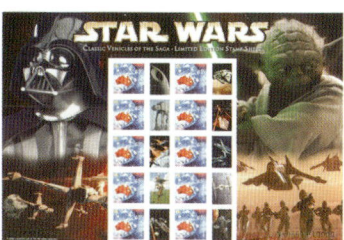 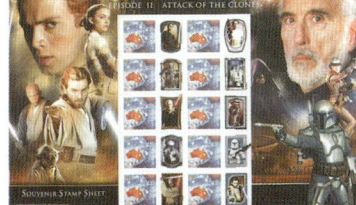  

479-01   479-02   479-03   479-04

 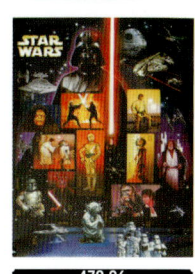   

479-05   479-06   479-07   479-08   479-09

Stamps

- ❏ Episode II stamp sheet [479-02] 20.00
- ❏ Episode III stamp sheet [479-03] 20.00

Japan Post (Japan)
- ❏ 30th anniversary sheet in folder [479-04] 55.00
- ❏ 30th anniversary sheet of custom stamps in folder [479-05] 45.00

SSCA
- ❏ First day cover collection $1.00 stamp on 3 different envelope designs with covers 20.00
- ❏ Stamp collection folder with sheet of nine $1.00 stamps, and sheet of three triangular $2.00 stamps 25.00

Stamp wallets.
- ❏ Darth Vader, gold [2:387] 50.00
- ❏ Darth Vader, silver [v1e1:398] 40.00
- ❏ Stormtrooper, gold [v1e1:398] 50.00
- ❏ Stormtrooper, silver [2:387] 40.00
- ❏ Yoda, gold [2:387] 50.00
- ❏ Yoda, silver [v1e1:398] 40.00

United States Postal Service
30th anniversary stamp sheets.
- ❏ Individual sheet [479-06] 20.00
- ❏ Sealed; digital color postmark packaging 20.00
- ❏ Canceled May 25, 2007 .... 35.00
- ❏ Unopened pack of 1,500 sheets 650.00
- ❏ Yoda stamps, sheet of 20, any of 8 plate positions [479-07] 10.00

Express mail prepaid mailers with first day covers.
- ❏ Darth Vader 25.00
- ❏ Obi-Wan Kenobi 25.00
- ❏ Yoda 25.00

Express mail prepaid mailers.
- ❏ Darth Vader 20.00
- ❏ Obi-Wan Kenobi 20.00
- ❏ Yoda 20.00

First day with envelope, hand canceled in Los Angeles, mounted with character profile. Listed by profile, any stamp.
- ❏ C-3PO and R2-D2 [v1e1:398] 35.00
- ❏ Darth Vader [v1e1:398] 35.00
- ❏ R2-D2 [v1e1:398] 35.00
- ❏ Stormtrooper [v1e1:398] 35.00
- ❏ Yoda 35.00

First day with envelope, hand canceled in Los Angeles.
- ❏ Anakin and Obi-Wan 15.00
- ❏ Boba Fett 15.00
- ❏ C-3PO 15.00
- ❏ Chewbacca and Han Solo 15.00
- ❏ Darth Maul 15.00
- ❏ Darth Vader 15.00
- ❏ Emperor Palpatine 15.00
- ❏ Luke Skywalker 15.00
- ❏ Millennium Falcon 15.00
- ❏ Obi-Wan Kenobi 15.00
- ❏ Princess Leia and R2-D2 .... 15.00
- ❏ Queen Amidala 15.00
- ❏ Stormtroopers 15.00
- ❏ X-Wing Fighter 15.00
- ❏ Yoda 15.00

Peter Mayhew Day, hand canceled in Granbury, TX, mounted with stamp sheet. June 6, 2007.
- ❏ Any stamp 50.00

Walsall Security Printers
- ❏ 6 sheet 35 cent horizontal stamps showing scenes from the movie, St. Vincent and Grenadines 15.00

3-sheet souvenir $2 triangular self-adhesive stamps. 3 designs: 1995 video artwork, St. Vincent and Grenadines
- ❏ 23 carat gold foil stamps 25.00
- ❏ .999 pure silver [4:281] 20.00
- ❏ Foil [479-08] 10.00

9 sheet $1 vertical self-adhesive foil stamps; 3 designs: 1995 video artwork, St. Vincent and Grenadines
- ❏ 23 carat gold foil stamps 25.00
- ❏ .999 pure silver 20.00
- ❏ Foil [479-09] 15.00

Standees

Mpire, tabletop.
- ❏ Anakin Skywalker [480-01] 8.00

Stationery

- ❏ Darth Vader [480-02] 8.00
- ❏ The Emperor [480-03] 8.00

20th Century Fox
- ❏ First time on DVD, Sept 21 [4:282] 95.00

Episode I: The Phantom Menace. Preorder standees.
- ❏ Approximately 5' [4:282] 45.00
- ❏ Countertop [4:282] 15.00

Advanced Graphics
Classic trilogy.
- ❏ Admiral Ackbar [4:282] 40.00
- ❏ Ben Kenobi [4:282] 40.00
- ❏ Boba Fett [4:282] 40.00
- ❏ C-3PO [4:282] 40.00
- ❏ Chewbacca [4:282] 40.00
- ❏ Darth Vader with lightsaber original [4:282] 40.00
- ❏ Darth Vader without lightsaber 40.00
- ❏ Emperor Palpatine 40.00
- ❏ Emperor's Royal Guard [4:282] 40.00
- ❏ Han Solo [4:282] 40.00
- ❏ Han Solo in Carbonite [4:282] 40.00
- ❏ Han Solo, stormtrooper disguise [4:282] 40.00
- ❏ Jawa [4:282] 40.00
- ❏ Luke Skywalker [4:282] 40.00
- ❏ Princess Leia [4:282] 40.00
- ❏ Princess Leia, Jabba's prisoner [4:282] 40.00
- ❏ R2-D2 [4:282] 40.00
- ❏ Stormtrooper [4:282] 40.00
- ❏ Tusken raider [4:282] 40.00
- ❏ Wicket [4:282] 40.00
- ❏ Yoda [4:282] 40.00

Episode I: The Phantom Menace.
- ❏ Anakin Skywalker [4:282] 40.00
- ❏ Battle droid [4:282] 40.00
- ❏ C-3PO [4:282] 40.00
- ❏ Darth Maul, Jedi duel [4:282] 40.00
- ❏ Darth Maul, Tatooine [4:282] 40.00
- ❏ Jar Jar Binks [4:282] 40.00
- ❏ Obi-Wan Kenobi [4:282] 40.00
- ❏ OOM-9 [4:282] 40.00
- ❏ Padmé Amidala [4:282] 40.00
- ❏ Queen Amidala [4:282] 40.00
- ❏ Qui-Gon Jinn [4:282] 40.00
- ❏ Watto [4:282] 40.00

Episode II: Attack of the Clones.
- ❏ Anakin Skywalker, 6'2" [4:282] 40.00
- ❏ Clone trooper, 6'1" [4:282] 40.00
- ❏ Jango Fett 6'1" [4:282] 40.00
- ❏ Mace Windu 6'3" [4:282] 40.00
- ❏ Obi-Wan Kenobi 5'11" [4:282] 40.00
- ❏ Padmé Amidala 5'6" [4:282] 40.00
- ❏ Yoda [4:282] 40.00
- ❏ Zam Wesell 5'7" [4:282] 40.00

Episode III: Revenge of the Sith.
- ❏ Anakin Skywalker [4:282] 40.00
- ❏ Chewbacca [4:282] 40.00
- ❏ Clone trooper [4:282] 50.00
- ❏ Clone trooper, yellow [4:282] 50.00
- ❏ Darth Sidious [4:282] 40.00
- ❏ General Grievous [4:282] 50.00
- ❏ Obi-Wan Kenobi [4:282] 40.00
- ❏ R2-D2 and C-3PO [4:282] 40.00
- ❏ R2-D2 and C-3PO, retouched 40.00
- ❏ Yoda [4:282] 40.00

Mini figures.
- ❏ Leia, Han Solo, Yoda, Darth Vader, Luke Skywalker, Chewbacca, Boba Fett, stormtrooper, C-3PO, and R2-D2 .... 30.00

Bantam Books
- ❏ C-3PO and jawas standee promotes Visual Dictionary and Incredible Cross-Sections books [480-04] 45.00

Cardboard Cut-Out Co. Ltd.
Desk Top Cut-Outs.
- ❏ Anakin Skywalker 12.00
- ❏ Chewbacca 12.00
- ❏ Darth Vader 12.00
- ❏ Final battle 12.00
- ❏ Stormtrooper 12.00

Disney Theme Park Merchandise
2010 Star Wars weekends. Characters shopping.
- ❏ Aurra Sing [480-05] 150.00
- ❏ Chewbacca [480-06] 150.00
- ❏ Darth Vader [480-07] 150.00
- ❏ Queen Amidala 150.00
- ❏ R2-D2 [480-08] 150.00

DK Publishing
Episode I: The Phantom Menace. 3D paper engineered.
- ❏ Battle droid [480-09] 150.00
- ❏ Destroyer droid [480-10] 200.00
- ❏ Pit droid [480-11] 150.00
- ❏ R2-D2 [480-12] 100.00

Factors, Etc.
- ❏ Boba Fett 65.00
- ❏ C-3PO 65.00
- ❏ Chewbacca 65.00
- ❏ Darth Vader 65.00
- ❏ R2-D2 .... 65.00

Frito Lay
Episode I: The Phantom Menace.
- ❏ Queen Amidala, "You Could Win …" [480-13] 80.00
- ❏ Qui-Gon Jinn, "Collect all 12 …" [480-14] 80.00

Kellogg's
- ❏ C-3PO cereal [480-15] 265.00

Movie Cards
Jayce' Carterie.
- ❏ Darth Vader [480-16] 15.00
- ❏ Luke Skywalker [480-17] 15.00
- ❏ Princess Leia [480-18] 15.00
- ❏ R2-D2 [480-19] 15.00
- ❏ Yoda [480-20] 15.00

Pepsi Cola
Episode I: The Phantom Menace.
- ❏ Boss Nass, Pepsi [480-21] 75.00
- ❏ Darth Maul, Mountain Dew [480-22] 75.00
- ❏ Jar Jar Binks, Mountain Dew [480-23] 75.00
- ❏ Mace Windu, Pepsi [480-24] 75.00
- ❏ Obi-Wan Kenobi, Mountain Dew [4:283] 75.00
- ❏ Queen Amidala, Pepsi [480-25] 75.00
- ❏ Qui-Gon Jinn, Pepsi [480-26] 75.00
- ❏ Watto, Pepsi [480-27] 75.00

Pizza Hut
- ❏ Darth Vader 6' with lightsaber standee promoting Pepsi during Star Wars special edition 100.00

Random House
- ❏ Darth Vader, promoted vintage reading products [480-28] 125.00

Sales Corp. of America
- ❏ C-3PO and R2-D2 .... 70.00
- ❏ Darth Vader and Emperor's Royal Guard [480-29] 70.00
- ❏ Wicket the Ewok 70.00

Scholastic
- ❏ Boba Fett (young) and Jango Fett, advertises Episode II era young reader books 45.00

The Empeiros Group
Episode I: The Phantom Menace. Desktop, approximately 12" tall.
- ❏ Darth Maul [480-30] 15.00
- ❏ Darth Sidious [480-31] 15.00
- ❏ Jar Jar Binks [480-32] 15.00
- ❏ Obi-Wan Kenobi [480-33] 15.00
- ❏ Queen Amidala [480-34] 15.00
- ❏ Sebulba [480-35] 15.00
- ❏ Watto [480-36] 15.00

Wizards of the Coast
- ❏ Star Wars roleplaying game, Han / Boba Fett [480-37] ... 75.00

Stationery
Continued in Volume 3, Page 344

- ❏ Stationery set, includes pencil, pen, ruler, eraser, sharpener, and decal [481-01] 10.00
- ❏ Stationery set [481-02] 20.00

481-01 | 481-02 | 481-03 | 481-04 | 481-05 | 481-06 | 481-07

481-08 | 481-09 Cover and Open | 481-10 | 481-11 | 481-12 | 481-13

Stationery

(UK)
- ❏ Stationery set, Clone Wars, ruler, pencil, sharpener, eraser [481-03] 10.00

Animations
11-piece stationery sets with portfolios, notebook, memo pad, pencil pouch, pencils, sharpener, ruler, eraser.
- ❏ Clone Wars [481-04] 10.00
- ❏ Star Wars [481-05] 10.00

Drawing Board Greeting Cards, Inc.
- ❏ Star Wars lap pack folder with droids on paper, plain envelopes; 10 sheets, 10 envelopes 30.00
- ❏ Star Wars R2-D2 die-cut paper; 18 sheets, 12 envelopes, boxed [481-06] 30.00
- ❏ Star Wars stationery with X-Wing on paper, battle envelope; 18 sheets, 12 envelopes, boxed [481-07] 35.00

HC Ford (UK)
- ❏ Character stationery, pencil topper, pencil, ruler, mini-memo notebook, eraser [v1e1:400] 65.00
- ❏ Fancy stationery set [481-08] 85.00
- ❏ Stationery—pencil top gift set, random pencil, eraser, mini memo, 2 toppers [v1e1:400] 50.00
- ❏ Stationery set, mechanical pencil, pencils, pencil sharpener, pencil caps, eraser, crayons, memo note pad [481-09] ..70.00

Innovative Designs
- ❏ 32-piece stationery assortment, 8 tattoo sheets, 8 memo pads, 8 push pencils, 8 markers [481-10] 10.00

Japan Star Wars Fan Club (Japan)
- ❏ Japan Star Wars Fan Club envelopes [481-11] 100.00

Letraset
- ❏ Envelopes, 12-pack, illustrated in front corner, and on rear [481-12] 45.00
- ❏ Space writing set, 15 envelopes, writing pad, rub down transfers, notebook [481-13] 120.00

Mead
16 envelopes, 15 sheets of paper.
- ❏ Boba Fett, C-3PO, Darth Vader, stormtroopers, Yoda 15.00

- ❏ Darth Vader 15.00
- ❏ X-Wings 15.00

Tokyo Queen Co., Ltd. (Japan)
- ❏ C-3PO and R2-D2 [v1e1:400] 35.00
- ❏ Darth Vader, lap pack [v1e1:400] 60.00
- ❏ Stormtrooper on Dewback [v1e1:400] 35.00

Statues and Busts
Continued in Volume 3, Page 345

5-packs, 2" busts, ceramic.
- ❏ Queen Amidala, stormtrooper, C-3PO, Darth Maul, alien [482-01] 15.00
- ❏ UFO, Jar Jar, Darth Vader, Anakin Skywalker, Yoda 15.00

Life-sized characters.
- ❏ Yoda, Blockbuster Video giveaway to promote Episode I video [482-02] 500.00

Yoda, life-sized by Lawrence A Noble.
- ❏ Artist proof, 6 produced ....OSPV
- ❏ Regular edition, 25 produced ....OSPV

Applause
- ❏ Bounty hunters, 5,000 produced [482-03] 135.00
- ❏ Clash of the Jedi diorama [482-04] 60.00
- ❏ Darth Maul [482-05] 50.00
- ❏ Darth Maul, Jedi duel, 20,000 produced, exclusive to Suncoast [482-06] 65.00
- ❏ Darth Vader in meditation chamber, 5,000 produced, exclusive to FAO Schwarz [482-07] 95.00
- ❏ Duel of Fates [482-08] 50.00
- ❏ Guardians of Peace, lights up [482-09] 125.00
- ❏ Han Solo Release from Carbonite, built-in light, 2,500 produced [482-10] 145.00
- ❏ Jabba with slave Leia, 5,000 produced [482-11] 80.00
- ❏ Leia's Rescue, 5,000 produced [482-12] 55.00
- ❏ Luke in Bacta tank [482-13] 95.00

- ❏ Obi-Wan Kenobi [482-14] 45.00
- ❏ Queen Amidala [482-15] 50.00
- ❏ Qui-Gon Jinn [482-16] 45.00
- ❏ Rancor, 5,000 produced [482-17] 75.00
- ❏ Sandtrooper and Dewback, 5,000 produced [482-18] ...70.00
- ❏ Shadows of the Empire, 5,000 produced [482-19] 70.00
- ❏ Wampa Attack, 3,000 produced [482-20] 80.00

Bespin duel characters on light-up bases.
- ❏ Darth Vader [482-21] 100.00
- ❏ Luke Skywalker [482-22] 100.00

Attakus (France)
2,500 produced, each. Individually numbered.
- ❏ Darth Vader 125.00
- ❏ Shadowtrooper 125.00
- ❏ Stormtrooper 125.00
- ❏ Wicket the Ewok 125.00

Japan editions. 200 produced, each.
- ❏ Boba Fett [v1e1:401] 300.00
- ❏ Darth Maul 300.00

Metal collection. Diorama figures, approximately 4" in scale. 2,500 produced, each. Individually numbered.
- ❏ C-3PO [482-23] 85.00
- ❏ Darth Vader [482-24] 85.00
- ❏ Obi-Wan Kenobi [482-25] 85.00
- ❏ R2-D2 [482-26] 85.00
- ❏ Stormtrooper commander [482-27] 85.00
- ❏ Stormtrooper marksman [482-28] 85.00
- ❏ Stormtrooper sentry [482-29] 85.00
- ❏ Stormtrooper vanguard [482-30] 85.00

Metal collection. Dioramas. 400 produced, each. Individually numbered.
- ❏ Death Star corridor 1,000.00
- ❏ Millennium Falcon, Han, Chewbacca, Luke, Leia exclusive figures [482-31] 2,300.00

Statues and Busts

Limited edition statuettes. Series 1.
- Boba Fett [482-32] 1,200.00
- Darth Maul [482-33] 450.00
- Han Solo in Carbonite [482-34] 260.00
- Princess Leia [482-35] 345.00
- R2-D2 [482-36] 215.00
- Yoda [482-37] 300.00

Limited edition statuettes. Series 2.
- C-3PO [482-38] 365.00
- Darth Vader [482-39] 365.00
- Emperor Palpatine [482-40] 445.00
- Emperor's Royal Guard [482-41] 365.00
- Jabba the Hutt [482-42] 950.00
- Jabba the Hutt and Princess Leia [482-43] 1,450.00
- Luke Skywalker X-Wing pilot [482-44] 300.00
- Stormtrooper [482-45] 365.00

Limited edition statuettes. Series 3.
- Chewbacca [4:284] 500.00
- Clone trooper [482-46] 300.00
- Darth Vader II 900.00
- Han Solo [482-47] 390.00
- Jango Fett [482-48] 400.00
- Jawa [482-49] 120.00
- Obi-Wan Kenobi [482-50] 390.00
- Padmé Amidala [482-51] 350.00
- Salacious Crumb [482-52] 250.00
- Salacious Crumb and Jabba's pipe [482-53] 390.00

Limited edition statuettes. Series 4.
- General Grievous 580.00
- TIE Fighter pilot 400.00
- Tusken raider 390.00
- Wicket W. Warrick 280.00
- Yoda, Episode II 300.00

Limited edition statuettes. Series 5.
- Bib Fortuna 400.00
- Gamorrean Guard 450.00
- Luke Skywalker Jedi Knight 400.00
- Oola 400.00
- Probe droid 460.00
- Sandtrooper sergeant [482-54] 475.00
- Sandtrooper squad leader 475.00
- Yoda, bronze, Fan Club excl., 250 prod. [v1e1:402]... 1,150.00

Bowen Designs Inc.
Bronze statues on granite bases. Limited to 100 pieces.
- Darth Vader 14.5" tall [482-55] 3,000.00

Bronze statues on granite bases. Limited to 50 pieces.
- Boba Fett 13.5" tall [482-56] 3,400.00
- Chewbacca 19.5" tall [482-57] 3,000.00
- The Rancor 15" tall [482-58] 3,000.00

Code 3 Collectibles
3D movie poster art.
- 10-year anniversary, Star Wars 80.00
- Empire Strikes Back 80.00
- Empire Strikes Back, excl. to Celebration III [482-59] 100.00
- Return of the Jedi 80.00
- Star Wars [482-60] 80.00

Compulsion Gallery
- Boba Fett [482-61] 750.00
- C-3PO [482-62] 700.00
- Darth Vader [482-63] 750.00
- R2-D2 [482-64] 700.00

Disney / MGM
- Boba Fett metal 3D [482-65] 65.00
- Darth Goofy, 600 produced, individually numbered ..175.00
- Jedi Mickey, Big Fig [482-66] 165.00
- Princess Minnie, 600 produced, numbered [482-67] 175.00
- Stormtrooper Donald, 600 produced, numbered 175.00
- X-Wing pilot Mickey, 600 prod., numbered [482-68]...175.00

Disney Theme Park Merchandise
Big Figs 2011. Include matching pin.
- Donald as Darth Maul [482-69] 95.00
- Donald as Stormtrooper [482-70] 95.00
- Goofy as Darth Vader [482-71] 95.00
- Mickey as Luke Skywalker, pilot [482-72] 95.00
- Minnie as Princess Leia [482-73] 95.00

Enesco LLC
- Stitch as Yoda, 3,000 produced [482-74] 100.00

Statues and Busts

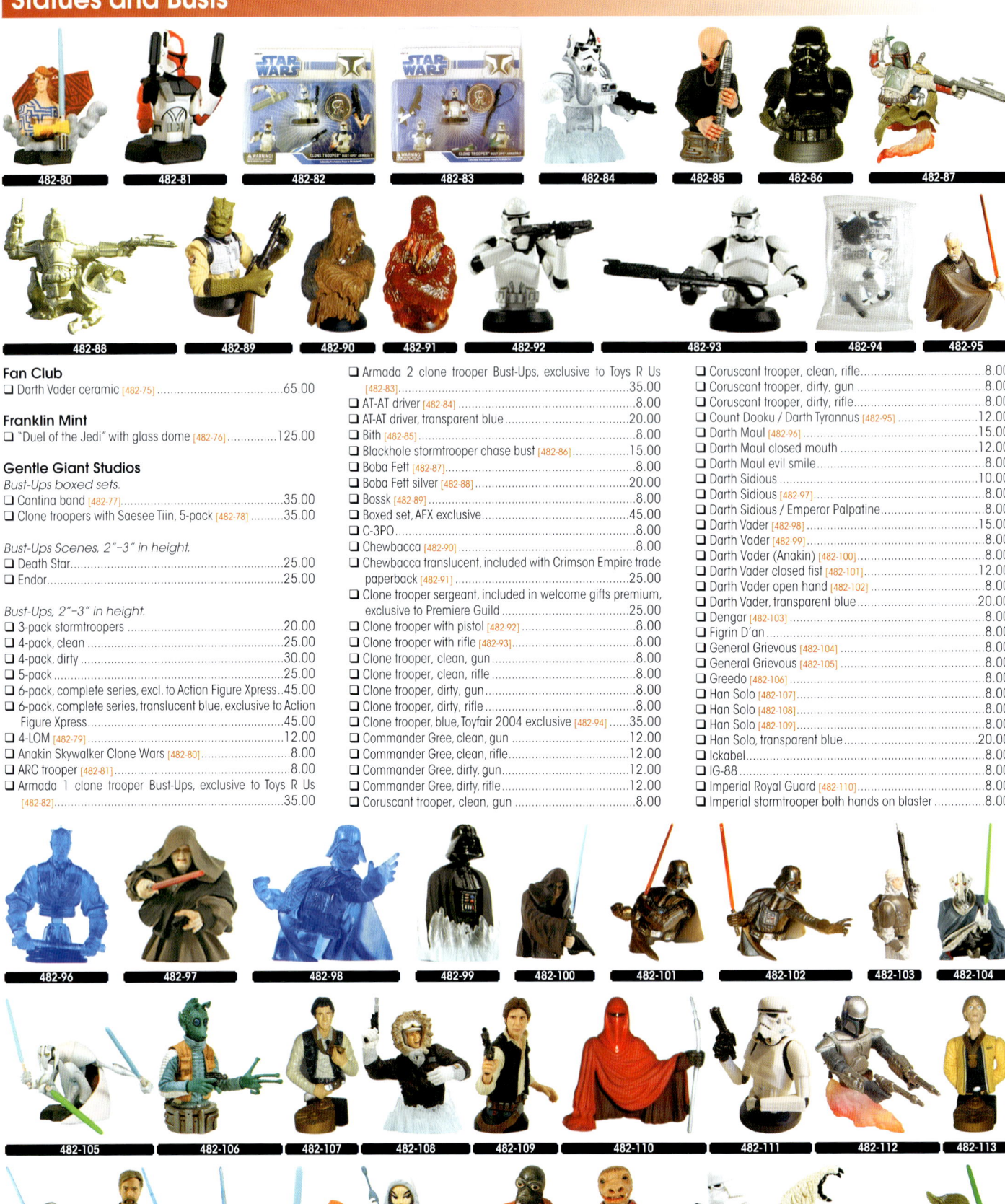

Fan Club
☐ Darth Vader ceramic [482-75] 65.00

Franklin Mint
☐ "Duel of the Jedi" with glass dome [482-76] 125.00

Gentle Giant Studios
Bust-Ups boxed sets.
☐ Cantina band [482-77] 35.00
☐ Clone troopers with Saesee Tiin, 5-pack [482-78] 35.00

Bust-Ups Scenes, 2"–3" in height.
☐ Death Star 25.00
☐ Endor 25.00

Bust-Ups, 2"–3" in height.
☐ 3-pack stormtroopers 20.00
☐ 4-pack, clean 25.00
☐ 4-pack, dirty 30.00
☐ 5-pack 25.00
☐ 6-pack, complete series, excl. to Action Figure Xpress.. 45.00
☐ 6-pack, complete series, translucent blue, exclusive to Action Figure Xpress 45.00
☐ 4-LOM [482-79] 12.00
☐ Anakin Skywalker Clone Wars [482-80] 8.00
☐ ARC trooper [482-81] 8.00
☐ Armada 1 clone trooper Bust-Ups, exclusive to Toys R Us [482-82] 35.00
☐ Armada 2 clone trooper Bust-Ups, exclusive to Toys R Us [482-83] 35.00
☐ AT-AT driver [482-84] 8.00
☐ AT-AT driver, transparent blue 20.00
☐ Bith [482-85] 8.00
☐ Blackhole stormtrooper chase bust [482-86] 15.00
☐ Boba Fett [482-87] 8.00
☐ Boba Fett silver [482-88] 20.00
☐ Bossk [482-89] 8.00
☐ Boxed set, AFX exclusive 45.00
☐ C-3PO 8.00
☐ Chewbacca [482-90] 8.00
☐ Chewbacca translucent, included with Crimson Empire trade paperback [482-91] 25.00
☐ Clone trooper sergeant, included in welcome gifts premium, exclusive to Premiere Guild 25.00
☐ Clone trooper with pistol [482-92] 8.00
☐ Clone trooper with rifle [482-93] 8.00
☐ Clone trooper, clean, gun 8.00
☐ Clone trooper, clean, rifle 8.00
☐ Clone trooper, dirty, gun 8.00
☐ Clone trooper, dirty, rifle 8.00
☐ Clone trooper, blue, Toyfair 2004 exclusive [482-94] 35.00
☐ Commander Gree, clean, gun 12.00
☐ Commander Gree, clean, rifle 12.00
☐ Commander Gree, dirty, gun 12.00
☐ Commander Gree, dirty, rifle 12.00
☐ Coruscant trooper, clean, gun 8.00
☐ Coruscant trooper, clean, rifle 8.00
☐ Coruscant trooper, dirty, gun 8.00
☐ Coruscant trooper, dirty, rifle 8.00
☐ Count Dooku / Darth Tyrannus [482-95] 12.00
☐ Darth Maul [482-96] 15.00
☐ Darth Maul closed mouth 12.00
☐ Darth Maul evil smile 8.00
☐ Darth Sidious 10.00
☐ Darth Sidious [482-97] 8.00
☐ Darth Sidious / Emperor Palpatine 8.00
☐ Darth Vader [482-98] 15.00
☐ Darth Vader [482-99] 8.00
☐ Darth Vader (Anakin) [482-100] 8.00
☐ Darth Vader closed fist [482-101] 12.00
☐ Darth Vader open hand [482-102] 8.00
☐ Darth Vader, transparent blue 20.00
☐ Dengar [482-103] 8.00
☐ Figrin D'an 8.00
☐ General Grievous [482-104] 8.00
☐ General Grievous [482-105] 8.00
☐ Greedo [482-106] 8.00
☐ Han Solo [482-107] 8.00
☐ Han Solo [482-108] 8.00
☐ Han Solo [482-109] 8.00
☐ Han Solo, transparent blue 20.00
☐ Ickabel 8.00
☐ IG-88 .... 8.00
☐ Imperial Royal Guard [482-110] 8.00
☐ Imperial stormtrooper both hands on blaster 8.00

436

Statues and Busts

- ☐ Imperial stormtrooper one hand on blaster [482-111] 8.00
- ☐ Imperial stormtrooper with heavy blaster rifle...............8.00
- ☐ Jango Fett [482-112].................8.00
- ☐ Luke Skywalker [482-113]..........8.00
- ☐ Luke Skywalker [482-114]..........8.00
- ☐ Luke Skywalker, transparent blue 20.00
- ☐ Nalan 8.00
- ☐ Obi-Wan [482-115]..........8.00
- ☐ Obi-Wan Kenobi [482-116]........8.00
- ☐ Obi-Wan Kenobi [482-117]........8.00
- ☐ Obi-Wan Kenobi spirit 25.00
- ☐ Padmé Amidala [482-118].........8.00
- ☐ Ponda Baba [482-119].............8.00
- ☐ Princess Leia, blaster up 15.00
- ☐ Princess Leia, pointing blaster 8.00
- ☐ Snaggletooth, blue 32.00
- ☐ Snaggletooth, red [482-120] 8.00
- ☐ Snowtrooper [482-121] 8.00
- ☐ Snowtrooper, transparent blue 10.00
- ☐ Spirit of the Rebellion, set of 4, summer convention exclusives, clear, 5,000 produced [v1e1:403] 45.00
- ☐ Spirit of the Rebellion, set of 4, summer convention exclusives, glow-in-the-dark, 500 produced [v1e1:403] ..75.00
- ☐ Stormtrooper army builder set 15.00
- ☐ Stormtrooper, long rifle..........8.00
- ☐ Tactical ops 501st trooper, clean, gun 8.00
- ☐ Tactical ops 501st trooper, clean, rifle 8.00
- ☐ Tactical ops 501st trooper, dirty, gun 8.00
- ☐ Tactical ops 501st trooper, dirty, rifle 8.00
- ☐ Tech 8.00
- ☐ Tedn 8.00
- ☐ Utapau trooper, clean, gun 8.00
- ☐ Utapau trooper, clean, rifle 8.00
- ☐ Utapau trooper, dirty, gun 8.00
- ☐ Utapau trooper, dirty, rifle 8.00
- ☐ Wampa [482-122] 8.00
- ☐ Wampa, transparent blue 20.00
- ☐ Yoda [482-123] 8.00
- ☐ Yoda [482-124] 8.00
- ☐ Yoda [482-125] 8.00
- ☐ Yoda clear, 5,000 produced [v1e1:403] 10.00
- ☐ Zuckuss [482-126] 8.00

Bust-Ups, 2"–3" in height. Convention exclusives.
- ☐ 2-pack Luke Skywalker and Han Solo in stormtrooper disguise [482-127] 25.00
- ☐ Darth Vader standing in flames [482-128] 35.00
- ☐ Jango Fett silver, exclusive to Comic-Con [482-129].......20.00

Busts 1:1.
- ☐ Bossk [482-130] 500.00
- ☐ Darth Maul 700.00
- ☐ Greedo 600.00

Busts.
- ☐ Darth Vader, pink for breast cancer awareness, exclusive to Comic-Con [v1e1:404] 75.00

Classics busts 2007–2009.
- ☐ 3-pack Royal Guard x 2, Senate Guard 150.00
- ☐ AT-AT driver [482-131]..........40.00
- ☐ Boba Fett [482-132]................40.00
- ☐ Boba Fett bronze, 50 produced, individually numbered, exclusive to Forbidden Planet, London [482-133] 100.00
- ☐ Jar Jar Binks [482-134] 40.00
- ☐ Kit Fisto [482-135] 40.00
- ☐ Lieutenant clone trooper, 3,000 produced, individually numbered, exclusive to Premiere Guild 65.00
- ☐ Momaw Nadon, 500 produced, numbered [482-136] 40.00
- ☐ Obi-Wan Kenobi (Episode III) [482-137] 40.00
- ☐ Queen Amidala, 500 produced, numbered [482-138].....40.00
- ☐ Snowtrooper, 500 produced, numbered [482-139] 40.00
- ☐ TIE Fighter pilot [482-140] 40.00

Kustomz. Rotocast vinyl with certificate of authenticity.
- ☐ Darth Vader on Imperial Star Destroyer 85.00
- ☐ Jawas in sandcrawler [482-141] 85.00
- ☐ Scout trooper on speeder bike [482-142] 85.00
- ☐ Speederbike, holiday with blue snowflake decor... 1,200.00
- ☐ TIE pilot with TIE Fighter [482-143]........85.00
- ☐ TIE pilot with TIE Fighter, red, exclusive to Star Wars Celebration Japan [482-144] 95.00

Life-sized character statues. Clone Wars.
- ☐ Captain Rex 1,500.00
- ☐ R2-D2 ....1,200.00
- ☐ Yoda [482-145] 850.00

Statues and Busts

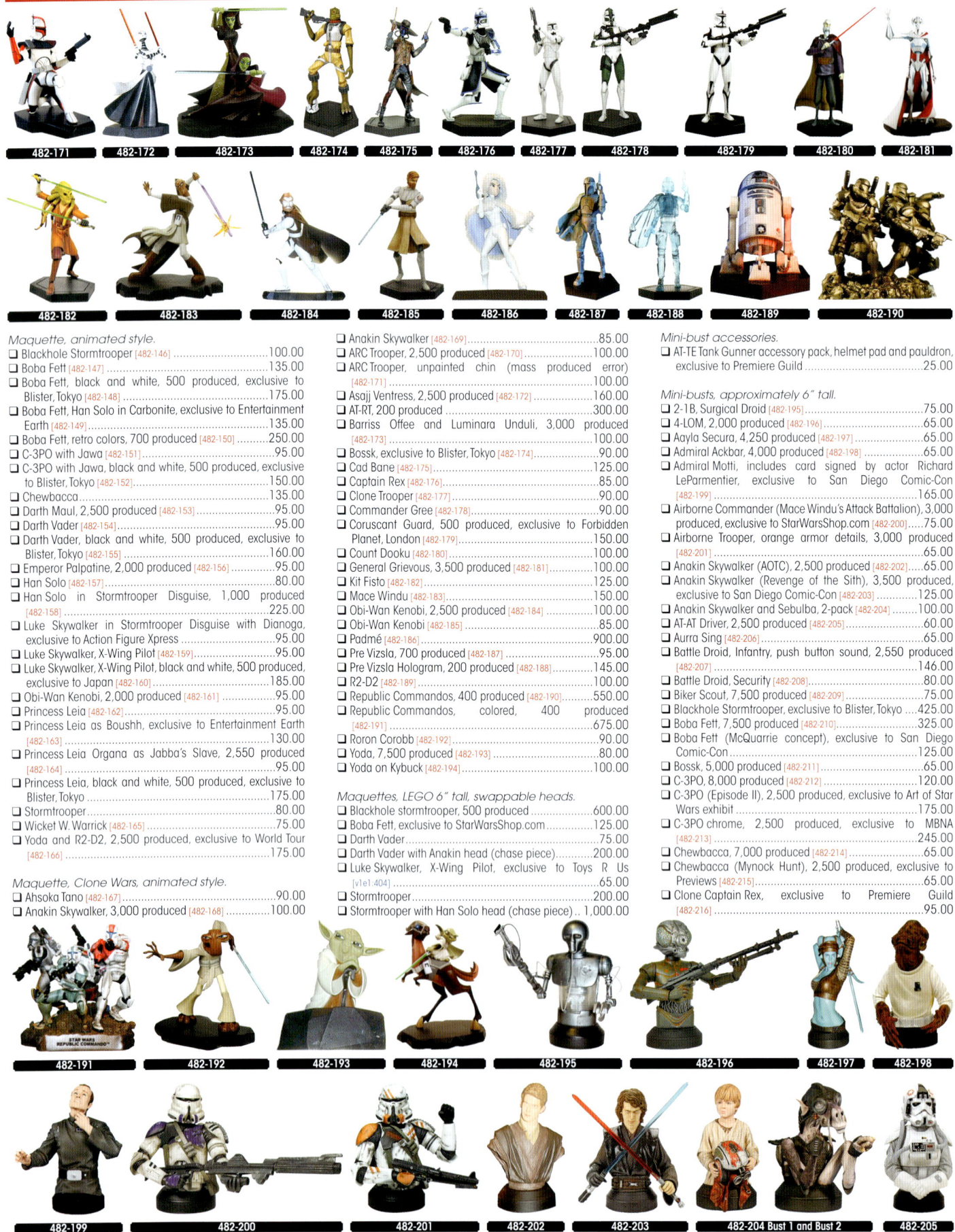

Maquette, animated style.
- Blackhole Stormtrooper [482-146] 100.00
- Boba Fett [482-147] 135.00
- Boba Fett, black and white, 500 produced, exclusive to Blister, Tokyo [482-148] 175.00
- Boba Fett, Han Solo in Carbonite, exclusive to Entertainment Earth [482-149] 135.00
- Boba Fett, retro colors, 700 produced [482-150] 250.00
- C-3PO with Jawa 95.00
- C-3PO with Jawa, black and white, 500 produced, exclusive to Blister, Tokyo [482-152] 150.00
- Chewbacca 135.00
- Darth Maul, 2,500 produced [482-153] 95.00
- Darth Vader [482-154] 95.00
- Darth Vader, black and white, 500 produced, exclusive to Blister, Tokyo [482-155] 160.00
- Emperor Palpatine, 2,000 produced [482-156] 95.00
- Han Solo [482-157] 80.00
- Han Solo in Stormtrooper Disguise, 1,000 produced [482-158] 225.00
- Luke Skywalker in Stormtrooper Disguise with Dianoga, exclusive to Action Figure Xpress 95.00
- Luke Skywalker, X-Wing Pilot [482-159] 95.00
- Luke Skywalker, X-Wing Pilot, black and white, 500 produced, exclusive to Japan [482-160] 185.00
- Obi-Wan Kenobi, 2,000 produced [482-161] 95.00
- Princess Leia [482-162] 95.00
- Princess Leia as Boushh, exclusive to Entertainment Earth [482-163] 130.00
- Princess Leia Organa as Jabba's Slave, 2,550 produced [482-164] 95.00
- Princess Leia, black and white, 500 produced, exclusive to Blister, Tokyo 175.00
- Stormtrooper 80.00
- Wicket W. Warrick [482-165] 75.00
- Yoda and R2-D2, 2,500 produced, exclusive to World Tour [482-166] 175.00

Maquette, Clone Wars, animated style.
- Ahsoka Tano [482-167] 90.00
- Anakin Skywalker, 3,000 produced [482-168] 100.00
- Anakin Skywalker [482-169] 85.00
- ARC Trooper, 2,500 produced [482-170] 100.00
- ARC Trooper, unpainted chin (mass produced error) [482-171] 100.00
- Asajj Ventress, 2,500 produced [482-172] 160.00
- AT-RT, 200 produced 300.00
- Barriss Offee and Luminara Unduli, 3,000 produced [482-173] 100.00
- Bossk, exclusive to Blister, Tokyo [482-174] 90.00
- Cad Bane [482-175] 125.00
- Captain Rex [482-176] 85.00
- Clone Trooper [482-177] 90.00
- Commander Gree [482-178] 90.00
- Coruscant Guard, 500 produced, exclusive to Forbidden Planet, London [482-179] 150.00
- Count Dooku [482-180] 100.00
- General Grievous, 3,500 produced [482-181] 100.00
- Kit Fisto [482-182] 125.00
- Mace Windu [482-183] 150.00
- Obi-Wan Kenobi, 2,500 produced [482-184] 100.00
- Obi-Wan Kenobi [482-185] 85.00
- Padmé [482-186] 900.00
- Pre Vizsla, 700 produced [482-187] 95.00
- Pre Vizsla Hologram, 200 produced [482-188] 145.00
- R2-D2 [482-189] 100.00
- Republic Commandos, 400 produced [482-190] 550.00
- Republic Commandos, colored, 400 produced [482-191] 675.00
- Roron Corobb [482-192] 90.00
- Yoda, 7,500 produced [482-193] 80.00
- Yoda on Kybuck [482-194] 100.00

Maquettes, LEGO 6" tall, swappable heads.
- Blackhole stormtrooper, 500 produced 600.00
- Boba Fett, exclusive to StarWarsShop.com 125.00
- Darth Vader 75.00
- Darth Vader with Anakin head (chase piece) 200.00
- Luke Skywalker, X-Wing Pilot, exclusive to Toys R Us [v1e1:404] 65.00
- Stormtrooper 200.00
- Stormtrooper with Han Solo head (chase piece) 1,000.00

Mini-bust accessories.
- AT-TE Tank Gunner accessory pack, helmet pad and pauldron, exclusive to Premiere Guild 25.00

Mini-busts, approximately 6" tall.
- 2-1B, Surgical Droid [482-195] 75.00
- 4-LOM, 2,000 produced [482-196] 65.00
- Aayla Secura, 4,250 produced [482-197] 65.00
- Admiral Ackbar, 4,000 produced [482-198] 65.00
- Admiral Motti, includes card signed by actor Richard LeParmentier, exclusive to San Diego Comic-Con [482-199] 165.00
- Airborne Commander (Mace Windu's Attack Battalion), 3,000 produced, exclusive to StarWarsShop.com [482-200] 75.00
- Airborne Trooper, orange armor details, 3,000 produced [482-201] 65.00
- Anakin Skywalker (AOTC), 2,500 produced [482-202] 65.00
- Anakin Skywalker (Revenge of the Sith), 3,500 produced, exclusive to San Diego Comic-Con [482-203] 125.00
- Anakin Skywalker and Sebulba, 2-pack [482-204] 100.00
- AT-AT Driver, 2,500 produced [482-205] 60.00
- Aurra Sing [482-206] 65.00
- Battle Droid, Infantry, push button sound, 2,550 produced [482-207] 146.00
- Battle Droid, Security [482-208] 80.00
- Biker Scout, 7,500 produced [482-209] 75.00
- Blackhole Stormtrooper, exclusive to Blister, Tokyo 425.00
- Boba Fett, 7,500 produced [482-210] 325.00
- Boba Fett (McQuarrie concept), exclusive to San Diego Comic-Con 125.00
- Bossk, 5,000 produced [482-211] 65.00
- C-3PO, 8,000 produced [482-212] 120.00
- C-3PO (Episode II), 2,500 produced, exclusive to Art of Star Wars exhibit 175.00
- C-3PO chrome, 2,500 produced, exclusive to MBNA [482-213] 245.00
- Chewbacca, 7,000 produced [482-214] 65.00
- Chewbacca (Mynock Hunt), 2,500 produced, exclusive to Previews [482-215] 65.00
- Clone Captain Rex, exclusive to Premiere Guild [482-216] 95.00

Statues and Busts

- ☐ Clone Trooper (AOTC), 7,500 produced [482-217] 65.00
- ☐ Clone Trooper (Revenge of the Sith), 15,000 produced [482-218] 65.00
- ☐ Clone Trooper 501st Special Ops 65.00
- ☐ Clone Trooper Captain (red), 7,500 produced [482-219] ... 85.00
- ☐ Clone Trooper Commander (yellow), 7,500 produced [482-220] 85.00
- ☐ Clone Trooper Coruscant, deluxe with interchangeable Jango and clone heads, 2,500 produced, exclusive to Action Figure Xpress [482-221] 75.00
- ☐ Clone Trooper Elite Corps, exclusive to Premiere Guild [482-222] 85.00
- ☐ Clone Trooper Lieutenant (blue), exclusive to San Diego Comic-Con International and WizardWorld Chicago [482-223] 450.00
- ☐ Clone Trooper Pilot, 2,500 produced, exclusive to Wizard World LA [482-224] 225.00
- ☐ Clone Trooper Sergeant (green), 2,500 produced [482-225] 180.00
- ☐ Clone Trooper Shock Trooper with shock trooper microbust, 3,500 produced, exclusive to San Diego Comic-Con .. 175.00
- ☐ Clone Trooper Utapau 65.00
- ☐ Commander Baraca, 2,000 produced [482-226] 145.00
- ☐ Commander Bly, 2,000 produced, exclusive to Forbidden Planet, London [482-227] 225.00
- ☐ Commander Bly (Clone Wars), exclusive to Action Figure Xpress [482-228] 50.00
- ☐ Commander Cody, 3,500 produced [482-229] 150.00
- ☐ Commander Cody, Holiday, wearing a scarf and holding a light-up snowman hologram 180.00
- ☐ Commander Fox, excl. to Premiere Guild [482-230] 155.00
- ☐ Commander Gree, 2,500 produced, exclusive to Star Wars Celebration IV [482-231] 165.00
- ☐ Commander Neyo, exclusive to Blister, Tokyo 225.00
- ☐ Count Dooku, 2,500 produced [482-232] 65.00
- ☐ Darth Malak, 2,000 produced [482-233] 125.00
- ☐ Darth Maul, 10,000 produced [482-234] 50.00
- ☐ Darth Maul (The Phantom Menace), exclusive to Premiere Guild [482-235] 150.00
- ☐ Darth Maul holographic, 2,500 produced 95.00
- ☐ Darth Nihilus, exclusive to PBM Express [482-236] 75.00
- ☐ Darth Revan, 3,850 produced [482-237] 85.00
- ☐ Darth Talon, 3,850 produced [482-238] 65.00
- ☐ Darth Vader, 3,500 produced [482-239] 200.00
- ☐ Darth Vader (Thank The Maker), Holiday, includes interchangeable hands and "Thank The Maker" mini-comic reprint. Holds C-3PO's head or a dove, recreating a Lucasfilm holiday card, exclusive to Premiere Guild [482-240] 250.00
- ☐ Darth Vader Revealed, 5,000 produced, exclusive to Entertainment Earth 65.00
- ☐ Darth Vader Revenge of the Sith, 20,000 produced [482-241] 90.00
- ☐ Darth Vader smoked, 4,000 produced, exclusive to MBNA 160.00
- ☐ Darth Vader, McQuarrie, 2,500 produced, exclusive to San Diego Comic-Con [482-242] 85.00
- ☐ Darth Vader, The Force Unleashed [482-243] 75.00
- ☐ Death Trooper, 2,500 produced [482-244] 80.00
- ☐ Death Trooper deluxe, removable armor parts and interchangeable arms, exclusive to Gentle Giant website [482-245] 100.00
- ☐ Dengar, 4,000 produced [482-246] 65.00
- ☐ Emperor Palpatine (Return of the Jedi) [482-247] 100.00
- ☐ Emperor Palpatine (Revenge of the Sith), 4,500 produced [482-248] 65.00
- ☐ Figrin D'an [482-249] 60.00
- ☐ Galactic Marine, exclusive to Forbidden Planet, London [482-250] 150.00
- ☐ Gamorrean Guard, 4,000 produced [482-251] 65.00
- ☐ Garindan [482-252] 65.00
- ☐ General Grievous, 7,000 produced [482-253] 65.00
- ☐ Grand Moff Tarkin, 6,000 produced [482-254] 65.00
- ☐ Greedo, 7,500 produced [482-255] 65.00
- ☐ Hammerhead [482-256] 75.00
- ☐ Han Solo, 8,000 produced [482-257] 65.00
- ☐ Han Solo, Hoth (blue coat), 650 produced, exclusive to Premiere Guild 95.00
- ☐ Han Solo, Hoth (brown coat), 2,200 produced 65.00
- ☐ Han Solo, stormtrooper disguise [482-258] 50.00
- ☐ IG-88, 5,000 produced [482-259] 50.00
- ☐ Imperial Gunner, exclusive to Action Figure Xpress [482-260] 100.00
- ☐ Imperial Storm Commando, exclusive to Premiere Guild [482-261] 100.00
- ☐ Jango Fett, 2,500 produced [482-262] 100.00
- ☐ Jango Fett, interchangeable heads, 9,000 produced [482-263] 65.00
- ☐ Jango Fett chromed, 5,000 produced, exclusive to MBNA [482-264] 225.00
- ☐ Jar Jar Binks and W. Wald, 2-pack, Holiday, 600 produced, exclusive to Premiere Guild [482-265] 150.00
- ☐ Jawa 2-pack, one with gun and one repairing R5-D4 head, 7,000 produced [482-266] 65.00
- ☐ Kit Fisto [482-267] 65.00
- ☐ Lando Calrissian (Empire Strikes Back) [482-268] 50.00
- ☐ Lando Calrissian in Skiff Guard Disguise, 4,000 produced [482-269] 65.00
- ☐ Lieutenant Renz, 2,500 produced, exclusive to RebelScum.com [482-270] 30.00
- ☐ Logray (Ewok Medicine Man) [482-271] 175.00
- ☐ Luke Skywalker, Hoth [482-272] 65.00
- ☐ Luke Skywalker, Jedi, 6,500 produced [482-273] 65.00
- ☐ Luke Skywalker, Stormtrooper Disguise, 3,500 produced [482-274] 175.00
- ☐ Luke Skywalker, Tatooine with lightsaber, 2,200 prod ... 60.00
- ☐ Luke Skywalker, Tatooine with T-16 Skyhopper model, 550 produced, exclusive to Premiere Guild [482-275] 125.00
- ☐ Luke Skywalker, X-Wing Pilot, 7,500 produced [482-276] 35.00
- ☐ Mace Windu, 2,500 produced [482-277] 80.00
- ☐ Mara Jade, 2,000 produced, exclusive to GenCon [482-278] 150.00
- ☐ Muftak and Kabe, 2-pack [482-279] 95.00
- ☐ Nien Nunb, 900 produced [482-280] 75.00
- ☐ Obi-Wan Kenobi, A New Hope, 6,000 prod. [482-281] .. 65.00
- ☐ Obi-Wan Kenobi, AOTC, 2,500 produced [482-282] 65.00
- ☐ Obi-Wan Kenobi (Revenge of the Sith), exclusive to Entertainment Earth [482-283] 100.00
- ☐ Obi-Wan Kenobi, Clone Trooper Armor, 5,000 produced [482-284] 65.00

Statues and Busts

- Obi-Wan Kenobi, Spirit of, light-up features, 2,000 produced, exclusive to Wizard Entertainment 65.00
- Oola, 2,700 produced [482-285] 65.00
- Padmé Amidala (AOTC), 2,500 produced [482-286] 65.00
- Padmé Amidala, Snow Bunny, holiday, 800 produced, exclusive to Premiere Guild [482-287] 175.00
- Plo Koon, 4,500 produced [482-288] 65.00
- Princess Leia, A New Hope, 6,000 produced [482-289] .. 65.00
- Princess Leia Organa (Mynock Hunt), 2,000 produced, exclusive to Previews [482-290] 75.00
- Princess Leia Organa in Hoth Fatigues [482-291] 65.00
- Princess Leia Organa, Jabba's Slave, 4,200 produced [482-292] 115.00
- Princess Leia, Boushh Disguise, 5,000 produced [482-293] 50.00
- Qui-Gon Jinn, 5,000 produced [482-294] 65.00
- Qui-Gon Jinn, Holographic, light-up features, exclusive to Star Wars Celebration Japan 135.00
- Rebel Fleet Trooper, 700 produced [482-295] 100.00
- Ree Yees [482-296] 90.00
- Republic Commando, light-up visor, 950 produced, exclusive to Premiere Guild [482-297] 95.00
- Republic Commando Boss, 200 of the numbered busts were sold as boxed sets of four commandos [482-298] 95.00
- Republic Commando Fixer, 200 of the numbered busts were sold as boxed sets of four commandos [482-299] 95.00
- Republic Commando Scorch, 200 of the numbered busts were sold as boxed sets of commandos [482-300] 95.00
- Republic Commando Sev, 200 of the numbered busts were sold as boxed sets of four commandos [482-301] 95.00
- Royal Guard, 6,667 produced [482-302] 65.00
- Salacious Crumb (with C-3PO head), 2,500 produced [482-303] 135.00
- Salacious Crumb, holiday, Santa hat and lights, 200 produced [482-304] 1,200.00
- Sandtrooper chromed, 200 produced [482-305] 1,375.00
- Sandtrooper Corporal (black pauldron), 2,500 produced, exclusive to Star Wars Celebration III 245.00
- Sandtrooper Sergeant (white pauldron), 15,000 produced 50.00
- Sandtrooper Squad Leader (orange pauldron), 15,000 produced [482-306] 35.00
- Senate Guard, 3,333 produced [482-307] 65.00
- Shaak Ti, 5,000 produced [482-308] 65.00
- Shadow Guard, 750 produced, exclusive to Premiere Guild [482-309] 150.00
- Shae Vizla, 2,500 produced [482-310] 75.00
- Snowtrooper, 2,600 produced [482-311] 65.00
- Snowtrooper, McQuarrie, exclusive to San Diego Comic-Con and Entertainment Earth [482-312] 90.00
- Starkiller, 2-pack, Galen Marek: Ultimate Good and Ultimate Evil Apprentice, exclusive to Action Figure Xpress [482-313] 175.00
- Stormtrooper, 10,000 produced [482-314] 100.00
- Stormtrooper (McQuarrie) deluxe, exclusive to San Diego Comic-Con [482-315] 150.00
- Stormtrooper chromed, 2,500 produced [482-316] 150.00
- Stormtrooper Commander, 2,500 produced, exclusive to StarWarsShop.com [482-317] 75.00
- Tedn Dahai Cantina Band [482-318] 65.00
- TIE Pilot, 3,500 produced [482-319] 55.00
- TIE Pilot, Black 3 with silver "Ace" stripes, packed 1:6 with basic Black 3 busts, 700 produced 100.00
- Tusken Raider, interchangeable arms allow for rifle or Gaffi stick poses, 5,000 produced [482-320] 65.00
- Watto [482-321] 70.00
- Wicket W. Warrick [482-322] 115.00
- Yak Face, Holiday, 800 produced, exclusive to Premiere Guild [482-323] 225.00
- Yoda (Empire Strikes Back), 15,000 produced [482-324] 65.00
- Yoda with lightsaber, 2,500 produced [482-325] 350.00
- Yoda, 3D Glasses, commemorates Episode I in 3D [482-326] 120.00
- Yoda, Spirit of with light-up features, 2,500 produced, exclusive to Convention 70.00
- Zam Wesell, 2,500 produced [482-327] 65.00
- Zuckuss, 5,000 produced [482-328] 65.00

Statues.
- Asajj Ventress and Count Dooku 250.00
- Bantha and Tusken Raider 275.00
- Bib Fortuna, mail-in premium, free with coupons from Jabba and Max Rebo statues [482-329] 375.00
- Boba Fett, 6,500 produced 200.00
- Boba Fett with Han Solo in Carbonite [482-330] 265.00
- C-3PO, 3,000 produced 185.00
- Chewbacca, collector club excl., 3,000 produced 180.00
- Darth Maul with Bloodfin, 2250 produced 225.00
- Darth Maul, international edition, 2,000 produced ... 175.00

Statues and Busts

482-285 · 482-286 · 482-287 · 482-288 · 482-289 · 482-290 · 482-291 · 482-292 · 482-293

482-294 · 482-295 · 482-296 · 482-297 · 482-298 · 482-299 · 482-300 · 482-301

- ❏ Darth Maul, US edition, 3,000 produced 175.00
- ❏ Darth Vader chrome, 2,500 produced, exclusive to Blister, Tokyo 450.00
- ❏ Darth Vader Kneeling, from Empire Strikes Back 200.00
- ❏ Darth Vader, 14", 7,500 produced 285.00
- ❏ Darth Vader, 15" chrome with light-up lightsaber, 2,500 produced 450.00
- ❏ Death Trooper 250.00
- ❏ Han Solo, 2,000 produced 195.00
- ❏ Han Solo on Tauntaun, 3,000 produced [482-331] 195.00
- ❏ Jabba the Hutt, 2,500 produced 395.00
- ❏ Luke and Tauntaun, 4,000 produced 185.00
- ❏ Luke Skywalker, Bespin 165.00
- ❏ Max Rebo Band, 2,500 produced [482-332] 200.00
- ❏ Obi-Wan Kenobi, Clone Wars 300.00
- ❏ Princess Leia as Jabba's prisoner, accessory pack with Leia, Jabba's arms, Hookah pipe, pillow, base 75.00
- ❏ Princess Leia as Jabba's Slave, 5,500 produced [482-333] 180.00
- ❏ Rancor, 2,000 produced 300.00
- ❏ Royal Guard [482-334] 185.00
- ❏ Sandtrooper and Dewback [482-335] 280.00
- ❏ Scout Trooper on Speeder Bike, 5,000 produced 200.00
- ❏ Senate Guard [482-336] 195.00
- ❏ Stormtrooper [482-337] 185.00
- ❏ Wampa, approximately 11" 165.00
- ❏ Yoda (Clone Wars), approximately 2' 575.00
- ❏ Yoda, Empire Strikes Back, 2,000 produced 150.00

VIP holiday exclusives.
- ❏ 2006 Max Rebo, musical with Santa hat and lights, 200 produced 1200.00

Gentle Giant Studios (Japan)
Bust-Ups, 2"–3" in height.
- ❏ 4-LOM 8.00
- ❏ Boba Fett 8.00
- ❏ Boba Fett silver 8.00
- ❏ Bossk 8.00
- ❏ Dengar 8.00
- ❏ Jango Fett 8.00
- ❏ Zuckuss 8.00

Hasbro
Cinemascape.
- ❏ Darth Vader, Revenge of the Sith [482-338] 150.00

Illusive Originals
- ❏ Admiral Ackbar, bust maquette, 10,000 produced [482-339] 95.00
- ❏ Boba Fett bust maquette, 10,000 produced [482-340] . 180.00
- ❏ Chewbacca maquette, 7,500 produced 125.00
- ❏ Darth Vader Reveals Anakin Skywalker maquette, 9,500 produced [482-341] 850.00
- ❏ Jabba the Hutt maquette, 5,000 produced [v1e1:406] .. 275.00
- ❏ Rancor maquette, 9,500 produced [482-342] 540.00
- ❏ Yoda maquette, 9,500 produced [482-343] 775.00

Kenner
Cinemacast.
- ❏ Darth Vader, 10,000 produced [482-344] 150.00
- ❏ Luke and Leia, movie poster pose [482-345] 150.00
- ❏ Luke and Leia, pewter, movie poster pose [482-346] 250.00

Kilian Enterprises
- ❏ Yoda, ESB 10th anniversary, 50 produced [3:385] .... OSPV

Legends in 3-Dimensions
- ❏ Gamorrean Guard, 14" tall, 3,000 produced [482-347] .. 155.00

9 inch tall busts, limited edition with certificate of authenticity.
- ❏ Boba Fett, 5,000 produced [482-348] 160.00
- ❏ Cantina Band Member, 2,500 produced [482-349] 125.00
- ❏ Emperor Palpatine, 2,500 produced [482-350] 65.00
- ❏ Greedo, 2,500 produced [482-351] 65.00
- ❏ Tusken Raider, 2,500 produced [482-352] 170.00

Lucasfilm
- ❏ Chewbacca, 2005 gift [v1e1:407] .... OSPV

Master Replicas
- ❏ C-3PO 149.00

Peltz Productions
- ❏ King Crab, X-Wing uniform, 500 produced 45.00

482-302 · 482-303 · 482-304 · 482-305 · 482-306 · 482-307 · 482-308 · 482-309

482-310 · 482-311 · 482-312 · 482-313 · 482-314 · 482-315 · 482-316 · 482-317 · 482-318 · 482-319

482-320 · 482-321 · 482-322 · 482-323 · 482-324 · 482-325 · 482-326 · 482-327 · 482-328 · 482-329

Statues and Busts

Pepsi Cola
- Ewok, 3,500 produced 735.00

Life-sized character statues.
- Anakin Skywalker 2300.00
- Darth Maul [v1e1:407] 2300.00
- Jar Jar Binks [v1e1:407] 2300.00
- Watto [v1e1:407] 875.00
- Yoda [482-353] 1400.00

Pepsi Cola (Japan)
Sound Big Cap sets.
- 1: Luke Skywalker and Darth Vader 45.00
- 2: Han Solo and Chewbacca 45.00
- 3: Princess Leia and stormtrooper 45.00
- 4: C-3PO and R2-D2 .... 45.00
- 5: Anakin Skywalker and Queen Amidala 45.00
- 6: Yoda and Emperor Palpatine 45.00
- 7: Obi-Wan Kenobi and General Grievous 45.00

Reds, Inc.
- Darth Vader 3', pre-painted [482-354] 830.00

Royal Tara
- Luke Skywalker, autographed C.O.A. [482-355] 350.00
- Obi-Wan Kenobi with crystal lightsaber [482-356] 500.00

Rubies
- Clone trooper helmet with base, 7,500 produced [482-357] 1,300.00
- Darth Vader helmet with base, 5,000 produced ... 1,300.00
- Jango Fett helmet with base, 5,000 produced 1,300.00
- Yoda bust, 5,000 produced [482-358] 1,300.00
- Yoda, Episode II life sized [482-359] 750.00

San Diego Padres
- Darth Vader Thunder, Pepsi sponsored, given out by the Lake Elsinore Storm (San Diego Padres affiliate) on May 19, 2005 .... 80.00

Sideshow Collectibles
Busts, 1:1 scale.
- Admiral Ackbar, 300 produced 500.00
- C-3PO 700.00
- Darth Maul 700.00
- General Grievous [482-360] 750.00
- Greedo, 300 produced [482-361] 650.00
- Yoda 600.00

Dioramas.
- Ambush on Hoth, 750 produced 425.00
- Anakin vs. Asajj 300.00
- Anakin vs. Asajj with switch-out alternate head for Asajj, 275 produced 350.00
- Diplomatic Mission 350.00
- Duel of the Fates [482-362] 300.00
- Duel of the Fates, faux bronze, 75 produced 450.00
- Look Sir—Droids 130.00
- Luke vs. Rancor, 400 produced [482-363] 250.00

442

Stickers

- ❏ Obi-Wan vs. Anakin, 1:9 scale, over 13 inches tall 300.00
- ❏ Padmé vs. Nexu, 750 produced 200.00
- ❏ Padmé vs. Nexu, faux bronze, 50 produced 200.00
- ❏ Sabotage, 750 produced 190.00
- ❏ Senate Duel, Yoda vs. Darth Sidious 450.00
- ❏ Space Slug Enviorama, 2,000 produced, exclusive to Star Wars Celebration IV 125.00
- ❏ Yoda vs. Count Dooku 200.00
- ❏ Yoda vs. Count Dooku, faux bronze, 100 produced ...375.00

Legendary scale busts.
- ❏ Commander Cody, 800 produced 300.00
- ❏ Obi-Wan Kenobi 300.00

Statues, bronze.
- ❏ Darth Vader, 30 produced ....OSPV
- ❏ Sistros and Braata: Secret Origins of the Sith, 25 prod...OSPV
- ❏ Boba Fett, 75 produced ....OSPV
- ❏ Darth Vader, 50 produced ....OSPV
- ❏ Jango Fett, 25 produced ....OSPV

Statues. 1:1 scale.
- ❏ Salacious B. Crumb, 600 produced 375.00

Statues. 1/4 scale.
- ❏ Anakin Skywalker 300.00
- ❏ Anakin Skywalker with alternate interchangeable Anakin as Sith Apprentice portrait 350.00
- ❏ Asajj Ventress, 500 produced 250.00
- ❏ Asajj Ventress with interchangeable portrait, 500 produced 300.00
- ❏ Aurra Sing, 750 produced 300.00
- ❏ Aurra Sing with lightsaber trophy case, 450 produced 350.00
- ❏ Ben Obi-Wan Kenobi, 2,250 produced 175.00
- ❏ Ben Obi-Wan Kenobi with exclusive Jedi training remote 290.00
- ❏ Boba Fett, 2,000 produced 350.00
- ❏ Boba Fett with wall-mountable Mandalorian artifact, 2,000 produced 400.00
- ❏ Count Dooku, 750 produced 350.00
- ❏ Darth Maul 300.00
- ❏ Darth Maul Cyborg 350.00
- ❏ Darth Maul Cyborg with exclusive interchangeable portraits 400.00
- ❏ Darth Maul with Sith probe droid 325.00
- ❏ Darth Talon, 1,500 produced 300.00
- ❏ Darth Talon with removable cape with wired hem, 650 produced 350.00
- ❏ Darth Vader with exclusive mouse droid, 2,000 produced 425.00
- ❏ Darth Vader, 2,500 produced 350.00
- ❏ General Grievous, 2,500 produced 475.00
- ❏ General Grievous with exclusive fabric cape and clasp 500.00
- ❏ Han Solo, 2,500 produced 230.00
- ❏ Han Solo with exclusive Yavin Medal of Honor, 250 produced 300.00
- ❏ Luke Skywalker and Yoda 350.00
- ❏ Luke Skywalker and Yoda, exclusive Darth Vader helmet 425.00
- ❏ Luke Skywalker Jedi Knight, 1,000 produced 300.00
- ❏ Luke Skywalker Jedi Knight with switch-out hand holding blaster pistol, 700 produced 350.00
- ❏ Luke Skywalker, 2005 Comic-Con exclusive for pickup, 500 produced 155.00
- ❏ Luke Skywalker, 2005 Comic-Con exclusive non-attendee, 500 produced 135.00
- ❏ Luke Skywalker, limited to 2,500 ....225.00

483-01

483-02

483-03

483-04

483-05

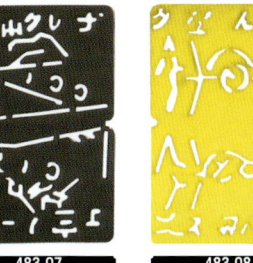
483-06
483-07
483-08

483-09
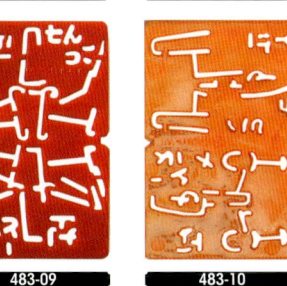
483-10

- ❏ Princess Leia with exclusive stormtrooper blaster, limited to 1,000 ....325.00
- ❏ Princess Leia, limited to 1,250 ....200.00
- ❏ Princess Leia, Slave 300.00
- ❏ Princess Leia, Slave with Salacious B. Crumb, 750 produced 350.00
- ❏ Scout Trooper, 550 produced 300.00
- ❏ Scout Trooper with E-11S sniper rifle, 300 prod........350.00
- ❏ Speeder Bike and Scout Trooper 920.00
- ❏ Speeder Bike and Scout Trooper, 1500 produced 800.00
- ❏ Tusken Raider, 750 produced 300.00
- ❏ Tusken Raider, interchangeable rifle, 500 produced..350.00
- ❏ Yoda and Clone Trooper, 1500 produced 400.00

Star Wars Celebration VI
Daily 6" resin maquettes.
- ❏ Darth Bane (Saturday) 65.00
- ❏ Death Trooper (Sunday) 65.00
- ❏ Mara Jade (Thursday) 65.00
- ❏ Quinlan Vos (Friday) 65.00

Takara TOMY A.R.T.S. (Japan)
Plaster statue collection.
- ❏ Chewbacca [482-364] 10.00
- ❏ Darth Vader [482-365] 10.00
- ❏ Han Solo [482-366] 10.00
- ❏ Han Solo in Carbonite (chase) [482-367] 10.00
- ❏ Luke Skywalker [482-368] 10.00
- ❏ Princess Leia [482-369] 10.00

Tomy (Japan)
Series 1. Approximately 6 cm tall. Miniature dioramas.
- ❏ AT-AT [482-370] 20.00
- ❏ Darth Vader and stormtroopers [482-371] 20.00
- ❏ Millennium Falcon [v1e1:408] 20.00
- ❏ R2-D2 and C-3PO [482-372] 20.00
- ❏ X-Wing [482-373] 20.00

Series 2. Approximately 6 cm tall. Miniature dioramas.
- ❏ Boba Fett with Carbonite Han [482-374] 20.00
- ❏ Darth Maul vs. Qui-Gon Jinn [482-375] 20.00
- ❏ Han Solo and Chewbacca [482-376] 20.00
- ❏ Luke Skywalker on sailbarge [482-377] 20.00
- ❏ Yoda on Dagobah [482-378] 20.00

Series 3. Approximately 6 cm tall. Miniature dioramas.
- ❏ Anakin on speeder bike [482-379] 20.00
- ❏ Gunship over AT-TE [482-380] 20.00
- ❏ Jedi Starfighter [482-381] 20.00
- ❏ Slave I [482-382] 20.00
- ❏ Yoda [482-383] 20.00

Stencils
Continued in Volume 3, Page 347

Maruka (Japan)
Each stencil available in black, blue, green, orange, red, and yellow.
- ❏ C-3PO [483-01] 35.00
- ❏ Darth Vader's TIE Fighter [483-02] 35.00
- ❏ Death Star [483-03] 35.00
- ❏ Landspeeder [483-04] 35.00
- ❏ Millennium Falcon [483-05] 35.00
- ❏ R2-D2 [483-06] 35.00
- ❏ Star Destroyer [483-07] 35.00
- ❏ TIE Fighter [483-08] 35.00
- ❏ X-Wing [483-09] 35.00
- ❏ Y-Wing [483-10] 35.00

Stickers
Continued in Volume 3, Page 347

- ❏ 1,000 stickers by the roll [484-01] 8.00
- ❏ 7 characters, 2 X-Wings, puffy [484-02] 15.00
- ❏ C-3PO and Imperial Cruiser look-alikes [4:288] 15.00
- ❏ Darth Vader [484-03] 10.00
- ❏ I am a Jedi like my father before me 5.00
- ❏ Let's See It In THX, 2" round, Star Wars Celebration '99, promotional [4:288] 2.00
- ❏ May the Floss Be with You [v1e1:409] 4.00

Automobile stickers.
- ❏ AT-AT [484-04] 8.00
- ❏ Bantha skull [484-05] 8.00
- ❏ Rebel Alliance 8.00
- ❏ Republic Cog [484-06] 8.00
- ❏ Suparatláta [484-07] 8.00

484-01

484-02

484-03

484-04

484-05

484-06

Stickers

  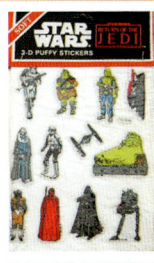     

484-62 | 484-63 | 484-64 | 484-65 | 484-66 | 484-67 | 484-68 | 484-69 | 484-70

484-71 | 484-72 | 484-73 | 484-74 | 484-75 | 484-76 | 484-77 | 484-78

❏ Darth Vader's TIE Fighter [484-32]...............20.00
❏ Imperial Cruiser [484-33]...............20.00
❏ Millennium Falcon...............20.00
❏ Millennium Falcon with Star Wars logo...............20.00
❏ TIE Interceptor...............20.00
❏ X-Wing Fighter [484-34]...............20.00

Barri-Shelli (Canada)
Sticker and Picture sets.
❏ Star Wars [484-35]...............280.00

Cedibra (Brazil)
❏ Star Wars, set of 120...............60.00

Creative Imaginations, LLC
Cardstock sticker sheets.
❏ Star Wars [484-36]...............10.00
❏ The Clone Wars [484-37]...............10.00

Chipboard sticker sheets.
❏ Clone Wars [484-38]...............10.00
❏ Empire Strikes Back, foil [484-39]...............10.00
❏ Star Wars [484-40]...............10.00

Chipboard stickers.
❏ Clone Wars [484-41]...............5.00
❏ Star Wars [484-42]...............5.00
❏ The Empire Strikes Back [484-43]...............5.00

Epoxy sticker sheets.
❏ Star Wars icons [484-44]...............10.00

❏ Star Wars phrase [484-45]...............10.00
❏ The Clone Wars icons [484-46]...............10.00
❏ The Clone Wars phrases [484-47]...............10.00

Layered sticker sheets.
❏ Clone Wars [484-48]...............8.00
❏ Star Wars [484-49]...............8.00

Scrapbook stickers, 12" x 12" sheet.
❏ Clone Wars [484-50]...............10.00
❏ Star Wars [484-51]...............10.00

Sticker sheets.
❏ Clone trooper [484-52]...............6.00
❏ Clone Wars logo [484-53]...............6.00
❏ Empire Strikes Back [484-54]...............6.00
❏ Han Solo [484-55]...............6.00
❏ Heroes [484-56]...............6.00
❏ Luke Skywalker [484-57]...............6.00
❏ Silhouettes [484-58]...............6.00
❏ Stormtrooper [484-59]...............6.00
❏ Stormtrooper [484-60]...............6.00
❏ Star Wars logo [484-61]...............6.00
❏ The Dark Side [484-62]...............6.00
❏ Yoda [484-63]...............6.00

Crystal Craft (Australia)
Return of the Jedi. 3D Puffy stickers.
❏ Han, R2-D2, Chewbacca, Leia, Paploo, X-Wing, Emperor, C-3PO, Wicket, Ackbar, Millennium Falcon, logo on right of header card. [484-64]...............16.00

❏ Stormtrooper, Gamorrean Guard, Boba Fett, Slave I, Bib Fortuna, TIE Fighter, Jabba, Royal Guard, Vader, AT-ST, logo on right of header card. [484-65]...............16.00
❏ Wicket the Ewok, 8 individual scenes, logo on right of header card. [484-66]...............16.00

Decopac
❏ Star Wars sheet of 24 for cupcake packaging...............5.00

Disney / MGM
❏ "Battle Station," Millennium Falcon...............20.00
❏ C-3PO, R2-D2, and MGM logos...............20.00
❏ "Commander Rebel Alliance," Luke Skywalker...............20.00
❏ "Headquarters—X-Wing Fighting Sqaudron"...............20.00
❏ "Imperial Lord—Darth Vader"...............20.00
❏ "Moon of Endor," Ewok village...............20.00
❏ Star Tours 3D holographic, 1 sheet of 9 stickers [484-67]...............35.00
❏ Star Tours logo, glow-in-the-dark...............30.00

Drawing Board Greeting Cards, Inc.
Empire Strikes Back 3D Perk-Up.
❏ Tusken raider, Cloud Car, TIE Fighter, Jawa, Darth Vader, stormtrooper, Lando Calrissian, Boba Fett [484-68]...............20.00

Ewoks.
❏ 7 individual stickers [484-69]...............15.00
❏ 8 individual stickers [484-70]...............15.00
❏ 8 individual stickers; 4 Princess Kneesaa, 4 Wicket [484-71]...............15.00
❏ 9 individual Scenes, Perk-up [484-72]...............15.00

   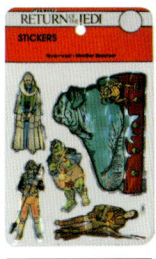     

484-79 | 484-80 | 484-81 | 484-82 | 484-83 | 484-84 | 484-85 | 484-86 | 484-87

484-88 | 484-89 | 484-90 | 484-91 | 484-92 | 484-93

Stickers

484-94 | 484-95 | 484-96 | 484-97 | 484-98 | 484-99

    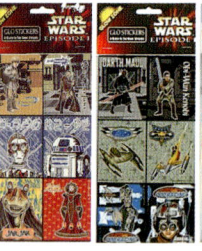 

484-100 | 484-101 | 484-102 | 484-103 | 484-104 | 484-105 | 484-106

Return of the Jedi. Perk-up or puffed.
- ❏ Bib Fortuna, Lando, C-3PO, Jabba, Darth Vader, Royal Guard, R2-D2, Princess Leia, Max Rebo Band [484-73].............10.00
- ❏ Biker scout, Paploo, Wicket, Klaatu, Chewbacca, Gamorrean Guard, Han, Luke, Yoda [484-74].....................10.00
- ❏ Chewbacca, Darth Vader, R2-D2, C-3PO, Luke, Yoda, X-Wing, cloud card, Boba Fett, Han Solo [484-75]......................15.00
- ❏ Han, R2-D2, Chewbacca, Leia, Paploo, X-Wing, Emperor, C-3PO, Wicket, Ackbar, Millennium Falcon [484-76].......15.00
- ❏ Royal Guard, Darth Vader, Bib Fortuna, Boushh, Gamorrean Guard, AT-ST, Wicket, Kneesaa x 2, stormtrooper, Boba Fett, Biker scout, TIE Fighter, R2-D2 [484-77].........15.00
- ❏ Shuttle, Death Star, B-Wing, Falcon, logo, speeder bike, X-Wing, TIE Fighter, AT-ST [484-78].......................10.00
- ❏ Stormtrooper, Gamorrean Guard, Boba Fett, Jabba's sail barge, Bib Fortuna, TIE Fighter, Jabba, Royal Guard, Vader, AT-ST [484-79].........15.00
- ❏ Wicket the Ewok, 8 individual scenes [484-80].............15.00

Return of the Jedi. Prismatic, large.
- ❏ C-3PO...10.00
- ❏ Darth Vader [484-81]..............................10.00
- ❏ Emperor's Royal Guard............................10.00
- ❏ Jabba the Hutt...................................10.00
- ❏ Millennium Falcon and X-Wing.....................10.00
- ❏ Princess Leia....................................10.00
- ❏ R2-D2..10.00
- ❏ Shuttle Tydirium.................................10.00
- ❏ Wicket...10.00
- ❏ Yoda...10.00

Return of the Jedi. Prismatic. Sheets of 5.
- ❏ Characters: Bib Fortuna, Jabba the Hutt, Gamorrean Guard, Lando Calrissian, Leia as Boushh [484-82].............25.00
- ❏ Ships: Death Star, X-Wing, imperial shuttle, TIE Fighter, Millennium Falcon [484-83]............................25.00

Return of the Jedi. Puffy.
- ❏ C-3PO [484-84]...................................10.00
- ❏ Darth Vader [484-85].............................10.00
- ❏ R2-D2 [484-86]...................................10.00

Drawing Board Greeting Cards, Inc. (Canada)
- ❏ Perk up: Princess Leia, Lando Calrissian, Luke Skywalker, X-Wing Fighter, Yoda, See Threepio, Chewbacca, X-Wing Fighter, Artoo Detoo, Han Solo, 3 sheets, 10 stickers, Star Wars decal [484-87]..................20.00

Dyna Mart
Produced in the US for French market. Classic trilogy and Episode I images. Set contains 200 cards, plus 150 sticker cards and 150 stickers. Additional images and checklist in 3rd edition, page 388.
- ❏ Stickers 1–150, each [484-88]....................2.00
- ❏ Complete set....................................90.00

     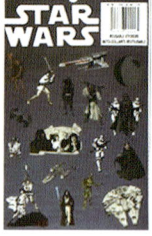   

484-107 | 484-108 | 484-109 | 484-110 | 484-111 | 484-112 | 484-113 | 484-114 | 484-115

484-116 | 484-117 | 484-118 | 484-119 | 484-120 | 484-121 | 484-122

484-123 | 484-124 | 484-125 | 484-126 | 484-127 | 484-128 | 484-129 | 484-130 | 484-131 | 484-132

Stickers

  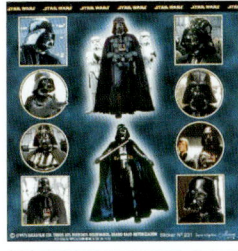   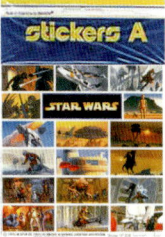 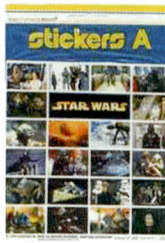

484-133　484-134　484-135　484-136　484-137　484-138　484-139

484-140　484-141　484-142　484-143　484-144　484-145　484-146　484-147　484-148

EnSky (Japan)
- 40 mini stickers [484-89] 8.00

Index seals.
- Classic, 2 sheets of 13 seals 10.00
- Prequel, 2 sheets of 12 seals 10.00

Fan Club
- Darth Vader, "Official Star Wars Fan Club" 12.00

Fascal (UK)
- 12 pouches, 12 stickers each, store display [484-90] ... 395.00
- Artoo Detoo [484-91] 10.00
- Chewbacca [484-92] 10.00
- Darth Vader [484-93] 10.00
- Han Solo [484-94] 10.00
- Imperial Troops [484-95] 10.00
- Luke Skywalker [484-96] 10.00
- Millennium Falcon [484-97] 10.00
- Obi-Wan Kenobi [484-98] 10.00
- Princess Leia [484-99] 10.00
- See Threepio [484-100] 10.00
- Star Wars logo 10.00
- The Force [484-101] 10.00

Flomo (UK)
- Vader / Death Star II, prismatic [484-102] 8.00

Fox Studios
DVD classic trilogy promotional. Walmart exclusives.
- A New Hope [484-103] 5.00

- Empire Strikes Back [v1e1.411] 5.00
- Return of the Jedi [v1e1.411] 5.00

Glow Zone
Six Episode I Glo stickers.
- Anakin, Qui-Gon, C-3PO, R2-D2, Jar Jar, Queen Amidala [484-104] 15.00
- Darth Maul, Obi-Wan, Trade Federation Fighter, Naboo Fighter, Sebulba, Anakin [484-105] 15.00

Hallmark
- 6 sticker sheets, 2 scene sheets [484-106] 15.00
- Episode I, Queen Amidala, Jedi, Jar Jar Binks, logo, Anakin Skywalker, Darth Maul, Jedi vs. Sith, Anakin and droids [484-107] 5.00
- Episode I sticker tablet, "over 280 stickers" 5.00
- Kids stickers: Luke, Leia, Han, Vader, logo, Yoda, C-3PO, R2-D2, Chewbacca, Ben, 4 sheets [484-108] 5.00
- LEGO Star Wars, Darth Vader, C-3PO, Boba Fett, Chewbacca, stormtrooper, R2-D2 [484-109] 5.00

Classic trilogy series.
- Empire Strikes Back [484-110] 8.00
- Return of the Jedi [484-111] 8.00
- Star Wars [484-112] 8.00

Hallmark Party
- Star Wars Generations, 4 sheets of 6 stickers [484-113] 5.00
- Star Wars Generations Villains, from 48-pack of party favors [484-114] 2.00

Heart Art Collection, Ltd. (Japan)
Makie stickers.
- Boba Fett [484-115] 5.00
- C-3PO [484-116] 5.00
- Darth Vader [484-117] 5.00
- Stormtrooper [484-118] 5.00
- Yoda [484-119] 5.00

Heartline
Episode I: The Phantom Menace.
- 8 stickers, 4 sheets 5.00
- 9 stickers, 4 sheets [484-120] 5.00

Hi-C
- Return of the Jedi, folded, Hi-C premium [484-121] 30.00

Innovative Designs
- 10-pack Clone Wars glow-in-the-dark stickers, exclusive to Target [484-122] 5.00
- 12 sheet value pack, glow-in-the-dark [484-123] 10.00
- Star Wars, 4 sheets, 16 stickers [484-124] 5.00

6-packs of 3D stickers, exclusive to Target.
- Clone Wars, exclusive to Target [484-125] 5.00
- Star Wars heroes [484-126] 5.00
- Star Wars scenes [484-127] 5.00
- Star Wars villains [484-128] 5.00

Kenner
- Fantastic Sticker Maker Star Wars refill kit, forty photos and machine tape refill [484-129] 25.00

 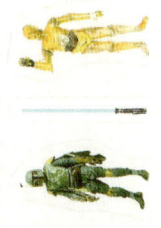   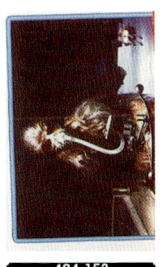   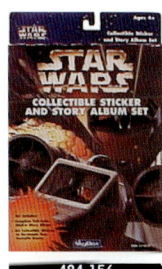

484-149　484-150　484-151　484-152　484-153　484-154　484-155　484-156

484-157　484-158　484-159　484-160　484-161　484-162　484-163　484-164

Stickers

Lucasfilm
Street art on vinyl.
- Darth Vader [v1e1:412] 4.00
- Yoda [v1e1:412] 4.00

M&M World
Mpire, prism background.
- Anakin Skywalker [484-130] 5.00
- Darth Vader [484-131] 5.00
- Emperor [484-132] 5.00
- Mace Windu [484-133] 5.00
- Queen Amidala [484-134] 5.00

MAUCCI S.A. (Argentina)
- Sheet of 10: Darth Vader [484-135] 10.00
- Sheet of 13: C-3PO x 4, Jawas x 2, Max Rebo Band, Gamorrean Guard, R2-D2, Cantina band, Rancor [484-136] 10.00
- Sheet of 13: Yoda, R2-D2, Jawas x 2, Ben, Luke, Han, Chewbacca, Boba Fett, stormtrooper, biker scout, Tarkin, Princess Leia [484-137] 10.00
- Sheet of 18: concept art [484-138] 10.00
- Sheet of 23: movie scenes [484-139] 10.00
- Sheet of 23: characters 10.00
- Sheet of 23: movie scenes 10.00
- Sheet of 6: Boba Fett, Darth Vader, biker scout, snowtrooper, stormtrooper, Emperor [484-140] 10.00
- Sheet of 7: vehicles art [484-141] 10.00

Merlin Publishing Internat'l Ltd.
- Bounty hunters, sheet of 6 [484-142] 12.00
- Droids, sheet of 7 [484-143] 12.00
- Imperial forces, sheet of 8 [484-144] 12.00
- Rebel forces, sheet of 8 [484-145] 12.00
- Star Wars, sheet of 17 [484-146] 12.00

Mimoco (Japan)
Mimobot promotional stickers, shaped.
- Boba Fett [v1e1:413] 5.00
- Chewbacca 5.00
- Darth Vader 5.00
- Luke Skywalker, X-Wing pilot [484-147] 5.00
- Princess Leia [v1e1:413] 5.00
- R2-D2 .... 5.00
- Stormtrooper 5.00

Paizo Publishing / Fan Club
- Dexter's Diner, Boonta Eve Classic, Outlander Club, Corellian Spice Freighters Guild [484-148] 5.00

Panini
Numbered stickers. 1-156, A-X, and s1-s36. Some images require 2-3 stickers to complete. Checklist in 3rd edition, page 389.
- 1-156, each [484-149] 3.00
- 1-156, set 85.00
- A-X, each 4.00
- A-X, set 90.00
- s1-s36, each [484-150] 5.00
- s1-s36, set 75.00

Panini / Skybox
66 stickers, numbered. Some images require multiple stickers to complete. Images in 2nd edition, page 392. Checklist in 3rd edition, page 389.
- 1-29: A New Hope, each [484-151 to 484-152] 2.00
- 30-55: Empire Strikes Back, ea. [484-153 to 484-154] 2.00
- 56-66: Return of the Jedi, each [484-155] 2.00
- Complete set 75.00
- Complete set with album [484-156] 95.00

Paper Magic Group
- Stick-R-Treats, Attack of the Clones, bag of 18 .... 10.00

Party Express
- Clone Wars, Yoda, oval [484-157] 2.00

4 sheets each pack.
- Classic trilogy [484-158] 5.00
- Clone Wars [484-159] 5.00
- Episode II: Attack of the Clones [484-160] 3.00
- Episode III: Revenge of the Sith 3.00
- Starships [484-161] 5.00

Pizza Hut
Episode I character stickers, 2" round.
- Anakin Skywalker [v1e1:413] 5.00
- Darth Maul [v1e1:413] 5.00
- Jar Jar Binks [v1e1:413] 5.00
- Nute Gunray [484-162] 5.00
- Queen Amidala [v1e1:413] 5.00
- Ree Yees Senator [v1e1:413] 5.00

Pizza Hut (Germany)
- "Get Into It!", Episode I, any color [484-163] 5.00

Rose Art Industries
- Fun with stickers [484-164] 15.00
- Sticker studio, over 200 stickers [484-165] 10.00
- Sticker value pack, over 145 stickers [484-166] 10.00
- Super sticker and tattoo station with case, black case [484-167] 20.00
- Super sticker and tattoo station with case, purple case 25.00

Revenge of the Sith.
- Fun with tattoos and stickers 20.00

Sandylion
- Saga removable stickers, 2 sheets [484-168] 5.00
- Sticker paradise, 6 reusable sticker sheets and sticker album [484-169] 10.00

Clone Wars, square.
- Anakin and Ahsoka 1.00
- Obi-Wan and Anakin 1.00
- Obi-Wan Kenobi [484-170] 1.00
- Yoda 1.00
- Yoda, Anakin, and clones 1.00

Clone Wars.
- 35 stickers [484-171] 8.00
- 48 stickers [484-172] 5.00
- 62 stickers, 2 sides, glow in the dark [484-173] 5.00
- Stickers [484-174] 5.00
- Super Sticker Set, 750 stickers [484-175] 8.00

Episode I collector series stickers. 3 in each pack.
- #1 Space Battle [484-176] 5.00
- #2 Ground Battle [484-177] 5.00
- #3 Podrace [484-178] 5.00
- #4 Jedi [484-179] 5.00
- #5 Villains [484-180] 5.00
- #6 Droids [484-181] 5.00

448

Stickers

Episode I: The Phantom Menace.
- ❑ 6 sticker sheet, Obi-Wan Kenobi [484-182] 5.00
- ❑ 7 sticker sheet, Darth Maul [484-183] 5.00
- ❑ 8 sticker sheet, Qui-Gon Jinn [484-184] 5.00
- ❑ 9 sticker sheet, Jar Jar Binks [484-185] 5.00
- ❑ 9 sticker sheet, Naboo Invasion [484-186] 5.00
- ❑ 9 sticker sheet, Queen Amidala [484-187] 5.00
- ❑ 10 sticker sheet, Heroes, 2 sheets per pack [484-188] 5.00
- ❑ 10 sticker sheet, Space Battle [484-189] 5.00
- ❑ 11 sticker sheet, Villains, 2 sheets per pack [484-190] 5.00
- ❑ 12 sticker sheet, Podracing [484-191] 5.00
- ❑ 21 sticker sheet, Create-A-Sticker Scene, starfighters and explosions [484-192] 8.00

Episode III: Revenge of the Sith, square.
- ❑ Chewbacca 2.00
- ❑ Darth Vader 2.00
- ❑ Epic Duel 2.00
- ❑ General Grievous [484-193] 2.00
- ❑ Obi-Wan Kenobi 2.00
- ❑ Yoda 2.00

Episode III: Revenge of the Sith. 8 sheets, each.
- ❑ 104 stickers [484-194] 5.00
- ❑ 56 stickers [484-195] 5.00

Sticker rolls, boxed.
- ❑ 1,000 Stickers by the roll 10.00
- ❑ Sticker Extravaganza, Episode I [484-196] 10.00
- ❑ Sticker Extravaganza, Episode II with sticker album [484-197] 10.00

Vendpack stickers. Episode I: The Phantom Menace.
- ❑ 1 Naboo Space Battle 5.00
- ❑ 2 Darth Maul 5.00
- ❑ 3 Anakin Skywalker (Podracer) 5.00
- ❑ 4 Battle Droid 5.00
- ❑ 5 Anakin's Podracer 5.00
- ❑ 6 Watto 5.00
- ❑ 7 Obi-Wan Kenobi 5.00
- ❑ 8 R2-D2 .... 5.00
- ❑ 9 Qui-Gon Jinn and Obi-Wan Kenobi 5.00
- ❑ 10 Queen Amidala [484-198] 5.00
- ❑ 11 Jar Jar Binks 5.00
- ❑ 12 Amidala's Royal Starship 5.00

Scion
- ❑ What Moves You, exclusive to Star Wars Celebration VI [484-199] 5.00

Smart
- ❑ Darth Vader for prepaid cell phone service, 1.5" x 3" lenticular 8.00
- ❑ Darth Vader for prepaid cell phone service, 4" round 5.00

Space World (Japan)
- ❑ Sheet of 15 [484-200] 25.00

Star Wars Celebration VI
- ❑ Star Wars Alphabet sticker sheet 20.00

Star Wars Insider
- ❑ "See You At Star Wars Celebration..." 3"x5" promotional 5.00

Stickeroni
- ❑ 30 icons, 2 sheets [484-201] 8.00
- ❑ Clone Wars pop-up scene with stickers [484-202] 5.00
- ❑ Clone Wars, 2 sheets of 10, Captain Rex, Ahsoka, Mace Windu, Obi-Wan, R2-D2, C-3PO, Anakin, Yoda, Jedi emblem, Republic emblem [484-203] 5.00
- ❑ LEGO Star Wars holographic, 13 stickers, 4 sheets [484-204] 5.00
- ❑ Star Wars, 100 stickers, 10 sheets [484-205] 8.00
- ❑ Star Wars, 26 stickers, 1 sheet [484-206] 5.00

Puffed stickers.
- ❑ Sheet of 9 characters, logo, Han Solo, Darth Vader, Boba Fett, Chewbacca, stormtrooper, C-3PO, R2-D2, Luke Skywalker [484-207] 10.00
- ❑ Sheet of 9 space, Millennium Falcon, moon, Slave I, logo, TIE Fighters, Vader's TIE, Star Destroyer, X-Wing Fighter, Death Star [484-208] 10.00

Super7
- ❑ Boba Fett, coming soon [484-209] 5.00

Tokyo Queen Co., Ltd. (Japan)
- ❑ Box of 48 sheets [484-210] 1,200.00
- ❑ Escape pod, May the Force be with you, Luke and C-3PO, TIE Fighter [484-211] 30.00

- ❑ Hildebrandt art, Chewbacca, May the Force be with you, stormtrooper [484-212] 30.00
- ❑ May the Force be with you x 2, stormtroopers, Vader, droids, Han and Chewbacca [484-213] 30.00
- ❑ X-Wing / Death Star, Darth Vader, See-Threepio [484-214] ... 30.00

Topps
- ❑ Empire Strikes Back Probot, Chewbacca, stormtrooper, R2-D2, Yoda, C-3PO, Boba Fett, and large Vader, puffed [484-215] 20.00

Topps (Canada)
Reusable stickers, 1 sheet of 10.
- ❑ Galactic Empire 10.00
- ❑ Rebel Alliance 10.00

Vending Supply
Die-cut stickers with prism background.
- ❑ C-3PO [484-216] 10.00
- ❑ Darth Vader [484-217] 10.00
- ❑ Death Star and Shuttle Tydirium [484-218] 10.00
- ❑ Jabba the Hutt [484-219] 10.00
- ❑ Princess Leia 10.00
- ❑ R2-D2 [484-220] 10.00
- ❑ Royal Guard 10.00
- ❑ Wicket the Ewok [484-221] 10.00
- ❑ X-Wing Fighter / Millennium Falcon [484-222] 10.00
- ❑ Yoda Jedi Master [484-223] 10.00

Fluffy Adorable.
- ❑ Return of the Jedi puffed, same art as Random House bookmarks [484-224] 20.00

Return of the Jedi stickers with reflective background.
- ❑ Admiral Ackbar [484-225] 12.00
- ❑ Ben Kenobi [484-226] 12.00
- ❑ Boba Fett [484-227] 12.00
- ❑ C-3PO [484-228] 12.00
- ❑ Chewbacca [484-229] 12.00
- ❑ Darth Vader [484-230] 12.00
- ❑ Emperor's Royal Guard [484-231] 12.00
- ❑ Han Solo [484-232] 12.00
- ❑ Jabba the Hutt [484-233] 12.00
- ❑ Lando as Skiff Guard [484-234] 12.00
- ❑ Luke Skywalker [484-235] 12.00

Stickers

  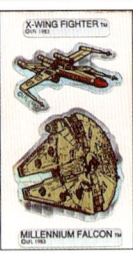      

484-220 | 484-221 | 484-222 | 484-223 | 484-224 | 484-225 | 484-226 | 484-227 | 484-228

484-229 | 484-230 | 484-231 | 484-232 | 484-233 | 484-234 | 484-235

484-236 | 484-237 | 484-238 | 484-239 | 484-240 | 484-241 | 484-242

- ❏ Princess Leia as Boushh [484-236] 12.00
- ❏ R2-D2 [484-237] 12.00
- ❏ Stormtrooper [484-238] 12.00
- ❏ Wicket [484-239] 12.00
- ❏ Yoda [484-240] 12.00

Vending Supply (Canada)
Black and white set of 6, unnumbered. Approximately 2" x 3".
- ❏ C-3PO [484-241] 20.00
- ❏ Chewbacca [484-242] 20.00
- ❏ Darth Vader 20.00
- ❏ Han Solo 20.00
- ❏ Luke Skywalker 20.00
- ❏ Princess Leia 20.00

Stickers: A New Hope

O-Pee-Chee (Canada)
Series 1–3. Stickers included with cards sold in wax packs.
- ❏ Series 1, stickers 1–11, each [485-01] 30.00
- ❏ Series 2, stickers 12–22, each [485-02] 25.00
- ❏ Series 3, stickers 34–55, each 25.00

Panini
256 numbered stickers. Some images require multiple stickers to complete. Checklist in 3rd edition, page 391.
- ❏ Stickers 1–256, each [485-03] 2.00
- ❏ Complete set 120.00

Topps
Series 1–5. Stickers included with cards sold in wax packs.
- ❏ Series 1, stickers 1–11, each 35.00
- ❏ Series 2, stickers 12–22, each [485-03] 30.00
- ❏ Series 3, stickers 23–33, each [485-04] 20.00
- ❏ Series 4, stickers 34–44, each [485-05] 20.00
- ❏ Series 5, stickers 45–55, each [485-06] 20.00

Stickers: Attack of the Clones

Daily Star
Episode II: Attack of the Clones. Round stickers.
- ❏ Sheet 1, 8 stickers [486-01] 8.00
- ❏ Sheet 2, 9 stickers [486-02] 8.00

Hallmark (UK)
Super Stickers. 2 sheets per package.
- ❏ Anakin, Jango Fett, Obi-Wan, Dooku, Zam Wesell, Mace Windu, Padmé, C-3PO, and R2-D2 .... 8.00
- ❏ Count Dooku, logo, Yoda, Slave I, Mace Windu, Anakin, Padmé, Jango, Jedi Starfighter, Obi-Wan 8.00
- ❏ Padmé, Episode II heroes, Episode I characters, Anakin .. 8.00
- ❏ Padmé, Obi-Wan, Jango, Anakin, Mace, C-3PO 8.00

Heartline
- ❏ Anakin, logo, Yoda, Dooku, Slave I, Jango, Obi-Wan, Jedi Starfighter, 4 sheets of 8 [486-03] 5.00
- ❏ Anakin, logo, Yoda, Dooku, Slave I, Jango, Obi-Wan, Jedi Starfighter, Padmé, Mace, space x 2, 4 sheets of 12 ... 5.00
- ❏ Jango Fett, 2 sheets of 1 [486-04] 8.00

Merlin (Italy)
Stickers depicting LEGO mini figures, Numbered L1-L8, each.
- ❏ L1 Zam Wesell 5.00
- ❏ L2 Anakin Skywalker 5.00
- ❏ L3 Count Dooku 5.00
- ❏ L4 Yoda 5.00
- ❏ L5 Jango Fett 5.00
- ❏ L6 Boba Fett 5.00
- ❏ L7 Obi-Wan Kenobi 5.00
- ❏ L8 Clone trooper 5.00

Merlin Publishing Internat'l Ltd.
- ❏ Unopened package of six stickers 20.00

Salo (Spain)
- ❏ Complete collection, collecting album, and stickers in a clear carry case [486-05] 50.00

Sandylion
- ❏ Heroes and villains, 2 sheets of 17 [486-06] 10.00

Foil background.
- ❏ Heroes, 1 sheet of 9 [486-07] 5.00
- ❏ Jedi, 1 sheet of 10 [486-08] 5.00
- ❏ Vehicles, 1 sheet of 8 [486-09] 5.00
- ❏ Villains, 1 sheet of 10 [486-10] 5.00

SmileMakers series, 2" x 2" square.
- ❏ Anakin Skywalker [486-11] 3.00

     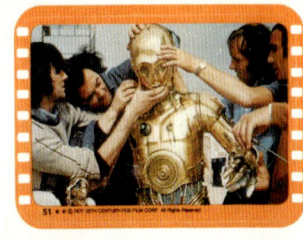

485-01 | 485-02 | 485-03 | 485-04 | 485-05 | 485-06

Stickers: Premiums

 486-01
 486-02
 486-03
 486-04
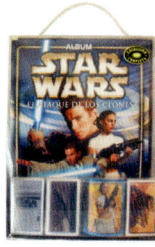 486-05
 486-06

 486-07
 486-08
 486-09
 486-10
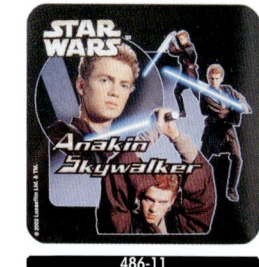 486-11
 486-12
 486-13
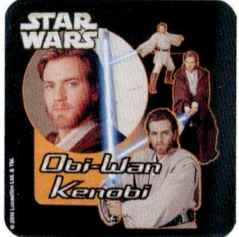 486-14

 486-15
 487-01
 487-02
 487-03
 487-04
 487-05
 487-06
 487-07

 487-08 Sample
 488-01 Sample
 488-02 Sample
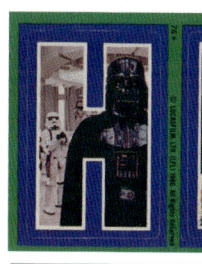 488-03 Sample
 488-04 Sample

- ☐ Count Dooku [486-12] 3.00
- ☐ Jango Fett [486-13] 3.00
- ☐ Obi-Wan Kenobi [486-14] 3.00
- ☐ Padmé Amidala [486-15] 3.00

Stickers: Clone Wars

- ☐ 4 sheets: Yoda, Ahsoka, Ahsoka, Yoda, Anakin, Anakin, Obi-Wan, Obi-Wan, Clone Wars logo 8.00

Animations
- ☐ 13 stickers [487-01] 8.00

Bondy Fiesta (Mexico)
60 stickers unnumbered. Distributed inside chewing gum wrappers.
- ☐ Any, each [487-02] 5.00
- ☐ Complete set 250.00

Hallmark Party
- ☐ Sticker boxes [487-03] 10.00
- ☐ Sticker sheets: Yoda, Captain Rex, Obi-Wan, Savage Opress, Anakin, General Grievous [487-04] 5.00

Innovative Designs
- ☐ 12 sheets, 120 stickers 5.00

Paper Magic Group
- ☐ General Grievous, Anakin, Obi-Wan, Yoda, Clones, jumbo lenticular [487-05] 5.00

Stickeroni
- ☐ Foil sticker sheets [487-06] 8.00

Topps
10 stickers, numbered from 90 card set.
- ☐ Stickers 1–10, each [487-07] 5.00

90 trading card stickers, numbered.
- ☐ Sticker cards 1–90, each [487-08] 3.00
- ☐ Complete set 35.00

Stickers: Empire Strikes Back

O-Pee-Chee (Canada)
Series 1-3. Stickers included with cards sold in wax packs.
- ☐ Series 1, stickers 1–33, each 20.00
- ☐ Series 2, stickers 34–66, each 20.00
- ☐ Series 3, stickers 67–86, each 15.00

Topps
Series 1-3. Stickers included with cards sold in wax packs.
- ☐ Series 1, stickers 1–33, each [488-01] 15.00
- ☐ Series 2, stickers 34–66, each [488-02] 15.00
- ☐ Series 3, stickers 67–86, each [488-03] 15.00

Yoplait (Spain)
50 stickers, numbered. Designed to be collected onto a poster instead of an album / loose.
- ☐ Stickers 1–50, each [488-04] 25.00
- ☐ Complete set 1,600.00

Stickers: Heritage

Topps
Alphabet stickers from retail distribution. Backs make up a picture of characters.
- ☐ Stickers 1–10, green, Anakin image, each 4.00
- ☐ Stickers 11–20, yellow, Obi-Wan image, each 4.00
- ☐ Stickers 21–30, blue, Droids image, each 4.00

Stickers: Parody

Hello Kitty / Star Wars mash-ups.
- ☐ Boba Kitty [v1e1:416] 5.00
- ☐ C3KO [v1e1:416] 5.00
- ☐ ChewKitty [v1e1:416] 5.00
- ☐ Han Kitty [v1e1:416] 5.00
- ☐ Luke Kitty [v1e1:416] 5.00
- ☐ Princess Kitty [v1e1:416] 5.00
- ☐ R2K2 [v1e1:416] 5.00
- ☐ Storm Kitty [v1e1:416] 5.00

Garbage Pail Kids
- ☐ Ashcan Andy [v1e1:416] 5.00

Stickers: Premiums
Continued in Volume 3, Page 350

20th Century Fox (Thailand)
- ☐ Attack of the Clones sheet of 8 [489-01] 15.00

Stickers: Premiums

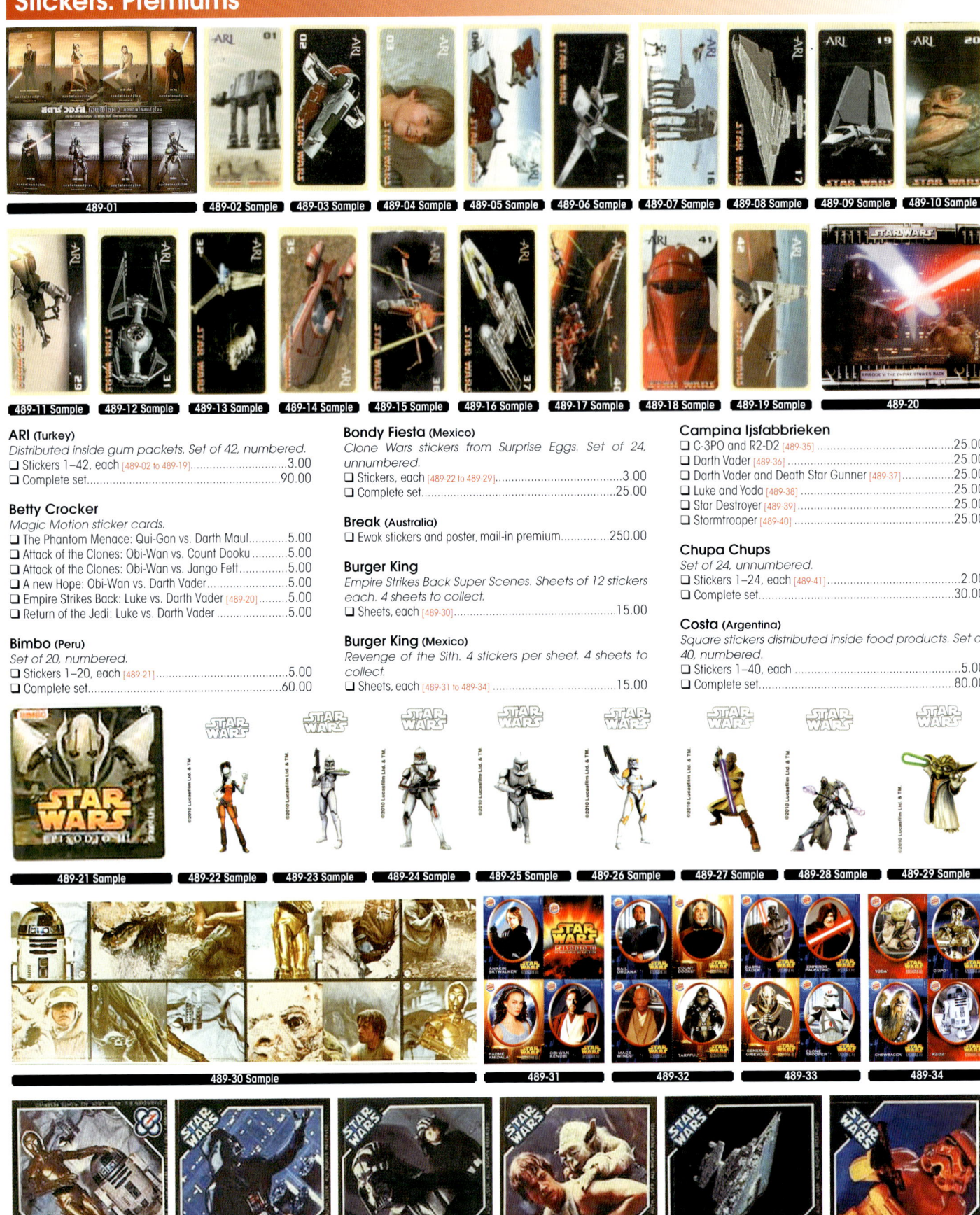

ARI (Turkey)
Distributed inside gum packets. Set of 42, numbered.
- Stickers 1–42, each [489-02 to 489-19]............3.00
- Complete set............90.00

Betty Crocker
Magic Motion sticker cards.
- The Phantom Menace: Qui-Gon vs. Darth Maul............5.00
- Attack of the Clones: Obi-Wan vs. Count Dooku............5.00
- Attack of the Clones: Obi-Wan vs. Jango Fett............5.00
- A new Hope: Obi-Wan vs. Darth Vader............5.00
- Empire Strikes Back: Luke vs. Darth Vader [489-20]............5.00
- Return of the Jedi: Luke vs. Darth Vader............5.00

Bimbo (Peru)
Set of 20, numbered.
- Stickers 1–20, each [489-21]............5.00
- Complete set............60.00

Bondy Fiesta (Mexico)
Clone Wars stickers from Surprise Eggs. Set of 24, unnumbered.
- Stickers, each [489-22 to 489-29]............3.00
- Complete set............25.00

Break (Australia)
- Ewok stickers and poster, mail-in premium............250.00

Burger King
Empire Strikes Back Super Scenes. Sheets of 12 stickers each. 4 sheets to collect.
- Sheets, each [489-30]............15.00

Burger King (Mexico)
Revenge of the Sith. 4 stickers per sheet. 4 sheets to collect.
- Sheets, each [489-31 to 489-34]............15.00

Campina Ijsfabbrieken
- C-3PO and R2-D2 [489-35]............25.00
- Darth Vader [489-36]............25.00
- Darth Vader and Death Star Gunner [489-37]............25.00
- Luke and Yoda [489-38]............25.00
- Star Destroyer [489-39]............25.00
- Stormtrooper [489-40]............25.00

Chupa Chups
Set of 24, unnumbered.
- Stickers 1–24, each [489-41]............2.00
- Complete set............30.00

Costa (Argentina)
Square stickers distributed inside food products. Set of 40, numbered.
- Stickers 1–40, each............5.00
- Complete set............80.00

452

Stickers: Premiums

   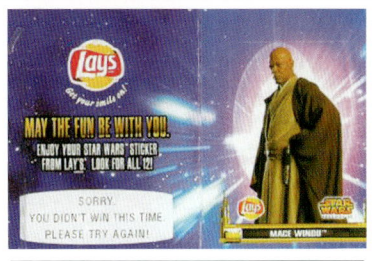 

489-41 Sample • 489-42 • 489-43 Sample • 489-44 • 489-45

Dark Horse Comics
☐ Star Wars Starfighter Crossbones 5.00

Doggis (Argentina)
Set of 4 distributed in hot dog packages.
☐ Anakin [v1e1:417] 15.00
☐ Count Dooku [v1e1:417] 15.00
☐ Mace Windu [v1e1:417] 15.00
☐ Obi-Wan Kenobi [489-42] 15.00

Felfont (Argentina)
Super Jack chocolate egg premiums. Sheets of 10 stickers. 28 sheets to collect, unnumbered.
☐ Sheets of 10, each [489-43] 5.00

Frito Lay
Episode III: Revenge of the Sith sticker game pieces. Set of 7, unnumbered.
☐ Chewbacca 3.00
☐ Darth Vader 3.00
☐ Mace Windu [489-44] 3.00
☐ Obi-Wan Kenobi 3.00
☐ Padmé 3.00
☐ R2-D2 [v1e1:417] 3.00
☐ Yoda 3.00

Fundy Star (Hungary)
Distributed inside candy bars. Set of 12, unnumbered.
☐ Anakin Skywalker [v1e1:417] 8.00
☐ Anakin's Podracer [v1e1:417] 8.00
☐ Battle Droid [v1e1:417] 8.00
☐ Darth Maul [v1e1:417] 8.00
☐ Droid Starfighters 8.00
☐ Gui-Gon Jinn (sic) [v1e1:417] 8.00
☐ Jar Jar Binks [v1e1:417] 8.00
☐ Naboo Starfighters [v1e1:417] 8.00
☐ Obi-Wan Kenobi [v1e1:417] 8.00
☐ Queen Amidala [v1e1:417] 8.00
☐ Space Battle [v1e1:417] 8.00
☐ Watto [489-45] 8.00

General Mills
Stick-on scenes. 4 mini-sets: character, creature, robot, scene. Characters.
☐ Ben (Obi-Wan) Kenobi [489-46] 10.00
☐ Han Solo [489-47] 10.00
☐ Luke Skywalker [489-48] 10.00
☐ Princess Leia Organa [489-49] 10.00

Stick-on scenes. 4 mini-sets: character, creature, robot, scene. Creatures.
☐ Chewbacca [489-50] 10.00
☐ Darth Vader [489-51] 10.00
☐ Jawa [489-52] 10.00
☐ Stormtroopers [489-53] 10.00

Stick-on scenes. 4 mini-sets: character, creature, robot, scene. Robots.
☐ Artoo-Detoo (R2-D2) [489-54] 10.00
☐ C-3PO and R2-D2 [489-55] 10.00
☐ Luke repairs C-3PO [489-56] 10.00
☐ See-Threepio (C-3PO) [489-57] 10.00

Stick-on scenes. 4 mini-sets: character, creature, robot, scene. Scenes.
☐ Attack on Darth Vader's Ship [489-58] 10.00
☐ Ben cuts off the tractor beam [489-59] 10.00
☐ Cockpit of the Millennium Falcon [489-60] 10.00
☐ Han Solo, Princess Leia and Luke [489-61] 10.00

General Mills (Canada)
Stick-on scenes. 2 mini-sets: character, creature. Characters.
☐ Ben (Obi-Wan) Kenobi 15.00
☐ Han Solo 15.00
☐ Luke Skywalker [489-62] 15.00
☐ Princess Leia Organa [489-63] 15.00

Stick-on scenes. 2 mini-sets: character, creature. Creatures.
☐ Chewbacca [489-64] 15.00
☐ Darth Vader [489-65] 15.00
☐ Jawa [489-66] 15.00
☐ Stormtroopers 15.00

Harpers (New Zealand)
Dog Chow. Set of 12, numbered.
☐ Bag sticker [489-67] 8,000.00
☐ 1 C-3PO, Chewbacca, Princess Leia [489-68] 500.00
☐ 2 Darth Vader [489-69] 500.00
☐ 3 Luke and Gamorrean Guards [489-70] 500.00
☐ 4 Salacious Crumb [489-71] 500.00
☐ 5 Gamorrean Guard [489-72] 500.00
☐ 6 Darth Vader, Luke Skywalker [489-73] 500.00

      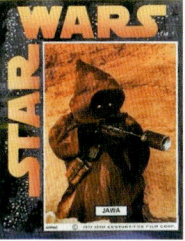

489-46 • 489-47 • 489-48 • 489-49 • 489-50 • 489-51 • 489-52

     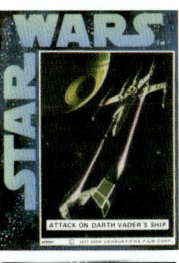 

489-53 • 489-54 • 489-55 • 489-56 • 489-57 • 489-58 • 489-59

  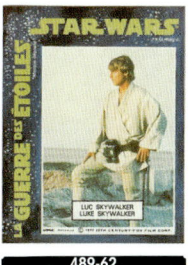   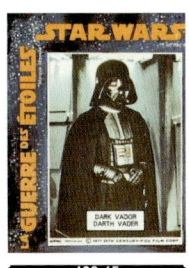 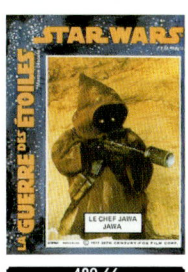

489-60 • 489-61 • 489-62 • 489-63 • 489-64 • 489-65 • 489-66

Stickers: Premiums

- ❑ 7 Wicket [489-74] 500.00
- ❑ 8 Han Solo [489-75] 500.00
- ❑ 9 Jabba the Hutt [489-76] 500.00
- ❑ 10 Luke Skywalker [489-77] 500.00
- ❑ 11 Stormtroopers [489-78] 500.00
- ❑ 12 B-Wing Fighters [489-79] 500.00

Henryx
Distributed inside chewing gum packets. Set of 7, unnumbered.
- ❑ Anakin's podracer 10.00
- ❑ AT-AT 10.00
- ❑ Count Dooku 10.00
- ❑ Darth Vader 10.00
- ❑ Jango Fett 10.00
- ❑ Sandtroopers 10.00
- ❑ X-Wing Fighters 10.00

Hollywood Chewing Gum (France)
Set of 20, unnumbered.
- ❑ Stickers 1–20, each [489-80] 5.00
- ❑ Complete set 50.00

Kellogg's
Stickers are adhered to trading cards for backing.
- ❑ 1 Luke Skywalker [489-81] 15.00
- ❑ 2 Han Solo [489-82] 15.00
- ❑ 3 R2-D2 [489-83] 15.00
- ❑ 4 C-3PO [489-84] 15.00
- ❑ 5 R2-D2 and C-3PO [489-85] 15.00
- ❑ 6 Yoda [489-86] 15.00
- ❑ 7 Ewok [489-87] 15.00
- ❑ 8 Darth Vader [489-88] 15.00
- ❑ 9 Chewbacca [489-89] 15.00
- ❑ 10 Princess Leia [489-90] 15.00

Kellogg's (Australia)
Set of 10, unnumbered. Free inside Kellogg's LCMs, Muesli Bars, and Crispix packs.
- ❑ Anakin Skywalker [489-91] 8.00
- ❑ Chewbacca [489-92] 8.00
- ❑ Clone Trooper 8.00
- ❑ Darth Vader [489-93] 8.00
- ❑ Emperor Palpatine [489-94] 8.00
- ❑ General Grievous [489-95] 8.00
- ❑ Obi-Wan Kenobi [489-96] 8.00
- ❑ R2-D2 and C-3PO [489-97] 8.00
- ❑ Senator Amidala [489-98] 8.00
- ❑ Yoda [489-99] 8.00

Kellogg's (Canada)
Stick'R Cards. 11–20 are card premiums.
- ❑ 1: Luke Skywalker [489-100] 15.00
- ❑ 2: Han Solo [489-101] 15.00
- ❑ 3: R2-D2 [489-102] 15.00
- ❑ 4: C-3PO [489-103] 15.00
- ❑ 5: C-3PO and R2-D2 [489-104] 15.00
- ❑ 6: Yoda [489-105] 15.00
- ❑ 7: Ewok [489-106] 15.00
- ❑ 8: Darth Vader [489-107] 15.00
- ❑ 9: Chewbacca [489-108] 15.00
- ❑ 10: Princess Leia [489-109] 15.00

Kellogg's (New Zealand)
Return of the Jedi sticker game pieces. Set of 12, unnumbered.
- ❑ Admiral Ackbar 15.00
- ❑ Bib Fortuna 15.00
- ❑ Chewbacca 15.00
- ❑ Darth Vader 15.00
- ❑ Ewoks 15.00
- ❑ Han Solo 15.00
- ❑ Jabba the Hutt 15.00
- ❑ Luke Skywalker 15.00
- ❑ Max Rebo 15.00
- ❑ Princess Leia 15.00
- ❑ See Threepio [489-110] 15.00
- ❑ Yoda 15.00

Kent (Turkey)
Rectangular artwork stickers distributed inside gum packets. Set of 112, numbered.
- ❑ Stickers 1–112, each [489-111 to 489-143] 5.00
- ❑ Complete set 150.00

Kortex (Australia)
- ❑ Return of the Jedi / May the Force be with you [489-144] 25.00

Meiji (Japan)
Candy roll premiums. Set of 18, unnumbered.
- ❑ Battle over Death Star [489-145] 40.00
- ❑ C-3PO [489-146] 40.00
- ❑ Chewbacca [489-147] 40.00

454

Stickers: Premiums

- ❏ Darth Vader [489-148]..................................40.00
- ❏ Darth Vader / Imperial Officer [489-149]........40.00
- ❏ Darth Vader and starfield [489-150]...............40.00
- ❏ Darth Vader surveys [489-151].....................40.00
- ❏ Detention corridor [489-152].........................40.00
- ❏ Millennium Falcon cockpit [489-153].............40.00
- ❏ Obi-Wan Kenobi..40.00
- ❏ Princess Leia and R2-D2 [489-154]..............40.00
- ❏ R2-D2 [489-155]..40.00
- ❏ R2-D2 and C-3PO [489-156].........................40.00
- ❏ Sandtrooper on Dewback [489-157]..............40.00
- ❏ Stopped at Mos Eisley [489-158]..................40.00
- ❏ Tusken raider and bantha [489-159].............40.00
- ❏ X-Wing / Logo [489-160]...............................40.00
- ❏ X-Wing / Logo [489-161]...............................40.00

MGM / UA
- ❏ Ewoks—The Battle for Endor sheet of six.........35.00

Nagatanien
- ❏ 1 Obi-Wan Kenobi [489-162].........................5.00
- ❏ 2 Anakin Skywalker [489-163].......................5.00
- ❏ 3 Jedi vs. Sith [489-164]...............................5.00
- ❏ 4 Darth Maul [489-165].................................5.00
- ❏ 5 Queen Amidala [489-166]...........................5.00
- ❏ 6 Jedi vs. Sith [489-167]...............................5.00
- ❏ 7 Jedi Master [489-168]................................5.00
- ❏ 8 Battle Droid and STAP [489-169]...............5.00
- ❏ 9 Duel on Tatooine Desert [489-170].............5.00
- ❏ 10 Jar Jar Binks [489-171]............................5.00
- ❏ 11 Lightsaber Duel [489-172].........................5.00
- ❏ 12 Gungan Army [489-173]............................5.00
- ❏ 13 Obi-Wan and Qui-Gon [489-174]...............5.00
- ❏ 14 C-3PO [489-175].......................................5.00
- ❏ 15 AAT (Tank) [489-176]................................5.00
- ❏ 16 R2-D2 [489-177].......................................5.00
- ❏ 17 Podrace [489-178]....................................5.00
- ❏ 18 Battle Droids...5.00
- ❏ 19 Yoda [489-179]..5.00
- ❏ 20 Naboo Starfighter [489-180]......................5.00

Nintendo Power Magazine
- ❏ Rogue Squadron [489-181]............................8.00

Pepsi Cola
- ❏ Jedi vs. Sith..5.00

Pepsi Cola (Argentina)
- ❏ Arturito (R2-D2)...80.00
- ❏ B-Wing Fighter [489-182]...............................80.00
- ❏ Darth Vader [489-183]...................................80.00
- ❏ Han Solo [489-184].......................................80.00
- ❏ Luke Skywalker [489-185].............................80.00
- ❏ See-Threepio [489-186]................................80.00
- ❏ Wicket [489-187]...80.00

489-100 | 489-101 | 489-102 | 489-103 | 489-104 | 489-105 | 489-106
489-107 | 489-108 | 489-109 | 489-110 | 489-111 Sample | 489-112 Sample | 489-113 Sample | 489-114 Sample
489-115 Sample | 489-116 Sample | 489-117 Sample | 489-118 Sample | 489-119 Sample | 489-120 Sample | 489-121 Sample | 489-122 Sample | 489-123 Sample | 489-124 Sample
489-125 Sample | 489-126 Sample | 489-127 Sample | 489-128 Sample | 489-129 Sample | 489-130 Sample | 489-131 Sample | 489-132 Sample | 489-133 Sample | 489-134 Sample
489-135 Sample | 489-136 Sample | 489-137 Sample | 489-138 Sample | 489-139 Sample | 489-140 Sample | 489-141 Sample | 489-142 Sample | 489-143 Sample | 489-144

Stickers: Premiums

PEZ Candy, Inc. (UK)
Stickers were distributed through PEZ refill packs.
- ❏ C-3PO [489-188]...5.00
- ❏ Darth Vader [489-189]...5.00
- ❏ Han Solo..5.00
- ❏ Luke Skywalker [489-190]...................................5.00
- ❏ Princess Leia [489-191].......................................5.00
- ❏ R2-D2 [489-192]..5.00
- ❏ Stormtrooper [489-193].......................................5.00
- ❏ Yoda [489-194]..5.00

(Russia)
Set of 37, numbered.
- ❏ Stickers 1–40, each [489-195 to 489-218]..........4.00
- ❏ Complete set...100.00

Schick
- ❏ Anakin Skywalker [489-219].................................5.00
- ❏ Darth Maul [489-220]...5.00
- ❏ Jar Jar Binks [489-221]...5.00
- ❏ Obi-Wan Kenobi [489-222]...................................5.00
- ❏ Qui-Gon Jinn [489-223]..5.00

Tip-Top (New Zealand)
Jedi Jelly.
- ❏ C-3PO surrounded by Ewoks [489-224]............20.00
- ❏ Warock [489-225]...20.00
- ❏ Wicket [489-226]..20.00
- ❏ Wicket, R2, and C-3PO [489-227].......................20.00

R2-D2 Space Ice.
- ❏ Death Star [489-228]..40.00
- ❏ Han and Chewie [489-229].................................40.00
- ❏ Han in Gunwell [489-230]...................................40.00
- ❏ Luke vs. Vader Painting [489-231].....................40.00
- ❏ Millennium Falcon in Docking Bay [489-232]....40.00
- ❏ Pilots in Hangar [489-233].................................40.00
- ❏ Princess Leia and R2 [489-234].........................40.00
- ❏ Purchase of the Droids [489-235]......................40.00
- ❏ Sandcrawler [489-236]......................................40.00
- ❏ These Aren't the Droids You're Looking For [489-237].....40.00
- ❏ TIE Pilot [489-238]...40.00
- ❏ Tusken Raiders [489-239]..................................40.00
- ❏ Vader on the Rebel Ship [489-240]....................40.00
- ❏ X-Wing Battle in Trench [489-241].....................40.00
- ❏ X-Wing in Trench [489-242]...............................40.00

Twinkies premiums.
- ❏ Chewbacca [489-243]...30.00
- ❏ Darth Vader [489-244].......................................30.00
- ❏ Luke Skywalker [489-245].................................30.00
- ❏ Princess Leia [489-246].....................................30.00
- ❏ See Threepio [489-247].....................................30.00
- ❏ Yoda [489-248]..30.00

456

Stickers: Return of the Jedi

    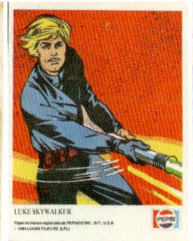  

489-181 489-182 489-183 489-184 489-185 489-186 489-187

 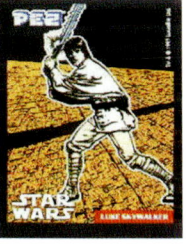    

489-188 489-189 489-190 489-191 489-192 489-193 489-194

UFO (Netherlands)
- ❏ C-3PO [489-249]...45.00
- ❏ Chewbacca [489-250]..45.00
- ❏ Princess Leia [489-251]..45.00
- ❏ Yoda [489-252]..45.00

Walkers (UK)
Square stickers are 1.5" x 1.5". Set of 7, unnumbered.
- ❏ Stickers, each [489-253 to 489-254].........................2.00
- ❏ Complete set..15.00

Stickers: Return of the Jedi

Butterfly Originals
Puffed stickers.
- ❏ Darth Vader, Luke Skywalker, Patrol (Star Destroyer), TIE Fighter, Galactic Emperor (Stormtrooper), Millennium Falcon [490-01] 25.00
- ❏ Princess Leia Organa, Han Solo, Lando Calrissian, Monster (Rancor), Wicket, Shuttle Tydirium [490-02]...................25.00
- ❏ R2-D2, Jabba the Hutt, Salacious Crumb, C-3PO, Chewbacca, Yoda [490-03]..25.00

C and D Visionaries, Inc.
- ❏ R2-D2 and C-3PO [490-04] 4.00

Campina Fun Products (UK)
Color plastic stickers are 4.5".
- ❏ 3-pack, random 40.00
- ❏ 6-pack, random 50.00
- ❏ Admiral Ackbar [490-06]..20.00
- ❏ Baby Ewoks [490-07]...20.00
- ❏ C-3PO [490-08]..20.00
- ❏ Chewbacca [490-09]..20.00
- ❏ Darth Vader [490-10]..20.00
- ❏ Gamorrean Guard [490-11].....................................20.00
- ❏ Jabba the Hutt and Salacious Crumb [490-12]...........20.00
- ❏ Klaatu [490-13] 20.00
- ❏ Paploo [490-14]..20.00
- ❏ R2-D2 [490-15]...20.00
- ❏ Shuttle Tydirium [490-16]..20.00
- ❏ Yoda the Jedi Master [490-17].................................20.00

Color puffed plastic stickers are 4.5".
- ❏ Admiral Ackbar..30.00
- ❏ Baby Ewoks [490-18]...30.00
- ❏ C-3PO..30.00
- ❏ Chewbacca..30.00
- ❏ Darth Vader..30.00
- ❏ Gamorrean Guard..30.00
- ❏ Jabba the Hutt...30.00
- ❏ Klaatu..30.00
- ❏ Paploo..30.00
- ❏ R2-D2..30.00
- ❏ Shuttle Tydirium..30.00
- ❏ Yoda the Jedi Master...30.00

   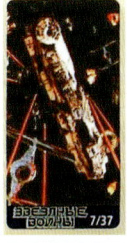       

489-195 489-196 489-197 489-198 489-199 489-200 489-201 489-202 489-203 489-204 489-205

489-206 489-207 489-208 489-209 489-210 489-211 489-212 489-213 489-214 489-215 489-216

489-217 489-218 489-219 489-220 489-221 489-222 489-223 489-224 489-225 489-226

Stickers: Return of the Jedi

Campina Fun Products (Italy)
Il Ritorno dello Jedi. Approximately 4.5 inches.
- 1 Luke Skywalker [490-19]..........30.00
- 2 Boba Fett [490-20]..........30.00
- 3 Guardia Gamorreana [490-21]..........30.00
- 4 Dart Fener [490-22]..........30.00
- 5 D3-BO [490-23]..........30.00
- 6 Max Rebo [490-24]..........30.00
- 7 Jabba [490-25]..........30.00
- 8 Bib Fortuna [490-26]..........30.00
- 9 Imperatore Galactico [490-27]..........30.00
- 10 Ciubecca [490-28]..........30.00

Stickers: Revenge of the Sith

- ☐ 11 Paploo [490-29] 30.00
- ☐ 12 C1-P8 [490-30] 30.00
- ☐ 13 Ben Kenobi [490-31] 30.00
- ☐ 14 Lando Calrissian [490-32] 30.00
- ☐ 15 Ammeraglio Ackbar [490-33] 30.00
- ☐ 16 Joda [490-34] 30.00
- ☐ 17 Ian Solo [490-35] 30.00
- ☐ 18 Leila Organa [490-36] 30.00

Rapport
Sheet of 3.
- ☐ C-3PO and R2-D2 [490-37] 30.00
- ☐ Darth Vader [490-38] 30.00

Rolf Schultz (Germany)
- ☐ Logra024, Leia, Yoda, Chief Chirpa, Han, X-Wing, lightsaber, Luke and Vader duel [490-39] 15.00
- ☐ Vader, Yoda, Royal Guard, Endor Heroes, Star Barrle, Heroes, Star Destroyer, Ewoks [490-40] 15.00

Topps
180 stickers, numbered. Some images require multiple stickers to complete. Checklist in 3rd edition, page 397.
- ☐ Stickers 1–180, each 1.00
- ☐ Complete set 90.00

Album stickers.
- ☐ 5-pack 15.00

Series 1–2. Stickers included with cards sold in wax packs. Images in 2nd edition, page 205. Checklist in 3rd edition, page 304.
- ☐ Series 1, stickers 1–33, each [490-41] 15.00
- ☐ Series 2, stickers 34–55 [490-42] 15.00

Ultra-Figus (Spain)
- ☐ El Regreso del Jedi set of 240 .... 80.00

Stickers: Revenge of the Sith

2.5" round. Walmart giveaways.
- ☐ Darth Vader 5.00
- ☐ Darth Vader (close-up) 5.00
- ☐ Obi-Wan vs. Anakin 5.00
- ☐ Obi-Wan vs. Anakin indoor 5.00
- ☐ Yoda 5.00

(France)
- ☐ Sheet of 8, rectangular [491-01] 5.00
- ☐ Sheet of 9, 1 long and 8 round [491-02] 5.00

Animations
- ☐ 13 stickers [491-03] 5.00

C and D Visionaries, Inc.
- ☐ Chewbacca [v1e1:421] 5.00
- ☐ Clone trooper [v1e1:421] 5.00
- ☐ Darth Vader Sith Lord [v1e1:421] 5.00
- ☐ Yoda, round [v1e1:421] 5.00

Round.
- ☐ Anakin vs. Obi-Wan [v1e1:421] 5.00
- ☐ C-3PO and R2-D2 [v1e1:421] 5.00
- ☐ Darth Vader [v1e1:421] 5.00
- ☐ Darth Vader (close-up) [v1e1:421] 5.00
- ☐ General Grievous [v1e1:421] 5.00
- ☐ Yoda [v1e1:421] 5.00

Shaped characters.
- ☐ Boba Fett [491-04] 8.00
- ☐ C-3PO [491-05] 8.00
- ☐ Clone trooper [491-06] 8.00
- ☐ Darth Vader [491-07] 8.00
- ☐ Darth Vader with lightsaber [491-08] 8.00
- ☐ Luke Skywalker [491-09] 8.00
- ☐ Obi-Wan Kenobi [491-10] 8.00
- ☐ Yoda [491-11] 8.00

Sheets of 8.
- ☐ Han Solo, droids, Obi-Wan, Death Star duel, C-3PO on Tatooine, Princess Leia, X-Wings, R5-D4 [491-12] 10.00

Sheets of 10.
- ☐ Darth Vader, Anakin, Darth Vader, Clones, epic duel, Anakin, Yoda, Darth Vader, Jedi, Darth Vader [491-13] 10.00
- ☐ Epic duel, Darth Vader, epic duel, Jedi, Vader in flames, Jedi, 4 small [491-14] 10.00
- ☐ Jabba, Death Star duel, X-Wing, ceremony, Obi-Wan, Luke, Han Solo, Princess Leia, logo, Death Star escape [491-15] 10.00

Skateboard stickers.
- ☐ Vader [491-16] 8.00

Stickers for Trick or Treaters.
- ☐ Box of 20 boxes 15.00

Fun Stuff
Sheets of 9.
- ☐ Obi-Wan, Yoda, Darth Vader, Boba Fett, Chewbacca, C-3PO and R2-D2, General Grievous, Clone trooper, Anakin [491-17] 10.00

Hallmark
- ☐ 55+ stickers, 2 sheets [491-18] 8.00

Heart Art Collection, Ltd. (Japan)
- ☐ Clone trooper, General Grievous, Yoda [491-19] ... 10.00
- ☐ Darth Vader [491-20] 10.00
- ☐ Darth Vader, Sith [491-21] 10.00
- ☐ Darth Vader, Vader [491-22] 10.00
- ☐ Posters Collection [491-23] 12.00
- ☐ Yoda Jedi Master [491-24] 10.00
- ☐ Yoda, Sith Lord, Darth Vader [491-25] 10.00

Mello Smello
- ☐ 60-count sheet [491-26] 5.00
- ☐ Stickers for Trick-or-treaters, 24 boxes bagged [491-27] ..15.00

Glittered stickers.
- ☐ 3-pack 10.00
- ☐ 501st Shock trooper [491-28] 5.00
- ☐ 501st Shock trooper, "First In, Last Standing" [491-29] ..5.00
- ☐ Anakin Skywalker [491-30] 5.00
- ☐ Chewbacca [491-31] 5.00
- ☐ Darth Vader [491-32] 5.00
- ☐ Darth Vader (helmet) [491-33] 5.00
- ☐ Epic Duel [491-34] 5.00
- ☐ General Grievous [491-35] 5.00
- ☐ Jedi Starfighters [491-36] 5.00
- ☐ Revenge of the Sith [491-37] 5.00
- ☐ The Emperor, "Power" [491-38] 5.00
- ☐ Yoda [491-39] 5.00

Unlicensed
- ☐ Sheet of 14, characters with glitter backgrounds [491-40] 10.00

Stickers: Saga

491-01 491-02 491-03 491-04 491-05 491-06 491-07 491-08 491-09 491-10 491-11 491-12

491-13 491-14 491-15 491-16 491-17 491-18 491-19 491-20 491-21 491-22 491-23

Stickers: Saga

Dyna Mart (France)
Produced in the US for French market. Classic trilogy and Episode I images. 150 sticker cards, numbered.
- ❏ Stickers s001–s150, each [492-01] 3.00

Stickers: The Phantom Menace

Episode I. Comic-style drawings.
- ❏ 5703 C-3PO, R2-D2/Luke, Yoda, Qui-Gon, Obi-Wan, Queen Amidala [493-01] 10.00
- ❏ 5703 Obi-Wan, Queen Amidala, Imperial logo, Qui-Gon vs. Maul, R2-D2, Jabba [493-02] 10.00
- ❏ CF372-1 R2-D2/C-3PO, Darth Maul, Queen Amidala, Rebellion logo, Obi-Wan, Qui-Gon [493-03] 10.00
- ❏ CF372-2 C-3PO, R2-D2/Luke, Yoda, Qui-Gon, Obi-Wan, Queen Amidala [493-04] 10.00
- ❏ CF372-3 Obi-Wan, Queen Amidala, Imperial logo, Qui-Gon vs. Maul, R2-D2, Jabba [493-05] 10.00

Sheet of 7.
- ❏ Maul/battleship/logo, Padmé/Obi-Wan, Rodarian, Anakin/logo, blaster, Gungan Sub, C-3PO [493-06] 10.00

Sheets of 9.
- ❏ Jar Jar, R2-D2, Battleship, Amidala/logo, TC-14, Maul, Royal Starship, Yoda, Watto [493-07] 10.00
- ❏ Sebulba, Maul, Sith Infiltrator, Anakin/logo, R2-D2, Nute Gunray, Droid, Blaster, Qui-Gon 10.00

(Spain)
Episode I characters, prismatic foil. Approx. 7″ tall.
- ❏ Anakin Skywalker [493-08] 10.00
- ❏ Ann and Tann Gella [493-09] 10.00
- ❏ Darth Maul [493-10] 10.00
- ❏ Jar Jar Binks [493-11] 10.00
- ❏ Mace Windu [493-12] 10.00
- ❏ Obi-Wan Kenobi [493-13] 10.00
- ❏ Padmé, queens attendant [493-14] 10.00
- ❏ Queen Amidala, battle dress [493-15] 10.00
- ❏ Queen Amidala, senate gown [493-16] 10.00
- ❏ Queen Amidala, senate gown with cape [493-17] 10.00
- ❏ Queen Amidala, travel gown [493-18] 10.00
- ❏ Qui-Gon Jinn [493-19] 10.00
- ❏ Sebulba the Dugg [493-20] 10.00
- ❏ Watto [493-21] 10.00
- ❏ Yoda [493-22] 10.00

Caltex (South Africa)
- ❏ Anakin Skywalker [493-23] 5.00
- ❏ C-3PO [493-24] 5.00
- ❏ Darth Maul [493-25] 5.00
- ❏ Jar Jar Binks [493-26] 5.00
- ❏ Obi-Wan Kenobi [493-27] 5.00
- ❏ Queen Amidala [493-28] 5.00
- ❏ Qui-Gon Jinn [493-29] 5.00
- ❏ R2-D2 [493-30] 5.00

Crazy Planet
Mega stickers. 32 stickers, numbered.
- ❏ Stickers 1–32, each [493-31–493-33] 5.00

Mini stickers. 24 stickers, numbered. Additional images and checklist in 3rd edition, page 399.
- ❏ Stickers 1–24, each [493-34] 3.00
- ❏ Complete set 65.00

Duncan
36 stickers, numbered. Additional images and checklist in 3rd edition, page 399.
- ❏ Stickers 1–35, each [493-35] 5.00
- ❏ Complete set 50.00

Linden (Chile)
Set of 40, numbered. Images in 3rd edition, page 400. Checklist in 3rd edition, page 399.
- ❏ Cards 1–40, each [493-36] 5.00
- ❏ Complete set 70.00

Meiji (Japan)
Distributed in boxes of chocolate. 24 stickers, numbered.
- ❏ Stickers 1–24, each [493-37] 5.00
- ❏ Complete set 95.00

Merlin (Italy)
Printed for Hasbro 1999 catalog. Set of 15 numbered H01–H15.
- ❏ Stickers H01–H15, each [493-38] 10.00
- ❏ Complete set 75.00

Merlin Publishing Internat'l Ltd.
244 numbered stickers. Checklist in 3rd ed., page 400.
- ❏ Stickers 1–244, each 2.00
- ❏ Complete set 70.00

491-24 491-25 491-26 491-27 491-28 491-29 491-30 491-31

491-32 491-33 491-34 491-35 491-36 491-37 491-38 491-39 491-40

String Dispensers

492-01 Sample | 493-01 | 493-02 | 493-03 | 493-04 | 493-05 | 493-06 | 493-07 | 493-08 | 493-09 | 493-10

493-11 | 493-12 | 493-13 | 493-14 | 493-15 | 493-16 | 493-17 | 493-18 | 493-19 | 493-20 | 493-21 | 493-22

Pepsi Cola
- Heroes 3.00
- Jedi vs. Sith 3.00
- Qui-Gon, Jar Jar, Maul, Amidala 3.00
- Sebulba, Anakin / Podracer [493-39] 3.00

Ricolino
Set of 24, numbered. Images in 2nd edition, page 398. Checklist in 3rd edition, page 401.
- Stickers 1–26, each [2:398] 5.00
- Complete set 75.00

Sabritas (Mexico)
Set of 39, numbered. Images in 2nd edition, page 399. Checklist in 3rd edition, page 402.
- Stickers 1–39, each [2:399] 3.00
- Complete set 50.00

Salo
Set of 176 stickers, numbered, plus foil stickers numbered A–W. Public service / PSA stickers inserted randomly. Images in 2nd edition, page 400. Checklist in 3rd edition, page 402.
- Game Pieces, each [2:400] 1.00
- Public Service Stickers, each [4:295] 1.00
- Stickers 1–176, each [2:400] 2.00
- Stickers A–W, each [2:400] 3.00

Unlicensed
- Sheet of 9: Nute Gunray, Darth Sidious, Sebulba, Qui-Gon, Obi-Wan, C-3PO and R2-D2, Watto, Jar Jar, Darth Maul ..15.00

Straws
Continued in Volume 3, Page 352

Applause
Sippers sold loose with tag.
- Jar Jar Binks [494-01] 10.00
- Pit Droid [494-02] 10.00
- R2-D2 [494-03] 10.00
- Watto [494-04] 10.00

Applause (UK)
Sold on cards.
- Jar Jar Binks Sipper [494-05] 15.00
- Pit Droid Sipper 15.00
- R2-D2 Sipper 15.00
- Watto Sipper [494-06] 15.00

Celebration III
- Darth Vader twisty [494-07] 15.00

Zak Designs
Packaged in plastic bags.
- Anakin Skywalker [494-08] 10.00
- Darth Maul [494-09] 10.00
- Jar Jar Binks [494-10] 10.00
- Queen Amidala [494-11] 10.00

Episode III: Revenge of the Sith. Boxed.
- Darth Vader [494-12] 15.00

String Dispensers

Sigma
- R2-D2 string dispenser with scissors [495-01] 185.00

     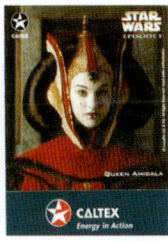  

494-01 | 494-02 | 494-03 | 494-04 | 494-05 | 494-06 | 494-07 | 494-08 | 494-09 | 494-10 | 494-11 | 494-12

493-23 | 493-24 | 493-25 | 493-26 | 493-27 | 493-28 | 493-29 | 493-30

493-31 Sample | 493-32 Sample | 493-33 Sample | 493-34 Sample | 493-35 Sample | 493-36 Sample | 493-37 Sample | 493-38 Sample | 493-39 Sample

461

Subway Tickets

     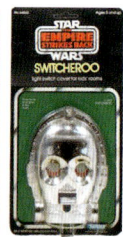  

495-01 | 496-01 | 496-02 | 496-03 | 497-01 | 497-02 | 497-03 | 497-04

  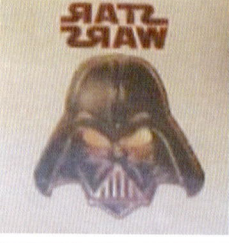   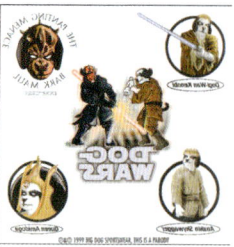

498-01 | 498-02 | 499-01 | 499-02 | 499-03 | 499-04

Subway Tickets

- ❏ Metro Passenger 75.00

SMRT
Classic trilogy.
- ❏ Empire Strikes Back style A [v1e1:424] 20.00
- ❏ Empire Strikes Back style B [v1e1:424] 20.00
- ❏ Return of the Jedi [v1e1:424] 20.00
- ❏ Star Wars style A [v1e1:424] 20.00
- ❏ Star Wars style B [v1e1:424] 20.00
- ❏ Ticket folder [2:402] 25.00

Episode I.
- ❏ Heroes [v1e1:424] 10.00
- ❏ Queen Amidala [v1e1:424] 10.00
- ❏ Sith Lord, Darth Maul [v1e1:424] 10.00
- ❏ Villains [v1e1:424] 10.00

Super Packs

Alligator Books (UK)
- ❏ Busy pack, reusable stickers, press-out figures, door hanger, book mark [496-01] 10.00

Antioch
Classic trilogy.
- ❏ Memo board with pen, 2 wallet cards, 1 tasseled bookmark, 1 die-cut bookmark, 1 doorknob hanger [496-02] 15.00

Episode I: The Phantom Menace.
- ❏ Memo board with pen, 2 wallet cards, 1 tasseled bookmark, 1 die-cut bookmark [496-03] 10.00

Switch Plates and Covers

- ❏ Turn-Ons, Boba Fett [3:404] 10.00

Hot Topic

- ❏ A New Hope movie poster art [497-01] 8.00

Kenner
Switcheroos.
- ❏ C-3PO [497-02] 250.00
- ❏ Darth Vader [497-03] 300.00
- ❏ R2-D2 [497-04] 250.00

Tape and Dispensers
Continued in Volume 3, Page 352

Butterfly Originals
- ❏ Darth Vader Return of the Jedi with 16 ft. of tape [498-01] 20.00

Sigma
- ❏ C-3PO, ceramic [498-02] 650.00

    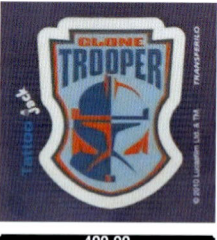  

499-05 | 499-06 | 499-07 | 499-08 | 499-09 | 499-10 | 499-11

499-12 | 499-13 | 499-14 | 499-15 | 499-16 | 499-17

499-18 | 499-19 | 499-20 | 499-21 | 499-22 | 499-23 | 499-24

Tattoos, Temporary

499-25 · 499-26 · 499-27 · 499-28 · 499-29 · 499-30 · 499-31

499-32 · 499-34 · 499-33 · 499-35 · 499-36 · 499-37 · 499-38

Tattoos, Temporary
Continued in Volume 3, Page 352

- "Star Wars," Darth Vader Comic-Con 2004 exclusive [499-01] 3.00

(Australia)
Episode III: Revenge of the Sith.
- Tattstack, 15 tattoos, storage tin, applicator [499-02] 20.00

Amulet Books
- The Secret of the Fortune Wookiee, the third book in the bestselling origami Yoda series [499-03] 3.00

Big Dog
- Dog Wars, sheet of 5 [499-04] 5.00

Cartoon Network
- Clone Wars, sheet of 6, Logo, Anakin Skywalker, R2-D2, Captain Rex, Yoda, Cartoon Network logo [499-05] 5.00

Del Rey
- Stormtrooper / Allegiance, given away during Timothy Zahn signing tour [499-06] 5.00

Felfont (Argentina)
Clone Wars. Chocolate egg premiums.
- Anakin and Obi-Wan [499-07] 3.00
- Capt Rex in cross hairs [499-08] 3.00
- Clone trooper [499-09] 3.00
- Clone trooper with blaster rifle [499-10] 3.00
- Obi-Wan Kenobi [499-11] 3.00
- Obi-Wan torso [499-12] 3.00
- Rex [499-13] 3.00
- Rex, "First In, Last Standing" [499-14] 3.00
- Yoda [499-15] 3.00

General Mills
Episode II: Attack of the Clones cereal premium.
- Anakin / Zam Wesell [499-16] 3.00
- Obi-Wan / Jango Fett [499-17] 3.00
- Padmé / Battle Droid [499-18] 3.00
- Yoda / Count Dooku [499-19] 3.00

Hallmark Party
- Clone Wars [499-20] 5.00
- Star Wars characters [499-21] 5.00
- Star Wars Generations [499-22] 5.00

Hasbro
- Get Revenge [499-23] 5.00

IMC Toys (UK)
- Clone Wars Tattoo Studio [499-24] 60.00

Innovative Designs
Sheets of 8.
- Classic characters 5.00
- Clone Wars [499-25] 5.00

Sheets of 12.
- Angry Birds characters, C-3PO, Wedge, Darth Vader, Luke, Han, Chewbacca, R2-D2, Luke Pilot, Obi-Wan Kenobi, Princess Leia, stormtrooper, Yoda [499-26] 5.00
- Classic characters, Chewbacca, Boba Fett, Darth Vader, stormtrooper, "Vader," Droids, Luke, Yoda, Han, Leia, Imperial emblem (tribal), Rebel Alliance emblem (tribal) 5.00

499-39 · 499-40 · 499-41 · 499-42 · 499-43 · 499-44 · 499-45 · 499-46 · 499-47 · 499-48 · 499-49

499-50 · 499-51 · 499-52 · 499-53 · 499-54 · 499-55 · 499-56 · 499-57 · 499-58

499-59 · 499-60 · 499-61 · 499-62 · 499-63 · 499-64 · 499-65 · 499-66 · 499-67

Tattoos, Temporary

499-68 · 499-69 · 499-70 · 499-71 · 499-72 · 499-73 · 499-74 · 499-75 · 499-76

449-77 · 449-78 · 449-79 · 449-80 · 449-81 · 449-82 · 449-83 · 449-84 · 449-85

Sheets of 28.
- ❏ Classic trilogy iconography, Ages 3+ [499-27] 8.00

Jedi Assembly
- ❏ I Survived Order 66 [499-28] 5.00

Lyons Maid
Ice cream premiums. Strips of 3, unused.
- ❏ Admiral Ackbar, Darth Vader, Bib Fortuna 25.00
- ❏ Chewbacca, Gamorrean Guard, R2-D2 ....25.00
- ❏ Greedo, stormtrooper, Han 25.00
- ❏ Jabba the Hutt, Obi-Wan, Princess Leia 25.00
- ❏ Wicket, Emperor, Luke 25.00
- ❏ Yoda, Boba Fett, C-3PO 25.00

McDonalds
Included with Clone Wars fingerboards premiums.
- ❏ Anakin Skywalker [499-29] 3.00
- ❏ Asajj Ventress [499-30] 3.00
- ❏ Cad Bane [499-31] 3.00
- ❏ Captain Rex [499-32] 3.00
- ❏ Commander Cody [499-33] 3.00
- ❏ General Grievous [499-34] 3.00
- ❏ Mace Windu [499-35] 3.00
- ❏ Obi-Wan Kenobi [499-36] 3.00
- ❏ Yoda [499-37] 3.00

Mello Smello
Classic trilogy.
- ❏ Boba Fett, Darth Vader, C-3PO, Chewbacca, Landspeeder, Millennium Falcon, Vader, Princess Leia, Darth Vader, Star Wars, X-Wing [499-38] 5.00
- ❏ Darth Vader, R2-D2, Jawa, Luke, TIE Fighter, Chewbacca, Vader's TIE, X-Wing, Vader, Han Solo, C-3PO, Princess Leia, Obi-Wan, Millennium Falcon, Star Wars [499-39] 5.00
- ❏ TIE, Jawa, X-Wings, Leia, Vader's TIE, Droids, Obi-Wan [499-40] 8.00
- ❏ X-Wing, Tusken Raider, Chewbacca and Han, Han Solo, R2-D2, landspeeder [499-41] 8.00

Revenge of the Sith.
- ❏ Darth Vader, Vader, Grievous, Jedi emblem, duel, Vader's helmet, Jedi, ARC-170, Vader, Jedi, Grievous, Grievous [499-42] 5.00
- ❏ Darth Vader, Vader, Jedi, Hero, Vader, helmet, Yoda, Jedi emblem, Sith, Sith Lord [499-43] 5.00
- ❏ Shield, Jedi Starfighter, Darth Vader, Sith, General Grievous, lightsaber battle, ARC-170, Jedi [499-44] 8.00
- ❏ Sith Lord 3.00
- ❏ Vader in flames, Anakin's Jedi Starfighter, Jedi symbol, Jedi, Sith, Republic symbol, Sith Lord [499-45] 8.00

Norben
- ❏ Skin Transfers reusable, Anakin and Sebulba [499-46] 10.00
- ❏ Skin Transfers reusable, Jedi vs. Sith [499-47] 10.00

Panini (UK)
- ❏ 1 Aayla Secura and Barriss Offee [499-48] 3.00
- ❏ 2 Plo Koon [499-49] 3.00
- ❏ 3 Mace Windu [499-50] 3.00
- ❏ 4 Kit Fisto [499-51] 3.00
- ❏ 5 Aurra Sing [499-52] 3.00
- ❏ 6 Bossk [499-53] 3.00
- ❏ 7 Cad Bane [499-54] 3.00
- ❏ 8 C-3PO [499-55] 3.00
- ❏ 9 Battle Droid [499-56] 3.00

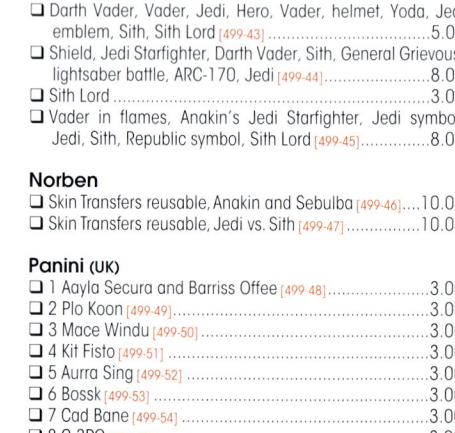

449-86 · 449-87 · 449-88 · 449-89 · 449-90 · 449-91 · 449-92 · 449-93 · 449-94

449-95 · 449-96 · 449-97 · 449-98 · 449-99 · TT100 · TT101 · TT102 · TT103

499-104 · 499-105 · 499-106 · 499-107 · 499-108 · 499-109 · 499-110 · 499-111 · 499-112

Tazos

      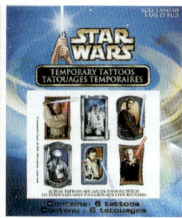 

499-113 | 499-114 | 499-115 | 499-116 | 499-117 | 499-118 | 499-119 | 499-120

- ❏ 10 Super Battle Droid [499-57].........................3.00
- ❏ 11 R2-D2 and C-3PO [499-58]...........................3.00
- ❏ 12 Ahsoka [499-59]...3.00
- ❏ 13 ARC trooper [499-60]...................................3.00
- ❏ 14 Anakin [499-61]..3.00
- ❏ 15 Trooper [499-62]..3.00
- ❏ 16 Obi-Wan [499-63]...3.00
- ❏ 17 Captain [499-64]..3.00
- ❏ 18 Savage [499-65]...3.00
- ❏ 19 Yoda [499-66]...3.00
- ❏ 20 Jedi emblem [499-67]...................................3.00
- ❏ 21 Republic emblem [499-68]............................3.00
- ❏ 22 Obi-Wan, Anakin, Yoda [499-69]...................3.00
- ❏ 23 Clone Commanders [499-70].........................3.00
- ❏ 24 Boba Fett [499-71]..3.00
- ❏ 25 Slave I [499-72]..3.00
- ❏ 26 Shaak Ti [499-73]...3.00
- ❏ 27 General Grievous [499-74]............................3.00
- ❏ 28 ARC trooper [499-75]...................................3.00
- ❏ 29 Savage Oppress [499-76].............................3.00
- ❏ 30 Yoda [499-77]...3.00
- ❏ 31 Captain Rex [499-78]....................................3.00
- ❏ 32 Yoda [499-79]...3.00
- ❏ 33 Ahsoka [499-80]..3.00
- ❏ 34 Clone trooper [499-81].................................3.00
- ❏ 35 Anakin Skywalker [499-82]...........................3.00
- ❏ 36 Captain Rex [499-83]....................................3.00
- ❏ 37 Droid Tri-Fighter [499-84]............................3.00
- ❏ 38 Obi-Wan Kenobi [499-85]..............................3.00
- ❏ 39 Delta Squad [499-86]....................................3.00
- ❏ 40 Saesee Tiin [499-87].....................................3.00
- ❏ 41 Anakin Skywalker [499-88]...........................3.00
- ❏ 42 Kit Fisto [499-89]..3.00
- ❏ 43 Chewbacca [499-90].....................................3.00
- ❏ 44 The Clone Wars [499-91]..............................3.00
- ❏ 45 Obi-Wan vs. Savage [499-92].......................3.00
- ❏ 46 Death Watch [499-93]...................................3.00
- ❏ 47 Vulture Droid [499-94]..................................3.00
- ❏ 48 Twilight [499-95]...3.00
- ❏ 49 Jedi Starfighter [499-96]...............................3.00
- ❏ 50 Y-Wing Fighter [499-97]................................3.00
- ❏ 51 Jedi Knight [499-98]......................................3.00
- ❏ 52 Pre Vizsla [499-99]..3.00
- ❏ 53 Savage [499-100]..3.00
- ❏ 54 Yoda [499-101]...3.00
- ❏ 55 Jabba the Hutt [499-102].............................3.00
- ❏ 56 Anakin and Obi-Wan [499-103].....................3.00
- ❏ 57 General Grievous vs. Anakin Skywalker [499-104].......3.00
- ❏ 58 Asajj Ventress [499-105]..............................3.00
- ❏ 59 Y-Wing Fighter [499-106].............................3.00
- ❏ 60 ARC-170 [499-107].......................................3.00
- ❏ Unopened packet [499-108]............................10.00

Party Express
- ❏ 5-pack: Vader helmet in flames, Jedi emblem, Darth Vader, Jedi Master, Vader 10.00
- ❏ Clone Wars [499-109].......................................5.00
- ❏ Star Wars: Rebel Alliance, TIE Fighter Squadron, Red Leader, troopers, Rebel, TIE Fighter, 2 sheets [499-110]...............5.00

Pepsi
Episode I: The Phantom Menace.
- ❏ Darth Maul / "Sith Lord" 5.00
- ❏ Queen Amidala / "Queen Amidala" 5.00
- ❏ Qui-Gon Jinn / Naboo Fighter 5.00

Revell
- ❏ Tattoo Set [499-111]..15.00

Rose Art Industries
- ❏ Fun with Tattoos [499-112]..............................15.00

Star Wars Celebration VI
Emblems.
- ❏ Empire [499-113]...5.00
- ❏ Mandalorians [499-114].....................................5.00
- ❏ Rebel Alliance [499-115]....................................5.00

starwars.com
- ❏ Ewok Village [499-116].....................................15.00
- ❏ Jawas and Droid [499-117]..............................15.00

Tapper Candies
- ❏ Episode I: The Phantom Menace, pkg. of 16 [499-118].....8.00
- ❏ Episode II: Attack of the Clones, package of 6 [499-119]...8.00

Topps
- ❏ Clone Wars Jedi Starfighter #7 [499-120].........5.00

Tazos
Continued in Volume 3, Page 354

ConAgra Foods (Peru)
Set of 20 Tazos, unnumbered.
- ❏ Tazos, each..3.00
- ❏ Complete set...40.00

Tazo (Australia)
20 Tazos, numbered 81–160 plus 3 special "Connect-a-Tazo" starship cards. Images in 2nd edition, page 404. Checklist in 3rd edition, page 405.
- ❏ Tazos 81–100 (3D motion), each......................2.00
- ❏ Tazos 101–130 (octagonal), each [500-01].......2.00
- ❏ Tazos 131–140 (3D), each................................2.00
- ❏ Tazos 141–160 (hologram), each.....................2.00
- ❏ Shuttle (Connect-a-Tazo) [500-03].................10.00
- ❏ TIE Fighter (Connect-a-Tazo) [500-04]...........10.00
- ❏ X-Wing (Connect-a-Tazo) [500-05].................10.00

Tazo (China)
40 Tazos, numbered. 15 holo foil Tazos throughout the set. Checklist in 3rd edition, page 406.
- ❏ Holofoil Tazo, any number, each.......................3.00
- ❏ Regular Tazo, any number, each.......................3.00

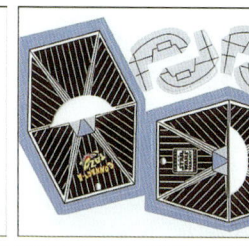 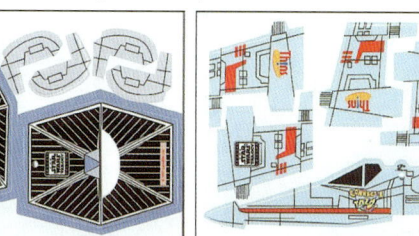

500-03 | 500-04 | 500-05

500-01 Sample | 500-02 Sample | 500-06 Sample | 500-07 Sample | 501-01

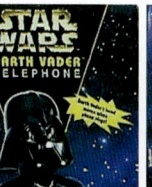       

501-02 | 501-03 | 501-04 | 501-05 | 501-06 | 501-07 | 501-08 | 502-01 | 502-02

Tazos

        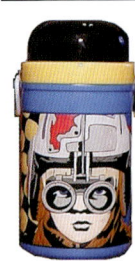

Tazo (Mexico)
50 numbered Tazo, plus one bonus Tazo. Images in 2nd edition, page 408. Checklist in 3rd edition, page 406.
- ❏ Tazos 1–50, each [500-06] 2.00
- ❏ Bonus Darth Vader Tazo 4.00

Tazo (Poland)
50 numbered Tazos. Checklist in 3rd edition, page 406.
- ❏ Tazos 1–50, each 3.00

Tazo (UK)
50 numbered Tazos. Checklist in 3rd edition, page 406.
- ❏ Tazos 1–50, each [500-07] 2.00

Telephones

American Telecommunications
- ❏ Darth Vader speakerphone [501-01] 95.00

Sound Trax
- ❏ Darth Vader [501-02] 150.00
- ❏ R2-D2 [501-03] 150.00

Telemania (UK)
- ❏ Darth Vader, Episode III Box [501-04] 165.00
- ❏ R2-D2, Episode I Box [501-05] 150.00
- ❏ R2-D2, Episode III Box [501-06] 150.00

Tiger Electronics
Compact phones.
- ❏ Darth Maul [501-07] 25.00
- ❏ Queen Amidala [501-08] 25.00

Tents
Continued in Volume 3, Page 354

Monkey Business
- ❏ Darth Vader [502-01] 25.00
- ❏ Epic duel [502-02] 25.00

Thermos
Continued in Volume 3, Page 354

- ❏ Darth Vader pop-up thermos [503-01] 260.00

Aladdin (Peru)
- ❏ Guerra de las Estrellas [503-02] 500.00

King Seeley-Thermos
- ❏ Star Wars: R2-D2 and C-3PO, blue [503-03] 35.00
- ❏ Star Wars: R2-D2 and C-3PO, red [503-04] 80.00
- ❏ Empire Strikes Back: Yoda, blue [503-05] 35.00
- ❏ Empire Strikes Back: Yoda, red [503-06] 35.00
- ❏ Return of the Jedi: Wicket, blue [503-07] 80.00
- ❏ Return of the Jedi: Wicket, red [503-08] 20.00
- ❏ Droids [503-09] 100.00
- ❏ Ewoks: Princess Kneesaa [503-10] 90.00

King Seeley-Thermos (UK)
- ❏ Empire Strikes Back: Darth Vader [503-11] 90.00

Star Wars Celebration V
- ❏ Stormtrooper [503-12] 25.00

Thermos Co.
- ❏ Clone Wars [503-13] 15.00
- ❏ Clone Wars portable beverage container [503-14] 10.00
- ❏ Darth Vader [503-15] 15.00
- ❏ Geonosis Duel 15.00
- ❏ Slave I [503-16] 20.00

Zak Designs
- ❏ Anakin and Sebulba with cup lid [503-17] 20.00

Sip N' Snack canteens.
- ❏ Anakin and Sebulba [503-18] 10.00
- ❏ Anakin and Sebulba with podrace cup [503-19] 12.00
- ❏ Anakin Skywalker [503-20] 8.00

Thimbles

Birchcroft
China thimbles, hand-painted collection 1.
- ❏ C-3PO [504-01] 10.00
- ❏ Chewbacca [504-02] 10.00
- ❏ Darth Vader [504-03] 10.00
- ❏ General Jan Dodonna [504-04] 10.00
- ❏ Grand Moff Tarkin [504-05] 10.00
- ❏ Han Solo [504-06] 10.00
- ❏ Leia Organa [504-07] 10.00
- ❏ Luke Skywalker [504-08] 10.00
- ❏ R2-D2 [504-09] 10.00
- ❏ Yoda [504-10] 10.00

China thimbles, hand-painted collection 2.
- ❏ Darth Maul [504-11] 10.00
- ❏ Darth Sidious [504-12] 10.00
- ❏ Exar Kun [504-13] 5.00
- ❏ Freedon Nadd [504-14] 5.00
- ❏ Naga Sadow [504-15] 5.00
- ❏ Obi-Wan Kenobi [504-16] 10.00
- ❏ Palpatine [504-17] 10.00

Toothbrushes

       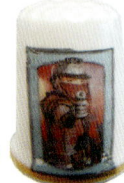 

❏ Senate Statue [504-18] 5.00
❏ Too-Onebee [504-19] 10.00
❏ Ulic Qel-Droma [504-20] 5.00
❏ Wicket [504-21] 10.00

China thimbles, hand-painted collection 3.
❏ Anakin Skywalker [504-22] 10.00
❏ Clone trooper [504-23] 10.00
❏ Count Dooku [504-24] 10.00
❏ Jango Fett [504-25] 10.00
❏ Mace Windu [504-26] 10.00
❏ Obi-Wan Kenobi [504-27] 10.00
❏ Yoda [504-28] 10.00
❏ Zam Wesell [504-29] 10.00

China thimbles, hand-painted collection 4.
❏ Ben Kenobi [504-30] 10.00
❏ Chewbacca [504-31] 10.00
❏ Darth Vader [504-32] 10.00
❏ Grand Moff Tarkin [504-33] 10.00
❏ Han Solo [504-34] 10.00
❏ Lando Calrissian [504-35] 10.00
❏ Luke Skywalker [504-36] 10.00
❏ MonMothma [504-37] 10.00
❏ Princess Leia [504-38] 10.00
❏ Yoda [504-39] 10.00

China thimbles.
❏ A New Hope movie poster art, hand painted [504-40] 10.00

Timers, Kitchen

Taito (Japan)
❏ R2-D2 [505-01] 100.00

Tissue Covers

Heart Art Collection, Ltd. (Japan)
❏ R2-D2 roll tissue cover [506-01] 45.00

Jay Franco and Sons
❏ Space battle scene printed on 2 sides [506-02] 15.00

Toasters
Continued in Volume 3, Page 355

Underground Toys
❏ Star Wars, toasts Vader image into bread [507-01] 60.00

Tooth Care
Continued in Volume 3, Page 356

Dr Fresh LLC
❏ Floss Picks [508-01] 10.00

Toothbrush Holders
Continued in Volume 3, Page 356

(UK)
❏ Toothbrush and light-up beaker set [509-01] 20.00

Grosvenor
❏ Darth Maul, electronic [509-02] 40.00
❏ Droid Fighter and Naboo Fighter, rotating [509-03] 35.00
❏ Jar Jar Binks, 3D [509-04] 20.00

Jay Franco and Sons
❏ Anakin / Sebulba 2 sided sculpt [509-05] 15.00

Sigma
❏ Snowspeeder toothbrush holder [509-06] 175.00

Toothbrushes
Continued in Volume 3, Page 356

Avon (Mexico)
❏ Anakin Skywalker [510-01] 12.00
❏ C-3PO [510-02] 12.00
❏ Padmé Amidala 12.00
❏ R2-D2 [510-03] 12.00

Colgate
Classic trilogy.
❏ Darth Vader [510-04] 8.00
❏ Droids on Tatooine [510-05] 8.00
❏ Luke Skywalker, X-Wing Pilot [510-06] 8.00
❏ Luke Skywalker, X-Wing Pilot (space battle) [510-07] 8.00
❏ Princess Leia [510-08] 8.00
❏ Princess Leia (Rebel insignia) [510-09] 8.00

The Phantom Menace.
❏ Anakin Skywalker [510-10] 8.00
❏ C-3PO [510-11] 8.00
❏ Darth Maul [510-12] 8.00
❏ Jar Jar Binks (Naboo) [510-13] 8.00
❏ Jar Jar Binks (Tatooine) [510-14] 8.00
❏ "Jedi vs. Sith" with Free Darth Maul Holder [510-15] 8.00
❏ Obi-Wan (Jedi vs. Sith) [510-16] 8.00
❏ Queen Amidala (Coruscant) [510-17] 8.00
❏ Queen Amidala (travel gown) [510-18] 8.00

The Phantom Menace. Sculpted character handle.
❏ Anakin Skywalker as podracer pilot [510-19] 10.00
❏ Darth Vader [510-20] 10.00
❏ Jar Jar Binks [510-21] 10.00
❏ Yoda [510-22] 10.00

The Phantom Menace. Sculpted character toothbrush holder.
❏ Anakin Skywalker / Anakin [510-23] 12.00
❏ Anakin Skywalker / R2-D2 [510-24] 12.00
❏ Jar Jar Binks (Naboo) / Jar Jar [510-25] 12.00
❏ Jar Jar Binks (Naboo) / R2-D2 [510-26] 12.00
❏ Obi-Wan (Jedi vs. Sith) / Darth Maul [510-27] 12.00
❏ Obi-Wan (Jedi vs. Sith) / R2-D2 [510-28] 12.00
❏ Queen Amidala (Coruscant) / Amidala [510-29] 12.00
❏ Queen Amidala (Coruscant) / R2-D2 [510-30] 12.00

Toothbrushes

Episode I: The Phantom Menace. Sculpted character head single brush toothbrush holder, toothbrush, and toothpaste.
- ❑ Darth Maul / Darth Maul [510-31].................20.00
- ❑ Jar Jar Binks (Naboo) / Jar Jar [510-32].................20.00
- ❑ Queen Amidala (Coruscant) / Amidala [510-33].................20.00

Colgate (Singapore)
Episode I: The Phantom Menace.
- ❑ Anakin Skywalker [510-34].................15.00
- ❑ Jar Jar Binks (Naboo) [510-35].................15.00
- ❑ Jedi vs. Sith [510-36].................15.00
- ❑ Queen Amidala (Coruscant) [510-37].................15.00

Grosvenor
- ❑ Jango Fett, figural [510-38].................25.00
- ❑ Lightsaber, handle blinks red [510-39].................10.00

H and A (UK)
- ❑ Yoda toothbrush set, glow-in-the-dark [510-40].................25.00

468

Towels: Bath

         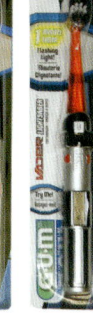  

510-54 | 510-55 | 510-56 | 510-57 | 510-58 | 510-59 | 510-60 | 510-61 | 510-62 | 510-63 | 510-64 | 510-65 | 510-66 | 510-67 | 510-68 | 510-69

511-01 | 511-02 | 511-03 | 511-04 | 511-05 | 511-06 | 511-07 | 511-08 | 511-09 | 511-10

Kenner
Battery operated.
- Star Wars [510-41] 385.00
- Wicket the Ewok [510-42] 355.00

Oral-B
On card back.
- C-3PO and R2-D2 [510-43] 40.00
- Chewbacca and Han Solo [510-44] ... 40.00
- Darth Vader [510-45] 40.00
- Ewoks [510-46] 40.00
- Luke Skywalker [510-47] 40.00
- Princess Leia [510-48] 40.00

Shrink wrapped without card back.
- 3-pack, any characters 200.00
- C-3PO and R2-D2 [510-49] 25.00
- Chewbacca and Han Solo [510-50] ... 25.00
- Darth Vader [510-51] 25.00
- Ewoks [510-52] 25.00
- Jedi Masters (premium) [510-53] 25.00
- Luke Skywalker [510-54] 25.00
- Princess Leia [510-55] 25.00

Oral-B (Canada)
Shrink wrapped without card back. English and French.
- C-3PO and R2-D2 [510-56] 30.00
- Chewbacca and Han Solo [510-57] ... 30.00
- Darth Vader [510-58] 30.00
- Ewoks [510-59] 30.00
- Luke Skywalker [510-60] 30.00
- Princess Leia [510-61] 30.00

Sunstar Americas Inc.
- Anakin and Vader [510-62] 10.00
- Yoda and Rex [510-63] 10.00

Battery-operated characters.
- Rex [510-64] 8.00
- Vader [510-65] 8.00

Battery-operated lightsabers.
- Anakin [510-66] 8.00
- Vader [510-67] 8.00
- Yoda [510-68] 8.00

Tiger Electronics
Tooth Tunes.
- Star Wars, 2 minutes of music, sound FX, and phrases [510-69] 12.00

Toothpaste
Continued in Volume 3, Page 357

Colgate
Galactic Bubblemint flavor.
- Anakin Skywalker [511-01] 5.00
- Darth Vader and Death Star [511-02] .. 5.00
- Droids on Tatooine [511-03] 5.00
- Jar Jar Binks [511-04] 5.00
- Jedi vs. Sith [511-05] 5.00

Tartar Control with free teen/adult toothbrush.
- C-3PO (The Phantom Menace) [511-06] ... 30.00
- Darth Maul [511-07] 30.00
- Darth Vader [511-08] 30.00
- Princess Leia [511-09] 30.00
- Queen Amidala [511-10] 30.00

Totes, Record and Tape

Buena Vista Records
- Return of the Jedi cassette tote [512-01] 30.00
- Star Wars / Empire Strikes Back record tote [512-02] 35.00

Towels: Bath
Continued in Volume 3, Page 357

Bibb Co.
- Boba Fett with Darth Vader and C-3PO, Cloud City, R2-D2, and Yoda 30.00
- Darth Vader, Boba Fett, Star Destroyer, Tauntaun with C-3PO, R2-D2, Leia, Han, Chewie, Falcon, copyright on image Black Falcon [2:410] 30.00
- Darth Vader, Chewbacca, Han, Leia, Luke, R2-D2, and C-3PO 30.00
- Darth Vader, Leia, Luke, R2-D2, and C-3PO ... 30.00
- R2-D2 .... 30.00
- Return of the Jedi bath towel and wash mitt set [513-01] 50.00

Character World Ltd. (UK)
- Poncho, Clone Wars [513-02] 20.00

512-01 | 512-02 | 513-01 | 513-02 | 513-03 | 513-04

Towels: Bath

 514-01
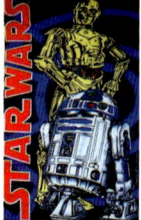 514-02
 514-03
 514-04
 514-05
 514-06
 514-07
 514-08
 514-09
 514-10

 514-11
514-12
 514-13
 514-14
 514-15
 514-16
 514-17
 514-18
514-19
 514-20

Idea Nuova
❑ Jedi towel sack 20.00

Jay Franco and Sons
❑ Darth Vader 2-piece bath set [513-03] 20.00

❑ Angry Birds X-Wing Pilot Luke bath towel, blue with red trim [513-04] 15.00

Towels: Beach
Continued in Volume 3, Page 357

❑ C-3PO and R2-D2 [514-01] 20.00

Classic trilogy. 30" x 60".
❑ C-3PO and R2-D2 [514-02] 20.00
❑ Darth Vader [v1e1:431] 20.00
❑ Return of the Jedi classic poster art [v1e1:431] 20.00

Episode I: The Phantom Menace. 30" x 60"
❑ Anakin Skywalker, Podrace [514-03] 20.00
❑ Darth Maul [514-04] 20.00
❑ Jar Jar Binks [v1e1:431] 20.00
❑ Naboo Space Battle [v1e1:431] 20.00
❑ Queen Amidala, Celebration [v1e1:431] 20.00
❑ Queen Amidala, Senate [v1e1:431] 20.00

Episode II: Attack of the Clones. 30" x 60"
❑ "Heroes," Anakin, Mace, Yoda, Obi-Wan, Padmé [v1e1:431] 20.00

❑ Jedi Starfighter [514-05] 25.00
❑ "Laser Fight," Anakin and Obi-Wan ... Vader vs. Kenobi [v1e1:431] 20.00
❑ "Villains," Palpatine, Maul, Dooku, Vader 20.00

(Austria)
❑ Darth Vader / Epic duel [4:301] 20.00

(Japan)
❑ Boba Fett [514-06] 35.00

Bibb Co.
❑ Boba Fett, Cloud City, Darth Vader, R2-D2 and C-3PO, snowspeeders, Yoda 30.00
❑ Boba Fett, Darth Vader, Chewbacca, Han, Leia, Luke, R2-D2 and C-3PO [4:302] 30.00
❑ Boba Fett, Darth Vader, Leia, Luke, R2-D2 ......30.00
❑ C-3PO, Chewbacca, Darth Vader, Han, Leia, Luke, and R2-D2 [v1e1:431] 30.00
❑ C-3PO, R2-D2, and planets [v1e1:431] 30.00
❑ Chewbacca with planets 35.00
❑ Darth Vader with planets 30.00
❑ Darth Vader, Death Star, Jawas, and stormtroopers 30.00
❑ Darth Vader, TIE Fighters, logo 30.00
❑ Main heroes circled by Ewoks, ships, Jabba's palace, and Darth Vader 30.00
❑ Max Rebo Band, R2-D2 and Wicket, Jabba the Hutt 30.00
❑ Return of the Jedi art, Luke and Darth Vader Duel in front of Darth Vader silhouette [514-07] 30.00
❑ Wicket the Ewok 30.00
❑ Yoda with Dagobah tree 30.00

Disney Theme Park Merchandise
❑ Jedi Knight legs 50.00

Franco Manufacturing Company
Exclusive to KMart.
❑ Darth Vader [514-08] 15.00
❑ Darth Vader, silhouette art [514-09] 10.00
❑ The Clone Wars [514-10] 10.00

Idea Nuova
Towel sacks, 30" x 60".
❑ Darth Vader / Sith Lord [514-11] 20.00
❑ Jedi [514-12] 20.00

Jay Franco and Sons
❑ Anakin Skywalker, podrace [v1e1:431] 20.00
❑ Boba Fett [514-13] 20.00
❑ Darth Vader [514-14] 20.00
❑ Droids on black background, white reverse 20.00
❑ Droids on white background, white reverse 20.00
❑ Princess Leia [v1e1:431] 20.00
❑ Queen Amidala, Coruscant [4:302] 20.00
❑ Stormtrooper "Freeze you rebel scum" 20.00
❑ The Phantom Menace movie poster art [514-15] 20.00
❑ Vader helmet, space battle [514-16] 20.00
❑ Vader on black background, white reverse 20.00

M&M World
Mpire characters.
❑ Darth Maul, "I feel the power of the Dark Side" [514-17] 25.00

 515-01
 515-02
 515-03
 515-04
 515-05
 515-06
 515-07
 515-08
 515-09

 515-10
 515-11
 515-12
 515-13
 515-14
 516-01
 516-02
 516-03

470

Towels: Washcloths

 517-01
 517-02
 517-03
 517-04
 517-05
 517-06
 517-07
 517-08
 517-09
 517-10
 517-11
 517-12

Pottery Barn
- Darth Vader and Boba Fett [514-18] 20.00
- Darth Vader and Boba Fett hooded beach wrap 30.00

Star Wars Celebration Japan (Japan)
- Celebration Japan logo on red towel [514-19] 25.00
- Stormtrooper 70.00

Star Wars Celebration V
- Star Wars Celebration V [514-20] 25.00

Star Wars Celebration VI
- Slave Leia 35.00

Towels: Hand
Continued in Volume 3, Page 358

3-piece washcloth and hand towel, Episode I: The Phantom Menace
- Anakin Skywalker [515-01] 20.00

Bibb Co.
- Boba Fett, Darth Vader, and snowspeeders [515-02] 25.00
- C-3PO and R2-D2 .... 25.00
- C-3PO, Leia, Luke, R2-D2 [515-03] 25.00
- Darth Vader and Dogfight 25.00
- R2-D2 .... 25.00

Heart Art Collection, Ltd. (Japan)
- Character print, repeats, black print on green [515-04] ... 25.00
- Character print, stormtrooper, R2-D2, Yoda, Darth Vader, C-3PO, black print on gray [515-05] 25.00

- Clone trooper pull, gray [515-06] 25.00
- Darth Vader, black vine print on red [515-07] 25.00
- R2-D2 and C-3PO under blossoming tree, black print on pink [515-08] 25.00
- R2-D2 flying over mountain, blue print on sky blue [515-09] 25.00
- Stormtroopers, black print on sky blue [515-10] 25.00
- Yoda, black vine print on green [515-11] 25.00

Tomy / Taito (Japan)
- Darth Vader, black on red [515-12] 25.00

Westpoint Stevens
2-piece washcloth and hand towel, Episode I: The Phantom Menace
- Anakin Skywalker 15.00
- Jar Jar Binks 15.00
- Queen Amidala 15.00
- Starfighters [515-13] 15.00
- Starships [515-14] 15.00

Towels: Hooded

- Darth Vader, exclusive to Target 15.00
- R2-D2, exclusive to Target 15.00

Franco Manufacturing Company
- Darth Vader, exclusive to KMart [516-01] 20.00

Jay Franco and Sons
Angry Birds.
- Chewbacca hooded poncho [516-02] 15.00
- X-Wing Pilot Luke hooded wrap [516-03] 15.00

Towels: Washcloths
Continued in Volume 3, Page 358

(Japan)
- Art: Dark Lord's Gambit 10.00

Basic Fun
Magic Washcloths.
- C-3PO and R2-D2 [517-01] 10.00
- Yoda [517-02] 10.00

Bibb Co.
Empire Strikes Back.
- Boba Fett and Darth Vader 20.00
- C-3PO and R2-D2 [517-03] 20.00
- Darth Vader [517-04] 20.00
- Hoth (Ice planet) [517-05] 20.00
- R2-D2 .... 20.00
- X-Wing Fighter 20.00
- Yoda [517-06] 20.00

Return of the Jedi.
- Luke, Leia, and Han [517-07] 20.00

Grosvenor (UK)
- Darth Vader, expandable flannel [517-08] 10.00

Tex (UK)
- Anakin Skywalker, podracer [517-09] 15.00
- Darth Maul [517-10] 15.00
- Jar Jar Binks [517-11] 15.00
- Queen Amidala [517-12] 15.00

 518-01
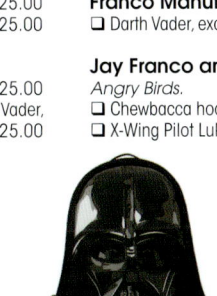 518-02
 518-03
 518-04
 518-05
 518-06
 518-07
 518-08
 518-09  518-10

471

Toy Storage

  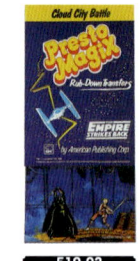     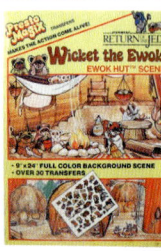 

519-01 | 519-02 | 519-03 | 519-04 | 519-05 | 519-06 | 519-07 | 519-08 | 519-09

519-10 | 519-11 | 519-12 | 519-13 | 519-14 | 519-15

Toy Storage

Neat Oh!
LEGO ZipBin storage toy cases.
- Battle bridge [518-01]..................................20.00
- Darth Vader [518-02]..................................25.00
- Death Star transforming toy box [518-03]........20.00
- Millennium Falcon [518-04]..........................15.00
- Millennium Falcon messenger bag [518-05]....20.00
- Stormtrooper [518-06]................................25.00
- TIE Fighter [518-07]...................................15.00
- Toy box [518-08].......................................25.00

Worlds Apart (UK)
Pop Tidy pop-up storage hampers.
- Clone Wars [518-09]..................................25.00
- R2-D2 [518-10]...45.00

Transfers

American Publishing
Presto Magix bagged sets. Empire Strikes Back.
- Asteroids [519-01]....................................18.00
- Beneath Cloud City [519-02]......................18.00
- Cloud City Battle [519-03].........................18.00
- Dagobah Bog Planet [519-04]....................18.00
- Deck of the Star Destroyer [519-05]............18.00
- Ice Planet Hoth [519-06]...........................18.00
- Rebel Base [519-07].................................18.00

Presto Magix bagged sets. Ewoks.
- Ewok Hut [519-08]....................................25.00
- Ewoks at Play [519-09].............................25.00

Presto Magix bagged sets. Return of the Jedi.
- Death Star [519-10].................................20.00
- Ewok Village [519-11]..............................20.00
- Jabba's Throne Room [519-12]..................20.00
- Sarlacc Pit [519-13].................................20.00

Presto Magix boxed sets.
- Battle on Endor [519-14]..........................80.00
- Ewok Village [519-15]..............................85.00
- Ewoks at Home [519-16]..........................85.00
- Jabba's Throne Room [519-17]..................80.00
- Star Wars Activity set [519-18]...................95.00

BSB
- Death Star corridor...................................45.00

Creative Imaginations, LLC
4 rub-down sheets.
- Clone Wars [519-19].................................15.00
- Star Wars [519-20]..................................15.00

 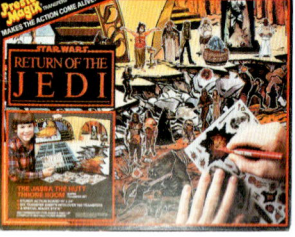  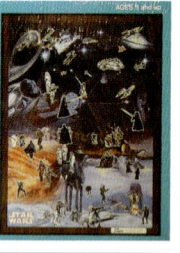  

519-16 | 519-17 | 519-18 | 519-19 | 519-20

519-21 | 519-22 | 519-23 | 519-24 | 519-25 | 519-26

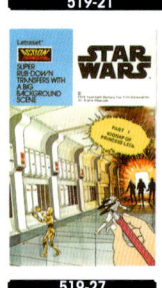       

519-27 | 519-28 | 519-29 | 519-30 | 519-31 | 519-32 | 519-33 | 519-34

Travel Kits

519-35   519-36   519-37   519-38   519-39

DR Editorio Magno (Mexico)
- Batalla en la Ciudad Nebulosa [519-21] 100.00

Kraft
Dairylea. Food premiums.
- Bespin Cloud City [519-22] 20.00
- Dagobag Bog Planet [519-23] 20.00
- Hoth Ice Planet [519-24] 20.00
- Space Battle [519-25] 20.00

Dairylea. Mail-in premiums.
- Empire Strikes Back bumper transfer pack [519-26] 85.00

Letraset
- 1 Kidnap of Priness Leia [519-27] 35.00
- 2 Sale on Tatooine [519-28] 35.00
- 3 Action at Mos Eisley [519-29] 35.00
- 4 Escape from stormtroopers [519-30] 35.00
- 5 Flight to Alderaan [519-31] 35.00
- 6 Inside the Death Star [519-32] 35.00
- 7 Prison Break [519-33] 35.00
- 8 Death Star Escape [519-34] 35.00
- 9 Rebel Base [519-35] 35.00
- 10 Last Battle [519-36] 35.00
- Part 1: Battle at Mos Eisley [519-37] 75.00
- Part 2: Escape from the Death Star [519-38] 75.00
- Part 3: Rebel Air Attack [519-39] 75.00

Nabisco Shreddies premiums.
- C-3PO, stormtrooper, TIE, Chewbacca, R2-D2, Vader [519-40] 20.00
- Han, R2-D2, X-Wing, Obi-Wan, stormtrooper, C-3PO [519-41] 20.00
- Leia, Luke, stormtrooper, TIE, Han, Chewbacca [519-42] ...20.00
- Luke, C-3PO, Obi-Wan, R2-D2, TIE, Vader [519-43] 20.00

Rose Art Industries
Presto Magix.
- Stick 'n Lift [519-44] 25.00

Thomas Salter (UK)
Bagged sets, English packaging.
- Ewoks [519-45] 30.00
- Jabba the Hutt [519-46] 30.00

519-40   519-41   519-42   519-43   519-44

Boxed sets.
- Ewok Village [519-47] 50.00
- Sarlacc Pit [519-48] 50.00

Boxed sets. Large.
- Ewok Village, giant [519-49] 80.00
- Ewoks at Home [519-50] 80.00
- Jabba the Hutt Throne Room, extra large [519-51] 80.00
- The Battle on Endor, extra large [519-52] 80.00

Thomas Salter (Italy)
- N. 21 - Il Ritorno Dello JEDI [v1e1.434] 60.00

Walls
Vintage, mail-away premiums.
- C-3PO [519-53] 15.00
- Chewbacca [519-54] 15.00
- Darth Vader [519-55] 15.00
- Jawas [519-56] 15.00

- Luke Skywalker [519-57] 15.00
- Obi-Wan Kenobi [519-58] 15.00
- Princess Leia [519-59] 15.00
- R2-D2 [519-60] 15.00
- Sand Person [519-61] 15.00
- Stormtrooper [519-62] 15.00
- TIE Fighter [519-63] 15.00
- X-Wing Fighter [519-64] 15.00

Travel Kits
Continued in Volume 3, Page 358

Adam Joseph Industries
Princess Kneesaa personal care bags.
- Blue with red trim [520-01] 120.00
- Lavender with purple trim [520-02] 135.00
- Pink with blue trim [520-03] 120.00
- Red with black trim [520-04] 120.00

519-45   519-46   519-47   519-48

519-49   519-50   519-51   519-52

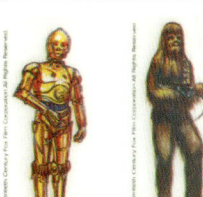         

519-53 519-54 519-55 519-56 519-57 519-58 519-59 519-60 519-61 519-62 519-63 519-64

Travel Kits

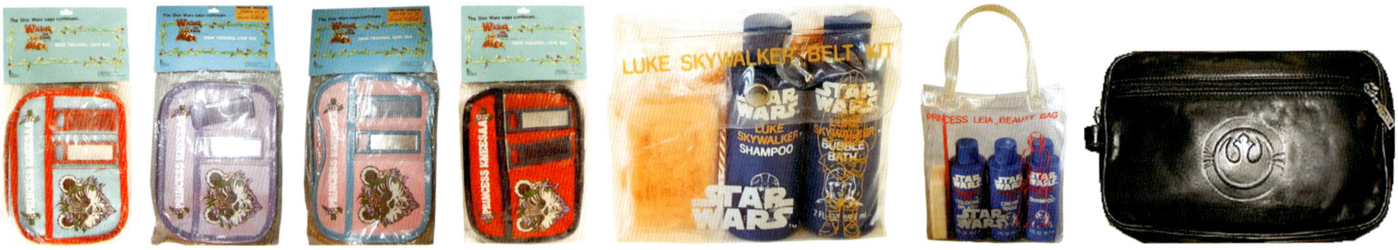

520-01 520-02 520-03 520-04 520-05 520-06 520-07

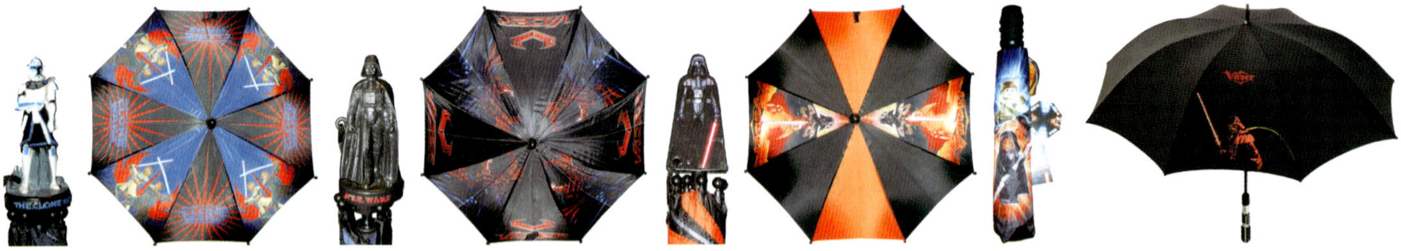

521-01 Handle and Canopy 521-02 Handle and Canopy 521-03 Handle and Canopy 521-04 521-05

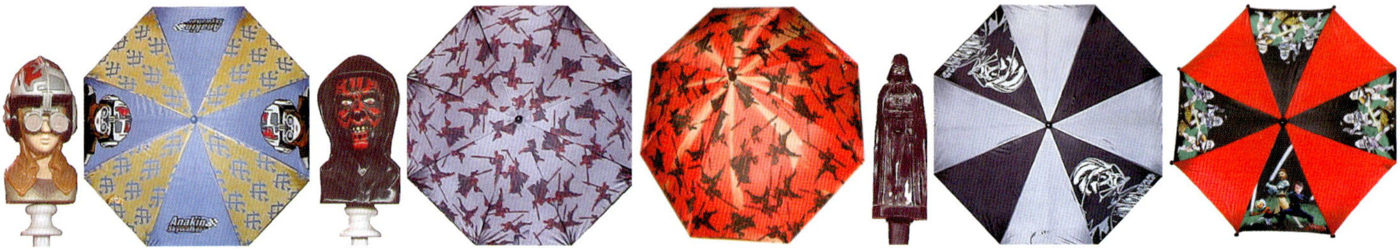

521-06 Handle and Canopy 521-07 Handle and Canopy 521-08 521-09 Handle and Canopy 521-10

Omni Cosmetics

- ❑ Luke Skywalker Belt Kit; clear vinyl with belt slots, bubble bath, shampoo, soap, comb, toothbrush [520-05]..........60.00
- ❑ Princess Leia Beauty Bag; clear vinyl with straps, shampoo, rinse, cologne, soap, comb [520-06]..........75.00

Sharper Image

- ❑ Zippered travel case with logo zipper keys and embossed rebel logo [520-07]..........45.00

Umbrellas

Continued in Volume 3, Page 358

ABG Accessories

Character represented on hood with sculpted figure on handle.

- ❑ Clone trooper [521-01]..........25.00
- ❑ Darth Vader [521-02]..........25.00
- ❑ Darth Vader (flat handle) [521-03]..........20.00

LEGO characters.

- ❑ Captain Rex..........20.00
- ❑ Obi-Wan and Darth Maul [521-04]..........20.00

Adam Joseph Industries

Clear plastic with characters on hood.

- ❑ C-3PO and R2-D2..........90.00
- ❑ Darth Vader and Emperor's Royal Guards..........90.00

B/W Character Merchandising

- ❑ Empire Strikes Back Storm Stick..........90.00

Happinet (Japan)

- ❑ Darth Vader [521-05]..........120.00
- ❑ Vader logo..........95.00

Museum Replicas

Lightsaber handle, colored rod, and emblem on cover.

- ❑ Darth Vader..........145.00
- ❑ Luke Skywalker, A New Hope..........145.00
- ❑ Luke Skywalker, Return of the Jedi..........145.00

Pyramid

Character represented on hood with sculpted figure on handle.

- ❑ Anakin Skywalker, podracing [521-06]..........25.00
- ❑ Darth Maul, gray, black, and red [521-07]..........25.00
- ❑ Darth Maul, orange, black, and red [521-08]..........25.00
- ❑ Darth Vader, gray and black [521-09]..........25.00

Trade Mark Collections Ltd. (UK)

- ❑ Clone Wars [521-10]..........25.00

USB Devices

Continued in Volume 3, Page 359

(Japan)

Moe light-up figures.

- ❑ Yoda..........45.00

Cube Works (Japan)

USB hubs.

- ❑ Darth Vader [522-01]..........90.00
- ❑ R2-D2 [522-02]..........90.00
- ❑ R2-Q5 [522-03]..........150.00

522-01 522-02 522-03 522-04 522-05 522-06

522-07 522-08 522-09 522-10 522-11 522-12 522-13 522-14 523-01

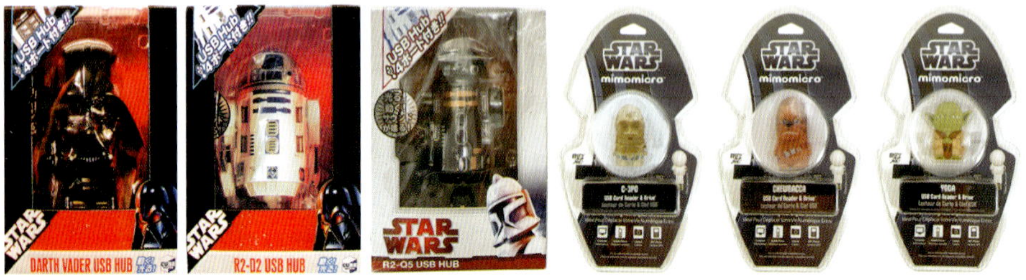

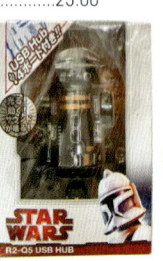

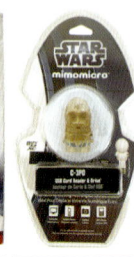

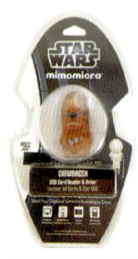

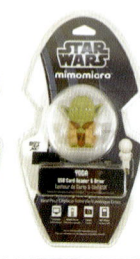

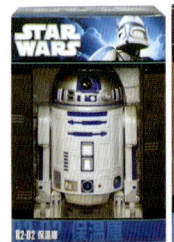

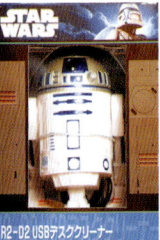

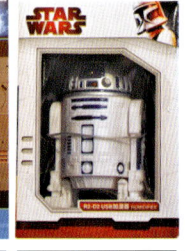

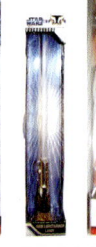

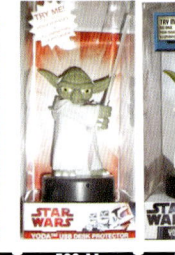

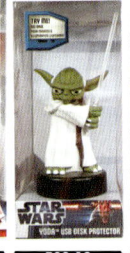

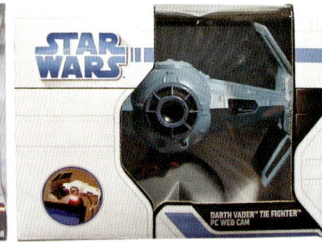

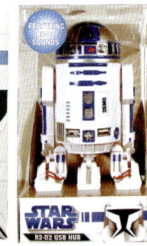

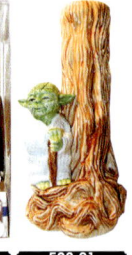

Vending Machine Translites

  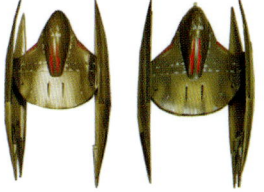 

524-01　　　　　　524-02　　　　　　524-03

525-01　　　　　525-02　　　　　526-01

   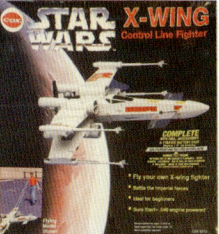  

525-03　　525-04　　525-05　　525-06　　527-01　　527-02

Mimoco
MicroSD card reader and drive.
- C-3PO [522-04] 30.00
- Chewbacca [522-05] 30.00
- Millennium Falcon 30.00
- Yoda [522-06] 30.00

Taito (Japan)
- R2-D2 can warmer [522-07] 45.00
- R2-D2 desktop vacuum [522-08] 35.00
- R2-D2 humidifier [522-09] 35.00

Underground Toys
- Lightsaber desk lamp [522-10] 40.00
- Yoda desk protector [522-11] 30.00
- Yoda desk protector [522-12] 30.00

Wesco Limited (UK)
- Darth Vader's TIE Fighter webcam [522-13] 80.00
- R2-D2 hub [522-14] 45.00

Vases

Sigma
- Yoda [523-01] 120.00

Vehicles, Display

Hasbro
Store displays.
- Millennium Falcon, 6' diameter [524-01] 1,400.00
- Naboo Fighter, 6' length [524-02] 600.00
- Trade Federation droid fighters, set of 2 [524-03] 400.00

Vehicles, Propeller Driven

Estes
Sterling model kit control line fighters without engine.
- X-Wing 35.00
- Y-Wing [525-01] 35.00

Estes / Cox
- Darth Vader's TIE Fighter kit with Cox engine 50.00
- Death Star Battle Station with X-Wing control line fighter kit, radio controller 160.00
- Landspeeder radio control vehicle kit with Cox engine [525-02] 125.00
- Naboo Fighter [525-03] 24.00
- Naboo Fighter electronic remote control with display stand 18.00
- Snowspeeder Fighter kit with Cox engine [525-04] 50.00
- Star Wars Combat Set, X-Wing and TIE Fighter with Cox engines 120.00
- Trade Federation Droid Fighter [525-05] 24.00
- X-Wing Fighter kit with Cox engine [525-06] . 50.00

Vending Machine Translites

Pepsi Cola
- Episode I Podracing [526-01] 95.00

 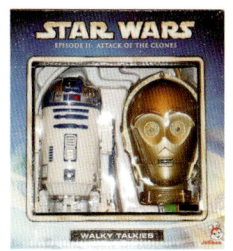 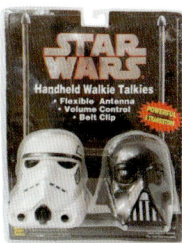    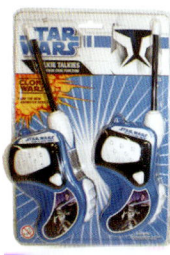

528-01　528-02　528-03　528-04　528-05　528-06　528-07

   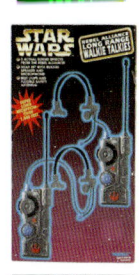   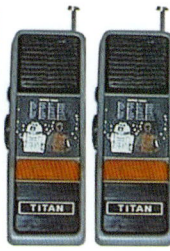

528-08　528-09　528-10　528-11　528-12　528-13　528-14 Boxed and Open

Vitamins

529-01 | 529-02 | 529-03 | 529-04 | 529-05 | 529-06 | 529-07 | 529-08 | 529-09 | 529-10

Vitamins
Continued in Volume 3, Page 360

Natural Balance
- 3-tablet vitamin promotional sample [527-01] 50.00
- 60-tablet vitamin bottle and box [527-02] 30.00

Walkie Talkies and Text Messengers

Hasbro
- Jedi Communicators [528-01] 25.00

Jollibee
- Episode II. R2-D2 and C-3PO [528-02] 35.00

Micro Games of America
- Darth Vader and stormtrooper helmets designed to be clipped to belt [528-03] 30.00

Mix 'n Match individual.
- Darth Vader [528-04] 35.00
- Stormtrooper [528-05] 35.00

Sakar International
SMS Text Messenger.
- Clone Wars [528-06] 25.00

TGA (Australia)
- Walkie Talkies with Morse code function [528-07] 30.00

Tiger Electronics
- Clone trooper and Jango Fett [528-08] 20.00
- Darth Vader voice changer [528-09] 25.00
- Imperial symbol over speaker with belt clips [528-10] ...20.00
- Jedi Comlink [528-11] 25.00
- Rebel Alliance long-range [528-12] 40.00

Tiger Electronics (UK)
- View Comm walkie talkies [528-13] 30.00

Titan
- Executive, R2-D2 and C-3PO, Morse code pad [528-14] ..85.00

Wall Decorations
Continued in Volume 3, Page 360

Fathead
Life-sized vinyl wall graphics.
- Boba Fett 80.00
- C-3PO 80.00
- Chewbacca 80.00
- Darth Vader 80.00
- R2-D2 ....80.00
- Stormtrooper 80.00
- Yoda 80.00

Priss Prints
Border Stick-Ups.
- Podrace [529-01] 10.00
- Space Battle [529-02] 10.00

Jumbo Stick-Ups.
- 25-piece: Podrace [529-03] 15.00
- 25-piece: Space Battle [529-04] 15.00
- 50-piece: Podrace and Space Battle [529-05] 25.00

RoomMates
Peel and stick appliques.
- Yoda, giant [529-06] 15.00

York Wall Coverings
Peel-and-stick appliques.
- Clone Wars [529-07] 25.00
- Clone Wars [529-08] 25.00
- Clone Wars lightsabers [529-09] 25.00
- Saga characters, 31 reusable accents [529-10] 25.00

Wallet Chains
Continued in Volume 3, Page 361

Rock Rebel
- Boba Fett [530-01] 15.00
- Darth Vader [530-02] 15.00

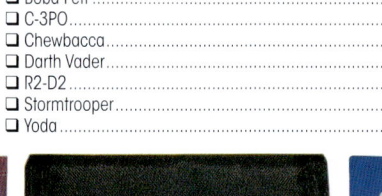

530-01 | 530-02 | 531-01 | 531-02 | 531-03 | 531-04 | 531-05 | 531-06

 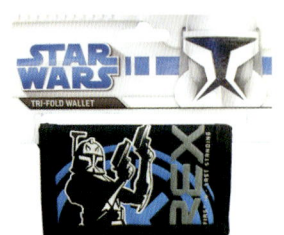     

531-07 | 531-08 | 531-09 | 531-10 | 531-11 | 531-12 | 531-13

     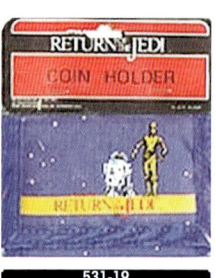

531-14 | 531-15 | 531-16 | 531-17 | 531-18 | 531-19

Wallets
Continued in Volume 3, Page 361

- ❏ Return of the Jedi, nylon and Velcro [531-01] 30.00
- ❏ The Power of Myth, Episode I [531-02] 25.00

Bi-fold printed wallets.
- ❏ A New Hope [531-03] 20.00
- ❏ Boba Fett [531-04] 20.00
- ❏ Darth Vader [531-05] 20.00
- ❏ Star Wars logo [531-06] 20.00

Clone Wars.
- ❏ Anakin and Obi-Wan [531-07] 15.00
- ❏ Captain Rex tri-fold wallet [531-08] 15.00

Episode I, tri-fold.
- ❏ Darth Maul [531-09] 20.00
- ❏ Jedi [531-10] 20.00
- ❏ Jedi vs. Sith [531-11] 20.00
- ❏ Podracing [531-12] 20.00
- ❏ Queen Amidala [531-13] 20.00

Episode I: The Phantom Menace.
- ❏ Darth Maul, zippered coin pouch 15.00

Episode III: Revenge of the Sith.
- ❏ Darth Vader / Epic Battle vinyl [531-14] 15.00

Adam Joseph Industries
Billfolds, vinyl.
- ❏ Darth Vader [531-15] 45.00
- ❏ Droids [531-16] 45.00
- ❏ Yoda [531-17] 45.00

Coin holders, nylon.
- ❏ Darth Vader [531-18] 50.00
- ❏ Droids [531-19] 50.00
- ❏ Yoda [531-20] 50.00

Wallets, nylon.
- ❏ Darth Vader [531-21] 50.00
- ❏ Darth Vader, Return of the Jedi band [531-22] 75.00
- ❏ Droids [531-23] 60.00
- ❏ Droids, Return of the Jedi packaging band [531-24] 75.00
- ❏ Yoda 50.00

Wallets, vinyl.
- ❏ Darth Vader 45.00
- ❏ Droids [531-25] 45.00
- ❏ Princess Kneesaa [531-26] 40.00
- ❏ Wicket the Ewok [531-27] 40.00
- ❏ Yoda [531-28] 45.00

Animations
- ❏ Darth Vader [531-29] 15.00
- ❏ Darth Vader wallet and mini-flashlight gift set [531-30] ... 25.00
- ❏ Darth Vader, crossed lightsabers, leather [531-31] 25.00
- ❏ Darth Vader, vinyl, exclusive to Target 15.00
- ❏ Star Wars logo on black nylon [531-32] 20.00
- ❏ Vader, exclusive to Target [531-33] 15.00
- ❏ Yoda, vinyl, exclusive to Target 15.00

Disney / MGM
- ❏ Jedi Training Academy [531-34] 25.00
- ❏ Star Tours logo 35.00

Hot Topic
- ❏ Darth Vader 15.00

Industrias CYS
- ❏ Droids 75.00
- ❏ Star Wars 60.00

Mana
- ❏ Darth Vader, "There's a little good in everybody" Jedi Club [531-35] 40.00
- ❏ Jedi Master / X-Wing [531-36] 40.00

Personajes Registrados
- ❏ Darth Vader 25.00
- ❏ R2-D2 .... 25.00
- ❏ Wicket 25.00

Small Planet Co. Ltd. (Japan)
- ❏ Stormtrooper print [531-37] 35.00

The Anthony Grandio Company
Debit card holders, printed fabric with leather. 250 produced of each, exclusive to Star Wars Celebration IV.
- ❏ Star Wars 30th anniversary 35.00
- ❏ Star Wars Celebration IV 35.00

Wallpaper

Border trim.
- ❏ Characters [532-01] 65.00

Crown Wallcoverings Limited
Based upon the cartoons and book art. 10.05 m rolls.
- ❏ Droids 400.00
- ❏ Ewoks 350.00

Imperial Chemicals
Border trim.
- ❏ Droids: based upon educational book art 120.00
- ❏ Ewoks: Wicket swings from the vine while Kneesaa and friends sit below [532-02] 90.00
- ❏ Return of the Jedi: alternating ovals with: 3 heroes, R2-D2, Chewbacca and C-3PO, Darth Vader, Ewoks, Rebo band [532-03] 95.00

Wallpaper rolls.
- ❏ Star Wars [532-04] 350.00
- ❏ Empire Strikes Back [532-05] 300.00
- ❏ Return of the Jedi [532-06] 280.00

Super7
- ❏ Imperial Forces [532-07] 200.00

Waste Baskets
Continued in Volume 3, Page 363

- ❏ Clone Wars 30.00
- ❏ Clone Wars, Clones [532-01] 30.00

BHS (UK)
- ❏ Podracer [532-02] 25.00

Waste Baskets

532-01

532-02

532-03

532-04

532-05

532-06

532-07

532-01

532-02 Side 1 and Side 2

532-03 Side 1 and Side 2

532-04 Side 1 and Side 2

532-05

532-06

532-07

532-08

532-09

532-10 Side 1 and Side 2

Chein Industries
- ❏ Ewoks animated scenes [532-03] 300.00
- ❏ Return of the Jedi Logo and collage [532-04] 65.00

Heart Art Collection, Ltd. (Japan)
- ❏ R2-D2 [532-05] 125.00
- ❏ R2-Q5, 250 produced [532-06] 175.00
- ❏ R2-R9 [532-07] 125.00
- ❏ R4-P17, 500 produced [532-08] 150.00

Jay Franco and Sons
- ❏ Classic characters, step [532-09] 50.00
- ❏ Naboo space battle, plastic [532-10] 30.00

Watches
Continued in Volume 3, Page 363

- ❏ C-3PO and R2-D2 on round face 45.00
- ❏ C-3PO and R2-D2, round silver face with yellow inner border 75.00

- ❏ Darth Vader's helmet, round white face 35.00
- ❏ Episode I college [v1e1:438] 25.00
- ❏ Imperial Cog, stainless steel 35.00
- ❏ Jedi [v1e1:438] 120.00
- ❏ Lightsabers, black face on silver [533-01] 45.00
- ❏ Princess Leia and R2-D2, round face, no numbers 25.00
- ❏ Queen Amidala clip-on [533-02] 45.00
- ❏ R2-D2, round white face 25.00
- ❏ Vader [v1e1:438] 120.00
- ❏ Yoda [v1e1:438] 25.00

(France)
- ❏ Star Wars, round face with lightsabers [v1e1:438] 30.00

(UK)
- ❏ Vader, lights up 40.00

3D Arts
Orange hologram character, round black face, white numbers, black band, clear 3D Arts case.
- ❏ Boba Fett [533-03] 45.00
- ❏ Darth Vader [533-04] 45.00
- ❏ X-Wing Fighter [533-05] 45.00
- ❏ Yoda [533-06] 45.00

A.H. Prismatic
- ❏ Darth Vader, green hologram, round black face, white numbers, black band with "Star Wars" and "Darth Vader" 45.00

Armitron
- ❏ X-Wing [533-07] 65.00

Avon
- ❏ Obi-Wan Kenobi, oval face, blue lightsaber second hand, plastic band [533-08] 16.00

Bradley (Germany)
- ❏ C-3PO and R2-D2, desert scene, octagonal face framed with screws [v1e1:438] 90.00
- ❏ C-3PO and R2-D2, desert scene, round dial on square face [v1e1:438] 85.00

533-01

533-02

533-03

533-04

533-05

533-06

533-07

Watches

   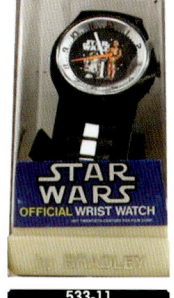 

533-08 533-09 533-10 533-11 533-12

Bradley Time
- C-3PO and R2-D2 in desert, Star Wars logo, round face, blue vinyl strap, gold casing, adult size 115.00
- C-3PO and R2-D2 in desert, Star Wars logo, round face, blue vinyl strap, silver casing, child size, watch stand packaging [533-09] 95.00
- C-3PO and R2-D2 in desert, Star Wars logo, round face, blue vinyl strap, silver casing, child size, enhanced trademark, clear cylinder packaging [533-10]................95.00
- C-3PO, R2-D2, Star Wars logo, round black face, red second hand, numbers on outer silver ring [533-11]................115.00
- C-3PO, R2-D2, Star Wars logo, round black face, white hands and numbers [v1e1:439] 85.00
- Darth Vader, Star Wars logo, round gray face, planets on outer time ring, white hands, black-and-silver band [533-12]...85.00
- Darth Vader, Star Wars logo, round gray face, white hands, black band [533-13]..................................80.00
- Darth Vader, Star Wars logo, round white face, red hands, black band [533-14]..................................65.00
- Ewok cartoon, round white face, stars and planet on outer time ring, red hands, black band [533-15]..............50.00
- Ewoks, Return of the Jedi logo, round green face, black hands [v1e1:439] 45.00
- Jabba, Return of the Jedi logo, round blue face, black band [v1e1:439] 60.00
- R2-D2, C-3PO, Star Wars logo, round black face, white hands, black band 75.00
- Yoda, Star Wars logo, round gray face, black hands, black band [v1e1:439] 65.00
- Yoda, Star Wars logo, round white face, brown hands, brown leather band [v1e1:439] 80.00
- Yoda, Star Wars logo, round white face, stars and planets on outer time ring, white hands, black-and-silver band [v1e1:439] 125.00

Clicks
Analog watches.
- Clone trooper [533-16] 20.00
- Darth Vader..................................20.00
- Darth Vader Sith Lord [533-17]..................................20.00
- Jedi (Yoda) [533-18]..................................20.00

ClicTime Holdings Ltd.
LEGO watches with matching LEGO mini-figure.
- Artoo-Detoo #9002915 [533-19]..................................25.00
- Boba Fett #9005466 [533-20]..................................25.00
- C-3PO #9001901 [533-21]..................................25.00
- Darth Vader #9002908 [533-22]..................................25.00
- Luke Skywalker #9002892 [533-23]..................................25.00
- Stormtrooper #9001949 [533-24]..................................25.00
- Yoda #9002076 [533-25]..................................25.00

Disney / MGM
- Lightsabers face in round padded box, Time Works.....75.00

Star Wars Weekends.
- 2003 Jedi Mickey and Yoda, 250 produced [533-26]...225.00
- 2004 Mickey and Minnie, 500 produced [533-27].......175.00
- 2005 Darth Vader / Mickey [v1e1:439]..................................75.00
- 2009 Mickey and Yoda [533-28]..................................150.00

Fantasma
- Battle of the Force, 7,500 produced..................................95.00
- Darth Vader, round black face, numbers on outer watch face, second hand is Sci-Fi Channel logo, black band, 7,500 produced, individually numbered [533-29].........95.00
- Darth Vader, round black face, numbers on outer watch face, second hand is TIE Interceptor chasing X-Wing, black band, 7,500 produced, individually numbered [533-30].........85.00
- Millennium Falcon, flip-open cover reveals round face with space battle scene, black band, 10,000 produced, individually numbered [533-31]..................................75.00

Fossil, Inc.
- 25th anniversary, classic scene, 2,000 produced [533-32]..................................175.00
- Artoo-Detoo and See Threepio, spiral background, blue and yellow highlights on face [v1e1:439]..................................135.00
- Boba Fett Collectors Watch, gold edition, individually numbered [533-33]..................................125.00
- Boba Fett Collectors Watch, silver edition, 10,000 produced, individually numbered [533-34]..................................85.00
- Boba Fett, brass finished face, brown strap with matching storage box, 10,000 produced, individually numbered [533-35]..................................85.00
- C-3PO and R2-D2, includes sculpted R2-D2 case, 500 produced, individually numbered [v1e1:439]..................................200.00
- C-3PO, gold finished face, brown strap with matching storage box, 10,000 produced, individually numbered [v1e1:439]..................................75.00
- Clone Wars, leather band [v1e1:439]..................................150.00
- Darth Vader (helmet) in flames, glowing face, black band, individually numbered..................................175.00
- Darth Vader (helmet) in flames, glowing face, silver band, 2,000 produced..................................170.00
- Darth Vader and his TIE, 23k gold plated with Vader head storage box, 10,000 produced, individually numbered.........120.00
- Darth Vader and his TIE, silver color all over with Vader head storage box, 15,000 produced, indiv. numbered..........95.00
- Darth Vader and Imperial insignia, 23k gold case, black strap with matching storage box, 10,000 produced, individually numbered..................................125.00
- Darth Vader DVD art face, 300 produced, individually numbered..................................250.00
- Darth Vader, silver finish face, black strap with matching storage box, 10,000 produced [v1e1:439]..................................75.00
- Star Wars logo, hinged box features frame with five movie poster miniatures..................................125.00
- Stormtrooper, silver color all over, 3,000 produced, individually numbered..................................145.00
- Stormtrooper, silver color all over with sculpted helmet storage box, 15,000 produced, individually numbered.........125.00
- Star Wars logo, Rebel insignia, and Imperial insignia with Death Star storage box, 10,000 produced [v1e1:439]....95.00

533-13 533-14 533-15 533-16 533-17 533-18 533-19 533-20

533-21 533-22 533-23 533-24 533-25 533-26 533-27 533-28

479

Watches

| 533-29 | 533-30 | 533-31 | 533-32 | 533-33 | 533-34 | 533-35 |

Episode II: Attack of the Clones.
- Boba Fett etched on silver dial with Mandalorian etched metal band, dog tag, trading card, 2,000 produced [v1e1:439] 95.00
- Gold logo on gunmetal face with black strap, 2,500 produced [v1e1:439] 100.00

GSX (Japan)
- Darth Vader, 300 produced, indiv. numbered 1,400.00
- Stormtrooper, individually numbered 600.00

Hope Industries
Quartz analog, gold tone buckle, gold Death Star storage case.
- Return of the Jedi [533-36] 35.00
- Star Wars: A New Hope 35.00
- The Empire Strikes Back [533-37] 35.00

Quartz analog, gold tone buckle.
- Return of the Jedi [533-38] 30.00
- Star Wars: A New Hope [533-39] 30.00
- The Empire Strikes Back [533-40] 25.00

ILM
- Industrial Light and Magic employee watch 300.00

Legendary Timepieces
- Lars Homestead [533-41] 150.00

Montreal
- R2-D2 character watch [533-42] 25.00

Nelsonic
Character watch with collectors storage tin.
- Anakin Skywalker podracer 25.00
- Darth Maul lightsaber [533-43] 25.00
- Darth Maul sculpted case [533-44] 25.00
- Jar Jar Binks rotating tongue 25.00
- Jar Jar Binks water filled analog [533-45] 30.00
- Queen Amidala [v1e1:440] 25.00
- Space Battle rotating starfighter disk [533-46] 30.00

Character watches.
- C-3PO skeletal case [533-47] 25.00
- Darth Maul holographic [533-48] 25.00
- Darth Maul sculpted case [533-49] 25.00
- Jar Jar Binks rotating tongue [533-50] 25.00

Laser dial character watches in collectors storage tin.
- Darth Maul [533-51] 25.00
- Queen Amidala [533-52] 25.00
- Qui-Gon Jinn [533-53] 25.00

Olympic Promotional Watches
- "Feel the Force—Back on the big screen," Pepsi Cola [533-54] 35.00

Seiko (Japan)
- C-3PO, 600 produced 1,375.00
- Darth Maul, 800 produced 1,375.00
- Darth Vader 1,425.00
- Stormtrooper, 500 produced 1,375.00
- Yoda, 600 produced 1,375.00

Skagen
Walt Disney Weekends 2006.
- Darth Vader with helmet box, 500 produced 175.00

Sony Ericsson
- Episode III watch in steel canister with lid [v1e1:440] 50.00

Star Movies
Attack of the Clones. Character watch in black stamped tin case.
- Anakin Skywalker [533-55] 35.00
- Padmé Amidala [533-56] 35.00

Super Live Adventure (Japan)
- Darth Vader, Super Live Action box [533-57] 400.00

Unlicensed
Children's watches with character on face and imagery molded into plastic band.
- Anakin Skywalker on face, starship, Yoda, logo, Anakin, clone commando on band, blue band 10.00
- Anakin Skywalker on face, starship, Yoda, logo, Anakin, clone commando on band, gray band [533-58] 10.00
- Anakin Skywalker on face, starship, Yoda, logo, Anakin, clone commando on band, red band 10.00
- Darth Vader on face, Yoda, Star Wars logo, Anakin Skywalker on band [533-59] 10.00
- Mace Windu on face, starship, Yoda, logo, Anakin, clone commando on band, gray band [533-60] 10.00
- Mace Windu on face, starship, Yoda, logo, Anakin, clone commando on band, yellow band 10.00

Watchit
- C-3PO and R2-D2 .... 25.00
- Darth Vader face with stormtrooper band [533-61] 25.00
- Star Wars movie poster face with logo band [533-62] 25.00

Coin Watches. Character raised on brushed brass-tone face. Episode I storage tin included.
- Darth Maul [533-63] 40.00
- Queen Amidala [533-64] 35.00

World Wide Licenses Ltd.
Watches include round, padded storage tin.
- Darth Maul communicator 35.00
- Droid Fighter, die-cast with leather band [533-65] 40.00
- Qui-Gon Jinn, hologram face with die-cast band 45.00

Zeon
- Anakin Skywalker / Darth Vader lenticular [533-66] 25.00
- Anakin Skywalker with lightsaber sweep hand 25.00

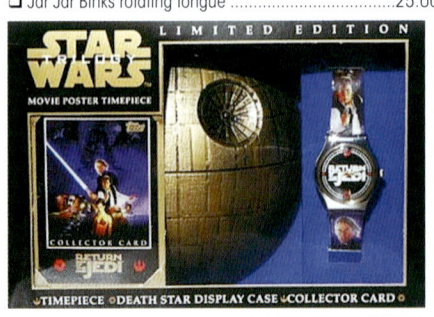 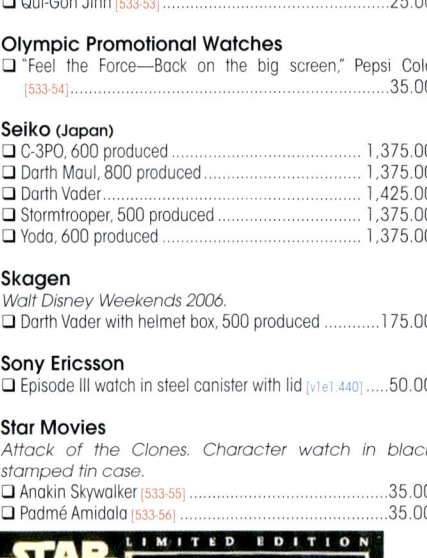     

| 533-36 | 533-37 | 533-38 | 533-39 | 533-40 |

| 533-41 Face and Back Side | 533-42 | 533-43 | 533-44 | 533-45 | 533-46 | 533-47 |

Watches: Digital

| 533-48 | 533-49 | 533-50 | 533-51 | 533-52 | 533-53 | 533-54 | 533-55 | 533-56 |

| 533-57 | 533-58 | 533-59 | 533-60 | 533-61 | 533-62 | 533-63 | 533-64 | 533-65 | 533-66 |

Watches, Pocket
Continued in Volume 3, Page 366

Nelsonic
- Darth Maul Sith Probe Droid [534-01] 25.00
- Space Battle [534-02] 35.00

Watches: Digital
Continued in Volume 3, Page 365

- C-3PO left, R2-D2 below, Chewbacca right, Return of the Jedi logo above display, 1 button, white band................115.00
- Han, Leia, Jabba, Return of the Jedi on white face......60.00
- Luke, AT-ST, and Speeder Bike trooper, Return of the Jedi logo on white face 60.00
- Projection Watch [535-01]..............................25.00
- R2-D2 watch face with alarm, timer, stopwatch, date indicator, 5,000 produced................................195.00
- Whizz watch controls R2-D2 toy via radio 35.00

Episode III: Revenge of the Sith.
- Darth Vader [535-02] 15.00
- Darth Vader with changeable faces [535-03]..............15.00
- Jedi [535-04]..15.00
- Sith [535-05]..15.00
- Yoda [535-06]..15.00

Episode III: Revenge of the Sith. Dome shaped packaging.
- Darth Vader [535-07]..................................15.00
- Darth Vader with changeable faces [535-08]..............15.00
- Jedi [535-09]..15.00
- Yoda [535-10]..15.00

Episode III: Revenge of the Sith. Tin box packaging.
- Changeable faces [535-11]............................25.00
- Darth Vader watch and clock.........................30.00

(UK)
Action sounds LCD watches.
- Clone Wars [535-12].................................20.00
- Darth Vader [535-13].................................20.00

Flip top watches.
- Clone trooper [535-14] 15.00

Lenticular strap watches.
- Clone Wars [535-15]..................................15.00

Reversible watches.
- Clone Wars [535-16]..................................15.00

BNS Marketing Network, Inc.
Episode II.
- Anakin Skywalker [535-17] 15.00
- Anakin, Padmé, Obi-Wan [535-18] 15.00
- Attack of the Clones, 5 interchangeable covers [535-19]...15.00
- Jango Fett [535-20] 15.00

Bradley Time
- Biker Scout quartz stopwatch [535-21]..................275.00
- C-3PO and R2-D2 below, Star Wars logo above, round black face, 1 button, black band, blister packed [535-22] 45.00

| 534-01 | 534-02 | 535-01 | 535-02 | 535-03 | 535-04 | 535-05 | 535-06 | 535-07 |

    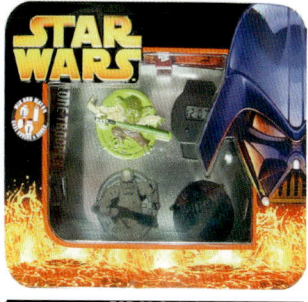 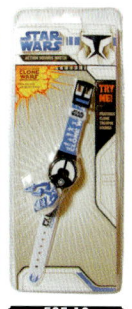 

| 535-08 | 535-09 | 535-10 | 535-11 Style 1 | 535-11 Style 2 | 535-12 | 535-13 |

Watches: Digital

- C-3PO and R2-D2 below, Star Wars logo above, round black face, 1 button, black band, clear case [v1e1:441] 60.00
- C-3PO and R2-D2 below, Star Wars logo above, round black face, 1 button, black band, Star Wars logo window box 65.00
- C-3PO and R2-D2 below, Star Wars logo above, round black face, 3 button, black band [v1e1:441] 50.00
- C-3PO and R2-D2 below, Star Wars logo above, round starfield face, 2 button, blue band [v1e1:441] 50.00
- C-3PO left, R2-D2 right, 2 X-Wings above, square starfield face, 1 button, black band [v1e1:441] 75.00
- C-3PO left, R2-D2 right, Star Wars logo above, round starfield face, 1 button, black band 60.00
- C-3PO left, R2-D2 right, Star Wars logo above, round starfield face, 2 button, black band, musical [v1e1:441] 95.00
- C-3PO left, R2-D2 right, Star Wars logo above, square starfield face, 1 button, black band 60.00
- C-3PO left, R2-D2 right, Star Wars logo above, square starfield face, 2 button, black band, musical 135.00
- C-3PO left; R2-D2 right; X-Wing, Star Wars logo, TIE Fighter above, square blue face, 2 button, black band, musical [535-23] 125.00
- C-3PO left; R2-D2 right; X-Wing, Star Wars logo; Vader's TIE Fighter above; musical alarm text below, square blue face, 3 button, black band, musical 135.00
- Clock and calculator ruler [535-24] 45.00
- Darth Vader below, black Star Wars logo above, round gray face, 1 button, black band [v1e1:441] 55.00
- Darth Vader below, black Star Wars logo above, round gray face, 3 button, black band [v1e1:441] 55.00
- Darth Vader below, blue Star Wars logo above, round gray face, 1 button, black band [535-25] 55.00
- Darth Vader, red Star Wars logo, white face, Vader holding time window, black vinyl band [535-26] 55.00
- Darth Vader/Star Wars logo changing image, round blue face, 1 button, black band 110.00
- Droids logo above, C-3PO right, R2-D2 below, square face, 1 button, black band [535-27] 50.00
- Ewoks below, Return of the Jedi logo above, round face, 1 button, black band [535-28] 45.00
- Jabba below, Return of the Jedi logo above, round face, 1 button, black band [535-29] 50.00
- Jabba below, Return of the Jedi logo above, square face, 1 button, black band 45.00
- Wicket the Ewok, Whistle Time [535-30] 450.00
- Yoda below, Star Wars logo above, round white face, 1 button, black band [v1e1:442] 55.00
- Yoda below, Star Wars logo above, square black and white face, 1 button, black band 45.00

Radio watch with headphones.
- R2-D2, Star Wars [535-31] 275.00
- Wicket, Return of the Jedi [535-32] 275.00

Burger King
Episode III: Revenge of the Sith DVD release promotion. Interchangeable watches with a collector's tin.
- 1 The Phantom Menace [535-33] 10.00
- 2 Attack of the Clones [535-34] 10.00
- 3 Revenge of the Sith [535-35] 10.00
- 4 A New Hope [535-36] 10.00
- 5 The Empire Strikes Back [535-37] 10.00
- 6 Return of the Jedi [535-38] 10.00

Casio
Revenge of the Sith.
- Darth Vader [535-39] 300.00
- Star Wars logo [535-40] 300.00

Clicks
Domed package.
- Darth Vader 10.00

Squared package.
- Darth Vader [535-41] 10.00
- Epic Duel [535-42] 10.00
- Yoda [535-43] 10.00

Disney / MGM
- Darth Vader helmet cover 25.00
- Star Tours, inaugural flight January 1987 [535-44] 85.00

       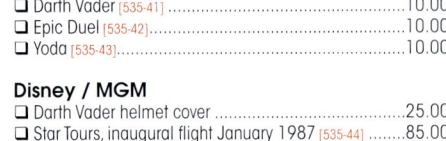

535-14 | 535-15 | 535-16 | 535-17 | 535-18 | 535-19 | 535-20

  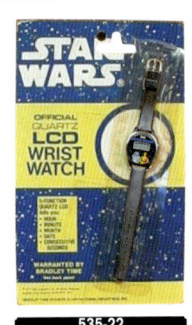  

535-21 Boxed and Open | 535-22 | 535-23 | 524-24

  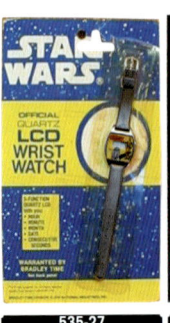    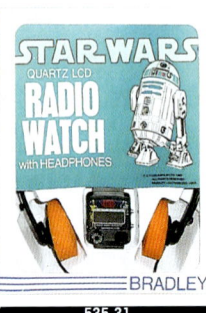 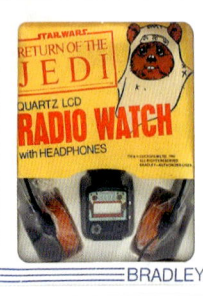

535-25 | 535-26 | 535-27 | 535-28 | 535-29 | 535-30 | 535-31 | 535-32

535-33 Side 1 and Side 2 | 535-34 Side 1 and Side 2 | 535-35 Side 1 and Side 2 | 535-36 Side 1 and Side 2 | 535-37 Side 1 and Side 2 | 535-38 Side 1 and Side 2

Watches: Digital

Duracell
- Digital Darth Vader SE art, promotional packaged with batteries [535-45] 75.00

Ecclissi
- Death Star face, sterling silver [v1e1:442] 350.00

FAB (Fashion Accessory Bazaar) Starpoint
- Captain Rex and Anakin [535-46] 15.00
- Clone Wars 15.00
- Obi-Wan and Anakin, sports alarm [535-47] 15.00

Hope Industries
- 2-pack Darth Maul flip top and Battle Droid flip top with collectors storage tin [535-48] 25.00
- 3-pack Sculpted Collection: Anakin, Jar Jar, Darth Maul with lightsaber case [535-49] 25.00
- 4-pack die-cast Battle Droid, Darth Maul, Pit Droid, R2-D2, boxed with magnet seal [535-50] 50.00

Collector timepiece. Death Star storage case.
- Boba Fett [535-51] 20.00

- Darth Vader [535-52] 20.00
- Stormtrooper [535-53] 20.00

Collector timepiece. Millennium Falcon storage case.
- Boba Fett [535-54] 20.00
- C-3PO [535-55] 20.00
- Darth Vader [535-56] 20.00
- R2-D2 [535-57] 20.00
- Stormtrooper [535-58] 20.00
- Yoda [535-59] 20.00
- Yoda, alternate coloring [535-60] 20.00

Die-cast watches in plastic case packaging.
- Battle Droid 15.00
- Darth Maul [535-61] 15.00
- Pit Droid 15.00
- R2-D2 .... 15.00

Episode I collector watch with lightsaber case, box packaging.
- Anakin Skywalker [535-62] 12.00
- C-3PO [535-63] 12.00

- Darth Maul [535-64] 12.00
- Jar Jar Binks [535-65] 12.00

Episode I collector watch with lightsaber case, sealed bubble packaging.
- Anakin Skywalker [535-66] 15.00
- C-3PO [535-67] 15.00

535-39   535-40   535-41

535-42   535-43   535-44   535-45   535-46   535-47   535-48

535-49

535-50

535-51

535-52

535-53   535-54   535-55   535-56   535-57   535-58

535-59

535-60

535-61

535-62

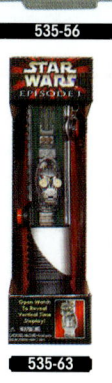
535-63

535-64   535-65

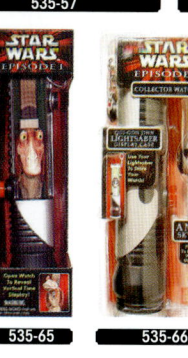
535-66

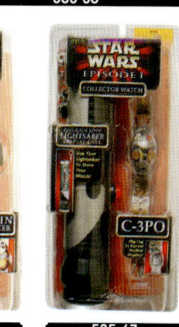
535-67

Watches: Digital

- ❏ Darth Maul [535-68] 15.00
- ❏ Jar Jar Binks [535-69] 15.00

Episode I die-cast watch with tin collector case, boxed, brass finish.
- ❏ Battle droid [535-70] 20.00
- ❏ Darth Maul [535-71] 20.00
- ❏ Pit droid [535-72] 20.00
- ❏ R2-D2 [535-73] 20.00

Episode I die-cast watch with tin collector case, boxed, steel finish.
- ❏ Battle droid [535-74] 20.00
- ❏ Darth Maul [535-75] 20.00
- ❏ Pit droid 20.00
- ❏ R2-D2 [535-76] 20.00

Flip-top watches.
- ❏ Anakin Skywalker [535-77] 10.00
- ❏ C-3PO [535-78] 10.00
- ❏ Darth Maul [535-79] 10.00
- ❏ Jar Jar Binks [535-80] 10.00
- ❏ Obi-Wan Kenobi [535-81] 10.00
- ❏ Queen Amidala [535-82] 10.00

Imperial Forces collector timepiece gift set, character watches with plastic Death Star storage case.
- ❏ 2-piece: Darth Vader and Boba Fett [535-83] 20.00
- ❏ 2-piece: Darth Vader and stormtrooper [535-84] ... 20.00
- ❏ 3-piece: Boba Fett, Darth Vader, stormtrooper 25.00

Rebel Alliance collector timepiece gift set, character watches with plastic Millennium Falcon storage case.
- ❏ 2-piece: C-3PO and R2-D2 .... 20.00
- ❏ 2-piece: C-3PO and Yoda [535-85] 20.00
- ❏ 3-piece: C-3PO, R2-D2, Yoda 25.00

Sculpted classic trilogy character flip-top watches.
- ❏ Boba Fett [535-86] 15.00
- ❏ C-3PO [535-87] 15.00
- ❏ Darth Vader [535-88] 15.00
- ❏ R2-D2 [535-89] 15.00
- ❏ Stormtrooper [535-90] 15.00
- ❏ Yoda [535-91] 15.00

Its About Time
- ❏ Battle Droid on STAP [535-92] 12.00
- ❏ Destroyer droid transforming watch / clock [535-93] .. 20.00
- ❏ Jar Jar Binks sticking out tongue [535-94] 12.00
- ❏ Jar Jar Binks talking watch [535-95] 20.00
- ❏ Obi-Wan on battleship [535-96] 12.00

Flip-top watches.
- ❏ Anakin Skywalker [535-97] 15.00
- ❏ Darth Maul, black band [535-98] 15.00
- ❏ Darth Maul, red band [535-99] 15.00
- ❏ Queen Amidala [535-100] 15.00
- ❏ Queen Amidala interchangeable [535-101] 20.00

JazWares, Inc
- ❏ Bounty hunter watch [535-102] 25.00
- ❏ Sith watch [535-103] 15.00

Joy Toy (UK)
Flip top watches.
- ❏ C-3PO / R2-D2 interchangeable [535-104] 15.00

535-68

535-69

535-70

535-71

535-72

535-73

535-74

535-75

535-76

535-77

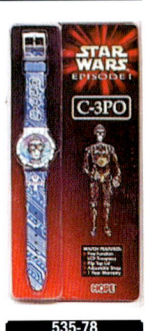
535-78

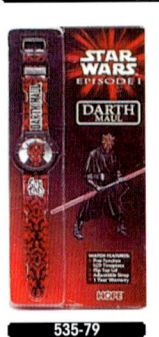
535-79

535-80

535-81

535-82

535-83

535-84

535-85

535-86

535-87

535-88

535-89

535-90

535-91

Watches: Digital

Montreal
Character watches.
- C-3PO, flip [535-105] 25.00
- C-3PO and R2-D2 [535-106] 25.00
- Han Solo [535-107] 25.00

Nelsonic
- Podracer turbine [535-108] 25.00
- Podracer watch with built-in compass [535-109] 25.00

Talking watch with tin collector case.
- Darth Maul [535-110] 25.00
- Jar Jar Binks [535-111] 25.00

Playworks
- Darth Vader with TIE Fighters on wristband [535-112] 15.00

Character head with face-cover.
- Boba Fett 7.00
- C-3PO [535-113] 7.00
- Darth Vader [535-114] 7.00
- Millennium Falcon [535-115] 11.00

- R2-D2 [535-116] 7.00
- Stormtrooper [535-117] 7.00
- Yoda 7.00

Seiko (Japan)
- R2-D2 .... 1,275.00

Taito (Japan)
- Ahsoka Tano [535-118] 18.00
- Anakin Skywalker [535-119] 18.00
- Asajj Ventress [535-120] 18.00
- Battle droids [535-121] 18.00
- Clones [535-122] 18.00
- Obi-Wan Kenobi [535-123] 18.00

Texas Instruments
- C-3PO and R2-D2 above, Star Wars logo below, square blue starfield face, 2 buttons, black band, 10 decals 95.00
- C-3PO and R2-D2 above, Star Wars logo below, square blue starfield face, 2 buttons, gray band [535-124] 95.00
- C-3PO and R2-D2 above, X-Wings and Darth Vader below, square starfield face, 2 buttons, black band 95.00
- Darth Vader and X-Wings above, Star Wars logo below, square face, 2 buttons, black band, blister packed [535-125] 95.00
- Darth Vader and X-Wings above, Star Wars logo below, square face, 2 buttons, black band, plastic case [535-126] 85.00
- Star Wars logo above and below, square silver face, 2 buttons, black band with R2-D2 and Darth Vader graphics 125.00

Toy Options
Silver metal flip-top watches.
- C-3PO [535-127] 40.00
- Darth Vader [535-128] 40.00
- Stormtrooper [535-129] 40.00

Watchit
- Destroyer droid transforming watch / clock [535-130] 25.00
- R2-D2, Light and Sound [535-131] 20.00

Flip-top watches.
- Boba Fett [535-132] 20.00
- C-3PO [535-133] 20.00
- Darth Maul [535-134] 15.00
- Darth Vader, musical [535-135] 25.00

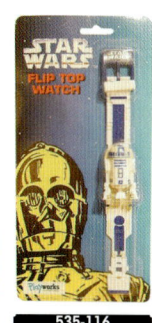

Watches: Digital

   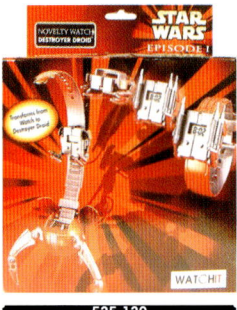  

535-127 535-128 535-129 535-130 535-131 535-132

        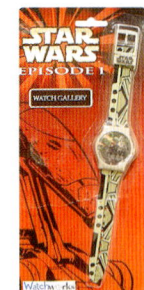

535-133 535-134 535-135 535-136 535-137 535-138 535-139 535-140 535-141

535-142 535-143 535-144 535-145 535-146 535-147 535-148 535-149 535-150

- ❑ Millennium Falcon [535-136] 20.00
- ❑ Queen Amidala [535-137] 15.00
- ❑ Queen Amidala, interchangeable [535-138]...................20.00
- ❑ R2-D2 ....20.00

Novelty LCD watches. Classic trilogy.
- ❑ C-3PO [535-139] 20.00

Novelty LCD watches. Episode I.
- ❑ Droid fighter 20.00
- ❑ Sith communicator 20.00

Watchit (Argentina)
- ❑ Darth Vader, flip top [535-140] 20.00

WatchWorks
- ❑ Battle droid [535-141] 15.00
- ❑ Destroyer droid transforming watch / clock [535-142].....25.00
- ❑ Droid fighter flip-up, sculpted [535-143] 15.00
- ❑ Jar Jar Binks [535-144] 15.00
- ❑ Jar Jar Binks talking watch [535-145] 25.00
- ❑ Obi-Wan Kenobi [535-146] 15.00
- ❑ Sith communicator 20.00

World Wide Licenses Ltd.
- ❑ Darth Maul sound and FX [535-147] 30.00

Zeon
- ❑ Episode II: Attack of the Clones animated talking watch [535-148] 25.00
- ❑ Star Wars [v1e1-444]..85.00

Flip top watches.
- ❑ C-3PO / R2-D2 interchangeable [535-149]....................25.00
- ❑ Jango Fett [535-150] 20.00

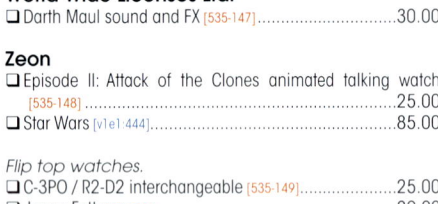

536-01 Views from 3 Sides 536-02 536-03 536-04 536-05 536-06 536-07 536-08 536-09 536-10 536-11

536-12 536-13 536-14 536-15 536-16 536-17 536-18 536-19 536-20 536-21 536-22

Water Bottles
Continued in Volume 3, Page 366

❏ Celebration III Anakin / Vader lenticular [536-01] 15.00

Animations
Mini with printed cozy, exclusive to Target.
❏ Chewbacca [536-02] 8.00
❏ Darth Vader [536-03] 8.00
❏ Yoda [536-04] 8.00

Disney / MGM
❏ Star Tours logo 35.00

Heart Art Collection, Ltd. (Japan)
❏ R2-D2 [536-05] 45.00

Koozie Sports Bottles
Lucas Arts.
❏ Rebel Assault 2 [536-06] 10.00

Masterfoods USA
Metal canisters with M&M character graphics. Nylon bags. China.
❏ Anakin Skywalker [536-07] 25.00
❏ General Grievous [536-08] 25.00

Pepsi Cola (Mexico)
Episode I: The Phantom Menace.
❏ Jar Jar Binks [536-09] 15.00
❏ Qui-Gon vs. Darth Maul [536-10] 15.00

Star Wars: Special Edition.
❏ C-3PO [536-11] 25.00
❏ Darth Vader [536-12] 25.00
❏ R2-D2 [536-13] 25.00
❏ Stormtrooper [536-14] 25.00

Seneca Sports Inc.
❏ R2-D2 ....10.00

Silver Buffalo
❏ Darth Vader / "You Don't Know The Power of the Dark Side", stainless steel, 25 oz. [536-15] 15.00

Spearmark International (UK)
❏ Clone Wars [536-16] 20.00
❏ Episode II Sports Bottle [536-17] 10.00

Star Wars Celebration V
❏ Boba Fett logo 20.00

Star Wars Celebration VI
❏ VaderAde [536-18] 25.00

Vandor LLC
Collapsible water bottles, exclusive to Target.
❏ Boba Fett [536-19] 10.00
❏ Darth Vader [536-20] 10.00
❏ R2-D2 [536-21] 10.00
❏ Stormtrooper [536-22] 10.00

Window Clings
Continued in Volume 3, Page 367

20th Century Fox
❏ Attack of the Clones Yoda, "Unlock the Saga" [537-01] ...50.00

Blockbuster Video
❏ Win Yoda April 9–14, 2-piece video promotion 65.00

Disney / MGM
❏ Jedi Training Academy [537-02] 15.00

Fan Club
❏ Star Wars cling [537-03] 30.00

KFC
Episode I character face with rectangle background.
❏ Jar Jar Binks [537-04] 25.00
❏ Queen Amidala 25.00

Window Clings

Episode I full-character figure 2-piece door cling.
❏ Queen Amidala 50.00
❏ Qui-Gon Jinn 50.00

Liquid Blue
❏ Anakin Skywalker 15.00
❏ Darth Maul with 2-sided saber 15.00
❏ Jedi vs. Sith 15.00
❏ Naboo space battle 15.00

Norben
❏ Anakin Skywalker 15.00
❏ Darth Maul 15.00
❏ Jedi vs. Sith 15.00
❏ Space Battle 15.00

Pizza Hut
❏ Darth Maul life-size 2-piece door sticker 65.00
❏ "Don't Leave Coruscant Without Them." (toys, large rectangle) 30.00
❏ "Don't Leave Coruscant Without Them." (toys, small rectangle) 30.00
❏ Mace Windu and Yoda 50.00
❏ Qui-Gon Jinn and pink alien from Jedi council 45.00
❏ "Welcome to Coruscant" 2-sided door cling 50.00

Taco Bell
18" x 24" advertising Star Wars Special Edition.
❏ Boba Fett, Empire Strikes Back [537-05] 60.00
❏ Chewbacca, Star Wars [537-06] 60.00
❏ Darth Vader, Return of the Jedi [537-07] 60.00
❏ Droids, Empire Strikes Back [537-08] 60.00
❏ Stormtrooper, Star Wars [537-09] 60.00

6' tall door decals.
❏ C-3PO [537-10] 75.00
❏ Chewbacca [537-11] 75.00
❏ Stormtrooper [537-12] 75.00

Feel The Force promotion. Window promotions.
❏ Vader: Win Millions of Prizes! [537-13] 45.00
❏ Yoda: Play the Feel the Force game! [537-14] 45.00

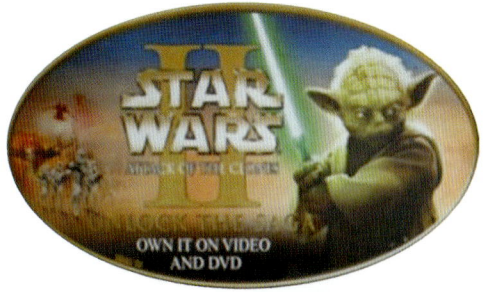
537-01

537-02

537-03

537-04

537-05

537-06

537-07

537-08

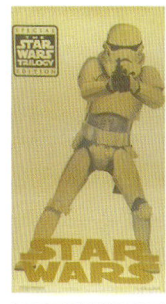
537-09

537-10

537-11

537-12

537-13 Side 1

537-14 Side 1

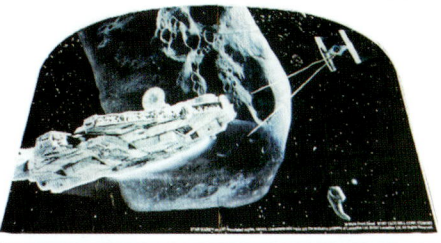
537-13 / 537-14 Side 2

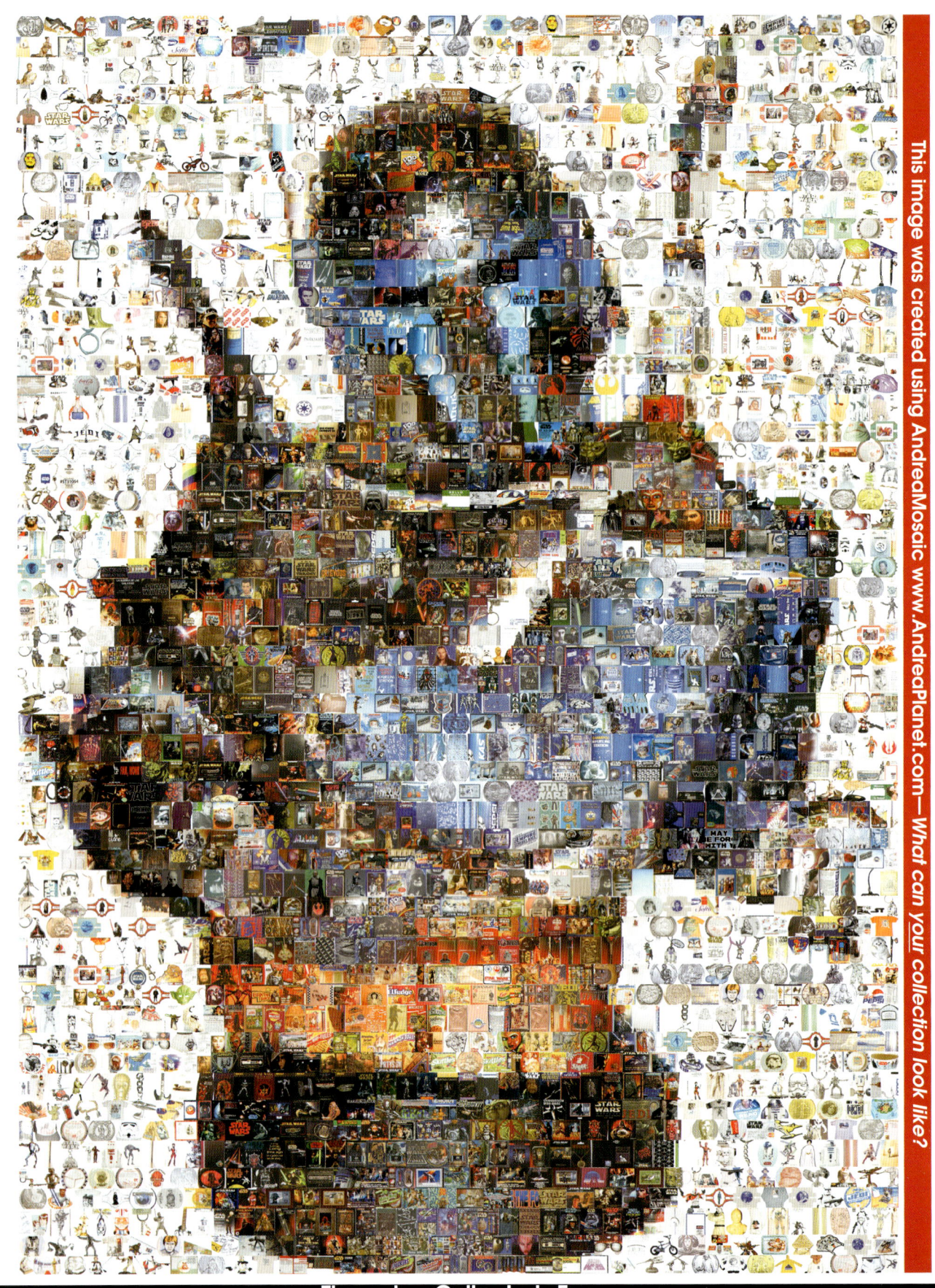

Through a Collector's Eye
Every image used above can be found elsewhere within this book.

STAR WARS CALENDARS ARE FOREVER!

The lessons: (1) Time gives perspective, and (2) Not every answer remains the same for all time. Calendars, planners, and datebooks used to devalue quickly. After all, in the year 2013, who would have wanted a predated planner from the year 2002? Printed materials are pricey at retail and typically have a fairly short life for usefulness. Calendars are usually valuable for "16 months" at the outside.

Fortunately, you can now take that old datebook that's on eBay for $6.00 and tuck it safely away knowing that will be useful to you again some day! You've got the answer key (below)!

Although there are only seven weekdays that any given year can start on, the odd number of days in a year coupled with leap years tossed in for good measure can make figuring out which years are fully compatible a bit tricky. You could open up the calendar on your computer or mobile device and scroll back and forth through the years, checking both January 1 and March 1 weekdays (darn you, leap year!!), or you can open your always-handy Star Wars Super Collector's Wish Book, Volume 1, 2nd Edition, turn to page 489 across from the eye-catching mosaic, and look up the compatible years to match up when you shop for a re-purposed calendar.

Leap years offer limited calendar options, so when 2028 rolls around, you'll have two choices: "Buy a new one" or go find a 2000 calendar before everyone else reads about this and buys them all up. Whichever you decide, make sure to hold onto it for 2056!

STAR WARS: PREPARING YOU FOR THE NEXT FIFTY YEARS

2027 will be the golden 50th anniversary for Star Wars, the original theatrical film later to be designated Episode IV: A New Hope. On its journey to documenting the half century of merchandising, the Star Wars **Super Collector's Database** crossed 150,000 unique entries in mid-2023. It was a day to be "*long remembered*" in Darth Vader's own words.

Information gathering has become easier with mobile phone cameras and online inventories—while at the same time, it is nearly impossible to document it all at the rate it is pr-oduced, sold, disseminated, and stored away in pursuit of the next new find. You need a reliable resource that stays updated regularly.

Whether you, as a fan and collector, need the application to track your super (or select) collection, or if you need a community to support and encourage your collecting efforts, the Star Wars **Super Collector's Database** would be "*honored to have you join us*" (Vader again).

It's a prepopulated database application for Windows and for Android mobile devices so you will always have your own collection close at hand. https://www.StarWarsDatabase.com

Interchangeable Calendar Years 1977–2060: Common Years

1977	1978	1979	1981	1982	1985	1986
1983	1989	1990	1987	1993	1991	1997
1994	1995	2001	1998	1999	2002	2003
2005	2006	2007	2009	2010	2013	2014
2011	2017	2018	2015	2021	2019	2025
2022	2023	2029	2026	2027	2030	2031
2033	2034	2035	2037	2038	2041	2042
2039	2045	2046	2043	2049	2047	2053
2050	2051	2057	2054	2055	2058	2059

Interchangeable Calendar Years 1977–2060: Leap Years

1980	1984	1988	1992	1996	2000	2004
2008	2012	2016	2020	2024	2028	2032
2036	2040	2044	2048	2052	2056	2060

Alfamart Coins: An Indonesia Exclusive

Collecting is one of the few passions where it can be exciting to have missed something ... once you discover it. A rarely known pair of coin sets was offered by Alfamart, a chain store in Indonesia.

Produced by "Red Enterprises," two sets of 40 mm coins were distributed in blind packs.

The first was for Rogue One. The set includes 36 base coins with varying (unpublished) levels of scarcity as determined by opening multiple cases to build sets. Also offered was a black-and-gold Darth Vader coin and a special gold colored K-2SO coin.

The following year, Alfamart offered another exclusive set of 50 coins from what was then all seven of the Star Wars theatrical films.

The coins were distributed in blind packs of three coins each, with the third coin either being a basic coin or else an advertising branded coin with a black finish.

There were 7 limited-edition Star Wars coins advertised that have not yet been discovered in the blind packs, leading to the speculation that they were either special offer or else a redemption set. Leaflets from the blind packs include unique voucher codes.

ROGUE ONE (2016)

- Death Trooper / Imperial Guard [500-01]
- Death Trooper [500-02]
- Defend the Galactic Empire / Darth Vader [500-03]
- Defend the Galactic Empire / Death Trooper [500-04]
- Defend the Galactic Empire / Krennic [500-05]
- Defend the Galactic Empire / Shoretrooper [500-06]
- Defend the Galactic Empire / Stormtrooper [500-07]
- Elite Enforcer [500-08]
- Join the Rebellion / Baze [500-09]
- Join the Rebellion / Cassian [500-10]
- Join the Rebellion / Chirrut [500-11]
- Join the Rebellion / Jyn [500-12]
- Join the Rebellion / K-2SO [500-013]
- K-2SO [500-14]
- Scarif Trooper [500-15]
- Scarif Troopers Elite Soldiers, Galactic Empire [500-16]
- Scarif [500-17]
- Scene: Darth Vader [500-18]
- Scene: Stormtrooper [500-19]
- Scene: The Galactic Empire [500-20]
- Scene: The Rebellion [500-21]
- Scene: TIE Striker [500-22]
- Scene: X-Wing vs. AT-ACT [500-23]
- Stormtroopers Elite Soldiers, Galactic Empire [500-24]
- The Galactic Empire / AT-ACT [500-25]
- The Galactic Empire / AT-ST Walker [500-26]
- The Galactic Empire / Death Star [500-27]
- The Galactic Empire / Imperial Star Destroyer [500-28]
- The Galactic Empire / Krennic Imperial Shuttle [500-29]
- The Galactic Empire / TIE Fighter [500-30]
- The Galactic Empire / TIE Striker [500-31]
- The Rebellion / U-Wing [500-32]
- The Rebellion / X-Wing [500-33]
- The Rebellion / Y-Wing [500-34]
- X-Wing Pilot Rebel Squadron [500-35]
- X-Wing Red Squadron the Rebel Alliance [500-36]

STAR WARS (2017)

- Admiral Ackbar / Rebel Alliance
- Anakin Skywalker / Jedi
- Anakin Skywalker / Sith
- Battle Droids / Separatists
- BB-8 / Resistance
- Boba Fett / Bounty Hunter
- C-3PO / Rebel Alliance
- Captain Phasma / First Order
- Chewbacca / Rebel Alliance
- Chief Chirpa / Bright Tree Village
- Clone Trooper Phase I / Galactic Republic
- Count Dooku / Sith
- Darth Maul / Sith
- Darth Vader / Galactic Empire
- Death Star / Galactic Empire
- Emperor Guard / Galactic Empire
- Finn / Resistance
- Flame Trooper / First Order
- General Grievous / Separatists
- Grand Moff Tarkin / Galactic Empire
- Han Solo / Rebel Alliance
- Jabba the Hutt / Grand Hutt Council
- Jango Fett / Separatists
- Jar Jar Binks / Galactic Republic
- Jawa
- Kylo Ren / First Order
- Lando Calrissian / Rebel Alliance
- Luke Skywalker / Jedi
- Mace Windu / Jedi
- Maz Kanata / Pirate
- Millennium Falcon / Rebel Alliance
- Obi-Wan Kenobi / Jedi
- Obi-Wan Kenobi / Jedi
- Padme Amidala / Galactic Republic
- Palpatine / Sith
- Plo Koon / Jedi
- Poe Dameron / Resistance
- Qui-Gon Jinn / Jedi
- R2-D2 / Rebel Alliance
- Rey / Resistance
- Sandtrooper / Galactic Empire
- Scout Trooper / Galactic Empire
- Snowtrooper / First Order
- Stormtrooper / First Order
- Stormtrooper / Galactic Empire
- Tasu Leech / Kanjiklub
- TIE Bomber / Galactic Empire
- TIE Fighter / Galactic Empire
- X-Wing / Rebel Alliance
- Yoda / Jedi

35 YEARS OF STAR WARS: MERCHANDISE AND COLLECTIBLES, 1977–2012

Collecting epochs are marked by different experience-changing events for most readers of this series. This book covers the 35-year pre-Disney era of Star Wars collectibles and merchandise. (Volume 2 covers the toys from the same period.)

The vintage years were from **1977–1985**, when the first wave of marketing for the original trilogy was active. Often remembered as the "toy years" for Star Wars, the original premise of this book series was to demonstrate that Star Wars was everywhere else in the home as well, many times in creative and surprising ways.

1993–1999 were the modern years (now classic) when Star Wars merchandising was revived and fans saw the Star Wars Special Editions (SW:SE) in the theater, which led up to the release of the prequel film trilogy, Episodes I–III. This also marked the dividing eras when Hasbro acquired Kenner and the legacy toy line evolved.

1999–2012 was a historic stretch seeing both the crash of the fan base accompanied by a glut of merchandise early in the period up through the reinvigoration of the fan and collector communities during the conclusion of the prequel films and popularity of the Clone Wars cartoons. Capping this span was the theatrical release of Episode I: The Phantom Menace in 3D.

2012 was the year Disney acquired Lucasfilm, which lead to the sequel trilogy, individually told story films, and streaming television series.

Prior to the Disney acquisition, the realm in which Star Wars games, comics, and novels were chronicled was officially named "The Expanded Universe." All non-canon (not seen in the films) material was determined by Disney to become known as "Legends," as the new owner of the franchise told new timeline stories in the time/space formerly occupied by the Expanded Universe.

By locking in those first 35 years, this book provides a visual exploration of the essence that came from the out-of-theater Star Wars exposure on the public and the role it played in establishing the foundation for what Star Wars is today in modern popular culture.

Ceramic snowspeeder toothbrush holder by Sigma "The Tastesetter"—1982/1983

"Let the Wookiee Win" (My Personal Star Wars Merchandise Journey)
By Cole Houston

When I was invited to pen an article for this edition of *The Star Wars Super Collector's Wish Book*, I had to take a moment to look back over the years and reminisce about the earliest merchandise based on that "Galaxy Far, Far Away" that was a part of my life in the late '70s. As an avid toy collector from the moment there were Star Wars toys, the impact of other merchandise on my life and collection was not as profound, but it was nonetheless a part of my history with the franchise.

A long time ago—in the late '70s—two things happened that would forever cement the name of young filmmaker George Lucas into the public consciousness. First, he was denied the opportunity to fulfill a dream of bringing Flash Gordon to the big screen, resulting in the creation of Star Wars as an alternative. And then there was the true spark of genius that set Lucas apart from everyone in Hollywood before and since: the retention of merchandising rights for his creation.

The effect of this was twofold. One, it increased revenues from the low-budget film that became a cultural phenomenon, and, for the most part, it imposed a level of quality control in which licenses to manufacture were granted and which were rejected outright. There are a few notable exceptions, the most glaring being the infamous and awkward C-3PO tape dispenser, but for the most part—at least initially—the Star Wars name was not simply slapped onto any product that wanted a brief edge in the marketplace. That said, from paper goods such as party invitations and Dixie Cups, to household items such as trash cans and cookie jars, to collectibles such as porcelain figurines, merchandise did flow out into the world from a variety of manufacturers. As the years turned into decades, the sheer volume of licensed Star Wars products has increased exponentially, though not always for the best.

Given the nature of licensing in those days, however, Star Wars merchandise was not nearly as pervasive in retail spaces as it would become in the years and decades that followed. Personally, the first piece of merchandise that I would discover was a now-obscure magazine titled *Star Wars Spectacular*. This special edition was published by Famous Monsters and was a surprise find in the grocery store magazine section. Tucked amid issues of *Car and Driver* and *Ladies' Home Journal* was a publication that called out for me—and a dollar and a quarter of my pocket money in the bargain! It was worth every penny since it expanded my connection with the film I had discovered that summer on a family road trip that would take over much of my life. Within those pages, amid the "Over 60 fantastic photos" promised on the cover was a close-up of the intrepid copilot Chewie with "Chewbacca, the Wookiee" in bold letters beside it, preceding a brief bio. By this time I had only seen Star Wars once and, as far as I knew, C-3PO had uttered the phrase "Let the monkey win!" This was the most profound of the numerous glimpses into the world of Star Wars that had only just begun to blossom.

It is certain that there are far more scholarly collectors out there who have delved deeply into the history of Star Wars merchandise, and I will leave that researched work to those with the passion to discover every aspect. For my part, and for this article, I will instead invite you on an all-too-brief journey into my own personal experiences with Star Wars merchandise, beginning in 1977 and perpetuating to this day. It all began, of course, with that aforementioned Star Wars publication that shared a kind of "starter's gun" status with Kenner's Star Wars Early Bird set, but that is more in the realm of toys, and this volume is about, well, everything else. So, with that in mind, the first significant element of the initial merchandising boom that impacted my own life was California Originals' unrivaled Chewbacca tankard!

Released in 1977, this was one of three rather sizable figural mugs licensed and produced by that manufacturer. Obi-Wan Kenobi and Darth Vader rounded out the line, and, while handsome pieces in their own right, they lacked the personal appeal to me of the Chewbacca model (which I still have to this day). Once touted as George Lucas's favorite example of Saga merchandise, the sculpt on this mug captures the true nature of the Wookiee far better than any product that followed over the years. There is a gentleness in the subtle expression rendered by the sculptor's hands, which, on film, was what made Chewie a far more approachable nonhuman character from the outset. Early on, it was a well-used, practical drinking vessel from the time it was first given as a Christmas gift, and it even, to the horror of many a reader, I am sure, had a few trips through the dishwasher before I decided it was better served as a display piece than a working mug. Breathe easy; it has never seen a beverage since!

As memories rise to the surface of merchandise that was important in my youth, two pieces that were proudly displayed in my bedroom spring to mind that reflect upon a couple of genres of collectibles that carried the Star Wars brand. The most prominent was the original Don Post Studios Darth Vader Helmet. Don Post was well known by the '70s for its amazing rubber masks featuring the likenesses of Universal Studios monsters as well as many an original creation. Being no stranger to licensing, the company was the go-to for high-end Star Wars costume elements in those early days. This was a major investment for a twelve-year-old, retailing for close to $45 in those days (I recall that it was a challenge to scrape together the funding), but worth every penny! Unlike the heavy latex rubber masks most common for this manufacturer's lines, Vader was presented in a two-piece hard-plastic form (this before *The Empire Strikes Back* and *Return of the Jedi* would reveal an even more complex three-part structure) with Velcro attached to the inner forehead and the inner helmet portions for a secure fit. A far cry from the flimsy rubber masks with thin plastic inserts—Stormtrooper and Sandpeople—that my younger brother and I found in a Colorado gift shop back in the day. This amazing helmet was proudly displayed when not put to rare use as a mask.

Vader's distinctive helmet stood upon a shelf of other masks—some Star Wars, some originals—from various manufacturers on a wall adjacent to my bedroom closet door. Upon that door from the age of twelve to eighteen was a Princess Leia poster featuring the intrepid heroine, blaster in hand, sporting a defiant yet alluring look, set upon a red background. To this day, it's a favorite image from the early years of my long relationship with Star Wars.

Many are the iconic images that prevail from the Saga, including variations of the X-Wing versus TIE Fighter battle. This classic was utilized on one of the facing panels of the original Star Wars lunchbox from Thermos. The opposite side featured the scene of Luke, Ben, and the droids being stopped by Stormtroopers at Mos Eisley. This was a favorite piece of merchandise for me, despite having reached that age where, apart from Arnold Horshack on *Welcome Back, Kotter*, most school kids had abandoned lunch kits in favor of paper bags. What was particularly curious about this particular lunchbox was that the side panels lacked any artwork in favor of a starfield motif. Later releases would correct this, bringing it in line with the more heavily illustrated lunch kits featuring popular movies and television themes. To rectify this rather bland presentation, I personally opted to festoon the sides of mine with stickers from Topps' early Star Wars trading card packs.

While trading cards as a product have been around for over a century, the original Star Wars line (which enjoyed five series in the '70s and five in the '80s between the two sequels) were produced at the tail end of the period, when a stiff, brittle, and bland stick of bubble gum was included in every waxy-wrapper pack. The gum was the bane of many a collector, because it inevitably left a rectangular stain on the back of the card at the bottom of the stack! But that never stopped avid collectors like a friend of mine and me during our pursuit of a full set of each early Star Wars wave—Blue, Red, Yellow, Green, and Orange! Between us, we easily bought a full box each over time and haggled over trades for missing card numbers. Even after his family moved out of state, the trading continued with lists of available trading cards that I would send to him as "Uncle Yoda's Used Card Lot" in the '80s. Ah, the thrill of the hunt back in those days!

Such a hunt often extended along many lines. My family missed out on one of the Holy Grails of Star Wars collectors, Sigma's R2-D2 cookie jar—a piece all too often found today minus the Astromech's head (lids of cookie jars are notorious victims of breakage, after all). One such specimen was given to my wife and me many years ago and was later gifted to the author of this very tome and brilliantly repurposed as a flower pot! School supplies, apparel, and especially bisque figurines were often illusive or simply cost-prohibitive in the pursuit to own a piece of the Saga in merchandise form. Fast food premiums such as posters and drinking glasses proved difficult to obtain due to scheduled releases not always coinciding with family decisions to "dine out"—and the added cost to the meal. Personally, I only recently completed my collection of Burger King glasses from all three Original Trilogy films.

In those days, some standouts in the merchandise realm were the jewelry of Factors, Etc. (which also produced posters in an era when everyone had one or more posters on their walls). Necklaces with long chains from which depended a Stormtrooper or Vader's helmet, an X-Wing Fighter, or unusual figural representations of Chewbacca, Artoo, or Threepio with loosely jointed features were the height of Star Wars fashion in the '70s.

Sadly, I no longer have my original Chewie necklace, but I managed, to this day, to maintain all of the unused pages from a book of Star Wars iron-on transfers published by Ballentine (the Jawas image being one of the few utilized to decorate the back of my pajama top in 1977). Other rarities of that period that I no longer have were cardboard stand-ups featuring the likenesses of favorite heroes and villains, which my parents discovered at a Dallas bookshop. We had C-3PO, Darth Vader, and Chewbacca, which, cleverly, were tacked to a bedroom ceiling to keep them free of dust and damage while acting as a decorative element.

From its arrival into the world vernacular, Star Wars has also had an impact on the publishing industry. Personally, the chance discovery of Marvel Comics' six-issue adaptation of what would become known as A New Hope in poly-bagged sets of the first and last three issues of that run sparked a collecting passion. After the initial run, the title departed the movie, and new adventures of the lead characters were told for many years. In those days, 7-Eleven was our comic shop, and finding every issue was nothing short of a challenge. Somehow, I did manage to keep up with the monthly publication schedule and amassed all 107 issues and three Annuals. However, that first Annual did escape my attention and was only discovered from seeing a page of original art for sale at a comic convention, thus spurring me to track down a copy of that previously missed issue!

Early into Star Wars, there was a slow entrée into the paperback book genre of publications. After the novelization of Star Wars, Alan Dean Foster's *Splinter of the Mind's Eye* became the first—and, for quite a while, only—example of what would become The Expanded Universe (long before it carried such a title). A series of young-readers novels focusing on Han Solo and Chewbacca would mark the first true story arc in Star Wars novels. Career scoundrel Lando Calrissian was also treated to a three-book arc before *Heir to the Empire* became the effective starting gun for a publication race that perpetuates to this day in fits and starts. Personally, I only ever owned and read *Splinter of the Mind's Eye* (which many in its day mistook as the "sequel to Star Wars" despite lacking Han and Chewie), but novels are no less an important aspect of Star Wars merchandise over the decades.

During the Sequel Era, the Don Post masks were among the most common merchandise to grace my personal collection. The company's Boba Fett helmet—though a bit lacking for not having a full-face screen but rather a thin strip of smoked translucent plastic up by the eyes—was no less a favorite in the line. I would also, as I could afford them on a high school student's budget, collect the Stormtrooper, X-Wing Pilot, and Emperor's Royal Guard helmets as well as another favorite, the Admiral Ackbar mask. The latter I purchased at, of all places, the Sears store at a local mall! Back in the '80s, for a few years anyway, Sears had an annual pop-up Halloween store that would appear out of nowhere in early October and was my resource for Don Post masks and helmets annually. To this day, the above all share a shelf in my studio room, proudly displayed decades later.

The list of merchandise solely from 1977 to 1983 alone is staggering in its size, so naturally I have refrained from a deep dive into everything outside of my ever-expanding toy collection in this article. Topps' candy-filled character heads and Applause's figural mugs of a variety of characters from the Saga are worth mentioning as more memorable, if not somewhat similar, examples of marketing during that period. While Star Wars became less marketable during the late '80s and early '90s, some products were still produced but with few standouts. With *Shadows of the Empire* and the Star Wars Special Editions, the promise of a continuation of that galaxy far, far away (and its requisite merchandise) loomed large and sparked something of a resurgence that never died down again.

Concentrating my collecting efforts primarily on toys has meant that so much of the merchandise of this era was not part of what I sought out personally. It would take the late '90s resurgence of Star Wars to ignite a passion for Star Wars merchandise anew. Applause produced a variety of affordable statues back then, including Han Solo in Carbonite flanked by Boussh with a light-up feature showcasing the captured hero, while another featured a remarkable trio of bounty hunters undoubtedly inspired by a Ralph McQuarrie illustration of the day, which became part of my "Statue Gallery." While that collection includes many other pop-culture properties, it is most heavily populated by Star Wars. Over a dozen Gentle Giant Mini-Busts flesh out this collection, along with French manufacturer Attakus's impeccable Princess Leia (Jabba's Palace) and Oola—prized pieces in the collection.

Christmas ornaments, especially those from Hallmark, have been a periodic aspect of my personal collecting habits as well. This in no small part due to the fact that the greeting card company licensed Star Trek with what became an incredibly rare USS Enterprise ornament over five years before the Millennium Falcon became the first electronic Star Wars ornament in the line! As if to make up for lost time, Hallmark released new ornaments annually side by side with those from Trek, a trend that continues to this day. Both electronic ornaments

(which attach to Christmas light strings) and standard solid ornaments have become a staple, with Momaw Nadon (a.k.a. Hammerhead) being a personal favorite, as this marked an unexpected incarnation of my favorite Mos Eisley character. And, speaking of that "wretched hive," a particular standout in Hallmark's offerings would have to be its Star Wars Celebration VI exclusive ornament set of Obi-Wan Kenobi wielding his lightsaber, Ponda Boba (a.k.a. Walrus Man), and the belligerent alien's severed arm as ornaments!

While on the subject of Star Wars Celebrations over the years, that convention, which began in 1999, saw the production of a tonnage of exclusive merchandise that is often difficult at best to obtain. My wife and I were fortunate enough to have been invited by Geoffrey T. Carlton to accompany him and a group of his close friends to help man his booth at Star Wars Celebration VI. I knew from some fan websites that one of the exclusive offerings would be a clever Gamorrean Guard piggy bank. At the time, only turnaround illustrations of the design were available, so I was impressed to discover that this $30 piece was not tiny and made of plastic but rather a sizable ceramic piece! Another exclusive bank by Diamond Select was a variation on its plastic R2-D2 bank, R2-Q5 in Imperial colors. What was not readily known was that this would be the rarest of its releases, with a mere 100 produced! I managed to procure three, one for myself, one for Geoffrey, and one—as it worked out—for one member of our group who had missed out due to that minimal quantity available. While quite scarce, convention exclusives like these are some of the most intriguing examples of Star Wars merchandise.

During my personal journey as a collector of Star Wars memorabilia, which began with a chance encounter with a fateful magazine, the volume of time and money expended in pursuit of a piece of the Saga is something rather staggering to contemplate. Yet, every moment, every penny spent has been fulfilling beyond words. Today there is Star Wars merchandise in nearly every corner of our house, from Star Wars logo bar stools in the kitchen, to art on the walls, to a copy of the Star Wars Spectacular on the wall over the sofa in my studio! While not my original copy, obtaining one later in life was something of a necessity. Set amid hundreds of toys that have been part of my life for nearly 50 years now is an equally smile-inducing volume of examples of how Star Wars became part of our lives through a bewildering variety of goods that show no sign of ever falling out of fashion.

Over the years and decades, R2-D2 has been a kitchen timer and an aquarium, Yoda has lent his trademark ears to a baseball cap bearing his name, Darth Vader and C-3PO have aided in switching lamps off and on as Clappers, and the Rancor Monster has been a bottle opener! Favorite characters have become shoes and slippers, Tiki-inspired drinkware, fridge magnets, and kitchen utensils. Waffle irons create breakfast treats in shapes like the Death Star or the Millennium Falcon, Luke Skywalker's ill-fated Taun Taun inspired an April Fool's joke that became an actual sleeping bag, and the hilt of Darth Vader's lightsaber is invoked as an umbrella handle!

These all are mere scratches at the surface of the sheer volume of products illustrated in this volume. As you peruse the pages, let it take you on your own personal journey through collecting Star Wars; from budding enthusiasts to veteran Super Collectors, all of us have many memories that will only be enhanced every time these pages are perused. When it comes to Star Wars merchandise, if Chewbacca might be considered the representative of the Saga, we simply have to "Let the Wookiee win!"

Cole "JediCole" Houston is an avid Star Wars collector with thousands of toys, statues, and collectibles concentrated in two rooms of his house as well as his "Statue Gallery" in the living room. He first crossed paths with the author of the Star Wars Super Collector's Wishbook *when the first edition was nearing publication, and has been a contributor of images and articles in many editions since. Based in the Dallas / Fort Worth area, he created, produced, and hosted the live podcast* The Rantcor Pit *for nine years. He is an active part of the local convention scene and has been producing and hosting game shows for one convention for nearly 20 years.*

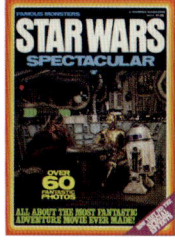

Super Collecting Source Books: An Archive of Knowledge for Your Library

Star Wars collecting is not a hobby for me. It is my life. I compile the Star Wars Super Collector's Wish Books. I maintain the Star Wars collector's database. I produce the Star Wars Blind Pack video series. I contribute to the archival works of others. I exhibit at conventions, speak at events, and perform sourcing identification, verification, and appraisals for Star Wars estates. Star Wars has challenged and entertained me for nearly 50 years. One day, somebody is going to have to take my place—perhaps for their next 50 years. This was my journey, provided as a starting point to promote you continuing on your own.

In 1977, when I was ten years old, I saw Star Wars for the first time in my hometown theater. My first encounter with merchandising was at Burger Chef enjoying a kid's meal on a Star Wars Fun Meal tray. My dad bought the Luke Skywalker poster for me that meal too. There were no toys to be had in the beginning, which led me to imprinting on the other available goods.

Until the merchandising revival of 1999 overwhelmed my collecting budget, my personal goal had been to own "one of everything." The Special Edition film releases of 1997 presented an era of opportunity, since they were a wake-up call to many people who had "Star Wars" lying around their house in boxes and closets from 20 years earlier. Most original collectors had gone on to other life pursuits and found themselves happy to turn their forgotten childhood stuff into a quick buck. It was this alignment of ages that sent me down the collecting path to position myself for where I am today.

Current collectors don't have the benefit of having gotten to start back at a Burger Chef on day one. What I once found at Woolworth's and Meyer's Toy World after school for a week's allowance is now actively sought out or bid upon feverishly as the collecting community snaps up every piece of vintage Star Wars that comes to market for fortunes more than the original retail cost. That adds volume to the new merchandise released almost daily, feeding a variety of interests and keeping the must-have keep-up market alive and well.

Even with the introduction of AI, the internet is incapable of reproducing the expertise of thousands of collectors evolving with individual and unique experiences that shape their focus and knowledge. With that in mind, the final bit I leave to you in the closing of this new edition of the first volume of the series is to reveal the answer to the question asked of me the most: *What books do I own in my own reference library*?

What follows isn't an exhaustive list. I won't delve into the more than 50 other price guide books and magazines that line my shelves that anyone can find at most common sites.

I don't dismiss the historical value of others who have also marked the way. Instead, this collection of titles represents the books of expertise that I have selected to immerse myself into that aren't typically known or available to casual collectors. You won't find the depths of their content on any website.

If you want to earn your degree in Star Wars super collecting, they are worth searching out and worthwhile to own. Perhaps more important than building a respectable collection is having a library of knowledge to access whenever either a mystery or an opportunity presents itself.

2015

2017

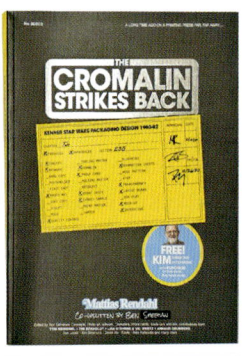
2020

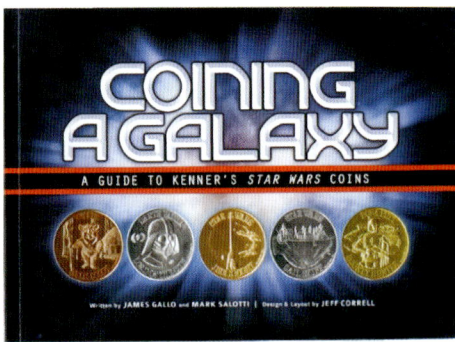
2012

2022

2012

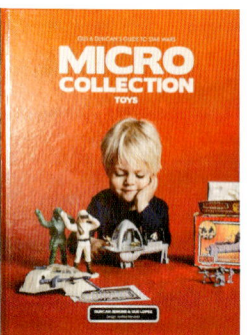
2015

2010

2016

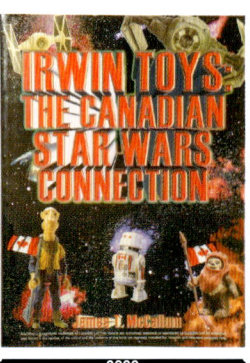
2000

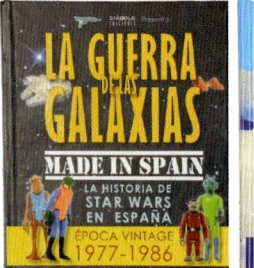
2017

2018

2006

2013

2016

2022

A New Proof
Kenner Star Wars Packaging Design 1977–1979
Mattias Rendahl, edited by Gus Lopez
Dear Publications, 2015
152 pages, 8" x 11"

A Saga on Home Video
A Fan's Guide to U.S. Star Wars Home Video Releases
Nathan P. Butler
2017
285 pages, 6" x 9"

Cromalin Strikes Back, The
Mattias Rendahl and Ben Sheehan
Dear Publications, 2020
256 pages, 8" x 11"

Coining A Galaxy
James Gallo and Mark Salotti
Enter the Arena Press, 2012
82 pages

Far Far Away
A Guide to Unlicensed Polish Star Wars Figures
Jakub Burzynski
2022
264 pages, 7" x 10", hardcover, dust jacket

Gus & Duncan's Guide to Star Wars: Cast & Crew Items
Duncan Jenkins and Gus Lopez
Completest Publications LLC, 2012
251 pages, 8.5" x 8.5", hardcover

Gus & Duncan's Guide to Star Wars: Micro Collection Toys
Duncan Jenkins and Gus Lopez
Completest Publications LLC, 2015
148 pages, 8" x 11", hardcover

Gus & Duncan's Guide to Star Wars: Prototypes
Duncan Jenkins and Gus Lopez
Completest Publications LLC, 2010
336 pages, 9.5" x 11.5", hardcover, dust jacket

French Touch
The Definitive Guide to French Star Wars Collectibles 1977–1987
Stephane Faucourt
2016
274 pages, 8" x 10.5"

Irwin Toys: The Canadian Star Wars Connection
James T. McCallum
CG Publishing Ltd., 2000
120 pages, 8" x 10.5"

La Guerra de las Galaxias Made in Spain
Volume 1, Epoca Vintage 1977–1986
Jose Gracia
Diabolo Ediciones, 2017
296 pages, 7" x 9.5"

La Guerra de las Galaxias Made in Spain
Volume 2, Epoca de Transicion y Renacimiento 1987–1996
Jose Gracia
Diabolo Ediciones, 2018
279 pages, 7" x 9.5"

La Guerre des Etoiles: Meccano to Trilogo
French to European Vintage Star Wars Action Figure Toys
Stephane Faucourt
2006
144 pages, 8.25" x 11.5"

Star Wars: The French Connection
Geoffrey Montfort
Createspace, 2013
232 pages, 8.5" x 11"

Stars Wars LEGO Minifigure Catalog
5th Edition
Christoph Bartneck
Createspace, 2016
204 pages, 6" x 9"

Star Wars Mini Guide
Identify Your Kenner Card Back Reverses 1977–1985
ReadFive Designs, 2022
238 pages, 6" x 8.5"

Star Wars PBP/POCH
Made in Spain Comprehensive Catalog
Volume II
Javier Ruilopez
Artes Graficas Palerom, 2019
261 pages, 8.5" x 12", hardcover

Star Wars PBP/POCH
Made in Spain Comprehensive Catalog
Volume III
Javier Ruilopez
Artes Graficas Palerom, 2021
253 pages, 8.5" x 12", hardcover

Star Wars Phenomenon in Britain
The Blockbuster Impact and the Galaxy of Merchandise, 1977–1983
Craig Stevens
McFarland & Company, 2018
359 pages, 7" x 10"

Star Wars Poster Book
Stephen J. Sansweet and Peter Vilmur
Chronicle Books, 2005
320 pages, 9" x 12", hardcover, dust jacket

Star Wars Toy Guide Volume 1
Kenner Action Figures 1977–1985
Gianni Venturini and Gregory Armstrong
ReadFive Designs, 2022
533 pages, 12" x 15", hardcover, dust jacket

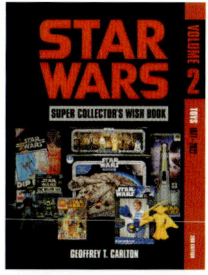
2023 / 464 Pages

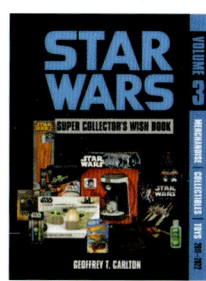
2023 / 464 Pages

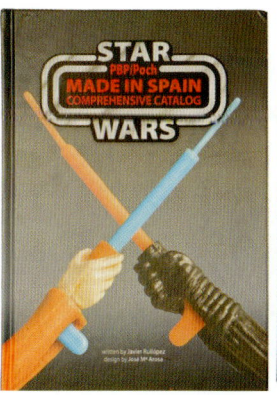
2019

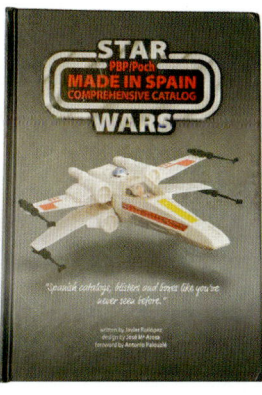
2021

2018

2005

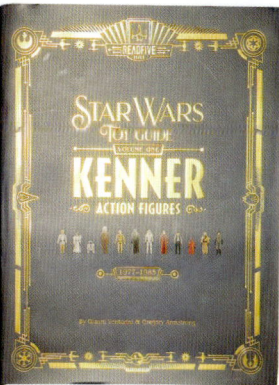
2022